The ASTD
Training and
Development
Handbook

Books in the ASTD Trainer's Sourcebook Series

Elaine Biech
CREATIVITY AND INNOVATION: THE ASTD TRAINER'S
SOURCEBOOK

Anne F. Coyle
LEADERSHIP: THE ASTD TRAINER'S SOURCEBOOK

Dennis C. Kinlaw
COACHING: THE ASTD TRAINER'S SOURCEBOOK

Dennis C. Kinlaw
FACILITATION SKILLS: THE ASTD TRAINER'S SOURCEBOOK

Lisa McLain
PROJECT MANAGEMENT: THE ASTD TRAINER'S
SOURCEBOOK

Herbert R. Miller
SALES: THE ASTD TRAINER'S SOURCEBOOK

Tina Rasmussen
DIVERSITY: THE ASTD TRAINER'S SOURCEBOOK

Sean T. Ryan
CUSTOMER SERVICE: THE ASTD TRAINER'S SOURCEBOOK

Judson Smith
QUALITY: THE ASTD TRAINER'S SOURCEBOOK

Cresencio Torres & Deborah M. Fairbanks
TEAMBUILDING: THE ASTD TRAINER'S SOURCEBOOK

Bobette Hayes Williamson
SUPERVISION: THE ASTD TRAINER'S SOURCEBOOK

John C. Wills
STRATEGIC PLANNING: THE ASTD TRAINER'S SOURCEBOOK

The ASTD Training and Development Handbook

A Guide to Human Resource Development

Fourth Edition

ASTD

Sponsored by the American Society for Training and Development

Robert L. Craig   **Editor in Chief**

McGraw-Hill

New York   San Francisco   Washington, D.C.   Auckland   Bogotá
Caracas   Lisbon   London   Madrid   Mexico City   Milan
Montreal   New Delhi   San Juan   Singapore
Sydney   Tokyo   Toronto

Library of Congress Cataloging-in-Publication Data

The ASTD training and development handbook : a guide to human resource
   development / Robert L. Craig, editor in chief ; sponsored by the
   American Society for Training and Development.—4th ed.
      p.   cm.
      Previous ed. published under title: Training and development
   handbook. 3rd ed. 1987.
      Includes index.
      ISBN 0-07-013359-X
      1. Employees—Training of.   I. Craig, Robert L.   II. American
   Society for Training and Development.   III. Training and development
   handbook.
   HF5549.5.T7T6648   1996
   658.3'124—dc20   96-4177
                                                                        CIP

McGraw-Hill

A Division of The McGraw·Hill Companies

        5 6 7 8 9 0   DOC/DOC   9 0 1 0 9 8

ISBN 0-07-013359-X

*The sponsoring editor for this book was Richard Narramore, the editing supervisor
was Jane Palmieri, and the production supervisor was Suzanne W. B. Rapcavage.
It was set in Palatino by Cynthia L. Lewis of McGraw-Hill's Professional Book
Group composition unit.*

Printed and bound by R. R. Donnelley & Sons Company.

American Society for Training and Development Handbook Advisory Board

Contents

Section 2   Program Design and Development

Section 3   Media and Methods

Section 4   Training Applications

Section 5   Resources

Foreword

As we go to press with this fourth edition of *The ASTD Training and Development Handbook*, it is in order to pause and reflect on the dramatic changes in the field since the first edition was published in 1967 and since ASTD's first days back in the 1940s. But at no time has change in our field been more profound than we are seeing now. Fierce new international competition, astounding new technologies, and deep shifts in the nature of the workforce all bring unprecedented challenges to those charged with improving workforce competence and productivity.

The role of ASTD members has shifted from conducting what was all too often considered nice-to-have programs to programs absolutely essential to organizational performance. ASTD members are at the leading edge of coping with international competition, advancing technology, and workforce change. Thus, ASTD itself occupies a more critical position nowadays since its role is to improve the performance of those who improve workforce performance. A major ASTD initiative in supporting and advancing the field is the development, collection, and dissemination of knowledge relevant to performance improvement, e.g., updating this handbook, a collection of the state-of-the-art; incorporating new technologies into the increasingly comprehensive ASTD Information Center; and building an aggressive program of professional publishing.

We hope that our efforts serve their purpose well.

Curtis E. Plott
CEO and President
American Society for Training and Development
Alexandria, Virginia

Preface

To preface this fourth edition of *The ASTD Training and Development Handbook*, I want to emphasize that never in the history of this handbook, or that of ASTD for that matter, has the demand for excellence in human resource development been so compelling. While the field of HRD has made magnificent strides in the past 50 years or so, the current and future economic environment of intense worldwide competition, rapidly changing technologies, and different kinds of employees all create a whole new order of challenges for developing our workforce performance. Workforce performance will determine which organizations prosper and survive in the marketplaces of the foreseeable future. So, we've tried to gather the best of HRD practices for this newest collection of the body of knowledge in the field.

The very notion of helping people prepare themselves to better achieve their own goals and those of their employers is simply common sense. But it also makes solid economic sense for society at large. That's why we've included even more material on the "bottom-line" aspects of HRD in this edition—dealing with how to measure results and obtain the feedback necessary for continuous improvement of the practice of improving human performance and how to show evidence of the "payoff" of HRD.

For example, we've added chapters on "Human Performance Technology" by Marc J. Rosenberg of AT&T; "Cost Accounting for Training" by Wesley W. Stillwagon of KPMG Peat Marwick; and "Measuring the Results of Training" by Jack J. Phillips, Performance Resources Organization.

Reflecting the global nature of today's employee training and education, past ASTD President Stephen H. Rhinesmith brings his extensive overseas experience to the chapter on "Training for Global Operations."

In the context of the increasing influence of government regulation and societal issues on HRD, we have new chapters on "Training and the Law" by lawyer Patricia Eyres; "Occupational Safety and Health Training" by National Safety Council President Gerard Scannell; and "Diversity Training and Development" by V. Robert Hayles, Vice President of Human Resources and Diversity, The Pillsbury Company, and Chairman of ASTD's Board of Directors.

A very important characteristic of this handbook is that it is largely the work of practitioners in the field, people who are accountable for the HRD performance in their organizations. A leading example is A. William Wiggenhorn, contributor of the chapter on "Organization and Management of Training." Bill heads up

Motorola University, which has a worldwide reputation for innovation and leadership in the field.

To ensure the authority of this collection of knowledge, I have called upon another group of senior practitioners as our advisory board. I owe them enormous thanks for all their help in selecting the contributors, reviewing and commenting on the draft manuscipts, and for their overall advice in producing this new edition. It has been especially rewarding to work with them.

I must also thank my wife, Skip, for her tolerance and help during the many months of putting this new edition together, and my son, Bob, for his support.

I hope that this new edition of the collection of HRD professional practices helps speed the field on its way to meeting the new challenges of improving human performance.

ROBERT L. CRAIG
Editor in Chief
Fairfield, Connecticut

SECTION 1

The Training and Development Function

1

The History of Training

Vincent A. Miller

Vincent A. Miller *is Vice President, MMT International, Ltd., a consulting firm specializing in management, motivation, and technical training. He was the 1974 president of ASTD and served on its board of directors from 1971 through 1979. He was the principal organizer and first director of the ASTD International Division which is now known as the International Professional Practice Area. Also, he was one of the organizers and first secretary-treasurer of the International Federation of Training Organizations (IFTDO). Miller is the recipient of two prestigious awards from ASTD; the Gordon M. Bliss Award in 1974 and the International Trainer of the Year Award in 1979. He is the author of three books, the most recent being* The Guidebook for Global Trainers.*

It is generally agreed that human beings began amassing knowledge at the beginning of the stone age. As they invented tools, weapons, clothing, shelter, and language, the need for training became an essential ingredient in the march of civilization.

History tells us that the fastest form of long-range transportation in the year 6000 B.C. was the camel caravan which traveled at an average speed of about 8 miles per hour. It was not until the chariot was invented about 1600 B.C. that the average speed of long-distance transportation was increased to about 20 miles per hour.

Whether our ancestors stumbled upon or invented these facets of civilization is of very little significance. What is more important is that human beings had the ability to pass on to others the knowledge and skill gained in mastering these circumstances. This was done, not by written words, but by deliberate example, by signs, and by words. We can surely say that here was the first on-the-job training. Through signs and words, the development process which we call training was administered; and when the message was received successfully by another person, learning took place and knowledge or skill was transferred.

Discovery, application, communication, improvement, and more discovery: that is the probable cycle of inventions in the early days of human history. As communication improved, discovery and invention took giant steps forward. Inventions or discoveries that might have taken 50,000 years to accomplish in the stone age, might be reduced to hours or even seconds with today's technologies.

Training's Beginnings

Most scholarly dissertations on the history of communication begin with a description of the early cave wall drawings which serve as a documentary record and textbook of the time. Isn't it conceivable that the etchings and paintings were also effective instructional illustrations, orienting primeval youngsters to such skills as fishing and hunting and how to protect themselves from the large wooly mammoths that roamed the land?

As archaeological excavations continue to unearth clay brick or stone tablets on which is inscribed information about the lives of people living 6000 or more years ago, the place of training in the skyrocketing development of knowledge and civilization has become dramatically more evident.

The Sumerian Palace of Kish in Mesopotamia, built in 3500 B.C. is an example of the ancient use of brick. The Bible tells us that the ancient Tower of Babel was also built of brick. The astounding architectural and masonry accomplishments of the craftspeople, embodied in the pyramids and ancient temples such as Solomon's First Temple are memorials to the stonemasons, the brickmasons, the carpenters, the artists, and the scientists of ancient times. But, let us keep in mind that thousands of people worked on these projects. The work could not have been accomplished without training; without transfer of knowledge from one person to another or from one person to many people.

It must be remembered that in these early civilizations, literacy reached neither the craftspeople nor the peasantry. The skills and knowledge of the crafts could be transmitted only by direct instruction from the skilled craftspeople to the not so skilled.

Historical Apprenticeship Data

Thus was developed an apprenticeship system whereby an experienced person passed along knowledge and skills to the novice, who after a period of apprenticeship became a journeyman, or yeoman. Provisions for governing apprenticeship were instituted as early as 1800 B.C. when such rules were included in the code of Hammurabi, who placed a code of his laws in the temple of Shamash (God of Justice) in Babylon.

The apprenticeship system was not restricted to artisans. The ancient temples taught religion and frequently taught art. The armies took the responsibility for training soldiers. In all walks of life, knowledge was passed from one person to another. Apprenticeship was the vehicle of instruction in medicine, law, and many other professions where the education is now in the domain of the colleges and universities. As recently as the 1920s, it was possible in the United States for a person to "read law in the office of an attorney." Following a period of study, the apprentice lawyer took a government-sponsored examination. A passing grade on the examination qualified the apprentice to practice law.

The apprenticeship system never seemed to work properly in colonial America. It involved a commitment of years, and imposed obligations and burdens on both the employer and the employee. It proved inadequate as an efficient source of labor, although it provided a temporary source of cheap labor. One reason it did not work well was that adult male labor was scarce. Most able-bodied men who would otherwise be candidates for apprenticeship were primarily on farms, or involved in the shipping trade.

Guilds

Another development in the Middle Ages was the formation of guilds, which were associations of people whose interests or pursuits were the same or similar. The first guilds known were in England before the Norman conquest (A.D. 1066). By the end of the twelfth century, guilds were spread throughout the cities of Europe. The basic purpose of guilds was mutual protection, assistance, and advantage. In essence, guilds created private franchises and at the same time established quality standards for products through quality standards for workmanship.

There were three classes of membership in the guilds: the master workers who owned the raw materials and the tools, and directed the work; the apprentices who usually lived with the master and who received practically no pay except maintenance and training; and finally, the journeymen who had passed through the apprenticeship stage but were not yet qualified as masters and received fixed wages for their labor.

The journeyman generally remained in the master's house. However, it was possible for the journeyman to save money, buy tools, and take an examination in his craft. Once the journeyman had passed the examination and had become a master craftsman, he could set up his own shop. However, as the markets expanded, more machinery and tools were required and becoming a master craftsman required a great investment, reducing the opportunities of a journeyman to become a master craftsman. As a result, journeymen banded together and formed yeomanry guilds. The yeomanry guilds were forerunners of today's labor unions.

During the peak of the guild system, which occurred between the twelfth and fifteenth centuries, the privileges of the members of yeomanry guilds were protected by strict regulation of hours, tools, prices, and wages. The system required that all have the same privileges and pursue the same methods. In the craft unions today, we still find restrictions as to the number of apprentices, regulations as to the quantity and quality of work, and the establishment of a base system of financial reward.

Craft Training

The nineteenth century ushered in an era of social legislation, and with it sizable changes in the concept of the workers' organizations. Through all of these changes, however, one constantly developing emphasis has been upon the quality of training received by workers and this has culminated in the staunch support of the unions for any legislation that provides a wide range of vocational education.

Industrialization meant two changes in work preparation. Specific training was now required before specific tasks could be performed. In the traditional craft and agrarian order, people had "grown up" into stable, lifelong occupations, while in the industrial setting they were trained to specialize in only one part of the total craft. The other change required a different work orientation. Work activity was now focused away from the individual, family, or small group and toward a large impersonal organization within a large, impersonal urban community. The industrial revolution required education for specific tasks, and education to function within the emerging corporate organization. This education, or training, was generally provided by the corporate organization.

One of the interesting sidelights in the history of education for business is that several of the early schools of business administration were established as a result of evening programs in business. It is commonly thought that the evening courses became an added service of existing schools of business, but in many instances the reverse is true. The evening courses sponsored by corporate organizations came first and were followed later by full-time colleges.

The history of the growth of training which accompanied the great industrial expansion is fascinating. As early as 1809, the Masonic Grand Lodge of New York, under the leadership of De Witt Clinton, established vocational facilities. Manual training began in the United States about 1825. However, most of the manual training schools that sprang up after 1825 were more disciplinary than vocational schools. The so-called state industrial schools were really places of incarceration for "bad boys." Nevertheless, the basic concept was correct. The schools gave idle hands training in such a manner that, in accompaniment with a trained mind, the pupils eventually would be able to make a contribution to society rather than constitute a liability to it.

The concept of the application of higher learning to practical affairs has flourished in the United States since the Rensselaer Polytechnic Institute broke the classical barrier in 1824 to become the first college of engineering. Instruction in agriculture, education, business administration, accounting, journalism, and a variety of other fields has followed, and gradually there has developed the general acceptance of the notion that there is a bona fide link between education and training.

We could wonder why the universities failed to embrace training in the 1800s. Way back in 1830, the trustees of Columbia University established a new scientific curriculum, in which no Latin or Greek was required, and voted to make the courses available to young men "employed in business and mercantile establishments." Apparently, employers were not of a mind to grant the necessary time off the job for their employees to study, and the program failed to materialize. The fact that there were no takers does not detract from the foresight of the Columbia trustees.

Cooper Union in New York instituted evening vocational classes in 1824. By 1886, private manual training classes were established in Cincinnati, Cleveland, Toledo, and Chicago, and public institutions of a similar sort were established in Philadelphia, Baltimore, and Omaha. One of the great steps forward in the effort to free workers from the limitations of their immediate craft requirements was the passing of the Land Grant Act in 1862. When Abraham Lincoln signed this act, he initiated a means of higher education for the average man's children, which previously could be enjoyed only by the wealthy.

The Industrial Era Emerges

The industrial revolution began in England about 1750, and spread from there to France and Belgium, then to Germany and the United States. After the revolutionary war, Americans eagerly turned their energy toward the pursuit of prosperity, through power-driven machinery, steam engines, and a factory system that put useful knowledge and new technology to work. This early American drive for industrialization was so successful that, for example, in 1807 there were 15 cotton mills in the country, and by 1815 mills utilizing 500,000 spindles were employing 76,000 workers. These men, women, and children were already being called "industrial workers."

The change from an agrarian to an industrial economy in the United States was manifested by the rapid increase in the number of patents issued by the U.S. Patent Office. An average of 77 patents were issued each year between 1790 and 1811, and an average of 192 patents were issued each year between 1812 and 1817.

Industry became employer, guardian, and patron of body and soul. Industry was willing to become involved in broad issues of education and quality of life. Manufacturers recruited farm maidens to work in their mills. Employers provided not only for a job, but for an entire set of living circumstances designed to nurture and educate. The girls lived in rambling boardinghouses, supervised by a matron. Literary evenings, elevating lectures, and circulating libraries were provided for them. They were expected to attend church on Sunday, and if they did not abide by stringent rules of conduct, they were dismissed from their job.

Male workers also labored under the strict eye of the mill owners, particularly regarding morals, health, and well-being. The new "working class" wanted the opportunities industry offered as much as industry wanted workers with a certain level of intelligence, skill, and resourcefulness. The new system of manufacture meant that the machines were skilled, not necessarily the operators of the machines. As viewed by the industrialists, craftsmanship belonged to the past, industrial education to the future.

There was no American system of public education to provide "useful knowledge" for potential young workers in those early days of the industrial era. Out of necessity, training had to be done within a company or in a trade group. Most companies did not turn to the educational system for help in training their people—a subject we discuss elsewhere in this chapter. However, the educational system continued to prepare people for jobs in industry. During the period between the Civil War and World War I the education of persons preparing themselves for jobs in industry came to be known as vocational education.

Since most trainers are aware that many of the new training techniques are an extension of other sound principles of training, we should not be too amazed to learn that training programs which we use regularly in our modern training were used many years ago. For example: people began playing chess thousands of years ago; the Prussians started to apply gaming situations to military training in the early 1800s. They used games consisting of highly detailed maps and utilized color-coded blocks to represent troops. Players determined troop movements and appropriate armaments. Following the game the players' decisions were discussed and critiqued. The war games became very popular and were adapted for military training throughout the world.

The case method of training was developed by Christopher Langdell at the Harvard School of Law in the 1880s. This nondirective training technique can be used with large or small groups. When the case method was introduced by Langdell, it slowly won acceptance in the schools of law, medicine, and business.

Another training technique that has been around longer than most people would be willing to believe is role playing. Psychodrama and role playing were originally designed about 1910 by Dr. J. L. Moreno in Vienna, Austria. The technique became more publicized in the 1930s, after Dr. Moreno came to the United States. He developed concepts of group play, role theory, and the use of creativity and spontaneity in therapeutic and educational contexts.

Factory Schools

One of the first factory schools established was in 1872 at Hoe and Company, a manufacturer of printing presses in New York City. The company had such a volume of business that it was forced to increase production. There was no time to train machinists by the apprenticeship method, and it was necessary to establish a factory school.

Similar factory schools were established at Westinghouse in 1888, at General Electric Company and Baldwin Locomotive Works in 1901, and at International Harvester Company in 1907. Such companies as Western Electric, Goodyear, Ford, and National Cash Register soon installed factory training schools. Other companies saw the advantages of having factory training schools, and they soon became a common practice.

Training Support from Other Sources

The YMCA was a key influence in the development of training. In 1892 the Brooklyn YMCA offered a course in freehand drawing. The Springfield, Ohio, YMCA offered trade training in patternmaking, toolmaking, and cabinetry. In 1905 the West Side New York YMCA offered 63 courses, 36 percent of which were commercial, and 26 percent industrial and scientific.

An innovation in education took place in the first decade of this century when Dean Schneider of the University of Cincinnati, College of Engineering, introduced cooperative education. Under this plan, the student would go to school for a time and work in the factory an equal amount of time. Then the student would repeat the process, going to school for additional training, and going back to the factory for more practical experience, until the student graduated from the university. This process required a contract or agreement between the university, the student, and the employer.

America first saw correspondence instruction when the Chautauqua Literary and Scientific Circle offered several classes in 1882. The University of Chicago sponsored the first college-level correspondence courses in 1890. The modern American correspondence school had its beginning in 1891, when Thomas J. Foster founded the International Correspondence Schools. The oldest date of an apprentice plan in conjunction with a correspondence school was 1903, when ICS worked out a plan with a southern railway system.

By 1850 American unions were actively concerned with the restriction of entry into the skilled trades. The unions were also fighting with the employers for control of the apprenticeship training. By 1900 the unions were setting up training schools that were sometimes in opposition to those set up by management. Nowadays, the unions and trade associations are utilized as educational resources by many employers. The unions have large training funds which are used for training and retraining the union workers. Sometimes, funds for retraining are built into the union contract with management.

The Ohio Mechanics Institute was started in Cincinnati, Ohio, in 1828. Horace Mann did much to improve the system of free public schools when he was a member of Congress from 1848 to 1852. However, despite all the grand arguments and some genuine reforms, the need for educated industrial workers continued. In 1876, while visiting the Centennial Exhibition in Philadelphia, President John D. Runkle of the Massachusetts Institute of Technology met Victor Della Vos, director of the Moscow Imperial Technical School. Della Vos had organized his school with shops for instructing boys in a definite method for each trade skill. He analyzed trades according to their component skills and devised a pedagogical order combining drawings, models, and tools into a graduate series of supervised exercises by which the students could become proficient in a trade. That same year, the Massachusetts Institute of Technology established instruction shops for engineering students and set up a new school of mechanical arts to offer education for industrial careers along with the scientific education curriculum.

Industry Association Support

By the early 1900s, vocational education was sufficiently extensive that there was a great need for mutual assistance in this field. The natural outgrowth was the realization that in unity of action there is strength. In 1906, a group of 250 key educators interested in industrial education met at Cooper Union in New York City, and formed the National Society for the Promotion of Industrial Education. This society later merged with others to become The American Vocational Association. In 1913 a meeting was held at New York University, and the National Association of Corporation Schools was formed. It started with 60 members representing 34 corporations. The association held four annual conventions. The first convention was held in Dayton, Ohio, in 1914. By the time the organization held their fourth convention in 1918, the main interest of the organization had changed to "personnel." The name was changed in 1920 to The National Association of Corporation Training. Shortly thereafter, it merged with the Industrial Relations Association of America to become the National Personnel Association. Less than three years later, in 1923, the name was changed to The American Management Association.

The National Society for the Promotion of Industrial Education, mentioned earlier, changed its name to the National Society for Vocational Education in 1918, and merged with the Vocational Association of the Middle West (founded in 1914) to become the American Vocational Association in 1925. The AVA membership is composed of more than 55,000 teachers, supervisors, administrators, and others interested in the development and improvement of vocational and practical arts education.

The National Vocational Guidance Association, organized in Grand Rapids, Michigan, in 1913 also supported the concept of training. It is now a division of the American Personnel and Guidance Association, which was founded in 1952. The National Association of Foremen was founded in 1925. This organization of business and industrial managers, from supervisory level to middle managers and above, was very involved on the training scene from the time they were organized through World War II. An indication of their involvement during the war years is their 1944 conference for educational directors in industry, which was held in Columbus, Ohio. Nearly 500 people from 28 states attended that conference. In 1956, the National Association of Foremen changed its name to the National Management Association.

Training: 1910 to 1920

By 1910, the Ford Motor Company had moved into a new plant at Highland Park, Michigan, and they had established a production line concept. However, it was not until 1913 that the "moving assembly line" was established, where an automobile began its journey as a bare chassis on one end of the line and ended up on the other end of the line as a finished Model T Ford automobile. Thus began the need for special training of the production line worker for a specific job, because each person on the assembly line needed to be skilled in only the tasks performed at that particular workstation.

World War I prompted a tremendous stimulus for training. Historically, training has always grown best where emergency is the dominant thought. On September 12, 1917, the Emergency Fleet Corporation of the United States Shipping Board set up an educational training section. There were 61 shipyards with 50,000 workers and there was an urgent need for 10 times as many workers but not many more trained workers were available. The only answer to the problem was training of new workers. Charles R. Allen, the head of the program, ordered that all of the training be done at the shipyards and that the instructors should be the supervisors at the shipyards.

Allen adopted the four-step method of "show, tell, do, and check" as his standard method of job instruction training to solve this World War I problem. Many lessons were learned during the war. The following statement was made at the time of the 1920 census: "The public is again reminded, through the census, of the lessons which the war should have taught regarding the tremendous loss in the ability of the public schools to reach out to all alike and give them the educational and training equipment necessary for a life career."

Training in the 1920s

After World War I, a series of factors combined to compel companies to provide a stable source of competent future management. Many colleges and universities responded to the industrial need for managerial-level personnel with business education programs. The loss of men in World War I and the inability of the economy of the late 1920s and early 1930s to support the surplus personnel required by the apprenticeship method of providing managerial talent caused that method (managerial apprenticeship) to die out. In fact, apprenticeship for the skilled trades faded away within some corporations.

The prosperity of the early 1920s tended to discourage the application of training to industrial situations. However, by this time, correspondence schools had gained recognition and acceptance and were serving the needs of the American wage earner. It was said that probably more men in American industry had gained the technical phases of their skills from correspondence schools than by any other means.

Sales training seemed to receive some stimulus during the postwar boom period of the roaring twenties. There were the years when the so-called modern appliances began to be heavily merchandised. Local radio stations were just beginning their broadcasts, and families were buying their first radios. The ownership of an electric refrigerator, or an electric range, or an electric wringer washer was indeed a status symbol in the 1920s. Many sales people were trained in door-to-door selling for these big-ticket items.

Training in the 1930s:
The Depression Years

As the economy plunged into the greatest depression in American history, more and more top-management people decided that training was not needed. The great number of workers whose jobs were terminated when businesses failed or were reduced in size provided an adequate supply of skilled and experienced workers. The depression years of the 1930s wrecked many internal training programs. Apprenticeship in the skilled trades was terminated in many industries. There were plenty of skilled workers waiting to be hired into any available job, and they voiced the cry: "Why train others, when we are here to do the job?"

On the other hand, a great influence to the furtherance of training was stimulated by this same set of depression-laden circumstances. Unemployed people had time on their hands and nothing to do with those hands. This problem became acute. A major effort to solve it was instigated by local, state, and federal governments. Perhaps the most widespread program was that involving the appropriation of federal funds for training in handicrafts. Hundreds of thousands of unemployed men and women occupied their spare time by learning leatherwork, weaving, art and painting, jewelry making, chair caning, and many other crafts. These people soon discovered that they could profitably occupy their time making some useful things, and in some cases they could provide income by selling the articles which they made. People became training-conscious, and likewise they became conscious of their own learning potential. The training tools of the 1930s generally consisted of chalkboards, writing easels or chart pads, "magic lantern" slides, and in the later years of the decade, some commercially prepared 16-millimeter sound motion picture films. It was the development of the 16-millimeter sound movie projector that first brought the audiovisual technology into practical prominence in the classroom. Of course, there were some enterprising trainers who were using "talking machines," both cylinder and disk, to give them some audio capabilities.

In the later 1930s, after Hitler sent his troops into Austria in March 1938, Britain and France began to increase their orders for defensive armaments, which were built in the United States. Likewise, the United States began to bolster its own defensive armaments. These "war" orders were eagerly accepted by American manufacturers and had much to do with improving the U.S. economy and reducing the size of the unemployment lines. The need for retraining on a massive scale was recognized, as people who had been unemployed or underemployed for years again returned to skilled jobs and workers without skills were hired to do work that required skills.

The 1940s and World War II:
Training Becomes a Profession

A number of national organizations gave support to training directors before the American Society for Training and Development (ASTD) was founded, but the National Society of Sales Training Executives became the first national society devoted strictly to training when it was founded in 1940.

There was registration for the draft in the United States late in 1940, and many people who had never before worked in a manufacturing plant eagerly answered the call to replace those who were being drafted into the armed forces. It was obvious to all that the United States was on the brink of war, and our involvement was imminent since we were supplying the Allies with ammunition and planes, guns, and tanks. The new people in industry needed to be trained as welders, machinists, and riveters in order to produce the war materials. The United States entered the war in December 1941.

Training was needed, but who would do it? By the time the United States entered the war, many of the vocational teachers had taken higher-paying jobs in industry, and in some cases those who were left in teaching positions were not familiar with the needs of the employers. At last, business came face to face with the reality that they had too long ignored. They had neglected training during the depression years of the 1930s and now they were in a bind. Suddenly, the training function of the supervisor became paramount. In fact, management found that without training skills, supervisors were unable to produce adequately for the war effort. Supervisors with training skills established new production records, using inexperienced, aged, handicapped, and women workers.

Training became a necessity, and soon the title of Training Manager was common in the management hierarchy. The wartime trainers suddenly needed to move vast numbers of people through orientation, attitude building, and technical instruction. To achieve their goal, they turned increasingly to training films, filmstrips, simulators, flip charts, flannel boards, and models which would help them get their message across. Role playing began to receive a lot of attention too. Today's trainer, looking at the training aids of the 1940s would declare them ancient, but they were the state of the art back then.

The actual training of supervisors to become job instructors was developed to classic simplicity by the Training Within Industry Service (TWI), which was established in 1940 by the National Defense Advisory Commission. On April 8, 1942, by presidential order, TWI became a part of the War Manpower Commission and operated under the Bureau of Training. By the time TWI ceased operations in 1945, it had been instrumental in training 23,000 persons as instructors and had awarded nearly two million certificates to supervisors who had gone through the TWI programs in more than 16,000 plants, services, and unions.

JIT, or job instruction training, was developed to train supervisors in defense plants in the skill of instructing their workers as rapidly as possible. Train the Trainer Institutes were held all over the United States. Initially, the institutes were three days long. Fifteen to thirty people attended. Later, the institutes grew to a 45-hour program. JIT was all-inclusive. It not only taught how to instruct but also put emphasis on the related problems of human relations between the supervisor and the worker and the equally important matter of determining the best job methods. It was quite natural then that other J programs followed, so we had:

JRT—Job Relations Training

JMT—Job Methods Training

JST—Job Safety Training

Each program was a specialized facet of the fundamentals inherent in the JIT card. Added to the J programs listed above was a program development course (PDT) which was developed for executives who were unfamiliar with training techniques.

The American Society for Training and Development was organized in the 1940s. Perhaps the most factual account of the founding of ASTD was written by its first president, Thomas S. Keaty. The following information is an edited account of a 1956 report which Mr. Keaty wrote describing those early days of ASTD.

The idea of having a national training society that would cut across all industries was suggested on April 2, 1942, at a meeting of the American Petroleum Institute Committee on Training, which was held at the Roosevelt Hotel in New Orleans. Tom Keaty was delegated to develop a constitution, and to secure charter members for the new organization. Copies of a proposed constitution were mailed to 25 prominent training directors in the mid-continent area on June 15, 1942, with a request for comments and an expression of interest. In the next six months, a total of 12 charter members from eight states was secured. The constitution was approved by the charter members. On January 12, 1943, the new society, which called itself the American Society of Training Directors (ASTD) met in

Baton Rouge, Louisiana, for the first formal meeting under the new constitution. Thomas S. Keaty was elected president; Dr. Andrew Triche, vice president; and J. W. Bowling, secretary and treasurer. By February 1944, the membership had grown to more than 100 members from 16 states. By late 1945, the membership had grown to almost 200 members from 28 states.

The first ASTD "Annual Meeting" was held in Chicago, September 27 and 28, 1945. Delegates of training associations from New York, New Jersey, Wisconsin, Illinois, Michigan, Louisiana, and Indiana were present to discuss affiliation of similar organizations. The decision was made at this meeting to accept other training associations as chapters of ASTD but also to accept memberships of individual members. The annual dues for individual membership was established at four dollars per year.

The first printed issue of *Industrial Training News* was published by ASTD in June 1945. All previous ASTD periodicals had been mimeographed. The name was changed to *Journal of Industrial Training* in June 1947, when it became a bimonthly journal. The name was changed again to the *Training Directors Journal* in 1958, when it became a monthly publication. It became the *Training and Development Journal* in 1966 and reached its present size of approximately 8½ by 11 inches in 1969. The name was changed to *Training and Development* in 1991.

The training laboratory has become a highly respected and widely used learning method since its inception at Bethel, Maine, in 1947. Led by Leland Bradford, Ronald Lippitt, and Kenneth D. Benne, the National Training Laboratory conducted its first summer session. Since then large numbers of training organizations have participated in NTL workshops, and this method of human relations training has spread throughout the world.

Training in the 1950s

The wire recorder was mentioned as being used for training purposes after World War II. Here for the first time, the trainer had the ability to record voice or music with a reasonable sound quality, and to rerecord over a used area of the wire to make corrections and changes. Those who used the wire recorders thought they were great. There was only one thing wrong with the system. At the most inopportune times, the wire would not wind onto the reel properly, and since it was like fine piano wire it would get tangled. Those who used the wire recorders would live in fear of getting the wire tangled. Despite all of its problems, it was the best recording equipment available to trainers until after 1952 when the 3M Corporation discovered the process for coating acetate and polyester tapes with metallic oxide. Now, magnetic recording, which was invented in 1899 by Poulsen, could be used by trainers. Most training departments began using the new reel-to-reel tape recorders.

It was not until 1956 that the first practical videotape recorder was made by the Ampex Corporation. It was originally used by broadcasters so they could record programs for later transmission. These original videotape recorders were large, complex, and expensive. Although, 10 years later, many large training departments were using reel-to-reel videotape which produced black and white pictures for some of their training, the videotape recorder was not a universally acceptable training tool until the videotape cassette and color video recorders were available to trainers in the 1970s.

The first permanent office for ASTD was opened in Madison, Wisconsin, in 1952. It is interesting to note that the reason the office was opened in Madison, Wisconsin, is because the secretary-treasurer, Russell Moberly, who kept all of the records, lived there. By this time, there were 32 chapters and 1600 members.

In the meantime, ASTD chapters were gaining experience with closed-circuit television, and with educational television broadcasts. In 1957, the New Jersey chapter participated in a novel experiment, using closed-circuit television to teach 2000 temporary postal employees the job they were hired to do for the Christmas season. By 1958, there were 32 educational television stations in operation. They were teaching courses in typing, shorthand, sales training, and almost any phase of technical and professional skills that one could think of.

Already, at the 1958 ASTD conference, there was a session titled "Human Factors in Automation." The session leader discussed what to do to overcome problems that follow progressive replacement of human labor by automation. Trainers started to pay more attention to the evaluation of training in the 1950s. Up to this time, only a few trainers bothered to evaluate the results of their training. Also in the 1950s, many top companies and schools began using business games in their training of managers. "In-basket" exercises and other decision-making simulation games were very popular. Role playing was used extensively for training salespeople and industrial managers.

Training in the 1960s

As we entered the 1960s, only one American business organization was using assessment centers, and even in the mid-sixties only a few companies were using assessment centers. The popularity of the training laboratory and other forms of sensitivity training increased tremendously during the 1960s. Trainers began to talk and write about their experiences with sensitivity training and behavioral change, and by the end of the decade assessment centers, sensitivity training, and behavioral change were tremendously popular. By far the most popular training technique used in training during the 1960s was programmed instruction.

On July 28, 1961, ASTD President Vernon Sheblak appointed a committee on teaching machine technology. (Remember, this is before computers were available.) The committee worked with other committees from government and education to exchange information, report on new developments, and prepare a set of recommendations. The recommendations of the joint committee appeared in the January 1966 *Training and Development Journal*. The National Society for Programmed Instruction, now known as the International Society for Performance Improvement, was organized in 1962, with many of its charter members holding membership in NSPI and ASTD. In the early and mid-sixties, great promises were being made about programmed instruction. Its popularity carried through the sixties, then seemed to die out. However, the development process and the learning and teaching fundamentals which were a part of programmed instruction can also be used to prepare other training programs.

By 1968 there were 10,000 videotape recorders in use. They were smaller now and more economical, although the cost was still $3000 to $7000 for a reel-to-reel black and white recorder. Although acceptance was growing and the need was great for videotape recorders, many training departments did not purchase them because there was no compatibility between one brand and another.

Some sophisticated teaching machines were developed. The machines and their circuitry were developed by computer, but the teaching machines themselves were electromechanical and might cost $30,000 to $50,000 to construct. Many reports were written about the benefits of computer-assisted instruction, and in most cases the reference was to an electromechanical training device that had been designed with the aid of a computer. The computer itself had not yet been miniaturized.

Throughout the 1960s there was a growing awareness of how necessary it is for a trainer to be well grounded in the role of training and to use needs assessment and evaluation techniques. Performance appraisal, which is another form of evaluation, also came into popular use in the 1960s.

The need for management training was recognized more than ever before. Management training was almost as popular a subject as programmed instruction. Trainers started to hear about the systems approach and organization development near the end of the decade. More attention was paid to motivation. Also, the training director's job was being analyzed and given more recognition.

A nationwide Job Development Program was announced by President Lyndon B. Johnson on February 1, 1965. This was the first of a series of government-sponsored programs aimed at helping the unemployed, the poor, the disadvantaged, the minorities, and the hard-core unemployable. The Manpower Development and Training Act (MDTA) was extended. The Job Corps, designed to train young men for jobs in industry, was operating in otherwise unused army camps. Special training centers were set up in metropolitan areas to train the hard-core unemployed. Special attention was paid to the rights of all minorities.

The first edition of the *Training and Development Handbook,* sponsored by ASTD and published by McGraw-Hill, was published in 1967. It was the most complete training reference ever assembled up to that time.

Training in the 1970s

By 1970, fifty-nine of the Job Corps centers had closed down and smaller in-city centers had been established to handle local trainees. In the meantime, much attention was being given to training the disadvantaged and hard-core unemployed. More trainers were being involved in this type of training from 1970 to 1972 than at any other time in history. Involvement with these social issues called for an added dimension to the professionalism of training, and ASTD urged its members to take action and use their knowledge to help solve these pressing problems. Gradually, the training concerns shifted to a concern for minorities as a total grouping. Under government pressure, most organizations began serious efforts to fulfill established quotas for hiring or involving women or racial minorities in responsible management positions. Much of the training in the first half of the decade was involved with training these minorities, and upgrading as many of them as possible to supervisory positions.

ASTD's first female board member, Frances M. Kidd, was elected to serve a 1957–1958 term of office. The next woman to serve on the board was Inez Lauderbach who became vice president of Region 6 in 1969 and served in that capacity until August 1970 when she became an adjunct board member. Since 1969, there has been an unbroken chain of female leaders on the board of directors. Jan Margolis, the first female president of ASTD, took office in 1979.

Trainers did become more professional during this decade. ASTD produced a *Professional Development Manual for Trainers.* Those who read the trade journals were bombarded with information about how to determine training needs, evaluation, management development, motivation, the training function, and training methods. Trainer involvement in the national society increased by about 17,000 members, and additional trainer involvement of local chapter members also amounted to about 17,000.

Organizational development (OD), which gained acceptance during the 1960s, became the most popular and the most talked about training technique or practice of the 1970s. OD was a combining of many interlocking components, including manager selection, personnel development, organization structure, management methods, interpersonal relations, and group dynamics. The trainers who became involved in OD were now concerned with much more than "people development," for which the name human resource development (HRD) had now been coined. Whereas, the personnel and training departments were concerned with people, the OD consultant was concerned with the well-being of the entire organization. Many senior trainers became internal or external OD consultants in the 1970s.

The work that had been done in the area of needs assessment, task analysis, and evaluation laid the groundwork for the introduction of competency-based learning, which came into popular use in the last half of this decade. Competency-based learning is concerned with having the trainees develop certain specified competencies that match the requirements of their job, while recognizing the fact that the trainee has certain competencies which fit the job requirements and do not require additional training.

There was a considerable amount of international training activity in the 1970s. ASTD received several contracts from the Agency for International Development (AID), starting in 1970. Operating under the various AID contracts, ASTD was able to assist in organizing a national training organization in Venezuela, hold the first world conference on training in 1972 in Switzerland, and follow through on the organization of the International Federation of Training and Development Organizations (IFTDO). The formal signing of the IFTDO charter took place at the third international conference in Oslo, Norway, in 1974. Without financing from AID through ASTD the IFTDO would never have survived. ASTD continued as the Secretariat for IFTDO until 1981 at no cost to IFTDO. Workshops were also conducted in Ethiopia, in Latin America, and in Asian countries, with the objective being the establishment of national training societies.

Another milestone for trainers was the opening of the ASTD Washington, D.C., office in 1975 to foster closer relationships with federal agencies on behalf of member interests. The first Washington office was just a branch office, while the headquarters location remained in Madison, Wisconsin. However, the board of directors approved the move of all offices to Washington, D.C., in 1981.

Many advances in training technology came as a result of improvements in training hardware. A few items which should not be forgotten are the variable-speed tape recorders, standardized videocassettes, availability of satellites for training use, and tremendous improvements in computers and availability of computer programs for training, although desktop computers were not yet available and anyone using computers for training had to tap into a mainframe computer.

The 1980s: Desktop Computers Become Popular

As we entered the 1980s, few people realized what an impact the computer would have on their lives before the decade was finished. In 1980, many training managers were struggling to get their secretarial pools on-line with word processing computers. Most of them did not have any experience with the new desktop computers. The IBM desktop computer, which was to become the standard format for most other desktops, was introduced in 1982, and shortly thereafter the market was flooded with "compatibles." By the end of the decade trainers and training managers were using computers for training, but computers were also on trainers' desks for communication, using fax and electronic mail.

It was in August of 1981 that ASTD moved its entire staff from Madison, Wisconsin, to Washington, D.C., and after several moves within the Washington area, they settled in their present location at 1640 King Street in Alexandria, Virginia. ASTD was still growing. The 1985 membership count showed 22,300 national members and 143 chapters, and there were also about 23,000 local members of ASTD chapters. The tremendous growth prompted a change in the governance structure of the society. Starting in 1984, a board of governors, made up of distinguished senior-level HRD practitioners, academicians, government executives, and HR executives, was established to set priorities and strategic direction for the society, while a smaller board of directors served as the decision-making body.

Trainers became more conscious of their expenditures as a result of the business recession. Many trainers were studying methods of reporting to show return on investment for the training they had done. Many systems for reporting return for investment in training were developed although no system seemed able to cover all types of training and all circumstances, but that is a challenge that will most likely be solved by a computer in the future.

Behavior modeling, which had been used in the 1970s, became more popular in the 1980s. Its greatest use was for management skills training, although it could be used for training in any skill. Actually, behavior modeling has been used since humans began to communicate with each other. In that sense (one person duplicating the behavior of another), it will be with us forever. However, the process is most likely to be integrated into training programs without mention that behavior modeling is taking place.

In October 1987, ASTD's first National Technical and Skills Conference was held in Cincinnati, Ohio. The conference provided three days of hands-on, practical information for high-tech trainers. The information was presented by some of the world's top experts in the field. The first technical and skills conference was a huge success, and that type of conference has been repeated each year since 1987.

There was renewed emphasis on career development during the 1980s. Perhaps this was a direct result of the chartering of the Career Development Division within ASTD. According to leading career development theorists, we must give continuing attention to career development because of the ever-changing makeup of the workforce and because of changing social patterns and job structures.

The Baldrige National Quality Award was established in 1987 by national legislation. This award focuses on Total Quality Management of American companies, and focuses attention on quality management, including quality training.

Near the end of the decade it was apparent that corporate needs were changing and many organizations realized that they must enter the global market place if they are to survive. As a result, ASTD placed more emphasis on supplying information that would inform trainers about how their training would be affected by a company's global operations.

The 1990s and Beyond

For at least the next 10 years, the demands of the global economy will continue to change the way businesses are organized and operated. Performance will be measured by standards set by customers, and the major new role for trainers will be to support the organization to achieve that performance.

Many HRD professionals will be engaged in helping organizations change and transform. Many of them will act as brokers for the constant learning that will make such changes possible. Others will help organize and facilitate work through process reengineering and Total Quality Management.

Learning professionals will work with many models of individual and organizational learning, especially those that describe how people learn in the context of work.

The power of technology to change the way information is created, stored, used, and shared will influence the design and delivery of training. Classroom training and courses led by instructors will frequently be replaced by computer-based instruction.

In their roles as agents of learning, trainers will shift their focus from themselves as teachers to their students as learners. The 1990s are full of many such challenges to tradition; they are certain to prompt many exciting developments in the area of workplace learning and performance.

2

Organization and Management of Training

A. William Wiggenhorn

A. William Wiggenhorn is President, Motorola University, and Senior Vice President of Training and Education at Motorola. He joined Motorola in 1981 as Director of the Training and Education Center with the responsibility for upgrading the Motorola workforce to meet the challenges of worldwide competition in the 1980s and beyond. Wiggenhorn has been at the forefront of the field and has established a leadership role for Motorola in workforce development. Prior to joining Motorola, he was Director of Training and Education and a sales and marketing executive at Xerox Corporation; college administrator at the University of Dayton; and member of the consulting firm Bergamo, Inc. Among his honors: 1990 McKinsey Award for best article, "Motorola U.: When Training Becomes an Education," Harvard Business Review, July–August, 1990, and the Penang State Award (Honorary 'Darjah Johan Negeri') for service in conjunction with the birthday celebration of the Head of State of Penang 9th July 1994. He has participated in The White House Conference on Productivity and The White House Conference on Aging, and has given testimony several times on training issues before Congress. Other affiliations have included Board of Governors, ASTD; Chairman of the Board of Trustees, Le Mans Academy; Management Development Board, United Technologies; Board of Trustees of the Society of Actuaries Foundation; Chair, National Issues Committee, ASTD; Quality Advisory Committee of ISVOR-Fiat, Turin, Italy; and Management Development Advisory Committee, Capital Holding Corporation. He has a B.A. in History and a master's in Public Administration from the University of Dayton. He has done postgraduate work in human resource management at Indiana University, Ohio State, The George Washington University, and Penn State.

Every human resource department worthy of the name must grapple with issues of employee performance, quality standards, and accountability. In our tool kit are program choices and results, cost control, and cost recovery: the essentials of training organization and management. The internally endorsed guidelines that hold the department manager's priority setting together and guide program facilitation are the rope tying together management decision making.

The rope is there so everyone can get a grip on the mission and task of the organization; so everyone can pull in one direction. The rope is politely called policy. Training policy gives consistency, direction, and common ground to all the players.

Training policy is priority setting in action. Training policy can help the department and its parent company cope with change management on every level: personal, professional, internal, external, global, competitive, industrial, and technical. Corporate realities guarantee that idealistic training policy is fluff and inflexible policy is unrealistic. Training policy must serve and support company mission, culture, markets, industry, and budgets, and recognize internal and external realities even as they change.

We will look at the *training* function of human resource departments separate from the many other services and functions they perform. This subject is more about HR *development* mission and policy than HR *department* mission and policy. This is about program strength and relevance to critical business issues. Our focus is on training and development expertise and resources brought to bear on people's skills as resources.

Our task here is not to argue for one specific mission or approach, but to encourage you to consider the issues and develop the policy tools which

> will help create a proper fit between your department's mission and task and that of your company

> are necessary for survival in the face of a reality that is changing more quickly than ever before

> make training value-added by providing solutions to critical business issues.

Ever more rapid change coming in the next century will make obsolete larger numbers of the workforce as never before. Human resource development is likely to become the major defense against obsolescence and ennui in the twenty-first century. We must start now to make policy that faces that reality.

Creating Training Policy in the Face of Change

The national and international social, economic, and technological factors influencing the practice, management, and even the definition of professional development and training are volatile and uncontrollable. The need for professional and professionally managed HR development was never more clear. But the role, practice, and evaluation of that profession must evolve, too. Human resource development as a discipline and human resource development professionals as individuals cannot pretend to be immune to the change all around them.

In another 10 or 20 years what we do may no longer be called "training" or "the Human Resource Department." But the deliberate development of people's skills as resources in business, industry, and society as a whole has only just begun.[1] Human resource department practice and self-image must evolve to take advantage of the potential those same volatile factors present. Those unstoppable changes must be seen as challenges and opportunities, not roadblocks or temporary blips in an orderly world.

We will discuss these issues with an eye on the opportunities you are likely to face and the choices you may need to make in the next 10 years. You will be asked by reality, employers, and employees to create realistic guidelines that can be changed as necessary, though not on a whim; guidelines that can cope with and adapt to change as it happens.

Establishing Broad Goals

Mission statements are intentionally broad. Policy serves to narrow the overall objective of a well-thought-out mission statement into measurable, achievable, relevant terms.[2] Training department policy should be a practical, adaptable, useful implementation tool; not a straightjacket or control device. A case must be made for the need and value of the creation and maintenance of properly integrated and actively pursued HR development *policy* that can meet the challenges of change on a regular basis.

Trainers and training managers cannot position themselves above the tidal wave of change. Human resource departments must lead the way into the essential and continuous accumulation and improvement of the skills we all need to navigate the uncharted waters of continuous change. Standing on the shore expecting that tidal wave to subside to normalcy will help no one.

Accepting the Fact of Change

As the twenty-first century dawns, no one doubts any more the wisdom of the observation that the only constant is change. Changing economies, changing geopolitical realities, and changing technology are a triple threat to everyone's adaptability. That threat exists on every level: personal, professional, and corporate. To survive we must revitalize humankind's oldest strength: adaptation through innovation.

Our view at Motorola is that the organization and management of the training function must be guided by policy that addresses the need for flexible, ongoing processes for identifying and adapting to that constant of change. Change management through training policy that supports and encourages innovation can be a major contributor to corporate stability and growth and employee loyalty.

Professional Value-Added Opportunities

Only by responding to the challenges before us will the organization and management of the training function be an ever more highly valued player in corporate America. Training department policy and mission must, of course, first of all dovetail with the parent corporation's mission.

To support your company's long- and short-term business goals, ask about the overriding philosophy of the business and review the current scope of your training operations.[3] Then look long and hard at what programs and policies need to be in place for the HR development function to be responsive to the changes occurring inside and outside your company.

This is not about the famous policy quoted by an overworked customer service representative who must explain on the phone to an unsatisfied customer why no refund will be forthcoming. This is about policies that serve as tools and strategies for all concerned to pursue and aid the mission of the department and, by extension, the mission of the company.

Motorola's fundamental objective is Total Customer Satisfaction. Any strategy, plan, process, tool, or policy that can aid and abet that objective will be entertained.

Motorola University's mission has evolved over the years as policies, processes, tools, and resources have evolved. That mission is now stated as:

> To be a major catalyst for change and continuous improvement in support of the corporation's business objectives. We will provide for our clients the best value, leading edge training and education solutions and systems in order to be their preferred partner in developing a Best in Class workforce.[4]

Policy must be a tool, not a burden; a collection of guides, not a handbook of rules. Training policy must observe and react to the entire mosaic of a department, both within the context of its corporate culture and its fit in the marketplace.[5] The training manager must ask about the training and education programs and objectives that exist now: Why do they exist? Why were they created and why are they being sustained?

Dare to ask what should exist. Dream about short-term needs and long-term applications. Ask yourself, your colleagues and your boss, other department heads, workers, and your board, even your company's customers, what does training mean to you?

Such questions are not intended as a detailed needs analysis in relation to any particular problem or opportunity. Instead, the perspective is much broader and seeks to define the mission, objectives, and place within the corporation of the training function. From this base, the various alternatives for organizing the function—and addressing the changing and evolving needs of that organization—can be explored.[6]

Defining Human Resource Development

Trainers and training managers need to be clear about their own definitions of the training function. Professional definitions of training can help determine what trainers should and should not agree to do in an organization. Clear definitions of training can facilitate choices that contribute to professional trainers' overall success.[7]

At Motorola University the board of trustees formulates training policy, sets priorities, allocates resources, and supports the joint ventures of the education and training community. This board is composed of senior corporate managers.

The board of trustees reviews Motorola University's performance against its strategic plans and formulates action plans accordingly. Our regional advisory boards, composed of senior corporate managers, provide geographically specific information which is combined with additional input from Motorola business units to help us define and deliver the highest quality and value in training and educational products.

By publicizing a definition of its mission, a training department can help educate managers and employees about what it can and cannot do. Such ongoing education of managers and employees can build the support for training that is lacking in so many companies.

By publicizing a clear set of policies attuned to that mission, a training department can help managers and employees achieve and maintain that mission. Regular success at making that connection to a mission that all are committed to, and recognition of that success, can motivate as nothing else can.

Nesting Policy in Mission

Creating connections between daily tasks and job satisfaction of all employees can be a major contribution of any HR department. Finding and supporting connections between business's mission and training can be one of the most interesting and important aspects of organizing relevant training efforts. Yet it is frequently minimized or totally ignored, even by seasoned professionals in the field.[8]

The potential payoffs of assuring a linkage between operations, mission, and training are enormous for both the business as a whole and the training function.[9] Well-utilized training and development expertise can spell the difference in survival for many organizations and personal careers. But the same accelerating rate of change that makes mainstreaming of the training mission essential also heightens the challenge and difficulties of performing that mission.

To meet that challenge, training and development practitioners will need broad-ranging professional development as much as their clients and customers. McCullough wrote in the previous edition of this *Handbook* (1987) that all of the field is relatively new and its core of knowledge is still being formulated.[10] In many ways this is still true, but a major cause of that sense of incompleteness is that the policy and mission of HR development as a profession and as a corporate partner has long been a moving target.

Not only are we constantly faced with new and better ways to provide learning opportunities (interactive videodiscs, computer-based instruction, and accelerated learning techniques, to mention a few), but we are also faced with tremendous changes in the workplace.[11] A corporate mission may change a little, tuned and tuned again over time. Department policy may change a lot. But the fundamental task of every organization is the integration of specialized knowledge into a common task.[12] The challenge of good policy making is to keep the focus of all programs, efforts, design, and learning on that common task.

Focusing the Team on the Forest, Not the Trees

New competitive realities are forcing corporate managers to question long-undebated strategies, corporate governance, work organization, and the very purposes and practices of management. Managers are learning to rethink old formulas in the light of new circumstances. Similarly, managers have to know how to test and evaluate new ideas and solutions, distinguishing what is genuinely helpful from what is mere hype.[13]

The human resource manager is charged with helping corporate managers and their staffs develop and sharpen those skills. Building such a learning organization is hard work. Incorporating continuous improvements into everything we do, encouraging employees—and ourselves—to acquire new skills and to work differently, and empowering them to make decisions never happens easily or quickly.

Maintaining an ongoing effort in that direction is a team effort: not just a training department team, not just an executive committee team. Determining a definition of training in an organization should not be a solitary activity. It should be developed through reiterations with management and members of the community.[14] (See Fig. 2-1 for Motorola sources of training requirements process model.)

Our entire society, and business context, is engaged in a long-term cultural transformation that requires unflagging commitment to and unwavering sponsorship of training and development on the part of senior management. In particular, the transformation challenges many managers to unlearn some of the

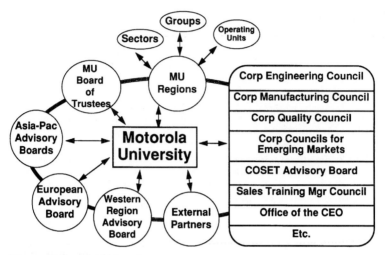

Figure 2-1.   Sources of requirements.

behaviors that previously made them successful. However, managers who embrace an empowering leadership style can expect to gain the commitment of their employees to their mission and policies.[15]

Training personnel and programs should model and encourage the creation of a workplace where employees are empowered to make a difference. But everyone does not draw the same values and goals from their experiences with and perception of their workplace's mission and culture. Observing mission and culture up close does not necessarily give everyone the same tools, the same expectations, or the same answers. Our policies must light the way.

What Should Policy Cover?

Because much of the modern organization is composed of specialists, each with his or her own narrow area of expertise, the organization's mission must be crystal clear. The organization must be single-minded or its members will become confused. They will each define results in terms of their own specialty and try to impose their values on the organization.

Only a focused and common mission will hold the organization together and enable it to produce. Without such a mission, the organization will soon lose credibility and, with it, its ability to attract the very people it needs to perform and prosper.[16] The interaction of training, expectations, and management style are the fabric of the corporate culture and the embodiment of the corporate mission. Training and development policy must aid them all.

Attracting and keeping the people needed must be a major part of what HR department policy addresses. The HR department should assist in the recruitment, retention, and socialization of employees at every level.

Defining Horizons of Change

A training mission statement identifies the principal reason for the existence of the training function and relates this reason to the overall mission of the business. Jerry Pittam wrote in this *Handbook,* third edition (1987), that training mission statements ought to look well beyond a 10-year horizon if they are to justify and contribute to a department's function and relevance.

Less than 10 years later we see that change—change in global realities, technology, educational needs, and much more—are so rapid that 10 years can now be considered dangerously over the horizon. Who would dare try to predict conditions even 10 years from now, of electronic imaging; international tariffs, and competition; computerized, roboticized production; satellite conferencing, training, and human development; virtual reality language immersion classes, vacations, or therapy; ad infinitum?

This is not to say that thinking about 10-year bites of time is useless. Far from it, but for most issues to be addressed by policy making as discussed here, 5-year spans are more than sufficient. The first thing Motorola University efforts taught us was not to look too far ahead. We came to realize that you do a disservice to all concerned by training people in skills they will probably not need for five years or more.[17]

Motorola's training and education policy reads, in part, "In order to ensure that Motorola develops and maintains a best-in-class workforce capable of meeting business needs, a minimum of five days of job relevant training and education will be required for every Motorola employee each year."

These numbers were not arrived at arbitrarily, nor is such an undertaking to be achieved inexpensively. We have more than 130,000 employees worldwide. We currently devote about $120 million per year worldwide to the development and delivery of programs and literature. Motorola University, alone, has 300 full-time training professionals and 600 contract associates. In 1993, 550,000 days of training were delivered to Motorola employees and suppliers' employees worldwide.

Motorola considers education and training an indispensable competitive advantage. Not only does it make possible the maintenance of a "best-in-class workforce," but it also enables our multipronged, effective entry into new and potential markets. The use of training as a marketing initiative in the recruitment and development of employees, partners, and suppliers has also proved, undeniably, to be value-added.

Skill Sets as Capital

As the job skills our changing business world requires become ever more complex, and as adaptability to new job functions and new technology is placed at more of a premium, the challenges inherent in recruiting and keeping skilled workers have increased as well.[18] The advantages of 5- and 10-year foresight require ongoing examination of a road map and the marshaling of skills and resources that your HR department will need to deliver skill sets training as they are needed.

You should try to look 5 to 10 years down the road in order to make decisions within 2 years about developing the training programs needed in 5 to 10 years. Simultaneously you must provide employees with tools and training that fit the situation and organization they deal with in the near future.

In an economy where the only certainty is uncertainty, the one sure source of lasting competitive advantage is knowledge. When markets shift, technologies proliferate, competitors multiply, and products become obsolete almost overnight, successful companies are those that consistently create new knowledge, disseminate it widely throughout the organization, and quickly embody it in new technologies and products. These activities define the knowledge-creating company, whose sole business is continuous innovation.[19] These activities should be defined and promoted by HR development and HR department policy.

Machines, warehouses, trucks, word processors, and factories don't innovate; people innovate. Motivated people dedicated to a mission and guided by intelligent policy, innovate. The most valuable capital is human capital; the most powerful technology is people.[20]

Valuing Intellectual Capital

The time has come to find ways to track and account for knowledge as an asset because it is rapidly becoming the essential ingredient of innovation. Using accounting systems that place values only on materials and labor ignores the primary engine of innovation: intellectual capital.[21]

Measuring and managing the intangible assets of skill and knowledge is not new. Knowing the value of hiring someone with five years' experience over someone with two years' experience proves that intellectual capital has had value as long as there have been résumés. The chief ingredient in this new approach is to consider such intellectual capital to be a measurable part of a corporation's assets.

Intellectual capital is produced when the application of ideas or skills produces higher-valued assets—often new assets, and opportunities, of enormous value. How did we get this far using accounting sheets without a column for intellectual capital?

One of the departments of a corporation that ought to have ideas, skills, and their applications as its stock and trade is the department in charge of human resource development. The primary process of HR development is location and preparation of appropriate knowledge and skill sets; the primary outcome desired by HR development is efficient, useful application of that knowledge. The business of helping people use their brains better is the business and capital of training and development.[22] If innovative HR development professionals can leverage that idea, their future is assured.

Creating Competence

If companies are to command any loyalty, they must include individual development as part of their innovation process. It is safe to assume that everyone will have to acquire new knowledge at the very most every 4 or 5 years or become obsolete.[23] Human resource departments must create policy that encourages and eases contiguous and continuous improvement.

Training is nothing less than the act of creating a superior competence than existed before. The training manager's ability to do so will determine the commitment of subordinates and superiors alike. When trainees look forward to training sessions because of the dynamic and engaging way your department conducts them, the end result will be employees who emerge with confidence and commitment; employees committed to improving themselves on an ongoing basis; employees who are able to perform, and, more important, want to perform the things you have taught them to do.[24]

Cyclical development encourages continuous evolution and reexamination of all training and development elements. Create tools, structure, awareness, and innovations that build and maintain the process as a cycle. Programs and teams can represent circles within circles. Time, resources, and goals can affect the cycle's scale and relationship to other departments and services. But cycles encourage momentum and innovation.

Don't treat policy making or any of these elements as linear. Linear development allows programs to be isolated from each other, from appropriate overview, from fitting into the development of human resources policy and implementation. Linear development leads to too many dead ends and isolated programs.

Building and managing the cycle of HR policy, development, and support that revolves around your company and department mission is how HR departments do their job best. Developing programs, content, and policy which consistently develop and motivate employees to be able and eager to perform well is what HR department *accountability* is about. The creation of successful training policy in the face of change can be seen as the cause and effect of that training success.

Demanding Accountability

Being held accountable; there's the rub. There have to be people who make decisions or nothing gets done. There have to be people who are *accountable* for the organization's mission, its spirit, its performance, and its results.[25] Part of the manager's task in every department and unit of a corporation is to define and tune policies that make good results possible.

What gets debated endlessly is just what is accountability; how to measure success and failure; how to assign and measure responsibility; and how to measure and account for the costs and paybacks of the programs in which we want our company, managers, and workers to invest their time and money. Nowhere are these issues more sensitive than in training and development.

Decisions have to be made about what programs to offer, how to pay for and justify them before the fact, and how to alter or redefine them after the fact. Let's look at the issues of training and development management accountability. What is it? Who is responsible for reporting accountability? Who and what controls training and development content? How carefully must we manage the control of policy and resources? How manageable are costs, and how can we measure the return on the training investment?

What Is Accountability?

Being accountable—for a department, a division, a team, or a unit—can mean keeping track of numbers and interpreting them, setting goals, and measuring results. This responsibility requires the necessary authority to perform those tasks effectively. Every M.B.A. can spout volumes about the proper assignment of accountability in all sorts of business units. But management is still struggling with the assignment of accountability for the products and results of the training function.

What management level should have final approval of course content; of overall training plans; of hiring and promotion; of budgets for course development; of training methodologies?[26]

Accountability for Training of Leaders

While senior management must have considerable authority, in the modern organization neither management in general nor training management in particular should define their job as the need to command action or obedience.[27]

Managers must motivate and lead, not push or demand. Management in the knowledge society of today and tomorrow should focus on nothing less than the encouragement of systematic organizational innovation.[28]

Human resource development departments must equip management to lead and employees to aid and implement innovation. Management at every level must learn to fashion policies, programs, and goals which benefit people and the company, which create encouragement. That is what training and development department accountability is about.

Being accountable for encouragement may seem the height of warm and fuzzy job descriptions and virtually unmeasurable. If training and development managers take on responsibility for encouragement, what happens to hard numbers and accountability?

Western society has granted corporations legal status similar to persons. We talk about a corporation having a mission, objectives, even personality. We have learned that companies can profit from being managed not as machines but as living organisms, organisms that to survive must learn, grow, and adapt.[29]

Much like an individual, a company can have a sense of identity and fundamental purpose. This is the organizational equivalent of self-knowledge—a shared understanding of what the company stands for, where it is going. The knowledge-creating company can be as much about ideals as it is about ideas, a fact which fuels innovation. The essence of innovation is to recreate the world according to a particular vision or ideal. Such an effort works best if that vision is shared by all the individuals involved.[30]

Thus, every employee, from factory floor to chairman of the board, who is consciously pulling as hard as she or he can in the agreed direction is being accountable. Everyone may not agree on what grip to use, how thick the rope should be, or what gloves to wear, but they must all pull together on the same rope. The HR department must provide strong, appropriate rope and enormous amounts of encouragement.

Knowing the Company Culture and Pulse

The best trainers and training managers take time to find sources of information that allow continuing examination of the structure, culture, and decision-making processes of their firm.[31] Many of the changes tracked may seem subtle, especially in the face of rapid changes in markets and technology. But this is like a master sailor listening to the creaks and groans of his ship at sea. Any noise that hasn't been heard before signals a change worth looking into. Such inspection and attention is necessary to know when any policy rope is wearing thin!

Don't dismiss company statements about missions, trends, policies, and strategic plans regardless of format. Everything from speeches by senior management to carefully phrased annual reports can offer information about hopes, intentions, temperature, and pulse. Documents intended for internal and external consumption can help clarify training and development needs, present and future.[32] Don't ignore the hopes and dreams postulated even in a high-flying press release. If you are to be accountable, if you are to provide the programs *most* needed and the policy rope for *all* to pull on, you must track current physical conditions *and* dreams and hopes.

The objective of all such pulse taking and subsequent training effort is nothing less than the creation of better products, better services, and better organizations. Getting maximum return on the investment of salary, benefits, facilities, and training from each employee requires full use of each employee's talents and ideas.[33] But that takes time and deliberate effort. Ways must be found to get employees, at every level, to be committed to their own corporate and professional goals.[34]

Peter Drucker didn't stop with the claim that modern management must not command. He went on to say that managers must inspire. Inspiration can be cultivated by policies that encourage enthusiasm and everyone pulling on the rope together.

Motorola instituted the Six Sigma Quality Program to accomplish that. In the late eighties we attempted to go from 6000 defects per million parts or steps to 3.4 defects per million in 5 years. While this goal looked like an enormous one, possibly unattainable, overall Motorolans have responded by being motivated, enthusiastic, and proud. In short, inspired. We went on to win the Malcolm Baldrige National Quality Award in 1988. The processes of that turnaround were the origins of Motorola University.[35] Today, MU is a major player in the Motorola product, service, and employee quality effort.

Taking Individual Pulses

Employees must be treated well, in ways that they expect and appreciate. If they are not, don't be surprised when many of your better people leave for the competition.[36] The management and training magazines and journals are full of case studies that demonstrate this fact over and over. Respect, reward, and recognition are paramount in retention efforts. Thoughtful, value-packed training and development programs are essential to that respect, reward, and recognition. Meanwhile, in the last decade of the twentieth century there are corporations, some actually profitable, who still deal with their employees as faceless cogs. This benefits no one.

Good treatment of employees means valuing their efforts and intentions, supporting them with internal resources that help them get their jobs done and help them learn to do their jobs better even as those jobs change. Measuring, tracking, and managing the training and development department's role in that process is another way for training managers to be accountable to the corporation and to individual customers.

Gaining Wide Support

Meeting the challenges of constant change and the promise of the twenty-first century means creating and managing new knowledge. That should be part of the mission of any training and development effort. Done well, creating new knowledge requires a virtually nonstop process of personal and organizational self-renewal.

Such a wide-ranging effort cannot be accomplished, let alone managed, by one department or isolated authority, whether marketing, strategic planning, executive committees, or training and development. Inventing new knowledge is not a specialized activity, but part and parcel of the whole-company mission and policy making that drives excellence and quality.[37]

Inventing, defining, and packaging new knowledge may be the primary mission of a training and development department, especially knowledge that boosts and even redefines competence. But an organization's context and resistance to new competencies can short-circuit the best of efforts. This is another reason for training and development managers to keep a finger on the pulse of every aspect of their organization's culture.

Your training programs may be elegant, the content welcomed, and the intent appreciated. But if the context of people's work lives does not also change, even your best training efforts will be seen by many as a waste of time.[38] Overcoming the attitude that training is usually a waste of time is a colossal undertaking.

At Motorola the development of training programs starts with the identification of critical business issues. This assures the clear and firm connection of training programs to reality and the true needs of the business. All that corporate mood investigation, culture awareness, pulse taking, and task research mentioned above can be directed at identification of those critical business issues.

Change management must be a corporatewide, systemwide effort. Accountability means doing all you can from your vantage point in training and development, as leader, scout, and team player. That includes managing the cultural underpinnings of an organization to encourage the policies and support necessary for pertinent and successful training and development. Devoting time and resources to that effort wastes no one's time, but the wider and deeper that support, the better.

The Value of Culture Awareness

Culture awareness serves another important function in your efforts to cultivate wide support. You may find yourself in a position of having to sell your programs and services internally. This situation is not necessarily bad if it is an understood element in the culture. Accountability then encourages measuring the sales success, product quality, and desirability of your training and development programs. These things are all worth taking time to document, but to sell well you have to know what audience will respond to what features and benefits. Learn about the players and their needs; recognize how things get done. Learn who has decision-making power over what issues.[39]

Your selling job becomes a matter of paving the way for ideas and programs and selling the benefits of attendance to your intended audiences. If staff and budget allow, follow up with evaluations, coaching and applications services to aid continuous improvement of trainees, trainers, and programs.

Human resource departments must cultivate support at all levels of the organization. This activity is not merely a defense against budget cutting, but it is essential in everyday efforts to market programs and services and to measure accountability. Widespread support can help guard against unexpected evaluation results, changes in funding, or disregard of efforts or programs in place.[40]

You must seek true support, however, not tolerance or lip service. Time spent by training managers to cultivate the support and participation of other managers is invaluable. If you have confidence in the quality and relevance of the programs you are selling, gaining manager participation, attendance, and support should pay dividends in many ways.

Middle Managers as Allies

Support should be sought and cultivated at every level, but do not minimize the support and resource value of middle managers in other departments. Middle managers are usually closest to the major information intersections of any company.[41]

They often have to mediate between what is and what should be, making them primary players in creating and managing change. This in no way is intended to dilute the power and impact of top management's commitment to change programs. But it is often middle managers who have the task of forging connections between reality and company vision.[42]

At Motorola, no one is above or beyond the need for training and development. Each Motorola manager owns the need and benefits of training for his or her people. The content, direction, depth, and application of that training is up to each employee and his or her supervisor.

Even in companies where much of the responsibility for training decisions and assignment is owned by other department managers and individual workers, every training program is a training department product of which you and your people must be proud. Every step in the process must show that. Every step should be addressed and enhanced by your marketing strategy.[43] The insights and support of middle managers should be recruited to accomplish this goal. Your department's control over program creation and presentation is a matter of accountability, responsiveness, and professionalism.

Your professionalism can also be used to get feedback from senior managers. Needs assessments need not be done only with surveys, think tanks, and focus groups. You can arrange meetings with department managers and senior managers, one or two at a time, to quite openly ask them about their departments' training and development needs. If they don't volunteer problems you can address, be prepared to question them about their critical business issues.

Controlling the Welcome Mat

The opposite of fighting those who seek to cut training budgets almost as a reflex is working with those who think that training can fix virtually anything. Controlling your training department's resources and owning whatever programs you do deliver also means knowing when to short-circuit unrealistic expectations.[44]

Expanding training department services should be encouraged. Trainers who can help managers at every level focus as much on organizational macrogoals as well as department microdynamics should be welcomed as professionals by other department managers. The middle managers at those intersections should be first in line. This is precisely the way in which accountability, resources, and authority are blended and managed across unit lines.

Managing Costs

One part of the control and accountability equation that consistently causes training managers nightmares is managing and justifying costs. Different organizations use different ways to track and account for their costs. Several means of tracking costs and income have been developed, including the return on investment (ROI).[45] The day is here when a basic program on a computer disk will be able to track and compute the full range of costs for trainers. Computing training's value can get complicated, but it cannot be ignored.

Development costs include needs assessments, writing and evaluation, materials research and program design time, materials development and production, writing and preparation, and more. These costs can then be spread over per-participant or per-program numbers. Repeat of a new program over time usually helps lower the scale of the investment.

A program intended for a cadre of 26 executives might require an investment of 100 hours to develop the materials and expertise to deliver it. Three months later another class of newly promoted executives may take the same program. Six months later that program could require substantial revision and updating to be used again. Was that 100-hour investment justified? Do you need policies to determine when an outside trainer-consultant should be hired? Or is each case worth analyzing on its own merits?[46]

Tracking Training Investment

The kinds of documentation that good trainers typically engage in can also be used to track and justify costs. Every planning step and resource used can be converted into a cost factor. But beware of record keeping that becomes so time-consuming as to become its own resource-gobbling line item.

There, currently, does not seem to be any accepted standard or "chart of accounts" for quantifying training costs. Lots of thought may have gone into this at hundreds, if not thousands, of organizations. But the computations for "training costs" at different organizations are rarely comparable with any accuracy. You might attempt to keep costs in the same format as other functions in your organizations. Confer with your budget chief, comptroller, or accounting department. They may open numerous doors of tracking opportunity for you.

Having regular quantification of all the time, energy, and expertise expended to produce programs, materials, and consulting services will be an excellent tool for justifying existing budgets. Justifying the value of the programs that your budget produces, however, is another matter entirely, discussed below under quality and relevance.

Cost justification is tied to program and department effectiveness. Does training program content get integrated quickly and smoothly into job performance? Are attendees more efficient, productive, or effective in any measurable way? Do training and development program attendance contribute to individual job satisfaction? Do your attendees and their supervisors think the attendees learned valuable skills or insights?[47]

Sometimes the answer to a lot of these questions is no, because the programs offered are too far ahead of expected changes. As we discussed earlier, preparing people for changes in market, strategies, products, or processes too long before those new skills are needed lessens the value and eventual application of the training. However, much of the cost of substantial and enthusiastically delivered training and development programs can be justified by something seemingly as simple as lowered absenteeism.

You can also measure and justify the investment in training through increased customer satisfaction and employee retention. You might need a control group to prove the true scale of the impact, but if you feel that the cost benefits are unquestionable, finding a way to quantify them consistently could be a very valuable exercise.

Customer *and* employee satisfaction and retention are valuable goals in every sense. The best training and development consistently works toward both simultaneously.

> The ultimate success of the Motorola University mission depends on the commitment of Motorolans—to take action to become a world-class workforce to ensure that Motorola remains Best in Class. This can and will happen through a dedication to continuous learning. Motorola University provides the means—Motorolans must provide the initiative.[48]

In a way, we have come full circle. Getting your own employees to exhibit the kinds of initiative mentioned here is similar to creating the encouragement discussed earlier. Encouragement produces initiative; initiative produces innovation, innovation produces effective change; successful change management produces increased job satisfaction and effective encouragement.

The Limits of Accountability

Many executives look to HR development to solve or resolve issues that they cannot seem to fix in other ways. Being professional, optimistic, and committed educators can take trainers and training managers a long way, both professionally and personally. But beware of targets and goals that are too small or too big: projects that offer only limited potential for organizational impact; goals that take on the sacred cows of a corporate culture.

This is not to say that organizational redefinition is impossible. After all, the millions of words written about change management aren't all wrong. But accountability without commitment from the controllers of all the resources and attitudes required to do the job will guarantee failure.

Those attitudes may be locked into the roles that people believe the organization requires of them. Some of that mindset is, of course, wrought by corporate culture, and that is a very difficult thing to change. But rewiring the organizational context can force people to experiment with new attitudes and behaviors.[49] Hopefully, the new behaviors will not be defensive. Part of your job is to help people avoid or overcome the natural reaction of defensiveness.

All these issues of context, accountability, cost, authority, and control are showcased very well in a case study reported in the November 1993 issue of *Bank Marketing Magazine*. Barbara Haas reported on a single bank's successful effort at completely overhauling the content, style, and organization of their training and development efforts. The existing programs had been bad-mouthed by employees for some time, and were created and delivered by three departments which fought over limited resources. The confusing training and lack of morale was defined as a marketing and public relations problem.

In mid-1989, management completely unpacked the existing system. A new department was created with a director who would report to the senior vice president of marketing. The new director was positioned in the organization on the same level as managers responsible for advertising, public relations–employee communications, quality service, and product management–marketing research.

The new department asked the employees what training they needed. New classes were created to meet those needs. Experienced employees were invited to be trainers and contribute to course content and design. Senior management fully supported these programs, sending positive signals that training was important.

Enthusiastic internal marketing of the programs and opportunities improved participation, attendance, and morale. This result was accomplished partly by the training manager's willingness to ask peers in advertising and public relations for assistance with print materials. Other department heads gained new respect for the trainer's presentation skills. Greatly expanded interdepartmental use of one another's expertise improved employee morale, integrated effort, and customer satisfaction. Cost justification was never an issue.

Making Development Pay

High-speed change is nothing new. Changes in technology have been accelerating since the early seventies and booming since the early eighties. Changes in political climate, international trade, and law have been in flux for decades and in turmoil since the late eighties. Corporate investment in some mix of training, education, and development is fast becoming a necessity. If your company decides to take a pass now, they will drown in their inability to attract and keep the personnel they need at *every* level, to compete and survive in the high-tech, instant access, global economy of the next one hundred years.

Your training department mission statement might be long-term and global, but your policies had better recognize and support aggressive, ongoing training and development if your career and your company are to have a future.

Those training and development efforts must be appropriate, relevant, and of measurable quality. Let's look at that now.

Guaranteeing Quality and Relevance

Quality, relevance, and broad support are the triumvirate of good training and development policy. Your policy concepts and program management must create and support all three. Many of the problems you may be having right now can be traced to missing pieces of one of those three elements.

Quality materials, instruction, and follow-up are all to be eagerly sought. But quality programs with irrelevant or mismatched content produce only hollow results.

The relevance of content can be guided with rich needs assessment. But excellent topic choices will fall flat if attendees find low-quality materials, exercises, presentation, or follow-up. Relevance, too, applies to topics and pre- and posttesting, materials, venues, trainers, and materials.

Relevant topics delivered to the wrong audience, or through the wrong choice of program style, will fail, costing you support, respect, and resources. Relevance requires attention to the needs of the individual; her or his career, the job that person is asked to do, the reality of the marketplace, the technology, and the social context that is changing so rapidly.

Broad Support Is an Equal Partner

Relevance and quality can both be more easily attained if you have taken the time to gain broad support. Support will get you more honestly answered needs assessment instruments and better quality and relevance feedback. But, as mentioned above, beware of support that throws problems in your lap, problems for which you cannot deliver solutions.

Cultivating broad support, consistent quality, and relevant topics, services, and details will drive you in the direction of rewards, recognition, and respect. Smart policies can help you in every category. Smart policies get all your people pulling on the right rope in the right direction. Quality and relevance come from creating and delivering training programs and development opportunities of the greatest use to your organization's mission. Assuring that connection has a lot to do with training department accountability.

Managing and Measuring Quality and Relevance

High expectations are all well and good. You should have them for your people and programs. Your boss is likely to have them for you. Delivering on high expectations is what keeps you in your job and keeps the rewards coming.

Managing department personnel, programs, and resources to meet those high expectations includes the care and feeding of appropriate policies.

Some companies have decided that relevance means creating remedial reading or writing programs because they can't hire enough people with basic communications skills. Other companies, such as Xerox, have decided that offering training to their suppliers' workers is an excellent way to improve product quality and customer satisfaction. A few companies, such as Motorola, create supplier-customer training partnerships in the shared quest for ever-improving quality.

Whomever the audience you are charged with serving, they are your training department's customers. Treat your training department programs as products that must provide customer satisfaction and you will find ways to measure and manage quality and relevance.

Funding People and Program Improvement

Needs assessments, focus groups, pre- and posttests, and surveys will help you use your resources to maximize your own customers' satisfaction. If one of your goals is continuous improvement of employee productivity, your training and education programs must also undergo continuous improvement.

Constant improvement may be a misnomer. What we're all doing is chasing the creation and maintenance of a perfect fit with an ever-changing reality. You may, however, be part of a corporate culture that says If it's not broken, don't fix it. Training programs that are seen as already excellent may get ignored when it comes to funding for improvement. The constant of change makes this oversight a serious error. Paul S. Adler in "Time and Motion Regained"[50] explores a training and development experiment which attempted to achieve three primary goals—the kind of thing I have called here "policies"—in a companywide training program. Every program has to (1) improve overall quality and productivity, (2) involve workers in the design of their work, and (3) capture and institutionalize continuous improvement. Such goals serve workers, management, and the viability of the whole organization. They can also make it possible to manage and measure quality and relevance.

Pursuing Relevance

No one can rebuild a corporate culture in a day. This fact has not stopped some people from trying. Adaptation to change and new learning does not occur in a vacuum. Getting to know your corporate culture can enable you to adapt more easily. If you know how to read between the lines, you will know which must-have outcomes really have priority. You can then manage your own department strategies and policies to match. Relevant, not to mention useful, programs result most often from clear program goals.[51]

Look carefully at your department's measures of success. Find ways to demonstrate their effect on the never-ending parade of critical business issues and the bottom line. Take time to communicate your successes internally; make sure management gets the message about training and development's place in the culture of respect, reward, and recognition.

Meanwhile, selling your programs by creating high expectations may increase your chances for successful programs. Those expectations have to be realistic, but they can help make significant gains in attendance and participation. Aggressively selling programs in advance stacks the deck of appreciation and relevance in your favor.

Use honest record keeping to back up your claims of success *and* relevance. Argue what the numbers mean, if you like, but clear all the categories with committees and superiors, and keep those records immaculately. Know in advance what reports for what audience are expected on an annual basis, and plan accordingly.[52]

Careful record keeping will not only allow you to generate appropriate reports as needed but will also enable you to perform market research on everything from demand and applicability to development costs. Your sales efforts, creation of truly relevant programs, and upgrading of existing programs in appropriate directions are all linked.

Funding Program Improvement

The key word is *improvement* as separate from program development. There are managers who readily approve expenditures for the development costs of wholly new programs before approving expenditures to fine-tune or improve the productivity of existing programs.

We are all learning to live with constant change, and the process of continuous improvement is certainly central to policies that organize and manage the training function. But throwing out your playbook every six months is not the answer. Incremental program improvement should be a standard, welcomed, recognized line item in every training department budget.

Motorola University continuously searches for innovative ways to leverage each and every employee's creativity and potential for learning for both personal and corporate benefit. Our commitment to continuous learning grows out of our conviction that Total Customer Satisfaction means to anticipate customer needs even as they change, as accurately and seamlessly as possible. Motorola University contributes to that mission by encouraging and supporting all the processes of continuous learning.[53]

Motorola defines personal and corporate continuous learning as a process of constant renewal. We provide our employees with the opportunity to acquire all of the knowledge, skills, and tools necessary to fulfill the corporate mission: Total Customer Satisfaction. We cannot ask Motorolans to dedicate themselves to such a rigorous effort unless we are willing to devote the resources necessary to give their efforts every chance to succeed. Thus, we strive to make every part of the trainee's experience best-in-class: materials, presentations, follow-up, evaluation devices, instructors, teaching strategies, delivery mechanisms, content, and facilities.

The culture, the resources, and the mindset of every department and function of Motorola, corporatewide and worldwide, is subject to the rigors of Six Sigma analysis: phone service, food service, factory floor, products, and customer satisfaction. Even the coffee offered during breaks in training has quality measures applied to it by the food service.

Managing Revitalization Processes

Managing the training and development process requires some of the same combinations of focus and intent as the managing of a corporate unit as a whole. These include coordination, commitment, and the development of new cooperative competencies; coordination of training product development opportunities; commitment to team accomplishment, that pulling on the same rope policy again; and the competencies that continually update the knowledge and skills needed to create and deliver training that is wanted and needed. When well done and properly coordinated, such effort can pay for improvement and virtually guarantee quality and relevance. It can pay for itself through increased productivity and job satisfaction for every unit and individual exposed to it.

Creating and Meeting Appropriate Expectations

Part of the selling of programs is creating appropriate expectations, which can start with needs assessments. Broad participation in the assessment of needs and programs can create positive feelings toward the value of the programs offered. In most larger firms, the broader the input solicited, the better received the resulting programs and their upgrading.[54]

Some revitalization efforts are enhanced by using recognized, external sources of expertise. This strategy is especially important when you are introducing more radical or controversial programs, even if the needs assessments has suggested that people are ready and willing to entertain such ideas.[55] Trying to champion controversial notions from inside an organization may wreak havoc on your hard-won broad support.

Some training departments restrict their customer definition by paying more attention to the attitudes and needs of the managers of departments than the practical needs of workers.[56] At Motorola University we feel that anyone whose skills, attitudes, or performance is expected to change as the result of participation in the training and education offered is our customer.

Managing Objectives

Processes and management styles legitimately vary from company to company. But your own department's productivity and impact should be measured by the results your programs have on morale and productivity. This goes back to the record keeping mentioned above. Managing a revitalization process requires finding ways to bring every member of every team up to speed, including management teams.

The Motorola Chief Executive Office and other senior managers are involved in making decisions about education, and they often facilitate training themselves. Advisory boards at corporate, regional, and unit levels ensure that Motorolans receive the right training, at the right time, in an environment conducive to learning. But this top-down commitment and involvement is intended to assure that training and its benefits are recognized and supported, not merely obeyed or enforced.

Feedback and input about specific needs are welcomed at every level and channeled through corporate council advisory boards in Quality, Manufacturing, Engineering, Software, and Science. This is symptomatic of the scope and scale of Motorola's commitment of resources to training, development, and education.

Building such companywide support has two primary benefits. One, any divergence between individual needs and top management's needs can be better minimized. The thorough attention that the Motorola corporate culture now pays to individual training and development helps assure alignment of personal and corporate goals and increases the value attributed to that educational effort.

Two, wide support is needed for long-term, consistent development of qualified, knowledgeable, resourceful people capable of creating and implementing innovation. Finding and keeping such employees has never been more important than now.

Aiming High

The training and educational opportunities that an employer offers should not only be first-rate, but should be integrated with reward, recognition, and other motivation efforts. Training that is valued by the recipients will build loyalty as well as productivity.[57] First-rate training builds in its own success.

The primary message of this chapter, if not this entire handbook, is that the speed of change already evident in technology and competition requires any corporation committed to excellence to pay at least equal attention to training and development as they do to markets and to product research and development.[58]

If broad support for quality training and educational programs and opportunities is not part of the culture of your organization, your organization is likely to fall ever further behind as the competitive environment continues to change around it. Half-hearted training becomes part of the problem, not the solution.

Guaranteeing Quality and Relevance

The regular appearance of innovation and offices and plants full of eager, delighted employees is all the evidence you need to prove the successful delivery of relevant and quality training. The training department can and should be both model and facilitator of innovation. To do that consistently requires the broad support mentioned above.

Does your HR department guide, if not control, recruitment? Is one of the prehire traits sought, across the board, the ability and willingness to grow, learn, and adapt? Is on-the-job training delivered, planned, and/or monitored by professional trainers?

Are people often managed by criticism? Are people rewarded and recognized for effort and innovation? Are goals and rewards worth striving for? Are worker reward programs seen as an unfair share of the benefits of extraordinary effort?

How can the training department overcome such obstacles to improvement and higher productivity? Employees at every level must feel that all and any rewards are equitable. This means that serving the corporate good must have personal benefits. All the talk about loyalty and teamwork will be hollow if individuals, at any level of the corporation, feel that they cannot personally share in the results of greater effort and success. The concern is not just about salaries and bonuses but intangible recognition and reward.[59]

There are still many companies at which such an undertaking is a large order. Whether the audience addressed or the support sought is blue collar, white collar, or clerical, or consists of supervisors, middle managers, or executives, the training department must lead the charge toward altering people's internal maps of reality. The communications expertise that trainers and developers are expected to have puts that task on their plate.

Training and development must communicate new insights, new knowledge, and new approaches in ways that help people see the world in sharper focus. The need for and measurement of quality and relevance of training and development grow directly out of your need for your audience to appreciate the value of the insights and knowledge you offer them.[60]

One way to accomplish this objective is to find ways for the employees to own the company mission and vision. Broad vision statements can help by allowing, if not encouraging, individuals to attach themselves to whatever word or phrase strikes their fancy. The company vision must be broad enough to offer employees room to prioritize their own goals.[61]

It's like that policy rope; not only does it not matter whether or not everyone wears gloves, it does not matter where on the rope they take hold. All that matters is that everyone is pulling on the same rope in the same direction.

Connecting Guarantees to Accountability

All this talk about training departments demonstrating leadership and innovation is not to suggest that the training department can be all things to all departments. Building broad support while also assuring quality and relevance may require recruiting content experts internally.

The training expert can judge if the content expert requires a little or a lot of coaching and support in delivery.[62] You need never be seen as passing the buck; be seen as a team player who knows when to pass the baton.

The contexts and interrelationships of sales, markets, laws, customs, borders, and technology are all moving. The only way to keep a high success rate is for your company, its people, and its policies to keep moving, too. However, change must not be made for its own sake but in response to targets that never stand still.

It has been said many times but has never been more true: if your company, your people, or your policies are standing still, they are losing ground. For any corporation to endure, its people must value the company. Training policy that serves management prerogatives, organizational mission, and individuals' needs in the face of continuous change is training policy that endures. Let's look at that endurance, now.

Creating Training Policy That Endures

The corporate mission that assumes continuous improvement in productivity, products, customer satisfaction, and employees must also assume continuous improvement in the quality, relevance, and support of training and development. Managing resources and leading people in the face of continuous change is accomplished by guiding continuous change toward improved strategies that serve the company's mission. That's the secret of responding to change with continuous innovation, not change for its own sake. The only way to keep up with moving targets and contexts is for companies, their people, and their policies to keep moving, too.

The modern corporation has been declared to be on its deathbed at least a dozen times in the last 30 years. The naysayers have predicted that virtually all large corporations will go the way of the dinosaur, largely replaced by thousands of small centers of production and specialization. Millions of individuals, they predict, will be working from home, using high-tech, low-cost computers, each doing work once done by office workers gathered by the hundreds and thousands in glass towers.

While much of that has come to pass, there still seems to be endeavors that only large, complex organizations can accomplish. The waves of change already upon us will certainly alter the height of corporate hierarchies and affect how work is organized, delivered, and measured. But I believe that corporations as some kind of organized entity will be with us for some time to come.

However, the nature of the relationships within corporations, the skills needed to manage them, and the policies needed to keep them viable must evolve. One hundreds years from now most successful corporations may be virtually unrecognizable to today's organization man or woman, but there will be corporations.

If the corporation as an idea is not to outlive its usefulness, the training and education of the people necessary to its viability must not outlive their usefulness. Well-done, relevant training, development, and education are essential. Human resource professionals must define and pursue their mission aggressively and with full institutional support, guided by training department policy that endures in the face of constant change.

Training Policy as Management Tool

The creation of enduring training and development policy should not suggest a search for a holy grail of policy or an immutable mission. Policy that endures means policies and policy-making machinery that recognizes and adapts to ever-changing challenges; policies that recognize the need to adapt to evolving reality and the need for change.

This means that HR development policy had better address the development needs of people at all levels of decision making and participation in the company, including human resource development professionals. As corporate hierarchies continue to flatten, managers will need broader skills to manage the remaining resources at their command. The workers, blue collar and white collar, experienced and newly recruited, will need broader skills and subsets of skills. The initiative to create innovation and adaptability to innovation will be paramount requirements.

A valued skill in training managers will be the ability to recognize and/or measure trainability and adaptability. The great managers of the twenty-first century will have to be organizers, planners, and teachers who can simultaneously empower their employees while encouraging ongoing development and training.[63]

Whether you consider your company's business to be global or local, motivating people to want to learn is part of the training and development mission. Encouraging the creation of the tools and opportunities for development should be embodied in policies integral to a culture of encouragement. Large-scale, institutionalized efforts are being made in this direction already, some very successfully.

At Motorola, we chose to call our major retraining and culture realignment effort a university. We wanted people to rethink their assumptions, to have high expectations for themselves, their training experience, and our training staff. Motorola University is charged, literally and figuratively, with working toward those goals of motivation and encouragement by selling and providing tools for personal and professional development.

The TSB Retail Banking and Insurance Company encouraged its human resources department to turn into a coaching and counseling department. This effort included encouraging managers to become active learners and instructor-guides to the people they supervise. The TSB HR department crafted new policies, in response, which would encourage an end to passive training, moving toward daily work experience examination techniques that foster continuous learning. They had to rewrite training policies, strategies, and structures, find new resources, and create new networks of support and encouragement. So far, their efforts have largely been met with enthusiasm and applause.[64]

Grappling with large corporate changes, even those recognized as necessary, means creating a climate that welcomes change. Such an undertaking includes accepting and learning from success and failure. Department and unit managers who are managing this effort successfully have usually learned to pick a compass point, not to specify solutions. Even at the training department level this method can mean using policy and tool choices to guide outcomes, not dictating the shape and color of those outcomes.[65]

Managers of change know that trying to define how the organization or process will look after those changes take place is very risky business. Part of the application and acceptance of innovation in response to change is to also accept that innovations are just another step in the change process, a process that never stops. The ongoing effect requires constant reality checks and needs assessments. Who would have guessed 20 years ago that in-house training departments would find it necessary to offer ongoing remedial reading and math classes as well as graduate-level management programs?

In that same 20 years we have seen workers at every level rise to seniority, if not leadership, who are being asked to master and apply skills that they probably never studied at all in their formal school years. In fact, for probably the first time in the history of western civilization, we have millions of experienced workers who must be taught to use skills, science, and technology that did not exist when they were in school.

The speed of change in our social and professional lives has already reached the point where specialty degrees such as accounting, and even advanced degrees such as an M.B.A., fade in practical value less than 10 years after graduation if degree holders do not regularly extend and exercise their skills.

For our organizations to thrive we must learn how to use training policy as a management tool. We must learn to gracefully abandon products, policies, and practices that are outdated or in other ways holding back achievement of our mission.[66] What training policy must never abandon is our people, their loyalty, their potential, and their need for encouragement.

Training Policy as an Organizational Tool

No matter what industry your firm is in or what the scope of the market you seek, you should constantly monitor the fit between your employee's talents and the corporate structure. In larger companies and multisite, let alone global, organizations this balancing act may be a delicate one.

As companies grow, key managerial functions tend to move away from the corporate center, toward the markets they serve. This course requires ever better lines of communication, reportage, and needs assessment if senior management and training and development are to best serve their own organization.[67]

Effective change management brings additional pressure for decentralization. Most companies are finding that change management must include quick responses to the changing reality that everyone is supposed to be watching so closely. What good does it do to observe and recognize change if your organization does not also cultivate the ability to respond quickly to those changes?

Peter Drucker suggests in *The Learning Imperative* that functions which tend to migrate away from the corporate center are moving closer to the market, and thus closer to opportunities for innovation.[68] Training and management policy should encourage that movement. Have the people closest to the problem at least participate, if not actually manage, the creation and implementation of solutions.

This idea does not apply only to global or multiplant operations, nor is it a new one. Remmele Engineering of Minnesota has encouraged their employees to want and to seek training on state-of-the-art equipment and concepts since its founding in 1949. They have taken to heart the idea that you can get the best performance and the most stable workforce by hiring the best potential applicants, supplying the right tools, and staying out of the employees' way. Remmele encourages its employees to decide how to do their jobs and allows them to change processes as necessary with a minimum of oversight.[69]

The nature and speed of change of the last 20 years has given Remmele management the challenge of tracking and providing the tools and training that fit their employees' view of what is needed to accomplish that continuous improvement. But their basic HR development philosophy has not needed to change.

Drucker, however, also insists that while a unit must be bonded by language, culture, history, or locality to be considered a community, he defines corporations by their tasks. The reality of specialized language, corporate culture and history, and even the sense of locale, can easily form bonds of community in any corporation's employees.

If you are seeking ways to reduce turnover and absenteeism, and to increase performance and loyalty, you must recognize the power and reality of that sense of community. Every organization has the potential to create a sense of community in its employees. Moreover, if that community consistently rewards and recognizes effort, innovation, and personal development, you'll get loyalty far beyond your expectations.

Look at the annual lists of so-called great places to work. Employees at these places, long-term and new, speak of a powerful sense of family and community. The employees at every level share a fierce loyalty engendered by many things, sometimes including vision and mission.

But the most common element at these places is the sense of being respected, recognized, and rewarded. Management at those companies is reaping that to which it has paid attention. This fact is why management by criticism doesn't work in the long term: you just get more of what you pay attention to.

No company can survive without the hundreds or thousands of workers who show up regularly and pay attention to doing a good job.[70] They keep doing it because they are recognized for doing it. They are loyal because their efforts are applauded and encouraged. Many people may feel like strangers in their own neighborhoods, but at work they have friends, support mechanisms, reward, and society. Their workplace is a community of values, people, and culture.[71]

The Fel-Pro Corporation's sense of community and intertwining of work, family, and community is so complete that they have created and funded on-site child care. They don't defend such an investment. They wonder why thousands of other companies are not doing the same thing.

Federal Express quickly built a culture of hard work and customer satisfaction. That the company grew quickly and shared the rewards doesn't hurt their loyalty index. But growing companies guard their success by hiring people who will contribute to their growth and by doing all they can not to hire people likely to be along just for the ride. Group, team, and personal contributing becomes part of the workplace culture. The success of the culture and the encouragement and recognition of individual contributions creates community.

Nabisco created an education initiative that put into action the primary findings of dozens of educational research field studies. Overall, the studies concluded, the more attention parents pay to their children's daily progress, the better the children do in school. Nabisco (as of late summer 1992) gives workers time off for their children's school activities, encourages parents' involvement in school issues, and trains employees to make contributions to those activities.

The benefits include happier working parents, loyal and enthusiastic workers, and people who see hope for their own future and that of their children. Nabisco has also contributed to the creation of future employees who will be better able to cope and perform against very stiff competition. Such a program, if supported, nurtured, and kept aligned with reality, will see some of its effects in the hiring prospects coming through their doors 10 and 20 years from now. Nabisco has defined its culture and created community, loyalty, and values with one program.

Seek out case studies, articles, and books about successful training management, philosophies, and programs that have helped companies thrive and prosper: Federal Express, Remmele, Fel-Pro, Motorola, Nabisco, Xerox, Arthur Anderson, Caterpillar, and many more. Each of these companies is learning to create training and development policies that can adapt and endure in the face of continuous and ever-more-rapid change. They are preparing for the twenty-first century.

Managing Policy in the Face of Continuous Change

The graceful abandonment of outdated products, policies, and practices can be a two-edged sword. If we rush change, we may give up on programs or products that only need a tune-up to gain new relevancy. The willingness to submit to change should not be used as an excuse to contribute regularly to the trash heap of abandoned ideas, programs, or materials.

Being willing to abandon virtually any effort means facing the reality that change management must be well integrated into the processes and culture of the organization. However, this ought not to be taken for deliberate fickleness or change for its own sake. Training and development leadership champions should focus on outcomes and mission, not on programs or policy. Human resource development professionals should champion reality checks, ongoing needs assessments and continuous learning; quality, relevance, and broad support; and respect, reward, and recognition. Policy and policy management are just tools to that end.

Building a motivated workforce and getting those encouragement processes running well can be very time-consuming.[72] Don't expect overnight results from anything discussed here. Bringing continuous learning programs and resources up to the speed of continuous change is a delicate process. Never forget that the very target we are tracking is by definition a moving target.

Tracking and adapting to continuous change is like trying to dock your capsule to an orbiting space station. You may eventually be linked to the space station, but your forward velocity, attitude, altitude, and the vectors of the stresses threatening to pull you apart are still changing.

The mission of training and development policies should be to make those stresses and forces as visible and as manageable as possible. We do so by bringing as many talents and resources to the job as we can muster.

Training department needs assessments and reality checks should tell us when it is time to act purely as training and development specialists and when it is time to act as change and communications consultants. We must pay attention to our own training and development so that if our readings of market reality and corporate needs assessment warrant it, we can also act as organizational development consultants. Chasing those moving targets means we, as HR development professionals, must be willing to move and change, too. We are faced with walking the line while influencing the line that we walk.

The policies, strategies, and mission of training and development programs and departments must respond to the organization they serve. If you are doing your job well, you will at certain times feel that you are functioning as the organization's metacognitive voice. Analyzing and dictating behavior even as you perform and change that behavior is corporate metacognition at its purest.

All efforts and strategies, all goal setting and objectives, must focus on customer and company needs as seen in the bright light of clear-eyed reality. Ever-changing policy serves best when it connects training and development solutions to those critical business issues and to the mission and culture of the company.

Conclusion

The image of policy as rope for all to pull on can easily be dismissed as effort spent creating rope that only ties down the champions, leaders, and innovators who need to be unleashed if change is to be met head on. I'm asking you to consider policy making and policy management as rope that creates handholds and support for all well-intentioned members of a corporate culture.

Training and development policy must create handholds not as restraints, but as a means to consistent direction: handholds that help employees pull in the same direction, and handholds that result from seeing employees as training department customers who must be well served. Training and development policy should help create happy and loyal employees who are also seen as training department customers to be kept satisfied and delighted.

Policy must be a living, developing tool, not something to get tangled in and tripped over. The organization and management of the corporate training function must be an integrated effort. I have argued here for an ever-growing role for human resources development personnel in all parts and functions of the corporation. Human resources professionals must actively pursue their own training and development in the direction of ever-greater input into the team psyche that literally organizes, manages, and motivates a company.

Such integration should result in an ever-growing central role for HR departments. That role should move ever closer to the center of policy making, accountability, and the personal development to be required of corporate personnel in the twenty-first century.

Human resource development professionals must learn to create policy to which their managers can commit. Managers at every level of the corporation must be willing to commit to training, retraining, education, and the idea that workers and their experience and insights are valued intellectual capital.

Corporate commitment to innovation means committing to the education and development of people who can create and implement innovation. Creating and keeping the loyalty and commitment of your employees will be your greatest asset, regardless of your industry, market, or playing field. Loyalty, community, and commitment will only come from your company's continuing investment in its employee's interpersonal and professional training and development.

The corporate commitment to training and development as an essential tool in the creation of innovation must become an integral part of corporate culture if those corporations are not to be drowned by the unavoidable waves of continuous change. Welcome to the twenty-first century.

References

1. Caudron, Shari, "HR Leaders Brainstorm," *Personnel Journal*, August 1994, pp. 54–61.
2. Pittam, Jerry, L., "Organization and Management of the Training Function," Chapter 2 in Robert Craig, ed., *Training and Development Handbook*, 3d ed., McGraw-Hill, New York, 1987, pp. 19–34.

3. Ibid.

4. *1993 Motorola Year End Report* (no author).

5. Drucker, Peter, "The New Society of Organizations," Part 1, Chapter 1, in Robert Howard, ed., *The Learning Imperative: Managing People for Continuous Innovation,* A *Harvard Business Review* Book, Boston, 1994, pp. 3–18.

6. Pittam, ref. 2.

7. Warshauer, Susan, *Inside Training and Development: Creating Effective Programs,* University Associates Inc., San Diego, 1988.

8. Pittam, ref. 2.

9. Ibid.

10. McCullough, Richard C., "Professional Development," Chapter 3, in Robert Craig, ed., *Training and Development Handbook,* 3d ed., McGraw-Hill, New York, 1987, pp. 35–63.

11. Ibid.

12. Drucker, ref. 5.

13. Howard, Robert, "Introduction," *The Learning Imperative: Managing People for Continuous Innovation, A Harvard Business Review Book,* Boston, 1993, pp. xiii–xix.

14. Warshauer, Susan, *Inside Training and Development: Creating Effective Programs,* University Associates Inc., San Diego, 1988.

15. Howard, Robert, "The CEO as Organizational Architect," Part 2, Chapter 4, in *The Learning Imperative: Managing People for Continuous Innovation, A Harvard Business Review* Book, Boston, 1993, pp. 133–156.

16. Drucker, ref. 5.

17. Wiggenhorn, William, "Motorola U: When Training Becomes an Education," Part 4, Chapter 2, in Robert Howard, ed., *The Learning Imperative: Managing People for Continuous Innovation, A Harvard Business Review* Book, Boston, 1993, pp. 233–254.

18. Yate, Martin, *Keeping the Best—And Other Thoughts on Building a Super Competitive Workforce,* Bob Adams, Inc., Holbrook, MA, 1991.

19. Nonaka, Ikujiro, "The Knowledge-Creating Company," Part 1, Chapter 3, in Robert Howard, ed., *The Learning Imperative: Managing People for Continuous Innovation,* A *Harvard Business Review* Book, Boston, 1993, pp. 41–56.

20. Yate, ref. 18.

21. Stewart, Thomas A., "Your Company's Most Valuable Asset: Intellectual Capital," *Fortune Magazine,* October 3, 1994, pp. 68–74.

22. Ibid.

23. Drucker, ref. 5.

24. Yate, ref. 18.

25. Drucker, ref. 5.

26. Pittam, ref. 2.

27. Drucker, ref. 5.

28. Howard, ref. 13.

29. Nonaka, ref. 19.

30. Ibid.

31. Warshauer, ref. 14.

32. Ibid.

33. Yate, ref. 18.

34. Ibid.

35. Motorola University (no author), *This Is Motorola University, Quality, Creativity, Renewal,* Motorola University Press, Schaumburg, IL, 1993.

36. Yate, ref. 18.

37. Nonaka, ref. 19.
38. Beer, Michael, Russell A. Eisenstat, and Bert Spector, "Getting from Here to There," Part 4, Chapter 1, in Robert Howard, ed., *The Learning Imperative: Managing People for Continuous Innovation*, A *Harvard Business Review* Book, Boston, 1994, pp. 217–232.
39. Warshauer, ref. 14.
40. Ibid.
41. Nonaka, ref. 19.
42. Ibid.
43. Warshauer, ref. 14.
44. Ibid.
45. London, Manuel, *Managing the Training Enterprise*, Jossey-Bass, San Francisco, 1989.
46. Warshauer, ref. 14.
47. Ibid.
48. Motorola University (no author), *A Catalyst for Change Through Continuous Learning*, Motorola University Press, Schaumburg, IL, 1992.
49. Beer, ref. 38.
50. Adler, Paul S., "Time and Motion Regained," Part 4, Chapter 3, in Robert Howard, ed., *The Learning Imperative: Managing People for Continuous Innovation*, A *Harvard Business Review* Book, Boston, 1994, pp. 255–276.
51. Warshauer, ref. 14.
52. Ibid.
53. Motorola, ref. 48.
54. Warshauer, ref. 14.
55. Ibid.
56. Pittam, ref. 2.
57. Drucker, ref. 5.
58. Heisler, W. J., and Benham, Philip O., "The Challenge of Management Development in North America in the 1990s," *Journal of Management Development*, vol. 2, no. 2, 1992, pp. 16–31.
59. Yate, ref. 18.
60. Brown, John Seely, "Research that Reinvents the Corporation," Part 2, Chapter 1, in *The Learning Imperative: Managing People for Continuous Innovation*, A *Harvard Business Review* Book, Boston, 1993, pp. 81–96.
61. Nonaka, ref. 19.
62. Warshauer, ref. 14.
63. Heisler, ref. 58.
64. Taylor, Sally, "Managing a Learning Environment," *Personnel Management*, October 1992, p. 54(4).
65. Beer, ref. 38.
66. Drucker, ref. 5.
67. Howard, ref. 15.
68. Drucker, ref. 5.
69. Fitpatrick, Robert, "Remmele Engineering: If It Ain't Broke...," *Training*, May 1994, p. 42(6).
70. Yate, ref. 18.
71. Howard, ref. 15.
72. Yate, ref. 18.

Suggestions for Further Reading

Boyett, Joseph H., and Henry P. Conn, *Workplace 2000, The Revolution Facing American Business*, Penguin Group, New York, 1991.

Campbell, Andrew, and Laurel L. Nash, *A Sense of Mission: Defining Direction for the Large Corporation*, Addison-Wesley, The Economist Books, Reading, MA, 1992.

Caudron, Shari, "HR Leaders Brainstorm," *Personnel Journal*, August 1994, pp. 54–61.

Galvin, Paul V., *The Idea of Ideas*, Motorola University Press, Schaumburg, IL, 1991.

Heisler, W. J., and Benham, Philip O., "The Challenge of Management Development in North America in the 1990s," *Journal of Management Development*, 2(2), 1992, pp. 16–31. An excellent overview of the relationship between training and education, and a prescription for encouraging both in corporations, training personnel, middle and upper managers, and in university and corporate cultures.

Howard, Robert, ed., *The Learning Imperative: Managing People for Continuous Innovation*, A *Harvard Business Review* Book, Boston, 1993. Source of much clarity and breadth on the issues of people and learning management. A collection of articles from many authors with many perspectives well worth exploring in detail. Excellent companion volume to both the 15-page Heisler and Benham article and the book by Boyett and Conn, both cited in this list.

Jennings, Marianne M., "Business Schools' Formula for Irrelevance," *The Wall Street Journal*, November 28, 1994, p. A18. An insightful indictment of university-based academic-think graduate business management and curriculum decision making with examples that may at first make you laugh. Then review the content of your own outsourced graduate program recommendations.

Randle, Wilma, "Workplace Education Is Missionary's Urgent Message," *Chicago Tribune*, May 13, 1994, Section 3, p. 3.

Santucci, Phillip J., "Put Training Where It Belongs," *Training and Development*, November 1993, pp. 4–6.

Stewart, Thomas A., "Your Company's Most Valuable Asset: Intellectual Capital," *Fortune Magazine*, October 3, 1994, pp. 68–74. Lessons on the cost of watching the parade go by. The article draws comparisons between those who jumped early on processes for assigning value to and managing intellectual capital as a resource, even a profit center, versus those now starting into it, and those still on the sidelines.

Taylor, Sally, "Managing a Learning Environment," *Personnel Management*, October 1992, p. 54(4).

Wisdom, Barry L., and D. Keith Denton, "Manager as Teacher," *Training and Development*, December 1991, p. 54(4).

3

Selecting and Developing the Professional HRD Staff

William J. Rothwell

William J. Rothwell *is an associate professor in the Department of Adult Education, Instructional Systems and Workforce Education on the University Park Campus of the Pennsylvania State University. He oversees a graduate degree program in Training and Development/Human Resources and HRD, and teaches courses on the subject. Accredited for life as a Senior Professional in Human Resources (SPHR) through the Human Resource Certification Institute, he earned an M.B.A. from Sangamon State University in Springfield, IL, and a Ph.D. in Human Resource Development from the University of Illinois at Urbana-Champaign. He consults with business, government, and nonprofit enterprises on HRD. Before entering academe in 1993, he worked from 1979 to 1993 as an HRD professional, first as a state government agency training director and later as a corporate Assistant Vice President and Management Development Director for a large insurance company. He has authored, coauthored, and edited numerous books and articles on HRD, including* Mastering the Instructional Design Process *(Jossey-Bass, 1992), the* ASTD Reference Guide to Professional Human Resource Development Roles and Competencies *(HRD Press, 1992),* The Complete AMA Guide to Management Development *(AMACOM, 1993),* Human Resource Development: A Strategic Approach *(HRD Press, 1994),* Planning and Managing Human Resources: Strategic Planning for Personnel Management *(HRD Press, 1994),* Improving On-The-Job Training *(Jossey-Bass, 1994),* Effective Succession Planning *(AMACOM, 1994), and* Practicing Organization Development: A Handbook for

48

Consultants *(Pfeiffer, 1995). A Registered Organization Development Consultant (RODC), he is a frequent presenter at ASTD international conferences and is a member of the National Society for Performance and Instruction, the Society for Human Resources Management, the American Management Association, the Organization Development Institute, and the Academy of Human Resource Development.*

Selecting and developing the professional human resource development (HRD) staff are more complex activities now than they were just a few years ago. Corporate downsizing in some organizations has reduced the cadre of professionals who are committed to an enduring occupational focus on HRD. Vacancies in HRD departments do not automatically translate into full-time professional replacements. Alternative staffing methods are often used instead. Among them: reliance on temporary workers, creative vendor assistance, outsourcing, job sharing, and work process reengineering to eliminate staffing replacement needs. HRD responsibilities are also being shifted, in whole or part, to operating managers or decentralized to operating departments. Some organizations have opted to make HRD assignments visibility-enhancing developmental opportunities for high-potential workers who have no lasting career interest in the field itself. Moreover, the nature of HRD work is changing, focusing less on traditional training methods and more on holistic human performance improvement and consulting.

Meanwhile, the occupational preparation of HRD professionals has never been more impressive. The results of a 1993 study by *Training* magazine indicated that 38 percent of the survey respondents held master's degrees, 39 percent held bachelor's degrees, 7 percent held doctoral degrees, and 16 percent were working without any college degree.[1] While planned company training has increased 45 percent from 1983 to 1991,[2] the *Academic Directory* published by the American Society for Training and Development lists a sizable number of possible educational preparatory programs for HRD professionals—some 70 certificate programs, 85 bachelor's programs, 108 master's programs, and 80 doctoral programs.[3] Demand for formal educational preparation of HRD professionals has been growing,[4] though some observers of the field have periodically called for occupational certification in HRD to verify competence.[5,6]

Against this complex backdrop, HRD managers and professionals are challenged to think and act creatively. HRD managers must not view selecting and developing a professional HRD staff as isolated activities; rather, they are options (among others) in addressing the larger issue of sourcing the talent necessary to meet present and future organizational needs. HRD professionals, on the other hand, must take responsibility for building their competence in line with their employers' needs and their own career goals.

This chapter will emphasize that selection and development are choices in a larger scheme for sourcing talent. The chapter will also explain why selecting and developing the HRD staff is important, provide a holistic model for carrying out those activities, and review each step of the model.

Why Is Selecting and Developing the Professional HRD Staff Important?

Devoting an entire chapter to selecting and developing the professional HRD staff may seem unusual in a book that is otherwise devoted to improving the performance of other employees. Such a chapter is even more remarkable at a time when many decision makers have chosen to explore multiple approaches to sourcing HRD talent. However, selecting and developing HRD professionals has never been more important. There are several reasons why this statement is true.

First, as the absolute number of HRD professionals has dwindled in the lean-staffed organizations of the 1990s, those who remain must be exceptionally skilled. Often they are asked to shoulder more and different work. They must also function under considerable job-induced stress and must be willing to work longer hours.[7]

Second, more HRD professionals find themselves forced to magnify their impact beyond their numbers. They are orchestrating organizational learning and developing high performance work organizations even as they must work harder and smarter. They must help their organizations anticipate and react to large- and small-scale change.

Third, HRD professionals must be selected and developed with care because the selection and development processes they use set important examples for their customers, clients, and stakeholders. After all, if HRD professionals are unable to demonstrate exemplary approaches to selecting and developing their own staff, they are less credible in advising others on these important matters. In short, they must "walk the talk."

Fourth, as many HRD professionals shift their emphasis from a narrow focus on designing and delivering training to a broader focus on holistic human performance improvement and consulting, they must acquire new competencies as they assume new leadership roles. Their efforts, while more visible, are also more risky because they are sometimes out of keeping with the traditional role expected of "trainers" as "corporate schoolteachers."

What Model Can Guide the Selection and Development Process?

Consider three fundamental issues before selecting and developing the professional HRD staff:

- What is the purpose of the HRD effort? (In this chapter, the term *HRD effort* refers to all parts of the organization that play a role in HRD. It is not limited to one HRD department.)
- How will the HRD effort carry out its purpose?
- How many—and what kind of—people should be sourced to carry out the plan and achieve the desired results?

The first two questions are, of course, appropriately determined through a strategic HRD planning process. A strategic HRD plan is necessary to ensure that the talents selected and developed for the HRD effort will meet organizational needs.

Use the model depicted in Fig. 3-1 to help you conceptualize these issues. Each step in this model is described in detail below.

Step 1: Clarify the Values Driving the HRD Effort

Values are "are deep-seated, pervasive standards that influence almost every aspect of our lives."[8] Values drive all organizational, and individual, efforts

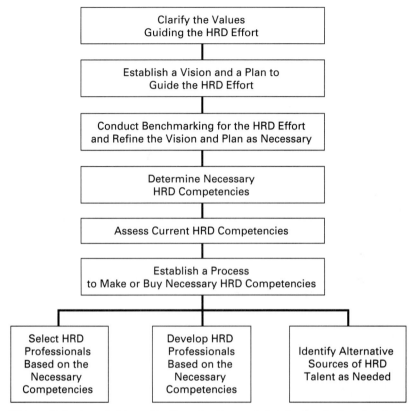

Figure 3-1. A model to guide the selection and development of professional HRD staff.

because they "are the bedrock of any organizational culture."[9] Values have greater depth than attitudes. They indicate preferences rather than absolutes.

Organizational values are embedded in corporate culture and are expressed through rites, rituals, and views about "right" and "wrong" ways of performing. Values affect, and are in turn affected by, the HRD effort as well as decisions about selecting and developing the professional HRD staff.[10] Therefore, values clarification is central to such activities as strategic planning, staff planning, selecting employees, developing employees, and improving human performance.

Before selecting and developing professional HRD staff, clarify the values driving the organization and the HRD effort. Seek answers to such questions as these:

- Who are the key stakeholders and "customers" of the HRD effort?

- What are the appropriate responsibilities of the stakeholders, customers, and employees of the HRD effort?

- What is the organization's definition of HRD? How widely is it shared? What HRD issues, if any, are controversial? Why are they controversial?

- When, in the opinion of key decision makers in the organization, should HRD activities be emphasized? Never? At the outset of employees' careers? In preparation for job or work changes? In organizational trouble spots? As solutions to existing performance problems? In anticipation of performance problems yet to surface?

- Where should HRD activities be carried out? Are they appropriately handled during work time or on employees' time? Will the organization pay overtime for employees who participate in HRD activities?
- How should HRD activities be designed, delivered, and evaluated?
- How much pressure exists to show financial or nonfinancial returns on HRD activities? Who is applying that pressure—and why?
- What is and what should be the role of HRD activities in improving performance and in encouraging individual learning?

As these questions are addressed, be sure to put the organization on the record about what it values and what it seeks from HRD professionals, line managers, learners, and other relevant stakeholder groups. Realize in this process that HRD professionals themselves are affected by perspectives and values that are unique to their line of work.[11]

Step 2: Establish a Vision and a Plan to Guide the HRD Effort

Visioning is the process of creating a compelling, achievable view of what the future will look like. As Lee writes, "the concept of vision has never been more important than in today's work of flattened, delayered, decentralized organizations."[12] While frequently associated with management by objectives and strategic planning,[13] visioning is a quintessential element in selecting and developing a professional HRD staff. After all, decision makers must have a sense of the desired destination of their efforts and the direction in which they are leading the organization before they can make informed decisions about what talent should be sourced to those ends. A vision crystallizes where the HRD effort is headed and galvanizes support, enthusiasm, and ownership.

When selecting and developing the professional HRD staff, HRD managers and others are required by visioning to address several important questions:[14]

- What trends inside and outside the organization affect the HRD effort?
- What should a successful HRD effort "look like"?
- What results is the HRD effort striving to achieve?

Take steps, then, to determine a unified vision for the HRD effort. Use the vision as the basis for a mission statement for HRD.[15]

Use the mission statement, in turn, as a point of departure for *planning for HRD*, which means "the process of changing an organization, stakeholders outside it, groups inside it, and people employed by it through planned learning so that they possess the knowledge and skills needed in the future."[16] The plan embodies and activates the vision. It provides concrete, but long-term guidance for making the vision a reality.

Selecting and developing the professional HRD staff should be carried out as part of the planning process. During planning, the HRD manager and staff should address such questions as these:

- What people are needed to help the HRD effort address trends inside and outside the organization?

- How many and what kind of people are needed to make the vision a reality?
- Through what combination of sources can the HRD effort find and use the talent needed to transform the vision into reality?

Step 3: Conduct Benchmarking and Refine the Vision and the Plan

Once decision makers have clarified the values, vision, and plan to guide the organization's HRD effort, they are well advised to do a reality check to ensure that they are on target. One way to do that is to carry out a benchmarking study to compare their HRD effort to world-class or industry-class best practices, typical practices, or desired practices. Information about HRD staffing, in particular, can be obtained from various sources. That information can give decision makers valuable clues about whether their vision is, or is not, well founded. It may also fire the imagination with new, different, and innovative approaches that could achieve more efficient, more effective, or even breakthrough results.

To conduct a benchmarking study, decision makers should first clarify what is to be benchmarked. They should then identify comparative or "best practices" organizations, decide how the information will be collected, conduct the study, and use the results. (For more information on benchmarking, see the chapter on benchmarking and other relevant sources that describe methods in more detail.[17])

Although issues for investigation in benchmarking may vary, of course, key HRD staffing issues for investigation may include any or all the questions posed in the worksheet appearing in Fig. 3-2. Use the questions appearing in the worksheet as a starting point. Add to the questions or modify them as necessary to seek information of particular relevance to your organization. (For instance, you may wish to add questions about salaries, job titles, and other information about HRD professionals.) Then use the worksheet to record information from several organizations. Summarize the results, feed them back to decision makers, and use them to refine the organization's vision and HRD strategic plan.

Benchmarking information about HRD staffing may also be obtained from the American Society for Training and Development's annual survey on Training Expenditures, which is conducted as part of the National HRD Executive Survey. Figure 3-3 summarizes the most recently available study results at the time this chapter was written. It depicts the average number of employees per company, the average number of full- and part-time training and development staff, and the average ratio of trainer to staff. Figure 3-4 indicates the respondents' perceptions about HRD staffing; Fig. 3-5 summarizes the percentage of HRD effort and programming that is devoted to different levels of employees; and Fig. 3-6 summarizes the most important trends affecting HRD staffing and work activities.

Step 4: Determine Necessary HRD Competencies

Once the vision and plan to guide the HRD effort have been established and refined, HRD managers should then decide what HRD competencies are necessary to transform the vision and HRD strategic plan into realities. That task requires comprehensive staff planning for the HRD effort. Such planning should not focus so much on the *headcount* or *work activities to be performed* as on *needed HRD competencies*.

Directions: Use this worksheet to benchmark HRD staffing practices in other organizations. Select organizations that are "world-class" by consulting appropriate written and other authoritative sources. Then contact representatives of the organizations. Pose the following questions over the phone or on-site visit to representatives of each organization. Finally, consolidate responses and identify common trends. Use the results in strategic planning for your organization's HRD effort.

Questions	Your notes
▪ What is the number of full-time HRD professionals in the organization? How are they defined as HRD professionals?	
▪ What is the number of part-time HRD workers in the organization? How are they identified?	
▪ How is the HRD effort structured? Does the organization have one or more centralized HRD departments? How many and what kind of people work in each one? What work do they perform? Does the organization have one or more decentralized HRD functions? How many and what kind of people work in each one? What work do they perform?	
▪ What is the ratio of full-time HRD professionals and part-time HRD practitioners to employees?	
▪ What education, experience, and other competencies are needed from the full-time HRD staff? From the part-time HRD staff?	
▪ What do decision makers in the benchmarked organizations perceive about the relative "fit" between the numbers and types of HRD professionals available and the quantity and type of work they perform? How well does staff competence match up to workload? To quality demands?	
▪ How are HRD activities evaluated?	
▪ How are HRD professionals recruited, selected, and developed? What practices seem to work the best, and why?	
▪ How does the organization identify and use sources of HRD talent other than full-time HRD professionals? What practices seem to work best in identifying, managing, and developing such alternative sources of talent?	

Figure 3-2. A worksheet for benchmarking HRD staffing.

Average number of employees per company	13,546
Average number of training and development staff in same function	11
Average number of *full-time* training and development staff in rest of company	30
Average number of *part-time* training and development staff in rest of company	109
Average of *total number* of training and development staff per company	137
Average ratio of trainer to staff	1 to 99

Figure 3-3. Staffing summary. (*Source: The National HRD Executive Forum, January 1995. Copyright 1995 by the American Society for Training and Development, Alexandria, VA. Reprinted by permission of ASTD.*)

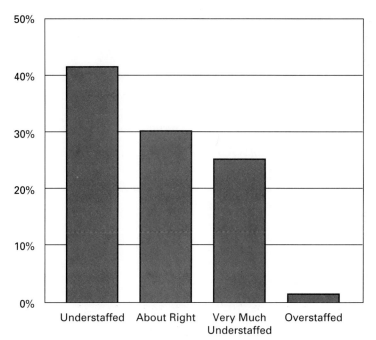

Figure 3-4. Perceptions about HRD staffing. (*Source: The National HRD Executive Forum, January 1995. Copyright 1995 by the American Society for Training and Development, Alexandria, VA. Reprinted by permission of ASTD.*)

Competencies are available from many sources, of course. They may be obtained, for example, from part-time line management assistance, retired HRD professionals from the organization, temporary workers, and external consultants. In this context, *competencies* should be understood to mean "underlying characteristics of an employee (that is, motives, traits, skills, aspects of one's self-image, social roles, or bodies of knowledge) which result in effective and/or superior performance in a job."[18] They are thus tied to *individuals* more than to *jobs*.

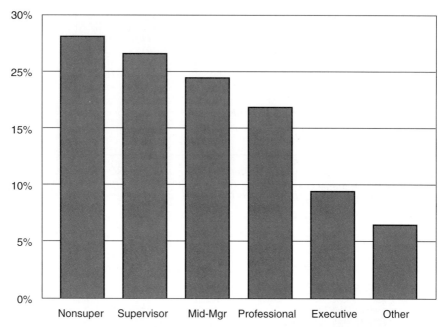

Figure 3-5. Percentage of training and development effort/programming that goes to employees. (*Source: The National HRD Executive Forum, January 1995. Copyright 1995 by the American Society for Training and Development, Alexandria, VA. Reprinted by permission of ASTD.*)

- Measuring the bottom-line payoff of training
- Doing more with less
- Adapting to the emerging technologies
- Executive support for training
- Managing an increasingly diverse workforce
- Providing alternatives to classroom instruction
- Downsizing
- Helping managers move from the mindset of "training" to the mindset of "performance improvement"
- Transfer of training
- Identifying and improving basic competency of workforce
- Globalization
- Accelerating the learning process

Figure 3-6. Trends affecting HRD efforts. (*Source: The National HRD Executive Forum, January 1995. Copyright 1995 by the American Society for Training and Development, Alexandria, VA. Reprinted by permission of ASTD.*)

To conduct comprehensive staff planning using competency assessment, begin by reviewing current HRD competency studies. From those studies, make a list of the HRD competencies that are needed by the organization to transform the vision and HRD strategic plan into reality. Then take stock of available competencies within the organization and identify competencies that are needed.

What follows is a brief review of HRD competency studies and a description of a process for identifying the HRD competencies needed by an organization to realize its vision and HRD strategic plan.

Reviewing Competency Studies of HRD

Many studies have been conducted to assess the roles, competencies, work outputs, ethical standards, and quality requirements of HRD work. These studies can be enormously helpful to HRD managers who are conducting staff planning for an organizationwide HRD effort or who are systematically selecting and developing individuals to fill existing or anticipated vacancies. These studies can also be helpful to line managers who oversee their own HRD efforts, individuals who are preparing to enter HRD work, faculty at universities who are planning curricula to guide undergraduate and graduate programs in HRD, and HRD professionals who are preparing themselves to achieve career goals inside or outside their employers or who are simply upgrading their skills to keep pace with rapid change.

Current thinking on HRD competencies dates from Leonard Nadler's 1962 doctoral dissertation, which examined the needs of selected training directors in Pennsylvania.[19] In an article published in 1967 as a follow-up to his dissertation, Nadler, writing with Gordon Lippitt, described training directors as filling three key roles: learning specialist, administrator, and consultant.[20] Learning specialists design and deliver training courses; administrators manage the training function; and, consultants assist line managers.

A 1976 study of training roles was conducted by the U.S. Civil Service Commission.[21] It identified five key training roles: (1) career counselor; (2) consultant; (3) learning specialist; (4) program manager; and (5) training administrator. The study also delineated the competencies necessary to enact each role.

Another 1976 study was conducted by the Ontario Society for Training and Development (OSTD) to examine the roles and competencies of Canadian trainers.[22] Four key training roles were identified: (1) instructor; (2) designer; (3) manager; and (4) consultant. To carry out these roles, training professionals should be able to demonstrate proficiency in 11 important competencies: (1) administration; (2) communication; (3) course design; (4) evaluation; (5) group dynamics process; (6) learning theory; (7) manpower planning; (8) person-organization interface; (9) teaching practice; (10) training equipment and materials; and (11) training needs analysis.

In 1978, the American Society for Training and Development commissioned a membership study to identify training activities. Spearheaded by Pinto and Walker,[23] the study resulted in a list of key activity areas of training work: (1) analyzing needs and evaluating results; (2) designing and developing training programs and materials; (3) delivering training and development programs and services; (4) advising and counseling; (5) managing training activities; (6) maintaining organization relationships; (7) doing research to advance the training field; (8) developing professional skills and expertise; and (9) developing basic skills and knowledge. Though focused more on work activities than on underlying competencies, this was the first in a line of several important competency studies of HRD work.

In 1983 ASTD published the results of a landmark study that established the pattern for professionally conducted competency studies ever since. Entitled *Models for Excellence*,[24] it was completed under the leadership of Patricia A. McLagan and resulted in (among other study results) the identification of 15 training and development roles, 31 competencies, and 102 work outputs. Training and development roles identified in the study were: (1) evaluator; (2) group facilitator; (3) individual development counselor; (4) instructional writer; (5) instructor; (6) manager of training and development; (7) marketer; (8) media specialist; (9) needs analyst; (10) program administrator; (11) program designer; (12) strategist; (13) task analyst; (14) theoretician; and (15) transfer agent. Competencies identified in the study included adult learning understanding, audiovisual skill, career development knowledge, competency identification skill, computer competence, cost-benefit analysis skill, counseling skill, data reduction skill, delegation skill, facilities skill, feedback skill, futuring skill, group process skill, industry understanding, intellectual versatility, library skills, model-building skill, negotiation skill, objectives preparation skill, organization behavior understanding, organization understanding, performance observation skill, personnel and HR field understanding, presentation skills, questioning skill, records management skill, relationship versatility, research skills, training and development field understanding, training and development techniques understanding, and writing skills. (The results of this study were reported extensively in Chap. 3, "Professional Development," by Richard C. McCullough in the third edition of this *Handbook.*)

In 1987, ASTD's board of directors authorized a new competency study to update *Models for Excellence.* The ASTD board chartered a Task Force on Competencies and Standards to begin the effort. The study results were compiled after numerous meetings and several rounds of questionnaires to over 800 experts in the HRD field. The results were published in five related volumes: *The Models,*[25] *The Research Report,*[26] *The Manager's Guide,*[27] *The Practitioner's Guide,*[28] and (separately issued) *The Academic Guide.*[29] Only the most important results of the first four volumes, collectively entitled *Models for HRD Practice,* will be described in this chapter.

HRD was defined by the study as "the integrated use of training and development, organization development, and career development to improve individual, group, and organizational effectiveness. Those three areas use development as their primary process, and are the focal point of this study."[30] It is an examination of HRD, rather than training and development, that distinguishes *Models for HRD Practice* from its predecessor *Models for Excellence.* HRD was placed in the larger context of a Human Resource Wheel (see Fig. 3-7) because "other human resource areas (human resource planning, for example) influence development [and] therefore suggest that HRD practitioners must at least be aware of these additional areas and their impact on individual, group, and organization development."[31]

Models for HRD Practice lists 11 HRD roles, 35 competencies, and 74 work outputs. To understand *The Models,* you must first understand key terms as defined in the study:

- *Role.* A common grouping of competencies. A role should not be confused with a job title.

- *Competency.* "An area of knowledge or skill that is critical for producing key outputs. Competencies are internal capabilities that people bring to their jobs; capabilities which may be expressed in a broad, even infinite array of on-the-job behaviors."[32]

- *Output.* "A product or service that an individual or group delivers to others, especially to colleagues, customers, or clients."[33]

- *Ethical issue.* "Key areas of ethical challenge that HRD practitioners frequently face"[34]

- *Quality requirements.* "The characteristics of a quality output."[35]

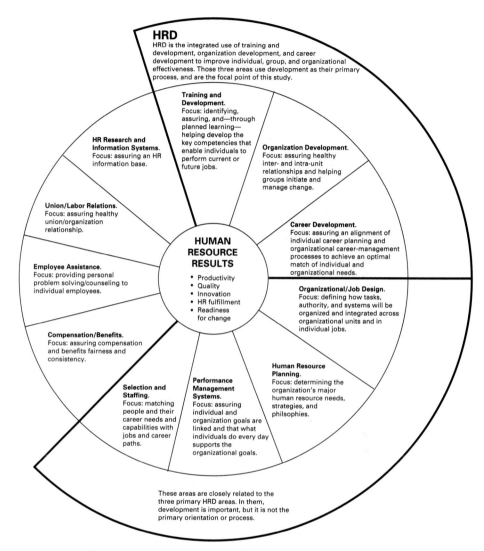

HRD
HRD is the integrated use of training and development, organization development, and career development to improve individual, group, and organizational effectiveness. Those three areas use development as their primary process, and are the focal point of this study.

Training and Development.
Focus: identifying, assuring, and—through planned learning—helping develop the key competencies that enable individuals to perform current or future jobs.

HR Research and Information Systems.
Focus: assuring an HR information base.

Organization Development.
Focus: assuring healthy inter- and intra-unit relationships and helping groups initiate and manage change.

Union/Labor Relations.
Focus: assuring healthy union/organization relationship.

HUMAN RESOURCE RESULTS
• Productivity
• Quality
• Innovation
• HR fulfillment
• Readiness for change

Career Development.
Focus: assuring an alignment of individual career planning and organizational career-management processes to achieve an optimal match of individual and organizational needs.

Employee Assistance.
Focus: providing personal problem solving/counseling to individual employees.

Organizational/Job Design.
Focus: defining how tasks, authority, and systems will be organized and integrated across organizational units and in individual jobs.

Compensation/Benefits.
Focus: assuring compensation and benefits fairness and consistency.

Human Resource Planning.
Focus: determining the organization's major human resource needs, strategies, and philsophies.

Selection and Staffing.
Focus: matching people and their career needs and capabilities with jobs and career paths.

Performance Management Systems.
Focus: assuring individual and organization goals are linked and that what individuals do every day supports the organizational goals.

These areas are closely related to the three primary HRD areas. In them, development is important, but it is not the primary orientation or process.

Figure 3-7. The Human Resource Wheel. (*Source: P. McLagan, The Models, ASTD, Alexandria, VA, 1989, p. 6. Copyright 1989 by the American Society for Training and Development, Alexandria, VA. Reprinted by permission of ASTD.*)

Figure 3-8 lists and defines the roles identified in the study; Fig. 3-9 lists and defines the competencies of HRD professionals; Fig. 3-10 relates competencies to roles; and Fig. 3-11 lists HRD work outputs. For the complete list of quality requirements, see *Models for HRD Practice.*

McLagan's 1987 study remains the preeminent competency study of HRD. It has spawned numerous follow-up studies, including an examination of the perceptions of chief executive officers about HRD roles,[36] a cross-cultural comparison of HRD roles in the United States and Taiwan[37] and numerous unpublished European studies.[38,39] McLagan's study has served the United

Roles	Descriptions
Researcher	The role of identifying, developing, or testing new information (theory, research, concepts, technology, models, hardware, and so on) and translating the information into implications for improved individual or organizational performance
Marketer	The role of marketing and contracting for HRD viewpoints, programs, and services
Organization change agent	The role of influencing and supporting changes in organization behavior
Needs analyst	The role of identifying ideal and actual performance and performance conditions and determining causes of discrepancies
Program designer	The role of preparing objectives, defining content, and selecting and sequencing activities for a specific intervention
HRD materials developer	The role of producing written or electronically mediated instructional materials
Instructor-facilitator	The role of presenting information, directing structured learning experiences, and managing group discussion and group process
Individual career development	The role of helping individuals to assess advisor personal competencies, values, and goals and to identify, plan, and implement development and career actions
Administrator	The role of providing coordination and support services for the delivery of HRD programs and services
Evaluator	The role of identifying the impact of an intervention on individual or organizational effectiveness
HRD manager	The role of supporting and leading a group's work, and linking that work with the total organization

Figure 3-8. The roles of HRD. (*Source: P. McLagan,* The Models, *ASTD, Alexandria, VA, 1989, p. 49. Copyright 1989 by the American Society for Training and Development, Alexandria, VA. Reprinted by permission of ASTD.*)

States in much the same way that other competency studies of fields related to HRD have served Australia[40] or England.[41]

Competency studies of HRD have been carried out since *Models for HRD Practice,* however. Among the most important of these were three related studies carried out under the sponsorship of The International Board of Standards for Training, Performance and Instruction (IBSTPI), which functions as a service organization for HRD professionals. The first study, completed in 1986, was entitled *Instructional Design Competencies: The Standards.*[42] Focusing only on the role of instructional designer, the study revealed that practitioners in that role perform the following activities: (1) determine projects that are appropriate for instructional design; (2) conduct needs assessment; (3) assess the relevant characteristics of learners-trainees; (4) analyze the characteristics of a setting; (5) perform job, task, and/or content analysis; (6) write statements of performance objectives; (7) develop the performance measurements; (8) sequence the performance objectives;

Figure 3-9. HRD competencies. (*Source: P. McLagan, The Models, ASTD, Alexandria, VA, 1989, pp. 43–45. Copyright 1989 by the American Society for Training and Development, Alexandria, VA. Reprinted by permission of ASTD.*)

TECHNICAL COMPETENCIES
(*Functional knowledge and skills*)

1. *Adult learning understanding.* Knowing how adults acquire and use knowledge, skills, attitudes; understanding individual differences in learning
2. *Career development theories and techniques understanding.* Knowing the techniques and methods used in career development; understanding their appropriate uses
3. *Competency identification skill.* Identifying the knowledge and skill requirements of jobs, tasks, and roles
4. *Computer competence.* Understanding and/or using computer applications
5. *Electronic systems skill.* Having knowledge of functions, features, and potential applications of electronic systems for the delivery and management of HRD (such as computer-based training, teleconferencing, expert systems, interactive video, satellite networks)
6. *Facilities skill.* Planning and coordinating logistics in an efficient and cost-effective manner
7. *Objectives preparation skill.* Preparing clear statements which describe desired outputs
8. *Performance observation skill.* Tracking and describing behaviors and their effects
9. *Subject matter understanding.* Knowing the content of a given function or discipline being addressed
10. *Training and development theories and techniques understanding.* Knowing the theories and methods used in training; understanding their appropriate use
11. *Research skill.* Selecting, developing, and using methodologies such as statistical and data collection techniques for formal inquiry

BUSINESS COMPETENCIES
(*Having a strong management, economics, or administration base*)

12. *Business understanding.* Knowing how the functions of a business work and relate to each other; knowing the economic impact of business decisions
13. *Cost-benefit analysis skill.* Assessing alternatives in terms of their financial, psychological, and strategic advantages and disadvantages
14. *Delegation skill.* Assigning task responsibility and authority to others
15. *Industry understanding.* Knowing the key concepts and variables such as critical issues, economic vulnerabilities, measurements, distribution channels, inputs, outputs, and information sources that define an industry or sector
16. *Organization behavior understanding.* Seeing organizations as dynamic, political, economic, and social systems which have multiple goals; using this larger perspective as a framework for understanding and influencing events and change
17. *Organization development theories and techniques understanding.* Knowing the techniques and methods used in organization development; understanding their appropriate use
18. *Organization understanding.* Knowing the strategy, structure, power networks, financial position, and systems of a specific organization
19. *Project management skill.* Planning, organizing, and monitoring work
20. *Records management skill.* Storing data in an easily retrievable form

INTERPERSONAL COMPETENCIES
(*Having a strong communication base*)

21. *Coaching skill.* Helping individuals recognize and understand personal needs, values, problems, alternatives, and goals
22. *Feedback skill.* Communicating information, opinions, observations, and conclusions so that they are understood and can be acted on

---

(Continued)

Figure 3-9. (*Continued*) HRD competencies. (*Source: P. McLagan, The Models, ASTD, Alexandria, VA, 1989, pp. 43–45. Copyright 1989 by the American Society for Training and Development, Alexandria, VA. Reprinted by permission of ASTD.*)

23. *Group process skill.* Influencing groups so that tasks, relationships, and individual needs are addressed
24. *Negotiation skill.* Securing win-win agreements while successfully presenting a special interest in a decision
25. *Presentation skill.* Presenting information orally so that an intended purpose is achieved
26. *Questioning skill.* Gathering information from stimulating insight in individuals and groups through use of interviews, questionnaires, and other probing methods
27. *Relationship-building skill.* Establishing relationships and networks across a broad range of people and groups
28. *Writing skill.* Preparing written material that follows generally accepted rules of style and form, is appropriate for the audience, is creative, and accomplishes its intended purpose

INTELLECTUAL COMPETENCIES
(*Knowledge and skills related to thinking*)

29. *Data reduction skill.* Scanning, synthesizing, and drawing conclusions from data
30. *Information search skill.* Gathering information from printed and other recorded sources; identifying and using information specialists and reference services and aids
31. *Intellectual versatility.* Recognizing, exploring, and using a broad range of ideas and practices; thinking logically and creatively without undue influence from personal biases
32. *Model-building skill.* Conceptualizing and developing theoretical and practical frameworks that describe complex ideas in understandable, usable ways
33. *Observing skill.* Recognizing objectively what is happening in or across situations
34. *Self-knowledge.* Knowing one's personal values, needs, interests, style, and competencies and their effects on others
35. *Visioning skill.* Projecting trends and visualizing possible and probable futures and their implications

(9) specify the instructional strategies; (10) design the instructional materials; (11) evaluate the instruction and training; (12) design the instructional management system; (13) plan and monitor instructional design projects; (14) communicate effectively in visual, oral, and written form; (15) interact effectively with other people; and (16) promote the use of instructional design.

A 1988 follow-up study, sponsored by IBSTPI, was entitled *Instructors' Competencies, Volume I: The Standards.*[43] Focusing on the instructor's role only, it revealed that practitioners in that role perform the following activities: (1) analyze course materials and learner information; (2) assure preparation of the instructional site; (3) establish and maintain instructor credibility; (4) manage the learning environment; (5) demonstrate effective communication skills; (6) demonstrate effective presentation skills; (7) demonstrate effective questioning skills and techniques; (8) respond appropriately to learners' needs for clarification or feedback; (9) provide positive reinforcement and motivational incentives; (10) use instructional methods appropriately; (11) use media effectively; (12) evaluate learner performance; (13) evaluate delivery of instruction; and (14) report evaluation information.

The third and final study sponsored by IBSTPI was entitled *Training Manager Competencies: The Standards.*[44] Published in 1990, the study revealed that

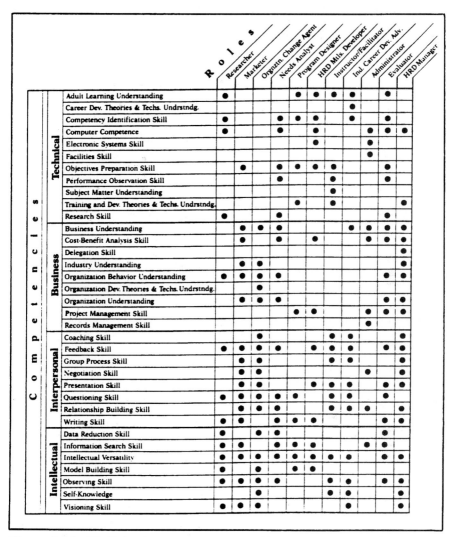

Figure 3-10. The Roles-Competencies Matrix. (*Source: P. McLagan, The Models, ASTD, Alexandria, VA, 1989, p. 61. Copyright 1989 by the American Society for Training and Development, Alexandria, VA. Reprinted by permission of ASTD.*)

managers of training should be able to: (1) assess organizational, departmental, and program needs; (2) develop plans for the department and programs; (3) link human performance to the effectiveness of the enterprise; (4) apply instructional design and development principles; (5) assure the application of effective training principles; (6) evaluate the instructional design, development, and delivery function; (7) apply the principles of performance management to their own staff; (8) think critically when making decisions and solving problems; (9) assure that actions are consistent with goals and objectives; (10) adapt strategies and solutions given change; (11) produce effective and efficient solutions; (12) develop

Figure 3-11. HRD work outputs. (*Source: P. McLagan*, The Models, *ASTD, Alexandria, VA, 1989, pp. 18–20. Copyright 1989 by the American Society for Training and Development, Alexandria, VA. Reprinted by permission of ASTD.*)

1. Concepts, Theories, or Models of Development or Change
2. HRD Research Articles
3. Research Designs
4. Data Analysis and Interpretations
5. Research Findings, Conclusions, and Recommendations
6. Information on Future Forces and Trends
7. Positive Image for HRD Products, Services, and Programs
8. Plans to Market HRD Products, Services, and Programs
9. HRD Promotional and Informational Material
10. Marketing and Sales Presentations
11. Contracts or Agreements to Provide Service
12. Sales and Business Leads
13. Teams
14. Resolved Conflicts for an Organization or Groups
15. Changes in Group Norms, Values, Culture
16. Designs for Change
17. Client Awareness of Relationships Within and Around the Organization
18. Plans to Implement Organization Change
19. Implementation of Change Strategies
20. Recommendations to Management Regarding HRD Systems
21. Strategies for Analyzing Individual or Organization Behavior
22. Tools to Measure Individual, Work Group, or Organizational Performance Discrepancies
23. Recommendations for Needed Change in Individual, Work Group, or Organizational Performance
24. Definitions and Descriptions of Desired Individual or Group Performance
25. Program/Intervention Objectives
26. Program/Intervention Designs
27. Graphics
28. Video-Based Material/Live Broadcasts
29. Audio-Based Material
30. Computer-Based Material
31. Print-Based Learner Material
32. Job Aids
33. Instructor-Facilitator Guides
34. Hardware-Software Purchasing Specifications
35. Advice on Media Use
36. Learning Environment
37. Presentations of Material
38. Facilitations of Structured Learning Events (such as case studies, role-plays, games, simulations, tests)
39. Facilitations of Group Discussions
40. Facilitation of Media-Based Learning Events (such as videotapes, films, audiotapes, teleconferences, computer-assisted instruction)
41. Test Delivery and Feedback
42. Group Members' Awareness of Their Own Group Process
43. Feedback to Learners
44. Individual Action Plans for Learning Transfer
45. Individuals with New Knowledge, Skills, Attitudes
46. Professional Counseling or Referrals to Third Parties
47. Career Guidance and Advice
48. Feedback on Development or Career Plans
49. Support for Career Transitions
50. Transfer of Development or Career Planning Skills to the Learner
51. Provision of Career Development Resources

Figure 3-11. (*Continued*) HRD work outputs. (*Source: P. McLagan, The Models, ASTD, Alexandria, VA, 1989, pp. 18–20. Copyright 1989 by the American Society for Training and Development, Alexandria, VA. Reprinted by permission of ASTD.*)

52. Behavior Change from a Counseling/Advising Relationship
53. Individual Career Assessments
54. Facility and Equipment Selections
55. Facility and Equipment Schedules
56. Records of Programs and Clients
57. Logistical Support and Service to Program Participants
58. On-Site Program Support and Staff Management
59. Functioning Equipment
60. Evaluation Designs and Plans
61. Evaluation Instruments
62. Evaluation Findings, Conclusions, Recommendations
63. Evaluation Processes
64. Evaluation Feedback
65. Work Direction and Plans for HRD Staff
66. Performance Management for HRD Staff
67. Resource Acquisition and Allocation for HRD
68. Linkage of HRD to Other Groups/Organizations
69. HRD Budgets and Financial Management
70. HRD Department Work Environment
71. HRD Department Strategy
72. HRD Department Structure
73. HRD Long-Range Plans
74. HRD Policy

and sustain social relationships; (13) provide leadership; (14) use effective interpersonal communication techniques; and (15) communicate effectively orally and in writing.

More recently, the trainer's role was examined in a 1993 report issued by the U.S. Department of Labor (DOL) and conducted by the Secretary's Commission on Achieving Necessary Skills (SCANS).[45] DOL researchers examined the "industry training specialist" role by interviewing only five job incumbents. The researchers concluded that training specialists must be able to demonstrate the competencies listed in Fig. 3-12.

At this writing, the most important recent competency study related to HRD was sponsored by the Ontario Society for Training and Development (OSTD) and conducted by a design team headed up by Valerie Dixon.[46] OSTD's design team "focused their energies on designing and producing documents that capture what they, as seasoned training practitioners, learned by trial and error over the years but wished they'd known earlier."[47] The study results defined five competency categories for training and development: (1) analyzing performance needs; (2) designing training; (3) instructing-facilitating; (4) evaluating training; and (5) coaching the application of training. Each competency category is further subdivided into core competencies, which total 31. The core competencies, in turn, are subdivided further into contributing competencies, contributing competency profiles, and learning blueprints.

Other competency studies have been conducted on training and development over the years[48–51]—and on the competencies required in such related fields as human resource management[52] and organization development.[53] However, the need is growing to update McLagan's 1987 study to help HRD professionals overcome the tendency to be all things to all people (what some call *occupational*

	Mean	Standard deviation
COMPETENCIES		
C10 Teaches others	5.00	.00
C07 Interprets and communicates information	4.80	.45
C01 Allocates time	4.60	.55
C12 Exercises leadership	4.60	.55
C05 Acquires and evaluates information	4.20	.84
C06 Organizes and maintains information	4.00	1.41
C11 Serves customers and clients	4.00	1.73
C14 Works with cultural diversity	4.00	.71
C16 Monitors and corrects performance	3.80	1.30
C15 Understands systems	3.80	.84
C18 Selects technology	3.60	1.14
C13 Negotiates to arrive at a decision	3.60	1.67
C08 Uses computers to process information	3.60	1.52
C17 Improves and designs systems	3.40	1.34
C04 Allocates human resources	3.20	1.64
C19 Applies technology to task	2.80	1.10
C03 Allocates material and facility resources	2.80	1.10
C20 Maintains and troubleshoots technology	2.40	.89
C02 Allocates money	2.20	.84
FOUNDATION SKILLS		
F13 Responsibility	5.00	.00
F02 Writing	5.00	.00
F05 Listening	4.80	.45
F06 Speaking	4.80	.45
F01 Reading	4.60	.55
F14 Self-esteem	4.40	.55
F11 Knowing how to learn	4.40	.55
F16 Self-management	4.20	.84
F15 Social	4.00	.71
F17 Integrity and honesty	3.80	.84
F12 Reasoning	3.80	1.10
F08 Decision making	3.60	.55
F09 Problem solving	3.60	.55
F07 Creative thinking	3.60	.89
F03 Arithmetic	2.40	.89
F10 Seeing things in the mind's eye	2.40	.55
F04 Mathematics	2.20	1.30

Figure 3-12. Competencies required for industry training specialists. (*Source: The Secretary's Commission on Achieving Necessary Skills*, Skills and Tasks for Jobs: A SCANS Report for America 2000, *U.S. Department of Labor, Washington, DC, 1993, pp. 3-145–3-146.*)

schizophrenia[54]), as a means to reinvent the field itself.[55] The aim should be to create a more expansive view of the HRD professional as one who has roles in holistic human performance improvement that transcend but include training interventions and who contributes to cultivating the research-based criteria tied to high-performance work organizations.[56,57] To that end, some believe that HRD competencies must encompass such performance improvement interventions as feedback, job design, organizational design, rewards and incentives, motivation, ergonomics, and many more.[58]

Identifying HRD Competencies Needed by an Organization to Realize Its Future Vision and HRD Strategic Plan

HRD managers should use the competency studies described in the previous section as a point of departure to identify the competencies needed by the professional HRD staff, and perhaps other stakeholders as well, in the organization to realize the future vision of the HRD effort and to implement the HRD strategic plan. This process is admittedly more art than science. Carry it out through brainstorming—or lead HRD staff members and/or HRD stakeholders in one or more small-group brainstorming exercises for that purpose. If possible, do that as part of the HRD strategic planning process.

To that end, you may find it helpful to construct a worksheet. (See Fig. 3-13.) In the left column of the worksheet, list HRD strategic objectives to be achieved by the HRD effort in the organization. Then, in the next column, list the work outputs tied to each objective. Be sure to clarify what products or services will be supplied to the customers or stakeholders of the HRD effort to achieve the objectives. Then, using the competency studies described in the previous section of this chapter, identify in the next column the competencies that must be demonstrated to achieve the desired work outputs. The result of this activity should be a chart that depicts the relationship among strategic objectives for the HRD effort (or department), work outputs, and necessary competencies that must exist in the professional HRD staff to achieve desired results.

Directions: Use this worksheet to relate HRD strategic objectives, work outputs, and competencies required of the professional HRD staff. In the left column below, list the strategic objectives of the HRD effort in the organization. Then, in the next column, list the work outputs keyed to each objective. In the third column, identify the competencies required of HRD professionals to achieve the strategic objectives and yield the desired work outputs. This activity should result in a chart that depicts the relationship among strategic objectives for the HRD effort (or department), work outputs, and the competencies required of professional HRD staff to achieve desired results. (*Add paper as needed.*)

Strategic objectives	HRD work outputs	HRD competencies

Figure 3-13. A worksheet for comprehensive HRD staff planning.

Step 5: Assess Current Competencies

Once you have identified the competencies necessary to achieve strategic objectives and work outputs desired of the HRD effort, take stock of current competencies. There is no "one right way" to carry out this process. It may call for using one or more approaches for assessing current competencies.

One approach is to use *The Manager's Guide* from *Models for HRD Practice. The Guide* provides detailed advice about ways to assess current competencies among HRD staff.

A second approach, which might be called the *top-down method,* is to prepare a worksheet that builds on the results of Fig. 3-13. The worksheet should list required HRD competencies in the left column and then require a *collective assessment* of current HRD professional staff competencies in the right column. Working with his or her staff, the HRD manager can then engage them in an interactive dialogue to take stock of collective staff competencies, identify needed competencies, and set priorities for sourcing needed talent. The approach is called *top-down* because it is led by the HRD manager and requires a collective assessment of staff competencies.

A third approach, which might be called the *bottom-up method,* requires a detailed examination of the *individual competencies* of HRD professional staff members. Assessment is performed individually using the worksheets from *The Practitioner's Guide* in *Models for HRD Practice* or tailor-made worksheets developed from other competency studies. Such assessments may take the form of 360-degree examination in which individuals are evaluated (as appropriate) by themselves, their peers, their organizational superiors, their organizational subordinates, customers, and other stakeholders.[59] The individual results, while separately arrived at, are eventually compiled into a collective chart that depicts the composite competencies of the entire HRD professional staff. That chart, in turn, can become the basis for taking stock of collective staff competencies, identifying needed competencies, and setting priorities for sourcing needed talent.

Step 6: Source Necessary Competencies

As the model appearing in Fig. 3-1 shows, three primary ways exist by which to source necessary talent (competencies): select staff, develop staff, or identify other sources of talent. In this section of the chapter we shall briefly review how these ways may be used to source the competencies necessary for the HRD effort to achieve its strategic objectives.

Selecting the Professional HRD Staff

Selecting is the process of matching human resource supplies to work demands. In the limited sense that the term is used in this chapter, it refers to the process of meeting necessary work requirements through full-time staff.

Select full-time professional staff for the HRD effort from inside or outside the organization only when HRD competencies are required that

- match HRD strategic objectives,

- cannot be presently acquired from within the organization and are too costly to build from within,

- can be cost-justified on a comparative basis with other approaches to staffing,
- are likely to be needed for some time, and
- are consistent with organizational policies and constraints on employee selection—such as existing hiring freezes or reductions in force.

Remember that the expenses associated with full-time staff members are not limited to salary alone. Additional, indirect expenses include supplies, equipment, and benefits.

To carry out the selection process using a competency-based approach, begin by clarifying the work requirement to be met or the problem to be solved. (Try to avoid thinking in "job-based" terms because that may be too limiting.) Consider:

- Is there a match between the work requirement or problem and the strategic objectives of the HRD effort? (*If the answer is no, then rethink whether selection should be carried out.*)
- How long will the work requirement or problem exist? Is the need short-term, long-term, or project-oriented?
- How does the work requirement or problem match up to the existing competencies available to the HRD effort? Can the requirement be met or the problem solved, in whole or part, with existing staff?
- What results are desired, and how soon are they needed?
- What work outputs will be tied to the results?
- What quality requirements will be linked to the desired work outputs?
- What competencies are required to achieve desired results and produce desired work outputs?
- What HRD role or combination of roles best captures the essence of the work outputs and competencies required?

Use the answers to these questions as the basis for preparing a work description to express the work requirements to be met or the problem to be solved. Rely on samples of job descriptions from other organizations if they are helpful and can save valuable time.[60] Then craft a work specification that outlines the education, experience, and other characteristics that will be necessary in order for people to learn the work.

Recruit inside and outside the organization as appropriate. For internal recruitment, use such methods as job posting, word-of-mouth recruiting, and requests for nominations from management employees. Consult the Human Resource Department about ways to link the opening to existing individual development plans, if carrying out the work will lead to a substantial developmental opportunity. For external recruitment, consider using, as appropriate, executive recruiters, the Job Service, employment agencies, newspaper (or professional journal) advertisements, and university placement offices.

Begin the screening process for a full-time position by first preparing a profile of the competencies of the ideal applicant. List those on a worksheet prepared for that purpose, if possible. Then comply with the normal screening procedures of the organization by asking for completed employment applications, résumés, and results of psychological tests. Review the applications, focusing in on education, experience, or other characteristics that could be reasonably expected to yield competencies needed to carry out the work. Narrow the applications to three or four. Then ask the applicants to interview for the position. If possible, involve more than one person in the selection process—and use the profile developed for the screening process as the basis for interview questions and ratings. Ask applicants to bring samples of their work and deliver on-site demonstrations or presentations to show what they can do.

Developing the Professional HRD Staff

Developing is the process of cultivating talents to ensure that people are oriented, trained, cross-trained, upgraded, and prepared for advancement. Like selecting staff, developing should be carried out in a way that helps the HRD effort realize its strategic objectives. It should also be realistically tied to the individual career aspirations of HRD professionals.[61]

Develop the professional HRD staff when HRD competencies are required that

- match HRD strategic objectives,
- can be acquired in a reasonable time and at a reasonable cost from within the organization,
- can be cost-justified on a comparative basis with other approaches to staffing,
- are likely to be needed for some time, and
- are consistent with organizational policies and constraints on developmental methods.

Development is appealing because it enriches the available supply of talent and lifts the morale of the professional HRD staff. It can end up making better use of competencies that are already available to the organization.

To carry out the developmental process using a competency-based approach, you may find it useful to balance the top-down and bottom-up approaches described in the preceding section of this chapter. First determine the competencies needed by the HRD effort to realize its strategic objectives. Then, perhaps in parallel fashion, ask professional HRD staff members to assess their individual competencies. Be sure to use a common frame of reference, such as the competencies listed in *Models for HRD Practice* or the competencies listed in some other research-based study. Identify the gaps between available and necessary competencies. Then prepare a developmental plan for the HRD effort (collectively) and for contributors (individually).

Particularly helpful in this process is an individual development plan (IDP). It should be prepared to guide the competency-building efforts geared to individual staff members. To prepare such a plan, begin by identifying the competencies that are needed for work requirements and that are already possessed by the individual. Then pinpoint specific competencies to be developed, the means of developing them, time frames for development, and methods of assessing how well they have been developed. A sample IDP is shown in Fig. 3-14.

Many developmental methods may be used to build HRD staff competencies. Such methods may focus around giving individuals access to appropriate assignments, hardships, people, and other events.[62] The methods may include:

- Sending individuals outside the organization to attend non-degree-related seminars or conferences
- Sending individuals outside the organization to attend degree-related classes
- Rotating individuals inside the organization so they are given useful exposure and can gain experience

Directions: Use this form to pinpoint specific HRD competencies that are to be developed for the staff member, the means by which they are to be developed, time frames for development, and methods of assessing how well they have been developed. First complete information about the individual staff member in Part I. Then, answer the questions appearing in Part II. Finally, ask for signatures from the staff member and his or her immediate supervisor in Part III. Update this form annually.

Part I

Employee's Name	Job Title
Today's Date	Developmental Plan for Period
Supervisor's Name	Job Title

Part II

What Competencies Should Be Developed? (List them below.)	How Should the Competencies Be Developed? (For each competency listed in the left column, indicate one or more methods for building it.)	Over What Time Frame Should the Competencies Be Developed? (For each competency listed in the left column, indicate the time span for development.)	How Can the Developmental Effort Be Evaluated? (For each competency to be developed in the left column, indicate how successful development will be assessed and measured.)

Part III

Signature of Employee	*Date*
Signature of Employee's Supervisor	*Date*

Figure 3-14. A sample individual development plan.

- Giving individuals new work assignments to "stretch" their abilities.
- Giving individuals selected reading materials or access to videotapes, audiotapes, or software
- Pairing individuals up with exemplary role models or on-the-job coaches

An important point to remember, however, is that organizationally sponsored development should be *planned*. It should also be accompanied by frank feedback about individual performance and prospects to keep expectations realistic.

Identifying Other Sources of Talent

Finding the appropriate talent to do the work at the right time and in the right way may call for innovative approaches to achieve desired work results. Although many such approaches are possible, the following discussion will briefly focus on two only: (1) selecting or developing part-time staff from inside the organization and, (2) selecting external HRD consultants.

Select or develop part-time staff from inside the organization when the organization requires HRD competencies that

- match HRD strategic objectives,
- can be acquired from within the organization,
- are not too costly to select or build from within,
- can be cost-justified on a comparative basis with other approaches to staffing,
- are likely to be needed only for a brief time, and
- are consistent with organizational policies and constraints.

Remember that part-time staff members, particularly those selected from operating departments, may bring with them credibility with other members of the organization. Assignments in the HRD effort may also be developmental experiences in their own right. However, part-time staff members may not bring with them the appropriate competencies to carry out HRD work. They may thus require extensive training.

Select consultants to provide assistance only when HRD competencies are required that

- match HRD strategic objectives,
- cannot be presently acquired from within the organization and are too costly to build from within,
- can be cost-justified on a comparative basis with other approaches to staffing,
- are likely to be needed for a short time only, and
- are consistent with organizational policies and constraints on consultant selection.

When contemplating the use of consulting assistance, begin the process by developing a request for proposal (RFP) that spells out exactly what the consultant will be expected to do. Then develop a rating sheet directly from the RFP. On the sheet, list the work requirements. Then rate consultants' proposals and qualifications against the work requirements. As in selecting full-time staff, try to involve more than one person in the process of selecting a consultant. Rely on the rating sheet as key in the decision-making process.

While consultants are being used more today than ever before—and they are particularly appropriate when the needs are short-term and require specialized expertise—they are sometimes misused. Moreover, consultant assistance may have disadvantages. For instance, consultants typically lack awareness of the organizational culture. They may thus require guidance to avoid making mistakes that would not be made by savvy employees. The hourly cost of consultant assistance may be two to three times what it costs to employ full-time employees. To rely on consultants for long time spans can be unnecessarily costly and will rarely be sustained by a cost-benefit analysis. Additionally, consultants do not bear the consequences of their decisions and actions as full-time employees do.

Summary

This chapter has described the processes of selecting and developing the professional HRD staff against the larger backdrop of HRD strategic planning. These processes should not be viewed (or conducted) in isolation; rather, they should be viewed in the context of answering such questions as these:

1. What values guide the HRD effort?
2. What vision and plan guide the HRD effort?
3. How can the vision and plan be refined and modified based on external benchmarking?
4. What HRD competencies are necessary for the HRD professional staff to achieve desired strategic objectives?
5. What are the current HRD competencies?
6. What processes may be used to make or buy needed HRD competencies?

Selecting and developing the professional HRD staff are just two processes by which to source the talent needed to achieve the strategic objectives of the HRD effort. Full-time professional HRD staff should be selected only when organizational needs will be enduring and when the organization lacks the HRD competencies to achieve its desired mission. Development should be continuous, tied to building the existing competencies of the professional HRD staff so that they match the competencies required to achieve strategic objectives. Other staffing approaches should be used as appropriate to hold down the costs of employing a full-time professional staff. Such approaches may include outsourcing some or all of the work, transferring employees into the HRD effort on a full-time or part-time basis, relying on contractual assistance, and using temporary assistance. When using such approaches, one goal of the organization should be to muscle-build the HRD competencies available to the organization.

The future of HRD is exciting. But it is also fraught with many challenges to be met and many obstacles to be overcome. Among them is broadening the scope of HRD work to include more than traditional training and development activities. As the future unfolds in the present, HRD professionals must learn to be flexible—and to strike an assertive stance in working toward their own development and helping their organizations use selection, development, and other staffing methods to best effect.

References

1. Froiland, P., "Trainers' Salaries," *Training,* November 1993, p. 30.
2. Carnevale, Anthony, and Ellen Carnevale, "Growth Patterns in Workplace Training," *Training and Development,* May 1994, p. S22.
3. Gaudet, Cynthia, and Joe W. Kotrlik, "Status of HRD Certificate Programs," *Human Resource Development Quarterly,* April 1995, pp. 91–99.
4. Casner, B., and W. Jordan, "Professional Trainers Go to School," *Training and Development Journal,* July 1989, pp. 77–79.
5. Cunningham, T., "Should Trainers Be Certified?" *Canadian Training Methods,* April 1976, pp. 6, 8, 14.
6. Bratton, Barry, "Professional Certification: Will It Become a Reality?" *Performance and Instruction,* February 1984, pp. 4–7.

7. Zemke, Ron, "The Ups and Downs of Downsizing," *Training*, November 1990, pp. 27–34.

8. Schmidt, Warren H., and Barry Posner, *Managerial Values and Expectations: The Silent Power in Personal and Organizational Life*, AMACOM, New York, 1982, p. 13.

9. Deal, Terence, and A. Kennedy, *Corporate Cultures*, Addison-Wesley, Reading, MA, 1982, p. 21.

10. Hansen, Carol, W. Kahnweiler, and A. Wilenski, "Human Resource Development as an Occupational Culture Through Organizational Stories," *Human Resource Development Quarterly*, October 1994, pp. 253–268.

11. Leach, Jim, "Characteristics of Excellent Trainers: A Psychological and Interpersonal Profile," *Performance Improvement Quarterly*, 1991, 4(3), pp. 42–62.

12. Lee, Chris, "The Vision Thing," *Training*, February 1993, pp. 25–34.

13. *Info-Line*, "How to Develop a Vision," July 1991, Issue 107.

14. Allen, Richard, "On a Clear Day You Can Have a Vision: A Visioning Model for Everyone," in Elwood F. Holton III, ed., *Academy of Human Resource Development 1995 Conference Proceedings*, Academy of Human Resource Development, Austin, TX, 1995, p. 5-4.

15. *ASTD Trainer's Toolkit: Mission Statements for HRD*, ASTD, Alexandria, VA, 1990.

16. Rothwell, William, and H. C. Kazanas, *Human Resource Development: A Strategic Approach* (revised ed.), Human Resource Development Press, Amherst, MA, 1994, p. 2.

17. Camp, Robert C., *Benchmarking: The Search for Industry Best Practices That Lead to Superior Performance*, American Society for Quality Control, Milwaukee, 1989.

18. Boyatzis, Richard E., *The Competent Manager: A Model for Effective Performance*, John Wiley & Sons, New York, 1982, pp. 20–21.

19. Nadler, Leonard, "A Study of the Needs of Selected Training Directors in Pennsylvania Which Might Be Met by Professional Education Institutions," *Dissertation Abstracts International*, 24(2), 1962.

20. Lippitt, Gordon L., and Leonard Nadler, "Emerging Roles of the Training Director," *Training and Development Journal*, 1967, 21(8), pp. 26–31.

21. *The Employee Development Specialist Curriculum Plan: An Outline of Learning Experiences for the Employee Development Specialist*, U.S. Civil Service Commission, Washington, DC, 1976.

22. *Core Competencies for Training and Development*, Ontario Society for Training and Development, Toronto, Canada, 1976.

23. Pinto, Patrick R., and James W. Walker, *A Study of Professional Training and Development Roles and Competencies*, ASTD, Madison, WI, 1978.

24. McLagan, Patricia A., and Richard C. McCullough, *Models for Excellence: The Conclusions and Recommendations of the ASTD Training and Development Competency Study*, ASTD, Washington, DC, 1983.

25. McLagan, Patricia A., *The Models*, ASTD, Alexandria, VA, 1989.

26. McLagan, Patricia A., *The Research Report*, ASTD, Alexandria, VA, 1989.

27. McLagan, Patricia A., *The Manager's Guide*, ASTD, Alexandria, VA, 1989.

28. McLagan, Patricia A., *The Practitioner's Guide*, ASTD, Alexandria, VA, 1989.

29. Dixon, Nancy, and Jim Henkelman, eds., *The Academic Guide*, ASTD, Alexandria, VA, 1989.

30. McLagan, Patricia A., *The Models*, ASTD, Alexandria, VA, 1989, p. 6.

31. Ibid., p. 5.

32. Ibid., p. 77.

33. Ibid.

34. Ibid.

35. Ibid.

36. Bengtson, Babs, "An Analysis of CEO Perceptions Concerning Trainer Roles in Selected Central Pennsylvania Manufacturing Firms," unpublished doctoral dissertation, Pennsylvania State University, University Park, 1994.

37. Lee, Shang-hou, "A Preliminary Study of the Competencies, Work Outputs, and Roles of Human Resource Development Professionals in the Republic of China on Taiwan: A Cross-Cultural Competency Study," unpublished doctoral dissertation, Pennsylvania State University, University Park, 1994.

38. de Rijk, R. N., M. Mulder, and J. Nijhof, "Role Profiles of HRD Practitioners in Four European Countries," paper presented in Milan, Italy, University of Twente, Twente, 1994.

39. Ginkel, Kemp, Martin Mulder, and Wim. Nijhof, "Role Profiles of HRD Professionals in the Netherlands," paper presented at the conference "Education and Training for Work," University of Milan, Milan, Italy, University of Twente, Twente, 1994.

40. *Workplace Trainer Competency Standards*, Competency Standards Body—Assessors and Workplace Trainers, Australia, 1994.

41. *National Standards for Training and Development*, Training and Development Lead Body, England, 1992.

42. Foshay, Wesley, Kenneth Silber, and Odin Westgaard, *Instructional Design Competencies: The Standards*, The International Board of Standards for Training, Performance and Instruction, Iowa City, IA, 1986.

43. Foshay, Wesley, Kenneth Silber, and Odin Westgaard, *Instructors' Competencies, Volume I: The Standards*, The International Board of Standards for Training, Performance and Instruction, Iowa City, IA, 1986.

44. Foshay, Wesley, Kenneth Silber, and Odin Westgaard, *Training Manager Competencies: The Standards*, International Board of Standards for Training, Performance and Instruction, Iowa City, IA, 1986.

45. The Secretary's Commission on Achieving Necessary Skills, *Skills and Tasks for Jobs: A SCANS Report for America 2000*, U.S. Department of Labor, Washington, DC, 1993.

46. Dixon, Valerie, Kathleen Conway, Karen Ashley, and Nancy Stewart, *Training Competency Architecture* and *Training Competency Architecture Toolkit*, Ontario Society for Training and Development, Toronto, 1995.

47. Dixon, Valerie, Kathleen Conway, Karen Ashley, and Nancy Stewart, *Training Competency Architecture*, Ontario Society for Training and Development, Toronto, 1995, p. xv.

48. Cameron, W. A., *Training Competencies of Human Resource Development Specialists in Tennessee*, Summary Report, Research Series No. 1, University of Tennessee, Knoxville, 1988.

49. Eaves, T. A., "Trainer Competencies: An Examination of Existing Research," paper presented at the National Adult Education Conference of the American Association for Adult and Continuing Education, Milwaukee, WI, November, 1985.

50. Marquardt, Michael J., and Dean W. Engel, *Global Human Resource Development*, Prentice Hall, Englewood Cliffs, NJ, 1993.

51. Rae, Leslie, *Evaluating Trainer Effectiveness*, Business-One, New York, 1993.

52. Lawson, T., *The Competency Initiative: Standards of Excellence for Human Resource Executives*, Golle and Holmes Custom Education, Minneapolis, 1990.

53. McLean, Gary, and Roland Sullivan, "Essential Competencies of Internal and External OD Consultant," Appendix in William Rothwell, Roland Sullivan, and Gary McLean, eds., *Practicing Organization Development: A Handbook for Consultants*, Pfeiffer and Co., San Diego, 1995.

54. Regalbuto, Gloria, "Recovery from Occupational Schizophrenia," *Training and Development*, May 1991, pp. 79–86.

55. Galagan, Patricia, "Reinventing the Profession," *Training and Development*, December 1994, pp. 20–27.

56. *Road to High-Performance Workplaces: A Guide to Better Jobs and Better Business Results*, U.S. Department of Labor, Office of the American Workplace, Washington, DC, 1994.

57. Dubois, David, and William J. Rothwell, *Developing the High-Performance Workplace Organizational Assessment Package,* Human Resource Development Press, Amherst, MA, in press.

58. Gilley, Jerry, and Amy J. Coffern, *The Role of the Internal Consultant: Where Do You Fit?* ASTD, Alexandria, VA, and Business-One, New York, 1993.

59. Cohen, Debra, "360-Degree Feedback Offers Varied Ways to Create Feedback Surveys," *HRMagazine,* 1993, *38*(11), pp. 32–38.

60. *ASTD Trainer's Toolkit: Job Descriptions in HRD,* ASTD, Alexandria, VA, 1990.

61. Stump, Robert W., and the HRD Careers Committee, *Your Career in Human Resource Development: A Guide to Information and Decision Making,* rev. 2d ed., ASTD, Alexandria, VA, 1990.

62. McCall, Morgan, W., Jr., *Developing Executives Through Work Experience,* Technical Report 33, Center for Creative Leadership, Greensboro, NC, 1988.

4

The Learning Organization

James D. DeVito

James D. DeVito *is Johnson & Johnson's Vice President of Educational Research and Services. He is responsible for identifying state-of-the-art educational methodologies, technologies, and delivery systems for the corporate setting. He coordinates educational benchmarking activities for Johnson & Johnson and participates in selected professional organizations to gain access to best practices in the human resource development field. He is responsible for the delivery of Credo Challenge Meetings and the Executive Luncheon Series and contributes to the design and planning of major company meetings. DeVito began his career as a secondary school teacher. Later, he became Executive Director of Special Programs at Long Island University in Greenvale, NY. His corporate experience also includes sales administration and educational administration at IBM. He has significant international training and consulting experience including activities in Asia and Europe. He organized international personnel conferences and has chaired his company's Training Council composed of operating company trainers and consultants. DeVito was recently elected to the board of directors of ASTD and is past Chairman of the Conference Board Council on Education, Training and Development.*

The learning organization is a relatively new concept that has had a profound effect on how we think about organizational life. The learning organization offers a set of propositions that has had dual appeal to line managers and human resource development professionals. In these early stages of its development, a special challenge is to be faithful to its original thought and yet demonstrate its usefulness to organizations.

This chapter is a conceptual guide to the learning organization: it explores how to think about the concept; how to apply it to organizational life; how to define the roles and systems needed to support it; how to measure progress over time; and finally, how to get started.

The Basic Concept

The learning organization concept challenges a company to use knowledge as a basis for its competitive strategy and to see organizational learning as the bedrock for its ability to be truly global. As a foundation for organizational transformation, the learning organization holds great promise, challenging the very individuals who are the enterprise in a personal way. It therefore has something to say to all organizations, regardless of size, industry, or purpose, whether they are profit or not-for-profit. The learning organization spans an enormous field: it can aid large corporations to be competitive globally while it offers each individual the opportunity to achieve his or her potential with support from a community of colleagues.

The learning organization as a concept tends to defy definition.

> Learning organization is a category that we create in language. Like every linguistic creation, this category is a double-edged sword that can be empowering or tranquilizing. The difference lies in whether we see language as a set of labels that describe a preexisting reality, or as a medium in which we can articulate new models for living together.
>
> When we speak of a "learning organization," we are not describing an external phenomenon or labeling an independent reality. We are articulating a view that involves us—the observers—as much as the observed in a common system. We are taking a stand for a vision, for creating a type of organization we would truly like to work within and which can thrive in a world of increasing interdependency and change.[1]

For some, this description may characterize the learning organization as a philosophical system or a world view; for others, it embodies a movement, a way of life. How adamant must one be to be faithful to its tenets? Does the learning organization commit the enterprise to a particular organizational ideology that replaces everything else? These are just some of the issues and questions asked by human resource development professionals and, to a greater extent, the line managers they support. Since it is a relatively new concept, and understanding of its practice is evolving, the learning organization provides an enormous opportunity for experimentation. Individuals and organizations will focus on a definition of the learning organization that responds to their most immediate needs. Line managers will likely consider its benefits out of a sense of pragmatism: "Here's something that might finally turn this place around!" The human resource development professional may likely follow a more altruistic path to the door of the learning organization. However one chooses to consider the opportunity, there is flexibility in the way one grasps the concept.

Think of the learning organization as an hourglass. (The construct of the hourglass is the author's own way of trying to simplify a complex philosophy of organizational life known as the learning organization.) There is the presence of two distinct but connected spherelike forms; there exists the capability of traveling into both spheres at either end without leaving the confines of its shapely structure. As a way to approach the learning organization, think of one end as "building capacity" and the other as "harnessing experience." Building capacity emphasizes becoming all that is possible. Here, a division, a department, or a team shares a common vision and acts to accomplish that vision. As they grow as individuals and as a team, their understanding and action increases, and they achieve more than they originally intended. Applications of the building capacity approach concentrate on developing individual and team potential.

Harnessing experience emphasizes capturing and sharing valued accomplishments. Harnessing experience stresses the retrieval of learning that can be shared with the rest of the organization. One cannot share everything, but those lessons that can be shared are in strategic areas such as core processes, technologies, and culture. Applications of the harnessing experience approach focus on building a network of information systems enabling the organization to retrieve and deploy valuable lessons.

Both concepts depend on learning and both are positive expressions of the intent of the learning organization. Most organizations will find that one of these orientations is more compelling than the other in responding to their current needs. Both orientations are legitimate expressions of the learning organization. Some companies will base their practice on the building capacity platform; others will be attracted to the harnessing experience orientation.

Although the organization thinks and acts in one sphere, eventually it will gravitate to the other end of the "hourglass" and explore new opportunities. These complementary options for work in learning organizations can attract different departments of the same organization to either sphere. In some cases, the pull will be because of a particular functional orientation; in others, the direction of choice will come from the state of the business. As the organization matures in its learning organization work, it will initiate projects in both spheres. Progress in one area will generate insights for pursuit in the other.

Peter Senge is the leading proponent of learning organizations. In his monumental work, *The Fifth Discipline*,[2] he describes the components of the learning organization that are portrayed above as building capacity:

> A simple definition [of the learning organization] is that a learning organization is a group of people, a community, continually enhancing their capacity to create what they want to create.[3]

He further expands this description by saying that the learning organization is

> where people continually expand their capacity to create results they truly desire, where new and expansive patterns of thinking are nurtured, where collective aspiration is set free, and where people are continually learning how to learn together.[4]

The learning organization channels the energy of like-minded individuals into the formation of a community. With a common understanding, they in turn direct that energy to the achievement of common organizational goals.

Peter Senge says that learning organizations are about building "communities of commitment." These communities are devoted to expanding and renewing the capacity of organizations to achieve their visions.

Communities also are devoted to the collective capacity of the individuals who comprise it. The community is more than the sum of the individuals, and the community experience has a profound effect on the development of each individual. It increases the performance of the whole while it increases the capacity of the individual.

Some organizations may find that this understanding of the learning organization is beyond their interest or their capability. The approach may be incompatible with their current culture. Others may argue that it taxes limited resources. The investment in time, people, and energy simply may be too great, even though they can appreciate its promise. While their assessment may be correct, the learning organization may be precisely what is needed.

Another starting point for learning organization work, harnessing experience, may be viewed as more pragmatic because its intent is to capture and share essential lessons across the enterprise. The harnessing experience approach may appeal to those who see in the learning organization the ability to gain competitive advantage, where lessons learned are quickly dispatched to the rest of the organization. For them, the payoff is in internal cooperation across disparate units.

David A. Garvin, the Robert and Jane Cizik Professor of Business Administration at the Harvard Business School, takes this pragmatic harnessing experience approach to the topic. He contends that managers need a firmer foundation for launching and building learning organizations, consisting of the "three Ms": meaning, management, and measurement.

> First is the question of meaning. We need a plausible, well-grounded definition of learning organizations; it must be actionable and easy to apply. Second is the question of management. We need clearer guidelines for practice, filled with operational advice rather than high aspirations. And third is the question of measurement. We need better tools for assessing an organization's rate and level of learning to ensure that gains have in fact been made.[5]

Garvin offers the following definition of the learning organization:

> A learning organization is an organization skilled at creating, acquiring, and transferring knowledge, and at modifying its behavior to reflect new knowledge and insights.[6]

Similarly, Perkins and Shaw offer a complementary description:

> It [organization learning] is the capacity of an organization to gain insight from its own experience, the experience of others and to modify the way it functions according to such insight.[7]

Here the emphasis is on capturing lessons learned globally so that others can learn from them and apply them locally. This approach eliminates the redundancies in research and execution that impede growth. Learning now becomes a new weapon in the competitive arsenal.

David Garvin goes on to identify the characteristics of learning organizations:

> Learning organizations are skilled at five main activities: systematic problem solving, experimentation with new approaches, learning from the experiences and best practices of others, and transferring knowledge quickly and efficiently throughout the organization....Many companies practice these activities to some degree. But few are consistently successful because they rely largely on happenstance and isolated examples. By creating systems and processes that support these activities and integrate them into the fabric of daily operations, companies can manage their learning more effectively.[8]

For organizations considering the learning organization as a change strategy, usually knowing what is useful and possible is more important than ideology. Practitioners know that they need to assess how to introduce organizational interventions. Timing is critical. It is also essential to gauge tolerance levels. This saves time, energy, and, in some cases, political capital. Ultimately, progress will be made, but true progress often depends on the painstaking building of its preconditions.

The hourglass imagery can be helpful in recognizing that the work of the learning organization is in both spheres, one more pragmatic and immediate than the other. As progress is made, it is appropriate to turn the hourglass over and explore new territory. Over time, both spheres will need attention to keep the learning organization in balance, much like the symmetrical form of the hourglass itself.

An overemphasis in one sphere could distort the ability of the organization to integrate learning for maximum business impact. Likewise, the organization's inability to deal with marketplace realities may not be improved necessarily because it has better trend information (harnessing experience) or because it is able to retrieve data in a superior way. There may be human barriers (building capacity) that prevent access or implementation. The learning organization works best when there is an interactive relationship between both spheres.

Responding to Changing Needs

There are four compelling reasons why the learning organization has come into prominence in the past decade.

1. Competitive Environment

The worldwide competitive environment of the last decade has pushed every organization to question the essential elements needed to sustain long-term growth. Likewise, the interdependence of organizations, countries, and global markets has forced businesses to create new ways of operating in a single worldwide economy. These organizations require systems and structures that support and facilitate its interdependent worldview. While most businesses are not multinational, they are influenced by an increasingly global marketplace.

2. Rate of Change

The rapid rate of change explains why organizations and individuals must find mechanisms to capture learning. Capturing crucial changes in its technology, processes, and culture allows for rapid dissemination to the rest of the organization. Speed is now a great advantage.

3. Personal Fulfillment

People today demand that their work life provides opportunities to express their talents and abilities. They are not content to let the organization determine how they can be fulfilled. They insist upon work experiences that stretch them in pursuit of their personal visions. In a learning organization, this approach is valued by the company, for ultimately it stands to benefit as a result.

4. Demand for Creativity and Innovation

There is an insatiable quest for innovation as organizations compete in worldwide markets.

> Innovation is everywhere. The problem is learning from it....It goes on at all levels of a company—wherever employees confront problems, deal with unforeseen contingencies, or work their way around breakdowns in normal procedures. The problem is, few companies know how to learn from this local innovation and how to use it to improve their overall effectiveness.[9]

These four reasons confirm the timely interest of organizations in the concept of the learning organization. Whether a company consciously chooses to create a "learning organization" as a strategy for change, it has no option but to be committed to organization learning. The global marketplace expects it as a precondition for continued growth.

Purpose

The purpose of the learning organization is to maximize the potential of individuals and the company in order to achieve ever-changing objectives. The community of learners is about creating. They are working (living) together not only to solve problems but to create solutions.

> The problem solver tries to make something go away. A creator tries to bring something new into being. The impetus for change in problem solving lies outside ourselves—in some undesired external condition we seek to eliminate.[10]

The learning organization presupposes that the appropriate metaphor for productive work is not the well-oiled machine, but a human system, a human organism. Taylorism, a new theory in the early twentieth century, held great promise as the organizing principle for a productive workforce. Reducing complex output into its component parts and having human labor subservient to the requirements of the production cycle was the best way to ensure growth. In time, this model was exchanged for an approach that relied on the creativity of people, the organization's most important asset.

The human organism with its regulating features is a more robust image for people at work. It illustrates the existence of systems, of processes, of balance, of unrealized potential, something which the machine imagery cannot hope to capture. The relationship of units, of processes, all working to sustain the whole, better describes the organization. Kofman and Senge succinctly state: "We are going through the process of learning that the world is composed of interrelationships, not things."[11]

Applications to the Business Environment

As theory intersects with practice, applying learning organization principles to fast-paced, highly competitive businesses is a challenge. What are the major components of the learning organization? What is the scope of the initiative? What should be targeted for learning? How can learning be captured, retrieved, and deployed?

Major Components

Depending on their initial approach, building capacity or harnessing experience, organizations will emphasize different components of the learning organization. Senge talks about the "disciplines of the learning organization"; Garvin speaks of its "building blocks."

While Peter Senge's work conforms more to the building capacity sphere and David Garvin's corresponds to the harnessing experience sphere, neither orientation is exclusive. Both speak to the whole domain; it is simply a question of emphasis.

Garvin's approach will be more acceptable in those organizations where a short-term, bottom-line culture exists. This is not to suggest that Garvin's approach is less desirable or that the "community of learning-based approach" proposed by Senge is too mystical for organizations to adopt. When it comes to application, the agenda is framed around what is needed but possible to implement.

The Disciplines of the Learning Organization. The word *discipline* means "to learn": "A discipline is a body of practice, based on some underlying theory or understanding of the world, which suggests a path of development or 'education' in its true sense of drawing out."[12] Peter Senge describes five disciplines: personal mastery, mental models, building shared vision, team learning, and systems thinking.

The purpose of the disciplines is to increase the capacity of individuals, teams, and, by extension, the entire organization to create a community realizing a deeply held vision shared by the members. Each of the five disciplines is briefly described.

Personal Mastery. "Personal mastery is the discipline of continually clarifying and deepening our personal vision, of focusing our energies, of developing patience, and of seeing reality objectively....Its roots lie in Eastern and Western spiritual traditions, and in secular traditions. Personal mastery is the discipline that connects personal learning and organizational learning."[13]

Mental Models. "Mental models are deeply ingrained assumptions, generalizations, or even pictures of images that influence how we understand the world and how we take action."[14] These models lie below our conscious thoughts. They explain our biases, our tendency toward stereotyping. Until individuals and teams are able to bring these assumptions to the surface, they typically are unable to make progress.

Building Shared Vision. This discipline takes individual visions and ties them into a shared vision, galvanizing a group to achieve its goal. This is not a flight from current reality; it sets up a creative tension that pulls current reality closer to the vision rather than having it diminish the vision.

Team Learning. According to Senge, "teams, not individuals, are the fundamental learning unit in modern organizations; unless the team can learn, the organization cannot learn."[15] Team learning starts with dialogue; it suspends assumptions and enters into a genuine thinking together. When there are no hidden agendas, teams gather new insights and knowledge.

Systems Thinking. This is called the fifth discipline because it ties the previous four disciplines together. "Systems thinking is a discipline for seeing wholes. It is a framework for seeing interrelationships rather than things, for seeing patterns of change rather than static snapshots."[16] It is an attempt to keep the four from becoming individual techniques; systems thinking creates a whole. This is the cornerstone of the learning organization. Systems thinking enables us to deal with the complexity of life in modern organizations.

Learning Organization "Building Blocks." Assuming that the organization begins its work in the harnessing experience sphere, the building blocks of the learning organization revolve around Garvin's five main activities:

Systematic Problem Solving. Using the quality movement as a basis, Garvin suggests the following organizational expertise:

1. Relying on the scientific method rather than guesswork
2. Insisting on data, rather than assumptions
3. Using simple statistical tools such as histograms, Pareto charts, etc.

Experimentation.   As distinguished from problem solving, experimentation is motivated by opportunity and expanding horizons, not by current difficulties. It takes two main forms:

1. Ongoing programs where incremental gains are realized from improvement strategies
2. Demonstration projects where ambitious undertakings are designed from scratch to develop new organizational capabilities.

Learning from Past Experience.   "Companies must review their success and failures, assess them systematically, and record the lessons in a form that employees find open and accessible."[17] The challenge for the vast majority of organizations is installing a databased system that catalogs learning so that lessons can be easily accessed.

Learning from Others.   In learning from others through benchmarking, "the greatest benefits come from studying practices, the way that work gets done, rather than results, and from involving line managers in the process."[18]

Transferring Knowledge.   "For learning to be more than a local affair, knowledge must be spread quickly and efficiently through the organization....A variety of mechanisms spur this process, including written, oral, and visual reports, site visits and tours, personnel rotation programs, education and training programs, and standardization programs."[19]

Companies committed to building the learning organization understand that it is not created overnight. The disciplines and building blocks cited above require the understanding and dedication of scores of individuals and teams over many years. Given their nature, they are never mastered. They will forever demand refinement.

Targeting What Gets Learned, Retrieved, and Deployed

Identifying the learning agenda requires planning and a personal and organizational commitment. The decisions that are agreed upon will determine how dedicated the company is to becoming a learning organization and how much benefit can be derived from its practice. It is a question of priorities: Does the company place greater value on the answers it receives to questions or on discovering how the organization processes information to arrive at those answers? If an organization is unable to determine how it learns, it can never get beyond incremental or adaptive learning. On the other hand, generative learning enables organizations to position themselves for major breakthroughs.

How does learning differ in generative organizations?

> The ability of an organization/manager to learn is not measured by what the organization/manager knows (that is the *product* of learning) but rather by *how* the organization/manager learns—the *process* of learning. Management practices encourage and reward those managers whose behaviors reflect five dimensions: openness, systemic thinking, creativity, a sense of efficacy and empathy.[20]

The chart entitled "Characteristics of Types of Learning Organizations" (see Fig. 4-1) should be examined on its face, but also with an eye toward the underlying dispositions that must be in place for an organization to excel in generative learning. Generative learning is likely only if the organization has invested sufficient resources in the building capacity orientation. The full benefits of the learn-

	Adaptive	Generative
Strategic Characteristics		
Core competence	Better sameness	Meaningful difference
Source of strength	Stability	Change
Output	Market share	Market creation
Organizational perspective	Compartmentalization (SBU)	Systemic
Developmental dynamic	Change	Transformation
Structural Characteristics		
Structure	Bureaucratic	Network
Control systems	Formal rules	Values, self-control
Power bases	Hierarchical position	Knowledge
Integrating mechanisms	Hierarchy	Teams
Networks	Disconnected	Strong
Communications flow	Hierarchical	Lateral
Human Resource Practices		
Performance appraisal system	Rewards stability	Flexibility
Reward basis	Short-term financial	Long-term financial and human resource development
Focus of rewards	Distribution of scarcity	Determination of synergy
Status symbols	Rank and title	Making a difference
Mobility patterns	Within division or function	Across divisions or functions
Mentoring	Not rewarded	Integral part of performance appraisal process
Culture	Market	Clan
Managers' Behaviors		
Perspective	Controlling	Openness
Problem-solving orientation	Narrow	Systemic thinking
Response style	Conforming	Creative
Personal control	Blame and acceptance	Efficacious
Commitment	Ethnocentric	Empathetic

Figure 4-1. Characteristics of types of learning organizations.

ing organization are realized not by choosing one or the other orientation. Eventually both, building capacity and harnessing experience, must be embraced.

Framing the Learning Agenda. The learning agenda is arrived at by pursuing three paths:

1. How things are done *around here* (and why they are done the way they are)
2. How things are done *out there* (and why they are done that way)
3. How things are done *within me* (and why)

Usually, how things are done around here, in my company, in my organization, may be more difficult than determining how things are done out there. In all organizations there are barriers to sharing information. Barriers can be structural, emotional, and political. Structural barriers are easier to address (companies prefer reorganization to most other types of reform) because restructuring avoids change that requires personal transformation. "How things are done around here" means capturing the technologies, norms, values, and core processes that make an organization work. These may neither be universally understood nor generously shared, nor are mechanisms always in place to retrieve them.

"How things are done out there" contains two major areas of potential learning. First, how do other organizations implement the core processes that are critical to our success? Second, what is going on out there in the external environment with customers, regulatory agencies, the superhighway, geopolitical developments that may cause us to think differently about the near future? Companies are motivated to seek improvements if their current approach is causing pain, but they also need to search in areas where they already believe they have superior performance.

Finally, "How things are done within me" contains the most fundamental kind of knowledge that the learning organization requires, particularly if the building capacity orientation is emphasized. Here is where "personal mastery" comes in. This concept involves more than skills acquisition, like adding credits to one's bank account. Knowing, facing, and accepting one's vulnerabilities along with one's abilities is a lifelong endeavor. "How do I learn; how do I resolve conflict; how do I establish and maintain relationships?" These are the issues that require a personal commitment; they are the issues that every honest person works on for a lifetime. This level of dedication is essential to the building of the learning organization, because it is only through this personal commitment to change and growth that the individual has the motivation to continue with the ongoing mission of learning truthfully how things are done around here and how things are done out there. When a person experiences the personal rewards of change and growth, as well as the tension and pain of achieving a personal vision through self-mastery, she has the motivation to do the work of the learning organization. She becomes a credible model of learning to those around her. The "walk" and "talk" are aligned; this is someone to listen to. This personal demonstration of learning dispels the skepticism that inevitably will arise after the initial enthusiasm of learning organization work fades.

Content of the Learning Agenda
Information, Trends, Capabilities. The organization's capacity to capture data and information is essential for decision making. But gathering and retrieving information by itself does not give the organization a competitive advantage. It must seek to use and organize the data in a way that gives it an

edge over the competition. For example, Peter Senge's insight into the meaning of capturing and retrieving experience reflects his building capacity orientation. The learning organization is much less about the acquisition of knowledge. True, it is captured, but for the purpose of identifying trends or expanding the capacity to create.

> So learning has very little to do with taking in information. Learning is a process that is about enhancing capacity. Learning is about building the capability to create that which you previously couldn't create. It's ultimately related to action, which information is not.[21]

Processes, Competencies.   Competitive advantage for an organization is in its ability to enhance what it uniquely does best and apply it to the next business opportunity.

> The real sources of advantage are to be found in management's ability to consolidate corporatewide technologies and production skills into competencies that empower individual businesses to adapt quickly to changing opportunities....Core competencies are the collective learning in the organization, especially how to coordinate diverse production skills and integrate multiple streams of technologies.[22]

An organization's capabilities, its technologies and work processes, are targets for learning. Transferring them from one environment to another is the organization's most critical and promising learning agenda.

Norms, Values.   The cultural norms of an organization and its values need to be learned and shared. Here managers need to be able to distinguish between core values and practices. In their book *Built to Last,* James Collins and Gerry Porras describe the dedication of senior management in visionary companies and the dedication to communicating the organization's values.[23]

Some companies have created their own difficulties because they were unable to distinguish between their core values and practices. Practices are changeable; core values ought not to change. Knowing the difference enables companies to move with the times while preserving their basic beliefs. Understanding, learning, and communicating an organization's core values are essential for the learning organization.

Roles and Systems to Support the Learning Organization

The intent of the learning organization is to build capacity and harness the organization's experience. These efforts are designed to foster change and transformation. The creation of a learning organization is an organizational change effort where change presupposes learning. Learning is a fundamental component of human life.

> I do not think we are in the business of inventing learning organizations. They already exist....We're not building an airplane here. We're developing the capacity of a community of people. We're creating an organization in which you cannot *not* learn because learning is so insinuated into the fabric of its life.[24]

Roles

However, how well do we learn? What are the consequences of inadequate learning for individuals and organizations? Organizational learning requires targeted support and an infrastructure to capture and deploy it. Therefore, organizations need to ask what the roles of the CEO, management, teams, and individuals are. What is the role of human resource development, education, and training in the pursuit of the learning organization? What systems are necessary and what is the role of electronic systems in support of the learning organization?

The Role of the CEO and the Management Team.   The enterprise leader, the CEO, and the management team are guides to the future. Gary Hamel and C. K. Prahalad speak to the level of investment top management must make to secure a place in the future:

> Our experience suggests that to develop a prescient and distinctive point of view about the future, a senior management team must be willing to spend 20% to 50% of its time over a period of months. It must then be willing to continually revisit that point of view, elaborating and adjusting it as the future unfolds.[25]

The CEO has a special responsibility to have the executive team engage in learning. This means more than endorsing executive education programs. It means that the executive team needs to address issues that prepare the organization for the future. In Johnson & Johnson, the executive team spends at least one week per quarter examining a major issue that will have strategic impact on the organization's future. This is part of an overall strategy for getting the company ready for new strategic opportunities, be they product-, region-, or technology-driven. They have been faithful to this process, called FrameworkS, for over three years now.

> The intent of the process was to expose the Executive Committee and other Company leaders to a wide variety of new information and new perspectives, for generating discussions about these perspectives and for identifying opportunities for actions. We decided to call this process "FrameworkS," with a capital "S," to emphasize the multiple views—or frames of reference—that needed to be generated.[26]

There is tremendous learning going on, but there is also action and decision making. The circle of inclusion was recently expanded in one FrameworkS session where all of top management, some 300 people, spent an entire week together in a learning mode. The tone was conversational; the work, deliberate. Personal and business unit agendas were set aside to deal with the strategic growth opportunities that faced the entire enterprise.

The top management team of any company sets the organization's agenda. The way it deals with that agenda either fosters solutions or generates further complexities, oftentimes unknowingly. Therefore, understanding their role in systems terms is the most generative contribution a senior management team can make to the organization.

McGill and Slocum succinctly describe the role of management:

> The primary responsibility of management and the focus management practices in a learning organization is to create and foster a climate that promotes learning. Management's task is not to control or be a corporate cheerleader or crisis handler; it is to encourage experimentation, create a climate for open communication, promote constructive dialogue, and facilitate the processing of experience. When management accomplishes this, employees share a commitment to learning.[27]

The Role of the Manager.   Supervisors and managers play prominent roles in creating the learning organization. How they choose to manage either will release the energies of their associates in the pursuit of their common vision or will inhibit their ability to contribute. Hierarchy is giving way to competence. Positional authority is only important to the person in authority who lacks competence.

The debates about adopting the right organizational structure or embracing the right management style in order to create the high-performance workplace have changed not because we have developed more insightful models or because we have developed better management theories. The shift has occurred primarily because technology has provided a capability that was never possible before.

Computer applications have enabled both younger and more mature managers to make relatively equivalent contributions to organizational productivity. What the younger manager lacks in experience he gains in computer literacy.

> Much of the technology that will give managers the freedom to shape their organizations is already being commercialized—expert systems, group and cooperative work systems, and executive information systems. Expert and knowledge-based systems (a subset of artificial intelligence technology) are rapidly appearing in commercial settings.[28]

Effective managers tend to be people-oriented individuals who thrive on personal contact. Computers can never replace human contact; they make it possible to establish connections to more people; they also make it possible to have new kinds of transactions between individuals and within teams. Properly used computers foster greater interpersonal contact.

The Role of Teams.   If the fundamental work unit has shifted from the individual to the team, team learning takes on extraordinary importance. As with individuals, all teams are not of the same heritage. Some are thrown together quickly to address an issue and then move on. This kind is the "problem-solving team."

> In the cluster organization, groups of people will work together to solve business problems or define a process and will then disband when the job is done. Team members may be geographically dispersed and unacquainted with each other, but information and communication systems will enable those with complementary skills to work together.[29]

Other teams are formed for more thoughtful considerations, perhaps serving in a planning, data-gathering, or strategy-formulation capacity to provide recommendations for others to act upon. This is the "analysis team." Their primary challenge is in accessing all the relevant information available in order to frame the recommendations without bias.

> While in the past computers primarily supported individual work, the computer systems of the future will also be geared toward groups.[30]

Organizations are already using meeting and groupware applications consisting of electronic brainstorming and group decision-making software. These technologies make it possible for an organization to deal with substantive issues regardless of level. The computer can keep the author of ideas anonymous; the best ideas survive and get attention regardless of organizational status or political influence.

Still other teams may be formed out of the departmental structure. They may be assigned specific project work that relies on the expertise of individual team members. Since the team members have their home base in the same department and usually have greater access to one another on an ongoing basis, they are generally able to interact for the purpose of their own learning and development. This is the "development team." Charlotte Roberts offers advice on the development of team learning:

> Team learning is also the most challenging discipline—intellectually, emotionally, socially, and spiritually. The process of learning how to learn collectively is unfamiliar. It has nothing to do with the "school-learning" of memorizing details to feed back in tests. It starts with self-mastery and self-knowledge, but involves looking outward to develop knowledge of, and alignment with, others on your team. Most of us have had no training in this. This discipline will lead you there. Do you have the necessary patience, with yourself and others?[31]

Team learning, either organized formally through training and educational experiences or informally through on-the-job team reflection sessions, is becoming an important component in a company's management development strategy. Donald Schon relates the interaction of learning and reflection:

> Team learning processes, listed below, call for integrated thinking and action:
>
> *Framing:* Framing is an initial perception of an issue, situation, person or object based on past understanding and present input.
>
> *Reframing:* Reframing is a process of transforming that perception into a new understanding or frame.
>
> *Integrating perspectives:* Divergent views are synthesized and apparent conflicts resolved, though not through compromise or majority rule.
>
> *Experimenting:* Experimenting is action undertaken to test a hypothesis or a move or to discover something new.
>
> *Crossing boundaries:* When two or more individuals and/or teams communicate, they cross boundaries.[32]

The truth is that *all* teams—the problem-solving team, the analysis team, and the development team—are, in fact, "learning teams." Their capacity to learn is highly influenced by the charter that brought them into being. Problem-solving and analysis teams contribute to the learning organization by harnessing experience; the development team builds capacity.

The Role of the Individual.   The learning organization is dependent on everyone in it. In the past, an organization could be successful if it had a sustainable core of motivated, intelligent individuals to steer it. Today, however, the high-performance organization depends on everyone. "They insist that everyone learn about customers, competitors, and the company's own operations, not just top management."[33]

Learning is a primary characteristic of fast-cycle companies in the pursuit of competitive advantage.

> Markets, products and competitors move so quickly today that organizations with centralized intelligence functions simply cannot keep up. This is why fast-cycle managers want active sensors and interpreters of data at every level of the company. And why they emphasize on-line learning, which is the catalyst for continuous process innovation.[34]

Paradoxically, while outsourcing keeps individuals wondering and worrying if their function will be next, those who remain are expected to play increasingly indispensable roles.

Lynda Applegate describes some of the characteristics of the workforce and work environment of the future:

> As top management seizes on its ability to monitor without restricting freedom, employees will have more control over their own work. There will be fewer rigid policies from a less visible headquarters....Workers will be less tied to any one organization, and building loyalty to a company will be harder than it is today....As companies pull together the resources they need on a project-by-project basis and as information and communication networks extend beyond the organization, company boundaries will be harder to define. Organizations may draw on expertise that lies in a supplier or an independent consultant if appropriate.[35]

Systems in Support of the Learning Organization

Systems in support of the learning organization are often initiated in human resources or are inspired by the emerging use of electronic systems.

Human Systems.   Human resource organizations have developed a variety of systems that are designed to foster the quality of work life. Communications programs, formal education, opportunities for personal development, team-based work systems, and increased responsibility strategies are all designed to enhance the individual's personal growth.

The human resource development (HRD) professional, a term encompassing anyone who is engaged in the development of the organization's human assets, often plays an initiating role in proposing that the organization embark on building the learning organization for the company. Absent a formal declaration to become a learning organization, most companies today will embrace its principles.

The term *learning architect* is useful to describe the role that the HRD professional plays in establishing the learning organization. This is an individual who knows her craft, the organization, and its strategic path. She is able to fashion learning situations that fit the culture and values of the organization. Clearly, the free expression she has suggests that this is one of today's most influential roles, having impact on many individuals and large systems. Given the downsizing and reengineering of many organizations today, several "stone masons" have been let go or redeployed. These same organizations, however, value the need for the learning architect who can craft the learning agenda. The advent of the learning organization has not increased the size of the training department; in most cases, personnel has been reduced. However, those individuals and functions involved in training, education, and performance improvement have more than doubled considering the performance support roles played by the information-technology group, senior management, the line organization generally, and organization development professionals. Although many traditional training and development HRD roles have been outsourced, the elevated learning architect's role is one that can have a dramatic impact on the organization's future, its very survival.

Electronic Systems.   "Successful learning organizations use technology to elicit, code, store and create knowledge."[36] What do "high-tech" electronic systems have to do with learning organizations, which most would consider to be "high-touch"? In fact, today's business enterprise cannot be successful if it lacks either element.

> When information from previously unrelated sources is structured in a meaningful way, human beings become capable of revolutionary thinking. Computers that use

their speed and memory to reveal patterns in raw data augment the extraordinary capacity of humans to recognize and assign meaning to patterns.[37]

The integration of electronic systems with the capacity of individuals and teams to achieve their vision is the formula for future success.

Nicholas Negroponte, Director of the MIT Media Lab, writes in *Being Digital,* "In the postinformation age, we often have an audience the size of one. Everything is made to order, and information is extremely personalized."[38]

The new postinformation age puts the choice for entertainment, information, and, finally, learning in the hands of the individual. The once-rigid line between work and personal life has become blurred. Learning takes place on one's own time, now that technology has made self-directed learning more possible. The ultimate customization occurs when the individual selects his or her solutions. This is also the ultimate customization for teams and management groups who now have at their disposal a wide array of options. Where do these options and solutions come from? They come from the power of technology to capture what is possible, based on the knowledge, insights, intuition, and experience of the individual or team.

> We define institutional learning as the process by which information models change, be they data models, forecasting models, or procedural models. Therefore, a good enterprise model should include a design for systematically changing these kinds of models based on signals received from the environment. That means an adaptive organization avoids running learning loops repeatedly over static information models....Using technology to integrate how an organization interprets "what's going on out there" with a codification of "how we do things around here" creates an intelligent corporation.[39]

Making it possible for individuals, teams, and units to access information when they need it requires institutional networked capability. This capacity to share enables teams to be more productive and enables individuals to engage in genuine teamwork.

There is no institutional transfer of learning from the individual unless the organization wires itself with the capacity to store the lessons and disseminate them, as needed, to the entire organization.

> In the networked organization, rigid hierarchies are replaced by formal and informal communication networks that connect all parts of the company. In the adhocracy, a set of project-oriented work groups replace the hierarchy.[40]

The building of the learning organization requires a parallel building of an infrastructure that can deliver lessons at the time the learner needs them. Our training and education paradigm is designed around the proposition that learning some predetermined information is important "just in case" you need it a few months from now. (See Figs. 4-2 and 4-3.) Alternate training delivery systems have now made it possible for people to access training, education, and learning closer to the time it is needed. By accessing a satellite broadcast program, playing a video disc, or using any other form of self-directed learning, it is possible to learn closer to the time of need. Here the individual has more control. There are other systems, be they electronic or otherwise, known as performance support systems that provide critical information to the learner at the time it is needed. Providing just enough knowledge, just in time, is the promise of performance support systems; they place the control of learning in the hands of the individual at the time of immediate need. Gloria Gery writes about electronic performance support systems (EPSS) as a set of tools that helps the individual

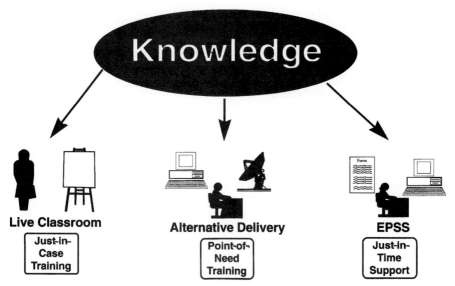

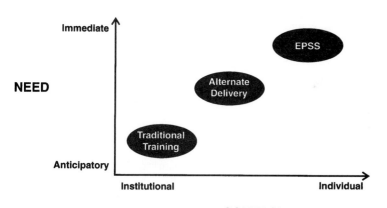

Figure 4-2.   Education-support systems.

Figure 4-3.   High-performance workplace providing education-support systems to enhance performance.

access or retrieve information or provides support to the user in achieving a performance objective.[41]

> The use of technology to transfer learning throughout the organization is a high priority of many global learning organizations, including Samsung, Xerox, and Singapore Airlines. Corning adds a new twist to technology transfer across locations, whether across the hall or across the ocean. They see it as a "process designed to identify the technical experts, capture their knowledge, and then transfer that knowledge to new generations of experts. Corning has made technology transfer a powerful tool in enhancing its corporate success on a global scale."[42]

The enduring benefits of the learning organization are best realized by using technologies to share the company's core processes and by providing the organization with the capability to retrieve what it has learned across the entire enterprise.

Measuring Progress

Measuring progress in building the learning organization can cause some dilemmas, particularly for training professionals. What can and should be measured? What are the barriers to success? What are the success indicators?

Care needs to be taken to select an approach that is appropriate. Most traditional training evaluation methods will not be helpful. While it is true that managers value what is measured, it is also true that what may matter most in the development of a learning organization is not easily measured. The temptation, of course, is to do it anyway, and risk having the evaluation process subvert that which you are trying to achieve. For example, presenting data on only those pieces of the process for which measures exist may simply distort the true progress that is being made. Bill O'Brien of Hanover Insurance offers this guide: "Time periods for measurement must be congruent with the gestation period of the learning."[43] Here are some additional admonitions:

1. Work in establishing the learning organization is tantamount to installing a new culture. Focus efforts into the start-up and leave the question of measurement aside for a few years.

2. Figure out why you want to measure. Does it arise out of a posture to "prove" that it is working? If so, it may simply reinforce the old culture.

3. Position your work in this area as "measuring progress" rather than evaluation.

4. Whatever you do in the area of "measuring progress," do it with the active participation of the line organization. Agree together on the criteria for measurement up front and involve them in the process.

Nature of the Measurement

Admitting that there are some difficulties in measuring the effectiveness of the learning organization is a healthy place to begin. Most learning organization assessment problems are generated by a lack of clarity about the organization's original purpose, namely, to build capacity and to harness experience.

Given our understanding of what the learning organization is and its purpose, determining what to measure should be client-centered. If the learning organization is about *building capacity,* the measurement will focus on the following:

- *Self and team reflection:* The capacity of individuals and team members to engage in reflection for the purpose of examining their progress.

- *Truth telling:* The ability of team members to speak their own minds and, in the presence of the team, to reflect the same truths.

- *Public works:* The capacity of individuals to speak and act in a public way as the work proceeds, as opposed to private actions and deliberations that only become public under certain controlled conditions.

- *Change-directed learning:* The ability of the team to direct its learning toward self, group, and organizational change.

On the other hand, organizations with a *harnessing experience* orientation, will be more interested in measuring the outputs of their efforts. Their outcomes and achievements can be appreciated and readily measured by outside observers. David A. Garvin provides a framework for measuring progress:

> Organizational learning can usually be traced through three overlapping stages. The first step is cognitive. Members of the organization are exposed to new ideas, expand their knowledge, and begin to think differently. The second step is behavioral. Employees begin to internalize new insights and alter their behavior. And the third step is performance improvement, with changes in behavior leading to measurable improvements in results: superior quality, better delivery, increased market share, or other tangible gains. Because cognitive and behavioral changes typically precede improvements in performance, a complete learning audit must include all three.[44]

Garvin specifically endorses the "half-life" curve developed by Analog Devices as a proven way to measure the value that short learning cycles have on organizational performance. Companies that take less time to improve must be learning more quickly than their competitors.

Clearly, in the early stages, it is important to point toward the impact of bottom line results. A focus group of 50 human resource development professionals cited the following indicators of success:

- Using action learning to solve business problems or seize business opportunities.
- Reflecting on learning experiences, such as asking what prevented or permitted seeing better solutions.
- Developing awareness of the gains that can be squeezed from mistakes and successes.
- Shortening competitive cycles, as in developing new products more quickly.
- Helping management to recognize learning as a factor that affects the bottom line.
- Increasing individual and group accountability for learning.
- Leveraging key learning points, such as learning to acquire the most critical data, not all data.[45]

Barriers to Success

Measuring learning organization progress can be greatly inhibited by individual and organizational factors. Immediate competitive pressures can become so powerful that the goal of building the learning organization may be abandoned since short-term responses may prove to be inadequate. Regulatory pressures, competing initiatives, impending reorganization, or any eventuality may become a convenient way to rationalize implementation problems.

There are two major barriers to measuring learning organization progress: human factors and technology-based factors. In the area of human factors, *self-interest* can play a role, most notably the inability to set aside one's own agenda when the team agenda should prevail. Secondly, it can take the form of *organization politics:* the inability to overcome internal pressures when a daring move is necessary sacrifices organization learning. It either delays what needs to be learned or it instills the learning of the wrong lesson. The human factors barrier can take on a third dimension, namely, the natural tendency toward *inward focus.* Learning progress is slowed when a reinforcing culture of norms and expectations are mistaken for competencies. The not-invented-here syndrome, which inhibits the introduction of necessary core technologies and processes from outside the immediate organization, will impede both learning and progress.

The human factors barriers to effective progress in the development of the learning organization are varied expressions of the larger difficulty that adults experience in their ability to learn. Chris Argyris believes that most people see learning as "problem solving" so they look outside of themselves for the answer. In addition, in discussing the reasons for adult learning deficiency, most often people blame poor motivation. Argyris argues that failed learning capability is not an emotional failure; it is a thinking failure, "the cognitive rules or reasoning they use to design and implement their actions."[46]

The second class of barriers to measuring progress is technology-based factors. Some organizations fail to create the systems for capturing what is learned and may then fail to create the capabilities for transferring what is learned. In most organizations these are hardware, software, and technology-based issues where the infrastructure does not exist to enable a complex organization to share its most valued prize with other organizational units—its own knowledge and experience. The importance of electronic systems in support of the learning organization was explored above.

Understanding the Barriers That Can Aid in Measuring Progress

The Individual.   *The Fifth Discipline* names seven myths that make organizations poor learners. We can gain insight about what we need to create by rejecting those beliefs that cause less-than-optimal behavior. The extent to which the following myths are absent can become a positive indicator of organizational progress. Following the statement of each myth is an adaptation of the appropriate reality, which is also based on *The Fifth Discipline*.

1. *Myth:* I am my position.
   Reality: I am part of a team that has specific value to add to the whole and can aid my team members in contributing their best.

2. *Myth* The enemy is out there.
   Reality: My ability to compete with the enemy "out there" usually depends on my ability to deal with the systems enemies "in here."

3. *Myth:* The illusion of taking charge (emotionally)
   Reality: Taking charge begins with seeing how we contribute to our own problems.

4. *Myth:* Fixation on events (as symptoms of causes)
   Reality: Threats to our success come from imbedded internal and external processes.

5. *Myth:* The parable of the Boiled Frog (where the frog is slowly boiled to death because it accommodates itself to increased heat and doesn't see the immediate danger)
   Reality: A highly perceptive competence to see the emergence of harmful trends

6. *Myth:* The delusion of learning from experience (at a time when experience is not predictive of future realities)
   Reality: The ability to understand that experience is a good teacher only if we have a long-enough view to see the larger processes behind our experiences

7. *Myth:* The myth of the management team (as a status motivator)
   Reality: A genuinely human team that can place the good of the whole above the ego and survival needs of the individual team members.[47]

The extent to which organizations are trapped by these myths is a revealing indicator of the work to be done. An assessment of the organization's ability to remove the myths and live the realities is a way for the enterprise to measure its progress.

The Organization.   Michael Marquardt and Angus Reynolds[48] have identified organizational barriers to learning:

> Organizations—structures, people, systems—may either help or hinder learning. Too often they hinder organizational learning and put up barriers through some or all of the following means:
>
> - Bureaucracy
> - Competitive atmosphere
> - Control
> - Poor communication
> - Poor leadership
> - Resource allocation
> - Rigid hierarchy
> - Size

Individuals can practice the principles of the learning organization but with limited success. True competitive advantage depends on the extent to which the entire organization can deal with the larger systems issues that are imbedded within each barrier.

Success Indicators

In a 1993 study conducted by the ASTD Learning Organization Network,[49] companies were plotted on a continuum of four variables, where each variable presented a polarity of accomplishment as described below. The four variables described characteristics of the learning organization:

1. *Single-strategy change effort vs. integrated strategy change effort.*   The change effort is focused on only one major element of the system such as training as opposed to the change effort focusing on major systems elements such as reward, structure, and culture.

2. *Local impact vs. system impact.*   The effort is localized to one unit—a plant, division, or department of an organization—as opposed to the effort involving the entire organization or directed to one department at a time until the entire organization is impacted.

3. *Single-loop learning vs. double-loop learning.*   The intent of the effort is to function more effectively within existing norms and toward established goals as opposed to seeking the transformation of the organization moving beyond existing norms and establishing stretch goals. In single-loop learning, individuals and organizations remain within known frames of reference regardless of how ineffective the outcomes may be. In double-loop learning people examine and challenge existing assumptions and look for solutions outside of their experience.

4. *Individual competence vs. team-system competence.*   The initiative is directed toward increased individual skill development and performance as opposed to team, department, or total system change. The intent of the researchers is to give the organization a gauge on its own progress. This scale when subject to the consensus of key players within the change effort can become an impor-

tant learning tool. By scoring a company's efforts according to the polarities described above, a company can get a sense of the progress it has made.

Measuring learning organization progress can focus on the entities where learning takes place, namely, teams, individuals, management, CEO, etc. For example, in the area of teams, Dechant and Marsick suggest in their *Team Learning Inventory* a more informal probing discussion of the following questions to be held by the team members themselves:

Organization and team conditions:
   To what extent:

- do team members have an opportunity to define and develop the team's objectives?
- is team effort valued over individual achievement?
- do senior managers support the outcomes of work teams?

Learning processes:
   To what extent:

- can team members drop their departmental frames and think from an organizational perspective?
- do team members seek out, listen to, and incorporate the perspectives of all team members in analyzing problems?
- does the team invite people from outside the team to present information and have discussions?

Capturing and transforming learning:
   To what extent:

- do members pass on what is learned to people outside the team through informal channels?
- are there mechanisms to convey the findings from work teams to the right people?
- are electronic bulletin boards used to ask for help?[50]

Measuring progress can guide the development of the learning organization if it is seen as a means to help establish a new culture. If evaluation becomes an end in itself, it will distract the organization from its primary work. That focus should be establishing the new culture to aid the organization in achieving its strategic objectives while providing satisfying work. Customized evaluating mechanisms may need to be developed, enabling the organization to measure its progress without succumbing to the dubious aspects of current evaluation schemes. Describing the journey the organization has made, revealing its progress and setbacks over time, may be far more important to the client organization than relying on more rigorous methods with their acknowledged limitations.

Developing Learning
Organization Competence

The learning organization describes the interaction between organizational learning and productivity. Developing competence in the practice of the learning organization requires some fundamental shifts in our understanding of how learning influences the way work is organized and how work is to be accomplished. We've seen that work is becoming more open and therefore more public;

it is always in progress and therefore subject to new influences. Therefore, all participants in organizational work are called to honesty and an ongoing dedication to their continued development.

Getting Started

Depending on the learning organization approach that is chosen, whether it be building capacity or harnessing experience, learning organization practitioners will be faced with three serious questions:

1. Is there a good fit between the company's needs and the promise of the learning organization?
2. Is the organization willing to secure the resources of time, energy, and commitment?
3. Do I believe in this vision myself; do my associates share this vision; and can we commit to a process that may place us at odds with existing belief systems?

With recognition that years of intense work are required, there must be an understanding that the promise of the learning organization holds something extraordinary for its members. Practitioners should assess how much work is needed to develop the preconditions for success. They should be prepared to approach its development deliberately, stringing together small successes that may lead to major breakthroughs. The vision will be built over time, for it needs to be shared by many.

Returning to the imagery of the hourglass and the approaches of Senge and Garvin, we find that there are some prescriptions for getting started. Surprisingly the first steps in either orientation, building capacity or harnessing experience, are quite complementary. The beginning can and should be quite modest.

The building capacity sphere calls for beginning with just one other person or with a team that is trying to solve a problem but is open to the prospect of examining its own process.

The first steps in the harnessing experience sphere are likewise quite straightforward. Garvin[51] identifies them in this way:

- The first step is to foster an environment that is conducive to learning. There must be time and reflection and analysis, to think about strategic plans, dissect customer needs, and assess current work systems and invent new products.

- Another powerful lever is to open up boundaries and stimulate the exchange of ideas among different organizational entities and functional groups.

Kofman and Senge infer a vision when they say that the learning organization ultimately needs to embody three capabilities that distinguish it from traditional business enterprises.

The learning organization must be grounded in three foundations:

1. A culture based on transcendent human values of love, wonder, humility, and compassion
2. A set of practices for generative conversation and coordinated action
3. A capacity to see and work with the flow of life as a system.[52]

This vision provides the ultimate description of a learning organization and eloquently describes the challenge necessary to begin building this kind of enterprise. However, the practitioner's initial vision will need to be suspended while the organization's vision is shaped over time by the collective insights of its major stakeholders.

The Work to Be Done

Given the infancy in our understanding of the theory and practice of the learning organization, organizations would make a serious error in thinking that becoming a learning organization is simply a matter of implementing what has been learned already. From the theory side of the equation, understanding the similarities and differences between individual and organizational learning is an ongoing research endeavor. Daniel H. Kim[53] addresses how individual learning is transferred to the organization.

From the practice, or experimentation side of the equation, chances are there are units already in one's organization that are becoming learning organizations with reasonable success. Their results should be quite obvious.

Ulrich, Von Glinow, and Jick in an article entitled "High-Impact Learning: Building and Diffusing Learning Capability," summarizes what is known and not known about learning organizations. The following accepted assumptions have become part of a new learning paradigm:

1. The concept of the learning organization is grounded in diverse streams of management history.

2. Learning matters.

3. Learning within organizations comes from both individuals and organizations.

4. Learning can occur along a continuum from superficial to substantial.

5. Learning comes from many small failures.

6. Learning often follows a predictable set of processes.[54]

While organizations have benefited greatly from the prolific work of Peter Senge and others, there are some things that are not known about organizational learning that the authors identify in terms of three challenges:

1. Learning organizations must avoid the trap of becoming all things to all people.[55]

Our understanding of the learning organization needs to be viewed as a progression of thought that begins with "T" (Training) groups in the 1950s and proceeds through such initiatives as MBOs (management by objectives) in the 1960s, strategic planning in the 1970s, and Quality Circles in the 1980s. Unless the learning organization can be identified with a set of concepts and practices that achieve general consensus, it will over time mean very little to most people.

2. Learning organization metaphors need to avoid concept clutter....The field is littered with conceptual and operational imprecisions.[56]

3. Management actions to improve learning capability need to be identified, tested and assessed through multiple research methods.[57]

As the authors reveal, there have been many thought papers on why learning matters rather than empirical research on how managers build their own learning capacity.

Peter Senge describes learning organizations as those that are continually enhancing their capability to create. This thought applies to those who have laid the groundwork for the development of learning organization thinking. Senge states: "By rough calculation, at least 100 years of work by some very fine minds produced the theories that underlie the five disciplines I describe in the book."[58] He credits Jay Forrester and Don Schon from MIT; David Bohm, a quantum physicist; Chris Argyris from Harvard; Robert Fritz, a talented musician whose thought contributed to personal mastery; and Charlie Kieffer, the founder of Innovation Associates, whose thinking contributed to shared vision.[59] Similarly, today's researchers and practitioners of the learning organization continue in that same pioneering spirit of thought and practice that will eventually lead to breakthroughs, perhaps in areas that are as much electronically driven as they are humanistically inspired.

At the outset, the hourglass was used as a metaphor for the learning organization. There is an eternal quality about the hourglass: in measuring time it can do so indefinitely, by simply being turned over. It is a finite tool that can measure the infinite. This reflects a reality about learning organization work, namely, the eternal renewal and continuous improvement that learning organization work is designed to achieve. The work is never-ending; building capacity through communities of commitment is continuous; harnessing experience to add value to the whole is an ongoing endeavor.

References

1. Kofman, Fred, and Peter Senge, "Communities of Commitment," *Organizational Dynamics*, Autumn 1993.
2. Senge, Peter, *The Fifth Discipline*, Doubleday Currency, New York, 1990.
3. Galagan, Patricia, "The Learning Organization Made Plain," an interview with Peter Senge, *Training and Development*, October 1991.
4. Calvert, Gene, Sandra Mobley, and Lisa Marshall, "Grasping the Learning Organization," *Training and Development*, June 1994.
5. Garvin, David, "Building a Learning Organization," *Harvard Business Review*, July–August 1993.
6. Ibid.
7. Shaw, R. B., and D. Perkins, "Teaching Organizations to Learn," *Organization Development Journal*, Winter 1991.
8. Garvin, David, "Building a Learning Organization," *Harvard Business Review*, July–August 1993.
9. Brown, John Seely, "Research that Reinvents the Corporation, *Harvard Business Review*, January–February 1991.
10. Kofman, Fred, and Peter Senge, "Communities of Commitment," *Organizational Dynamics*, Autumn 1993.
11. Ibid.
12. Galagan, Patricia, "The Learning Organization Made Plain," an interview with Peter Senge, *Training and Development*, October 1991.
13. Ibid.
14. Ibid.
15. Ibid.
16. Ibid.
17. Garvin, David, "Building a Learning Organization," *Harvard Business Review*, July–August 1993.
18. Ibid.

19. Ibid.

20. McGill, M. E., J. W. Slocum, and D. Lei, "Management Practices in Learning Organizations," *Organizational Dynamics*, Summer 1992.

21. Vogt, Eric, and Nancy Gottlieb, "An Executive Introduction to Learning Organizations," Micromentor, Inc., Cambridge, MA, pp. 1–12.

22. Prahalad, C. K., and G. Hamel, "The Core Competence of the Corporation," *Harvard Business Review*, May–June 1990.

23. Collins, J., and G. Porras, *Built to Last*, HarperCollins, New York, 1994.

24. Senge, Peter, "The Learning Organization Made Plain," *Training and Development*, October 1991.

25. Hamel, G., and C. K. Prahalad, "Competing for the Future," excerpt from *Fortune*, September 5, 1994.

26. Larsen, R. S., Memorandum, *Johnson & Johnson*, July 22, 1994.

27. McGill, Michael E., and John W. Slocum, "Unlearning the Organization," *Organizational Dynamics*, Autumn 1993.

28. Applegate, Lynda M., "Information Technology and Tomorrow's Manager," *Harvard Business Review*, November–December 1988.

29. Ibid.

30. Ibid.

31. Roberts, Charlotte, "*The Fifth Discipline Fieldbook: The Art and Practice of the Learning Organization*," Doubleday, New York, 1994.

32. Watkins, Karen, and Victoria Marsick, *Sculpting the Learning Organization*, Jossey-Bass, San Francisco, 1993.

33. Bower, Joseph, "Fast-Cycle Capability for Competitive Power," *Harvard Business Review*, November–December 1988.

34. Ibid.

35. Applegate, Lynda M., "Information Technology and Tomorrow's Manager," *Harvard Business Review*, November–December 1988.

36. Marquardt, Michael, and Angus Reynolds, *Global Learning Organization*, Richard D. Irwin, New York, 1994.

37. Haeckel, Stephan, "Managing by Wire," *Harvard Business Review*, September–October 1993.

38. Negroponte, Nicholas, *Being Digital*, Alfred A. Knopf, New York, 1995.

39. Haeckel, Stephan, "Managing by Wire," *Harvard Business Review*, September–October 1993.

40. Applegate, Lynda M., "Information Technology and Tomorrow's Manager," *Harvard Business Review*, November–December 1988.

41. Gery, Gloria J., *Electronic Performance Support Systems*, Ziff Institute, Cambridge, MA, 1991.

42. Marquardt, Michael, and Angus Reynolds, *Global Learning Organization*, Richard D. Irwin, New York, 1994.

43. Senge, P. M., C. Roberts, R. B. Ross, B. J. Smith, and A. Kleiner, *The Fifth Discipline Fieldbook*, Doubleday Currency, New York, 1994.

44. Garvin, David, "Building a Learning Organization," *Harvard Business Review*, July–August 1993.

45. Calvert, Gene, Sandra Mobley, and Lisa Marshall, "Grasping the Learning Organization," *Training and Development*, June 1994.

46. Argyris, C., "Teaching Smart People How to Learn," *Harvard Business Review*, May–June 1991.

47. Senge, Peter M., *The Fifth Discipline*, Doubleday Currency, New York, 1990.

48. Marquardt, Michael, and Angus Reynolds, *Global Learning Organization,* Richard D. Irwin, New York, 1994.

49. ASTD Learning Organization Network, *Portrait of the Learning Organization: Stories from Early Adopters,* ASTD, Alexandria, VA, 1993.

50. Marsick, Victoria J., and Karen E. Watkins, *Sculpting the Learning Organization,* Jossey-Bass Publishers, San Francisco, 1993.

51. Garvin, David, "Building a Learning Organization," *Harvard Business Review,* July–August 1993.

52. Kofman, Fred, and Peter Senge, "Communities of Commitment," *Organizational Dynamics,* Autumn 1993.

53. Kim, Daniel H., "The Link Between Individuals and Organizational Learning," *Sloan Management Review,* Fall 1993.

54. Ulrich, D., M. A. Von Glinow, and T. Jick, "High-Impact Learning: Building and Diffusing Learning Capability," *Organizational Behavior,* Autumn 1993.

55. Ibid.

56. Ibid.

57. Ibid.

58. Senge, Peter M., *The Fifth Discipline,* Doubleday Currency, New York, 1990.

59. Galagan, Patricia, "The Learning Organization Made Plain," an interview with Peter Senge, *Training and Development,* October 1991.

5

Diversity Training and Development

V. Robert Hayles

V. Robert Hayles, *Vice President, Human Resources and Diversity, Pillsbury, A Grand Metropolitan PLC Company. He is the human resource executive for Technology, Tax, and Treasury and also responsible for leading diversity work worldwide in GrandMet food organizations (e.g., Pillsbury, Green Giant, Häagen-Dazs, GrandMet Foods–Europe) to achieve exceptional business results by valuing and achieving the contributions of all people. He was formerly Director of Human Resources for the Pillsbury Technology Center. Prior to that, he was Manager, Valuing Differences, Digital Equipment Corporation and led strategies to leverage diversity for productivity-profitability by working effectively across all differences (e.g., age, culture, function, gender, geography, and style). Other previous positions: Associate Professor of Engineering Administration at George Washington University; Director, Research and Human Resources, Office of Naval Research; and Research Scientist, Battelle Human Affairs Research Center. Dr. Hayles was the first behavioral scientist to manage the U.S. Department of Navy Technology Base (an annual budget of over $1 billion). He has been a diversity consultant to many public, private, and civic organizations including the Urban League, World Bank, Internal Revenue Service, Stanford University, Exxon, Hewlett-Packard, Prudential, and Monsanto. Dr. Hayles has an undergraduate degree in the behavioral and physical sciences, a doctorate in social science, and postgraduate education in business. Hayles serves on the ASTD Board of Directors.*

This chapter begins with definitions of key terms related to diversity and diversity work. It next addresses a broad range of reasons for engaging in such work.

This is followed by a description of what must be done as preparation for conducting diversity work. Selected models and tools that guide training and development are described at the individual–small group and organizational levels. Selection criteria for facilitators are covered along with guidelines for the delivery of education and training. A discussion about evaluation is provided, followed by comments on cotraining, burnout, and rage.

What Is Diversity?

To experientially define diversity a group might divide itself by moving to different sides of an open space based on visible and invisible descriptors such as: likes to cook, likes to fish, eye color, parental status, introvert-extrovert, tenure in the group, and other characteristics. Discussions of comfort, new learnings about each other, invisible differences, and commonalities are worthwhile during the experience.

Individuals might then describe situations where they were with a group of people similar to them in some significant and self-defined way. Feelings associated with these experiences should also be shared. This process should be repeated for experiences where each person was different from every one around them. Participants produce at least 80 percent positive feelings about experiences with people like them (e.g., understanding, acceptance, camaraderie, fun, common bonds) and 80 percent negative feelings about experiences where they were different (e.g., anxious, uncomfortable, conspicuous, uneasy, afraid). Furthermore, when people are different, their behavior is often interpreted as aloof, hostile, stupid, or rude.

The above experiences provide the basis for defining diversity. We are all "different" and have experienced the pain of being treated negatively as a result of some differences. The goal of diversity work is to acknowledge that everyone is different while behaving in ways that cause everyone to feel the positive feelings associated with sameness or being around people we perceive to be like us.

Most organizations define diversity with a long list of characteristics. They include differences we frequently can see but cannot control such as age, disabilities, sex, race-ethnicity, and other genetically determined characteristics. They also include ones that we cannot typically see nor control such as sexual orientation and cultural origins. Partially self-determined differences like educational background, language, lifestyle, and job specialty are included by the most extensive diversity initiatives. No listing seems complete. An excellent video resource for defining diversity is *A Tale of O.*[1]

Diversity Is "All the Ways in Which We Differ"

Diversity work includes activities at both the personal and organizational levels. Comprehensive personal work addresses knowledge, behavior, and attitudes. Comprehensive organizational work addresses both human resource and business (e.g., decision-making, cross-functional, teamwork, and globalization) systems. The work addresses similarities *and* differences and seeks unity without uniformity.

Personal Diversity Work

1. *Head.* Knowledge, facts, information
2. *Hand.* Behaviors, skills, abilities, actions
3. *Heart.* Feelings, emotions, attitudes

Organizational Diversity Work

1. Business systems (synergizing across functions)
    a. Research and development
    b. Purchasing
    c. Customer service
    d. Sales
    e. Other systems
2. Human resource systems
    a. Recruitment
    b. Development
    c. Compensation and benefits
    d. Promotion
    e. Other systems

Why Conduct Diversity Training and Development?

Because people differ in motivational needs, there is no single reason that will convince everyone to engage in diversity work. Therefore, multiple categories of reasons are noted below. The change agents or persons making the case for diversity should custom-fit the justification to the audience. Fortunately, a wide range of resources are available to make this case. Summary statements for six categories of reasons are:

1. Personal Effectiveness

We know, from numerous anecdotes and decades of research, that people who learn to live and/or go to school with people who are significantly different develop better communication skills across those differences. Cook[2] summarized research focused on educational settings and described documentable positive outcomes. Children in integrated schools acquired greater social skills and achieved more personal growth than students in segregated schools. Integration did not cause declines in academic performance. Cox[3] describes how a climate of fairness and equity motivates individuals to maximize their individual performance and contributions to an organization. Ramirez[4] has reported research on individuals who can function in two or more cultures and think in two different styles (one that ignores the context and one that is especially sensitive to it). These individuals are measurably more effective in leading small multicultural groups to resolve complex problems. Deshpande and Viswesvaran[5] describe the positive impacts of intercultural training on expatriate managers. Beyond these empirical studies, the author has heard many individuals describe how their effectiveness as parents, colleagues, supervisors, community leaders, and other roles has increased following diversity education and training.

2. Social and Demographic Changes

Organizations that successfully address these changes are more successful with their clients, customers, and consumers. Excellent descriptions of how diversity work supports success by addressing social and demographic changes can be found in Morrison's[6] chapter titled "Achieving Benefits from Leadership Diversity" and in Popcorn's[7] report. They show the advantages of dealing proactively with increasing ethnic diversity, social changes like spending more time at home, and the impacts of a rising average age.

3. Litigation

Pain is not the most effective long-term motivator of change. When you inflict pain to achieve results, recipients of the pain will tend to seek redress whenever possible. Litigation is painful and usually produces short-term effects. It is included here because it is a reality. Examples of diversity litigation reported in the media during 1992 include:

1. *State Farm Insurance.* Class action for failure to fairly promote women settled for $239 million.
2. *Texaco.* Gender bias in the failure to promote one woman resolved for $17 million.
3. *IDS.* Class action suit over age bias settled for $35 million.
4. *USX.* Class action suit involving race discrimination settled for $42 million.
5. *Shell.* Wrongful termination suit based on sexual orientation settled for $5 million.

Other growing areas of diversity litigation include national origin, religion, disability, and workers' compensation for excessive stress. The U.S. Equal Employment Opportunity Commission received over 100,000 charges regarding diversity issues (not including workers' compensation for stress) in fiscal year 1993.

4. Fairness and Equity

When people are treated unfairly and inequitably they will usually complain. If the complaints are heard, some satisfaction is experienced by the complainant. If, on the other hand, complaints do not seem to be heard, unfortunate events frequently occur. These counterproductive events include everything from an increase in questionable expense reports to civil disturbances.

5. Productivity

Many anecdotes and research findings currently available show that diverse groups frequently outperform homogeneous groups. This higher performance occurs both in quality and quantity. Excellent factual anecdotes can be found in Adler.[8] A review of small-group performance literature regarding diversity was done by Ziller.[9] Ziller concluded that on simple tasks, groups heterogeneous in terms of personality, race, gender, etc., perform as well as and sometimes better than homogeneous groups. On complex tasks that require creative problem solving, heterogeneous groups significantly outperform homogeneous groups.

6. Profitability

Numerous anecdotes and research projects demonstrate the profit value of diversity. Organizations that have and value diversity avoid making many types of mistakes. For example, when Gerber decided to sell their baby-food product in Africa, they changed the white baby on their label to black and brown ones. The product still did not sell. Upon further investigation they discovered that it was customary to put a picture of the contents on the label—not the intended consumer. Gerber had to relabel its jars and apologize for suggesting that their consumers were cannibals. This mistake could have been avoided by having and valuing participation from someone with product experience in that part of the world. This is not a commercial specifically for hiring an African; anyone with the knowledge could have saved Gerber from this loss. There are hundreds of additional examples like this in the marketing literature and media.

With more empirical work, several excellent studies show that companies having progressive human resource practices (including diversity work) show more sales growth, more profit growth, better financial performance in a downturned economy, and overall better long-term financial performance than their less-progressive peers. These studies[10,11,12] have examined performance covering 5 to 20 years.

Progressive human resource practices are also an integral part of the best quality initiatives. Data on the outcomes of quality initiatives from Malcolm Baldrige Award competitors shows significant positive impacts on organizational performance (see Fig. 5-1).

Summary

WE NO LONGER NEED TO ALLEGE OR SPECULATE—AVOIDING DIVERSITY WORK HAS MAJOR NEGATIVE CONSEQUENCES. ADDRESSING DIVERSITY PRODUCES SUBSTANTIAL AND MEASURABLE POSITIVE RESULTS.

Figure 5-2 on the following page summarizes the case for diversity.

	Percent improvement
Annual average market-share boost	13.7
Average customer complaints drop	11.6
Employee turnover decline	6.0
Order-processing time reduction	12.0
Defect decline	10.3
Employee suggestions increase	16.6
Lost workday rates improved	1.8
On-time delivery rate rise	4.7
Overall customer satisfaction growth	2.5
Customer retention, return on assets, and return on sales increases	1.0

Figure 5-1. Quality does count as indicated by the survey results of Malcolm Baldrige National Quality Award competitors. (*Source:* The Wall Street Journal, *June 4, 1991.*)

1. *Personal effectiveness.* People who engage in diversity work are more effective in both personal and professional areas of life.
2. *Social and demographic changes.* Diversity work facilitates effective adaptation to these changes and leads to enhanced customer satisfaction, consumer relations, and marketplace success.
3. *Litigation.* Organizations that conduct diversity work experience significant reductions in external litigation and internal unresolved complaints.
4. *Fairness and equity.* Diversity work nurtures fairness and equity. It leads to fewer unresolved complaints, protests, riots, and misappropriations. A climate of fairness and equity enhances the motivation to perform and contribute.
5. *Productivity.* Laboratory and field research have demonstrated that on complex tasks well managed diverse teams outperform well-managed homogeneous teams in both quantity and quality. Diversity directly contributes to enhanced productivity.
6. *Profitability.* Organizations that conduct comprehensive diversity work are more profitable. Current research shows this to be true over 2-, 5-, 11-, and 20-year periods of analysis.

Figure 5-2. Making a case for diversity: six major elements.

Preparing to Conduct Diversity Training and Development

This section outlines the major elements of diversity prework and deals with gaining organizational commitment and assessing individual and organizational needs.

Getting Support from Organizational Leaders

While diversity efforts are often initiated in parts of organizations, the fastest-moving and most successful efforts gain support early from formal and informal leaders. Whether this is done in one-to-one sessions, executive briefings, introductory workshops, or other creative approaches, the two elements (what and why) outlined below are present.

What Is Diversity?

A broad, inclusive definition of diversity explicitly declares that *everyone will benefit* from diversity work (e.g., shy people, nongolfers, men, nonexempt employees, executives, salespeople, people with disabilities, and parents). It also requires that *everyone must engage* in diversity work (e.g., younger employees, managers, scientists, people of color, and secretaries). Discussion of the definition also makes the point that diversity work is about similarities *and* differences. Major similarities will be the organization's vision, mission, goals, and objectives. The work is about *unity without requiring uniformity.*

Since many people think race and gender when the word *diversity* is used, special effort is required to articulate a broad, inclusive definition of diversity. Some organizations use other words to facilitate the acceptance of this view of diversity. Some talk about pluralism, globalization, reengineering focused on processes, or organizational development and effectiveness.

Equal opportunity, affirmative action, and diversity will often be raised in the same context. View them as working partnership with one another. Equal opportunity guarantees equality and fairness and provides complaint resolution processes. Affirmative action proactively works to create diversity where it is lacking or insufficient. It can conceptually be applied to any situation where a group or perspective is underrepresented. For example, if the sales department has no senior managers with backgrounds in marketing, use affirmative action to address it. If there are not Spanish-speaking employees in the customer service department which serves Spanish-speaking clients, use affirmative action.

Why Engage in Diversity Work?

Once the definition has been presented, discussed, examined, and at least intellectually accepted, rationales for directing resources into diversity work must be shared. Because people differ in motivational needs, multiple categories of compelling reasons must be noted. The change agents or persons making the case for diversity should fit the justification to the audience. Six key elements to make the case for diversity are listed in Fig. 5-2. More details and sources are provided in the section called "Why Conduct Diversity Training and Development?"

In each of the above areas, examples from the organization being addressed are helpful. Internal information on employee attrition, missed opportunities in the increasingly diverse marketplace, marketing successes and blunders, litigation, and complaints help make the case. The next-best examples come from the same industry or type of organization. Diversity professionals who specialize in making the case to management keep current data and examples for this purpose.

Needs Assessment

Before diversity work can begin, the organization should be assessed to determine its strengths, weaknesses, and opportunities. The organization's stage of development regarding diversity should also be determined. This assessment is necessary to guide the design of diversity work. At least three areas should be examined.

1. Representation.   An excellent guide for this part of the assessment can be found in most any city, state, federal, or other government equal-opportunity or affirmative-action audit. Examine the organization to see if diversity is evident at all levels in all functions. Are hiring opportunities, promotions, performance appraisals, training opportunities, recognition and awards, pay, and all other benefits of employment distributed fairly and equitably? This analysis is primarily a statistical one focused on possible differential treatment related to race, gender, age, disability, marital status, or any characteristic of interest. Having an external resource conduct or at least be involved in these analyses adds credibility.

2. Climate.   The purpose of assessing the climate is to determine whether or not the experience a person has in the organization is impacted by differences. Some quantitative indicators of differing climates for different groups are attrition, internal complaints, litigation, and unexcused absences. Qualitative indicators of climate include employee perceptions about their quality of work life. This includes questions asked in standard organizational surveys about issues such as satisfaction with supervisor, perceptions about discrimination, beliefs about fair application of disciplinary procedures, and views about equity regarding the issues listed in the section above (e.g., promotions and performance appraisals). Methods for assessing climate include observation, interviews, focus groups, surveys, and questionnaires.

3. "Bests."   This part of the assessment means evaluating the organization relative to peer organizations. (Also see Chap. 19, Benchmarking for Best Practices.) A growing literature evaluates and describes the best places to work for people in general, mothers, Hispanics, African-Americans, and so on. Sample sources include:

1. *Good Housekeeping* (August 1990) lists the "69 Top Companies for Working Mothers."
2. *Fortune* (February 8, 1993) lists "America's Most Admired Corporations."
3. *Business Week* (August 6, 1990) describes "The Best Companies for Women."
4. *Hispanic* (January–February 1992) presents the 100 best places for Hispanics to work.
5. *The Advocate* (June 16, 1992) offers the "Top 10" places for gay men and lesbian workers.
6. *Black Enterprise* (February 1992) identifies "25 Best Places for Blacks to Work."

There are a significant number of benchmarking studies regarding diversity. An excellent and comprehensive one is reported in *The New leaders: Guidelines on Leadership Diversity in America* by Ann Morrison.[6]

Ideally, the assessor designs a tool to evaluate his or her organization relative to the above three areas. The best places to work and benchmarking literature provide reference points and standards of performance. One organization, The Pillsbury Company, developed a "Diversity Index" based on the above three areas which covers seven key areas. Thomas A. Gordon (Thomas A. Gordon & Associates, Inc., Philadelphia, Pennsylvania) made significant contributions to the design of this index. The seven key areas addressed in this index are described in Fig. 5-3.

Once an assessment is done, the results should be fed back to the organization. Areas that are not likely to be addressed or at least discussed should not be included in data collection that is directly from members of the organization. As with any such survey or interviews, confidentiality must also be protected. Feedback methods should match the culture and style of the organization and may range from informal small-group discussions to formal large-scale, high-technology methods. In general, the process should include two-way dialogues and involve written, visual, and spoken mediums.

Models and Theories to Guide Workshop Design

The author's first experience with leading diversity work came when a senior military officer indicated that "we need a race relations officer for this post and I'm designating you as that person." The author thanked the officer for that opportunity and requested additional guidance. The answer was quite clear. "You're the one with a doctorate in psychology—use it!" The author proceeded to apply research and theory-based knowledge about attitude change, behavior modification, communication, and organizational change and/or development to the issue of race relations. Since then, applications have been made to many diversity issues. The materials presented below are samples of social science models and tools that guide and enhance the effectiveness of diversity work.

Sponsorship. Powerful, influential, credible leaders must understand, own, and champion our diversity initiative. They must create and sustain a climate of belief in the concept and its multiple rationales.

Support. At least 5 percent of our people must become both conscious and competent about diversity. These ambassadors must lead by example, train, educate, and coach all employees to routinely apply relevant diversity concepts to the conduct of our business.

Strategy. Diversity-relevant activities and resources must be integrated with organizational goals, priorities, and values. Sponsors must lead in communicating our vision and strategy.

Skills. All employees must participate in education and training to develop general and specific knowledge about the culture and skills to succeed in a diverse workforce and marketplace. All employees should also have opportunities to develop understanding (emotional) to enhance usage of the above knowledge and skills.

Staffing. Diversity must be visible in every part and at all levels of our organization. Staffing processes must explicitly reflect this goal.

Systems. Every business and human resource system (process and content, formal and informal, internal and external) must include diversity.

Scanning. To effectively lead our diversity initiative, we must sense, measure, and monitor both the external (customer, consumer, competitor, investor, legislative, etc.) and internal (employee) environments. Results of these scans will help guide continuous improvement.

Figure 5-3. Diversity index: seven key areas.

H-cubed. A very basic model comes from the literature on personal development. That literature uses terms like cognitive, behavioral, and affective to describe what must be addressed.

The author uses the expression H-cubed, which refers to the head, hand, and heart (knowledge, behavior, and feelings). Effective diversity training addresses all three aspects in appropriate developmental sequences. The proportion of each is determined by needs assessments and the willingness of participants to engage in the more intrusive work which involves feelings. Good diversity work includes attention to knowledge and behavior. Excellence in diversity can be achieved by including emotional (attitudinal, feeling, affective) material. While the head and hand work can be required, heart work must be voluntary. Of the three elements, heart work also requires the highest level of counseling and facilitation competency.

Examples of each of the above elements might be useful. Head work consists of activities aimed at increasing knowledge about diversity issues. Historical or demographic material, facts about specific cultures, data on the costs of discrimination, and a business case for diversity are knowledge-oriented. This work can and should occur in early developmental stages. Hand work addresses what we do and say. It might involve discussions of appropriate and inappropriate behavior in a certain context followed by some role playing or "practice." This occurs best once the topic has been thoroughly introduced and a constructive climate established. Heart work should be voluntary and only done after appropriate introductory and climate-setting work. It includes higher-risk (requiring higher trainer skill) activities like examining stereotypes, discussing personal prejudices, and surfacing disagreement between spoken beliefs and actual behaviors. Many "heart work" activities are described in Fowler and Mumford,[13] Thiederman,[14] and Walker.[15]

Intergroup Contact. Another significant body of research that can guide diversity education and training deals with the conditions under which people work effectively together. Some conditions have been demonstrated to be especially effective in reducing prejudices. The *contact hypothesis* described by Amir[16] summarizes those conditions as when:

1. groups have equal status;
2. positive perceptions of the other group occurs;
3. other majority-group members are involved;
4. activities involved require intergroup cooperation;
5. situations entail interdependence or superordinate goals;
6. contact is more intimate than casual;
7. authority and/or social climate promotes intergroup contact; and
8. contact is pleasant or rewarding.

These conditions should be created inside and outside of the education and training situation.

Developmental Stages. Another powerful theoretically based collection of frameworks for designing diversity education and training comes from the literature on how we grow and move to more mature stages of development regarding awareness, sensitivity, or identity. A well-known model is Bennett's Developmental Model of Intercultural Sensitivity.[17] Its stages are denial, defense, minimization, acceptance, adaptation, and integration. Bennett describes the first three stages as ethnocentric, focused on one's own ethnic group as the central point of reference, and the last three stages as ethnorelative, where others are merely different and not necessarily inferior.

A developmental model more focused on identity has been created by Cross[18] and is called the Black Identity Transformation Model. Its stages include preencounter, encounter, immersion-emersion, internalization, and internalization-commitment. There are parallel models for other identifiable groups. For example, a model described by Airall[19] addresses whites and is called the Racial Identity for Whites Model. Its stages are naiveté, acceptance, resistance, redefinition, and internalization.

Developmentally sequenced education and training initiatives are the most sophisticated approaches available. They are designed to move participants progressively forward from their present stage. Models like those presented above provide sound theoretical guidance. See Hayles[20] for a more extensive listing and description of education and training techniques based on social science research. He includes techniques such as belief similarity, cathartic processes, complexity training, culture assimilators, and self-insight generation.

Diversity Organizational Development

There are also models that go beyond the individual or small-group level and address the organization's stage of development. Well-developed models have been presented by Armour (Transcultural International: Toronto, Canada, and Amsterdam, The Netherlands), Bailey Jackson (University of Massachusetts at Amherst), and Judith H. Katz and Frederick A. Miller (Kaleel Jamison Consulting

Group, Inc., Cincinnati, OH). While each model has its own unique vocabulary, they all describe the stages through which an organization goes as it moves from a monocultural-exclusive stage through some transitional times and ultimately to an inclusive-pluralistic-transformed stage. Education, training, and development efforts along with other actions should be appropriate for the current stage and implemented to move the organization forward toward a more pluralistic stage. The authors of the above models have also developed specific action recommendations suited to each stage of development. As an organization moves through these stages, education and training should move from awareness-knowledge and broadly defined diversity issues to attitudes-feelings and behaviors regarding complex challenging issues (e.g., sexism, racism, and sexual orientation).

Trainer Selection and/or Development

Use internal trainers to the greatest extent possible. External resources are to be used strategically and when adequate internal talent is not available. Criteria for selecting external trainers are noted first, followed by a process appropriate for selecting and developing internal resources.

Selecting External Trainers.   Two general types of expertise must be examined. First, look for the competence to deliver general introductory sessions regarding diversity defined inclusively. Second, look for in-depth competencies regarding specific diversity issues (e.g., ageism, antisemitism, cross-functional teaming, disabilities awareness, homophobia, intercultural issues, language, racism, sexual harassment, and sexism). Individual trainers will not be highly qualified in more than a few specific areas.

In addition to being able to deliver introductory diversity workshops or sessions making the case for diversity work, prospective trainers should be able to answer the following questions. The nature of a competent response is briefly noted in parentheses following the questions.

1. How is the education and training that you will deliver designed? (Knowledge, awareness, and skills; developmentally sequenced; based on the results of needs assessments; adaptive regarding different participant learning styles; cognitive and behavioral work is required; and affective or emotional work is optional.)

2. How do you handle questions about why we are doing this?   (Reiterating the business case for diversity with concrete data and relevant examples of successes and failures; exploring costs and benefits of diversity work; and reaffirming an inclusive definition of diversity.)

3. What else do we need besides education and training?   (Address diversity in our human resource, functional, and business systems.)

4. What human resource areas do we need to address when it comes to diversity?   (Practices and policies covering recruitment through retirement; removing barriers and inequities; rewards and incentives for diversity work and/or progress; and evaluation of effectiveness.)

5. What does it mean to address diversity in business and functional systems? (Targeted marketing; cross-functional team building; studying and using marketplace demographic data; and involvement of employee resource groups in business activities.)

6. How do you deal with resistance and backlash? (Developmental sequencing; inclusive definition of diversity; balancing challenge and support to participants; responding at the mental, behavioral, and emotional levels; and active listening.)

7. Who should conduct diversity training? (Cotraining is ideal; cotrainers should differ in at least gender and ethnicity or style; and having passion around the issue but personal rage under control.)

8. What are your diversity education and training competencies regarding specific issues such as antisemitism, French-Canadian/Anglo-Canadian conflicts, and black-white racial matters? (Have done personal emotional work on the issue; historical knowledge; demographic information; can describe appropriate and inappropriate behaviors; counseling skills; and facilitation skills.)

9. What personal competencies support your success in diversity work? (Abilities to deal with psychological stress, effectively communicate, and build interpersonal relationships. These were factors analytically identified by Hammer.[21])

10. What are your education and training credentials? (Academic background, postdegree professional development, professional organization participation, experience, references, examples of excellence in challenging situations, and learnings from failures.)

Selecting Internal Trainers. The criteria successfully used by Grand Metropolitan, a public limited company (PLC), to select internal trainers were: (1) have good basic communication skills; (2) at least "meet expectations" in the regular job; (3) receive support from their managers; and (4) show a personal commitment to diversity and diversity work. Criteria 1 to 3 are typical standards for additional work opportunities. Criteria 4 is somewhat unique to diversity work. If you are an accountant who does an excellent job at work but has difficulty balancing your checkbook, there is no reason to limit your employment opportunities. If, however, you do excellent diversity work at the office and then are seen by fellow employees engaging in antisemitic, sexist, or racist behavior away from the office, your credibility for diversity work is seriously damaged. Therefore, a personal commitment is required.

Once the above criteria are met, then the internal talent pool must be developed to deliver the desired results. The basic model for such development entails the following steps for prospective internal facilitators.

1. Going through the workshops to be conducted as a participant. This step should be done more slowly and to a greater depth than the actual sessions to be led by these "trainees."

2. Going through the workshop in a "train the trainer" mode with full explanations of the rationales for each element of the session. Trainers must understand the models which determine the content, sequence, and processes used.

3. Practicing delivery of the workshop with participants suitable for facilitators who are just beginning to gain experience. Detailed constructive feedback from participants and the person(s) leading the internal development process is essential.

4. Delivery of the workshop in a cotraining mode with an experienced trainer. Ample feedback is required.

5. Continue cotraining with experienced professionals until both the new trainer and experienced trainers agree that competency is sufficient to work with less experienced trainers or alone.

6. Seeking and reviewing feedback continues to occur for all facilitation work. Be alert for signs of burnout.

Trainers can resign, be asked to resign, or take an extended break whenever their effectiveness declines. Trainers should also absent themselves when they find the work overly stressful or no longer rewarding.

Training Delivery Guidelines

Facilities

The facilities in which diversity training is conducted should be healthy, flexible learning environments.

Healthy means: nutritious food with variety sufficient to meet diverse dietary preferences; physically safe in terms of access and security; convenient diverse exercise options; pleasing to the senses; clean and safe (air, water, sanitation); and comfortable (temperature, humidity, seating).

Flexible means: large rooms and breakout rooms; adjustable and movable chairs and tables; adjustable meal times and serving locations; meeting space available 24 hours a day; convenient transportation arrangements to nearby terminals; a convenient rental car resource; and all Americans with Disabilities Act guidelines should be exceeded.

Learning environment includes: modern audiovisual equipment; telecommunication link; computer resources on-site; diverse supplies for writing, drawing, crafting, and other creative activities; stimulating mind-expanding reading materials; and access to on-line research resources.

See Fig. 5-4 for a brief checklist.

Participant Selection and Group Size

Who Goes First? Successful diversity initiatives usually start with senior management and then proceed with all employees. Starting with the senior

---

1. Food quality, variety, and service flexibility
2. Exercise resources
3. General safety and security
4. Clean (air, water, sanitation)
5. Comfortable (heating, cooling, seating, bedding)
6. Flexible meeting spaces (e.g., size, seating arrangements)*
7. Easy transportation access
8. Modern audiovisual equipment and training tools
9. Computer resources (e.g., research, writing, communicating)
10. Mind-expanding (scenic, with library and creativity resources)

*Americans with Disabilities Act guidelines should be exceeded.

Figure 5-4. Ten-item facilities checklist.

group demonstrates a leadership commitment. It also affirms that everyone must do her or his own personal work in this area. It cannot be delegated. Working with the senior group makes it easier to obtain resources to continue the work.

Voluntary or Mandatory Participation?   Invitations to diversity work-shops should come form the appropriate senior manager with language such as "strongly encouraged," "significant for your/our success," or "of personal and organizational benefit." Using language like "required" or "mandatory" often sets an antagonistic tone that takes time to overcome. The work should feel necessary and important but not be directly communicated. Informational and behavioral work should be done with everyone. Work that addresses feelings, attitudes, and deeply held values should remain voluntary.

Group Size.   One-way communication can occur in virtually any size group given the appropriate audiovisual and communication technologies. In order for developmental personal learning to occur, interaction or dialogue is usually beneficial. Such dialogue occurs best when the group has no more than 15 to 20 participants. Everyone present should be a participant. Observers interfere with the learning atmosphere. Observers can threaten confidentiality, raise apprehension about being evaluated, and inhibit disclosure.

Integrated or Segregated Groups?   Should you work with intact work teams or mix participants across functions, work groups, or even organizations? The goal is to create the best possible individual and group learning environment. If trust levels and communications are already good within a work group, then doing diversity work as a group can facilitate team building as well as progress regarding diversity. Low trust levels and poor communication will be impediments to diversity work within the team. When this situation is evident, team and trust-building activities should be conducted before addressing diversity directly. An alternative is to mix participants across work groups so that poor communication and trust histories are not present.

Another meaning for segregated versus integrated refers to grouping people by demographic characteristic (e.g., age, nationality, gender, ethnicity, disabilities status, or job level). While some forms of diversity will be present in every group, care should be taken to do work with seemingly homogeneous groups only when it will strengthen the participants and ultimately enhance their participation in the larger, more diverse world. This statement reflects the values of the author and highlights the belief that diversity work is not value-free or even value-neutral.

Cotraining.   The best learning situations for facilitators and participants occur when there is diversity on the facilitator team. Having two or more facilitators allows one person to present and facilitate while others pay attention to process and environmental issues (e.g., confused-looking participants, unasked questions, discomfort, audiovisual equipment, lighting, heating and cooling, noise). Cotraining with someone different (in at least ethnicity, gender, and style) produces greater learning among participants.

Follow-Up Sessions

Once a foundation or introductory workshop has been conducted, additional sessions dedicated to specific issues should be held (on racism, sexism, style, intercultural, cross-functional issues). If an organization begins with issue-specific sessions, it is very likely to see more resistance and backlash. A foundation session (with a broad definition of diversity and cogent justification for doing diversity work) tends to prevent backlash and eliminate resistance.

Topics

The topic selection remains somewhat subjective. The first topic addressed after the foundation session should be one that meets the following criteria: (1) obviously significant for all or at least the vast majority of participants (e.g., style and gender are typical starting points); (2) is either very obvious or has been identified in a needs assessment; and (3) does not go too far outside the initial comfort zones of most participants (e.g., sexual orientation is likely to be too great a challenge for the first session).

Sequencing

After a few sessions, most participants learn how to learn about diversity issues. As they do, the particular sequence of topics becomes less important and the necessity to conduct formal sessions declines. Self-directed learning will continue to provide progress.

Possible Session Sequence

1. Introductory diversity workshop (foundation for all differences)
2. Style (e.g., Myers-Briggs Type Indicator*)
3. Sexual harassment
4. Gender
5. Racism/color
6. Cross-functional team building
7. Age, disabilities, sexual orientation, etc.
8. Intercultural issue workshop (e.g., American-French)

Structure

A general agenda for postintroductory sessions includes:

1. Introductions, icebreakers, preview and/or overview
2. Reminder: Diversity is "all the ways in which we differ."
3. Statement that this session deals with one of those ways
4. What is it? (e.g., ageism, sexism, functional stovepiping)
5. How did it get started?

Note: Use of Myers-Briggs Type Indicator instruments requires certification.

6. What sustains it today?
7. What can we do organizationally to change it?
8. What can we personally do to change it?
9. Practical exercises and applications of learnings
10. Summary, evaluation, and closure

Selection and/or Development of Trainers

Before getting trained to facilitate follow-up sessions, facilitators must deliver several successful introductory sessions. If they choose to continue developing additional skills, they then go through specialty workshops as participants. From that point, "train the trainer" follows the same path as for the introductory session. A basic rule is that a person must do his or her own personal work on an issue before facilitating others' development on that issue.

Moving from Awareness to Skill Building

The introductory work is primarily aimed at awareness, gaining commitment, reducing resistance, and preventing backlash. Follow-up sessions contain skill-building exercises and practical applications. They are intended to increase behavioral effectiveness of participants. Designers and facilitators must apply knowledge about learning styles and learning (cognitive processes, physical memory, reinforcement, etc.) to this skill-building work. Excellent examples of activities for building culture-specific skills are presented on pages 103 to 111 in Brislin.[22] Helping participants learn how to learn will maximize the effectiveness of follow-up sessions and facilitate self-directed continuing education.

Self-Directed Continuing Learning

Once an organization has initiated diversity education and training, it should provide means for self-directed continuing education. An internal diversity library or bibliographic resource is useful at this point. A communications system that informs participants about external events that can educate is also appropriate. Sources for diversity learning are virtually unlimited. See Fig. 5-5 for specific suggestions.

Evaluation

Purposes

Education and training evaluations to examine the outcomes of the work can be used to assess the effectiveness of the design, indicate needed modifications, and track participant progress over time.

1. Arts, entertainment, and cultural events
2. Audiotapes and videotapes (training and general interest)
3. Books (fiction and nonfiction)
4. Discussion or dialogue groups
5. Documentaries, movies, films, and public television
6. Journals (focused on cultural and diversity topics)
7. Magazines (e.g., ethnic and special interests)
8. Travel (local, regional, international)
9. University, college, and/or school courses
10. Volunteer work

Figure 5-5.   Ten sources for diversity learning.

Approaches

All approaches should be based on the objectives of the education and training initiative. If possible, the best evaluations include preassessments, postassessments, and follow-up assessments over time. Observations by others complement self-evaluation and should be included whenever possible. Major foci of the program evaluation are design, specific activities, learning materials, environment, and facilities. Foci of the facilitator evaluation are subject-matter knowledge, facilitation skills, and actual behavior relevant to the workshop topic. Written forms and interview or focus-group questions should be custom-designed for each program. A general professional resource for conducting evaluations is the *Handbook of Evaluation Research*.[23] (Also see Chap. 14, Evaluation, and Chap. 15, Measuring the Results of Training.)

Term

Change regarding awareness can occur relatively quickly and therefore may be measured soon after an introductory diversity session. Change regarding feelings and behaviors typically takes longer and should be measured over months and years. Measuring changes of behavior or feelings immediately after a workshop will suggest that there has been little change—when in reality the seeds for longer-term change have been planted and might become evident over time. Caution must be exercised in drawing conclusions about the effectiveness of a session based only on a short-term evaluation.

Special Issues

A. Cotraining

The most effective diversity education and training is done by teams of at least two individuals. During the 1970s the author conducted internal research (in civilian organizations within the Department of Navy and the U.S. Government) regarding the impact on learning of the composition of the education and training team. Pre- and posttests were given to participants in an equal-opportunity training program. The facilitators were always two-person teams. The teams were systematically varied according to gender (same or different) and ethnicity (same or different). Teams that were diverse in terms of ethnicity or gender

1. Seek unity in objectives, diversity in styles.
2. Get to know your cotrainer as a person.
3. Share and/or discuss both strengths and development needs.
4. Commit to give caring feedback to each other.
5. Switch content and process leadership roles as needed.
6. Demonstrate valuing diversity with your partner.
7. Show how differences can create synergy.

Figure 5-6. Seven tips for cotrainers.

produced significantly more learning among participants than teams homogeneous in gender or ethnicity. Teams that were diverse in terms of both gender and ethnicity produced the most learning of all possible combinations. Both sets of results were statistically significant.

Additional tips for effective cotraining are noted in Fig. 5-6.

DIVERSITY WORK IS MEASURABLY MOST EFFECTIVE WHEN FACILITATED BY DIVERSE TEAMS.

B. Burnout

Successful facilitators must use their heads, hands, and hearts. This total commitment and involvement often leads to burnout. Doing difficult, intimate work of this nature tends to drain one of mental, physical, and emotional energy. Feelings of too little progress over too much time, so much need and too few resources, so much ugly behavior among so many people, and other generalized feelings of fatigue and hopelessness occur. Symptoms include uncontrolled anger, frequent complaints of fatigue, passivity, martyr behavior, and monotone speech when passion seems appropriate.

The cure is mental, physical, and emotional renewal. This recovery should be designed to suit the characteristics of the burned-out individual. It is important to engage all three aspects (head, hand, and heart) in the renewal process. Many of the activities that cure burnout also prevent or increase resistance to it. Specific curative activities are suggested in Fig. 5-7.

C. Rage

Many diversity trainers experience pain and severe anger (rage) about things that are said and done to people. Over time this feeling can grow and be observed as rage—emotional pain displayed as anger. This emotion often surfaces when a certain phrase is used that brings up repeated injustices or meanness (e.g., "you're great, you think like a man," said to a woman; "you're not like other Hispanics," said to a Latino; "your English is as good as most Americans," said to a fourth-generation Chinese-American; "can you jew down the price," said to a Jewish person; "you're a good dancer for a white person," said to a Caucasian; etc.).

Rage can incapacitate a trainer and therefore learning to manage one's own rage is part of preparing to be a diversity facilitator. Working with someone different makes it unlikely that all members of a facilitator team will feel rage at the same time. This setup allows cotrainers to be supportive of one another and intervene in a problem situation, if necessary.

HEAD:
Different work
Reading that is fun
Organizing small physical things (books, music, marbles)
Playing mentally challenging games
Planning a celebration

HAND:
Physical exercise
Review and possibly change eating habits
Fix some heavy broken things
Build, draw, paint, sculpt, etc., something
Rest

HEART:
Spend time with people who love you
Play with children or others that you love
Spend time in a place you love
Read and/or write words of joy and love
Dream

Figure 5-7. Burnout cure ideas.

RAGE ACCOMPANIES PERSONAL COMMITMENT.
RAGE OFTEN MOTIVATES ONE TO LEAD DIVERSITY WORK.
RAGE DOES NOT CREATE COMPETENCE.

Conclusion

Diversity training and development is a significant contributor to individual and organizational effectiveness. If it is done well, everyone involved in it grows. If it is done poorly, personal and organizational damage will be done. The knowledge and experience base that is currently available supports the conduct of increasingly effective diversity work. A part of the physician's oath is appropriate for guidance.

"FIRST, DO NO HARM"

References

1. Goodmeasure, Inc., *A Tale of O: On Being Different, A Training Tool for Managing Diversity*, Cambridge, MA, 1993.
2. Cook, Stuart W., "Social Science and School Desegregation: Did We Mislead the Supreme Court?" *Personality and Social Psychology Bulletin*, 1979, vol. 5, no. 4, pp. 420–437.
3. Cox, Taylor, Jr., *Cultural Diversity in Organizations: Theory, Research and Practice*, Berrett-Koehler Publishers, San Francisco, 1993.
4. Ramirez, Manual III, *Cultural Democracy, Bicognitive Development and Education*, Academic Press, New York, 1974.

5. Deshpande, Satish P., and Chockalingam Viswesvaran "Is Cross-Cultural Training of Expatriate Managers Effective?: A Meta Analysis," *International Journal of Intercultural Relations*, vol. 16, 1992, pp. 295–310.

6. Morrison, Ann M., *The New Leaders: Guidelines on Leadership Diversity in America*, Jossey-Bass, San Francisco, 1992.

7. Popcorn, Faith, *The Popcorn Report*, Harper Business, New York, 1992.

8. Adler, Nancy J., *International Dimensions of Organizational Behavior*, Kent Publishing Co., Boston, 1986.

9. Ziller, Robert C., "Homogeneity and Heterogeneity of Group Membership," in C. G. McClintock, ed., *Experimental Social Psychology*, Holt, Rinehart and Winston, New York, 1972, pp. 385–411.

10. Kanter, Rosabeth Moss, *The Change Masters: Innovation and Entrepreneurship in the American Corporation*, Simon & Schuster, New York, 1983.

11. Kravetz, Dennis J., *The Human Resources Revolution*, Jossey-Bass, San Francisco, 1989.

12. Levering, Robert, *A Great Place to Work*, Random House, New York, 1989.

13. Fowler, Sandra, and Monica Mumford, eds., *The Intercultural Sourcebook: Cross-Cultural Training Methods*, Intercultural Press, Yarmouth, ME, in press.

14. Thiederman, Sondra, *Bridging Cultural Barriers for Corporate Success: Manage the Multicultural Work Force*, Lexington Books, Lexington, MA, 1991.

15. Walker, Barbara A., "Valuing Differences: The Concept and a Model," in Mary Ann Smith and Sandra J. Johnson, eds., *Valuing Differences in the Workplace*, published by the University of Minnesota and ASTD, Minneapolis and Alexandria, VA, respectively, 1991, pp 7–17.

16. Amir, Yehuda, "The Role of Intergroup Contact in Change of Prejudice and Ethnic Relations," Chapter 8 in Phyllis A. Katz, ed., *Towards the Elimination of Racism*, Pergamon, New York, 1976, pp. 245–308.

17. Bennett, Milton J., "A Developmental Approach to Training Intercultural Sensitivity," *International Journal of Intercultural Relations*, vol. 10, no. 2, Summer 1986.

18. Cross, W. E., "The Negro-to-Black Conversion Experience: Towards a Psychology of Black Liberation," *Black World*, 1971, vol. 20, pp. 13–27.

19. Airall, Angela M., "How Whites Can Grow in Racial Identity," *Cultural Diversity at Work* (newsletter), Seattle, September 1992, vol. 5, no. 1.

20. Hayles, Robert, "Inter-Ethnic and Race Relations Education and Training," in D. S. Hoopes, P. B. Pedersen, and G. Renwick, eds., *Overview of Intercultural Education, Training and Research*, Society for Intercultural Education, Training and Research, Washington, DC, May 1987.

21. Hammer, Mitchell R., "Behavioral Dimensions of Intercultural Effectiveness: A Replication and Extension," *International Journal of Intercultural Relations*, vol. II, 1987, pp. 65–88.

22. Brislin, Richard, and Tomoko Yoshida, *Intercultural Communication Training: An Introduction*, Sage Publications, Thousand Oaks, CA, 1994.

23. Streuning, Elmer L., and Marcia Guttentag, eds., *Handbook of Evaluation Research*, vols. I and II, Sage Publications, Beverly Hills, CA, 1975.

6

Training for Global Operations

Stephen H. Rhinesmith

Stephen H. Rhinesmith *is one of the world's leading experts on global business strategy implementation and human resource development. For over 25 years, he has worked with business, government, and private organizations to help managers and international teams improve their effectiveness and productivity. As an executive, consultant, trainer, diplomat, author, and lecturer, he has experience leading and motivating people in more than 60 countries. Dr. Rhinesmith is a consultant to many* Fortune *100 corporations on globalization and the development of global mindsets, competencies, and corporate cultures. His recent book,* A Manager's Guide to Globalization: Six Keys to Success in a Changing World, *is being used in management development programs throughout the United States and abroad to help managers gain a more global perspective in their work. He brings to his present work 20 years of senior international management experience, 15 of which were as president of three different service corporations—the AFS International Student Exchange Program, Holland America Cruise Lines, and Moran, Stahl & Boyer, a consulting firm specializing in cross-cultural training for businesspeople. Dr. Rhinesmith was the first American appointed to head an area of specialization at a Russian university, serving as founder and Chair of the Department of Organizational Sociology from 1992 to 1995. In 1994, he was Chairman of ASTD's board of directors. He received his B.A. from Wesleyan University in 1965 and his M.A. and Ph.D. in Public and International Affairs from the University of Pittsburgh in 1966 and 1972, respectively.*

The recent globalization of many of the world's corporations has raised new training challenges for human resource organizations. Not only are there *new* training needs, such as training people in headquarters to deal with customers and suppliers around the world, but traditional training like expatriate preparation are expanding and more urgent than ever.

In this chapter, we will explore the implications of these changes for various global training target populations, examine seven different types of global training, discuss cultural influences on global training designs outside the United States, explore the development of global trainers, and outline the management of an overall global training strategy.

Target Populations for Global Training

The number of people needing some form of global training today is very different from 10 years ago. In general, we can talk about four different target populations.

1. Expatriates

An expatriate includes *anyone* who is assigned outside his or her home country. In global organizations, these persons may be transferred from any one of 100 countries to any one of another 99 countries. Providing relevant training from headquarters or a regional training department presents new challenges, since a trainer must be familiar with the expatriate's home culture as well as the culture to which they are being transferred. When companies operated only out of their home country, with expatriates only from that country, the training equation was easier.

Training expatriates for relocation increasingly includes spouse and children over the age of eight. This means that even a three-day predeparture program for an expatriate must include not only business perspectives but also local adjustment orientation for the spouse and a special program to help children understand what it will be like to be a foreigner in another culture with children their own age.

2. People Traveling Internationally

There has also been a change in training needed by people traveling internationally. In former times, those traveling internationally were primarily senior executives or salespeople.

In today's global organization, however, many people are engaged in multicultural task forces. These groups meet around the globe on a periodic basis to discuss functional coordination across geographic regions, global product policies, or cross-functional coordination of matrix operations. *Many* more people are involved in cross-cultural interaction than ever before.

3. Headquarters Personnel

Third, with a greater number of companies globalizing their operations and creating matrix structures, many employees are finding themselves in multiple reporting relationships with people outside their own countries. Therefore, a plant manager working in Milwaukee may report to a North American manager and global operations manager of a German parent company based in Frankfurt.

Similarly, many staff functions are now interacting internationally. The legal, tax, and finance departments examine global joint ventures. People in accounting try to figure out how to deal with accounts receivable in Saudi Arabia, Colombia, Indonesia, and Norway. And the purchasing department considers bids from suppliers in all corners of the world.

All of these people, many of whom will never leave headquarters, need some form of orientation regarding how to work and live in a multicultural global organization.

4. People Involved in Technology Transfer

Finally, there are many more people involved in international training and technology transfer today. Classically, these people have traveled abroad as expatriates to transfer new ideas and methods to populations in developing countries. In today's global world, however, people are transferring technology from their own plants and offices to trainees who have been brought in from around the world.

These efforts to "globalize" foreign employees involve programs and ways to increase their understanding of the company while giving them the needed skills and mindsets necessary to operate in their home country.

The Walt Disney Company, for example, trained 150 Americans in Orlando to work with the French as part of their start-up of Euro-Disneyland. Most of these Americans, however, never traveled to France. They worked with French trainees coming to Orlando for training prior to the opening of the European theme park.

Types of Training Needed for Global Operations

The types of training needed for global operations has also expanded greatly from earlier days. Previously, the primary types of international training were expatriate adjustment and in-country technology transfer. Today there is a wide range of international training needs in new global organizations. There is a need to develop global perspectives in headquarters personnel; build multicultural teams for persons working together from around the world; provide global functional training in areas such as sales, marketing, manufacturing, and finance; develop global networks of senior executives to manage matrix organizations; and ensure cultural self-awareness for those working with people from many countries around the world. Let's examine each of the seven types of global training for today's global world.

1. Expatriate Adjustment Training

The most common form of global training continues to be *predeparture* training for expatriates. While this form of training is becoming more widespread, it is estimated that approximately 70 percent of American businesspeople who are sent abroad *still* do not receive any predeparture orientation![1]

Those who do conduct such training, however, find it an important part of their efforts to reduce costs by reducing expatriate early returns and facilitating more rapid adjustment to the new culture.

Expatriate adjustment training usually takes place during predeparture for a manager and his or her family. The typical program is three days, but it can be much longer if language orientation is involved. There are a number of suppliers who specialize in providing this kind of training on a customized basis for a reasonable price.[2]

Some companies have found it useful to provide an additional two-to-three-day program for larger groups of expatriates during their assignment abroad. This training provides an opportunity for expatriates to examine their adjustment process and to determine ways they can improve their effectiveness in local country interactions.

This *in-country training* is best done after an expatriate has had some time in-country to become aware of his or her adjustment challenges. The best timing is between six months and the end of the first year of a typical three-year assignment.

The most innovative training for expatriates, offered by only a handful of companies, is *reentry training* prior to the employees' return. Studies have found that many expatriates suffer a certain amount of "reverse culture shock" when returning home.

Reentry training helps expatriates and their families anticipate the potential problems they may face when they return home to a much faster pace of life with people who are less interested in their overseas experience than they might expect. It also emphasizes the reverse adjustment process and prepares them for a period of transition from their assignment abroad. This reentry training is ideally done while the expatriate and his or her family are abroad, but it can also be done within the first few weeks after return.

Reentry training has proven to be helpful in retaining expatriates after their return. Many companies report that in the past their expatriates returned to their home country, became disillusioned with the company for not utilizing their expertise, and eventually resigned or were not given positions which could use their knowledge and experience. These are issues which can be explored in reentry training and which the expatriate can prepare to overcome.

2. Technology Transfer Training

Technology transfer training addresses the particular challenges of teaching and coaching across cultures. The major emphases are on different cultural approaches to the student-teacher relationship, cross-cultural communications, and different perspectives on authority and hierarchical relationships.

For example, trainees from group-oriented societies will be less predisposed to ask questions, reveal what they don't know, and engage in learner-centered learning. Many American specialists on the other hand assume a greater partnership in technology transfer. Americans, being from a more individualistically oriented society, will expect a trainee to take responsibility for his or her own learning and to be intimately involved in setting learning objectives and determining training needs. This will not work in many more hierarchically oriented cultures of the world.

These differences in formality and teacher- vs. student-centered learning are many times compounded by differences in thinking patterns and the ability to make ideas concrete and simple when working through an interpreter or in a second language. Expatriates need training in how to communicate across these differences, both from a cultural and technical perspective.

Technology transfer training also needs increasingly to be applied to people in headquarters who are training those from abroad as well as to expatriates traveling abroad for the purposes of transferring technology into another country on-site.

3. Global Mindset Training

A new form of training which has emerged with the evolution of global organizations is training aimed at helping managers work in a global matrix organization. Sometimes, referred to as matrix management or global mindset training, this training is aimed at helping employees operate in a more complex organization. Emphasis is placed on balancing global and local needs, and operating cross-functionally, cross-divisionally, and cross-culturally around the world.

This training also helps employees understand the uncertainty and ambiguity of operating in a global matrix framework and the kinds of conflicts which arise from the interaction of people from different functions, product lines, and countries. Each of these persons have their own perspectives.

Global functional managers (manufacturing, human resources, finance, etc.) are interested in transferring best practices around the world within their function to achieve the best products at greatest efficiency. Global product managers are interested in reducing costs by standardizing purchasing and production on a global basis. Both of these global interests conflict with local country managers who are concerned about ensuring that there is as much customization of products, processes, and services as possible to meet the particular needs of their local population.

Global matrix management involves creating "matrix minds" for these people so they can see their conflicting priorities and negotiate accordingly in trying to achieve overall corporate objectives.

4. Multicultural Team Building

With globalization there has been a sharp increase in the use of multicultural teams. These teams, comprising people from different national cultures, are faced with working together across differing management styles and preferences and different management structures, strategies, and corporate cultures.

The rise of global teams stems from an increase in cross-functional and cross-country coordination. Global functional teams meet annually or more frequently to coordinate global and local interests in product development, engineering, design, and delivery or in staff meetings to ensure common approaches to finance, human resources, information systems, and other functions which must be coordinated globally.

Many of these teams require training and team-building activities to help them function more effectively. A typical intervention would involve a one- to two-day training program aimed at helping a team understand the influence of cultural differences on leadership, problem-solving, decision-making, and communications styles.

These team-building activities can be run when a new global product-development team or joint-venture team is being formed for a new global venture. A training session to help these people develop ways of working together across their cultural differences can be very useful.

Equally useful is a team-building meeting after a team has been functioning for six months or so, in order to help them reflect on the work they have been doing together. In this case, the team analyzes their past experiences to understand some of the personal, cultural, and team factors which have played a role in their problems and successes.

Both approaches are useful, and many teams find that some attention to process on at least an annual basis is helpful in ensuring that cultural differences are understood and dealt with rather than being ignored and eventually building into misunderstandings that can affect the group's functioning and productivity.

5. Global Functional Training

Many international companies have found that it is important to offer functional courses on the implications of doing business in different areas. The AT&T School of Business, for example, offers a wide range of courses in subjects like Global Marketing, Strategies for Global Finance, Global Pricing and Selling Policies, Global Purchasing, and Global Human Resource Development.

All of these courses are aimed at providing people with specific information needed to operate within their function on a global basis. These programs are a supplement to the more generic global courses on Global Business Strategy, New Country Investment Strategies, and Global Mindset Training which we described earlier.

6. Cultural Self-Awareness Training

A new form of cultural training has emerged from the era of globalization which is called cultural self-awareness training.

The need for this training has evolved from the need to train managers who could work in many different countries within the course of any given year. In global companies, more and more managers are being asked to operate in Brazil one week, Australia the next, Japan the week after that, and then go to Europe or the Middle East the next month to conduct business in three or four more countries.

Unlike expatriate training, which concentrates on providing skills and knowledge about one country to which a person has been assigned, cultural self-awareness training helps people understand what it is to be from their own culture so that they can be sensitive to the differences which may exist between themselves and others when traveling in a wide range of cultures throughout the world.

A typical cultural self-awareness program can be run in two days. Emphasis is usually placed on a number of variables that are contrasted across different cultures throughout the world. For example, in the United States there would be a discussion of individualism versus group-oriented cultures, differences in attitudes toward time, structure, hierarchy, communications, and other factors on which one can compare Americans with other cultures. The objective is to demonstrate that the American approach is really a minority viewpoint when compared with most countries of Asia, Africa, Latin America, and even a good deal of Europe.

These variables are then applied to specific business situations which can be tailored to a specific industry or company or which can be taught within a general global context, thereby demonstrating differences between American and other countries' approaches.

In this way people learn an analytical framework for understanding American culture and its relation to other countries around the world, which can increase their cognitive ability to operate when abroad. This knowledge does *not* necessarily, however, guarantee that their emotional or behavioral skills will be improved. Understanding differences, however, is many times the first step in dealing with them.

7. Executive Development: Action-Reflection-Learning

Action-reflection-learning (ARL) is the most multifaceted and sophisticated means of global training. It is used for middle to senior executives in order to help corporations build a cadre of managers who can work across functions, organizational divisions, and cultures.

The basic design, developed by the MiL Institute in Lund, Sweden, involves teams of executives, usually no more than six to a team, who are mixed by function, organization, and geography and given a series of training experiences over a six- to twelve-month period.

These one-week training programs (typically four) are conducted in four different countries on three to four different continents (when possible) so that participants gain a first-hand understanding of the complexities of doing business in different cultures around the world.

At the same time, the teams are given real business problems to solve within their organization. These problems, sponsored by a senior executive on an issue which he or she would like to have addressed (but does not have the resources or expertise to deal with it), are important opportunities for the participants to apply the knowledge they gain in a real-time situation.

At the end of the program each team makes a report to senior management with recommendations on how to solve the problems. In almost all cases, the recommended actions lead to cost savings or revenue increases which offset the *total* cost of the training.

The program results in the development of a network of people from around the world with a more global mindset, skills in working in multicultural teams, a capacity to see problems across functions and cultures, and a network of relationships throughout the organization which can be the key factor in the success of operating in a global matrix environment.

These are the seven different kinds of global training in which people are engaged in this new global world. It is a very different world from the past when most global training meant only expatriate training and technology transfer. There is a rich new field and new challenges for people interested in international training. Now that we have discussed the need, let us look at some of the approaches and design and methodology issues which arise in responding to the different training needs we have outlined.

Designing and Training Outside the United States

Global training is a sophisticated business, which is one of the reasons why many companies outsource this function. There are very few companies in the United States that design and conduct their own predeparture expatriate training programs, and only the very large corporations conduct their own training around the world. The major reasons for this are the need to adjust training designs for cultural differences when training outside the United States, and the need for modifications in trainer behavior when working in foreign cultures.

Cultural Influences on Training Design

The major cultural influence on training outside the United States has been explored by Geert Hofstede, the Dutch researcher who has conducted seminal research on the impact of culture on management. In his book, *Cultures and Organizations: Software of the Mind,*[3] he identifies a range of variables which also affect instructional design in different world cultures.

One of his dimensions is power distance, or the degree to which a society places emphasis on *differences* in status and authority relations. Hi-power distance represents the degree to which a society emphasizes authority differences, and lo-power distance is the degree to which egalitarian relations govern instruction.

The implications of this power distance for trainer-participant relations can be very important. The following list outlines some of the variables affected by power distance differences:

Hi-Power Distance	*Lo-Power Distance*
Formal relationships	Informal relationships
High dependence	Low dependence
Teacher-oriented	Learner-oriented
Highly personal	Impersonal
Status emphasized	Equality emphasized
Fixed approach	Variable approach
Conformity	Experimentation

As can be surmised, in hi-power-distance cultures, there is an emphasis on more traditional teacher-student relations. In such a situation, one major factor to be contended with is student initiative. One can assume that in hi-power-distance cultures, students will expect the teacher to take the initiative and that it will not be natural for students to volunteer their opinions or participate in classroom discussions without being explicitly called upon. Another option is to give them an opportunity to meet first in groups and then speak on behalf of the whole group in report outsessions rather than speak on behalf of themselves.

One trainer conducted a seminar in Japan and spoke for 13 hours straight over two days without a question! He had been told in advance that this was the way the audience would prefer to operate and that there would be questions at the end of the session after small groups had a chance to discuss ideas presented in the seminar. Admittedly, this seminar was for a large audience, but in smaller training circumstances in hi-power-distance countries it is also necessary to make modifications to training approaches to take into account different teacher and student initiatives.

This fact does not mean that one cannot do experiential training in high-status cultures. There are never any absolute rules in cross-cultural interaction, but the nature of such interaction suggests that if you want more interactive training in more formal cultures, you should plan to do it later in the program design rather than using it as an "ice-breaker."

Certain "proprieties" will also need to be followed in high-status cultures. These include allowing older participants to be called by their last names, even while calling younger participants by their first names; not placing people in role-play situations in which they might "lose face" before the group; and in general using a more structured design where expectations are clear and methods and procedures are more explicit.

These guidelines concerning teacher-oriented versus learner-oriented training preferences, while affected by culture, are also affected by personal learning styles. David Kolb developed a learning styles theory in the 1970s which has had a great influence on training design for the last 20 years.[4]

Kolb maintains that a learning experience requires four components: experience, reflection, theory, and application. He believes therefore that experiential learning, which stresses experience and reflection, is inadequate without the introduction of theory and the planning of back-home application. Likewise, he argues, the traditional academic approach of theory and application is inadequate for full learning unless it is augmented by some experience and reflection during the training experience.

Kolb's theory has been very influential over the years as a guide to training design. It has led instructional designers to ensure that a total learning segment has theory and practice as well as time for reflection and application.

Kolb goes further, however, and suggests that different people have different learning styles. As a result, some people prefer to enter the learning cycle from an experience, some from reflection, some from a listening to a lecture, and some from anticipating problems and challenges they may have in the future. He advocates that learning sequences alter their starting points to attract different types of learners at different points in the training program. This results in a training design which reaches people with very different learning preferences to ensure motivated learning from everyone in a group.

While Kolb's theory is true on an international basis, what we have said about hi-power-distance and lo-power-distance cultures would indicate that some cultures may have a predominant bias for one style over another. For example, Americans tend to prefer *experience* as a starting point whereas Japanese, as we have noted, prefer to start with *theory* through some form of lecture or presentation.

Finally, it is important to remember that more power-distance cultures will also be sensitive to the instructor's *knowledge* base. It may therefore be useful to begin training with some sort of formal presentation which demonstrates academic and theoretical knowledge of the field and establishes one's *expertise* in the traditional sense of an academic discipline before engaging in a more informal approach to discovery learning. In high-status cultures, people want to know that the trainer is an expert in addition to being a good facilitator of the learning process.

Sylvia Odenwald suggest six guidelines in adapting training to local conditions:[5]

1. Provide opportunities for trainees to apply the material to their own cultural situation through case studies and role plays (where appropriate).

2. Listen to feedback from trainees from more than just the verbal perspective and be aware that nonverbal behavior will probably mean very different things in different cultures.

3. Look for opportunities to take advantage of cultural differences, asking questions about how various ideas and practices would be modified to fit local cultural conditions.

4. Be flexible in adapting to local cultural learning methods. If the culture stresses memorization of lists, then "go with the flow" and provide an opportunity for them to do that in addition to more experiential methods. Meet participants halfway—at least!

5. Learn about the local region and its technology so that training designs can anticipate everything from local facilities to the degree to which the training can take advantage of local resources in developing the learning experience.

6. Most importantly, as an outsider, remember that the trainer will never fully understand local cultural styles, and therefore be prepared to change any training design during the program if assumptions made about appropriate methods do not prove correct.

Developing Global Trainers

It should be apparent by now that being a global trainer has certain requirements. The requisite experience is hard to gain and requires a somewhat odd mixture of traditional expertise and authority combined with facilitative learning skills and strong global experience that can be adapted to local conditions. While there are more global trainers today than ever before, they are in great demand and hard to develop.

Developing Global Trainers

Most global trainers are domestic trainers who through international experience have learned to adapt their training designs and personal styles to different global populations. There are many routes that people have taken to become global trainers.

One way to develop global skills is through a series of international living experiences which result in sufficient sensitivity to cultural differences that can be used in training. Many global trainers started as Peace Corps volunteers, exchange students, or the children of professionals posted overseas, and through these experiences they gained intercultural sensitivity at a young age.

Another route to becoming a global trainer is to be given professional opportunities to train internationally and to work consciously to modify training designs and styles to international audiences.

It is only in the last five years that there has been much literature developed to help global trainers think about how they need to modify their approaches for international audiences.

A third way to develop global training skills is through one of the limited number of graduate programs which take into account global training and education methods and practices, but these are relatively new.

Guidelines for Global Training

Joyce Rogers, an international training specialist with MCI, has the following guidelines for global trainers:[6]

1. Be concerned with:

   Perceptions—How people see the world.
   Assumptions—Underlying beliefs and values.
   Experiences—That things will be a certain way.

Trainers need to have cultural self-awareness, they need to understand the influence of their own culture on their approaches to training and education and be sensitive to how their trainees may have different perceptions, assumptions, and expectations about the training experience.

2. Solicit help from people who have effectively trained in other cultures to create appropriate case studies and critical incidents.

Ensure that materials are adjusted to reflect local situations, value systems, and realities. Use examples that exist in the local context and avoid examples from foreign cultures that may not fit the local trainee population.

3. Be reflective, observing, and ready to adjust.
4. Maintain a moderate rate of speech.

Check with trainees from time to time to ensure they are understanding you. To accomplish this, it is better *not* to ask people if they understand what you are saying, because they can't answer appropriately. Instead, it is more effective to ask them to explain back to you something you have said. Many trainers have been misled by asking people who do not understand English well whether they understand what the trainer just said!

5. Find a local informant to be translator of language and culture.

It is important not to assume that your local interpreter understands the local culture. It is possible to have an interpreter who is very good as a translating machine but who does not have cultural self-awareness of what it is like to be from their own culture. When looking for a cultural informant, be sure that you find someone with an adequate outside perspective on their own culture and someone who can explain this to you in terms that make sense from your own cultural perspective.

6. Study some local language to gain empathy but not fluency.

It is more important to have studied *any* language for a few years than to be fluent in every language of the countries where you will be working. Since many global trainers are training in many countries throughout the world, it is unrealistic to expect them to be fluent in every country in which they operate. It *is* important, however, that global trainers have studied some language and are empathic to the difficulties that people experience when they are trying to listen and speak in a foreign language. Fatigue is one of the most usual experiences of people who work in a second language during a training program but otherwise use their first language for work experiences.

7. Use written words, graphics, visuals, and pictures whenever possible to reinforce your message.

Communications studies reveal that listeners remember 7 percent of what they hear, 35 percent of what they see, and 75 percent of what they experience. It is important, therefore, to reinforce communications through as many forms as possible.

8. Keep everything open for discussion.

There is no room in global training for rigidity. Flexibility, patience, and good listening skills are probably as important as any other characteristics. Global trainers must be highly enough skilled and comfortable enough with their material that they can make major last-minute adjustments to deal with unexpected situations, participant interests, and changes of facility.

Global Trainer Competencies

In addition to training guidelines, there are trainer competencies. One list contains the following personal attributes for trainers:[7]

1. Tolerance for ambiguity
2. Cognitive and behavioral flexibility
3. Personal self-awareness and a strong personal identity
4. Cultural self-awareness
5. Patience
6. Enthusiasm and commitment
7. Interpersonal sensitivity and relationships
8. Tolerance for differences
9. Openness to new experiences and people
10. Empathy
11. A sense of humility
12. A sense of humor

These 12 competencies are well-chosen. While at first they seem like any other "walk-on-water" list, closer examination and comparison against the demands of global training reveal that they are in fact a well-defined series of competencies related to specific training capabilities necessary for good program design and execution.

Developing global trainers is not easy. They remain a scarce resource, but there are an increasing number of qualified people who can provide assistance in this ever-growing field of education.

Developing a Global Training Strategy

Sylvia Odenwald, in *Global Training*, suggests the following seven steps in setting up a global training strategy:[8]

1. Assess global training needs.
2. Assist management in thinking globally.
3. Create a global training strategy.
4. Design guidelines for multinational training.
5. Develop a global training curriculum.
6. Select and train global trainers.
7. Manage the multinational training system.

Let us use this as a framework for discussing an integrated, strategically driven global training effort.

1. Assess Global Training Needs

The starting point for assessing global training needs, oddly enough, is not with your target populations, but with your CEO and his or her business strategy.

Global training is, by definition, business-driven, because it inevitably is linked to the future development of the business. For this reason, one begins with an examination of the company's business strategy for development. This plan may include expansion in emerging markets, penetration of mature markets, or restructuring from a multinational structure with highly decentralized operations to a global structure with global product lines and a matrix organization. A training strategy is very much dependent upon what direction the business is taking. So, first and foremost global training is *business-driven* and *strategically linked*.

Against this business assessment, there then needs to be an assessment of training needs. This effort may involve any of the types of training discussed at the beginning of this chapter: expatriate, technology transfer, global mindset, multicultural team building, global management, cultural self-awareness, or global action-reflection-learning. The best combination of training will depend on the strengths and weaknesses of managers and employees to fulfill the global strategy of the organization.

2. Assist Management to Think Globally

It is clear that one starting point for actual implementation of training will probably involve senior management. Very often even the most senior management will not know the difference between an international, multinational, and global company and will be unclear about the global mindsets and skills needed for their strategy.

A briefing or one-day seminar can be conducted with an outside consultant to make top management aware of the implementation implications of their global strategy. Unfortunately, experience reveals that many senior managers develop a business strategy without an organizational strategy which spells out how the business strategy will be implemented and aligned through the organization's corporate culture, systems, and people. If this plan has not been made, and it is more than likely that it will not have been, global training should point this fact out and assist senior management in developing an implementation strategy.

3. Create a Global Training Strategy

A global training strategy needs to be varied, targeted to different populations with different needs, and time-phased over several years to support the global business strategy. Priority of implementation will parallel business needs and will be driven by whether the business is moving rapidly into new areas of the world or restructuring itself for global operations in a way which involves new people in global thinking and management.

Beginning with the business priorities, therefore, a training strategy should be developed which combines the different kinds of training discussed earlier. A company restructuring that results in reorganizing the company along global product lines would require the following kinds of training programs.

- *Global mindset training* for senior management and all those working in the new matrix organization;
- *Cultural self-awareness training* for everyone working in international settings, with international suppliers, customers, or colleagues, and conducting training and development of people from other countries.
- *Technology transfer training* for people going abroad or transferring technology in their home workplace to a foreign trainee;
- *Action-reflection-learning training* with cross-functional, cross-cultural, and cross-product teams to integrate the company and provide an understanding of how to manage a matrix organization.

This is obviously a full plate, and the reorganization will need to be planned not only according to the types of training but also the number of people who need to be trained.

In many large organizations, there is a cascaded training process necessary which could involve thousands of people in some of the basic skills like cultural self-awareness. Developing an appropriate schedule and obtaining the necessary resources will only be possible if such training is directly linked to the global strategy and driven by business needs.

4. Design Guidelines for Multinational Training

There are several guidelines for multinational training which should be followed.

First, as much training as possible should be done in groups of mixed nationality. If one is going to train an American group about cultural self-awareness, it is best if at least 25 percent of the participants can be foreigners flown in from overseas operations. The reverse is also true. Single-culture global training loses much of the richness that can be gained from a multinational group.

Obviously, the budget implications of multinational training are great, and it will take a well-reasoned training plan to gain the additional resources to bring people in from other countries. It is well worth the effort, however, in the benefits gained not only in enriching classroom material and discussions but in also building the global network of personal relationships ultimately necessary to make any global organization work.

A second guideline for multinational training is that there should be a mixture of functional training and mindset and culture training. In other words, when there is global marketing, business, and finance training, there also needs to be general training in cross-cultural thinking and relations. People should be exposed to both the "business side" of global operations and the "human side," because experience proves that the latter is many times more important than the former in ultimate success globally.

Finally, multinational training requires support from the very top of the organization. There needs to be a clear statement from the CEO that this training is considered an integral part of the business strategy and that it is a priority in the company. If possible, mandated and cascaded training of certain levels of the organization is the best way to approach global training, because the end objective is a corporate culture change which requires a certain mass of people to learn to think in new ways. Hit or miss training offerings for people who are interested will never achieve the kind of business payoff that senior management needs from a globally focused training effort that it linked to the business strategy.

5. Develop a Global Training Curriculum

The most critical question with a global training curriculum is whether to buy or develop it. As indicated earlier, most companies buy the talent necessary for global training because it is such a specialized area. Different kinds of training may result in different combinations of inside-outside resources.

Normally, cultural training is contracted out. Sales, marketing, finance, and other functional training is many times done by company trainers, adapting some of the training programs which are taught in the home country.

If the decision is to develop, rather than to outsource, then the guidelines noted previously should be followed. The best resource to consult in adapting home-country training programs to different regional and local cultures is *Global Human Resource Development* by Marquardt and Engel, Section Two, "Roles and Practices of Global HRD."[9]

Another approach taken by some companies is to develop regional training advisory councils. These councils, comprised of HRD and line managers, can assist in modifying training materials for local practices and providing local case studies and critical incidents which will make the training more relevant to different world regions.

In other cases, some companies have chosen to establish regional training centers where local HRD trainers adapt headquarters training programs and design and develop their own training programs based exclusively on local training needs.

While regional training centers may be possible for larger organizations, smaller organizations that cannot afford this route at times seek out strategic alliances with local training institutions. These institutions under a long-term contract can come to know your organization and its needs and develop a curriculum tailored to the needs of your company and the needs of the local or regional population.

6. Selecting Outside Global Trainers

In selecting outside trainers for global programs, a number of steps are suggested by Gary Wederspahn from Moran, Stahl and Boyer's International Division:[10]

1. Obtain multiple referrals of three clients that have worked with the person being considered.

2. Check with the Society for Intercultural Education, Training and Research (SIETAR), 808 17th Street, NW, Suite 200, Washington, DC 20006 for referrals.

3. Look for someone who has been in the business at least five years.

4. Ask in how many countries has the trainer had first-hand experience and in what capacity.

5. Ask what the consultant's ongoing professional development and research interests are to determine how they are keeping up with the field.

6. Look for global trainers who are personally warm and would be good at establishing interpersonal relations since these attributes are more important in training in many other parts of the world than the United States.

SIETAR is a particularly useful resource, as is the Intercultural Press in Yarmouth, Maine, which publishes many books on cross-cultural and global training and development.

7. Manage the Multinational Training System

In the end, global training must be a *system*. It should be business-driven and part of the organization's strategy to achieve its objectives. It must be part of the strategy to develop the corporate culture, mindsets, skills, and behavior to help the company achieve its global objectives.

If at all possible, one should avoid running training programs for the sake of having global training. General training courses in global thinking and operations for open enrollment many times will be undersubscribed. It is an irony that during these times when so many people need to be trained for global operations, few people see themselves as appropriate candidates for such training.

For example, many of the target populations we noted earlier in this chapter, such as headquarters personnel who do not travel abroad, do not see themselves as "global managers" or as people in need of global training. Yet these people are very much part of the "globalization" of a company and need global training as much as people traveling internationally.

There is therefore a great need to ensure that senior management understands that global training is a significant driver of the corporate culture change necessary for a globalizing company to achieve its corporate objectives. The global mindsets and skills to be competitive in today's world are increasingly dependent on the ability of HRD specialists to identify global training needs and deliver effective training programs throughout the world.

This is a time of great challenge and opportunity in global training and a time for people willing to rise to the occasion to find new and meaningful experiences as *global* human resource developers.

References

1. Marquardt, Michael, and Dean Engels, *Global Human Resource Development,* Prentice Hall, Englewood Cliffs, NJ, 1993, p. 5.

2. Odenwald, Sylvia, *Global Training: How to Design a Program for the Multinational Corporation,* American Association for Counseling and Development, Alexandria, VA, 1988. In this excellent book, she lists categories and suppliers of global training programs. Some sample program titles and their suppliers are outlined below. For a full listing of courses and the contact information, see *Global Training,* pp. 68–104.

   Category 1: Cultural awareness
   1.1 Global Interface Skills Training [Moran, Stahl and Boyer (MS&B) International, Boulder, CO]
   1.2 Going Global [International Training Associates of Princeton (ITAP), NJ]
   1.3 Doing Business Internationally [Training Management Corporation (TMC), Princeton, NJ]
   1.4 Cultural Awareness Program (INSERVE, Dallas, TX)
   1.5 Cross-Cultural Technology Transfer (Moran, Stahl and Boyer International)

   Category 2: Multicultural communications
   2.1 Communications Skills for Foreign-Born Professionals (Intercultural Development, Inc., Solana Beach, CA)
   2.2 Communications Strategies for the Non-Native Speakers of English [International Orientation Resources (IOR), Northbrook, IL]
   2.3 Language and Culture of American Business (Global Interact, Dallas, TX)
   2.4 International Protocol and Presentation (Pachter and Associates, Cherry Hill, NJ)
   2.5 Working with International Visitors or New Citizens (Intercultural Development, Inc.)
   2.6 Cross-Cultural Training and Orientation (Bennett Associates, Chicago, IL)
   2.7 Cross-Cultural Teamwork (TMC)

2.8 Business Basics for the Foreign Executive (Global Interact)

Category 3: Country-specific training
3.1 Pre-Departure Orientation (Moran, Stahl and Boyer International)
3.2 Family Adjustment to an Overseas Assignment (Global Dynamics, Inc., Randolph, NJ)
3.3 Expatriate Reentry (Clarke Consulting Group, Inc., Redwood City, CA)
3.4 International Briefing (ITAP)
3.5 Regional/Country Business Briefing (TMC)
3.6 Business Briefings and Seminars (Bennett Associates)
3.7 Working with the Japanese (Clarke Consulting Group)

Category 4: Executive development
4.1 Global Business Briefings (IOR)
4.2 The Effective Global Manager (TMC)
4.3 International Executive Seminars (ITAP)
4.4 Global Project Team Management (TMC)

Category 5: Language courses
5.1 Language Tracing (MS&B International)
5.2 Language Programs (IOR)
5.3 Language Tutoring Services (LinguaCall International, Inc., Glenside, CA)

3. Hofstede, Geert, *Cultures and Organizations: Software of the Mind*, McGraw-Hill, London, 1991.

4. Kolb, David A., *Learning Styles Inventory*, Prentice Hall, Englewood Cliffs, NJ, 1973, p. 21.

5. Odenwald, Sylvia, op. cit., pp. 50–51.

6. Rogers, Joyce, see Odenwald, Sylvia, op. cit., pp. 143–144.

7. Odenwald, Sylvia, op. cit., p. 155.

8. Ibid., p. 169.

9. Marquardt, Michael, and Dean Engel, *Global Human Resource Development*, Prentice Hall, Englewood Cliffs, NJ, 1993.

10. Wederspahn, Gary, see Oldenwald, Sylvia, op. cit., pp. 144–145.

Bibliography

Austin, Clyde, ed., *Cross-Cultural Re-entry*, Abilene Christian University Press, Abilene, TX, 1986.

Evans, Paul, Ives Doz, and Andre Laurent, eds., *Human Resource Management in International Firms: Change, Globalization and Innovation*, St. Martin's Press, New York, 1990.

Harris, Philip R., and Robert T. Moran, *Managing Cultural Differences*, 3d ed., Gulf Publishing Co., Houston, TX, 1991.

Hofstede, Geert, *Culture's Consequences: International Differences in Work and Related Values*, Sage Publications, Beverly Hills, CA, 1980.

Landis, Daniel, and Richard W. Brislin, *Handbook for Intercultural Training*, vol. I, Pergamon Press, Oxford, England, 1983.

Marquardt, Michael and Dean W. Foster, *Global Human Resources Development*, Prentice Hall, Englewood Cliffs, NJ, 1993.

———, and Angus Reynolds, *Global Learning Organization: Gaining Competitive Advantage Through Continuous Training*, Irwin Professional Publishing, Burr Ridge, IL, 1994.

Miller, Vincent A., *A Guidebook for International Trainers in Business and Industry*, Van Nostrand Reinhold, and ASTD, New York, 1979.

Moran, Robert T., Philip R. Harris, and William G. Stripp, *Developing the Global Organization: Strategies for Human Resource Professionals*, Gulf Publishing Co., Houston, TX, 1993.

Odenwald, Sylvia, *Global Training: How to Design a Program for the Multinational Corporation*, Business One, Irwin, Homewood, IL, 1993.

Pedersen, Paul, *A Handbook for Developing Multicultural Awareness*, American Association for Counseling and Development, Alexandria, VA, 1988.

Phillips, Nicola, *Managing International Teams*, Irwin Professional Publishing, Burr Ridge, IL, 1994.

Reich, Robert B., *The Work of Nations: Preparing Ourselves for 21st Century Capitalism*, Alfred A. Knopf, New York, 1991.

Rhinesmith, Stephen H., *A Manager's Guide to Globalization: Six Keys to Success in a Changing World*, Business One, Irwin, Homewood, IL, 1993.

Tung, Rosalie, *The New Expatriates: Managing Human Resources Abroad*, Ballinger Publishing, New York, 1987.

White, Bren, *World Class Training*, Odenwald Press, Dallas, TX, 1992.

7

Quality of Training

Brenda B. Sumberg

Brenda B. Sumberg is Director of Motorola University for the Americas. In that capacity, the United States (Central, East, Southwest, West, and Hawaii) and the Latin America Regional Motorola University offices report to her. She has worked with Motorola, Inc., since 1982, first as a consultant and, since 1984, in a number of Motorola University staff positions, including Director of Design, Director of International Distribution, and Director of Quality. She has served as a member of the Executive Committee of Motorola Corporate Quality Council, the Advisory Council to the Total Quality Forum Leadership Steering Committee, and as a member of the review panel for the National Science Foundation Transformations to Quality Organizations program. Prior to working with Motorola, Sumberg held a variety of positions in public school teaching and administration as well as in social service agencies. She holds a B.S. degree in Mathematics from the University of Illinois and an M.Ed. degree in Guidance and Counseling from Texas Christian University.

Are you in the "business" of quality training? Are you applying quality concepts to your "business"? Even many of those of you who answered "yes" to the first question may have had difficulty answering affirmatively to the second. Why? Historically, training organizations have either not collected any data about their quality or have collected some data but have considered it irrelevant. (And it may have been.) Frequently, evaluation data has been collected but not really put to use to provide any kind of information or basis for change. Perhaps it is because no one has required you to focus on the quality of training, or you have tried and not been successful, or you don't know how to start. It may even be that you don't consciously or consistently think of your organization as a business.

Whatever the reason, it may become an increasingly important issue with which to grapple. There are several reasons for this. They include:

- The world around you is working on quality and it is, therefore, becoming an assumed condition.
- You may have taught quality to the rest of your world; how does your nonapplication of your own teaching impact your credibility?
- The increased emphasis on accountability and "customer focus."

It is only a matter of time until these issues apply to your organization. After all, you really are running or are part of a business. Regardless of your structure, affiliations, or funding model, training organizations have revenues, costs, and budgetary responsibilities as well as customers or markets, products, and services.

Key Elements of Quality

All the specific suggestions for applying quality to training in this chapter take place within the context of a quality system appropriate for any environment. Some key elements:

- Identification of the current organizational culture and understanding of how change occurs within it and what changes need to occur;
- Development of a roadmap to accomplish that change;
- Leadership support;
- Employee involvement;
- Consistent modeling and reinforcement of the importance of quality; and
- Transfer of the appropriate skills and knowledge to the people involved.

These elements are as important in a training organization as anyplace else.

Underlying some of these points is the fact that it is important to determine who is driving the quality process in your organization. Is it the right person or group so that change will occur? Quality must be a regular part of the way you do business. While there may be people identified as facilitators of the process, the whole organization—from top to bottom—must be involved and actively behave in ways that prove support. There must also be a clear set of expectations. If people expect this process to be a one-time "shot" with a relatively short cycle time, they will be disappointed. What you are talking about is a major culture change which is never-ending. As soon as you think you have finally "gotten it right," a new expectation will appear.

While not a specific topic addressed here, the use of benchmarking to identify best practices that can then drive goals and changes to accomplish them should be an integral part of any quality system. (Also see Chap. 19, Benchmarking for Best Results.)

The Customer Focus

The idea of being "customer focused" is a good place to start. Perhaps, the first thing that needs clarification is the link between quality and customer. From my perspective, quality refers to doing right the first time those things that are important to your customers. Spending time and resources improving things from which your customer derives no benefit is not what I am talking about when I speak of quality. With that in mind, in order to concentrate on the quality of training, you must know who your customers are. Do you? Would everyone in your organization agree with your list? My experience is that most people initially view this concept as a simple one, but when they attempt to reach consensus with their colleagues, they realize that it is actually very complex. An important first step in a quest for quality is to include all stakeholders in agreeing on who the customers are.

When we first attempted this at Motorola University, we expected it to be a very quick exercise. However, it took several meetings with multiple groupings of people for input until we could finalize a list on which we could agree. We originally identified 13 different customer segments. Our initial quality efforts focused on five of these segments because we realized that we could not do everything at once. These five were the CEO, the Motorola University board of trustees, decision-making managers (those who decide who should go to what training and ultimately pay for it), participants, and other training professionals in Motorola but outside Motorola University. These were chosen because they are the segments that place the most demands upon us. We periodically review the entire list and update it, as needed.

Identify Products and Services

The next step in the process is to identify the products and services you provide to your customers. Again, depending on the scope of responsibilities of your organization, this may not be as simplistic a task as you first imagine. But simple or complex, it is an important step. Obviously, if you are going to improve the quality of your products and services, you must have an agreed-upon, precise, consistent idea of what they are. This process should help to focus your efforts in a couple of different ways. Which of these products and services are really important to your customers? Are there some that should be eliminated? Some that are not important enough to your customers to deserve the time and attention being paid them? Are some outside your core areas of competence? Or in the opposite direction, are there some products and services that are very important to your customers but that have no clear champions in your organization? Is a reallocation of resources needed?

Our experience with this exercise at Motorola University was an interesting one, to say the least. When we brainstormed our first list of products and services, we ended up with about 75 items. By combing and grouping into categories our customers would recognize as distinct, we ended up with a list of 16. These ranged from program design and content to delivery, trainer certification, research, translation, and conference planning. The process did cause us to question whether or not we should be doing everything we were at the time and helped us to focus on the need to keep asking that question.

Once all stakeholders have reached consensus on your customers and products and services, it is helpful to identify which customers use what products and services. One way to do this is through the use of a matrix (see Fig. 7-1).

Customer Requirements

Once you have this information, it is necessary to determine your customers' requirements for each of these products and services. What does the customer

Customers, Products and Services

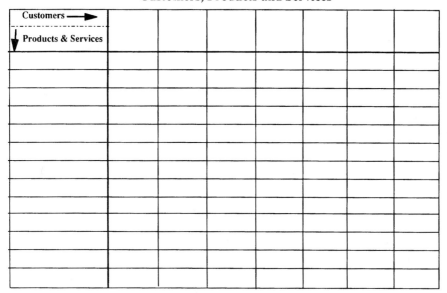

Figure 7-1. Customers and products and services matrix.

feel it is important to do well? What does the customer consider "quality"? These customer perceptions may or may not be what you would assume them to be. Depending on the nature of your organization, it is sometimes helpful to document what your associates believe to be the customer requirements for each of these products and services before gathering the information from the customers. This list can ultimately serve as either a positive reinforcement of their knowledge of their customer base or an "Aha!" that they really don't have a very good understanding of their marketplace.

There are several ways to gather this customer information which may range from what courses you should be designing, developing, or delivering to factors concerning your actual accomplishment of each of those activities or any others in which you are engaged. Do you have some process for regular contact with those whom you have identified as customers in order to gather their requirements? Those processes need to be established. It may be that there are existing infrastructures within your environment that can become the starting point for such processes, or it may be that you have to establish the process from "scratch." The important thing is that you clearly identify your customers' needs and respond to them rather than making isolated decisions based on assumptions of what the requirements are.

Holding focus groups of various segments to find out what the customers think is important about specific products and services can be very effective. It can also be a preliminary step. Focus-group input can be used to develop a structured instrument for a much broader survey of your customers to determine those factors that are most important to them.

Over the years, Motorola University has used a variety of methods for gathering customer requirements. The process has been and still is an evolving one with the goal of continuous improvement. We have always had regular input from a group of very senior managers (general managers and assistant general managers of Motorola's major businesses, senior executives of key staff functions, and a member of the CEO). This group has evolved from an executive advisory board to a board of trustees with their focus shifting from advice on a relatively tactical level to direction of major focuses and policies. This group meets three or four times each year for day-long meetings to make clear their requirements for us.

Corporate Councils and Advisors

Another set of requirements came originally from functional advisory councils we formed to include senior functional managers from each of the Motorola businesses. Each of these councils identified their needs to support their functional goals. As the corporation formed functional corporatewide councils with charters broader than training, we dissolved ours. Now we have members of the Motorola University staff working very closely with these councils to identify their training requirements.

We have also established advisory boards in geographic regions of the world where Motorola has major employee populations. These regional boards are composed of the general managers of the major facilities in each region and their role is to identify their training requirements across that region. There is also direct contact between personnel in the Motorola University regional offices and the business and training managers in each region to further define and identify requirements.

The members of the chief executive office work directly with us to determine executive education needs. A summary of the sources of input is provided in Fig. 7-2.

As you might imagine, all of this input may result in very different or even conflicting requirements from different segments. Resolving those differences or conflicts becomes critical as does having a process for prioritizing in order to

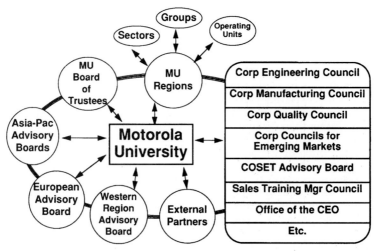

Figure 7-2.   Sources of input.

balance needs and resources. Figs. 7-3*a* and *b* show a tool we have used to help accomplish this.

We have taken a first step in defining requirements other than specific program needs through the development of a Customer Satisfaction Survey. This instrument asks customers from various segments to rate the importance of a number of criteria connected with our products and services. I will discuss this instrument in more detail later in this chapter.

Customer Satisfaction Is Level 1 Evaluation

A new learning for us in this regard is the recognition that the traditional Kirkpatrick Level 1 evaluation, which has always been viewed as participant reaction or perception, is really a Customer Satisfaction Survey of the particular customer segment comprising participants in our training. While the instrument I will discuss in the measurement portion of this chapter was designed to give us the information we thought we needed, it is now being redesigned to address those elements that our customers consider important to the quality of the experience. Interviews and focus groups are being conducted to gather that information which will then be incorporated into the items to be evaluated. Similar techniques have been used to determine the areas on which it is important to focus in the management of our training facilities.

Once your customers define their requirements, it is necessary for you to determine what you must have to meet those requirements or to make some harder decisions. Does your charter or mission need to change? Do you need to manage expectations more carefully?

For instance, when our board of trustees directed us to provide training and education support to our expanding business in China, it became necessary for us to shift resources and establish business plans to support a regional office in China. When one customer segment told us that it was not important to have their telephone communication with someone in their locality, we were able to collapse resources into a single 800-number system. Our customers' consistent requirement for a user-friendly registration and tracking system has been the driver for us to source and implement a new training management system. Because this system will meet their expressed needs, our customers have been very supportive of this decision.

Define Key Processes

With customer requirements always kept in mind, an important step is the defining of all of the key processes required to produce your products and services. First, decide what the key processes used in your business are. Then, several levels of definition can occur. The ultimate goals are:

- To reduce variation by having replicable processes, thus eliminating opportunities for error
- To remove non-value-added steps, again reducing opportunities for error and also reducing cycle time
- To identify issues created by the process

Motorola   **Project Request**
Training & Education   **Business/Group Submitting**

---

1. Business goal (in specific, measurable terms, e.g., $$$, %, Sigma)

---

2. Specific problem to be addressed by training

---

3. Scope   Corporatewide ☐   Local ☐

4. Time frame   Current-oriented issue ☐   Future-oriented issue ☐

---

5. Factors (nontraining) contributing to current/anticipated performance problem

---

6. Potential measurable impact of training on goal

Revenue/cost savings
$ _____

Cycle-time reduction
_____ %

Quality-level improvement
_____

Performance improvement
_____

Customer satisfaction
_____

---

7. Specific request
   Training needs assessment   ☐
   Training program   ☐   Part of _____ curriculum
   Curriculum   ☐

---

8. Population

Job category to be trained	No. Committed	No. Potential

---

9. Critical people

Requestor(s) decide to	Sponsor(s) (senior manager)	Client(s) (those who can send people)

---

10. Subject-matter experts
   Identified   ☐   Who? _____
   Contacted and willing to participate ☐   Need external SME ☐

OVER, PLEASE

Figure 7-3a. Project request (page 1).

---

11. Known content requirements
(what participants have to know or be able to do)

---

12. Market conditions/constraints (if any)

Cost _____

Length _____

Opportunity window _____

Delivery mechanism/considerations _____

---

13. If you know of any existing programs that would meet this request, please identify.

Please print or type

Completed by	Date
Location	Phone

06/12/91   Form also available from Training Managers and Competency Center Managers on diskette.

Figure 7-3b.   Project request (page 2).

At the most basic level, a process may be documented by simply listing the tasks or steps required. An addition to this list might be the person(s) or function(s) responsible for each step. Fig. 7-4 is an example of such a list.

A second technique for defining a process is flow charting. This allows identification of relationships between tasks and may include decision-making steps that can lead to alternative process steps (see Fig. 7-5).

Probably the most helpful technique is the cross-functional mapping of key processes. This allows you to see the relationships of the process steps as well as the people or functions involved in each step and provides the most complete information for reaching the goals of this phase of your road to quality (see Figs. 7-6a and b).

- Build Sponsor Table
- Build and maintain Course Table
- Build and maintain Test Table
- Build and maintain Objective Table
- Build and maintain Training Session Table
- Order Assessments
- Include target population description and learning objectives in back of Participant Guides
- Administer assessments during training
- Mail Assessments to Evaluation Department
- Scan, import, produce reports and return assessments

Figure 7-4. Participant assessment process.

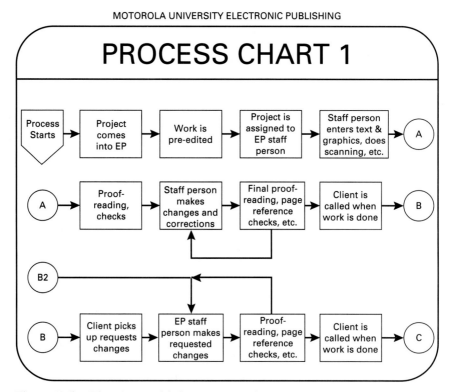

Figure 7-5. Electronic publishing process chart.

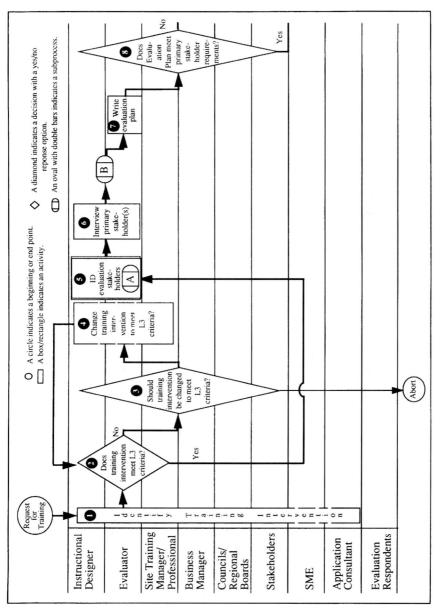

Figure 7-6a. Level 3 Evaluation new-program planning map (version 1).

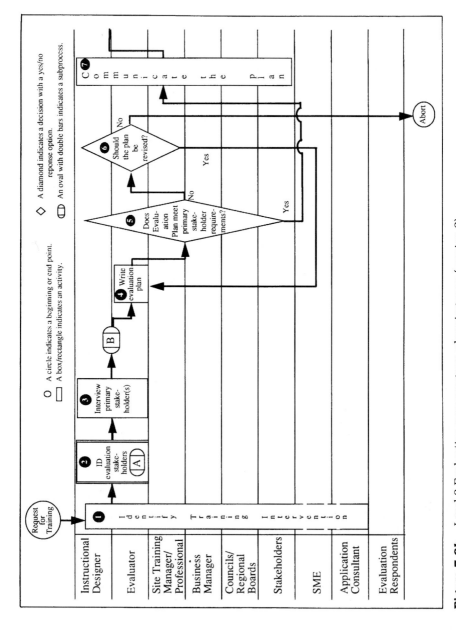

Figure 7-6b. Level 3 Evaluation new-program planning map (version 2).

Whichever of these techniques is used, there are several keys to success. Among them are:

- The people who actually do the work must be involved in defining the process.
- It is important to initially define the process as it is, "warts" and all.
- Once the "as is" is defined, considering issues raised during the definition, customer requirements, and the goals, redefine the process as it "should be."

"As Is" versus "Should Be"

A cross-functional team from Motorola University just recently redefined a process that was causing dissatisfaction for our internal and end-user customers. Using cross-functional mapping to define the "as is" and "should be," the process was reduced from 92 process steps to 40, from a theoretical cycle time of 61 days to 30 and from an actual cycle time that reached as high as three years to a maximum-to-date of 51 days.

A key element in improving the quality of training is to identify some key areas of focus and establish metrics (quantitative measurements, e.g., time, dollars, number of errors) so you know your baseline performance and can determine whether improvements are needed and, if they are attempted, what the impact is. Another way to think about this task is to use measurements to establish a baseline, set improvement goals, and track progress in reaching those goals. It is probably wise to choose just a few key things that are important to your customers and that are either impacted across departments or through multiple layers of a single department. It is important that everyone be clear on his or her role in reaching the goal. Once the key areas have been identified, the method for gathering the data and reporting results must be designed.

Level 1 Evaluation

It is in this context that traditional training evaluation techniques can play a role. As I indicated earlier, level 1 evaluation can be used to measure the satisfaction of participants with factors they have identified as important. After all, when dealing with customers, perception is reality. If what they perceive as important is not satisfactory, how likely are participants to work to gain the knowledge and/or skills addressed, much less try to use them in the workplace? First of all, be sure to measure those things that are important to the customers and then design the instrument to give the best data possible.

We recognized the design issues several years ago and made several changes in our evaluation forms. These included:

- Reformatting so that responses were not in a straight line that encouraged mindless "checking"
- Identifying an anchor for every response to reduce the variation in interpretation and to clarify whether the response indicates satisfaction or dissatisfaction.
- Making responses specific to the item
- Making items more specific to reduce variability in interpretation; i.e., focusing on specific objectives instead of one general objectives question

MOTOROLA UNIVERSITY

Level 1
PARTICIPANT ASSESSMENT

Course Name: ________ Instructor Name: ________ Course Date: ________

Control Number

0 1 2 3 4 5 6 7 8 9

○ AECG ○ UDS
○ CODEX ○ PWDG
○ LMPS ○ SPS
○ CORP ○ SUPPLIER/CUSTOMER
○ GSTG ○ OTHER
○ GSS/CELLULAR

My job matches the target audience description located on the last page of the Participant Guide.

Yes ○ No ○ Expect To Match Within 1 Year ○

MARKING DIRECTIONS

- **Fill in the circle completely.**
- **Do not make any stray marks on this form.**

Correct Mark ○●○○ Incorrect Marks

Directions: Please fill in the circle which most closely describes your reactions to the training program you have just attended. Your feedback is important to Motorola University as we continually strive to reach total customer satisfaction. Thanks very much for your participation!

1. The course content met my expectations.

Exceeded ○ Met ○ Not Met ○

2. The course has increased my capability of performing current or future job tasks.

Strongly Agree ○ Agree ○ Disagree ○ Strongly Disagree ○ Unable to Judge ○

Please help us to understand why you disagree or strongly disagree.

____

3. With respect to my current or future job needs, the course was available to me . . .

Too Early ○ Just in Time ○ Too Late ○

4. I had the skills or knowledge I needed to begin this course.

Strongly Agree ○ Agree ○ Disagree ○ Strongly Disagree ○ Unable to Judge ○

5. The degree to which I feel I met the course objectives is . . .
(See last page of the Participant Guide for description of objectives)

	Very High	High	OK	Low	Very Low
Objective #1	○	○	○	○	○
Objective #2	○	○	○	○	○
Objective #3	○	○	○	○	○
Objective #4	○	○	○	○	○
Objective #5	○	○	○	○	○

6. The examples presented for me to understand the content were . . .

Very Helpful ○ Helpful ○ OK ○ Not Helpful ○ Useless ○ Unable to Judge

7. The course activities, simulations, or games were . . .

Very Helpful ○ Helpful ○ OK ○ Not Helpful ○ Useless ○ None Used ○

If you responded not helpful or useless, how would you improve them?

____

8. The variety of course activities was . . .

Too Much ○ OK ○ Not Enough ○

Please continue on the other side.

Figure 7-7*a*. Participant assessment form (page 1).

- Identifying responses from intended target population so that data not be contaminated with perceptions of "noncustomers" for that product

Examples of these changes may be seen in Fig. 7-7*a* and *b*.

As indicated earlier, this form is under revision. The change will be to focus on those items considered important by the customers.

9. The course was taught in a logical sequence.

Strongly Agree	Agree	Disagree	Strongly Disagree
O	O	O	O

10. The time allotted for me to practice what I learned was ...

Too Much	OK	Not Enough	Not Applicable
O	O	O	O

11. The time allotted for questions was ...

Too Much	OK	Not Enough
O	O	O

12. The course length was ...

Too Many	OK	Too Few
O	O	O

13. The information in the Participant Guide (Class Materials) is easy to read and understand.

Strongly Agree	Agree	Disagree	Strongly Disagree
O	O	O	O

14. All of the information included in the Participant Guide was presented in the course.

Yes	No	Unable to Judge
O	O	O

15. The instructor was well prepared.

Strongly Agree	Agree	Disagree	Strongly Disagree
O	O	O	O

16. The speed at which the instructor provided information was ...

Too Fast	OK	Too Slow
O	O	O

	Outstanding	Above Average	OK	Poor	Unsatisfactory
17. The subject matter knowledge of the instructor was	O	O	O	O	O
18. The instructor's presentation skills are	O	O	O	O	O
19. The instructor's ability to encourage participation during the class was	O	O	O	O	O
20. The instructor's ability to communicate the material was	O	O	O	O	O

21. The training facility or laboratory provided a quality environment to support the training experience.

Strongly Agree	Agree	Disagree	Strongly Disagree
O			O

22. The appearance and format of the printed materials was ...

Outstanding	Above Average	OK	Poor	Unsatisfactory
O	O	O	O	O

23. Overall, I was satisfied with the course.

Yes	No
O	O

24. What would you consider to be the strong points of the course? _____

_____

25. What part(s) of the course do you feel need to be expanded? _____

_____

26. What area(s) do you feel should be removed from the course? _____

_____

27. What do you feel should be added to the course to make it better? _____

_____

28. GENERAL COMMENTS: _____

_____

Figure 7-7b. Participant assessment form (page 2).

Using such instruments as data-gathering tools, metrics can be developed for those items deemed to be most important or requiring improvement or impacted by particular departments. Items reflecting design decisions may provide data for metrics appropriate for the departments that design the training, while items focusing on delivery may drive metrics most appropriate for the departments with those responsibilities.

Using the Data

There are several ways to use the information. For instance, if relevance is a critical area and you track the percentage of customers satisfied with the relevance of the courses you deliver, you may find a wide range of percentages. By using a pareto analysis, you can determine which of the courses are causing most of the problems. It may be possible to focus even further by identifying whether there are particular instructors for whose classes satisfaction seems to be particularly low. Another possibility may be to focus on the delivery sites to determine whether there is a significant difference between them. Another focus could be the particular item in the group of items impacting relevancy that seems to be particularly troublesome. By further focusing the information in this way, determining possible action steps for improvement is made easier. It is these action steps that are important. The metrics simply point to the weed and track progress. If no action is going to be taken, don't bother measuring.

Sometimes, additional information may be necessary before action plans for improvement can be determined. That may indicate the use of focus groups to get further clarification or the use of supplemental survey instruments for the same purpose (i.e., a set of more specific questions on the subject distributed to the next several groups of participants in that course).

Level 2 Evaluation

Level 2 evaluation is a means of gathering information on the quality of the learning occurring in the classroom. This information can then be used to drive an appropriate metric and resulting actions.

Within Motorola University, we decided to use level 2 evaluation to judge the quality of the course rather than the quality of the student. We set goals for the learning required in a pilot test before a course could be released. This minimum goal was established as 80 percent of the participants achieving 80 percent of the objectives of the course. If this didn't occur at pilot, the course needed revision before release, just as the corporation's products must meet a certain minimum quality goal before release. Following release, the metric established was the percentage of courses meeting the established learning goal (80 percent/80 percent or higher). The goal of the measurement was that 100 percent of the courses delivered would meet the learning goal established for that course. Any time a course does not meet that goal, investigation of the root cause is undertaken. A process for analyzing based on the history of a particular instructor delivering that course or the delivery of that course within certain regions, target populations, item analysis, etc., was established. This kind of investigation can lead to a remedy and improvement of the learning.

Levels 3 and 4 Evaluation

It is also possible to establish metrics involving level 3 evaluation. At the time the evaluation is planned, the customer should identify the level of transference expected. The metric then becomes the number of courses evaluated that meet the customers' expectations.

The same kind of approach can be taken with level 4 evaluation.

Another type of metric may be established around the satisfaction of customer segments other than participants. As mentioned earlier, we developed a

Customer Satisfaction Survey instrument that measures both the importance placed on certain criteria by customers and their rate of satisfaction with our performance against that criteria. The reason that both pieces of information is required is that you should put your energy into improving those areas that are most important to your customer. You may be doing something very well that your customer says is not important and you may be doing some things poorly that are very important to your customer. This might indicate that a shift in resources is needed. This type of information can form the basis for metrics, goals, and action plans to meet those goals. The metrics will show whether or not improvement is occurring by periodically resurveying your customers. Fig. 7-8 shows a portion of a Customer Satisfaction Survey.

1. When *making decisions* about training and education…												
a) What importance do you attach to the following criteria? (Please complete column a for all criteria before completing the ratings in column b.) b) How do you rate Motorola University?	a) How important are these criteria to you: 0 = not a criteria 1 = not important 3 = somewhat important 5 = highly important						b) How do you rate MU in its ability to satisfy the criteria? 1 = not acceptable 3 = acceptable 5 = best-in-class					
Criteria	0	1	2	3	4	5	1	2	3	4	5
A. Training to support your business plans											
B. Motorola culture training											
C. Training to accomplish change											
D. Training to enable leading-edge technology											
E. Institutes											
F. Senior executive programs and conferences											
G. Program tailoring to meet specific needs											
H. Functional curricula and training roadmaps											
I. Customer-supplier training											
J. Special events											
K. Value received for price paid											
L. List and rate other criteria you consider important											

Figure 7-8. Portion of customer satisfaction survey.

Cycle-Time Improvement

As part of your continuous improvement efforts, it may be that reduced cycle time is one of your customers' requirements. I spoke before about the opportunities afforded in this arena by cross-functional process mapping. It is important to understand the beginning and end of the cycle you are measuring and not to optimize one subprocess at the expense of the whole cycle. The collection of data may consist simply of tracking when key activities actually occur.

For instance, Motorola University had a need to reduce the cycle time of design and development of courses. However, if we focused only on getting a course to the point of first delivery, it really didn't solve the problem. The whole process starts with the customers' recognition of a training need and ends with performance of all target population changed appropriately. Because we have global responsibility, if we take into consideration our total global target population during analysis and design, the actual design and development process cycle time is increased but the implementation cycle time is reduced so that the total process is reduced.

It is important to establish a baseline; set an improvement goal; track against that goal, identifying barriers or process steps that prevent achievement of the goal; and revise the process accordingly. Again, make sure that in revising the process you are not ignoring customer requirements.

Decision Making

As you establish metrics and report on them, they must be the basis for determining when, where, and how to make improvements. There must be consistency in the reporting and subsequent actions. Leadership support and reinforcement must also be consistent, and the metric should be used as information for decision making, not as a basis for any kind of punitive action. You don't want to "shoot the messenger."

Deciding on which metrics to use is sometimes difficult. Don't wait until you are sure you have identified the "right" ones. Start someplace! If they aren't the best ones, you'll find that out and can try others until your customers begin to see a difference.

Again, remember that this is a never-ending journey because as you begin to do the right things right, your customers will expect even more. However, that's a nice problem to have.

For those of you involved in teaching other organizations how to apply quality concepts, simply be creative about how you can do the same things within your own organization. What is generally observed in organizations that really do improve their quality is a surge of pride and confidence. In addition, the organization will have increased credibility with its customers and peers.

8

Training Records and Information Systems

Alfred J. Walker

Alfred J. Walker *is a Principal with Towers Perrin, in their Saddle Brook, NJ, Office. He is the National Practice Leader of Human Resource Information Management (HRIM) practice which includes Human Resource Systems and Human Resources Reengineering. This practice specializes in computer-based technology for human resource and management functions and examines new organizational models for more effective and efficient HR service delivery. The work includes reengineering HR processes, developing requirements for human resource systems, assisting clients with project management and systems architecture problems, vendor evaluation, and determining more effective methods of utilizing mainframe and micro-based technology in personnel and payroll applications. Recent clients include Air Products and Chemicals, American Airlines, BASF, Coca-Cola, Exxon, GTE, IBM, International Paper, Marriott, Mars Inc., and Sears. Before joining Towers Perrin, Walker directed the human resource systems work at AT&T for over 17 years. In addition, he was with Alexander & Alexander and Information Science, Incorporated, for five years. He is a well-known author and lecturer, founder and board member of both the Human Resource Systems Professionals organization and the Human Resource Planning Society and adjunct university professor. His HRIS Development is considered the seminal text in HR systems and his newest book is* Handbook of HRIS: Reshaping the Human Resource Function with Technology, *McGraw-Hill. He has a B.S. and an M.B.A. in economics and has*

done postgraduate work in operations research. He was the
1994 Summit Award winner of the HRSP organization achieve-
ment over a lifetime to the human resource field.

Today's forward-looking companies like AT&T, DuPont, Florida Power & Light, Motorola, and others have automated much in the way of the administration that accompanies training and development. In addition, other companies and organizations of more modest size are also embracing technology to help with the operational details.

This chapter traces the history of training record-keeping systems, outlines the features of such systems, and provides some guidance on how to develop them.

Historical Perspective

Technology to assist with student enrollment and training participation traces its lineage to personnel data systems. Such systems include computer-based payroll-personnel systems now more frequently referred to as human resource information systems (HRIS). These systems have been in existence for over 30 years and during that time have grown from very simple record-keeping systems to complex, interactive, knowledge-based environments with visual and auditory components often deployed on a global basis. While earlier systems were limited in scope and initially intended to track basic demographic information on employees such as department, name, salary, and so on, today's fully integrated HRIS brings together the full spectrum of data regarding an individual, including benefits, compensation, and work history, among others, as well as information pertaining to that person's training and development. It is this integration of data that has finally led the training and development modules of the HRIS to become as useful as they are today since the information relating to an employee's career goals and job requirements can now be automatically linked to training that may be essential or even mandated. In earlier systems the linkage simply was not possible due to several factors: system and database size and cost constraints; the central nature of the HRIS architecture; data collection and manual input which called for paper-based records to be sent to a central data entry function (inherently slow and cumbersome but which was the model that most organizations used to collect training records); and the fact that for many employee groups there was no HR program nor incentive to plan for the training and development of the workforce, so little formal training was conducted. What training was recorded was limited to the technical workforce.

This training, for engineers, scientists, computer programmers, and certain craft positions, was recorded "after the fact," and the computer database updated with the course number, title of the course, along with the date and location of the course itself. These were the courses "that mattered" according to management 20 years ago, as there really were few broad-based issues or courses that were extended to all employees. The highly technical employees were the group that were of greatest concern and, therefore, courses for them were the ones that got delivered and tracked by the training systems or personnel data systems that were then in existence. For the vast majority of the employees, there was no need to invest in systems and therefore no history of training courses was computerized. If a nontechnical employee did go to a company course, the record of that attendance was filed in the supervisor's file for that employee or it was sent "to personnel" for filing in the employee's records. But in the main, there was no tracking of all courses for all employees, much less other types of developmental experiences as we will discuss later in this chapter.

From a conceptual standpoint, training and development was viewed as one of the basic modules of the overall human resource system, as shown in Fig. 8-1. Things changed, however. In the late 1970s the very large companies like Ford Motor Company, Xerox, and IBM had such extensive course offerings and training departments that they soon found that it was more efficient to develop computerized training systems or modules of the HRIS due to the efficiencies they offered. These systems were either a full component of an HRIS, as shown in Fig. 8-1, or were connected to the central payroll-personnel systems and had their own databases, input forms, and outputs (see Fig. 8-2). If they were sepa-

Figure 8-1. Major HRIS modules, 1960s–1970s.

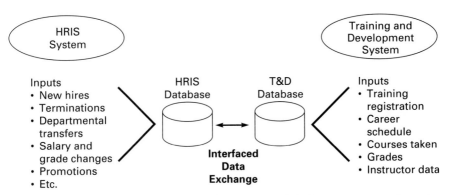

Figure 8-2. Late 1970s–1980s—Interfaced approach linking training systems to the HRIS.

rate systems, they would be interfaced to the central HRIS for new hires, terminations, and/or transfers and the like.

The outputs of such interfaced systems were course catalogs, class rosters, training completion notices, trainer schedulings, classroom assignments, and the like, similar to the outputs of the T&D module of an HRIS. Whether the training systems were modules of an HRIS or were separate systems usually depended upon factors such as the size of the database which, in turn, was a function of the population and frequency of training, the standardization of the data itself, the usage of the data, and the ease of developing a stand-alone solution. For large companies offering hundreds of courses, the projects and systems were too large and complex to incorporate in a single HRIS system. In any event, by the mid 1970s full computerization of training records had arrived for many organizations. And still it was the technical areas that were leading the way with this trend, continuing well into the 1980s.

Changing Demand

Driven by competition, new markets and new products and customer demands, the engineering and/or the computer areas were dealing with constant change and technology obsolescence. Training, therefore, was of utmost importance to the management of these departments. For these work groups, scheduling classes and assignments and tracking employees who were scheduled to attend or who did attend training were time-consuming and difficult tasks. However, with the HRIS initiatives under way, the premise of help through automation was such that these groups were more than willing to participate in the process of moving the records from paper to electronic media. The difficulties arose though when standards began to be applied. For example, if two departments or groups both offered courses substantially the same, could they be listed as the same course? Other questions arose as well such as Why have the same course offered at the same location by two or more instructors when one would suffice? Even more basic questions were surfaced as the training area was computerized, such as What constitutes training that should be tracked? A one-day course? Two days? Is there a completion requirement? How does one record attendance at a course? How about self-paced courses? Do we need to track down on the instructor? How do the EEO requirements get factored in? These and other related issues and problems were dealt with by those involved in automating training and developing. Where successful, though, the teams were able to develop integrated or stand-alone systems to help with the administration. Often though, the issues these questions raised by standardization got in the way, thwarting even the best of intentions and resulting in the training area being able to automate only a portion of the system or only extend it to those units that fit the ultimate design.

Those projects that did succeed in automating training and development were able to do so due to a set of criteria similar to the following:

- They had a strong mandate from senior management which was used to break logjams.
- Sufficient staff and funding was available to complete the project.
- Strong project management discipline was evident throughout.
- Scope was broad enough to gain acceptance but small enough to be accomplished.
- Users and participants wanted the project to succeed and assisted the effort.

In the 1970s and into the 1980s these systems were primarily tracking systems, recording training taken and usually not linking developmental work other than formal training or assisting with the larger issues of workforce productivity, quality, customer satisfaction, and cost containment since the more progressive ideas of linking training with development or increasing productivity were still on the horizon for most employers.

The Business Needs Define the New Training and Development Systems

Most trainers would agree that increasing individual and organizational productivity through a performance-based training strategy is one of the underlying reasons, if not *the* most important, behind training and development. Other drivers include closing gaps in performance, increasing bench strength, developing better methods for satisfying customers, and identifying and developing better team performance. These drivers, though, are all related to the basic goal of winning in the marketplace. And, over a long period of time those who continuously increase productivity through better performance will win in their markets given the correct management guidance and overall business strategies. The training and development strategy therefore, if it is to be successful, must recognize and, of course, complement the business strategies but go beyond them to focus on increasing individual and organization productivity. Hence, the phrase "a learning organization." But how to get to an organization that constantly renews itself and keeps pace with new work and new skills? This can be done in a variety of ways ranging from identifying and developing individual and group core competencies to implementing skill-based programs or customer-driven approaches. All of these methods are outlined elsewhere in this handbook.

Regardless of the approach taken by management to meet these needs, the workforce must keep pace with the newer technologies and market demands, and that involves life-long learning. And, the training and development methods of the late 1990s and early 2000s necessarily are being altered to meet these needs with new ideas and products to keep the workers productive in their jobs. Scheduling and tracking the development needs and learning that is required, however, has become a more difficult task. For example, how does the employee, work group leader, or supervisor keep pace with the training and development needs? Faced with constant demands on one's time for more productivity, more sales, better customer service, and higher quality at reduced costs, how can one also learn new skills and competencies that may be required in the future? The complexity of constantly assessing current skills, scheduling training, recording the new knowledge, comparing it to a core competency requirement, and determining the training and/or development experience to an overall development plan that may be laid out for an employee has now become a daunting task for supervisors that have wide span of control. Also, the training departments and HR functions have need for the same data.

The answer to these problems, to a large degree, lies in the newer training and development systems that are being developed. Among other features, these newer systems help target specific training for employees based upon their existing skills and the position requirements, keep all the data on a historical basis, and link all HR plans and programs such as the development plans with training data.

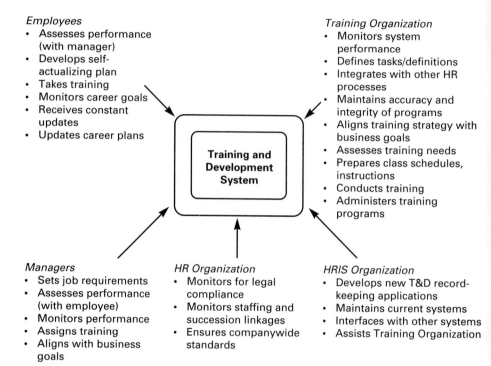

Employees
- Assesses performance (with manager)
- Develops self-actualizing plan
- Takes training
- Monitors career goals
- Receives constant updates
- Updates career plans

Training Organization
- Monitors system performance
- Defines tasks/definitions
- Integrates with other HR processes
- Maintains accuracy and integrity of programs
- Aligns training strategy with business goals
- Assesses training needs
- Prepares class schedules, instructions
- Conducts training
- Administers training programs

Training and Development System

Managers
- Sets job requirements
- Assesses performance (with employee)
- Monitors performance
- Assigns training
- Aligns with business goals

HR Organization
- Monitors for legal compliance
- Monitors staffing and succession linkages
- Ensures companywide standards

HRIS Organization
- Develops new T&D record-keeping applications
- Maintains current systems
- Interfaces with other systems
- Assists Training Organization

Figure 8-3. Advanced training and development record-keeping system.

The Vision

As depicted in Fig. 8-3, the newer T&D systems call for all employees and managers to have direct on-line access to all training programs and data pertaining to performance of their units and groups as well as individuals, with the ability to know about career opportunities and possible jobs. They automatically handle a variety of activities that are still manual in many companies.

The Goal

The goal of all T&D systems is to support a performance-based training strategy in a learning organization. Figure 8-4 shows how Motorola and others are handling their training and development needs with their new T&D system.

As shown in Fig. 8-3 and outlined in the case study, the newer systems help assess and evaluate the individuals' competence in their existing job and match the employees' strengths and weaknesses with a prescribed level of competence or standard that must be achieved. Courses and other measures for closing any gaps in performance can be viewed and the employees and/or managers can choose the appropriate course based upon schedules, cost, and long-range development goals of both the employee and other team members. The system can be used to enroll the employee in the training; monitor any precourse work that needs to be completed; track attendance; book travel and hotel rooms, if appropriate; and document the course when completed. These systems go far beyond the older model of merely tracking the training already taken and helping with

TEDS Project as Case Study

Working in a collaborative effort with several other large employers—companies such as Bell Atlantic, Florida Power and Light, Dupont, Motorola, and others—have installed an advanced training and development system that has integrated the needs of the employee, supervisor, and the training administration staff. The system helps manage the individual's training and development as specified by the roles and tasks the employer performs, or is being prepared to perform, and the system takes this data along with other information to provide, upon demand, an up-to-the-minute status on each person in the system. In addition, normal statistics and data on courses, instructors, facilities, and such are automatically tracked for the administrators who are managing the training functions. It is based upon software "TEDS" supplied by a vendor, CBM Technologies, and has a modular structure as follows:

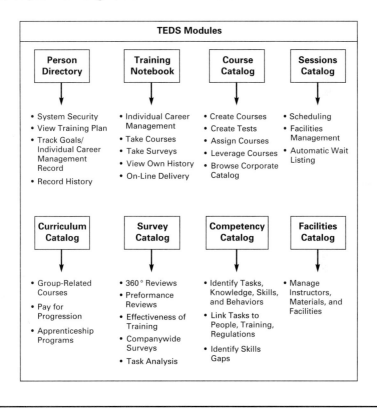

Figure 8-4. TEDS project as case study.

the administrative end. They help define the needed competencies, assess performance, present options on how to close any performance gaps, and document the training as delivered. Progress through a series of training programs (progression training) is also noted by these systems. They help deliver training and development, not just record it.

The impetus for the newer systems which follow an integrated approach has been made possible by a number of factors including newer regulations which in many cases are now mandated by federal or state safety, health, transportation, and environmental agencies; newer available, cost-affordable, local area network (LAN) technology, such as networks with client-server approaches, faxes, and imaging, etc.; the increasing emphasis on quality, including ISO 9000 standards; and the push to streamline and redefine work into its component parts, thereby keeping costs low.

Developing the System

The first step in developing such systems connecting performance to training is to define the work based on tasks and to regroup the work so it can be taught and assessed more easily. Redefining work into a series of steps or tasks has been getting widespread attention for some time through initiatives such as reengineering and competency-based performance. These disciplines flow out the steps of a process and redesign it to eliminate redundancies and waste, increase customer service, and cut time and cost. These redesigned processes are then subjected to a duty-task analysis and repackaged into newer jobs made up of a series of these tasks. An inventory of such tasks is a key component of the new T&D systems and the link is then made by the system to determine the training necessary to teach these tasks. They can also inform the job analysts and trainers if the training program exists now. The system will also know which employees can already perform the tasks.

The next step then is to link the tasks to the training on an ongoing basis. Confusion regarding similar training titles and programs yet different tasks can now be greatly reduced since the work is brought down to the task level. Tasks and learning events, which teach those tasks, are specified on a corporatewide basis or down to a level where the commonality between job tasks and the learning events exist and can be validated.

Managers and employees can then use this tool to track competencies, assess skills and abilities, and build upon them as required. When job content changes due to technology or business conditions, the duty-task analysis team can investigate the changes and examine the learning events to determine their relevancy and need for new training. The underlying philosophy here is that much of the training in organizations is generic, and there is little need for different training and learning events when slight organizational differences in work exist. If fundamental principles and knowledge is obtained then on the job, training can augment the base training. Here's where the inventory of tasks and learning events is critical; the system can provide the tools to categorize and maintain the inventory for the base tasks and training for the use by the training organization and even beyond this team for use by managers and the employees directly.

With the integrated T&D system, the end users become the line managers and employees themselves who are able to perform a series of developmental activities in addition to the assessment of base training and do not have to rely upon the training organization or HR function for help.

Manager and Employee Involvement

The system provides planning tools to help managers and employees jointly outline a program for development based upon their assessment of the primary job, its tasks and the position requirements, the long-range goals of the employee, and the organizational gaps that may exist. This annual or more frequent employee development planning exercise has long suffered due to lack of job aids and integration with other HR processes. The new T&D system contains job briefs for the "core" jobs, the tasks that make them up, and the base requirements for them. The system helps the manager and employee to determine the fit between what competencies they may possess and those needed if they were to aspire to a different job. This achievement is possible since past history of all training taken is maintained by the system and, therefore, it is easy to determine what training and experiences would be applicable to the new work. This "degree of fit" is highly useful for both parties, as it outlines a possible course of action and shows any unrealistic expectations that either party has.

The manager and employee then agree to a sequence of developmental steps, taking into account current job needs and gaps; how these map to the organization gaps, if any; and the long-term career goals of the employee.

Since the new T&D system is integrated with the staffing and succession planning processes, other linkages are made possible as well. As jobs become open and are posted and electronically broadcast throughout the unit or organization, the hiring manager can be automatically notified of any employees who have shown interest in the position during their development sessions with their current managers. The "degree of fit" model can then be drawn by the hiring manager which shows the strengths and weaknesses of the employee in relation to the open job. Contact with the employee or current manager can then take place if the hiring manager wants to pursue the employee for an interview.

Connectivity with the succession planning process can be aided with the new system as well. For the "high-potential" (HIPO) employees who need developmental assignments, the management or HR executive resources staff can determine the next logical moves based upon assessment of strength versus core job-task requirements and intervene in the staffing process as appropriate to provide the HIPO employees the development and other exposures they need to build the managerial bench strength of the company.

Measuring Training

The new T&D system also provides management with the ability to measure the effectiveness of its training and development programs. Analysis of groups of employees or individuals can be made to ascertain if they do in fact meet the mandated requirements, if specified, or the position requirements as outlined by the direct supervisor. Where incumbents do not meet the requirements, the database contains the information of the number of modules or units of instruction taken, the number passed, the number failed, the number of retries, the timeframes, etc., for management's use.

There is a deeper analysis thought to get at the issues relating to productivity improvements of individuals or teams over time; correlation of performance to work group size and efficiencies and longitudinal studies of work teams are where the system will show it has great potential. These types of investigations are almost impossible today with paper-based records or, in most cases, no records at all. The following are concerns related to the training strategies: What effect does training have over time? When should you retrain? When should work schedules be shifted in relation to certain conditions? What forms of training are most effective over short or long periods of time? The effectiveness of training begins and ends with many companies' ability or inability to measure it. One axiom is, If you can't measure it, you can't manage it! Therefore, the ability to measure various forms of training must be built into the processes and the delivery-tracking systems.

It goes without saying that not all training or learning will be delivered by this system; in fact, most will not since it is informal. Most learning and training will take place as it does today—through a combination of two kinds of experience: (1) hands-on, on-the-job experience gained at the desk, laboratory, on the line, in the field, and/or through interaction with the supervisor, other workers, and/or customers, and (2) actual experience augmented by other media such as classroom instruction, mentoring, etc. But the system will aid with planning for the training-development and assessment of training results. It will also help with measurement and documentation of much of the training and development that can be recorded and the assessment and certification of the workers who take the training. And it will be an integral component of the evidence required to meet the legal requirements as dictated by regulatory agencies. Further, these new systems are more efficient since they combine many features of stand-alone systems with advances not available until now in areas such as process and work-flow improvement, standards and codification, and the latest technology.

A more modest approach is to utilize a training component of a broader scope HRIS as shown in Fig. 8-1. Using this approach, the user can still tie the training needs to the individual development plan but the technology may not be as advanced nor as grounded in competencies to the degree that more elegant solutions might be. However, they do provide most of the administrative assistance such as recording the courses taken, helping with certification requirements, tracking career paths, and the like.

Recently, some fairly low-cost desktop local area network (LAN) systems have been appearing on the commercial HRIS and training marketplace with fairly extensive capabilities including tuition billing and accounting and full registration features. These are stand-alone systems which can be made compatible with the baseline HRIS and payroll systems and offer an attractive alternative for small midrange companies.

Some companies have made good use of systems such as e-mail and voice-response systems to help announce course offerings or help with registration.

Technical Considerations

Since the record-keeping systems are primarily computer-based information systems, there are several considerations that organizations need to consider in planning for and implementing a training and development system. These include at least the following, as outlined in Fig. 8-5, and are more fully explained below:

I. Developing the System Requirements

The requirements should be specified in as much detail as possible in order to price out the project and present to the users and management the benefits and the costs of the endeavor. The major components of the requirements include:

a. Objectives and Scope.   What the project entails; why is it being undertaken; what is good or bad about the current environment; why a new system is required; what population is covered; how processes would work (e.g., how users enter and engage the system); how users use the system and when and

I. Developing the requirements for the system
   a. Objectives and scope
   b. Standards and definitions
   c. Resource needs
   d. Time frames
   e. Cost-benefits
   f. Integration with other HR processes
   g. Integration or interface with other systems
   h. Functional processes and data content

II. Defining the system development and operating environment
   a. Development approach
   b. Technical platform
   c. Modules, components, applications
   d. Administrative needs
   e. Accuracy program and measurements
   f. Backup, retention, and security
   g. Schedule

III. Conversion and implementation strategy
   a. Database population coverage
   b. Pilots and trials
   c. Rollout
   d. Ongoing maintenance and releases

Figure 8-5. Considerations in planning for and implementing a training and development system.

under what conditions; how it fits with other initiatives and projects underway; legal issues and system boundaries.

b. Standards and Definitions. What the structure of the system will be from the user's standpoint, i.e., data standards, codes, graphical user interfaces and presentation formats; user requirements regarding course numbers; definitions of terms, e.g., course descriptions, numbering conventions the users must follow, meaning of items such as tasks, jobs, teams; any U.S. versus international definitions (ISO 9000).

c. Resource Requirements. The number of people and backgrounds needed to develop and operate the system; how the new role of manager, team leader, and employee is laid out and how each person will use the new system; what staff levels changes are required, if any; the development roles and maintenance roles of the HRIS team, IS organization, and the user group.

d. Time Frames. How long it is expected to take to develop and implement the system and any dependencies on other projects.

e. Cost-Benefits. Quantitative analysis of the investment and payback (if any) of the project on a phase-module-component basis, i.e., where organization is financially after the investment in Phase I or first deliverable; after Phase II, etc.

f. Integration with Other HR Processes. How the new T&D system would work with other HR processes and systems such as the compensation, performance management, staffing, and succession planning processes.

g. Integration or Integration with Other Systems.   How the T&D system would interact with other technical systems, and how data would pass between them. This would include "factory floor" and other managerial systems that every manager may have access to as well as e-mail systems, the HRIS or other payroll-personnel systems, and other training and development systems.

h. Functional Processes and Data Content.   The content of the system beginning with an enterprise data model for training and development. This would include the entities and the data that support them, e.g., courses, customers, students, instructors, jobs, and tasks. In addition, if reengineered workflows have been developed, then a set of relationships and functional users can be depicted as to what data they require to complete their tasks and/or functions under the new system. These would be described in a functional manner here and also set forth in a technical manner in Section II below.

II. Defining the Development and Operating Environment

Once the system requirements have been agreed upon and the project given the "go-ahead," then the system can be defined in more detail. This detail will differ from company to company based upon the standards for systems development but should include the following:

a. Development Approach.   How the system will be developed, i.e., steps, tools, programming and documentation standards; testing steps; whether to build or buy (if product available in market) and which system commercially available might be purchased or adopted.

b. Technical Platform.   What specific technologies and approach will be used, i.e., hardware, operating system, user interface, CASE tools; database management system that is proposed; and what the environment will be, i.e., client-server, networks, and telecommunications needs.

c. Modules, Components, and Applications.   The specifics of each of the applications that will be built. The functionality needed grouped by module or component would be described here in great detail. For example, the layout and content of each display panel, course delivery screens, data content, functions, reports; course catalogs; and how each module, such as the career development, would perform. This includes data definitions, edits, defaults, etc.

d. Administrative Needs.   The project management structure needed for the project would be laid out here. This includes team-reporting relationships, budgeting needs, space needs, testing, etc., required to build and maintain the system.

e. Accuracy Program and Measurements.   How the information will get into the system and remain accurate to the point of delivery and on into history; how the training and development processes will be measured in the future.

f. Backup, Retention, and Security. How user's privacy and security will be maintained (log-ons, passwords), and how the system will be protected from intrusion, viruses, and catastrophes. Also, how data would be retained, i.e., what data is kept for how long. How the system will be backed up and with what frequency—daily, weekly, etc.

g. Schedule. The development schedule and resources needed to meet the user requirements.

III. Conversion and Implementation Strategy

Concurrent with the definition phase, a conversion and implementation plan should be drawn up to include the following points:

a. Database Population Coverage. How the data will get into each field both initially and thereafter. Will there be a feed from the HRIS? Will each employee put in his or her past training? How will an audit-verification take place?

b. Pilot or Trial. Will there be an initial group to put in data and use the system to refine it and to work out the new procedures? If so, for how long? What are the roles and responsibilities? How to test the new system?

c. Rollout. What is the plan to take a tested and trialed-piloted module to the larger population? Is it best done by geography, by unit, or by type of employee, e.g., all hourly employees first with managers next?

d. Ongoing Maintenance-Release. What is the plan for maintaining the system once rolled-out and how will changes and new releases be handled? How will the employees be trained?

T&D System Applications

The following are major application areas or modules in a T&D system that should be considered.

Course Scheduling

This task begins with a listing of possible courses and training needs derived from the development plans submitted by employees and supervisors as well as historical input from the training organization based on past demand. There also may be corporate or business issues that will influence the scheduling of courses. From this demand, an overall course schedule is developed. The training curricula would display the range of courses offered, whether taught on-site, at local schools or universities, or with company trainers or adjunct facility; whether self-paced or instructor-led.

The display can be both in electronic form or in printed course catalogs. The display should list the date, location, course syllabus, instructors, prerequisites, credit hours, and tuition.

Instructor Scheduling

At the same time the overall schedule is prepared the selection and assignment of qualified instructors needs to be accomplished. The T&D system must supply the training staff with information regarding each potential instructor's background, qualifications and certifications, past course evaluations, availability to teach, and current schedule.

Student Registration

The T&D system must allow students, employees, supervisors, and/or others to enroll themselves or authorized staff in one or more courses. The enrollment would take into account capacity of the class; any allocations based upon job, department, or other factors; any training prerequisites and/or job qualifications; and potential conflicts such as having taken the same or a similar course before. Invoices would be established and sent along with any prereading or prework that needs to be completed. Enrollment confirmations are also prepared and mailed or routed when enrollment is finalized.

Preparation for Training

While the registration is taking place, training rooms can be assigned for classroom courses based upon the type of course, audiovisual requirements, size of class, location, etc. Wait lists are maintained if the classes are oversubscribed; cancellations are noted either with or without penalty as required. There is often need to swap students from one class to another or to reassign instructors if classes are merged or additional classes or schedules are shifted. The system can track videos, materials on loan, and other items necessary for training to assist the training support staff.

Conduct Training

The T&D system must print the class rosters, permit daily sign-on's, keep track of costs and materials used, maintain evaluations, and print and mail grade notices and completion certifications. Final invoices are prepared based upon any outstanding amounts. Interim evaluations and tests can sometimes be tracked as well.

Reporting, Analysis, and History

Because the database can maintain an almost unlimited history of courses, instructors, students, costs, sites, etc., they can be mixed and merged in an endless variety of ways. Many reports will be triggered by events such as the finalization of enrollment or course completion, and therefore invoices and rosters need to be automatically produced and tracked. In this sense the T&D system is an operational, production-type system interfacing with the budgeting, general ledger, accounts payable, and receivables systems. But because of advanced technology the queries and analyses that can be performed permit the training organizations to analyze registrations, course enrollment patterns, student or instructor ratings and biases, among other considerations, as they are being conducted as well as after the fact. Certifications and legal requirements can also easily be monitored since the linkages with job requirements and sensitive positions and the training can be made.

Critical Success Factors in Training Systems Design

In order to ensure the most efficient and effective training and development system, there is usually a set of issues, objectives, or goals that are the most important to have go well for the system to be a success. These are referred to as critical success factors (CSFs). They will differ from company to company, depending on the particular issues, needs, cost imperatives, systems architecture, and related considerations. The CSFs should be developed and agreed upon by the users, management, and the development team to help guide the project development and help in prioritizing modules and allocating resources. The CSF approach will enable the developers to gain a consensus on the project goals and objectives and use that direction and "buy-in" throughout the development cycle when differences in opinions arise or key trade-off decisions that inevitably arise need to be made.

The following are some examples of CSFs in the training and development area that should be considered.

Support Training Programs

The primary goal of any T&D system is to automate and assist in the effective delivery of knowledge to the participants.

Integration of Human Resource Plans and Programs

The T&D system should help bring about a closer tie to the career development, performance management, training, and staffing programs, among others. Because information systems can automatically "bring up" items for attention at selected times or events, the plan connectivity can be enhanced with a well-designed system. Examples of such integration include training courses that are earmarked to be taken for an individual which can be noted by the system and routed to the supervisor for action, and performance management analyses which can be supported by certain courses.

Increase Management Effectiveness

The management team of today and tomorrow must be ensured to be as strong as it can be to meet the competitive challenges of the marketplace. The T&D

system can identify and track management performance and help schedule development and training programs to close gaps.

Acquire, Retain, and Develop Top Talent

The system can help managers find suitable candidates for positions based upon their "fit" with job requirements and their background, experience, and training. Once they are in the job, their development and training are easily tracked. Dimensions of the talent needs include the people mix to ensure that the work groups are sufficiently diverse to meet market needs. This diversity is essential for most companies in terms of marketing, customer support, and team performance. The T&D system can help track the key characteristics from both in a compliance and business perspective, and ensure that developmental opportunities are being afforded to women and minorities as well as white males.

Meet Regulatory Requirements

Meeting all of the training, certification, and qualification requirements in a large organization is almost impossible without a systematized approach to defining and tracking the jobs, skills, training, and documentation needed by the various state and federal agencies. This information must be in such a format as to be accessible by team, individual, location or site, date, certification type or skill, or item such as hazardous material or piece of equipment.

Support Employee-Manager Self-Sufficiency

Enabling the supervisor and/or employee to know about the job requirements, job opportunities, and T&D options that are available and to assist with the appropriate selection sequence, timing, cost, and enrollment of the training or development program. Assisting with this self-sufficiency helps reinforce the concept that the worker and manager themselves are in the best position to decide the specific type of training needed, only involving the human resource specialists when necessary.

Streamline the Work First

Using process flows and reengineering concepts, the developers and users should ensure that the enrollment, delivery, and tracking processes are as streamlined and efficient as they can be before automating them. In this way the computerization will support the desired or reengineered process and not merely automate the old method. Paperwork, unnecessary steps, and other waste should be kept to a minimum.

These CSFs can then be matched with the corporate objectives and/or business strategies to ensure that they are aligned. For example, suppose a company was embarking on a major new marketing initiative by entering new territories and also desired to keep operating costs low while simultaneously ensuring ongoing customer satisfaction, maintaining product quality, and complying with all laws

Critical success factors	T&D Systems Alignment Grid				
	Corporate Goals				
	Support new marketing program	Keep Costs low	Comply with all regulations	Maintain product quality	Customer satisfaction
Support training programs overall	X	X	X	X	X
Integrate HR plans and programs		X	X		X
Acquire, retain, and develop top talent	X			X	X
Increase management effectiveness	X	X			
Meet regulatory requirements		X	X		
Support employee-manager self-sufficiency		X		X	
Streamline the work		X	X		

Figure 8-6. T&D Systems Alignment Grid.

and regulations. While doing so, the team could produce an alignment grid to test the T&D system with these corporate goals. That grid would look something like the one shown in Fig. 8-6.

Conclusion

Training and development record-keeping systems have become an integral component in most training departments and will be even more indispensable in the years ahead. Even in the smallest companies it is not unusual to find tracking of courses and grades taking place either through their HRIS systems or their own training tracking systems. Because of the emphasis being placed on performance management and competency-based programs as well as the legal and regulatory needs, the requirement to integrate these HR programs through these systems as well as maintain complete and accurate data has never been more important. Indeed, as we move forward with even more types of training and development in the future through telecommunications and worldwide networks, the job of selecting, delivering, and tracking suitable training will be all but impossible without such systems.

Bibliography

Abratrain, Training Administration System, Abra Software, St. Petersburg, FL 33702 (800-847-2272).

Burke, Michael J., and Gary Kaufman, "Internal Information for Managing HR Programs," *Managing HR in the New Information Age,* Bureau of National Affairs, 1991, pp. 100–106.

Empire/SQL, Humanic Design Corp., Mahwah, NJ 07430 (201-825-8887).

Genesys, Genesys Software Systems, Inc., Methuen, MA 01844 (508-885-5400).

Ingenium for Windows, Meliora Systems, Rochester, NY 14618 (800-388-7332).

Latimer, Robert L., *Managing Diversity for Strategic and Competitive Advantage,* Doubleday/Dell, New York, 1994.

PeopleSoft/HRMS, PeopleSoft, Inc., Walnut Creek, CA 94596 (800-947-7753).

Registrar, Historian, Scheduler, Silton-Bookman Systems, Cupertino, CA 95014 (800-932-6311).

Selinger, Olivia, "Implementing a Career Development System," *The Review, Association of Human Resource Systems Professionals,* February–March 1995, pp. 22–27.

Skopos HRS/PRO, Anchor Software, Los Altos, CA 94022 (415-903-4785).

TD/2000, Spectrum Human Resources Systems Corp., Denver, CO 80202 (800-477-3287).

TEDS, The People Resource Planning Solution, CBM Technologies, Atkins, VA 24311 (703-783-6991).

Walker, Alfred, J., *Handbook of Human Resource Systems,* McGraw-Hill, New York, 1992.

9

Training
and the Law

Patricia S. Eyres

Patricia S. Eyres *is a licensed California attorney with over 17 years civil litigation experience. As founder and President of Litigation Management and Training Services, Inc., in Long Beach, Eyres consults with business owners and government agencies on legal issues affecting the workplace. She conducts a variety of training programs to sensitize management and human resource professionals to legal liabilities arising in the workplace. Her workshops focus on preventing costly lawsuits or minimizing disruption when unavoidable claims occur. As both an attorney and training professional, she has developed a unique expertise on the liabilities which arise in the context of training and developing employees. She has presented workshops on avoiding corporate and personal liability for the design and delivery of training at national conferences of ASTD, International Society for Performance Improvement, and many other trade and professional groups. She teaches "Training and The Law" at California State University at Long Beach, Extension Services, and "Labor and Employment Law" at the University of California, Irvine. She has authored numerous articles including "Keeping the Training Department Out of Court" (Training, September 1990), and is the author of* Training and Legal Issues: The Law and How It Relates to Training *(HRD Press, 1994) and is contributing author to the* Handbook of Human Performance Technology, *Chapter 35, "Legal Ramifications of Human Performance Technology" (Jossey-Bass, 1992). Prior to founding Litigation and Training Services, Inc., Eyres was supervising partner of a law firm's civil litigation department. She is also a member of the State Bar of California and the American and Long Beach Bar Associations and has served as 1990 President of Women Lawyers of Long Beach.*

Criminal conduct. Professional liability. Training liability. Gross negligence. Malpractice. The legal concepts are virtually interchangeable. The economic and career consequences can be serious. No matter which term is used, the realities of assessing risks and managing legal compliance in regulated work environments are causing increasing concern for managers, human resources specialists, and trainers. Indeed, legal exposure for professionals is no longer the exclusive province of physicians and lawyers. Training and development professionals in hazardous work environments, and technologically complex work sites, are being held accountable for injuries or damages to people, property, and the environment.

A maze of federal and state laws now govern the process of training employees, adding to the burden of regulating the workplace both profitably and legally. In the next decade, increasing numbers of multicultured and multiabled workers will enter the workforce. Many will need basic English literacy instruction. Others with no technical experience will require advanced skills training. Administrative agencies will continue to regulate training programs in public- and private-sector workplaces, particularly industries involved with hazardous workplace conditions.

In many high-risk industries, executives, managers, and trainers are recognizing that the costs of comprehensive training programs are significantly less than the ultimate costs of litigating after an accident or injury. For example, Arco Refinery recently paid $3.5 million in fines for a July 1990 explosion at a Texas plant. In announcing the payment, which was to that point the largest Occupational Safety and Health Act (OSHA) settlement in history, Arco officials said "the company believes...its interests are better served by focusing on improving workplace safety rather than by contesting or litigating the differences it may have with OSHA."

Lawsuits involving training typically run the gamut from regulatory penalties and lawsuits for failure to train or inadequate methodology to negligence in managing the training facilities. However, these traditional areas of training liabilities are by no means the only source of legal exposure. In addition to workplace diversification, rapidly developing technology is challenging traditional assumptions about the selection of trainees for advanced skills and management programs. Employers need to document their selection criteria carefully to avoid discrimination claims by older employees, women, and others based upon inappropriate—and unlawful—assumptions about technical abilities which deprive those employees of equal opportunities. Time-honored methods of testing and evaluation are also being subjected to increasing scrutiny by regulatory agencies and, ultimately, by a judge or jury.

The tangible costs of discrimination claims is also significant. The most recent statistics from the Equal Employment Opportunity Commission (EEOC) for the fiscal year ending 1994 reflect a record pace of discrimination claims. The EEOC expected to top 90,000 charges of employment discrimination in the fiscal year 1994, breaking the all-time high of 87,942 in 1993.[1] A significant number involve gender, ethnicity, and disability based on denial of access to entry-level training. Many of the age discrimination cases focused on allegations that older workers were passed over for advanced automation training. An analysis of charges through April 30, 1994, reveals that approximately 13 percent of disability discrimination claims under the Americans With Disabilities Act (ADA) are based on neurological impairments, which includes learning disabilities and other disorders affecting the training function.[2]

Many employers faced with criminal or civil actions have reached settlements which include not only monetary awards but also commitments to increase the scope of training. One recent case involving ergonomic workplace hazards was brought against New York Intercontinental Branded Apparel for one willful violation of agency regulations for "exposing employees to hazards of repetitive motion job tasks that could lead to the development of cumulative trauma disorders." The OSHA investigation which led to the citation was triggered by an employee complaint rather than by any specific injuries or illnesses at the work site. In the settlement, the employer agreed, in part, to establish employee and supervisor training on cumulative trauma hazards and medical management of those disorders. OSHA reports that the settlement is comparable to other ergonomic settlements it has reached with employers throughout the country.

This chapter will provide an overview of the most significant legal issues affecting the training of employees in the 1990s and beyond. This includes an explanation of the interrelationship of statutory and common-law issues directly impacting the training and development area, including health and safety, equal employment opportunity, labor standards and compensation, and copyright. The chapter will also highlight the most critical legal compliance issues involving mandated training, review the most significant risks for criminal prosecution and civil litigation, and survey the emerging issues of discrimination in training.

Interrelationship of Statutory and Common Law

In the context of training, three sets of legal requirements apply: statutory law, administrative regulations, and common law.

Statutory Law

Statutes are laws enacted by political policy-making bodies, including laws enacted by Congress on the federal level, by state legislatures, and by municipalities. In most instances, a statute will specify the nature of the required conduct (such as training to be conducted), the time requirements for the conduct, and the penalties for noncompliance. The statute may impose criminal sanctions, civil penalties, and/or obligations to make "restitution" to injured victims. The statute may specify that it provides an exclusive governmental remedy, thereby precluding a private right of action for damages by an injured person. The terms *law, code, ordinance, Act,* and *legislation* are used interchangeably to describe statutory law.

Examples of statutes which involve or address workplace training in the health and safety context include the Occupational Safety and Health Act (OSHA); Resource Conservation and Recovery Act of 1976 (RCRA); Comprehensive Environmental Response, Compensation and Liability Act of 1980 (CERCLA/Superfund); Emergency Planning and Community Right to Know, Superfund Amendments and Reauthorization Act (SARA); Toxic Substances Control Act; and Drug-Free Workplace Act of 1988.

In another arena, the federal Equal Employment Opportunity (EEO) statutes are frequently invoked by employees for discrimination claims involving selection criteria for training opportunities, content, methodology, and delivery of training. These include the Civil Rights Act of 1964, Title VII, as amended in 1991; Age Discrimination in Employment Act (ADEA); and the Rehabilitation Act of 1973 and Americans With Disabilities Act (ADA). Still other EEO-type statutes mandate notice and instruction to employees regarding their rights under the law, particularly the Family and Medical Leave Act of 1993 (FMLA).

Elements of a Crime.   In order to withstand constitutional scrutiny, every criminal statute must set forth the basic compliance requirements, specifically, the elements of conduct which violate the statute and the range of penalties for violation of the law. Most criminal statutes require a specific level of culpability in the form of "intent" to violate the law, such as *willful* safety violations under OSHA. Congress was poised to enact amendments to the Occupational Safety and Health Act which would have imposed criminal sanctions against employers whose workplace safety violation "recklessly" causes death or serious injury to an employee. Those proposals have been carried over in each successive term since 1991.

In state prosecutions for workplace fatalities, the standard is frequently lower, such as *gross negligence,* which is typically the case with state manslaughter laws. Illinois-based Film Recovery Systems was prosecuted under a state penal code for involuntary manslaughter after an untrained, non-English speaking worker died from cyanide exposure. The standard of culpability (intent) supporting the ultimate conviction was gross negligence. Then, on appeal, the convictions were reversed and remanded to the trial court for retrial. The basis for the reversal was the issue of "intent." The appellate court noted that the same conduct supported the indictments for murder and reckless conduct, but the two offenses require mutually exclusive mental states—murder requires an intentional act and reckless conduct is unintentional.

At the other end of the spectrum is California's Corporate Criminal Liability Act.[3] This statute is unique; it arguably imposes criminal penalties on managers who fail to warn or train employees about workplace hazards, even if the failure is due to *simple negligence.* The act provides, in part, that liability is generally dependent on a manager's actual knowledge of a serious concealed danger. For purposes of the act, the term *actual knowledge* is defined to mean that a corporation or individual manager has information that would convince a reasonable person in the circumstances in which the manager is situated that serious concealed danger exists.

One of the early prosecutions under the California act involved a failure to train. In February 1992, Reclamation Services hired an 18-year-old day laborer and ordered him to move a desk with a forklift. Unfortunately, the employee had no training in forklift operations, and the forklift tipped over on top of him and killed him. The California division of OSHA assessed a penalty for serious and willful violations. The district attorney then charged the company with violating the Criminal Liability Act. The company eventually pleaded guilty and agreed to pay a fine.

Civil Statutes.   In contrast to criminal statutes, some legislation imposes remedies which are civil in nature. These penalties can include civil fines and court-ordered injunctions or hazard abatement, but *not* criminal fines or jail terms. The distinction is critical, because criminal convictions may result in jail terms for individual managers or executives, harsher penalties ("megafines"), and/or "probation" for repeat offenders. An employer receiving a criminal "conviction" under federal law is subject to the mandatory provisions of the Federal Sentencing Guidelines, which may result in long-term compliance or remedial orders. Probation under sentencing guidelines may result in conditions placed upon ongoing operations and/or increased penalties for subsequent convictions.

Elements of a Civil Infraction.   As with criminal laws, civil statutes specify the elements of conduct required for violation, the degree of culpability (intent) required, and the penalties for single and multiple infractions. Like criminal laws, civil statutes have penalties that can include assessment of fines and/or abatement orders. However, unlike criminal laws, civil codes may also require violators to compensate victims of their unlawful conduct for damages caused by the conduct.

At the federal level, the equal employment opportunity laws (antidiscrimination statutes) call for civil remedies against employers who engage in discriminatory conduct. In contrast to criminal statutes, which *must* specify the precise nature of required intent, the scope of conduct required for an infraction under civil statutes has been the subject of extensive interpretive judicial decisions. These decisions are rendered in cases brought by the EEOC or by individual claimants seeking relief for employers' violations of the particular statute.

Private Rights of Action. A civil statute may specifically authorize a private right of action for damages by an aggrieved individual. Thus, an employee victimized by the violating conduct may seek redress in the courts. In a discrimination case, a claimant may file an administrative claim with the EEOC. The agency will then investigate and decide whether to proceed with an enforcement action. If the agency decides not to pursue action on behalf of the claimant, that individual will be given an opportunity to pursue an independent lawsuit.

Still other statutes provide for civil remedies but have no enforcement mechanism *other than* a private lawsuit for damages by an injured party or an aggrieved individual. This type of suit typically involves claims for damages by "third parties" rather than by employees, as the latter enjoy the protections of health and safety, environmental, and even state workers' compensation statutes. Thus, regulatory agencies may bring action on behalf of an aggrieved employee, just as that employee is also accorded private action rights under certain statutes.

The fact that a civil statute provides a "remedy" through a governmental enforcement agency does not automatically create a private remedy for an injured person. The federal Occupational Safety and Health Act, for example, does not in any way affect workers' compensation laws or any other common-law or statutory rights, duties, or liabilities of employers or employees under any law pertaining to employment-related injuries, diseases, or death. This means that an injured employee or his or her surviving heirs cannot bring a civil action for damages based exclusively on a violation of an OSHA general-duty training requirement or the hazard communication standard.

Specialized Orders. Some statutes that do not impose criminal sanctions or civil penalties permit a court to devise specialized court orders to fit the circumstances. These remedies are in the nature of civil penalties, but they usually require either ceasing conduct (abatement) or positive action (affirmative-action plans) by the violator rather than payment of damages to compensate for past injuries.

In the context of training, health and safety statutory violations may result in specialized orders mandating training programs and/or further safety measures. For example, Phillips 66 Company reached an agreement with OSHA after the Houston Chemical Complex explosion. To resolve citations and civil penalty issues, Phillips has agreed to institute process safety management procedures at several facilities. As part of the agreed order, Phillips has agreed to provide training for both direct-hire and contractor employees to educate them in specific work-site hazards. The order is quite specific regarding content and timing of training and goes well beyond the existing OSHA training mandates. Similarly, EEOC now regularly requires training on discrimination avoidance as part of its conciliation orders when workplace bias cases are resolved.

Personnel Administration Statutes

Fair Labor Standards Act. The Fair Labor Standards Act (FLSA), as amended, is a federal statute of general application that establishes minimum wage, overtime pay, child labor, and equal-pay requirements. In general, the FLSA covers all employees of any enterprise engaged in interstate commerce or in the production of goods for interstate commerce.

With respect to training, employers who require individuals to obtain certain training before they are formally hired are required to compensate them at least the minimum wage. If they are not considered employees, they need not be compensated.

Trainees need not be compensated under the FLSA if the following conditions are met: (1) the training, even though it includes actual operation of the employer's facilities, is similar to that which would be given in a vocational school; (2) the training is for the benefit of the trainees or students; (3) the trainees or students do not displace regular employees, but work under their close observation; (4) the employer that provides the training derives no immediate advantage from the activities of the trainees or students, or on occasion its operations may actually be impeded; (5) the trainees or students are not necessarily entitled to a job at the conclusion of the training period; and (6) the employer and the trainees or students understand that they are not entitled to wages for the time spent in training.

The Department of Labor has promulgated guidelines for determining whether training time is compensable under the FLSA. Attendance at lectures, meetings, training programs, and similar activities need not be counted as working time if the following four criteria are met: (1) attendance occurs outside the employer's regular working hours; (2) attendance is voluntary; (3) the course, lecture, or meeting is not directly related to the employee's job; and (4) the employee does not perform any productive work during such attendance.

Job Training Partnership Act.   The Job Training Partnership Act (JTPA),[4] enacted in 1982 as the successor to the Comprehensive Employment and Training Act (CETA), is a comprehensive federal program with provisions that include job-training and employment assistance and training to fulfill affirmative-action obligations. The purpose of the JTPA is to establish programs to prepare youth and unskilled adults for entry into the labor force and to afford job training to economically disadvantaged individuals and those facing barriers to employment. The JTPA relies heavily on private industry to design, choose, deliver, and monitor the types of training programs funded by the law. Under the JTPA, up to 50 percent of eligible employees' wages are paid directly to the employer in recognition of the employer's costs to train the individuals. The act also provides that employers receiving payments under the law "shall establish and maintain a grievance procedure for grievances or complaints about its programs and activities from participants, sub-contractors and other interested persons."[5]

Statutes that Protect Intellectual Property.   Training frequently involves development and distribution of written materials, artwork, or other "intellectual property." Such materials include participants' implements, workbooks, or other documentary resources used in the training program. The materials may be a stand-alone product or part of a presentation. Whatever type is used, the creator of the materials should take certain legal steps to protect that work from infringement. The intellectual property of a business has intrinsic and commercial value which should be protected.

In addition, instructors frequently use materials from other sources as part of their training materials or in conjunction with their presentation. The creators of those works may have protections against the unauthorized use of the materials, if they have obtained copyright protection. The subsequent unauthorized use of the material may give rise to a claim for infringement. The remedies in this context may also be civil or criminal.

A copyright is a legal device that provides the creator of a work that conveys information or ideas the right to control how the work is used. The Federal Copyright Act of 1976 grants authors a wide range of intangible, exclusive rights over their work. These rights include: (1) reproduction right (the right to make copies of a protected work); (2) distribution right (the right to sell or otherwise distribute the work publicly or privately); (3) derivative (the right to create derivative work, to prepare new work based on the protected work or to create adaptations of the original or derivative work); and (4) display rights (the right to display or perform work in public).

Type of Protection. Copyright protects an author's words to the extent that they are original. The primary objective of copyright protection is to encourage the creation of new intellectual and artistic works. There is no reason to protect works whose creation is a purely mechanical or clerical act such as a form or a phone book. However, if the form encompasses a unique process, design, or model which is part of the author's consultation services, it should be protected from infringement, particularly if it is an integral part of the services or product the trainer offers.

A work need not be entirely new to be capable of protection under the Federal Copyright Act. Copyright protects new material an author adds to a previously existing work. Such material is known as a *derivative work*. A derivative work is one that is created by adapting or transforming previously written material into a new work of authorship, such as a screenplay based on a novel.

Notice. A copyright automatically comes into existence the moment an author fixes his or her words in some tangible form. It is prudent for training professionals (both internal and external consultants) to include a copyright notice on all published works so that potential copiers will be informed of the underlying claim to copyright ownership. A sample copyright notice is as follows:

> Copyright © 1995 [author/business name]. All rights reserved including the right to reproduce these materials in any form, in whole or in part, without the express written permission of the copyright holder.

Registration. Prompt registration in the U.S. Copyright Office makes the copyright a matter of public record and provides several advantages if it is ever necessary to go to court to enforce it. To register a work, the owner-author must complete a registration form and deposit copies of the work with the Copyright Office.

Limitations on Protection. Several significant limitations have been placed on copyright protection of original works. First, ideas and facts are not protected. Copyright only protects the words which the author expresses as facts and ideas. Copyright does not protect the facts or ideals themselves; these are free for anyone to use. For example, when Charles Darwin published *The Origin of the Species* he was only able to protect his words, not to prevent anyone from writing about the concept of evolution.

Second, there is a fair-use exception to copyright protection. An author is free to copy from a protected work for purposes of criticism, news reporting, teaching, or research so long as the value of the copyrighted work is not diminished for the author. Proper citations should be used at all times, to avoid passing the work off as original (a concept known as plagiarism). The best practice is to obtain written consent from the copyright holder to use the materials, even in an educational program. However, there is a protection available to use such materials in the training context; despite that fact, it is prudent to be sure all citations or other attribution to the copyrighted work are included.

Third, works in the public domain are not subject to copyright protection. Any work that is not protected by copyright is in the public domain, which includes works in which the copyright was lost or expired or works authored or owned by the federal government.

Computerized Material. Electronic databases are a new source of research, data, and ideas for valuable material in a training program. An electronic database or bulletin board is a body of facts, data, or other information assembled into an organized format suitable for use in a computer. The variety of information contained on electronic databases is expanding quickly. Everything from government documents to stock quotes to magazine and journal articles may be accessed. A database consisting of unprotectable facts or data (names, addresses, numerical data) is a compilation of facts and is not protected by the copyright laws.

However, a database that contains individually protectable works (such as full text of copyrighted articles) is a *collective work.* This is a special type of compilation, which is created by selecting and arranging into a single whole work preexisting materials that are separate and independent works entitled to copyright protection in their own right. There may be protection for the selection and arrangement of the materials making up the collective work.

Obtaining Permission for Use. Trainers need to obtain permission to use a copyrighted work. Such permission must be in writing. Situations in which permission must be obtained include: (1) when taking an author's words or the particular sequence of words that comprise the author's expression; (2) when the work is not in the "public domain"; and (3) when the intended use goes beyond the bounds of "fair use." Under the fair-use privilege, you are permitted to make *limited use* of an author's prior work without asking for written permission. All authors and other copyright holders are deemed to give their automatic consent to the fair use of their work by others so long as proper acknowledgement is given and a full citation to the copyrighted material is set forth.

Copyright Infringement. The Copyright Act imposes penalties for unauthorized use of copyrighted materials. Such use is an infringement of protected intellectual property. Infringement occurs when a person other than the copyright owner exploits one or more of the owner's exclusive rights without express written permission. Such unauthorized use is sometimes called *piracy.* An author has the legal remedy of an infringement lawsuit to stop further infringement and for damages due to past infringement. The objective of such a suit is to restore the copyright owner to the same position he or she would have been in had the infringement not occurred.

Violations of Law. There are a number of penalties for copyright infringement. Willful copyright infringement is a federal crime. The U.S. Attorney General has the power to prosecute infringers. A convicted infringer may also be ordered by a federal court to pay a copyright owner restitution, which is a form of compensation to reinstate what was lost by the holder. Finally, the holder of the copyright can file his or her own action for damages and an order to cease further unauthorized use of the copyrighted material for commercial or private gain.

Federal Preemption of State Laws. Some federal statutes are so comprehensive in their regulation of a particular subject that the individual states have not attempted to legislate in the subject area. The Copyright Act is an example. In many other areas, however, the states have also enacted laws to regulate employers. Particular states are free to enact laws which provide for additional regulations over all employers for particular industries.

Some states, like California and Florida, have adopted state OSHA statutes which provide *more stringent* penalties than the federal OSHA. Others have enacted industry-specific statutes mandating training and documentation requirements which surpass federal OSHA requirements, such as the California Refinery and Chemical Plant Worker Safety Act of 1990.

Must employers in some states meet higher standards than others? What about employers with multiple work sites in states with differing requirements? A frequent question raised by employers is which laws control? The primary area in which conflicting or overlapping federal and state requirements must be evaluated by training and development professionals is in the domain of health and safety and employment rights laws. Workplace activities are governed by a variety of statutes. Some are overlapping. Others may even contain conflicting provisions. Accordingly, employers frequently must determine which laws apply to their activities and when those standards are applicable.

A state law can be preempted by federal law or regulation expressly or by implication. Express preemption occurs when Congress legislates comprehensively, thereby leaving no room for states to supplement. Implied preemption occurs when a state law "stands as an obstacle to the accomplishment and execution of the full purposes and objectives of Congress."

Alternatively, a federal statute may expressly state that it is *not* the Congressional intent to occupy the field, thereby leaving it to the states to set their own standards. For example, while Congress is poised to expand criminal sanctions under federal OSHA, it will not preclude enforcement of state laws. Federal OSHA has such provisions with respect to certain high-risk hazard training such as chemical hazard communication requirements. So do the federal workplace civil rights statutes which expressly state that it is the intent of Congress that the statutes *not* preempt state or local laws.

Administrative Regulations

Regulations provide the implementation procedures for compliance with a statute. The regulations provide guidance to the administrative agencies and the courts when a violation of the statute is alleged. For example, federal OSHA, EEOC, and DOL must look to regulations specifying how to implement the legislation they enforce. For example, the ADA provided that within one year after its enactment, the EEOC was to promulgate regulations to enforce the ADA's employment provisions. OSHA, EEOC, DOL, and other administrative agencies also promulgate enforcement guidances for enforcement personnel which do not have the force of law but which may be invoked when an inspection or audit of a work site is undertaken.

Common Law

In contrast to statutes, common law is enacted by judicial precedents on both the federal and state levels. Common-law liabilities are created in two ways: (1) by judicial interpretations of a statute (such as Title VII or a state statute), or (2) by state common-law doctrines. When interpreting a statute, the court must determine whether the statute applies to a particular set of facts. In such an instance, the court may extend, as common-law interpretation, the reach of a particular statute. For example, Title VII prohibits sex discrimination but does not specify on its face all of the factual circumstances which may constitute such discrimination. The cases then "flesh out" the statute, but the underlying claim is still based on a statutory right. In contrast, state common law is based primarily on tort and contract theories, for which there may not be a particular statute underlying the claim. A "tort" action is a personal-injury or property damage claim and is to be distinguished from a claim based on a contract.

In most states, the claimant files a civil action, which proceeds to a conclusion by the trier of fact. The trier of fact may be a jury, a trial court judge, or an arbitration panel. The dissatisfied party may file an appeal.

While written opinions by federal trial courts are relatively common, state trial court decisions are rarely in writing. When the trial court verdict is appealed to a state court of appeals, a panel of judges renders a written decision, or "opinion." Under limited circumstances, an appeal may proceed to the highest state court or to the U.S. Supreme Court. The latter are discretionary; the high court may decline to review the matter, thereby leaving the appellate decision as precedent. Because appeals to the highest courts (U.S. Supreme Court or state courts of highest jurisdiction) are discretionary, the appealing party must demonstrate an issue of national (or statewide) significance or one in which there is a conflict in the decisions of the lower courts.

The court's written opinion establishes the precedent. The decision is generally binding on future cases in the same jurisdiction and is often persuasive in jurisdictions which have no contrary precedents. The basic pattern of legal reasoning is by example. It is reasoning from case to case. It is a three-step process described as the doctrine of precedent in which a proposition descriptive of the first case is made into a rule of law (common law) and then applied to the next similar situation.

Common-law theories in the training context typically include allegations of lack of training or inadequate training methodology. This is usually one of several areas of liability asserted by the claimant, for instance, employee training, supervision, work practices, or equipment maintenance. As a result, a jury may determine that alleged training deficiencies were either a primary or a secondary cause of the injury. After the evidence is presented, the jury is instructed about the level of proof required for each element of the claim. The claimant cannot prevail unless each element is proved. For example, in a negligence action, the plaintiff must prove each of the elements of duty, breach of duty, proximate cause, and damages.

In the training context, the level of proof means that the injured employee must prove that the employer or trainer owed him or her a duty of reasonable care, that the duty was breached, that the breach was a legal (proximate) cause of his or her injuries, and that he or she suffered damage in a certain amount. The determination of whether a duty of care exists is generally a question of law for the courts to decide; whether the defendant breached this duty of care by acting unreasonably under the particular circumstances is a question for the trier of fact. In most civil cases, either party may request a jury trial. If a jury is waived by both parties, the trier of fact will typically be a single judge.

The employer's *duty* may legally be established in one of three ways:

1. It may be based on the standard of care *for trainers in a particular industry.*

For example, a physician has a duty to provide medical care for patients which is within the accepted standards practiced by members of the medical profession in the area where the particular physician practices. Likewise, an attorney must provide competent legal services in accordance with standards followed by lawyers similarly situated. When the service provider holds him- or herself out as a specialist, such as a cardiologist or a patent attorney, a higher standard of care is imposed commensurate with the level of expertise expected of such a specialist.

In essence, standard of care is often defined as the level of conduct expected of similarly trained professionals working in the same field. In the training context, the program developer must comply with the applicable standard of care for similar training programs in the industry. The element of "duty" may be established by the mandates of a statute, industry-specific standards, employer policies, and/or expert testimony by persons experienced in the industry.

2. *A minimum standard of care may be established by a statute or other regulatory scheme which governs the particular subject or industry.*

Although an OSHA violation does not create a private right of action, it may establish a minimum or threshold standard of care. In these instances, the requirements of the legislation establishes the standard of care and satisfies the element of "duty." In particular industries, such as hazardous-waste control or nuclear facilities, the standard of care (duty) may be more stringent than the statute itself. When this occurs or when there is no governmental regulation, the standard of care may be imposed by judicial decisions, by the employer's own safety policies, or by a combination of these elements.

3. *A duty of care may be established by an employer's own policies and practices, particularly when there is evidence that the employer exceeded minimum statutory requirements.*

An example of a practice which may create an employer duty of care is a detailed performance management or process safety training program designed and delivered internally for the organization. The bases on which courts have found a legal duty and actionable breach of that duty, in the context of negligent and/or inadequate training or similar common-law claims will be addressed in detail later in this chapter.

Legal Liabilities Arising from Training

There are five primary areas of training liabilities: (1) noncompliance with mandated training under statute; (2) civil liabilities for failure to train, inadequate training, and/or common-law negligence; (3) workers' compensation and personnel-related claims; (4) training that fails to meet special needs of multilingual and/or disabled employees; and (5) discrimination in training opportunities, content, or delivery.

Mandated Training

The most explosive area of training liabilities continues to be noncompliance with requirements to educate employees about workplace hazards. The federal OSHA general-duty clause spells out required training on general hazards and workplace safety rules. Most approved state plans do the same. However, Hazard Communication Standards (the right to know and to understand) provide the framework for much broader liability.

The issue boils down to three employee rights: the right to know, the right to understand, and the right to act. These rights are addressed in Chap. 44, Occupational Safety and Health Training.

Civil Lawsuits Seeking Monetary Damages

Legally supportable training involves more than something to read. It is especially important for supervisors to understand that effective training involves much more than simply giving employees something to read. They must be alert to the special needs of subordinates with poor reading skills or English language difficulties (e.g., see Chap. 39, Basic Workplace Skills). Likewise, training to a blind level of confidence (e.g., six hours of simulator training) without determining the trainee's competence level is probably insufficient. On the surface, the documentation may seem complete, but the important evaluation element is missing. *Job task analysis, performance-based instruction, and performance-based evaluation are vital.*

In addition to criminal penalties and fines, employers and individual trainers may be subjected to civil lawsuits. These lawsuits are generally based on tort theories of negligence for *failure to train* or *inadequate training* or on tort *failure to warn* claims. Common-law tort actions can support awards for compensatory damages, to compensate losses suffered by an aggrieved party, or punitive damages, to punish a wrongdoer's fraudulent, oppressive, or malicious conduct.

Failure to Train.   In the training context, an organization must comply with the standards that apply to similar training programs in its industry. Sometimes a minimum standard of care is established by statute. In this situation, evidence of a statutory violation might be introduced to establish negligence per se. This is negligence as a matter of law. In other words, the element of duty is met without further required proof. Where negligence per se exists, duty and breach of duty are automatically established. However, the plaintiff *still* must prove that the breach of duty was the legal (proximate) cause of the injury. He or she must also prove the nature and amount of damages. In other states, the statutory violation may be accepted for the limited evidentiary value of establishing a minimum standard of care. Thus, duty is *not* established as a matter of law. The trier of fact would then weigh evidence of the statutory training requirement against any conflicting evidence to determine the standard of care.

In some industries, particularly high-risk employers, the standard of care may be based on industry standards or employer policies, even where they substantially exceed the minimum requirements of a statute. The elements of industry standards and expert-witness opinions to establish standard of care were addressed by the Alabama Supreme Court in *Thompson v. Liberty Mutual Insurance Company*.[6] The court relied upon the affidavit of a professor of mechanical engineering who concluded that industry standards were not followed with respect to the instruction and training of an injured worker on a piece of equipment.

In the absence of a statute, employer policy, or guiding case precedent, most states measure the standard of care by what the "reasonable person" would do under all the circumstances, balancing the risks and the objectives. In essence, the trier of fact, typically a jury, will decide whether the employer met the standard of care required in the particular work setting. Frequently, expert witnesses are called to provide opinions on what training the reasonable employer in the industry would conduct. The jury then weighs the credibility of conflicting experts by looking at their education, experience, credentials, and knowledge of relevant workplaces.

Negligence Resulting in Injuries to Third Parties.   Courts have recognized a cause of action for an employer's negligent training of its employees that results in injury to a third person. For example, California courts have recognized that a medical university owes a duty to patients who are under the care of residents to see that the residents have received proper training and supervision. In the case of *County of Riverside v. Loma Linda University,*[7] the court concluded that the university was negligent in discharging its contractual duties to educate and train the residents and to supervise their training.

Similarly, in 1992, in a case called *Stacey v. Truman Medical Center,*[8] the center had a policy on fire evacuation procedures but a particular nurse had not been trained. The nurse failed to remove a patient from a room on fire and the patient died. The court found that the center had a duty to train its nurses in the proper (and effective) performance of their job. When they fail to do so, the resulting damages to a third party are recoverable in a civil lawsuit under the common law of negligence.

In *Estate of Arrington v. Fields,*[9] a security guard company was sued after a scuffle in which one of its employees shot a patron at a convenience store, believing the man was a thief. The guard had been issued a handgun, but had not been given training in its use. This fact alone, the court concluded, constituted negligence.

Negligence Resulting in Injuries to Employees. In the majority of states, the workers' compensation codes provide an exclusive remedy. The injured employee cannot file a civil lawsuit for damages outside of the workers' compensation forum unless she or he can prove that the employer's conduct was willfully or grossly negligent. However, these exclusivity provisions have been riddled with exceptions in some states. Exceptions frequently are established by evidence that the employer *knew* of specific or general hazards and failed to undertake timely or effective training. In addition, the element of "willfulness" is defined differently from state to state. In some jurisdictions, an employer is found to be "willful" if the risk of harm is foreseeable; others require a showing of actual knowledge.

The common law of most states provides remedies for injuries to employees in some instances where the exclusive provisions of workers' compensation codes do not apply. Texas, for example, has recognized that an employer owes a duty to furnish reasonably safe tools with which the employee is to work, including knowledge and training on use of the equipment and safe work practices.[10] In the most recent discussion of the issue, the court in *Delaney v. University of Houston*[11] found an employer liable for negligent implementation of company policies which failed to prevent a violent act. The duty to properly implement company policies includes the duty to provide training designed to prevent workplace violence, where the violence is foreseeable.

Inadequate Training. Sometimes total absence of training is not the issue. When some training has been done but an injury nevertheless occurs, the issue may be the scope of the training, the adequacy of the methodology, and/or the qualifications of the instructor. Then the common law of a state, handed down in judicial decisions, will often come into play. In these cases, the claimant may try to prove that although a company met the minimum requirements of a statute, the circumstances demanded additional training or a different instructional approach to the training.

Most statutes—certainly OSHA, SARA, and CERCLA ones—mandate the content and timing of training but *not* the methodology. Congress has left that decision to the training professionals. Most state civil statutes do the same. The decision on training methodology must be based on the needs and rigors of the particular job for which the training is being conducted. Once again, what would the "reasonable employer" under all the circumstances provide? Even when an employer complies with the minimum standards prescribed by a statute, a court may find that the employer has breached the standard of care by providing inadequate or ineffective training.

In 1995, the Occupational Safety and Health Review Commission (OSHRC) upheld a serious charge against a bridge-painting and sandblasting firm for failure to properly instruct employees in the recognition and avoidance of hazardous conditions they would encounter and the need to use safety belts while working at heights more than 10 feet above the ground. An employee who was not wearing a safety belt was fatally injured when he fell from a suspended scaffold while removing paint from the bridge. Although the employer had a work rule instructing employees to wear belts and lifelines, the rule did not satisfy the training requirements because it did not explain the hazards employees would encounter that would require the use of protective equipment. The conclusion that the training was inadequate was supported by a coworker's testimony that he did not consider the height at which they were working to be hazardous and did not think that safety belts were necessary when working at a height of less than 25 feet above the ground.

Employers and trainers may defend themselves by being prepared to demonstrate that their training was adequate to provide the trainee with necessary information to perform the job safely. Significantly, in one OSHRC case, willful charges of failure to provide employees with information and training on hazardous chemicals was vacated on the ground that the employer had communicated general information about its hazard communication program on the employee bulletin board, provided specific training on the use of personal protective equipment, and furnished copies of the settlement containing hazard communication information and training for employee review (*Atlantic Battery Co., Inc.*, OSHRC, Dec. 1994).

Liability for Vendors-Suppliers. An employer *may not* escape liability for damages resulting from a complete failure to train or from inadequate training by asserting that it released control over program content to instructors (either internal or external consultants) or to an outside subcontractor or vendor. In most states, when an employer mandates or sponsors the program the principle of "agency" will apply. The instructor or vendor acts on behalf of the employer. Additionally, the duty to train under most statutory schemes is not a delegable duty. This precludes the employer from claiming that it delegated the appropriate training to an outside vendor.

In addition to agency relationships, most states' common law of negligence imposes a duty on the employer to conduct an appropriate investigation before retaining an instructor, contractor, or vendor. Particularly with hazardous communications training, an employer is responsible for ascertaining the instructor-vendor's qualifications, experience, and skills before making a selection.

Thus, the training department of the employer organization is charged with the additional responsibility of making selections of instructors and vendors cautiously to avoid a claim of negligence in the selection process. Sometimes the regulatory statute will specify required instructor qualifications. Some industries require certifications. In the absence of guidance from the legislation, expert testimony on the appropriate standard of care would be placed in evidence.

To minimize liability, safety records for outside skills training programs should be examined and the investigation process carefully documented. In addition, references should be contacted for every instructor or vendor. Finally, representatives from the employer's training or human resources department should monitor the scope, content, and delivery of the training to assure that the necessary substantive topics are covered effectively.

On-the-Job Injuries.   Most cases of on-the-job injuries are covered by the exclusive jurisdiction of a state Workers' Compensation Code. This precludes a private tort action, unless an exception for willfulness or intent exists, which may include employer knowledge that the employee was inadequately trained. An example of a strict interpretation of this rule is *Reed Tool Company v. Copelin,*[12] in which a widow sought damages for the death of her husband, alleging in part that the employer *actually knew* her husband was inadequately trained. The court rejected this level of intent as an exception to the exclusivity of workers' compensation and dismissed the case. Contrary results have been reached in many other states where workers' compensation cases have been riddled with exceptions and lowered "willfulness" thresholds.

In recent years, a number of work-related stress disability claimants have focused on their alleged lack of training as a cause of their stress-related disabilities. Likewise, employees who have been injured as a result of inadequate training have turned to workers' compensation statutes for compensation. Two primary examples are in the area of cumulative trauma disorders (repetitive motion injuries) or other ergonomic hazards and injuries sustained in high-risk training exercises such as emergency response.

Many jurisdictions will now allow common-law claims against employers for injuries sustained at work, because the codes often provide that an employee's exclusive remedy is found in the state's workers' compensation laws.[13] Some state courts have examined the nature of the injury suffered, finding that if the injury is physical it will be subject to the exclusive provisions of the workers' compensation codes, but if it is a mental injury, the plaintiff will be allowed to proceed with a state common-law action for damages based on negligence or intentional wrongdoing.

Violence and Threats of Violence in the Workplace.   Unfortunately, the incidents of violence in the workplace seem to be increasing. In 1992, the National Institute for Occupational Safety and Health (NIOSH) identified homicide as the third leading cause of death from injury in the workplace nationwide. Occupational homicides accounted for approximately 7600 deaths during that period.[14] The second national census of fatal occupational injuries undertaken by the Bureau of Labor Statistics of the U.S. Department of Labor found that homicide accounts for 17 percent of all occupational fatalities, making it the second leading cause of job-related deaths.[15] The National Safety Council figures, published in its annual *Accident Facts* booklet in 1993, revealed that 16.5 percent of the 9100 workplace fatalities in 1993 were due to workplace violence.[16]

Federal law generally requires employers to provide their employees with a place of employment that is "free from recognized hazards that are causing or are likely to cause death or serious physical harm to…employees."[17] Encompassed within this general requirement is an employer's obligation to do everything that is reasonably necessary to protect the life, safety, and health of employees, including the furnishing of safety devices and safeguards and the adoption of practices, means, methods, operations, and processes reasonably adequate to create a safe and healthful workplace.

Homicide and other violent acts account for the highest number of work-related fatalities in California, according to the Division of Occupational Safety and Health. Violent incidents in the workplace can be divided into three major types. The first type involves an agent with no legitimate relationship to the workplace who usually enters the workplace to commit a robbery. Employers must develop systems for ensuring that employees comply with work practices designed to make the workplace more secure and provide training in the steps to take during an emergency and how to diffuse hostile situations.

For the second type of violent incident, involving customers, current or former clients, patients, and/or passengers, control of physical access through workspace design is highlighted. California's OSHA has prepared special guidelines for implementing an effective workplace security program for health-care and community service workers.

Training is again highlighted in the third type of violent event, where the assailant has an employment-related involvement with the workplace, such as being a current or former employee, supervisor, or manager. Employers may soon be expressly mandated to establish a clear antiviolence management policy, apply the policy consistently, and provide appropriate employee training in violence prevention.

New state OSHA guidelines advise that employers who are "at risk" for workplace violence must implement and maintain an effective security plan which includes, in part, "a system to communicate with employees about security hazards, which includes procedures to enable employees to inform the employer of security hazards without fear of reprisal," and "training and instruction regarding: (a) how to recognize workplace security hazards, (b) measures to prevent workplace assaults, and (c) emergency and post-emergency procedures."

Other Workplace Conduct.   Until recently, the primary area of statutorily mandated training has been in the health and safety area. However, some states are beginning to mandate other types of workplace training and are imposing business penalties for failure to comply. In Maine, for example, a new statute, the Maine Human Rights Act, took effect on October 9, 1991. It requires all employers, both public and private, to take specific steps to ensure a workplace "free of sexual harassment."[18] In workplaces with 15 or more employees, the employer *must* conduct an education and training program for all new employees within one year of commencement of employment that includes information on their rights and responsibilities. Additional training for supervisory and managerial employees must include specific responsibilities and methods they must take to address sexual harassment claims. Similarly, in February 1993, Connecticut enacted comprehensive regulations mandating sexual harassment training for employers with 50 or more employees to provide at least two hours of training and education to all supervisory personnel.[19]

Another example of a new federal statute mandating notification and education of employees regarding their rights under the law is the Family and Medical Leave Act (FMLA). It *mandates* that employees be instructed on their rights under the FMLA. This includes posting in conspicuous places on the premises a notice that explains pertinent provisions of the law and information about filing a charge of violation of the law. The regulations provide that where a significant portion of the workforce is not literate in English, the employer must provide the required information "in a language in which the employees are literate."[20]

Delayed Injury or Illness from Exposure.   Long-term health problems from occupational exposures is a significant issue on the horizon. High-risk jobs pose a unique hazard to the American workforce. One of the thorny issues of the 1990s involves employee allegations of ill health due to long-term exposure to toxic substances through ingestion, inhalation, or skin absorption. This type of injury can be quite expensive for the employer, taking the form of lost workdays, increased workers' compensation benefits, and lost productivity from other employees who begin to perceive themselves at risk. Sometimes, the adverse health effects are not detected until many years after the exposure. When the information becomes known to the employer, a duty may exist under state common law to notify former workers who are at risk, even though Congressional attempts to impose a notification mandate have not mustered enough support. According to a Bureau of National Affairs (BNA) Special Report entitled *Occupational Safety and Health: Seven Critical Issues for the 1990's,* some federal agencies already are drafting notification programs for former employees. The report says, for instance, that the U.S. Department of Energy (DOE) plans to notify former workers who may face a high risk of respiratory disease from exposure to beryllium.

Another emerging issue of the 1990s is *repetitive stress injuries*, sometimes called *cumulative trauma disorder*. The common terminology to describe this type of injury is "ergonomics." Injuries that result from repetitive job motions and cumulative trauma disorder are on the rise. OSHA has issued new guidelines for training in this area. It is critical, OSHA says, for employees to be well informed not only of the ergonomic hazards to which they may be exposed on the job, but of the steps being taken by their employers to reduce that exposure. Informed employees, according to the OSHA guidelines, are better able "to participate actively in their own protection." Training recommendations range from formal instruction on the ergonomic hazards associated with a particular job, to orientation and hands-on training of new and reassigned employees. OSHA also recommends that supervisors and managers be trained in the safety and health responsibilities associated with their positions.

OSHA has recently released the revised draft of its proposed ergonomics standards. The new draft reduces the number of workers potentially covered from 6.1 million (issued in June 1994) to 2.6 million. It also requires employers to provide training for employees in high-risk jobs and to develop medical management programs for musculoskeletal injuries.

Safety Training that Meets Special Needs. Safety training is vital for two reasons: (1) successful completion by each employee required under statutory mandates fulfills the employer's compliance requirements; and (2) employees who are effectively trained, satisfying the right-to-know and right-to-understand laws, will work more safely, thereby increasing productivity and reducing injuries and downtime. For training to be effective, and legally defensible, the employer must assure itself that the training has been satisfactorily completed. This is a significant challenge when portions of the worker population have special needs.

It has been estimated that as much as 15 percent of the U.S. population have some type of learning disability. Dyslexia is one of the common disabilities, involving difficulty in reading. Dysgraphia is the inability to write. Other learning disabilities make it difficult to distinguish shapes and colors, while others affect hand-eye coordination. Finally, attention deficit disorder (a clinically diagnosable disorder) results in short attention span, easy distraction, impulsive behavior, and hyperactivity. The presence of employees with such learning disabilities in a training class on safety or health-related issues places a significant challenge on the instructor. Thus, training materials, presentation, and post-training evaluation must be modified, where necessary, to accommodate individuals to assure that they are adequately prepared to work safely.

Further, trainees and workers with learning disabilities are protected from discrimination under the Americans With Disabilities Act and many comparable state antidiscrimination statutes. These EEO laws require the employer to make reasonable accommodations to the known disabilities of employees, where possible and appropriate. This assures balance between meeting health and safety requirements and adherence to antidiscrimination laws.

Under the ADA, employees are protected from discrimination in *all* the benefits of employment. This includes preemployment selection criteria, ability to participate in job-specific training, as well as generalized training provided to the entire workforce. *Disability* is broadly defined as any condition or illness which substantially impairs one or more of life's major activities: walking, sitting, standing, moving, manipulating, dexterity, talking, seeing, hearing, learning, and working.

Thus, employees with physical impairments as well as cognitive learning disorders are covered. A person becomes a "qualified disabled candidate or employee" when he or she can perform the *essential functions* of the job with or without reasonable accommodation.

Although the ADA provides that an individual with a disability may be excluded from a job when (1) she cannot perform the essential functions of the job, with or without a reasonable accommodation, or when (2) she presents a direct threat of harm to herself and others, this standard is quite hard to meet. Indeed, the EEOC has specifically stated in its *Technical Assistance Manual* for ADA compliance:

> An employer may require that an individual not pose a direct threat of harm to his or her own safety or health, as well as to the health or safety of others. However…such determinations must be strictly based on valid medical analyses or other objective evidence related to this individual.…A determination that a person might cause harm to himself or herself *cannot* be based on stereotypes, patronizing assumptions about a person with a disability, or generalized fears about risks that might occur if an individual with a disability is placed in a certain job. Any such determination must be based on evidence of specific risk to a particular individual.[21]
>
> Where there is a significant risk of substantial harm to health or safety, an employer must still consider whether there is a reasonable accommodation that would eliminate this risk or reduce the risk so that it is below the level of direct threat.[22]

Examples of accommodations for learning disabled employees include allowing extra time to complete a test or examination, administering an oral exam rather than a written test, and providing computer-enhanced material and alternative presentation formats for sensory-impaired trainees.

The ADA does not override health and safety requirements established under federal or state laws. For example, if a standard is required by another federal law, the employer must comply. The need to satisfactorily pass required safety training is job-related and consistent with business necessity. Therefore, the employee's successful completion of mandated hazard communication training may be used to evaluate whether a trainee is a qualified disabled employee (e.g., can perform all essential functions of the job with or without a reasonable accommodation). EEOC has concluded, however, that "an employer still has the obligation under the ADA to consider whether there is a reasonable accommodation, consistent with the standards of other federal laws, that will prevent exclusion of qualified individuals with disabilities who can perform jobs without violating the standards of those laws."[23]

Reasonable accommodations may include, but are not limited to (1) making facilities readily accessible to and usable by handicapped persons; (2) job restructuring, part-time or modified work schedules; (3) acquisition or modification of equipment or devices used on the job; (4) appropriate adjustment or modification of examinations; and/or (5) the provision of readers and interpreters and other similar actions.

Finally, employers in many Western states are experiencing difficulty in training limited-English- or non-English-speaking employees. While Title VII of the Civil Rights Act of 1964 prohibits discrimination against individuals due to their national origin, there is no comparable "reasonable accommodation" requirement to the ADA's requirements. Nevertheless, professionals who design and deliver training, particularly safety-related instruction, should assure themselves that the material is understood and absorbed by the limited-English-literate employee. Failing to do so may result in common-law negligence claims if an injured employee claims he did not receive "adequate" training to perform safely in a particular work environment.

Discrimination in Training Programs

Although workplace safety is vital, employers are required to balance the need for safety with the individual rights of employees to be free from improper discrimination in America's workplaces. Many training programs, and the selection criteria for participation in training opportunities, are under judicial and regulatory scrutiny. Time-honored methods of testing and evaluation will be closely monitored by the EEOC and parallel state commissions.

Since 1964, with the passage of expanded civil rights legislation, employers are obligated to maintain a discrimination-free workplace. The premise of all federal equal employment opportunity legislation, and many state statutes, is that an employer must not permit its managers and supervisors to make employment decisions on the basis of an employee's gender, race, color, religion, national origin, age, or disability. Such decisions include those regarding training such as selection for advanced training, availability of on-the-job training, and the content of training.

Disparate Treatment
Discrimination in Training

The general guidelines concerning litigation of disparate treatment cases were initially set forth by the U.S. Supreme Court in *McDonnell Douglas Corp. v. Green* in 1973. McDonnell Douglas was accused of racial discrimination because it refused to rehire a former employee. The court sought to clarify the standards of proof by requiring that the plaintiff first establish a prima facie case showing that he was a qualified minority-group person who was rejected for an available position.

In the training context, disparate treatment cases usually involve an allegation that the reason a particular employee did poorly at a job, which led to discipline, downgrading, or termination, was that the supervisor did not provide sufficient training. In that type of case, the proof is generally the testimony of the employee, the supervisor, and other employees who allegedly received more training.

Many of the challenges to training on the ground of disparate treatment involve on-the-job training. Certain deficiencies can easily lead to job discrimination problems, such as upper management assuming that supervisors are training new employees or the lack of a system for conducting training or monitoring its successes and failures. For example, management found itself liable for unlawful discrimination where it was demonstrated that an employee was fired for poor job performance because he was not adequately trained due to the discrimination of those in charge of training.

Discriminatory Selection Procedures
for Advanced Training

Many of the discrimination cases in training involve allegations of disparate treatment or disparate impact arising from the methods of selecting employees for special training programs. Disparate-treatment cases involve employer treatment of one individual (or group) differently from another because of race, color, religion, sex, national origin, or age. Proof of discriminatory intent is critical in disparate-treatment cases. However, in some cases a discriminatory intent may be *inferred* from the mere fact that differences in treatment occurred. Thus, ill-will or "malice" are not required.

Disparate-impact cases occur in situations where the employment practice is neutral on its face but impacts more severely one protected group. The disparate impact cannot be justified by business necessity. Proof of discriminatory motivation is not generally required in a disparate-impact case. Instead, the key is whether the requirement is job-related.

Typically, these programs are intended to upgrade participants, but the controversy regarding selection often involves disparate impact. The basic approach to analyzing the legality of a selection procedure is to evaluate whether the selection criteria are applied consistently to all employees and then to determine whether the procedure results in disproportionate rejection of any Title VII–defined group. If a selection procedure does have a disparate impact, the procedure must be shown to have a business necessity.

Accordingly, an employer may use any selection criteria as long as they are applied evenly and do not have a discriminatory effect. To avoid potential liability under EEO laws, criteria must be job-related and should consist of objective measures wherever possible. If nondiscriminatory criteria are used, even if the employer misjudged the qualifications of an applicant, there should be no violation of Title VII.

Most managers and training professionals would agree that refusal to select a female for advanced training because she "might" decide to take an extended pregnancy leave is unlawful under Title VII. Yet many employers have been charged with similar discrimination under the Age Discrimination in Employment Act (ADEA) when they pass over an individual for advanced training on the premise that the employee's potential retirement will prevent the company from recouping its training investment. Even worse, stereotypes about the aging process have led trainers to discriminate against employees protected under ADEA by refusing to train them on advanced automation equipment because of a concern that the employees are "too set in their ways" or otherwise unreceptive to change. In addition, older workers have complained that they are treated differently in training and are singled out for "ageist" comments by instructors. Such claims are flooding the EEOC and state enforcement agencies.

Discrimination can also occur in the assignment of jobs that provide training necessary for future promotions. The law requires that individuals be given the opportunity to compete equally for jobs on the basis of job-related criteria. Thus, in a case involving a fire department, the court found discrimination where minority employees were not assigned the administrative jobs that provided on-the-job training for promotions.[24]

There are no uniformly acceptable or unacceptable selection criteria for advanced or on-the-job training opportunities. Whether the criteria are found to be nondiscriminatory may depend on several factors. Statistical evidence of discrimination, the structure of the selection system, the particular training program or job in question, the relationship between the criteria and the job, and the consistent application of the criteria to all employees frequently are more important than the actual criteria. Among the selection criteria which have been upheld by the courts are experience (if the requirement is job-related), skills, productivity, absenteeism-tardiness, and disciplinary records.

Age discrimination is prevalent in training cases. Although a lack of training is a legitimate basis for selection for layoffs, when the lack of training is age-related an indirect violation of the ADEA can be found. For example, two long-term field engineers had been denied training on newer equipment because they had the most experience on the old equipment that was being phased out and the employer felt it could not afford to take them out of the field to train. Their layoff violated the ADEA.[25]

The Environmental Protection Agency settled a discrimination suit filed by a senior agency attorney who claimed she was not promoted because of her age and gender and then retaliated against for filing a bias complaint.[26] The plaintiff alleged that after she filed EEO complaints, her supervisors retaliated against her by denying her training and travel opportunities and downgrading her performance evaluations. Similarly, in *Franci v. Avco Corporation*,[27] an employer's criterion for selecting employees for layoff (economic savings which eliminated older, higher-salaried employees) disparately affected employees within the statutorily protected age group. The employer violated the ADEA.

In establishing selection procedures, the employer should consider instituting the following policies to insure that the system is as objective as possible: (1) provide those responsible for the selection of trainees with written guidelines specifying the weight to be given to each selection criteria; (2) publicize training opportunities; and (3) make sure all employees are aware of the requirements they must meet for admission to the training program.

Remedial and Affirmative-Action Programs

Title VII contains a specific provision prohibiting employers from discriminating in their apprenticeship and training programs. Training programs can be a powerful tool in the affirmative-action process. Because of this fact, some employers have been led to provide more openings in training programs to members of protected groups. Because federal government contractors have specific obligations to meet affirmative-action goals under the Rehabilitation Act of 1973, remedial training programs aimed at upgrading female and minority workers may be defensible. In fact, both the courts and employers have frequently fashioned remedial training programs for affirmative-action purposes.

The most significant case addressing remedial programs involved Kaiser Aluminum and Chemical Corporation.[28] The plaintiff, Brian Weber, attacked the program on the ground that it discriminated against him as a Caucasian employee. The U.S. Supreme Court's decision found that Kaiser and the Union did not violate Title VII when they voluntarily (in contrast to a court order) set aside 50 percent of the openings in the craft training program for black employees. The *Weber* decision is not a comprehensive discussion of affirmative action and reverse discrimination.

In addition, the scope of affirmative-action regulations, and the role of OFCCP in auditing compliance with affirmative-action goals and timetables, is under review at the federal level. Similarly, many states are assessing their requirements for affirmative-action and related programs for employers who do business with government agencies. The requirements to include effective training, mentoring, and coaching opportunities for underrepresented employees, in applicant and promotional pools, will remain a part of affirmative-action compliance; however, the extent of liabilities for failure to establish goals or meet timetables will continue to be refined by the legislative and judicial actions in the next decade.

Emerging Issues in Diversity Training

In the discrimination arena, the subject of diversity training has become a significant issue. Diversity training programs have become popular staples in many organizations. (Also see Chap. 5, Diversity Training and Development.) Indeed, when properly designed and presented, they are an essential component to many affirmative-action programs and initiatives valuing diversity. When not appropriately designed—or worse, when delivered in a discriminatory manner—such programs are both ineffective and legally indefensible.

There are three primary dangers of diversity programs from a legal standpoint: (1) racial, ethnic, or sex-based remarks made in diversity training sessions may be used in later employment discrimination litigation as evidence of management bias; (2) the potential that employers will be forced to disclose the results of their "diversity audit" in pretrial discovery; and (3) the diversity program process may serve to encourage groups or individuals to seek a litigated resolution to perceived or actual unfair treatment.

Content of the Program.   Where an employer's diversity training materials contain candid remarks by managers that could be construed as racial or sexual bias, or where an employer's "diversity scan" reflects unfavorably (statistically or through anecdotal evidence) on the employer's record with minorities or women, admission of such information in a subsequent discrimination lawsuit can be damaging to the employer's case.

One example is *Stender v. Lucky Stores, Inc.*[29] In 1988, Lucky Stores sought to determine the cause of the glaring lack of promotions for women and minorities within the organization. As part of its attempt to remedy the situation, the company conducted an in-house diversity training session for all store managers. As part of the training, the managers took part in an exercise that is commonplace in many diversity training seminars—they were asked to list various stereotypes that they had heard about women and minorities. The stereotypes listed by the store managers included assumptions that women will not work late shifts because their husbands will not let them, customers might object to seeing a woman in management, women are afraid to work at night, women seem to step down a lot after being promoted, women do not go into management because they are not accepted, men do not want competition from women, the crew will not accept women, and women cry more.[30]

Subsequently, the female employees filed a class-action suit alleging sex discrimination based on lack of promotions for females. In pretrial discovery, over the objection of Lucky Stores, the court ordered production of the notes from the in-house diversity training session containing the store managers' stereotyped comments. The court rejected Lucky's contention that the notes were protected by the self-evaluative and attorney-client privileges.[31] The court said the self-evaluative privilege did not apply because the qualified evidentiary privilege to which self-critical affirmative-action-related materials are entitled must be interpreted narrowly. The programs were for the purpose of training and informing managers about Lucky's affirmative-action plans.

The court relied on the notes as evidence that Lucky's managers had discriminatory attitudes toward women. The court considered these comments to be evidence of sex discrimination among the managers, ruling that the comments were *not just portrayals of social stereotypes, but reflections of what many Lucky managers believed.* Hence, the court concluded that the notes constituted "evidence of discriminatory attitudes and stereotyping of women" by Lucky's managers.

Sexual Harassment in Training Content and Delivery.   Another frequent source of recent Title VII complaints in the training context have been cases alleging sexual harassment in the *content or presentation* of training. These cases stem from written materials, verbal content (jokes and banter), and related conduct in the presentation of the instruction which involve sexually offensive material. Two significant cases are currently pending on appeal. The first involves a program for police department recruits in which the content of the slide presentation included graphic sexual pictures. The instructor's defense was that he simply wanted to capture the attention of the trainees in an otherwise dry, technical subject area, which was unpersuasive to the initial trier of fact.[32] A second case was brought by a male student who objected to the content of a professor's lecture and language in a class taught through extension services of a public educational system.[33]

Training Methodology. Of course the training methodology must be appropriate to meet the learning objectives and must not itself create a separate basis for significant liability. To professional trainers this point seems obvious, but there is a new sexual harassment case with a training twist.

On September 2, 1994, in the case of *Hartman v. Pena,* 11 air traffic controllers filed a sexual harassment lawsuit against the U.S. Department of Transportation arising out of a mandatory racial and gender diversity workshop they were required to attend in June 1992. The male plaintiffs allege that the program created a hostile and offensive working environment in an attempt to "turn the tables on the men": they were forced to walk through a line of female controllers who fondled them and rated their sexual attributes. Specifically, they allege that one by one, the men were forced to walk through the throng of women and were subjected to "touching, groping and other demeaning and unwelcome sexual harassment."[34]

If the allegations prove true, the government as employer may face the very liability for gender discrimination that the training was designed to combat. The Air Traffic Controllers Association filed a grievance over the programs, and settled in late September with the FAA. Controllers who say they were harmed by the training can seek restoration of sick leave they used or reimbursement for medical expenses. The union's executive vice president, Mike McNally, estimates this compensation could apply to as many as 4000 workers. Additionally, one union member identified as Controller A in the settlement, who has been on leave without pay due to emotional problems allegedly aggravated by the work-shops, will receive $75,000 and the chance to return to full-time duties. The civil lawsuit is still pending in Chicago.

This case is potentially significant because, if proven, the allegations relate *directly to the training methodology.* A finding of liability would fall squarely on the training program itself, rather than on discrimination evidenced by participants in the workshop.

The *Hartman* case differs from the discrimination case against Lucky Stores, where the substantive reactions of the trainees in a diversity training program were used *as evidence* of management bias. In *Stender v. Lucky Stores, Inc.,* the female employees of Lucky Stores filed a class-action sex discrimination lawsuit based on the lack of promotions for females over a period of years. The FAA case involves the *training methodology.*

Another case that involved methodology in a workshop was *Fitzgerald v. US West Communications, Inc.*[35] The Tenth Circuit Court of Appeals addressed the issue of diversity training in a slightly different context. US West Communications was found liable for compensatory damages as a result of racially charged comments made by its in-house training instructors to a US West executive when she was selecting outside facilitators to conduct the company's diversity work-shops. The court addressed the emerging and challenging issues involved in content-methodology in diversity workshops:

> This developing area of diversity training has, at its motivating core, highly emotional areas of interpersonal relationships with real and potentially volatile strong conflicts, and its purpose is to cause those involved to recognize and deal appropriately with such as they find within themselves and others....

Unfortunately, the very workshop format which was designed and intended to expose strong, unacceptable emotions and responses so that they could be examined and controlled…engendered an emotional response that while not uncommon, was one that [the employee] was unable to deal with.[36]

Religious Discrimination in Training. "New-age" programs are as diverse as the name implies. These programs do not involve typical classroom instruction but rather nontraditional training techniques and methods. Training objectives range from "unleashing human potential," to leadership skills, risk taking, and motivational decision analysis. Unlike conventional business training, the so-called new-age workshops claim to transform participants, not simply improve their job-related skills.

The programs vary in their approaches. Workshops designed to improve motivation, cooperation, or productivity through the use of meditation, yoga, and biofeedback have raised concerns about conflicts with personal philosophies and even injury to the employee's psyche. The more unconventional programs utilize techniques based on Eastern occultism and mysticism to change the way employees think. Still others consider such unorthodox methods to be what they have described as "witchcraft in the nuclear age."[37]

Critics of new-age programs say that the programs often lead people to unknowingly accept a mystic world view. Thus, they have been principally challenged on grounds of conflict with fundamental religious beliefs. New-age training programs have been hit by several dozen lawsuits for discrimination. Some employees have also sought damages for personal injuries, alleging psychotic breakdowns and even suicides.

The most common legal pitfall is the mandatory program which conflicts with religious beliefs. Techniques such as meditation, self-hypnosis, and other "mind-altering" experiences have been challenged for conflicting with the rights of employees to the free practice of their religious beliefs (or lack of beliefs). When employees or supervisors have refused to participate in mandatory programs, their subsequent dismissals have been successfully overturned. This has led the EEOC to promulgate specific guidelines disapproving of new-age techniques which violate Title VII's proscription against religious discrimination.

As possible ways to accommodate employees, the EEOC suggests substituting an alternate technique "not offensive to the employee's belief" or excusing the employee from either a particular part of the training or the entire program. However, employers must be aware that excused employees still have the right to be free from discrimination which places them at an unfair disadvantage in acquiring skills which may lead to job advancements or promotional opportunities. Accordingly, such a program should not be implemented if it is the *sole* opportunity for skills development which will lead to advancement opportunities. To do otherwise results in a disparate impact on employees who exercise their rights to be free from religious discrimination.

References

The citations to legal precedents in this chapter use the format found in the official statutes and case reports. This is the most effective way to locate the full text of a statute or description of the case or administrative decision. This is the only way to locate the statute in the law library. "29 U.S.C." is Title 29 of the United States Code; state statutes are similarly cited by their official code format for immediate access through a law librarian or on-line database.

Although the names of cases are also indexed alphabetically by the name of the claimant (the first name on the case caption), the text of the case opinion can only be found by locating the official case *Reporter*. The official *Reporters* can be found in hardcopy format in most law libraries. They can also be searched by the citations on-line through the LEXIS/NEXIS database as well as specialized databases on the Internet.

Federal cases are cited by the official *Reporter* citations. For example, a trial court decision would be in the *Federal Supplement*; 25 *F. Supp.* 1040 (N.D. Cal. 1994) is volume 25 of the *Federal Reporter*, page 1040, from the trial court in Northern California in 1994. Similarly, Opinions of the Federal Intermediate Courts of Appeals are in the *Federal Reporter:* 18 F. 2d 111 (9th Cir. 1994) is volume 18 of the *Federal Reporter*, 2d series, page 111, from the Ninth Circuit (Western U.S.) Court of Appeals in 1994.

Throughout these references, state cases are cited to the most commonly accessible *Reporters*. For example, "S.W." refers to the *Southwest Reporter*, with each cite referencing the volume number, page, and date. Likewise, "Cal. App. 3d" is the third series of California Appellate.

1. Equal Employment Opportunity Commission, cited in BNA *Employment Discrimination Report* (1994).

2. Equal Employment Opportunity Commission, cited in BNA *Employment Discrimination Report* (1994).

3. California Penal Code §387.

4. 29 U.S.C. §§1501–1781 (1982).

5. 29 U.S.C. §1554 (1982).

6. 552 So.2d 129 (Ala. 1989).

7. 118 Cal. App. 3d 300, 317 (1981).

8. *Stacey v. Truman Medical Center* (1994).

9. 578 S.W.2d 173 (Tex. Civ. App. 1979).

10. *Farley v. MM Cattle Co.*, 529 S.W.2d 751, 754 (1975).

11. 835 S.W.2d 56 (Tex. 1992).

12. 689 S.W.2d 404 (Tex. 1985).

13. *Chinnery v. Virgin Islands*, 865 F.2d 68 (1989) [negligent hiring and retention claims]; *Dickert v. Metropolitan Life Ins. Co.*, 428 S.E.2d 700 (So. Carolina Sup. Ct. 1993) [Court upheld dismissal of a claim of negligent retention and supervision of a supervisor accused of sexual harassment, on the ground the victim's injury was the result of work-related injury under South Carolina law]. Similar conclusions have been reached by courts in Indiana, California, Wisconsin, and New York.

14. National Institute of Occupational Safety and Health Surveys (1992).

15. Bureau of Labor Statistics, USDL-94-384 (August 10, 1994).

16. *BNAC Communicator*, Spring-Summer 1995 (page 11).

17. 29 U.S.C. §654(a)(1).

18. Human Rights Commission Regulation: Maine Human Rights Act., Me. Rev. Stat. Ann. Title V, §§4511–4632 (1979, Supp. 1991).

19. Connecticut Fair Employment Practices Act, Conn. Gen. Stat. Ann. §§46a–51. The Connecticut Commission on Human Rights and Opportunities enacted the regulations pursuant to Public Act 93-85, empowering the commission to develop the regulation.

20. *Federal Register*, vol. 58, no. 106, 31,830 (June 4, 1993); 29 C.F.R. §2619; §825.300(c).

21. *ADA Technical Assistance Manual*, Section 4.05; emphasis in original (1992).

22. *ADA Technical Assistance Manual*, Section 4.05.

23. *EEOC Technical Assistance Manual*, Section 4.6, example 1.

24. *Wilmore v. City of Wilmington,* 699 F.2d 667 (3d Cir. 1983).

25. *Coates v. National Cash Register Company,* 433 F. Supp. 655 (W.D. VA 1977).

26. *Kirk v. Browner* (D.C. Wash., no. C93-584R, July 26, 1994).

27. 538 F. Supp. 250 (D.C. Conn. 1982).

28. *United Steelworkers of America v. Weber,* 443 U.S. 193 (1979).

29. 803 F. Supp. 259 (N.D. Cal. 1992).

30. 803 F. Supp. 259, 292–93 (1992).

31. The self-evaluative or critical analysis privilege is based on the concern that disclosure of documents reflecting candid self-examination will deter or suppress socially useful investigations and evaluations of compliance with the law voluntarily undertaken by a company. *Hardy v. New York News, Inc.,* 114 F.R.D. 633 (S.D.N.Y. 1987).

32. *Welte v. Los Angeles Police Dept.* (1994).

33. *San Bernardino Community College v. Gallegos,* Civ. no. 8444 (1995).

34. *Bureau of National Affairs Employment Discrimination Report,* vol. 3, no. 10, p. 300 (Sept. 14, 1994).

35. No. 93-1142 (10th Cir., Jan. 31, 1995).

36. *Ibid.*

37. *Fortune,* July 6, 1987, p. 69.

10

Cost Accounting for Training

Wesley W. Stillwagon

Wesley W. Stillwagon is an Internal Consultant, Educational Design Technology, KPMG Peat Marwick LLP. Prior to this position, he was self-employed in Instructional Design and Technical Publications. He was engaged in projects for AT&T; The Competency-Based Pay programs of Blue Cross and Blue Shield of New Jersey, Inc.; a large retailer; and for a major New Jersey health-care center. He was the Generation Training Manager for Pennsylvania Electric Co. (Penelec/GPU). He was honored with the President's Award for developing an integrated training concept. He held training management positions for RCA (four manufacturing divisions). He holds a B.S. and an A.A.S. and has held a number of instructor-teacher certifications. He has authored: "New Approach Speeds Simulator Design and Procurement," Power Engineering magazine, April 1987; (with Roland Burns, University of Plymouth, UK), presenter, Operations Management Association, June 1992, United Kingdom, "Improving the Competitive Edge Through the Application of Human Performance Engineering," published 1993 in "Achieving Competitive Edge, Getting Ahead Through Technology and People," (Springer-Verlag); "Improving Manufacturing Competitiveness Through the Application of Human Performance Engineering," International Journal for Technology Management and UNESCO. Subject of Biographical Record in Who's Who in the World, Who's Who in Finance and Industry, and Who's Who in U.S. Executives.

Upon completion of this chapter, assuming the reader has direct-training development experience, he or she will have conceptual tools (perhaps not the only ones) with which to establish and effectively utilize a training cost accounting system, including:

- A working knowledge at an organization officer's level, of training return-on-investment issues to improve cost reporting
- An understanding of life-cycle costing
- Costs associated with individual learning objective–driven program elements
- The cost relationship of learning objectives to training method
- Suggested procedure for projecting training program development and delivery costs
- Methods of improving training program economics using the cost accounting system

Introduction to Cost Accounting for Training

Many of us are responsible for dozens of training programs that are in any number of development, delivery, or maintenance stages. As such, we need an easy-to-manage training cost accounting system. At the ideal extreme, an organization should be able to meet its labor-intensive performance goals with no costs associated with performance improvement. Regardless of the task, the assigned employee should be able to achieve a worthy performance level such that the value of the accomplishment equals or exceeds the costly behavior.[1] This would imply the performance equation shown in Fig. 10-1. In the performance equation:

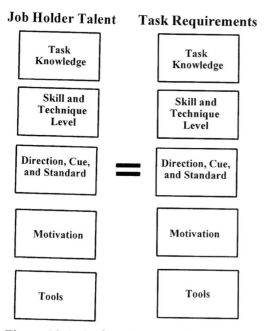

Figure 10-1. Performance equation.

The knowledge necessary to achieve worthy performance held by the job holder equates to the knowledge required by the task.

The skills and technique of the job holder equals the skills and techniques required of the task.

The job holder has been properly charged for the task with supervisor instruction, cue, and standards.

The motivation of the job holder equates to the motivation to achieve worthy performance for the task.

The tools and support necessary to the task are provided for the job holder.

Training can support many of the equation elements and performance improvement goals, but training is only a tool or service that provides presentation, guidance, and counsel to the performance improvement goals. It shouldn't be construed as the only means to the goals. The primary responsibility for performance improvement must remain with the job holder and his or her immediate supervisor. (In many organizations, the primary accountability for supervisors is the development of the skills and ability of the job holder.) The training cost accounting system should be developed under that philosophy.

Specifically, a realistic cost accounting system for training would be based upon a sound training development process. Many problems within an organization related to training support (including the opinion held by officers of the value of "training" within an organization's performance improvement efforts) can be attributed to the failure to utilize a sound training development process,[2] thereby making it impossible to monitor costs because of the inability to

- distinguish between information goals within the training program and those actually serving a *training* need;
- distinguish the consequence of the training experience on performance improvement from other factors; or
- apply sound cost accounting procedures that enable good performance improvement or training management decisions.

Improperly developed training programs, in addition to being ineffective and inefficient, are difficult, if not impossible, to track with a reliable cost accounting system. As a result, the economic relationship between costs in development, presentation, and overhead and the benefit to the organization or the trainee is obscured.

If training as a profession is to achieve respect as a direct contributor to improved profit, better performance, or effectiveness within an organization, a solid cost accounting system that explicates all relationships between level of performance and performance improvement efforts is a necessity. Such an accounting system is only possible when it has solid processes upon which to construct.

Training Cost Accounting, Direct and Indirect Training Economics

It shouldn't surprise anyone that while a suitable system for training cost accounting is needed, with no commonly accepted training course creation or revision standard, or systematic way to determine training course content, its development would be difficult to impossible to achieve (especially since any *accounting* depends upon the validity of the structure). When decision makers (who are increasingly pressured by our very dynamic economy) have tools such as spreadsheets and relational databases with which to analyze utilization of resources (including human resources), the pressure on the trainer to account for actions, plans, program direction, method, and the like is growing. With such high-tech tools, a trainer's justification of training expenditure using such hard-to-refute factors as "human factors fog" is coming to an end. Trainers are increasingly challenged to relate the expenditure of resources in the name of *training* to the consequence and to do so in bottom-line (dollar and cents) terms.

Bottom-Line Training Accounting Elements

What are the elements of training cost economics and how do they impact the bottom line? An understanding of training economics starts with the abstract and moves to the concrete (see Table 10-1). The most abstract considerations for training cost economics require:

1. Calculating all costs of training program development and delivery
2. Comparing the resulting figure to the benefit in improved performance
3. Comparing the resulting figure against alternative methods of achieving the same goals
4. Comparing the resulting figure against doing nothing

The rather abstract equation in Table 10-1 appears deceptively simple, but consider the right-side components:

Improved performance. Measurement of performance at an elementary production level is a relatively simple process, so comparing the performance against concrete standards is also simple. But when the tasks associated with performance move from the simpler production level to the more complex, this comparison becomes much more difficult. And transposing the elements to training cost indicators is correspondingly difficult. (See Fig. 10-2.)

We all know that job descriptions and accountability systems are completely objective only with tasks that are inarguably observable and overtly measurable. But how do we measure performance (and thereby calculate costs or determine value) within tasks for which no starting cue, procedure, or stan-

Table 10-1. Training Cost Economics.

Cost, $	Comparison/benefits
	Improved performance
Training program development and delivery	Compared with alternative method(s) of achieving the same performance goal
	Cost savings
	Not doing anything at all

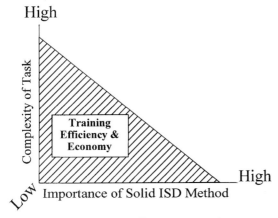

High

Complexity of Task

Training
Efficiency &
Economy

Low

High

Importance of Solid ISD Method

Figure 10-2. Training effectiveness and economy.

dard for worthy performance has been defined? And if we cannot do this, how can we tell if or how performance improvement was achieved and how it impacts training costs?

The areas of job performance requiring the most serious improvement initiatives, measurement, cost controls, and investment are usually the ones requiring the most complex and innovative economic considerations.[3]

Alternative methods. If we are unable to track or interpret the costs of more complex tasks, how, in the concrete sense, can we determine if an alternative method to achieving the same goal will favorably compare?

Cost saving. With the same logic (above), we are equally handicapped when defining the cost savings related not only to training but to any directed effort involving performance improvement.

Not doing anything. In questions of managing cost accounting for training, an often ignored question is whether, within the context of the organization's goals, it would have been more fiscally responsible to do nothing over the development and delivery of a performance improvement training program (considering the decision would have to be supported with dollar-and-cents-based evidence). Certainly it would be easy when supporting simple production tasks, but when the task requires consideration for the more complex human faculties, knowledge, abilities, interpersonal effectiveness, and dynamics, the formula for cost accounting economics becomes considerably more complex and demanding.

How can we really consider an ideal training cost accounting system when we haven't considered a training development and presentation structure within which economic factors can be applied and compared? Such an ideal training development and presentation structure-system will have to be able to efficiently and effectively develop, present, and test those performance-enhancing elements necessary to fill the gap between the actual performance level and the worthy performance level. (There really is no other fundamental reason for *training* to exist as an organizational entity.)

The accomplishment of the abstract cost comparison is possible only when all economic elements at the more concrete levels are available, such as the preprogram and program development economic elements.

Preprogram Development Economic Elements:

- *Cost of problem analysis.* Includes the design, execution, and results analysis. The problem-analysis focus is used to clearly define the gap between what the performance should be (worthy performance level) and what the performance level actually is. Filling the gap through whatever means should result in dollar savings because then the costly behavior would equal or exceed the value of the accomplishment.[4] Figure 10-3 represents the normal *complex*[5] of elements that contribute to performance problems. With this consideration, it should be easy to see that a *training* program consisting of just relevant textbook information on the technology or an attempt to transfer knowledge can't completely fill the gap.

  Many times the costs associated with developing and delivering training programs have been saved through sound problem analysis. The problem analysis looks at the issues represented in Fig. 10-3 and, in addition to naming where training resources be applied for the most good, names areas not training-related or resolvable (sometimes recommending other resources for this resolution).

  "A well designed training program should be directed to nothing but the improvement and maintenance of job performance."

  T. F. Gilbert[6]

- *Cost of performance.* This element includes:

  Process analysis. The product of the performance analysis is the "know-whats and know-hows" that form the foundation of the learning objectives.

  Development of learning objectives. Once the learning objectives are defined, the training program should take on a new appearance, that is, a structure made up of learning blocks to which a sound cost accounting system may be applied. The sum-total learning blocks become the more abstract *training program*. Each learning block has its own cost accounting requirements that

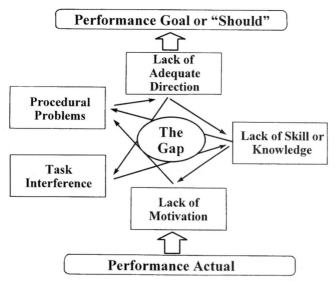

Figure 10-3. Normal complex of performance problems.

contribute to the final balance sheet totals. Seen individually, there may be some losers and winners. The competent training cost accounting practitioner can demonstrate the relationship between the loser learning objective segment and the program success. (The segment may be a necessary prerequisite for a subsequent, performance-related objective-segment.)

- *Cost of developing and approving training program conceptual plan.* This element includes:

Needs analysis. Where the presentation and critiquing method or methods are selected for each learning objective.

Cost-benefit analysis. Where the economic benefit of the entire program versus the cost of development and delivery is calculated for prediction and decision-making support. Since some learning objectives are prerequisite in nature and should not be considered for their stand-alone economics, the cost accounting totals here should be evaluated for the program.

Program Development Economic Elements:

- *Costs of developing the program presentation.* This element involves critiquing elements to economically and soundly meet the learning objectives. The individual learning objective represents the elemental building block of a training program. The learning objective and all program work is focused on that goal. Each learning objective is a stand-alone segment with its own cost considerations. The final program costs are therefore a summation of the learning objective element costs.

The next concrete cost consideration calculates the cost relationship between the development effort and the training presentation. This concrete cost is evaluated in terms of effectiveness; in other words, How effective and appropriate was the training method for each learning objective? The more effectively presented the training material, the simpler the program appears. In actuality, the smoother and more effective the program, the more creativity and effort was expended in its development. Like a poorly developed speech or presentation, a stumbling, inappropriately focused program usually indicates very little preprogram research and poor development work. This situation may be the result of so many experts in a field erroneously assuming that their subject-matter expertise automatically qualifies them to train. In some situations, we are referring to one or two program developers working for a limited period of time on a program that will impact hundreds or thousands of trainees yearly through the life of the program (life-cycle consideration). This being so, it makes sense, that even if you doubled the amount of program development work (one or two program developers), and as a result, saved a small percentage in time, overhead, and resources on the delivery end (perhaps halving the training program length), or improved the performance, resulting in increased revenue from hundreds (or thousands) of trainees, the effort may result in considerable savings, profit, or reduction of overhead. Of course, there is a point at which increasing the program development-delivery costs will not achieve a proportional return in effectiveness, especially when the whistles, bells, and buzzers of the presentation outshine the original intent of the program. We've all experienced such programs in our careers.

Some of the factors to consider in building a training cost accounting system at this level are:

- Learning objective soundness and relationship to performance goals
- The appropriateness of the learning objective and the presentation and critiquing method(s)

At the lowest level of consideration (these costs are the easiest to calculate) are the labor, material, and overhead costs associated with the development, delivery, and support for the program. More often than not, the following are the only elements considered in analyzing training cost accounting:

- Cost of program development, including: (1) Labor and overhead of developer(s); (2) Labor and overhead of auxiliary and administrative support personnel; (3) Costs of material, travel, contractors, subcontractors, and relevant overhead.

- Cost of delivery, facilities, and support; also costs of labor, overhead, travel, and supplies for participants

- Costs associated with follow-up (when considered)

In summary, the training cost accounting system is founded upon a sound program development process, and at the top level we consider the economics of program development and delivery and compare them with the benefits of program delivery and alternative approaches to problem resolution and against not doing anything at all.

Questions About Training Cost Accounting

Answers to the following abstract questions are impossible to develop without considering certain preprogram development processes and economics.

- What are the benefits (expressed in dollars and cents) in improved performance as a direct result of training program development?

- How can we compare the benefits (expressed in dollars and cents) from training program development and delivery against alternative methods of achieving the same goals?

- What are the cost savings (expressed in dollars and cents) to the organization directly related to training program development and delivery?

- How can we predict the impact upon the organization if we do nothing at all in the face of the performance problem?

Such processes must concretely define the problem, cull out the training resolvable solutions, make suggestions regarding alternative solutions (that are counted among training assets), define the know-whats and the know-hows for each task, define the learning objectives and measurement standards, develop the conceptual training plan that would most economically meet the learning objectives, and acquire approval for the approach.

Once the approach is approved, the objective-based modules must be developed and presented. Measure the results at the end of *training* and after returning to the job to determine economic benefit.

Lastly, the most important part of a sound training cost accounting system is the basic (nuclear or archetypal) element, the learning objective–based module. The learning objective–based module has an intrinsic cost structure, and the accumulation of economic considerations for each module will result in the economic data necessary for the concrete valuation of the program.

A Sample Training Cost Accounting

Going back to the highest economic tier or cost consideration for a training program, we find that the spreadsheet should appear similar to the simplified one in Fig. 10-4.

In our hypothetical example of a performance improvement problem affecting 2000 employees, the training developer and the sponsor of the program [consisting of three modules, learning objective (LO) numbers 1, 2, and 3] chose an Instructional System Design (ISD)-guided instruction-demonstration, critique, and feedback approach for resolution of their performance improvement problem. Module LO 1 covered essential prerequisite material for modules 2 and 3, so no performance improvement could be attributed directly to that segment. Module 2 cost $15,000 to develop but could be shown to result in an annual performance improvement increase or savings of $540,000. Module 3 cost $7800 to develop and resulted in an improvement or savings of $112,000 per year.

The alternative methods considered were on-the-job training, a CBT program, and a self-paced guided instruction program. Each was considered for the cost of development and delivery (see Fig. 10-5) for each learning objective and the expected performance improvement resulting from the instructional module presentation.

Regarding the cost of doing nothing (even though doing nothing costs nothing to develop), if we simply consider the hidden costs of doing nothing compared with benefits of performance improvement resulting from a formal ISD training approach, the cost to the organization can be at least equal to the cost of developing the improvement program. Unchecked performance problems can, through time, (1) grow, often logarithmically; (2) remain a consistently costly burden; or (3) go away, perhaps through some divine intervention (very rare). Experience shows that performance problems usually grow and rarely remain consistent or go away. This means that if the organization chooses to do nothing and thus avoid an intervention by a competent training professional, the related and often hidden costs of a growing performance problem are usually many

Training Program				
Module	Development/ delivery costs, $	Performance improvement, $	Alternative method, $	Doing nothing, $
Module 1/LO 1	$6,400.00	$0.00		
Module 2/LO 2	$15,000.00	$540,000.00		
Module 3/LO 3	$7,800.00	$112,000.00		
Totals	$29,200.00	$652,000.00		
Profit/Loss	$622,800.00			
VS. ALTERNATIVE METHOD				
VS. DOING NOTHING	($652,000.00)			

Figure 10-4. Simplified spreadsheet.

times the cost of the training intervention. Avoiding actions can be costly. The hidden costs of doing nothing should not be ignored or buried and are often much greater than the cost of training. (Also see the previous section, "Bottom-Line Training Accounting Elements.")

Training Program Suggested Development Sequence

To maintain better control over costs, the accounting system should use the same time-milestones as the program development, delivery, and maintenance procedure. It should allow management queries to milestones or time markers on PERT (Project Evaluation and Review Technique) or Gantt charts (the most likely time when such an inquiry or interest would surface). Having a uniform program development procedure when numbers of programs are being monitored, while not essential, makes managing costs and predicting budget easier and more reliable, especially for the new training manager. Today, such tracking tasks can be dramatically improved by using one of the new project management applications available for computers. It is the opinion of the author that the use of such tracking tools is a requirement for managing a reliable training cost accounting program.

The flow diagram presented in Fig. 10-5 is a suggested training development, delivery, and maintenance system that would work well with training cost accounting tasks. It follows the flow of program development and maintenance most frequently observed (when a training program development system exists at all) in U.S. business and industry: starting with the request, then through the analysis, to the learning objectives, to the plan, to the development, the delivery, and finally to the closed loop through which feedback and posttraining analysis ultimately impact the learning objectives. Until the learning objectives are distin-

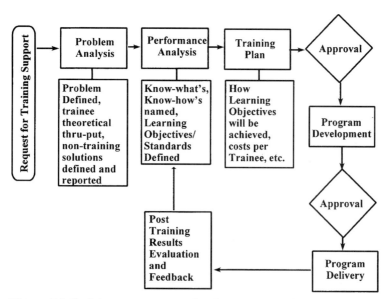

Figure 10-5. A training program development procedure.

guished by the problem and performance analysis, the cost accounting is handled as a single entity. Each learning objective–focused segment has its own cost accounting structure. When all of the modules are combined into a *program*, a single cost accounting path can again occur (that is a summation of all learning objective cost elements). When you are in the loop, you are in program maintenance, which also enables single-path cost accounting. (See Fig. 10-5.)

The process can now be used with spreadsheets, Gantt, or PERT charts to visualize the placements of cost impacting elements. Use the Fig. 10-5 procedure-flow as a guide: The process starts with a request for training (normally from a nontraining management person). The wise trainer will treat the training request as an acknowledgment of a problem for which the requestor believes training may be a solution.

The first step for which cost accounting may be considered in the flow (see Fig. 10-6), is the problem analysis. The problem is thoroughly defined at this point, the expected trainee throughput is calculated, and the nontraining resolvable issues named and reported. The costs associated with this step are spread over all of the module–learning objective segments. In our hypothetical example on page 208, the costs of that step are included under development and delivery costs for modules 1, 2, and 3. (In reality, the total costs for the problem-analysis tasks are stored, since at this point they are to be spread among the number of learning objectives yet to be determined.)

One of the products of the problem analysis is the naming of some of the performance gap elements for which training may be the solution. (The others are the gap elements for which nontraining solutions must be applied.) The performance gaps require an analysis aside from the problem analysis, although the latter analysis may be expedited with data from the former. The objectives, focus, or perspective required for success is different. The trainer now focuses only on the performance issues. Other issues, highlighted in the problem analysis, are no longer relevant to the work of the trainer. The performance analysis, therefore, only considers relevant *performance issues*. Here, the *know-whats, know-hows*, and standards are defined in detail. In the next step, the learning objectives are created from those definitions. The costs of this work eventually will also be spread into the individual module development-delivery totals.

Performance analysis reviews the task from outside of the context of a problem and objectively defines the technical and the human side of the procedure, including the validity of the standard of worthy performance. (Perhaps the

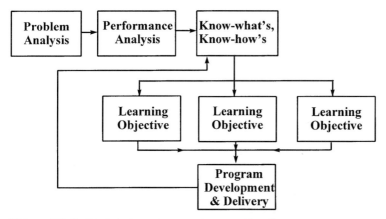

Figure 10-6. Training program cost accounting flow.

performance goal is not realistic and the *performance actual* is, thereby reducing or eliminating the need for training.) The cost of producing and delivering a training program that can never achieve an unrealistic performance goal, which leads to frustration on the part of trainers, trainees, and field supervisors, is a staggering waste. Such training experiences reduce the vision of training as a contributor to organization productivity, profit, and utility.

The product of the performance analysis is the *know-whats* and *know-hows* for worthy performance. They will be used to create learning objectives and measurement standards, each having its own training-learning method, medium, and critique, and each having its own cost-tracking system. At this point, the single-path cost accounting branches to the individual learning objective segments. Each learning segment is directed to the support of performance improvement on a job-related task. This rule is necessary if a direct (test of details) correlation between the learning experience and performance improvement at the job-site is to be established. If a direct correlation is not practical or desirable, an analytical correlation may be established.[7] The segment of the spreadsheet devoted to the learning objective–focused segment should look similar to the one in Fig. 10-7.

In our example "Presentation Costs" spreadsheet (see Fig. 10-8):

- The "cost of materials, tools, supplies expended per course presentation and per trainee" was mostly attributable to the development and delivery of a handout workbook that provided reinforcement and reference for the trainees that completed the program.

- "Depreciation," or recoupment of the cost of an asset through deductions based upon the asset's life,[10] on capital equipment (i.e., building and fixtures), including depreciation of classroom furniture, fixtures, and videotape players and monitors, should be tracked in at least two sets of records:

    1. One set should reflect the required depreciation under the provisions of *Generally Accepted Accounting Principles* (*GAAP*, commonly called *book depreciation*) and is calculated on a straight-line method (i.e., the depreciation is proportional to the prescribed life of the item).
    2. The other set is maintained for tax purposes. Whoever is responsible for tax (typically the tax director) would maintain the tax depreciation records. Tax depreciation (specifically, federal) is not normally calculated using a linear or straight-line approach. The greatest loss in value is incurred during the first full year of use, and this nonlinear loss is so reflected in the tax depre-

Characteristic	Segment 1	Segment 2	Segment 3
Problem analysis[8]	$500.00	$500.00	$500.00
Performance analysis	$2,500.00	$2,500.00	$2,500.00
Training plan	$500.00	$500.00	$500.00
Segment development	$2,900.00	$11,500.00	$4,300.00
Totals	$6,400.00	$15,000.00	$7,800.00
Presentation costs[9]			
Grand total	$29,200.00		

Figure 10-7. Learning objective segment of spreadsheet.

Factor	Description	Cost, $
Replenishables	Cost of materials, tools, supplies expended per course presentation and per trainee	$30,000.00
Depreciation (book and tax, see below)	On capital equipment (facilities, if applicable)	$18,000.00
Instructor wages, overhead, and expenses (when applicable)	For 226 training days, including prep time	$38,029.02
Trainee wages, overhead, and expenses (when applicable)	For 2000 trainees divided into 167 twelve-person classes in one year	$240,384.00
Other presentation expenses	Classroom-laboratory rental, rental for equipment, and other overheads	$8,000.00
	Totals	$334,413.02

Figure 10-8. Presentation costs spreadsheet.

ciation. A tax depreciation is determined from tables and publications such as the one issued by the Internal Revenue Service. They list depreciable items, the life of the items, and the depreciation percentage for the annual or quarterly depreciation deduction.[11]

- "Instructor wages" was based upon an annual salary of $35,000 plus a 25 percent benefit package; if the instructor were to travel to the trainees, costs of travel expenses would be included here.

- "Trainee wages, overhead, and expenses" for the 2000 trainees was based upon a $25,000 annual average wage plus a 25 percent benefit package. (If the trainees had to travel to the training site, travel expenses would be included here.)

- Under "other presentation expenses" was an estimate of incidental material such as pencils for note taking, etc.

Conclusion

Clearly, with every cost within organizations being carefully scrutinized, people with training responsibilities will be expected to develop and maintain sound training cost accounting systems. Industry will have to recognize the importance of solid adult training methodology and become more adept at including more than technical information in their programs; and institutions of higher learning will have to become more flexible and poised to quickly and effectively respond to industry training needs (something not traditionally done). Each side has lessons to learn from the other one about the training issue, the technique, and the adult learning principles.

Greater specialization and economic considerations in program development and delivery is clearly in our future, and training-on-demand for specialized, individual needs for the highest-complexity tasks will stretch us. A working example of a cooperative, cost-effective effort between business and education is at the University of Plymouth, Plymouth Teaching Company Centre, United Kingdom, under the direction of Dr. Roland Burns. The Teaching Company Centre represents a fruitful, cost-effective connection between training in business and industry and institutions of higher learning. Such relationships, given the cost-effectiveness, are predictable.

References

1. After Gilbert, Thomas F., *Human Competence, Engineering Worthy Performance,* McGraw-Hill, New York, 1978.

2. [Regarding standards to revise or create training programs]: "No standard in American industry is met so poorly." [Regarding standards for determining training program comment]: "A well-designed training program should be directed at nothing but the improvement and maintenance of job performance. The greatest criticism that could be made about training in American industry is that it fails to do this job in any systematic way. Examine most industrial training courses and you will find that at least half of their content does not seem to be directed specifically to any job performance. Typically when a course of training is devised, its objectives (on the rare occasions when they are clearly stated) are guided by subject matter as it appears in the textbooks or in the heads of subject matter specialists and not as the job requires it." Thomas F. Gilbert, Ph.D., from a noncopyrighted report of results on an evaluation of an integrated training system.

3. "The human resource component of operational finances is poorly managed now because it isn't counted or measured well enough to allow for its true control," (p. S-6). "Traditional accounting methods treat people only as expenses, so funds used to train people are computed as expenses," (p. S-7). "Japanese and European managers spend three to five times as much on worker training," (p. S-6). *Economic Accountability for Training: Demands and Responses,* "Return on Investment: Accounting for Training," Anthony P. Carnevale and Eric Schulz, Supplement to the *Training and Development Journal,* July 1990. Reprinted with permission. All rights reserved.

4. After Gilbert, Thomas F., *Human Competence, Engineering Worthy Performance,* McGraw-Hill, New York, 1978.

5. The term *complex* is used here because performance problem elements are often interdependent, and nudging one will affect the others.

6. From an uncopyrighted evaluation of an integrated training system.

7. A direct training cost accounting correlation between learning segment-experience and on-the-job task worthy performance level exists when a proportional and solid relationship exists between per-trainee cost of training and the improvement in performance. An *analytical* training cost correlation exists when the cost-benefit relationship can only be comparatively implied.

8. *Problem analysis* and *performance analysis* costs are typically spread evenly throughout all segments because the total number of learning objective segments and the cost-benefit impact of each are unknown until these important steps are completed.

9. *Presentation* costs for our example include the annual costs of replenishables, depreciation on training equipment, instructors' time, trainee time, classroom-laboratory rental, and/or other overheads.

10. Your tax professional will also consider depreciation for intangible property such as goodwill, going concern, covenant-not-to-compete, patents, franchises, and intellectual property.

11. Suggestions from Tracy L. Curran, KPMG, New York, NY.

SECTION 2

Program Design and Development

11

The Behavioral Sciences

Harold M. F. Rush

Harold M. F. Rush *is a member of the organization and management discipline of Gemini Consulting. His background includes consulting, research, teaching, and the management of human resources in the private and public sectors. He has consulted for many transnational corporations based on six continents and in a wide variety of businesses and he is a recognized authority on international communication and cross-cultural training. Rush directed international human resources, covering 45 countries worldwide, and the organization and executive resources function for Avon Products. With Exxon Corporation, he was responsible for manpower and organizational development at the world headquarters and, successively, headed personnel resources, planning, and development for the Europe-Africa and Asia-Pacific regions and for Exxon Minerals Company. He was* Raoul de Vitry d'Avoucourt Professor of Human Resource Management *at INSEAD, the European graduate school of business, and he has lectured extensively at universities and schools of business worldwide. Rush served at The White House, as a member of a small team of executives, creating and managing the first effort of business, government, community leaders, and social activists concerned with the hiring and training of minorities. He served as Associate Director of the Mayor's Office of Operations for New York City, leading a team of internal consultants from the public and private sectors. Rush established and headed The Conference Board's behavioral sciences and organization development function, and he was a founding member of the International Quality of Worklife Project. He is author of six books on management and organizational behavior as well as numerous articles and monographs.*

Managers are commonly described as leaders who enable people to work most effectively by performing the work of planning, leading, and controlling.

Of the four basic managerial functions, none is more crucial to the success of the organization than leading, for it is in performing this function that the manager's ability to manage is put to the acid test. It is in leading, more than in any other function, that the manager must deal directly with the human resources of the organization, and as any experienced manager knows, this is often a complex and difficult job, requiring knowledge and skill beyond that which the average person naturally possesses. People are variable; their behaviors are sometimes predictable, and sometimes not; people both think and feel; what worked well for management in the past often seems less effective when dealing with a more mobile, better-educated, more aggressive, and more affluent workforce.

For these reasons, the managerial profession has looked outside the traditional business disciplines for insights and guidance in formulating strategies to manage the "people" part of the enterprise. Increasingly, the assistance is sought from a loosely bound collection of academic disciplines referred to as the *behavioral sciences,* which may include sociology, anthropology, socioeconomics, the various subspecialties within psychology (clinical, social, experimental, etc.), and a host of other disciplines concerned with human behavior in social settings—in this case, the world of work and the work environment.[1]

While the coming together of management and the behavioral sciences has been a gradual process that continues to evolve even today, the heightened interest on both sides of the fence can be traced back only about four decades. However, there are some significant series of events which can be identified as precursors of the contemporary behavioral science-business interface. Principal among them are the so-called Hawthorne studies, the emergence of group dynamics research, and the group theory of organization.

The Hawthorne Studies

If one seeks the genesis of the behavioral sciences in business, one must consider the Hawthorne studies the watershed event. Beginning in 1927 and continuing for five years, the Hawthorne studies were conducted at Western Electric's Hawthorne plant near Chicago. A group of social scientists from Harvard was brought into the plant to study "the relation between conditions of work and the incidence of fatigue and monotony among employees." To do so, they set out to assess the influence of physical and environmental influences such as temperature, light, and humidity at the workplace and the relationship of rest periods to subsequent efficiency on the job. They selected experimental groups of employees, manipulated work conditions, and recorded the results. While they were able, in some instances, to determine cause-and-effect relationships between work conditions and efficiency, they also found that, almost regardless of what changes they made in the work environment, efficiency increased among their experimental groups of workers. This gave rise to what is called the *Hawthorne effect,* that is, the theory that employees perform more efficiently simply because they are given special attention.

More significant than the findings based on the original premise that physical conditions at the workplace affect efficiency were the unexpected findings that were gleaned from the Hawthorne studies. Because the researchers were, in effect, set back each time they tried to relate the various physical conditions to worker efficiency, the project, which was designed to last only one year, extended to five years. The reason: There were influences affecting efficiency and productivity much more strongly than working conditions—namely, group social structures, group norms, and group pressures. The researchers found, for example, that employees were more productive when working in groups than when working in isolation and that wage incentives alone did not determine product output, even on a piecework basis. Workers would sacrifice greater output for group acceptance.[2] Modern managers will find this no surprise, since they know and understand what happens to "rate-busters," but in the late 1920s—when most of industry was influenced heavily by "efficiency experts," time and motion studies, and incentive plans that were based on purely economic considerations—the social-group influences and interpersonal factors that were operating came as a surprise both to management and to the social scientists.

Group Dynamics Research

Although the principles of gestalt psychology had been applied to other areas of behavioral research, it was not until Kurt Lewin, the German-born American psychologist, and his colleagues began their experiments on interacting, face-to-face groups that the gestalt was adapted to social units or groups. The *gestalt* principle, most simply stated, is that the whole is greater than the sum of its parts. With this orientation as an underlying theoretical framework, Lewin and his colleagues made studies of groups as phenomena that were quite different from studies of individuals who compose groups. The research findings suggest that groups do, indeed, take on a distinct personality that supersedes the aggregate personality of its members, and for the first time in the history of social psychology, such terms as "group feeling," "group atmosphere," and "group goals" had an established scientific basis.

Moreover, it was found that the behavior of individuals acting in group situations is determined partially by the group's interaction and behavior, while influencing the norms and behavior of the group. In other words, there is a dynamic interaction, a give-and-take which occurs whenever groups function, that gives rise to what is referred to as *group dynamics*. Lewin and his associates studied group dynamics in the context of the "field" or "life space" in which the behaviors take place, and they posited that behavior can be understood only in the context of this field, thereby creating an analogy, however tenuous, to field theory in the physical sciences. Field theory in social psychology has been variously expressed in mathematical formulas, but the equation $B=f(PE)$, or behavior as a function of personality plus environment, underscores the situational nature of group dynamics and field theory. The personality of individuals may have many determinants, including heredity, early maturational experiences, beliefs, needs, etc., but any given behavior is a function of that personality *plus* the environment or field in which the individual interacts with others—therefore, behavior is changing and dynamic.[3]

Group Theory of Organization

Group dynamics research, which later produced the learning techniques of laboratory training (discussed later), clearly reinforced and gave explanation to the social-group phenomena that the Hawthorne research uncovered in factory work groups. It also formed the basis for large-scale research by Likert, Pelz, et al. on the roles of leadership and work groups, commonly referred to as the *group theory of organization*.

Prior to the Hawthorne studies, supervisors generally dealt with employees as individuals, using a corresponding managerial style designed to supervise on a one-to-one basis. With the research which demonstrated that organizations are actually composed of distinct and identifiable social groups, both formal and informal, and the complementary research on group dynamics and group behaviors, behavioral scientists—mainly from the University of Michigan—undertook extensive action research to identify where these groups exist in organizations, the patterns of group interaction in work situations, and the factors that encourage or impede group cohesion and effectiveness, the relationship of particular groups to other groups, and the individual's role in the several groups and subgroups to which he or she belongs.

Consistently it was demonstrated that the key to successful leadership lies in managers' recognition that they are not managing a collection of individuals— that they must couch their managerial strategies in terms of their relationships to the various groups to which they belong and particularly to the groups they supervise. This may involve an understanding of the function of informal groups in the organization, whose influence may be greater than is indicated by the work grouping that appears on the formal and official organization charts.

Since an organization is more than a large collection of individuals it is actually a series of overlapping groups—groups with the characteristics of individuals (norms, beliefs, values, feelings, inputs, outputs, etc.) but reinforced and modified by group interaction in any given situation. Crucial to the effective manager's role in relationship to these groups is the matter of *perception*—the way the manager perceives his or her role with the groups and the way the groups perceive the manager.

Behavioral Theories and Theorists Influencing Contemporary Management

With the backdrop of the foregoing breakthrough research findings, the behavioral sciences have produced a wealth of subsequent research and theory that have special relevance to the management of modern organizations. Some of these were produced quite independently from business organizations and were adapted by business enterprises because the problems they address are common in business organizations; others were carried out as developmental or action research in and for business organizations. It is impossible in this space to discuss in detail even the most significant findings, let alone others that may have made contributions to the growing body of behavioral research. However, some of the theories and research which seem to have most influenced the managerial process can be treated briefly in overview here.[4]

Since the work of some pioneers in the behavioral sciences first began to capture the interest of leaders, there have been noticeable, and sometimes dramatic, changes in the way organizations are viewed and managed. The influence of the behavioral sciences has been a steady one, and the business school graduates of today have been exposed to the field as a regular and routine part of their education for management. Some of the theories and research described here are no longer startlingly new to leaders and managers, but the contribution of the behavioral sciences to the overall body of knowledge and practice known as "management" is inescapable and undeniable.

Certainly, too, the research and contributions of behavioral scientists have expanded and evolved over the years, including those intervening years since the previous edition of this handbook was published. Limitations of space require some decisions and selectivity. We have chosen to deal with some of the fundamental theories, rather than with later refinements because it is important to know the seminal influences on what today has become a widely accepted "new" discipline known as organizational behavior.

Clearly there are some behavioral science concepts and applications that caught the attention of leaders at one time but which are no longer seen as relevant or particularly useful. Further, there has been within the training and development discipline, indeed within the larger field of management, a long-standing tendency to embrace new, imaginative ideas, only to discard them later, resulting in accusations of "faddism." Transactional analysis (TA), which enjoyed considerable vogue in the 1970s, comes readily to mind. TA is, in fact, an easily grasped and practical construct for analyzing human interaction and communication and it is useful as a model of communication in organizational life, particularly in providing insight into boss-subordinate and peer relations and in conflict management. Yet one rarely encounters TA's conscious usage in organizations these days.

For these reasons, in this chapter, we have chosen not to deal with certain programs, techniques, and theories that may be "past their prime," albeit seen as useful and relevant at another time. Doubtless, some of the behavioral science contributions that are discussed here will seem passé by the time the next edition of this handbook is published, and likely newer contributions will replace them.

What we shall deal with are some of the basic foundations of the behavioral sciences because their influence is inestimable in stimulating or "seeding" subsequent organizational behavioral research and the development of techniques for managing more effectively. For this reason, many of the publications cited in this chapter's footnotes are not recent; instead, they represent the "classics" or seminal works in the field of behavioral sciences as applied to organizations and, as such, are *sine qua non* for one who wants to grasp the impact of these earliest theorists. Moreover, an appreciation of them is necessary for understanding current behavioral research and to comprehend contemporary theories in the proper context. However, we shall also deal with some more recent contributions from the behavioral sciences that are currently in wide application or that are now emerging and seem to be especially promising contributions.

Kurt Lewin

As mentioned above, the group dynamics research which was headed by Kurt Lewin has had a weighty impact on subsequent behavioral science applications in contemporary organizations. The most widely applied facet of this research is one that has special interest to executives concerned with training and development: *laboratory training*.[5]

Laboratory training is the generic term for a variety of educational experiences designed (1) to increase individuals' sensitivity to their own motives and behavior, (2) to increase their sensitivity to the behavior of others, (3) to give them an understanding of how others perceive their behavior and are affected by it, and (4) to determine what factors facilitate or impede group effectiveness. The most common method of laboratory training used by business organizations, especially since the early 1960s, has been *sensitivity training* labs, the heart of which is the *T group* ("T" for training).[6]

While there are many variations on the basic T group, the traditional or "classic" one involves about 12 participants, usually strangers to one another, who meet for two weeks in an isolated spot without agenda and without hierarchical status to interact in face-to-face groups. Although designed to be an educational experience, the sessions are intended to encourage emotional or visceral learning, as contrasted with intellectual or "head-level" learning, which characterizes more traditional education. Further, there is no appointed leader or teacher, though an experienced "trainer" may act in the role of process observer and interpret the behavioral interactions of participants. The group's behavior is both the content and the process of the learning experience—totally experiential in nature. Participants learn to give and receive feedback on a completely candid and instantaneous basis, and the behaviors of individuals and the larger group are reacted to in terms of the "here and now," thereby underscoring Lewin's emphasis on understanding behavior in the "field" in which it occurs.[7]

Laboratory training is still widely used as a developmental technique, though in recent years organizations have tended to replace laboratory training or to supplement it with exercises designed to bridge the gap between the "pure" lab experience and on-the-job problems and situations.[8]

Rensis Likert

The name of Rensis Likert looms large in social psychology. Likert is widely known as the developer of one of the most popular opinion and attitude measurement scales. His research and contributions to organizational theory, however, are more germane to training and development because these address organizational behavior, organizational climate, and leadership effectiveness. Out of extensive longitudinal research on organizations, Likert developed his *linking-pin* concept, with the complementary *interaction-influence* principle, and his four-systems typology of organizations.

The *linking-pin concept* concerns the manager's role in relation to the groups he or she supervises and the group's perception of their manager. The manager serves as a vital link between subordinates and his or her peers and superiors. Thus the manager is the channel of communication between organizational levels; the interpreter of objectives, policies, directives, etc., for subordinates; and the representative and advocate of the members of the work group for his or her peers and superiors. There is nothing new here, so far, since this is a primary function of *any* manager. The difference—and a crucial one—is that the linking pin is a *member* of at least two groups, and thus his or her behavior reflects the values, norms, and objectives of both groups. Usually the manager is the subordinate in one group (e.g., top management) and the superior in the other (e.g., middle management). Further, in order to be an effective linking pin, the manager must be perceived by both groups as a real member of the group, with corresponding identification with each group's activities, problems, accomplishments, etc.[9]

Interaction-Influence Principle.   Even if the behaviors and perceptions of both groups are favorable in relation to the so-called linking pin, the *interaction-influence principle* must also be operative for the manager to be effective in an organization composed of overlapping and interfacing groups. Research on leadership styles and managerial effectiveness supports the necessity of a positive operation of the interaction-influence principle, with two essential variables at work.

First, the amount of influence a manager (linking pin) exerts upward in an organization directly determines the amount of influence he or she exerts downward. Stated simply, the more a manager is respected and listened to and can influence peers and superiors, the more effective he or she will be in managing subordinates. Managers who carry little weight with higher levels of the organizational hierarchy are apt to have little influence on the work groups that report to them.

Second, the more that managers allow themselves to be influenced by their subordinates, the more influence they, in turn, exert on subordinates. For example, in making decisions that will affect subordinates, the manager is more apt to get commitment and involvement from the work group in carrying out the decision if the work group has had some voice in determining the course of the decision. (See Fig. 11-1 for a graphic presentation of the linking pin and the directions of interaction and influence.)

The Four Systems.   The interaction-influence principle clearly has strong implications for the development of a managerial style that is participative and involves the work group. And this is the style that Likert champions in his exposition of the *four systems of organization,* which is a comparative analysis of organizational and performance characteristics of four distinct types of organization. The systems are arranged on a continuum as follows:

System 1: Exploitive-authoritative

System 2: Benevolent-authoritative

System 3: Consultative

System 4: Participative-group

Several organizational variables are analyzed in terms of their existence in organizations typified by the respective systems and their corresponding organizational climates and management styles, including such variables as leadership processes used, character of motivational forces, communication processes, decision-making processes, and control processes. The four-system construct can be used to identify and describe organizations that are characteristic of the various points on the continuum, as well as to provide a model for normative organizational change.[10]

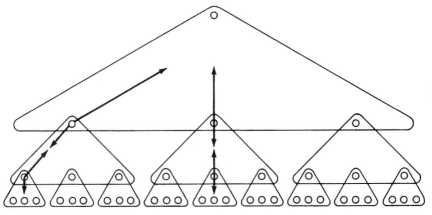

Figure 11-1. The linking-pin function. (*Source: Rensis Likert,* New Patterns of Management, *McGraw-Hill Book Company, New York, 1961. Used with permission.*)

Douglas McGregor

Although Douglas McGregor made contributions to the body of behavioral research and had an active career as professor of management, management consultant, writer, and college president, his name is most often associated with his formulation of philosophical views of mankind, which he called *Theory X* and *Theory Y*.[11]

Theory X, basically a negativistic set of beliefs, includes the following assumptions (paraphrased):

1. People have an inherent dislike for work and will avoid it whenever possible.
2. Because they dislike work, people must be coerced, controlled, directed, or threatened with punishment in order to get them to exert sufficient effort toward organizational objectives.
3. People prefer to be directed, want to avoid responsibility, have little ambition, and seek mainly security.

Theory Y, in contrast, is an optimistic view of human nature:

1. Physical and mental work are as natural as play and rest.
2. People will exercise self-direction and self-control in achieving objectives if they are committed to the objectives.
3. Commitment to objectives is a function of the rewards associated with their achievement.
4. Under proper conditions, people learn not only to accept but also to seek responsibility.
5. Creativity, ingenuity, and imagination are *widely* distributed among the population; most people are capable of directing these abilities toward solving organizational problems.
6. Under conditions in most existing organizations, the average person's intellectual potentialities are being utilized only partially.

McGregor called the sets of assumptions *managerial cosmologies,* and he recognized that they represent only two of many possible "cosmologies"—a term related to *weltanschauung,* which is used in psychology and philosophy to denote a comprehensive conception of the world. They are therefore fundamental orientations or perceptions about the basic nature of human beings, particularly in relation to work and organizational life. While managerial styles and strategies logically are based on these theories, McGregor insisted that he was not proposing a "cookbook" for managing. He adds, however, that Theory X most nearly sums up the view traditional management has taken toward the workforce, while Theory Y represents an enlightened view of how most people are constituted, based on a considerable storehouse of research on human behavior.[12]

"Consensus" Management? Any management style starts with one's beliefs about the nature of people, and in most cases the sets of beliefs or assumptions held by managers become self-fulfilling prophecies when it comes to actual managing. If one's beliefs about people are consonant with those of Theory X, there is only one way to manage: by exerting external control on subordinates. On the other hand, if one views people in a way characteristic of the Theory Y assumptions, there is the possibility of allowing people to exercise self-control.

This is what McGregor stated in his compilation of Theory Y, not a "soft" or "consensus" management, though critics often have leveled this charge.

There are qualifiers in Theory Y, and they are important to an understanding of what McGregor intended. For example, he specifies that people will exercise self-control and self-direction *if* they are committed to the objectives; people will accept and seek responsibility *under proper conditions.* McGregor realized that not all people are psychologically mature and that work is, in fact, a burden to some people, and he also realized that some people are passive and dependent and need to have external control. He adds, however, that people are not like this by nature; instead, their experiences in organizations have made them this way. While McGregor's own style and purpose reflected a Theory Y view of human nature and a management style consistent with Theory Y, he realized that if the manager cannot create the conditions that will lead people to use their creativity or if he cannot gain commitment and involvement, authority and imposed control must be exercised. The key to understanding the differences between the two theories is rigidity versus flexibility. Theory X allows for no flexibility in managerial style, while Theory Y suggests a wide range of styles, depending upon the workforce and the situation.

McGregor argued that managing requires a special kind of skill and expertise because the manager's success is dependent upon effective utilization of the talents, minds, abilities, and efforts of other people. He therefore advocated a professional management founded upon scientifically obtained knowledge of human motivations and behaviors.[13]

Leadership.   Although he uses "manager" as a generic term, throughout McGregor's work there is a recurring theme of leadership. Particularly in his latter years he was principally concerned with understanding and describing the characteristics of effective leaders. Leadership has also been a long-standing interest of one of McGregor's protégés, Warren Bennis, who has written extensively and often provocatively on the subject of leadership. Bennis, one of the key figures in the behavioral science movement himself, makes a marked distinction between managing and leading, arguing that many organizations are managed well but led poorly. He has identified requisite personal traits and behaviors of effective leaders as well as organizational factors that must be present or be created by the leader in order for a would-be leader to lead, positing that leadership can be learned.[14]

Abraham H. Maslow

Maslow, a leader of the humanistic psychology movement, was concerned primarily with the fullest development of human potential; thus his burning interest was the study of superior people. He did not set out to develop a model of employee job motivation, though his theory of human personality has become probably the most influential conceptual basis for employee motivation to be found in modern industry. It is based on Maslow's theorizing and research into how the personality develops and grows and on the cardinal relationship of growth to motivation.

Starting with the assumption that human beings are wanting animals and are forever striving for goals of various kinds, Maslow posited that people want because they *need* these goals. Furthermore, while the finite expression of these needs may vary from individual to individual and from culture to culture, there are certain fundamental stages of need and growth common to all human beings—or at least the potential is present in everyone. Whether a person reaches the upper plateaus of these potential stages of growth depends upon the degree to which lower-level needs are adequately fulfilled. In fact, Maslow categorized these needs into a conceptual hierarchy, called, logically enough, the *hierarchy of needs*.[15] The five levels of the hierarchy, here represented in their ascending pattern of emergence, are

- self-actualization needs
  - esteem needs
    - love and belongingness needs
      - safety needs
        - physiological needs

Physiological needs.   These are the needs for food, warmth, sleep, sex, and other primarily bodily satisfactions.

Safety needs.   These include the need to be free from actual danger, as well as the need for psychological assurance of security.

Love and belongingness needs.   These are the basic needs for other people, social acceptance, and group membership, as well as the need to give and to receive love and affection.

Esteem needs.   These include the need to have the respect and esteem of others, as well as the need for self-esteem.

Self-actualization needs.   These are the needs to realize one's potential fully, to become what one is capable of becoming, and to actualize the real "self," which is more than the basic organism.

The hierarchy implies that needs occur in the order in which they are presented, with physiological needs appearing first, then safety needs, etc. (see Fig. 11-2). This theory of personality and maturation states that until one level of need is fairly well satisfied, the next higher need does not even emerge. Moreover, once a particular set of needs is fulfilled, it no longer motivates. One is not driven to find safety if one is already safe, although if safety is taken away or threatened, it once again becomes the person's driving force or motivation, just as a fish is not motivated to seek water unless it is taken out of water. Stated simply, people are not motivated to achieve goals that they have already reached.

While Maslow posits these five sets of needs as inherently possible for all people, there are impediments of various kinds that can cause a person to reach a certain level of the hierarchy and cease to grow further. Even in relatively mature people, the lower-level needs remain and must be constantly maintained in order for motivation to be directed at the upper-level social and egotistic levels. In fact, the necessity of keeping the lower, more basic and primitive needs satisfied is a key factor in the Maslow model of personality and motivation. Because the lower-level needs are more immediate and urgent, if they are not constantly satisfied, they again come into play as the source and direction of a person's motivation. For example, a person who has climbed up the emotional ladder of the hierarchy of needs to the level of "esteem" will fall back to satisfy the safety needs if his or her safety is threatened.

While Maslow posits a serial nature of needs, it is important to keep in mind that an individual's motivation is not static, fixed, or "set in concrete." Whatever need is operative at a given time becomes the focus of an individual's striving to achieve satisfaction. Despite the tendency to fall back to a lower level if a lower-level need is insufficiently met, this lasts only until the need is satisfied. Then the individual's

Figure 11-2. Maslow's hierarchy of needs.

motivation is once again directed at the appropriate higher-level need. Maslow states explicitly that a person can be identified as being primarily at a given level—the level of prime motivation—at any given point in life. Emotionally healthy and mature persons are found striving to satisfy upper-level needs.

Self-Actualization Is Rare. However, while everyone may have a self-actualizing potential, Maslow's study of superior people indicates that few reach the level at which self-actualization is their prime motivation. Truly self-actualizing people are rare specimens. They are realistically oriented and are accepting of themselves, other people, and the natural world for what they are; they are greatly spontaneous; they are problem-centered, rather than self-centered; they have an air of detachment and a need for privacy; they are autonomous and independent; they have a fresh, rather than stereotyped, appreciation of people and things; they have had profound mystical or spiritual experiences, though not necessarily religious ones; they identify with all human beings rather than a subgroup; they have intimate relationships with a few specially loved people, and these relationships tend to be profound rather than superficial; they possess democratic values and attitudes; they do not confuse means with ends; they have a philosophical, rather than hostile, sense of humor; they have a great fund of creativeness and resist conforming to the culture; and they transcend the environment, rather than merely coping with it.[16]

Frederick Herzberg

Many managers, though intrigued and fascinated by Maslow's theory of personality and motivation, find it difficult to translate into concrete on-the-job application. However, the research and subsequent job redesign prescriptions of Frederick Herzberg and his colleagues are seen by large numbers of managers as a practical and workable means of increasing employee motivation. Yet the work of Herzberg can be understood only in terms of its extrapolation from Maslow's work, although on some fine points the connection is tenuous or represents an interpretation somewhat different from that of Maslow.

Herzberg's research, which has captured the imagination and loyalty of a host of followers (and has infuriated and alienated many others), began not as an inquiry into job redesign as such, but as an investigation of job factors and their relation to employee mental health. Herzberg and his colleagues were attempting to identify which kinds of on-the-job sequences contribute to job satisfaction and which ones cause dissatisfaction.

They found that rarely were the same sorts of events listed as sources of both satisfaction and dissatisfaction. In fact, allowing for some overlap, the things that caused satisfaction had a distinctly different character from that of the things reported as causing dissatisfaction.[17]

Two-Factor Theory. Herzberg hypothesized, then, that the opposite of dissatisfaction is not satisfaction, but simply no dissatisfaction, and that the absence of satisfaction is not dissatisfaction, but no satisfaction. His postulating these sets of factors as different in character, separate, and discrete caused the theory to be called the *Herzberg two-factor theory of job satisfaction*. A listing of the basic factors—which he called *satisfiers* and *dissatisfiers*—may illustrate the substantive differences in their character, though not necessarily in order of importance within each set of factors.

Satisfiers (Job Content Factors or Growth Needs)

Achievement

Recognition

Responsibility

Work itself

Growth

Advancement

Dissatisfiers (Job Context or Hygiene Factors)

Working conditions

Policies and administrative practices

Supervision

Interpersonal relations

Salary (all forms of financial compensation)

Status

Job security

Personal life

Job Enrichment versus Job Enlargement. Building on this model, Herzberg and his colleagues coined the term "job enrichment" to describe the process of redesigning work in order to build in or emphasize the motivators. They prefer the term "job enrichment" over the older term "job enlargement" because, in their view, enriching the job is quite a different thing from increasing the number of tasks. In fact, they refer to job enlargement as *horizontal job loading*, meaning that the job is redesigned to include additional tasks or operations of about the same difficulty as the core job. They insist that little, if any, real motivation will result from this kind of job redesign, since none of the motivators are accounted for, and that adding additional boring jobs to what is already a boring job may even decrease motivation. In contrast, job enrichment, or *vertical job loading*, involves building into the job the motivators by delegating some of the planning and controlling aspects, as well as the "doing" of the job.[18]

There has been widespread criticism of the theory from within the professional ranks of psychology as well as from practitioners in business and industry. Critics charge that the research design is simplistic and that people tend to tell an interviewer what they think the interviewer wants to hear. Perhaps a more telling criticism is based on people's innate ego-defensiveness, which may make them attribute satisfaction or success to themselves and dissatisfaction or failure to the environment or to other people.

Chris Argyris

A recurring theme in research and writing is the effects of organizational life upon the human personality. Because people are social animals, they construct organizations, formal and informal, to meet their need for social contact and to accomplish objectives that individuals cannot accomplish. Since the industrial revolution, there has been an ever-increasing tendency to institutionalize and formalize the aspects of organizations that capitalize on the economy of scale in order to increase output of goods and services.

One outcome, according to Argyris, is the alienation of the persons who make up the organization—a result of the fact that the view of "economic man" underlies and determines the operation of organizations. Ironically, the social and egoistic needs of the people in the organization are largely ignored, when taking them into account could result in the tapping of vast resources of creativity and in the obtaining of employee commitment to organizational objectives. Argyris states that modern organizations are often the source and *cause* of human alienation, apathy, and antagonism because such things as formalized structures, rigid channels of communication, prescriptive job designs, and pyramidal or hierarchical levels of authority are imposed on people in most organizations.

Individual or Organizational Needs?   Chris Argyris is one of the era's most prolific authors of books on management and organization development. His studies through the doctoral level combined economics and psychology and he argued that a degree in only one of these disciplines was not reflective of his broader work and interests. Therefore, he persuaded his university to award him a "new" degree and he is believed to be the first person to receive his doctorate in the field now commonly known as "organizational behavior." Argyris sees a fundamental dichotomy between individual and organizational needs, and because individuals by nature tend to place their own needs before those of the organization, neither their needs nor those of the organization are optimally fulfilled. Argyris argues that this will always be the case if individuals perceive that the organization's needs are given precedence over their own, and he contends that this is the case almost universally in contemporary organizations. He proposes as a solution a radical revamping of organizational practices to allow individuals the opportunity for self-realization in order for their psychological energy to be directed more toward organizational objectives.[19]

Argyris's complex prescription for improved organizational health includes an "open" organization, in which there are challenging goals for its members, work that permits some self-actualization, a highly developed sense of trust and supportiveness, interpersonal competence, a democratizing of decision making, and a decentralization of influence and authority, plus an awareness throughout the organization of the interdependence of its parts. He stresses, too, the dynamic nature of organizations, as opposed to a static view. Furthermore, for increased individual and organizational effectiveness, the dynamic nature of both must always be maintained by keeping the organization flexible enough to change, grow, modify, and adapt its internal structure, roles, processes, practices, and objectives to cope with pervasive change in its members and the environment in which it exists.

David C. McClelland

"Achievement" and "motivation" are ubiquitous concepts in the literature of the behavioral sciences that address themselves to the world of work. While some theories posit a connection between the two concepts, e.g., Herzberg's categorization of achievement as a motivating factor, there is a group of behavioral scientists whose central subject is the motivation to achieve. The best known of these researchers and theorists is David C. McClelland, noted for his studies of the degree of *need for achievement* in persons with varying personalities and social histories.[20]

McClelland and his colleagues have over the years studied individuals to determine how strong their need for achievement is. The research is based not so much on empirical observation of the subjects as on their response to several projective tests commonly used by psychologists in assessment of personality traits and in clinical diagnosis, notably H. A. Murray's Thematic Apperception Test (TAT). From among the 20 cards composing the TAT, which are untitled pictures, McClelland selected those with implicit "achievement imagery." The subject taking the TAT is given each card in succession and is asked to study each card and to imagine who the people in the picture are, what their relationships are, what the scene depicts, what led up to this scene, and what will happen afterward. Essentially the subject projects himself or herself into the picture and becomes one of the "actors" in the scene. The interviewer is alert to the various themes that emerge from the subject's narrative. An important theme, of course, is the need to achieve, a weighty personality and behavior variable.

Relevance of Need Achievement. In McClelland's model, persons are characterized as having either high or low need for achievement (nAch), which may be determined by the overall culture in which he or she was raised, familial relationships and experiences, interpersonal relationships, life experiences, etc. The nature of the nAch, as interpreted by McClelland and others who study achievement motivation, is a strong determinant in occupational choice and in the way people respond to the challenges or tasks that arise out of the job. For example, entrepreneurs predictably test out with high nAch, and among nonentrepreneurial types salespeople tend to demonstrate a high degree of need achievement.

People with high nAch typically are found to:

1. Prefer situations in which they can take personal responsibility for finding solutions to problems
2. Tend to set moderate and realistic achievement goals and to take "calculated" risks
3. Want concrete feedback on how well they are doing

There is a tendency for these people to make decisions themselves, not only to have better control over the outcome but to gain personal satisfaction from achieving. They usually are not given to sharing responsibility or to gambling on chance.

In setting moderate—or what they perceive as realistic—goals, people with high nAch are again selecting situations in which their need for achievement can be satisfied. If the goal is too easy to reach, they gain little sense of achievement; if it is too difficult, they are likely to fail and thus derive no sense of achievement.

The desire for concrete feedback on how they are doing is merely another example of such persons' need to do and achieve. Without the feedback, they do not know whether they are successful.

People with high nAch more frequently resume interrupted tasks after interpolated failure than after interpolated success. Once their need for achievement is satisfied—in this case, returning to a task repeatedly until they have completed or mastered it—they tend to go on to other challenges. On the other hand, people with low nAch tend to resume or to repeat tasks after success rather than after failure.

Cultural Determinants of nAch.   The achievement motive, as already noted, can be determined by a complex interaction of experiences. The research indicates that the degree of emphasis placed upon achievement per se may vary from culture to culture; e.g., some Native Americans test out with higher nAch than others, and the test results underscore the relative emphasis that the respective tribal nations place on achievement. But within a given culture or subculture there are discernible differences between individuals in terms of need for achievement, e.g., how much or how little the parents stressed achievement, what opportunities the individual encounters for psychological success, and how he or she copes with these opportunities. Regardless of the degree of nAch, two significant findings stand out in the diagnostic research on the achievement motive and the empirical research that correlates with the clinical assessments: (1) Rather than being an innate characteristic, the need for achievement is *learned* through a series of reinforcing learning experiences, and (2) it can be taught under the right circumstances.[21]

These two points are the most pungent parts of the achievement-motive research and theory. By first determining the degree of nAch in the individual and then ascertaining the maturational and other learning experiences that were responsible for it, new influences, experiences, and emotional climates can be created to raise the need for achievement. Whereas persons with high nAch require freedom to take risks, pursue challenging goals, and receive their gratification from successful completion of tasks, people with low nAch tend to be more concerned with acceptance by their peers, superiors, and subordinates; with affiliation; and with material rewards for relatively unchallenging tasks. People with high nAch more often seek the *intrinsic* rewards, represented by higher-level needs (à la Maslow), while people with low nAch tend to be motivated by the *extrinsic* rewards that are represented by lower-level needs.

B. F. Skinner

Sporadically throughout the history of psychology as a recognized discipline, the behaviorist school of thought has enjoyed a vogue, only to fall into disfavor with the majority of psychologists after a period of popularity. Virtually every introductory course in psychology includes a review of the early psychological experiments of Pavlov, the Russian physiologist, and his work with dogs. Other names associated with the behaviorist approach, Watson and Thorndike notably, are probably familiar to the layperson too.

Behaviorist psychology, also known as *stimulus-response* (or *stimulus-organism-response*) psychology, is actually a branch of experimental psychology (as contrasted with other branches, such as social and clinical) which is concerned with the kinds of stimuli that will produce a given response or responses and under what conditions. Members of this school tend to be interested in behavior per se and are not very concerned with the more abstract aspects of psychological theory—unconscious motivation, genetic predisposition, etc. Rather, they study the effects of the various stimuli and their ability to induce or modify certain behaviors by accompanying the stimuli with some kind of reward. Once a desired behavior or behavioral pattern is achieved through response to stimuli and rewards, the organism (or subject of the experiment) tends to maintain the behavior, even after the reward is taken away. All that is required, once the behavior is "locked in," is the stimulus associated with the reward, which produces a *conditioned response.*

For example, in the famous Pavlov research, there is the oft-cited experiment in which a bell was sounded simultaneously with the presentation of meat to the dog in his laboratory. After the dog had come to associate the repeated stimulus (bell) with the repeated reward (meat), Pavlov discovered that he could cease providing the meat, and the dog's response (salivation) would still occur each time the bell sounded.

Roots in Stimulus-Response Psychology. The work of B. F. Skinner follows generically the stimulus-response approach, though with some considerable modifications. Like his fellow behaviorists, he is concerned only with overt behavior that can be observed, predicted, and changed. He does not deny the existence of unconscious processes and motives or of genetic and cultural determinants of personality or behavior. He simply does not attempt to study them or take them into account in his highly scientifically controlled research. He states that modification of such things as genetically produced motivations is an extremely difficult and long-term task—because they are fundamentally resistant to change—while modification of overt behavior is relatively much more simple. He feels, therefore, that the minds, energies, and talents of psychologists ought to be directed toward changing behaviors, rather than delving into complex or metaphysical origins of behavior. Moreover, even when it can be shown that some aspect of behavior is due to season of birth, gross body type, or genetic constitution, the fact is of limited use. It may help in predicting behavior, but it is of little value in an experimental analysis or in practical control because such a condition cannot be manipulated.

Focus on Modifying Behavior. Skinner's chief interest is thus the manipulation and control of behavior. He proceeds on the assumption that all behavior is orderly and lawful and that the greater the understanding of cause and effect, the greater the potential for behavioral change, or, to use his term, *behavioral modification.* So far his position is not unlike that of other stimulus-response psychologists. The principal difference, however, is Skinner's emphasis on the *operant,* which he defines as "a response that operates on the environment and changes it." Operants are factors not necessarily directly associated with an applied stimulus—for example, a direct response to a stimulus, after the response has been sufficiently conditioned, such as the reflex of dropping a hot coal. Operants, while also logical and stimulated by something in the environment, cannot always be traced to an observable stimulus—for example, crossing from one side of the street to the other.[22]

The crux of Skinner's method of behavioral modification is *reinforcement.* Whenever a desired behavior occurs, whether in direct response to an applied stimulus or to an operant, it is rewarded, in order to increase the probability of its recurrence. This is positive reinforcement. Conversely, whenever an undesired behavior occurs, it is punished, in order to decrease the probability of recurrence. Frequent reinforcement of the operants will cause the behavior to become conditioned; therefore, the theory is often referred to as *operant conditioning* or *operant reinforcement*. The behavior becomes "locked in" if the reward (or punishment) follows the behavior immediately, because the subject more readily associates the reinforcing factor with the behavior. While this is an important factor in operant reinforcement, an almost equally important consideration is the schedule of reinforcement. Once the subject has associated the reward with the behavior, rewards are withheld and given irregularly. For instance, rather than administer the reward after each demonstration of behavior (which could lessen the subject's association of the operant and its reinforcement), one gives intermittent rewards, which are apt to increase the rate of response: the subject keeps performing the behavior until he or she is rewarded. Variable or intermittent rewards further tend to make the learned response more resistant to extinction.

While most of Skinner's research has been in laboratories using animals, mainly rats and pigeons, he and his disciples show no trepidation in extrapolating and generalizing the applicability of their findings to human behavior. In fact, the Skinnerian model has been adopted in a wide range of applications, including missile control, aspects of space technology, educational technology, treatment of the mentally ill, behavioral assay of psychoactive drugs, and the development of experimental cultures and societies.

Programmed Learning.   Another widespread application of Skinner's work is in training and development, especially in job-skills training, though sometimes not identified as such. The training and development professional is likely to be familiar with at least one educational technology that can be traced to Skinner, not only for its rationale and methodology, but also for its actual development as well. One of the first examples of "programmed learning" was developed by Skinner and his associate, J. G. Holland.[23] The Skinnerian principles are readily discernible in programmed learning systems in which the learner gets immediate feedback on the solution to a problem or the answer to a question. The learner is usually told when an answer is correct (desired response) and instructed to continue (reward), but if the answer is incorrect or insufficient, the instruction is to try again or revert to previous material (punishment). Moreover, until the desired response is given, the learner may not proceed, and no further material will be supplied. In practice, programmed instruction or programmed learning techniques may be used in individual or group training, employing a variety of instructional methodologies. Increasingly, a method of self-instruction is being used in the form of computer-assisted learning, or CAL. CAL is one of the clearest examples of the application of programmed instruction. (Also see Chap. 26, Interactive Multimedia Training Systems, and Chap. 40, Computer Skills Training.)

Recently there has been an upsurge of interest in operant reinforcement and behavior modification in business organizations, quite apart from interest in programmed learning. Increasingly, companies are applying Skinnerian techniques to improve on-the-job performance in a systematic way. Employees get instantaneous feedback on, and evaluation of, their performance of daily tasks. If a job is done well, the employee is rewarded for it, possibly by direct recognition from a superior, or possibly by the posting of his or her accomplishments for peers to see. The "reward" may also take the form of giving the employee a preferred work assignment. And in some instances companies are trying to effect that often-heralded ideal of tying financial rewards and promotion to *actual* performance and, further, of associating performance with reward in employees' minds.[24]

Stratified Systems Theory

Stratified systems theory (SST) developed from the work of Elliott Jaques, whose early interest was in studying the nature of tasks and their complexity with a view toward establishing equitable rates of pay in industrial organizations. It has evolved to a somewhat complex theory of organization and organization behavior with special implications for organization planning and structure, job design, career pathing and development, and personal competency.[25]

SST is basically a systematic theory of work in social organizations. Based on extensive study of organizations with a wide variety of purposes, it appears that there are fixed and observable hierarchical levels in most organizations, regardless of the nature or purpose of the organization and regardless of the environment or culture in which it exists. These levels or strata develop because the character of the work at successively higher levels is fundamentally different and more complex than at lower levels. For a given level to function properly, it must bring to bear a degree of thinking, perspective, and scope that not only builds upon the work of lower levels but integrates it into a larger and more complex framework. As one climbs the hierarchy one finds a greater number and a more complicated set of variables to deal with, and each successively higher level must have the capacity to integrate the work of the levels immediately below it.

Time-Span and Time-Frame. Although it is impossible in this space to discuss even simplistically all the concepts embodied in SST, it is essential to look at some related principles which are used to determine the nature of work at the respective organizational strata and for assessing the capability of people to perform well at each strata. Among the key concepts of SST are *time-span* and *time-frame*. Time is the common variable in both because, among the many ways of describing work and its structuring, the time factor is easily understood and readily measured.

Time-span refers to the task with the longest duration at respective hierarchical levels. Within the lower strata these tasks are of relatively short duration and are therefore completed within a brief time-span. At the highest levels, by contrast, the time-span encompasses strategic decisions and actions, which by necessity have very long time-spans. At lower strata even the longest task may have relatively short duration, and its consequences will be seen immediately. At higher strata the duration and the impact are truly long-range.

Whereas time-span describes the tasks to be done in performing work and meeting job objectives, the related term *time-frame* is used to denote the complexity of the longest task people are capable of handling. Time-frame is a measure of the level or strata of work that people do. All work has certain prescribed limits or requirements which specify what a person must or must not do to accomplish the work. The qualifier in this construct is "discretion" in performing the work. The more complex the task, and therefore appropriate at higher organizational levels, the more discretion a person has in how to do the work and the more ambiguity he or she must deal within in exercising discretion in its performance.

In other words, most jobs involve a variety of tasks, but the time-span is based on which task takes the longest to complete. However, the longest tasks may not be the majority of the tasks to complete, but they are the most crucial measure of the work. Time-frame is a measure of the ability of an individual to perform at various hierarchical levels with increasing complexity. Another way of looking at time-frame is to assess how long a person can be left unsupervised to perform a task without veering off-course or causing problems for the organization.

Implications for Management.   Interest in applying the concepts of SST has waxed and waned over the past three decades and there has been a small but passionate coterie of devotees. There has, within the past few years, been a resurgence of interest in SST on the part of organizational theorists and developmental specialists, and Jaques' work has attracted new adherents including several small OD consulting firms and at least one organization whose previous work was rooted in psychoanalytically oriented psychology. This may be due partly to the special language employed by its theorists, language that sometimes seems unclear to a casual reader. It may also be due to people's not looking beyond the *prima facie* theory of hierarchical organization structures. There is some evidence, too, that the behavioral sciences have had sufficient influence on management and that there is a trend to push decisions down to the point of their impact rather than have data travel upward through organizational levels for decision making or "blessing," then travel downward to the locus of the problem or opportunity. If one considers the management implication of stratified systems theory, it not only appears consistent with decentralization and decision making at lower organizational levels but mandates an enriching of managerial jobs at lower strata.[26]

Figure 11-3 illustrates the various strata or levels of work, with time-spans ranging from 3 months to 50 years. This chart shows the seven levels that exist in most business organizations, with roughly analogous levels in military organizations. (Figure 11-3 includes military organizations because Jaques' work in most recent times has been with validation of his theories within the military.) The description of the work appropriately done at corporate or strategic levels differs in its fundamental character from the work at "operations" and "comprehensive" managerial levels. In SST the highest level of "direct command" appears to be at Stratum V, and, while there are *official* reporting levels at Strata VI and VII, the actual relationships are most often that of colleagues who may possess complementary skills and who are properly concerned with long-range issues. From Stratum V and downward, clear boss-subordinate relationships, in the traditional hierarchical sense, obtain.

Dysfunctional Organizations.   Even in the most patently hierarchical organizations it is not uncommon to observe managers at the "strategic" level becoming involved in day-to-day operating matters, sometimes resulting in a truncating of the lower managers' authority (and motivation) and at the same time taking higher-level managers themselves away from their jobs of charting and managing major change.

SST posits that the hierarchical levels—usually seven though theoretically eight in very large organizations—exist because they evolve naturally to advance the organization's purpose. They are not arbitrary levels or strata. If a higher level does not have the capability of and the responsibility for processing and integrating the work of lower levels, it serves no useful purpose. SST research has shown repeatedly that, regardless of the content of the work, a manager at a given stratum cannot effectively assess or integrate the works of others at the same stratum, let alone those with higher-level time-spans and time-frames. Yet many organizations are dysfunctional because they try to organize themselves and function with disregard for these principles.

Stratum or Level of Work	Time-span		Description	Civilian Organization	Military Organization
	50 years				
VII			Strategic design; development; deployment of complex systems	Corporation	Joint Chiefs of Staff
	20 years	Strategic			
VI			Direct deployment of complex systems	Group	Corps
	10 years				
V			Complex system; encompassing operating systems and modifying context	Subsidiary	Division
	5 years	Comprehensive			
IV			Alternative operating systems— general management	General Management	Brigade
	2 years				
III			Direct-operating systems— management of a mutual recognition unit	Unit	Battalion
	1 year				
II		Operational	Direct operating methods— supervision of a mutual knowledge system	Section	Company
	3 months				
I			Direct operating tasks	Shop Floor	Squad

Figure 11-3. Levels of work in civilian and military organizations.

For example, in some regionalized and decentralized organizations one finds research scientists, whose time-frame may be quite advanced and whose work has a time-span of 10 or more years, reporting to a unit manager whose time-span may be only 2 or 3 years. One result may be scientists who feel (and often are) misunderstood and unappreciated, and who nevertheless must defer to the management decisions of the unit manager (at Stratum III).

Another example of inefficiency and ineffectiveness may be found when one examines the various planning systems of many organizations. Typically, corporate-level management (Strata VI and VII) has responsibility for so-called long-range planning, whether or not there is a corporate staff department charged with this responsibility. Corporate strata may undertake to plan for the next 10 years or beyond, while "general" management (Strata IV and V) may do 3-year plans, and divisional management (Stratum III) may develop 18-month or 2-year plans. All these plans get reexamined, restated, and revised annually. SST research, using sophisticated trend extrapolation procedures and complex forecasting models, suggests that planning is most effective when it is tied to the median time-frame for each stratum. Further, there is a mathematical deterioration in the probability of accuracy with most planning tools and methods beyond 7 years. Moreover, the planning that usually occupies the corporate strata is not only inaccurate but unhelpful and dysfunctional, because the thinking, planning, and decision making that go on at corporate strata are extrapolative and linear. SST theory states that the "planning" at the top strata ought to go beyond linear forecasting. Instead, the corporate strategy ought to be concerned with environmental scanning, anticipating major events and trends, and creating the future that is wanted or needed. Then linear planning is left to lower strata, where its impact is felt and managed.[27]

Redundant Levels and Positions.   Despite some indications of new and experimental forms of organization, most organizations still hold on tenaciously to some traditional principles of span-of-control. SST proponents claim that if "true" strata are built into organizational design, span-of-control can be expanded appreciably. Not only does SST prescribe the basic seven managerial levels but it states that more levels or strata are unnecessary, even in *very* large organizations. (In the military whole, intact, fighting armies are managed by brigadier generals, Stratum IV managers.)

Myers-Briggs Type Indicator

The groundbreaking research of Carl Gustav Jung (1875–1961), the Swiss psychologist and psychiatrist, on the origins and development of personality must be described as monumental. Yet for a very long time, the contributions of Jung were eclipsed by those of his contemporary, sometime colleague, sometime adversary, Sigmund Freud. Each, along with Alfred Adler, was the founder of a school of psychology that stressed the importance of unconscious influences on feelings and behavior, as contrasted with the behavioral schools that stress observable behavior to the virtual exclusion of nonconscious motivations. Jung's position as a scientist has been derogated as unscientific by some persons who otherwise acknowledge his unique contributions to the study of humankind, possibly because of his interest in and use of the occult. Ironically, it can be argued that Jungian theories lend themselves more readily to verification, to controlled research, and to validation than those of many of his colleagues, notably his theories, and supporting research, into "racial memory" or the "collective unconscious." Similar beliefs, practices, and behaviors occur in disparate cultures, widely dispersed and having no common history or contact with each other.

Like Freud with the terms "id, ego, and superego," and Adler with his "inferiority and superiority complexes," some of the basic language of Jung's collection of work and theory, called "analytic psychology," have entered the common vocabulary without the average person's being aware of the origin of the terms. Two words that readily come to mind are *introversion* and *extroversion*, denoting fundamental differences in personality and behavior.[28]

The concepts of extroversion and introversion also happen to be key elements in one of the most dynamic and influential forces in the contemporary behavioral sciences, called the *Myers-Briggs Type Indicator* (MBTI). In a relatively short time MBTI has captured the interest of psychologists, psychotherapists, educators, clergy, and others in the "people professions." Not least among those attracted to MBTI and its multiple applications are businesspeople, especially those concerned with individual and organizational behavior, including training and organization development specialists. The MBTI is a psychometric instrument that, at the same time, depends completely upon Jung's work, while elaborating the basic concepts and adding related theoretical constructs that help to translate Jungian thought into a practical and useful tool.

The Two Attitudes.   Carl Jung observed that all people are *constitutionally* disposed to view life differently, in either of two modes, *extroversion* or *introversion*, called *attitudes*. Because these terms have been adopted in popular language, it is useful to clarify what Jung actually intended them to mean. To the average person, an extrovert is someone who is outgoing, easily accessible, open, and epitomized by the old-time salesman. And the introvert is commonly thought of as someone who is quiet, maybe somewhat shy or withdrawn, closed, and epitomized by the scholar or "bookworm." Directionally at least, these stereotypes are not without basis, but they are only stereotypes and often not descriptive of either the personality or behavior of persons characterized by either attitude.

The crucial element in understanding what is meant by introversion and extroversion is the flow of *energy*. Extroverts derive most of their energy from phenomena outside themselves, from events, things, environment, and other people. In the introvert energy comes from within themselves, and the energy is more often subjective than objective. Extroverts interact with the environment and *need* externals, including people. Introverts draw more on inner strengths and function quite well alone. Extroverts deal in empirical, concrete things. Introverts are charged by ideas and concepts.

All humans have the capacity for extroversion and introversion, but people typically develop a basic attitude or predisposition to *prefer* either an extroverted or introverted mode of existence. Well-developed extroverts deal very effectively with perceptions and ideas, and well-developed introverts deal ably with the external world when necessary, but introverts are usually more comfortable with reflection and what is inside them. *Preference* is the key to understanding these differences. These preferences develop *very* early in life, determined possibly by genetic or social factors—or both. The average person has two hands, and both are used constantly, but most people are decidedly right-handed or left-handed, a function of a fundamental predispositional makeup. A given reality or event may be experienced by two people, but the extrovert tends to deal with the immediacy of the event and its impact, while the introvert may be more interested in the implications of the event than in its observable consequences.

Behavior is often situational, and the empirical behavior of a person does not *necessarily* indicate his or her basic attitude, whether it be extroversion or introversion. For example, extroverts may deal with concepts very effectively; and introverts may excel in certain professions that involve constant and close contact with other people. Some of the popular confusion about the terms may be due to Jung's choosing introversion to describe an attitude that connotes inward orientation, and people sometimes use it as a synonym for introspection, implying an inability to look beyond oneself.

It is important to note that, because all people possess the capacity for both extroversion and introversion, Jung acknowledged that rarely, if ever, does one find a "pure" introvert or extrovert, certainly not in mentally healthy people. Further, the extent to which a person uses extroversion or introversion may change to accommodate circumstances, but the fundamental predisposition or preference does not change.

The Functions.   While a grasp of the concepts of extroversion and introversion is absolutely essential to any understanding of Jung's work or to the Myers-Briggs Type Indicator, the two attitudes cannot stand alone. They must be complemented by what Jung referred to as "conscious psychological functions," which are, in a sense, subdivisions or subclassifications of the two basic attitudes. The functions are kinds of psychic activity that theoretically remain the same in varying circumstances.

Jung identified four psychological functions or modes of action:

1. *Thinking:* rational processes that elicit purpose or *meaning* from the object we observe, thereby forming a concept of it.
2. *Feeling:* informs us of the *value,* or use, of the object or occurrence.
3. *Sensing:* informs through the *senses* of sight, touch, smell, hearing, etc.
4. *Intuition:* the time dimension that points to *possibilities* that lie ahead.

In each of the above functions the key word in the definition is in italics. Additional clarification might include: *thinking* refers to conscious, objective, thought processes; *feeling* is highly subjective and highly individual; *sensing* is immediate and empirical; *intuition* refers both to vision of the future as well as to the often vague, sometimes undefined, "knowledge" on something of an instinctive level.

Just as humans possess introverted and extroverted attitudes, they also possess simultaneously all four functions, according to Jung. And, typically, people perceive life and its experiences predominately through one of the four functions, supported usually by a secondary function. In other words, we typically develop one function (and to a lesser degree another one) while neglecting the others in most instances. All are present in all of us, but we typically *prefer* one of the functions as our mode of dealing with events and ideas. Moreover, he saw the functions as two pairs of opposites, that is, sensing *or* intuiting, feeling *or* thinking.

Jung's typology describes a personality first in terms of introversion or extroversion, then in terms of the four functions. The result is eight basic types, e.g., extroverted thinker or introverted thinker; extroverted feeler or introverted feeler, and so on.

Origins of MBTI.   Jung admitted that *possibly* there are more than four functions, but in his direct experience and from his extensive research into psychological types in many cultures, he could discover only four basic functions.

At first independent of Jung's work, but later influenced by it and revising her work to incorporate it, Katherine Briggs began in the first quarter of this century to develop her own psychological typology, mainly from biography. When Jung's typological theories were published in English (in 1923), her interest in psychological type intensified. Katherine Briggs introduced typology into her family and profoundly influenced her daughter Isabel, who later married and kept her surname as well as that of her husband.

Isabel Briggs-Myers over a long lifespan collected data on psychological type, at first on an anecdotal basis and later with large research populations. Having received encouragement and some concrete support from principals in a major consulting firm and a developer of psychometrics, she eventually was able to test students in a public school system, using the early forms of what later was refined into the current MBTI instrument. Subsequently she had access to a medical school and tested the psychometric instrument on 10,000 nurses and 5000 medical students.

Her data bank grew and the instrument was modified several times to reflect subsequent findings. But Isabel Briggs-Myers found little interest and support among psychologists. This was due to several factors, among them a lack of general acceptance of the feasibility of measuring basic personality through psychometric instruments (more often the instruments used are projective techniques), the unpopularity of typological theories of personality per se, and surely the credibility of Briggs-Myers. Despite her diligent research, she was not a psychologist. She was basically self-taught in statistics and psychometrics. She persisted and gradually gained support from a handful of supporters. In 1962, Educational Testing Service published her test for research purposes but did little to promote it. Support and acceptance in the professional and academic communities continued to come slowly, but some support was forthcoming from a few respected academics. In 1975 publication of the MBTI and administration manuals was transferred to Consulting Psychologists' Press. The Center for Applications of Psychological Type was established to carry out further research and to provide service to users of the MBTI.

The MBTI has been validated on a variety of populations, including students, teachers, nurses, physicians, marketers, administrators, and managers, among others.

As validation studies have progressed, variations and extensions of the basic instrument have been developed. The form in widest current usage remains the 126-item questionnaire, which is scored by a certified professional. The Center for Applications of Psychological Type, The Association for Psychological Type, and others are experimenting with some more elaborate forms of the MBTI instrument, including one long one that attempts to break down the 16 fundamental types into subsets in order to describe more fully the nuances of the basic types or to understand the seeming anomalies in the personality types of certain individuals. For example, the ostensible paradox of the shy extrovert, or the person who tests out as a strong intuitor but who is expert at proofreading, a skill normally associated with sensors.

Going Beyond Jung. A significant departure from Jung, or possibly a further refinement of Jungian theory, is Myers-Briggs' addition of two extra dimensions to the total picture of a given psychological type. The MBTI incorporates these two dimensions as an integral part of the personality type. They are *perceiving* and *judging*.[29]

Perceiving is defined as a process of becoming aware of things, people, occurrences, and ideas, of gathering data. *Judging* includes the process of coming to conclusions about things that are perceived.

These two dimensions are viewed by Briggs-Myers as not only complementary to the Jungian personality theory but essential to a fuller understanding of the theory itself and to a more complete understanding of human personality. She posits that the methods of *perceiving* actually explain and make operational the *sensing* or the *intuiting*. In other words, intuiting and sensing are two different ways of perceiving.

In a similar vein, Briggs-Myers sees *feeling* and *thinking* as two different ways of reaching conclusions about reality or *judging*.

People with a marked preference for perceiving are more comfortable with open-ended situations, to gathering more data. Those with a judging preference more readily make interpretations of data, reach conclusions, seek closure.

In summary, the MBTI typology comprises 16 basic types of personality, determined by one's basic predispositions toward:

- Extroversion (E) or Introversion (I)
- Intuiting (N) or Sensing (S)
- Thinking (T) or Feeling (F)
- Judging (J) or Perceiving (P)

The parentheses after each preference show the initials used in shorthand descriptions of each preference. With the exception of N for intuiting (to avoid confusion with the I for introversion) they are the first letter of each preference. The 16 types are described by the four letters that describe, respectively, each type; e.g., ISFP is an introverted, sensing, feeling, perceiver. The exact opposite on each dimension is an ENTJ, an extroverted, intuiting, thinking, judger. The 16 types can, and do, include various combinations of descriptive letters, each one of which describes a major modification in preference and type. There are ESFJs, ISFJs, ENTPs, INTPs, ESTJs, etc.

The Four Temperaments. While each of the 16 basic types contains significant differences on each dimension of choice or preference, there is a further grouping of type components called *temperaments*. While they may have considerable differences, their common preferences and behaviors are said to outweigh the differences. For example, an ESFP may be quite different from an ISTP, but they share the SP preferences and are likely to be more akin than different, the extroversion-introversion scale and their other differences notwithstanding, because they are sensing perceivers. The grouping of type components into the temperaments and the accompanying labels from Greek mythology is primarily the work of David Keirsey and Marilyn Bates. Many users of the MBTI agree with this categorization, but the temperaments construct and its assertion that the groupings are logical is not universally accepted as integral to MBTI thought or application.

The four temperaments have been variously described, but they are popularly described and labeled with the names of Greek gods of mythology, with whom they share preferences and behaviors.[30]

1. *Dionysian (SP)*. Seek freedom, value spontaneity, and resist being constrained or obligated. Do things because the *process* of doing them is pleasing, regardless of the goal or outcome. Action-driven, here-and-now, thrive on crisis situations requiring immediate action or response. Often optimists. Not easily controlled.

2. *Epithean (SJ)*. Strong affiliation needs, sense of duty and obligation, keepers of traditions, get satisfaction from serving and giving, strong work ethic. Want, but often cannot request, recognition and appreciation for what they perceive as merited. Often pessimists. Group acceptance serves as control and elicits conformity to group norms.

3. *Promethian (NT)*. *Must* understand, predict, explain, and harness phenomena. Value competence above all else, in themselves and others. Thrive on challenge and strive to control a variety of situations. Most self-critical of all, and constantly set higher and higher goals of perfection; therefore, aware of own shortcomings and never satisfied with accomplishment. Embarrassed by praise.

4. *Apollonian (NF)*. Sets extraordinary goals, even transcendent ones, that are hard even for NFs to explain. Strive for "real" or "truest" self, and are always

in process of "becoming." Work, relationships, efforts must be imbued with "meaning." Hard workers, if cause is deemed worthwhile, and tireless in pursuit of a cause. Can be a gadfly in pursuing one goal after another.

Dominant and Auxiliary Processes.   In MBTI theory, everyone can be described by one of the 16 types, written as four-letter profiles. Just as people possess all of the type components but typically learn and prefer to use some processes more than others, they also have dominant and auxiliary processes within their own type. For example, ESFP describes someone who is an extroverted, sensing, feeling, perceiver. However, not all four letters play an equal part in determining the type and its resultant modes of behaving. In the ESFP person, the dominant mode is S for sensing, with the auxiliary F for feeling. By contrast, the ESTJ is characterized as having a dominant T for thinking, with the S for sensing as auxiliary.

There are several ways to find the dominant and auxiliary processes for each of the 16 basic types, some of them fairly complicated. True to form, the extrovert's dominant process is more evident than the introvert's, because introverts do not show their dominant type in outward behavior. Even their dominant preference is introverted or hidden from others. For quick reference a chart showing the 16 types appears as Fig. 11-4. The dominant process for each type is circled.

Indicating Type.   To ascertain a person's type, the psychometric instrument can be used that is a series of questions with multiple-choice answers, complemented by a group of word pairs. Persons being tested are told to choose their answers without second thoughts, on the assumption that initial reactions or choices are apt to be more spontaneous and therefore more indicative of the person's true preferences. There are no right or wrong choices, since the instrument is not normative. Rather it is intended to get a reading of the person's basic type, without any judgments or prescriptive biases.

Results of the MBTI will type a person into one of the 16 basic types. It is important to note, however, that there are scales for each dimension; e.g., one person's S may be more pronounced than that of another person who also comes out an S.

The instrument has gone through several revisions and modifications, as validation data has been amassed and analyzed over the years. The instrument comprises written questions and is self-administered. The form in widest current usage consists of 126 items or questions. The MBTI is scored by a trained professional, and feedback is given to the respondent. There is also an abbreviated version with 50 items that can be self-scored.

ST	SF	NF	NT
I(S)TJ	I(S)FJ	I(N)FJ	I(N)TJ
IS(T)P	IS(F)P	IN(F)P	IN(T)P
E(S)TP	E(S)FP	E(N)FP	E(N)TP
ES(T)J	ES(F)J	EN(F)J	EN(T)J

Figure 11-4. Dominant processes in MBTI (dominant process for each type circled).

Although the Myers-Briggs type indicator (MBTI) is intended for "normal" or healthy populations and does not attempt to diagnose or otherwise deal with psychopathology, it is a controlled test, and the publishers try to restrict administration to those specially trained and approved for access to the test.

Socialization, Language, Culture.   Jung maintained an abiding interest in the study of many cultures, including Asian and African as well as European and western civilizations. Indeed, he posited that his basic theories of personalities transcend cultural barriers, though he offered little explanation or insight about how his types evolved. One theory is that type is innate, since topological preferences emerge very early in a person's life and do not change appreciably throughout one's lifetime. However, on at least one dimension of the MBTI, some women will show a marked preference for thinking over feeling, although when they were still girls they may have shown a preference for feeling. It is widely believed that these women were always thinkers but that they were socialized into feeling behaviors which were thought more "appropriate" for females in western societies. Though probably less frequently, some males are "socialized" into stereotypical behaviors and may demonstrate a thinking preference as boys but show a natural preference for feeling as adult males.

Some validation research has investigated the possible role society and culture play in determining type. Indeed, there are some cultures in which certain type profiles predominate beyond the expected distribution among populations, even to the extent of suggesting a quasi-"national" type.

The MBTI was developed on and for an English-speaking, fundamentally North American population. The MBTI instrument has been translated into several languages including French, Spanish, and Japanese (with much of the slang and colloquial terms that appear in the English-language versions removed) and the instrument is in wide usage in many parts of the world. But still more research is needed to explain, with any acceptable degree of certainty, the relative weight culture should be given in determining type.

Applications and Uses of MBTI.   In a relatively short time the MBTI has been adopted by a variety of professions. It is, arguably, the most widely used psychometric test for nonclinical, nonpsychiatric populations although it was not in popular usage until the early 1980s.

Although it is a relatively uncomplicated instrument that yields quick and easily understood data, aside from statistically controlled reliability and validity studies, users and proponents rate the MBTI as an unusually accurate descriptor of personality and behavior. While acknowledging that individuals are unique and that even among those whose type is described by the same four letters there are marked differences, the MBTI is nevertheless amazingly predictive of behavioral traits and predispositions. Given a particular event or phenomenon, observed or experienced by a variety of people, those with the same MBTI type have a high probability of interpreting and acting on the stimulus in a recognizably similar manner, because they share a constellation of personality components.

The MBTI has found widespread usage in formal education, from early school through higher education; individual, couples, family, and group counseling; career guidance; and communications, to name but a few.

Organizations, including business organizations, have found the MBTI especially useful in training and development and organization development, because of its relevance and applicability to a host of concerns, including selective placement, career pathing, management style and leadership, team and intergroup development, management of individual differences, conflict resolution, and adult learning methodologies.

Appreciative Inquiry

"If it ain't broke, don't fix it" is a popular and telling adage in our culture. People around the globe, and especially in western civilizations, have a proclivity for concentrating on negative aspects of situations. We value problem solving, trouble shooting, and the ability to detect the hidden flaw and to locate errors or dysfunctional elements. In activities and behaviors ranging from child rearing to managerial style, we tend to concentrate on what one should *not* do, and most rules and regulations are couched in terms of what is unacceptable or forbidden. Too rarely do we articulate what one should do or what in a given situation is going well. Even in so-called organizational improvement or organizational development interventions, ostensibly designed to move the organization in a positive direction, we most often concentrate on fixing things that are wrong rather than identifying what is right.

Appreciative Inquiry is an emerging behavioral science technology, based on an action-research model and clearly normative, that approaches organizational diagnosis from the standpoint of understanding what are positive events or characteristics in the organization, analyzes and operationalizes them, and develops models that will reinforce and multiply them throughout an organization. Once a positive phenomenon is understood, it can be emulated, replicated, and taught as a means of achieving the organization's desired goals and behaviors. Among professionals who are using Appreciative Inquiry, the common advice is "catch someone doing something right." While concentrating on positive occurrences, Appreciative Inquiry (AI) is more than just "positive thinking." It is a means of social inquiry and resultant training and organization development that has more in common with Skinner and "operant conditioning" than it does with Norman Vincent Peale and later self-improvement gurus. It shares with Lewin's action research the belief that, in seeking to cause behavioral change, one must recognize that there are positive and negative forces at play in any given situation and that one's probability of achieving the desired change is greater if one reinforces the positive or "driving" forces.[31] Although AI has some fairly complex psychological underpinning, its technology and its techniques are easily grasped and applied. Despite its emphasis on the affirmative aspects of a situation, the stimulus for introduction of Appreciative Inquiry's methodology is often a perceived problem.

The potential for application of the technology is virtually limitless, as two disparate examples illustrate. AI is currently being used as the principal OD technology, and in subsequent training programs, in a large Latin American company whose representation of women in management is minimal and whose management wants to create an organizational climate that will be more supportive to the few women managers in the company and more conducive to attracting other capable women. AI is also being utilized by consultants who are working with Ugandan villages in an attempt to change behaviors in a positive direction and to help to halt the spread of AIDS. Clearly, in both of these examples, a problem precipitated the introduction of AI, but in both instances the change being sought is mainly dependent upon positive reinforcement. Both incorporate individual and group training as an essential part of the change strategies.

Evolution and Organizational Systems

As the behavioral sciences have evolved over the years, the extent to which they have had real influence and been useful in providing insight and tools to assist management has depended, in large part, on the user's "gestalt" view of organizations, i.e., the extent to which one takes a systems view of organizations and organizational change. There are many ways of analyzing and describing organizations but the more useful models include the belief that organizations, like humans, are complex and comprise a network of mutually dependent and interacting parts and systems. Although the organization has been described in different ways, most systems theory posits that *any* organization, regardless of its structure or purpose, has at least three basic systems:

1. *Technical or operating system:* the fundamental tasks, the know-how, the processes that the organization performs or produces; the reason the organization exists.
2. *Administrative system:* the ways the organization does its business; policies, procedures, rules, norms.
3. *Social system:* the people who make up the organization; individual and group behavior.

Systems theory includes the belief that if one intervenes or changes something in one of these systems, the other two are affected. Some of the earliest attempts to change organizations, including primitive forms of industrial engineering and time-and-motion studies, often worked only in the technical or administrative systems while ignoring the social system. On the other hand, many applications of the behavioral sciences concentrated on the social system to the exclusion of the technical and administrative systems and attempted organization change via social interventions exclusively.

Reengineering and TQM

In recent years, there have been several influential movements in organizational life that, at least in part, have recognized the need to address the organization's three systems and become more integrative. Two that come to mind readily are the *Total Quality Management* movement and organizational *reengineering.*

Total Quality Management (TQM) usually incorporates methodologies that address the technical system and often the administrative system while utilizing its human resources in fuller, more creative ways. Typically, it uses small-group problem-solving methods to achieve its objectives, which include increased emphasis on quality in the products or services of the organization and often a major emphasis on customer-client service.

Reengineering, ideally at least, addresses the technical-operating system and the administrative system and it often includes consideration of the social system. Reengineering usually incorporates such venerable methods as industrial engineering and "short-interval scheduling" while utilizing rational problem solving, small-group process, and sociotechnical inputs to achieve major change in the way organizations are structured and manage work flow.[32]

Paradigm Shifts and "Jobless" Organizations

Regardless of the change being sought, there is increasing evidence that one's "mindset" toward the change must undergo radical reorientation. People speak of changing or shifting one's *paradigm.* A paradigm is defined simply as a pattern or model involving concrete reality as well as one's perception and belief systems about what one perceives or experiences. Paradigms include sets of rules and regulations that are used to set boundaries and inform people on how to think and behave inside those boundaries for psychological success. Regarding change in individuals and organizations, a shift in paradigms means the ability to step outside a given situation and look at it anew through different eyes—to "get out of the box"—in order to evolve a new model, a whole new way of organizing perceptually the reality of belief.[33]

Paradigm shifts take place frequently but usually through a complex process of changing one's beliefs and attitudes, whether planned or not, whether as a result of conscious action or as a result of a new and different experience. For example, until after World War II, many people held a paradigm of the Japanese as a backward, bellicose people who produced cheap goods. Today's paradigm of Japan as a (arguably *the*) dominant economic power in the world and by far the front runner in many forms of technology could hardly have been imagined not long ago.

Similarly, paradigm shifts occur on a personal level and certainly in the life of organizations, and these are usually complex, too. For example, after decades of theorizing and talking about it, many organizations are actually setting up self-managed work groups. In addition to the selection of the group's members and concomitant reengineering of certain work-flow processes, often a paradigm shift is required first. Likely, this involves a radical paradigm shift on the part of management who must, minimally, discard some traditional views about managerial control and shift to a new paradigm that includes trust in people's intelligence, integrity, creativity, and a sense of responsibility, in order to organize work groups in which the group itself manages individual and group behavior, quality, output, and productivity. In this case, to paraphrase, the paradigm shift is from a Theory X to a Theory Y view of people at work. Equally, a paradigm shift may be required on the part of people who do the work, who are trained to plan, organize, do, and control themselves—activities traditionally performed by their bosses.

In fact, there is evidence that a major paradigm shift is occurring in relation to the basic social contract between employer and employee. This shift has come about through the creation of a more flexible workplace and organizations that have realized they can function—indeed, even be *more* productive—without the boundaries that have for so long defined the workplace. Organizations are realizing that where and when one performs work is not necessarily the determinant of either the quantity or quality of the work. "Flextime" programs, with myriad variations, have been part of organizational life for more than 40 years in much of western Europe. Finally flextime is catching on in other parts of the world. There are several rationales for adopting flextime, including a more independent and better educated workforce; the need to grant people more control over their work lives; higher levels of motivation and commitment; an organization's wish to be more available to their clients and customers; and integrity, creativity, and sense of responsibility in order to organize work groups in which the group itself manages individual and group behavior, quality, output, and productivity. In this case, to paraphrase, the paradigm shift is from Theory X to a Theory Y view of travel and environmental concerns, dual-career couples, and other work-family issues. Though still not the norm, flextime is increasingly being instituted by organizations, and those who have had experience with it overwhelmingly report gains in productivity and increases in employee job satisfaction.[34]

The paradigm shift about ways of working is in the process of taking place, and it may even include new forms of organizing and performing work which are more dramatic than flextime. These means include telecommuting (working all or part of the time away from the traditional workplace, usually connected via computers, phones, fax, etc.), multiple-organizational careers that replace older cradle-to-grave employment expectations, "executive temps" and other forms of contract employment as an alternative to "employee" status, job sharing, and even large numbers of people working without any of the regular physical office or the accoutrements of a traditional job but rather in what is called a "virtual office." The wide variety of alternative means of working brings the long-held paradigm of holding a job into question.[35]

Revolution and Transformation

The emphasis and focus of the so-called behavioral science movement began with interventions aimed at individual behavior. Soon organizations realized that, laudable as individual growth may be, what they really needed was development of the organization, giving rise to organization development. Great strides were made in effecting organizational change through group methods but a coldly objective assessment of much of what has been called organization development usually addressed change in small groups within the larger organization. This situation is easily understandable since the technology that gave birth to organization development and other applications of the behavioral sciences was rooted in small-group psychology.

There were very few examples of successful total-organization change and even fewer examples of large-scale change projects that have lasted over time. These interventions most often brought about only incremental change, albeit worthwhile. What was missing was the ability to bring about total organizational change, including integrated and complementary change, in all the various "systems" of the organization. Even if the technology had been developed and if the professional change agents had the skill to effect total change, there still remained one essential element: the mandate to create revolutionary change. That mandate can only come from the leader of the organization.

Enlightened leadership must, first, have a vision of the organization's future, then the skill to instill that vision in the people of the organization, matched by a strong commitment to create the future the organization desires.[36] Clearly, this type of leadership involves more than merely administering or managing the business, it is more than addressing discrete problems within the organization, it is more than making modifications or adjustments within the old paradigm. Instead, it involves having the courage to make truly *radical* changes in *all* the complementary systems and processes of the organization, a *holistic* approach to change that is nothing less than a total transformation of the organization.

The long-heralded communication age has finally arrived; the world is, in fact, rapidly becoming a "global village" and competition is at an all-time high. Passive adaptation to the lightning speed of environmental change will not be enough to survive, let alone create and sustain aggressive growth. Organizations must change, grow exponentially, or die. Recognizing the necessity of radical change, the avant garde organizations and their leaders have reached out to utilize all the skill they and their organizations can muster and they have gleaned the best contributions from many relevant and germane disciplines including the considerable contribution of the behavioral sciences and the behavioral sciences' special insight into people in organizations. There are already such organizations. Their stories are dramatic examples of transformation and their number is increasing.[37]

Summary

Any review of the behavioral science research and writings reveals that there are many aspects to the complex subject of human behavior. There are differing points of view concerning the facets of personality that are the most relevant to human motivation, a point that usually comes through strongly, even in a cursory overview of a few of the leading theories, such as the one presented here. However, it becomes equally clear, despite the variety of approaches, that all are concerned with gaining greater understanding of the causes and forms of human behavior, especially in the context of organizations.

In some instances the contributions of the behavioral sciences offer specific guidelines or "how-to" action steps for improving the motivational climate. In other instances the contributions are in the forms of insights into the inner workings of personality and behavior, which are translations of research findings but which remain in the realm of theory. Even these theoretical or "philosophical" contributions can be useful, insofar as they provide a conceptual framework for understanding people and the behaviors they exhibit.

This is no small consideration for the manager, who, by definition, accomplishes objectives through and with the efforts of other people. In fact, the manager's skill is greatly dependent upon his or her ability to look beyond the overt behaviors of people into the sources and causes of those behaviors. Most managers who are successful in their jobs exhibit an understanding of the human as well as the material side of enterprise. To do this one need not be an "armchair psychologist" or an "office sociologist," although in managing today's workforce the inputs of the behavioral sciences are in many ways as relevant as the physical or material concerns facing the manager.

Despite the tremendous advances of modern technology, successful management of the enterprise is greatly dependent upon effective utilization of the most important asset of any organization—the human resources.

While the process of motivation is always complex and often elusive, it is incumbent upon the manager, *at the very least,* to work toward removing the demotivating factors in the organization's culture and in his or her own interpersonal style in dealing with peers, superiors, and subordinates. This is not an easy task, regardless of the degree of sensitivity and insight the manager possesses, but at the heart of the matter is a recognition that motivation is inextricably linked with individual growth and development.

Development of subordinates is properly a line responsibility. But the training and development professional has a special role to fulfill in the process, which consists in keeping abreast of the developments within the field of human behavior and in serving as a valuable resource for the manager who is trying to create a climate in which motivation flourishes.

References

1. Rush, Harold M. F., "What Is Behavioral Science?" *The Conference Board Record,* January 1965.

2. Roethlisberger, F., and W. J. Dickson, *Management and the Worker,* Harvard University Press, Cambridge, MA, 1939. Also, Roethlisberger, F., and W. J. Dickson, *Counseling in an Organization: A Sequel to the Hawthorne Research,* Harvard University Graduate School of Business, Boston, 1966.

3. Lewin, Kurt, *Resolving Social Conflicts: Selected Papers on Group Dynamics,* Gertrude W. Lewin, ed., Harper & Row, New York, 1948. Also Cartwright, Dorian, and Alvin Zander, eds., *Group Dynamics: Research and Theory,* 2d ed., Harper & Row, New York, 1960.

4. Rush, Harold M. F., *Behavioral Science: Concepts and Management Application,* National Industrial Conference Board, New York, 1969. This book deals in greater depth with the nature and contributions of the various behavioral sciences, the work and writings of most of the theorists discussed in this handbook, and three approaches to behav-

iorally oriented training. It includes 10 case studies of business applications of behavioral science technology.

5. Schein, Edgar H., and Warren G. Bennis, *Personal and Organizational Change Through Group Methods,* John Wiley & Sons, Inc., New York, 1965.

6. For a discussion of typical sequences of events in T groups for business people, see Rush, Harold M. F., *Behavioral Sciences: Concepts and Management Application,* Chap. 3.

7. Marrow, Alfred J., *Behind the Executive Mask,* American Management Association, New York, 1964. Marrow discusses the rationale for laboratory training for managers and gives an excellent narrative account of behavioral interaction in a "classic" T group.

8. For a discussion of organization development, see Chap. 29 of this handbook. See also Rush, Harold M. F., *Organization Development: A Reconnaissance,* The Conference Board, New York, 1973.

9. Likert, Rensis, *New Patterns of Management,* McGraw-Hill, New York, 1961.

10. Likert, Rensis, *The Human Organization: Its Management and Value,* McGraw-Hill, New York, 1967.

11. McGregor, Douglas, *The Human Side of Enterprise,* McGraw-Hill, New York, 1960. Although McGregor wrote many articles for business and professional journals, *The Human Side of Enterprise* is his only book-length work published before his death. Its influence on the behavioral science movement within the business community is inestimable.

12. McGregor, Douglas, *Leadership and Motivation,* W. G. Bennis, E. H. Schein, and C. McGregor, eds., The M.I.T. Press, Cambridge, MA, 1966.

13. McGregor, Douglas, *The Professional Manager,* Catherine McGregor and Warren G. Bennis, eds., McGraw-Hill, New York, 1967.

14. Bennis, Warren G., *An Invented Life: Reflections on Leadership and Change,* Addison-Wesley, Reading, MA, 1994. Also Bennis, Warren G., "Why Leaders Can't Lead," *Training and Development Journal,* April 1989.

15. Maslow, Abraham H., *Motivation and Personality,* 2d ed., Harper & Row, New York, 1970.

16. Maslow, Abraham H., *Toward a Psychology of Being,* 2d ed., Van Nostrand Reinhold, New York, 1968. Also Maslow, Abraham H., *Eupsychian Management: A Journal,* Dorsey Press, Homewood, IL, 1965.

17. Herzberg, Frederick, *Work and the Nature of Man,* World Publishing Company, Cleveland, 1966.

18. Rush, Harold M. F., *Job Design for Motivation: Experiments in Job Enlargement and Job Enrichment,* The Conference Board, New York, 1971.

19. Argyris, Chris, *Integrating the Individual and the Organization,* John Wiley & Sons, New York, 1964. Also *Interpersonal Competence and Organizational Effectiveness,* Dorsey Press, Homewood, IL, 1962.

20. McClelland, David C., et al., *The Achievement Motive,* Appleton-Century-Crofts, New York, 1953.

21. McClelland, David C., and David J. Winter, *Motivating Economic Achievement,* The Free Press, New York, 1969.

22. Skinner, B. F., *Science and Human Behavior,* Macmillan, New York, 1953.

23. Holland, J. G., and B. F. Skinner, *The Analysis of Behavior: A Program for Self-Instruction,* McGraw-Hill, New York, 1961.

24. Skinner, B. F., *Beyond Freedom and Dignity,* Alfred A. Knopf, New York, 1972. This bestseller is a defense of Skinner's position on the use of operant reinforcement as a means of control over people to accomplish broad social goals of societies and cultures. It is also an excellent exposition of operant reinforcement theory and method, couched in lay terms.

25. Jaques, Elliott, and Kathryn Cason, *Human Capability: A Study of Individual Potential and its Application,* Cason Hall & Co., Falls Church, VA, 1994.

26. Jaques, Elliott, and Stephen D. Clement, *Executive Leadership: A Practical Guide to Managing Complexity,* Cason Hall & Co., Falls Church, VA (2d printing), 1994.

27. Jaques, Elliott, *Requisite Organization: The CEO's Guide to Creative Structure and Leadership,* Cason Hall & Co., Falls Church, VA, 1986.

28. Jung, C. G., *The Collected Works of C. G. Jung,* vol. 6, *Psychological Types* (*Bollingen Series*), Princeton University Press, Princeton, NJ, 1971.

29. Briggs-Myers, Isabel (with Peter Myers), *Gifts Differing,* Consulting Psychologists Press, Palo Alto, CA, 1980.

30. Keirsey, David, and Marilyn Bates, *Please Understand Me: Character and Temperament Types,* Prometheus Nemesis, Del Mar, CA, 1978.

31. Srivastva, Suresh, and David L. Cooperrider, *Appreciative Management and Leadership: The Power of Positive Thought and Action in Organizations,* Jossey-Bass, San Francisco, 1990.

32. Westbrook, Jerry D., "Organizational Culture and its Relationship to TQM," *Industrial Management,* January–February 1993.

33. Barker, Joel A., *Paradigms: The Business of Discovering the Future,* Harper-Collins, New York, 1993. Also Stucker, Jan Collins, "The Business of Paradigms," *Business and Economic Review,* vol. 38, no. 2, January–March 1992.

34. Olmsted, Barney, and Suzanne Smith, *Creating a Flexible Workplace,* 2d ed., AMACOM (American Management Association), New York, 1994.

35. Bridges, William, *Job Shift: How to Prosper in a Workplace Without Jobs,* Addison-Wesley, Reading, MA, 1994.

36. Tichy, Noel M., and Mary A. Devanna, *The Transformational Leader,* John Wiley & Sons, New York, 1990.

37. Gouillart, Francis J., and James N. Kelly, *Transforming the Organization: Reframing Corporate Direction, Restructuring the Company, Revitalizing the Enterprise, Renewing People,* McGraw-Hill, New York, 1995.

12

Adult Learning

Malcolm S. Knowles

Malcolm S. Knowles *is Professor Emeritus of Adult and Community College Education of North Carolina State University. Previously, he was Professor of Education at Boston University, Executive Director of Adult Education Association of the U.S.A., and Director of Adult Education for the YMCAs of Boston, Detroit, and Chicago. He received his A.B. at Harvard College in 1934 and his M.A. and Ph.D. from the University of Chicago in 1949 and 1960, respectively. Since his retirement in 1979, he has been actively engaged in consulting and conducting workshops with business and industry, government agencies, educational institutions, religious institutions, voluntary agencies, and ASTD chapters and conferences in North America, Europe, South America, Australia, Japan, Singapore, Thailand, and Korea. He is the author of 17 books, the most recent being* The Adult Learner: A Neglected Species, *Gulf Publishing, rev. ed. 1984,* Andragogy in Action, *Jossey-Bass, 1984, and* The Making of an Adult Educator, *Jossey-Bass, 1989, and over 230 articles.*

Wherefore Pedagogy?

All formal educational institutions in modern society were initially established exclusively for the education of children and youth. At the time they were established there was only one model of assumptions about learners and learning—the pedagogical model (derived from the Greek words *paid,* meaning "child," and *agogus,* meaning "leader"; so "pedagogy" means literally "the art and science of teaching children").

This model assigned full responsibility for making all decisions about what should be learned, how it should be learned, when it should be learned, and if it had been learned, to the teacher. Students were given the role of being submissive recipients of the directions and transmitted content of the teacher. It assumed that they were dependent personalities, that they had little experience that could serve as a resource for learning, that they became ready to learn what they were told they had to learn (to get promoted to the next level), that they were subject-centered in their orientation to learning, and that they were motivated by extrinsic pressures or rewards. The backbone methodology of pedagogy is transmission techniques.

As educational psychologists started researching educational phenomena around the turn of the century they were governed largely by these assumptions, too. But they were not really looking at learning; they were investigating reactions to teaching. And the more they found out about how teachers could control learners' reactions, the more controlling teaching became. Pedagogy was king.

When adult education began to be organized systematically in the first quarter of this century, pedagogy was the only model teachers of adults had to go on, with the result that until recently adults were taught as if they were children. I believe that this fact accounts for many of the troubles adult educators encountered, such as a high drop-out rate (where attendance was voluntary), low motivation, and poor performance. When training began emerging as a specialty within the general adult education movement almost half a century later, this was the only model available to trainers, as well.

Then Came Andragogy

The first inkling that the pedagogical model may not be appropriate for adults appeared in a book by Eduard C. Lindeman, *The Meaning of Adult Education,* in 1926.[1] Based on his experience as both an adult learner and a teacher of adults, Lindeman proposed that adults were not just grown-up children, that they learned best when they were actively involved in determining what, how, and when they learned. But it was not until the 1950s, when we began getting empirical research on adults as learners, that the notion that there are differences between youth and adults as learners began being taken seriously.

A seminal study by Houle[2] spawned a crescendo of studies (Tough,[3,4] Peters,[5] Penland,[6] and others) of how adults learn naturally (e.g., when they are not being taught). These studies document the fact that adults do indeed engage in more intentional learning outside of formal instruction than in organized programs and that they are in fact highly self-directed learners. Meantime, knowledge about adult learners was coming from other disciplines. Clinical psychologists were providing information on the conditions and strategies that promoted behavioral change (which is what education should be about, too). Developmental psychologists were illuminating the development stages that adults experience throughout the life span, which are a main stimulus of readiness to learn. Sociologists were exposing the effects that many institutional policies and practices have in inhibiting or facilitating learning (especially the inhibiting effects of rules and regulations, requirements, registration procedures, time schedules, and the like). Social psychologists were revealing the influences of forces in the larger environment, such as social attitudes and customs, reward systems, and socioeconomic and ethnic stratification.

Early in the 1960s European adult educators were feeling a need for a label for this growing body of knowledge about adult learners that would enable them to talk about it in parallel with the pedagogical model, and they coined the term (or actually rediscovered the term that had been coined by a German adult educator in 1833) *andragogy.* It is derived from the Greek word *aner,* meaning "adult" (literally, "man, not boy"). It was initially used to mean "the art and science of helping adults learn," but, as will be shown later, the term has taken on a broader meaning. It is a term that is now widely used around the world as an alternative to pedagogy.

What Do We Know About Adults as Learners?

The research cited above leads to the following assumptions about adults as learners, on which the andragogical model is based:

1. *Adults have a need to know why they should learn something.* Tough[4] found that adults would expend considerable time and energy exploring what the benefits would be of their learning something and what the costs would be of their not learning it before they would be willing to invest time and energy in learning it. We therefore now have a dictum in adult education that one of the first tasks of the adult educator is to develop a "need to know" in the learners—to make a case for the value *in their life performance* of their learning what we have to offer. At the minimum, this case should be made through testimony from the experience of the trainer or a successful practitioner; at the maximum, by providing real or simulated experiences through which the learners experience the benefits of knowing and the costs of not knowing. It is seldom convincing for them to be told by someone (like the boss) that it would be good for them.

To practice what I preach, let me try to make a case for your learning about "Treating Adult Learners as Adults." Let me quote from an article I wrote for the *Training and Development Journal* of September 1976, "Separating the Amateurs from the Pros in Training":

> When I first got into training in 1935 the assumption was made that one didn't need to have qualifications much different from any other administrative role to do a good job as a training director. The role was defined essentially as that of managing the logistics of organizing and operating activities for various groupings of individuals. If one had any experience in planning schedules, building budgets, getting out promotional materials, hiring people, and filling out reports, he [there were no she's at that time] was qualified. We were all amateurs....But no longer. During the intervening years there has been a body of knowledge about how adults learn and a body of technology for facilitating that learning that is changing the role of trainer and requiring that he or she know things few teachers know and probably none of his or her associates knows. The trainer must know *andragogy*—the art and science of helping adults learn—and how it differs from *pedagogy*—the art and science of teaching youth....This is the mark of the pro.

I am assuming that all who are reading this chapter want to be pros.

2. *Adults have a deep need to be self-directing.* In fact, the psychological definition of "adult" is one who has achieved a self-concept of being in charge of his or her own life, of being responsible for making his or her own decisions and living with the consequences. At the point at which we arrive at this self-concept we develop a deep psychological need to be seen and treated by others as being capable of taking responsibility for ourselves. This fact creates a special problem for us in adult education and training in that although adults may be completely self-directing in most aspects of their lives (as full-time workers, spouses, parents, and voting citizens), when they enter a program labeled "education" or "training," they hark back to their conditioning in school and college and put on their hats of dependency, fold their arms, sit back, and say, "Teach me." The problem arises if we assume that this is really where they are coming from and start teaching them as if they were children. We then put them into an inner conflict between this intellectual map—learner equals dependent—and their deeper psychological need to be self-directing. And the way most people deal with psychological conflict is to seek to withdraw from the situation causing it. To resolve this prob-

lem adult educators have been developing strategies for helping adults to make a quick transition from seeing themselves as being dependent learners to becoming self-directed learners. My little paperback book, *Self-Directed Learning: A Guide for Learners and Teachers*[7] describes some of these strategies.

3. *Adults have a greater volume and different quality of experience than youth.* Except in certain pathological circumstances, the longer we live the more experience and more varied experience we accumulate. The greater reservoir of experience affects learning in several ways:

- Adults bring into a learning situation a background of experience that is itself a rich resource for many kinds of learning for themselves and for others. Hence, in adult education, the greater emphasis on the use of experiential learning—techniques, such as discussion methods and problem-solving exercises, that tap into the accumulated knowledge and skills of the learners, or techniques, such as simulation exercises and field experiences, that provide learners with experiences from which they can learn by analyzing them.

- Adults have a broader base of experience to which to attach new ideas and skills and give them richer meaning. The more explicit these relationships (between the old and the new) are made—through discussion and reflection—the deeper and more permanent the learning will be (see Boud et al., 1985).

- It is predictable that a group of adults, especially if there is an age mix, will have a wider range of differences in background, interests, ability, and learning styles than is true of any group of youth. Adult groups are heterogeneous groups. Accordingly, increasing emphasis is being placed in adult education on individualized learning and instruction, through contract learning, self-paced multimedia modules, learning resource centers, and other means.

- But there is a potentially negative consequence of this fact of greater experience—it tends to cause people to develop habits of thought and biases, to make presuppositions, to be less open to new ideas. (How often have you heard somebody react to a new proposal, "It won't work. We tried it five years ago and it didn't work"?) Some techniques have been developed to try to counter this tendency—sensitivity training, open-mindedness scales, creativity exercises, and others.

But the difference in quality of experience adults bring with them is also significant. Few youths have had the experience of being full-time workers, spouses, parents, voting citizens, organizational leaders, and of performing other adult roles. Most adults have. Accordingly, adults have a different perspective on experience: it is their chief source of self-identity. To youth, experience is something that happens to them. But adults define themselves in terms of their unique experiences. An adult's experience is who he or she is. So if adults' experience is not respected and valued, is not made use of as a resource for learning, they experience this omission not as a rejection of their experience but as a rejection of them as persons. Evidence indicates that this phenomenon is especially characteristic of undereducated adults.

4. *Adults become ready to learn when they experience in their life situation a need to know or be able to do in order to perform more effectively and satisfyingly.* The pedagogical model makes the opposite assumption—that people become ready to learn what they are told by some authority figure (teacher, trainer, boss), that they have to learn because it's good for them or the authority figure demands it. Adults experience "being told" as infringing upon their adulthood—their need to be self-directing—and tend to react with resentment, defensiveness, and resistance. Adults learn best when they choose voluntarily to make a commitment to learn.

This principle is often difficult to apply in business and industry, since, rightly or wrongly, employer-provided training tends to be perceived as employer-required training. Indeed, often attendance is compulsory. When I sense that there are people in one of my activities who have been "sent," I do two things to try to reduce the resistance it induces. First, I make it public that I realize that there may be some people in the room who aren't there because they want to be, and that I am sorry about this because it tends to get in the way of learning. But, I explain, there is nothing I or you can do to change this at this time, so let's accept it as a given and see if we can't have a pleasant and profitable time together anyway. More importantly, I try to involve them in discovering for themselves—through participating in simulation exercises, self-diagnosing their learning needs through competency-based rating scales, or observing role models of superior performance—the value for their own lives of learning what the program has to offer.

One of the richest sources of readiness to learn is the transition people make when moving from one developmental stage to another. As Havighurst[8] points out, as we confront having to perform the development tasks of the next stage of development, we become ready to learn those tasks; and the peak of our desire to learn them he calls the "teachable moment." A typical sequence of developmental tasks in work life would be (1) to begin a process of career planning, (2) to acquire competencies required for a first job, (3) to get a first job, (4) to become oriented to the first job, (5) to master the competencies required to perform excellently in the first job, (6) to plan and prepare for a next-step-up job, and so through a cycle of career development. The final developmental task would be to prepare for retirement from a career. A main implication of this concept is the importance of timing our educational offerings to coincide with the worker's developmental tasks. Indeed, some of the great goofs of training have occurred as a result of forcing people into training activities before they are ready for them—as, for example, pushing people into supervisory training programs before they feel they have mastered the work they are to be supervising.

5. *Adults enter into a learning experience with a task-centered (or problem-centered or life-centered) orientation to learning.* Children and youth have been conditioned by their school experience to have a subject-centered orientation to learning; they see learning as a process of acquiring the subject matter necessary to pass tests. Once that is done, their mission is accomplished. This difference in orientation calls for different ways of organizing the content to be learned. In traditional education the content is organized into subject-matter courses—such as Composition I, in which the rules of grammar are memorized, Composition II, in which sentence and paragraph structures are memorized, and Composition III, in which rules of outlining, syntax, and the like are memorized. In adult education the content is organized around life tasks: Composition I becomes "Writing Better Business Letters," Composition II becomes "Writing for Pleasure and Profit," and Composition III becomes "Improving Your Professional Communications."

I have found that this principle is commonly violated in orientation programs, in which the sequence of topics might be (1) The History and Philosophy of XYZ Co., (2) The Market and Products of XYZ Co., (3) The Personnel Policies of XYZ Co., and so on, instead of starting with a census of problems and concerns, along with problems and concerns of the organization and trainer. But I strongly urge trainers to review their entire programs and restructure the units around tasks, problems, or life situations. The participants will see the program as much more relevant to their lives and they will learn the content with the intention of *using* it.

6. *Adults are motivated to learn by both extrinsic and intrinsic motivators.* One of the most significant findings of the research into adult learning is that adults are

motivated to learn. Allen Tough,[4] the researcher who has to date accumulated the largest volume of information about how adults learn in normal life, has yet to find a subject in his research who had not engaged in at least one major learning project (a minimum of seven hours of intentional learning) in the preceding year, and the average number of learning projects was over seven. The problem (and our challenge) is that they may not be motivated to learn what we want to teach them; hence the importance of following through on the first assumption above—developing a need to know.

The pedagogical model màkes the assumption that children and youth are motivated primarily, if not exclusively, by extrinsic motivators—pressures from parents and teachers, competition for grades, diplomas, and the like. Adult learners respond to extrinsic motivators—wage raises, promotion, better working conditions, and the like—up to the point that they are reasonably well satisfied. But the more potent and persistent motivators are such intrinsic motivators as the need for self-esteem, broadened responsibilities, power, achievement, and the like (Wlodkowski[9]). The message here, as I read it, is to appeal to both the desire for job advancement and life enrichment in promoting your programs.

Implications for Practice

The assumptions of pedagogy and andragogy have a number of implications for what we do as human resource developers. One basic implication is the importance of making a clear distinction between a *content plan* and a *process design*.

When planning an educational activity, the pedagog thinks in term of drafting a content plan, and he has to answer only four questions to come up with a plan: (1) What content needs to be covered (the assumption being that they will only learn what he transmits, and therefore he has to cover it *all* in the classroom)? So he draws up a long laundry list of content terms. (2) How can this content be organized into manageable units (one-hour, three-hour, etc., units)? So he clusters the content items into manageable units. (3) How can these content units be transmitted in a logical sequence (rather than the sequence in which the learners are ready to learn it)? So he arranges the units in a sequence according to chronology (history, literature, political science) or from simple to complex (science, math). (4) What would be the most effective methods for transmitting this content? If unit 1 is heavily loaded with information, the method of choice will probably be lecture and assigned reading; if unit 2 involves skill performance, the method of choice will probably be demonstration by him and drill, drill, drill by them. By answering these four questions, he ends up with a content-transmission plan.

The andragog, on the other hand, when she (get the gender change?) undertakes to plan an educational activity, sees her task as being twofold: first, and primarily, to design and manage a process for facilitating the acquisition of content by the learners; and only secondarily to serve as a content resource (she perceives that there are many content resources in addition to her own—peers, supervisors, specialists, and a variety of materials in the learner's environment, and that an important part of her responsibility is to keep up to date as to what these resources are and to link learners with them). So the andragog has to answer a very different set of questions to come up with a process design. (Notice that it is not a matter of the pedagog's being concerned with content and the andragog's not being concerned with it; rather, the pedagog is concerned with transmitting the content and the andragog is concerned with facilitating the acquisition of the content by the learners.)

The questions raised by the andragog have to do with implementing the following elements of an andragogical process design:

1. *Climate setting.* A prerequisite for effective learning to take place is the establishment of a climate that is conducive to learning. Two broad aspects of climate must be considered: institutional climate and the climate of training situation.

Among the questions that might be raised regarding institutional climate are: Do the policy statements of the institution convey a deep commitment to the value of human resource development in the accomplishment of the mission of the institution? Does the budget of the institution provide adequate resources for the support of significant human resource development (HRD) efforts? Is the HRD staff involved in the decision-making process as regards personnel policies and programs? Are adequate physical facilities for HRD activities provided? Does the reward system of the institution give credit for the achievement of personal growth on the part of individuals and their supervisors?

As regards setting a climate in a training situation, these are the conditions that I think characterize a climate that is conducive to learning, and the questions that might be asked in creating a process design to achieve those conditions:

- A climate of mutual respect. I believe that people are more open to learning if they feel respected. If they feel that they are being talked down to, embarrassed, or otherwise denigrated, their energy is diverted from learning to dealing with these feelings. I do several things to try to bring such a climate into being: First, I provide name tents—5 by 8 cards with their names printed on them with bold felt pens—so that I (and they) can start calling on them by name. Then I put them into small groups of five or six persons (preferably sitting around tables) and ask them to share their "whats" (their work roles); their "whos" (one thing about themselves that will enable others to see them as unique human beings); any special knowledge, skill, or other resources they would be willing to share with others; and any questions, problems, or concerns they are hoping will be dealt with in this program. I ask one person in each group to volunteer to give a high-point summary of this information about each group. I feel that this hour is the most important hour in the whole training event, since it starts the process of creating a climate that is conducive to learning.

- A climate of collaborativeness rather than competitiveness. The above sharing exercise causes the participants to start seeing themselves as mutual helpers rather than rivals. For many kinds of learning, the richest resources are within their peers, hence the importance of making these resources available.

- A climate of supportiveness rather than judgmentalness. I think I largely set this climate by being supportive in my own behavior, but the opening exercise also tends to establish peer-support relationships.

- A climate of mutual trust. In order to reduce the instinctive mistrust with which people typically react to authority figures, in presenting myself I emphasize who I am as a human being rather than as an expert, and I urge them to call me by my first name.

- A climate of fun. Learning should be one of the most joyful things we do, and so I do everything I can to make the experience enjoyable. I make a lot of use of spontaneous (not canned) humor.

- A human climate. Learning is a human activity; training is for dogs and horses. So I try to establish a climate in which people feel that they are being treated as human beings, not objects. I try to care for their human needs—comfortable chairs, frequent breaks, adequate ventilation and lighting, availability of coffee or cold drinks, and the like.

The first question an andragog asks in constructing a process design, therefore, is "What procedures should I use with this particular group to bring these climatic conditions into being?"

2. *Creating a mechanism for mutual planning.* A basic law of human nature is at work here: people tend to feel committed to a decision or activity to the extent that they have participated in making the decision or planning the activity. The reverse is even more true: people tend to feel uncommitted to the extent they feel that the decision or activity is being imposed on them without their having a chance to influence it.

In planning a total program—all the courses, workshops, seminars—of an institution, the usual mechanism is a planning committee, council, or task force. To be effective, it is critical that it be representative of all the constituencies the program is designed to serve. (See Houle[10] for helpful guidelines.)

For a particular program, such as a course or workshop, I prefer to use teams of participants, with each team having responsibility for planning one unit of the program.

The fullest participation in planning is achieved, however, through the use of learning contracts, in which case the learners develop their own learning plans (see Knowles[7,11,12]).

The second question the andragog answers in developing a process model, therefore, is "What procedures will I use to involve the learners in planning?"

3. *Diagnosing the participant's learning needs.* The HRD literature is rich in techniques trainers can use for assessing training needs as perceived by individuals, organizations, and communities (Boone,[13] Brown and Wedel,[14] Davis and McCallon,[15] Knowles,[16] McKenzie and McKinley,[17] Mager and Pipe[18]). These needs are the appropriate source of goals for a total program (Knowles,[16] pp. 120–126). But in a particular training event involving particular individuals, a learning need is not a need unless so perceived by the learner. One of the highest arts in training is creating the conditions and providing the tools that will enable learners to become aware of their training needs and therefore translate them into learning needs. A new body of technology is being developed for facilitating this process, with emphasis on such self-diagnostic procedures as simulation exercises, assessment centers, competency-based rating scales, and videotape feedback (Knowles,[16] Wlodkowski[9]).

So the third set of questions the andragog asks in constructing a process design is "What procedures will I use in helping the participants diagnose their own learning needs?"

4. *Translating learning needs into objectives.* Having diagnosed their learning needs, participants now face the task of translating them into learning objectives—positive statements of directions of growth. Some kinds of learning (such as machine operation) lend themselves to objectives stated as terminal behaviors that can be observed and measured (Mager[19]). Others (such as decision-making ability) are so complex that they are better stated in terms of direction of improvement (Knowles,[11] pp. 128–130).

So the fourth question the andragog asks is "What procedures can I use for helping participants translate their learning needs into learning objectives?" (For suggested procedures, see Knowles,[7] pp. 25–28.)

5. *Designing and managing a pattern of learning experiences.* Having formulated the learning objectives, the trainer and the participant then have the task of

designing a plan for achieving them. This plan will include identifying the resources most relevant to each objective and the most effective strategies for utilizing these resources. Such a plan is likely to include a mix of total group experiences (including input by the trainer), subgroup (learning-teaching team) experiences, and individual learning projects. A key criterion for assessing the excellence of such a design is, how deeply involved are the participants in the mutual process of designing and managing a pattern of learning experiences?

So the fifth question the andragog asks is "What procedures can I use for involving the learners with me in designing and managing a pattern of learning experiences? (For suggested procedures, see Knowles,[16] pp. 235–247.)

6. *Evaluating the extent to which the objectives have been achieved.* In many situations institutional policies require some sort of "objective" (quantitative) measure of learning outcomes (Kirkpatrick,[20] Scriven,[21] Stufflebeam[22]). But the recent trend in evaluation research has been to place increasing emphasis on "subjective" (qualitative) evaluation—finding out what is really happening inside the participants and how differently they are performing in life (Cronbach,[23] Guba and Lincoln,[24] Patton[25,26,27,28]). In any case, the andragogical model requires that the learners be actively involved in the process of evaluating their learning outcomes (Knowles[12]).

The sixth question, therefore, that the andragog asks is "What procedures can I use to involve the learners responsibly in evaluating the accomplishment of their learning objectives?"

By answering these six sets of questions, the learning facilitator emerges with a *process design*—a set of procedures for facilitating the acquisition of content by the learners.

But Not Andragogy *versus* Pedagogy

When I first began conceptualizing the andragogical model I perceived it as being antithetical to the pedagogical model. In fact, in the book in which I first presented the andragogical model in detail, *The Modern Practice of Adult Education,*[16] I used the subtitle "Andragogy versus Pedagogy." During the next few years I began getting reports from elementary and secondary school teachers saying that they had been experimenting with applying the andragogical model in their practice and finding that children and youth also learn better in many situations when they are involved in sharing responsibility. And I got reports from teachers of adults that they had found situations in which they had to use the pedagogical model. So when I revised the book in 1980 I used the subtitle, "From Pedagogy to Andragogy."

As I see it now, whereas for 13 centuries we had only one model of assumptions and strategies regarding education—the pedagogical model, now we have two models. So we have the responsibility now of checking out which set of assumptions is realistic in which situation, and using the strategies of whichever model is appropriate for that situation. In general, the pedagogical assumptions are likely to be realistic in those situations in which the content is totally strange to the learners and in which precise psychomotor skills are involved, as in machine operation. But even in these situations, elements of the andragogical model, such as climate setting, might enhance the learning. And I use elements of the pedagogical model, such as reinforcement, in my andragogical practice. So my stance now is not either-or, but both—as appropriate to the situation.

Program Design and Development

Preparing for the Future

In the third quarter of this century we accumulated more research-based knowledge about adults as learners than was known in all of previous history. In the past decade that body of knowledge has at least doubled. I am confident that the present body of knowledge will at least double in the next decade. My colleagues in the biological sciences assure me that their disciplines will contribute some of the major breakthroughs, especially as regards the physiological, chemical, and neurological (such as right-brain, left-brain) processes involved in learning. The technology of making resources for learning available is already in a state of revolution, especially with the development of computers and communications satellites. My own conviction is that by the end of this century most educational services will be being delivered electronically to learners at their convenience in terms of time, place, and pace.

What a challenge we in human resource development face if we are to avoid the obsolescence of our workforce. I can foresee this challenge requiring that we reconceptualize a corporation (or any social system) as a system of learning resources as well as production and service-delivering system and redefine the role of HRD away from that of managing the logistics of conducting training activities to that of managing a system of learning resources. We would then ask a very different set of questions from those we have traditionally asked in training and development. The first question would be, "What are all of the resources available in this system for the growth and development of people?" Then we would have to ask, "How well are these resources being utilized now, and how might they be more effectively utilized?" We might come up with a chart that looks something like Table 12-1.

If nothing more is done than what has been described so far, the quality of human resource development in a corporation would probably be improved. But learning would still be episodic, fragmented, and disconnected. It can be made more systematic, incremental, and continuous through the use of learning contracts or development plans (Knowles[12]).

A contract simply specifies what an individual's objectives are for a given learning project, what resources will be used in fulfilling the objectives, what evidence will be collected to demonstrate that the objectives have been fulfilled, and how that evidence will be validated. In one corporation the contract is negotiated between the individual and the HRD staff; in another, it is between the individual and his or her supervisor; in another, it is between the individual and a team consisting of the supervisor, a representative of the HRD department, and a peer. Progress toward fulfilling the contract is monitored, and the evidence is validated by these same parties. Several corporations with a management-by-objectives program have incorporated the contracting process into the MBO process.

Several things happen when a systems approach is adopted. A heavier responsibility is placed on the line supervisors and managers for the development of their personnel than traditionally has been the case. This integrates the HRD function more closely with the operating function, and line supervisors and managers derive added self-esteem and job satisfaction from their developmental role once they have become adept at it.

Employees find that their personal and professional development are more integrated with their work life. A much wider range of resources for learning are available to them, and employees are more directly involved in planning and achieving their own development—adding to their self-esteem and satisfaction.

For HRD professionals, the systems approach represents a major shift in role. They are less concerned with planning, scheduling, and conducting instructional activities, and are more concerned with managing a system. One of their major

Table 12-1. Managing a System of Learning Resources

Resources	Strategies for enhancing their utilization
Scheduled training activities (courses, workshops, seminars)	Revise time schedule so as to make activities more accessible to employees
	Revise programs so as to make them more congruent with adult learning principles
	Train presenters in adult education methods
Line supervisors and managers (the most ubiquitous resources for day-in-and-day-out employee development)	Build responsibility for people development into their job descriptions
	Build into supervisory and management training programs sessions on principles of adult learning and skills in facilitating learning
	Give credit in personnel appraisals for performance as people developers
Libraries, media centers (printed materials, audiovisual and multimedia programs)	Arrange to be open during hours accessible to all employees
	Make information about resources available to all employees
	Provide help in using them
Individual employees, specialists, and technicians (many people in organizations have knowledge and skills others would like to learn)	Store this information in a data bank and make it available to employees through an educational brokering center
Community resources (courses, workshops, specialists, etc., in colleges and universities, community organizations, professional associations, commercial providers, etc.)	Include in the above data bank

responsibilities is to serve as consultants to the line—a closer and more functional relationship, and one more central to the operation of the business.
How much more fulfilling a role!

References

1. Lindeman, Eduard C., *The Meaning of Adult Education,* New Republic, New York, 1926.
2. Houle, Cyril O., *The Inquiring Mind,* University of Wisconsin Press, Madison, 1961.
3. Tough, Allen, *Learning Without a Teacher,* Ontario Institute for Education, Toronto, 1967.
4. Tough, Allen, *The Adult's Learning Projects,* 2d ed., Ontario Institute for Education, Toronto, 1979.
5. Peters, John M., and S. G. Gordon, *Adult Learning Projects: A Study of Adult Learning in Urban and Rural Tennessee,* University of Tennessee, Knoxville, 1974.
6. Penland, Patrick R., *Individual Self-Planned Learning in America,* Final Report of Project 475AH60058 under grant No. G007603327, U.S. Office of Education, Office of Libraries

and Learning Resources. Unpublished manuscript, Graduate School of Library and Information Sciences, University of Pittsburgh, 1977. Available as ERIC document. Also available from the University of Pittsburgh bookstore under the title *Self-Planned Learning in America.*

7. Knowles, Malcolm S., *Self-Directed Learning: A Guide for Learners and Teachers,* Cambridge Book Co., New York, 1975.

8. Havighurst, Robert, *Developmental Tasks and Education,* 2d ed., David McKay, New York, 1970.

9. Wlodkowski, Raymond J., *Enhancing Adult Motivation to Learn,* Jossey-Bass, San Francisco, 1985.

10. Houle, Cyril O., *The Effective Board,* Association Press, New York, 1960.

11. Knowles, Malcolm S., *The Adult Learner: A Neglected Species,* 3d ed., Gulf Publishing Co., 1984.

12. Knowles, Malcolm S., *Andragogy in Action,* Jossey-Bass, San Francisco, 1984.

13. Boone, Edgar J., ed., *Serving Personal and Community Needs Through Adult Education,* Jossey-Bass, San Francisco, 1980.

14. Brown, F. Gerald, and Kenneth R. Wedel, *Assessing Training Needs,* National Training and Development Service Press, Washington, DC, 1974.

15. Davis, Larry N., and Earl McCallon, *Planning, Conducting, Evaluating Workshops,* Learning Concepts, Austin, TX, 1974.

16. Knowles, Malcolm S., *The Modern Practice of Adult Education,* 2d ed., Cambridge Book Co., New York, 1980.

17. McKenzie, Leon, and John McKinley, ed., "Adult Education: The Diagnostic Procedure," *Bulletin of the School of Education,* vol. 49, no. 5, Indiana University, Bloomington, 1973.

18. Mager, Robert, and Peter Pipe, *Analyzing Performance Problems,* Fearon Publishers, Belmont, CA, 1970.

19. Mager, Robert, *Preparing Instructional Objectives,* Fearon Publishers, Belmont, CA, 1962.

20. Kirkpatrick, Donald L., *Evaluating Training Programs,* ASTD, Washington, DC, 1975.

21. Scriven, N., ed., *Evaluation in Education,* McCutchan Publishing Corp., Berkeley, CA, 1974.

22. Stufflebeam, Daniel, et al., *Educational Evaluation and Decision Making,* Peacock Publishers, Itasca, IL, 1971.

23. Cronbach, Lee J., et al., *Toward Reform of Program Evaluation: Aims, Methods and Institutional Arrangements,* Jossey-Bass, San Francisco, 1980.

24. Guba, Egon G., and Yvonne S. Lincoln, *Effective Evaluation: Improving the Usefulness of Evaluation Results Through Responsive and Naturalistic Approaches,* Jossey-Bass, San Francisco, 1981.

25. Patton, Michael Q., *Utilization-Focused Evaluation,* Sage Publications, Beverly Hills, CA, 1978.

26. Patton, Michael Q., *Qualitative Evaluation Methods,* Sage Publications, Beverly Hills, CA, 1980.

27. Patton, Michael Q., *Creative Evaluation,* Sage Publications, Beverly Hills, CA, 1981.

28. Patton, Michael Q., *Practical Evaluation,* Sage Publications, Beverly Hills, CA, 1982.

Additional Reading

Boud, David, Rosemary Keogh, and David Walker, eds., *Reflection: Turning Experience into Learning,* Nichols Publishing Co., New York, 1985.

Brookfield, Stephen D., *Understanding and Facilitating Adult Learning,* Jossey-Bass, San Francisco, 1986.

Cross, K. Patricia, *Adults as Learners,* Jossey-Bass, San Francisco, 1981.

Houle, Cyril O., *The Literature of Adult Education: A Bibliographic Essay,* Jossey-Bass, San Francisco, 1982.

Knox, Alan B., *Adult Development and Learning,* Jossey-Bass, San Francisco, 1977.

Merriam, Sharan B., and Phyllis M. Cunningham, eds., *Handbook of Adult and Continuing Education,* Jossey-Bass, San Francisco, 1989.

Peters, John M., et al., *Adult Education: Evolution and Achievements in a Developing Field of Study,* Jossey-Bass, San Francisco, 1991.

Smith, Robert M., et al., *Learning to Learn Across the Life Span,* Jossey-Bass, San Francisco, 1990.

13

Designing Instructional Systems

Michael Molenda

James A. Pershing

Charles M. Reigeluth

Michael Molenda *has been a member of the Instructional Systems Technology faculty at Indiana University since 1972. He teaches courses in instructional design, evaluation and change processes, media applications, and instructional technology foundations. He served on the board of directors of the Association for Educational Communications and Technology from 1988 to 1991. His corporate consulting work includes work with LG Group (Korea), AT&T Global Information Solutions, and Citibank. He is coauthor of* Instructional Media and Technologies for Learning, *5th ed. (1996), and "Educational Technology in Elementary and Secondary Education" in* International Encyclopedia of Education *(1994). He has lectured and consulted with education agencies in Spain, the Netherlands, Indonesia, Swaziland, Qatar, Kuwait, Jordan, and Venezuela. He has served as a senior Fulbright lecturer in Peru. He holds a Ph.D. in instructional technology from Syracuse University.*

James A. Pershing *is a faculty member in the Department of Instructional Systems Technology at Indiana University. He teaches courses in survey research, evaluation, project management, and the economic dimensions of training and development. He holds a Ph.D. and master's degree in education and economics, respectively, from the University of Missouri. He has published articles and made professional presentations on* *strategic planning and policy analysis, evaluation, and instructional development. Dr. Pershing has lectured and consulted with government agencies and corporations in Canada, Chile, Mexico, Puerto Rico, Korea, and the United States. His corporate consulting includes work with Arthur Andersen, AT&T, Delco Electronics, Eli Lily, Hunts Food, Hoosier Energy, LG Group, Samsung (Korea), and the National Bank of China.*

Charles M. Reigeluth *has been a Professor, Instructional Systems Technology Department, Indiana University, since 1988 and served as chairman of the department from 1990–1992. He is founder and Director of the Restructuring Support Service at Indiana University and President of the Division for Systemic Change in Education in the Association for Educational Communications and Technology (AECT). He has also served as instructional consultant for corporate, health, public, and higher education institutions, and as educational restructuring consultant for state and local education agencies. He taught secondary-level science for 3 years and spent 10 years on the faculty of the instructional design program at Syracuse University, culminating as chair of the program. Dr. Reigeluth's interests include reinventing public education and designing high-quality educational resources. He has published 6 books and over 60 articles and chapters on those subjects and has produced several educational software programs. He has developed a vision of a new educational system to better meet the needs of learners in the information society of the twenty-first century, and he has developed and refined guidelines for the change process to help educational stakeholders to bring about the changes most appropriate for their community. He is the major developer of several instructional design theories including the elaboration theory and simulation theory. Two of his books received an AECT "outstanding book of the year" award. He has a B.A. in economics from Harvard University and a Ph.D. in instructional psychology from Brigham Young University.*

This chapter deals with processes for the design of instruction that fits within the training program of an organization. We begin with the rationale for approaching instructional design systematically and a discussion of models of the instructional design process. Second, we describe the procedures of the conventional instructional systems development (ISD) model. Third, we propose and explain an updated model, the Business Impact ISD Model, that addresses the new realities of training in today's business context.[1] It ties the instructional design process more closely to other business processes, shifting the focus from training per se to improving organizational productivity through performance improvement. The functions of needs analysis, evaluation, and implementation—already present in the conventional model—are expanded in the Business Impact ISD Model. These are the functions by which the instructional design process can be more strategically aligned with the larger business system.

Why Design Instruction?

To be a vital element of any organization, the training program must be integrated into the business operations of the organization, it must provide valuable outputs, and it must do so in a cost-effective manner. In most cases, not only must the instruction be effective, but it must be consistent in content and quality over time and across different work sites. For years these criteria have been applied to other business processes such as production and sales, but only in recent years have they been applied with rigor to training programs. As the demands for training results have increased, the search for efficient, effective instructional systems has increased. This has led to instructional design processes that resemble product-design processes, entailing market analysis, planning, engineering, development, testing, and eventual mass production and installation.

Why Instructional Design Models?

Since the 1970s there has been a proliferation of models of instructional design (ID). The purpose of a model is to convey key concepts and processes to be included in a particular approach. Models, whether verbal, visual, or a combination of both, are a shorthand method of communicating what the authors believe to be the critical success factors in their approach to instructional design. Models are sometimes meant to be followed literally as step-by-step procedural blueprints, but more often they are offered as general guides to critical operations and their sequence. The most common terms applied to the ISD process are *model* and *road map*. Both words imply fidelity to reality, but both emphasize that the model-map is a metaphor. The road map and model both implicitly portray the element of time: the map indicates in inches how far it is from point A to point B and makes possible an inference of how long it takes to get there; the ID model portrays events (mental, behavioral, or physical) that will occur in the duration of a good project.

Interestingly, in no case that we know of has an instructional design model been promulgated as a *description* of what expert practitioners do. Rather, it is an idealized guide that suggests what to do and when to do it, usually without being very specific about *how* to do it. Unfortunately, critics have often set up a "straw man," implying that instructional design models are, or ought to be, descriptions of expert practice. They then observe or interview experts and discover—*voilà!*—that experts do the job very differently from the step-by-step logic specified in the model. Critics then treat this finding as a proof that the model is invalid. In the design of instruction, as in other lines of work, there is a good deal of craft and art. The intuitive shortcuts developed with experience inevitably lead the expert away from the "cookbook" and toward improvisation. But for the apprentice chef (not to mention the manager of the restaurant), the cookbook is the vital link to maintaining quality and consistency from day to day and project to project.

The ISD Model

There are different "families" of ID models, but the most prevalent and most widely adopted type is known as instructional systems development (ISD). This family of models places highest value on the following qualities:

1. *Systematic:*   the steps are carefully prescribed and follow a logical order
2. *Systemic:*   the steps are intended to cover all processes critical for success; the designer is constantly aware of the interdependence of the elements of the

total instructional system (learners, instructors, materials, environments, job demands, etc.)

3. *Reliable:*   the steps are spelled out in sufficient detail that the intellectual processes can be carried out with great similarity from one designer to another, one site to another, one project to another, and over time

4. *Iterative:*   it is expected that the cycle of analysis-design-development-testing-revision will be repeated a number of times during any given project

5. *Empirical:*   data gathering is built into the process and decisions are made on the basis of data

The main elements of the ISD model are *a*nalysis, *d*esign, *d*evelopment, *i*mplementation, and *e*valuation; thus it is sometimes referred to as the *ADDIE* Model (see Fig. 13-1).

Limitations of the ISD Model

McCombs[2] conducted an extensive analysis of the implementation of the ISD approach up to that time, especially in the U.S. military. She identified four principal problem areas:

1. Gaps in the prescriptions offered in ISD models

2. Inadequate knowledge and skills of designers using the models

3. Incomplete or inadequate application of the model

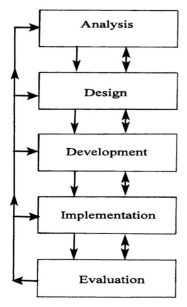

Figure 13-1. The ADDIE Model.

4. "Overproceduralization" (designers filling out forms for their own sake) as a consequence of models that specify highly detailed procedures

The implication of McCombs' analysis is that ISD models do not substitute for human imagination and creativity, nor do they fully compensate for lack of prior design experience. They can provide useful guidelines, especially to novices, but they cannot make those novices experts instantly.

The ISD Process Today

The Present

What does the ISD process look like today? There is no single authoritative source to answer this question. The closest thing to a consensus probably is the set of Instructional Design Competencies issued by the International Board of Standards for Training, Performance, and Instruction (IBSTPI).[3] IBSTPI's list of competencies for instructional designers implies the processes of ISD that are considered essential by practitioners:

1. Determine projects that are appropriate for instructional design.
2. Conduct a needs assessment.
3. Assess the relevant characteristics of learners-trainees.
4. Analyze the characteristics of a setting.
5. Perform job, task, and/or content analysis.
6. Write statements of performance objectives.
7. Develop the performance measurement.
8. Sequence the performance objectives.
9. Specify the instructional strategies.
10. Design the instructional materials.
11. Evaluate the instruction-training.
12. Design the instructional management system.

The Future

By the mid-1990s the ISD approach has come to be more popular than ever in corporate education. Ironically, the same forces of technological innovation and rapid organizational change that made ISD necessary are also threatening its hegemony. Because of the short shelf-life of information and even of the products and services offered by some companies, there is a growing resistance to the whole notion of formal classroom instruction, not to mention the potentially lengthy and labor-intensive process of designing that instruction.

There is much speculation about embedding expert systems into the work environment (e.g., with electronic performance support systems), delivering "just-in-time learning" to the desktop, and converting classroom instruction to on-job apprenticeships. Options such as these are explored in other chapters of this handbook. It is most likely, though, that these alternatives will be added to, rather than replace, systematically designed instruction.

The Logic of the ISD Model

The basic engine of the ISD model is the systems approach: viewing human organizations and activities as systems in which inputs, outputs, processes (throughputs), and feedback and control elements are the salient features. Designing instruction can proceed in an orderly and systematic way if the processes are carried out in a logical order and the output of each setup provides the input for the next. For example, the output of the needs analysis is a set of performance deficiencies (such as errors being made by workers). In the task analysis these deficiencies are broken down to determine what ought to be taught. This output is converted into statements of performance objectives. The objectives are analyzed to decide on sequencing of instruction and instructional strategies. Materials are then designed to implement these strategies, and so on.

Procedures of the Conventional ISD Model

Detailed procedures for ISD are elaborated in several widely used and respected textbooks, such as Romiszowski,[4] Kemp et al,[5] Dick and Carey,[6] Gentry,[7] and Leshin et al.[8] In this chapter we summarize the procedures at a general level.

In the conventional ISD model, the major phase—analysis, design, development, implementation, and evaluation—are typically subdivided into a number of procedural steps, as shown in Fig. 13-2.

Needs Analysis

To justify embarking upon an instructional development project, there must be evidence of a performance deficiency of such a type and of such a scope as to require training. Typically, business activities or reports are the first indicators of performance problems. A drop in market share could signify deficiencies in customer service. The purchase of new manufacturing technology indicates a need for operator training. Lawsuits could be triggered by discriminatory practices.

How must employee performance change to overcome the deficiency? The success of training can be measured according to how well the trainees *use* their newly acquired skills on the job. These transfer-of-training attainments can be established as the goals of the design effort.

The steps of needs analysis are:

1. *Define "system of interest."* Whose problem is going to be solved? Are we interested in the whole organization, one department, or one function within the department? State clearly who will be affected by the anticipated training—individuals, teams, or the organization as a whole.

2. *Determine performance deficiencies.* Are people performing below acceptable standards? Is the business expanding to offer new services and take on new employees? Is a new product being introduced that sales and maintenance staff are not yet informed about? These questions generally lead to gathering data. Interviews, focus groups, surveys, document review, and observation are all common methods for identifying or confirming performance deficiencies. Some information might be generated in the normal course of business: phone response rates, defective parts inventories, and documented compliance errors,

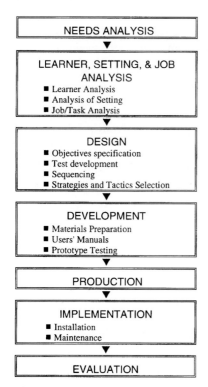

Figure 13-2. Breakdown of phases and steps
in the ADDIE ISD Model.

for example. Other information might be gathered especially for needs analysis,
by methods such as

- training-needs survey

- competency study

• performance analysis

- task analysis

3. *Separate incentive, management, and ignorance problems.*   Once performance
deficiencies are identified, the *source(s)* of those deficiencies must be identified.
That is, are they caused by ignorance (for which training may be the cure) or are
they rooted in other causes that are beyond the reach of training? There are three
broad possibilities. First, people may lack the knowledge or skill to do the job
effectively (ignorance problem). Second, people know how to do the job but fail
to do so because they are not motivated to do so (incentive problem). Third,
people *know* how to do the job and *want* to do the job but are prevented from
doing so by inadequate tools, poor communications, or obstructive organizational structures (management problem). Again, data must be gathered to carry
out this analysis (referred to by Harless as "front-end analysis");[9] methods might
include observation, interview, or analysis of records. The point is that only those
performance deficiencies that can be attributed to ignorance ought to be candidates for training.

4. *State problem to be solved.* Having identified one or more ignorance problems, you have some assurance that training may be a feasible solution to your problem. The next step is to state explicitly the problem to be solved.

5. *Determine cost-benefit payoff.* Training may not be justified if the projected benefits are less than the projected costs. Both costs and benefits may be measured in "soft" terms (e.g., effort and creativity expended) as well as in hard monetary terms. For example, one of the costs is opportunity cost: What other opportunities are being neglected to pursue this one? The calculation of costs and benefits is likely to be a rough "back of the envelope" estimation, but some effort at analysis must be made.

Learner, Setting, and Job Analysis

Learner Analysis. Designers consider it essential to take into account the characteristics of the people to be trained, the learners. What are their backgrounds, job experiences, aptitudes, motivations, and styles of learning? It is well recognized that people differ in many respects. It is not possible to know or cater to all differences, so the challenge is to decide which characteristics are most crucial to the instructional decision-making process.

1. *Entry competencies.* Probably the single factor that will make the largest impact on design decisions is the knowledge and skills of the trainees upon entering the program. What do they already know? Do they have the prerequisite knowledge and skills needed to enter the new training? Do they come in with misconceptions or biases about the subject? This information influences the entry point, complexity, pace, and emphasis of the instructional content.

2. *General characteristics.* Next in importance is a description of the learners in terms of personal qualities that define their role in the workplace. What are their ages? What are their job types? Where do they fit in the organizational hierarchy? Where are they located geographically? This data will suggest their motivation level—their eagerness or reluctance to take part.

3. *Learning styles.* There are numerous theories about how to classify people according to learning style (see Kolb,[10] and Myers and McCauley,[11] and Butler[12]). No one theory has been proven to be superior in giving guidance to designers. All these theories agree, though, that in any given group of adults a wide variety of styles is represented: people who prefer visual to verbal representation, people who prefer working in groups to individually, people who approach tasks sequentially versus those who take large intuitive leaps, and so on. In most situations it is not feasible to assess design for all the different learning styles. What is feasible, though, is to make sure that your instructional strategies provide a range of *options*—self-study or small-group work, reading a manual or exploring a computer database, viewing a video demonstration or doing hands-on manipulation. Given alternatives, learners can choose an approach to learning that best suits their preferences.

Analysis of Setting. The setting in which training is to be developed and delivered has a significant impact on how development and delivery is done. The resources and constraints of the organization (time, money, people, equipment) and its culture (values, mission, policies) will affect the development time, the delivery method, and the time and place of instruction.

Designers working inside their own organization usually know the resources available and the constraints, although they usually seek explicit guidelines on the budget and timelines for new initiatives. Outside consultants, though, must determine what the resources and constraints are in a given setting. Client reports, observation, and interviews with informants can supply data to clarify such factors as

- Organizational philosophy
- Preferred delivery methods
- Human resources available for instructional design
- Time
- Money
- Equipment and facilities

Job-Task Analysis.   Having established a need for training and having surveyed the characteristics of the trainees and the training setting, the analyst must develop a thorough understanding of the job or task to be learned. This task entails analysis of the parts of the job, their sequence, the frequency of performance, their criticality to successful performance, and accompanying bodies of information.

These analyses typically are conducted by observing expert performance, interviewing experts, and scrutinizing technical documentation. The major challenge for the designer is to select the most appropriate analytical tool for each situation, Jonassen and Hannum[13] identify some 30 task analysis techniques; Zemke and Kramlinger[14] provide instructions for about two dozen, ranging from behavior algorithms to the critical incident technique; and Swanson[15] discusses needs and task analysis in the context of performance improvement. It is beyond the scope of this chapter to describe these.

Design

Objectives Specification.   Completion of job-task analysis provides the designer with a detailed breakdown of what needs to be taught and learned. The last step of analysis and the first step of design is to specify clearly the performance objectives. Performance objectives describe what the learner will be able to do at the conclusion of instruction. In addition, they usually state the conditions under which the new capability will be displayed and the criteria by which successful performance will be judged. Clearly stated objectives can

- Establish clear-cut instructor and student goals
- Provide a basis for criterion-referenced measures
- Guide the selection of teaching-learning strategies

However, specifying objectives can be very time-consuming. It is usually cost-effective to specify them in performance terms for the terminal objectives and perhaps one or two levels of breakdowns of those objectives, but seldom is it productive to do so all the way down to enabling objectives.

The acronym ABCD can be used as a reminder of the major steps in the development of objectives statements:

1. *Audience:*   Describe the target population of learners.
2. *Behavior:*   Specify the performance expected after the learning experience. Use action verbs to describe observable behavior. If necessary, clarify the rele-

vant skill by adding a qualifying verb, e.g., "Demonstrate, by *calculating* according to the formula...."

3. *Conditions:* Describe the conditions under which the behavior is to be exhibited, including any resources given to or withheld from the learners. Describe the working environment under which the task will be performed. State what resources will be given or withheld, e.g., Can trainees use notes taken in class? What tools will they be working with? Job aids? Technical manuals?

4. *Degree* or standards: Specify the quantitative or qualitative criteria by which the performance will be judged. The standards may specify *quantitative* requirements, e.g., the number of steps that must be covered, the number of features that output must contain, the minimum acceptable percent correct, or tolerances. Standards may specify *qualitative* requirements for the output, such as "smoothly," "logically," or "as evaluated by experienced judges."

Test Development. Having specified the higher-level objectives in performance terms, it is relatively easy to take the next step, to specify the means for assessing whether learners have attained those objectives often referred to as performance measures. Development of performance measures at this point in the ISD process will help to clarify any uncertainties in the performance objectives. Additionally, performance measures will guide the design of instruction by focusing training efforts on the desired outcomes.

In general, there are three classes of performance measures: written tests, role-play and simulation exercises, and observation of on-job performance. Written tests are effective for assessing knowledge objectives, but not so effective for assessing the ability to apply that knowledge or assessing the attainment of desired attitudes. Role-play and simulation activities can assess more effectively those objectives dealing with applied skills, especially interpersonal skills such as communication, management, and sales. They are also relevant to assessment of attitude objectives, by allowing behaviors to be observed that presumably are the manifestations of an internal (unobservable) "attitude." Assessment of hands-on tasks can be accomplished by observing on-job performance. For reasons of convenience, cost, and safety, artificial approximation—in the form of role-plays or simulations—are often used to assess hands-on skills. The trade-off is a reduction in the real-life fidelity of the conditions under which the skill is displayed.

The steps of performance measurement are:

1. *Select type of assessment.* Choose the type of performance measurement to be used, beginning with the categories of written tests, role-play and simulations, and on-job performance observation.

2. *If test is a written one, select type of test.* If a written test will provide adequate assessment of your objective, choose the type(s) of items to be used: true-false, multiple-choice, matching, short answer, or essay.

3. *If role-play is used, devise a problem.* If the learning task requires a more realistic venue for measurement, devise a problem or situation that is realistic and typical for performance of the task.

4. *Include* conditions *and* degree. These should have been specified in the objective.

5. *Devise recording system.* Develop a concrete means for recording the results of your performance measurement. For example, for written tests an answer sheet is usually used; for role-play, a debriefing guide and observation form (including a scoring system of some sort); for on-job performance, a criterion checklist or other sort of observation form.

Sequencing.   After objectives and tests have been developed, the learners' end state should be clear. The next step is to determine the order in which the knowledge, skills, and attitudes will be taught. At this stage, collaboration with one or more subject-matter experts (SME) is indispensable. Sequencing is not critical if the content of the lesson is quite small, but it becomes more crucial as the length and complexity of the training increase.

There are a number of methods for sequencing content:

1. *Lower-level to higher-level skills.*   This is based on Gagne's theory of hierarchical organization[16] which assumes that the learning of higher-level skills depends on the mastery of all prerequisite lower-level skills.

2. *Start to finish.*   This applies to procedural skills, based on the order in which the steps are performed in real life.

3. *First to last.*   This applies to chronological or historical information, based on the time order of events in real life.

4. *Simple to complex.*   This is based on Reigeluth's Simplifying Conditions Method,[17] a part of the Elaboration Theory which proposes that complex skills can best be mastered by experiencing a graduated set of cases, in which the problems become more and more complicated.

Sequencing decisions can be made through the following steps:

1. *Judge importance of sequencing.*   Decide if the content is large and interrelated enough to be concerned about sequencing. If the total instructional time is less than one hour, sequencing is probably not critical. If the topics of the lesson or course are not interrelated but are independent, sequencing probably is not important.

2. *Decide which sequencing method(s) to use.*   If the task is fairly simple and is procedural, select a *start-to-finish* type of sequence—teaching the first step first, then the second step, and so on. If any individual steps are above the entry level of the learners, use the *lower-level to higher-level* skills sequence— teaching the lower-level prerequisite skills first. If the task is fairly complex and nonprocedural, select a *simple-to-complex* sequence—teaching the simplest complete version of the task first, then the next more complex version, and so on. In addition, use the start-to-finish type of sequence if appropriate to sequence within each version of the task. If the task does not fit any of these profiles, examine the tasks and content to find a fit with another sequencing method.

3. *Implement the sequencing method(s).*   Detailed procedures for different sequencing methods can be found in Leshin et al.[8] or Kemp et al.[5]

Strategies and Tactics Selection.   Before the development phase can begin, the designer must decide on the overall strategy, the midlevel approaches, and the detailed tactics for helping learners progress from where they are to where they must be. Strategic decisions are large-scale issues that affect the entire course, such as

- Learning environment, which can be on-job, in-classroom, or informal (e.g., at home)

- Instructional strategy, of which there are many options, including: case study, in which students analyze real-world cases; project-based learning, in which students conduct one or more projects and do readings or discussions as needed to help them with their project; and sequential topics, in which students typically do assigned readings about a topic, followed by lectures, discussions, and/or exercises

Midlevel decisions deal with issues that affect "units" of a course, such as

- Grouping, which can be individual, small group, or large group
- Control system, which can be teacher-led, media-controlled, or learner-controlled
- Realism, which can be real-world, simulated, or decontextualized
- Pedagogical approach, which can be anywhere on a continuum from discovery through guided discovery to expository

(*Note:* If any of these decisions are applied to the entire course, it is a strategic decision rather than a midlevel decision).

Tactical decisions affect small pieces of the instruction, typically a lesson or part of a lesson. They include

- Methods, such as lecture, tutorial, discussion, self-study, laboratory, etc.
- Media, such as print, video, computer, human, etc.
- Message design, including visual factors, spatial factors, time-based factors (including interactional design), and human factors
- Routine tactics, which are routinely used for a given type of learning, such as presenting, demonstrating, providing practice, giving feedback, etc. (see Leshin et al.[8])
- Supporting (or secondary) tactics, which are used depending on the difficulty of the task for the learners, such as attention-focusing devices, mnemonics, alternative representations (see Leshin et al.[8])

(*Note:* If any of these decisions are applied to a whole unit of the course, it is a midlevel decision rather than a tactical decision.)

Specifying an appropriate combination of strategies and tactics can be a complicated matter because there are many options to consider. It is often difficult to know where to begin. However, in actual practice the decision making is usually simplified by one or more of the following factors. First, these elements are often strongly interrelated. For example, having chosen large-group grouping and teacher-led control, the options for pedagogical approach, environment, method, and media are severely narrowed. Second, practical constraints often dictate some of these decisions. For example, it may be impractical to pull 40 software engineers off their jobs into a central training facility, so the choices might narrow rapidly to computer-mediated delivery in self-study form.

Development

Materials Preparation. In the development phase, the actual products to be used in the teaching-learning process are created, at least in prototype form. Most training is designed to be guided by print or audiovisual materials rather than left to the extemporaneous impulses of the instructor. Embedded in tangible materials, the lesson can be repeated with more or less predictable results. Training materials should be constructed so that they deliver on the specifications outlined in the design stage; follow accepted principles of human learning; present pertinent information; and provide opportunities for the practice and feedback needed to attain mastery of the specified knowledge, skills, and attitudes.

Regardless of the format or combination of formats, the materials must contain all the ingredients necessary to carry out the learning experiences specified in the strategic, midlevel, and tactical design decisions. An approach to materials development that focuses on performance outcomes will start with development of the practice-feedback activities. Be sure to incorporate the supporting tactics and message design features called for by the design specifications. This should result in first drafts or storyboards of role-play materials, interactive video programs, computer-based instruction, worksheets, and the like. The other routine tactics should be developed next (presentations, demonstrations, etc.). With the practice activities clear, it is easier to develop the supporting tactics that will best prepare the learner for the practice. Again, be sure to incorporate the supporting tactics and message design features called for by the design specifications. This should result in first drafts or storyboards of videos, print materials, lecture outlines, overhead transparencies, slide or tape programs, and so forth. Such an approach will yield a lean, short training program focused on take-away skills.

Manuals.   The learner's manual contains the directions needed for using the resources in the total instructional system. The manual relates the purpose of the training, lists specific objectives, and tells the trainees what they will be doing at each step of the learning process.

The instructor's manual describes the total system and its purposes. It provides an overview of the structure of the activities and materials—how they relate to one another. Objectives are spelled out and related to the various system components. Specific step-by-step directions for conducting teaching-learning activities are the heart of the instructor's manual. Worksheets and other job aids guide instructors in planning and monitoring their activities. The manual also contains the tests or other performance measures.

Prototype Testing.   The prototype instructional materials and manuals should be checked at various stages so that errors detected in the early stages can be remedied before large investments of time and money are made. This type of testing is also referred to as formative evaluation—evaluation of the instruction while still in the formative stages (as opposed to summative evaluation—the assessment conducted after revisions have been made and materials have been mass-produced). In practice, testing of prototypes is often quite informal and small-scale. The first step is to have a few people who are representative of the target audience work through the materials in a one-on-one tryout with an evaluator. They are encouraged to think aloud and to report any problems.

After revisions are made on the basis of one-to-one tryouts, small-group tryouts involving larger numbers of representative learners are sometimes conducted. Here more formal evaluation procedures are usually followed: a pretest, use of the prototype, a posttest to determine learning, and reactionnaires or interviews to determine learners' feelings about the instruction. At this point, the designer develops and uses the performance measures (written tests, role-plays, or on-job observation) that were specified earlier in the design phase.

Revisions are made in the prototype depending on the performance and expressed feelings of the tryout learners. Specific formats for efficient analysis of tryout data are suggested in Dick and Carey[6] and Gentry.[7]

Formative evaluation usually includes expert appraisal, that is, critiques of the draft materials by subject-matter experts and media or methods specialists. This assessment is done because content errors or inadequate methodology may not be detected by learners.

Production

After the prototype materials have been tested and revised, they are ready to be produced in large enough numbers to serve all intended learners. Most ISD models lack any significant discussion of the production process, since it is assumed this will be accomplished by media production specialists (who may be quite separate from the instructional design team). In many organizations this task is subcontracted to an outside agency. In other cases it is done by an in-house production center. In any case, the production process is considered to be a routine activity in which the production personnel are basically replicating the materials and manuals designed, tested, and revised by the design team.

Implementation

Installation. The transition from completed product to full installation and use can be difficult. In any organization there are numerous sources of resistance to new ideas or new ways of doing things. The introduction of a new course into an existing system can trigger "rejection" responses from one or more parts of the system. For example, new courses usually require some instructor training, especially if the instructors are not on the design team. If there is insufficient time or trainers for instructor training, instructors may experience difficulties, become frustrated with the course, and undermine it. Installation requires these steps:

1. *Secure vocal support from sponsor.* Acceptance of the instructional innovation by those responsible for the target system is a prerequisite to installation. Public support from the responsible decision maker(s) will give legitimacy to the solution.

2. *Identify informal opinion leaders and enlist their support.* An outsider might need advice from insiders, or other sorts of data, to identify those people within the target system whose opinions are influential among the other members. Leverage the influence of *informal* leaders by persuading them to support your efforts. Tactics might include asking their help, informing them about the benefits of your innovation, or arranging a demonstration for them. After some influential individuals buy in, encourage them to talk to others.

3. *Train the trainers.* Organize and conduct training sessions for those responsible for delivering the new course or instructional system.

4. *Procure and install equipment and other resources.* Usually, existing equipment and facilities need to be reconfigured or new ones procured and installed. Other resources, ranging from lighting to pencils, need to be procured or otherwise prepared for the instruction.

Maintenance. Instructional designers' responsibilities for an innovation typically end with initial installation, but the quality and longevity of the innovation may decline rapidly if no attention is given to longer-term maintenance. For example, those originally trained to deliver the course may move on. Their replacements may receive little or no training and may deliver the course poorly or change it arbitrarily. Further, someone must decide when the course needs revision or replacement. This decision may be made arbitrarily unless there is some mechanism for monitoring the operation of the course or other innovation.

Installation is not complete until the innovation receives continuing funding and is incorporated in the forms and procedures by which the target system is managed. In some cases, special equipment, facilities, or personnel will be necessary. These arrangements, too, need to be embedded into the routine. Installation and maintenance procedures such as these are spelled out by Gentry.[7]

Evaluation

Evaluation at the end of the process is primarily of a summative type—to provide evidence to sponsors and potential users about the value of the solution. Kirkpatrick [18] differentiates four levels of evaluation:

Level 1: Reaction. How participants react to an instructional program.

Level 2: Learning. The extent to which participants improve knowledge, skill, or attitude as a result of participation.

Level 3: Behavior. The extent to which on-the-job behavior is changed or skills are transferred to the work setting.

Level 4: Results. The final results or business impact that occurred because of participation.

Kirkpatrick,[18] Newby,[19] and Kemp et al.[5] suggest specific procedures for gathering and analyzing summative evaluation data to respond to each of these levels of evaluation. (Also see Chap. 14, Evaluation, and Chap. 15, Measuring the Results of Training.)

A Business Impact ISD Model

Rationale

Corporate education specialists and instructional technologists view the ISD process differently than in the past because of the changing business environment brought about by global competition, Total Quality Management, and corporate reengineering. These influences, which gained strength throughout the 1980s and crested in the 1990s, forced human resources people to begin to focus seriously on the *business impact* of their work. It became clear that only those processes that could be demonstrated to have a direct effect on profitability (or another measure of organizational success) were going to survive.

This new emphasis has caused instructional designers to expand the boundaries of their models to incorporate features of the larger environment that affect and are affected by instruction. ISD's "systemic" view required not only a look at the human resources system, but link-ups with the other systems in the organization—production, sales, accounting, and so on. Successful organizations no longer view training as a staff or support function; it must contribute to the bottom line. Training must focus on business needs—performance problems or business opportunities. Training is now done "for impact" rather than "for activity," as argued persuasively by Robinson[20] and Newby.[19]

Further, it is now recognized that training is inextricably linked with organizational change. Training that takes place in isolation is largely unproductive. For training to be transferred and applied to the workplace it must be accompanied by changes in the workplace—job redesign, incentive systems, supervisor support, new tools, and so on. New skills and attitudes gained in the classroom shrivel rapidly unless used and supported on the job. This means that the workplace must be readied at the same time as the trainees. Nontraining interventions—job aids, self-directed work teams, and the like—have to be developed along with training interventions. Change management has become a regular feature of organizational life and must be articulated with training. Contrary to first appearances, integration of new training into the organizational routine cannot be left until the end of the development cycle. Ultimate acceptance of new or revised training depends on decisions made starting from the very first stages.

We propose a Business Impact ISD Model to incorporate these issues and new emphases. The model is an enlargement and refinement of the conventional ISD model and is shown in Fig. 13-3.

Features of the Business Impact ISD Model

The major theme of the Business Impact ISD Model can be summed up in the statement "training alone doesn't solve performance problems." Almost *all*

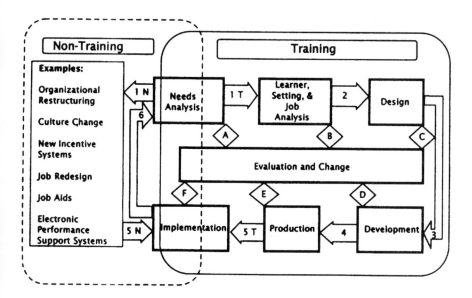

Legend

1N Performance improvement plan, non-training interventions	Process Evaluation	Evaluation Criteria
	A Strategic alignment	Social/business impact
1T Performance improvement plan, training interventions	B Context evaluation	Transfer of training
	C Expert judgment	Participant learning
2 Goals and Objectives	D Learner tryout &	Participant reaction
3 Blueprint/Specifications	usability testing	
4 Tested prototype	E Planning program	Activity accounting
5N Non-training interventions		budgeting system
5T Training interventions = the	F Summative	Overall assessment
instructional system	evaluation	of worth
6 Performance improvement system = the solutions		

Figure 13-3. Business Impact ISD Model.

performance problems faced by organizations are multidimensional. They are rooted in more than one cause or barrier, and training may or may not be part of the solution.

What is most distinctive about the Business Impact ISD Model is that evaluation and change concerns are addressed explicitly *at each stage*. The model shows explicitly how training and nontraining interventions relate to each other, springing from a common needs analysis and intersecting in a common implementation process. This dictates a more complex graphic depiction, but a depiction that accords with the reality of instruction designed for business impact.

Evaluation Is a Driving Force.   At each stage in the model, the instructional designer uses different methods to evaluate activities and outputs. These evaluation activities provide quality assurance throughout the process. Additionally, important program evaluation criteria and standards are contemplated and specified at each stage of the ISD process rather than at the end. By doing so, decision-making processes are integrated into each stage of instructional development. Decision making stays focused on the ultimate target of instructional development—business impact.

Change Management Is a Driving Force.   The resolution of problems and the actualizing of business opportunities by their very nature mean change. Thus managing change is critical to program success. There are important change management tasks to address at each stage of the model, as there are for evaluation. Executives, managers, supervisors, and line and staff personnel impacted by the changes being advocated must buy into the program and actively support and participate in its success. Buy-in is required to accomplish two goals. First, support and resources are necessary in order to address the noninstructional components of the business intervention. As instructional development proceeds, so do the processes to diagnose and find solutions to the noninstructional needs. Ideally, these instructional and noninstructional activities take place in parallel and are coordinated and articulated. Second, changes will be required in the workplace to facilitate the needs of the newly trained worker. There must be preparations to facilitate the transfer and application of new knowledge and skills. Some of these activities occur before, some during, and others after the training.

Outcomes at Each Stage.   Identifiable products emerge from each stage of the process in this model. These "outputs" ideally become "inputs" for subsequent stages. However, the process is not unidirectional. Processes and products from earlier stages of development are often revisited and modified during later stages. This process of iteration is necessary since the development process is dynamic. Although progress is ongoing, it is not unusual to take two steps forward and one step back. Unanticipated findings in early stages of the ISD process can lead to decisions to modify a project or even to abandon it.

Strata of Training Evaluation

The Business Impact ISD Model uses a taxonomy of training evaluation based on the strata of impact ranging from stratum 0, where only attendance is counted, with no pretense of measuring the learning outcomes, to stratum 5, measuring the impact of the training program on the general society in which the organization plays a part. These strata are an extension of Kirkpatrick's[18] levels. At each stratum the evaluation has a different target:

Stratum 0: Activity accounting. Counts the volume of training conducted or the number of trainees, regardless of the quality or impact of the training.

Stratum 1: Participant reactions. Measures participants' satisfaction with the training and is sometimes referred to as "smile tests."

Stratum 2: Participant learning. Attempts to assess the extent to which learners accomplish the objectives of the program; do they exhibit the intended knowledge, skills, and attitudinal behaviors at the completion of training?

Stratum 3: Transfer of training. Focuses on job performance; do the participants use their new skills on the job?

Stratum 4: Business impact. Examines the ultimate impact on the success of the organization; does the improved employee performance make a difference to profitability (or other criterion of success)?

Stratum 5: Social impact. Attempts to ascertain the impact of the organization's changed performance on society.

None of these targets is inherently more correct or more worthy than any other. In different circumstances different targets—and sometimes multiple targets—may be justified.

1. *Example A.* A newly developed orientation program for new hires is developed. The need arises from exit interviews with employees who left the organization within six months of being hired. They indicated confusion about the goals of the company and did not feel part of the team. Targeting evaluation on stratum 1, participant reaction, makes sense given the importance of emotional response. Assessing the business impact (stratum 4) is also critical given the potential cost savings associated with reducing employee turnover, particularly among recent hires.

2. *Example B.* Plant safety has become a problem. Government regulators are insisting that shop workers be trained on safety procedures and be certified that they have taken the training and passed a competency examination. Stratum 2, learning, is central to such a certification program. Stratum 3, transfer, is also critical. Reductions in accidents can be monitored before and after the program. Stratum 5, social impact, could be of interest if the company encourages trained workers to work with local school, churches, and social service agencies to improve their safety practices.

3. *Example C.* A program on recycling scrap and waste is initiated. Executives want all employees to view a training video promoting and explaining recycling. Stratum 0, activity accounting, is necessary to monitor compliance with the goal of having all employees view the video. Stratum 4, business impact, would be important if revenues are expected from sorting and selling scraps and waste products. Stratum 5, social impact, may be important if the volume at the local landfill diminishes significantly because of the program.

As these examples indicate, the evaluation strata do not constitute a hierarchy of importance or desirability. Different strata may be used, depending on the nature and scope of the program. In the past, thinking of evaluation in "levels" has perpetuated a belief that higher levels of evaluation are more difficult and costly to implement than lower levels. This idea too is incorrect. Difficulty and cost depend on circumstances. For complex and hierarchical learning, it can be very difficult and costly to design and develop valid and reliable performance tests (stratum 2). Benefits or the return of investment (stratum 4) for a program that reduces rework or recalls of a product are quite easy to measure in monetary benefits. Program cost data is also relatively easy to calculate for most programs.

Procedures of the Business Impact ISD Model

Needs Analysis

Initiating a Needs Analysis.   Needs analysis can be approached either in a reactive or proactive mode. In the reactive mode, executives, managers, supervisors, or workers directly convey information to the analyst. The information conveyed may be in the form of a performance problem or business opportunity, or it may be in the form of a request for training. In the latter case, those making the request have already resolved the issue of need. They have made a judgment that training is part or all of the solution to their needs.

In the proactive mode the analyst takes the initiative. Much like a detective, the individual employs a variety of strategies to identify performance problems and business opportunities. Information regarding needs in the proactive mode can be gathered in a number of ways. The review and analysis of data and information from organizational documents is one technique. Annual business reports, long-term planning documents, and speeches by executives are examples of formal documents to focus upon. Less formal or informal documents may include in-house production and sales records, accident reports, personnel documents, meeting minutes, and reports documenting activities in research and development. By interacting with other personnel formally and informally, the analyst can construct hypotheses about needs. Volunteering for task forces, strategic planning groups, and personnel recruiting teams can also reveal information about emerging needs.

How the Business Impact ISD Model Differs.   In a business environment, the purpose of needs analysis is to identify performance problems or business opportunities. Ascertaining the nature and extent of needs and their causes and solutions is at the heart of the needs analysis. Typically, as a needs analysis unfolds, multiple causes and multiple solutions to a problem or opportunity will emerge. These problems and solutions can be broadly classified as training or nontraining interventions. The Business Impact ISD Model explicitly incorporates nontraining interventions into the model. These can be subsumed under three categories: organizational development (OD), human resource development (HRD), and technical systems development (TSD).

- *Organizational development.*   OD deals with strategy, the structure of an organization, its systems, competence, and culture. Strategy refers to the broad set of business objectives and guidelines for achieving long-term competitive advantage. Structure is with the functional relationships among people, facilities, and equipment. Systems include technical, human, financial, and information resources. The boundaries of subsystems and their interrelationships define an organization's overall system. Competence compares the employees' knowledge and skills to the requirements of their roles in the organization. Culture is the theme or pattern of rules and norms that control and influence the way people behave. For an organization to be effective, work culture must be aligned with strategy and structure.

- *Human resource development.*   HRD deals with people, including the ways in which people are selected and placed in jobs. It also covers employee incentive and motivation systems as well as employee health and safety. Employee education, development, and training are integral to HRD and are considered to be training interventions.

- *Technical systems development.* TSD includes ergonomics, which focuses on problems arising from the relationships among people, jobs, equipment, and the work environment by applying anatomical, physiological, and psychological knowledge. TSD deals first of all with the machines, tools, and facilities which make up the physical parts of a production system. It also deals with the whole range of job aids that guide employees in the mechanical and conceptual processes of the organization. These may include expert systems and electronic performance support systems as well as paper documents.

Needs Analysis Process Evaluation. Strategic alignment is the key in evaluating the needs analysis process. There are two major concerns. First, are the questions that evolved, data collected, and analyses used supportive of the strategies and policies of the organization? Second, does the performance improvement plan that evolved from the needs analysis relate to performance problems or business opportunities which are directly aligned with the visions and directions of the organization?

Needs Analysis Outcome Evaluation. At the needs analysis stage the design team ought to establish the criteria by which the total project will be judged. These criteria usually focus on targets at stratum 4, business impact, and stratum 5, social impact.

- Business impact criteria:

  Increasing productivity, market share, quality, savings, etc.
  Decreasing costs, downtime, errors, waste, accidents, absenteeism, etc.

- Business impact assessment tools:

  Pre- and posttraining data
  Cost-benefit analysis or return-on-investment analysis

- Social impact criteria:

  Contributions of training to local, regional, national prosperity
  Matching of trained manpower to local, regional, national needs
  Improved organizational climate, improved socioeconomic indicators, greater equality of opportunity, etc.

- Social impact assessment tools:

  Cost-benefit analysis, value analysis, organizational climate surveys, statistical indicators of socioeconomic conditions, human resources accounting, etc.

Assessing Payoff. The final purpose of a needs analysis is to identify the *criteria* to be used in judging how proposed interventions will yield payoff. In the Business Impact ISD Model it is critical for the design team and sponsor to agree "up front" about the criteria for success. In short, what is the potential "bottom line" for the organization? In business terms, this translates to costs and benefits. Costs are the resources (time, facilities, money, etc.) to be invested in implementing proposed interventions. Benefits are the returns attributable to those investments. If designer and sponsor can agree on how costs and benefits will be measured, the designer can make sure that these factors *are* measured during the subsequent phases of the project. Delivering benefits greater than costs makes corporate heroes of designers.

Change Activities.   The seeds for ultimate acceptance and use of the solution are planted at the beginning of the ISD process. Some of the most critical change activities begin during the needs analysis stage. The important actors at this stage are the sponsor—the person(s) who must approve the whole project—and the other key decision makers. The latter might include supervisors of the employees to be trained, subject-matter experts, or customers. The goal is to identify the key people, think about how the solution to the problem (for example, a new course) will affect each of them, and begin to pursue their buy-in.

The steps involved are:

1. As the problem is clarified, identify potentially key adopters (whose acceptance is critical to successful implementation).
2. Determine what would appeal to key adopters: How will it affect each of them personally? Different attributes of the solution will appeal to different sets of potential adopters (e.g., CEOs will be attracted to high-impact training, plant managers may be attracted to short and practical interventions, supervisors are looking for training that changes on-job performance, and customers are seeking better service).
3. Begin to involve the key people, especially informal opinion leaders. ("People support the ideas they help create.")

Outcome.   The major outcome of a needs analysis is a performance improvement plan. As shown in Fig. 13-3, this plan has two components: nontraining interventions (1N) and training interventions (1T). The former might include organizational restructuring, job redesign, altered systems for performance appraisal, new incentives, and job aids. The latter typically include courses, self-study modules, apprenticeship experiences, and other structured learning activities.

Learner, Setting, and Job Analysis

How the Business Impact ISD Model Differs.   While analyzing learners, settings, and job tasks, the Business Impact ISD Model adds two functions (1) to continue to look for ways to take care of the *nontraining* aspects of the overall intervention, and (2) to seek information regarding barriers to the *transfer of training* to the job.

Broad and Newstrom[21] recommend devising strategies for transfer of training that can be implemented before, during, and after training. A few examples follow:

Before Training

- Plan the timing carefully, avoiding seasonal or cyclical busy times.
- Provide trainees with pretraining assignments, such as readings or on-job problems to bring to the training session.
- Review proposed training with supervisors; discuss the training objectives and how they will impact work.

During Training

- Send work units as a group rather than as individuals.
- Provide a substitute on the job so the trainee will not be "swamped" with accumulated work upon return.

- Simulate on-job conditions as much as possible.
- Ask trainees to visualize themselves applying their new skills.
- In small groups, discuss the pros and cons of using the new skills; develop an action plan.

After Training

- Debrief supervisor and/or coworkers.
- Schedule regular meetings to discuss progress and any remediation needed.
- Provide an information or support hotline.

Process Evaluation.   The task is to ensure that the findings (the characterization of the learners, the description of the work setting, the breakdown of jobs and tasks) are on target. The goal is accomplished by sharing the findings with the sponsor and affected workers and their supervisors. Encourage them to react to your descriptions. Most importantly, ask supervisors to examine the proposed training objectives and rate them as to the value of the trainees attaining them.

Outcome Evaluation.   The analyst develops the criteria and methods for a stratum 3 evaluation, focusing on transfer of training to determine if trainees are actually applying their new knowledge and skills on the job. Some methods for gathering data about actual performance include:

- On-site observation of performance by trained observers
- Interviews with supervisors, trainees, coworkers, or subordinates
- Check-up on action plans made during training

Change Activities.   As the requirements for the new performance become clear, the designer should work with the supervisors and trainees to effect the workplace changes necessary to support the trainee's new performance. That is, supervisors must accept the learning of the knowledge and skills proposed in the job analysis and the changes that must be made in the work setting to enhance the probability that employees will use their new skills. Most of these changes entail nontraining interventions, including

- Supervisor observation and reward of new skills
- Job redesign
- Changes in organization, e.g., work teams instead of individual performers
- Upgraded tools or facilities
- Informational job aids or electronic performance support systems
- Reinforcement and follow-up by supervisors or the training department

Outcome.   The main outcome of this phase is a clear identification of the goals and objectives of the project. The purpose of all the analysis is to provide clear guidelines for the size and shape of the solution. Writing performance objectives in the ABCD format encourages the designer to be clear about the audience, the conditions, the performance, and the measurement standards.

Design

How the Business Impact ISD Model Differs.   The Business Impact ISD Model does not differ significantly from the ADDIE Model in terms of the activities carried out in the design phase. There is a bias in this model, though, toward instructional strategies that are most likely to yield mastery of new skills and transfer of those skills to the workplace. Active learning in the form of apprenticeships, role-plays, simulations, and embedded training is emphasized. Further, the designer coordinates the training design with the design of job aids, performance support systems, and any other nontraining interventions. The final intervention plan, incorporating training and nontraining elements, should be designed as a single unit so that the numerous changes throughout the organization occur at the proper times and each change reinforces the effectiveness of the whole intervention.

Outcome Evaluation.   The major evaluation concern at the design stage is to prepare the criteria and methods for stratum 2 evaluation, learning. Methods are discussed earlier under "Test Development." The difference in the Business Impact ISD Model is, again, one of emphasis, with the Business Impact ISD Model having a bias toward performance measures that relate closely to the stated program objectives. What was learned? Is that learning directly relevant to the identified performance problems?

Change Activities.   During the design stage, the principal change concern is to visualize an instructional system that is going to be accepted by subject-matter experts (SMEs), instructors, and learners. Unless the training experience is appealing to those most affected by it, it will not be used. So the main change management task at this stage is to pursue buy-in by these key actors through activities such as

1. When content and sequencing decisions are being made, check these decisions with supervisors and potential trainees to determine if this content is considered relevant to the job and worthwhile spending time and energy mastering.
2. When strategies and methods decisions are being made, check with SMEs and instructors to determine what sorts of pedagogical approaches are most likely to be successful. Not only is their expert advice helpful, but by collaboration they deepen their commitment to the solution.
3. When media decisions are being made, involve media production specialists, not only to determine the feasibility of a particular delivery system, but also to be sure that they will support and work enthusiastically to produce the solution being pursued.

Outcome.   The outcome of the design stage is a blueprint or set of specifications for the instructional system and for the performance measures (tests) to be developed (shown as 3 in Fig. 13-3).

Development

How the Business Impact ISD Model Differs.   At the development stage, the Business Impact ISD Model differs from the conventional ISD model primarily in regard to the approach taken to formative evaluation and the addition of planned change activities. As discussed below, the formative evaluation activities are expanded to include usability testing in addition to learner verification. At this stage, evaluation focuses on stratum 2 (participant reaction) and stratum 3 (learning). Usability testing is added in this model because of the model's emphasis on attracting acceptance by learners and instructors. The design team wants to discover early if there are features of the instructional system that are difficult to use or repellent to users.

Evaluation for Usability. In usability testing, a sample of end users actually uses the prototype while being observed by designers, who record reactions with an eye toward possible revisions. The benefits of usability testing are: (1) difficulties are detected and remedied before full production (2) over time, designers become more sensitive to user needs and thus better at designing user-friendly products.

Usability testing typically takes the form of prototype testing, conducted either in a lab setting or the actual intended work environment. The number of users involved may vary between 5 and 20 people who are representative of the potential users, beginning with a small sample and continuing until feedback becomes redundant, at which point testing ceases. Evaluators often use a think-aloud protocol in which users are encouraged to speak continuously as they work with an instructional product, providing insights into their expectations and reactions. Prototype testing is repeated after each major modification.

The sorts of questions addressed in usability testing are:

1. Are the directions easy to follow?
2. How long does it take to use specific parts of the product?
3. How many errors do people make in using the product?
4. Do people like the product?

These questions may be answered by direct observation, interview, focus-group discussion, or reactionnaire.

Change Activities. The main thing to be done at the development stage to enhance acceptance of the product is to create a product that is appealing to the users—instructors and learners. People are more likely to accept a solution that has certain attributes:

- Relative advantage—a clear personal payoff
- Compatibility with existing habits and values—doesn't require too much personal change
- Simplicity—the main features are easy to see and understand
- Cultural compatibility—the tone and examples are in line with the audience members' expectations and preferences
- Pedagogical appeal

The last point, pedagogical appeal, has been elaborated in Keller's Motivation Model.[22] This model recommends specific strategies for gaining and sustaining attention (e.g., novelty, questions, human interest, humor) and increasing relevance (e.g., give examples of utility, allow learners to feel ownership, use familiar examples and analogies). Keller's model also provides prescriptions for promoting learners' confidence (e.g., challenging, successful experiences) and satisfaction (e.g., let them see they can solve real-world problems, give ample positive feedback). The point of all these design features is to make the instructional experience appealing and thus more likely to be accepted by learners.

Outcome.   The outcome of the development stage is a tested prototype—a complete version of the instructional system, including the teaching and learning materials, all learning activities, and all user manuals (shown as 4 on Fig. 13-3).

Production

How the Business Impact ISD Model Differs.   At the production phase, the Business Impact ISD Model adds a concern for accounting to the customary activities designated in the conventional ISD model. This is a reflection of the model's focus on deriving business benefits from any costs expended.

Process Evaluation.   Production processes, whether conducted in-house or contracted out to a media production agency, must be carefully managed and monitored. An approach often applied to managing complex projects, as multimedia productions often are, is Planning, Programming, and Budgeting System (PPBS). PPBS is a systematic approach to allocating scarce resources to accomplishing an objective. Planning deals with setting objectives and priorities. Programming refers to selecting and organizing specific activities to accomplish the objectives. Budgeting matches programs with resources—a spending plan. Through mechanisms such as PPBS the design team can maintain control of production processes and weigh the value of product received for the money spent.

Change Activities.   Typically, "train the trainer" activities are conducted during the time that the instructional system is in production. These activities are discussed below as part of the implementation phase.

Outcome.   The instructional system that finally emerges from the production process (5T in Fig. 13-3) is the outcome of this phase. If prototype testing and revision took place at the development phase, the designer can have some confidence that this instructional system will be effective in helping people learn and will be viewed positively by instructors and learners.

Implementation

How the Business Impact ISD Model Differs.   In the conventional ISD model, implementation activities focus on "train the trainer" operations and persuasion strategies to win acceptance from key players. These are also included in the Business Impact ISD Model. In addition, though, the Business Impact ISD Model specifies that this phase includes a set of activities to merge and consolidate the training and nontraining interventions. The merger is shown in Fig. 13-3 in the form of arrows 5N and 5T shown feeding into the implementation phase.

Outcome Evaluation.   At the implementation phase, the focus of evaluation shifts to a summative judgment about the overall worth of the interventions. What, in the final analysis, was done and what was its value to the organization? This may include assessment of stratum 0 (activity accounting) and strata 4 (business impact) and 5 (social impact) phenomena.

Stratum 0, activity accounting, can be a legitimate and helpful type of evaluation. It asks: How many people experienced which activities at what cost? This information can serve three purposes: (1) an internal review to be used in planning and controlling routine operations, (2) an analysis that can help in formulating major plans and policies, and (3) a report to external parties about compliance to regulations.

Stratum 4, business impact, evaluation can be carried out by gathering actual cost and benefit data. In the needs analysis phase it was recommended that the designer and sponsor agree on a definition of what would be a successful yield of benefits. Benefits may result from either of two changes: (1) reduced inputs to the production processes of an organization (e.g., reduced personnel costs for goods or services delivered), or (2) increased outputs from the production processes (e.g., higher-quality goods or services).

The two methods outlined below are commonly used to demonstrate the business return of a program. The first is the benefit-to-cost ratio (BCR). The BCR uses total program benefits and total program costs. The BCR formula follows:

$$BCR = \frac{\text{Program benefits}}{\text{Program costs}}$$

The second is the return on investment (ROI) method. In calculating the ROI of a program, the total costs are subtracted from the total benefits to produce the net benefits. Net benefits are then divided by total program costs and multiplied by 100. The ROI formula follows:

$$ROI\ (\%) = \frac{\text{Net program benefits}}{\text{Program costs}} \times 100$$

For example, if a program has benefits of $160,000 and costs $40,000, the BCR is calculated as follows:

$$BCR = \$160,000 \div \$40,000 = 4, \quad \text{or 4 to 1}$$

In other words, for every $1 invested, $4 in benefits are returned.

The ROI is based on net benefits ($160,000 minus $40,000, or $120,000), so the calculation follows:

$$ROI\ (\%) = (\$120,000 \div \$40,000) \times 100 = 300\%$$

This means that for each $1 invested, there is a $3 return in net benefits.

Note that these formulas assume that all costs for development and delivery of an intervention, and the benefits, can be calculated in monetary terms and occur in one year. However, if a program has a lasting impact, significant benefits may continue after the first year. If so, development costs are prorated over a number of out years and compared to benefits for those out years.

The task of the design team at this last step, then, is to calculate the total costs of the performance improvement interventions and the total benefits yielded by the change. This, of course, is not always a clean or easy task, but it is far easier to accomplish if there was agreement at the beginning on the criteria.

Change Activities.   The challenge at the implementation phase is to tie together the nontraining interventions and training interventions and ensure that they are accepted, installed, and maintained within the organization. As recommended earlier in the context of the conventional ISD model, the design team can cultivate both formal and informal channels of influence to promote acceptance by securing vocal support from the sponsor and other formal leaders and persuading informal opinion leaders to support these changes. These installation and maintenance activities must be coordinated between the instructional design team and whoever is responsible for the nontraining interventions. Integration is the key.

Outcome. The outcome of the implementation phase (shown as 6 in Fig. 13-3) is the complete performance improvement system, the combination of training and nontraining interventions that were specified earlier in response to the deficiencies identified in the needs analysis. The amalgamation, installation, and maintenance of the performance improvement system completes the cycle.

Conclusion

The current business environment, brought about by global competition, Total Quality Management, and corporate reengineering, is forcing training and development people to focus seriously on the *business impact* of their work. This requires instructional designers to expand the boundaries of their traditional ISD models to consider features of the corporate and societal environments. Training must focus on business needs—performance problems or business opportunities. This chapter has presented the conventional ISD model and contrasted it with a Business Impact ISD Model to help meet this need.

References

1. Many of the concepts and elements of the Business Impact ISD Model grew out of three summers of collaboration between the authors and training managers of the LG Group (Korea) as we discussed ways to adapt the LG training process to the demands of today's competitive global business climate.
2. McCombs, Barbara L., "The Instructional Systems Development (ISD) Model: A Review of Those Factors Critical to Its Successful Implementation," *Educational Communications and Technology Journal,* Summer 1986, pp. 67–81.
3. IBSTPI (International Board of Standards for Training, Performance, and Instruction), *The Professional Reference Guide to the Competencies,* n.d., c. 1989.
4. Romiszowski, A. J., *Designing Instructional Systems,* Nichols, New York, 1981.
5. Kemp, Jerrold E., Gary R. Morrison, and Steven M. Ross, *Designing Effective Instruction,* Merrill, New York, 1994.
6. Dick, Walter, and Lou Carey, *The Systematic Design of Instruction,* 3d. ed., HarperCollins, New York, 1990.
7. Gentry, Castelle G., *Introduction to Instructional Development,* Wadsworth, Belmont, CA, 1994.
8. Leshin, Cynthia B., Joellyn Pollock, and Charles M. Reigeluth, *Instructional Design Strategies and Tactics,* Educational Technology Publications, Englewood Cliffs, NJ, 1992.
9. Harless, J. H., *An Ounce of Analysis (Is Worth a Pound of Objectives),* Harless Performance Guild, McLean, VA, 1975.
10. Kolb, D., *Self-Scoring Inventory and Interpretive Booklet,* McBer, Boston, MA, 1985.
11. Myers, I. B., and M. H. McCauley, *Manual: A Guide to the Development and Use of the Myers-Briggs Type Indicator,* Consulting Psychologists, Palo Alto, CA, 1985.
12. Butler, Kathleen A., *Learning and Teaching Style: In Theory and Practice,* Learner's Dimension, Columbia, CT, 1987.
13. Jonassen, David H., and Wallace H. Hannum, "Analysis of Task Analysis Procedures," in Anglin, G., ed., *Instructional Technology: Past, Present, and Future,* Libraries Unlimited, Englewood, CO, 1991.

14. Zemke, Ron, and Thomas Kramlinger, *Figuring Things Out,* Addison-Wesley, Reading, MA, 1982.
15. Swanson, Richard A., *Analysis for Improving Performance,* Berrett-Koehler, San Francisco, 1994.
16. Gagne, Robert M., Leslie J. Briggs, and Walter W. Wager, *Principles of Instructional Design,* 4th. ed., Harcourt Brace Jovanovich, Fort Worth, 1992.
17. Reigeluth, C. M., "Elaborating the Elaboration Theory," *Educational Technology Research and Development,* 40(3), pp 80–86.
18. Kirkpatrick, Donald L., *Evaluating Training Programs: The Four Levels,* Berrett-Koehler, San Francisco, 1994.
19. Newby, Tony, *Training Evaluation Handbook,* Pfeiffer and Company, San Diego, 1992.
20. Robinson, D. G., and J. C. Robinson, *Training for Impact,* Gulf Publishing, Houston, 1991.
21. Broad, Mary L., and John W. Newstrom, *Transfer of Training: Action-Packed Strategies to Ensure High Payoff from Training Investments,* Addison-Wesley, Reading, MA, 1992.
22. Keller, John M., "Strategies for Stimulating the Motivation to Learn," *Performance and Instruction,* October 1987, pp. 1–7.

Bibliography

Branson, R. K., and G. Grow, "Instructional Systems Development," in Robert M. Gagne, ed., Instructional Technology Foundations, Lawrence Erlbaum Associates, Hillsdale, NJ, 1987, pp. 397–428.

Branson, R. K., G. T. Rayner, J. L. Cox, C. J. Furman, F. J. King, and W. H. Hannum, *Interservice Procedures for Instructional Systems Development* (5 vols.). TRADOC Pam 350-30 and NAVEDTRA 106A, Fort Monroe, VA, U.S. Army Training and Doctrine Command (NTIS no. ADA-019 486 through ADA-019 490), 1976.

Brinkerhoff, Robert O., *Achieving Results from Training,* Jossey-Bass, San Francisco, 1991.

"Essentials for Evaluation," *Info-Line: Practical Guidelines for Training and Development Professionals,* ASTD, Alexandria, VA, 1986 (Stock No. 8601).

Gagne, Robert M., ed., *Instructional Technology: Foundations,* Lawrence Erlbaum Associates, Hillsdale, NJ, 1987.

Gustafson, Kent L., *Survey of Instructional Development Models,* 2d. ed., Clearinghouse on Information Resources, Syracuse University, Syracuse, NY, 1991.

Holcomb, Jane, *Making Training Worth Every Penny,* Pfeiffer & Co., San Diego, 1994.

"How to Collect Data," *Info-Line: Practical Guidelines for Training and Development Professionals,* ASTD, Alexandria, VA, 1990 (Stock No. 9008).

"How to Conduct a Cost-Benefit Analysis," *Info-Line: Practical Guidelines for Training and Development Professionals,* ASTD, Alexandria, VA, 1990 (Stock No. 9007).

"Measuring Attitudinal and Behavioral Change," *Info-Line: Practical Guidelines for Training and Development Professionals,* ASTD, Alexandria, VA, 1991 (Stock No. 9110).

Olsen, John R., and V. B. Bass, "The Application of Performance Technology in the Military," *Performance and Instruction,* July–August 1982, pp. 32–36.

Phillips, Jack J., ed., *In Action: Measuring Return on Investment,* ASTD, Alexandria, VA, 1994.

———, *Handbook of Training Evaluation and Measurement Methods,* Gulf Publishing, Houston, 1991.

Reiser, Robert A., "Instructional Technology: A History," in Robert Gagne, ed., *Instructional Technology: Foundations,* Lawrence Erlbaum Associates, Hillsdale, NJ, pp. 11–48.

Shrock, Sharon A., "A Brief History of Instructional Development," in Gary J. Anglin, ed., *Instructional Technology: Past, Present, and Future,* Libraries Unlimited, Englewood, CO, 1991, pp. 11–19.

Shrock, Sharon A., and William C. C. Cosarelli, *Criterion-Referenced Test Development: Technical and Legal Guidelines for Corporate Training,* authors, Weymouth, MA, 1989.

"Statistics for HRD Practice," *Info-Line: Practical Guidelines for Training and Development Professionals,* ASTD, Alexandria, VA, 1991 (Stock No. 91101).

14

Evaluation

Donald L. Kirkpatrick

Donald L. Kirkpatrick *is Professor Emeritus at the University of Wisconsin Management Institute where he spent 30 years conducting conference and seminars for all levels of management. His business experience includes Personnel Manager, Bendix Products, Aerospace Division and Training Director, International Minerals and Chemical Corp. He served on the National Board of Directors of the American Society for Human Resource Management (SHRM) and is a past national president of ASTD. He has written six management books including* How to Train and Develop Supervisors, How to Manage Change Effectively, How to Improve Performance Through Appraisal and Coaching, No-Nonsense Communication, *and* How to Plan and Conduct Effective Meetings. *His 1994 book is entitled* Evaluating Training Programs: The Four Levels. *He frequently speaks at national programs of ASTD, SHRM, and AMA. As a consultant, he conducts workshops in the United States and the Far East. He has developed and published eight supervisory-management inventories. His latest is* Management Inventory on Leadership, Motivation, and Decision-Making. *He received his B.B.A., M.B.A., and Ph.D. at the University of Wisconsin, Madison. His dissertation was called* Evaluating a Human Relations Course for Supervisors. *Kirkpatrick is an Elder at Elmbrook Church and active member, Gideons International.*

Effective training directors will make an effort to evaluate all their training activities. The success of these efforts depends to a large extent on a clear understanding of just what "evaluation" means. This chapter will attempt to accomplish two objectives: (1) to clarify the meaning of evaluation and (2) to suggest techniques for conducting the evaluation.

These objectives will be related to "in-house" classroom programs, one of the most common forms of training. Many of the principles and procedures can be applied to all kinds of training activities such as performance review, participation in outside programs, programmed instruction, and the reading of selected books.

The following quotation from Daniel M. Goodacre III is most appropriate as an introduction:

> Managers, needless to say, expect their manufacturing and sales departments to yield a good return and will go to great lengths to find out whether they have done so. When it comes to training, however, they may expect the return—but rarely do they make a like effort to measure the actual results. Fortunately, for those in charge of training programs, this philanthropic attitude has come to be taken for granted. There is certainly no guarantee, however, that it will continue, and training directors might be well advised to take the initiative and evaluate their programs before the day of reckoning arrives.[1]

Evaluation Clarified

Nearly everyone would agree that a definition of evaluation would be "the determination of the effectiveness of a training program." But this has little meaning until we answer the question: In terms of what? We know that evaluation is needed in order to improve future programs and to eliminate those programs which are ineffective. The problem is how to begin.

Evaluation changes from a complicated, elusive generality into clear and achievable goals if we break it down into logical steps. These steps can be defined as follows:

Step 1: Reaction.   How well did the conferees like the program?

Step 2: Learning.   What principles, facts, and techniques were learned? What attitudes were changed?

Step 3: Behavior.   What changes in job behavior resulted from the program?

Step 4: Results.   What were the tangible results of the program in terms of reduced cost, improved quality, improved quantity, etc.?

With this clarification of the meaning of evaluation, training directors can now begin to pinpoint their efforts at evaluation. They better realize what they are doing, and they recognize the limited interpretations and conclusions that can be drawn from their findings. As they become more experienced and sophisticated in evaluation design and procedures, they slowly begin to obtain more meaningful results on which future training can be based.

These four steps will now be defined in detail with examples and suggested guidelines. It is important to stress that the described *procedures* and *techniques* can be used in almost any organization. It is also important to stress that the *results* from one organization cannot be used in another organization. Obviously, there are many factors that would influence the results. These variables include the group, the conference leader, and the approach to the subject.

Step 1: Reaction

Reaction may best be defined as how well the trainees liked a particular training program. Evaluating in terms of reaction is the same as measuring the feelings of the conferees. In fact, it is measuring "customer satisfaction." It is important to emphasize that it does not include a measurement of any learning that takes place.

Guidelines for Evaluating Reaction

1. Determine what you want to find out.
2. Use a written comment sheet covering those items determined in step 1.
3. Design the form so that the reactions can be tabulated and quantified.
4. Obtain honest reactions by making the forms anonymous.
5. Encourage the conferees to write in additional comments not covered by the questions that were designed to be tabulated and quantified.

The comment sheet shown in Fig. 14-1 was used to measure reaction at an ASTD summer institute that was planned and coordinated by the staff of the Management Institute, University of Wisconsin.

Those who planned this ASTD program were interested in reactions to subject, technique (lecture versus discussion), and the performance of the conference leader. Therefore, the form was designed accordingly. The conferees were asked to place a check in the appropriate spaces so that the reactions could be readily tabulated and quantified.

In question 3, concerning the leader, it was felt that a more meaningful rating would be given the leader if the conferees considered items A through F before checking the overall rating. This question was designed to prevent a conference leader's personality from dominating group reactions.

Question 4 encouraged the conferees to suggest any improvements that came to mind. The optional signature was used so that follow-up discussions with conferees could be done. In this ASTD summer institute, about half of the conferees signed their names. With this type of group, the optional signature did not affect the honesty of their answers, in all probability. It is strongly suggested that unsigned sheets be used in most in-house meetings, however.

In most cases, a simpler comment sheet is sufficient. Figure 14-2 shows a form that obtained significant information on reaction and requires minimum time from participants. This form can be used for each leader. Of particular importance is the separation of "subject" from "leader."

To evaluate a total program that includes a number of sessions, a final comment sheet (Fig. 14-3) can provide additional valuable information for improving future programs. So that "standards of performance" can be established for the quality of instruction, the reactions can conveniently be converted to numerical ratings. For example, on the forms shown in Figs. 14-2 and 14-3 the following ratings can be used: excellent = 5, very good = 4, good = 3, fair = 2, and poor = 1. An example of reactions from 27 participants might be:

10 Excellent	$10 \times 5 =$	50
10 Very good	$10 \times 4 =$	40
5 Good	$5 \times 3 =$	15
1 Fair	$1 \times 2 =$	2
1 Poor	$1 \times 1 =$	1
27 Total participants		108 Total points

Dividing 108 (total points) by 27 (total participants), we get a rating of 4. Experience in a particular organization can provide data for the establishment of a standard of performance for all instructors.

I firmly believe in getting a comment sheet on each subject and each leader. In the case where the same leader is conducting a series of meetings with the same

---

ASTD INSTITUTE

Leader _____ Subject _____

Date _____

1. Was the subject pertinent to your needs and interests?

   ☐ No ☐ To some extent ☐ Very much so

2. How was the ratio of lecture to discussion:

   ☐ Too much lecture ☐ O.K. ☐ Too much discussion

3. Rate the leader on the following:

	Excellent	Very good	Good	Fair	Poor
A. Clarifying objectives					
B. Keeping the session alive and interesting					
C. Using audiovisual aids					
D. Maintaining a friendly and helpful manner					
E. Illustrating and clarifying points					
F. Summarizing					

What is your overall rating of the leader?

☐ Excellent ☐ Very good ☐ Good ☐ Fair ☐ Poor

4. What would have made the session more effective?

_____

_____

_____

_____

_____
Signature (optional)

Figure 14-1. Reaction form.

group, it may not be necessary to get reactions after each session. In a nine-session program, for example, it may be sufficient to obtain reactions after the third, sixth, and ninth sessions. A final comment sheet should also be used to get an evaluation of the entire program.

In cases where several leaders instruct for short periods of time, a form such as Fig. 14-4, should be used instead of using a separate reaction form for each leader. This form provides a great deal of information and takes a short time to complete.

It has been emphasized that the form should be designed so that tabulations can be readily made. In my opinion, too many comment sheets are still being

REACTION SHEET

Please give us your frank reactions and comments. They will help us evaluate this program for possible improvement in future programs.

Leader _____ Subject _____ Date _____

1. How do you rate the subject content?

      ☐ Excellent   COMMENTS:
      ☐ Very Good
      ☐ Good
      ☐ Fair
      ☐ Poor

2. How do you rate the conference leader?

      ☐ Excellent   COMMENTS:
      ☐ Very Good
      ☐ Good
      ☐ Fair
      ☐ Poor

3. What benefits do you feel you got from this session?

      ☐ New knowledge that is pertinent.
      ☐ Specific approaches, skills or techniques that I can apply on the job.
      ☐ Change of attitude that will help me in my job.

      OTHER:

4. What would have made this session better? (Use other side if necessary.)

Figure 14-2. Reaction form.

used in which the conferees are asked to write in their answers to questions. A form of this kind makes it very difficult to summarize comments and to determine patterns of reaction.

How to Supplement the Evaluation of the Conferees

At the Management Institute of the University of Wisconsin, sessions are always evaluated in terms of the reactions of the conferees. Occasionally the coordinator of the program felt that the group reaction was not a fair evaluation of the effectiveness of the program. Sometimes the conference leader's personality made such an impression on the group that this person received a very high rating. In other sessions, the conference leader received a low rating because he or she did not have a dynamic personality. Therefore, some members of the Management Institute

FINAL REACTION SHEET

NAME OF PROGRAM _____ DATE _____

1. How would you rate the overall program?

      ☐ Excellent   COMMENTS:
      ☐ Very Good
      ☐ Good
      ☐ Fair
      ☐ Poor

2. To what extent will it help you do a better job for your organization?

      ☐ To a large extent
      ☐ To some extent   COMMENTS:
      ☐ Very little

3. What were the major benefits you received? (Check as many as you wish.)

      ☐ Helped confirm some of my ideas.
      ☐ Presented new ideas and approaches.
      ☐ Acquainted me with problems and solutions from other companies.
      ☐ Gave me a good chance to look objectively at myself and my job.

    Other benefits:

4. How were the meeting facilities, luncheon arrangements, etc?

      ☐ Excellent   COMMENTS:
      ☐ Very Good
      ☐ Good
      ☐ Fair
      ☐ Poor

                     (OVER)

Figure 14-3. Final reaction sheet.

adopted a procedure by which the conference leader was rated by the coordinator as well as by the group. The form shown in Fig. 14-5 was used.

This procedure in which the coordinator of the program also evaluates each conference leader was also used in an ASTD summer institute. It was found that a coordinator's rating was usually close to the group's rating, but in some instances it varied considerably.

It is suggested that the training director in each company consider this approach. A trained observer such as the training director or another qualified person would fill out an evaluation form independent of the group's reactions. An analysis of the two would give the best indication of the effectiveness of the program.

5. What would have improved this program?

6. Would you like to attend future programs of a similar nature?

    ☐ Yes
    ☐ No
    ☐ Not sure

7. Other comments and suggestions for future programs:

Signature (optional) _____

Figure 14-3. (*Continued*) Final reaction sheet.

Conclusions About Reaction

The first step in the evaluation process is to measure the reactions to training programs. It is important to determine how people feel about the programs they attend. Decisions by top management are frequently based on one or two comments made by people who have attended. A supervisory training program may be canceled because one superintendent told the plant manager that "this program is for the birds."

Also, conferees who enjoy a training program are more likely to obtain maximum benefit from it. According to Spencer, "for maximum learning you must have interest and enthusiasm." In a talk given by Cloyd Steinmetz, of Reynolds Metals and a past president of ASTD, he stressed: "It is not enough to say, 'here is the information, take it?' We must make it interesting and motivate them to want to take it."

Reaction Sheet

Please give your frank and honest reactions:

Scale: 5 = Excellent   4 = Very good   3 = Good   2 = Fair   1 = Poor
(insert appropriate number)

Leaders	Subject	Presentation	Discussion	AV Aids	Overall
Tom Jones					
Gerald Ford					
Luis Aparicio					
Simon Bolivar					
Mohammad Ali					
Chris Columbus					
Bart Starr					

Facilities   Rating _____   The overall program   Rating _____

   COMMENTS: COMMENTS:

Meals   Rating _____   Suggestions for future programs:

   COMMENTS:

Figure 14-4. Leader rating sheet for several leaders.

To evaluate effectively, training directors should begin by doing a good job of measuring the reactions and feelings of people who participate. It is important to do this in an organized fashion, using written comment sheets which have been designed to obtain the desired reactions. It is also strongly suggested that the form be so designed that the comments can be tabulated and quantified. In the experience of the staff of the Management Institute, it is also desirable to have the coordinator, training director, or another trained observer make his or her own appraisal of the session in order to supplement the reactions of enrollees. The combination of these two evaluations is more meaningful than either one by itself.

An instructor who has effectively measured the *reactions* of conferees and finds them to be very favorable can feel extremely proud. However, the instructor should also feel humble because the evaluation measurement has only begun. Even though he or she has done a good job of measuring the reaction of the group, there is still no assurance that any learning has taken place. Neither is there any indication that the behavior of the participants will change because of the training program. And still further away is any realistic way of judging any results that can be attributed to the training program.

Step 2: Learning

It is important to recognize that a favorable reaction to a program *does not assure* learning. All of us have attended meetings in which the conference leader or speaker used enthusiasm, showmanship, visual aids, and illustrations to make a presentation well accepted by the group. A careful analysis of the subject content would reveal that the speaker said practically nothing of value—but said it very

COORDINATOR'S RATING OF LEADER

Name of leader_____Subject_____

Date _____

	Very much so	To some extent	No
A. PREPARATION 1. How well prepared?			
2. Preparation geared to group?			
B. CONDUCTING 1. Held interest of group?			
2. Was enthusiastic?			
3. Used audiovisual aids?			
4. Presented material clearly?			
5. Helped the group apply the material?			
6. Adequately covered subject?			
7. Involved the group?			
8. Summarized during and at end?			

C. CONSTRUCTIVE COMMENTS
What would you suggest to improve future sessions?_____

_____

_____

D. ADDITIONAL COMMENTS

_____

_____

_____

Figure 14-5. Leader rating sheet for single leader.

well. It is also important to recognize that an unfavorable reaction probably assures no learning. It takes effort to learn, and "turned-off" participants won't try.

Learning Defined

For the purpose of evaluation, learning is defined as follows: attitudes that were changed, and knowledge and skills that were learned. It does not include the on-the-job use of the attitudes, knowledge, and skills. This application will be discussed later in this chapter in the section on behavior.

Guidelines for Evaluating in Terms of Learning

Several guidelines should be used in measuring the amount of learning that takes place:

1. The learning of *each conferee* should be measured so that quantitative results can be determined.
2. A before-and-after approach should be used so that any learning can be related to the program.
3. Where practical, a control group (not receiving the training) should be compared with the experimental group which receives the training.
4. Where practical, the evaluation results should be analyzed statistically so that learning can be proved in terms of correlation or level of confidence.

These guidelines indicate that evaluation in terms of learning is much more difficult than evaluation in terms of reaction, as described earlier. A knowledge of statistics, for example, is desirable. In many cases, the training department will have to call on the assistance of a statistician to help plan the evaluation procedures, analyze the data, and interpret the results.

Suggested Methods

Classroom Performance.   It is relatively easy to measure the learning that takes place in training programs that are teaching skills. The following programs fall under this category: job instruction training, work simplification, interviewing skills, reading improvement, effective speaking, and effective writing. Classroom activities such as demonstrations, individual performance of the skill being taught, and discussions following a role-playing situation can be used as evaluation techniques. The training director can organize these in such a way that he or she will obtain a fairly objective evaluation of the learning that is taking place.

For example, in a course that is teaching job instruction training (JIT) to supervisors, every supervisor will demonstrate in front of the class the skills of JIT. From their performance, the training director can tell whether the supervisors have learned the principles of JIT and can use them, at least in a classroom situation. In a work simplification program, the conferees can be required to fill out a "flow process chart," and the training director can determine whether they know how to do it. In a reading improvement program, the reading speed and comprehension of the participants can be readily determined by their classroom performance. In an effective speaking program, each conferee is normally required to give a number of talks, and an alert training director can evaluate the amount of learning that is taking place by observing the individual's successive performances.

Thus in situations like these, an evaluation of the learning can be built into the program. If it is organized and implemented properly, the training director can obtain a fairly objective measure of the amount of learning that has taken place. He or she can set up before-and-after situations in which the conferees demonstrate whether they know the principles and techniques being taught. In every program, therefore, where skills of some kind are being taught, the training director should plan systematic classroom evaluation to measure the learning.

Paper-and-Pencil Tests.   Where principles and facts are taught rather than skills, paper-and-pencil tests can be used. In some cases, standardized tests

---

SUPERVISORY INVENTORY ON HUMAN RELATIONS

1. Anyone is able to do almost any job if he or she tries hard enough.   A   DA
2. Intelligence consists of what we've learned since we were born.   A   DA
3. If a supervisor knows all about the work to be done, he or she is
   therefore qualified to teach others how to do it.   A   DA
4. A well-trained working force is a result of maintaining a large training
   department.   A   DA
5. In making a decision, a good supervisor is concerned with his
   employees' feeling about the decision.   A   DA
6. The supervisor is closer to his or her employees than to management.   A   DA
7. The best way to train a new employee is to have him or her watch a
   good employee at the job.   A   DA
8. Before deciding on the solution to a problem, a list of possible
   solutions should be made and compared.   A   DA
9. A supervisor should be willing to listen to almost anything the
   employees want to say.   A   DA

Figure 14-6. Test to measure learning. (*Copyright © 1993 by D. L. Kirkpatrick. Published by Dr. D. L. Kirkpatrick, 1920 Hawthorne Drive, Elm Grove, WI 53122.*)

can be purchased to measure learning. In other cases, training directors must construct their own.

To measure the learning in human relations programs, for example, the *Supervisory Inventory on Human Relations* might be used. Sample test items are listed in Fig. 14-6 (answered by circling A for "agree" or DA for "disagree").

Standardized tests are also available in such areas as communications, time management, managing change, leadership, decision making, modern management, and safety. In following the guidelines that were suggested in the beginning of this chapter, this kind of standardized test should be used in the following manner:

1. The test should be given to all conferees prior to the program.

2. If practical, it should also be given to a control group which is comparable with the experimental group.

3. These pretests should be analyzed in terms of two approaches. In the first place, the total score of each person should be tabulated. Second, the responses to each item of the inventory should be tabulated in terms of right and wrong answers. This second tabulation not only enables a training director to evaluate the program but also provides some tips on the knowledge and understanding of the group prior to the program. This means that in the classroom, the training director can stress those items most frequently misunderstood.

4. After the program is over, the same test or its equivalent should be given to the conferees and also to the control group. A comparison of pretest and posttest scores and responses to individual items can then be made. A statistical analysis of this data will reveal the effectiveness of the program in terms of learning.

One important word of caution is necessary: Unless the test or inventory accurately covers the material presented, it will not be a valid measure of the effectiveness of the learning. Frequently a standardized test will cover only part of the material presented in the course. Therefore, only that part of the course covered in the inventory is being evaluated. Likewise, if certain items on the inventory are not being covered, no change in these items can be expected.

Many training directors and others responsible for programs have developed their own paper-and-pencil tests to measure learning in their programs. For example, the American Telephone and Telegraph Company incorporated into its Personal Factors in Management program a short test measuring trainee sensitivity and empathy. First, each individual was asked to rank, in order of importance, 10 items dealing with human relations. The participants were then assigned to groups which worked 15 minutes at the task of arriving at a group ranking of the 10 statements. Following this 15-minute "heated discussion," each individual was asked to complete a short inventory, which included the following questions:

1. *a.* Were you satisfied with the performance of the group? Yes ____ No ____

   b. How many will say that they were satisfied with the performance of the group?

2. *a.* Do you feel that the discussion was dominated by two or three members? Yes____ No ____

   b. How many will say that they thought the discussion was dominated by two or three members?

3. *a.* Did you have any feelings about the items being ranked that, for some reason, you felt it wise not to express during the discussion? Yes ____ No ____

   b. How many will say that they had such feelings?

4. *a.* Did you talk as often as you wished to in the discussion? Yes ____ No ____

   b. How many will say that they spoke as often as they wished?

The successive class sessions then attempted to teach each conferee to be more sensitive to the feelings and ideas of other people. Later in the course, another "empathy" test was given to see whether there was an increase in sensitivity.

In Morris A. Savitt's article entitled "Is Management Training Worthwhile?"[2] he described a program that he evaluated. He devised a questionnaire which was given at the beginning of the program "to determine how much knowledge of management principles and practices the conferees had at the beginning." At the end of the 10-week program, the same questionnaire was administered to test the progress made during the course. This is an example of a questionnaire tailored to a specific program.

Paper-and-pencil tests can be used effectively in measuring the learning that takes place in a training program. It should be emphasized again that the approach to this kind of evaluation should be systematic and statistically oriented. A comparison of before-and-after scores and responses can then be made to prove how much learning has taken place.

Conclusions About Learning

It is easy to see that it is much more difficult to measure *learning* than it is to measure *reaction* to a program. A great deal of work is required in planning the evaluation procedure, in analyzing the data that is obtained, and in interpreting the results. Wherever practical, it is suggested that training directors devise their own methods and techniques. As has been pointed out in this section, it is relatively easy to plan classroom demonstrations and presentations to measure learning where the program is aimed at the teaching of skills. Where attitudes, knowledge, and skills are the objectives of the training program, it is advisable to use a paper-and-pencil test. Where suitable standardized tests can be found, it is easier to use them. In many programs, however, it is not possible to find a standardized test, and training directors must use their skill and ingenuity in devising their own measuring instruments.

If training directors can prove that their programs have been effective in terms of learning as well as in terms of reaction, they have objective data to use in selling future programs and in increasing their status and position in the company.

Step 3: Behavior

A personal experience may be the best way of introducing this section. When I joined the Management Institute of the University of Wisconsin, one of my first assignments was to sit through a one-week course called "Human Relations for Foremen and Supervisors." During the week I was particularly impressed by a foreman named Herman from a Milwaukee company. Whenever a conference leader asked a question requiring a good understanding of human relations principles and techniques, Herman was the first one who raised his hand. He had all the answers in terms of good human relations approaches. I was very much impressed, and I said to myself, "If I were in industry, I would like to work for a man like Herman."

It so happened that I had a first cousin who was working for that company. And oddly enough Herman was his boss. At my first opportunity, I talked with my cousin Jim and asked him about Herman. Jim told me that Herman might know all the principles and techniques of human relations, but he certainly did not practice them on the job. He performed like the typical "bull of the woods" and had little consideration for the feelings and ideas of his subordinates. At this time I began to realize there may be a big difference between knowing principles and techniques and using them on the job.

Five requirements must be met for change in behavior to occur:

1. Desire to change
2. Know-how of what to do and how to do it
3. The right job climate
4. Help in applying the classroom learning
5. Rewards for changing behavior

The third requirement refers primarily to the boss of the person being trained. If he or she has established a preventive or discouraging climate, no change in behavior is likely to occur even if the trainee is anxious to change and has acquired the necessary knowledge and skill. If the climate is neutral or encouraging, the change in behavior is apt to take place.

Several guidelines are to be followed in evaluating training programs in terms of behavioral changes:

1. A *systematic* appraisal should be made of on-the-job performance on a *before-and-after* basis.
2. The appraisal of performance should be made by one or more of the following groups (the more the better):
   a. The person receiving the training

 b. The person's superior or superiors
 c. The person's subordinates
 d. The person's peers or other people thoroughly familiar with his or her performance.
3. A statistical analysis should be made to compare performance before and after and to relate changes to the training program.
4. The posttraining appraisal should be made three months or more after the training so that the trainees have an opportunity to put into practice what they have learned. Subsequent appraisals may add to the validity of the study.
5. A control group (not receiving the training), if practical, should be used.

A "Supervisory Skills" Institute[3]

At the Management Institute, University of Wisconsin, a three-day institute called "Supervisory Skills" was evaluated. The institute covered six topics: order giving, training employees, appraising employee performance, preventing and handling grievances, decision making, and initiating change. A questionnaire was completed by each supervisor who attended the institute to obtain information on the participant, the company, and the participant's relationship with his or her immediate boss. Specific information was obtained on:

1. The participant: job, experience, education, age, reasons for attending the program, and what he or she hopes to learn

2. The company: size, type, and climate for change

3. The participant's boss: years spent as boss, the climate he or she sets for change, and involvement in sending the person to the institute

 Interviews were conducted with each participant within two to three months following the institute. The interviews were conducted in the participant's company to obtain information regarding changes in behavior that had taken place on the job. In addition, interviews were conducted with the participant's immediate supervisor as another measure of changes in the participant's behavior.
 Examples of specific questions are shown in Fig. 14-7. In addition to measuring changes in behavior, determining what results were achieved was also attempted. Questions asked of both the participant and his or her boss are shown in Fig. 14-8. Although the design of the evaluation was relatively simple, it provided data to indicate that significant changes in both behavior and results were achieved.

Conclusions About Behavior

The future of training directors and their programs depends to a large extent on their effectiveness. To determine effectiveness, attempts should be made to measure in objective terms. Measuring changes in behavior resulting from training programs usually involves a complicated procedure. But it is worthwhile if training programs are going to increase in effectiveness and their benefits are to be made clear to top management.
 It is obvious that very few training directors have the background, skill, and time to engage in extensive evaluations. It is therefore frequently necessary to call on industrial psychologists, research people, and consultants for advice and help.

Training employees	Yes		No		Not sure
a. *Since* the supervisor attended the program, are his or her new or transferred employees better trained?					

Training method	Participant always	Participant usually	Participant sometimes	Participant never
b. *Before* the program, who trained the workers?				
c. *Since* the program, who trained the workers?				

Progress in training effectiveness	Does not apply	Much more	Some-what more	No change	Some-what less	Much less	Don't know
d. *Since* the program, if someone else trains the employees, has the supervisor become more observant and taken a more active interest in the training process?							
e. *Since* the program, if the supervisor trains the employees, is he or she making more of an effort in seeing that the employees are well trained?							
f. *Since* the program, is the supervisor more inclined to be patient while training?							
g. *Since* the program, while teaching an operation, is the supervisor asking for more questions to ensure understanding?							
h. *Since* the program, is the supervisor better prepared to teach?							
i *Since* the program, is the supervisor doing more follow-up to check the trainees' progress?							

Figure 14-7. Examples of supervisor interview questions in Kirkpatrick study.

1. To what extent has the program improved the supervisor's working relationship with his boss?

☐ To a large extent
☐ To some extent
☐ No change
☐ Made it worse

2. Since the program, how much two-way communication has taken place between the participant and his subordinates?

☐ Much more
☐ Somewhat more
☐ No change
☐ Somewhat less
☐ Much less
☐ Don't know

3. Since the program, is the participant taking a more active interest in employees?

☐ Much more
☐ Somewhat more
☐ No change
☐ Somewhat less
☐ Much less
☐ Don't know

Figure 14-8. Interview questions for supervisor and boss in Kirkpatrick study.

Step 4: Results

The objectives of most training programs can be stated in terms of results such as reduced turnover, reduced costs, improved efficiency, reduction in grievances, increase in quality and quantity of production, or improved morale. From an evaluation standpoint, it would be best to evaluate training programs directly in terms of results desired. There are, however, so many complicating factors that it is extremely difficult, if not impossible, to evaluate certain kinds of programs in terms of results. Therefore, it is recommended that training directors evaluate in terms of reaction, learning, and behavior first and then consider results.

Certain kinds of training programs, though, are relatively easy to evaluate in terms of results. For example, in teaching clerical personnel to do a more effective typing job, you can measure the number of words per minute on a before-and-after basis. If you are trying to reduce grievances in your plant, you can measure the number of grievances before and after the training program. If you are attempting to reduce accidents, a before-and-after measure can be made. But a word of caution: A difficulty in the evaluation of training is evident at the outset, technically called "the separation of variables"; that is, how much of the improvement is due to training as compared to other factors? This is the problem that makes it very difficult to measure results that can be attributed directly to a specific training program.

4. On an overall basis, to what extent has the supervisor's job behavior
   changed *since* the program?

Supervisory Areas	Much Better	Somewhat Better	No Change	Somewhat Worse	Much Worse	Don't Know
a. Order Giving						
b. Training						
c. Decision Making						
d. Initiating Change						
e. Appraising Employee Performance						
f. Preventing and Handling Grievances						
g. Attitude toward Job						
h. Attitude toward Subordinates						
i. Attitude toward Management						

5. In regard to the following results, what changes have been noticed *since* the participant's
   attendance in the program?

Performance Bench Marks	Much Better	Somewhat Better	No Change	Somewhat Worse	Much Worse	Don't Know
a. Quantity of Production						
b. Quality of Production						
c. Safety						
d. Housekeeping						
e. Employee Attitudes and Morale						
f. Employee Attendance						
g. Employee Promptness						
h. Employee Turnover						

Figure 14-8. (*Continued*) Interview questions for supervisor and boss in Kirkpatrick study.

A "Cost-Reduction" Institute

A number of years ago, two graduate students at the University of Wisconsin
attempted to measure the results of a cost-reduction institute conducted by the
Management Institute. Two techniques were used. The first was to conduct depth
interviews with some of the supervisors who had attended the course and with their
immediate superiors. The other technique was to mail questionnaires to the remaining enrollees and their supervisors. Following is a brief summary of that study:

Depth Interviews

Interview with Trainees

1. Have you been able to reduce costs in the few weeks that you have been back
   on the job?

   Replies: 13—Yes
              3—No
              2—Noncommittal or evasive
              1—Failed to answer

2. How? What were the estimated savings? Different types of replies indicated that the 13 people who said they had made cost reductions had done so in different areas. But their ideas stemmed directly from the program, according to these trainees.

Interview with Superiors.   Eight of the cost-reduction actions described by the trainees were confirmed by the immediate superior, and these superiors estimated total savings to be from $15,000 to $21,000 per year. The specific ideas that were used were described by superiors as well as by the trainees.

Mailed Questionnaires.   Questionnaires were mailed to those trainees who were not contacted personally. The results on the questionnaire were not nearly as specific and useful as the ones obtained by personal interview. The study concluded that it is probably better to use the personal interview rather than a questionnaire to measure results from this type of program.

Conclusions About Results

The evaluation of training programs in terms of "results" is progressing at a very slow rate. Where the objectives of training programs are as specific as the reduction of accidents, the reduction of grievances, and the reduction of costs, we find that a number of attempts have been made. In a few of them, the researchers have attempted to segregate factors other than training which might have had an effect. In most cases, the measure on a before-and-after basis has been directly attributed to the training even though other factors might have been influential. An article called "Evaluating Training Programs: Evidence vs. Proof"[4] describes a philosophy and approach that are appropriate for most programs.

Summary

One purpose of this chapter is to stimulate training people to take a penetrating look at evaluation. Their own future and the future of their programs depends to a large extent on their ability to evaluate and use evaluation results.

Another objective has been to clarify the meaning of evaluation. By breaking it down into reaction, learning, behavior, and results, the training professional can begin to do something about it and can gradually progress from a simple subjective reaction sheet to a research design that measures tangible results.

Articles on evaluation will continue to appear in *Training and Development* and other magazines. Some of these articles are well worth studying because they describe effective principles, procedures, and methods of evaluation.

This chapter has not provided the answers to the training director's problem of evaluation. It has attempted to provide an understanding of principles and methods. Better understanding will come from continued study of new principles and methods that are described in articles written in professional journals. Needless to say, skill in using proper evaluation methods can come only with practice.

References

1. Goodacre, Daniel M., III, "The Experimental Evaluation of Management Training: Principles and Practices," *Personnel,* May 1957.

2. Savitt, Morris, "Is Management Training Worthwhile?" *Personnel,* September–October 1957.

3. Kirkpatrick, Donald L., "Evaluating a Training Program for Supervisors and Foremen," *The Personnel Administrator,* September–October 1969.

4. Kirkpatrick, Donald L., "Evaluating Training Programs: Evidence vs. Proof," *Training and Development Journal,* November 1977.

Special Reference

The following book contains more details on the four levels of evaluation described in this chapter. In addition to guidelines, principles and techniques, it includes case studies of applications including those at IBM, Motorola, Arthur Andersen, First Union National Bank of North Carolina, St. Lukes Hospital, and Kemper Insurance. It is a valuable reference for anyone seriously interested in evaluation.

Kirkpatrick, Donald L., *Evaluating Training Programs: The Four Levels,* Berrett-Koehler Publishers, San Francisco, 1994.

Bibliography

Basarab, David J., Sr., and Darrell K. Root, *The Training Evaluation Process,* Kluwer Academic Publishers, Boston, 1993.

Holcomb, Jane, *Make Training Worth Every Penny,* Wharton Publishing, Del Mar, CA, 1993.

Kirkpatrick, Donald L., *How to Train and Develop Supervisors,* AMACOM, American Management Association, New York, 1993.

Phillips, Jack J., *Training Evaluation and Measurement Methods,* Gulf Publishing Co., Houston, 1991.

Robinson, Dana Gaines, and James C. Robinson, *Training for Impact,* Jossey-Bass, San Francisco, 1989.

15

Measuring the Results of Training*

Jack J. Phillips

Jack J. Phillips *has 30 years of human resource development and managerial experience. He has served as training manager, senior human resources officer, executive, and now faculty member at Middle Tennessee State University. Through Performance Resources Organization, he consults with clients in manufacturing, service, and government in the United States and abroad. He has served as President, Retail Banking Division, Secor Bank, Federal Savings Bank, a large regional savings bank. He joined Secor as Senior Vice President, Human Resources, and progressed through several assignments to President. Dr. Phillips has served in a human resource management development position in banking, construction materials, metals, textiles, and aerospace. He received an associate's degree in electrical engineering with highest honors from the Southern College of Technology and a B.S. in physics and mathematics, summa cum laude, from Oglethorpe University. His graduate work includes an M.S. in decision sciences from Georgia State University and a Ph.D. in human resource management from the University of Alabama.* He has authored or edited HRD Needs Assessment *(with Ed Holton), 1995;* Measuring Return on Investment, *1994;* Handbook of Training Evaluation and Measurement Methods, *2d ed., 1991;* The Development of a Human Resource Effectiveness Index, *1988;* Recruiting, Training, and Retaining New Employees, *1987; and* Improving Supervisors' Effectiveness, *1985. In 1986, his Jossey-Bass*

---

*Portions of this material were taken from Phillips, J. J., ed., In Action: Measuring Return on Investment, vol. 1, ASTD, Alexandria, VA, 1994, and Phillips, J. J., Handbook of Training Evaluation and Measurement Methods, 2d ed., Gulf Publishing, Houston, 1991.

book, Improving Supervisors' Effectiveness, *won an award from the Society for Human Resource Management. He has authored over 75 articles and serves as series editor of the new case studies publication,* In Action: Case Studies, *ASTD.*

Few topics in the human resource development field are as frustrating, illusive, and important as measuring training results. The techniques for measuring training results have been developed for years, yet the process has not been fully adopted, explored, or utilized to the extent that it should be. One recent report shows some movement to wide-scale adoption when it is reported that 47 percent of all industries are measuring business results of training in 44 percent of their courses.[1] Removing some of the mystery of measuring training results is the primary goal of this chapter. It presents the different elements and components, piece by piece, in a simplified format, including an approach to calculate the return on investment (ROI), that is not confusing and complex. This chapter fully explores the evaluation process and the strategies needed to implement an overall measurement and evaluation program.

Measurement Trends

In any direction one chooses to take in the human resources development (HRD) field, the pressure to measure the results of training is increasing. In developing countries as in fully developed nations, the issue is a hot topic. At some time or another, virtually every organization will tackle this important issue in a comprehensive manner. The pressure to measure the results from training may come from line managers, the internal customers of HRD who must support HRD, or from top executives who must allocate resources to those functions in the organization that are contributing to the bottom line. Four important trends are visible on the HRD horizon. Collectively, they provide evidence of the pressure for increased use of measurement and evaluation.

Training and Development Budgets Are Increasing

There is clear evidence of the increase in training and development budgets. In the United States, budgets for 1994 were up 5 percent over 1993.[2] Budgets are also increasing in other countries, particularly where training expenditures are tied to government legislation. As budgets increase, so does the need for accountability. Large (and growing) budgets become big targets for critics and skeptics. When HRD receives significant funding increases, it is usually at the expense of other parts of the organization that do not receive similar increases. As the percentage of operating expenses allocated to HRD continues to increase, the HRD budget will continue to be a target of those who question its existence or its ability to enhance organizational effectiveness.

HRD Is Linked to Competitive Strategies

Many organizations are utilizing HRD as a competitive weapon to create a distinct or unique advantage. In some situations, training is seen as the most critical competitive weapon. Whether the organization is experiencing tremendous growth, restructuring, rightsizing, or changing markets and locations, training is seen as an important vehicle to implement these changes. HRD has become a powerful change management tool to help organizations successfully meet the challenges of the future. Ambitious HRD efforts, linked with competitive strategies, enable organizations to increase market share, introduce new products, improve delivery and customer service, reduce cost, become more efficient, and improve the response times and increase productivity. When training takes on the highly visible role, such as implementing parts of the strategic plan, with it comes pressure for accountability. Top executives and other significant groups want to ensure that all competitive tools are accountable and measurable.

Accountability of All Functions Is Increasing

Virtually every function in an organization is being subjected to increased accountability. Functions previously taken for granted as necessary and unmeasurable, such as public relations, are now required to show a contribution. This is especially true for staff support functions. Even the internal audit function, which several years ago never dreamed of being held accountable for their success, are now adapting measurement processes and in some cases turning audit functions into profit centers. In this respect, HRD is just one of many functions responding to pressures to show their contribution in measurable terms.

Top Executives Requiring Training Results

Chief executives and top administrators, struggling to make their organizations lean, profitable, and viable are demanding accountability with all expenditures. They are encouraging, and sometimes requiring, the HRD staff to measure training results. In some cases, executives issue ultimatums to show the value of HRD or take a budget cut, as happened at IBM.[3] In other cases, top executives use subtle hints and suggestions.

These four trends are occurring in all types of the organizations and are placing renewed demands on the HRD staff to show its contribution in measurable, quantitative terms. This pressure creates a need to measure the results of training so that management will have confidence that there is an adequate return on all programs. Even executive education programs offered by universities, which were previously untouchable on the accountability issue, are now facing tremendous pressure to show their results. A recent comprehensive report on executive education in *The Wall Street Journal* revealed many problems with executive education.[4] The report asks the question, "Would you spend millions of dollars without knowing what, if anything, you are going to get for it?" Incredibly, this is what is occurring with most executive education programs. The HRD staff must meet the challenge and find ways to measure training results.

The Ultimate Level of Evaluation: ROI

Perhaps it is helpful to briefly review the different levels of evaluation, a concept developed more than 35 years ago by D. L. Kirkpatrick, and modified by various organizations and individuals.[5] (See Chap. 14, Evaluation.) Although Kirkpatrick presented four levels, today's environment requires at least one other level, the return on investment, to compare costs versus benefits.

The Five Levels of Evaluation

The recommended levels, presented in Fig. 15-1 are somewhat modified from Kirkpatrick's levels to adjust to current trends and practices in place in many organizations. Figure 15-1 shows which questions are addressed at a specific level. At the first level, reaction and planned actions are measured. This level focuses on how the participants are satisfied with all facets of the program and captures their planned actions as a result of the program. At the second level, measurements concentrate on what participants have learned in the program. Learning is usually measured by tests which determine the degree to which skills, knowledge, or attitudes have changed. At the third level, the focus is on job applications and usually involves behavioral changes. It measures the extent to which participants have actually utilized what was learned in the program. The fourth level represents an important area, business results, which includes the actual contribution of the program to the organization. Still, the fourth level is inadequate in the current environment of increased demand for accountability. A fifth level is needed where ROI is measured, requiring business results to be converted to a monetary unit and the added value of the program is compared to its costs.

Figure 15-2 shows the relationships and characteristics of these five levels. The value of information derived from this process is highest at level 5 and lowest at level 1. The power to show results is greatest at level 5 and decreases at lower levels, with almost no possibilities at the reaction level. Almost all organizations conduct reaction evaluations to measure participant satisfaction, but very few conduct evaluations at the results level and ROI level, perhaps because reaction evaluation is easy, whereas business results and ROI calculations are very difficult. The return on investment from HRD usually rests with this infrequently used, valuable, and difficult fifth level of evaluation.

Although business results are desired, it is very important to evaluate the other levels, as well. There is some evidence of a chain of impact among the levels, which indicates that if measurements are not taken at each level, it is difficult to conclude that the results achieved were actually caused by the HRD program.[6]

Although it is important to produce business results and measure ROI with HRD programs, it is difficult to measure at those levels. This leads to two impor-

Level	Questions
1. Reaction and planned action	What are participants' reactions to the program and what do they plan to do with the material?
2. Learning	What skills, knowledge, or attitudes have changed and by how much?
3. Job applications	Did participants apply on the job what they learned?
4. Business results	Did the on-the-job application produce measurable results?
5. Return on investment	Did the monetary value of the results exceed the cost for the program?

Figure 15-1. Evaluation levels.

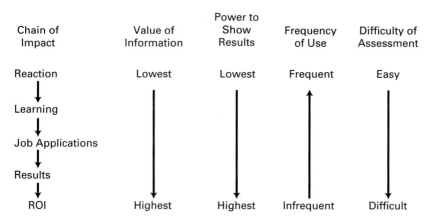

Figure 15-2. Characteristics of evaluation levels.

tant questions. What is the appropriate strategy? Is anything short of level 4 or 5 evaluation acceptable? The answers are not easy. Level 4 evaluations are not for every program; the calculation of a return on investment should be reserved for only a few programs. Some organizations wrestling with this issue develop specific strategies for ROI calculations which often hinge on two specific actions: setting targets and sampling.

Setting Evaluation Targets

Recognizing the complexity of the evaluation levels, as described in Fig. 15-1, some organizations attempt to manage the process by setting targets for the percentage of HRD programs measured at each level. For example, it is easy to measure reaction, and many organizations require 100 percent evaluation at that level. The second level, learning, is another relatively easy area to measure and the target is high, usually less than 100 percent but greater than 50 percent. This decision is specific to the organization, based on its desire to measure learning and the nature and types of programs. At the on-the-job application level, measurement targets are lower because the follow-up process is time-consuming. At the business results level, the target is relatively small because of the difficulty of measurement. The numbers are even smaller for the fifth level, the ROI process, which commands significant resources and budgets. Table 15-1 presents an example of evaluation targets from a large electric utility.

Table 15-1. Targets for Percentages of
Programs to Be Evaluated

Level	Percentage
Participants' satisfaction	100
Learning	70
On-the-job applications (behavior)	50
Results	10
ROI	5

Setting evaluation targets has several advantages. First, it provides measurable objectives for the HRD staff. Second, adopting targets focuses more attention on the accountability process, communicating a strong message to the HRD staff about the commitment to measurement and evaluation. Finally, focusing on targets at all levels helps realize benefits of the chain of impact. For all level 4 evaluations, there is usually a requirement for evaluations at the previous three levels. This requirement enhances the organization's ability to show that the results obtained at level 4 are caused by the HRD program and not other factors.

Sampling

If ROI calculations are needed for some, but not all, courses, each organization must attempt to find that desired level of ROI calculations. There is no prescribed formula, and the number depends on many variables, including:

- Staff expertise in evaluation
- Resources that can be allocated to the process
- The organization's commitment to measurement and evaluation
- Pressure from others to show ROI calculations
- The nature and types of HRD programs

A few organizations use a sampling process to select a small number of programs for ROI calculations. Most organizations, however, settle for evaluating one or two sessions of their most popular programs. For example, the U.S. Office of Personnel Management developed an ROI calculation for one of its most popular courses, Introduction to Supervision. Other organizations pick a program from each major training segment. For example, in one large bank with six academies, ROI is calculated for one program selected from each academy each year. If an organization is implementing ROI for the first time, it is recommended that only *one* program be selected for a calculation.

Although it is important to take a statistically sound approach to the sampling process, it is more important to consider a trade-off between available resources and the level of sampling and analysis that management will accept for ROI calculations. Sometimes the objective is not to convince the HRD staff that their programs work but to show top management that HRD makes a difference. In this case, it is important that the sampling plan be developed with the input and approval of top management. In the final analysis, top management must be comfortable that the process yields a satisfactory assessment of the HRD function.

Data Collection Tools

To measure training, data must be collected and there are a variety of data collection tools that can be used at the various levels of evaluation and the various stages in the process. Some data collection tools are used before the program, others during, and still others after the program. Collectively, they provide the evaluator with a full array of helpful and useful tools to collect all types of data to measure the results of training. A brief description of each type is presented here.

Questionnaires

Probably the most common form of data collection tool is the questionnaire. Ranging from short reaction forms to detailed follow-up instruments, questionnaires come in all sizes. They can be used to obtain subjective information on participant reaction as well as document measurable results for use in an economic analysis. Basically, there are five types of questions:

- *Open-ended question.* Has an unlimited answer. The question is followed by an ample blank space for the response.
- *Checklist.* A list of items where a participant is asked to check those that apply to the situation.
- *Two-way question.* Has alternate responses, a yes-no or other possibilities.
- *Multiple-choice question.* Has several choices, and the participant is asked to select the most correct one.
- *Ranking scales.* Requires the participants to rank a list of items.

A questionnaire may contain any or all of these types of questions.

Attitude Surveys

Attitude surveys represent a specific type of questionnaire with several applications for measuring the results of HRD programs. A program may be designed to change employees' attitudes toward work, policies, procedures, the organization, and even the immediate supervisor. Before-and-after program measurements are often needed to show changes in attitude. Sometimes an organization will conduct an attitude survey to assess employees' attitudes toward one of the areas listed previously. Then, based on these results, HRD programs are undertaken to change attitudes in areas where improvement is needed. In addition, attitude surveys can help evaluate HRD when they are used to

- Provide feedback to managers on how well they are balancing their various managerial and supervisory responsibilities
- Build a database that can inform the organization of the content and processes of selecting, developing, and training managers
- Assist in the design and modification of human resource policies, management systems, and decision-making processes, thereby improving overall organizational effectiveness
- Provide a way to assess progress during periods of change
- Assess the organization's internal employee relations climate and monitor the trends[7]

Measuring attitudes is a complex task. It is impossible to measure an attitude precisely, since information gathered may not represent the participant's true feelings. Also, the behavior, beliefs, and feelings of an individual will not always correlate. Attitudes tend to change with time, and there are a number of factors that form an individual's attitude. With recognition of these shortcomings, it is possible to get a reasonable fix on the attitude of an individual.

Surveys alone are not the only way to measure attitudes. Interviews and observations, two other ways to check attitudes, are discussed later.

Tests

Testing is important in program evaluations for measuring learning. Preprogram and postprogram comparisons using tests are very common. An improvement in test scores shows the change in skill or knowledge of the participant which should be attributed to the program. By any measure, there was a dramatic increase in the use of tests in the 1980s and the trend continues for the 1990s. One source has identified more than 3000 commercially available tests.[8]

Several types of tests are used in the HRD field and there are three different ways in which tests can be classified. (Also see Chap. 16, Testing.) The first way is based upon the medium used for administering the test. The most common media for training tests are paper and pencil; performance tests, using simulated tools or the actual equipment; and computer-based tests, using computers and video displays. Written tests are by far the most common type of knowledge and skills tests used in the training process. Performance tests are usually more costly to develop and administer than written examinations. Computer-based tests and those using interactive video are relatively new developments in testing. A computer monitor or video screen presents the test questions or situations. Trainees respond by typing on a keyboard or touching the screen. Interactive videos have a strong element of realism because the person being tested can react to images, often moving pictures and video vignettes, that reproduce the real job situation.

The second way to classify tests is by purpose and content. In this context, tests can be divided into aptitude tests or achievement tests. Aptitude tests measure basic skills or innate or acquired capacity to learn an occupation. An achievement test assesses a person's knowledge or competence in a particular subject. It measures the end result of education and training.

A third way in which to classify tests is by test design. The most common are oral examinations, essay tests, objective tests, norm-referenced tests, criterion-referenced tests, and performance tests. Oral examinations and essay tests have limited use in HRD program evaluation. They are probably more useful in academic settings. Objective tests have answers which are specific and precise, based on the objectives of a program. Attitudes, feelings, creativity, problem-solving processes, and other intangible skills and abilities cannot be measured accurately with objective tests. A more useful form of objective test is the criterion-referenced test.

Performance testing, a very common approach, allows the participant to exhibit a skill (and occasionally knowledge or attitudes) which has been learned in an HRD program. The skill can be manual, verbal, or analytical, or a combination of the three. Performance testing is used frequently in job-related training where the participants are allowed to demonstrate what they have learned. In supervisory and management training, performance testing comes in the form of skill practices or role-plays. Participants are asked to demonstrate discussion or problem-solving skills they have acquired. The principles of test development are similar to the design and development of questionnaires and attitude surveys. More detail is presented in other sections of this handbook.

Interviews

Another helpful evaluation instrument is the interview, although it is not used as frequently as the other methods. Interviews can be conducted by the HRD staff, the participant's supervisor, or an outside third party. Interviews can secure data not available in performance records or data difficult to obtain through written responses or observations. Also, interviews can uncover success stories that can be useful in the overall evaluation. Participants may be reluctant to describe their results in a questionnaire but will volunteer in the information to a skillful interviewer who probes for it. The interview process will uncover changes in behavior, reaction, and results. In some programs, the interview process comprises the total evaluation, although it's not recommended.[9]

A major disadvantage of the interview is that it is time-consuming. It can also require the training or preparation of interviewers to ensure that the process is conducted in an effective manner. The same principles involved in designing questions for a questionnaire can also apply to the interview.

Focus Groups

Focus groups are particularly helpful when in-depth feedback is needed for training program evaluation. For many cost-conscious trainers, the focus-group process is becoming the evaluation instrument of choice.[10] The focus group is a small-group discussion conducted by an experienced facilitator. It is designed to solicit qualitative judgments on a particular topic or issue. Group members are all required to provide their input, and individual input builds on group input.

For years, the HRD profession has largely ignored the focus-group potential for evaluating training. In other types of research—particularly marketing research—the focus group has long been used to generate quality information on which to make decisions. Marketing researchers have used the focus group to test new products, marketing campaigns, and questionnaire wording. It is also used to collect information for training needs analyses, secure input for changes in company policies, and provide feedback on problems and concerns within an organization.

The focus group is particularly helpful when information is needed about the quality of a training program or an assessment of behavior change resulting from a training program. For example, the focus group can be used in the following situations:

- To evaluate the training design and the training process in a pilot test program
- To evaluate the reactions to specific exercises, cases, simulations, or other components of a training program
- To assess the overall effectiveness of the program as perceived by the participants immediately following a program
- To assess the impact of the program in a follow-up evaluation after the program is completed

Essentially a focus group is helpful when evaluation information is needed which cannot be collected adequately with simple, quantitative methods.

Observations

Another useful evaluation instrument is observation. This process involves observing the participant either before, during, or after an HRD program to record changes in behavior. The observer may be a member of the HRD staff, the participant's supervisor, a member of a peer group, or an outside party. The most common observer, and probably the most practical, is a member of the HRD staff, although this choice may appear to be self-serving.

Several types of observation methods are available to use in HRD evaluation. They include:

- Behavior checklist, which is useful for recording the presence, absence, frequency, or duration of a participant's behavior as it occurs
- Coded behavior record, which contains a predetermined code of behaviors that can be used in a checklist format
- Delayed report method, where the observer does not use any forms or written materials during the observation but records the observed behavior at particular time intervals during the observation period
- Video recording, where video cameras capture actual behavior of participants
- Audio monitoring, where on-the-job conversations are monitored to assess skills

The observation method has some disadvantages. In some situations the behavior observed is not typical or representative of the actual behavior on the job. Also, video or audio monitoring may create concern about invasion of privacy. This process is effective, however, for capturing behavior as it is displayed on the job. It is particularly useful in customer service and sales training where secret customers or mystery shoppers are often utilized to determine the degree to which customer service or sales skills are being utilized.

Performance Records

In every organization records are available which reflect performance. Although it may appear awkward to refer to performance records as evaluation instruments, in the context of evaluation, they serve the same purpose as tests or attitude surveys. They enable management to measure performance in terms of output, quality, costs, and time and are necessary for an accurate evaluation system. Table 15-2 lists common performance records or measurements for an employee or group of employees.

During determination of the use of records in the evaluation of an HRD program, the first consideration should be existing records. In most organiza-

Table 15-2. Examples of Performance Records

Absenteeism	Percent of quota achieved
Accident costs, accident rates	Processing time
Break-in time for new hires	Production schedules
Budget variances	Productivity
Complaints, employee and customer	Project schedule variations
Cost reduction	Rejects, scrap
Costs, overhead	Reports completed
Costs, unit	Sales (dollars and number)
Downtime	Sick leave costs
Efficiency	Supervisor bonuses
Employees promoted	Tardiness
Equipment use	Terminations, employees
Errors, employee	Time card corrections
Grievances	Total output
Inventory adjustments	Transactions completed
New accounts	Turnover
On-time shipments	Work backlog
Overtime	Work stoppages

tions there will be records suitable for measuring the improvement expected from an HRD program. If not, additional record-keeping systems will have to be developed for analysis and measurement. At this point, as with many other points in the process, the question of economics enters. Is it economical to develop the record-keeping system necessary to evaluate an HRD program? If the costs are greater than the expected return for the entire program, then it is meaningless to develop them.

There are a variety of data collection tools available. Table 15-3 summarizes the features of instruments presented here. Each type is listed with the appropriate level of evaluation and the advantages and limitations. This table can serve as a guide to compare the various types of instruments used in evaluation. It is adapted in part from an aide developed by the U.S. Office of Personnel Management. For additional information on these instruments, see other works.[11]

Measuring Training Service

In addition to the five levels of evaluation described earlier, several other areas of measurement are possible and are recommended. Sometimes regarded as training service, these measures ensure that the appropriate training is delivered on a cost-effective basis within the time frame needed by the client. Four of the most common training service measures are briefly described below.

Measuring Customer Satisfaction

Although program participants are often regarded as customers, this measurement involves other clients, usually those who request or support the program. (Participant satisfaction is measured at level 1 with reaction and planned action.) As organizations place increased emphasis on satisfying customers, and as some HRD departments move closer to a profit center concept, it is important to ensure that customers are satisfied with the services of the HRD staff. Target groups for this type of measurement are:

- Individuals who request the initial training program
- Supervisors of the participants who attend the program
- Senior managers who must allocate resources to support the overall training effort
- Other employees who must work with the results of the training program

A simple questionnaire sent routinely to a part or all of these groups can be helpful in measuring the level of satisfaction. A recommended approach is to sample a group of these customers to check their level of satisfaction each year. As an alternative, the customer satisfaction check may be tied to a specific program, particularly when it is regarded as a significant new program.

Measuring Response and Delivery Times

Time is a critical factor and many organizations enjoy a competitive advantage because of their response time, delivery time, or time to develop new products and services. The HRD function is often regarded in the same way. The HRD staff must develop programs in a timely manner. One measure of delivery time is the time from the request for training until the program is actually delivered.

Table 15-3. Instrument Features

Instruments	Evaluation Levels				Advantages	Limitations
	Reaction	Learning	Behavior	Results		
Questionnaire	*		*	*	■ Low cost ■ Honesty increased ■ Anonymity optional ■ Respondent sets pace ■ Variety of options	■ May not collect accurate information ■ On-job responding conditions ■ Respondent sets pace ■ Return rate rarely controllable
Attitude survey	*		*	*	■ Standardization possible ■ Quickly processed ■ Easy to administer	■ Predetermined alternatives ■ Response choices ■ Reliance on norms may distort individual performance ■ May not reflect true feelings
Written test		*			■ Low purchase cost ■ Readily scored ■ Quickly processed ■ Easily administered ■ Wide sampling possible	■ May be threatening to participant ■ Possible low relations to job performance ■ Reliance on norms may distort individual performance ■ Possible cultural bias
Performance test		*	*		■ Reliability ■ Simulation potential ■ Objective-based	■ Time-consuming ■ Simulation often difficult ■ High development costs
Interview	*		*	*	■ Flexible ■ Opportunity for clarification ■ Depth possible ■ Personal contact	■ High relative effects ■ High cost ■ Face-to-face threat potential ■ Labor-intensive ■ Trained interviewers necessary
Focus groups	*		*		■ Flexible ■ Low cost ■ Good qualitative responses ■ Personal contact	■ Effectiveness rests with facilitator ■ Subjective ■ Sometimes difficult to summarize findings

Method			Advantages	Disadvantages
Observation	*		• Nonthreatening to participants • Excellent way to measure behavior change	• Possibly disruptive • Reactive effect • Unreliable • Training observers necessary
Performance records	*	*	• Reliability • Objectivity • Job-based • Ease of review • Minimal reactive effects	• Lack of knowledge of criteria for keeping or discarding records • Information system discrepancies • Indirect nature of data • Need for conversion to usable forms • Records prepared for other purposes • Sometimes expensive to collect

Another measure is the timing of training relative to when it is supposed to be delivered to support new technology or new products. This just-in-time training is critical for organizations to gain and maintain a competitive advantage. Also, the time it takes for the target audience to complete the program is another important measure.

Tracking and Comparing Costs

Training costs are very important and should be monitored at different stages and compared to what has been accomplished previously or to other alternative delivery methods. It is recommended that costs be tracked by individual program and by four functional areas:

- Analysis
- Development
- Delivery
- Evaluation

Cost can easily be monitored by charging them to a particular account classification and allocating them to one of the four areas above. Analysis costs are important because they will clearly show the amount of cost involved in conducting the needs analysis. Sometimes management is concerned about excessive analysis expenditures. Development costs are critical because they can be used to compare with a potential program purchase or with previous development time. Delivery costs are usually the greatest costs, and the delivery cost per person is a critical factor in measuring the overall efficiency of the training effort. Finally, evaluation costs are important because they show the HRD staff how much it is spending to improve the training process and increase training effectiveness. This figure will normally be very low, in the range of 5 percent or less of the total training budget, even for some of the companies with the most comprehensive measurement and evaluation systems. Combining costs with response and delivery times enables the HRD staff to compare one training approach to another, for example, externally versus internally developed programs. Also, the data will enable a comparison of classroom versus computer-based training, or conference discussion versus on-the-job training. These comparisons are critical as organizations attempt to deliver training in an efficient and effective manner.

Measuring Entry Capability

Some HRD staffs measure the ability of participants as they enter a training program or series of programs. The action is not necessarily for excluding participants, but to determine at what level the training should begin or if remedial training is needed (or if the training can be skipped altogether). Too often organizations train individuals for tasks they are already familiar with. They have the skills or knowledge from previous courses or experiences. Also, on the other extreme, sometimes participants attend training programs when they are not capable of fully comprehending the process. Measurement of entry capability will help in the placement of trainees and in the pacing of the program to ensure that the other measures of training effectiveness are appropriate.

Measuring Participant Performance: Level 1 and 2 Evaluations

Measuring participant performance during the program is important, but it should not be the end of the evaluation process. This measurement focuses on levels 1 and 2 of the five-level model presented earlier. Although specific techniques involved in measuring these two levels were discussed in an earlier part of this handbook, a few additional points are included here.

Measuring Reaction and Planned Actions

Participant reaction is critical and is necessary to judge the overall reaction to programs. Reaction should include information on program content, instructional materials, out-of-class assignments, method of delivery, instructor-facilitator, facilities and learning environment, and overall evaluation. In addition, it is important to show planned improvements. Here, participants are asked to indicate what they will do with the material, how they will apply it, and the success they expect to achieve. If possible, this process should be taken a step further to show the value of the improvement to the department or work unit. Also, the confidence level can be included to illustrate the level of confidence in the estimates. Requesting planned actions has several advantages. It clearly communicates to participants that something is expected after training. The act of writing planned actions enhances the possibility that those actions will occur. Also, if a follow-up is planned, this document provides a basis to compare in the follow-up process.

Measuring Changes in Knowledge and Skills

At level 2, measures are taken to determine the extent to which participants have learned what has been presented, either new skills, knowledge, or in some situations, attitudes. It is important to measure, even if informally, the degree to which the learning has occurred. In addition to the variety of tests which are described earlier in this handbook, some less-threatening methods can be used. These include:

- Self-reports
- Exercises
- Observations during training programs
- Checklist by facilitators
- Team assessments

Because of the likelihood of a chain of impact with the five levels of evaluation, it is important that measures be taken at every point, even if not in a formal, structured test. Informal methods will help ensure to the facilitator and program designer that learning has occurred.

Measuring Job Applications and Business Results: Level 3 and 4 Evaluations

Several approaches are available to collect data after a program is conducted. All are focused on gathering information to determine the extent to which the program has been successful. The six approaches described below show the range of possibilities.

Using a Follow-Up Assignment

Perhaps the easiest, and simplest, approach is to require participants to complete a task, project, or assignment after the program has been conducted and return the assignment to the training and development department. The participants' supervisor may or may not be involved in the process. When management support is not very strong, this technique may be the most successful approach. Participants usually are not aware of the follow-up assignments before the program begins. The results should be reported to the participants' supervisor, although they may not be involved in approving or participating in completing the project. This simple technique can help ensure transfer of training and provide the opportunity for a success story. Occasionally a participant will have an outstanding accomplishment that can be highlighted in other types of communication.

Planning a Follow-Up Assessment with Surveys, Interviews, Observations, and/or Focus Groups

A very common approach is to use some specific follow-up technique to determine exactly what has been accomplished since the training program has been conducted. This may involve one-on-one interviews conducted on a sampling basis, direct observation by an HRD staff member or third party, utilization of focus groups to determine what has been accomplished, or the implementation of questionnaires or surveys. Each specific type of data collection process has its advantages and disadvantages, as presented earlier. A very common arrangement is a follow-up questionnaire designed to measure job applications and business results after the program was completed. The questionnaire contains many of the same or similar questions used on the end-of-program reaction questionnaire. The follow-up probes, in detail, specific accomplishments and provides an opportunity to identify reasons for lack of results. A follow-up, if utilized, should be scheduled and the information should be shared with other participants. A variety of strategies are used to ensure that there are high rates of participation. Completing follow-up questionnaires should be required, not optional.

Integrating Action Planning into the Program

By far the most common technique for measuring results at levels 3 and 4 is the use of action plans. In this process, the action plans are actually developed in the HRD program and approved by the program facilitator. After the program is completed, participants work on the action plan and document the progress made toward the measurable objectives in the plan. The planning process may or may not involve the participants' supervisor but in all cases it is recommended that the supervisor receive a copy of the completed plan. In some organizations the plans are audited; others require the plans to be submitted to the HRD department to substantiate the results obtained in the program. The unique feature about this process is that the participants are briefed on the action plan process during the program. A specific session or module is devoted to this process and participants are usually presented with an example of an appropriate action plan. They develop plans following specific guidelines distributed in the session and the facilitator determines if the plans are feasible and appropriate. Action plans come in a variety of formats tailored to the organization and the specific types of data collected as well as reporting formats. An example is presented as Fig. 15-3.

Implementing Performance Contracting

A special type of action plan is a performance contract, which is a preprogram agreement between the HRD staff and the participants and each participant's supervisor. With this approach, all parties involved in the contract meet before the program is conducted and set specific objectives to accomplish which are related to the material in the program. Specific and measurable objectives are established and the contract is discussed during the program. The reporting mechanisms can follow the same arrangement as indicated in the action planning process.

Conducting a Special Follow-Up Evaluation Session

One of the most effective approaches is to reconvene the participants at a predetermined time after the program has been conducted in a special follow-up session. Usually one to three months after the program has been completed, participants attend the session and report on specific accomplishments. The documentation of these accomplishments shows evidence of level 3 and 4 evaluation. In addition, these sessions provide opportunities for additional training, particularly on advanced techniques or to refine specific skills and practices taught in the program. They also provide an opportunity to indicate specific barriers or problems to obtaining results.

Tracking Performance Data After the Program

Finally, the most credible process is to track department, work-unit, or individual performance data after the program is completed utilizing common measures of output, quality, costs, and time. It is essential to track data that is influenced or enhanced by the training program. This process involves going to the records of the organization, division, plant, or department to measure before- and after-program performance.

Collectively these six approaches provide a complete array of postprogram follow-up methods which organizations use to determine actual performance from the training program.

Name		Title

Department	Location	Telephone #

Today's Date	Start Date	Completion Date	Major Event Dates

This plan is for _____

Total Annual Value of Improvement $_____	**Significant Non-Monetary Improvements**

Significant Non-Monetary Improvements
1. _____
2. _____
3. _____
4. _____
5. _____

I. Improvement Area _____

Target Performance _____ Current Performance _____

Net Improvement _____ Annual Value of Improvement _____

	Action Items	Target Date	Completion Date
1.			
2.			
3.			
4.			
5.			
6.			
7.			
8.			
9.			
10.			

Calculations:	Non-Monetary Improvements 1. 2.

Figure 15-3. Action plan.

Measuring ROI: Level 5 Evaluation

The model shown in Fig. 15-4 presents an overall framework for developing the ROI. The framework serves as a simple and useful tool for developing ROI. It tracks the steps from data collection to calculating the actual monetary return. The model assumes that costs to compare with monetary benefits will be developed. Also, it assumes that each program will have intangible benefits that are not converted to monetary values but nevertheless are reported as benefits.

The ROI process begins with postprogram data collection methods, described above, which are at the heart of any evaluation system, and moves to the actual ROI calculation. Two very important steps, isolating the effects of training and converting data to monetary values, are described later.

Two formulas are often used to determine the return of a program—the benefit-to-cost ratio (BCR) and ROI:

$$BCR = \frac{\text{Program benefits}}{\text{Program costs}} \qquad ROI\,(\%) = \frac{\text{Net program benefits}}{\text{Program costs}} \times 100$$

The BCR utilizes the total benefits and costs. In the ROI formula, the costs are subtracted from the total benefits to produce the net benefits, which are then divided by the costs. For example, for an HRD program having benefits of $600,000 and a cost of $200,000 the BCR is calculated as follows:

$$BCR = \frac{\$600,000}{\$200,000} = 3\,(\text{or 3 to 1})$$

For every $1 invested, $3 in benefits are returned. The net benefits are $600,000 − $200,000 = $400,000, so the ROI is

$$ROI = \frac{\$400,000}{\$200,000} \times 100 = 200\%$$

This ROI means that for each $1 invested, the ROI is $2.

The benefits are usually annual benefits (the amount saved for a complete year). Although savings may continue after the first year if the program has lasting effects, the amount begins to diminish and is usually omitted from calculations. In the total program cost, it is recommended that development costs be included in the first year of the program unless the development is very expensive. An alternative is to prorate development costs over the projected life of the program.

The values for ROI in HRD are usually quite large, in the range of 150 percent to 400 percent of the initial investment, which illustrates the significant results of successful programs. In a recent casebook, ROI values range from 150 percent to 2000 percent.[12]

Isolating the Impact of HRD

A step that is often overlooked in evaluation is the process of isolating the effects of HRD—determining the extent to which the HRD program is linked to the improved results. At a very minimum, an evaluation report should acknowledge that other factors influenced results and should list the factors. Doing so adds credibility to the process, even if no attempts are made to isolate the influence. Fortunately several strategies can be helpful to isolate the impact and are briefly presented here.

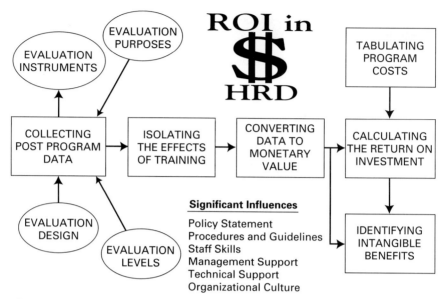

Figure 15-4. ROI model.

Use of Control Groups

The use of control groups is the most effective way to isolate the effects of an HRD program. In this arrangement, a control group that is nearly identical to the group involved in the HRD program is established. The performance of the two groups are compared and if the groups are similar and subject to the same external influences, the differences in the performance of the group can usually be attributed to the HRD program. Other variations of the control-group paradigm are described elsewhere.[13] When control groups are not feasible or practical, other possibilities are available.

Control-group arrangements show up in many settings. A recent review cited a Federal Express analysis as a good example of the state of the art in measuring ROI.[14] The study focused on 20 employees who went through the company's two-week training program soon after being hired to drive company vans. Their performance was compared with a control group of 20 other new hires whose managers were told to do no more (nor less) on-the-job training than normal. Performance was tracked for the two groups for 90 days in categories such as accidents, injuries, time-card errors, and domestic air-bill errors. The 10 performance categories had dollar values assigned by experts from engineering, finance, and other groups.

Trend-Line Analysis

Sometimes trend lines can predict where an output performance variable would be without the program. A trend line can be drawn using a series of preprogram measures. This is not an exact process, but provides an estimation. The predicted values from the trend line are compared with measures taken after the program, and differences are attributed to the program.

Figure 15-5 shows an example of a trend-line analysis for a reject rate. As can be seen in the figure, there was a downward trend on the reject rate prior to the

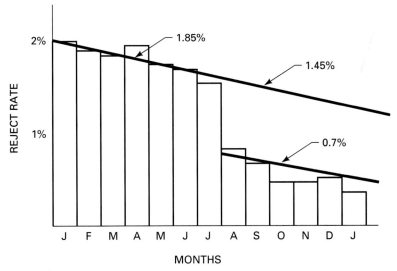

Figure 15-5. Trend-line analysis.

program. Although the program apparently had a dramatic effect on the reduction of rejects, the trend line shows that rejects would have continued to reduce based on the trend that had been previously established. It is tempting to measure the improvement by comparing the average six months prior to the program to the average six months after the program. A more accurate comparison is to use the six months' average after the program and compare it to the trend-line value at the midpoint of the six-month period after the program (October–November value). In this example the difference is 0.75 percent. Although this process is not exact, it gives an approximate value for the actual impact of the program.

Forecasting Methods

A more analytical approach to the trend-line analysis is to use a variety of forecasting methods to determine the expected level of an output that would be variable in the future if the program were not undertaken. There are several forecasting models that can take into account variations such as seasonal and cyclical fluctuations. They can develop reasonably accurate predictions of future values of the variable. Although a detailed discussion of forecasting methods is beyond the scope of this book, interested readers can find information on the different models and processes in other works.[15]

Participants' Estimates of Training's Effects

It may be helpful to have participants estimate the percentage of their improvement attributable to the HRD program. The participants are very close to the improvement and may know how much of the improvement each factor caused. Their collective estimates can be reliable and carry much credibility with the management group.

Participant estimation can be obtained by following a series of questions after describing the improvement:

- What percentage of this improvement can be attributed to the application of training program?
- What is the basis for this estimation?
- What confidence do you have in this estimate?
- What other individuals or groups could estimate this percentage or determine the amount?
- What other factors contributed to this success?
- Can you estimate the contribution percentage of each factor in a table or chart?

Table 15-4 shows an example of this approach.

To be very conservative, a confidence level can be factored into the percentages. In this approach, the level of confidence, expressed as a percentage, is multiplied by the estimate. For example, if a participant allocates 50 percent of the improvement to the training program but is only 70 percent confident in this estimate, the confidence level is multiplied by the estimate to provide a usable value of 35 percent. This adjusted percentage is multiplied by the amount of the improvement to isolate the portion attributed to training. The data is then ready for conversion to monetary values and, ultimately, used to calculate the return on investment.

As an added feature, management may approve the amounts that have been estimated by participants. For example, in an HRD program involving the performance management training program for Yellow Freight Systems, participants estimated the amount of savings which was attributed to the program.[16] Managers at the next two levels above participants reviewed and approved the estimates. So, in essence, the managers actually confirmed participants' estimates.

Management's Estimates of Training's Effects

In some cases, upper management or supervisors of participants can estimate the percentage of improvement attributable to the HRD program. Although this process is subjective, the source of the estimate is the group who may be most familiar with the situation and are aware of the other influences which affect performance. In a case involving Litton Guidance and Control Systems, management subtracted out any factors known to have contributed to the improvements in productivity and quality.[17] Then, to arrive at a conservative estimate, management applied a subjective factor, in this case 60 percent, to determine the portion

Table 15-4. Example of Participant Estimations

Factor which influenced improvement	Percent of improvement caused by	Confidence expressed as a percentage
1. Training program	50	70
2. Change in process	10	80
3. Adjustment in standards	10	50
4. Revision to incentive plan	20	90
5. Increased management attention	10	30
Total	100	

of results that could be attributed to the HRD program. Although this process was subjective, the 60 percent factor was decided on in a meeting of top executives, so the group had confidence in this value and was comfortable with the resulting calculations. Ideally, one should have estimates from both participants and management and combine them in some creative, helpful way.

Calculating the Effects of Other Factors

Although not appropriate in all cases, there are some situations where it may be feasible to calculate the impact of factors (other than training) which influenced the improvement and then conclude that training accounts for the remaining portion. In this approach, training takes credit for improvement that cannot be attributed to other factors. An example will help explain the approach. In a consumer lending program for a large commercial bank, a significant increase in consumer loan volume was generated after a training program was conducted for consumer loan officers.[18] Part of the increase in volume was due to the training program and the remaining was due to other factors during the same time period. Two factors were identified: loan officers' production improved with time and production increased because of falling interest rates. As loan officers make loans, their confidence improves. They will utilize consumer lending policy manuals and they gain knowledge and expertise through trial and error. The amount of this factor was estimated by using input from several internal experts. Industry sources were utilized to estimate the relationship between increased consumer loan volume with falling interest rates. Information from a national trade group provided some indication of what additional volume could be expected for every quarter of a percent of interest rate reduction. These two estimates accounted for a certain percent of increased consumer loan volume. The remaining improvement was attributed to the training program.

The Use of Customer Input

A very helpful approach in some narrowly focused situations is to solicit input directly from customers concerning the impact of training. In these situations, the customers are asked to indicate why they have chosen a particular product or service or how their reaction to the product or service organization has been influenced by individuals and their skills and abilities. This approach focuses directly on what the training program is often designed to improve. For example, after a teller training program was conducted, following a bank merger, market-research data showed that the percentage of customers who were dissatisfied with teller knowledge was reduced by 5 percent when compared to market survey data before training.[19] (Teller knowledge was increased by training.)

Therefore, 5 percent of the reduction of dissatisfied customers was directly attributable to the training program.

Although these approaches are subjective (except for perhaps the control-group and forecasting methods), they provide useful information that helps focus on the effects of HRD. The results can be more accurate than the results obtained from evaluating other functions. Consider, for example, the difficulty of isolating the effects of an organization such as an advertising program, a public relations function, a new purchasing policy and procedure, a new cost-accounting program, or a new engineering design. In each case, subjective input and decisions are required to estimate the impact. This is an area that will need additional research and application in the future.

Converting Data to Monetary Values

It is sometimes helpful to divide the collected data into hard data and soft data. Hard data is

- Objectively based
- Easy to measure and quantify
- Relatively easy to assign dollar values
- Common measures of organizational performance
- Very credible in the eyes of management

  Soft data is

- Subjectively based in many cases
- Difficult to measure and quantify, directly
- Difficult to assign dollar values
- Less credible as a performance measure
- Usually behaviorally oriented

This distinction helps in the data analysis and conversion processes. All hard data is usually converted to monetary values, whereas soft data may or may not be converted, depending on the difficulty of making the conversion and the credibility of the output. Hard data usually includes quantity, quality, cost, and time. Soft data focuses more on attitudes, work climate, work habits, and other items that are behaviorally based and subjective.

Converting Hard Data

Converting hard data is a relatively easy task. The output values are translated into profit units, which are converted to monetary values. Cost savings can usually be transferred directly to the ROI formula, although the money value of time may alter the exact amount. A cost savings will need to be discounted to obtain a present value to compare to program costs. Quality measures are a little more difficult because there are so many factors which can be affected by quality improvements. Table 15-5 shows the specific items that may be influenced by a change in quality. The value of time savings needs some attention, too. Sometimes the salary of the individuals whose time has been saved is an appropriate measure. At other times, as shown in Table 15-6, the value of time savings derives from any of several different factors.

Table 15-5. Factors Involved in Converting Quality Data to Monetary Values

- Scrap or waste
- Rework
- Customer or client dissatisfaction
- Product liability
- Inspection and quality control
- Internal losses
- Employee morale

Table 15-6. Factors Involved in Converting
Time Savings to Monetary Values

- Wages or salaries
- Better service
- Penalty avoidance
- Opportunity for profit
- Training time

Converting Soft Data

Perhaps the most difficult conversion is determining the monetary value of a soft-data improvement, and many organizations do not attempt this process. Several strategies can provide reliable estimates of the value of soft-data improvements, however.

Historical Costs

Some organizations track the costs of certain soft-data items. If these costs are available, they should be utilized when developing monetary values for improvements in those variables. Unfortunately, for most soft-data items, historical costs are not available, which creates a need for reliable estimates. A case in a petroleum company illustrates the use of costs in soft-data conversion in a training program for dispatchers. The value of improvement (reduction, in this case) in customer complaints was converted to a monetary value based on historical records. The time it took to resolve a complaint was monitored, and the cost was derived using the salaries and benefits of the individuals involved. This approach used internal cost data (i.e., salaries) in a soft-data conversion.

Expert Opinion

Sometimes the best estimates of the value of a soft-data improvement may come from experts in the field. Experts who have studied, analyzed, and developed these estimates previously may come from within the organization. There may also be external experts who have researched the topic across organizations. For example, information on the cost of a grievance might be obtained from a labor relations staff member internally, or from an external expert who studies the costs of grievances in several organizations and industries.

External Studies

For some soft-data items (e.g., turnover, absenteeism, tardiness, and customer complaints), studies that place a value on a unit of improvement are available. When such studies are available, they should be utilized. For example, there have been many studies to calculate the cost of absenteeism both by industry and in specific organizations.[20] The value in the studies may need to be adjusted to apply to a particular organization.

Participants' Estimates

The individuals involved with an improvement may have some sense of the value of the improvement and should be asked directly. Sometimes participants in an

HRD program are asked to place a value on a particular unit of improvement that will serve as a measure of the program's success. For example, in a program with supervisors aimed at reducing absenteeism, participants, all of whom were supervisors, were asked to estimate the cost of a single absence in their work units. After discussion of the factors that contributed to the cost, the supervisors provided estimates. The average value for the group was used in the final analysis to estimate the value of the reduction in absenteeism. In some cases this approach may not be feasible, because participants are unable to provide estimates. In other cases, however, this may be the richest source of information available.

Management's Estimates

It is assumed that managers or supervisors of participants have more knowledge of the process than the participants; because so many think this is so, managers can be asked to place a value on a unit of improvement. This approach increases management support and buy-in for the evaluation.

HRD Staff's Estimate

The last, and probably the least credible, source of estimates is HRD staff. In this approach, the HRD staff uses whatever information is available to estimate the value of the improvement. This attempt is risky because the value may be perceived to be self-serving and not very credible.

What It Means

A typical reaction to these conversion strategies is that they are so subjective that the conversion is virtually worthless. This is not the case. Subjective assignments appear in all aspects of business. Data developed in organizations is often based on estimates or subjective assessments. The HRD staff should not have to apologize for the subjectiveness of the soft-data conversion. The best strategy is to use all of the input from people who are knowledgeable, clearly identifying the sources and assumptions when the results are communicated to audiences. Program evaluators seem hesitant to use the above strategies to convert the values of soft-data improvements to monetary values. This is an area that will need increased attention in the future.

Measurement Challenges: More Standardization and Thoroughness

After the literature is researched, dozens of cases reviewed, and issues with HRD professionals explored, several conclusions concerning measurement and evaluation begin to emerge. These are presented as challenges to the profession.

Cost Standards

The methods organizations use to track costs vary considerably. What one organization assumes is a cost of training, another may not. The HRD field needs standard cost data. Although there have been several attempts at standardization, most of the efforts have failed. It is becoming increasingly difficult to compare costs from different programs. This issue is particularly important as the U.S. government attempts to require, or encourage, employers to invest more in training. When the specific makeup of an organization's investment becomes a crucial measure, standardization can help. In the interim, components in the total costs for programs should be discussed and described.

Evaluation Designs

Many organizations do not focus enough attention on evaluation design. Although a control group, the preferred approach, was presented in this chapter, this paradigm is infrequent in practice. Yet it can be used without the disruption, problems, and inconvenience that are usually feared by practitioners. In addition, the use of pre- and postcourse measurements does not appear to be as frequent as it should be. Other design schemes, such as time-series measurements, are also useful but are largely ignored.

Isolating the Effects of HRD

In far too many situations, the improvement in an output variable after an HRD program is conducted is assumed to be caused by the implementation of the program. In reality, several variables affect output and performance. Many practitioners are not taking the extra step to attempt to isolate the influence of the program on the overall results. As presented earlier, there are a variety of strategies available, but examples of their actual use are very rare. This is an excellent area for future research and is an important challenge for the HRD field.

Standardized Methodology

Evaluation methods and techniques vary. There are only so many ways in which data can be collected; however, the number of processes for data analysis is finite. Data collection methods are often used without regard to their advantages and disadvantages. Additional efforts to standardize and publicize these methods would be helpful to the field.

Statistical Techniques

Although most HRD practitioners want to avoid statistics, many conclusions require statistical analysis. Even top executives, who may not understand a sophisticated statistical analysis, need to know that conclusions are based on a certain confidence level, supported by appropriate methodology. In many evaluation projects, the concept of statistical power is largely ignored. Some sample sizes are so small that the results cannot be considered to be supported statistically. This factor does not receive enough attention with practitioners.

Converting Data to Monetary Values

Because of the subjective nature of the conversion, the results from HRD programs are not converted to monetary values. It is an essential step for an ROI calculation. Although this step was included in most of the cases in this chapter, many other evaluations do not compare benefits with cost. Conversion to monetary values should be a fundamental requirement.

The challenges described here represent a mandate for the HRD field. Standardization and consistency are needed to continue to make progress with measuring training results. Perhaps the different groups involved in HRD should attempt to develop standards or generally accepted guidelines. Although development and acceptance of standards will take a long time, the HRD field will be much better off if such an effort is undertaken, and there will be many more successes in the future.

Conclusion

This chapter has presented workable solutions and appropriate methods to tackle one of the most challenging and important issues in human resource development: measuring training results. Although the process is complex, it can be simplified when it is broken down into various strategies, levels, models, and techniques. The result is a manageable process modest enough for even the smallest HRD departments.

This chapter presented a brief summary of the tools used to collect data for evaluation. Levels of evaluations were outlined and specific techniques for measuring at each level were explored and developed. Four ways to measure training service were presented and this represents a growing area of interest among HRD professionals. Developing a return on investment was explored along with two important areas essential for calculating this return. Techniques to isolate the effects of training are often omitted and ignored but yet are essential for an effective ROI calculation. Seven workable strategies were covered. Also, converting data to monetary values is necessary to compare the value of training with training costs. Although much progress has been made with all these techniques and strategies, there are many challenges left to make measurement and evaluation a mainstream function in HRD departments.

References

1. "Industry Report," *Training*, October 1994, *31*(10), p. 29.

2. Ibid., p. 29.

3. Gallagan, P. A., "IBM Gets Its Arms Around Education," *Training and Development Journal*, 1989, 43, p. 37.

4. Fuchsberg, G., "Taking Control," *The Wall Street Journal*, September 10, 1993.

5. Kirkpatrick, D. L., "Techniques for Evaluating Training Programs," in D. L. Kirkpatrick, ed., *Evaluating Training Programs*, ASTD, Alexandria, VA, 1975.

6. Alliger, G. M., and E. A. Januk, "Kirkpatrick's Levels of Training Criteria: Thirty Years Later," *Personnel Psychology*, 1989, 42, pp. 331–342.

7. Rosen, N., "Employee Attitude Surveys: What Managers Should Know," *Training and Development Journal*, November 1987, pp. 50–52.

8. Lee, C., "Testing Makes A Comeback," *Training*, December 1988, p. 49.

9. Fetterol, E., "Did the Training Work? Evaluation by Interview," *Training News*, December 1990, pp. 10–11.

10. Erkut, S., and J. P. Fields, "Focus Groups to the Rescue," *Training and Development Journal*, October 1987, pp. 74–76.

11. Phillips J. J., *Handbook of Training Evaluation and Measurement Methods,* 2d ed., Gulf Publishing, Houston, 1991.

12. Phillips, J. J., ed., *In Action: Measuring Return on Investment,* vol. 1, ASTD, Alexandria, VA, 1994, p. 262.

13. For example, see Pedhazur, E. J., and L. P. Sehmelkin, *Measurement, Design, and Analysis: An Integrated Approach,* Lawrence Erlbaum Associates, Hillsdale, NJ, 1991, and Fitz-Gibbon, C. T., and L. L. Morris, *How to Design a Program Evaluation,* Sage Publications, Beverly Hills, CA, 1987.

14. Hassett, J., "Simplifying ROI," *Training,* September 1992, p. 54.

15. For example, see Makridakis, S., *Forecasting Methods for Management,* 5th ed., John Wiley & Sons, 1989, and Jarret, J., *Business Forecasting Methods,* 2d ed., Basil Blackwell, Cambridge, MA, 1991.

16. Phillips, J. J., ed., *In Action: Measuring Return on Investment,* vol. 1, ASTD, Alexandria, VA, 1994, p. 262.

17. Ibid.

18. Ibid, p. 187.

19. Rust, R. T., A. J. Zahorik, and T. L. Keiningham, *Return on Quality: Measuring the Financial Impact of Your Company's Quest for Quality,* Probus Publishers, Chicago, IL, 1994.

20. Martocchio, J. J., and D. A. Harrison, "To Be There or Not to Be There? Questions, Theories, and Methods in Absenteeism Research," in G. R. Ferris, ed., *Research in Personnel and Human Resource Management,* vol. II, JAI Press, Greenwich, CT, 1993.

16
Testing

Mary L. Tenopyr

Mary L. Tenopyr *is Measurement and Selection Systems Director at AT&T Corporation. She was graduated with a doctorate with specialty in psychological measurement from the University of Southern California. She is immediate past president of the Division of Evaluation, Measurement, and Statistics of the American Psychological Association. She has been president of the Society for Industrial and Organizational Psychology, also a division of the American Psychological Association. Dr. Tenopyr is a past member of the Army Science Board and on the editorial boards of several journals. She is a Fellow of the American Psychological Society and the American Psychological Association. She has received the Society for Industrial and Organizational Psychology award for outstanding professional practice.*

This chapter is designed to define testing, explain the various roles testing has in relation to training, describe and relate information about the testing's most important characteristics, describe developments in selection testing, relate information about the status of achievement testing, and provide a summary of the topics covered.

Definition of Testing

Testing is a process whereby one obtains a quantifiable estimate of some aspects of performance at a given point in time. Although the term *quantifiable* implies numerical measurement, it also applies to categories such as "excellent" or "good," to letter grades such as "A" or "B," and to gross categories, such as "pass" or "fail." All these categories can be translated into numbers. The term *performance* in the definition of testing is not meant to imply that actual hands-on work is required to define a test. Most tests consist of constructed tasks upon which performance is measured. For example, both the task of answering questions about job knowledge and the handling of simulated in-basket materials are constructed tasks.

Although the distinction is not always clear, tests may be divided into two general categories. First there are tests of maximum performance, in which the examinee is instructed to do his or her best. The typical training test is in this category. The other type of test is a habitual performance test in which the examinee reports in terms of what he or she believes or feels or how the person would habitually act in a given situation. Most of the instruments used to measure personality, character, interests, or attitudes fall in this category. In terms of training, these habitual performance instruments are of limited interest; however, they are probably most useful in evaluating training designed to change beliefs and attitudes.

Various Roles of Testing

Testing, essentially, has five roles in training. These are (1) selection of trainees, (2) diagnosis of training needs, (3) evaluation of training adequacy, (4) evaluation of trainee achievement, and (5) use as criterion for selection test results. A purpose of this chapter is to relate clearly the interdependence of testing and the training development and delivery processes. Testing cannot be considered in isolation from the total training system, and testing in one of its roles cannot be considered apart from the way it functions in its other roles. This chapter also gives an overview of current knowledge relative to each of the roles of testing and indicates the relationships among roles and the implications of the law for each of these roles.

Appropriate testing in training cannot be accomplished unless one considers the context in which training is embedded. Despite the fact that test development and application are important, basically a test can be no better than the training upon which it was based. Of course, the training can be no better than the needs analysis upon which the training was designed. In turn, the needs analysis depends upon adequate definition of the job for which training is to be developed, followed by appropriate measurement of job performance or other job behaviors, so that training needs can be adequately delineated. The role of diagnostic testing here depends upon the allocation of the tasks which the organization decides need to be done to achieve its goals.

Thus, the situation in its simplest form is a chain: organizational goals, task definition to achieve these goals, task allocations to jobs, job definition, performance measurement, needs analysis (possible diagnostic testing), training development, training delivery, and testing.

Any inadequacies along this chain will render the final process less than perfect. For example, if a job is poorly defined or performance on it is not measured adequately, any training needs analysis will suffer, the training will be poorly developed, and any measurement of trainee success may have little relevance with respect to performance of the job and, in turn, achievement of the goals of the organization.

Also, one can conceptualize the simple chain configuration relative to training as being complicated by various feedback loops which are characteristic of a system. For example, training can result in a situation in which the job is redefined, because of different skills of job incumbents after training.

Furthermore, training and related testing are intricately involved with other personnel practices of the organization. For example, changes in wage rate may affect the general skill level of job applicants and dictate the need for different training. Conversely, the fact that an organization offers the opportunity for training may affect the wages the employer has to offer to attract job applicants.

Examples could be given of many other interactions with the equipment procurement system or with a production control system. What has been presented here, of course, does not represent the totality of the many interactions training and its associated testing can have in the systems and subsystems within an organization or those impinging on an organization, but it should be sufficient to indicate that training testing does not exist in a vacuum. Training testing is highly dependent upon many factors within and outside the organization and cannot be developed or evaluated without consideration of its whole role in the total organization.

The ensuing discussion of the roles of testing in training will have a more narrow focus than the preceding material; however, the reader is cautioned to keep in mind that testing is usually a reflection of the steps that preceded test development and the interactions of those steps with many processes within and outside the organization.

Testing Characteristics

Validity

The important concept relative to test use is validity, which refers to the accuracy of inferences made from test scores.[1] Test validation is a process of investigation, relative to determining such accuracy. Various types of investigation may be involved, depending upon the exact situation, but in all cases the type of investigation is dependent upon the use to which the test is to be put. It is inappropriate to speak of "validating" a test; one investigates the validity of a test for a particular use. It is equally inappropriate to speak of a "valid test"; rather one should speak of "valid test use." A test which is used validly for one purpose may not be used validly for another. Although there are various strategies for investigating validity, it is important to recognize that validity is essentially a unitary concept related, of course, to the specific use. Since 1954[2] there has been a tendency to categorize validity into categories. This trend unfortunately has led to a situation in which various types of validity have been discussed separately by numerous writers and the underlying unity of validity has been, for the most part, ignored.

It is common now to speak of three strategies for investigating validity; however, the use of different strategies for validation does not define different types of validity. The three strategies are criterion-related, content, and construct. Depending upon the use to which a test is to be put one may wish to emphasize one of those strategies more than others; however, this action does not constitute using one "type" of validity.

Standards for validation may be found in *Standards for Educational and Psychological Testing*,[3] a document that is currently under revision by the American Educational Research Association, the American Psychological Association, and the National Council on Measurement in Education. The standards should become available from the American Psychological Association in the late 1990s.

Criterion-Related Validity. The criterion-related strategy is used when one specifically wants to relate test use to some outcome called a criterion. The criterion may be singular, such as grades in training, or it may be a composite of several outcomes, such as training time, job performance, and tenure. In any event, the criterion is the primary variable of interest and it is the relationship of the test with the criterion one wishes to investigate. For example, one may establish training time as a criterion and wish to know how well aptitude tests given at time of hire relate to later training time. The relationship is usually expressed numerically through a statistic called a *coefficient of correlation* or some variation thereof. In the validation situation, these coefficients are often referred to as validity coefficients. A typical validity coefficient is a unit-free index number, not to be confused with a proportion, and it can take on values from +1.00 to −1.00. A coefficient of +1.00 indicates a perfect positive correlation: that is, the person who scored highest on the test scored highest on the criterion. The person who scored second highest on one scored highest on the other. With a coefficient of correlation of +1.00, the same relationship exists point for point throughout the two sets of data. In work with testing, this degree of relationship rarely, if ever, occurs. A coefficient of correlation of zero indicates a pure random relationship between the test and the criterion. In this situation, the best prediction of criterion performance one can make from the test score is to say that regardless of test score, every examinee will be average in criterion performance. This is, in practical terms, equivalent to no prediction at all. A coefficient of correlation of −1.00 means the same as one of +1.00; only the relationship is reversed. The person who scores highest on the test does poorest on the criterion. In testing, a negative coefficient of correlation is most likely to occur when the "good" ends of the test and the criterion scales are in different directions. For example, aptitude tests often correlate negatively with training time, because high test scores are "good" and high training time is "bad." When scales are in the same direction, correlations between aptitude tests and training success criteria are usually positive. They are also usually of moderate size, roughly in the range from .15 to .60. Coefficients of correlation of this magnitude, whether they be positive or negative, indicate that test scores are useful in making predictions of criterion performance.

Earlier writings[4] differentiated between types of criterion-related validity depending upon the type of design used in the validation study. The most common differentiation was between "predictive" and "concurrent" validity. The term *predictive* was used to describe studies in which job applicants are hired regardless of test score (predictor), and criterion data (e.g., course grades) is collected later. The term *concurrent* was reserved for use in situations in which the predictor and criterion data are gathered at approximately the same point in time. In organizations, the latter type of design usually involves testing of present employees and gathering criterion data (e.g., supervisors' ratings) at the same time.

Later writings[5,6] have indicated that the distinction between the two types of design is not always clear and that many design variations are possible. Also Schmitt, Gooding, Noe, and Kirsch[7] have indicated that there are relatively small differences in the validity estimates for three classes of design.

Content Validity. A second type of validation strategy is the content-oriented strategy. It consists mainly of investigating a domain of content such as a collection of job tasks, sampling from that domain, and building a test on the basis of that sample. This strategy relies heavily on systematic use of expert judgments, although some numerical techniques may be used in developing a content-oriented test. The content-oriented strategy is the one most meaningful for training achievement tests. It is the method most used for diagnosing training needs and evaluating training and trainees. It is also important in selecting trainees when the objective is to select those who already have some knowledge or ability in the area in which training is to be done. Another use is to develop criteria for validation studies involving selection tests.

The first step in content-oriented test construction is to define a content domain. In training, defining the domain theoretically consists of all the steps in the chain preceding testing, as presented earlier, however, in measuring trainee achievement, one usually starts with the training as it has been developed and delivered. In other words, the domain is what has been taught.

This raises an interesting philosophical question: What if the training itself is not valid? Questioning the validity of the training process could lead to an almost infinite regress. One could question the needs analysis, the performance measurement on the job, the delineation of job tasks and requirements, and so on. Failures in any of these could serve to make the final training test, based on training content, not valid for making inferences about job performance or other job-relevant behavior.

The training organization should not assume that training tests are valid for inferences about later job behavior unless the total training system is well developed and every link in the chain of events leading to the training test is properly performed. The best test construction cannot compensate for poorly developed or delivered training. The moral of the story is to avoid the question of whether the training itself is valid by following professional techniques in training development and delivery and by influencing those in charge of job design and other facets of the organization relevant to the training situation to perform their functions properly.

Defining an appropriate job domain upon which to base training developments almost always requires careful job study. Many methods have been advanced for job analysis. Some are more useful than others in training development. Some of the recent writings on this subject are contained in Bemis, Belenky, and Soder[8], Gael[9], Levine[10], and McCormick.[11]

After the job domain is defined and appropriately narrowed by a needs assessment, the objectives of training set, and the training developed and delivered, one is ready to speak of a training domain. This is the total content of the training as it is actually delivered. It is this training domain, the content domain, which should be the basis for developing training tests for diagnoses, trainee evaluation, and use as a criterion for selection tests.

The second step, after defining the content domain, is the sampling from that domain to obtain the tasks, knowledges, skills, or abilities which are to be the basis for actual test questions or other tasks. Many methods can be used for sampling, but the basic guide to sampling should be the course objectives.

In some cases, it is critical that trainees know some material taught extremely well whereas other parts of the material need not be known so well. Developing a test which reflects differences in criticality of content is usually best achieved by sampling extremely heavily from the more critical areas and less heavily from those areas of lesser importance. The instructor may wish to engage the services of independent subject-matter experts to determine criticality at this point; however, the judgment as to what is critical should have been done during training development and the steps which preceded it.

For some jobs, such as airline pilot, the notion of sampling has little meaning. When everything the trainee does is critical, every aspect of the training domain should be subject to testing.

Content sampling should result in a sample sufficient in size to provide later a test which will yield stable measurement. This matter is basically a question of test reliability, which is the degree to which test scores are free from errors of measurement.[3] Reliability will be discussed in more detail later; however, in general, longer tests provide more freedom from one type of error of measurement; this fact does not mean that inappropriate lengthening of a test is advisable. The inclusion of irrelevant material in the content sample just for the sake of lengthening the test is not a justifiable procedure.

Content sampling also should be cast, if possible, in terms of what the examinee has to do later on the job. Samples should be described in terms of "action" verbs (e.g., "*Records* the trouble call number to line 5 of Form 220").

If one follows the standard prescriptions for writing training objectives,[12] the sampling should follow directly from the objectives. Writing the description of the members of the sample in this way will also help preclude the development of a test which is based upon rote memorization of facts.

Content sampling should not be heavily based on the ease with which test items can be written for a particular subject. Often the most critical parts of training have required the most creative test writing. Especially to be avoided is oversampling in areas in which it is easy to write questions with simple numerical answers which are subject to rote memorization.

The content sampling is best summarized in a document variously known as a *test outline* or *test budget*. Various procedures for developing this document have been proposed, but there is no evidence that any format other than the traditional outline format as taught in elementary school is necessary. However, for organizational training purposes there are several criteria this document should meet: (1) it should be closely allied with the course objectives, i.e., it should accurately reflect what was taught; (2) it should deal in actions at every step in the outline; (3) it should be broken down into fine-enough units so that the number of test tasks to be developed for the finest outline unit is small (some recommend that the units should be so fine that no more than five test questions are assigned to any given unit); and (4) it should provide a training-relevant test as long as is reasonable and feasible.

When a training test is used in a way that will have any effect on a trainee's future in the organization, it might be wise to have the test budget reviewed by one or more independent subject-matter experts and their judgments recorded. This not only will serve as a quality-control measure but will also aid in possible later legal defense, if the test is challenged in civil rights litigation.

Construct Validity.   The third major strategy is construct validation. This strategy focuses primarily on the test score as a measure of a psychological characteristic of interest. The term *construct* is used because one is trying to measure something intangible that has essentially been constructed. In the mental ability area, one can speak of characteristics such as logical reasoning or computational ability. In the personality area, terms like friendliness and sociability are often used as if they were constructs.

Early conceptions of construct validation, such as that of Cronbach and Meehl[13] implied that every construct had to be embedded within a complex and continually developing theory. This idea was developed through the years and refined.[14] The use of the term *construct*, however, came to be applied without all the theoretical support that early writers had contemplated. Possibly in recognition that ideals would never be fulfilled, later writers have looked upon constructs as requiring less rigorous definition. However, few writers would disagree that a construct has to be embedded in a conceptual framework and have a body of empirical evidence supporting its definition. Terms implying constructs are in use in everyday language. Conversations are sprinkled with terms like *drive, enthusiasm,* or *introversion*. Yet many of these terms do not have the research-based empirical support to justify their use in testing or in precisely describing individuals. One should be cautious in applying such labels and also examine carefully any claims that a test "measures" such abstract constructs.

A language of constructs has not been agreed upon by psychologists. Throughout psychology one can find a proliferation of terms used to describe people. However, definitions of the same term often vary from researcher to researcher, and there seems to be no clear path to truth. The situation is complicated by the fact that even very narrow personal characteristics, such as the ability to type, can be considered constructs.[15] Thus, one can conceive of an almost infinite number of constructs.

Unless one resorts to construct validation, one has little evidence about the meaning of test scores beyond the specifics of the exact training situation. One may know that scores on a certain test requiring reading correlate with success in a course designed to train retail clerks; however, one cannot explain the reasons for this relationship without invoking constructs. It is highly likely that certain constructs affect both performance on the test and performance in training, but without further evidence, we do not know what those constructs are and hence cannot fully discern the meaning of the relationship.

Construct validation takes on particular importance in training when one engages in efforts designed to change attitudes, leadership abilities, or other such characteristics which are hard to define. For evaluation of trainees and training, there is often a tendency to select commercial tests on the basis of the label applied to the test or unsupported claims in the test manual. Often labels are misleading; test names may suggest some relationship to the objectives of the training course, but the same test name can be used for a number of tests which are not highly related, and the test user has no guarantee that the test chosen has any relationship to the objectives of a given training course.

In situations where the trainer is dealing with constructs, he or she is well advised either to choose commercial tests carefully or to avoid their use. An alternative is to base training measurement on the content of the training course. The distinction between content and construct validity is not always an easy one to make. Content-oriented test construction strategies can form strong evidence of construct validity.[15,16] The training developer, however, may have to conduct considerable research to ensure that the content of the course is relevant to the constructs he or she wants to develop in trainees.

Reliability

Classical Reliability Theory.   Reliability refers to the freedom of test scores from errors of measurement or, in more general terms, to their consistency of measurement. As it is inappropriate to speak of the validity of a test, it is equally inappropriate to speak of the reliability of a test. Reliability is essentially a generic term, and different reliability coefficients are appropriate, depending upon a purpose. The commonest ways of estimating reliability are (1) to administer the same test to the same people a second time and obtain the coefficient of correlation between test and retest results, (2) to administer an alternate form of the test to the same people and obtain the coefficient of correlation between forms, and (3) to determine the coefficients of correlation among items or other parts of a test administered only once and estimate the reliability on the basis of these coefficients. The latter method yields what is commonly known as an estimate of internal consistency.

Each of these methods or variations thereof is useful for different purposes. For example, the stability of test scores over time is best estimated by test-retest with a suitable time interval between test administrations.

Possibly the most common ways of estimating reliability for training tests are the various internal consistency methods.[17] Because they depend upon only one administration of the test and do not require the development of an alternate form of the test, they are the least expensive to use. All these methods depend on the degree of homogeneity of response to the content of the test. The source of unreliability indicated by internal consistency methods is differences in response to different parts of the test. This source of unreliability may often be traced to different content in different parts of the test.

The internal consistency methods do not indicate other possible sources of unreliability, such as examinee's changing their responses to items on a retest or differences in content between two forms of a test. The internal consistency methods, because of their convenience and cost, tend to be used at times when other reliability estimation methods may be more appropriate. For highly speeded tests, the use of internal consistency methods may lead to a falsely high estimate of reliability. When the content within a test varies widely, as might be the case for a beginning building maintenance test which might involve several subjects such as electricity, carpentry, and plumbing, an internal consistency method might yield a lower estimate of reliability than other methods.

One of the more recent developments relative to reliability is generalizability theory, which has been developed by Cronbach, Gleser, Nanda, and Rajaratan.[18] This theory's use is becoming more common and accepted.

Reliability in testing is most important for its support for validity. Generally, a test which is not reasonably reliable cannot be very valid. Reliability is never a substitute for validity. The fact that a test gives consistent results does not mean that it is measuring the right thing.

Special Reliability Considerations in Achievement Testing. When tests are developed to be criterion-referenced[19] (i.e., developed to determine mastery of a training subject), as opposed to norm-referenced (i.e., designed to communicate the person's standing relative to some group), classical reliability theory is often not applicable. Although many organizational training tests can provide both norm-referenced and criterion-referenced interpretations, when a training test is designed to be interpreted only in terms of specified performance standards (e.g., "can [or cannot] assemble a widget correctly in 90 seconds"), special reliability formulas may apply. These have been summarized by Berk.[20,21] A review of methods for estimating the reliability of mastery-nonmastery classifications in criterion-referenced testing has been prepared by Subkoviak.[22]

The literature relative to the reliability of criterion-referenced tests continues to develop. The reader is advised to monitor the educational research literature continually.

Selection for Training

Basics of Selection

In selecting persons for training, there are two approaches. When, in general, training is to start at a low level of mastery and relatively untrained people are to be selected, the use of aptitude tests supported by the results of criterion-related validation is appropriate. When training is to start at a higher level of mastery and trainees are to be selected on the basis of current level of learning, an achievement test may be appropriate. The distinction between aptitude tests and achievement tests is not clear. The difference is usually cast in terms of the way the test is used. When the test is used to predict, it is usually referred to as an aptitude test. When a test is used to reflect past events, such as the amount of material previously learned, it is called an achievement test.

The distinction between aptitude and achievement is not in test content. Obviously, answering simply arithmetic questions on a test which is called a numerical aptitude test requires some past learning, but if the test is used to predict later learning success, the test is properly referred to as an aptitude test. Also, when tests indicating specific training content mastery are used to predict later performance, such as degree of achievement in a higher-level training source, they are essentially being used as aptitude tests. However, despite being somewhat inappropriate, in the ensuing discussion the term *achievement* will denote tests which are direct reflections of degree of mastery of training content and the term *aptitude* will be reserved for tests of the more general abilities usually used to predict later training or job success.

In selecting for training, it is often difficult to establish clear-cut roles for aptitude and past achievement. The question of what action to take with regard to a person who has had some previous training but cannot pass validly used aptitude tests often arises. No test is a perfect predictor; consequently this situation can occur in the case of some individuals. The only solution to the dilemma imposed is thorough criterion-related investigation involving both the aptitude tests and a measure of training achievement.

Relative to aptitude tests used for trainees selection, evidence of criterion-related validity is usually necessary. This need is supported not only by principles of good professional practice[3,4] in psychology but also by federal government guidelines on testing,[23] numerous state and local regulations on testing, and a developing body of case law.

It should be emphasized that conducting criterion-related validation studies requires a great deal of rigor and knowledge. Earlier writings, however, suggested that any little study would be sufficient. This is not the case. Those wishing to conduct such studies are advised to seek the assistance of an industrial psychologist or a psychometrician.

Recent Developments

There have been a number of recent developments in selection testing. Some render older ideas meaningless. For example, it has been shown[24] that to detect validity one needs much larger samples of persons to study than was previously believed. The typical test validation study as historically done (i.e., one involving 30 to 100 people), will often not give validity results which even approximate the "true" validity. Rather than do small studies which may be meaningless, one is advised to seek expert advice and seek approaches other than criterion-related validation in the exact situation.

One such approach which has recently emerged is based upon the validity generalization literature.[7,25,26,27,28] The authors of this research assert that all aptitude tests are validly used for predicting success in all jobs. This fact does not mean, however, that all tests are equally valid for any job or any purpose. It means only that in all likelihood any aptitude test will offer at least a minimum level of prediction for the usual job and training success criteria. In other words, this does not mean that any test for selecting trainees is valid enough to be useful for any course. Validity, as mentioned previously, is not an all-or-none phenomenon, and the closer the value of the validity coefficient to $+1.00$, the more accurate is the prediction and the more useful the test, in general. The trainer should seek expert advice to achieve the highest validity he or she can in selecting trainees.

The fact that certain tests are generally highly valid for selecting clerical employees has been demonstrated; the literature does not seem so conclusive relative to blue-collar jobs. Also managerial selection on the basis of aptitude tests needs further study to determine the degree of generalizability of selection tests in this situation.

The question of possible discrimination against various groups in the population has been a subject of much heated debate and research over the past two decades. The definition of discrimination in selection has essentially been agreed upon by professionals.[29] Discrimination is not a matter of differences in passing rates on selection tests; rather, it is a question of whether differences in scores on selection tests are reflected in differences in job or training performance. In other words, do groups who score low on the test also do poorly in training, and vice versa? Using this kind of definition, the research literature indicates that racial discrimination on selection tests is, in general, not a major problem[29,30] in employment or education settings. The research literature with respect to gender differences is not conclusive. However, gender differences on most selection tests are often not of any practical significance, except in mathematical reasoning and spatial visualization tests.

Another area which has received considerable attention during the last decade is the utility of tests. The term *utility* refers to the cost-effectiveness of use of tests or other human resources interventions. Determination of savings from the use of tests or any other personnel practice has always been difficult; however, for selection tests, new methods of estimating utility have been developed and are being widely used.[31,32] Such methods can also be used to determine the cost-effectiveness of training itself.

A final area in which research results have become fairly conclusive is choosing among various selection procedures.[7,28] It is clear that aptitude tests, along with work samples and peer ratings, are the best-known predictors of measures of job success, including training success. Traditional selection procedures like interviews and education and experience evaluations are relatively poor predictors of job or training performance. Also the typical validity found for aptitude tests, based on all the published literature and much of the unpublished literature, is high enough to afford good prediction of job success. Furthermore, aptitude tests predict training achievement even better than they do job performance. Consequently, for most situations in which there is to be selection for training, it is advisable to use aptitude tests rather than some other selection method.

Measuring Training Achievement

Types of Achievement Testing

Training achievement tests can be used in any of the five roles of testing: (1) selecting trainees, (2) diagnosing training needs, (3) evaluating training needs, (4) evaluating trainee achievement, and (5) serving as criteria for validating selection tests.

How one develops and evaluates achievement tests depends upon the philosophy of training in the organization and the specific policies and goals affecting the training organization. The selection of training test development procedures may at times depend also upon the nature of a specific course's overall objectives.

It is in the organizational training area that classical test theory and the newer test theories are most likely to be at least philosophically different. Classical test theory involves norm-referenced testing in which an individual's test performance is related to one's standing in some reference group. Criterion-referenced testing, on the other hand, is purposely constructed to provide measurements relative to specific performance standards. Although it is not necessary to do so, most criterion-referenced tests are usually interpreted in terms of mastery or nonmastery, and the standards for mastery are usually specified in the course objectives.

Regardless of what type of achievement test, norm-referenced or criterion-referenced, the instructor sets out to develop, a wide number of tests development guides are available (e.g., Green[33]; Gorth, O'Reilly, and Pinsky[34]; Gronlund[35]; Hopkins and Antes[36]; Martuza[37]; Popham[38]; Rahmlow and Woodley[39]; Smith[40]; Swezey[41]; Thyne[42]; and Tuchman[43]). More advanced treatments of criterion-referenced testing may be found in Berk,[44] Berk,[45] Popham,[46] and Hambleton, Swaminathan, Algina, and Coulson.[47] These are only a small sample of the hundreds of publications on the subject. There is little doubt that criterion-referenced measurement has become and will continue to be a major force in American education. The methods of test construction have become well developed, and the psychometric questions are being answered, although there is still some debate.

Test Standards

The question of setting standards for criterion-referenced testing was well covered in a 1978 special issue of *Journal of Educational Measurement,* that was edited by Lorrie A. Shepard. Livingston and Zieky[48] have provided a useful manual for setting standards.

A special problem in standards setting is the situation in which everyone masters training and training time is the only variation among trainees. Here, although subject-matter experts may be asked for judgments, it is often useful to do a criterion-related study to determine the relationship between training time and an appropriate measure of later job behavior. The same technique may be used for a combination of degree of mastery and training time.

Validity of Achievement Tests

The questions of validity of criterion-referenced test score use are essentially the same as those for norm-referenced test score use. The test score use must be validated with reference to the inferences to be made from it.[16,49] In organizational training, however, there are many practical problems in achieving ideal validation. If training was developed on the basis of careful needs assessment and job study and the tests were developed on the basis of course objectives, one may make a claim for content validity when one's goal is to measure training achievement. It is recognized, however, that ideal development of training achievement tests on such a systematic basis is not always possible. Also when a published test is used as a measure of training achievement, content-oriented methods often will not suffice; furthermore any claim that a particular test is relevant to some construct must be strongly supported. Certainly, test names and unsupported claims in promotional literature in test manuals are not evidence of construct validity.

Many inferences made from training achievement tests, such as those about future job performance, are often best supported by criterion-related evidence. When a training test is used for selection or otherwise affects a trainee's career, the question of whether the test predicts later behavior on the job becomes paramount. In this situation, the trainer is often faced with a dilemma. As mentioned previously, a study on a small number of trainees may fail to detect validity. Also, adequate measures of job performance or other job behavior are often not available, and one is sometimes faced with judging a good test on the basis of its relationship to a bad criterion. In many cases, a small sample study involving a hastily developed supervisor's rating criterion or an unreliable production measure may be worse than no study at all. If one is to do criterion-related studies on training achievement, they must be done in the same careful manner as those for trainee selection tests.

A further complicating factor is that when training and associated training tests are used for selection, they fall under the purview of government guidelines on testing.[23] According to the guidelines, if the use of such tests results in different passing rates for different race, ethnic, or sex groups, the user of the tests should be prepared to submit evidence of validity to the government.

There is no question that many training achievement tests indicate different levels of achievement for different groups. An obvious solution is to devote extra attention in training to those who have difficulty in mastering the training material, so that most members of the affected groups master the courses. Another course of action is to implement a valid trainee selection program, so that those who cannot master training are likely to be screened out before training or given remedial training. These solutions, it should be noted, merely shift the burden of validation to the employment organization instead of the training organization.

However, satisfying legal requirements does not relieve the training organization of the responsibility for valid measurement of achievement. Valid measurement is necessary for all uses of training achievement tests. Possibly the best course of action for a training organization to achieve valid measurement of training achievement is to concentrate on test development and ensure content validity. When it is feasible to conduct appropriate criterion-related studies, one should probably do so.

Certainly, however, it is necessary to mount an integrated effort to achieve effective training measurement. Content appropriateness, quality of the measuring instruments, and appropriateness of the tests relative to the various inferences which may be made from test results must all be considered.

Summary

It has been emphasized that training and the steps preceding it are intertwined with testing. Good training is a necessary but not sufficient condition for having a good test. However careful the test construction, testing will probably not serve its intended purposes unless the training upon which the testing was based is appropriate. This applies in all of the five roles of testing in training.

Selection research has progressed in the past two decades. It was once believed that validity associated with aptitude tests was specific to the situation. Summaries of the research now indicate that there is much more generality to validity than previously believed. One the basis of the literature, it is possible to choose tests for selecting clerical trainees; however, relative to blue-collar workers and managers, the literature is less conclusive. It has been found that employee selection tests, in general, do not technically discriminate on the basis of race. Results with respect to gender are less conclusive. There were more problems than heretofore believed in doing validation studies on small samples, and cost benefits of testing can be more easily estimated than previously thought.

Also it has been found that among traditional selection procedures, tests are among the most validly used for predicting training achievement, and education, interviews, and experiences are relatively poor predictors. In measuring training achievement, criterion-referenced testing is nearing maturity. Many techniques for developing tests and analyzing test data are available in such form that a practitioner can use them. Various aspects of criterion-reference testing are still a subject of debate.

The field of testing should not be considered to be without further need for research and reasoned contemplation. Despite the notable developments in the last two decades in selection research and achievement testing, there are still many questions, and the reader is advised to keep current on further developments.

References

1. Cronbach, Lee J., "Test Validation," in Robert L. Thorndike, ed., *Educational Measurement*, 2d ed., American Council on Education, Washington, DC, 1971, pp. 443–507.

2. American Psychological Association, American Educational Research Association, and National Council on Measurement in Education, "Technical Recommendations for Psychological Tests and Diagnostic Techniques," *Psychological Bulletin,* vol. 51, 1954 (supplement).

3. American Educational Research Association, American Psychological Association, and National Council on Measurement in Education, *Standards for Educational and Psychological Testing,* American Psychological Association, Washington, DC, 1985.

4. American Psychological Association Division of Industrial/Organizational Psychology, *Principles for the Validation and Use of Personnel Selection Procedures,* Berkeley, CA, 1980.

5. Barrett, Gerald, James S. Phillips, and Ralph A. Alexander, "Concurrent and Predictive Validity Designs: A Critical Reanalysis," *Journal of Applied Psychology,* vol. 66, 1981,pp. 1–6.

6. Guion, Robert M., and Charles J. Cranny, "A Note on Concurrent and Predictive Validity Designs: A Critical Reanalysis," *Journal of Applied Psychology,* vol. 67, 1982, pp. 239–244.

7. Schmitt, Neal, Richard Z. Gooding, Raymond A. Noe, and Michael Kirsch, "Meta Analyses of Validity Studies Published Between 1964 and 1982 and the Investigation of Study Characteristics," *Personnel Psychology,* vol. 37, 1984, pp. 407–422.

8. Bemis, Stephen, Annholt Belenky, and Dee Ann Soder, *Job Analysis: An Effective Management Tool,* Bureau of National Affairs, Washington, DC, 1983.

9. Gael, Sidney, *Job Analysis: A Guide to Assessing Work Activities,* Jossey-Bass, San Francisco, 1983.

10. Levine, Edward L., *Everything You Always Wanted to Know About Job Analysis,* Mariner Publishing, Tampa, FL, 1983.

11. McCormick, Ernest J., *Job Analysis: Methods and Applications,* AMACOM, New York, 1979.

12. Mager, Robert F., *Preparing Instructional Objectives,* Fearon Publishers, Palo Alto, CA, 1962.

13. Cronbach, Lee J., and Paul E. Meehl, "Construct Validity in Psychological Tests," *Psychological Bulletin,* vol. 52, 1955, pp. 281–302.

14. Ghiselli, Edwin E., John P. Campbell, and Sheldon Zedeck, *Measurement Theory for the Behavioral Sciences,* W. H. Freeman, San Francisco, 1981.

15. Tenopyr, Mary L., "Content-Construct Confusion," *Personnel Psychology,* vol. 30, 1977, pp. 47–54.

16. Messick, Samuel A., "The Standard Problem: Meaning and Values in Measurement and Evaluation," *American Psychologist,* vol. 30, 1975, pp. 955–966.

17. Guilford, Joy P., and Benjamin Fruchter, *Fundamental Statistics in Psychology and Education,* 6th ed., McGraw-Hill, New York, 1978.

18. Cronbach, Lee J., Golda C. Gleser, Harinda Nanda, and Nageswari Rajaratan, *The Dependability of Behavioral Measurements: Theory of Generalizability for Scores and Profiles,* John Wiley & Sons, New York, 1972.

19. Glaser, Robert, and David J. Klaus, "Proficiency Measurement: Assessing Human Performance," in Robert M. Gagne, ed., *Psychological Principles in Systems Development*, Holt, Rinehart and Winston, New York, 1962, pp. 419–474.

20. Berk, Ronald A., "A Consumer's Guide to Criterion-Referenced Test Reliability," *Journal of Educational Measurement*, vol. 17, 1980, pp. 323–349. Erratum, vol. 18, 1981, p. 131.

21. Berk, Ronald A., "Selecting the Index of Reliability," in Ronald A. Berk, ed., *A Guide to Criterion-Referenced Test Construction*, Johns Hopkins University Press, Baltimore, 1984, pp. 231–266.

22. Subkoviak, Michael J., "Estimating the Reliability of Mastery-Nonmastery Classifications," in Ronald A. Berk, ed., *A Guide to Criterion-Referenced Test Construction*, Johns Hopkins University Press, Baltimore, 1984, pp. 267–291.

23. Equal Employment Opportunity Commission, Civil Service Commission, Department of Labor, Department of Justice, "Adoption by Four Agencies of Uniform Guidelines on Employee Selection Procedures," *Federal Register*, vol. 43, 1978, pp. 38290–38315.

24. Schmidt, Frank L., John E. Hunter, and Vern W. Urry, "Statistical Power in Criterion-Related Validation Studies," *Journal of Applied Psychology*, vol. 61, 1976, pp. 473–485.

25. Schmidt, Frank L., and John E. Hunter, "Development of a General Solution to the Problem of Validity Generalization," *Journal of Applied Psychology*, vol. 62, 1977, pp. 529–540.

26. Callender, John C., and H. G. Osborn, "Development and Test of a New Model for Validity Generalization," *Journal of Applied Psychology*, vol. 65, 1980, pp. 543–558.

27. Raju, Nambury S., and Michael J. Burke, "Two New Procedures for Studying Validity Generalization," *Journal of Applied Psychology*, vol. 68, 1983, pp. 382–395.

28. Hunter, John E., and Ronda F. Hunter, "Validity and Utility of Alternative Predictors of Job Performance," *Journal of Applied Psychology*, vol. 96, 1984, pp. 72–98.

29. Linn, Robert L., "Single Group Validity, Differential Validity, and Differential Prediction," *Journal of Applied Psychology*, vol. 63, 1978, pp. 507–512.

30. Schmidt, Frank L., and John E. Hunter, "Employment Testing: Old Theories and New Research Findings," *American Psychologist*, vol. 36, 1981, pp. 1128–1137.

31. Schmidt, Frank L., and John E. Hunter, "Individual Differences in Productivity: An Empirical Test of Estimates Derived from Studies of Selection Procedures Utility," *Journal of Applied Psychology*, vol. 68, 1983, pp. 407–414.

32. Boudreau, John W., "Effects of Employee Flows on Utility Analysis of Human Resource Productivity Improvement Programs," *Journal of Applied Psychology*, vol. 68, 1983, pp. 396–406.

33. Green, John A., *Teacher-Made Tests*, Harper & Row, New York, 1963.

34. Gorth, William P., Robert P. O'Reilly, and Paul D. Pinsky, *Comprehensive Achievement Monitoring: A Criterion-Referenced Evaluation System*, Educational Technology Publications, Englewood Cliffs, NJ, 1975.

35. Gronlund, Norman E., *Constructing Achievement Tests*, 2d ed., Prentice-Hall, Englewood Cliffs, NJ, 1977.

36. Hopkins, Charles D., and Richard L. Antes, *Classroom Measurement and Evaluation*, F. E. Peacock, Itasca, IL, 1978.

37. Martuza, V. R., *Applying Norm-Referenced and Criterion-Referenced Measurement in Education*, Allyn & Bacon, Boston, 1977.

38. Popham, W. James, ed., *Criterion-Referenced Measurement: An Introduction*, Educational Technology Publications, Englewood Cliffs, NJ, 1971.

39. Rahmlow, Harold F., and Katheryn K. Woodley, *Objectives-Based Testing: A Guide to Effective Test Development*, Educational Technology Publications, Englewood Cliffs, NJ, 1974.

40. Smith, Fred M., *Constructing and Using Achievement Tests in the Classroom: A Competency-Based Test*, Peter Lang, New York, 1984.

41. Swezey, Robert W., *Individual Performance Assessment: An Approach to Criterion-Referenced Test Development*, Reston Publishing, Reston, VA., 1981.

42. Thyne, James M., *Principles of Examining*, John Wiley & Sons, New York, 1974.

43. Tuchman, Bruce W., *Measuring Educational Outcomes: Fundamentals of Testing*, Harcourt Brace Jovanovich, New York, 1975.

44. Berk, Ronald A., *Criterion-Referenced Measurement: The State of the Art*, Johns Hopkins University Press, Baltimore, 1980.

45. Berk, Ronald A., ed., *A Guide to Criterion-Referenced Test Construction*, Johns Hopkins University Press, Baltimore, 1984.

46. Popham, W. J., *Criterion-Referenced Measurement*, Prentice-Hall, Englewood Cliffs, NJ, 1978.

47. Hambleton, R. K., H. Swaminathan, S. Algina, and D. B. Coulson, "Criterion-Referenced Testing and Measurement: A Review of Technical Issues and Developments," *Review of Educational Research*, vol. 48, 1978, pp. 1–47.

48. Livingston, Samuel A., and Michael Zieky, *Passing Scores: A Manual for Setting Standards of Performance on Educational and Occupational Tests*, Educational Testing Service, Princeton, NJ, 1982.

49. Linn, Robert L., "Issues of Validity in Measurement for Competency-Based Measurement," in Mary A. Bunda and R. Sanders, eds., *Practices and Problems in Competency-Based Measurement*, National Council on Measurements in Education, Washington, DC, 1979, pp. 108–123.

17

Backyard Research in Human Resource Development

Richard A. Swanson

Richard A. Swanson *is Professor and Director of the Human Resource Development Research Center at the University of Minnesota and Senior Partner of Swanson & Associates, Inc. Swanson is recognized internationally as an authority on organizational change, human resource development, analysis and evaluation of work behavior, forecasting financial benefits of HRD, and trainer training. In his 25 years in the field, he has performed consulting work for several large corporations in strategic human resource planning, personnel training, organization development, and quality improvement. He has designed management development programs, produced self-instructional technical training materials, conducted organizational culture studies, and initiated quality improvement in organizations producing goods and services. Clients have included CIGNA HealthCare, AT&T, 3M Corporation, Pemex, Champion International, General Motors, Honeywell, Marathon Oil, Medtronic, and Citicorp. Recently, he studied quality improvement, organization development, and training practices in Japan, Germany, and the Netherlands. Swanson has published over 175 articles on HRD. He is coauthor of* Performance at Work: A Systematic Program for Analyzing Work Behavior *(John Wiley & Sons, 1986),* Forecasting Financial Benefits of Human Resource Development *(Jossey-Bass, 1988), and* Performance Appraisal: Perspectives on a Quality Management Approach *(ASTD, 1990). His 1994 book is titled* Analysis for Improving Performance: Tools for Diagnosing Organizations and Documenting Workplace Expertise. *He has served as editor of the* Journal of Industrial Teacher Education *and the* Performance and Instruction Journal *and is the founding*

editor of the Human Resource Development Quarterly. *In 1996,
he assumed the presidency of the Academy of Human Resource
Development. In 1993, Swanson received the ASTD professors'
network national award for his "Outstanding Contribution to the
Academic Advancement of Human Resource Development." He
received his doctoral degree from the University of Illinois.*

There is nothing so practical as good research. I believe this, and I think you will
too, once you take a minute to think about it. Proven principles and theories are
as close to truth as we get. They allow us to predict the future better. Without the
operating principles and theories—the fruits of research—we have to start over
with every problem we face as though it is the first time this has ever happened.
Too many human resource development personnel operate this way on the job.
For them, every project is approached as a start-up project with a "how shall we
do this?" mode—without principles and theories to guide the effort. In this
manner, without research and its use in practice, inefficiencies in the profession
can continue for long periods of time.

Practical Benefits of Research

We know from research that trainees' *satisfaction* with training is not necessarily
related to the amount of their learning or their subsequent on-the-job performance.[1] Satisfaction, learning, and performance are separate and worthy *domains*
of human resource development evaluation but not *levels* of evaluation. As such,
they need to be conceptualized separately. While the domains have some relationship, they are not linear or hierarchical. Each domain is driven by different
assumptions that must be taken into account separately.

At minimum, basic research thinking helps the practitioner describe and align
human resource development (HRD) inputs, processes, and outputs.[2] Just this
practical application of system theory in everyday work would cause an enormous increase in the effectiveness and efficiency of the HRD profession.

From my experience in the profession, it is clear that thoughtful practitioners
do indeed apply research findings in their day-to-day work decisions. Whether
they are *advancing* HRD theory and practice is another matter. Yet, thoughtful
practitioners are in a perfect position to advance the profession through what I
am calling *backyard research*. Backyard research is systematic investigation and
inquiry that is embedded in the ongoing work of the organization. Backyard
researchers are perfect partners in the cycle of research and development (see
Fig. 17-1). Rigorous developmental activities that many practitioners engage in
are just a breath away from being research. Development is the process of
perfecting a new kind of product or activity. With a tier of inquiry added to the
process, legitimate research emerges!

Definition of Research

Research is often thought of in terms of a job. Actually, research is a *process*
having a specific type of outcome. *The outcome of research is new knowledge that is*

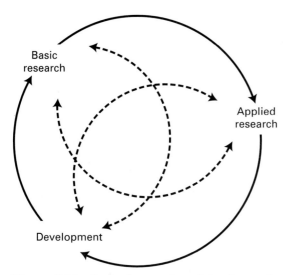

Basic research

Applied research

Development

Figure 17-1. Cycle of research and development.

obtained through an orderly investigative process. The dictionary definition of research is clear and simple. Research is

1. Scholarly or scientific investigation or inquiry
2. Close and careful study[3]

Each of you reading this chapter has most likely done research and may even do research on a regular basis in certain arenas of your work and/or personal lives. You may not call it research. Even so, the psychological barriers to research remain and are typified by (1) the pressures of time limitations and/or (2) the concern over being criticized as to the significance, method, or conclusions. I smile as I note these two barriers, because these same concerns haunt the most experienced researchers throughout their work. They are part of the human side of the research process. Researchers talk about the importance of humility and skepticism as attributes of a scholar. Certainly the press of time and the potential of criticism help keep the researcher humble. Internal skepticism keeps the researcher motivated. Researchers are the crème de la crème of skeptics. When somebody says, "I know everything will turn out well," the researcher will retort, "Not necessarily." When somebody says, "I know everything will go badly," the researcher will similarly retort, "Not necessarily." Untested generalizations do not satisfy the researcher. They are the beginnings of research, not the conclusions.

You, the Researcher

How do you approach this notion of being a researcher? Do you view it as a transition, analogous to the transition from a caterpillar to a butterfly? Or, do you view doing research as a compartmentalized segment of human activity? The first part of the title of this chapter, "Backyard Research," presents the assumption that you can engage in research in a compartmentalized manner and within a small or specific realm. Remember, many backyard cooks and backyard mechanics are terrific at what they do even though they do not engage in the activity day in and day out. The lower risk of the "backyard" often allows the activity to be enjoyed more and usually demands that it be conducted on a smaller scale. These are concepts that the neophyte and/or part-time researcher should keep in mind as a project is being planned. Don't make it too risky, keep it small, and have fun.

Practical Problems Worth Researching

There are different ways to categorize the many practical problems facing human resource development professionals today. Four general problem areas that practitioners face, and that researchers should pursue, are problems of impact, alternatives, importance, and explanation. The four problem statements are as follows:

Practical Problem 1: The Problem of Impact. What impact will the HRD intervention have? The researcher is driven to answer questions having to do with effectiveness and efficiency of HRD interventions in comparison to alternatives, criteria, and/or norms.

This most basic practical problem is the focus of the backyard research methodology presented as an example in this chapter. The other three problems are as follows, and readers wanting methodology help in these areas are directed to the *Research Handbook for Human Resource Development.*[4]

Practical Problem 2: The Problem of Alternatives. Once you are given a problem and all the alternative HRD interventions, what intervention should be selected? The researcher is driven to answer questions having to do with effectiveness and efficiency of processes by which HRD problem formulation, problem definition, and solution selection take place.

Practical Problem 3: The Problem of Importance. Given all the HRD issues, what one(s) is most important? The researcher is driven to answer questions of significance through scanning and forecasting the issues HRD could reasonably address in light of missions and goals at the organizational, process, and individual levels.

Practical Problem 4: The Problem of Explanation. Given all of our knowledge about HRD, how do you explain what can be expected? The researcher is driven to answer questions having to do with explaining and/or generalizing HRD or HRD-related phenomena through theory building and meta-analysis.

Researching the Impact of HRD

The literature on research methodology is very extensive. It is not the purpose of this chapter to try to capture all that knowledge. Rather, the purpose is to capture a limited number of how-to-do-it methodologies that have utility and appeal to a backyard researcher. These how-to-do-it options are presented in context of the basic problem of *impact* that faces human resource development professionals.

Remember, the problem of impact asks, What impact will the HRD intervention have? And, the researcher is driven to answer questions having to do with effectiveness and efficiency of HRD interventions in comparison to alternatives, criterions, and/or norms. Approaching this problem of impact is fairly straightforward.

Sales Training Example

Will a particular sales training program be effective? Let's call it Super Sales Training (SST). First, think about the basic system model: input, process, and output (I→P→O), and then begin to think about aligning the components as you plan your research. SST, the training program, is considered the *treatment* or *independent variable*, the variable being studied. In this case, SST is the *process* component of the I→P→O model. The categories of potential *outputs* for HRD (and SST in particular) include performance, learning, and satisfaction (PLS) (see Fig. 17-2).

Let's pull these elements together into a fairly simple research plan. In research, experimental research design is considered to be a very sound approach and conceptually is very simple.[5] Experimental design closely parallels the I→P→O system thinking. In experimental research, and the SST example, you have an experimental training treatment X_{SST} that is delivered and followed by an observation or evaluation of the effects or output: O_{PLS}. Over time it looks like this: $X_{SST} \rightarrow O_{PLS}$. Yet, without a basis of comparison, it is impossible to interpret the meaning of posttreatment evaluation data: O_{PLS}. It is conceivable that the posttreatment data is identical to the pretreatment data, with the conclusion being that the SST was a waste of resources. Without a comparison, you cannot determine the results. In order to get some basis of comparison, the basic one-group plan can be extended and/or a second comparison control group can be added.

Extending the one-group design is done by adding an outcome preassessment, O_{PLS}^1. This addition allows for pre- and posttraining comparisons. Adding a second postassessment at a later time, O_{PLS}^3, allows for long-term effects:

$$O_{PLS}^1 \rightarrow X_{SST} \rightarrow O_{PLS}^2 \rightarrow O_{PLS}^3$$

As you might imagine, the results of such a study could be very interesting. For example, there could be high satisfaction, moderate learning, and no improvement in workplace performance immediately following the training; there could be average satisfaction, high learning, and moderate improvement in

---

PERFORMANCE
- **Business results**...*organizational, process, or individual units*
- **Financial results**...*benefits in terms of money or monetary ratios*

LEARNING
- **Knowledge**...*mastery of the information and concepts*
- **Expertise**...*demonstration of workplace expertise*

SATISFACTION
- **Participants**...*those people directly involved in the intervention*
- **Sponsors**...*of the participants and/or intervention.*

Figure 17-2. *PLS Evaluation Model:* A three-domain—Performance-Learning-Satisfaction—evaluation taxonomy for performance improvement and human resource development. (*Copyright ©1995 by Richard A. Swanson.*)

workplace performance immediately following the training; or there could be gains from O^1 to O^2 followed by a drop-off from the O^2 levels at the later O^3 assessment in any or all of the domains—satisfaction, learning, or performance.

A true experimental design research study has at least two groups, and the participants are each randomly assigned to one of the groups. In symbols it looks like this:

Random (R) *SST* Group $O^1_{PLS} \rightarrow X_{SST} \rightarrow O^2_{PLS}$

No-treatment group $O^1_{PLS} \longrightarrow O^2_{PLS}$

For many reasons, it is rare to be able to conduct a true experimental design study involving people in a functioning organization. A recent experimental study reported in the literature tests the effectiveness of various forms of team building and is worth reviewing.[6] An optional two-group experimental research study is one that is spread over time. Individuals are not assigned to the groups randomly. Instead, they are in groups that evolve for other practical reasons within an organization. The preassessments O^1_{PLS} between the two nonrandom groups are compared to help establish the equality of the two groups.

First, the no-treatment group data O^1_{PLS} and O^2_{PLS} is collected for baseline data; then the treatment group baseline data is collected. (Of course, the no-treatment group, after it has served its research role as the control group, could receive the treatment.) In symbols it looks like this:

No-treatment group $O^1_{1(PLS)} \rightarrow O^2_{2(PLS)}$

SST Group $O^1_{1(PLS)} \rightarrow X_{SST} \rightarrow O^2_{2(PLS)}$

For our Super Sales Training (SST) example, think of having twelve events with four receiving no training (during the research period), four receiving the traditional sales training, and four receiving the experimental SST. This is a very practical three-group study (each group being made up of four events) because important questions about whether the new training makes a difference in comparison to both no training and the traditional training are being answered.

It was noted earlier that basic research thinking helps the practitioner align HRD inputs, processes, and outputs. This practical application of system theory in everyday work would cause an enormous increase in effectiveness. The research plans presented thus far help confront the system's "disconnects." For example, let's say that sales volume has been dropping off the past three years while the sales force has been stable during the same period. Why would you expect sales training to improve performance? A deeper analysis may reveal that the product lines have almost totally changed in the past three years, that the product knowledge of the sales force is very low, and Super Sales Training (SST) is about new-product knowledge. The logical connections from good HRD practice help shape the research design and the execution plan.

Quality of the Experimental Treatment

The treatment as well as the whole study should be well specified and replicable. In our example of Super Sales Training (SST), the content and method of the treatment need to be specified, controlled during implementation, and detailed to the level that another researcher could replicate it. For example, what if the instructor of one SST group is a superstar presenter, and the second group is taught by an excellent salesperson without any trainer training? Are the results really a measure of SST? Or are they a measure of instructors? Without knowing, you could end up eliminating SST and its excellent content because the research treatment was convoluted. The opposite could also be true. If SST was supposed to be designed in a way that excellent salespeople from the field can teach the course with little or no preparation, then a poorly designed study—one using highly skilled trainers—could have you thinking SST, as intended, really works.

Quality of the Participants

Researchers call individual participants who receive treatments *subjects*. The larger ideas having to do with conducting sound research have to do with populations and samples. The population is specified first and then the sample.

The subjects make up the sample. It is important to specify and control your population and sample. The population is the total group to which you want to generalize. Examples could include all employees of the organization; all employees of the organization that work in The Netherlands; all exempt employees; or all major-account sales personnel in the United States. Defining the population is not a silly undertaking. I have experienced many examples that undermine HRD program effectiveness. For example, what about the corporate training class unexpectedly having 25 percent non-English speaking employees? Then there's the training program designed for a particular group of employees but which was offered to all employees in a companywide elective format. The class eventually was filled, and not one of the intended workers was enrolled.

The sample of participants should be taken from the defined population. The research *ideal* is that samples be randomly selected. If subjects are randomly assigned to groups, the researcher can infer that the two groups start off being equal. Without this, it is difficult to compare the groups at the end if they started from different points. To be random, *every* member of the population must have an *equal chance* of being a member of the sample. This ideal is usually out of reach. Even so, you can make sure that participants are members of the defined population, and you can compare the two nonrandom groups on their average pretest scores for the purpose of providing evidence as to their equality.

Quality of the Measures

Measures need to be reliable and valid. A reliable measure yields consistent results. Valid measures truly evaluate what they purport to measure.

What if you stepped on your bathroom scale one minute and it read 150 pounds, and you stepped off and immediately on again for a second time, and then you weighed 158? The scale is not reliable. When a measurement device is inconsistent—unreliable—the question of validity is moot. A test must be reliable first before it can be valid. Even so, a perfectly reliable test can be invalid. For example, suppose you get on and off the scale 10 times with every reading being exactly 141 pounds. The scale is perfectly reliable. But the truth is that you weigh 161 pounds! This scale consistently (reliably) measured your weight wrong. Thus, a measurement device can be consistently wrong. It is reliable, but not valid. Thus, determining if the scale is correct, or valid, is an additional matter. You could take your bathroom scale to the doctor's office and compare it against the two higher-quality scales they use in their work. You'd be dealing with three scales all designed to measure the same thing. They should agree. If the two medical-center scales read 161 and yours reads 141, either use the medical-center scales as your measure or recalibrate your bathroom scale.

Assuring the reliability and validity of measures is an important phase of research. There are two major strategies for the "backyard researcher" to use in assuring the reliability and validity of the measurements used in research. The first method is to use an existing appropriate measurement instrument that already has established reliability and validity. Since you are most interested in the experimental treatment (in our example, it was SST), you will most likely be more concerned about dealing with SST rather than designing and defending instruments.

The second method is to take action to build the validity and reliability and then check it out. These strategies have a logical side and a statistical side. The logical side of validity is to build it through planning tools and reviews that ensure that the instrument is relevant and that its content matches the desired outcomes and/or dimensions of the treatment. This is called *content validity. Face validity* is simply how a measure is perceived by the stakeholder in terms of its form and relevance. Reliability is increased by reviewing the measurement items and/or process in terms of clarity and reasonableness and by increasing the numbers of observations in terms of items and/or times. Specific statistical techniques for assessing reliability and validity can be applied.[7]

Quality of the Administration

The conduct of any study is up for disruption even under the best of conditions. Thus, thinking the entire study through in terms of events, personnel, required resources, and sources of contamination can result in large rewards. Good management as a practitioner and as a scholar are not that different. There are numerous project planning and documentation tools that can be applied to research.

Quality of the Data Analysis

Data analysis can be intimidating to some backyard researchers. With the resources available today, this is becoming less of an issue. Easy-to-use software, information specialists in the company, and readily available help on the outside should disarm these fears. Here are two data-analysis concepts useful in getting further help: (1) tests of means and (2) correlations.

Tests of Means

Means are the average scores for groups. *There is no significant difference between the mean (average) expertise of those trainees who had the training and the mean (average) expertise of those who did not have the training.* The preceding sentence is a research hypothesis—specifically, a null hypothesis. A null hypothesis sets up a condition that you can support or not. In testing this hypothesis, each participant is required to take a test of the intended job expertise resulting from the training program at the end of the program. The scores of each of the participants are combined into an average score for their group. The average score from one group is statistically compared to the average score on the same measure from the other group. Hypotheses are either supported or not by the data analysis, and to some level of confidence. Thus, the idea of being 95 percent sure that the results are attributable to the treatments comes into play. These statistical manipulations end up on a common confidence reporting scale. If you are 95 percent sure, statisticians say you have tested the hypothesis at the .05 level (95 percent surety). Without this test, the differences may be a result of something other than the treatment being investigated.

Correlation Coefficient

Correlations are the relationships between variables. The purpose of the correlation coefficient is to express in mathematical terms the *degree of relationship* between any two variables. Correlations do not infer causation. Because one variable is highly correlated with another does not mean that one causes the other. It simply means that when one exists, you can reasonably predict the other. Ice cream sales could be highly correlated with soda sales. And, it could be that the underlying cause is the outside temperature. Even so, you can predict that when ice cream sales go up, soda sales will also go up without really knowing that the root cause is outside temperature.

Correlations are expressed on a +1.0 to −1.0 scale. Two variables can be perfectly correlated in a positive way (+1.0), perfectly correlated in a negative way (−1.0), not related at all (0.0), and anywhere else on the scale. At the beginning of this chapter research was cited that indicated that there was little correlation between trainee satisfaction and job performance.

Quality of the Reporting

If a tree falls in the forest and nobody is there, does it make any sound? Remember that philosophy puzzler? Oddly, the dissemination of research findings poses a similar problem. If research is conducted and it is not disseminated, is there new knowledge? Reporting the results is the last step in a research project. There are two threats to never completing this last step in the research process. One has to do with the human frailties of the researcher, and one has to do with the dissemination outlets.

The researcher has learned what he or she wanted to learn and is ready to move on, has found no significant differences (actually this is a very valuable knowledge), or is still worried about facing external criticism. These personnel barriers often leave very valuable data unreported.

The dissemination outlets create what appear to be ominous barriers with unfamiliar manuscript and publication requirements. The advice for how to deal with these obstacles takes on three aspects. One is to get a partner—someone who can provide assistance and who has been through the hoops. Sources of help are suggested in the following section. Another option is to submit your final report to the ERIC Clearinghouse (see reference in the next section, "Getting Help with Your Research"). This clearinghouse is a massive database of studies that come in a variety of formats and are made available to the public on microfilm. The third option is to produce an executive one-page summary. Some people will be interested in the full report, more will be interested in a journal article report, and most will be interested in the summary.

Getting Help with Your Research

While research can be a lonely process of investigation, there is no reason to be alone in the effort. There are many sources of help. The following are selected lists of organizations, people, and references available to you. I recommend that you use them.

Organizations

There are many organizations capable of assisting you in your research. Almost every university has an office of research and individual faculty members capable and interested in partnering with you. There are a limited number of organizations dedicated to human resource development research. Three of them are

Academy of Human Resource
  Development
8140 Burnet Road, P.O. Box 9589
Austin, TX 78766
Phone: 512-323-2736
Fax: 512-454-4221

Center for Workplace Education
American Society for Training and
  Development
1640 King Street, P.O. Box 1443
Alexandria, VA 22313
Phone: 703-683-8100
Fax: 703-683-8103

Human Resource Development Research
  Center
University of Minnesota
1954 Buford Avenue
St. Paul, MN 55108
Phone: 612-624-8481
Fax: 612-624-4720

People

The new book cosponsored by the Academy of Human Resource Development and the ASTD Research Committee, *Research Handbook for Human Resource Development: A Scholar's Response to Practitioner Questions,* published by Berrett-Koehler Publishers,[4] includes a list of 15 HRD researchers. They represent a ready resource to you and include the following alphabetically listed group of professionals:

Dr. Timothy Baldwin
Indiana University
Phone: 812-855-0221
Fax: 812-855-8679

Dr. Jan deJong
University of Utrecht (Netherlands)
Phone: 31-30-534-803
Fax: 31-30-534-803

Dr. Ronald Jacobs
Ohio State University
Phone: 614-292-5037
Fax: 914-292-7812

Dr. Michael Leimbach
Wilson Learning
Phone: 612-828-8645
Fax: 612-828-8835

Dr. Victoria Marsick
Columbia University
Phone: 212-678-3754
Fax: 212-678-4048

Dr. Gary N. McLean
University of Minnesota
Phone: 612-624-4901
Fax: 612-646-2391

Dr. Martin Mulder
University of Twente (Netherlands)
Phone: 31-53-893-652
Fax: 31-53-329-136

Dr. Wim J. Nijhof
University of Twente (Netherlands)
Phone: 31-53-893-590
Fax: 31-53-329-136

Dr. Wayne Pace
Brigham Young University
Phone: 801-378-5020
Fax: 801-378-8098

Dr. Richard A. Swanson
University of Minnesota
Phone: 612-624-9727
Fax: 612-624-4720

Dr. David L. Passmore
Pennsylvania State University
Phone: 814-863-2583
Fax: 814-863-7532

Dr. Richard J. Torraco
University of Nebraska
Phone: 402-472-3853
Fax: 402-472-5907

Dr. Catherine M. Sleezer
Oklahoma State University
Phone: 405-744-9197
Fax: 405-372-9189

Dr. Karen Watkins
University of Georgia
Phone: 706-542-4355
Fax: 706-542-4204

Selected Publications

The number of publications available to backyard researchers is overwhelming. The following limited list of references is presented as a small but helpful list and as a bridge to the larger library of sources.

Research Methods

Borg, W. R., and M. D. Gall, *Educational Research: An Introduction*, 5th ed., Longman, New York, 1989.
Campbell, D. T., and J. C. Stanley, *Experimental and Quasi-Experimental Designs for Research*, Houghton Mifflin, Boston, 1963.
Swanson, R. A., *Research Handbook for Human Resource Development: A Scholar's Response to Practitioner Questions*, Berrett-Koehler, San Francisco, 1995.

Summaries and Reporting of Existing Research

Annual Review of Psychology, American Psychological Association, Washington, DC.
Encyclopedia of Educational Research, Macmillan, New York.
ERIC Clearinghouse, 3900 Wheeler Avenue, Arlington, VA 22304; 1-800-227-3742.
Handbook of Industrial and Organizational Psychology, Rand McNally, Chicago, IL.
Human Resource Development Quarterly, Jossey-Bass, San Francisco, CA.
Human Resource Management Quarterly, John Wiley & Sons, New York.
Performance Improvement Quarterly, ISPI, Washington, DC.

Data Collection Methods and Instruments

Buros, O. M., *Mental Measurements Handbook*, Eighth Edition, Gryphon Press, Highland Park, NJ.
Hayes, B. E., *Measuring Customer Satisfaction: Development and Use of Questionnaires*, ASQC Press, Milwaukee, WI, 1992.
Mosier, N. R., "Financial Analysis: The Methods and Their Applications to Employee Training," *Human Resource Development Quarterly*, 1(1), 1990, pp. 45–63.
Zemke, R., and T. Kramlinger, *Figuring Things Out*, Addison-Wesley, Reading, MA, 1982.

The Final Comment

People often talk about theory-to-practice. In my opinion, the *practice-to-theory* is equally true. I am very respectful of the fact that theory often has to catch up to sound practice—that practitioners can be ahead of researchers! Thoughtful practitioners often do things that work, and scholars learn how to explain the successes at a later time. For an applied field such as HRD, the concept of the HRD practitioner being a backyard researcher is legitimate and crucial to the maturity of the profession.

References

1. Dixon, N. M., "Relationship Between Trainees' Responses on Participant Reaction Forms and Their Posttest Achievement Score," *Human Resource Development Quarterly,* 1(2), 1990.

2. Swanson, R. A., *Analysis for Improving Performance: Tools for Diagnosing Organizations and Documenting Workplace Expertise,* Berrett-Koehler, San Francisco, 1994.

3. Morris, W. I., *American Heritage Dictionary,* Houghton Mifflin, Boston, 1982, p. 1051.

4. Swanson, R. A., *Research Handbook for Human Resource Development: A Scholar's Response to Practitioner Questions,* Berrett-Koehler, San Francisco, 1995.

5. Campbell, D. T., and J. C. Stanley, *Experimental and Quasi-experimental Designs for Research,* Houghton Mifflin, Boston, 1963.

6. McClernon, T., and R. A. Swanson, "Effects of Computer-Based Support on Team Building with Management and Work Groups," *Human Resource Development Quarterly,* 6(1), 1995.

7. Gronlund, N. E., *Constructing Achievement Tests,* Prentice-Hall, Englewood Cliffs, NJ, 1988.

Bibliography

Beer, M., and Walton, A. E., "Organization Change and Development," *Annual Review of Psychology, 38,* pp. 339–367.

Bennis, W. G., "A New Role for the Behavioral Sciences: Effecting Organizational Change," *Administrative Science Quarterly, 8,* pp. 125–165.

Brinkerhoff, R. O., *New Directions in Program Evaluation: Evaluating Training Programs in Business and Industry,* Jossey-Bass, San Francisco, 1989.

Camp, R. C., *Benchmarking: The Search for Industry Best Practices that Lead to Superior Performance,* Quality Press, Milwaukee, WI, 1989.

Campbell, J. P., "Training Design for Performance Improvement," in J. P. Campbell and R. J. Campbell, eds., *Productivity in Organizations,* Jossey-Bass, San Francisco, 1988, pp. 177–215.

Campbell, J. P., and R. J. Campbell, eds., *Productivity in Organizations,* Jossey-Bass, San Francisco, 1988.

Demeuse, K. P., and S. J. Liebowitz, "An Analysis of Team Building Research," *Group and Organizational Skills, 6*(3), 1981, pp. 357–378.

Druckman, D., and R. Bjork, eds., *In the Mind's Eye: Enhancing Human Performance,* National Academy Press, Washington, DC, 1991.

Dunnette, M. D., ed. *Handbook of Industrial and Organizational Psychology,* John Wiley & Sons, New York, 1983.

Fitz-Enz, J., *Human Value Management,* Jossey-Bass, San Francisco, 1990.

Flanagan, J. C., "The Critical Incident Technique," *Psychological Bulletin, 28,* 1954, pp. 28–35.

Frederick, W., and L. Preston, *Business Ethics: Research Issues and Empirical Studies,* JAI Press, Greenwich, CT, 1990.

Gagne, E. D., et al., "The Role of Student Processing of Feedback in Classroom Achievement," *Cognition and Instruction, 4*(3), 1987, pp. 167–186.

Gradous, D. B., ed., *Systems Theory Applied to Human Resource Development,* ASTD Press, Alexandria, VA, 1989.

Harrington, J. H., *Business Process Improvement,* McGraw-Hill, NY, 1991.

Hayes, B. E., *Measuring Customer Satisfaction: Development and Use of Questionnaires,* ASQC Press, Milwaukee, WI, 1992.

Herrnstein, R., and C. Murray, *The Bell Curve: Intelligence and Class Structure in American Life,* Free Press, New York, 1994.

Hirokawa, R. Y., "Group Communication and Decision-Making Performance: A Continued Test of the Functional Perspective," *Human Communication Research, 14*(4), 1988, pp. 487–515.

Jacobs, R., *Structured On-the-Job Training: Unleashing Expertise in the Workplace,* Berrett-Koehler, San Francisco, 1995.

Johnson, S. D., "Cognitive Analysis of Expert and Novice Troubleshooting Performance," *Performance Improvement Quarterly, 1*(3), 1988, pp. 35–54.

Kusy, M. E., "The Effects of Types of Training on Support of Training Among Corporate Managers," *Performance Improvement Quarterly, 1*(2), 1988, pp. 23–30.

Latham, G. P., "Human Resource Training and Development," *Annual Review of Psychology, 39,* 1988, pp. 545–582.

Lavrakas, P. J., *Telephone Survey Methods,* Sage, Newbury, CA, 1987.

Mager, R. F., *Measuring Instructional Results,* Lake Publishers, Belmont, CA, 1984.

McLean, G. N., *Construction and Analysis of Organization Climate Surveys,* University of Minnesota Training and Development Research Center, St. Paul, 1988.

McLean, G. N., S. R. Damme, and R. A. Swanson, *Performance Appraisal: Perspectives on a Quality Management Approach,* ASTD Press, Alexandria, VA, 1990.

Miller, D., and S. Barnett, eds., *Doing Research in Human Resource Development,* ASTD Press, Alexandria, VA.

Mosier, N. R., "Financial Analysis: The Methods and Their Application to Employee Training," *Human Resource Development Quarterly, 1*(1), 1990, pp. 45–63.

Murphy, B. P., and R. A. Swanson, "Auditing Training and Development," *Journal of European Industrial Training, 12*(2), 1988, pp. 13–16.

Nadler, D., M. Gerstein, and R. Shaw, *Organizational Architecture: Designs for Changing Organizations,* Jossey-Bass, San Francisco, 1992.

Nicholas, S., and R. W. Langseth, "The Comparative Impact of Organization Development Interventions on Hard Criteria Measures," *Academy of Management Review, 7*(2), 1982, pp. 531–542.

Parker, B. L., "Summative Evaluation in Training and Development," *Journal of Industrial Teacher Education, 23*(2), 1986, pp. 29–55.

Phillips, J. J., *Handbook of Training Evaluation,* Gulf Publishing, Houston, 1991.

Phillips, J. J., *In Action: Measuring Return on Investment,* ASTD Press, Alexandria, VA, 1994.

Robinson, D., and J. Robinson, *Training for Impact: How to Link Training to Business Needs and Measure the Results,* Jossey-Bass, San Francisco, 1989.

Schuster, J. R., and P. K. Zingheim, *The New Pay: Linking Employee and Organizational Performance,* Jossey-Bass, San Francisco, 1992.

Sleezer, C. M., ed., *Improving Human Resource Development Through Measurement,* ASTD Press, Alexandria, VA, 1989.

Sleezer, C. M., and R. A. Swanson, "Is Your Training Department Out of Control?" *Performance and Instruction Journal, 28*(5), 1989, pp. 22–26.

Sleezer, C. M., and R. A. Swanson, "Culture Surveys: A Tool for Improving Organization Performance," *Management Decision, 30*(2), 1992, pp. 22–29.

Stolovitch, H. D., and E. J. Keeps, eds., *Handbook of Human Performance Technology,* Jossey-Bass, San Francisco, 1992.

Swanson, R. A., "Industrial Training," in W. H. Mitzel, ed., *Fifth Encyclopedia of Educational Research,* Macmillan, New York, 1982, pp. 864–870.

Swanson, R. A., "Research and Development (and Other Life and Death Matters)," *Performance Improvement Quarterly, 1*(1), 1988, pp. 69–82.

Swanson, R. A., and D. B. Gradous, *Forecasting Financial Benefits of Human Resource Development,* Jossey-Bass, San Francisco, 1988.

Swanson, R. A., and C. M. Sleezer, "Determining the Financial Benefits of an Organization Development Program," *Performance Improvement Quarterly, 2*(1), 1989, pp. 55–65.

Swanson, R. A., and C. M. Sleezer, "Measurement Practice Meets Measurement Science," in C. M. Sleezer, ed., *Improving Human Resource Development Through Measurement,* ASTD Press, Alexandria, VA, 1989, pp. 1–4.

Swanson, R. A., and C. M. Sleezer, "Training Effectiveness Evaluation," *Journal of European Industrial Training, 11*(4), 1987, pp. 7–16.

Weisbord, M., *Productive Workplaces: Organizing and Managing for Dignity, Meaning, and Community,* Jossey-Bass, San Francisco, 1990.

Wexley, K. N., and T. T. Baldwin, "Management Development," *1986 Yearly Review of Management of the Journal of Management, 12*(2), pp. 277–294.

Wilkins, A. L., and W. G. Dyer, "Toward Culturally Sensitive Theories of Culture Change," *Academy of Management Review, 13*(4), 1988, pp. 522–533.

18

Human Performance Technology*

Marc J. Rosenberg

Marc J. Rosenberg *is District Manager, Learning Strategy, Corporate Human Resources, AT&T, and is responsible for strategic planning for education, training, and performance improvement for AT&T, including the development of a learning technology and performance support strategy for the corporation. Dr. Rosenberg is a past President of the International Society for Performance Improvement (formerly National Society for Performance and Instruction/NSPI) and is on the editorial board of the society's research journal,* Performance Improvement Quarterly. *He has spoken at the White House and at over 100 professional and business meetings; has authored over 30 articles in the field; and has been quoted in several major publications including* Forbes A.S.A.P., Management Review, Training, *and* The Learning Enterprise *where he was featured as a "leading light" in 1995. He is coeditor of* Performance Technology: Success Stories *(ISPI, 1992) and a contributor to ISPI's* Handbook of Human Performance Technology *(Jossey-Bass, 1992). He is the recipient of numerous awards for his professional service and contributions in the areas of training, performance management, and electronic performance support.*

The challenge of competitiveness and high productivity is dominating the HRD field like never before. Looking for new ways to assure responsiveness to organizational needs, the human resources field is increasing its use of human performance technology (HPT), a practice that helps link business strategy and goals,

---

*The opinions expressed in this chapter do not necessarily represent those of AT&T Corporation.

and the capability of the workforce to achieve them, with a wide array of human resource interventions which include but are certainly not limited to education and training.

HPT is both a systematic process and a way of thinking that helps people look at performance improvement in a new light. It focuses on the analysis of performance problems (or opportunities) and their underlying causes, two diagnostic activities that assure that solutions selected are the best choices for any particular performance improvement challenge. And, it provides for the evaluation of success on the business terms senior managers are looking for.

This chapter describes human performance technology in detail, the steps in the process, and its relationship to quality improvement. It also looks at the impact human performance technology is having on the education and training field, focusing on the changes the field needs to make, as well as the opportunities HPT offers to the profession. Several definitions of HPT, examples of performance technology in action, and a list of recommended resources are also provided.

Introduction

> The nation's ability to compete is threatened by inadequate investment in our most important resource: people.
>
> *Business Week* (cover)
> September 19, 1988

It's taken a long time, but human performance has finally risen to the top of the business agenda. The *Business Week* cover story of September 19, 1988, was one of the first clear indications of a new sense of urgency regarding performance and productivity that continues today. Faced with intense competition and constant change, large and small companies, both local and global, have recognized that their people are their most sustainable and strategic asset. Today, organizations know that technological innovation provides only a temporary advantage, that cost-cutting can only go so far, and that trade barriers provide a false and fleeting sense of security. But the ability to recruit, develop, and retain a high-performing workforce can sustain competitive advantage long after the value of those other levers has diminished.

Compounding the challenge of building a high-performing workforce is the changing nature of work itself. In the past, jobs were more easily defined. Processes and procedures lasted longer and were better documented. People knew what they were supposed to do, and what they did didn't change much over time. Today, change is accelerating. The interdependence of work, and workers, combined with the constant change in job, customer requirements, and technology, put organizations in a never-ending race to keep up with new ways to accomplish work faster, better, and cheaper than before. Flatter, downsized organizations, coupled with the rapid rise of small-supplier businesses and the emergence of outsourcing as a key business strategy, has added to the challenge.

The response to these dramatic changes has seen the rise of training within organizations. From the proliferation of corporate universities to an emphasis on organizational learning, from dramatic expansion of tuition assistance programs to training requirements included in collective-bargaining agreements, businesses have rushed to meet the human performance challenge through expanded educational offerings. *Training Magazine* (1995), in their most recent study of training in the United States, reports $52.2 billion spent on formal training by U.S. organizations in 1995, an increase of 3 percent over 1994. This equates to some 49.6 million individuals receiving training and 1.6 billion hours of training delivered during the period.[1]

Clearly, training is big business. There is no doubt that training plays a key role in the development of high-performing workers and corresponding increases in productivity. But we have recently become keenly aware that not only is training expensive, it may not always be the best way to achieve performance goals. And, we have also learned that training alone certainly is not as effective as when it is combined with other performance-enhancing strategies. In light of our tremendous investment in education and training, we must ask what else we can do to improve performance in ways that cost less and work better, while at the same time enhancing the effectiveness of the training we do. While we build and manage training facilities and begin to deliver learning using alternative technologies we also need to link our work into a comprehensive process that leverages a much wider array of performance improvement interventions.

Focusing on performance rather than training or other approaches that Rummler and Brache[2] refer to as "piecemeal approaches [p. 2]" is essential if we are to enhance productivity and organizational capability in a sustained and meaningful way. As Rummler and Brache continue, "Whether the concern is quality, customer focus, productivity, cycle time or cost, the *underlying* issue is *performance* [italics added, p. 2]." Thus, we need to augment learning and instructional technology with a new "technology," one that is more strategic and focuses directly on performance improvement. Human performance technology provides such a framework. While the practice of HPT continues to evolve, and the reader is encouraged to explore other HPT models and approaches,* this chapter offers a good introduction and foundation to this new and important field.

What Do We Know About Performance?

From classrooms to the battlefield to the assembly line, we have studied performance, and how to improve it, for a very long time. The business literature is filled with articles and books on theories X, Y, and Z, on empowerment, competition, leadership, and even training. One very interesting way to look at performance that is very useful in understanding how to improve it was provided by Spitzer (as cited in Rosenberg)[3] as three fundamental theorems:

1. *Performance will* never *improve by itself.*   People find a level of performance that they are comfortable with. If we don't do anything—if we don't train them, don't correct their mistakes, don't tell them what we expect, don't improve their tools, etc.—we should expect that their performance will never improve.

2. *Once deteriorated, performance becomes* increasingly resistant *to improvement.* When performance begins to slip, and we take notice of it, correction is relatively easy and inexpensive. However, when performance deteriorates significantly, without notice or attempts at improvement, correction becomes much more difficult and costly. If this deterioration becomes severe enough, the organization may not have the resources to overcome the problem and could fail entirely.

---

*A list of resources is provided at the end of this chapter.

3. *Performance will only stay improved if there is* continuing support *from the performance improvement system.* Once we have improved and can maintain a high level of performance, our job is not finished. Efforts need to continue to keep performance high, least theorem 2 (above) come into play. Organizations or teams that work to improve performance, succeed, and then disband, believing their work is over, run the risk of being called back in the not-too-distant future when the unsupported high performance begins to deteriorate again.

These three theorems of performance improvement form the basis of our understanding of how human performance technology is used and why it works.

What Is Human Performance Technology?

To most people, the term *technology* conjures up images of computers and other types of hardware systems. Yet the primary definition of the word centers *not* on nuts and bolts and wires and chips, but around *systematic processes.* When we apply this definition to people, we can consider HPT as systems thinking applied to human resource activities. This is a good first definition.

Rosenberg, Coscarelli, and Hutchison,[4] in their analysis of the origins and evolution of the field, note that HPT grew from several major influences, including

- *Systems.* This influence provides a framework by which HPT can be implemented. Within this framework, we can view instructional technology as a subsystem to HPT, and we can see HPT as a subsystem within an organization's overall management system.[5] The critical nature of a systems view is underscored by Rummler,[6] Rummler and Brache,[2] and Senge[7] who focuses on systems thinking as an essential building block to a true learning organization. The complexity of individuals is magnified by their interrelationships with other people and their environment. Improving their performance (no small task!) requires a framework to see these larger systems, these "patterns of change rather than static 'snapshots.' [p. 68]."[7]

- *Behavioral and cognitive psychology and instructional systems design.* These influences provide a framework for how people learn—a fundamental ingredient to HPT. Rosenberg, Coscarelli, and Hutchison[4] note the general agreement that the roots of HPT ultimately stem from behavioral psychology (p. 16). They note the work of many behavioral and cognitive psychologists such as Skinner, Crowder, Gilbert, Bloom, Glasser, Bruner, and Gagne, who laid the foundations about programmed instruction and instructional technology and in 1962, formed the National Society for Programmed Instruction* to further development in this area.

- *Analytical systems.* These influences provide a framework for diagnosing problems relating to the performance of people. As early as the 1960s, learning psychologists like Mager, Gilbert, Rummler, and Harless used newly developed analysis techniques to show that instruction was not always effective in improving performance (Rosenberg, Coscarelli, and Hutchison, pp. 18–19).

---

*In the 1970s, the organization changed its name to the National Society for Performance and Instruction. In 1995, the name was changed again to the International Society for Performance Improvement (ISPI). In this chapter, the ISPI name will be used.

This finding led to extensive work to determine just what else might be more effectively used toward this end. It was this realization that led to the founding of the performance technology* movement.

Options for Improving Performance

As practitioners in the emerging field of HPT began to realize that there are many different ways, including training, to improve performance, a number of organizing structures began to emerge. One way to understand the options that are available for improving performance is to look at the arenas where performance may be changed and the factors that can be manipulated to affect performance improvement.

Essentially there are only three arenas for performance improvement. We can change or improve

- *The work.* We can change the things that people do—their jobs. This task might include restructuring organizations, changing manufacturing processes, splitting or combining jobs, using quality management techniques, etc.

- *The workplace.* We can create better work environments, provide better tools and improved information, introduce telecommuting and other "quality-of-life" enhancements, etc.

- *The worker.* We can hire, replace, transfer, or train people.

Within these three arenas, Gilbert's Behavior Engineering Model[8] (p. 88), modified slightly here, provides for six performance improvement factors that can be manipulated to enhance individual, group, and organizational performance:

1. *Consequences, incentives, and rewards.* Motivation, in the form of consequences, incentives, and rewards can have both a positive *and* a negative impact on performance. Negative or low compensation is an obvious demotivator. People can be well trained but not perform because they believe they are not adequately rewarded for their efforts. Sometimes, rewards are not performance-based or poor performance is rewarded. If, for example, the desired performance is to expand your company's products into new geographic markets where your competition is established but the compensation system continues to reward selling in secure, established territories, the old behavior is reinforced despite any training to the contrary; although there is "performance," it may not be considered "valued" or "worthy."**

2. *Data and information.* It is often the case that performance can be improved simply by telling performers the level of performance that is expected as well as helping them understand and eliminate deviations from acceptable performance. There are a number of ways to accomplish this low-cost intervention. Job or performance *standards* let workers know the level of proficiency that is expected of them. *Feedback,* from supervisors, peers, customers, etc., helps performers understand how well they are doing and where they need to improve. User-friendly performance or job *documentation* and *job aids,* either paper-based or on-

---

*The "human," as in *human* performance technology, is often omitted but always implied.

**For an excellent discussion of valued, or worthy, performance, see Gilbert,[8] pp. 15–25.

line, can provide essential information necessary for individuals, groups, or entire organizations to improve their performance. *Combining* standards, feedback, and documentation often enhances performance even more.

3. *Resources, tools, and environmental support.* The axiom that a bad environment will overcome a good performer is often true when attention is not paid to the resources, tools, and other environmental obstacles placed in the performer's way. Despite what people *learn* to do, or *want* to do, their performance will be substandard if there is a shortage of people, money, time, or materials, etc., which will not *allow* the work to get done. As with the individual who goes to training to *learn* new computer software only to return to the job and discover that there is no money to *buy* the software, the lack of resources and tools can be a huge demotivator to performance. People quickly learn that there is a disconnect between what they are *told* (trained) they are supposed to do and what they actually *can* do. The situation is compounded if management is not supportive of the new level of performance. Providing an environment where high performance can flourish goes beyond the necessary tools and resources to management's leadership and commitment to make high performance rewarding, fulfilling, and enjoyable.

4. *Individual capacity.* After the tools, incentives, and support are in place, performance can still come down to the *capabilities* of individual performers. Sometimes there is a true mismatch between performer and work. Not everyone can be a successful salesperson, a competent engineer, or a brilliant physicist. Matching individuals to jobs is a *complex* process, involving level of education, personal interests and traits, career aspirations, academic capability, physical capability, etc. Mistakes can be made; individuals may not be able to perform to standard no matter what performance improvement intervention is tried. In such cases, perhaps a *job redesign* is called for, splitting the job or adding more people to a job. Also, increased emphasis on *selection*, including improved assessment of incoming workers to determine job match and capability, may often prove to be a better solution than other interventions, including the training of poorly qualified candidates. In addition, job reassignment is an important alternative when it is clear that there is a mismatch between actual and expected performance levels. Finally, although painful, termination of nonperforming employees may be necessary.

5. *Motives and expectations.* Critical to high performance and closely tied to capacity are worker's internal views of themselves and their jobs. Factors such as self-esteem, work ethic, values, quality orientation, etc., all play a major role in determining if workers can perform to standard. Other individual characteristics, such as fear of failure or punishment, and risk taking and avoidance can also influence performance levels. For example, some individual performers might know how to sell a product or service, be promised handsome rewards for doing so, and have the tools, resources, and management support to be successful, but they might not succeed if they exhibit a high level of anxiety about rejection.

6. *Skills and knowledge.* It should be clear that the five previous performance system factors can contribute a great deal to performance improvement, especially when used in combination, and should be considered more often. But there are a great many occurrences where a lack of skill and knowledge is, at least in part, a contributor to lowered performance levels. After all, it is not possible for people with the right motivation, performance standards, resources, tools, support, capacity, and motives to be successful performers if they *don't know how* to perform. Here is where *education* and *training* come into play. Even more important is that the parameters of the education and training field are expanding to include *information* delivery as well (see the second performance factor, data and

information, above). Education is seen as learning for the long term, while training is viewed as job- or competency-specific. The growth area for the field, information, is designed to meet the immediate and ever-changing knowledge needs of performers. With the boundaries of knowledge exploding outward and the useful life of information shrinking, performers have a greater need for more education, training, and information than ever before, delivered faster than ever before. In addition, the success of any education, training, or information initiative is enhanced when the other performance factors are *aligned* to support it.

The Performance Technology Model

Organizations are composed of interdependent *systems* such as manufacturing, marketing, finance, and others. To one degree or another, organizations also implement performance improvement systems which seek to maximize the effectiveness of an organization's human resources.

Unfortunately, the performance improvement system in many organizations is quite unsystematic. Activities such as training, hiring, compensation, job design and technological support, and documentation are often organized into "chimneys," with little or no collaboration. This traditional perspective can cause problems for front-line managers who seek to improve the performance of their people (Fig. 18-1).

With walls built between HR groups, managers are often forced to seek help from each group individually, and then they must make some decisions about how to piece the puzzle together to get the results they need. Furthermore, the benefits of collaboration are often lost on the HR groups themselves. Because of the way they are structured in traditional organizations, there is little opportunity for them to work together to create comprehensive solutions to improve performance. For example, the barriers between training and documentation that are found in many organizations often result in extensive redundancy of work. Instead of information being developed once, it's often rewritten many times, as user manuals are converted into instructor guides, student guides, job aids, on-

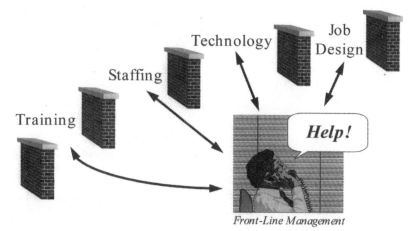

Front-Line Management

Figure 18-1. Traditional relationship between human resources and front-line management.

line databases, etc. There are also cases where cooperation is replaced by competition, as groups of specialists seek to "sell" their solution to the organization.

Applying a performance technology framework to the solving of performance problems, or the realization of performance improvement opportunities, offers an opportunity to systematically link various HR activities, or interventions, together in such a way as to provide more comprehensive solutions to the organization from the start (Fig. 18-2).

Now, managers who seek to improve the performance of their people can interact with a collaborative set of solutions rather than struggling to determine for themselves which of any number of separate solutions would be appropriate. Such a framework can be described in a performance technology model (Fig. 18-3).*

The performance technology model depicts the steps and activities of a performance improvement process or system.** Within the model, there are three major activities that are essential if we are to assure that the right performance improvement solutions are designed and implemented. They are performance analysis, cause analysis, and the intervention selection itself.

Performance Analysis

Performance analysis involves determining the organization's performance requirements in light of its objectives and its capabilities. Harless[11] uses the term *front-end analysis* to describe much the same activity (p. 106). Performance analysis is a *critical* component of the performance technology model because it concerns the determination of *what* we are trying to do, for example, solve a performance problem (e.g., decreasing productivity, increasing errors, lower sales) or realize a performance improvement opportunity (e.g., using new technology, forming alliances) before we determine *how* to do it (e.g., training).

---

*This HPT model was developed by the author and published in Deterline and Rosenberg[9] (ISPI, 1992).

**For other views on performance technology models, see Rosenberg et al. (1992), pp. 25–28, and Rummler et al.[10], pp. 32–49.

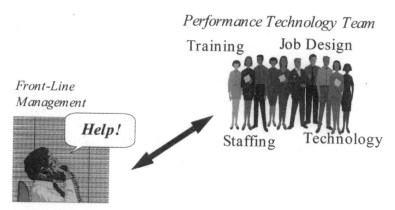

Performance Technology Team

Training   Job Design

Front-Line Management

Help!

Staffing   Technology

Figure 18-2. Systematic, HPT view of the relationship between human resources and front-line management.

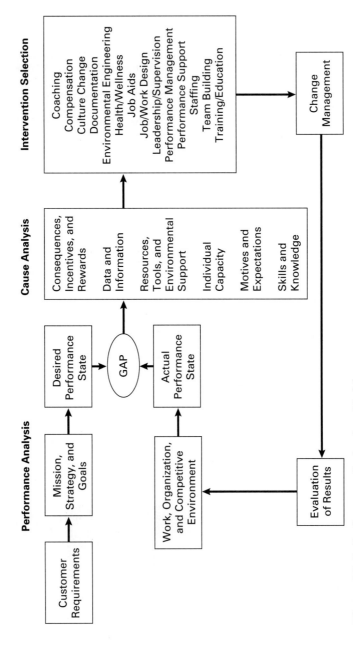

Figure 18-3. Performance Technology Model.

The goal of performance analysis is to determine the *gap* between what people are *supposed* to do (desired state) and what they currently are *able* to do (actual state.)[12] The desired state is determined from the workforce requirements (i.e., competencies and abilities necessary to achieve the organization's goals) as set forth in its mission and business strategy. These, of course, are derived from a careful assessment of customer requirements. The actual state is determined from a continuing assessment or scan of the current capabilities of the workforce, the efficiency of the organizational structure, the competitive position of the organization, and so on. There are a variety of tools and techniques that can be used to analyze performance, ranging from a review of existing organizational information, to interviews, focus groups, and observations with subject-matter experts, customers, suppliers, and exemplary and typical performers.[13]

Rossett[12] also suggests that it is important to gauge the feelings that key stakeholders (senior management, job performers, supervisors, etc.) have about the performance problem and related solutions (p. 100). Attitudes, possibly reflective of the broader organizational culture, can have an impact, both positive and negative, on the perceptions people have on the importance of the problem, the value of solving it, and the likelihood of success.

The resulting performance gap is defined as the *difference* between the desired and actual performance levels of the workforce being examined. The objective of performance technology then, is to determine what interventions, or combination of interventions, would most effectively and efficiently move the actual performance level toward the desired performance level, thus significantly reducing or eliminating the performance gap.

For example, a computer company wishes to develop and sell a new-model laptop computer. It has surveyed its customers' requirements and developed a business strategy to deliver a product that the organization hopes will succeed in the marketplace. Based on these requirements, the performance analysis yields a set of tasks, competency models, productivity levels, etc., that define how workers in product design, manufacturing, marketing, sales and service, etc., should function. It has also looked at the current capabilities of its design team, production personnel, and marketing and sales force, as well as the actual quality of service being offered to customers. From this analysis, a detailed description of the current readiness of the organization to meet the business objective is developed. The difference between the workforce requirements necessary to successfully design, build, sell, and service this new laptop computer and the actual ability of the firm to "pull it off" is the performance gap. Complicating matters is the real possibility that the gap is different for different segments of the workforce. Perhaps the company has a crack design team that is fully capable of designing to requirements, and perhaps the sales force has enough experience selling desktop computers to indicate that their performance gap may be minimal. But if the company has never built a laptop computer before, the gap in manufacturing may be quite significant. Thus, not only does performance analysis help in determining performance gaps, it focuses the organization on the level of severity of the gap, from function to function, which helps determine how the performance improvement investment should be distributed.

Cause Analysis

One of the most common mistakes made when seeking to improve performance is to move too quickly to the solution or intervention. "We need training," "let's have a team building day," or "the organization's culture needs to change" are examples of statements we all often hear. Even when a performance analysis is done, we are still not ready to design a solution because sometimes the analysis identifies symptoms of the problem rather than unmasking the real cause.

Take our laptop computer example. Suppose the laptop is built and available for sale. Focusing our continuing performance analysis on the sales function, we notice that the sales force is still selling the older desktop model when, in fact, the customer could benefit more from the laptop version (not to mention that the margins are higher for this laptop). So the performance gap would appear to indicate that salespeople are not selling the new machine, resulting in missed sales targets as defined in the overall sales strategy and goal statements. Why is this happening? Perhaps the sales force does not know enough about the new hardware. Perhaps the new laptop is not as good as the marketing department would have us believe. Or, perhaps a competitor's model is underpricing ours. To understand why the performance gap exists and how it can be closed, we need to examine not only the symptom (poor sales) but also the underlying cause.

Cause analysis, the second phase of the performance technology model, is the *bridge* between performance analysis, i.e., the determination of the performance gap, and the selection of the appropriate intervention(s) that will reduce or eliminate the gap. Here is where the six performance improvement factors, discussed previously, come in. The cause of a performance gap will almost always be found here. The key is to look at the gap from the variety of viewpoints provided by these six factors.

Again, the laptop example. Did the sales force have enough skills and knowledge necessary to successfully sell the product? We might look at the training records and performance of salespeople. In our example, we find that most of the sales force received training on the new hardware and demonstrated the competencies and knowledge necessary to sell it. Maybe the laptop was a poor performer. But reviews in PC magazines and test markets give the laptop high marks. It's also competitively priced, so pricing is not the cause. Going further with our hypothetical analysis, we learn that the compensation for selling the old desktop is greater than the compensation for selling the new laptop. Neither additional training, or product redesign, nor a lower price would have as much impact on the performance gap as changing the compensation plan for this product.

Thus cause analysis is critical to the application of performance technology because it enables us to look "under" the performance gap to discover its "roots." Then, we select intervention(s) that are most appropriate to both feed the high-performance roots and eliminate the roots that caused the performance gap.

Intervention Selection

Once the performance gap and its underlying causes are known, interventions can be selected. In our laptop computer example, a change in the reward and compensation structure would be required to accelerate desired performance. But what about the factory? Can it build the laptop? Perhaps it can, but not to the quality, cost, and customer requirements necessary for success. What should be done? Retrain the workers? Replace the workers? Outsource production? Perhaps all three interventions, used appropriately, would be best for this example.

Because, as Rummler (in Dixon,[14] p. 6) notes, performance problems are often "multicausal." More than one intervention may be needed; interventions often work best in combinations. Use of an electronic performance support system or a newly designed user manual may be enhanced by a redesigned work environment that makes access to these resources easier. The recruitment of new employees may be more successful when these new hires are assigned an effective coach. But what about the times when training is called for? There are many cases where performance can be improved by enhancing the skills and knowledge of workers. In most of these cases, however, performance can be improved even more, and maintained for a longer period of time, when the training intervention is coordinated with other interventions across the performance technology spectrum. So, when we combine training with the right supports on the job, such as the right tools, documentation, and other resources to get the job done, and when we can be sure that management is also well trained and supportive of the new learning, the likelihood that the training will be more successful and effective is increased.

Spitzer,[15] noting that intervention design is a planning process (p. 115), suggests 11 excellent intervention design principles that, when used, may increase the likelihood of a successful intervention:

1. *Design should be based on a comprehensive understanding of the situation.* This is reflective of the critical importance of the performance and cause analysis steps that precede intervention design.

2. *Interventions should be carefully targeted.* It is important to assure not only that the right people are targeted for the intervention but also that the intervention itself will yield enough impact to be *worth* the investment in time, people, and resources.

3. *An intervention should have a sponsor.* This person is different from the client or customer and is most likely to be the one making the largest financial and organizational commitment to the project. The importance of sponsorship is emphasized by Zemke (in Dixon[14]), who notes, "The farther up the organization you have to go to find out why the problem is worth fixing, the more likely it *will* get fixed; or at least someone will be willing to spend some money tying to fix it [p. 53]."

4. *Interventions should be designed with a team approach.* The interdisciplinary nature of HPT will usually call for expertise that is not generally found in one individual (this point is discussed later in this chapter).

5. *Intervention design should be cost-sensitive.* Solving performance problems with the *least cost* solution (that works) should be a paramount consideration.

6. *Interventions should be designed on the basis of comprehensive, prioritized requirements.* It is important to design interventions on the basis of what is most important, what is most possible, and what is most needed.

7. *Intervention options should be investigated.* The cost of interventions is usually too high *not* to consider reuse of previously used programs or the purchase of off-the-shelf products, if appropriate.

8. *Interventions should be sufficiently powerful.* Simplistic or short-term solutions may simply result in long-term client (and sponsor) dissatisfaction. Try to be as comprehensive as resources will allow.

9. *Interventions should be sustainable.* Again, those with a short-term view may make the mistake of implementing a program, "declaring success," and then disbanding the team. Interventions that are truly successful are sustained over a longer period of time by fully integrating them into the organizational culture and work processes. This, as Rummler (in Dixon[14]) suggests, is the difference between "wishing for performance and managing/engineering performance [p. 7]."

10. *Interventions should be designed with development and implementation in mind.* Simply stated, don't recommend interventions that can't be built and put into use. Elegant solutions may fail because they cost too much, conflict *too* much with the culture, or are too complex for the stakeholders, especially the job performers and their managers, to undertake.

11. *Interventions should be designed with an iterative approach.* Constant trial and revision (e.g., rapid prototyping) should be a feature of every design effort (pp. 116–122).

Just how many different types of interventions are there? This depends on your categorization scheme. Some practitioners combine all interventions into three areas: training/education, motivation, and environment. Rosenberg[3] suggested that interventions can be categorized into four major areas:

1. *Human resource development.* Concerned with improving the performance of individuals (e.g., training, career development, and individual feedback, incentives, and rewards).

2. *Organizational development.* Concerned with improving the performance of groups or teams (e.g., organizational design, team building, culture change, and group feedback, incentives, and rewards).

3. *Human resource management.* Concerned with managing and coaching the performance of individuals and groups, as well as with recruitment and staffing (e.g., supervision, leadership, succession planning, personnel selection).

4. *Environmental engineering.* Concerned with providing the tools and facilities that support improved performance (e.g., ergonomics, job aids, electronic performance support, sociotechnical systems design, job design, facilities design).

The performance technology model (Fig. 18-3) lists about 14 interventions that appear to be used often in large corporate environments. However, this list is by no means complete. Coleman[16] lists over 80 different interventions (p. 636) which even he says is far from complete.

Implementation and Change Management

So far, the performance technology model has emphasized analysis of problems and causes, and selection of solutions. Obviously, these solutions must be designed, built, and implemented in the organization. It is important not to overemphasize analysis at the expense of implementation; a good solution, poorly implemented, is really no solution at all.

Critical to successful implementation of a performance technology intervention is change management. Performance technology interventions often represent organizational and individual change, sometimes simple, often dramatic. Implementation can fail when change issues are not addressed adequately. Training can be wasted when the returning workers are given no support from management when they try to do what they've learned. A health and wellness program can be defeated by a poor selection of food in the cafeteria. Recruitment and staffing programs may not work if new hires cannot do the work they were hired to do because of a bad work design or lack of guidance.

Table 18-1. Attitude Change in Move from Change Avoidance to Change Acceptance

Change avoidance	Change acceptance
▪ Why?	▪ What new opportunities will this provide?
▪ How will this affect me?	▪ What problems will this solve?
▪ We don't do it this way.	▪ What would this look like?
▪ When will this change be over so we can get back to work?	▪ How can I help?
▪ Who gave you permission to do this?	▪ Who can help us?

In many cases, resistance to change, including change about performance, can be very strong. From the performance technologist, to senior management, to the actual performers themselves, we need to help people move from change avoidance to change acceptance.* (See Table 18-1.)

Dormant[17] focuses on change agentry as a key to HPT success. She suggests that HPT practitioners need to be both skilled in and at the forefront of change, noting, "successful implementation of interventions depends on a sound innovation, organizational readiness, leadership support, user acceptance, and—working quietly and effectively behind the scenes—an implementation team facilitated by an HP technologist who has the skills and knowledge of a change agent [p. 186]."

Daryl Conner, an Atlanta-based change consultant, has noted that "flawless execution cannot compensate for implementing the wrong solution."** This certainly applies to performance technology, where good analysis drives what we do. But it is also true that even when we do the right things, for the right reasons, we can fail if we don't heed the message and the challenge of organizational change.

Evaluation of Results

Once successfully implemented, the performance technology intervention is monitored to determine its impact on the organization. Because performance technology starts with the identification of the business problem, i.e., the performance gap, it gives the organization an improvement target to shoot for. This is where the *value* of the intervention is illustrated as we look to determine its impact on performance improvement. Using Kirkpatrick's[18] four levels of evaluation, it is possible to develop a comprehensive evaluation strategy to measure the effectiveness of the intervention:

▪ *Level 1: Reaction.* How do the various workforce constituencies (worker, management) feel about the intervention and its impact on them? What about customers and suppliers: how do they feel about it?

---

*Thanks to Patricia Shaffer, Apple Computer, Inc., for providing this viewpoint on change to the author in a discussion in the spring of 1994.

**From a keynote speech at the 1989 NSPI conference in Atlanta.

- *Level 2: Learning or capability.* What are people able to do after the intervention that they couldn't do before? What do they know now that they didn't know before?

- *Level 3: Transfer.* Are the interventions impacting the way work is being done? Are new skills, tools, processes, etc., being used on the job?

- *Level 4: Results.* What is the impact of the intervention on the performance gap? Are changes in the performance gap positively correlated to positive business performance and the "bottom line"?

The data from the evaluation efforts is fed back into the continuing organizational scan to determine changes in the actual performance of the workforce and to see if the actual performance approaches the desired performance, thus closing the performance gap. It is valuable information for the organization that helps it monitor the effectiveness of performance technology solutions.

When performance gaps go unspecified, it is almost impossible to show the organizational benefit of an intervention. Too often, training falls short in this area many times because the "course" was designed and implemented without a true understanding of the specifics of the performance gap it was to address. With evaluation linked to an identified performance gap, the ability of an intervention to show level-4 impact is greatly enhanced.

Benefits of HPT

Use of the performance technology model allows for a systematic, organizational effort to improve performance rather than a more simplistic "spray-and-pray" approach. The model assures that

- Performance problems, or performance improvement opportunities, are based on a thorough analysis of organizational goals, based on customer requirements and business strategy and the capabilities of the organization to achieve those goals.

- True causes of performance problems are addressed, rather than just symptoms, assuring a greater likelihood that the performance gap will be reduced or eliminated.

- Intervention selection is based on a complete analysis of the situation, and a *wide array* of interventions is considered.

- In all likelihood, more than one intervention will be systematically implemented, which will have a greater positive impact than any single intervention used alone.

- Attention is paid to the impact these interventions will have on the existing organizational structure and culture. Focusing on change management helps increase the long-term success of the overall performance improvement plan.

- Evaluation of performance is based on true business results, i.e., the reduction or elimination of the performance gap.

There has been some concern raised about the ability of any one individual, or even a team of professionals, to maintain expertise in all the possible interventions that are possible within the performance technology framework. This has led to some criticism of HPT that it is impossible to master the associated skills.

Hutchison[19] recognized that this dilemma could present problems in defining the field. She proposes two types of practitioners. First, the *performance technologist*, who is a specialist in performance and cause analysis, evaluation, and overall project management of the intervention(s) being implemented. This person is also probably the "keeper" of the HPT process itself. A second practitioner, the *intervention specialist*, is an expert in the design and implementation of one or more solutions. Instructional designers, organizational effectiveness consultants, compensation specialists, information systems experts, etc., are all examples of intervention specialists.

The challenge for the performance technologist, and the feature that makes that role so unique, is to be able to bring together a variety of intervention specialists necessary to solve a performance problem, manage this unique team, and continually form new teams as new problems or opportunities warrant. Although performance technologists may also be expert in one or more interventions, it is unlikely that anyone will be expert in enough solutions such that a team of intervention specialists would not be required. This mating of the performance technologist and the intervention specialist, together with a dynamic or "virtual" view of intervention teams, makes it easier to manage the variety of expertise necessary to make HPT successful.

New Definitions

Through use of the performance technology model, performance improvement becomes a well-structured, systematic process that leads to a more detailed definition like this one, developed by ISPI:

> A systematic set of methods and procedures, and a strategy, for solving problems, or realizing opportunities related to the performance of people. It may be applied to individuals, small groups and large organizations. [in Deterline and Rosenberg,[9] p. 3]

Another good definition is provided by Harless (in Geis[20]):

> The process of selection, analysis, design, development, implementation, and evaluation of programs to most cost-effectively influence human behavior and accomplishment. [p. 1]

Performance Technology and Quality

There is a strong relationship between performance technology and quality. Both are systematic processes, based on analysis. Both seek to improve organizational outputs, with quality referring to outputs of all kinds while HPT refers primarily to people. And both have similar process steps, as Table 18-2 shows.

In the chart (Table 18-2), each quality step has a corresponding performance technology step. Sometimes it is difficult to "sell" HPT in organizations already swamped with a wide variety of new processes and structures. When an organization has an established quality process, it may be easier to implement HPT within that process; Table 18-2 shows how close the two are. In fact, the similarity between quality and performance technology points to another helpful definition for HPT: the quality process applied to human resources.

Table 18-2. Relationship Between Quality and Performance Technology

Typical quality management process	Performance technology process
Establish process management responsibilities.	Identify owners of performance problem or performance improvement opportunity.
Define process and customer requirements.	Describe desired performance state.
Define and establish measure.	Define competence measures (standards).
Assess conformance to customer requirements.	Describe actual performance state.
Identify improvement opportunities.	Identify performance gap(s).
Determine root causes.	Conduct cause analysis.
Implement quality improvement.	Select and implement intervention(s).

Examples of HPT in Action

Performance technology is moving from the development of a conceptual framework to real applications in a variety of settings, several examples of which were identified by ISPI (in Deterline and Rosenberg[9]):

- One of the nation's largest real estate companies wanted to lower the costs associated with the high turnover of sales associates in local offices. If new associates became productive faster, their motivations with their career choice would be enhanced and they would be more likely to stay on with the firm. Self-paced training, supported by an in-office coaching system, helped sales associates learn the business and the local community faster. The use of the coach was the key to improved productivity. Special consideration was given to the selection of the right people to be coaches and the development of proper incentives for the coaches. The HPT solution of training, combined with extensive coaching, resulted in a 50 percent reduction in the time new sales associates got their first listing and a tripling of gross commissions by new hires who went through the program.

- A major overnight package delivery company also had to deal with a vast influx of new people, not resulting from turnover, but from growth. Productivity was being severely hampered by removing workers from the job to take classroom training in a centralized location. Decentralizing the training, using technology, resulted in a reduction of over 60 percent in off-the-job training time. But the training alone was not enough. To motivate workers to learn as much as possible, a pay-for-knowledge program was instituted, with appropriate incentives (e.g., bonuses, promotions) established to encourage workers to use the system effectively. The results included a better understanding of the job, coupled with a faster promotion rate and improved employee job satisfaction.

- The transportation department of a school district in one of the nation's largest cities was being deluged by complaints about poor service. Initially, training, in the form of a new manual, was introduced in an effort to improve performance and service. But the training solution did not achieve the necessary results. An in-depth performance analysis revealed additional causes of the performance problem ranging from inadequately defined job responsibilities, a poor communications system, and a general lack of involvement in decision making on the part of those who could have the most impact. The HPT approach of starting with performance and cause analysis uncovered many more opportunities to remedy the problem than was first believed. The results included a clear and dramatic decrease in the number of service complaints, and improved personal and working relationships on the part of the workers.

- A major retail chain discovered that to keep their people informed of all the processes and procedures of the business required millions of pages of documents in over 100 reference manuals. Employees were frustrated in their time-consuming search for information and angry when they sometimes learned that the information, once found, was inaccurate. Instead of training people to do a better job of finding the information, or training the information providers to improve the level of information accuracy, the company applied HPT to job redesign and implemented an electronic performance support system. Placing the information on-line greatly eliminated the "version control" problem and improved accuracy dramatically. In addition, through extensive computerized navigation tools, the time it takes to find the required information dropped significantly. Thus the use of technology in redesigning the job helped improve performance to a far greater extent than would be possible by training people to better cope with the existing process.

- A large insurance company was concerned about its succession plans at all levels of management. As top positions were filled, there was little attention paid to building the "bench strength" of talent at lower and middle management. Attention to development was weak, job descriptions were inadequate, and measurable competencies were lacking. Without these tools, the firm's ability to identify strong candidates for specific key jobs was in jeopardy. To remedy this situation, the company applied its management process, which is based on quality fundamentals, to developmental planning. Through use of the process, management competencies were developed and associated training was identified. Individual and organizational gaps were identified by the process and interventions to reduce the gaps were implemented. The competencies needed by the organization, along with the current identified skill gaps, were fed into the selection system to assure that the company would seek out and hire people who could fill an identified need. Thus the firm took its management process, the way it ran its business, and refocused it on the development of its people, in essence building a performance technology system. The results include competence models for key jobs, linked to development, earlier detection of skill gaps, and a reemergence of people development as "serious business" within the company.

These brief case studies sound a lot like reengineering. In fact, there is new insight that positions HPT as a reengineering process (Ray and Sword[21]; Stolovitch, Keeps, and Rodrigue[22]). These examples of HPT in action, as with many others that are emerging, show two unique characteristics of the process that at first glance may seem conflicting but actually showcase the real value of HPT. First, each example used a *similar* approach to improving performance: in-depth analysis of problems and causes. But each also showcased *differing* interventions or solutions to the problem(s). The power of HPT is such that this single systematic process can yield such a wide variety of approaches and possibilities. Use of HPT, therefore, gives organizations *more* options, rather than less, in the continuing quest to develop competitive advantage by identifying, developing, and retaining a high-performing workforce.

The Relationship Between
HPT and Training

Although one of the major roots of performance technology is in the areas of learning psychology and instructional systems design, HPT transcends these fields as a broader, more comprehensive concept. Rosenberg[23] noted that training practitioners found instruction alone less than effective in many cases where performance improvement was needed. Try as they might, they could not fit *their* solution into every opportunity, and they quickly discovered that other solutions were more effective and less costly. The realization that lack of skill and knowledge was only one of many possible causes of a performance gap helps the education and training profession in that it assures that

- *Problems are addressed by the* least cost *solution.* Training is expensive. When a less-costly intervention, such as a job aid or performance standards, will work, there is no need to spend money on training *unless* there is also a skill-knowledge deficit (and determining if there is a skill-knowledge deficit is one key reason why performance analysis is so critical). If money is not wasted on performance problems that are not skill-knowledge related, the "cost-benefit perception" of training is enhanced.

- *Success is* enhanced *by matching the best intervention to the deficiency.* Again, the likelihood of performance actually and *measurably* improving and *staying* improved is greatly increased by applying HPT analysis techniques.

- *Training is relieved from* inappropriate *tasks.* When a proper match of performance gap, cause, and intervention is made, not only is success more certain but also the "track record" of training will be improved since it will be less likely to be called upon to solve problems that aren't related to skill and knowledge. Thus, the utilization of expensive education and training resources becomes more cost-effective and *justifiable*.

- *Training can concentrate on* skill-knowledge *deficiencies.* Through HPT, education and training focuses more on what those interventions were *designed* to do. Efficiency and effectiveness increase, as does the morale and motivation of training professionals as they see a high success rate and organizational acceptance of their value.

- *Clients are better* satisfied. Education and training is focused on what it does best, and the results are easily recognized by those who pay the bills.

The implications of HPT for trainers and the education and training function are important:

- *Instructional design and technology are not* overarching *processes.* Educators should not assume that instructional technology or instructional design is the cornerstone of performance improvement. While there are certainly many similarities, instructional design assumes that an instructional intervention is called for. HPT makes no such assumption from the start.

- *Training is not a cure-all.* "If performance is down, give 'em training. If it's still down, give 'em more training." Many a training organization has been eliminated in a downsizing even though classes are full. The lesson here is *not* that training works, but that it only works on problems related to skill and knowledge. Applying training alone, even lots of it, in other areas is both wasteful and risky to the training organization.

- *Training must be totally integrated into the* business mainstream. While there is little question that good training results in learning, it does not necessarily follow that a high amount of learning results in an equally high level of performance. Therefore, measuring learning gain is good but insufficient. Educators must assess their results against identified performance gaps which are more closely aligned with customer requirements and the business's mission and goals.

- *Training professionals must become* performance technologists. Training will not be going away any time soon. In fact, the need for high-quality sophisticated education and training will only increase in the future. Yet it is likely that the utilization of other interventions will grow even faster. Even more important, the pressure for measurable, bottom-line results will require critical decisions at the *performance* level rather than at the learning level. In terms of organizational impact, increased responsibility, and career enhancement, performance technology is *the* growth market.

This paradigm shift from training to performance will accelerate over the next few years as organizations look for new ways to improve productivity and competitiveness. Lyau and Pucel[24] suggest that this shift will create some internal competitive challenges, noting that "it has become increasingly apparent that in order for training to retain current funding levels and/or receive larger amounts of organizational resource, it must be viewed as a competitor with other types of investments the organization might make to increase productivity [p. 75]." Whether training primarily competes with, or is systematically integrated into these other options, the shift is already under way, encompassing five major transitions that will impact both the training and the HRD field (see Table 18-3).

Moving from a training to a performance orientation not only requires a shift of ideas but a change in the skills sets for many practitioners. Stolovitch, Keeps, and Rodrigue[22] report on and offer a number of ways to define HPT skills. Today, many universities teach at least one course on HPT, and the marketplace is full of workshops on various aspects of the field, especially performance analysis. Perhaps what is needed next is the integration of HPT principles directly into internal and external corporate management and leadership programs.

Table 18-3. Five Major Transitions That Will Impact Training and HRD

From	To
Learning as an end in itself	Valued performance as the primary measure of effectiveness
Training and other interventions as tactical responses to somewhat larger tactical problems	Performance technology as a strategic response to strategic needs relating to people and productivity
A view of training as overhead and support, susceptible to budget cutting and downsizing	Performance technology as a competitive resource, perhaps even more important during business downturns
Interventions placed in HR functional chimneys that do not communicate with one another	An integrated performance improvement system that is *systemic* throughout the organization
A focus on educational results, e.g., learning	A focus on organizational and business results, e.g., the bottom line

A Final Definition

The paradigm shift from training to performance is not something that just the education and training function should experience. Anyone in the organization can and probably should develop this new perspective. In this regard, we cannot relegate HPT to specialized staffs, either inside or outside the training department. We need to build these skills into our sales managers, plant supervisors, senior executives, etc. Performance technology can be a part of the general management process and the use of HPT can be reflected in effectiveness measures of front-line managers in all functions of the organization.

In the final analysis, human performance technology is not only a systematic process and a set of skills but it may also be an attitude about how to get the best out of everyone. With this viewpoint, HPT can be defined as *a perspective* or *way of thinking* about how individual and organizational performance can be enhanced. This definition, while not as prescriptive as the others, may be the most important, because it can be ascribed to *anyone* in the organization, not just to HPT specialists. And when these people, from sales managers, to customer-care supervisors, to product managers and vice presidents, think and act like performance technologists, *that* will be the most exciting time for the HR field.

The Future of Training, Training Departments, and HPT

As organizations focus more and more on the performance of their people as a strategic competitive advantage, training departments will invariably transform into performance improvement departments. What would a performance improvement department look like and how would it be different from a training department?

First of all, performance improvement departments would devote significantly more time and resources to performance analysis. They would become human performance "problem identifiers," working closely with line management and senior executives. They would seek out opportunities to positively impact performance in the workplace, rather than waiting to be asked to develop training. To demonstrate their capabilities, they would aggressively look for opportunities to apply performance technology. Sometimes, these opportunities are not large or strategic, but they are the "low-hanging fruit," opportunities with a high likelihood of success. Starting small, the departments would build relationships with line managers who are willing to try new ways to improve performance. And they would showcase these successes in ways that draw positive attention to these new capabilities.

Performance improvement departments would also devote considerable resources to evaluation and measurement of interventions, showing, in a manner consistent with the goals of the organization, how performance technology contributes to business success. They would work to help the organization define performance gaps and show them how to measure their own success. In doing so, they would build partnerships with the line, transferring their skills to line managers and serving as HPT consultants so that performance technology becomes a part of the organizational culture.

Performance improvement departments would abandon the "anything you want is OK with us" approach to serving their clients. They would question unsubstantiated requests for training, even when it would be the easy thing to do, and try to steer clients away from solutions that are not appropriate for the problem. Of course, when training is called for, they would develop a comprehensive measurement plan that clearly goes beyond the "smile sheet" and relates directly to the impact on the business. And, prior to implementing training or other solutions, they would assure that the appropriate work environment, incentive and feedback system, and long-term support is in place.

Performance improvement departments would become more customer-focused. They would venture out more often from the training center into the cold reality of the front-line business. They would support such processes as product development, marketing, sales, and quality so as to enhance the effectiveness of those processes. By sharing the risks and the rewards of the marketplace with the organizations they serve, they become a value-added component of a successful enterprise, and HPT slowly becomes recognized as a strategic *business* tool.

Can training departments become performance improvement departments? Can they have greater influence on the success of an organization? Will training departments prosper in the "performance age"? The answer to these questions depends a great deal on the perspective of those who seek to make the transition from training to performance.

To wit, a short story. In the first half of the twentieth century, railroads carried the overwhelming majority of inter-city passenger traffic in the United States and were making great sums of money doing it. During this time, small fledgling airline companies began flying passengers from city to city and state to state. It was expensive, uncomfortable, and dangerous. The railroads looked at this emerging alternative to their business and contemplated what to do. They could have bought into these new airline companies for pocket change, but they did not. For, in their analysis, they determined that they were in the *railroad* business, not the *transportation* business. Today, only a small minority of the people travel by rail and those risky airlines of the first half of the twentieth century now dominate transportation as we enter the twenty-first century.

The lesson of this story should not be lost on the education and training profession. There will always be a need for high-quality education and training, simply because the times demand *more* learning, not less. But trainers must see themselves in the performance business, not just the training business. Learning, while extremely valuable, is insufficient unless people can apply what they are learning in ways that are valuable to the organization. Moving from training to performance, through a human performance technology framework, will maintain the leadership of our field in seeking new and better ways to improve competence, productivity, and competitiveness in the workplace.

References

1. "1995 Industry Report," *Training, 32*(10), October 1995, pp. 37–82.
2. Rummler, G. A., and A. P. Brache, "The Systems View of Human Performance," *Training, 24*(9), 1988, pp. 45–153.
3. Rosenberg, M. J., "Performance Technology: Working the System," *Training, 27*(2), February 1990, pp. 12–15, 33.
4. Rosenberg, M. J., W. C. Coscarelli, and C. S. Hutchison, "The Origins and Evolution of the Field," in H. Stolovitch and E. Keeps, eds., *Handbook of Human Performance Technology,* Jossey-Bass, San Francisco, 1992, pp. 14–31.
5. Mager, R. F., *Making Instruction Work,* David S. Lake, Belmont, CA, 1988, p. 10.

6. Rummler, G. A., "Organizational Redesign," in M. E. Smith, ed., *Introduction to Performance Technology*, NSPI, Washington, DC, 1986, pp. 211–235.

7. Senge, P. F., *The Fifth Discipline: The Art and Practice of the Learning Organization*, Doubleday, New York, 1990.

8. Gilbert, T. F., *Human Competence: Engineering Worthy Performance*, McGraw-Hill, New York, 1978.

9. Deterline, W. A., and M. J. Rosenberg, eds., *Workplace Productivity: Performance Technology: Success Stories*, ISPI, Washington, DC, 1992.

10. Rummler, G. A., and A. P. Brache, "Transforming Organizations Through Human Performance Technology," in H. Stolovitch and E. Keeps, eds., *Handbook of Human Performance Technology*, Jossey-Bass, San Francisco, 1992, pp. 32–49.

11. Harless, J. H., *Guiding Performance with Job Aids*, in M. E. Smith, ed., *Introduction to Performance Technology*, NSPI, Washington, DC, 1986, pp. 106–124.

12. Rossett, A., "Analysis of Human Performance Problems," in H. Stolovitch and E. Keeps, eds., *Handbook of Human Performance Technology*, Jossey-Bass, San Francisco, 1992, pp. 97–113.

13. Rossett, A., *Training Needs Assessment*, Educational Technology Publications, Englewood Cliffs, NJ, 1987.

14. Dixon, G., ed., *What Works at Work: Lessons from the Masters*, Lakewood Publications, Minneapolis, 1988.

15. Spitzer, D. R., "The Design and Development of Effective Interventions," in H. Stolovitch and E. Keeps, eds., *Handbook of Human Performance Technology*, Jossey-Bass, San Francisco, 1992, pp. 114–129.

16. Coleman, M. E., "Developing Skills and Enhancing Professional Competence," in H. Stolovitch and E. Keeps, eds., *Handbook of Human Performance Technology*, Jossey-Bass, San Francisco, 1992, pp. 634–648.

17. Dormant, D., "Implementing Human Performance Technology in Organizations," in H. Stolovitch and E. Keeps, eds., *Handbook of Human Performance Technology*, Jossey-Bass, San Francisco, 1992, pp. 167–187.

18. Kirkpatrick, D., ed., *Evaluating Training Programs*, ASTD, Alexandria, VA, 1975.

19. Hutchison, C. S., "A Performance Technology Process Model," *Performance and Instruction, 29*(3), 1990, pp. 1–5.

20. Geis, G. L., "Human Performance Technology: An Overview," in M. E. Smith, ed., *Introduction to Performance Technology*, NSPI, Washington, DC, 1986, pp. 1–20.

21. Ray, J. A., and S. M. Sword, "Reengineering and Human Performance," *Performance and Instruction, 32*(7) pp. 29–35.

22. Stolovitch, H. D., E. J. Keeps, and D. Rodrigue, "Skill Sets for the Human Performance Technologist," *Performance Improvement Quarterly, 8*(2), 1995, pp. 40–67.

23. Rosenberg, M. J., "Our Instructional Media Roots," *Performance and Instruction, 21*(3), 1982, pp. 12–15, 33.

24. Lyau, N., and D. Pucel, "Economic Return on Training Investment at the Organizational Level," *Performance Improvement Quarterly, 8*(3), 1995, pp. 68–79.

Recommended Resources

The following books, journals, articles, and professional associations are recommended for additional insights into human performance technology:

Deterline, W. A., and M. J. Rosenberg, eds., *Workplace Productivity: Performance Technology Success Stories*, International Society for Performance Improvement (ISPI), Washington,

DC, 1992.* A good introduction and overview of performance technology, with 12 case studies of performance technology applications.

Fournies, F. F., *Why Employees Don't Do What They're Supposed to Do…and What to Do About It*, McGraw-Hill, New York, 1988. A short, easy-to-read book with 16 common reasons why people don't, can't, or won't perform and practical suggestions for dealing with them. Straightforward and practical; concerned with *performance technology* without mentioning the term.

Gilbert, T. F., *Human Competence: Engineering Worthy Performance*, McGraw-Hill, New York, 1978.** A classic. A brilliant work that lays the foundation for performance technology.

Mager, R. M., and P. Pipe, *Analyzing Performance Problems*, Lake Publishing, Belmont, CA, 1985. An easy-to-read book that lays out a clear path for thinking about and conducting performance analysis activities.

Performance Improvement Quarterly, published by the Learning Systems Institute of Florida State University in cooperation with ISPI. Contains in-depth conceptual and research-based articles on all aspects of human performance technology.

Robinson, D. G., and J. C. Robinson, *Performance Consulting: Moving Beyond Training*, Berrett-Koehler, San Francisco, 1995. Focuses primarily on training solutions but provides a wealth of how-to information on performance analysis.

Rosenberg, M. J. "Performance Technology: Working the System," *Training, 27*(2), February 1990, pp. 42–48. Article links performance technology to business issues.

Rossett, A., *Training Needs Assessment*, Educational Technology Publications, Englewood Cliffs, NJ, 1987. A well-written, more in-depth discussion of performance analysis. A good follow-up to Mager and Pipe.

Rummler, G., and A. Brache, *Improving Performance: How to Manage the White Space in the Organizational Chart*, Jossey-Bass, San Francisco, 1991. A systems approach to performance technology that leans heavily on a business, productivity, and results context.

Stolovitch, H., and E. Keeps, eds., *Handbook of Human Performance Technology*, Jossey-Bass, San Francisco, 1992. A complete and extensive guide to the broad field of performance technology. A virtual "who's who" of thinkers in the field and a great reference.

In addition, the International Society for Performance Improvement (formerly the National Society for Performance and Instruction, or NSPI) sponsors educational programs, conferences, and publications dealing with human performance technology. ISPI, Suite 1250, 1300 L Street NW, Washington, DC 20005, Phone: 202-408-7969. FAX: 202-408-7972.

*NSPI has recently changed its name to the International Society for Performance Improvement.

**Currently out of print. The second edition is to be published soon by HRD Press.

19

Benchmarking for Best Practices

Christopher E. Bogan

Michael J. English

Christopher E. Bogan *is president and founder of Best Prac-*
tices Benchmarking and Consulting, LLC. Based in the Chapel
Hill–Durham area of North Carolina, Best Practices is a profes-
sional services company providing information, consulting, exec-
utive education, and research service in the field of best-practices
benchmarking and continuous performance improvement. Bogan
received his M.B.A. degree with honors from Harvard Business
School and his bachelor's degree magna cum laude from Amherst
College. He was a Nieman Fellow at Harvard University,
1981–1982. His work has focused on Total Quality Management
and best-practices improvement strategies. He is coauthor of
Benchmarking for Best Practices: Winning through Innovative
Adaptation, *McGraw-Hill, 1994, and* The Baldrige: What It is,
How It's Won, and How to Use It to Improve Quality in Your
Company, *1982. He has consulted with a wide range of compa-*
nies including Marriott, GTE, American Express, AT&T, Chevron,
Siemens, MONY, Exxon, and KPMG Peat Marwick. Bogan led the
consulting teams that assisted both GTE Directories and Federal
Express to become winners of the Malcolm Baldrige National
Quality Award in 1994 and 1990, respectively. He has developed
case studies and teaching notes for the Harvard Business School
and for the National Institute of Standards and Technology which
administers the Malcolm Baldrige National Quality Award. Prior
to founding Best Practices, Bogan was principal and founding
member of The TQM Group, Ltd., a Boston-based consulting firm,
and he worked at various media companies, including Times
Mirror Corp., Knight-Ridder Inc., Howard Publications, and
Cowles Publishing Co. He has contributed many articles to peri-
odicals such as The Harvard Business Review, Time, Planning
Review, The Los Angeles Times, *and* The Boston Globe.

394

Michael J. English is Director of Quality and Customer Service at GTE Directories, winner of the 1994 Malcolm Baldrige National Quality Award. Prior to that he served as Director of Quality Positioning, Director of Quality Measurement, and Director of Service Program Management during his 22-year career with GTE. His responsibilities have included developing and implementing companywide customer satisfaction measurements systems, benchmarking techniques, the GTE President's Quality Awards, customer service delivery methods, systematic continuous improvements, Baldrige Quality Award Criteria assessments and applications, and ISO 9000 Quality management plans. He is a popular speaker, writer, and authority in the fields of service quality management, customer satisfaction, measurement, and benchmarking. English has served as an examiner for the Malcolm Baldrige Quality Award since 1993. He is a 1970 M. A. (economics) graduate of California University at Sacramento.

Benchmarking Is an Essential Business Concept

In a world where common sense prevailed, benchmarking would seem prosaic. It is quite simply the systematic process of searching for best practices, innovative ideas, and highly effective operating procedures that lead to superior performance. What could be more straightforward? No individual, team, or operating unit—no matter how creative or prolific—can possibly parent all innovation. No single department or company can corner the market on *all* good ideas.

In view of this reality in which human limitations are recognized, it makes eminently good sense to consider the experience of others. Those who always go it alone are doomed to perennially "reinvent the wheel," for they do not learn and benefit from others' progress. By systematically studying the best business practices, operating tactics, and winning strategies of others, an individual, team, or organization can accelerate its own progress and improvement.

The history of innovative adaptation is arguably as old as humankind. For millennia people have observed good ideas around them and adapted those ideas to meet their needs and situations. Fred D. Bowers, Digital Equipment Corporation's benchmarking program manager, muses that "the second person to light a fire" is humankind's first benchmarker. Bowers' logic: the second fire-starter observed the first fire-starter and then borrowed the practice.

The obvious wisdom of studying others' best practices would seem self-evident. Learning by borrowing from the best and by adapting their approaches to fit your own needs is the essence of benchmarking. Surely there is nothing new or revolutionary in this prescription for improvement. Or is there?

For every example of innovative adaptation that graces the halls of history, there are many more examples of organizations, groups, and people that have declined to look outside of themselves for solutions. The fact is not remarkable that people have on many noteworthy occasions been inspired through the benchmarking process. By exposing organizations and people to new ideas and approaches, the benchmarking experience often spurs extraordinary insights and breakthrough thinking.

What *is* truly remarkable is that benchmarking has not sooner been embraced as a fundamental business process and skill. Benchmarking has broad applications in problem solving, planning, goal setting, process improvement, innovation, reengineering, strategy setting, and in various other contexts. Quite simply, benchmarking is a fundamental business skill that supports quality excellence.

Benchmarks and Benchmarking

Benchmarking's linguistic and metaphorical roots lie in the land surveyor's term, where a *benchmark* was a distinctive mark made on a rock, wall, or building. In this context, a benchmark served as a reference point in determining one's current position or altitude in topographical surveys and tidal observations. In the most general terms, a benchmark was originally a sighting point from which measurements could be made or it implied a standard against which others could be measured.

In the 1970s, the concept of a benchmark evolved beyond a technical term signifying a reference point. The word migrated into the lexicon of business where it came to signify the measurement process by which to conduct comparisons. In the early 1980s, Xerox Corporation, a leader in the business process of benchmarking, referred to benchmarking in rather narrow terms that focused primarily on comparisons with one's primary competitors. "Benchmarking is the continuous process of measuring products, services, and practices against the toughest competitors or those companies recognized as industry leaders," observed former Xerox CEO David Kearns.

During the decade of the eighties, the definition of benchmarking grew in scope and focus. No longer were the metrical objects or benchmarks of primary interest. Benchmarking came to refer to the outreach activity of comparing yourself against others. Various practitioners offered the following definitions:

> A process for rigorously measuring your performance versus the best-in-class companies and for using the analysis to meet and surpass the best-in-class. [Kaiser Associates, a management consulting firm that has actively promoted benchmarking.]

> A standard of excellence or achievement against which other similar things must be measured or judged. [Sam Bookhart, former manager of benchmarking at DuPont Fibers.]

> Benchmarking is the search for industry best practices that lead to superior performance. [Robert C. Camp, a Xerox Corporation manager, author of *Benchmarking: The Search for Industry Best Practices,* and one of the foremost benchmarking experts at the Xerox Corporation.]

The distinction between *benchmarking* and *benchmarks* continues to perplex many managers. In the authors' view, benchmarking is the ongoing search for best practices that produce superior performance when adapted and implemented in one's own organization. Emphasis should be placed on benchmarking as an *ongoing* outreach activity; the goal of the outreach is *identification* of best operating practices that, when *implemented,* produce *superior performance.*

Benchmarks, in contrast to benchmarking, are measurements to gauge the performance of a function, operation, or business relative to others. In the electronics industry, for instance, a benchmark has long referred to an operating statistic that allows you to compare your own performance to that of another or to an industry standard. Operating statistics employed as benchmarks provide incomplete comparisons. In a sense, they are "superficial," for they draw attention to performance gaps without offering any evidence or explanation for why those gaps exist. At times, the performance gaps surfaced through benchmark comparisons may reflect significant differences in operating systems and procedures; on other occasions, benchmark variances may reflect differences in the way different organizations track and measure the performance of their systems. The root causes of operating differences usually cannot be discerned from the "benchmarks" alone. In this respect, the benchmarks are like divining rods that lead the organization to hidden opportunities to innovate and improve performance. Benchmarking is the actual process of investigation and discovery that emphasizes the operating procedures as the things of greatest interest and value. Consequently, "best-practices benchmarking" can be described as the process of seeking out and studying the best internal and external practices that produce superior performance. One measures this performance through various financial and nonfinancial performance indicators. (Figure 19-1 illustrates the relationship of benchmarks and benchmarking.)

Best-practices benchmarking, which includes but isn't limited to the study of statistical benchmarks, can—and *should*—be applied at many levels of the organization and in many different contexts. For instance, many benchmarking projects have targeted critical technical functions such as distribution and logistics, billing, order entry and fulfillment, and training. However, benchmarking is also an advanced business concept with general management applications for high-level functions such as strategic planning, restructuring, financial management, succession planning, and supplier and joint-venture management.

Managing Change

Benchmarking teams, with a mandate to look far and wide for better operating practices, are arguably one of the best sentinels senior management can post

Benchmarking for Best Practices

Metrics	⬌	Processes
Benchmarks	⬌	Benchmarking
Operating Statistics	⬌	Practices

BEST PRACTICES

Winning Through Innovative Adaptation

Figure 19-1. Benchmarks and benchmarking.

along the watchtowers of the organization. They can sound the alarm when the first signs appear on the horizon that the organization has fallen behind the competition or has failed to take advantage of important operating improvements developed elsewhere. Best-practices benchmarking provides employees and managers with the tool, the rationale, and the process to accept change as constant, inevitable, and good. "Change has no constituency," observes General Electric CEO Jack Welch, who has established benchmarking for best practices as an essential part of GE's ongoing management and improvement efforts. "People like the status quo. They like the way it was."[1]

The ongoing adaptation of best practices helps an organization avoid being ambushed by unexpected change. A company can accelerate its own rate of improvement by systematically studying others and by comparing its own operations and performance with the best and most effective practices of highly innovative and successful companies. The search for best practices quickly draws you outside the confines of your own culture and personal habits. Best-practices benchmarking is therefore a pragmatic approach to managing change and performance improvement.

Many organizations have demonstrated the power of best-practices benchmarking. For example, General Electric currently embraces a best-practices program that is descended from several earlier management initiatives. More than 40 years ago, then-GE Chairman Ralph Cordiner pursued a best business practices strategy when he assembled an internal team of top managers and instructed them to identify and institutionalize the era's best operating practices.

> In 1951, [Cordiner] assembled a brainy team of GE executives, plus consultants and professors, including Peter Drucker, to recommend ways to improve GE's management. They studied fifty other firms, pored over the personnel records of 2000 GEers, did time-motion studies of executives at work, and interviewed countless GE managers.

> Two years later, they emerged with a Blue Book, a five-volume 3463-page management bible. Buried in endless pages of stultifyingly elaborate prescriptions are such powerful concepts as management by objective—as well as some of the most revolutionary ideas [current GE CEO Jack] Welch would later espouse. This discussion of decentralization, for instance, sounds a lot like Welch's principle of speed: "A minimum of supervision, a minimum of time delays in decision making, a maximum of competitive agility, and thus maximum service to customers and profits to the company."[2]

GE's *Blue Book* and every other best-practices compendium face the same challenge: How do you avoid bureaucracy when codifying and institutionalizing today's most-effective operating practices? The easiest way to fully leverage an identifiable best practice is to declare it a mandatory SOP (standard operating procedure). Paradoxically, an organization risks turning its current best practices into future bureaucratic tendencies as soon as it rigidly mandates and codifies them in hefty operating manuals. The road to competitive ruin is paved with once-effective operating procedures that have outlived their time. Companies implementing best-practices strategies must carefully balance the benefits of current SOP compliance with the benefits of future innovation. Tomorrow's best practices will inevitably evolve beyond or diverge from today's best practices. By their nature, best practices are dynamic and progressive. For this reason, best-practices benchmarking is often called an "evergreen" process: it renews the organization each time it is repeated. Consequently, best-practices champions regard benchmarking as an ongoing business process that is fully integrated with continuous improvement in their organizations.

Three Primary Benchmarking Types

Benchmarking has gained tremendous influence and currency in the nineties. Correspondingly, front-line employees and operating managers have applied basic benchmarking skills in scores of different business situations. Among these applications, three distinct types of benchmarking have proliferated: (1) process benchmarking, (2) performance benchmarking, and (3) strategic benchmarking.

Process Benchmarking

Process benchmarking focuses on discrete work processes and operating systems such as the customer complaint process, the billing process, the order-and-fulfill-ment process, the recruitment process, or the strategic planning process. This form of benchmarking seeks to identify the most effective operating practices from many companies that perform similar work functions. In recent years, process benchmarking has grown in stature in the United States. Many of the most impressive American benchmarking success stories refer to process bench-marking. Its power lies in its ability to produce bottom-line results. If an organization improves a core process, for instance, it can then quickly deliver performance improvements. These performance improvements may be calculated through increased productivity, lower costs, or improved sales, but their net effect frequently translates into improved short-term financial results. For this reason American managers, seeking performance improvements that will show up on their quarterly scorecards, embrace process benchmarking.

Performance Benchmarking

Performance benchmarking enables managers to assess their competitive positions through product and service comparisons. Performance benchmarking usually focuses on elements of price, technical quality, ancillary product or service features, speed, reliability, and other performance characteristics. Reverse engineering, direct product or service comparisons, and analysis of operating statistics are the primary techniques applied during performance benchmarking. The automotive, computer, financial services, and photocopier industries, among others, regularly employ performance benchmarking as a standard competitive tool.

Strategic Benchmarking

In general terms, strategic benchmarking examines how companies compete. Strategic benchmarking is seldom industry-focused. It roves across industries seeking to identify the winning strategies that have enabled high-performing companies to be successful in their marketplaces. Numerous Japanese corporations are accomplished strategic benchmarkers. A U.S.-based management consultant who specializes in working with Japanese corporations operating in the United States tells this story:

> My clients begin by asking, "What companies are really good?" Then we set up a trip in which the chairman or CEO of my client will go to visit these really good compa-

nies. Unlike American companies that begin a benchmarking project by determining what specific activity or process they want to examine, my Japanese clients are interested in fundamental lessons and winning strategies. They feel as if they already understand their processes.

It is not surprising that Japanese corporations, which characteristically focus on long-term horizons, should be most interested in strategic benchmarking. Strategic benchmarking influences the longer-term competitive patterns of a company. Consequently, the benefits may accrue slowly. Organizations seeking short-term benefits, such as those reflected in quarterly performance reports, usually find that process benchmarking produces results more rapidly.

Applications and Benefits

Benchmarking is a remarkably versatile business tool. Roland Loesser, the chief financial officer of the Sandoz Corporation's American operations, observes: "Benchmarking is powerful because it can be applied to virtually every function in our companies." Moreover, front-line managers are using it in many new and creative ways. The following are some of the more frequent applications.

Setting and Refining Strategy

Today's markets are in a dynamic state of flux. Consequently, important insights can be gleaned by studying the experiences and competitive strategies of others. Bath Ironworks in Maine, for instance, benchmarked the strategies and operations of 10 shipyards in Holland when the Cold War's end rendered the 108-year-old shipyard's business strategy completely out of date. Bath, the United States' fourth-largest shipyard and Maine's largest private employer, had assumed that the country's need for combat vessels would remain strong for the rest of the century. (Since 1977, 86 percent of the vessels Bath delivered were naval combat ships.) To quickly rethink its strategy and adjust to the "sea change" in the post–Cold War economy, Bath studied the strategy of the Royal Schelde shipyard in Vlissingen, Holland. Royal Schelde and other Dutch shipyards had already reorganized to accommodate merchant-ship building and the manufacturing of other complex structures such as bridges. "Contingency plans can be developed and implemented much faster and at far less cost [through benchmarking] than if developed from scratch," observes Bath Ironworks' manager of quality improvement William R. "Tip" Koehler.[3] The strategic lessons learned by other organizations and industries can help your own company refine its strategy, project the possible outcomes of changing its present course, and forecast potential cataclysmic shifts brought on by changing market circumstances.

Reengineering Work Processes and Business Systems

Benchmarking is a necessity for companies engaged in reengineering their processes and systems. Benchmarking gives you the ability to see things differently. It is like setting up a satellite dish outside your offices. Suddenly, signals from throughout the world can penetrate your organization. Benchmarking enables a company to get outside its conditioned responses or customary structures of thinking. When GTE reengineered eight core processes of its telephone operations, it examined the best practices of some 84 companies from diverse industries to help the company rethink the rules of the game for each of its core functions.

Reengineering without benchmarking is likely to produce flat 5 to 10 percent improvements, not the spectacular 50 to 75 percent performance improvements often seen with radical redesign. Benchmarking enables true reengineering. Through the study of outside best practices, a company can identify and import new technology, new skills, new structures, new training, and new capabilities.

Continuous Improvement of Work Processes and Business Systems

Not every benchmarking project or initiative will yield major-magnitude change and system breakthroughs. Benchmarking also provides a potent source for incremental changes and improvements. Benchmarking exchanges frequently yield "golden nuggets" that are weighed in ounces rather than pounds. KPMG Peat Marwick, the Big Six accounting firm, borrowed the concept of a supermarket's express checkout to start an express line in its word processing pools. The change enabled work teams with minor document changes to go through an expedited process. This small change was of great value to word processing departments that handled high-volume work orders. It solved the long-standing and nettlesome problem of work assignments with small changes being stalled in long work queues. Moreover, this innovative adaptation of a supermarket operating practice improved cycle time and boosted internal customer satisfaction. Additionally, it can be applied to many other service functions, such as copying, graphics production, and research.

Strategic Planning and Goal Setting

The unexpected missteps of blue-chip organizations such as IBM, American Express, Westinghouse, and General Motors have provided the world an important lesson: In the 1990s, market changes can be swift and powerful, economically hobbling even the most powerful corporations. Consequently, a growing number of companies undergoing a strategic planning and goal-setting process do so through benchmarking. Benchmarking helps organizations anticipate market changes and validate goals and targets. One can only wonder how much sooner these battered giants might have responded to shifting market realities if they used benchmarking as an integral part of their strategic planning and goal-setting process.

By reviewing the products, prices, practices, strategies, structures, and services of competitors and other industry front-runners, managers can validate the adequacy of their own goals, plans, and strategies. For instance, Mutual Life Insurance Company of New York requires all executives to find benchmarking information on their primary and secondary competitors as part of the company's newly revamped planning process. Says MONY Quality Officer Jan Howard: "Planning without awareness of what your competitors are doing is like flying a plane over the Alps in heavy fog without any instrument controls."

Problem Solving

Benchmarking frequently demonstrates its value in the problem-solving process. Ironically, most corporate problem-solving processes do not methodically look outside the team or organization for solutions. Standard problem-solving processes provide a structure that makes work groups more effective; they also prompt teams to root their analysis in empirical data, which supports management by fact—rather than by fancy. But most problem-solving processes indirectly encourage teams to reinvent the wheel because they seldom encourage work groups to consider external experience in developing their solutions. As an enabling tool for problem solving, benchmarking frequently produces elegant answers for thorny operating issues. Consider the following case from the Xerox Corporation, where benchmarking has been deeply integrated into the organization's fundamental quality and problem-solving efforts.

Plagued by high associate turnover in its corporate legal department, Xerox looked for solutions both internally and externally. Internal analysis revealed various causes for the problem; external analysis, however, turned up important insights. Xerox's benchmarking partners shared the same recruitment and selection process and all suffered from the same high associate turnover. Once recognizing that its essential recruitment strategy produced suboptimal results, Xerox adjusted it recruitment strategy rather than trying to fine-tune the process. In retrospect, this decision makes excellent sense because the best and brightest law students are usually geared to work for high-paying and high-powered law firms—not for corporate law departments. Many fine lawyers decide to move to corporations after practicing for several years at a firm. The common experience of all the benchmark partners gave Xerox confidence to move away from traditional recruitment on law-school campuses to a more radical strategy. This strategy emphasizes recruitment of experienced lawyers, who wish to make lateral career moves away from law firms and into corporate practices. Arguably, Xerox would never have gleaned this insight if not for its benchmarking investigation.

Education and Idea Enrichment

A Zen-like management riddle asks: "How does a fish know it is wet?" The fish spends all its life in water and knows no other condition. The riddle probes how people, who grow accustomed to operating in certain ways, know there are other approaches—perhaps better ways—of performing the same task. Benchmarking is a tool for achieving idea enrichment and general education. By regularly benchmarking critical functions, organizations ensure that they remain open to new ideas, changing trends, and evolving technology. If seeing is believing, then benchmarking is an effective process to ensure that managers and front-line operators see other approaches to accomplishing the activities over which they preside.

Market Performance Comparisons
and Evaluations

Human nature encourages people to reflect positively on the organizations and colleagues with which they work. Naturally, people want to validate their efforts. Correspondingly, organizations and individuals frequently presume the products and services that they provide to customers are also of high quality. Yet without carefully comparing those products and services to competitors' offerings, they cannot fairly evaluate their relative standing. However, fancy gives way to fact when you benchmark your company's products, features, and performance against competitors'. This type of performance benchmarking is common in many industries. Mortgage bankers, for instance, compare their interest rates, service fees, and product types on a weekly basis. *Consumer Reports* has long evaluated the features of various products, and J. D. Powers has "benchmarked" customer satisfaction levels among automobile owners. All these industry and professional ratings provide a fact-based market performance test that employs the essential skills of benchmarking. By heeding these and other types of performance benchmarks, organizations can assess the adequacy of their products, services, features, and performance. Such information can help them manage by customer-focused facts.

Catalyst for Change

Al Kuebler, of AT&T Universal Card Services, 1992 Malcolm Baldrige National Quality Award winner, observes an operating truth that every benchmarking manager has observed: "Tell me and I forget, show me and I remember, involve me and I understand."[4] Benchmarking is an effective catalyst for change because it involves employees in the personal discovery of more effective operating practices. Benchmarking exposes people to new approaches, systems, and procedures. It is first-person experience that helps an employee visualize the final goal of prospective change. In this respect, benchmarking demystifies change, making it more tangible and less threatening. Consequently, benchmarking helps manage organizational change.

A Utilitarian Tool

Managers and employees are inundated with a series of highly abstract yet exceedingly important challenges. These include general mandates to oversee such intangible concepts as change management, innovation, creativity, organizational learning, speed or cycle-time reduction, process simplification, and reengineering. For many managers concerned with such matters as serving customers, meeting daily deadlines, reducing costs, and growing revenues, these concepts seem perplexing. It's difficult to get your thoughts and your hands around these high-sounding but abstract concepts.

Benchmarking is an easily grasped, functional tool. As utilitarian as a fireplace poker, it can test and probe the hottest management concepts. Benchmarking doesn't support abstract postulations about arcane management concepts. It promotes the active discovery of systems that embody the concepts in real-world situations. Don't sit in isolation, for instance, while meditating how to compete through cycle-time reduction. Study the best practices of other organizations that have learned to perform critical functions more quickly than your own company. Benchmarking offers a kind of low-tech "virtual reality" for organizations eager to simulate operational experiences in their own environments. What better way to project a system's impact in your own company than to examine the performance effects of that system already implemented in another organization? "Ideas are a commodity," observes Dell Computer CEO Michael Dell. "Execution of them is not."[5] As a managerial tool, benchmarking provides a double benefit: it provides a way to access new ideas and to test or evaluate the implementation challenges they may present in your own organization.

A full list of benchmarking benefits cited by practitioners reaches as high as Everest. Bottom-line summaries almost always suggest that benchmarking does the following:

- Improves organizational quality
- Leads to lower-cost positions
- Creates buy-in for change
- Exposes people to new ideas
- Broadens the organization's operating perspective
- Creates a culture open to new ideas
- Serves as a catalyst for learning
- Increases front-line employees' satisfaction through involvement, empowerment, and a sense of job ownership
- Tests the rigor of internal operating targets
- Overcomes front-line employees' natural disbelief that they can perform better
- Creates an external business view
- Raises the organization's level of maximum potential performance

Finally, benchmarking for best practices generates one more benefit that is arguably the most important of all: it teaches organizations new lessons in competitiveness. "Benchmarking taught the managers how to compete," observed Sam Bookhart, formerly benchmarking manager at E. I. DuPont de Nemours & Company, Inc. "It wasn't just the marketing manager. It was the technical manager and the manufacturing manager and the accounting manager. It taught them how to compete and that resulted in dramatic changes in culture and in improved product and service quality."[6]

In the rough-and-tumble marketplace of the 1990s and beyond, few organizations can afford to ignore these lessons of competitiveness. There's a simple litmus test to determine benchmarking's applicability to your organization. Ask yourself: *Can my organization afford to stop improving? Can my organization afford to stop learning? Can my organization afford to stop competing for its position in the marketplace?* It's difficult to imagine many organizations—public or private, for-profit or nonprofit—that can respond "yes" to these inquiries. Every organization strives to maintain and enhance its position over time. That is the essence of competitiveness. That's also why benchmarking for best practices might also be defined as the art and science of winning through innovative adaptation!

The Whys and Hows of Benchmarks

As in any revolution, confusion often reigns among those engaged in the front lines of change. Many managers puzzle over the difference between benchmarks and benchmarking. The confusion is revealed, for instance, when a sales management team undertakes a "benchmarking" project and then articulates its project goal as identifying sale termination rates. The simple metric or benchmark describing terminated sales may provide a useful reference point against which to compare their unit's sales performance, but the metric alone provides no insight into the root causes of performance differences. Without such knowledge of operating practice differences, this sales management team will find it difficult to spearhead performance improvement. Unwittingly, this team continues to worship at the altar of the old bottom-line management philosophy that studies financial results without regard for what differences in organizational sales processes underlie the differences in sale termination rates. Identifying *benchmarks* takes a team only part-way to its ultimate goal of enhancing performance. In turn, an improvement team will also lose its bearings if it navigates by just studying practice or process differences. Without accompanying benchmarks that contrast the relative performance levels produced by different operating approaches, the team cannot easily evaluate the merits of different practices and systems.

Successful best-practices improvement strategies marry the study of metrics and processes; they unite benchmarks and benchmarking. Consequently, a successful benchmarking team will very early determine the benchmarks—the operating statistics or metrics—by which to evaluate two or more system or operating approaches. One hallmark of a well-designed set of project benchmarks is that they enable measurement and comparisons across systems. Trouble quickly ensues for benchmarking teams that choose esoteric or one-dimensional operating statistics that do not translate well across different organizations and systems. A flexible set of benchmarks reflect full process or system capabilities. Performance indicators may include dimensions such as cost, productivity, cycle time, yields, error rates, waste, and turnover.

Some important lessons emerge from the experiences of active benchmarkers:

1. *Do not strive to benchmark everything at best-in-country or best-in-world levels.* No company can be best in every function. "If you chase too many rabbits," observes a Japanese adage, "you will catch none." Companies that set out to be best in every function—without regard for the function's strategic importance—dilute their resources and their focus.

2. *Seek best-in-class benchmarks for core processes and functions of the highest strategic importance.* World and country leadership benchmarks require greater time, resources, and effort to develop. Apply them to strategic or core processes of businesses that compete daily in national or global markets.

3. *Seek internal, regional, or industry benchmarks for secondary and support processes.* For some processes and business activities that are not critical to the organization's strategic advantage, internal, regional, or competitive benchmarks may be most appropriate.

Benchmarking Critical Success Factors

Successful benchmarking projects bear a triple-A brand: *a*dopt, *a*dapt, and *a*dvance! After searching out and examining highly effective operating practices, experienced benchmarkers adopt the best, adapt them to their own work environments, and advance performance through careful implementation and continuous refinement of the practices. Several critical success factors enable triple-A benchmarking processes. A well-designed performance measurement and benchmark system is essential, of course. Other critical success factors include

- Senior management support
- Benchmarking training for the project team

- Useful information technology systems
- Cultural practices that encourage learning
- Resources, especially in the form of time, funding, and useful equipment

Designing Your Benchmarking Process

Newcomers to the field of benchmarking often puzzle over the great variation among benchmarking processes used at different companies. Some organizations use a four-step benchmarking process while others use a six-step process, seven-step process, eight-step process, or some other variation. The differences are cosmetic. Most companies employ a common approach that helps them plan the project, collect and analyze data, develop insights, and implement improvement actions. However, each company breaks this process into different numbers of steps, depending on how much detail they wish to describe at each step of their template. The best approach reflects common sense: Adopt a benchmarking process that suits an organization's culture and existing quality-improvement initiatives! Successful benchmarkers have found that it is far more important to build upon the managerial foundation and culture in place than to blindly adopt another organization's specific process. One company's effective benchmarking process design may even fail at another organization with different operating concerns. Indeed, organizations that excel in benchmarking almost always customize their own benchmarking process to reflect the organization's culture, infrastructure, and leadership philosophy.

The Simple, Consensus Model

Successful implementation frequently favors simplicity. Consequently, the authors employ for discussion purposes a very simple benchmarking process. One such model, articulated by the members of the Strategic Planning Institute's (SPI) Council on Benchmarking, is a loosely knit confederation of corporate benchmarking managers (see Table 19-1).

The SPI model shown in Table 19-1 represents a user-friendly template for designing your own benchmarking process. It is deliberately articulated in generic terms so that virtually any benchmarking process can be mapped into its five phases.

Table 19-1. The SPI Council on Benchmarking Model

Step	Description
1	Launch
2	Organize
3	Reach out
4	Assimilate
5	Act

The Launch Phase

At the outset, management must decide what improvement opportunity areas have the greatest impact or potential for the organization. This decision where the benchmarking team should set its sights is addressed immediately in the *launch* phase. (Figure 19-2 illustrates the process, purpose, and individual steps that compose the simple five-step benchmarking process.) Frequently benchmarking projects arise when senior executives identify high-level needs during senior management activities. Consider a few examples:

- During the strategic planning process, management must evaluate business factors critical for the organization to sustain its competitive advantage.
- During monthly and yearly operating assessments of core business processes and functions, management identifies opportunities for continuous improvement.
- Current benchmarking projects trigger awareness of additional opportunities.

The Organize Phase

During the second benchmarking phase, the *organize* phase, management organizes the project to ensure a clear project focus. At this time, senior-level managers identify important issues, weaknesses, and improvement opportunities; they prioritize the specific functions or processes to be studied; they obtain approval and support from process owners and stakeholders; and they assign the project to a benchmarking team that usually comprises front-line employees from all functions that help manage the process under study. The team then prepares a benchmarking project plan to serve as a roadmap. A benchmarking plan often includes the following components:

- Statement of purpose
- Justification for the study
- Statement of problem(s) or opportunities to be addressed
- Baseline survey or poll data from those involved in the process or practice
- Relationship of the project to company business priorities and goals
- Proposed benchmark measures
- Statement about benefits of the benchmarking study
- Methodology and scope statement, sketching what level of benchmarking is optimal for the circumstances (internal organizations, competitors, regional companies, industry leaders, functional or best-in-class leaders without regard for industry)
- A resources planning statement, identifying the time, people, and equipment resources needed, as well as estimates of study and implementation costs

The Reach-Out Phase

During the third phase of a benchmarking project, the team reaches out to understand its own and other organizations' processes. During the *reach-out* phase, the team

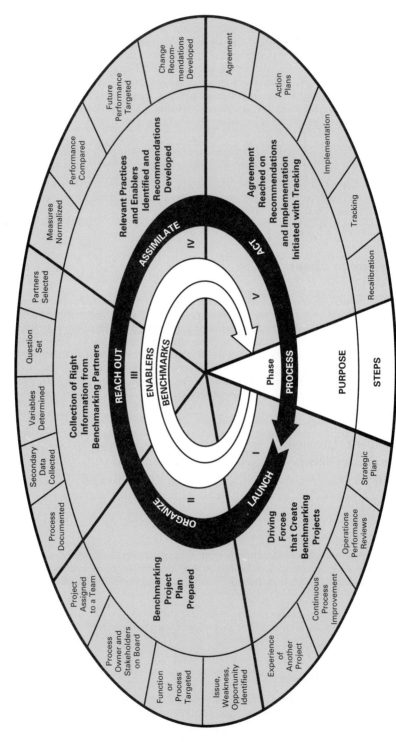

Figure 19-2. Benchmarking process.

- Documents the process to be studied (based on customer needs)
- Collects secondary data
- Determines the variables by which to evaluate performance
- Designs a questionnaire through which to solicit performance information from other organizations
- Conducts telephone interviews and general information gathering
- Selects benchmarking partners
- Conducts on-site visits among the best-performing partners

Understanding the Process. After project formation, team members usually immerse themselves in an intensive effort to operationally understand the process or practice they will benchmark. This immersion process begins with the team's reviewing—or even learning for the first time—about the process or practice area's mission, goals, and objectives and how they fit within the context of the corporate strategic plan. The team then identifies the customers who receive the process's product or output, and the team further defines the customers' needs and requirements for the process.

Next, the team gathers critical performance measures that enable benchmarking team members to evaluate the relative performance excellence of similar processes among different organizations. Finally, by observing, discussing, and chronicling the practice area with the front-line operators or process "owners," the team creates a functional flowchart, often including finely detailed subprocesses, operational boundaries, and hands-off points.

Performing Research. Once the team thoroughly understands the target process, it collects information about prospective benchmark partners and their best practices in the study area. The first line of research on best-practices partners is usually mined from among four primary sources: internal corporate information, public-domain information, information from outside experts, and original research.

Don't underestimate the wealth of information that resides within your own organization. Corporate libraries, databases, competitive reports and published papers, current studies, and market-research analysis are often gold mines of information. The human resource department's list of internal experts, including long-range planners, technical experts, and fellow employees who have worked for other leading organizations, represents a potentially rich information source.

Public-domain information (usually available through local public or university libraries) includes articles published in various journals and periodicals, position papers, business directories, conference proceedings, and company publications such as prospectuses and annual reports. Other external best-practices information sources include trade and professional societies, consultants, industry experts, academics, trade journalists, Wall Street analysts, vendors and service bureaus, and public seminars. Many benchmark teams also conduct original research, including telephone interviews with prospective benchmarking partners; surveys mailed to experts, customers, and suppliers; personal interviews with subject-matter experts; third-party studies; reverse engineering; and, of course, on-site observation.

Recognizing Benchmarking Partners. Answering a few fundamental questions can help the benchmarking team identify those partners whose experiences are likely to be most relevant. Consider the following generic questions that benchmarking teams will want to address before selecting benchmarking partners:

- Is the benchmark partner comparable financially (similar revenues, sales, profits)?
- Is the benchmark partner comparably sized (similar number of employees and market share)?
- Does the partner engage in comparable functions (similar work process, methods, practices)?
- Does the partner have comparable outputs (similar products and services)?
- Does the partner have comparable requirements (similar customer expectations)?
- Does the partner have comparable logistics (similar set-up and work flows)?
- Does the benchmark partner have comparable inputs (suppliers and ingredients)?
- Is the benchmark partner part of a comparable industry (similar products and markets)?
- Does the partner have comparable organizational and divisional structures?
- Is the partner part of a comparable market sector (public, private, governmental)?

Reach Out.   After the benchmarking team organizes completely, a smaller subteam often visits a few select benchmarking partners to collect on-site information and view operations. Frequently this detailed, on-site review helps the benchmarking team learn what specific practices and operating principles enable the partner to achieve its superior performance.

Conducting Site Visits.   To gather more detailed information than that developed in telephone interviews or surveys, many companies conduct site visits. The most interesting and credible method of gathering information, the site visit, affords firsthand feedback. Site visits also often result in long-term relationships that foster an ongoing exchange of information between benchmarking partners. When compared with surveys and telephone interviews, site visits are the most time-consuming and expensive means of information gathering due to the travel required. However, they produce the highest-quality information because companies view work processes, methods, and practices in action. The following guidelines can help your site-visit teams be more effective:

Collect and absorb information about the partner before the visit.

Prepare a question set in advance to guide and structure your team's visit.

Prepare the benchmarking partner for your team's visit.

Use a questionnaire to structure your site visit and discussions.

Travel in pairs or small groups during the site tour.

Arrange for follow-up conversations should there be additional questions.

Conduct a postsession debriefing to discuss the team's observations and ideas.

Prepare a trip report summarizing site-visit findings and conclusions.

Send a thank-you note and confirm the accuracy of site-visit notes describing the benchmark partner's operations.

The Assimilate Phase

During the fourth phase, the benchmarking team assimilates the best-practices information it has developed and prepares this information and corresponding improvement recommendations for senior management's review. During the assimilation phase, the team normalizes any measures that may still be in different reporting formats, studies and highlights performance gaps produced by different operating approaches, targets future performance goals, and develops change recommendations. The outcome of the assimilation phase is a best-practices report.

The Act Phase

During the fifth and final benchmarking phase, the team works with management and the process owners to prioritize recommendations and agree on an implementation strategy. Agreement leads to formalization of action plans, implementation schedules, measurement and tracking mechanisms, and recalibration plans. When the action plans are completed, ongoing responsibility for managing the improvement efforts often shifts to an implementation team. The benchmarking team still supports the implementation team by helping to establish tracking mechanisms and develop process standards, cycle-time measures, quality measures, and statistical control charting. Over time, the process of system is continuously fine-tuned and improved. Meanwhile, the organization must eventually recalibrate its benchmarks based on the newly established best practices.

A Call to Action

The call to action for the successful twenty-first century organization is a call to make best-practices performance improvement a cornerstone of the organization's approach to conducting business. Best-practices performance improvement is much more than just a business tool. For the twenty-first-century organization, it represents a fundamental approach to competing and managing. The best-practices strategy complements traditional continuous-improvement efforts. The best-practices strategy sets out to leverage the learning and experience of the best, rather than merely reforming the practices of the worst, which has been the traditional path of performance improvement. The best-practices approach is behaviorally powerful and compelling. It concentrates on performance improvement through organizational learning, effective management of intellectual assets, and leverage of others' proven experience.

In the twenty-first century, the effective use of intellectual capital will increasingly become a prerequisite of marketplace success—perhaps even of survival. Successful organizations will therefore employ best-practices benchmarking as a primary catalyst of fast learning; best-practices benchmarking will be regarded as a power tool for leveraging internal and external experience. In the future, return on intellectual assets will be equally as important a performance indicator as return on physical assets. In this new era which is dawning, best-practices benchmarking will be the long-handled level of the knowledge age. It will be a primary instrument helping the twenty-first century organization achieve the full benefits of intellectual leverage: By creatively adapting the best proven ideas, practices, and approaches of others, an organization can leverage their partners' people, knowledge, resources, and experience with very little capital investment.

Innovative adaptation creates a compounding effect on the internal rate of improvement; it produces a high-yield knowledge dividend. Consequently, best-practices benchmarking represents the ultimate competitive weapon: a low-investment organizationwide renewable resource that produces rapid learning and performance improvement by leveraging others' learning and most effective practices. Unleashed in a global marketplace, this approach to management and continuous improvement promises rich returns. And that is why, for so many organizations throughout the world, the best-practices revolution has just begun.

References

1. "Jack Welch's Lessons for Success," *Fortune,* January 25, 1993, pp. 86–93.
2. Tichy, Noel M., and Stratford Sherman, *Control Your Destiny or Someone Else Will,* Double-day, New York, 1993, p. 37.
3. Biesada, Alexandra, "Strategic Benchmarking," *Financial World,* September 29, 1992, p. 30.
4. Kuebler, Al, "The Quest for Excellence 5," annual conference of Baldrige Award winners, AT&T Universal Card Services presentation, February 15–17, 1993.
5. Sherman, Stratford, "The New Computer Revolution," *Fortune,* June 14, 1993, p. 60.
6. Bookhart, Samuel, "Benchmarking: A Powerful Management Tool," a speech made at the "Benchmarking Against the Best" conference sponsored by the International Research Institute, June 13, 1991.

SECTION 3

Media and Methods

20

Coaching for Growth and Development

Madeline F. Finnerty

Madeline F. Finnerty is president of Finnerty International, a consulting practice specializing in organization development. Her clients include manufacturing and service industries and public-sector organizations in the United States and New Zealand. Formerly, she was General Employee Involvement Manager with Sprint United Telephone Company, responsible for implementing a Total Quality Management process in Ohio and Indiana. She has also worked for the National Exchange Carrier Association, Inc., and New England Telephone Company. Her experience includes training, organization development, and employee involvement as well as operations management. In the ASTD, Finnerty has been a member of the National Nominating Committee and the Quality Symposia Advisory Committee. She is the recipient of the Women's Network Professional Leadership Award and the 1990 Distinguished Contribution to Employer/Client Award. Finnerty is also past national director of the ASTD Women's Network and past member of the Multi-cultural Network Executive Committee. A frequent public speaker, Finnerty has presented at ASTD National Conferences, the AQP National Conference, and the ASTD Quality Symposia. Her education includes a B.A. cum laude from Newton College of the Sacred Heart and an M.B.A. from Ashland University. She is pursuing a Ph.D. from the Fielding Institute in human and organization development. In 1988, she traveled as a People-to-People Delegate to the People's Republic of China and Hong Kong. She has also traveled extensively in Europe, Asia, and the South Pacific.

We are all familiar with the concept of coaching from our experiences as participants or observers of athletic events. The coach is the person who is able to inspire and direct athletes to their peak performance. However, the concept of coaching in the workplace is one which is undergoing a profound change. In traditional industrial-era organizations, coaching was the enlightened approach we took to correct deficient performance. It was an alternative to punitive discipline. Coaching was one of many management tools sitting in the kit, waiting to be selected for an appropriate application. Today, the information age has brought a rapidly changing business environment. The direction in which it is heading (see Fig. 20-1)[1] is clearly toward coaching, not only as a tool, but as a basic management role.

This chapter is designed to provide a broad understanding of coaching as a skill for helping others grow and develop in the workplace. For a manager or trainer thinking about doing a program on coaching, there are specific ideas for developing skills and knowledge and a step-by-step process for coaching. The introduction helps clarify why one would develop such a training program (the objective). Counseling for problem behavior, including difficult situations and consequences, is addressed in this chapter. Because being a coach requires good self-management skills, this chapter includes a self-inventory for coaches and talks about control and ego. A section focuses on the logistics of coaching: who coaches, when to coach, and where to coach (time and place). Finally, the chapter includes information on specific coaching relationships such as mentoring, peer coaching, and executive coaching. Throughout the chapter, a number of useful illustrations and references to resources provide additional information about coaching from a variety of different perspectives.

What Is Coaching?

The definitions of coaching reflect the varied interpretations of the role. Any of the following definitions, for example, are appropriate:

> The face-to-face process…to redirect a subordinate's behavior to solve a performance problem: to get the subordinate to stop doing what he shouldn't be doing or to start doing what he should be doing.[2]

> Face-to-face leadership that pulls together people with diverse backgrounds, talents, experiences and interests, encourages them to step up to responsibility and continued achievement, and treats them as full-scale partners and contributors.[3]

> Coaching is the ongoing guidance and instruction, used on a daily basis by a manager, to improve work performance and build competency.[4]

> Coaching is the process by which one individual, the coach, creates enabling relationships with others that make it easier for them to learn. The coach helps other people set and achieve performance goals at levels higher than those at which they are currently performing.[5]

> Coaching refers to the management activity that creates, by communication alone, the climate, environment and context that empowers individuals and teams to generate results. The root meaning of the verb "to coach" is "to convey a valued person from where he or she is to where he or she wants to be."[6]

The important thing is to be clear about how you define coaching. If you are planning to improve your own coaching skills or those of your employees, know

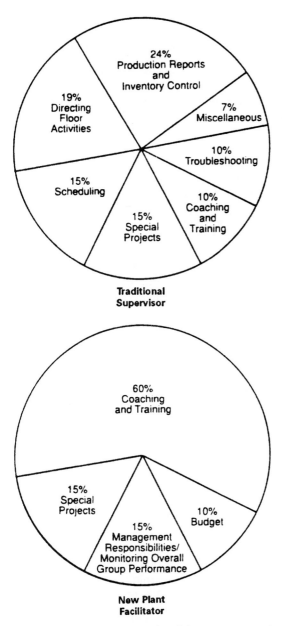

Figure 20-1. Changing role of the supervisor at
Bectin, Dickinson and Company.[1]

what you see as the scope of the "coach" role. If you are developing training for your organization, be sure you understand what your customers expect. If you create a wonderful program geared to teach managers how to hold coaching discussions with employees who are not performing and your organization has been looking for skills in a self-directed work-team environment, there will be a mismatch. Understand what you mean by coaching and clarify what your audience means by coaching. As the definition expands, and evolves, there is a potential for different interpretations.

Why Is Coaching Important?

The changes that have brought about a need for expert coaching skills are connected to the shift from the paradigms of the industrial era to the paradigms of the information age. We are seeing an all-encompassing revolution in the way businesses are managed. Supporting the need for managers to coach are macro-level changes brought about by global competition and technology (see Fig. 20-2). In the industrial era, businesses hired employees for their hands. Today, organizations must have the capacity to learn quickly to respond to the demands created by global competition and rapid changes in technology. This requires using the minds of employees. Coaching is the management skill that enables organizations to engage the minds of employees.

Imagine a football play where the defensive tackle lost his footing and created a different situation than the offense had anticipated. Do you think the players' manual would tell the ball carrier how to respond? Would the coach say, "Hold it! Stop right there. Let me tell my players what to do?" Of course not. Yet managers have been expected to direct every aspect of employee behavior. When the assembly line has "lost its footing" or a customer has had a problem, either the manager has intervened to make a decision or a manual has told employees what to do. Management systems built for efficiency and control have not expected or invited employee participation in decision making. Coaches, on the other hand, expect players to think. To meet the demand for high-quality and innovative products, delivered quickly and with excellent service, we need a management system that asks and trusts employees to think and solve problems "on the field." We need coaches.

Technology

Technology creates a demand for managers who can coach in two respects. The first relates to the rapid pace of technological change that creates an environment where employees are constantly faced with new learning. Managers can help employees successfully master new tools, programs, or work processes by providing performance observation and feedback. A greater part of the manager's role will be to coach for new learning. Additionally, many jobs today require greater competence because of the more complex technology involved. Employees need training and coaching to develop the skills to meet these higher demands. In another respect, technology has redefined the manager's job by automating many traditional managerial functions. Processes such as control, analysis, oversight, and coordination are now done by computers, making redundant the need for a manager to engage in such tasks. This innovation does not, in itself, redefine the manager's job as coach. However, it creates the need to rethink the manager's role.

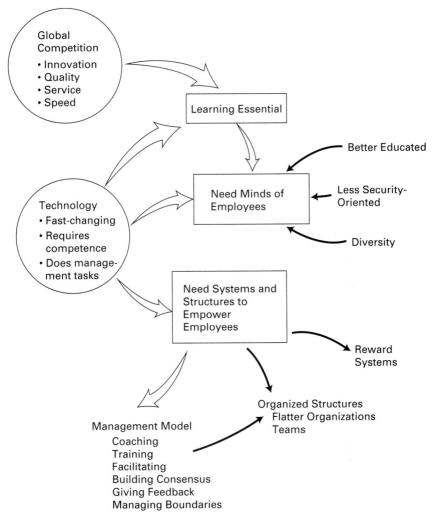

Figure 20-2. Factors effecting the shift to coaching as a key management role.[2]
(*Copyright 1995 by Finnerty International. All rights reserved.*)

Workforce

Managers today are confronted with a workforce that is more responsive to being coached than being controlled. Although employees may lack technological competence, they are better educated as a group. Participating in problem solving and decision making, using their heads to provide service and improve quality, is a reasonable expectation for them. Employees today are less security-oriented than those who lived through the depression and world wars. In "Employee Coaching: The Way to Gain Commitment, Not Just Compliance," Frankel and Otazo[7] propose that "today's workers feel that in exchange for coming to work, they should be stimulated, challenged and recognized for their efforts."

Diversity

Diversity is another characteristic of the workforce that dictates the need for good coaching skills. Understanding different needs and motivations of employees is essential to creating an environment that enables performance improvement. With the increase of women and nonwhite men in our organizations, all managers have to be skillful in detecting behaviors that stem from cultural differences. Working with people who have disabilities presents another opportunity to broaden one's ability to understand differences among coworkers and create an enabling environment. Coaching skills involve attentiveness to personal differences which are then incorporated into the success of the team.

How to Coach

Coaching in the narrowest sense is the process of helping a single employee improve a particular aspect of his or her performance. In the broadest sense it is the management role associated with high-performance teams. As such, it extends to training, facilitating, consensus building, conflict resolution, and boundary management. The skills, knowledge, and steps described here apply to the coach who deals with an individual learning the job for the first time or trying to improve a weakness. They also apply to the coach who works with a team to improve performance or reach a new goal. However, the scope does not encompass other functions that may be associated with the new management role called "coach."

Coaching Skills

To be a successful coach, managers, team leaders, or peers need several basic skills. As one coaching definition states, "Coaching is the management activity that creates, by communication alone, the environment...."[8] *Communication* skill is absolutely essential. As one is collecting data about performance in order to reflect and recommend changes, *listening* skills and *observation* skills come into play. The coach must then use *analyzing* skills to assess what the problem might be and what might correct it. Then comes the art of *giving feedback*. Finally, in the discussion about what the coach has observed and what the employee wants or needs come the *negotiation* skills. Together these skills are essential for coaching.

Coaching Knowledge

The coach must also have knowledge to assist the employee in achieving results. Expert knowledge of the task enables the coach to describe and demonstrate the desired behavior and to observe the employee performing the task and give feedback. Few athletic coaches would succeed if they were not intimately familiar with their game, from the basic movements of each player to the complex plays of the team of players. Similarly, the manager who coaches understands what is expected of each employee and is able to communicate that expectation.

Adult Learning Theory. To develop employees effectively, the coach should understand basic ideas from adult learning theory. In *Developing High-Performance People: The Art of Coaching*, Mink, Owen, and Mink devote an entire chapter to "Understanding How People Learn and Grow." They cite six factors which Brookfield (1986) identified as influencing adult learning:

1. More learning takes place if learning is seen as voluntary, self-initiated activity.

2. More learning takes place in a climate of mutual respect.

3. The best learning takes place in an environment characterized by a spirit of collaboration.

4. Learning involves a balance between action and self-reflection.

5. Effective coaching involves facilitation of critical reflection.

6. People learn best when their learning is self-directed.[9]

Another excellent reference in this area is *The Adult Learner: A Neglected Species* by Malcolm Knowles (1984). (See Chap. 12, Adult Learning.) Adult learning theory provides assumptions that have been proven to contribute to successful coaching, but the important thing is for the coach to be aware of his or her own assumptions about how employees learn. The inventory from *Developing High-Performance People: The Art of Coaching* (see Fig. 20-3) offers one way to assess your assumptions about adult learning.[10]

Motivation Theory. Familiarity with motivation theory is another useful knowledge area for coaches. Abraham Maslow's needs hierarchy proposes that people have varying levels of needs and must satisfy the more basic needs for food, shelter, safety, and belonging before they can focus on self-esteem and growth. Fournies[11] argues that trying to determine what needs level is motivating an employee places coaches in the role of amateur psychologist. It is valuable for coaches to know, however, that "when an environment enables people to meet their needs for esteem (competence, power, purpose, uniqueness) and growth (actualization through creative accomplishment), people become connected to that environment."[12] Creating the right environment can build commitment.

In *Coaching for Improved Work Performance,* Fournies[13] also discusses the motivation theories of McGregor and Herzberg. McGregor[14] classified management approaches as Theory X and Theory Y (see Fig. 20-4) and theorized about the outcomes of the two styles. Fournies suggests that the important knowledge for coaches is realizing that we treat employees according to what we believe about employees. The section on "Managing Self as Coach" (below) discusses this in greater detail. Frederick Herzberg looked at factors which satisfy or dissatisfy workers. He learned that the absence of a dissatisfier such as low pay or dirty working conditions does not create a satisfier or motivator. According to Herzberg (1966), the top two motivators for employees are achievement and recognition. Coaches understand the need for employees to achieve and provide them with knowledge about the task, observations, and feedback to help them achieve. Coaches also recognize the need for recognition and offer frequent praise. *The One Minute Manager* by Ken Blanchard (1982) offers one formula for effectively praising employees.

Steps for Coaching

Preparation for coaching a single employee or a team involves work related to the task and work related to the people. The coach must define the goals he or she hopes to lead the employees to achieve. The goals should be clarified in terms

Purpose

This exercise develops increased understanding of your assumptions about learning and how these assumptions affect your coaching.

Directions

Respond to each of the following statements by circling the number that most accurately explains your assumptions about learning and the learner. Use the following scale to describe your specific beliefs:

1	2	3	4	5	6	7	8	9
Never		Occasionally		Frequently		Often		Always

1 2 3 4 5 6 7 8 9	1. I believe all learners are different.
1 2 3 4 5 6 7 8 9	2. I believe that given enough time and proper instruction, learners can learn anything.
1 2 3 4 5 6 7 8 9	3. I give my learners opportunities for frequent practice.
1 2 3 4 5 6 7 8 9	4. I break instruction down into reasonable steps.
1 2 3 4 5 6 7 8 9	5. When I coach, I give clear instructions.
1 2 3 4 5 6 7 8 9	6. The pace of learning is determined by the learner.
1 2 3 4 5 6 7 8 9	7. The learner progresses to new material when she has mastered a particular step.
1 2 3 4 5 6 7 8 9	8. I explain carefully how the associate's job fits into the rest of the organization.
1 2 3 4 5 6 7 8 9	9. I provide many incentives for learning.
1 2 3 4 5 6 7 8 9	10. I influence the learning environment.
1 2 3 4 5 6 7 8 9	11. I make the learning experience enjoyable.
1 2 3 4 5 6 7 8 9	12. I get to know the learner.
1 2 3 4 5 6 7 8 9	13. I enjoy coaching.
1 2 3 4 5 6 7 8 9	14. I enjoy people.
1 2 3 4 5 6 7 8 9	15. I believe people like to learn.

The ideal response for each of these statements would have been a "9." You may recognize this to be true but may have honestly and appropriately rated yourself lower on many of the statements. If that is the case, then rewrite the statements so that you could honestly respond with a 9. What are your assumptions about learning and the learner?

Figure 20-3. Assumptions about learning and learners.[10]

Theory X	Theory Y
Most people are lazy.	People like to work.
Most people need to be controlled.	People have self-control.
Most people need to be motivated.	People motivate themselves.
Most people are not very smart.	People are smart.
Most people need encouragement to do good work.	People want to do a good job.

Source: Adapted from the work of Douglas McGregor, especially *The Human Side of Enterprise* (New York: McGraw-Hill, 1960).

Figure 20-4. Differences in management assumptions.[14]

of what (knowledge), how (skills), and why (value). The coach may also want to identify any resources for learning and improvement that will be necessary for the employees to utilize. The second part of preparation involves observation and analysis. The coach collects data about the current competencies and performances of the employees. In addition, the coach analyzes the environment for factors which influence employees' performance. Coaching is not the answer, for example, if performance is hindered by malfunctioning equipment.

Fournies has developed a precoaching analysis format that also considers the possibility of negative consequences for performance or positive consequences for nonperformance.[15] For example, is an employee who consistently performs well rewarded with extra work? Again, these are problems in the system that will not be fixed by coaching.

Equipped with clear goals and a thorough analysis of the situation, coaches develop a plan. In setting expectations, the coach sets high standards and, at the same time, is realistic about what he or she believes the employees can achieve. A schedule for the coaching process will include initial meetings, ongoing observations, and feedback. Coaching is a process that takes place over time.

Meeting with the individual or team, the coach lays out the learning goals. Relating the goals to feedback about existing performance helps establish a need to learn. For some tasks, basic training methodology is used: tell them, show them, and let them do it while you observe and give feedback. It is useful to stress the key points of the learning. Where the task is more complex, like solving a quality problem, the coach uses questions as a way of helping the team or individual explore possibilities. The Socratic method, asking questions, is an essential coaching strategy. (See the section on Counseling.) In addition, it is useful to explain the boundaries that go with the performance being learned or improved. For example, boundaries might include what resources will be available and what level of responsibility and decision making a team can exercise.

As with any new skill, practice is key to mastery. Coaches need to observe practice and performance regularly. Imagine a coach who instructs her basketball team for the first few practices and then retreats to her office to await the results of the game. Upon reading of the team's loss in the newspaper, she calls the team in for a "coaching" session and tells the team, "You came in third. What happened? Try harder!" The value of coaches is that they are constantly providing new information to their players. Observations about an employee's performance coupled with analysis based on the coach's expertise creates valuable information. This helps the employee clarify what is right about her performance and what needs to change. In addition to giving feedback while improvement is in progress, the coach conducts periodic follow-up to maintain the goals achieved.

There are many variations on the steps in the coaching process, but all follow a similar format. The steps include:

- Define performance goals.
- Identify necessary resources for success.
- Observe and analyze current performance.
- Set expectations for performance improvement.
- Plan a coaching schedule.
- Meet with the individual or team to get commitment to goals, demonstrate the desired behavior, and establish boundaries.
- Give feedback on practice and performance.
- Follow up to maintain goals.

Counseling

Counseling is a particular type of coaching that helps individuals evaluate their current behavior and discover and learn more productive behavior patterns. Employee performance can fall short of expectations for any number of reasons. As more organizations attend to quality, Deming's principles (Deming, 1986) help us see that the root cause of performance problems often lies within the system, not the employee. Is there a negative consequence, a missing resource, a lack of training, a time constraint that is preventing optimal performance? Coaching starts with identification of the problem and may require spending more time in the work setting to find out what is really happening. Once the manager is sure that the employee needs to be coached, the coaching process can be initiated.

Steps for Counseling

The face-to-face coaching session includes several steps. Identifying the problem behavior—what is not being done or what is being done that shouldn't be?—is the starting point. Get agreement from employees that a problem does exist based on the consequences of the existing behavior. In environments where there is limited feedback or cultural differences, employees may not know or believe that there is a problem. The coach can help them see the problem by drawing the connection between the behavior and the negative consequences. Using a Socratic method of asking leading questions can be very effective in getting an employee to admit that there is a problem. For example, if an associate were 20 minutes late today, the coach might ask, "How do you think your tardiness affects getting the job done? And what happens then? How do you think the rest of the team feels about your being late? What do you think that makes them do?"

Once you have agreement that there is a problem, help the employee figure out how to solve it. The coach needs to be clear about expectations but does not have to suggest the solution. The coach can question the employee in a way that leads to solutions. For example, perhaps an undependable automobile is the reason for tardiness. The coach might ask, "How else could you arrange to get to work? Could you fix the car to make it dependable? How? What would it take? When? How else can you get to work in the meantime?" Then, develop an improvement plan and gain commitment to the plan. If the employee has helped develop the solution, then he or she has a vested interest in the plan.

As with all coaching, feedback is essential. Any improvement, for example, being tardy by 5 minutes instead of 15, should be praised. The coach then expects continued improvement until the goal is reached. Attempts to improve which fall short are part of learning. When we are criticized for failing, we find it hard to continue. Coaches are willing to tolerate the time it takes to reach the desired goal. They observe and report on progress so that their employees know what they are doing right and where to correct behavior. They do not give criticism which simply judges the employee's behavior as succeeding or failing. Rather, they give true feedback: information that can be used to continue learning. Once the employee has met the target performance, periodic follow-up helps.

Consequences

The objective of counseling is a win-win situation where the employee achieves the desired performance. The intent is not to discipline or terminate. However, it is important during the coaching discussion to be clear about natural consequences of continuing the substandard behavior. Should a coach intervene and protect the employee from failure? One possible model for dealing with excuses comes from *Developing High-Performance People: The Art of Coaching:*

1. Did your associate fail? If you answer no, congratulate your associate for her success. If you answer yes, go to the next step.

2. Was your associate's failure due to a lack of attempting to carry out the steps in the plan? If you answer yes, find out what your associate wants and recommit to the plan. If you answer no, go on to the next step.

3. Was your associate's failure because the plan was too difficult? If you answer yes, simplify the plan by reworking the steps in the plan. If you answer no, go to the next step.

4. Be careful to discriminate clearly between circumstances that are clearly beyond a person's control and those that are not. Was your associate's failure due to circumstances beyond her control? If you answer yes, redesign the plan. If you answer no, go to the next step.

5. Was your associate's failure due to inability to perform? If you answer yes, teach the individual. If you answer no, allow the natural consequences to take place.[16]

The benefit of using the coaching process in this way is that it unhooks the emotion of having to deliver discipline to an employee who chooses not to perform. Each employee understands in advance what the consequences are and makes his or her own choice. As the manager-coach, you can wish the outcome were otherwise, but you don't have to own the guilt of having created it. The responsibility for the choice lies squarely with the employee.

Difficult Situations

Occasionally, we are faced with an employee who carries serious "battle scars" from previous experiences in life. In these situations it is particularly important to remember to deal with performance from the perspective of what behavior we see and what behavior we want to see. Coaches should not accuse or even suggest a problem they are not trained to diagnose. For example, we may suspect that a person is an alcoholic after repeated morning absences due to incidental illness or alcohol on the breath after lunch. What the coach can safely deal with is the resulting behavior, that is, "Your incidental absence is unacceptable. It makes it difficult for the department to meet schedules. What can we do about it?" Implying that the person is an alcoholic is inappropriate. This can place the coach at legal risk for damaging a person's reputation. Stick to the observed job performance and coach for an improvement in that area.

If coaching fails, there may be alternatives to termination, depending upon the organization. Some companies have employee assistance programs that can intervene. In other cases, the human resources department may have a way to provide assistance. Some performance problems involve temporary situations which the employee can master over time, like a divorce or financial crisis. Others are more serious long-term problems. The Mink, Owen, and Mink chapter "Coping with Failure"[17] offers more ideas for coaching people who have failed, including the healing process, forgiveness, letting go, and self-renewal. Good coaching is able to inspire many employees to satisfactory or exceptional performance. However, in rare cases, the counseling a person needs far exceeds the ability of a coach.

Training Coaches

As with any other training, coaching should begin with a needs assessment. Identify the knowledge and skills a coach should exhibit. This chapter offers one set of options. Numerous books and articles offer other variations. Assess potential students to determine their starting level of competence. As mentioned at the beginning of the chapter, there are many definitions of coaching and the role is evolving to fit the information age. It is not as critical that you select the "right" approach to coaching as it is that you select the model that fits where your organization is now or wants to be in the immediate future. What do you want people to be able to do and what are they capable of doing now?

Coaches need to have a knowledge of themselves, assumptions about people, ability to construct productive relationships with people, and a life which models their beliefs. Training can provide self-assessment tools to clarify student's beliefs about those they coach and feedback instruments to assist them with evaluating how well they model their beliefs. Many organizations today employ tools to solicit 360-degree feedback for managers from their employees, their peers, their supervisors, and their internal customers. A "Coach-the-Coach" Survey (see Fig. 20-5) developed by Frankel[18] is one example of such a feedback form. Accepting feedback ourselves models our belief in the positive value of being coached.

Methods

Because coaching is a behavior, training for coaching should provide ample experiential opportunities. The what and why may be delivered through short lectures and interactive discussions. You can also use the Socratic method to deliver knowledge and skills about coaching. Ask the students what they know and fill in the gaps. They could also be assigned research on coaching. Since coaching is a facilitating skill and requires an understanding of adult learning, these less traditional approaches more closely model the skills to be learned. In other words, the students are being coached to learn about coaching rather than being told pedagogically. The how of coaching clearly should be demonstrated and practiced. Role-plays, case studies, and simulations provide lessons in applying coaching skills.

Resources

Numerous training programs are on the market that teach coaching skills. Some are available for in-house trainers to use; others come with an instructor. Books, resource materials, and numerous periodicals describe coaching for those who want to create their own program. ASTD, located in Alexandria, Virginia, is an excellent resource for training materials. Again, evaluate the materials you plan to use for a match with your organization's needs and values. Some programs reflect the traditional industrial-era organization. Others are very much oriented to a self-directed, team-based environment.

Dealing with Resistance

If you are training managers to coach as part of their new role in a redesigned, information-age organization, expect resistance. Remember, many traditional

The person giving you this form is interested in knowing how well he or she is succeeding with coaching you toward your best performance. Please answer the questions below as candidly as possible using the scale provided.

Scale: 1 = Does a good job of this or does this to a satisfactory degree for me.
2 = Doesn't do enough of this or could do more of this for me.
3 = Does this too much or could do less of this for me.

——— 1. Lets me know on a regular, informal basis how I'm doing.
——— 2. Gives me immediate feedback on my performance, both positive and negative.
——— 3. Doesn't just tell me to change, but helps me to understand how to achieve required performance changes to improve my competence.
——— 4. Talks to me about my career goals.
——— 5. Shows genuine interest in me as a human being, not just a worker.
——— 6. Makes me feel comfortable speaking about personal problems that may impact my work.
——— 7. Doesn't hesitate to tell me when I'm doing something that could negatively impact my career.
——— 8. Treats me fairly.
——— 9. Treats me with respect.
——— 10. Helps me and my coworkers to function as a team, not just a group of individuals.
——— 11. Shows that he or she has my best interest at heart even when we may not agree.
——— 12. Doesn't use his or her authority to get me to achieve my goals, but rather talks things through with me.
——— 13. Helps me to set clear goals for myself.
——— 14. Helps me to understand how my work fits into the overall goals of the department.
——— 15. Treats me according to how I want to be treated.
——— 16. Doesn't try to control how I do my work—lets me accomplish my tasks as I see best.
——— 17. Listens to me about my feelings, ideas, and concerns.
——— 18. Knows what really motivates me to do my best work.
——— 19. Provides me with adequate training and/or developmental opportunities.
——— 20. Models the same behavior he or she expects from me.

What one thing would you like to see this person do more of that would help you to achieve your personal best at work? _____

While you do not have to sign this, you may do so if you wish in order to help this person better understand what you need from him or her.

Figure 20-5. Coach-the-Coach Feedback Form.

managers believe that command and control is their divine right. Halson's "Teaching Supervisors to Coach" suggests that "those who have been performing satisfactorily for many years may need substantial encouragement to accept that they still have something to learn. Being 'sent' on a course may well imply criticism, which can itself create resistance to learning."[19] Additionally, where teams of employees will be taking over many of the supervisory duties, managers are unclear about the coaching role and feel that their status is threatened. Geber's "From Manager into Coach" cites several examples of managers feeling less important in their new roles as coach. Comments such as "What am I going to tell my mother?" (from a middle manager without a college degree) belie a loss of self-esteem with the transition from manager to coach. As one training manager observed, "A lot of them felt they weren't as important as in the past. They'd earned their stripes and all of a sudden we were taking their leadership role away. Their career path seemed broken."[20] Recognize that training for managers who are becoming full-time coaches should be structured to address these emotional issues. Students will be unable to focus on coaching skills until they have vented their personal fears and concerns.

Managing Self as Coach

Being a good coach requires a certain amount of self-knowledge and self-management. In *Developing High-Performance People: The Art of Coaching,* coaching effectiveness is seen as a combination of skills, values, and job knowledge. Perhaps the most critical component, and the one most often overlooked, is values.[21] To be a good coach, a manager needs to understand his or her values about people and work. Many of us still operate in organizations where "authority typically means the ability to command and control subordinates and to make all the tough decisions...sometimes called the 'divine right of managers.'"[22] It is easy to be influenced by institutional values. However, when managers seek to empower employees to make decisions, problem-solve, and participate on teams, this authoritarian style is ineffective. If managers believe they have to be in command in order to be perceived as effective they are not likely to succeed as coaches. Take the time to assess your beliefs.

Doing a Self-Inventory

Douglas McGregor developed the classifications of Theory X and Theory Y management style. These styles are based on two different sets of assumptions about human nature. Ferdinand Fournies states, "The most important conclusion that can be drawn from McGregor's concept of Theory X versus Theory Y is not about workers, but about managers: MANAGERS DO WHAT THEY DO FOR OR TO WORKERS BECAUSE OF WHAT THEY BELIEVE ABOUT WORKERS."[23] Understanding what you believe about workers is key to becoming a successful coach. One quick check for values that makes for effective coaching is McGregor's theory (see Fig. 20-4). Another coaching inventory, developed by Frankel and Otazo[24] (see Fig. 20-6), looks for coaching behaviors that reflect a combination of skill and values. Any survey which asks one to reflect on values about people and work will serve to create awareness and focus personal growth as a coach.

Giving Up Control

The new roles of management, the ones referred to as "coach," include the ability to delegate, facilitate, resolve conflicts, and encourage consensus decision making. Many of these skills require that we challenge our own assumptions about control, caretaking, and learning. "The boss thinks he's there to make decisions—all the decisions," writes Tom Brown in "Boss—Or Coach?"[25] Coaches know that their teams are capable of decision making, particularly if the boundaries are clearly defined. "The boss likes to keep people in the dark" and "sees himself as a solitary guardian of the key departmental numbers," he says. Coaches, on the other hand, share information generously. What are your assumptions about controlling decisions and information? Many managers fear letting go because employees might make a mistake. Do you see a mistake as

Scale: 1 = To a Great Extent
             2 = To a Fairly High Extent
             3 = To Somewhat of an Extent
             4 = To a Small Extent

To what extent do you:

_____ 1. Ask others for feedback about how your behavior impacts them?
_____ 2. Know how others describe you?
_____ 3. Read books or attend programs which focus on your interpersonal skills vs. your technical skills?
_____ 4. Feel comfortable with receiving feedback about your performance or behavior?
_____ 5. Take the time to think about how you could be a better model for your employees?
_____ 6. Feel confident about your ability to coach employees?
_____ 7. Think that you can articulate your strengths and weaknesses?
_____ 8. Exhibit the same behaviors as you expect from your employees?
_____ 9. Feel comfortable admitting to your employees that you've made a mistake?
_____ 10. Feel comfortable talking about your feelings as opposed to your ideas?
_____ 11. Recognize how others feel, as opposed to think, about things?
_____ 12. Feel comfortable dealing with people who disagree with you?
_____ 13. Believe that you are as capable, if not more capable, than the next person?
_____ 14. Feel comfortable interacting with people at work on a personal or social level?
_____ 15. Take time to assure that the method used to achieve the end product is considered as carefully as the product itself?
_____ 16. Think that you could accurately write your own performance review from your boss's perspective?
_____ 17. Believe that the behavior of others may be a reaction to your behavior?
_____ 18. Take time during your work day to reflect on your actions and their impact on others?
_____ 19. Objectively observe and assess your own behavior?
_____ 20. Admit personal mistakes, learn from them, and correct them?

If you score between:

    20–40   You're in good shape! Continue your exercise program as you have to date.
    41–60   You're in training; Stretch yourself in those areas that you currently have some discomfort in order to achieve *your* personal best.
    61–80   You're out of shape, coach. Gradually begin exercising in those areas that you feel most comfortable and begin to build your stamina for coaching.

Figure 20-6. Getting in Shape for Coaching Inventory.

evidence of attempted learning with feedback, an opportunity (the Japanese view) for problem solving or improvement? Or does your organization see mistakes as something to cover up or blame on someone else? To be a successful coach, you have to realize that you don't play the game, your team does. Your job is to "review the game films" and look for as many errors as you can find because that is where the improvement will come.

Managers often act as a parent to their employee child, trying to prevent the child from making mistakes. Peter Block explores the shift from patriarchy to partnership in his book *Stewardship*. He writes, "Dependency rests on the belief that there are people in power who know what is best for others, including ourselves. We think the task of these leaders is to create an environment where we can live a life of safety and predictability."[26] Letting go of the need to be the leader who provides this safety and predictability for others is essential for coaches. Caring, but not caretaking, is key to empowering others to take risks, try new things, learn, and grow.

Setting Ego Aside

Successful coaches have a quality of humility. Max DePree in *Leadership Jazz* speaks of leaders being vulnerable. "Vulnerable leaders," he says, "trust in the abilities of other people; vulnerable leaders allow the people who follow them to do their best. An invulnerable leader can be only as good as her performance—what a terrifying thought!"[27] This is not an easy concept for managers to practice when we have been schooled in institutions that value being in control and being right. As Robert Haas, CEO of Levi Strauss, put it, "It had been difficult for me to accept the fact that I don't have to be the smartest guy on the block....In reality, the more you establish parameters and encourage people to take initiatives within these boundaries, the more you multiply your own effectiveness by the effectiveness of other people"[28] Consider your tolerance for being vulnerable and the effect that has on your ability to coach.

Who Coaches?

When we think in terms of coaching in the workplace, we normally think in terms of a supervisor coaching a directly reporting employee. Others who coach include mentors, hired coaches for executives, and the relatively new phenomenon of peer coaches. Occasionally, employees coach the boss.

Today, with an increasing number of team-based organizations, there are likely to be a greater variety of coaching relationships. Team leaders are likely to coach team members who are their peers as they strive to solve problems and manage their own work. Where they are providing support and encouragement to perform a new skill, the role may be comfortable. Where a team member needs to be counseled, the role becomes uncomfortable. Providing the team leader with training for coaching skills can help. Where the problem is a serious one, the manager may need to intercede and do the coaching or coach the team leader to coach. A questionnaire developed by Frankel (see Fig. 20-7)[29] can help a manager or a team leader assess whether he or she is the most appropriate person to coach an employee.

Where and When to Coach

Coaching is not the only key to performance improvement, so when is it appropriate? Coaching is appropriate for giving feedback on specific performance, clarifying the level of authority and responsibility when delegating work and problem-solving situations related to employee performance or where the employee is challenged to solve a problem. Gary Topchik offers several examples of when to coach (see Fig. 20-8).[30] The Center for Management and Organization Effectiveness suggests (see Fig. 20-9)[31] that coaching discussions may be related to an administrative situation or a task or project. Additionally, people need to hear positive feedback when they do the job well. Ken Blanchard (1982) addresses the practice of regular, specific, and brief praise in *The One Minute Manager*.

You may take the following inventory in order to determine whether you are the best person to coach a particular employee:

True	False	
———	———	1. I am comfortable giving any kind of feedback to this employee.
———	———	2. I not only trust this employee, I also like him or her.
———	———	3. We respect each other's capabilities.
———	———	4. I feel I am the most capable person to coach this employee in this particular area.
———	———	5. I treat this employee consistently with how I treat other employees.
———	———	6. I believe this employee is capable of making the behavioral changes I expect.
———	———	7. I've reviewed the situation and have determined that the responsibility for change is with the employee.
———	———	8. My relationship with this employee is purely professional.
———	———	9. The employee is not someone who threatens me.
———	———	10. The employee has a good working relationship with my boss.

If you answer false to *any* of these questions then there are some serious potential barriers to an effective coaching relationship with this employee. Any one of the above items can threaten the outcome of successful coaches. This is not to say that an answer of false precludes your ability to ultimately coach the employee, only that it's a clear sign that you have to go back and get in shape for coaching before you can do it effectively.

Figure 20-7. The Manager-as-Coach Checklist.

Here is a list of situations in which coaching might be an effective management tool:

- An employee needs skill development.
- Interpersonal behavior change is needed.
- A person is not working up to standard.
- A person is meeting standards but expresses a desire to improve.
- An employee is violating company policy.
- Job procedures or criteria change.
- An employee is not in tune with the culture or value system of the organization.
- An employee is ready for career advancement.
- An improvement or growth plan is developed as a result of information shared in an appraisal interview.
- A subordinate seems unmotivated or has a morale problem.
- After formal training, an employee needs help in implementing a new skill.
- A task is not being performed as effectively as it could be.

Figure 20-8. When to coach.[30]

Time and Place

Timing and location are also important when coaching. For the employee to believe that you care about his performance, you need to schedule adequate time to conduct a coaching session and arrange to be uninterrupted. Particularly in counseling sessions, you may have no idea, entering the session, what the employee will want to discuss. Cutting someone off in the middle of an emotional negotiation hurts your chances of being successful. In terms of location, giving praise publicly and delivering negative feedback in a private setting

---

Situations That Require Coaching to Improve Performance

Coaching discussions may be initiated as a result of an administrative situation or because the manager has become aware of an event or incident of concern in relation to a task or project.

Administrative Situations

- Setting objectives
- Performance reviews
- Salary discussions
- Career planning-development discussions
- Job posting and bidding discussions

Project or Task Situations

- A specific project or assignment problem:
  Delays
  Quality problems
  Quantity problems
  Lack of follow-through on commitments
- Absenteeism and/or tardiness
- Deficiency in effort or motivation
- Behavior which causes problems, i.e., abrasiveness
- Training: opportunity or assignment
- When someone joins your group or team
- Conflicts between employees or groups
- Communication problems or breakdowns
- When your own supervisor makes you aware that one of your employees has a problem

---

Figure 20-9. Coaching situations.[31]

is generally a good rule. However, with a culturally diverse workforce, it may be wise to ask your employees how they would like to be praised. To some cultures, such as the Native American, public praise is inappropriate, creating embarrassment rather than pride. Where coaching is related to skill building, it is also important to allow adequate time and to conduct the session in an area free of interruptions and distractions.

Mentoring

Mentoring is a specialized form of coaching. Typically, mentoring involves a relationship between a more senior manager and a new or less-experienced employee. In Homer's tale *The Odyssey,* Mentor was a friend of Odysseus entrusted with the education of his son, Telemachus. The mentor, then, is a trusted friend, given to assist with the education of their charge. This differs from the relationship one has with a supervisor. Some organizations establish formal mentor programs to assist high-potential employees with their careers. For example, newly hired college interns might be assigned a senior manager as their mentor. Other organizations have established mentor programs to assist disadvantaged populations, such as women and people of color. AT&T was one of the first organizations to do this in the early 1970s. This type of program provides the employee with a coach other than her own supervisor.

Mentors provide employees with information and feedback they might otherwise not have. Often, employees will make mistakes because they do not understand the "unspoken rules of the game." A mentor, for example, can advise a protégé that the reception for a departing vice president is a "command performance" and an opportunity to meet other company executives. The junior employee might at first have intended to skip the event, thinking that he wouldn't be missed. Knowledge of the organization's norms, values, and culture are key to success but usually not included in any training. Mentoring can fill the void.

Mentors can also watch for problems and provide timely feedback to prevent serious errors. When something goes wrong, they do damage control. Mentors have access to other senior-level managers on a basis that the employee's supervisor is not likely to enjoy. Often involved in the succession planning process, the mentor is also in a position to speak as an advocate for his or her mentee.

If an organization does not have a formal mentor program, mentoring is still possible. With all of the advantages to having one's own coach, employees may want to seek their own mentors. Discussing the choice of a mentor with one's supervisor can help assure a positive outcome. Then it is as simple as asking the mentor to fill the role. Most senior managers are flattered to help with someone's corporate education and development, although the employee may have to clarify what she needs from her mentor. Good mentor relationships can become trusted friendships, where roles actually reverse on occasion. Senior managers value trusted feedback, but their own direct reports are often reluctant to be the bearers of bad news and peers may be competing for a top position. Mentoring up can become an excellent coaching source for senior management.

Peer Coaching

Peer coaching is relatively new. Traditional, vertically structured organizations have looked to the formal, boss-subordinate relationship as the focus for growth and development. Even in the team-based organization structure, the team leader has a measure of accountability and responsibility for the team members' performance. Peer relationships where neither colleague holds position power over the other is a new arena for formal coaching strategies. However, it is a logical next step when one considers the evolution to more networked, collaborative organization structures.

In "Peer Training: Not Just a Low-Budget Answer," Daniel Rickett[32] describes an example of a strategic use of peer coaching. At Partners International, training manager Diane Mundy recruited key staff people to become experts at specific applications for their new computer system. These colleagues worked together to teach one another, specialize, and eventually facilitate learning for the rest of the employees through ongoing coaching and day-to-day interactions on the job. "The genius of peer training as an instructional method," Rickett states, "is that it mirrors the way people actually learn in the workplace. As Mundy discovered, most people prefer not to rely on manuals, self-instructional guides, or even 'help' menus in software programs. Whenever possible, they'd rather use managers and fellow workers as sources of information and help." Working with peers, people do not hesitate to ask for help for fear of appearing ignorant or having too small a problem to trouble a manager. "Another big advantage of peer training is that there is no superfluous teaching," says Rickett. "People learn what they need when they need it." While we usually think of coaching as a response to individual performance needs, this is an example of peer coaching as a company's strategy for training and development.

A trusted peer can be an excellent source of feedback, expertise, and support. Responding with appreciation and fact-finding questions to clarify the feedback allows a peer to comfortably give additional information in the future. Arguing the validity of feedback or becoming defensive is sure to discourage honesty from peers in the future. To make the most of peer feedback, colleagues can be asked to take a coach's role and provide ongoing support as you seek to improve performance. Some organizations provide 360-degree feedback instruments to solicit feedback from peers as well as supervisors and reportees.

Executive Coaching

Senior managers often have difficulty obtaining good, objective feedback about their performance. Since mentor programs often are focused on coaching less-experienced employees, the senior manager is left without a coach. Today, senior managers can hire a coach. "The Executive's New Coach,"[33] describes various types of executive coaches who provide everything from programs such as The Center for Creative Leadership's Awareness Program for Executive Excellence to the "clairvoyant" who provides instant personal assessments. Marilyn Moats Kennedy in "Good Coach, Bad Coach" suggests that before hiring an executive coach, managers should have a good idea of what the problem is, how long to work on it, and how much to spend on it. She also recommends considering the effect of hiring a coach on subordinates (fear) and peers (jealousy). Based on analyzing people's experiences with executive coaches she sees that "low-profile coaches with limited missions are more effective and less likely to create political fallout. So are those with tact and pinpoint focus on the problems to be solved."[34]

Summary

Coaching is an essential skill for anyone who has the responsibility for assisting others to perform well in a particular arena, be it sports or the workplace. Increasingly, those who coach in the workplace look more like athletic coaches. As Kouzes and Posner wrote:

> Coaches don't wait until the season is over to let their players know how they are doing; the same should be true in your business. Coaching involves the on-the-job, day-to-day spending of time with your people, talking with them about your game strategies, and providing them feedback about their efforts and performance. And when the game is over, you get together with the players and analyze the results of your efforts. Where did we do well? Where do we need to improve our efforts? What will we have to do differently, better, or more of the next time? And then it's practice and getting ready for the next game.[35]

This chapter presents some of the basic ideas to consider when assessing or training yourself or others for coaching. The main points in the chapter include the following:

- Coaching is defined in a variety of ways which reflect different perspectives on coaching.

- Coaching is becoming a key management role as a result of global competition, technological change, and a better-educated diverse workforce.

- Coaching is a process that requires specific skills and knowledge and which follows a definable plan.

- Counseling is a form of coaching applied to performance problems.

- Training for coaches can be structured to model the coaching process and should meet the organization's needs.
- Self-knowledge is a key component to successful coaching.
- Coaching is not limited to supervisor-employee relationships.
- The time and location of a coaching session are important.
- Mentoring, peer coaching, and executive coaching are specific types of coaching relationships.

References

1. Reprinted with permission of Bectin, Dickinson and Company.
2. Fournies, F. F., *Coaching for Improved Work Performance*, Liberty Hall Press, New York, 1987, p. 134.
3. Peters, T. J., and N. K. Austin, *A Passion for Excellence: The Leadership Difference*, Random House, New York, 1985, p. 325.
4. Cappozzoli, T., "Developing Productive Employees," *Supervision*, October 1993, pp. 16–17.
5. Mink, O. G., K. Q. Owen, and B. P. Mink, *Developing High-Performance People: The Art of Coaching*, Addison-Wesley, Reading, MA, 1993, p. 2. Copyright © 1993 by Addison-Wesley Publishing Company, Inc. Reprinted by permission of the publisher.
6. Darraugh, B., ed., "Coaching and Feedback," *Info-Line*, 9006, ASTD, Alexandria, VA, June 1990, p. 1.
7. Frankel, L. P., and K. L. Otazo, "Employee Coaching: The Way to Gain Commitment, Not Just Compliance," *Employment Relations Today*, Autumn 1992, pp. 311–320 (quote on p. 312).
8. Darraugh, B., ed., "Coaching and Feedback," *Info-Line*, 9006, ASTD, Alexandria, VA, June 1990, p. 1.
9. Mink, O. G., K. Q. Owen, and B. P. Mink, op. cit., pp. 133–134.
10. Mink, O. G., K. Q. Owen, and B. P. Mink, op. cit., pp. 142–143.
11. Fournies, F. F., op. cit., p. 31.
12. Mink, O. G., K. Q. Owen, and B. P. Mink, op. cit., p. 136.
13. Fournies, F. F., op. cit., pp. 32–41.
14. McGregor, D., *The Human Side of Enterprise*, McGraw-Hill, New York, 1960.
15. Fournies, F. F., op. cit., p. 132.
16. Mink, O. G., K. Q. Owen, and B. P. Mink, op. cit., pp. 180–181.
17. Mink, O. G., K. Q. Owen, and B. P. Mink, op. cit., pp. 190–207.
18. Frankel, L. P., *Coaching Corporate Players*, Unpublished manuscript, 1995.
19. Halson, B., "Teaching Supervisors to Coach," *Personnel Management*, vol. 22, pp. 36–39, 53.
20. Geber, B., "From Manager into Coach," *Training*, February 1992, pp. 25–31 (quote on p. 28).
21. Mink, O. G., K. Q. Owen, and B. P. Mink, op. cit., p. 8.
22. Katzenbach, J. R., and D. K. Smith, *The Wisdom of Teams: Creating the High-Performance Organization*, Harvard Business School Press, Boston, 1993, p. 131.
23. Fournies, F. F., op. cit., p. 23.
24. Frankel, L. P., and K. L. Otazo, loc. cit.
25. Brown, T., "Boss—Or Coach?" *Industry Week*, June 4, 1990, p. 8. Reprinted with permission of *Industry Week*. Copyright Penton Publishing, Inc., Cleveland, OH.
26. Block, P., *Stewardship*, Berrett-Koehler, San Francisco, CA, 1993, p. 8.
27. DePree, M., *Leadership Jazz*, Doubleday, New York, 1992, p. 220.

28. Howard, R., "Values Make the Company: An Interview with Robert Haas," *Harvard Business Review,* September–October 1990, pp. 132–145 (quote on p. 135). Reprinted by permission of *Harvard Business Review.* Copyright © 1990 by the President and Fellows of Harvard College. All rights reserved.

29. Frankel, L. P., loc. cit.

30. Topchik, G., "When to Coach (A Short Course for Managers)," *Training and Development,* May 1994, p. 24.

31. *Coaching Skills Resources,* The Center for Management and Organization Effectiveness, Salt Lake City, 1984, p. 7.

32. Rickett, D., "Peer Training: Not Just a Low-Budget Answer," *Training,* February 1993, pp. 70–72. Reprinted with permission from the February 1993 issue of *Training* Magazine. Copyright 1993, Lakewood Publications, Minneapolis, MN. All rights reserved. Not for resale.

33. Smith, L., "The Executive's New Coach," *Fortune,* December 27, 1993, pp. 126–134.

34. Kennedy, M. M., "Good Coach, Bad Coach," *Across the Board,* September 1994, pp. 11–12. (Marilyn Moats Kennedy publishes a monthly newsletter, *Kennedy's Career Strategist.* For a sample copy write 1150 Wilmette Ave., Wilmette, IL 60091; phone: 708-251-1661.)

35. Kouzes, J. M., and B. Z. Posner, *The Leadership Challenge: How to Get Extraordinary Things Done in Organizations,* Jossey-Bass, San Francisco, 1990, p. 257.

Bibliography

Blanchard, K., and S. Johnson, *The One Minute Manager,* Morrow, New York, 1982.

Brookfield, D., *Understanding and Facilitating Adult Learning,* Jossey-Bass, San Francisco, 1986.

Deming, W. E., *Out of the Crisis,* MIT Press, Cambridge, MA, 1986.

Herzberg, F., *Work and the Nature of Man,* The World Publishing Company, Cleveland, 1966.

Knowles, M. S., *The Adult Learner: A Neglected Species,* 3d ed., Gulf Publishing Company, Houston, 1984.

Maslow, A. H., *Motivation and Personality,* Harper & Row, New York, 1954.

21

Classroom Instruction

Ruth Sizemore House

Ruth Sizemore House *joined BellSouth in 1994 as a Manager of Organizational Change. Since that time, she has developed and delivered consulting interventions to minimize the strategic and tactical risks of major organizational change. Dr. House also teaches courses in organizational behavior and in managing organizational change at Atlanta campuses of Keller Graduate School. Before joining BellSouth, Dr. House was President and Lead Consultant of the Paradigm Corporation, a firm that provided deskside consulting and training to help clients manage the human side of technical projects—including the design and delivery of technical instruction. She wrote* The Path of Project Success: From Failure Analysis to Interpersonal Action in The 1992 Project Management Institute Seminar/Symposium Proceedings *(The Project Management Institute, Drexel Hill, PA 1992);* The Human Side of Project Management *(Addison-Wesley, Reading, MA, 1988), coauthored, with Martin Broadwell,* Supervising Technical and Professional People *(John Wiley & Sons, 1986), and coauthored two books with Dugan Laird:* Interactive Classroom Instruction *(Scott Foresman, Glenview, IL, 1984), and* Training Today's Employees *(Scott Foresman, Glenview, IL, 1983). She is active in the Project Management Institute and ISPI. She was named Atlanta's Woman in Project Management in 1993 by the local PMI chapter and subsequently featured in* PMNetwork. *She has made over 30 presentations to national meetings of ASTD, ISPI, and others.*

Most people can remember one instructor (at least) who made a subject come alive—crackle with excitement. Many can remember one (at least) who made the subject struggle unsuccessfully for life—fizzle and go flat. What makes the difference? A comparison between the two might look as it does in Table 21-1.

Table 21-1. Comparison Between Two Types of Instruction

When the instruction crackled	When the instruction fizzled
▪ Learning the subject matter seemed relevant. In some cases it was relevant to a job; in some cases it was relevant to the enjoyment of the class.	▪ Learning the subject matter seemed pointless. Concentrated effort paid off neither back on the job nor in the class itself.
▪ The instructor knew the subject matter well enough to have an in-depth, note-free *conversation* about it—and could have had that conversation with equal ease in the classroom or over lunch.	▪ The instructor knew the subject only well enough to deliver a superficial, note-bound *lecture* about it. No conversation about the subject would have been possible without the classroom props of notes or off-the-shelf videotapes.
▪ The students felt the energy of the instructor directed at and invested in them.	▪ The students felt their energy drained by the instructor. The instructor was sustained by their feigned attention.
▪ Students participated responsibly in the learning by discussing ideas, by asking questions, by completing activities.	▪ Students dodged participation if possible by withholding ideas, by stifling questions, by dragging their feet during activities.
▪ Students knew where they were headed and could recognize their progress in that direction.	▪ Students had no idea where they or the class was going. They didn't know if they were progressing or just going around in circles.
▪ Students left the experience feeling energized and optimistic.	▪ Students left the experience feeling drained and discouraged.

Engineering "crackle" rather than inducing "fizzle" takes balance: balance between freedom and discipline for both instructor and learner. To achieve that balance an instructor can

1. Plan around learner outcomes
2. Prepare and then prepare some more
3. In the beginning, set the stage
4. In the middle, encourage interaction
5. In the end (and before), assess progress
6. Leave the learner feeling good about the experience and good about her- or himself

Glenda Rose and Westleigh Adams are new instructors in general management at Housewell Engineering Corporation (HEC). They will follow these steps to plan a course for technical people who will lead interdisciplinary teams.

1. Plan Around Learner Outcomes

An in-depth assessment has been conducted at HEC; the new trainers have a detailed report along with a task analysis of team leadership. But Glenda and Westleigh must still reframe the information around two basic questions—in the plainest possible language—before they design the first classroom activity.

A. What will the learner do differently back on the job?

B. What must the learner do in class to show he is ready to perform on the job?

And their design should answer this additional question:

C. How can instruction help?
  - What can learner participation deliver?
  - What can visual or other aids provide?
  - What can the instructor provide?

A. What will the learner do differently back on the job?

The technical staff at HEC is accustomed to working in functional groups—engineers leading groups of engineers, computer specialists leading groups of computer specialists, architects leading groups of architects. Now they will be working in interdisciplinary teams. An engineer, for example, might be the team leader of a group including engineers, computer specialists, and architects.

Glenda and Westleigh can define the *purpose* of training by answering with one sentence the question: What will an engineer be expected to do after training that she could not have done or would not have done before training?

> After training, technical people will lead interdisciplinary teams to produce products and services for clients.

They can identify the *"must-haves"* for the training by answering the question: What must participants know and what skills must participants have in order to accomplish the purpose of training?

Participants will know
  - How project team leadership is different from line management
  - What characteristics high-performing project teams demonstrate
  - What specific things a project team leader can do to encourage these high-performing characteristics

Participants will be able to
  - Establish the team infrastructure required for high performance
  - Direct the energy of team members to the task or to the team itself as required
  - Handle conflict to encourage responsible participation and open discussion of disagreement

Glenda and Westleigh can identify the *"nice-to-haves"* for training by asking the question: What other information or skills would help participants better understand or accept the training?

> The technical people at HEC might better understand the training if they had information about the market requirements that have led to the establishment of customer-focused teams. And they might better accept the new demands on them if they had improved skills in stress management.

B. What must the learner do in class to show she is ready to perform on the job?

How can Glenda and Westleigh be sure that participants can lead interdisciplinary teams? By watching them do just that in class. They can be sure that participants can establish team infrastructure, direct team energy, and handle conflict in the same way—by watching the participants do those things in class.

To handle conflict in class, for example, participants can deal with a real-life conflict situation and demonstrate

- Active listening
- Assertive responding
- Negotiation skills

Where it is impossible to actually replicate the outcome in class, a simulation is second choice. If for some reason a simulation is unworkable, then a case study, a case incident, or some other approximation of the outcome would be in order.

C. How can instruction help?

Classroom activities that demonstrate learner outcomes are the starting point for the lesson plan Glenda and Westleigh will develop. To ensure a continued focus on learner outcomes, their lesson plan will outline—*in this order:*

- *Learner activities* that teach and demonstrate the desired learner outcomes

- *Visual and other aids* that can teach and demonstrate the desired learner outcomes

- *Instructor input* that supports or demonstrates the desired learner outcomes

The order here is different *and* important. Traditionally, instructors have begun their plans with a detailed description of what they themselves will do and say. From the beginning, these instructors invest energy in themselves—not in the learner. And in the resulting plan, these instructors draw attention to themselves—not the learner.

Glenda and Westleigh will keep their eyes on the learner; in fact, to the extent possible, they will see through the eyes of the learner. The lesson plan form that they use will help:

Learner activity	Visual/other aids	Instructor says or *does*
1. Conduct problem-solving session on conflict issue.	1. Video: "Out in the Open."	1. a. INTRODUCE AND SHOW VIDEO. In this video you'll see how… b. EXPLAIN ACTIVITY. In a series of three exercises we will now… c. DEMONSTRATE ACTIVITY WITH VOLUNTEER. Now, before we go into a fourth exercise, I'll demonstrate with a volunteer… d. ANSWER QUESTIONS AND DISCUSS COMMENTS. What questions do you have now about…

Glenda and Westleigh can develop the "Instructor says or *does*" column of the lesson plan at whatever level of detail they choose. If their lesson plan will be used by other instructors later, they may want to include an actual script. An inexperienced instructor or someone new to the subject matter could study the script in detail. After an instructor had instructed the workshop several times he or she might only need to track the "Learners Do" column to manage classroom activities.

2. Prepare and Then Prepare Some More

After the design of learner activities, prepare learner-controlled aids.

When Glenda first mentioned to Westleigh that she prepared learner-controlled aids *before* she prepared her own visuals and wrote out her own script, he was shocked. She developed materials in the exact *opposite* order that Westleigh had used. Her rationale? Actually, she admitted, she had used this approach the first time when she was under such a tight deadline to get student materials to the printer that she had no choice. She found to her surprise that as a result

- The entire workshop design was more learner-focused
- The design time was reduced by one-third to one-half of the usual time
- The production cycle for materials was much more efficient

Over time Glenda continued to use the approach and found that more and more she was able—early on—to see the classroom design unfold through the eyes of the learner. She weighted the learner materials more and more with the actual delivery of content (and, where possible, of feedback). She used

- Simulations
- Action mazes
- Idea mazes
- Games and exercises
- Calculations
- Minicases
- Ratings
- Inventories
- Discussion questions
- Charts and tables to be completed by learners
- Structured notes

Prepare trainer-controlled aids next.

When Glenda had put as much learning as possible into the hands of the learners themselves, she went on to instructor-controlled materials.

She built content and feedback into visual aids. She included

- Instructions for activities
- Discussion questions
- Answer keys
- Survey results
- Complete charts and tables

She identified videos that could help deliver content, short audiotapes that could trigger brainstorming, and journal articles that could help stimulate discussion.

Prepare trainer input.

Last, Glenda developed what she would need to say and do to make all the other avenues to learning work. She was more producer and director than "star." She was there to focus attention on the learner and the learning, not to be the focus of attention herself. Not only was it an effective role as far as the learner was concerned, it was a liberating role as far as Glenda was concerned. She was now free to concentrate on the learners: to watch, encourage, and give feedback to them.

Where her input was needed, she developed it accurately and in detail. She limited her input sessions to not more than 20 minutes each, and she interspersed even that 20 minutes with responses and short activities by the learners. Where her support was needed, she noted the steps she would need to take.

Test learner activities.

Some learner activities required almost precision timing. (Glenda would have a kitchen timer on hand for these.) Others would need just the right intervention from Glenda in order to work. Some would depend on skillful debriefing to drive the learning point home. Glenda did not want to try these activities "cold" for the first time during the workshop. So she enlisted the help of a few coworkers to "test-drive" a couple of the activities. One activity—whose content was both generic and nonproprietary—she practiced with neighbors she invited over for Saturday brunch.

Record input.

Glenda recorded her input on an audiotape. She listened to it two or three times on her car tape player as she drove to work. (When she "couldn't stand to listen to it anymore," she was ready for a rehearsal without her notes.) She rehearsed some of the input in front of a mirror or videotape.

Have conversation about the subject matter.

Eventually, Glenda felt she could have an informed *conversation* about her subject. If someone asked questions, she could answer most of them. If the conservation skipped unpredictably from one topic to another, Glenda could keep up with the changes in direction and keep up the pace. She didn't need to use notes; she just needed to use her head—where she had random access to the information. She was ready for the classroom.

3. In the Beginning, Set the Stage

In the garden and in the classroom, climate is important. Living things need freedom (psychological and physical space) to permit growth, and they need nourishment to stimulate growth.

Westleigh has been preparing for his session as Glenda has prepared for hers. His first workshop session is tomorrow. He wants to prepare both physical and psychological space to cultivate learning. Before the first learner arrives, he will

- Arrange physical space that is well-suited to the learners and to the training design
- Prepare himself to nurture learning relationships

And as the first participants arrive, he will immediately begin to

- Focus his attention on the learners
- Cultivate a learning relationship with each person from the very beginning

Arrange physical space.

Physical space that provides room for learners to grow will

- Permit learners to complete tasks without physical barriers or limitations
- Protect learners from distractions
- Be comfortable

Many learning tasks require interaction. Westleigh will interact with the learners. They will interact with him and with one another. Anything that prevents Westleigh from seeing or being seen by each learner is a serious limitation. A typical "classroom" style arrangement has many blind spots. So Westleigh will choose one of these alternatives:

A U-shaped arrangement will permit every learner to see Westleigh without looking over someone else's head. And learners will have a good chance of making direct eye contact with one another. But there are still some shadows (spots hidden—or nearly hidden—from Westleigh's view). If he chooses this arrangement, he will make a conscious effort to maintain eye contact with learners in the shadowy four corners of the U.

Westleigh could eliminate all of the shadows by using a circle. If Westleigh is part of the circle, he and the learners can have maximum eye contact. But he plans to use visual aids. So if he uses this arrangement, he will be sure the tables and chairs are lightweight enough for learners to shift them back into a U. Otherwise, the visual aids will be out of sight for half of the group.

When learners are working in small, leaderless groups, Westleigh can put *himself* in the shadows. If learners are seated around conference tables, Westleigh can stay out of the learners' line of sight so they will work independently. Round or square tables allow good eye contact between members of small groups and give no member extra status like "head of the table."

If no writing is necessary or if lapboards are provided, Westleigh can remove the tables and arrange chairs in circles throughout the room.

L-shaped rooms, long narrow rooms, and rooms with posts or niches present built-in barriers to line-of-sight and to movement. A rectangular room with a width-to-length ratio of about 3 to 4 will allow Westleigh the most flexibility. He will select a room that allows at least 25 square feet per person and, where writing will be required, he will allow at least 9 square feet of desk surface per person.

Some leaner distractions stem out of the learner's regular job: phone calls, messages from supervisors, and heavy traffic or coworkers near the training room. So Westleigh's first choice will be a training room away from the regular work site. Even with a separate location, he will limit disruptions (except in the case of emergencies) by having telephone messages posted on the door rather than brought into the classroom.

Noise is another typical frequent distraction. Westleigh will avoid the room near the noisy office equipment as well as the one in the line of traffic to the snack room.

Anxiety about the facility itself can also be distracting. So Westleigh will review safety procedures with the group. What is the safest exit in case of fire? Where can learners find the necessities: Phone? Restrooms? Food? Are there special protocols they should know? What are the provisions for learners with physical handicaps?

Comfortable chairs, comfortable temperature, and adequate ventilation are important. Westleigh isn't entirely satisfied with *any* of the company training rooms here. So he will

- Alternate seated activities with those that allow movement
- Suggest layered clothing that will allow learners to adjust to room temperature
- Schedule periodic "fresh-air breaks" to allow people to get out of the stuffy room into fresher air space

Prepare to nurture learning relationships.

Westleigh knows that relationship building starts the moment the learners enter the classroom. And participants won't feel welcomed by the sight of his back if he is still cramming content, moving furniture, or shuffling paper when they arrive. So Westleigh has last-minute studying, classroom arrangements, and paper shuffling out of the way at least 30 minutes before class begins. He is unhurried and relaxed when he greets the first learner—and every learner after that.

Focus on the learner.

As the first learners arrive, Westleigh personalizes his greeting with information he learned from the course roster:

"Mike, you came all the way from Washington State, didn't you?"

"Ellen, I understand you are an engineer. You worked on the St. Paul project, didn't you?"

As other learners arrive, Westleigh makes whatever introductions he can among them. He associates what he has learned about their special interests or their reasons for being in the session:

"Ellen, Mike Jones, who was on a similar project in Olympia, is also in this session. There he is....Ellen, this is Paul."

When Westleigh introduces himself, he shares the reasons he is looking forward to this particular session:

"I especially enjoy the diversity we have in this group: engineers, chemists, and biologists."

"It's really exciting to be a part of the first program of this kind at HEC."

Even before class starts, Westleigh will cultivate learning. He will model one of the most important learning roles: the role of listener.

Westleigh won't...	Westleigh will...
Pay attention to that little voice in his head that every now and then says "What a dumb comment!" or "I hope I can get back to the office in time to pick up my paycheck."	Put himself "on hold." Pay attention only to the voice of the learner.
Get distracted.	Stand between 2 and 3 feet from the learner and look him or her in the eye. It will be hard to notice anything else.
Turn a learner off with quick advice ("If you ask me, you should go straight to your labor relations officer with the problem.") or with a personal reference ("A similar thing happened to me back in 1982.").	Allow time for what the learner has said to sink in before he responds. Westleigh will wait 5 or 10 seconds to reply.

4. In the Middle, Encourage Interaction

Throughout the workshop, Westleigh will encourage interaction. He will

- Generate discussions by the group
- Ask questions that stimulate participation
- Handle conflict to encourage responsible participation and open discussion of disagreement
- Administer interactive activities to deliver content

Generate discussion by the group.

The key to learning is *responsible* participation by instructor and learners. One form of responsible participation is to talk about the purpose and the content of the session. That sounds simple enough. But Westleigh has found it's not always easy. In some groups open dialogue will just happen. In many groups it will not. So Westleigh has planned structured discussion sessions throughout the workshop:

1. In order to allow ample "air time" for all participants, Westleigh divides the class into discussion groups of five or six people. (Seven is too many.)

2. To ensure even participation by all members of the discussion groups, Westleigh asks each group to select a gatekeeper, a timekeeper, a historian, a conscience, and a facilitator.

> The *gatekeeper* sees to it that everyone in the group has the opportunity to listen and to speak. The gatekeeper might say, for example, "John, thanks for the helpful input. We haven't heard from Ellen for a while. Ellen, what do you think?"

> The *timekeeper* simply posts the group periodically on time elapsed and time remaining. At first, he or she might speak up at 15-minute intervals. During the last 15 minutes before the deadline, he or she might want to shift to every 5 minutes.

> The *historian* reminds the group of what has already been accomplished and what is left to do. The historian might say, for example, "We have already identified the executives who can sponsor this change. Before we leave, we need to develop a plan for approaching each one."

> The *conscience* keeps the group on track. The conscience might post a blank easel sheet on the wall and refer to it as the "bucket": "That's an important issue. But if we pursue it now, we might not finish with the planned items on our agenda. I'll write the topic over here so we won't lose it. If we have time left when we have finished our agenda items, we can take it out of the bucket and deal with it."

> The *facilitator* watches the whole process and sees to it that nothing falls through the cracks. She listens for everything that is said—and not said; he watches for everything that is done—and not done.

3. Westleigh walks around the room listening in on each group. If any group appears to get stuck, he allows them some time to work it through on their own. If they get stuck a third time or if they stay stuck too long, he may intervene. He might ask the group some questions to stimulate a different train of thought. He might simply listen to factions in a group and summarize the opposing opinions.

Ask questions that stimulate discussion.

Even when the entire class group is together, Westleigh uses questions to stimulate discussion and to check for understanding.

He uses *open questions* to stimulate discussion. Open questions have no one specific "correct" answer. Open questions encourage learners to draw on their own experiences and apply them to the content of the workshop. For example:

"How do you feel about...?"

"What experiences can you share about...?"

"How would you...?"

"What can you tell us about...?"

"Where might we use this information?"

"What are the pros and cons of this approach?"

Westleigh uses *direct questions* to check for understanding or to test for consensus. Direct questions have a limited number of possible answers. (Some direct questions like "What is your name?" would have a different correct answer for each person.) They direct the learner's mind to a specific, verifiable bit of knowledge or experience. The function of a direct question is to *focus*. (The function of an open question is to *explore*.) Westleigh uses direct questions to

- Review material already covered
- Check for understanding of information and concepts
- Pinpoint areas of agreement or disagreement

Handle conflict to encourage responsible participation and open discussion of disagreement.

As Westleigh wanders around the room during small-group discussions, he observes this behavior in Jan's group:

- Jan has pushed his chair back, crossed his legs away from the group, and started staring "out into space."
- Mary, red-faced, is talking in a strained whisper to George.
- George has turned the side of his face to Mary. He is maintaining some eye contact by cutting his eyes in her direction even though his face is "aimed" somewhere else.

Westleigh can feel his heart moving up to his throat. That little voice in his head is saying, "I *told* you this exercise wouldn't work, but you used it anyway! Now that group is going to explode and it's too late for you to do anything about it! You're going to look like a real Bozo and everyone in HEC will hear about it." Westleigh knows he shouldn't approach the group until he has dealt with his own little voice. So he takes the "all or nothing" phrases and the "doom and gloom" words out and substitutes more realistic, positive expressions. He is programming himself to intervene successfully when he says back to his little voice:

> This exercise *is* difficult, but it will work. The group is tense; so I will help them relieve the tension. Working this through could be the most beneficial part of the workshop for them.

As Westleigh walks over to the group, he relieves some of his own tension with a quick deep-breathing exercise. He

- Breathes in to the count of three
- Holds his breath to the count of twelve
- Exhales to the count of six
- Repeats this sequence three times before he reaches the discussion group

When Westleigh reaches the group, he makes a simple one-sentence statement like: "It looks like you might be stuck." Then he waits for someone in the group to reply. When someone speaks up, Westleigh:

- Puts himself on "hold" long enough to really listen to what is being said
- Leans toward the group—using his body to screen out distractions
- Pauses for 5 to 10 seconds after someone has spoken to let what has been said "sink in."
- Summarized the feeling content and the factual content of what he has heard: "George, you feel frustrated because you believe the issue is just too complex to resolve here in 20 minutes. Mary, you feel frustrated because you feel the group could accomplish *something* if you would just work together on it."

In some cases, Westleigh's summary of opposing points of view is enough, by itself, to get the group going again. Members of different factions will hear something in a different way than they heard before and find a way to work through the conflict.

In this particular case, Westleigh makes three attempts, but the group remains stuck. So he directs some next steps himself. He might narrow the scope of the original assignment so the group can accomplish at least part of the task in the time remaining. Or he might redefine the task entirely by asking them to talk about how they got "stuck" and what they could do about it. Perhaps they could apply some group problem-solving model to their own effort to work together.

Administer interactive activities to deliver content.

Westleigh will engage the responsible participation of learners in the development of content. He encourages open discussion throughout the session, but he also incorporates other structured interaction into the workshop through the use of

- Case studies
- Role-plays
- Team tasks

A case study is a description of a situation that leads to any of several interactions by learners:*

- Discussion
- Group problem solving
- Group action planning
- Group role-play

A case study can be as short as a few sentences or as long as a book chapter. Westleigh has constructed several that range in length from one paragraph to two typewritten pages. One of Westleigh's cases can illustrate a variety of uses:

> You are leading a task force to recommend the design and the strategy of a new organization that will soon be formed by the merger of two existing units. When you were given the assignment, your management seemed both enthusiastic and optimistic.
>
> Task force members began the effort with zeal. Subgroups met after hours and on weekends to fine-tune some excellent proposals. They didn't seem to mind the extra hours because they were so excited about the potential results.
>
> But management sent several proposals back for minor technical changes. The groups grew disheartened but continued to work hard. You feel so good about the proposals that you've begun to doubt management's willingness to commit. The task force is still getting together, but more and more people are missing meetings. Those present go through the meetings robotlike, but their excitement has gone. Fewer and fewer people you meet in the hall or see in the cafeteria come up to talk. Some—yourself included—are still working on revision after revision, still trying to bolster morale, still trying to rally around the effort. At the same time, you are getting closer to exhaustion, closer to disillusionment.

*Also see Chap. 24, Case Studies.

Westleigh has given this case out along with a Project Path Analysis Worksheet and these three questions:

- What path is this project taking?
- How could you steer it back on course?
- Pick one of two key people in this project. Do a quick "market analysis," filling in details that fit with your own experience. Then develop an actionable assertive statement.

Westleigh explains the objective of the case study—to analyze the path a project is taking, to decide how to steer it back on course, and to script an approach to one of the key people on the project. He recommends that people read the case study and then individually analyze the situation using the project path analysis. Afterwards they will take 20 minutes to discuss the case in small groups (of five or six people) before each group reports out to the class as a whole.

Many people bring a great deal of experience into the classroom. But the worksheet Westleigh has distributed along with the case study ensures that even inexperienced team members can contribute—with no "gotchas"! It is unlikely that Westleigh will need to add much input as an instructor. He can record key findings of each group on an overhead or flipchart (or have group historians do that). Then he can help consolidate the combined findings of all groups, identify points of unanimity, and discuss points of disagreement. The worksheet has provided enough structure to ensure relevant responses.

This case study can lead easily into a role-play.* When teams have developed an assertive script, the stage is set for action. Westleigh subdivides the groups into pairs and triads. One person can act out the scripted part, another can play the role of the key person being approached, and—in triads—the other can observe. The observer can use a checklist Westleigh has prepared to note certain responses and behaviors by the role-players.

Westleigh keeps an eye on role-players just as he did on discussion groups. In the discussion following the role-play he sees to it that

- The role-players themselves have an opportunity to talk first about their enactment.
- Observers give clear, direct feedback about what each person did well.
- The number of suggestions for change is limited to three suggestions per role-player.

After the first round of role-playing, teams can rotate roles so that each person has an opportunity to enact and, in the triads, each person has an opportunity to observe.

When it is time for whole-group discussion. Westleigh asks questions like

- What did you find especially difficult about using the script your team developed?
- What went especially well?
- How do you feel about using this approach back on the job?

The role-play in this case can lead to an additional team task. For example, the small groups could develop lists of actions they might take to boost morale under the case circumstances.

*Also see Chap. 25, Instructional Games, Simulations, and Role-Plays.

5. In the End (and Before), Assess Progress

Know where you are going before you start.

From the beginning, Glenda and Westleigh have focused on learner outcomes. They can assess progress by answering these questions (variations on the questions they asked in the planning stages):

- What has the learner done in class to show she or he is ready to perform on the job?
- What will the learner do differently back on the job as a result of this training?
- How are the instruction and the instructor helping?

They already know that they will look for indicators that learners know:

- How project team leadership is different from line management
- What characteristics high-performing project teams demonstrate
- What specific things a project team leader can do to encourage these high-performing characteristics

And they already know that they will look for indicators that learners can:

- Establish the team infrastructure required for high performance
- Direct the energy of team members to the task or to the team itself as required
- Handle conflict to encourage responsible participation and open discussion of disagreement

Clearly distinguish between those measures that help the learner learn and those measures that help others evaluate the learners' potential.

What they measure is determined by learner outcomes. *How* they measure will depend also on the way the measures will be used. If measures of progress will be used to evaluate the learners' potential, then the measures must be managed by the instructor or by a third party. If the measures of progress will be used to help the learners learn and to improve performance, then they are best managed by the learners themselves. (Some psychologists refer to the first type of measure as *summative* and the second type of measure as *formative*.)

Glenda and Westleigh clearly intend to maximize learning and to improve performance. So they will select methods that are

- Goal-related
- Immediate
- Self-administered
- Visual
- Measurable

Relating *feedback* to a learning goal will be easier for Westleigh and Glenda because they have already related each *activity* to a specific learning goal. But they must still be on guard not to let extraneous observations intrude on feedback designed to improve learning. In an activity related to active listening, for example, this feedback from Glenda would be appropriate: "Anne, you did a good job of maintaining steady eye contact with Dan—even though what he said was somewhat surprising." But even though Westleigh also teaches HEC's business grammar course, this remark would *not* be appropriate during the active-listening exercise: "George, you should have said 'If she *were* going to do that...' not 'If she *was* going to do that."

Engineering feedback that is immediate is somewhat trickier. The only way for feedback to be instantaneous is for the learner to hear, see, or feel a consequence of his or her behavior right away. Immediate feedback could be in the form of a simulation in which a consequence is experienced immediately; a computer program that administers "bleeps" or fanfares appropriately; or a biodot that instantly registers stress. Westleigh and Glenda will also use some *almost* immediate feedback like the replaying of videotaped exercises right after the exercises are completed and the debriefing of other activities right after the activities are concluded.

To the extent possible, Westleigh and Glenda have built self-administered feedback into the activities they designed. For example, participants will watch the videotape of their active-listening exercise with a checklist in hand. They will each use the checklist to observe their own behavior during the activity. They can rate themselves on how well they

- Showed readiness by leaning toward the speaker
- Showed involvement by maintaining steady eye contact
- Showed understanding by summarizing the feeling and the factual content of what had been said

The videotape provides feedback that is *visual* and the checklist makes the feedback *measurable* as well. For example, a learner could tally the number of times he appropriately summarized what the other person had said.

Provide feedback that helps the learner learn throughout the learning experience.

Valuable feedback comes in time for the learner to make adjustments in her behavior and succeed in the training. Pilots say that a plane can be off course over 90 percent of a given flight and still arrive within 5 miles of its destination at the appointed time. *Almost* instant feedback will tell the plan it's veering to the north of its course, then veering to the south of its course, and so on. But the feedback comes continuously and in small increments. An on-time flight is the result of moving forward with almost constant small adjustments to the course. Training should be the same. Westleigh and Glenda won't wait until the end of a session to let some learners know they have been off course all along. As they move forward, they will help learners make incremental adjustments that assure they will arrive at their destination by the end of the session.

Provide for assessment beyond the classroom.

The real payoff for training, of course, comes outside the classroom. Daily, Glenda asks learners to complete these two statements:

The most useful thing I did or learned today was...

Back on the job I can apply what I learned today by...

At the end of each workshop. Westleigh has learners translate the daily lessons learned into a six-wheel action plan. The learners

- List their top three to five lessons learned
- List their action ideas for each one
- Commit to action dates for each item
- Identify someone they will share their action plans with within 48 hours

Learners complete these action plans on three-part no-carbon-required paper. They leave two copies in a self-addressed envelope with Westleigh. Six weeks after the training session, Westleigh mails each participant his or her own action plan. The participant then adds comments about progress, sends one copy back to Westleigh, and keeps one copy for his or her own records.

6. Leave the Learner Feeling Good About the Experience and About Him- or Herself

Throughout the workshop, Glenda and Westleigh have provided positive feedback and encouragement. At the same time, they have been consistently straightforward with learners about the work left to be done. They end the session on a positive note for the whole group, thanking the group for their participation and wishing them well. The well wishing might take the form of three wishes, of a mock toast, or of a positive quotation.

As participants leave, Westleigh and Glenda personalize the good wishes with individual comments like:

"John, you have a good plan now for approaching Engineering with your concerns. I'll look forward to hearing how it goes."

"Mary, you're ready to deal with the foreman from the Toledo plant, now. If you want to call me for a pep talk right before you meet with him, please do so."

At the end of a successful session, participants have learned, they have learned how to learn more, and they have the self-confidence to apply what they have learned.

For Further Reading

Centra, John A., *Determining Faculty Effectiveness,* Jossey-Bass, San Francisco, 1979.

House, Ruth Sizemore, *The Human Side of Project Management,* Addison-Wesley, Reading, MA, 1988.

Laird, Dugan, and Ruth House, *Interactive Classroom Instruction,* Scott, Foresman, Glenview, IL, 1983.

Lefrancois, Guy R., *Psychology for Teaching: A Bear (Always, Usually) Sometimes Faces the Front,* Wadsworth, Belmont, CA, 1979.

Mager, Robert F., *Goal Analysis,* Fearon, Belmont, CA, 1972.

22

Self-Directed
Learning

George M. Piskurich

__George M. Piskurich__ is a consultant in instructional design and training systems and is based in Chapel Hill, North Carolina. In 20 years in the field, he has been involved in most every aspect of training and HRD. Dr. Piskurich has worked in both the public and private sectors as a stand-up trainer, designed integrated training systems for small and large organizations as a corporate training director, developed and taught workshops ranging from communications theory to computer-based training techniques, and been responsible for the assessment, development, instruction, and evaluation of managers and supervisors. A specialist in self-directed learning techniques, he uses print, slide, video, and computer-based formats to develop individualized packages on a number of topics including the biological sciences, techniques of instruction, supervisory skills, and various types of technical training. He has a bachelor's degree in biology from Penn State and a master's and doctorate in instruction from the University of Pittsburgh.

Self-directed learning (SDL) covers a wide range of activities, from reading a book to using the newest multimedia program. It occurs in learning centers, on the job, after work, at the local YMCA, and even in the classroom, though the last is often an unintentional occurrence.

As an instructional design it can be effective in circumstances where no other training design will be. These situations are often characterized by factors such as large employee populations with diverse training requirements, a need for individualized development, multiple training sites where the same instruction must occur concurrently, the need for a high degree of training consistency, and high turnover rates which require continuous training.

As a learning style, or perhaps a learning theory, it is the basis for concepts such as self-directed work teams and learning organizations. No matter what you find in your current situation, self-directed learning is likely to fit somewhere in your training and development matrix.

SDL in HRD and Academic Environments

The term *self-directed learning* is used to describe a number of different concepts in the training and development field. These concepts range from instructional designs to learning styles, and from individualized programs to distributed learning that may reach thousands of trainees.

Academic practitioners of SDL state that it encompasses applications from offering two or three methods for students to learn a particular concept to having the students choose the material they want to learn and how they are going to learn it. They use terms such as contract learning, individualized instruction, student-centered learning, and prescriptive learning to conceptualize SDL in their environment. Because of the nature of training, from both an informational and efficiency point of view, many of these concepts are not as relevant in business settings as they are in academic ones.

However, current academic research has also focused on SDL as a learning style, exploring in detail the concept of self-directedness in individuals. Self-directedness has a number of applications in HRD.

Due to space limitations, and the nature of this handbook, the majority of this chapter will concentrate on SDL as an instructional design. However, because of the emerging importance to HRD of SDL as a learning style, we will begin this chapter with a look at some of SDL's more theoretical applications, particularly as they relate to HRD. You can find further information on all aspects of SDL in the cited references.

SDL as Learning Theory: The Concept of Self-Directedness

The self in self-directed learning became more appropriate to HRD with the advent of the learning-center concept. In these facilities large numbers of training programs, even entire developmental systems, are available to meet company and individual needs. Learning centers increase the importance of trainee choice in the training process. This in turn creates the need for greater "self-directedness" on the part of the trainee, that is, the ability to make proper self-motivated learning decisions and then follow through with them.

The newest self-directed learning processes include the combining of the learning-center concept with modern technology to produce another choice intensive learning process often labeled *desktop learning*. This methodology is basically a "learning center at your desk," in the form of a computer workstation with access to hundreds of programs ranging from software instructions to relaxation videos. Again, the emphasis is placed on employee self-directedness to take advantage of this capacity.

Self-Directedness and Performance Interventions

While the above processes demand increasing amounts of self-directedness, they are overshadowed by the level of self-direction necessary for newer HRD concepts such as lifelong learning, employee empowerment, self-directed work teams, and the disciplines of the learning organization.

Constantly reinventing the learning organization through continual learning by the individual employees who comprise it, and by the teams that have been empowered to recreate it as part of the Total Quality Management (TQM) process, requires that the team members and through them the teams themselves exhibit high degrees of self-directedness.

Self-directedness, and its importance in performance interventions, is relatively new to HRD. The notion that people may or may not be self-directed, and that there are levels of self-direction which can be enhanced or decreased, depending upon factors such as proper preparation, self-direction support systems, and previous success in self-directed projects, is seldom considered when a corporation decides to move toward a culture that requires self-directedness. Yet, the success or failure of corporatewide empowerment, continuous improvement, and other quality initiatives often rests on the self-directedness of the individuals involved.

For example, while self-directed work teams are a major component of TQM, the self-directedness of the individuals placed in these teams is seldom considered. If the team is going to be self-managed, and if team empowerment is going to produce significant results, then its members must be able to set goals, be inner-directed, achievement-motivated, accommodating, and able to make decisions based on appropriate information gathering and proper evaluation.

These are all characteristic of people who show a high degree of self-directedness. In other words, for a quality team to perform in a self-directed manner, the team members must be strongly self-directed. If the team members do not exhibit high self-directedness, an unofficial leader often emerges, and the team devolves into a traditional work group, but with a pseudomanager who has no real authority.

Self-Directedness in the Learning Organization

In a much broader context, if as Senge suggests the next incarnation for business is to become a learning organization with such diverse disciplines as personal mastery, mental models, and team learning being necessary for everyone, then the importance of understanding, and if possible enhancing, self-directedness is critical for these evolutions to occur. A predisposition toward lifelong learning, grounded in well-developed reading, listening, and observational abilities, and the skill of reflection, is basic for the continuous-learning needs of the learning organization's members. These skills and abilities are once again characteristics of individuals with high levels of self-directedness. (Also see Chap. 4, The Learning Organization.)

Unfortunately, companies that have begun to move toward a continuous-learning environment are finding that to achieve the five disciplines through job-connected learning, now being termed *on-the-job learning*, or OJL, requires employees to have self-learning skills, what we've termed self-directedness, that many of them do not possess.

Self-Directedness in Individuals

For years we have believed that everyone will be self-directed if just given a chance, that each employee can and wants to take responsibility for his or her own learning, that we will all be lifelong learners because we want to be. However our experiences, and now research, is showing these assumptions to be in error. We are not all self-directed. There are various degrees of self-direction, among people, even within an individual, depending on current job circumstances and internal basics such as present levels of self-esteem.

The lack of self-directedness isn't normally due to any genetic or psychological limitation. Rather, it seems to be an acquired response to a society in which learners are "spoon-fed" and "hand-held" during the formative years of their learning.

This learning acculturation process is why many people have difficulties being self-directed. If you spend 12, 16, or more years being told what, when, and how to learn, it becomes rather disconcerting to be told "you're on your own." Even if somewhere in the past it was once your natural way of learning, you may no longer be comfortable with the idea.

Determining Individual Self-Directedness

To deal with the lack of self-directedness in employees we need to first determine the level of self-directedness, and then to augment it if possible.

Determining self-directedness can be accomplished through a number of instruments, one of the most accepted of which is the Gugliamino Self-Directed Learning Readiness Scale (SDLRS). This instrument considers factors such as innerdirectedness, achievement motivation, goal-setting skills, and listening ability, all of which we've already noted are important to the new performance interventions. It also includes other characteristics of self-directedness such as self-confidence and observational ability which may have a more indirect relationship.

The SDLRS has been validated in a number of research studies; it has also been translated into six languages, lending a strong multicultural aspect to its usefulness and to the entire concept of self-directedness. It has been found to correlate with such wide-ranging factors as creativity, job performance, life satisfaction, and need for structure, all of which in turn relate to the basic characteristics of self-directedness. In two studies with major companies, the SDLRS has been used to predict management success and as a tool in selection processes.

There are other instruments for measuring self-directedness as well, though they have not received the extensive multicultural and validity testing of the SDLRS. The important point is that if a company plans an intervention that requires high levels of self-directedness, there are instruments available to appraise the readiness of the individual employees for this process.

Enhancing Self-Directedness

After analysis, the question becomes, Is it possible to enhance individual and therefore corporate self-directedness? Research seems to indicate that it is not only possible but also quite achievable.

There are three components to this process. The first is to provide those involved with adequate preparation for the SDL experience. Whether your intervention is as simple as an SDL workbook, or as complicated as changing the corporate culture to that of a learning organization, preparation is necessary on all levels. Many individuals are simply not ready for self-direction, so they must be introduced to it gradually with a formalized preparation plan. Don't make the mistake of one corporate training manager who said, "But it's self-directed, they'll just do it."

Preparation for self-directed processes is not limited simply to participants. It should include supervisors and managers and the training and HR departments as well. A number of self-directed initiatives have failed because the people who staff these functions, and who fill key roles in allowing self-direction to happen, were not prepared adequately for the changes that were entailed. Preparation as part of developing self-directed learning is discussed in detail later in this chapter.

The second component of enhancing self-directedness is to develop support systems of live facilitators or counselors who will help the participants through the transition to self-direction. These individuals add external structure to self-direction. This type of personalized structure may seem to be the opposite of what you're striving for in trying to produce higher levels of self-direction in your employees, but it is often necessary for those who have been forced out of a self-directed way of thinking and are striving to recapture it.

Finally, success in SDL projects builds self-directedness. Strive to make sure that the first SDL projects assigned to individuals or teams are those they can succeed at. Don't start with reinventing the company, or redefining a department's function as the introduction to self-direction. Simple SDL tasks that provide a measure of success and build a feeling of confidence in the participants will increase their self-directedness and make them ready for the more complicated processes.

All three of these components can be effectively handled through the use of a self-directed learning center. In such a facility preparation for self-direction can take place through assessments of employee self-directedness. An SDL support system is created through the center itself and the center facilitator who functions as SDL expert, mediator, and guide. Finally, the center is a place where SDL projects can be successfully completed. Small ones such as single-concept packages will lead to larger and larger successes, until each employee becomes as self-directed as his or her own pace and job needs dictate.

As interventions become more complex, we tend to lose sight of the individual. Considering the need for self-direction on the part of the employees involved in our interventions will help to guard against forgetting that the basic factor in any HRD process is the human factor.

Defining SDL as an Instructional Design

Before learning organizations and self-directedness theory, SDL was, and still is, an effective and efficient instructional design. Even within this aspect it has many different definitions and characterizations. However, to simplify the issue we will limit ourselves in this discussion to a general instructional design definition. Thus, self-directed learning can be defined as *a training design in which trainees work at their own pace, without the aid of an instructor, to master predetermined material.*

Dissecting the Definition

In this definition, "predetermined material" signifies that the trainees cannot choose the material they want to learn. This statement is not meant to suggest that the academic definitions which stress choice in learning style or subject matter are wrong. However, in the business environment decisions such as what material needs to be learned or how the training will be available are often made by others, usually subject-matter experts (SMEs) in conjunction with the SDL designer.

The term *training design* indicates that SDL is only one of a number of approaches that can be employed to deal with a training problem. Other alternatives might be stand-up instruction, mentoring, or on-the-job learning. Thus, the choice to use SDL is a design decision, usually made after you've completed your analysis of a performance problem.

Master specifies the evaluation criteria for SDL. It indicates that a certain level of expertise must be exhibited by the trainees through the process of criterion-referenced evaluation.

The phrase "without the aid of an instructor" means exactly that. An instructor is neither needed nor desirable for a good SDL process.

Finally, "trainees work at their own pace" is also self-explanatory, though in the business environment this is often achieved within certain limitations that are set by the day-to-day needs of the company.

Using this definition we will now look at a systematic process for developing SDL.

Analysis and Assessment for SDL

SDL, like every other instructional intervention, begins with analysis. Performing this aspect adequately is probably more important than in most other formats due to the amount of time spent in design and development for SDL. In fact, much of this "extra" development time is spent in performing analysis processes.

SDL Advantages and Disadvantages (A Need Analysis)

The first step in SDL analysis is to determine if SDL is the right design. You do this by considering your training needs in relation to SDL's particular set of advantages and disadvantages. For example, if you need individualized development in your training process, SDL has that as an advantage, of if you have employees in many locations, you might want to use SDL as your design.

On the other hand, if you have little time for development, SDL is at a disadvantage, or if your material requires a high degree of group synergism, you might think again about using SDL. A list of the advantages and disadvantages of SDL that you can use in your analysis can be found below.

Advantages of Self-Directed Learning

Trainee

Available when trainee is ready	Trainee works at own pace
Individual choice of material	No surprises
Immediate feedback	Provides review and reference

Trainer-Developer

No constantly repeated classes	Less time on road
More time to develop	

Corporation

Multiple-site training	Reduced trainer travel cost
Requires fewer trainers	Reduced meeting room cost

Eliminates trainee travel costs   Just-in-time training

Downtime training   Capture SME knowledge

No training classes when busy   Easier shift training

Cross-training possible   Training consistency (quality)

Development programming   Less aggregate time spent

Disadvantages of Self-Directed Learning

Trainee

Not used to being a self-directed learner   Lack of an instructor

Not comfortable relying on objectives   Needs synergism of group

Trainer-Developer

Difficult to develop properly   Choice of media limited

Must revise more often   Selling concept harder

More trainee preparation needed   Control needs greater

Development time greater

Corporation

Production costs higher   Distribution costs

Reproduction costs   Revision costs

Possible logistics problems

Implementation Analysis

If your analysis of advantages and disadvantages seems to indicate that an SDL design is warranted, you next need to assess the best method for implementing your training. In self-directed learning the way you implement has a large bearing on how you develop. There are two basic implementation strategies in SDL: the learning center and distributed implementation. Basically, if you have or will have a learning center, you'll normally design your self-directed learning to be used there. If you aren't using a center, your SDL will most likely be used on the job, so you will need to design and develop with that fact in mind. This is often a distance learning situation, and is termed a "distributed" SDL implementation.

Format Analysis

Next you need to do a format analysis. Format refers to the media form you will use. This could be anything from paper and pencil to multimedia, depending on what media resources you have available or what funds you have to buy equipment and talent. You must consider your media capabilities, weigh in your implementation plan, and then choose your format within the limitations imposed upon you by these factors.

For example, you may be an excellent designer of computer-based training, but if only half of the 300 work sites where you need to do training have computers, you'll probably want to consider a different format, unless you have a lot of capital funding available. This fact may seem elementary, but many good SDL plans have failed because the hardware was not convenient at the training site or in the learning center, thus negating one of the prime advantages of SDL: availability when the trainee needs it.

Facilitator Analysis

Another assessment you need to perform is a facilitator analysis. In this analysis you look at who will be facilitating your SDL process, either in your learning center or, if you are using a distributed implementation, at your training sites. The facilitators' skills, abilities, and particularly their time and motivation will be limiting factors in how you design your program, so you need to consider them carefully before you begin.

For example, in a distributed implementation done for the 78 branch offices of a national insurance company, a performance evaluation was to be monitored and graded by the facilitators who were the branch managers. The designer found out much too late that the managers were too busy to spend the necessary time and so were delegating the task to subordinates who were not trained to evaluate performance and not current on the correct methods of doing the reports. Thus the evaluations were poorly done, the trainees undertrained and so unable to perform the tasks correctly on the job, and the SDL program was labeled a failure, all because the designer didn't find out if the chosen facilitators had the time to facilitate.

Trainee Analysis

Your final analysis is an assessment of the trainees for whom you're producing SDL. As in classroom instruction, your trainees have certain characteristics and experiences that will determine some of the parameters of your program. The problem is that you will not be able to ascertain these characteristics as you teach and so modify your lesson plan accordingly. By the time the trainee interacts with your SDL, modifications will be impossible, so you must be aware of these characteristics and experiences before you begin developing material.

Literacy and Reading Level.   The most obvious trainee characteristic for any self-directed learning is literacy. If your trainees are unable to read, they are going to have a difficult time in almost any SDL setting.

Reading Levels.   If absolute literacy is a significant consideration, then degree of literacy, commonly referred to as reading level, is also important, perhaps more so, as it affects more of your trainee population. Many studies have been done on reading levels, and plenty of tools are available for checking the level of newly created material. It is your responsibility to analyze your trainees and then decide for yourself what the proper reading level is.

A sixth-grade level is very common for SDL, though technical jargon may raise the level a grade or two. Most development work is now done on word processors and there are instruments available for them that can automatically compute reading level. You should check the level periodically as you write the content to save extensive revision.

Computer Literacy.   While reading skills are important, if you have been thinking about computer-mediated media formats, you'll need to estimate your trainees' computer skills as well. Even small problems such as the inability of a trainee to understand what you mean by a DOS command can negate your entire program. Menus might be necessary, with automatic boots, particularly if you are going into a highly distributed environment with no facilitator available.

Trainee Experience.   As in any training design, the experience a trainee brings to the training tells you where to start and how deep you need to go. Once again, you can't adjust your perceptions later when you see trainees giving you confused looks, so you must analyze correctly now. A poorly done analysis of this factor may lead you to develop a package that is not based on a foundation of information that *every* trainee has already mastered.

Your analysis should try to find the lowest common denominator, that is, the knowledge that you are sure every trainee will bring to the training. This is the point at which you start writing content. Because it is self-directed learning, more advanced learners will quickly move through the basics they already know. Meanwhile your less knowledgeable trainees will be able to take their time going through the entire package, learning everything they need.

Developing and Evaluating SDL

Once your assessment is completed you can begin development. For our discussion of SDL as an instructional design, the SDL package will be considered the main development product of this process. While the connotation of "package" is normally a paper-and-pencil workbook, here we are using it generically as the basic unit of self-directed learning, whether your media is paper, video, or computer. There are four major steps in developing SDL: job analysis, objectives, content, and criterion referencing. Each step is discussed in detail below.

Job Analysis

The first step in development is yet another analysis, the job analysis. A job analysis is one of four critical factors in building a good SDL package. Simply stated, if you are unable or unwilling to do a proper job analysis, your SDL package will not work! Once again, space limits the amount that can be said here about job analysis, but there are other books that discuss the process in detail. For SDL, the product, not the process, is important, and that product is a complete listing of all the tasks that must be mastered for the topic that will be covered in your SDL package.

Objectives

The second critical factor is the writing of trainee-centered objectives and subobjectives, each one directly related to a task in your job analysis. These objectives take the place of the classroom instructor. They guide your trainees through the package, indicating what information is most important and what they must master.

Once again, the same word of caution applies. If you are unable or unwilling to write proper trainee-centered objectives, do not attempt self-directed learning! Nothing has caused more SDL packages to fail than the slighting of this step. It would be akin to a classroom design without an instructor.

As an SDL developer, you must continually remind yourself that your package has to stand on its own. There will be no instructor to explain things, to stress key points, to augment what the developer missed. The trainees go through your package using only the guidance you give them, and the most important aspect of that guidance is the objectives. You *must* take the time to make sure the objectives cover all of the tasks in your analysis, with proper verbs so the trainees understand exactly what is expected of them.

Your objectives should follow a logical sequence, and be repeated often enough for the trainee to key in on them. When your objectives are done, review them. Have a subject-matter expert review them—and another designer do so as well. Make sure they are as clear, concise, and useful as possible, because once they are in the trainee's hands, they will make or break your SDL package.

Content

Your next task is to develop the content for your package. If you've chosen a print medium, this will be what the trainees read to help them to master the objectives. In videotape or slides it's the script; in computer-based training, the text screens. Whatever media your format analysis demands, the important point here is to use your objectives to write the material.

This, as you may have guessed, is the third critical factor in building a good self-directed learning package. Your content must relate directly to your objectives and cover them in enough detail for the trainees to achieve mastery. You may be able to write the content yourself, or you may need a subject-matter expert (SME) to perform this function. Either way, if you've developed good objectives, and developed them based on the job analysis, writing your content directly from the objectives should be the easiest part of the entire process.

As time is money, particularly in an SDL environment where training is often occurring during small packets of "downtime," try to keep away from too much "nice-to-know" information when you write. Your goal is to make your content as concise as possible yet still give the trainees what they need to master the material or skills that the objectives demand. A good review process, particularly a proper pilot which will be discussed later, will help insure that you have reached this goal.

Chunking.   After writing your content you need to break it into smaller, "digestible" pieces that the trainee can easily absorb. This process is called *chunking*. Chunks are separated by review and practice activities. They have various titles, depending on the particular SDL systems. Often the largest are termed *modules*. In a print format a module is usually an entire book. Other terms for smaller chunks are chapters, units, parts, or sections. There are no absolute definitions or accepted delineations for these terms. It's basically up to the SDL designer and the needs of the system. For example, a package, as we have been using the term, is usually a large discrete chunk, with smaller chunks contained within.

Since it's the smallest chunks that directly relate to the trainee's learning, these should be developed with the most consideration and planning. The larger chunks often become self-evident as you look for ways to combine your small ones. A good rule of thumb is that your smallest chunk should normally contain between three and five objectives. Of course realization of this goal is dependent on how much material is covered by an objective, but if you did a good job of developing enough objectives to guide the trainee adequately, this rule should serve you well.

Chunks usually begin with a restatement of the objectives that will be covered in them and directions on how to go about the learning. These directions are normally boilerplate and simply remind the trainee of the most efficient way to do the learning, based on how the material has been developed. Chunks typically end with some form of separator that provides a summary or review. Often this review includes a self-test in which the trainees answer questions and then check their own answers. There might also be some type of skills practice, if the objectives are more performance-based in nature.

This formalized beginning and ending, with some modification, is essential for all sizes of chunks, from the largest to the smallest. Whether it's a module, book, section, videotape, or new series of computer screens, the chunk should always begin with a statement of the objectives that will be covered in the coming material and end with a way for the trainees to evaluate their learning. This preorganizer and postevaluation helps the trainees develop a sense of responsibility for their own learning, one of the important elements of SDL.

Media Formats.   With your chunking done, you now need to produce the pieces that will make up your SDL package. Depending on your format, you'll probably have media to develop and a layout to plan.

Paper and Pencil.   If you're using a simple paper-and-pencil format, you need to plan how your book will look. Plenty of white space is a must, to make for easy reading. Graphics, if they are the right graphics, are also important. Special techniques such as blocking, shading, boarders, different size fonts, etc., all add to the readability and effectiveness of your package.

To accomplish these effects you need a good desktop publishing program combined with a high-quality laser printer and digital scanner. This equipment not only makes the material more usable for your trainees but it also gives you an edge when you show your completed package to the executive committee and ask for their support in making self-directed learning a reality in your organization. Many good SDL programs have been given extra credibility when the CEO notes that he is impressed by how the package "looks."

Slide-Tape and Video.   If you're using slide-tape or video as your format, you may feel that you can ignore these "print hints." However, in SDL, both of these formats require a companion print segment, with objectives, instructions, activities, and evaluation measures. That piece needs to look as good as the rest of your program—and be just as usable as any stand-alone print process.

Along with the print segment, you'll need to develop the visuals for a slide-tape or video format. Here you must guard against cognitive dissonance. Cognitive dissonance is the displaying of a visual while the trainee reads, hears, or is otherwise told about something different from what the visual shows. Once again, in SDL there is *no one* to provide clarification if the trainee becomes confused because your visual uses different terminology, or is too complex, or simply wasn't visible long enough to be digested. So be sure that all visuals match your verbiage, and that the trainee is given enough time to benefit from them. As with objectives and content, a strong systematic review process is important for your media.

Computer Formats.   Everything we've discussed so far concerning media formats goes double for computer-based training, interactive video, multimedia, and all the other exotic designs that are so useful for SDL. While these processes provide their own print component in the form of a computer screen, the rules and techniques of good print formatting apply to these screens in the same way as they apply to the written page. And don't forget the cardinal rule for any computer-mediated format: *Never develop an electronic page turner.* If you are going to add video or digital effects to your CBT, the rules of basic graphics and video apply as well, so use them.

Computers are marvelous instruments for SDL, and their uses are almost limitless, but hi-tech does not make up for poor development. Content and graphics must fit together, and be of the highest possible quality, whether your format is as simple as a print booklet or as complicated as multimedia.

Packaging.   One final thought on print formats also has applicability to any SDL process. When a print package is nearing completion one of the last steps is to plan for its binding. Your decision on the type of binding requires a consideration of what it will cost, how it will look, and most importantly, your program's need for revision. If you have to make a lot of copies, and they have to be revised often, cheap binding such as staples or hot glue might be best. On the other hand, they look cheap and are not as durable. For programs that will require a lot of single-page revisions, a ring binder, while initially expensive, may be cheaper and more practical in the long run.

Such "revision necessities" may affect your other media formats as well. For example, before you decide that interactive video is the only logical approach for your SDL package, you should consider how often you may have to revise it and how much it's going to cost each time you do. This might change your mind about the "most logical approach."

Choosing and developing your evaluation methodology is the next process to consider. There are two types of evaluations in SDL: evaluation of the trainee and evaluation of the package or system.

Trainee Evaluation

Evaluation of the trainee is done through mechanisms such as self-quizzes, which were mentioned earlier as chunk separators; written exams; and performance evaluations. In SDL these trainee evaluations are developed under a strict set of guidelines. Each question must relate directly back to an objective, thus guaranteeing that the answer is covered in the material that you developed from them. Cognitive objectives demand cognitive questions that expressly ask for the behaviors identified by the objectives' cognitive verbs. Performance objectives require performance evaluations. These techniques must measure the trainees' ability to accomplish the tasks that were delineated by the objective practiced in the activities and exemplified in the material.

Criterion Referencing.   This "criterion referencing" of trainee evaluation questions is the fourth and final critical factor (the others being job analysis, objectives, and content) in the development of a good SDL package. SDL test questions and evaluations are not formulated to trick the trainee. They are not developed to look for those "certain intangibles" that a "really good" test question can discern. They are written directly from the objectives and can be answered directly from the material. There are no hidden meanings or trick questions. The information is all there, right in front of the trainees, and keyed so they can find it and learn it. The concept of criterion referencing is relatively simple yet difficult for developers to achieve unless they continually remind themselves of its importance.

Criterion referencing is also the reason that self-directed learning can be considered a mastery process, thus completing the earlier definition. If the trainees know what's expected, can find it in an efficient manner, and are evaluated on that and that alone, they can master the materials on their own, and at relatively high levels. Eighty-five percent mastery on a good SDL package is common, and 95 percent is not unusual.

Question Reviews.   Once you have developed your questions, they need to be reviewed to insure that they are criterion-referenced. For best results, each question should be reviewed at least twice. The first review should consider how well each question relates to its objective and to the rules of good question writing. This task needs to be done by an instructional designer other than the original developer who understands these processes and knows what to look for.

The second review should be done by an SME whose task is to make sure the answers can be found in the material, and that both questions and answers are accurate. Once again the original developer, even if he or she is an SME, should not do this review. A fresh viewpoint from someone less involved in the writing will provide better results.

This review can be part of the SME review that you always perform on each of your packages after you have completed development. The SME has a number of responsibilities in the review process, depending on the needs of the SDL system you have developed, content accuracy, currency, and question relevance, to name a few.

A final review of your questions, to determine if the trainees themselves can answer them accurately, should occur as part of the piloting process that you do before any SDL package is distributed. Use subjects for your pilot who are as closely matched to your target trainees as possible in terms of knowledge and learning characteristics. If your package requires that the material be done on the job, you will have to take your package to the trainees, on the job, for the pilot. Observe how the trainees work through your package, and where they have problems. After they have finished, ask them questions based on your observations. Analyze their answers to the test questions to determine what they missed and why.

The second aspect of SDL evaluation is evaluation of the package or system (if you have a group of packages). This occurs after the program is in use and can be broken down into five parameters:

1. *Sufficiency.*   With this parameter, you consider if all the information the trainee needs to complete the objectives is available in the package. Your pilot and other reviews should have caught most of the problems here, but by asking those who have completed the package and, more importantly, used the information back on the job, you may find unsuspected areas that need augmentation. This parameter takes on more importance in an SDL system where you will want to know if you have all of the packages out there that you need.

2. *Usability.*   With this parameter, you try to determine if your packages are as easy to use as possible. Once again, you will need to ask the users, and the facilitators as well, to get this information.

3. *Currency.*   With currency, you consider whether the information in your package is up to date. For this you need to talk to SMEs and have them review the package for changes that have occurred since it was distributed.

4. *Compliance.*   With compliance, you consider whether the packages are actually being used in training as they were designed to. Once again, facilitators and users are the people to ask, but for you to really do a good job in this area, the best method is personal observation.

5. *Effectiveness.*   Simply stated, with this parameter you consider if the trainees have mastered the objectives. You have already developed evaluation measures to assess this as part of the user evaluation, so you only need to collect the data from these evaluations and analyze it using good statistical technique.

Preparing for SDL

Before you actually implement your self-directed learning you need to lay the groundwork for it by preparing various levels of the organization.

Preparing the Company and Company Management

The first step in preparing management for SDL is to talk to them at meetings. If you've done your development work well, you should have good-looking, user-friendly packages to exhibit. You'll need to explain what management's role is in the SDL process and how the control measures that your programs need will function. Then ask for management's commitment to the enforcement of the discipline that will make the system work.

This process starts with top management, and should work its way down as far as you can logically go. Don't miss a chance to go to any meeting and talk. Stress the advantages of SDL. If your organization is so large that you can't get to the lower management levels personally, train other people to do so. The best approach is to explain the program to a manager's direct superior and have him or her explain it to the manager. Develop fact sheets concerning the system that your surrogates can follow in their presentations to help them do the job effectively.

Preparing Direct Supervisors

The second group that you need to prepare for an SDL implementation is the direct supervisors of your trainees. These individuals can have a great effect on your system in how they help to prepare the trainees. They also influence compliance with your program as a whole. Basically, supervisors can supply some of the external motivation and guidance that the learners perceive as otherwise missing in the self-directed learning process.

An effective method for supervisor preparation is a self-directed learning package on self-directed learning. This concept is particularly useful when you have large numbers of supervisors in many different locations, as you might find in a distributed implementation. An SDL-on-SDL package can explain the basic concepts of your system to the supervisor while he or she is actually experiencing it.

After completing the package, the supervisors will have the background necessary to formally discuss the process of self-directed learning with the trainees. This basis will help move them to a state of readiness for self-direction as well as clarify what SDL really means to the company and to each position. Such discussions should also detail what the trainees' responsibilities are in the system. This step is all part of the trainee preparation process.

Preparing Trainees for SDL

To prepare trainees well, we need to understand them well. The learner is the one factor that is common to all forms of self-directed learning and, as noted earlier, most learners have one thing in common—they are usually *not* prepared to engage in SDL. The key to preparing a trainee for self-directed learning is to develop a systematic plan for this purpose that helps her or him to get comfortable with the idea of SDL.

One aspect of this plan is to sell the trainee on the advantages of self-directed learning: working at your own pace; availability when you need it; structure to help you learn easier; long-term reinforcement and review; and the many others we listed earlier.

The concept "sell" is the real purpose of trainee preparation. You must first interest the trainees in the idea of self-directed learning; then you must convince them of its usefulness by helping them envision using it. As the envisioning becomes comfortable, questions will occur that need to be answered. This is a classic representation of the selling process, and it should be the designer's goal in trainee preparation.

Most effective plans have the common factor of being instructor-mediated, preferably by the designated SDL facilitator-implementor. It may sound a bit illogical to have an instructor-led process prepare for self-directed learning. However, if you reconsider our earlier discussions concerning enhancing self-directedness, you'll understand why trainee preparation is best handled by a live instructor.

Four Steps for Trainee Preparation

No matter how you decide to execute your plan, there are four steps that usually make up the process:

Step 1: Definition.   You first state your overall definition of self-directed learning, then discuss that definition as it relates to the trainees. The leader should point out the differences and similarities to what the trainees are used to as far as training is concerned. Finally, the things that will be easier to do thanks to the self-directed learning system are explored. The primary task is to get the trainees interested.

Step 2: Advantages and disadvantages.   Next, the advantages and disadvantages need to be emphasized. The most important advantage, working at your own pace and without the aid of an instructor, should be discussed first. The freedom to personally control your learning, combined with the responsibility of being your own guide, exemplifies this concept nicely. On the negative side, it should be noted that if results don't quite match expectations, there is no one to blame but yourself. Other advantages that flow from these concepts, such as the ability to repeat material until mastery is achieved and the personal control of content flow, should be discussed next. This is where the trainees will begin envisioning themselves using the packages.

Step 3: Package mechanics.   With the vision begun, the third area details the mechanics of the learning package and implementation system. This step will solidify the envisioning process.

Step 4: Summary and reinforcement.   The final area begins with another reinforcement of the advantages of the new system. (Skip the disadvantages this time; trainees have heard them, and this is the time for a little less fairness and a little more propaganda.) Be sure that all questions have been fully answered. Then conclude by restating how to get started.

Developing good, well-planned trainee preparation that presents the advantages of SDL in ways that help develop and enhance those possibly atrophied self-directedness characteristics is part of your job as an SDL designer. It will make your implementation of self-directed learning easier and more effective.

Implementing SDL

With your package(s) completed and preparation under way, you now need to implement your SDL plan as determined during your implementation analysis. As noted earlier, there are two basic implementation strategies for SDL: the learning-center approach and distributed implementation, which is normally a distance-learning technique.

The Self-Directed Learning Center

Learning centers have many names. Designations such as Resource Center, Individualized Instruction Center, Learning Laboratory, and Training Facility are all used to denote a learning center, and a learning center can be a process that goes well beyond simple self-directed learning. For this discussion we will define a learning center as a specified location where SDL packages are stored and used.

A learning center for self-directed learning can be of any size or shape, located in a basement or a closet, as simple as a room with a table, or as complex as a simulator in a nuclear plant. However, it has two basic characteristics that make it a learning center. First, its *primary purpose* is to be a location where self-directed learning occurs. Second, an easily accessible facilitator is always on duty when the center is in operation. This second characteristic doesn't necessarily mean that the center must have its own staff. It does mean that when the center is open, a person whose first responsibility is to staff it must be available.

The terms *first* and *primary* in the preceding paragraph are important. Both the learning center and the facilitator may fill other roles. Neither of them has to be exclusively dedicated to the completion of SDL packages. However, if an SDL need arises, it takes precedence for both.

The main advantage of using a learning center is its physical presence. Because it's there, with your packages in it, your trainees can take advantage of the materials you've created when they are ready to learn. Its "being there" also means that as an SDL developer you can use its strengths in your package design. These strengths might include

- Particular equipment that it has available, so you can format a package in the most effective way

- A centralized location that all your trainees can access and that you can control

- Growing trainee comfort in going there to use your packages as they meet with success in their first SDL endeavors

- A facilitator

You can't overrate the advantage of knowing you'll have a knowledgeable facilitator available when you are designing your packages and developing materials. He or she can help start the trainees off properly, watch for problems, provide equipment, evaluate, and do a multitude of other tasks that might be necessary to the success of your packages. The facilitator will also help you to control your SDL process more closely, in itself an advantage of the learning center.

Disadvantages of a learning-center approach include the expense and time involved in setting up the center, the salary cost of the facilitator, and its lack of flexibility when on-the-job performances are practiced.

When developing a learning center, you need to consider location and facilitation and other factors such as budget, furniture and equipment, control of trainee flow, hours of operation, publicity, and evaluation of the center's effectiveness.

Distributed SDL Implementation

The other major implementation strategy for self-directed learning is distributed implementation. While usually characterized by multiple sites, which makes it a distance-learning process, a distributed self-directed learning implementation is best distinguished by where it takes place, or who is responsible for it, than by how many locations it takes place in. It is possible for a company with a single location, like a hospital, to need a distributed implementation strategy.

There are a number of factors that indicate the need for a distributed implementation. The first one is elementary. If you will not have an actual learning center, you will need to use a distributed implementation for your SDL packages. But you need to consider this carefully: There are many different forms of learning centers, ranging from whole buildings to closets. If you have a learning center, no matter how underfunded or understaffed, and you put your packages there, you are using a learning-center implementation. Even if people take your programs home from your center, it's not necessarily a distributed implementation.

On the other hand, if you plan to ship your programs out from a centralized location to sites that are not learning centers, you have a distance-learning process and will probably use a distributed implementation.

A more subtle, and perhaps more important, indicator of the need for a distributed implementation than the lack of a learning center relates to what you design into your self-directed learning packages. If your objectives and activities include practice in a work environment, you're probably going to need a distributed implementation system.

Work environment practice (you might stretch the point a bit by calling it *on-the-job training*) usually needs to be done on the job. This means that your packages are not used in a training center, but rather in a store, on the manufacturing floor, in the office, or wherever the job is done. Your packages and implementation must be designed to take these less-formalized training settings into account.

A third indicator is your training population. If the self-directed learning must go to them on the job, because that's the only place that logistics allows, you will have a distributed implementation. This type of SDL implementation might be chosen because of the number of trainees you need to train, the distances you have to cover, the time span in which the training must occur, turnover considerations, or simply corporate finances.

Problems to watch for in a distributed SDL implementation include cost and logistics of distribution of the SDL packages, control measures to ensure they are completed the way you designed them to be, revision logistics, and evaluation of both the trainees and package effectiveness.

There is no singular reason for choosing one SDL implementation over the other. Rather, as with the development of your SDL packages, you need to do a careful analysis of all the factors, and ask yourself, or your SMEs, the proper questions. Most important, take nothing for granted. Wait until all the facts are in before making your decision, then be flexible enough to change it if necessary.

Distance Learning Through Other Formats

Since we've already discussed distance learning in terms of a distributed SDL implementation, let's look at some other distance-learning methods.

Telephones

The most prevalent use of telephones for distance learning is in teleconferencing. Teleconferencing is seldom a formal learning intervention, as there are usually no trainee-based objectives or systematic design to the process. That's not to say that learning does not occur, but it is more from chance than from plan. Teleconferencing is good for simultaneous distribution of information, great for brainstorming, and can even be used as a lecture method in very limited situations.

Augmentations such as the use of fax machines and electronic blackboards or individual tablets for graphics can increase the effectiveness of formal telephone training but at substantially increased complexity and cost as well. Speaker phones or individual headsets free the trainees' hands for note taking but create noise and compatibility problems.

If you plan on using some form of telephone-mediated training, objectives, trainee guides, workbooks, and facilitators at the training sites will enhance your program considerably.

When designing, take advantage of the interactive capacity of the telephone, and develop questions, role-plays, and other interactive techniques.

When using telephone conferencing, guard against extraneous noise, be sure to have all speakers identify themselves each time they speak, and, as in a classroom situation, be prepared for "dead air" after you ask a question. Instantaneous transmission or not, it still takes people time to think.

Video (Satellite) Conferencing

Video conferencing, often referred to as teletraining, has become the most recognized form of distance learning. It is usually associated with a satellite uplink-downlink process, though some video distance learning is done through land-based microwave transmission and even through hard-wire (now more fiber-optic) cables.

Early use of video distance learning was usually for a lecture process, but as it became less a novelty and more a training tool, better instructional designs have been replacing the "talking head" in satellite broadcasts. These designs require the same type of detailed analysis that you would do for any training program, which were discussed earlier in this chapter. Your materials should include comprehensive student workbooks, designed to make the process as interactive as possible. Objectives are once again paramount, particularly if the system you are using does not allow for two-way communication.

Satellite instructors need to be well prepared, and rehearsals before the live broadcast are a must. Demonstrations must be planned and practiced meticulously. Even the instructor's clothing, jewelry, and gestures have to be planned out to ensure that they do not become distractions.

The trainees need to be prepared as well, with at least a fact sheet that explains what should and should not be expected during the training and what their responsibilities are.

One of the keys to a good teleconferencing learning process is the site facilitator. These individuals need to be trained in their role, given strong support, and used effectively. This process includes providing facilitators with proper course materials and rosters (a last-minute fax addendum is always a good idea), making them as much a part of the rehearsals as possible, providing them with basic technical information in case of problems, and designing interactions into the instruction in which facilitators can take part. This latter activity might be as simple as fielding questions for later discussion or as complex as leading role-plays and simulations. Facilitators can also play an important role in the evaluation and critiquing of the trainees and the program.

There are many levels and complexities to video distance learning, from a self-directed video that you mail to trainees in a distributed SDL implementation to the most modern in two-way voice and video teleconferencing. As in SDL itself, the key is to analyze your needs and determine which, if any, of its advantages serves your training processes best. Then design and develop your instruction systematically so it takes advantage of the strengths of the system and minimizes its weaknesses.

Computer Distance Learning

Another form of distance training involves the use of computers. As with video learning, there are many levels of this process as well, ranging from a distributed SDL approach to live computer network interactive conferencing. In between are self-directed learning programs available on computer networks (desktop learning), bulletin-board approaches where the interactions are not immediate, and even instructor-led interactions.

Use of computers for distance learning, particularly if networks are already in existence, costs less than use of a video satellite distribution. It allows for more interaction as well. Depending on the system in use, you can even use slow scan or in some cases live-action video through the computers. Compared to telephones, computers allow for easier use of graphics and are not as noise-sensitive.

Design, particularly objectives, is still the key issue. Control is also important, particularly in a multiparticipant, two-way interactive process. If you plan on a more systematized approach with some form of instructor or discussion leader, the same design and implementation hints detailed for video conferencing will serve you well for computer distance learning.

Bibliography

Bynum, M., and Nate Rosenblatt, "Self-Study: Boon or Bust?" *Training*, November 1964, pp. 61–64.

Cox, John H., "A New Look at Learner-Controlled Instruction," *Training and Development Journal*, March 1982, pp. 90–94.

Feeney, Edward J., "Beat the High Cost of Training Through LCI," *Training and Development Journal*, September 1981, pp. 41–43.

Hammond, M., and R. Collins, *Self-Directed Learning: Critical Practice*, Nichols/GP Publishing, New York, 1991.

Hiemstra, R., and B. Sisco, *Individualizing Instruction*, Jossey-Bass, San Francisco, 1990.

Kearlsey, G., *Training for Tomorrow: Distributed Learning Through Computer and Communications Technology*, Addison-Wesley, Reading, MA, 1985.

Kerr, E., "Electronic Leadership: A Guide to Moderating Online Conferences," *IEEE Transactions: Professional Communications*, 29(1), pp. 12–18.

Knowles, M. K., "How Do You Get People to Be Self-Directed Learners?" *Training and Development Journal*, May 1980, pp. 96–99.

Levine, T. K., *Teaching Telecourses: Opportunities and Options*, The Annenberg/CPB Project, Washington, DC, 1987.

Long, H., "Truth Unguessed and Yet to Be Discovered," in H. Long and Associates, *Self-Directed Learning: Emerging Theory and Practice*, Norman, OK, University of Oklahoma, 1989.

Long, H., "Changing Concepts of Self-Direction in Learning," in H. Long and Associates, *Advances in Research and Practice in Self-Directed Learning*, Norman, OK, University of Oklahoma, 1990.

Mentzer, Dean, *The Effect of Response Mode Upon the Achievement and Retention of Student Nurses Taught Life Science by Audio-Tutorial Instruction*, University Microfilms International, Ann Arbor, MI, 1974.

Ostendorf, V. A., *Teaching Through Interactive Television*, Virginia A. Ostendorf, Inc., Littleton, CO, 1989.

Piskurich, G., "Ensure Quality and Quality Training Through Self-Directed Learning," *Training and Development Journal*, September 1991.

Piskurich, G., "Individualized Media Instruction: A Dream Come True?" *Training and Development Journal*, December 1983, pp. 68–69.

Piskurich, G., *A Partially Centralized and Partially Decentralized Training System in a Health Care Setting*, University Microfilms International, Ann Arbor, MI, 1985.

Piskurich, G., *Self-Directed Learning: A Practical Guide to Design, Development, and Implementation*, Jossey-Bass, San Francisco, 1993.

Penland, P., "Self-Initiated Learning," *Adult Education, 29*, pp. 170–179.

Romiszowski, A. J., *Developing Auto-Instructional Materials*, Kogan Page, Ltd., London, England, 1986.

Rowntree, Derek, *Teaching Through Self-Instruction*, Kogan Page, Ltd., London, England, 1986.

Steinberg, E. R., *Teaching Computers to Teach*, Lawrence Erlbaum, Hillsdale, NJ, 1984.

Young, Deborah, *An Explanatory Study of the Relationship Between Organizational Climate and Self-Directed Learning Among Organizational Managers*, Kansas City, MO, University of Missouri, 1986.

Zimmer, M. B., "A Practical Guide to Videoconferencing," *Training and Development Journal*, April 1988, pp. 84–87.

23

Meetings!

Edward E. Scannell

Edward E. Scannell is Director of the Center for Professional Development and Training in Scottsdale, Arizona. He has been active in both civic and professional organizations, having served on the boards of directors of a number of groups including ASTD, the Tempe Chamber of Commerce, Meeting Professionals International (MPI), and the National Speakers Association. He was elected National President of ASTD in 1982 and later served a two-year term as Executive Chairman of the International Federation of Training and Development Organizations. An active member of the National Speakers Association (NSA), and its national president in 1991–1992, he earned his C.S.P. (Certified Speaking Professional) from NSA. He has given over 1000 presentations, seminars, and workshops across the United States and in several overseas venues. He has also given presentations to dozens of ASTD chapters and has appeared at both national and international HRD conferences. He has written or coauthored several books and over 100 articles in the field of HRD. His best-selling Games Trainers Play series is used by speakers, trainers, and meeting planners around the world. Scannell was formerly Director of the University Conference Bureau at Arizona State University; he also taught at the ASU College of Business and previously at the University of Northern Iowa.

In days gone by, it seemed there were only two sure things, death and taxes! Today, however, ask most anyone in any size or type of organization, and they will most certainly add a third item to that dubious list—that being meetings! And it's almost another certainty that we hold all three with the same amount of enthusiasm!

Whether we're talking about two people discussing an office problem, a regional manager conducting her quarterly sales meeting, an HRD manager facilitating a three-day team-building program, a professional speaker addressing 400 people at an incentive meeting, or a CEO opening a firm's annual international congress at an overseas venue, we're all involved in this world of meetings.

Meetings are indeed "big business"; consider a recent study by the American Society of Association Executives which suggests that the meetings industry is a $75-billion-a-year business! And that figure is based only on those dollars spent on meetings held by state and national associations. Couple that figure with one from ASTD which estimates that over $200 billion is expended for employee education, and you begin to get the picture: Meetings are big business!

Overview

Because meetings are so all-encompassing, this chapter will address the many and varied facets of the different types of meetings. Indeed, since the term *meeting* itself could be used to correctly identify anything from a quick 15-minute get-together to discuss that office problem to a chief executive officer pounding the gavel to begin an International Congress, it's important we begin by setting forth definitions for some of the more commonly used types of meetings.

We'll devote some time to the smaller staff, sales, or board meeting and also cover the basics of meeting planning for the larger-scale meeting, conference, or convention. We'll also include a number of checklists that will be helpful in developing, designing, or delivering any type of meeting.

Purpose of This Chapter

While we realize that most HRD professionals are not likely to be charged with orchestrating large-scale conferences on a daily basis, it is becoming increasingly evident that we all spend considerable time in "meetings." One study, in fact, suggests that people in middle management and higher may well spend 63 percent of their time in meetings!

The major purpose of this chapter is simply to identify the different types of meetings and to offer concrete, practical tools and techniques to make any type of meeting more productive and cost-effective.

Why People Attend Meetings

What if you gave a party and nobody came? What if you planned a meeting and nobody came? Well, certainly, if you're the boss and called a meeting for Tuesday morning at 10, more than likely, most everyone would attend. That's a given in the corporate world. But such attendance is not necessarily the case when it comes to association meetings, public seminars, or even voluntarily attended training programs.

So the question, "Why attend meetings?" is a germane one. Turning our attention to the large-scale annual association conference, let's look at some attendant reasons people come. Alvin Toffler (of *Future Shock* fame) suggests that people come to meetings for one or more of the reasons discussed below.

1. Information

The audiences of the 1990s are quite different from their counterparts of even a few years ago. They are hungry for content, i.e., they want information. They want to learn new concepts, skills, or knowledge that will help them today, not 10 years from now. State-of-the-art information is a part of the learning organization. This is not to imply that the days of "fun and games" are passé; on the contrary, people certainly want to have an enjoyable and even a fun experience, but they also want to learn something at the same time. Many HRD professionals are well aware that indeed learning can be fun, but content must be the most important ingredient of any meeting.

2. Networking

Not surprisingly, we find that many people choose to attend meetings and conventions because of the partnering, networking, and overall collegiality they will find among fellow attendees. Perhaps they haven't had a chance to share "war stories" with their counterparts from around the country or even the globe. Whatever the reason, frankly there are heavy numbers who attend meetings simply to see friends! This may not be all bad. Many HRD professionals would acknowledge that perhaps as much, if not more, "learning" takes place in these hallway conversations, during coffee breaks, etc., as occurs in the general or concurrent sessions.

Few of us would not agree to this premise. Perhaps we're facing a particular pressing problem, the answer to which is evasive, until we are casually discussing the world in general, and the conversation turns to our respective jobs and their challenges. Often, we find that George or Mary just experienced a similar situation and we discover that the way they handled it may well work for us. We get back to the office and—eureka! It did!

We often find that senior members of the association tend to believe "they've heard it all" and won't admit they can still learn new concepts. Obviously, this occurrence shouldn't happen, but it most assuredly does. Sell them on networking. Often, these very people can be "sold" on attending by having them contribute as panel members, speakers, hosts, or mentors. Use their experience!

3. Recreation

"All work and no play..." That's right; some people attend meetings just for the fun of it. That "fun," of course, may take a variety of forms such as golf, tennis, jogging, etc. Whatever the case, the astute meeting professional may build these types of recreational activities into the program. Indeed, in certain kinds of meetings, namely incentive meetings, the major thrust may be devoted to golf, tennis, and other outdoor activities. Although there will likely be some program time to cover business issues or topics, the primary purpose of the meeting is recreation.

It is also important to consider the geographic venue when scheduling program time. For example, when holding meetings in Hawaii, it is common to begin the program early in the morning hours, with the afternoons left open for optional activities. For example, when it's 6 a.m. in Hawaii, it's already 11 a.m. or 12 p.m. (depending on the time of year) in New York. Take advantage of this time differential and schedule accordingly. (But, please don't forget, this also works in reverse! Maybe a 7 a.m. program start time is acceptable for a program in New York, but that's also 4 a.m. on the West Coast!)

Some Additional Factors to Consider

Certainly, the three reasons listed (information, networking, and recreation), are factors we can relate to in our own decision-making process. However, for most of us, there are numerous other factors to consider.

A recent study by Virginia Polytechnic Institute and State University on this question brought forth an interesting array of responses: "What's the most important factor for attendees in selecting a conference?" The top five responses looked like this:

1. Hearing practicing industry speakers
2. Developing business and professional contacts
3. Keeping up with changes
4. Hearing well-known speakers in related fields
5. Exchanging new ideas

Conspicuous by its absence in this research project is one item that most experienced meeting professionals would definitely add, that being "location." For many attendees, the venue selected plays a major role in deciding whether or not to attend.

As is readily apparent, your attendees will have their own criteria in deciding to attend your meeting. Certainly, there will be some correlation with the items listed here. But the true HRD professional understands that no one single factor will necessarily be a selling point to all participants. Therefore, the more of these items we can build into our promotional efforts, the more likely will we be able to increase attendance.

Program Planning

The term *marketing concept* suggests that everything one does in any organization is geared toward the final end, i.e., the consumer. Well tested in both theory and practice, the concept states that essentially all marketing functions start with that "customer" and that myriad and varied activities emanate from, and to, that target market. Applying this marketing concept to your programming and meeting planning efforts appears to be a relevant and instructive task. That is to say, all your training programs, meetings, conferences, etc., must be aimed at your target market. Indeed, your employee, attendee, or colleague is your "customer"!

Although this is an obvious and seemingly evident truism, we still find too many situations in our field where this simple truth is overlooked. We've come a long way since Henry Ford's classic statement, "Give them any color they want, as long as it's black"! We still find those cases where programming and marketing are done at the whims and wishes of the marketer rather than the market.

The Marketing Mix

To provide a vehicle to use in building more effective meetings, workshops, and conferences, let's again revert to our marketing-concept theme. With some editorial paraphrasing, we'll borrow another marketing term known as the *marketing mix*. The marketing mix identifies the so-called Four P's of marketing, namely product, place, promotion, and price. With some additional modification, we'll propose the "program mix" or the "meetings mix" as follows. We'll start our process, of course, with our customer or the first "P," the participant. The meeting or training program must be designed in terms of his or her needs, wants, background, education, experience, etc. Our meeting mix looks as in Fig. 23-1.

Figure 23-1. Meeting mix.

The proper marketing mix consists of the following:

1. *The participant.* As suggested, all planning must start with your participant, whomever that "customer" might be. Recognizing that most organizations have a diverse workforce, you should learn as much as possible about the people coming to your meeting. Because of the diversity, this, of course, is much easier said than done! Needs assessment, observation, focus groups, surveys, and other types of informal research will help you to get some idea as to the profile of the prospective audience.

2. *The product (program).* For our purposes, we'll substitute the "program" for the product. After all, the program really is the item we're selling! This is the real heart of our meeting mix! The program content, the speakers, topics, etc., are important factors in one's choosing to attend a meeting. With the continued emphasis in the 1990s toward the learning organization, our customers demand state-of-the-art information.

3. *The place.* In retailing, experts tell us the three most important parts are location, location, and, of course, location! While one might debate the transferability of that premise to meetings, location is, without question, a critically important factor. With ever-increasing costs of travel and lodging, centralized locales may bring higher attendances. However, in many cases, coast-to-coast airfares are less than those for intermediate stops! For corporate meetings, many HRD professionals will opt to use a local hotel rather than using in-plant facilities.

4. *Promotion.* The old adage about building "a better mousetrap" never was and never will be true. Your best programs or meetings will go for naught if nobody knows about them! Simple as that sounds, we still find colleagues who forget all about "selling" that meeting. A continuing promotional effort is important in getting the word out.

5. *The price.* In these days of accountability and continual references to the bottom line, it is imperative to give quality and value in all offerings. As indicated above, costs continually escalate, and ways must be discovered to make every meeting cost-effective. On the other hand, people tend to equate price with value, so bear in mind that it is quite possible to price something too low; e.g., a prospective participant may believe "at that price, it can't be very good"—and not attend a meeting! You see our point.

6. *The plan.*   Although listed here as the last item in our mix, the plan is also the very first. For it is with the overall marketing or meeting plan that we begin our activities. What are the objectives of the meeting? What about the theme? Food functions? These are but a few of the ingredients that go into this part of the blending.

The Mix.   You should use these elements in the proper mix. It is not unlike a skillful chef taking the proper ingredients and making a masterpiece out of them, whereas another person, using the same ingredients, comes out with a different result. So too with the HRD professional—the skillful blending of these six elements will help ensure effective programming.

Effective Meetings

What makes an effective meeting? What are the skills and areas of expertise that professional meeting planners possess that enable them to orchestrate excellent meetings?

An intensive study, "Achieving Excellence in Meetings and Meeting Management," published by Meeting Professionals International (MPI) addressed those questions and arrived at some interesting answers.

In response to the question about what makes an effective meeting, MPI found there was no single answer, but rather each of four constituencies, the sponsoring organization, the attendee, the supplier (hotel, airline, exhibitor, etc.), and the meeting planner, all had different perspectives! Top management felt a meeting was successful when the meeting's goals or objectives were achieved. The attendees felt somewhat similar, but were frankly, and not surprisingly, more interested in their own personal goals and expectations rather than the meeting's goals. Suppliers felt a meeting was successful when the needs of the group were communicated in advance and if all parties were satisfied. The meeting planner obviously liked positive feedback and felt content if things went according to plan, with no last-minute surprises.

In regard to competencies needed for meeting planners, it was reported that meeting managers must possess over 50 skills and attributes! These tend to fall into the following five areas:

1. Cognitive style
2. Interpersonal style
3. Work habits and organization
4. Organizational style
5. Technical knowledge and skills

The Many Facets of Meeting Planning

Rather than recite the litany of the dozens of skills referred to in the MPI study, let's pick out several that are central to any meeting and therefore critical to the success of that particular event.

Admittedly, such a brief listing may exclude certain areas that are key ingredients for your program. We recognize the importance of exhibits as an integral part of many conferences and conventions. (Take, for example, the hundreds of booths at the ASTD International Conferences which also offer educational value to the conference.) But for most local or regional HRD meetings, we don't get involved with large-scale trade shows.

In planning any event, we can refer back to the often-used "5 W's" to remind us of a few factors that are always important. These are:

1. *Who*—Who will be coming to the training session or meeting?
2. *What*—What is the program? What are the goals?
3. *Where*—Where should we hold it? On-site? At a hotel?
4. *Why*—Why are we doing this? Why should people come?
5. *When*—When should the meeting be held? For how long?

Don't be misled by the simplicity of these five points. They can be real allies for you in your planning process.

In addition to the 5 W's, some more of the necessary functions include the items below, along with a few attendant questions:

1. *Needs assessment.* Since most HRD practitioners are familiar with needs assessment, it's a comfortable, as well as logical, place to begin. Because there is continued emphasis on cost-effective meetings, the first question to ask is simply, "Is this meeting necessary?" Don't be surprised if you get an awkward silence when you ask your colleagues, "Why are we having this meeting?" (Incidentally, the answer "because we always have this annual sales meeting" is not good enough!)

2. *Objectives.* In our HRD field, you've heard the saying, "You can't get lost if you don't know where you're going!" By the same token, unless we have specific, measurable goals, how can we possibly know if we've achieved them? Sadly, most meetings do not have goals or stated objectives. If you doubt that, tell us about the goals for your last meeting. What were your objectives? Did anyone else know what they were?

3. *The program.* The program is, of course, the real heart of any meeting. Because today's audiences want information, make sure your program is filled with relevant, timely content. However, don't forget about information overload. Balance your meeting time with adequate breaks, meal functions, and perhaps even some time for recreation. Sprinkle lecture-type sessions into your planning, but allow heavily for small-group sessions with interaction and participative techniques built in.

4. *The attendees.* Find out as much as possible about the participants. Are they newcomers or veterans in the field? What about their backgrounds and experience? What is their average age? Educational background? How about their expectations? Are they bringing spouses, partners, or families? Obviously, you'll never learn as much as you may want about the profile of your attendees, but the more you know about them, the better you'll be able to target their needs, wants, and expectations.

5. *Site selection.* In choosing a venue for your meetings, there are literally dozens of factors to be taken into consideration. Many HRD people prefer to take even their internal meetings to a local or closeby hotel or conference center. Although there are merits, of course, in conducting the training programs on-

site, there are often too many interruptions, people running back to the office, etc.

A recent study of corporate and association meeting planners conducted by *Meetings and Conventions,* a leading industry publication, ranked these items as the top five factors in selecting a city or location:

Availability of suitable hotels, facilities, etc.

Ease of travel to city

Travel costs

Distance from attendees

Climate

Obviously, there are several other criteria to be considered, for example, working with unions, the amount of tax on hotel rooms, recreation facilities, and image of the city. As you can readily see, site selection is a time-consuming process but one of the most important elements in meeting planning.

6. *Negotiations.* "Everything is negotiable," or so the saying goes. While it is true that the costs of lodging are almost always negotiable, depending on the room block desired, the time of year, the time of the meetings (weekend versus weekday), whether it is repeat business, etc., don't fall into the trap of pushing beyond the point of fairness. Don't forget that the hotel, airlines, ground services company, etc., are also in the business of making money. Be candid and be fair. Negotiation is a two-way street, so be prepared to compromise on certain issues. If you have flexibility with your meeting dates, this puts you in a great position to negotiate. Typically, food and beverage costs leave little margin in which to negotiate, but you may still find ways to save costs on these functions by working with the catering department of the hotel.

7. *Working with speakers.* The use of professional speakers will ordinarily help ensure the quality of your meeting, but make sure they will tailor their remarks to your group! If budget is a problem, you may be able to negotiate a portion of the honorarium by having the speaker do multiple sessions, e.g., perhaps a general session, followed by a breakout. If you're working with speakers from your own organization, make sure they're afforded some training in platform skills and proper use of audiovisual equipment and materials.

As indicated earlier, this is only a handful of the many areas that make for an effective meeting. Your skills in their proper use will assure you of an excellent meeting.

Conducting Board, Staff, Team, and Committee Meetings

How does one keep that board meeting from becoming a "bored" meeting? The same question, of course, could be posed for staff, sales, committee, or for that matter, just about any kind of group get-together. How is your team functioning? Could your meetings with your team members be more productive?

Ask most any colleague about any of these, or any other kind of meeting, and you'll likely get a response clearly less than positive. In fact, many of us would emphatically state that far too many meetings are clearly a waste of time. Unfortunately, in many organizations, they truly are! Far too many meetings miss their mark simply because of lack of planning or preparation. One study of over 1000 middle managers identified the top three reasons why meetings fail:

1. Getting off subject
2. Lack of agenda or goals
3. Last too long

Sound familiar? How about that meeting you ran the other day? How much time and money is wasted every day in meetings that are unproductive? To give you an idea of the volume we're talking about, consider that every single business day, these scenes are repeated—far too often with the same negative results.

Whether we're talking about training programs, staff meetings, committee or board meetings, it will be helpful to review some of the basics we often tend to overlook. The purpose of this section is to identify some types of meetings, review a few other reasons why meetings fail, and then offer several concrete, usable ideas that will make your next meeting more effective.

Types of Meetings

Since we're using the term *meetings* in its most generic sense, let's categorize them into these areas:

1. *Information.* This type of meeting includes a two-edged sword of both *giving* and *getting* information. Many training programs fall into this category since they may be providing cognitive information for new skills, knowledge, or attitudes. It is sharing experiences that the astute facilitators can use to further develop their trainees and colleagues.

2. *Action.* This type of meeting could be as small as two people addressing a specific problem and getting closure and action.

3. *Problem solving.* This type of meeting could be a group or team effort that gets together to attack a single problem. Perhaps conflict resolution is the goal.

4. *Brainstorming.* With the increasing use of Total Quality Management (TQM), we're seeing a real resurgence of the creative group-think process. The typical ground rules—e.g., no criticism, the wilder the better—are the bases for these creative exercises.

This brief listing, of course, is not meant to be exhaustive. There are not clearcut lines, for example, that necessarily distinguish or differentiate one type of meeting from another.

Why Meetings Fail

The reasons cited earlier (straying from the subject, no agenda or goals, and too lengthy) are ones to which we can all relate. In addition, several other factors can contribute to an ineffective meeting.

1. *Lack of planning.* Regardless of the type of meeting desired, preparation is always imperative. Obviously, even the novice trainer would not think of conducting a session without adequate planning. Why then, would anyone be so naive as to think any meeting could be conducted without ample preparation?

The answer is obvious, but too many of our colleagues (or bosses!) forget this basic point.

2. *Lack of objectives.*   Are there any of us in HRD who have not heard the phrase, "You can't get lost if you don't know where you're going"? Regardless of the kind of meeting desired, objectives must be stated and "bought into" by those in attendance.

3. *Lack of agenda.*   Just as a lesson plan or outline is an integral part of a training module, the agenda must be a critical part of any meeting. In the worst-case scenario, an outline on a flipchart is the minimum acceptable standard. Far better is the agenda that is sent out in advance to all attendees.

4. *Wrong people.*   Have you ever sat through a meeting wondering "What am I doing here?" or "Why did I have to attend this?" Make sure the people attending your meetings are the proper persons to be there. Do they have the background, experience, or expertise to contribute to the desired outcomes? Meetings are costly vehicles; if a number of attendees shouldn't be there, those costs rise measurably.

5. *Wrong place.*   There are times when the wrong meeting site can kill an otherwise effective meeting. Corporate retreats are often held away from the office. There is real merit in considering off-site meetings, both in the physical as well as the psychological sense. With fewer interruptions, phone calls, etc., the business at hand can usually be conducted more efficiently.

6. *Wrong times.*   Doubtless, there is not a reader who cannot, at this moment recall a meeting in which the timing was not the culprit. Maybe it was the day of the week—or even the time of day. But timing can also work to your advantage. It is amazing how quickly decisions or problems can be handled with an 11:30 a.m. meeting! Or better yet, if you really want action, schedule one for next Friday at 4:30 p.m.!

Making Meetings Work

With all this rhetoric about why meetings fail, how do we make them better? Consider these ideas as starters and you'll see how they can really work for you.

1. Agenda

As already stated, you need a game plan (agenda) for any meeting. It should be sent out in advance so participants can be prepared for discussion on those items. A sample agenda for a committee or board meeting might take a form like Fig. 23-2.

2. Expectations

To ensure that the stated objectives are in sync with those of the attendees, why not simply ask them? While not necessarily appropriate for weekly staff meetings or other events of an hour or so, such questioning is an excellent idea for longer sessions. Experienced facilitators always incorporate this technique at the early stages of their meetings.

EXECUTIVE COMMITTEE
MEETING PLANNERS INTERNATIONAL
Orlando, Florida

June 9

8:00 a.m.–11:45 a.m.

AGENDA

TIME	ITEM	PERSON RESPONSIBLE	ACTION
8:00	Welcome–Intros	Scannell	—
8:03	Objectives	Scannell	Info
8:08	Roll Call	Sklar	—
8:10	Review Agenda	Scannell	—
8:13	Additional Items	All	Vote
	1._____		
	2_____		
	3._____		
	4._____		
8:20	Secretary's Report	Sklar	Vote
8:25	Treasurer's Report	Trombino	Vote
8:30	Annual Budget Review	Trombino	Vote
10:00	BREAK		
10:15	EVP Report	Heath	Info
10:20	EVP Performance Review	Scannell	Vote
11:00	Old Business "To-Do List"	Scannell	Info
11:25	New Business	All	Info
11:40	Announcements		
11:45	Adjourn		Vote

Figure 23-2. Sample agenda.

Here's how it works. Initially, after the traditional welcome and introductions, an overview of the program or schedule is given. The objectives are then identified, at which time the group is asked, "Okay, you know my objectives. But to make sure your goals are similar to my goals, tell me what your objectives are for this meeting. In other words, what has to happen between now and four o'clock this afternoon to really make sure your goals or objectives are met?"

Since participants may be reticent or hesitant to respond individually, get them in groups of three or four and ask them to synthesize their comments. Ask a spokesperson from each group to list two or three of these objectives and post them on a flipchart. Make adjustments as necessary and appropriate, and add them to the agenda as scheduled meeting time allows. Now, *your* meeting is *their* meeting.

3. Facilitator

The term *facilitator* is continually being used in our profession. All but unknown a decade ago, it has become the "in" thing for trainers. To paraphrase Carl Rogers, we really cannot "teach" anyone anything, all we do is facilitate their learning. Many trainers, in fact, have abandoned their "trainer" hats and termed themselves "facilitators" instead.

For meetings, the role of the facilitator is an important one. Essentially, this task is one of a "chauffeur" who is the driver of the meeting, but in a very subtle way. The facilitator, typically from outside the group or organization, plays a neutral role and helps "steer" the meeting toward its destination, i.e., its stated objective. He or she keeps things going and ensures that all sides of an issue are heard. The facilitator has no vote and always maintains that middle-ground position.

By using an outside facilitator, the presiding officer can concentrate on the discussion and is an active listener. Because they don't have to worry about the "order" or conduct of the procedures, they can give full attention to the motion on the floor.

4. Consent Calendar

In most associations and professional organizations, there is always a multitude of items that, according to their bylaws, must be voted on by the board. As surprising as this may seem, these might include the secretary's report, membership reports, committee updates, etc. All too often, needless time is wasted on these somewhat mundane items, but since it is mandated by policy, the board plows through these, one by one, in slow, methodical fashion.

An effective and efficient way to handle these items is by use of the consent calendar. As its name implies, it requires the consensus or consent of the entire governing body. Here's how it works. Well in advance, the president, secretary, and chief staff officer of the association or society survey all the items on the agenda. They discuss these and make a thoughtful judgment on which items would likely be passed with little or no board discussion. These items are all compiled and listed on a "consent calendar."

At the board meeting, each item is announced individually. If even one person raises a question or comment on any item, it is automatically removed from the consent calendar. Remember, its purpose is to save board time but not to "railroad" things too quickly. Therefore, only those items that are approved with no question of any kind can stay on the consent calendar. Experience with this method over the past several years by the author with several boards of directors meetings has proven it to be a valuable timesaver.

5. Living Minutes

This tool is an excellent one to use for small-group, staff, board, or committee meetings. It entails a skilled recorder (*not* the presider or facilitator) to keep a running (living) documentation of the discussions. Using a flipchart, the recorder listens intently to the comments as each item is under discussion. As points are verbalized, the recorder succinctly and briefly captures the essence or key words of the comments and writes these on the flipchart. It is imperative that these words reflect the very intent of the contributor's comments, and the recorder should ensure that is being done with questions such as "Is this what you're saying?" or "Is this okay?"

As these outline-type sheets are filled, they are removed from the chart and affixed to the walls where everyone can see them. (*Caution:* Make sure you've received approval from hotel staff if you tape sheets to walls. Some hotels don't allow this.)

Another benefit of this method is that if someone leaves the room during discussion, all he or she needs to do is to glance at the chart to see what transpired during his or her absence.

6. Walking Meetings

You've probably been involved in a meeting where things got a bit "hot and heavy." Here's another tool you can use to prevent such an occurrence. For example, let's say an item comes up on the agenda which proves to be very sensitive. Before things get out of hand and pandemonium breaks loose, suggest a "walking meeting." Assign groups of two or three people to a team. If possible, get adversaries on the same team. Their task for the next 15 to 20 minutes is to "take a walk" to discuss the issue at hand and come back at the prescribed time with either a compromise, suggested solution, or another idea to reach consensus.

Some Final Thoughts

Here are some additional thoughts that might be of use:

1. *Motion sickness.* Far too many groups catch "motion sickness." While it's important to have parliamentary procedures, don't get carried away with it. Some items don't require a motion. Get agreement and move on.

2. *Starting times.* Why not call a meeting for 2:03 p.m. rather than 2:00 p.m. or 10:37 a.m. rather than 10:30 a.m.? People tend to remember odd starting times more easily and tend to be more punctual as well. If practical, state the starting and ending times and, although it goes without saying, we're going to say it: start and end *on time!*

3. *Stand-up meetings.* Why not try a meeting room with no furniture? Try it and you'll be surprised how fast things move along. Stand-up meetings are great for small-group meetings.

4. *Discussion time.* Limit discussion time on issues. More time is wasted on needless "discussion" where someone takes 15 minutes to simply echo someone else's position. Research suggests that, when presented an issue, 60 percent of the group will make up their minds—one way or the other—within 60 seconds! Obviously, don't curtail relevant and necessary discussion, but don't waste time! Differentiate between someone who has something to say from one who has to say something!

Conference Room Checklist

The sample Conference Room Checklist, shown as Fig. 23-3, is a format you will find workable for most of your meetings. It is a generic form that you will want to alter as necessary and make sufficient copies to use as a staging guide.

Directions: On the top right corner ("Page ____ of ____ Pages"), fill in one sheet for each day of your meeting, e.g., for a three-day conference, you would complete three separate sheets, with the first page being Page 1 of 3 pages. Complete the name of the conference or meeting as shown, along with the site, such as "XYZ Hotel," "Training Room 4," etc. Show the inclusive date(s) of your meeting on that line. The heading "Today's Date" is very important. It is all too easy to mix up the correct day along with an incorrect date, so this will help avoid that problem.

Time: Show the starting and ending times for each event.

Page ____ of ____ Pages

Conference _____

Today's Date ____, ____, 199__
        Day Month Date

Site _____

Director _____

Meeting Dates _____

Phone _____

Fax _____

Time	Event No.	Session	Room Name	Setup Style	Est. No.	A.V. ✓	Comments

Room Setup Style

A. Theater

Room _____

B. Classroom

Room _____

C. Conference

Room _____

D. Other

Room _____

Figure 23-3. Conference room checklist.

Event No.: Start a numerical sequence for each event. For example, if Registration starts on Monday morning, you might assign "M-1" to that event. The use of the respective day's first letter (T-Tuesday) is helpful.

Session: List here each activity by name, e.g., "Registration," "Opening Session," and "Managing Change."

Room Name: Show the exact room name for each respective event.

Setup Style: Refer to the lower part of the form ("Room Setup Style"). If, for example, Session W-2, the Opening General Session, will be set theater style, merely indicate an A in that column.

Estimated Number: Write in the anticipated number of attendees for each event.

Audiovisual: List whatever audiovisual (AV) needs are required for that time slot, e.g., 35-millimeter projector, overhead projector with LCD panel, remote, and 8 × 10 screen. Merely check (✓) after AV has been ordered from vendor.

Comments: Note any items relative to that line that will serve as a later reminder or checkpoint.

Room Setup Style: It is strongly suggested that a room layout be actually sketched out in the respective boxes showing the approximate stage area, audiovisual placement, tables, and chairs, etc. Write the names of the respective rooms requiring the prescribed room setup. (These drawings are particularly helpful to hotel setup crews since their instructions from their convention services department may not always be in line with your instructions.) Make additional copies of these drawings as needed.

Checklists*

On the following pages, you will find a number of checklists designed to save you time, effort, and perhaps even a headache or two along the way. All of these have been field-tested, refined, and revised for your use. Adapt them as necessary to fit your own meetings. These are generic forms and, depending on the size of your meeting, you will, of course, want to make the necessary adjustments in scope and schedule.

Appendix A. The Master Timetable is your complete meeting guide that provides a timetable for each of the varied activities for your upcoming meeting. These guidelines will assure leaving "no stone unturned" and not worrying as much about "Murphy's Law"!

Appendix B. The Hotel Review File is a quick summary sheet for use in your initial site inspection.

Appendix C. Following the initial negotiations concerning the property, this detailed form will help you secure most everything you and your participants will need to know in working with the staff.

Appendix D. As you walk through the meeting rooms assigned for your events, use this Meeting Room Inspection Checklist to check everything.

*These checklists are abstracted from *The Complete Games Trainers Play* (McGraw-Hill, 1995) and are used with permission.

Appendix E.   This Setting-Up-the-Room Checklist will enable you to cover all the intricate and individual details you need.

Appendix F.   The Key Meeting Coordination Listing is an important roster of key contacts. Home phones may be added for some individuals.

Appendix A:
Master Timetable

Minus One Year

Discuss meeting concept with executives directly involved.

Consider who will attend.

Set objectives.

Develop theme.

Set date.

Announce the dates.

Consider tentative sites.

Estimate time (days) for program.

Rough out staff responsibilities.

Minus Nine Months

Select hotel or facility.

Negotiate with hotel or facility for rooms and services.

Make list of printing needs.

Set up schedule for "promotion."

Create list of staff assignments.

Consider program for spouses (if invited to attend).

List subjects to be covered at meeting.

Choose company speakers best qualified to participate in program.

Clear company speakers with their superiors.

Create list of physical requirements.

Create checklist for each meeting segment.

Create a "teaser" advance mailing for promotion.

Minus Six Months

Invite company top executives.

Invite local dignitaries, board members, or VIPs.

Negotiate with outside speakers.

Reach understanding on types and length of speeches.

Get list of AV equipment needed by all speakers.

Inventory needs against company supplies.

Order buses for special transportation needs.

Get bids on decorations and/or special services.

Confirm all agreements in writing—speakers, company executives, suppliers, etc.

Confirm all meeting assignments in writing.

Plan for transportation of attendees to meeting city.

Create art theme for mailings and use in meeting room.

Mail advance program to participants.

Minus One Month

Reproduce materials to be distributed.

Make or order final visuals.

Send rooming list to hotel or facility.

Arrange for photographer.

Set timetable for ground transportation.

Mail information to attendees, including:

- Dates, times, locations
- Travel
- Parking
- Attire
- Expense reimbursement

Order necessary signs.

Alert press, if coverage is desired.

Make detailed arrangements chart for each session.

Arrange for recording of sessions.

Purchase souvenirs or theme giveaways.

Arrange for shipping materials.

Arrange for necessary reproduction of papers or forms at site.

Minus Two Weeks

Assemble materials for meeting.

Submit final VIP list to hotel or facility with instructions for special attention.

Check on shipping of materials.

Confirm meeting details with suppliers.

Reconfirm agreements with individuals on program.

Submit detailed list of materials and services required to hotel or facility.

Confirm specific hours and duties of hotel or facility personnel to service meeting.

Establish deadlines for completion of all hotel or facility and supplier services.

Assemble list of gratuities to be paid.

Order locked storage space at hotel or facility.

Arrange for receiving and shipping goods at hotel or facility.

Confirm menus, coffee break timing, and receptions, and clarify instructions.

Minus One Week

Prepare name badges.

Rehearse company speakers.

Prepare releases for invited press.

Make up meeting supplies package.

Minus Two Days

Schedule final rehearsals.

Review plans with hotel or facility department heads.

Check on arrival of shipped materials.

Check on delivery of rented AV equipment.

Place all materials and equipment in secured storage.

Order flowers, wine, fruit as gifts for outside speakers or VIPs.

Alert press, if coverage is desired.

Turn over *final* list of all attendees to hotel or facility.

Meet with entire facility department heads to confirm key arrangements.

Minus One Day

Reconfirm plans with registration desk.

Check weather reports for possible effects on arrivals.

Check out operation of AV equipment.

Review plans with electrician and maintenance staff.

Check handout materials.

Arrange to meet speakers and guests.

Meet again with convention services manager to finalize plans.

Distribute duplicate room setup plans to your staff.

Carry out final briefing for your staff on their responsibilities.

Reconfirm meal guarantees.

Reconfirm coffee break times and menus.

Reconfirm hospitality room arrangements.

Reconfirm credit and check cashing agreement with hotel or facility.

Clarify how to handle messages with telephone operators.

Have product displays set up.

Go through dress rehearsal of entire program.

Minus Two Hours

Check room setup.

Check ventilation and temperature.

Check mikes and PA system.

Check AV equipment.

Check registration desk setup.

Arrange handout material for use.

Corroborate availability of support staff.

Confirm that signs are in place.

Minus One Hour

Introduce outside speakers to fellow speakers.

Check on photographer.

Check on place cards.

Have honorariums ready.

Check on tape recorder operator.

Check lectern light and stage props.

Give last-minute instructions to program participants.

During the Meeting

Note audience response to content and meeting format.

Record questions raised by audience.

Keep record of attendance at meals.

Inventory liquor.

Pick up pagers and AV material left in meeting rooms.

Check all bills and record them on budget sheet.

Day of Meeting Plus One Day

Hold critique session with hotel or facility department heads.

Check all charges.

Arrange for shipping displays and materials.

Return rental AV equipment.

Issue gratuities.

Day of Meeting Plus One Week

Critique meeting with executives present and/or involved.

Send answers to field staff on questions raised at meeting.

Send thank-yous to meeting participants.

Prepare written report of meeting.

Make up dos and don'ts report for next year's planning committee.

Plan follow-up mailings to implement meeting objectives.

Appendix B: Hotel Review File

DATE _____

NAME OF HOTEL _____

ADDRESS _____

CONTACT _____ PHONE _____

NUMBER OF ROOMS _____ NUMBER OF SUITES _____

OTHER TYPES OF SLEEPING ACCOMMODATIONS_____

NEAREST TOWN _____ DISTANCE _____

NEAREST AIRPORT _____ DISTANCE _____

CHECK-IN TIME_____ CHECK-OUT TIME _____

AIR-CONDITIONED   [ ] ROOMS   [ ] PUBLIC SPACE   [ ] MEETING ROOMS

PARKING [ ]   INSIDE [ ]   OUTSIDE [ ]   SELF-PARKING [ ]

VALET PARKING _____ COST

AUTO RENTAL [ ] YES [ ] NO   NAME OF COMPANY _____

TRANSPORTATION	*FROM AIRPORT*	*FROM TRAIN*
COST OF TAXI	_____	_____
COST OF LIMOUSINE	_____	_____
COST OF CHARTER BUS	_____	_____
LAUNDRY SERVICE [ ] ONE-DAY	[ ] OTHER	
VALET SERVICE [ ] ONE-DAY	[ ] OTHER	
BABY-SITTERS [ ] YES	[ ] NO	
CONTACT _____	COST _____	

Appendix C: The Potential Meeting Site Questionnaire

Addendum for Hotel Meeting Facilities

1. What will be the room reservation cutoff date?
2. What are the current hotel rates? Any projections?
3. Do you provide transportation to and from the airport? The train? Cost?
4. Are meeting room walls removable? Soundproof? Time required to move?
5. What deposits do you require?
6. Does the hotel supply microphones? Current costs?
7. Do you have paging and/or general announcement capabilities?
8. Is a message center service available to the meeting?
9. Where can we obtain keyboarding, copying, and office facilities?
10. What is the cost for room setups?
11. What is your complimentary policy? VIP policy? Is it negotiable?

12. How many suites do you have? May we have floor plans? Current prices?

13. Where do meetings usually register?

14. Can you supply reference or client lists? Supply name of person (and number) who has used the facility within the past year.

15. Special services, for example, VIP treatment? Extras?

16. Check-in time? Check-out time?

17. How many extra meals do they prepare above the guarantee? What percent set over? Time to change guarantee?

18. Nearby recreational and sports facilities? Hotel health club? Swimming pool—indoor or outdoor? Hours?

19. Are screens or chalkboards in meeting rooms?

20. Do you have easels for signage available? Number?

21. Is baby-sitting service available?

22. Is there a charge for cribs? Rollaways?

23. Are there shops available in the facility? Nearby?

24. What is the cost for children in a room?

25. Are meeting rooms available 24 hours a day? Can materials be left in rooms overnight?

26. What credit cards do you accept?

27. What is your check cashing policy?

28. Are there special liquor laws? Corkage fees? Sunday service?

29. Is entertainment available in the hotel? What type? When?

30. What hours is room service available?

31. Will the registrant receive a confirmation? How long does this take?

32. Are there meeting room charges? Are they negotiable? What is not included?

33. Can buffets be served in meeting rooms? Certain number of people required?

34. What is the proximity of meeting space to sleeping rooms? Main desk? Food service? Rest rooms?

35. What are dining room hours?

36. Are the meeting rooms free from visual obstruction?

37. When will meeting room setup occur?

38. At what temperature is your meeting room thermostat usually set? Can it be changed in the room?

39. Can flipchart pages be taped to walls?

40. Do you have vending machines on hotel floors?

41. Are there airline reservation, car rental, and tour services in the hotel?

42. Can you provide flipcharts and markers? Number? Cost?

43. Are all facilities accessible to disabled persons?

Appendix D: Meeting Room Inspection Checklist

To inspect a meeting room properly, you should have a 50-foot steel measuring tape and a transistor radio. Your first job is to decide whether the room will meet your physical requirements. That's where you'll use the tape. A transistor radio will give you warning of acoustics problems. Place the radio outside your meeting room with the volume turned up and then go back into the meeting room, closing the door. How clearly can you hear the radio? Do the same thing for movable walls. How clearly can you hear through those "soundproof" walls?

Check these other factors which can affect your meeting:

Room air-conditioned?   _____

Individual controls for cooling and heating?   _____

Dimmer switch?   _____

Pillars or other obstructions?   _____

Will doors be at the rear of your meeting setup?   _____

Will chandeliers shine light into a speaker's eyes?   _____

Shine light into the eyes of the audience?   _____

Interfere with movie or slide projections?   _____

Can coffee be served in a nearby room?   _____

Is there a foyer?   _____

Can food be served in the meeting room?   _____

Distance to nearest elevators   _____

Distance to freight elevators   _____

Distance to nearest escalators   _____

Distance to checkroom facilities   _____

Distance to nearest public phone   _____

Distance to nearest rest rooms   _____

Is there a phone in the room?   _____

Can it be disconnected?   _____

Capacity of electrical outlets   _____

Alternating or direct current (ac or dc)?   _____

Do window curtains darken the room sufficiently?   _____

Chairs padded?   _____

With armrests?   _____

How many extra temporary seats available?   _____

Are there mirrors on the walls?   _____

Can they be covered, if necessary?   _____

Is there a PA system?   _____

Is there a permanent stage?   _____

If no stage, can a speaker's platform be created?   _____

Appendix E: Setting-Up-the-Room Checklist

- Arrive an hour early to set up and check the facility.
- Arrange the tables in the chosen training seating arrangement.
- Provide chairs for each participant and the trainer, and several extras at the back for visitors.
- Obtain a table on which to place the leader's guide and training materials.
- Provide water for participants' tables.
- Check that sufficient extension cords are available.
- Test-run equipment to ensure that all components are functioning.
- Remove all ashtrays from the room (optional).
- Verify that lunch and break food will be delivered on time.
- Confirm that workbooks, handouts, and forms have arrived at the training facility.
- Provide pencils and pads for participants.
- Place participants' workbooks or manuals on tables, noting that all are intact in binders.
- Check that flipchart paper and markers are available.
- Be sure that you have a watch or clock to know when to break for meals, etc.
- Prepare participant listing.
- Bring extra copies of workbooks, manuals, etc., to the seminar for unexpected arrivals.
- Verify that sufficient program evaluation forms are available.
- Have paper on hand to jot down comments made by the group.

Appendix F: Key Meeting Coordination Listing

Program name _____ Location _____ Date(s) _____

Names of staff   Telephone numbers

General Manager _____ _____

Sales Manager _____ _____

Convention Manager _____ _____

Reservation Manager _____ _____

AV Manager _____ _____

Front-Desk Manager _____ _____

Catering Manager _____ _____

Food and Beverage Manager_____ _____

Maitre d'Hotel _____ _____

Chef _____ _____

Dining Room Captains _____ _____

Room Service Manager _____   _____

Bell Captains   _____   _____

Setup—Meeting Rooms _____   _____

Housekeeper   _____   _____

Florist   _____   _____

Photographer   _____   _____

Social Director   _____   _____

House Physicians   _____   _____

Public Relations Manager _____   _____

24

Case Studies

Jay Alden

Judith Kirkhorn

Jay Alden is the Chair of the Information Strategy Department for the Information Resources Management College of the National Defense University. In previous positions, he was responsible for executive-level graduate programs in management at the University of Maryland and managed training development and evaluation groups at Xerox Corporation and other high-technology companies. He was Vice President for Research and Development of the National Society for Performance and Instruction (NSPI) and a member of that organization's Senior Advisory Panel and Emerging Technology Committee. Dr. Alden holds a Ph.D. in education research from Hofstra University.

Judith Kirkhorn is Director of Executive Programs, Graduate School of Management and Technology, University of Maryland. In previous positions, she directed the design and implementation management and leadership development systems in the AT&T Corporate Human Resources Organization and led curriculum development projects at the Union for Experimenting Colleges and Universities, the University of Kentucky College of Allied Health, and University of Wisconsin adult and teacher education programs. She was NSPI 1989–1991 Vice President, Technology Applications, and held leadership positions on several NSPI committees. Dr. Kirkhorn holds a Ph.D. in adult education and psychology from the University of Wisconsin.

What do you picture when you think of case studies? Someone spending hours pouring over pages and pages of details about a company, trying to find *the* key that will break the case? Discussions, maybe even arguments, between individuals or teams about what should have been done, or when it should have been done, or who should have done it? An instructor who listens more than she talks and asks

497

more than she states? Perhaps, a sense of understanding about what it was really like, or a fear that "that could happen to me," or the notion that "I think I could have done it better," or maybe all three of these feelings at the same time. Case studies engender many of these images because cases come in various packages and can be conducted in all sorts of ways. This chapter explores the enormous diversity in case studies, the rich variety of forms in which they are presented, and explains why and when they should be used. You'll come to appreciate the different strategies for conducting cases and the crucial role that the instructor plays no matter how it is done. You'll also gain insights into the many options for obtaining case studies, including a host of sources for finding existing cases and techniques for building them yourself. But first, what is a case study?

Characterizing Cases

What Is a Case Study?

Many differing kinds of learning exercises are often referred to as cases:

1. A predicament facing an organization is explained in great detail and students are expected to pose a solution or strategy for dealing with that complex situation.

2. A story is told about how some person or persons or some organization dealt with a difficult situation, and students analyze and critique the actions taken, indicating what was appropriate and what might have been done differently.

3. Students are placed in a dynamic situation in which things change as a result of their actions and they work the situation toward a satisfactory outcome.

These three kinds of exercises are all called *cases* from time to time because they all involve descriptions of particular *case situations*. However, within the context of this chapter, only the second kind of learning exercise is defined as a *case study*.

Problem-Solving Exercises.   The first type of exercise described above is a decision-forcing case often called a *problem-solving exercise*. In this type of exercise, the students are provided with a description of a problem situation and are required to pose a solution to the problem which satisfies some preconceived solution or meets the requirements of a defined model. The problem may occupy a single paragraph or be contained in 30-plus pages with tables, graphics, and exhibits, but the essence of the exercise is for students to analyze the problem and identify an appropriate solution to it. This type of exercise is very useful as a practice activity accompanying or following some other instructional method, or as a mechanism for evaluating student capability. But a problem-solving exercise may be inefficient and possibly ineffective as an independent instructional device. Suppose you were given a problem to solve in a discipline for which you have limited knowledge and experience—for example, preparing a legal defense for an accused criminal. Where would you start? How many hours would you need to study other source materials before being able to pose a reasonable defense strategy? Yes, you might learn a great deal from the ensuing discussion of solutions posed by other, more knowledgeable students, but your preparation time could have been used in more worthwhile and less frustrating pursuits. Of the three kinds of exercises discussed here, problem-solving exercises are probably the easiest to produce; they are useful as practice and evaluation activities but are least valuable as a technique for providing instruction.

Case Studies.   A case study, as defined here, looks like a problem-solving exercise. It includes the description of a complex situation, but embedded in the situation is an in-depth historical record—a *story*—of a set of actions that some-one took while facing that situation. The students must assess those actions in light of the given situation and aren't told that a problem exists. They must recognize and define it for themselves—that is, if a problem does in fact exist. After all, this retrospective type of case might demonstrate how such situations *should* be handled. Since there is no preconceived answer, the appropriateness of the students' analysis is based on their ability to justify their response. Image a case study dealing with the preparation of a legal defense for an accused crimi-nal. The case would provide the background information, the defense strategy, and the means by which the defense team developed their strategy, perhaps even the jury verdict. The case study would take more effort to develop than a prob-lem-solving exercise, but it would serve as a more effective learning experience for students. Case studies are useful as learning and practice exercises during instructional programs. However, they are not totally effective as evaluation mechanisms since *critiquing* is often a less demanding behavior than *doing*. Case studies can be combined with problem-solving exercises by having the students assess the actions already taken and then recommend what should be done about the resulting situation.

Simulations.   The third type of exercise, often called a *simulation* or game, has a dynamic quality. After students are briefed about a background situation, they are placed in an environment with changing real-time events. They must recognize whether or not a problem exists and then take appropriate action. Unlike problem-solving exercises and case studies, the situation changes as a result of their actions so they must continuously interact with the evolving events. A legal defense strategy simulation might involve a criminal trial in a courtroom situation in which the student plays the role of the defense attorney and the simulation models the prosecutor, witnesses, and judge. The exercise typically continues until the student obtains a *correct* solution (acquittal), meets with failure (conviction), or time runs out. Since a simulation comes close to real-world performance, it is probably the best type of exercise to use for evaluation. Also, since a simulation provides students with immediate feedback about their actions, it can be useful as a learning exercise—although failure is probable in the early attempts. The major problem associated with simulations is the effort required to build models that truly reflect reality.

In summary, case studies can be differentiated from problem-solving exercises and simulations. The heart of a case study is a story describing a series of events in which a person or group of people take action. Students analyze the events and critique the actions. Cases can be effective teaching and practice mechanisms but are only mildly useful for evaluation. Compared to the other types of exer-cises, case studies can be developed with moderate effort—more effort than required to produce a problem-solving exercise but much less than a simulation.

How Are Case Studies Used?

Case studies can be used for a variety of instructional purposes.

Icebreaking.   The case is used to quickly get the students actively involved in the course or program. The substance of the case may or may not be related to the content of the course. No actual *learning* is expected to result from the case. It's there at the beginning of a course solely for its "process" benefits—to get the students talking in class and ready to tackle the real instruction to come.

Thought-Provoking. The case aims at changing the *attitude* of the students or, at least, opening their minds to major problems that may occur in organizational settings. There's no expectation that the student will acquire a new skill from the case exercise. Rather, students discover they may have to learn a new skill or to look at a common situation in a new light.

Vicarious Learning. Students acquire information or a new capability from the case. They learn. Even though no one gave them direct instruction or a step-by-step procedure, when the discussions about the case are over, the students have learned a technique or strategy for coping with similar problem situations. At the very least, they should have learned how *not* to handle a particular kind of problem.

Practice Application. Students apply a capability recently acquired in the course. After students receive direct instruction for dealing with a situation, they gain practice by assessing how well someone in the case study put that capability to use.

Participant Testing. The case is used to test student knowledge. The instructor reviews the student's or team's assessment of a given case and makes a judgment about the quality of that assessment. The individual or team receives a formal grade or at least *feedback* concerning the goodness of their case analysis.

Some courses of instruction are taught almost entirely by case studies—this is referred to as the *case method*, as taught in institutions such as the business school at Harvard. Virtually, from the first day of the course to the last, students study increasingly complex cases having a range of instructional purposes. Students taught by the case method tend to become adept at analyzing case studies. In other courses, case studies of differing purposes are used selectively and are intermingled with other methods of instruction. One section of the course might precede tutorial instruction with a thought-provoking case to gain the students' interest in the topic; another section could rely on a case study to teach the fundamental approach that is then practiced in a simulation or problem-solving exercise.

The size and range of issues covered by a case study depends on the purpose of the case and the complexity of the issue being covered. Case studies used for vicarious learning, practice application, or participant testing of a complex behavior tend to be lengthy and have a broad focus. For example, a case study used to either teach, afford practice, or evaluate a capability in *business process redesign* would have to include information about a wide variety of organization departments, people, functional disciplines, and performance indicators and may require several hours of classroom time. On the other hand, a case used to provide instruction, practice, or testing of a concentrated task such as *counseling a problem employee* would have a narrow focus in terms of people, disciplines, and contributing factors and could probably be conducted in less than an hour. Icebreaking and thought-provoking cases usually have a narrow focus and are limited in size.

How Are Cases Structured?

Case study materials vary greatly. However, most cases often include several of the components discussed below.

Opening Scenario. This introductory section sets the stage for the case information. It describes the problem and recaps the major actions. The critical characters might be introduced at this point. The opening scenario provides just enough detail to make the case situation tantalizing. The following is a sample scenario for a short case called the *Overtime Grievance* case:

> You are the head of the Special Programs Branch which includes a critical Research Section. Because of a special rush project, the Research Section has been working 10 hours overtime for each of the last three weeks. You've left the assignment of overtime to *Nancy Davis* since it's her section that's responsible for getting the work out. The contract with the union calls for overtime to be allocated on an equitable basis among all qualified employees desiring to work overtime. In this case, a grievance is lodged about the way the overtime is being distributed and you need to decide what action to take.

Questions. This section provides the explicit questions that the students are required to answer in their analysis. Questions may either precede or follow the details of the case. If they are at the beginning, they serve to sensitize students to important factors within the case and guide the initial reading of the case. If questions are at the end, the students tend to treat all case details with equal attention. The questions then guide the review of the case in subsequent readings. Three kinds of questions may be asked, which either:

1. Cause the students to summarize and translate what they have observed: What went on here? Who are the main characters? How are they related? What is the nature of the problem they faced? These types of questions are useful with complex situations and can be used to evaluate the students' understanding of concepts and principles.

2. Involve an assessment of the situation and the actions taken by the characters: How well was the situation handled? What should participants have done differently? How could the problem have been avoided in the first place? These kinds of questions lay at the heart of a case study. They focus the students' attention on the story and the appropriateness of the behaviors and strategies exhibited in the case for the given situation.

3. Focus on the current decision point as the students attempt to resolve the situation: What should they do now? For example, as the branch head in the scenario listed above, How would you handle the grievance—let the union proceed with their action or direct Nancy to change her method of assignment?

Most case studies combine several types of questions. If a case only asks the third type of question, the learning activity would be better defined as a problem-solving exercise.

References. This section calls attention to background documents on the case. The documents are not included with the case; they are merely referenced. These references could include such items as policies, regulations, procedures, standards, and reports. For example, in the *Overtime Grievance* case, the students might be referred to the appropriate section of the union contract and the section of the personnel manual dealing with overtime.

Case Information. This section provides the details of the story. Here's the case information for the narrowly focused *Overtime Grievance* case:

> You've just finished the monthly status report when *Ralph Knapp,* steward in the Special Programs Branch, asks to talk with you about a first-stage grievance.
>
> RALPH: I've just talked to some of the guys in Nancy's section about the way overtime is being assigned down there. *O'Farrell* claims that he was bypassed last week in favor of *Hicks* who already worked overtime that week. What good is a contract if you guys won't stick to what it says? Can we settle this in the branch or do we run it on up through the grievance procedure?
>
> After discussing the matter with Nancy Davis, you put the apparent picture together. Short deadlines and an overload of work have forced Nancy to assign overtime to those employees she feels can give her the greatest work output. She claims she has considered sharing overtime equally, but only when the choice was narrowed to her most productive employees.
>
> NANCY: Frankly, we'd never make it if I assigned overtime to some of the deadwood. Sure, all my employees are technically qualified to do the overtime work, but if you reverse me on this one, we're dead as far as meeting the schedule goes. Let 'em push the grievance up through the channels. By the time it gets resolved by the top brass or an arbitrator, we'll be over the crisis and it won't matter. Just don't put the clamps on my shop now! Besides, if you shoot me down, how will that make me look to my people? Please, please give me some support on this one! You know, our budget is already stretched and having to pay overtime to a GS 9 like O'Farrell won't help it any. Several of the GS 7's such as Hicks can wind this project up in half the time if only you'll let me assign them the overtime.
>
> As you ponder your recent conversations with Ralph and Nancy, you again look at the status report and note that the Branch is only one day behind schedule with the special project. It *must* be completed on schedule, but the budget won't allow for more overtime than the 10 hours per week they've been averaging.

Exhibits. This section of the case study includes actual samples of materials that convey important information about the case: promotional materials, memos, letters, mission and vision statements, newsletters, plans, policies, procedures, standards, tables, photographs, graphics, reports. These kinds of material enhance the realism and complexity of the case situation. For the *Overtime Grievance* case, materials might include the Research Section's time sheets for the past three weeks, the project status report, and last year's performance evaluation of O'Farrell and Hicks. Note that exhibits differ from references in that they are provided with the case so the student doesn't have to look them up somewhere else.

Some case studies will include all five components listed above, but most will not. Many of the cases purchased from the Harvard Business School Press only include *case information* which the purchasers augment with their own questions to suit their purposes. One interesting structural variation provides case information solely through the use of *exhibits*—no narrative story is written.

How Are Cases Packaged?

Print. Most people picture case-study materials being provided on paper, a page or so, a booklet, a part of a textbook, or even an entire book. The students *read* the story and review the exhibits, individually, at their own pace. Recently, other forms of packaging are being used to present case information.

Video.   For some situations, it helps to put all or part of the story on video-tape. The students see the characters' expressions and hear their tone of voice. They visualize a dynamic process that would be difficult to describe in writing. Video is more interesting than the printed page. Try to picture a case study of a confrontational meeting. Did the subject of the case handle himself effectively? Was his response ethical? It is likely that a case of this sort would work better on video than paper. Not only would the video capture the students' attention, it would convey the intangibles connected with the meeting, the feelings, doubts, and concerns inherent in the situation. Of course, not all case situations lend themselves to video. Factual quantitative data and long chronologies are better presented by a print medium. Also, unless all students have copies of the video, information must be presented during class time (although, sometimes this could be an advantage over students taking a wide range of times to read a case during a class). The cost of producing a video case is also a concern. However, videos can be reasonably purchased to present cases of historical significance and cases related to generalizable ethical dilemmas and interpersonal communications.

Live.   Another means of presenting case information is to use "live" story-tellers, especially a key person or a panel of people who were directly involved in the case. They relate events from their perspective and answer questions to clarify points in the minds of the students. This strategy has been used extensively at the Wharton School in Pennsylvania. Besides telling their stories, the case participants can also be available to assess and comment on the student analyses. The most compelling aspect of this approach is the credibility that the speakers bring to the case. Students become enraptured with the storytelling—during the pauses, you can hear a pin drop. The greater the stature of the speaker, the more intense the crisis, the more relevant to the students' job situation, the more unforgettable the students' experience. The downside of this approach is the difficulty of scheduling the speakers, especially if the case has to be repeated with multiple classes.

Software.   Computer systems are now being used to present cases. Multimedia text, data, graphics, animation, video, and sound combine to make interesting storytelling. In addition, interactive computer systems can add a fascinating dimension. Students do not have to view all the case information in a linear fashion. They can pick and choose what information to view and the sequence in which to view it. One student might start by studying a particular exhibit, and then hear the opinion of one of the key subjects, and then access an external audit on the organization, and so forth, while another student takes an entirely different path. With this approach, the assessment of the students may include their ability to select key information or to come to a conclusion using the minimum amount of information from the overabundance of available details. Use of computer systems can also expand the conduct of case studies to environments outside a single classroom. Students can converse with the instructor and other students even though they log on at different times from different places. The reports from the various teams and class discussion could easily be accommodated over the network. The downside is that such computer-supported case studies require a technologically proficient student body and a resource-rich environment.

When Should Cases Be Used?

There is not a great deal of empirical research on the use of case studies. Studies comparing cases to lectures and cases to simulations have revealed mixed results. The studies have tended to use small numbers of students; results apparently have been affected by the content being taught and, perhaps, by the preferences of the teachers. There is general agreement on two points: (1) case studies are an effective means for developing problem-solving skills, but (2) they add no value when trying to increase factual knowledge. Rossett and Emerson[1] surveyed 52 training managers who used case studies. The top five reasons for using case studies were

1. Exercising problem-solving skills
2. Simulating real life
3. Sharpening decision-making skills
4. Generating discussion
5. Developing judgment

These results suggest that case studies are particularly useful for teaching "soft" skills, skills that have the following characteristics:

> Task competencies requiring interpretation and processing of a large amount of information concerning a problem situation for which there are numerous possible solutions of varying effectiveness.

In other words, cases sharpen higher-order intellectual skills—analysis, synthesis, and evaluation—which are often required by managers, physicians, lawyers, and other professionals. If, on the other hand, the required behavior is primarily prescriptive in nature, the learner would probably be better served by a *drill and practice* method of instruction.

There are, however, conditions which constrain the use of case studies, even for teaching soft skills. The course of instruction must provide the opportunity for students to prepare and discuss their analysis of the case. Either in class or out, students must have the time and the motivation to complete their analyses. Also, student interaction is a requisite component of case studies, so face-to-face or electronic communication among students must be arranged either during or after normal class hours. Finally, because the stress is on student involvement, the learners cannot be inexperienced or immature. They must be willing and able to dig deeply into the details of the case and to articulate and defend their positions.

Benjamin Franklin once said, "Experience keeps a dear school, but fools will learn in no other." Case studies provide a safe learning alternative to experience. Cases assure a high level of involvement of the learners with situations having real-world relevance, but no one ever died or was fired because of decisions made in case studies. Students can learn through the experience of others.

Administering Cases

You might think that conducting case studies offers the instructor a break from the hard work of making formal presentations. After all, it is the students who seem to carry most of the burden in case studies: they analyze the case, prepare and present their findings, and engage in the case discussion. The instructor merely sets up the process and then sits back and watches it all take place. If you think this is the way it is, you're greatly mistaken. Administering a case study—at least, doing it effectively—is much more difficult and stressful than presenting a block of information. The instructor in a case study is somewhat like the leader of a jazz combo. He or she orchestrates the piece, sets the tempo, brings in the various individual performers on cue, and allows them the freedom of innovation but assures their harmony as a group. And, what makes it even harder, not all the musicians are professionals or even good at what they do. What does the leader do when a *sour note* is heard—ignore it, cover it with other notes, get the musician to realize he's off-key, or treat it as a new, unique, possibly even ground-breaking sound? Instructors are central to successful case studies—they have four crucial roles in the administration of cases: orchestrating, overseeing, conducting, and evaluating.

The Orchestrating Role

The instructor sets up the process and assures that the students have the appropriate information and know what is expected of them.

Orientation. First, the instructor should orient the students about the case exercise. What is the purpose of the case in the course—icebreaking, thought-provoking, etc.? What are the roles of the students and what can they expect from the instructor? What procedures will be followed and how long should they take? How will the students be evaluated? The need for an orientation is especially strong during the initial cases and diminishes thereafter as students become more experienced with the case method.

Briefing. Second, the instructor decides and communicates how the students will acquire the case information. The case information can be presented to the students using (1) a *self-study* strategy where the students read or view the case by themselves or (2) a *group-paced* strategy where the instructor or guest speakers convey the information, possibly supported with audiovisual materials, to the entire class at the same time. A self-study briefing permits students to review the information at their own pace, repeating or skimming through sections as they see fit. A self-study strategy is called for when the case information is lengthy and there are insufficient classroom hours to devote to the briefing. A group-paced briefing assures that all students are exposed to the same information in the same sequence, including points of clarification made by the instructor. Even when there is ample classroom time for a self-study briefing, a group-paced strategy avoids the awkwardness associated with students' differing greatly in the amount of time they require to review the case information.

The Pigors[2] propose a briefing strategy called the *Pigors Incident Process* which combines self-study and group-paced techniques. The instructor provides a brief narrative of an incident, usually in one page or less. It is the students' responsibility then, as a group, to ask for specific additional details about the case to which the instructor responds. This process often takes about 20 to 30 minutes. If no one asks the "right" question, that information is withheld, and the students may have to conduct their analysis without some key information.

Assignment. Third, the instructor assigns the responsibilities for the case analysis to the students. What questions do they have to answer? Will they be expected to work individually, where the students must do the work on their own, or as members of a team of students who analyze the case and prepare a report together? An assignment to *individuals* helps assure that all students will review and analyze the case information and will be uniformly prepared to present their findings. Conversely, an assignment to *teams* permits students to specialize and possibly go deeper into certain facets of the case. They also practice teamwork and communication and can learn strategies for case analysis from one another. Assignment to teams requires that the case analysis go on in the classroom during normal hours or that the students get together or communicate with one another after hours. If the purpose of a case is practice application or participant testing, assignment to individuals is more typical.

The Overseeing Role

Student preparation is key to an effective case study. Students must thoroughly familiarize themselves with the case details and give a great deal of thought to the assessment of activities taken by the characters in the case. The instructor usually has an important role in monitoring the students while they analyze the case and prepare reports. She has to encourage extensive student preparation, especially if the students conduct their analyses away from class. The instructor might have to be available for questions after hours or to check preparation by the students upon their return to class. If the case goes on during classroom hours, the instructor should observe these activities from time to time and be prepared to gently intervene at signs of trouble or undue frustration. For some cases, the instructor might have a direct role in the student analysis by eliciting student opinions in an ongoing discussion immediately after the case information is presented. This latter approach is used sometimes with students inexperienced in case analysis.

The Conducting Role

The case discussion is the heart and soul of the case study. The instructor's role in leading the class discussion is the most challenging aspect of an effective case study. Here is where the instructor has to think on her feet—questioning, steering, clarifying, expanding, controlling, protecting, synthesizing, and summarizing—so that the class discussion builds to a successful learning outcome for most, if not all, the students. Much of the hardship associated with administering cases occurs during this stage:

> They [the students] are active and animated: offering ideas, raising questions, building on each others' statements, constructing a collective analysis, reframing the discussion, challenging the teacher, learning with and from each other as much as, or more than, from him or her. The teacher is also active, and frequently mobile: initiating discussion and drawing the class into it, inviting engagement with the issues, amplifying some students' comments and summarizing others', writing *their* words on the chalk board, relating separate remarks and pointing out opposing views, feeding the group's thinking back to it, pulling the threads of conversation together and tying them into the course's themes; in short, structuring and facilitating the student's work rather than delivering information, giving explanations, or providing answers.[3]

This conducting role of the instructor is more of an art than a science. There are few if any prescriptive formulas for facilitating the case discussion, but there are some guidelines.

Starting Out.   Begin by framing the discussion. What is the purpose of the case? Why was it selected for the course, and why is it being conducted now? Remind students of what they have previously learned and how that learning will be extended with the discussion of the case. The opening question might be the first question previously assigned to the students, if it is sufficiently broad in scope. Typically, the opening question with long and involved cases gets the students to summarize and interpret the overall situation: What went on here? Who are the main actors and what are their interests? How are they related? What options do they have? Boehrer[4] suggests starting out with "static" questions of this sort that call for brief responses since they tend to encourage wide participation among students at the onset of the discussion. However, he also suggests switching quickly to "dynamic" questions such as "Which of the different actors' views of this situation do you find most compelling?" in order to liven up the discussion.

Building Up.   Your intent during the discussion is to assure that the critical issues embedded in the case are brought to the surface and explored in depth. Yet, you want to draw out the issues and a variety of interpretations, not just your preconceived conclusions about the case, from the students. How much control should you exert in this process? "The professor has to navigate between two extremes: on the one hand, being too heavy-handed in steering the discussion in an unresponsive class and on the other hand, being too soft in steering a rambunctious discussion."[5]

Certainly, you should encourage discussion among students:

1. Reflect questions directed to you back to the class: Well, how would *you* answer that question?

2. Refrain from stating your position on the issues until late in the session, as this will otherwise quickly curtail any debate.

3. Don't worry too much about silences following your questions. If you answer too soon, the students will quickly learn to wait for you to answer your own question. View the silence as a time for the students to collect their thoughts; besides, it shows that the ball's in their court.

4. If students tend to be unresponsive, ask the class to rate some factor on a scale of 1 to 10 by a show of hands: How serious is this situation? Then call on volunteers or particular students to explain their ratings.

5. Listen actively to what students say and show respect for their positions. Thank them for their contributions; write what they say in view of the class, using precise phrasing whenever possible; connect their comments to other points made previously by students, naming names of who said what.

6. If it suits your purpose, extract more from the student's comment than is actually spoken, but don't overdo it.

7. To help animate a discussion, engage in a role-play with one of the students, having him or her take on the more senior character.

8. It sometimes helps to remove yourself from the discussion, taking a seat in the back of the room and merely observe the interaction among students. In fact, Chhokar[6] recommends an *unstructured* case discussion for mature students in which the instructor acts as one of the participants and students are encouraged, and even forced, to clarify and resolve doubts themselves rather than looking to the instructor to do it for them.

9. Gently defuse hostile and dominant students, who can sometimes choke off case discussions, by steering the discussion to other students and back to the

issues of the case. For example, in response to a monopolizing student: "We understand your position clearly; now we are going to see what others have to say about the issue." And, in response to an aggressive student: "I will think about what you are saying; you may be right."[7]

Concluding.   It is important to come to some type of closure before the session ends. Students express great frustration when the discussion of issues expands and grows and then just terminates without any resolution or conclusion. This doesn't mean that you should provide the "right" answer or the "school" answer, even though the students may request one. There is no such answer to a case. You could comment on the discussion, showing how the points raised relate to the course content, and where the discussion was exceptionally relevant and where it could have gone deeper. The points you recorded during the discussion could help in this process, especially if they were organized around some structured model. You also could ask a student—one of the more active ones—to summarize and pose conclusions to the case discussion and then add your own thoughts or elicit comments from other students. Conversely, you could state your own view or describe the actual decision made or follow-up actions taken in the case, and then ask students to offer their support or criticism. Regardless of what you do, the students should leave the class with a sense of accomplishment and completeness. Yet, the package shouldn't be wrapped too tightly; it's healthy when the discussion among the students continues on in the hallways and during the breaks.

If one instructor were to administer the identical case to different groups of students giving the same orientation and using the same administrative decisions, you would be amazed at the enormous variation in resulting discussions and conclusions. This is because the competent case teacher attends "to the journey more than to the destination; the process, more than the content."[8] The students control the case as much as, if not more than, the instructor; so it's a learning experience for everyone involved.

The Evaluating Role

The fourth crucial role of an instructor in administering cases is evaluation. Evaluation of student performance in the analysis of a case is a perplexing problem. First of all, the essence of a case study is that there is no single "right" answer so that assessment must be a matter of interpretation and judgment. Second, in the typical case exercise, student performance initially occurs in either individual or small-group preparation activities and then again as part of a full class discussion. How can an instructor, who must concentrate on his role as a facilitator of the learning process, simultaneously observe and measure individual student activity? It isn't easy, but there are several possibilities. The instructor can require students to prepare written reports or oral presentations prior to the class discussion and possibly even a final report or presentation following the class discussion. Both reports or presentations can be graded when it is convenient for the instructor. If the extent or quality of student participation in the small-group analysis of a case is part of the evaluation, the instructor could request an assessment of each student by his or her team members. Team members are usually brutally frank in such assessments. If evaluation of student participation in the "live" full class discussion is appropriate, the instructor could try to make notes during or immediately after the discussion or, better yet, enlist the help of a teaching colleague or assistant who can objectively observe the discussion. The evaluation role for instructors is beneficial for all kinds of cases, but it is essential when the purpose of the case is practice application or participant testing.

Obtaining Cases

So, how do you obtain case studies that will suit your instructional aims and foster an exciting and memorable learning experience for the students? Clearly, you have two fundamental options: (1) develop a new, unique case yourself or arrange for someone to do it for you, or (2) search for an existing case that you can adopt or adapt for your purpose. There are a host of other decisions to be made within each of these options, but the *make-or-buy* decision comes first. This concluding section will help you make this decision about how to obtain a case study. It describes the kinds of actions you have to take for each option since the level of effort and possibility of success are major considerations in the make-or-buy decision. But first, the section will concentrate on specifying the goals and constraints for the *ideal* case. Then, you can decide whether you would be better off developing a new case or searching for an existing one.

Defining Case Specifications

Anytime you plan to buy something expensive and important, you probably spend some time first thinking about the particular requirements for that item. Since your total investment in acquiring and conducting a case study can be quite sizable, it pays to lay out its specifications as well. Specifications for a case study can include such factors as *instructional goals, administrative constraints,* and *situational preferences.*

Instructional Goals.   At the very least, case specifications should describe the following pedagogical requirements:

1. *Objectives.*   Which learning objective(s) will the case study support?
2. *Purpose.*   What role should the case study serve relative to the learning objectives: Icebreaking? Thought-provoking? Vicarious learning? Practice application? Participant testing?
3. *Conceptual issues.*   What key topics, issues, or behaviors should be represented?
4. *Target audience.*   What important attributes of the learners should be considered in selecting or creating study materials (e.g., position, experience, number, learning style)?

Together, these requirements define the instructional goals that the case study must satisfy, whether it is to be constructed or purchased.

Administrative Constraints.   The acquisition of a case study must also consider the following practical restrictions.

1. *Required date.*   When must the case study be administered to actual students?
2. *Available resources.*   How much labor and/or funding can be devoted to the development or purchase of the case study?
3. *Administrative times.*   How many hours of classroom time can be devoted to administering the case study? How much after-hours time will students devote to case preparation?
4. *Acceptable packaging.*   Must any type of instructional media (print, video, etc.) be used or avoided?

Constraints such as these dictate size and complexity of the case, as well as the decisions for how to administer the case (briefing, assigning, reporting). These specifications, therefore, weigh heavily in the make-or-buy decision.

Situational Preferences.   There are several ways in which cases can be framed. To the extent that you feel strongly about these issues, articulate your own preferences before deciding whether to construct or buy a case study:

Degree of Integration.   To what extent should the case study be an independent exercise that focuses on a particular topic or part of an all-encompassing, ongoing case that builds as the course develops? Proponents for *independent* cases say they can be more readily focused on critical issues and more easily located in an existing form. Besides, they say, multiple independent cases offer a wider variety of circumstances and are inherently more interesting than a single running case. On the other hand, supporters of *running* cases point to their ability to deal with a more complex, real-world situation. They also believe that these kinds of cases make more efficient use of classroom time because a previous case discussion provides the background for the next installment.

Degree of Job Specificity.   To what extent should the case study be a totally realistic *job-specific* representation of the kinds of people in this organization, the particular problems they face, what they would really do and say, and the specific information to which they would have access, or an exercise that deals with the kinds of issues faced by people in this organization but presented in a different, more neutral setting? Many people favor job-specific cases. They argue that a high level of relevance captures the students' attention better and that learned skills more easily transfer to job performance. Detractors for job-specific cases make some interesting points. They say that case details must be completely realistic, because an incidental, trivial inaccuracy will detract from the main focus of the case ("come on, the briefcases aren't brown, they're black"). Also, if job specificity is required, you might as well forget about trying to search out an existing case study; it will have to be built from scratch. It is also difficult to make a case job-specific when the students in the class have a variety of jobs. The detractors believe that students will attend objectively to the issues in a case that is not job-specific and still transfer the learning to their own situation.

Degree of Actuality.   To what extent should the case study report *actual* events, data, and quotes, and provide actual exhibits, or invent *hypothetical* events, data, and quotes to suit your specific purpose? Most college professors feel strongly that cases should be *real,* even if the names of the people and organizations have to be disguised. The rationale for their preference deals primarily with the credibility of the details. It would be unlikely, they believe, to construct a complex case so that all the events and facts realistically hang together. And, if the story or organization is recognizable, the case has built-in plausibility and interest. Another reason for using and naming actual organizations, people, and events is that the students may include additional details about the case from their own knowledge and research. Some people feel that it is easier to be a *reporter* than a *writer of fiction.* Proponents of hypothetical cases prefer the flexibility and freedom they offer. An imagined case situation can combine a wide variety of circumstances or events that could conceivably have occurred but just haven't happened yet—at least to your knowledge. Perhaps one hypothetical case would suffice where, otherwise, several real cases would be required for the same degree of coverage. Also, a made-up case can be as long or as short, as broad or as focused as the course requires. If a new case has to be constructed, and the case writer is knowledgeable and experienced, it is faster to create a story than to report on an actual event.

Situational preferences aren't design specifications for a case study in the same vein as instructional goals and administrative constraints. Yet, if you feel strongly about any of these issues, define your preferences before you consider whether to purchase or construct the case study.

Case Development

Suppose you've decided that it would be best to meet the case specifications by constructing a brand-new case study. Here's a five-phase process for case development:

1. Select Story to Tell. Your first action is to identify a particular story—real or hypothetical—that will serve as a good teaching case. Newspaper or television accounts, stories in magazines, recent or historical novels, investigative reports, your own recollection of some classical event, or anecdotes recounted by colleagues are all sources of ideas for the story to tell in the case study. But what makes for a good case story? Dorothy Robyn[9] of the Kennedy School of Government at Harvard suggests five criteria:

1. *Pedagogic utility.* The issues or theory illustrated in the story will clearly serve the instructional goals of the case study.
2. *Conflict-provoking.* The story involves a controversy that will likely invoke disagreement among members of the target audience.
3. *Decision-forcing.* Embedded in the story is at least one crucial decision point for which a question can be raised to lend a sense of immediacy to the case and requires students to view the situation from a first-person perspective.
4. *Generality.* The issues portrayed by the story will be generalizable to situations that the students might face in their own work situation. (Incidentally, if you plan to report actual events, then the story should have recently occurred or be ageless in its applicability.)
5. *Brevity.* The story can be told in a time frame that is consistent with the administrative constraints placed on the exercise. (It is interesting to note that the Kennedy School reduced the average case size to 15 single-spaced pages about 10 years ago and has since further cut the size to half that amount.)

Another criterion for selecting the story for a case should involve your access to data: How practical will it be for you to flesh out the details of the case?

2. Gather Information. The next phase in the developmental process is to obtain the details of the story. For case studies based on actual stories, this activity typically involves a cyclical process including (1) *interviewing participants* for their perspectives on the events, (2) *obtaining exhibits* from the participants that disclose further details about the story, and (3) *researching documents* that can identify more details and still other participants to be interviewed. The cycle continues until there is adequate information to prepare an effective case study. How will you know when you've reached this critical juncture? Of course, you won't know for certain. The stopping point in information gathering is a matter of judgment and experience. One possible indicator is that the last interview or so revealed no new details about the case. Or, perhaps you've exhausted all your sources—there are no other participants or exhibits available to investigate. In some respects, the exact stopping point isn't so critical. A few excess or omitted details concerning the story makes the case exercise quite realistic. After all, problem-solving analysis in the real world is never limited to just the essential details—or even includes all the essential details—concerning the case situation. There's always some peripheral information that can lead you astray, and you never have all the necessary facts at your disposal—this is what makes the exercise interesting. If you're planning to create a hypothetical case based on your past experiences, you've probably already gathered the appropriate information. However, you also might consider doing some additional research and interviews on similar situations, just to make the story more current.

3. Prepare Story Outline.   This activity actually goes on concurrently with the previous phase. As you're gathering information about the case, you record your findings or creations in an outline that portrays the critical case details in a chronological order. The outline links the *details* and *exhibits* to each *milestone* in the story.

Milestones	Details	Exhibits
Events	Behaviors	Reports
Decision points	Measures/results	Memos/letters
Actions	Quotes	Samples

4. Decide on Administrative Issues.   With a sense of the story in mind and with knowledge of the case specifications (*instructional goals, administrative constraints,* and *situational preferences*), you're now in position to decide how the case study will be presented. These decisions are made just before preparation of the actual case materials:

Case Presentation Media.   What combination of media will be used to present the story: Printed materials? Video? "Live" presenters? Computer? The selection is based in part on the availability of media and on the nature of the story to be told.

Orchestration of the Exercise.   How will the students be briefed on the case? Will the students work individually or in teams? Where will the students conduct their analysis? How will the students report their findings? These decisions are made on the basis of such factors as the presentation media, the available classroom and after-hours time, and the complexity of the case.

5. Prepare Case Materials.   A four-step activity is recommended for writing the case (other media will of course require additional production steps):

Construct Exhibits.   Assemble the exhibits you will either make reference to or package along with the case materials. Remember, this can include such items as articles, goals, graphics, job descriptions, letters, memos, maps, mission statements, newsletters, organization charts, plans, policies, procedures, promotional materials, standards, photographs, reports, tables, and vision statements. Arrange the items in the order in which they will be read.

Write the Story.   If you plan to have a narrative description of the story accompanying the exhibits, start with some background history that might be necessary to set the context for the story or could shed some light on the events to follow. Then, take each of the story milestones in turn and describe them—simply, objectively, and factually. Try to use an informal storytelling style. Keep it interesting, but avoid funny disguised names for people and organizations since they usually distract from the storyline. Provide the perspectives of different characters, occasionally including *verbatim* conversations among them. A *flashback* to an earlier event is an interesting literary device, but it can confuse the chronology of events. Keep in mind, that the story may include some irrelevant information—even some *red herrings* to keep the students off balance—and that the details may be incomplete. The story should end at some critical decision point for a key player in the case.

Write the Case Questions. Now, with the entire story in front of you, prepare a handful of key questions to guide the students' analysis. If the story is long and complex, begin with one or two questions that require short answers, but get the students to summarize the main issues. *Who are the main characters and how are they related? What problems, if any, do they face?* Then move to a few questions that require the students to assess the actions of the main characters. These questions should be broad in scope and puzzling in nature to create some tension within the students and encourage a wide range of diverse answers. Finally, ask the students to suggest a means for resolving the decision point at the end of the case. If the questions are to be positioned between the opening scenario and the case information they should be somewhat general. On the other hand, if the questions are to be asked after the presentation of the complete story, they can and should reference explicit case details.

Write the Opening Scenario. Finally, construct an interest-provoking introduction to the case. Describe the confounding situation facing the main player in the case at the concluding decision point and briefly—very briefly—summarize how he or she came to this difficult point. Remember, you're just trying to grab the students' attention and provide the necessary orientation to the case details. For example, you could introduce the main players or, if there are too many of them, provide a roster of characters to help students. If the case questions are provided before the story is told, the opening scenario must convey enough information to make the questions meaningful. Typically, the opening scenario occupies a single paragraph and rarely extends beyond one page.

Sources of Existing Cases

Now suppose that, instead of building a new case, you'll first spend time searching for an existing case. Where can you find appropriate existing case studies? There are a wide variety of sources.

Harvard Business School (HBS). HBS is often mentioned as the pioneer in the use of cases for management education. Besides using cases in their own school, they've built up quite a business in marketing business cases to other users. Every year they update their catalog of over 3000 business cases which they will send to you for a nominal charge. The catalog is also available in a software version, for about the same price, that includes a keyword search facility. The cases, developed by the faculty and their teaching assistants, are divided into 17 subject areas: for example, accounting and control, business ethics, computers and information systems, entrepreneurship, finance, human resource management, marketing. Each case costs only a couple of dollars for degree-granting institutions and twice that price for other buyers. This cost holds whether the case is 1 page or 30 pages. Many of the cases include in-depth teaching notes which can also be purchased at the same price as the case itself. A few video cases and software cases are offered at a variety of prices. Some copy centers around the country have special arrangements with HBS such that they will copy a Harvard case—in the quantities you require from the original that you supply—and collect a smaller royalty figure than the direct purchase cost. (Harvard Business School Publishing: 1-800-545-7685)

Other Schools.   A number of other schools offer case studies. Each has a particular market niche that it serves:

The Kennedy School.   The John F. Kennedy School of Government at Harvard University offers over 1000 cases dealing with public policy and public administration. Their cases are listed under such classifications as strategy and organizational leadership, political management, managing organizational production and operational capacity, policy analysis and design, public values and professional ethics. The cases and notes available from the Kennedy School cost a couple of dollars each for everybody. They also have arrangements with Copyright Clearance Centers, Inc. (508-744-3350), who collect a small royalty charge per copy. Besides a printed catalog, they also offer a case selection consulting service which they priced at about $40 in their last catalog. (Case Program Sales Office: 617-495-9523)

Institute for the Study of Diplomacy.   The Edmund A. Walsh School of Foreign Service at Georgetown University contains the Pew Case Study Center. This center, which originated in 1991, currently offers over 200 case studies associated with international affairs. Specific subject areas include conflict resolution and mediation, defense and security, diplomatic history, ethics and international affairs, global resources and the environment, and international political economy. The cases, which include teaching notes, cost a few dollars each. The Pew Case Study Center allows customers to order up to five examination copies at no charge. (Pew Case Study Center: 202-687-8971)

Hartwick Humanities in Management Institute.   Hartwick College sells cases containing an excerpt from a classic literary text packaged with one or more contemporary articles on a leadership issue that is manifested in the excerpt. For example an excerpt from Herman Melville's classic *Billy Budd, Sailor* is combined in a case with an article by Warren Bennis on *Rebuilding Leadership.* A segment from Arthur Miller's *Death of a Salesman* is packaged with *Lessons for Success* by Jack Welch, CEO of General Electric. Most of the cases are less than 30 pages and sell for about $4 each; the teaching notes cost about $10 each. (Hartwick Humanities in Management Institute: 1-800-94-CASES)

Books and Videotapes.   Cases are included in many textbooks as separate chapters and appendixes or are embedded in relevant chapters. Some texts are devoted specifically to case studies concerning a particular subject area (*Cases in…*) and some entire books—both fiction and nonfiction—can be viewed as case studies. Also, many instructional videotapes include segments dramatizing a short case, and other videotapes of feature films and documentaries can be easily adapted as a case study. But, how do you find a specific book or video that will suit your purpose? You could stroll through the stacks at a local university library or Blockbuster Video, quickly scanning the contents. Or, you could obtain catalogs of textbooks and videos from the publishers and producers and review the abstracts. Or, you could try to access appropriate databases (*Books in Print*) and search the titles and possibly the contents. You could also check with colleagues and professional associates for their ideas on published stories and existing videos that might serve as case studies. Finally, consider adapting investigative reports that have already been published in professional journals or business periodicals (*Business Week, Fortune*) or by auditing agencies (General Accounting Office), or which have been broadcast on television (*Nightline, 60 Minutes*). Often the reports can be obtained from the publisher or producer at a nominal price.

Note that all existing *copyrighted* case materials, regardless of the source, cannot be copied and distributed to the students without the expressed permission of the copyright owner. There are no exceptions. Even though the case might be used for a nonprofit educational purpose, the fair-use doctrine does not apply when you're planning to use the material class after class. Copying materials almost always deprives the copyright owner of potential revenue. Either buy one per student or write for permission to copy.

The Make-or-Buy Decision

Should you spend your time searching for an existing case or developing an entirely new one? Practicality almost always favors a "buy" decision. Therefore, after preparing the case specifications, you need to answer the following question:

> Is it likely that an accessible and affordable case study—with the appropriate level of job specificity—already exists that can be used "as is" or adapted to meet the instructional goals and administrative constraints?

Considering the likely sources of existing cases, if your answer is Yes, then spend the time—at least some time—searching for an appropriate case. If you're successful, the case will cost only a few dollars per student. In most situations, that's a bargain. If you come up empty after a reasonable period of time, you can reconsider your decision. Sometimes, you can answer No to the question above, right away, because you need a job-specific case or the conceptual issues to be embedded in the story are unique. Then, you can immediately embark on the five-phase case development process (select story to tell, gather information, etc.) without bothering to first search existing sources.

Conclusion

Case studies are well-suited for teaching higher-order intellectual skills to mature professionals. The students like them, they get involved, they learn from them, they talk about them when class is over, and they remember them. Few instructional techniques yield these kinds of results.

References

1. Rossett, A., and T. Emerson, *The Case for Cases in Instruction,* Presentation at the Annual Conference of the National Society for Performance and Instruction, Los Angeles, 1991.
2. Pigors, P., and F. Pigors, "Case Method," in R. Craig, ed., *Training and Development Handbook,* 3d ed., McGraw-Hill, New York, 1987, pp. 414–429.
3. Boehrer, J., and M. Linsky, "Teaching with Cases: Learning to Question," in M. D. Svinicki, ed., *The Changing Face of College Teaching,* New Directions for Teaching and Learning series, Jossey-Bass, San Francisco, 1990.
4. Boehrer, J., "On Teaching a Case," *International Teaching Notes,* 19(2), Spring, 1994.
5. Saint-Jean, S., and L. Lapierre, "Taïeb Hafsi and the Case Method," in H. E. Klein, ed., *Innovation through Cooperation with Cases, Simulations, Games and other Interactive Methods,* World Association for Case Method Research and Application, Boston, 1993, pp. 4–14.
6. Chhokar, J. S., "Learning How to Learn: The Use of Unstructured Case Discussion and Seminar," in H. E. Klein, ed., *Problem Solving with Cases and Simulations,* World Association for Case Method Research and Application, Boston, 1990, pp. 125–130.

7. Saint-Jean, S., and L. Lapierre, "Taïeb Hafsi and the Case Method," in H. E. Klein, ed., *Innovation through Cooperation with Cases, Simulations, Games and other Interactive Methods*, World Association for Case Method Research and Application, Boston, 1993, pp. 4–14.

8. Barnes, L. B., "Case Method Leadership: Some Thoughts of an Ignorant Expert," in H. E. Klein, ed., *Problem Solving with Cases and Simulations*, World Association for Case Method Research and Application, Boston, 1990, pp. 3–9.

9. Robyn, D., *What Makes a Good Case* (N15-86-673), Kennedy School of Government, Harvard University, Boston, 1986.

Bibliography

Bocker, F., "Is Case Teaching More Effective than Lecture Teaching in Business Administration? An Exploratory Analysis," *Interfaces, 17*(5), September–October 1987, pp. 64–71.

Gentile, M., *Field Interviewing Tips for the Case Researcher* (9-391-041), Harvard Business School, Boston, 1990.

Gomez-Ibanez, J. A., *Learning by the Case Method* (N15-86-1136.0), Kennedy School of Government, Harvard University, Boston, 1986.

Knirk, F. G., "Case Materials: Research and Practice," *Performance Improvement Quarterly, 4*(1), 1991, pp. 73–81.

Lemmon, D., T. Vagoun, and R. Gibson, "Supporting the Case Method through Computer Mediation," in H. E. Klein, ed., *Innovation through Cooperation with Cases, Simulations, Games and other Interactive Methods*, World Association for Case Method Research and Application, Boston, 1993, pp. 241–248.

McDade, S. A., *An Introduction to the Case Study Method Preparation, Analysis, and Participation*, Harvard College, Boston, 1988.

Pfeiffer, J. W., and A. C. Ballew, *Using Case Studies, Simulations, and Games*, University Associates, Inc., San Diego, 1988.

Smith, G., "The Use and Effectiveness of the Case Study Method in Management Education: A Critical Review," *Management Education and Development, 18*(1), 1987, pp. 50–61.

Stolovich, H., and E. J. Keeps, "Selecting and Writing Case Studies for Improving Human Performance," *Performance Improvement Quarterly, 4*(1), 1991, pp. 43–54.

Trostel, A. O., and J. G. Buckeye, "Three Propositions for Writing Better Cases with Greater Impact," in H. E. Klein, ed., *Managing Change with Cases, Simulations, Games and other Interactive Methods*, World Association for Case Method Research and Application, Boston, 1991, pp. 188–195.

25

Instructional Games, Simulations, and Role-Plays

Sivasailam Thiagarajan

Sivasailam Thiagarajan *is president of Workshops by Thiagi, an organization that works with corporate managers and employees to improve their organization's performance, productivity, and profits. Thiagi's clients include more than 50 different organizations in high-technology, financial services, and management consulting areas. For these clients, Thiagi has consulted and conducted training in such areas as rightsizing, diversity, creativity, teamwork, customer satisfaction, Total Quality Management, and organizational learning. He has published 20 books, 60 games and simulations, and more than 200 articles. He has made hundreds of presentations and keynote speeches at professional conferences. He has been the president of the North American Simulation and Gaming Association and the National Society for Performance and Instruction. Internationally recognized as an expert in multinational collaboration and active learning in organizations, Thiagi has lived in 3 different countries and has consulted in 21 others. Thiagi has a Ph.D. in instructional technology.*

These instructional techniques are based on two important premises: (1) People learn better through active experience than passive listening; and (2) people learn better through interacting with one another than working alone.

Several other related instructional techniques share these basic premises—and incorporate additional ones. These related techniques include accelerated learning, behavioral modeling, experiential learning, groupware, interactive lectures, learning teams, and team building. Most of the principles and procedures discussed in this chapter also apply to these techniques.

Trends and Causes

Recent years have seen a rapid increase in the use of interactive, experiential training. Train-the-trainer workshops emphasize facilitation skills on a par with presentation skills.

Some of the factors that have contributed to this significant expansion in experiential learning are shown below.

Teaming of Employees

In recent years, many organizations have flattened their managerial hierarchies, empowered their employees, and created cross-functional teams. It makes sense that people who will work in teams should be trained in teams.

Diversification of the Workforce

Multicultural groups are eager to understand and communicate with one another. Disillusioned by the failure of rational approaches to diversity training, facilitators and trainers are turning to experiential activities that provide powerful avenues to empathy and insights.

Seriousness or Playfulness

Corporations are discovering the limitations of systematic and rational problem-solving approaches. Along with Tom Peters, they realize that crazy times call for crazy organizations. They are rediscovering the fact that playful approaches produce more powerful solutions.

Organizational Learning

Senge[1] and his associates have emphasized the importance of continuous learning by organizations that want to compete, survive, and thrive. All strategies for creating and sustaining learning organizations require that employees interact with one another and explore the changing world through what-if simulations. (See also Chap. 4, The Learning Organization.)

Learning About Learning

Advances in cognitive sciences have identified the limitations of traditional IQ test scores and verbal approaches to teaching and training. Gardner's[2] theory of multiple intelligences and Epstein's[3] Cognitive Experiential Self-Theory clearly indicate the need to balance traditional training with accelerated approaches.

Changing Preferences of Learners

Newer employees who have been brought up on television shows such as *Sesame Street* and *MTV* are increasingly intolerant of passive approaches to learning.

Most trainees who have enjoyed interactive instruction are unwilling to return to the traditional data-dump approaches.

The Microcomputer Revolution

Computers have made it easier to design and to deliver interactive training. Fast, authentic simulations that use complex quantitative models and present the results in a variety of graphic forms are now readily available. These simulations are far superior to those that required mainframe computers only a few years ago.

Interactive, experiential training techniques are likely to see increased use in the future. Even when their novelty wears off, it is unlikely that the pendulum will swing all the way back to the traditional approaches to teaching and learning.

Categories, Characteristics, and Variations

This section examines the critical characteristics of instructional games, simulations, and role-plays and explores their variety. This section is not intended to provide a conceptual framework but to expand your awareness of the range of application of these techniques.

Instructional Games

An instructional game is an activity that is deliberately designed to result in learning outcomes. This activity incorporates the following five critical characteristics of a game:

1. *Conflict.* Games specify a goal to be achieved and throw in obstacles to its achievement. A game may involve competition among players or teams. Alternatively, it may involve cooperation among players to work against barriers to a common goal. In a game, the players may be in conflict with previous scores, probability, computer programs, mechanical devices, or the ingenuity of the game designer.

2. *Control.* Games are governed by rules that specify such things as how each player takes a turn, makes a move, and receives the consequences. The rules of a game may be implicit or explicit, simple or complex, rigid or flexible.

3. *Closure.* Games have a special rule for coming to an end. A game may end because time has run out, because a player has reached the target score, or because all players but one have been eliminated. In a zero-sum game, one player or team wins at the expense of the others. Most effective instructional games use multiple criteria for closure and permit different players (or teams) to win along different dimensions.

4. *Contrivance.* Games contain elements that prevent people from taking the games too seriously. The degree of playfulness may vary from one game to another. Some games involve chance elements to motivate the learner while others focus on rewarding demonstrated competency.

5. *Competency base.* The fifth critical characteristic is designed to help players improve their competencies in specific areas. Instructional games can be used

with a variety of learning objectives ranging from rote recall to complex problem solving. Objectives may deal with motor, informational, conceptual, interpersonal, and affective domains.

Variations Among Instructional Games.   Instructional games range widely along several dimensions:

1. *Events of instruction.*   Instructional games can be used during different events of instruction. For example, a game may be used as an introductory activity to increase the learner's readiness. Another may be used to provide practice and feedback to people who have mastered basic concepts and skills. At a higher level, an instructional game may be used to provide insights and integrate learning.

2. *Combinations.*   An instructional game may be a free-standing activity or combined with other media and methods. An interactive lecture, for example, incorporates game elements with a traditional presentation. Adjunct games add practice and feedback to the instructional content provided through print, audiotape, or videotape.

3. *Formats.*   Just as recreational games use a variety of formats, instructional games use different formats. Here are some typical game formats, along with an example of each:

    Card games.   In a game called Incentives Rummy, players exchange cards and try to assemble sets of incentives that belong to the same type.
    Paper-and-pencil games.   In Customer Complaints, players list five complaints on a piece of paper. Their score depends on how many other players come up with the same complaint.
    Verbal games.   In Rapid TQM, teams recall technical concepts related to the measurement of quality and take turns calling them out. Teams score a point for each term found in an official list.
    Solitaire games.   In a puzzle called Definition Drop, a player attempts to unscramble a set of letters and arrive at the correct definition of a technical term.
    Quiz games.   In Hazmat Tournament, players collect points by answering questions dealing with hazardous materials.
    Board games.   In Teller's Life, players throw dice, pick up cards, answer questions related to being a bank teller, and advance along a board.

Simulation Games

An instructional simulation game has a critical characteristic in addition to the five mentioned previously: It is the *correspondence* between aspects of the game and selected aspects of reality. For example, the rules of a game may reflect real-world processes and the game artifacts may represent real-world products. It must be emphasized, however, that simulation games do not reflect reality but only a model of reality as perceived by the game designer. Thus, various simulation games individually designed by a behaviorist, a communications specialist, and a cultural anthropologist to reflect the same phenomenon will differ significantly.

Variations Among Simulation Games.   Simulation games vary along the factors discussed earlier. Here are some additional variations:

1. *Degree of correspondence.*   High-fidelity simulations authentically reflect several aspects of the relevant reality. Most computerized flight simulators are examples of high-fidelity simulations. High-fidelity simulations are especially

useful for training specific procedures such as landing an airplane. Low-fidelity simulations metaphorically link the game with reality. For example, a playing card in a simulation game may represent an act of sexual harassment. Low-fidelity simulations are especially effective in transferring principles over a wide variety of situations.

2. *Formats.* Simulation games fall into a few standard formats. Here are brief descriptions and examples of some popular formats:

- Decision-making simulations require players to allocate limited resources to achieve different goals and to face the consequences of their decisions. For example, National Budget requires the teams to allocate the tax revenues of a mythical country.
- Production simulations involve the manufacture of a product. In Page 1, teams are given graphics, typewritten copy, and a scribbled editorial, and must prepare a camera-ready copy of the first page of a newsletter.
- Procedural simulations are primarily dress rehearsals. In Site Visit, employees of an organization prepare for an inspection by three visitors from the funding agency.
- Troubleshooting simulations require the players to find the causes of a problem and to fix it. In Debug, different teams race against each other to discover why a software program keeps making the computer crash.
- Disaster simulations require the players to cope with natural or organizational disasters such as earthquakes and downsizing. In Violence, an emergency response team decides how to handle a simulated hostage situation in a supermarket.
- Interpersonal simulations focus on interactions among people. In Me and My Team, participants negotiate within teams to divide points between themselves and a team pool.
- Empathy simulations enable players to realize the plight of different social groups. In SH, participants experience the frustrations of the powerless and appreciate how it feels to be sexually harassed.
- Insight simulations are brief metaphorical activities that enable players to understand fundamental principles. In Dollar Auction, players learn about the nature of addiction.

Role-Plays

In a role-play, players spontaneously act out characters assigned to them in a scenario. Like simulation games, role-plays reflect selected aspects of reality. However, there are some important differences between these two instructional techniques: A simulation focuses on the situational (stimulus) variables, while a role-play focuses on the response variables. A simulation tends to use a detailed scenario, while a role-play may be initiated by a couple of sentences. Response choices are limited in a simulation but wide open in a role-play. A simulation usually focuses on physical factors, while a role-play concentrates on interpersonal factors. In a simulation, the consequences of a player's move depend on a quantitative model of reality. In a role-play, these consequences depend on the subjective reactions of other people.

Variations Among Role-Plays. Role-plays take several different forms. Here are some possible variations:

Media. The scenario for a role-play may be presented through a printed handout, an audiotape, or a videotape.

Characters.   The characters in a role-play may be identified in terms of job functions, personality variables, or attitudes. Some role-plays may require people to play their own roles in a different situation (as in a lifeboat survival exercise).

Responses.   Most role-plays involve face-to-face conversations among the characters. When appropriate, role-plays can be conducted over the telephone (as in the case of telemarketing). You can also use written memos as the mode of interaction among the players. Cross-cultural role-plays may focus entirely on gestures and body language.

Mode of usage.   A large group can be divided into pairs to conduct parallel role-plays. Alternatively, two people may act out the roles while the others observe. You may replace the role-players from time to time with other participants. You may also assign coaches to the role-players.

Number of players.   While role-plays usually involve two characters, you can stage a session in which several participants act out roles. At the other extreme, you can conduct a behavior-rehearsal with just one participant, using an empty chair to represent the other person.

Replay.   You can increase the effectiveness of role-plays through judicious repetition. You can have the role-players participate in different scenes of the same story. You can follow one role-play with another by changing the personality or attitudes of the players. You can increase the intensity of conflict from one role-play to the next. You can also reenact the same role-play with the players reversing their roles.

Computerization: Good News and Bad

The increasing availability of microcomputers has profoundly changed interactive instructional techniques. Here are some of the advantages of using computers:

They are highly motivating. The addictive effect of arcade games demonstrates the powerful impact of graphics and sound effects.

They permit solitaire play. Learners can schedule and pace instructional sessions to suit their preferences. Players can make errors in total privacy.

They overcome the limitations of space and time. On the Internet, players from different countries can participate in the same activity, at different times.

Computers take care of keeping scores. For example, they can use a complex formula to award points on the basis of speed, accuracy, difficulty level, and other such factors.

Computers permit multiple branching. Depending on the player's current choice and previous history, computer simulations can provide rapid branching along alternative pathways.

The use of computers is not without limitations and potential dangers. Here are a few of them:

It is tempting to use the computer for inappropriate purposes. For example, most solitaire simulations of social processes miss the point.

Computers may distract the players. The bells and whistles may direct the learner's attention to the wrong details.

Computer simulations are expensive. An interactive simulation with sound and graphics can cost millions of dollars to develop.

Some people are still frightened of computers. For the next several years, computer illiteracy and phobia will still be issues.

Conducting Instructional Games, Simulations, and Role-Plays

This section provides practical guidelines for conducting an instructional activity.

Three Important Principles

Before discussing the procedure for conducting the activity, let's briefly discuss three basic principles.

1. The Flow of the Activity.   The major difference between facilitating an activity and making a presentation is the saliency of your presence. When conducting an activity, you should intervene only when absolutely necessary. Games and role-plays acquire a life of their own. Get out of the way and let the players' behaviors determine the flow of the activity.

2. Planning and Implementation.   In using instructional activities, plan with your left brain and implement with your right. Be prepared for all contingencies, and be flexible to exploit serendipitous events. Have alternative sets of rules and switch from one to the other in the middle of your activity. To paraphrase Carse,[4] play with the rules of the game rather than playing within the rules of a game.

3. "Failure" as Data.   Your activity cannot fail. Whatever happens during the activity—and at its end—is useful data. Even if the outcomes are not what you expected, you have valuable experiences for reflection, debriefing, and learning. You can always say, "This is surprising! Let's discuss why the results are so different from those we got the last time we played."

A Procedural Framework

We can explore the procedure for conducting an activity within a commonsensical three-phase framework: before, during, and after the activity.

Before conducting the activity, prepare the play area, the materials, yourself, and the players. Brief the players and let the game begin.

During the activity, your major responsibility is to maintain a balance between competition and cooperation, between a tight and a loose structure, between a slow and a fast pace, between individuals and teams, and other such extremes.

After the activity, your critical responsibility is to conduct a debriefing discussion to enable players to reflect on their experiences and share their insights. You also need to integrate the outcomes of the activity with other elements of your instructional plan.

Let's discuss these phases in some detail.

Before the Activity

The following are some guidelines for three critical activities just before conducting an activity.

Positioning the Activity.   The words *game* and *role-play* have negative or frivolous connotations to most people. A simple positioning strategy is to avoid these words and to use more dignified synonyms such as *a modified Delphi technique* or *a behavior rehearsal*.

Sometimes, it is important to present a rationale for your using an interactive technique. You may want to briefly mention the reasons you chose an interactive instructional technique, without being defensive or presenting a lengthy justification. Here are a few rationales that seem to reassure trainees:

Task-based.   On-the-job training (OJT) is obviously the most effective training approach. Simulation games and role-plays bring the learners close to OJT while reducing or removing potential risks.

Job-based.   Most jobs involve joint decision making among different employees. Interactive training techniques prepare people for these activities.

Organizational.   Most organizations are moving toward self-directed work teams. Games and simulations reflect this mode.

Motivational.   Action and interaction attract and focus the learners' attention. Participants find interaction more interesting than passive instructional techniques.

Responding to the Participants' Objections.   While briefing your participants, you may be confronted with objections to the games. Here are some suggestions on how to respond to participant comments and questions that indicate resistance:

Objection 1: This topic is too serious for a game.
Suggested response: Playing a game (or participating in a role-play) permits us to step outside the box and take a creative look at the situation. This activity does not reduce the importance of the topic but permits us to look at it from different perspectives.

Objection 2: What can I learn about my job by playing with paper airplanes?
Suggested response: If we confront familiar job-related problems, we can become too concerned with details to see the forest for the trees. Also, a job-related situation that is specific to one participant may appear irrelevant to another. The use of real-world situations may trigger strong emotional reactions. In contrast, by using an abstract, metaphoric task, we can focus on the critical steps of the process and ignore the distracting details. At the end of the activity, we will conduct a debriefing discussion to connect our play experiences to real-world action planning.

Objection 3: This is a waste of time. We can learn much more information if you just make a presentation.
Suggested response: If my objective were to present a lot of information, I could have given you a handout or an audiotape. My objective is to help you actively explore key principles and procedures. This activity will give you the necessary skills and knowledge in a realistic context. It will also give you the confidence that comes out of actually using these skills and knowledge.

Objection 4: I don't want to work with the others. They don't know any more than I do.
Suggested response: In the workplace, it is increasingly important for you to interact with others and function as a member of a team. Your work team is likely to be very diverse. In this activity, as a member of a diverse team, you learn to appreciate alternative viewpoints and pick up critical skills related to functioning effectively as a team member.

Introducing the Activity. An important principle in conducting a game or role-play is to get the participants playing as quickly as possible. This means that you should keep explanations and instructions to a minimum. Remember, you do not have to explain all the rules in complete detail at the beginning. Start with a minimum set of rules and use a just-in-time approach to explain the other rules as needed.

Here are some alternative approaches for introducing the rules of your activity to the players:

- Walk through the rules using a set of transparencies.

- Distribute a handout with a minimum set of rules and ask the participants to study them. Clarify the rules and answer questions from the participants.

- Use a videotape to demonstrate how the game is played.

- Begin the game with a selected group of players and ask the others to watch. Later, have everyone get into their groups and play the game.

Whichever approach you take, anticipate some degree of confusion among the players. Tell the players that this is normal and explain that the rules will become clearer as the game progresses.

During the Activity

An effective activity is a transparent one. The participants do not notice any aspect of the activity but merely participate. To make your activity transparent, you should maintain a balance among different dimensions. The following are some specific guidelines for this balancing act.

How to Conduct an Activity: A Checklist

- As you introduce new rules and implement them, try to maintain a balance between a tight and a loose structure. If the players tend to be sloppy, suggest that they take the rules more seriously. If they get uptight, suggest that they have fun rather than being obsessed with the rules.

- Monitor the pace of the game and maintain a balance between fast and slow. Make sure the pace is a comfortable one. If the pace is noticeably slow, speed it up by adding time limits. If the pace becomes hectic, slow it down by insisting that players think before making moves.

- Monitor the intensity of competition. If it becomes too intense, modify the rules and change the activity into a cooperative event. Introduce multiple criteria for winning and permit different players or teams to win. On the other hand, if there is not enough competition to motivate the participants, keep announcing scores and comparing team progress. Announce a prize for the winning team.

- Monitor the playfulness among the participants. If the participants become too playful, stop the activity and conduct a midcourse debriefing to identify learning outcomes. On the other hand, if the players take the activity too seriously, introduce game elements such as bonus scores and chance factors.

- Monitor how teams deal with individual needs. If they appear to ignore the slower participants, reorganize the teams so they become groups of equal strength. Also pair up each player with a partner.

- Monitor the focus of the group's attention. If individual players dominate the teams, isolate them and give them additional responsibilities (such as keeping score or observing other players' behaviors). Encourage nonassertive participants by providing them with additional information.

- Monitor how much the participants depend on you. If they totally ignore you, blow a whistle or turn the lights off to get everyone's attention. Project the new rules on the screen and explain them. On the other hand, if the group becomes excessively dependent on you and asks too many procedural questions, refer the questions back to the group with a nondirective query such as, "What would you like to do?"

- In addition to monitoring and maintaining these balances, keep moving among the participants, communicating with individuals and teams whenever needed. During the activity, observe the participants' behaviors and take notes on important events for later debriefing.

- As the activity nears the end, get ready for its termination.

After the Activity

When a game or role-play concludes, it is not the end of the instructional activity. People do not automatically learn by participating in a simulation game or role-play. At the end of the activity, participants may be excited, frustrated, or even confused. With low-fidelity simulations and intensive role-plays, many participants may be wondering, "What's the point?" To ensure maximum learning, you must follow up your experiential activity with a debriefing. Failing to do so would be both inefficient and unprofessional.

Debriefing is the process of helping people make sense of their experiences and share their insights with one another. Debriefing can be used after a simulation or a real event.

A Structure for Debriefing.   A suitable structure for debriefing involves six phases, each with a specific purpose and a key question. These phases are described below and illustrated with sample questions related to the simulation game called Barnga. In this game, which deals with cross-cultural communication, players at different tables are led to believe they are playing a card game by the same rules. Later, when players are reassigned to different tables, they are frustrated by the other players' apparent misunderstanding of the rules. At the start of the debriefing, the facilitator reveals that the rules among different tables were slightly different and this subterfuge was incorporated in the simulation to highlight the dangers of making hasty assumptions.

How do you feel?   The purpose of this phase is to provide the participants with an opportunity to vent their feelings and emotions. The questions used are designed to help the players to more objectively analyze their experiences during the later phases of debriefing.

Sample questions in this phase include the following:

- How do you feel about the results of the card game?

- How did you feel when you discovered that the other players were not following the same rules?
- How did you feel about not being able to talk to one another?

What happened?   The purpose of this phase is to collect basic data. The questions in this phase encourage participants to recall their experiences and discover similarities, differences, and patterns.
Here are some sample questions from this phase:

- What strategies did you use to learn the card game?
- Who won the first round?
- What happened when you moved to another table?

What did you learn?   The purpose of this phase is to encourage participants to come up with generalizations and to test them. Begin this phase by offering some hypotheses and encouraging the participants to discuss them.
Here are some sample generalizations from this phase:

- When the other players don't follow the rules, your first thought is that they did not understand them.
- Not being able to speak makes it difficult to reconcile differences.
- Everyone feels that his or her set of rules is the correct one.

How does this relate to the real world?   The purpose of this phase is to relate the simulation game experiences to real-world experiences. The questions encourage the participants to relate their experiences in the activity to their experiences in their organization. Here are some sample questions:

- Does this game remind you of incidents from your workplace?
- If Barnga were a metaphor for some real-world event, what would this event be?
- How does the behavior of players from the other tables reflect the behavior of employees from other branch offices?

What if?   The purpose of this phase is to encourage the participants to extrapolate from their experience. The questions deal with what would happen if the simulation game's rules or conditions were altered. Here are some sample scenarios from this phase:

- What if the players were permitted to talk to one another throughout the game?
- What if a more complex card game were used in the simulation?
- What if the winning partnership in the card game received a large cash prize?

What next?   The purpose of this stage is to encourage action planning based on the insights from the activity. Questions encourage the participants to share their thoughts on how they would play the simulation game again. They are also encouraged to suggest changes in their behavior in the workplace.
Here are some sample questions from this phase:

- If we played the same game again, how would you behave differently?

- How would you change the way you behave in similar situations in the real world?

- What advice would you give to a friend who is about to participate in this simulation game?

Alternative Approaches to Debriefing.   The basic six-phase structure described above can be incorporated in a variety of debriefing approaches. As the facilitator, you can set aside a specific period of time and ask the players to share their experiences and insights. You can divide the players into smaller groups to encourage more participation. You can provide each group with a questionnaire based on the six-phase debriefing approach. You can record critical segments of the players' behaviors on videotape and replay them during the debriefing. You can ask the players to keep a journal to record their personal experiences, reflections, and analyses.

Designing Simulations, Role-Plays, and Instructional Games

Now that we know how an instructional game, simulation, or role-play is conducted effectively, we are in a better position to discuss the design of these instructional activities.

The design of these types of instructional activities is similar in some ways and different in others. In this section we will discuss the design of instructional games and simulations separately while stressing the common elements among them.

There is a major difference between the approaches used by instructional developers and game designers. Instructional developers prefer to use the Instructional Systems Design (ISD) Model, which begins with a needs analysis and proceeds systematically through the steps of instructional analysis, planning, design, production, evaluation, revision, and implementation. Game designers prefer a solution-initiated approach in which they begin with an existing game and modify it for use in other contexts. In this section, we discuss both of these approaches and illustrate them with sample applications.

Designing Simulation Games: The ISD Approach

Simulation games can be efficiently designed by using the ISD Model. The core activities in this approach—as applied to the design of the simulation games—are defining the instructional context, constructing a model of reality, and converting the model into a simulation game.

Let us explore this approach by reviewing how it was used to design the simulation game Barnga.

Defining the Instructional Context.   During the initial analyses, we decided that facilitators would use Barnga in multinational corporations to train employees on international assignments. Typically, from 10 to 40 participants would play the game. The facilitators would have lived in different countries and have considerable cross-cultural experience. The simulation would be played and debriefed in about an hour. Because it could be conducted in a developing nation, the facilitators might not have access to audiovisual equipment or computers. In terms of play materials, the simulation had to depend on what was commonly available in different parts of the world.

Creating a Model of Reality.   The subject area of the simulation game was cultural anthropology, specifically cross-cultural communication. We felt that the game should reflect the following principles:

- Cross-cultural conflicts arise not from the obvious differences between cultures but from subtle ones.

- Cross-cultural clashes occur when people overgeneralize from a few similarities and assume that everything will be the same.

- When people are surprised by the way others behave, they tend to attribute these differences to ignorance or dishonesty of the "foreigners" rather than to cultural differences.

- Language problems exacerbate cross-cultural conflicts. In Barnga, we wanted to depict cross-cultural interactions that are governed by rules and involve both cooperation and competition. The time frames for these interactions would be variable, and the same type of interaction would be repeated several times.

Converting the Model into a Simulation Game.   To permit maximum generalization of the principles, we decided to keep the simulation game at a high level of abstraction. We felt that the use of specific cross-cultural situations would encourage the participants to behave in a politically correct fashion. To trap the participants into being themselves, we decided to use a game within the simulation. We chose a simple card game to represent rule-based interactions. We could standardize and repeat the game to reflect repeated interactions. The scoring system for the simulated interactions would be the scoring system for the card game. The game could involve partners and opponents to represent people from one's own culture and from different cultures. By slightly changing the rules of the card game at different tables, we could simulate the subtle differences among different cultures. Once we had chosen the card game as the core activity, we decided to use this sequence: enculturation (cooperatively learning the game), indoctrination (playing the game at the original table), initial cultural clash (first tournament), and expanded clashes (second tournament).

Designing Role-Plays

The ISD Model can also be used to design a role-play. Once you have created a model of reality, you can prepare an outline for the scenario and select a suitable medium (print, audiotape, or videotape) for presenting it. You can then identify the major characters in the role-play and decide how they will interact.

Limitations of the ISD Model

The ISD Model can be used effectively for creating instructional games, simulations, and role-plays—just as it can be used to create other types of instructional materials. However, this model has certain limitations. For one thing, design activities seldom proceed in a linear fashion, and attempts to force a step-by-step approach result in an uninspired and mechanical final product. In the design of games, the premium is on creativity. It is unlikely that the linear ISD process can produce exciting games. It is not surprising, therefore, that interviews with designers of popular instructional games reveal only a limited use of the ISD Model. An alternative approach used by experienced game designers is presented below. Rather than explain this approach in isolation, the description incorporates a discussion of the design of nonsimulation games.

Designing Instructional Games: The Framegame Approach

All games include procedures and content. A framegame is deliberately designed so that you can unload the content and replace it with the content of your choice. A framegame is like a picture frame. You can remove the original picture and put a different picture in the same frame.

Gamegame 1: A Sample Framegame Application.   Here is an example of a game created through the framegame approach. Gamegame 1 is a nonsimulation game used to highlight the fact that different people have different opinions about games. Here are the steps in conducting this game:

1. Give each participant four blank index cards and ask him or her to write four different responses to this prompt: What are some common opinions about the use of games and simulations with adult employees?

2. After about five minutes, collect the cards, shuffle them, and randomly distribute three cards to each participant. Ask everyone to study the opinions on the cards and to arrange them in order of personal preference.

3. Place the extra cards on a table. Ask the participants to use these cards to replace cards from their hand that they don't like.

4. Ask the participants to exchange cards with one another. Every participant should exchange at least one card and may exchange any number. Stop this activity after about three minutes.

5. Ask the participants to form themselves into teams of any size. The members of each team should review their cards and select the three they all like the best.

6. After an appropriate pause for the teams to discuss and discard, instruct each team to prepare a graphic poster to reflect its three final cards.

7. Ask each team to display its poster and read its three final cards.

8. Have a judge select the teams to receive awards for the best presentation and for the greatest internal consistency among the selected cards.

Group Grope as a Framegame.   By changing the prompt in the first step of Gamegame 1, we can use the frame of the game for different purposes. The generic framegame is called Group Grope. Here are some examples of how Group Grope has been loaded with different content:

Total Customer Focus.   This game is used to get employee inputs to improve customer satisfaction. The prompt is, In what ways can we delight our customer? A typical suggestion card may read: Reward employees who delight customers.

ET: Effective Teams.   This game is used during the first meeting of a newly created work team. The prompt is, What factors contribute to the effectiveness of a team? A typical factor card may read: Shared relationship.

What Did You Learn Today? This game is used as a review and feedback activity every day during the last 30 minutes of a five-day training workshop. The prompt is, What important things did you learn today? A typical feedback card may read: How to listen to the customer.

More About Framegames. Group Grope is the appropriate framegame for helping participants to analyze a concept and share initial understandings; to explore a controversy and surface people's feelings; to demonstrate diversity and highlight different opinions; to conduct a needs analysis and obtain participant inputs; or to establish a baseline of entry knowledge and attitudes. In spite of its versatility, Group Grope cannot be used to help participants to learn problem-solving skills, factual information, or interpersonal skills. However, other framegames can be used with other types of learning. Several recreational games, party games, and TV games can also be used as framegames for the design of instructional activities.

Once you have located a suitable framegame, your next job is to take it apart, remove the original content, and plug in your content. Here are some guidelines for this activity:

- Analyze the game. Review a printed description of the game and locate its frame.
- Specify the procedure. Identify the steps, moves, and rules of the game. List them in an outline.
- Identify the content. Specify the type of topics and the type of instructional objectives that are most suited for this framegame.
- Select new content. Make sure it fits the frame.
- Develop the new game. Prepare the play materials to incorporate your content.
- Modify the game. Anticipate likely problems. Change the steps and rules of the game to suit your resources and constraints.

The framegame approach can be used to the design of simulations—but a little less effectively. You can use the different templates described earlier to create your simulations.

A major danger with the framegame approach is the use of inappropriate frames to teach all types of content. Most participants will get tired of repeatedly playing variations of Monopoly or Jeopardy! to learn different skills and concepts. To maintain the power of framegames, it is important to select the most appropriate frame for your instructional objectives, needs, resources, and constraints.

The Realities of Games, Simulations, and Role-Plays

The field of simulation gaming is replete with myths and superstitions passed on from one person to another as the absolute truth. By way of review, we would like to conclude this chapter by refuting nine of these myths.

Myth 1: They are all the same.
Reality: Games, simulations, and role-plays differ from one another in some critical respects—and are similar in other respects. In addition, there are different types of games, simulations, and role-plays.

Myth 2: They all involve competition.
Reality: Simulations and role-plays may involve competition if the "reality" they reflect involves competition. All games have conflict, which need not be the same as competition among players. For example, a cooperative game could have conflict between a challenging goal and limited resources.

Myth 3: They are all temporary fads.
Reality: Games and simulations have been with us ever since the dawn of civilization. Judging from important trends (including teams, diversity, and interactive media), they are likely to be with our descendants forever in the future.

Myth 4: Effective facilitators explain all the rules before conducting a game, simulation, or role-play.
Reality: Explaining all the rules merely makes the players confused and anxious. Effective facilitators start the activity with a minimal set of rules and introduce additional rules in a just-in-time fashion.

Myth 5: Effective facilitators stick to the rules.
Reality: Effective facilitators are flexible. They focus on playing with the rules rather than playing within the rules. They continuously adjust the level of competition, playfulness, and several other factors even in the middle of an activity.

Myth 6: The end of the activity is the end of instruction.
Reality: The end of the activity is the beginning of the debriefing session. With games, simulations, and role-plays, the activity merely provides an experiential base for reflection and learning. It is possible to spend three hours debriefing a three-minute activity.

Myth 7: Effective designers use a systematic approach to design games, simulations, and role-plays.
Reality: The systematic approach is one alternative for designing games, simulations, and role-plays. Creative design is often chaotic. Many designers begin with a solution and work backwards to a suitable problem to solve.

Myth 8: There is one best type of game, simulation, or role-play for all situations.
Reality: There is no single best type of simulation or any other activity. The choice of the most appropriate type of activity depends on several factors, including the nature of the objectives, the level and types of learners, and the needs of the facilitator.

Myth 9: Simulations reflect reality.
Reality: Simulations reflect a model of reality from the point of view of the game designer. Different designers may view the same situation from different perspectives.

A final myth suggests that the design and use of games, simulations, and role-plays is a serious and complex task. Nothing could be farther from the truth. The reality is that it is easier and more enjoyable to design and use an activity than to prepare and make a presentation. If you approach these techniques with an open mind and in a playful mood, you will have an enjoyable time and gain important insights—and so will your learners.

References

1. Senge, Peter M., *The Fifth Discipline: The Art and Practice of the Learning Organization,* Doubleday, New York, 1990.

2. Gardner, Howard, *Frames of Mind: The Theory of Multiple Intelligences*, Basic Books, New York, 1993.
3. Epstein, Seymour, *You Are Smarter Than You Think*, Simon and Schuster, New York, 1993.
4. Carse, James P., *Finite and Infinite Games*, The Free Press, New York, 1986.

Bibliography

Boud, David, Rosemary Keogh, David Walker, eds., *Reflection: Turning Experience into Learning*, Kogan Page, London, 1985.

Ellington, Henry, Eric Addinall, and Fred Percival, *Case Studies in Game Design*, Kogan Page, London, 1984.

Fripp, John, *Learning Through Simulation: A Guide to the Design and Use of Simulations in Business and Education*, McGraw-Hill, London, 1993.

Gredler, Margaret, *Designing and Evaluating Games and Simulations*, Gulf Publishing, Houston, 1992.

Greenblatt, Cathy Stein, *Designing Games and Simulations*, Sage Publications, Newbury Park, CA, 1988.

Jones, Ken, *Simulations: A Handbook for Teachers and Trainers*, Kogan Page, London, 1987.

Jones, Ken, *Interactive Learning Events: A Guide for Facilitators*, Kogan Page, London, 1988.

Jones, Ken, *Imaginative Events for Training: A Trainer's Sourcebook of Games, Simulations, and Role-Play Exercises*, McGraw-Hill, New York, 1993.

Newstrom, John W., and Edward E. Scannell, *Games Trainers Play*, McGraw-Hill, New York, 1980.

Pfeiffer, J. William, ed., *The Encyclopedia of Group Activities: 150 Practical Designs for Successful Facilitating*, University Associates, San Diego, 1989.

Scannell, Edward E., and John W. Newstrom, *More Games Trainers Play*, McGraw-Hill, New York, 1983.

Scannell, Edward E., and John W. Newstrom, *Still More Games Trainers Play*, McGraw-Hill, New York, 1991.

Schwarz, Roger M., *The Skilled Facilitator: Practical Wisdom for Developing Effective Groups*, Jossey-Bass, San Francisco, 1994.

Thiagarajan, Sivasailam, and Barbara Steinwachs, *Barnga: A Simulation Game of Cultural Clashes*, Intercultural Press, Yarmouth, ME, 1990.

Thiagarajan, Sivasailam, *Framegames by Thiagi*, Workshops by Thiagi, Bloomington, IN, 1994.

Thiagarajan, Sivasailam, *Diversity Simulation Games*, HRD Press, Amherst, MA, 1995.

van Ments, Morry, *The Effective Use of Role-Play: A Handbook for Teachers and Trainers*, Kogan Page, London, 1983.

26

Interactive Multimedia Training Systems

Jeffery J. Howell

Larry O. Silvey

Jeffery J. Howell is Director of Technology Services Group, Arthur Andersen & Co. SC where he supervises the design and development of computer-based training and interactive multimedia programs. He works with Andersen Consulting and the Andersen business units to support their worldwide practice in the planning and implementation of technology-based training solutions. Howell joined Andersen in 1990 as a Senior Education Manager. He has over 15 years experience in developing technology-driven solutions to performance and training problems. Prior to Andersen, positions he held include Midwest Division Manager, Applied Science Associates; Senior Instructional Designer, Microtel Ltd., part of GTE; CBT Author for McDonnell Douglas Astronautics Company; Training Analyst/Course Developer for Arabian American Oil Company; and Instructional Media Production Manager, U.S. Department of Health, Education and Welfare Research and Development Center at Indiana University. He received his M.S.Ed. in instructional systems technology from Indiana University. He is a member of ASTD and the International Society for Performance Improvement (ISPI) and on the board of directors of Interactive Multimedia Association's Compatibility Project. Howell is the author of "Expert Systems and Simulation for Training Test Desk Analyzers" in Advances in AI and Simulation (Society for Computer Simulation International) and coauthor of a chapter, "The New Teaching Paradigm Meets the New Generation of Technology: Achieving the Objective of Lifetime Learning" in Critical Thinking, Interactive Learning and Technology: Reaching for Excellence in Business Education (Arthur Andersen & Co., 1992).

Larry O. Silvey *is a Partner and Managing Director of Andersen Consulting Education. He joined Andersen in 1979, became Manager in 1980, was promoted to Principal in 1986 and to Partner in 1989. Silvey is presently responsible for the design, development, and delivery of all Andersen Consulting's centrally developed global training programs. Under Silvey's leadership, the company has received several awards for excellence in training and education. Most recently, Andersen Consulting's Business Practices Course, a 40-hour multimedia product, has been featured several times in the business press and received several national awards. Silvey also led in the development of Andersen's training development methodology. Before joining Andersen, he worked in the private sector as a productivity and training consultant. He received both a bachelor's degree in journalism and a master's degree in instructional technology from the University of Missouri. He completed additional postgraduate work at the University of Missouri at Kansas City. Silvey is a member of the International Society for Performance Improvement (ISPI) and sits on its Advocates Advisory Panel. He is also a member of ASTD's National Issues Committee.*

Interactive Multimedia: AV, CBT, and More

Interactive multimedia training programs represent a synergistic marriage of audiovisual (AV) media and computer-based training (CBT). These programs are designed to integrate text, graphics, animation, audio, and motion video so that each unit of content can be delivered in the medium that's best for it. Because these programs are computer-based, learners can interact with them and go through them in a sequence and depth that meets their particular requirements. And because their delivery systems are designed primarily for micro or personal computers, interactive multimedia training programs can be used at point of need.

For example: An instructional program for managers on employee performance reviews might utilize still-frame graphics to show evaluation forms and to chart the relationship between effective reviews and performance improvement. It might call up motion video with audio to model good manager behaviors in giving reprimands. It would allow the learner to customize the instruction to provide those skills he or she needs to acquire: say, goal setting and compliance with the Americans With Disabilities Act. It would provide the learner with immediate and continuous feedback and make recommendations for additional instruction based on the learner's performance. And it could be used by a manager the day before he or she must conduct a review.

Learner-Centered, Performance-Improving Training

This marriage of AV to CBT has created a whole that is very different from the sum of its parts. The interactive multimedia program provides a truly learner-centered, performance-improving experience that cannot be compared directly to any other form of training.

Besides enjoying all the benefits of standard audiovisual tools, users of interactive multimedia systems gain the dynamic advantage of interaction, with many happy results. The interactive multimedia program does the following:

1. Meets the individual needs of many learners, accommodating users at all levels of expertise

2. Lets each user work at the pace that best suits him or her

3. Offers the best presentation for different subjects

4. Reverses the traditional student-teacher ratio, bringing many teachers or experts to the individual student

5. Provides "creative" learning experiences that give each student a continuing functional reason to learn, beyond merely studying for a test

6. Can be designed to encourage learners to explore a topic rather than simply seek a single right answer

7. Allows learners at different levels to bring their own expertise and creative capabilities into the learning process

8. Can create a "virtual classroom" wherever a microcomputer or workstation can be placed

9. Permits small groups of two or three learners to engage in team problem-solving activities

10. Can function as an in-class electronic performance-support system, containing the information, guidance, and tools needed to complete complex case activities

Beyond offering the best presentation medium for each type of content, interactive multimedia training achieves a powerful synergy by making media reinforce each other. For example, an Audubon Society program on birds describes their songs with text and provides corresponding examples with audio. Having heard the songs the text describes, learners identify birds in the field more accurately. Knowing text descriptions for certain sounds, learners apply terms for birdsong characteristics (like "high-pitched" and "warble") more accurately.

Some interactive multimedia training programs are actually integrated into computer systems used by workers, so that small units of training can be delivered the moment they are needed to support job performance. In fact, the training functions of these systems are often difficult for a user to distinguish from its operational aspects.

For example: Bell Atlantic's data entry system for its telephone customer service representatives "coaches" them through incoming calls. It offers reps order forms at beginner, intermediate, and expert levels, with appropriate instructional cues, and it provides quick tutorials that enable reps to answer customers' questions about products and services where they may have previously lacked familiarity. When reps are not taking incoming calls, the system helps them organize their workloads and prompts them to initiate sales calls to selected customers. The system helps the reps to sell successfully during these calls by providing them with customers' histories and descriptions of products that should appeal to these customers.

Training Systems for Today's Business World

To sum up, interactive multimedia training programs can move training beyond teaching into the realm of direct-performance improvement. That makes these programs very important in today's business world. This is particularly so because the global economy is moving from an orientation to production toward an emphasis on converting information to knowledge.

In his 1991 book, *The Work of Nations*, Robert Reich says, "Even the most impressive of positions in the most prestigious of organizations is vulnerable to worldwide competition if it entails easily replicated routines. The only true competitive advantage lies in skill in solving, identifying, and brokering new problems." In other words, the future belongs to the "knowledge worker."

Traditional approaches to training mirrored the assembly line of an earlier industrial era, by stressing repeated memorization of answers and progression from one "course" to the next higher one. Learners "stored up" the knowledge they acquired in these courses for future use. They often found themselves unable to apply that knowledge when the time came, however, because facts without practice don't translate well to skills required in the workplace.

Continuous Need for Innovation Demands a "Learning Organization"

The shortcomings of traditional training are much more serious now than they were in the past, because today's business world presents workers with a continuous need to innovate in the process of solving problems. There are even fewer "right" answers that can be ingested before the fact. So learning too must be continuous, and take place when and where it's needed.

For continuous learning to be able to happen, the learner must control the learning process, to be able to analyze the problems that face him or her, work them through, and arrive at reasonable solutions in a systematic way. Furthermore, the learner must have "metacognitive" skills, that is, know how to initiate and complete his or her own learning successfully. In fact, with every worker in a company facing the need to learn in this manner, that company must put in place processes and systems that make it essentially a "learning organization."

For example: AT&T has set several precedents and standards in employing advanced-technology multimedia programs to train employees throughout its businesses. Like many high-technology customer-service companies, AT&T faced shrinking shelf life of technical information, ballooning costs of providing centralized training to international workforces, and increasing business risks associated with taking employees away from their customers for training. The company reengineered its training approach to combine distance learning with *cascaded learning,* a train-the-trainer concept that empowers supervisors to provide direction on the kind of training needed by their own workforces. Thus, training is targeted, tailored, and delivered to the right purpose and audience.

Video teletraining, audio and/or graphic teletraining, and hypertext are all used in the AT&T scheme, as well as face-to-face presentations. The company is also bringing video conferencing to desktops, providing employees with on-line, point-of-need access to live expert support. AT&T expects to make wider use of corporate broadband audio and video networks in the future.

Interactive multimedia programs can play a vital role in powering those processes and systems that make a company a learning organization (which, experts agree, AT&T is rapidly becoming). These programs are probably unmatched in their ability to transfer knowledge and develop skills at the same time, to allow the learner to develop a skill by acquiring knowledge and refine that knowledge by applying the skill.

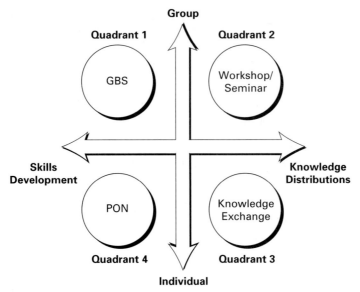

Figure 26-1. Training environment classifications. (*Andersen Consulting.*)

In addition to providing experience that's immediately transferable to the job and helping knowledge workers to manage problem solving, these programs empower users to manage *themselves* in a way that makes them more productive.

Just where and how interactive multimedia programs impact the change dynamic in the world of training can be seen in the diagram in Fig. 26-1, which shows an architecture of four training environments. Traditionally, training has been focused on providing group knowledge distribution, via the type of centralized, classroom-based activities represented in Quadrant 2 of the diagram. As training strategies are being reengineered today, the focus is shifting to a new paradigm reflected largely on the left side of the diagram, in Quadrants 1 and 4. Here, interactive multimedia systems support group skills development with simulation and Goal-Based Scenario (GBS) learning experiences, while supporting individual skills development in point-of-need contexts.

Meanwhile, knowledge distribution will change from a group experience to an individual one (i.e., in a shift of focus from Quadrant 2 to Quadrant 3), as companies leverage and disseminate their knowledge capital and operating experiences via electronic "knowledge exchanges" that use sophisticated network technologies, databases, and techniques. Interactive multimedia can be used to integrate training into knowledge exchanges, to extend their role from information access tool to integrated performance support environment.

But by no means are interactive multimedia programs the only training solutions for today and tomorrow. Merely because focus of training is shifting away from Quadrant 2 in Fig. 26-1 doesn't mean that Quadrant 2 will atrophy and disappear.

Classroom instruction, paper-based lessons, live role-plays, linear film and video, and on-the-job learning will continue to be relevant and useful; and interactive multimedia can be best understood, appreciated, and used as it fits into and enhances the continuum of training resources.

Nor is interactive multimedia technology a solution by itself. Interactive multimedia programs are like other training instruments: they will not be effective if they are not designed well. As we'll see, interactive multimedia gives instructional designers a literally marvelous opportunity to apply new design skills to break old design paradigms and develop new ones even as they use the latest ones. But the proof of the pudding still lies in the design, not in the technology. And it always will.

How Did Interactive Multimedia Get That Way?

A quick look at the forerunners and components of interactive multimedia can help put the strengths of these new systems in perspective.

Flipcharts have probably been around as long as paper has and they seem the farthest cry imaginable from multimedia programs. Yet flipcharts were really the first interactive audiovisual training instruments, because they could be developed and modified in the presence of learners. They reflect learners' ideas and enable instructors to tailor presentations for learners' benefit. They are inexpensive and useful for groups of two to perhaps two hundred learners. But they aren't durable and aren't really usable by anyone except for the instructors who create them. And since flipchart illustrations are usually drawn "on the fly" by instructors, they are neither graphically sophisticated nor reliably accurate.

"Magic lanterns" were used in training by both armies in the Civil War, and their descendants, called *overhead projectors* (OHPs), are still popular. OHP visuals are usually prepared in advance. That preparation allows them to be more sophisticated than flipchart drawings but results in slightly less interactivity than flipcharts offer (although OHP visuals can be altered in training sessions). Like flipcharts, OHPs are used primarily to support instructors. They can, however, be used by more than one instructor.

Slides permit very sophisticated visuals, including color photographs, but slide-based visuals are relatively inflexible. Usually, they can be altered for specific learner needs only by changing the order of the slides or inserting new ones. This medium introduced another kind of interactivity, though. Slides synchronized with audiotapes can be used by individuals for self-paced self-study. Today, graphics software programs can generate slidelike visuals for computer-based presentations. These visuals can also be converted to photographic slides.

Training films were used widely by the mid-1920s. They gave learners a keen sense of the dynamics of job tasks involving motion. With sound, added to film in 1927, the depiction of a job task could be enhanced by a narrator's or operator's commentary and a "role-play" could include the words as well as the movements of the players. These films were expensive to produce and duplicate. They couldn't be stopped or searched easily for examination and analysis of particular moves. They were cost-effective only for fairly large audiences, but they made it possible for the first time to "package" motion and sound-based instruction for wide-scale dissemination.

With the introduction in the early 1970s of narrow-gauge *videotape* in cassettes, motion media acquired a small measure of interactivity and became suitable for self-study and small-group use. The tape could be "paused" on a single "frame" of video, then moved forward or back frame by frame. But resolution of single frames on videotape is poor, which makes it hard to study small details in the picture. And because video signals on tape were (until recently) analog, it was impossible to access individual frames at random. Production costs for videotape programs are high, though not as high as those for film.

A New Interactivity

Development of *computer-based training* (CBT) increased markedly with the introduction of microcomputers in the early 1980s. For the first time, interactivity in
media-based instruction was able to take on the characteristics of a continuous
dialogue between learner and program.

For example: An early CBT simulation program developed by Andersen
Consulting asked learners to double the throughput of an on-line transaction
processing system. The program added learners' changes to an on-screen
schematic of the system, calculated increases or decreases in throughput resulting from these changes, and explained why the changes caused those particular
throughput variations. Learners discovered that attractively obvious single
changes like doubling CPU speed could actually *reduce* throughput. Effective
solutions (more than one) required well-thought-out combinations of upgrades
in CPU speed, disk and memory capacity, etc.

As the above example shows, the level of learner-program interactivity in
computer-based training made it possible for learners to explore a subject rather
than prepare for a test on it. However, because the personal computers of that
day lacked interfaces for motion media and had very limited data retrieval and
processing capacities, graphics were simple and static (limited to a schematic in
the example), and many programs were based on the "page-turner" or "read-
and-repeat" design paradigms: "Here's a question; answer it; I'll tell you if
you're right or wrong; if you're wrong, try again; if you're right, we'll proceed to
the next question."

In the mid-1980s, a series of advances in audiovisual and data processing technologies greatly expanded the versatility of computer-based training. Digital
codes and video on 12-in "laserdiscs" made it possible for computer programs to
instantly access over 50,000 still frames, or any point in half an hour of motion
footage. With the aid of an adapter, the computer display monitor could show
both computer-generated and video visuals. Adapters could also connect touch
screens, mice, and sensor-equipped replicas of job equipment to computers.
These interfaces enabled learners to communicate with programs and their visuals in ways that simulated real-life involvement with tasks being learned.
Advancements in large-scale random data storage increased processing power,
and other hardware and software components allowed microcomputers to
accommodate nonlinear trips through subject matter by learners. Combining
these components produced the first true computer-based interactive multimedia training systems.

These hybrid systems had all the strengths of interactivity embodied in earlier
media, and they brought all the teaching capabilities of audiovisual media to
learner-centered instruction, integrating motion, graphics, and text as learners
required. They could serve diverse, widely scattered populations accommodating both individuals in self-study and groups of learners.

There were drawbacks, though. Complex interfaces of up to half a dozen
pieces of hardware were required. These "hookups" were cumbersome and
expensive (initially costing some $20,000 for each system), and were very prone
to malfunctioning. They could not be easily placed at job sites for point-of-need
learning. High costs, low flexibility, and lower reliability slowed the adoption of
interactive multimedia by the training world.

And Then...The Door Opened

Those drawbacks started to disappear in the early 1990s, as "integrated" microcomputer systems appeared in greater and greater numbers. CD-ROM ("compact

disc/read-only memory") technology brought more efficient audiovisual components to interactive multimedia systems. Compact discs and their drives are smaller than laserdiscs and laservideo players. CD-ROM equipment is less expensive and easier to operate. It can be built into desktop computers—and even notebook computers—without significantly increasing their size. At the same time, better design, more efficient manufacturing techniques, and keen competition have driven prices for microcomputer hardware and software down precipitously. The door has opened to an era of high-tech training that has the potential to save companies millions of dollars while revolutionizing the way their workers acquire skills and use knowledge.

What Makes Interactive Multimedia Succeed? It's the Design!

A textbook downloaded to a computer and dressed up with graphics, video, and sound is *not* interactive multimedia training. Good design is the key to harnessing the unique instructional strengths of this medium: comprehensive learner control of the learning process and the ability to "hyperlink" content represented in media in infinitely variable relationships.

Challenging as they may be, these strengths permit instructional designers to set new standards for training effectiveness by breaking free of traditional design paradigms and creating and testing new ones. For instance, interactive multimedia programs needn't be restricted to a rigid learning path. Rule, example, or practice can be selected in any order that suits the learner.

Another design paradigm that no longer reigns unchallengeable is the ideal-circumstances model. Because of their versatility, interactive multimedia programs can immerse learners in simulations of the real world in all its surprising and messy complexity.

For example: The J.C. Penney Company trains its customer service representatives with an interactive multimedia system that simulates a full range of scenarios, with "customers" that might be courteous, neutral, irate, or abusive. A designer of the system pointed out that no other training instrument, even classroom role-plays using fellow students as "customers," can truly replicate the unpredictability of the real world. Penney reps, he says, "leave [the system] ready to do the job rather than ready to learn on the job." He adds that they reach peak proficiency in about a third less time than they did using other training methods.

As we look at five basic guidelines for effective design of interactive multimedia systems, you'll recognize that they are not radically different from those you might have used to develop training of other types. The nature of interactive multimedia, however, can require that they be understood and followed in nontraditional ways.

1. Begin by Determining Goals

The goal's the thing! Every other design aspect of an interactive multimedia training program derives from it as is the case with other types of training. And everyone on the program team must agree on what is to be achieved before development can get under way.

Interactive multimedia programs are often assigned goals that fall into four categories of achievement:

1. Transfer of Knowledge. The learner acquires information and learns what to do with it. This could be the goal for a program on compliance with federal regulations, in which text presents the regulations themselves while graphics and experts on video illustrate compliance procedures.

For example: Aetna chose CD-ROM-based interactive multimedia as the means for delivering *The Right to Know: OSHA Hazard Communications Standard* to more than 600 employees companywide. This Aetna program integrates text, sound, graphics, and slides. It also incorporates testing modules and record-keeping capabilities to facilitate compliance with OSHA's testing standards. Four requirements combined to make multimedia the appropriate delivery choice for this program. First, Aetna needs OSHA training media with a strong company orientation. Second, 20 percent of the material varies among different job functions, making very desirable a presentation that is both "seamless" in appearance and customized in content. Third, centralized classroom training on this subject would be expensive and difficult to schedule for Aetna, since the learner population is spread over three work shifts. Finally, because companies must prove to OSHA that they have trained their employees adequately, the training program must provide learner-centered tests and generate reliable, relevant test data and records.

2. Skill Building. The learner acquires certain capabilities by learning steps that directly address performance. Simulation is one vehicle for achieving this goal.

For example: Learners complete the American Heart Association's simulation-based interactive multimedia course in cardiopulmonary resuscitation (CPR) by watching maneuvers on video and repeating them on a mannequin equipped with 106 sensors. Combined feedback from the sensors ensures that learners develop CPR techniques with the precision required for CPR to save lives.

3. Performance Support. The worker acquires the skill or knowledge to solve a specific job problem without leaving the work environment. Bell Atlantic's customer phone reps' system, described earlier, addresses this goal.

Enhancement of Collaboration. Collaboration programs enable workers to improve their performance by communicating with experts, knowledge bases, and each other. These programs are especially useful in leading-edge technological fields, where development of formal training often can't keep up with the pace of change. Workers can collaborate in "logical" time (i.e., time represented by access to computer databases rather than by the duration of a face-to-face meeting), by posting questions or comments on electronic bulletin boards, or by entering them into "groupware" information structures, such as Lotus Notes or a knowledge exchange. Interactive multimedia support can make collaboration programs significantly more effective. This is essentially an indirect, or secondary, instructional goal for multimedia, but a valid one nevertheless.

4. Integrating Goals. Although paper-based and classroom training can integrate goals, it is the unique strength of interactive multimedia programs to "package" a classroom environment that supports goal integration and deliver that environment to the desktop.

For example: Andersen Consulting's *Business Practices* course integrates knowledge transfer with skill building in a multimedia self-study experience that supplants 60 hours of text study and 40 hours of classroom training. The basis of the course is a simulated consulting assignment at a book publishing company. Learners "work" in the various functional areas of the business (cash management, sales, product development, cost accounting, human resources, distribution, etc.). Graphics show critical documents, and video provides department tours, interviews with key executives, and expert assistance. Whenever learners encounter terms they don't know, they can access a reference system that defines and explains them (see Fig. 26-2). Learners then return to the simulation and see how the terms apply. The psychological effects of choosing to access the reference system, and being able to use the new terms immediately, enables learners to retain terms and their meanings significantly better than they would with define-terms-first-use-them-later instruction.

For example: ITT Hartford's *Underwriter Information Workstation* integrates knowledge transfer, skill building, and performance support. This program is stored in a networked system and fed directly to computers on underwriters' desks. Its core function is business application: enabling underwriters to prepare insurance policies and programs. That function has been augmented by wider access to information, hypertext definitions explanation, and tutorials for things that underwriters don't understand. Creating *Underwriter Information Workstation* "wasn't a matter of developing performance support and slapping it onto an existing application," says the program's instructional designer. "The content of the functional application [was] completely redesigned, and the content of the performance support—while much of it was in pre-existing manuals—was also redesigned." By integrating knowledge transfer, skill building, and performance support, *Underwriter Information Workstation* improves performance of underwriters, reduces training costs, increases productivity and quality of work, and enhances the company's capacity to apply automation to business problems more broadly.

Some skill-building simulations can replicate reality so closely, and in such little time, that they enhance performance-support goals.

For example: Minisimulations of emergency scenarios, designed into power-plant control systems, train operators in normal circumstances and support them in emergencies. These simulations may function individually in performance support and may be combined to deliver plant management and control skills. They are effective in performance support not only as aids to problem solving but as review and practice for operators who have trained with them.

Combining goals in novel ways typifies the kind of adventure in paradigm busting that interactive multimedia makes possible. It's the synergy that makes interactive multimedia very different from the sum of its parts.

2. Understand Your "Buyers," Particularly the Learners

Having identified a training goal, and determined that an interactive multimedia program can achieve it most effectively, you must decide if you can "sell" your idea. That requires understanding the various "buyers" for the program, the people in the organization who can and will influence the technical sophistication of the end product, the creativity that goes into it, and the costs that come out of it. These buyers include members of management, information systems technologists, subject experts, other instructional designers, and most important, the learners themselves.

The basic fact you'll need to know about your buyer populations is their willingness to accept innovations in technology and training. For instance, there was once a widespread tendency in business organizations to relegate contact with computers to subordinates and clerical personnel. There's less and less of this as time goes by, but it may still prove a significant factor in considering high-tech training solutions. Another example of a potential acceptance issue is that some subject experts may regard innovative training delivery systems as a threat to the integrity of their material.

Figure 26-2a–d. Four screens from Andersen Consulting's *Business Practices* course. The 40-hour interactive multimedia product is used by about 3500 learners each year. It puts Andersen's professionals in the simulated world of a consulting engagement at a printing and publishing company. (*Andersen Consulting.*)

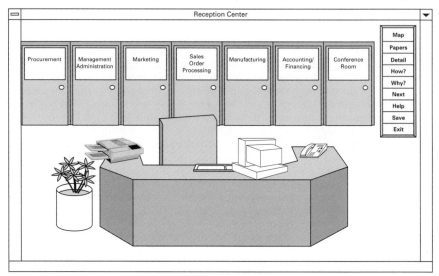

Figure 26-2a. Each module represents one of several task areas within a department of the client company. This introduction screen simulates the company's main reception center. Doors behind the reception desk access the company's "departments" (actually, learning modules).

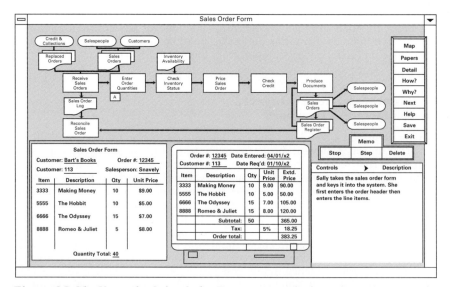

Figure 26-2b. Using the Sales Order Entry screen, the learner processes a sales order through the department. The tutorial-backed flowchart explains work and documents flow through the department. Text in the lower right corner describes what actually happens to documents.

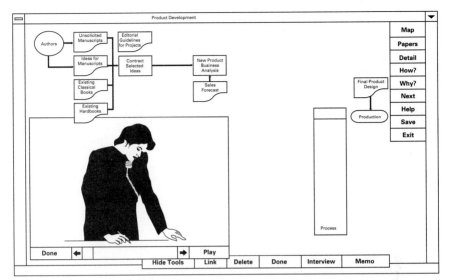

Figure 26-2c. In the Product Development module, the user learns interviewing techniques and department functions by watching a video clip of a phone interview with the client's product-development manager, conducted by an Andersen senior consultant. Behind the video window, a chart shows product-development work flow.

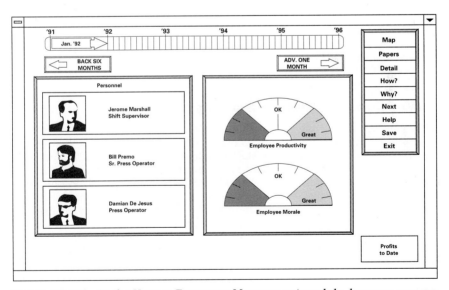

Figure 26-2d. In the Human Resources Management module, learners assume the role of the company's HR manager (even though Andersen professionals wouldn't do that in real life). The learner hires, fires, promotes, trains, evaluates, etc., and monitors the consequences on meters gauging morale, productivity, and profits.

It's also critical to understand how learners think. Do they prefer to consider concepts first, or do they like to be immersed in process and use that immersion to develop an understanding of what it means? Although multimedia can be designed so that learners have a choice, their bias or preference could influence program design.

3. Decide On Best Learner Experience

Knowing your goals, you can determine what type of learner experience will best achieve them.

Learning via interactive multimedia is often distinguished as "experiential." Actually, *all* learning is experiential, even classroom learning, which may not always deliver desired results. Interactive multimedia systems should be distinguished as being able to deliver the *right* experiences.

For example: Arthur Andersen's *Analytical Skills*, a CD-ROM multimedia program for new auditors, provides an unusual, if not unique, simulation: There's no video! The program takes the learner through a corporate audit in complete detail. The learner must complete a specific role in the simulated audit, as he or she would on an actual engagement. Video was not required in this training, even though it was to be a simulation, because there is very little that's "motion-critical" about a corporate audit.

Not having to accommodate video's major claims on development money and disc space, course designers were able to focus their resources on making the audit simulation greatly lifelike in every other way. This is a genuine multimedia program, but instead of video, its visuals are still-frame audit documents and photos. Voice-only audio delivers examples of on-the-job coaching and mentoring provided to staff auditors by their supervisors. The branching capabilities of the system enable the learner to simulate his or her own role in the audit, by creating documents and making decisions and experiencing the consequences of these analytical efforts.

4. Key Design to Content Stability

Until recently, interactive multimedia training programs were known for long development times: three months to two years or more. That made it advisable to use them to deliver relatively stable content. Today, with more robust technologies, experienced development teams, and refined methodologies, interactive multimedia courses are being produced from start to finish in one to six months. It's still prudent, however, to factor in the likelihood of content change when creating a course design. The question to consider: Is content likely to change in time cycles that are shorter than the redevelopment period dictated by this design approach? That question is particularly important when the design being considered involves audiovisual elements, which require more extensive production.

5. Use a Team Approach

To fully exploit the capabilities of interactive multimedia, you need to solicit, combine, and resolve many points of view and types of expertise. In that regard, interactive multimedia programs are like feature films.

One indispensable member of the team is the learner. Any design strategy should include a plan for involving the learner throughout the process. It's especially important that the design strategy allow for learners to test the program prototype: to react to the logic, user interface, and content. That's because the complexity of interactive multimedia can transcend "mere" English. Designers cannot be sure that the written specifications in a design document have been translated successfully into program performance until there's been hands-on use of the product.

How Much Do Interactive Multimedia Programs Really Cost?

Interactive multimedia programs can require substantially higher development and capital costs than other types of programs addressing the same goals. They may, however, deliver better training more cost-effectively.

To determine when interactive multimedia offers a cost advantage, it's necessary to understand and be able to work with all the cost factors. It's not sufficient to "spreadsheet" costs for interactive multimedia training in a conventional "dollars per hour of instruction" matrix.

Any effective assignment of costs to an interactive multimedia program should be built on a *cost per learner* for the proposed program and for alternative training instruments (including the existing one, if any). Cost per learner is delivery cost plus development cost, amortized over the life expectancy of the course and divided by the total number of learners who will use the program.

Key variables in determining costs per learner are planning, design, development, media production, and conduct costs for all types of program considered; number of learners in the target population, learner travel and lodging costs for central and regional schools and other "remote" sessions; equipment costs and course maintenance costs; and number of years before major content elements will require significant updates.

For example: Andersen Consulting's *Business Practices,* described earlier, is a 15-module product that cost more than $4 million to develop and put into service. It replaces some 60 hours of text-based self-study and 40 hours of classroom training. It is expected to function for five years without significant updates. About 3500 learners each year will take the course in their own offices or homes, instead of traveling to one of three Andersen Consulting training centers around the world. This switch from regional school to interactive multimedia is expected to save Andersen more than $45 million. This equates to $2571 savings per learner. It eliminates costs for travel, housing, and faculty, and it reduces learner payroll dollars by teaching the same content more effectively in less than half the time.

A *life-cycle cost-benefit analysis* can also be developed if costs per learner for an interactive multimedia program can be balanced against the performance improvement it will create, and the same sort of relationship can be established for alternative training instruments. This is probably the most rigorous assessment that can be applied to a proposed multimedia program.

"Make or buy" can be an important cost consideration with interactive multimedia programs, as it is with other types of training. If an existing multimedia program can fulfill your needs, development costs can be avoided. Development costs can be minimized by using existing programs that can be modified or expanded to meet your training needs, software frameworks, or "shells." The latter provides standard user interfaces and overall structures for navigating among various multimedia components (text, video, audio, and graphics). Content can be placed in each component and assembled within the shell structure.

There are two major guidelines for determining equipment costs:

1. Sophisticated computer equipment can now be bought at such reasonable prices that it may be more cost-effective to invest "up front" in fully equipped systems, with powerful and capable hardware available, than it would be to upgrade in mid–life cycle.
2. The life cycle of microcomputers and peripheral equipment is now about three years. That is the length of time that this machinery can be expected to operate reliably and be reasonably current in terms of performance. This fact means that it may not be possible to synchronize equipment replacement with updates or redesigns of programs.

Hardware specifications for interactive multimedia programs change constantly. Today's "numbers," if quoted here, would be out of date well before this book is superseded. The latest specifications are available from the Multimedia PC Marketing Council and the Software Publishers Association. General specifications include size of random-access memory (RAM); processor power and speed; hard-drive capacity; performance capabilities of CD-ROM drives; and characteristics of sound and video processing facilities.

What's *Different* in Producing Interactive Multimedia?

Although the process of producing interactive multimedia programs (see Fig. 26-3) parallels those for other types of training products at a high level, it is essentially different from start to finish in the details. This difference derives from the fact that decisions in all phases of the process (planning, design, and development) are more complex and harder to repair or reverse later. That's principally because so many of those decisions involve media, hardware, and software.

The process of creating interactive multimedia training is significantly more iterative (relying much more extensively on continuous testing of both software and learner reaction) throughout, and it calls for more types of multidisciplinary individuals (e.g., video producer, author, programmer, and graphics artist) on teams. These requirements are major cost drivers. They add to the weight borne by each step in each phase of the creation process.

Planning

This phase differs from its counterparts for other types of training programs principally because it requires resolution of more concrete, or cost-specific, issues than are usually addressed this early.

In addition to establishment of goals and assessments of costs and benefits, the planning phase involves a series of high-level design decisions in which the type of multimedia program is determined and "platform" issues concerning hardware and software are addressed.

During planning, the final shape of the development team should be considered. Makeup of the team is critical. Key members include the project manager,

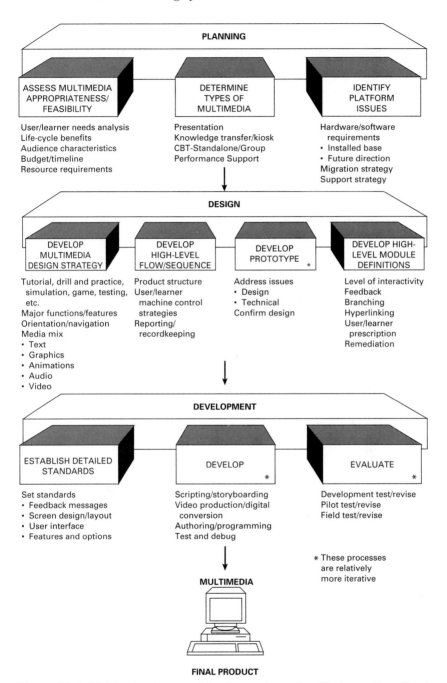

Figure 26-3. Multimedia design and development overview. (*Andersen Consulting.*)

an instructional designer who can design interactive products, interactive media programmers, authors, a graphic artist, and a media producer. "Crossover" talents are a significant plus. The more each team member knows about aspects of multimedia development outside his or her specialty, the more smoothly the project will function.

Design

This phase of a multimedia project involves decisions about media, learner control, branching, and interactivity that are not usually found in corresponding phases for paper-based and classroom training.

High-level module definitions are critical to the success of the program. And designers must pay significantly greater attention to media than they would in other kinds of projects since the media "mix" (types of media chosen and their relationship to one another) to achieve learning goals is the basic element of an interactive multimedia program.

Multimedia design must include creation of a program prototype and testing it with learners. Prototypes can be low-fidelity paper-based models to high-fidelity parts of working multimedia systems. For paper-based and classroom instruction, prototyping usually takes place fairly late in the development phase. But before development of a multimedia program can proceed, the following issues must be considered *early* on:

1. The delivery logic: the way in which the technology will achieve the desired goal

2. The delivery platform: the compatibility and performance of hardware and software

3. The learner interface: how the learner navigates the system

Prototype testing during design also shows whether or not learners will be able to use and accept the program as planned.

Development

Development of interactive multimedia is distinguished by inclusion of the actual creation of the software dynamics that power the course and production of the courseware and media.

Detailed design standards derived from prototype testing are established for screen design, feedback, features, and options. Production includes such steps as scriptwriting, recording and editing of video and audio, preparation of graphics and artwork, construction and programming of the delivery system and user interface, and conversion of all media to a digital format.

When video and audio segments produced or selected for the program are digitized, they are also compressed to occupy minimal disk or drive space while still retaining a good level of visual and audio quality. Many multimedia managers prefer to use a separate budget for media production—especially if video is involved.

Media producers may work on their own while designer-programmers create a software "skeleton" for the course, with each group advising the other as needed. The two groups then collaborate actively when it's time to integrate their products and create a finished program.

The multimedia workstation that supports a common digital format is key to successful development. This user-development system is usually based on a high-end microcomputer. Special hardware for multimedia production includes a multimedia playback board (a card inserted into the computer) and a multimedia capture module.

Detailed descriptions of hardware and software, and steps in production and programming, can be found in a variety of high-quality technical reference books available in the market today (see the bibliography at the end of this chapter).

The Future: Powering the "Virtual World"

Interactive multimedia training will soon play a vastly wider role in performance improvement and personal self-development. That's because interactive multimedia will power the forthcoming revolution in the influence of electronic media in our lives: the emergence of a "virtual world." We are about to see the electronic media we now use combine in one pervasive support system that delivers voice communications, data communications, facsimile transmissions, motion pictures, live entertainment, remote shopping, and education.

Because this system will be user-centered in terms of selection (i.e., the user has almost unlimited control over what to select), interactive multimedia training will help us interface successfully *with* it, in addition to providing us with means for acquiring skills and knowledge *through* it.

In this scenario for the future, development of interactive multimedia training programs will increase geometrically. Training and performance support will overlap more and more. The training effectiveness of collaborative systems will improve. In fact, the concept of "a separate time for training" will diminish in relevance and finally disappear from the business world, due in great part to the development and spread of interactive multimedia. Multimedia can be made available at any time, any place, including on the job.

These same dynamics will apply to formal education, from kindergarten through graduate school. Many elementary and secondary-school buildings may come to serve primarily as places for socialization and pursuit of athletics and lively arts, while students acquire skills and knowledge via home communications centers. Conventional baccalaureate and graduate programs that require long periods of residence on campus may serve significantly smaller segments of the general community and the business world.

Our ubiquitous electronic communications and computing system will provide access to a single and comprehensive information superhighway, sometimes called "the Net." To support interactive communications and learning, the Net will incorporate full motion and other forms of advanced visualization. Practically anyone will be able to provide content by feeding applications into the Net, although creating engaging and effectively interactive programs will still be a skill to be mastered with effort and talent.

Interactive multimedia programs on the Net will revolutionize business marketing. Direct mail, advertising, focus groups, and other conventional forms of communications between businesses and their markets will be superseded by a complex of dialogues with consumers, from which emerge guidelines for making products that satisfy manufacturers and customers equally. Business productivity will be significantly enhanced through ongoing dialogues between businesses and their stakeholders. In fact, the distinction between business, consumer, and financial worlds will blur and may even functionally disappear.

As more and more people use the Net, the instructional value and effect of collaborative learning will burgeon. Problems will be clarified by the scope and force of communications rather than through conventional patterns of learning such as study. "Virtual rap groups" that are time-shiftable will derive their educational value from being able to involve so many more participants than could communicate with one another in real time.

Business executives will play multiuser games over the Net, expanding their product and industry knowledge by "competing" with consumers, representatives of other companies, etc. These games, which constitute a type of collaborative program, are sometimes called "MUDs." (The term derives from "multiuser dungeons.") They feature characters who represent certain kinds of behavior, as in Dungeons and Dragons. This can be extended to any type of character, including characters in business simulations. Players can compete with resident characters or with each other, or with combinations of "live" and "system" opponents.

The future of media delivery is uncertain. CD-ROM technology, and CD-ROM-based information and entertainment products, may become less important in the future, as more material is sourced through the Net or available on interactive television. The environment will be competitive; but whether there will be a "winner" medium, and what that might be, is not apparent today.

Of all the technological innovations expected to enhance interactive multimedia in the virtual world, virtual reality (or VR) is probably the most fascinating because of its well-known capacity to expand or alter our awareness. VR programs are actually the ultimate in interactive multimedia.

For example: Many VR instructional programs are now being planned and developed for surgeons and other medical personnel. These programs improve doctors' understanding of disorders by reorienting the conventional relationship of the doctor to the affected body part. This reengineering might involve giving the doctor-learner a trip through a blood vessel as if he or she were walking a subway tunnel. Or, the system might give the doctor-learner a chance to reconstruct the object he or she is studying (a blood cell, for instance) as a model that has color-coded compartments, can be disassembled like a Lego construction, and provides customized feedback via language and sound effects as the doctor manipulates it.

Interactive multimedia programs, and the communications network they serve, have the potential to realign society in new communities; communities that appear whenever people congregate electronically, to work, shop, play, and learn. This realignment has already begun, and there is every reason to believe that it will be consummated within the next two decades in most of the advanced nations of the world.

Interactivity and interoperability will be so ubiquitous on the network that it will appear to be "seamless." Our use of the network and the interactive multimedia programs on it will be so much a part of our private and public existences that we will find it difficult to imagine what life was like before them. This exercise in imagination has been compared to wondering today what life was like before the telephone. It will actually be more intense than that: more like contemplating life before Gutenberg developed the printing press.

How Can Trainers "Get Ready"?

Trainers can position themselves to function effectively in the virtual world by getting involved in it as it develops. This doesn't require any particularly revolutionary *form* of participation. A practical first step is to read widely, beginning with the publications listed in the bibliography at the end of this chapter. Next, become familiar with the delivery systems. That might involve purchasing

CD-ROM-equipped microcomputers and off-the-shelf CD-ROM training programs, to develop an operational "feel" for multimedia dynamics. A good follow-up to that might be experimenting with the capabilities of multimedia design software (keeping in mind the advantage to be gained from developing combined skills in this area, like instructional design and programming).

Keeping current by active networking can be a matter of going to conferences held by familiar professional organizations. Most of their annual or international meetings have multimedia tracks. These organizations include: The ASTD (phone 703-683-8100); The International Society for Performance Improvement (ISPI; phone 202-408-7969); and the Association for Education and Communications Technology (AECT; phone 202-347-7834).

Some organizational resources that may not be quite so familiar to trainers are the Interactive Multimedia Association (IMA; phone 410-626-1380); Worldwide Web address http://www.ima.org); the Society for Applied Learning Technology (SALT; phone 703-347-0055); the Association for Multi-Media International (AMI; phone 813-960-1692); and the International Interactive Communications Society (IICS; phone 503-579-4427; e-mail iicshq@aol.com).

Finally, it would be a good idea to plunge into the very crucible of the virtual world. Join the Internet. It's full of conferences and other dialogues that deal with multimedia.

Bibliography

Books

Ambron, Sueann Robinson, and Kristina Hooper, eds., *Learning with Interactive Multimedia: Developing and Using Multimedia Tools in Education*, Microsoft Press, Redmond, WA, 1990.

Ambron, Sueann Robinson, and Kristina Hooper, eds., *Interactive Multimedia*, Microsoft Press, Redmond, WA, 1988.

Bunzel, Mark J., and Sandra K. Morris, *Multimedia Applications Development: Using Indeo Video and DVI Technology*, McGraw-Hill, New York, 1994.

Burger, Jeff, *The Desktop Multimedia Bible*, Addison-Wesley, Reading, MA, 1995.

Burger, Jeff, *Multimedia for Decision Makers: A Business Primer*, Addison-Wesley, Reading, MA, 1995.

The Concise Guide to Multimedia, Asymetrix Corporation, Bellevue, WA, 1994.

Multimedia Demystified, Random House, New York, 1994.

Reich, Robert, *The Work of Nations*, Knopf, New York, 1991.

Schank, Roger C., *Tell Me a Story: A New Look at Real and Artificial Memory*, Macmillan, New York, 1990.

Vaughn, Tay, *Multimedia: Making It Work*, Osborne McGraw-Hill, Berkeley, CA, 1993.

Periodicals

CBT Solutions, SB Communications, Hingham, MA.

Educational Technology, Educational Technology Publications, Inc., Englewood Cliffs, NJ.

Multimedia Monitor, Future Systems, Inc., Falls Church, VA.

Multimedia Producer, Knowledge Industry Publications, Inc., Los Altos, CA.

New Media Magazine, Hypermedia Communications, Inc., San Mateo, CA.

WIRED, Wired Ventures Ltd., San Francisco, CA.

27

Job Aids and Electronic Performance Support Systems

Allison Rossett

Allison Rossett is a Professor of Educational Technology at the San Diego State University and a consultant to corporations, government agencies and school systems in the design, development, and evaluation of performance and training systems. Her work focuses on needs assessment, individual, and organizational learning and instructional design strategies. Rossett was the recipient of the Association for Educational Technology, Division of Instructional Development Book of the Year Award in 1989 for Training Needs Assessment. Her book, A Handbook of Job Aids, won the National Society for Performance and Instruction's 1991 top book award and the Association for Educational Technology, Division of Instructional Development Design Tool of the Year Award. Rossett has published dozens of articles on needs assessment, training systems, and educational technologies; she has also edited journals, offered seminars, evaluated programs, and managed corporate contracts and federal and state grants. Her research, teaching, and consulting was featured in a profile in Training magazine. From 1988 to 1990 she was the Vice President for Research and Development for the National Society for Performance and Instruction. In 1991, she received one of eight Outstanding Faculty awards at San Diego State University. Rossett's client list includes EXXON, Texas Instruments, AT&T, Apple Computer, GTE, San Diego City Schools Integration Programs, Federal Emergency Management Agency, Home Insurance, International Paper, EDS, Century 21

International, British Columbia Telephone Company, IBM, the Getty Conservation Institute, Digital Equipment Corporation, and many others.

This chapter is about on-the-job performance support, an emerging trend that radically enlarges the professional sphere of the trainer. It is exemplified by this brief interaction:

> CLAIRE, A VICE-PRESIDENT: When my salespeople are in training they're not selling products. Last year it was 8 days away from the job at classes! This year, it looks to me like we're talking about 10 days or even more. I know these are complicated products we're rolling out, but can't we do something else? Is all that seat-time necessary?

> MACK, ANOTHER VP: I feel the same way. My accountants and clerks ought to be professors by now—after all the time they've spent in classes. What I want is something different, something they can use when they're on the phone or sitting at their computers or meeting with a customer. I know they need help, but is a class what they need? Is it all that they need?

Claire and Mack are typical 1990's customers for training and development. Because the workplaces, workers, and work are changing, these line executives recognize that something must be done to support their people and assure effective performance. They are, however, hesitant to send employees to settings that are literally and figuratively removed from customers and work and skeptical about their return on investment for training. Given new perspectives and reengineered processes in virtually every work environment, they are urging human resources and training professionals to figure out new and better ways of supporting employees. In Pechter,[1] David Ulrich, a University of Michigan professor and consultant, acknowledges the perception of training programs where supervisors perceive their employees as "kidnapped" into participation. Ulrich's solution is for human resources to focus more on problems that matter to line managers, on assisting executives to execute their business strategy, and on increasing organizational efficiency, employee commitment, and the company's capacity for change.

What Ulrich and many others (Garfield,[2] Harbour,[3] Rosenberg,[4] Gery,[5] Pechter,[1] Rossett[6]) tout is an expanded conception of the role of the trainer. No longer defined primarily as a stand-up instructor in a classroom, the training and development professional becomes responsible for assessing, designing, developing, and brokering larger performance systems that often include training, but are by no means limited to it. Table 27-1 presents the changes.

These changes represent a broader ken for trainers, with increased expectations regarding analysis, matching solutions to problems and opportunities, a perspective that includes both the needs of the organization and the individual, and a much wider array of interventions that *transcend the classroom and are riveted to the workplace*. Examples of this last transformation are job aids and electronic performance support, the topics for this chapter.

Why the Move Toward Job Aids and Electronic Support?

Many forces are combining to increase reliance upon on-the-job information and support:

Table 27-1. The Expanded Role of the Training Professional in the 1990s

Historical focus	Current and emergent focus
Training center	Workplace
Training event	Process that supports performance
Centralized service provider	Closer affiliation to the line and to the contexts in which work gets done
Development of materials used primarily during training	Development of materials that are referred to on-the-job
Focus on students in classes	Focus on students and others in surrounding work environment
Focus on teaching and learning	Focus on performance
Focus on individual	Focus on individual and organization
Success based on ability to teach	Success based on ability to coordinate, broker, and manage
Training is the means and the end	Performance is the end; training is one means among many
Priority is orchestration of effective class	Priority is orchestration of systems, materials, and environment that enables employee to do the job

1. *Quality.* The quality movement is characterized by a focus on the customer, cross-functional collaboration, and increased participation in decision making by employees at all levels. These emphases are dependent upon providing employees with ready access to information, common standards, and shared procedures and perspectives.

2. *Reengineering.* Hammer and Champy[7] have popularized a word and a concept that has swept across American organizations: *reengineering.* Reengineering establishes the expectation that all assumptions are off and that radical organizational redesign and change is desirable. This has led to aggressive examination of jobs, processes, technologies, and relationships—in fact, the very systems that combine into organizations. Critical aspects of reengineering are the provision of more information to more people in the organization through technology and nontraditional functional collaborations.

3. *Decentralization.* Akin to the emphasis on customer focus, many staff organizations are being pressed to move closer to line organizations. Customers want their services, including education and training, as close as possible to where the work gets done.

4. *Flattening.* Rossett and Gautier-Downes[8] note that a world of fewer managers creates a void, one being filled by on-the-job performance support. For example, the back of IBM employees' identification cards includes key perspectives to keep in mind when approaching customers. Another example is provided by the roaming field-service representatives who, porting palm-held computers, check travelers in when they return rental cars. Supervisors aren't there as these employees roam—but performance support is.

5. *Less money for training, when needed the most.* The workforce of the future is often depicted as likely to suffer from problems in math, science, and inadequate English-language skills, resulting in increased need for on-the-job training. Will

organizations provide it? The work that Carnevale and Gainer[9] did for the ASTD suggests not. They found that U.S. organizations currently offer training and development opportunities to only 35 percent of their employees, and that minorities, a burgeoning portion of the emerging workforce, are less likely to be recipients of those opportunities. While they urge an expenditure of 4 percent of payroll on training and development, they estimate that U.S. organizations are currently spending only 1.4 percent. This creates enormous pressure for desktop tools and systems that specify policies and perspectives and coach performance—at work and at prices organizations perceive as affordable.

6. *Technology.*   In the past, cost and capacities made it impossible to rely on technology for critical and widespread on-the-job support. That is no longer the case. Gery[5] touts the speed, capabilities, and cost of technology and the potential it offers for blurring the distinctions between training and work and work and the challenges of serving customers. Technology-based performance support is discussed later in this chapter.

7. *Integration of work and support.*   Traditional training is often perceived as separate and distinct from the world of work. Marguerite Foxon, in a presentation at San Diego State University in 1991, sketched two cliffs, one small and one large. The large cliff represents the world of work. The small cliff represents the training enterprise. Between the cliffs was a great chasm. This visual captures the problem: the traditional distance and distinction between training and the real world of work. What performance supports, like job aids and electronic systems, do is embed themselves in work. There is no distinction. There is no problem of authenticity because the work provides it. There are no problems of transfer from training to the workplace, because the support is provided on the job where the challenges and customers reside.

What Is a Job Aid?

In Rossett and Gautier-Downes' 1991 book on the topic,[8] the job aid is defined as "a repository for information, processes or perspectives that is external to the individual and that supports work and activity by directing, guiding and enlightening performance" [p. 4]. Some examples are useful: an index card with notes for a speech; a favorite cookbook; a booklet that prompts changing the message on an answering machine; a manual that provides the details of how to use software; a computerized help system that includes treatment and legislation for hazardous materials; a workbook that coaches a manager through orienting a new employee; and a poster that reminds employees of what to do if a chemical spills.

Job aids are mundane, hardly noticed by us, yet central to getting through a day. Examples abound, like a phone number scratched on the corner of a napkin, a shopping list, and hidden notes that list passwords providing access to computer systems. Job aids are also sublime, for example, elegant documentation for a new security system or an electronic performance support system for customer service agents. Job aids have a number of critical features; namely, they

- Store information, perspectives, and examples.
- Are called upon by individuals when and where they need them.
- Exist in the environment.
- Diminish the need to rely on memory.

Comparing Job Aids and Training

The distinction between training and job aids helps clarify both concepts. Ideally, training happens *before* the need for it arises and for the purpose of building *capacity within people*. Training is a planned experience enabling the acquisition of skills and knowledge to enhance a person's ability to perform. It often involves presentation, practice, and feedback and ideally results in a change in the mental state of the individual. For example, doctors, cosmetologists, and urban planners attend training to develop their abilities to handle many and occasionally unforeseen challenges.

Job aids, on the other hand, usually exert their influence as references *when the need to know arises*. Employees turn to job aids to support performance when a chemical splashes on somebody, when a glass of red wine spills on beige carpeting, or when a customer asks to be referred to a Spanish-speaking salesperson.

A particularly interesting difference between training and job aids has to do with the limitations of human memory. If we could remember everything, we wouldn't need job aids.

We can talk about two kinds of memory: long-term memory (LTM) and short-term memory (STM). Long-term memory represents information that is stored, encoded, and retained in our brains as networks. Thus, memories are stored in LTM, whether they are recollections about cooking rhubarb pie with Grandma, the history of the Philippines, the definition of *craven*, or a favorite brand of cereal. Training is conventionally interested in engineering experiences that enhance the movement of information from STM into LTM, from disorganized bits of data into meaningful networks. If the data gets into the network where it can be retrieved (remembered), we call that learning.

Short-term memory, also referred to as *working memory*, is limited. A good illustration of the limits on STM is what it takes to remember somebody's phone number or the prices for a product. While it is easy to retain these numbers briefly, something usually intervenes and the numbers are forgotten, unless they have been rehearsed over and over again and over time, a substantial expenditure of resources. Should those numbers be committed to memory or should some environmental support system be employed?

This is akin to the decision that professionals and executives like Claire and Mack confront when figuring out how to improve performance and make training stick. Should we spend and do what it will take to enable people to know their jobs *by heart*? What portion of each job or task must be stored in memory? Should we be looking beyond training, to various forms of performance support, to enable people to work at increasingly complex and changing jobs? Many professionals, including Puterbaugh, Rosenberg, and Sofman[10]; Clark[11]; and Gery[5], applaud the value of performance support. Clark[11] wrote:

> Designers should encourage learners to use their working memory to *process* information, *not* to store it. For example, as learners first practice a new procedure, give them access to clear written summary steps for reference so all working memory can be directed toward executing the procedure. The use of job aids, in the form of a written procedure table in this instance, can be especially powerful for this purpose. With enough repetition of the task, it will become automatic and bypass working memory. Then the job aid will become unnecessary. (p. 19)

Linking Job Aids and Training

While training and job aids are conceptually different, in practice they are often intertwined. As Clark points out above, and as Rossett and Gautier-Downes[8] emphasize, job aids and training need each other. Consider the years of education that enable a doctor to make proper use of the *Physician's Desk Reference*. Not too long ago, a friend described how her large computer company undertook the painful process of reducing its workforce. Prior to laying off thousands of employees, the company recognized that managers and supervisors were both emotionally and cognitively unprepared to do the deeds that lay before them. They conducted a needs assessment and parsed the job between training and job aids. The basic rationale, perspectives, and effect would be handled during training sessions rich with presentations, practices, and feedback. Critical procedures, regulations, and some trouble-shooting was supported through job aids. While nobody applauded the situation, several friends who delivered the bad news to laid-off workers said the system provided the support they needed. The training *prepared* them for the painful task through explanations, role-playing, and discussion. The job aid kept them on track *during* those difficult interactions.

When Are Job Aids Appropriate?

Harless[12] and Pipe[13] provide useful suggestions for when and where to use job aids. Building on their work, Rossett and Gautier-Downes[8] provide the following guidelines for when job aids are appropriate:

1. *The performance is infrequent.*   Job aids should be used when the individual can't be expected to remember how to do it because he or she rarely has to. Whether it is reliance upon aids to provide the details of an acquaintance's address or to compare product specifications or carry out the procedure for cleaning the heads on the VCR, job aids boost *infrequent* performance.

2. *It is a complex, multistep or multiattribute situation.*   Increasing complexity and government regulation surround the world of work. Job aids now support individuals who confront lengthy, difficult, and information-intensive challenges. How does an employee secure data in the computer system in such a way that certain employees will have access but others won't? How do employees activate new features of the numerical control lathe? What factors must a manager keep in mind when terminating an employee? Many employers will choose to answer these questions by providing their staff with job aids.

3. *The consequences of error are high.*   If a salesperson promises compatibility between an existing mainframe computer system and a large new system and a client purchases it and the compatibility just isn't there....If an accountant initializes a disk and that initialization wipes out valuable data....If a commercial jet maintenance employee fails to notice that the fuel tank is nearly empty, even though the gauge shows a three-quarters-full tank....If an employee is using computerized analysis to determine and match blood types and she isn't certain exactly how to do it....All of these circumstances point individuals towards reliance upon job aids in situations where you can't afford to get it wrong.

4. *Performance relies upon a large body of information.*   Getting jobs done in the Information Era depends upon ready access to large amounts of information on people, places, things, and policies. With access to references from the Yellow Pages, and to the extraordinary storage capacity of CD-ROM and CD-Interactive, individuals will increasingly rely upon print and automated job aids to answer questions about who, what, when, and where.

5. *Performance relies upon knowledge, procedures, or approaches that change frequently.*   Information challenges transcend large data sets; they extend to the

shelf life of knowledge, procedures, and approaches. In the past, an employee could feel relatively comfortable once he or she had settled into a position. That isn't true today. The contemporary salesperson is trying to stay abreast of changing products, features, and compatibilities.

6. *There is high turnover and the task is simple.* Organizations are less willing to invest in training when employees are seen as just passing through and the performance challenge is judged to be minimal. A friend's position provides a good example. She publishes a small, commercial directory of goods and services. Her sales force is active for only a few months each year, turns over frequently, and handles a very simple product line with a rate card that does not change frequently. She relies upon job aids because she wants her salespeople in the field, not at training sessions [pp. 31–32 in *A Handbook of Job Aids*].[8]

7. *Employees are expected to act in an empowered way with emphasized or new standards in mind.* Training professionals in the 1990s are increasingly influenced by cognitive perspectives (Clark,[14] Merrill[15]). In keeping with this critical shift, job aids are now being used to coach improved approaches to work and lives outside of work. For example, a manager refers to a series of guidelines and examples for how to support a grieving employee returning from the funeral of a loved one. Or a teacher is more prepared to explain a particular testing program to concerned parents because of being able to refer to prepared questions, answers and examples.

8. *There is little time or few resources for training.* Harless[12] and Duncan[16] believe that job aids save money. If the use of job aids enables a reduction in time devoted to training and performance is constant or improves, then it is obvious that money is both saved and made. Most executives accept as gospel that job aids are positive for their bottom line.

If one or several of these eight conditions are in place, it is likely that job aids will be appropriate—likely, but not guaranteed. Four factors press towards reliance on education and training and away from the use of job aids:

1. Threats to professional credibility, as in the way it looks for a teacher to refer to notes to answer a question that students expect him or her to know by heart

2. The need for speedy performance, as in an emergency response situation or when the organization demands high production or throughput

3. When fluid performance is a must, such as when a tennis player must respond to a tricky serve or a veteran eye surgeon to a medical emergency that occurs during surgery

4. When novel and surprising conditions present themselves

Rossett and Gautier-Downes[8] put it like this:

> Job aids aren't particularly good at supporting individuals when they confront novel and largely unpredictable circumstances. Those are the situations that demand an intangible ability to handle surprises, stress and new challenges. Whether confronted by a parent of a school child who is hysterical about test results or a flight combat situation, the school district and the Navy expect "good judgment" from employees. Fritz Brecke[17] explored the topic of training to instill judgment in pilots. He provides a useful definition of judgment as the "right stuff" evoked in situations that include uncertainty, lack of complete information, stress, task difficulty, cognitive complexity and time constraints. Brecke complains that military training in the early 1980's was characterized by an emphasis on correct completion of prescribed procedures and compliance with rules. While compliance with procedures can be comfortably

supported by job aids, it is not likely to clinch victory in the skies. That victory is the result of good judgment. If good judgment in a topsy-turvy world is a goal, job aids will not be major players in assuring the high end of that kind of performance. [p. 34]

Kinds of Job Aids

One of the most exciting aspects of job aids is the many ways that they can be used to support on-the-job performance. Typical job aids enable access to information and procedures, removing responsibility from the user's long-term memory and placing it instead on an external source, like a computerized help system, a telephone book, or a user manual. These familiar job aids help the user *at the moment of need* when, for example, the computer freezes and a bomblike icon appears on the screen, a family hungry for Hunan Chinese food turns to the local directory for assistance, or a teacher at the front of a class is desperate to make the video system work.

This chapter suggests an expanded view of job aids and electronic performance support systems, one that encourages their use to coach ways of thinking about the work in addition to databases and procedures. Timing is also an interesting aspect of job aids. This chapter encourages a broader window of opportunity for their use. Table 27-2 depicts these expanded views.

Beyond conventional support at the moment of need, coaching job aids can influence performance 5, 10, or even 30 minutes *prior to action*. An example is an audio job aid that was developed for a real estate sales training system. As the real estate agent drives to visit the prospective customer, he or she is listening to a tape about making a listing presentation. It reminds the agent about the concerns of people contemplating selling their homes and the critical factors in the decision to list with one agent over another. It provides sample objections and counters. It focuses on the perspectives of the successful listing agent. While this audio job aid is nowhere in sight during the listing presentation, its influence is felt.

Coaching and decision-making aids can improve performance *after* performance too. Parallel to the contemporary interest in empowerment, quality, and employee reflection, coaching aids encourage self-assessment. For example, after the listing presentation, the real estate agent consults a checklist that captures the key features of a successful presentation. The agent reviews the list in light of the recent interaction and is able to identify strengths and weaknesses and ponder strategies to employ next time.

Type One: Job Aids for Informing

A job aid that informs is one that diminishes uncertainty about some thing or some task, for example, the name of a veterinarian open on Sunday or a code

Table 27-2. Kinds of Job Aids.

	Traditional	Expanded view
Uses:	To provide information To support procedures	To provide information To support procedures To influence perspective and decision making
When:	During performance	During performance Just prior to performance Just after performance

associated with a computer peripheral. Informational job aids make data useful because they

- Answer *who, what, which, when,* or *where* questions
- Respond to the user's frame of reference, function, or subject-matter structure

Life is full of informational job aids. Here is just a portion of a day full of information aids: Belle begins her day by opening her calendar to see her appointments and obligations for the day. She then sits down at the computer to work on a book chapter, discovering that she is overusing the word *focus*. She turns to the automated thesaurus to seek alternative words. In a week, Belle will be visited by her three nieces, ages 9, 11, and 13. Concerned about her adult-oriented furniture, she rents bean-bag chairs through a search of the Yellow Pages. A friend comes for lunch, and because she didn't prepare anything, she decides to call out for food, using one of the menus collected to provide that information. In the afternoon, she gets a call from a colleague who is about to visit London. She lends him a favorite informational job aid, Richard Saul Wurman's *London Access*.[18] Wurman's guide is different from other guidebooks because he made a calculated decision that visitors want information by geographical location. His overarching structure is the places and districts of London, assuming that people find themselves in sections of town and then seek other meaningful categories like shops, galleries, parks, restaurants, etc.

In Fig. 27-1, Mary Predenkoski of the National Cryptologic School provides a classic example of an information job aid that supports use of FrameMaker 4.0.

Type Two: Job Aids for Supporting Procedures

A procedure, according to *Webster's*, "is a prescribed way of doing something." Procedures are associated with getting money out of automatic teller machines, applying for marriage licenses, and determining an account balance. Job aids that support procedures tell and show actions, order, and results.

Effective procedural job aids do the following:

- Answer the question, How?
- Answer the question, When?
- Present actions as steps, in order, with results that signal the next step

Lynn Edwards, a graduate student at San Diego State University, developed a procedural job aid for saving a file in Adobe Photoshop. It is presented as Fig. 27-2.

Examples of procedural job aids are everywhere. Look at the documentation that supports computer hardware and software. Look at the booklet that accompanies a VCR and answering machine. There are procedural job aids on bags of pasta. They are the meat and potatoes in every cookbook.

Type Three: Job Aids for Coaching Perspectives

The third kind of job aid, coaching aids, prompts ways of thinking about jobs and tasks. They coach heuristics. Heuristics are best defined by comparing them to algorithms. Algorithms, as defined in Rossett's *Training Needs Assessment*,[19] are

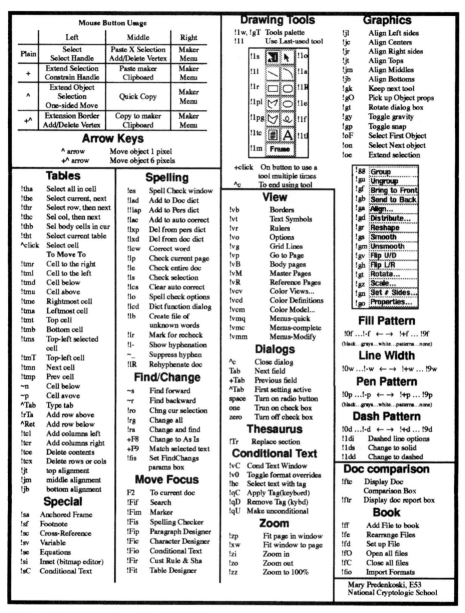

Figure 27-1. An information job aid.

straightforward. They are unvarying steps in an order that handles a narrow class of problems. Most computer programs represent algorithms, where the steps, order, decisions, alternatives, and results are concrete. Applying for a marriage license and preparing a room for painting are examples of algorithms. Heuristics, on the other hand, guide ways to think about the ambiguous areas of life and work. Heuristics provide guidelines and suggestions for topics that

Step 4

Saving the File

1. Under "File" on the top menu bar, drag down to "Save."

2. Save the final photo in one of two modes:
    a. For a photo used only on the screen or in Hypercard, save it as a PICT file.
    b. For a photo that will be output to a printer, save the file as a TIFF file.
    c. Name the file and click on "Save."

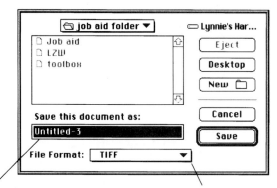

Type in the file name   Drag down to find the PICT or
                                         TIFF mode for saving the file

When you save the file as a TIFF file, another dialog box appears after you click on the "Save" button, allowing you to compress the file to save file space. Clicking on the LZW box when saving the file will compress the file without any loss of detail or degradation.

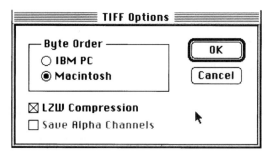

Click "OK." The file is now finished and ready to import into a page layout program or other program for use. Or, go on to Step 5 if you just want to print a copy.

Figure 27-2. A procedural job aid.

plunge people into gray areas, into questions and problems that lack straightforward answers. In place of the comfort of specified steps are heuristics or rules of thumb that can be considered before, during, or after the challenge. Heuristics are what we draw on when we confront life's thorny problems, for example, getting ready for a job interview, deciding whether to move to take that job, or analyzing whether buying or renting makes sense.

Algorithms give birth to procedural job aids; heuristics are the grist for job aids that coach perspectives and decisions. Coaching aids crystallize what it is that employees ought to ponder as they confront a challenge.

Effective coaching job aids do many of the following:

- Answer the question, Why?

- Answer the question, How?, but only as in How might I think about or approach that?

- Emphasize thoughts and feelings

- Define quality standards

- Encourage interaction with the aid, pressing the individual to skip a consideration, add or highlight factors

Consider two examples. The first coaching aid example is found in many classrooms at Motorola University. Like most training centers around the country, participants in classes at MU are expected to write their names on name-card tents. What's unusual is the job aid that appears in print on the back of every card. It reminds participants to ask questions, apply the material to their own situation, volunteer ideas and examples, etc. As students sit in class with their tent cards in front of them, they can't miss the job aid that prompts effective engagement with the instruction. Another example is provided by a friend's tennis coach. She created an audiotape that intones what to keep in mind when about to enter a match and when confronting various conditions during games.

Six Formats for Job Aids

Rossett & Gautier-Downes[8] expanded on Joe Harless's early work on job aids to establish six formats for job aids. These formats are often combined:

1. Steps Job Aids

The steps format, as its name suggests, represents actions in a particular order. When a developer selects the steps format, he or she wants to assure a flow of actions, in a particular order, for a narrowly defined purpose. Steps job aids include numbers, verbs and objects that often appear as a procedure manual, a to-do list, or a computer help screen.

Bob Hoffman, an instructor at San Diego State University, produced the following job aid in about three minutes for a very appreciative colleague who was desperate to connect a new little computer to the existing desktop system:

1. TURN OFF both computers and the printer.

2. DISCONNECT cable from the printer.

3. CONNECT that cable to the new portable computer.

4. TURN ON both computers.

5. PULL DOWN Apple menu on the portable.

6. SELECT Chooser.

7. SELECT Appleshare.

8. DOUBLE CLICK on Allison R.

9. TYPE username and password.

10. SELECT disks you wish to access. CLICK OK.

Additional examples can be found in cookbooks, where users are coached to slice, dice, and parboil with almost no training at all.

2. Worksheet Job Aids

The worksheet format is also characterized by steps in order. The critical difference is that the user is required to participate in substantive written responses, usually in the form of calculations. Worksheet job aids are used when employees need a result, often a numerical answer, such as taxes owed to the government, seed needed for reseeding a lawn, or how much money an individual must save for her or his retirement. Roger Addison, an executive with Wells Fargo Bank, presents a worksheet for cost justification. It is presented as Fig. 27-3.

3. Array Job Aids

Arrays present bodies of information through clear, accessible, and orderly structure. The user of an array job aid is attempting to answer all or some of the who, what, where, or when questions. Who is the congressperson from Chula Vista and how do I contact that person? What is the product code for a particular printer? What is the zip code in Ames, Iowa? On what day of the week will Yom Kippur fall in 1997? Familiar job aids are automated databases, telephone books, and price and shopping lists.

4. Decision Table Job Aids

Decision tables represent "if-then" situations. This format allows the user to identify solutions for given problems based on conditions that present themselves in several ways. Gautier-Downes, contributing to Rossett and Gautier-Downes' *Handbook of Job Aids*,[8] provides an example, an easy way for personnel clerks to identify the appropriate benefits brochure to give employees, as shown in Fig. 27-4.

5. Flowchart Job Aids

Flowchart job aids present an orderly sequence of questions that can be answered through a simple yes or no. After making the binary selection, the user is directed to the next step or to a proper course of action, until enough information is gathered to reach a conclusive end.

The topic of job aids offers an apt example. What format of the six should the trainer select? Figure 27-5 answers that question through a flowchart job aid.

COST JUSTIFICATION WORKSHEET   Project _____   Svc. Mgr. _____

CURRENT COST	PROPOSED COST (AFTER)	CURRENT COST (BEFORE)	PROPOSED COST (AFTER)
1. Calculate labor costs for each employee: Emp #1 HRS/WK ON TASK =$____ A HOURLY SALARY =$____ B BENEFITS @ 30% =$____ C A x [B+ C] x 52 WKS =$____ D Emp #2 HRS/WK ON TASK =$____ A HOURLY SALARY =$____ B BENEFITS @ 30% =$____ C A x [B+C] x 52 WKS =$____ D ADD ALL D's TO CALCULATE TOTAL ANNUAL LABOR $____ E	1. Calculate proposed labor costs: Emp #1 HRS/WK ON TASK =$____ A HOURLY SALARY =$____ B BENEFITS @ 30% =$____ C A x [B+ C] x 52 WKS =$____ D Emp #2 HRS/WK ON TASK =$____ A HOURLY SALARY =$____ B BENEFITS @ 30% =$____ C A x [B+C] x 52 WKS =$____ D ADD ALL D's TO CALCULATE TOTAL ANNUAL LABOR $____ E	4. Calculate operating costs for items such as postage, rent, utilities, computer time, cross-charges: ITEM # 1 WEEKLY USAGE =$____ A ITEM COST =$____ B A x B x 52 WKS ____ C ITEM #2 WEEKLY USAGE =$____ A ITEM COST =$____ B A x B x 52 WKS ____ C TOTAL ANNUAL SUPPLIES $____ E	4. Calculate proposed operating costs: ITEM # 1 WEEKLY USAGE =$____ A ITEM COST =$____ B A x B x 52 WKS ____ C ITEM #2 WEEKLY USAGE =$____ A ITEM COST =$____ B A x B x 52 WKS ____ C TOTAL ANNUAL SUPPLIES $____ G
2. Calculate supplies cost for all supplies used in the task that must be replaced. Do not calculate if current proposed costs are the same: ITEM # 1 QUANTITY USED/WK =$____ A ITEM COST =$____ B A x B x 52 WKS =$____ C ITEM #2 QUANTITY USED/WK =$____ A ITEM COST =$____ B A x B x 52 WKS =$____ C TOTAL ANNUAL SUPPLIES $____ E	2. Calculate proposed supplies cost: ITEM # 1 QUANTITY USED/WK =$____ A ITEM COST =$____ B A x B x 52 WKS =$____ C ITEM #2 QUANTITY USED/WK =$____ A ITEM COST =$____ B A x B x 52 WKS =$____ C TOTAL ANNUAL SUPPLIES $____ G	(X)	5. Calculate one-time costs for construction, moving, and new equipment: ITEM #1 ONE-TIME COST $____ A ITEM #2 ONE-TIME COST $____ A TOTAL ONE-TIME COST $____ G
3. Calculate cost of equipment rental, lease, and maintenance only if equipment will not be used in proposed costs: ITEM # 1 ANNUAL COST $____ A ITEM # 2 ANNUAL COST $____ A TOTAL ANNUAL EQUIP/MAINT $____ E	3. Calculate proposed equipment cost: ITEM # 1 ANNUAL COST $____ A ITEM # 2 ANNUAL COST $____ A TOTAL ANNUAL EQUIP/MAINT $____ G	6. Total current costs: Add all the E Figures: TOTAL ANNUAL LABOR $____ TOTAL ANNUAL SUPPLIES $____ TOTAL ANNUAL EQUIP. $____ TOTAL ANNUAL OPER. $____ TOTAL CURRENT COSTS: $____ F 7. ANNUAL NET SAVINGS Calculate the difference between the current and proposed total costs: F ____ H ____ F minus H =$____ Annual Net Savings Determine hard and soft dollar costs: Hard $ savings =$____ Soft $ savings =$____	6. Total proposed costs: Add all the G Figures: TOTAL ANNUAL LABOR $____ TOTAL ANNUAL SUPPLIES $____ TOTAL ANNUAL EQUIP. $____ TOTAL ANNUAL OPER. $____ TOTAL ONE-TIME COSTS $____ TOTAL PROPOSED COSTS $____ H

Figure 27-3. Worksheet job aid from Wells Fargo Bank.

Department	Hourly employee	Benefits brochure no.
Maintenance	Yes	123
	No	50
Housekeeping	Yes	136
	No	52
Food Service	Yes	148
	No	53
Sales	Yes	152
	No	54

Figure 27-4. Decision table job aid.

6. Checklist Job Aids

This format distinguishes itself through its main purpose which is to prompt the user to reflect on something in light of specified attributes or characteristics. Checklist job aids list critical information for the user to consider or verify before, during, or after performing a job or task. The checklist job aid is most often used for coaching job aids, for example, when it is desirable for employees to think about a task in a particular way. Rossett and Hoffman provide an automated tool for needs assessment that prompts trainers to consider a series of sources and activities and then to select those perceived as most appropriate for the situation. Figure 27-6 is a sample screen from "Needs Assessment Naturally."

Checklist job aids do not result in a single answer or number. What they do is coach an individualized approach to a complex problem based on a common core of considerations.

Developing Motivating Job Aids

As popular as job aids are, there are problems with their use or, more precisely, their nonuse. The problems are familiar. There's the job aid that gets ignored because it doesn't help do anything the employee thinks is important. There's another job aid that becomes useless because it isn't updated. And there's the job aid that is on somebody else's desk when you need it. Or the job aid that is almost too heavy to lift. Or the organization that calls job aids "cheat sheets," ignoring the volatile and large data sets involved, and expecting knowledgeable employees to know "everything" by heart.

In an article in *Performance and Instruction,* Tilaro & Rossett[20] addressed these concerns. Adapting some of Keller's[21,22] work on motivation, Tilaro and Rossett presented coaching job aids that advise on how to build, install, and maintain job aids. Figures 27-7, 27-8, and 27-9 target the work, worker, and workplace and anticipate obstacles to initial and continuing use of job aids.

Effective job aids boil down to customer focus, functionality, elegance, and immediacy. Technology, then, with its ability to go where the work gets done, when the challenges present themselves, has unique potential for job aids. The remainder of this chapter looks at the rich potential for the relationship between job aids and emergent technologies.

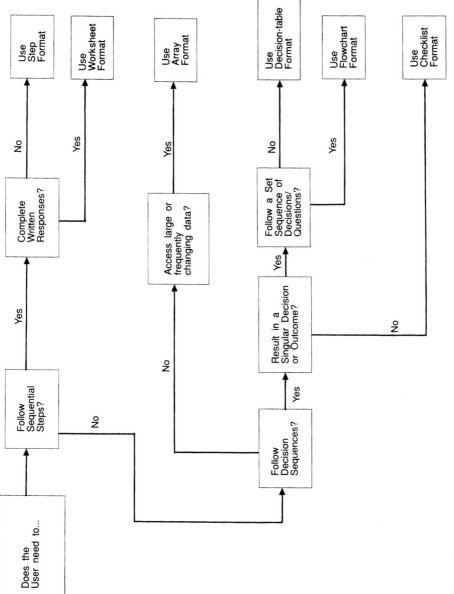

Figure 27-5. Flowchart job aid.

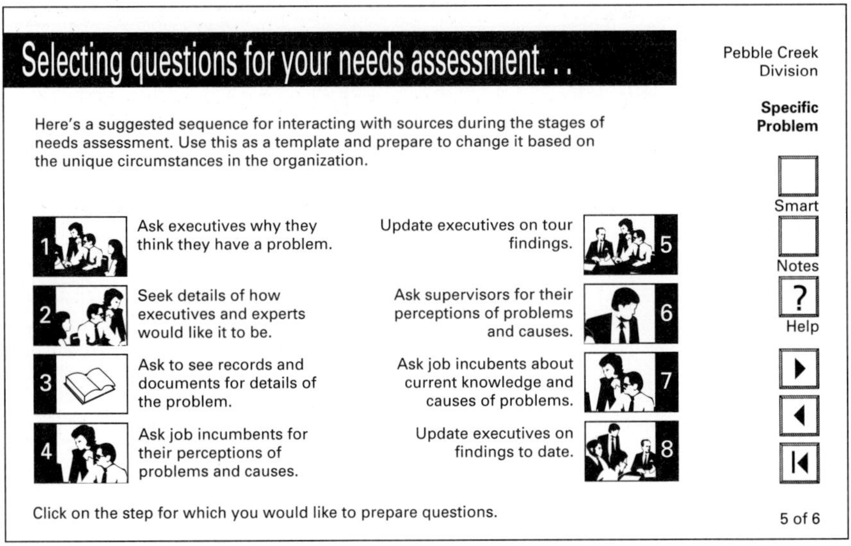

Figure 27-6. Automated needs assessment stages.

WORKER:

☐ Is the job aid designed from the workers' point of view?
☐ Have potential problems with workers been examined and specific strategies devised to counteract those problems?

WORKPLACE:

☐ Are there ways to link the job aid with performance and/or bottom-line results?
☐ Are there ways to link improved performance with organizational incentives and/or rewards?
☐ Has management been involved for "buy-in" and support?
☐ Has the job aid been pilot-tested at the work site?
☐ Have SMEs and management signed off on the rough draft of the job aid?

WORK:

☐ Have key elements been logically and naturally grouped and chunked?
☐ Has need-to-know information been included and nice-to-know material eliminated?
☐ Is critical information first?
☐ Is it possible to replace words with pictures?
☐ Can readability be improved by using color coding, highlighting, white space, bullets, or outlines?
☐ Is the job aid user-friendly, attractive, and aesthetically pleasing?
☐ Have typographical errors been eliminated?
☐ Can the job aid be simplified?
☐ Do design and function complement each other?

Figure 27-7. Building motivating job aids. (*From Angie Tilaro and Allison Rossett, "Creating Motivating Job Aids,"* Performance and Instruction, 32 (9), pp. 19–20, National Society for Performance and Instruction, Washington, DC. Copyright © 1993, National Society for Performance and Instruction.)

WORKER:

☐ Have sessions been scheduled to train end users in the use of the job aid?
☐ Have workers been shown the advantages and disadvantages of using the job aid?
☐ Has "change anxiety" been addressed?
☐ Will workers receive feedback on how well they are performing?

WORKPLACE:

☐ Have environmental stumbling blocks been eliminated?
☐ Has the final version of the job aid been pilot-tested for compatibility with the work site?
☐ Has use of the job aid been linked with performance and/or bottom-line results for management "buy-in"?
☐ Are incentives and/or reward systems in place for improved performance?
☐ Have SMEs and management signed off on the final product?

WORK:

☐ Is there an established method for evaluating use of the job aid after installation?

Figure 27-8. Installing motivating job aids. (*From Angie Tilaro and Allison Rossett, "Creating Motivating Job Aids,"* Performance and Instruction, 32 *(9), pp. 19–20, National Society for Performance and Instruction, Washington, DC. Copyright © 1993, National Society for Performance and Instruction.*)

WORKER:

☐ Is there an established system for introducing new employees to available job aids?
☐ Is there a designated "owner" responsible for future updating?
☐ Are there incentives for an employee to take on the responsibility of ownership?

WORKPLACE:

☐ Is there an established system for submitting changes for future updates?
☐ Has a revision schedule for future updates been prepared?

WORK:

☐ Is there a list of what job aids have been created?
☐ Is there a list of who has received job aids?

Figure 27-9. Maintaining motivating job aids. (*From Angie Tilaro and Allison Rossett, "Creating Motivating Job Aids,"* Performance and Instruction, 32 *(9), pp. 19–20, National Society for Performance and Instruction, Washington, DC. Copyright © 1993, National Society for Performance and Instruction.*)

Electronic Performance Support Systems

Job aids will increasingly involve technology, especially three kinds of technological supports: help systems, expert systems, and the souped-up, integrated version of them all, electronic performance support systems.

Help Systems

Accessible at the desktop and embedded in software, help systems provide *just-in-time* support to the worker. For example, a help system becomes important to the user when he or she is attempting to use a new piece of software. This is an opportunity to hit the Help key. An array of help options then appears. Other help systems are the thesaurus and spelling checker included in many word processing programs.

A help system offers the following:

- *Help lines:* This is the customary assistance at the bottom of the screen, available in a pull-down menu or through hitting a Help key or a question mark (?).

- *Documentation:* Here the computer is the repository for hard-copy documentation. Historically, access to this on-line documentation is through nested and often tedious menus. More frequently now, access and browsing occur through natural language searching. Users key in a phrase or name and are whisked to the relevant sections. Apple's HyperCard is an example of this emergent tool. For example, Jeff Brechlin and Allison Rossett developed a HyperCard orientation program for Apple Computer, Inc. A user enters Command-F or clicks the mouse on Find, enters a natural language choice like "Ethiopian restaurant," or "travel reimbursement," or "Newton," and is swiftly taken to the desired information.

- *Error detection and correction:* The user makes an error; independently, the help system notices and in typical job-aid format, prompts the procedure that corrects the error. Few on-line help systems do this currently.

- *Tutoring:* On-line help systems can also tutor users by offering definitions, examples, and small drill and practices.

Current on-line help systems serve primarily as information and procedural job aids. "Intelligence," however, is what most users desire, where the software infers and anticipates individual user problems from pauses and keystrokes and offers appropriate suggestions, a functionality akin to expert systems.

Expert Systems

Expert systems, like on-line helps, exist to support the user during work. However, unlike helps, expert systems take better advantage of the power of the computer, serving as intellectual assistant, advisor, and coach, rather than as a passive encyclopedia of information and procedures. Expert systems can be applied to most challenges, for example, suggesting approaches to a needs assessment (see Fig. 27-6), supporting inventory control, and diagnosing medical problems presented in an x-ray.

An expert system offers the following:

- *The wisdom of experts.* It's important to understand where expert systems come from. They come from experts and are derived by eliciting and codifying what they know that makes them experts. Consider successful real estate agents. The job of the expert-system producer is to find out how expert agents query and qualify potential customers, what the line of questioning and reasoning is, what information is critical to lending and home selection, and what aspects of the database of housing stock are most influential in pairing the customer with a prospective home. Once this information is gleaned, the challenge is to create software that represents this collected wisdom and makes it accessible to less expert people.

- *Coaching.* Through a question-and-answer process available on the computer screen, expert systems guide the user. By giving novices access to experts' approaches to real estate or medical diagnosis, the system enables less-experienced employees to act as if they are more experienced.

- *Patient, omnipresent support for employees.* The computer program is infinitely patient and never tires of prompting, interpreting, and running what-if scenarios.

- *Coaching for ambiguous conditions.* Expert systems are important to human resources professionals because they help employees solve complex problems in murky domains like interpersonal skills and customer service. The expert system can make a single recommendation, or in some cases, a range of recommendations, each of which is often presented with a confidence rating. For example, the real estate system provides confidence ratings related to the size of a loan for which a particular client might qualify.

- *Explanations relating to recommendations.* Welsh and Wilson[23] describe systems that inform the user about recommendations that were derived. This powerful option makes overt the facts, heuristics, and inferences that have influenced suggestions, with implications for building the novice's ability to reflect on the situation.

- *Friendly interface.* While a database, complex rules, syntax, and code are the muscle and bones of expert systems, these details are, unless sought out, invisible to the user. Optimally, what the user experiences is a painless and familiar experience with questions, answers, and suggestions.

Electronic Performance Support Systems (EPSS)

Electronic performance support systems go by many names: integrated performance support, performance support tools, and fully loaded expert systems, to name a few. The choice of name is not critical. What counts is what these powerful on-the-job systems offer to users and their organizations.

EPSSs embody all three kinds of job aids: they provide information; they support procedures; and they serve as coaches for decision making. In addition, EPSSs provide a way to access education about the topic at hand. Figure 27-10 presents the relationship between EPSS and the other technology-based job aids, highlighting EPSS as the system that encompasses the others and extends their reach by promising an educational function as well.

Puterbaugh, Rosenberg, and Sofman[10] of AT&T define EPSS as "software designed to improve worker productivity by supplying immediate on-the-job access to integrated information, learning opportunities and expert consultation—with scope and sequence controlled by the user" [p. 2].

What Is Special About EPSS?

- EPSS offer access to large databases that can be searched through natural language commands.

- EPSS include the opportunity to learn something. Puterbaugh, Rosenberg, and Sofman claim that this feature goes beyond the traditional drill and practices that are a part of on-line helps to also include cases, examples, exercises, and simulations. Some EPSSs do not include computer-based education but instead refer the user to modules and lessons available in print or video formats.

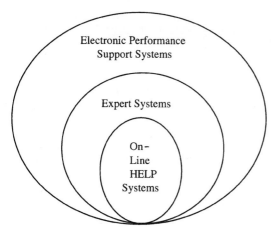

Figure 27-10. Technological job aids.

- EPSSs are expert systems that coach the user by presenting questions, assessing the answers, judging responses, and then making recommendations about a course of action. The advice can range from a suggestion about what houses the potential buyer might like and qualify to purchase to which diseases appear to be indicated by the data.
- EPSSs are recognized by their friendly, speedy, and nonclunky interface. Through it, the EPSS functions of information, education, and coaching smoothly connect to one another and are simultaneously accessible to the user. With a few keystrokes, the user can move from a hypertext database for a tutorial to a simulation back to the database and onto a session with the coach.

Rossett and Hoffman built an EPSS "Needs Assessment Naturally" (NAna) to support training professionals when they conduct needs assessments. It does the following:

1. It educates users on needs assessment and provides materials to help users explain and justify needs assessment to customers.

2. It provides a database of questions for needs assessment geared to sources of information like executives, experts, managers, and job incumbents.

3. For given needs assessment situations, like a request for training or the desire to upgrade the skills of a group of employees, it coaches the user in appropriate needs assessment steps, sources, and questions.

4. It enables users to select relevant approaches and questions and to alter the system to match the particular circumstances confronted by the trainer.

5. It coaches the development of reports and briefings that aid in communication with customers and colleagues. Figure 27-11 is another screen from this EPSS. It shows the part of the program that helps the user create a report.

EPSSs are technology-based job aids. Their growing stature in the marketplace is derived from their ability to deliver information, education, and consultation, with speedy connectivity, where the work gets done. Such desirable capacities should ensure that EPSSs are revolutionizing the workplace. Are they?

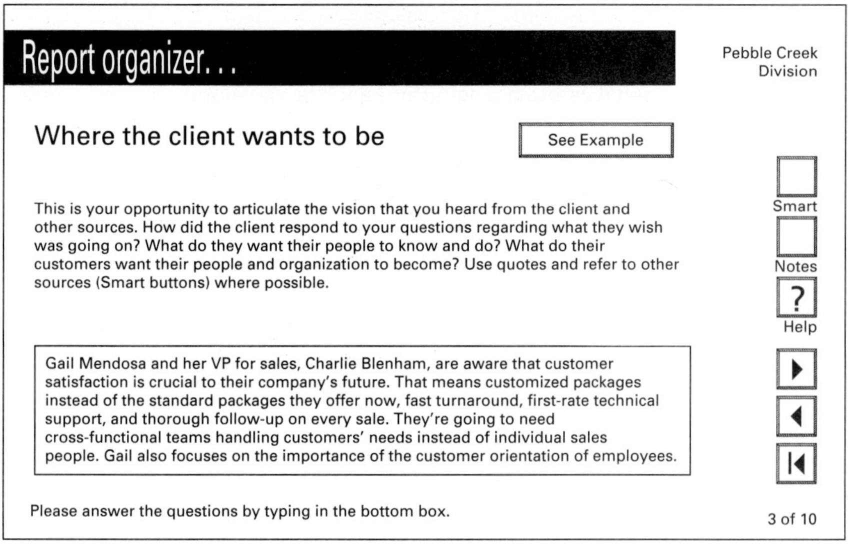

Figure 27-11. Automated needs assessment report generator.

Not yet. Although there are keynote speeches and even distinct conferences devoted to the topic of EPSSs, they are still more promise than reality. The reasons for their halting entry into the workplace deserve attention, as they have implications for many interventions to which training and development professionals turn:

- *Lack of cross-functional coordination.* In describing experiences with EPSSs at AT&T, Marc Rosenberg described complex challenges that necessitate working across functional boundaries. It's not unusual to confront a situation like this. The volatile data in the database is "owned" by two organizations. The experts are spread across three units, and there is interest in involving several external consultants. The individual who initiated the effort has just been given other responsibilities and his replacement isn't particularly committed. Nobody expected the effort to cost this much. And most of the participants don't understand why the training department is so interested. Some executives want to turn it over to management information systems (MIS) since it involves computers.

- *Interface frustrations.* Jeff Brechlin of Apple Computer believes that EPSSs rise and fall on the quality of the interface. In the *Harvard Business Review,* Davenport[24] complains of technocratic solutions that "often specify the minutiae of machinery while disregarding how people in organizations actually go about acquiring, sharing and making use of information. In short, they glorify information technology and ignore human psychology" [p. 119].

- *Lack of user preparedness.* Clark[25] reminded training and development professionals that not all individuals are equally able to avail themselves of EPSS, that not everybody knows what they don't know or knows how to rely upon reference tools to get their jobs done.

- *Absence of organizational infrastructure.* In many sites, the necessary technological delivery systems are not in place. Can computers communicate with one another within buildings and across miles? Do users have automated workstations? Sufficient telephone lines?

- *Absence of high-level sponsorship.* Successful new ways of working and cross-functional collaborations must be galvanized and nurtured by a high-level corporate executive. When you are lucky enough to find one, the luck must hold throughout what is often a lengthy analysis, development, and implementation effort.

- *The cost of EPSS.* Who is going to pay for EPSS? Because these systems are new, inherently cross-functional, and very expensive, this is not a trivial matter. It is difficult to garner resources to support functions that cross over traditional department lines and lack immediate payoff. If the ultimate goal is an integrated and full-service tool, including information, education, and advice, then units representing training, methodology, planning, personnel, marketing, compensation, engineering, research and development, media services, documentation, and others must cooperate to support the effort.

- *Resistance to innovations, particularly to innovations that involve new roles and rewards.* The union of technology and job aids introduces new ways of thinking about technologies and the role of the training professional. EPSSs, if they succeed in supporting performance at the desktop, alter and perhaps reduce the need for classroom instruction. This raises immediate questions about conventional reimbursements for training that are based on bodies in seats.

Conclusion

Remember Claire and Mack? They are the executives who opened this chapter with concerns about training and the workplace. They expressed dissatisfaction with training-as-usual, though they weren't sure what they wanted instead.

One thing that Claire and Mack and most executives are seeking is a closer link between training and work, one that brings the support and development to the customer, where the work gets done. Job aids and technology-based job aids, the topics for this chapter, do just that. From the lowliest reference card to a high-end electronic support system, they provide information, prompt procedures, and offer advice when and where users want it.

On-the-job performance supports enable training and development professionals to expand the reach of their services. They also support a sharpened customer focus for training and for the materials that participants take back to work with them. Sharpe Healthcare in San Diego, for example, structures some of its training around job aids and asks participants to build job aids during training. When participants return for refresher training, they bring these job aids for discussion and updating. Note that the assumptions here are different. No longer is the emphasis on the training event. Instead it shifts to developing employee capacity to seek assistance from materials that are provided and that they create themselves.

A technological example also drives home the point. Performance Mentor is software built by a Palo Alto company. What it does is help trained managers and supervisors conduct performance appraisals. It coaches preparation for the review meeting with the employee, provides notes for the interaction, and then prompts the manager to consider and rate how it went. This feedback is processed by the expert system to alter guidance for when this manager conducts appraisals in the future. Training and technology come together in philosophy and customer focus.

Job aids and EPSSs represent a similar paradigm with a very different price tag. What's important here is the paradigm, a paradigm that furthers critical changes in training and development—resulting in systems over events, consultation over presentation, functionality over subject matter, workplace over class-room, desktop over module, and reference over memory. Claire and Mack would say that it is about time and about place.

References

1. Pechter, K., "Forming a New Union," *Human Resource Executive,* July 1994, *8*(7), pp. 18–20.

2. Garfield, C., *"Second to None: How Our Smartest Companies Put People First,"* Business One, Irwin, Homewood, IL, 1992.

3. Harbour, J. L., "Increasing Efficiency: A Process-oriented Approach," *Performance Improvement Quarterly,* 1993, *6*(4), pp. 92–114.

4. Rosenberg, M. J., "Performance Technology: Working the System," *Training,* 1990, *27*(2), pp. 42–48.

5. Gery, G. J., "The Quest for Electronic Performance Support," *CBT Directions,* 1989, *2*(7), pp. 21–23.

6. Rossett, A. "Electronic Job Aids," *Data Training,* June 1991, *10*(7), pp. 24–29.

7. Hammer, M., and J. Champy, *Reengineering the Corporation,* HarperCollins, New York, 1993.

8. Rossett, A., and J. H. Gautier-Downes, *A Handbook of Job Aids,* Pfeiffer & Company, San Diego, 1991.

9. Carnevale, A. P., and L. J. Gainer, *The Learning Enterprise,* ASTD, Alexandria, VA, 1989.

10. Puterbaugh, G., M. Rosenberg, and R. Sofman, "Performance Support Tools: A Step Beyond Training," *Performance and Instruction,* November–December 1989, *28*(10), pp. 1–5.

11. Clark, R. C., "Part I: Task-general Instructional Methods," *Performance and Instruction,* 1986, *25*(3), pp. 17–21.

12. Harless, J. H., "Guiding Performance with Job Aids," in *Introduction to Performance Technology,* National Society for Performance and Instruction, Washington, DC, 1986, pp. 106–124.

13. Pipe, P., "Ergonomics and Performance Aids," in *Introduction to Performance Technology,* National Society for Performance and Instruction, Washington, DC, 1986, pp. 129–144.

14. Clark, R. C., *Developing Technical Training,* Addison-Wesley, Reading, MA, 1989.

15. Merrill, D. M., *Instructional Design Theory,* Educational Technology Publications, Englewood Cliffs, NJ, 1994.

16. Duncan, C. S., "Job Aids Really Can Work: A Study of the Military Applications of Job Aid Technology," *Performance and Instruction,* 1985, *24*(4), pp. 1–4.

17. Brecke, F. H., "Instructional Design for Aircrew Judgment Training," *Aviation, Space and Environmental Medicine,* 1982, *53*(10), pp. 951–957.

18. Wurman, R. S., *Information Anxiety,* Doubleday, New York, 1989.

19. Rossett, A., *Training Needs Assessment,* Educational Technology Publications, Englewood Cliffs, NJ, 1987.

20. Tilaro, A., and A. Rossett, "Creating Motivating Job Aids, *Performance and Instruction,* 1993, *32*(9), pp. 13–20.

21. Keller, J. M., "Motivational Designs of Instruction," in C. M. Reigeluth, ed., *Instructional Design Theories and Models: An Overview of Their Current Status,* Lawrence Erlbaum, Hillsdale, NJ, 1983, pp. 386–434.

22. Keller, J. M., "Strategies for Stimulating the Motivation to Learn," *Performance and Instruction,* 1987, *26*(8), pp. 1–7.

23. Welsh, J. R., and B. G. Wilson, "Expert System Shells: Tools to Aid Human Performance," *Journal of Instructional Development,* 1987, *10*(2), pp. 15–19.

24. Davenport, T. H., "Saving IT's Soul: Human-centered Information Management," *Harvard Business Review,* 1994, *72*(2), pp. 119–131.

25. Clark, R. C., "EPSS—Look Before You Leap: Some Cautions About Applications of Electronic Performance Support Systems," *Performance and Instruction,* 1992, pp. 22–25.

Bibliography

Brechlin, J., and A. Rossett, "Orienting New Employees," *Training,* 1991, *28*(4), pp. 45–51.

Chinell, David F., *System Documentation: The In-line Approach,* John Wiley and Sons, New York, 1990.

Cohill, A. M., and R. C. Williges, "Retrieval of HELP Information for Novice Users of Interactive Computer Systems," *Human Factors,* 1985, *27*(3), pp. 335–343.

Diamondstone, J., "Beyond the Band-aid: One Company's Use of CBT as a Corporate Strategy," *The CBT Digest,* March 1988, *2*(1), pp. 4–9.

Feigenbaum, E., P. McCorduck, and H. P. Nii, *The Rise of the Expert Company,* Vintage Books, New York, 1988.

Gery, G. J., *Making CBT Happen,* Weingarten Publications, Boston, 1987.

Gery, G. J., *Electronic Performance Support Systems,* Weingarten Publications, Boston, 1991.

Harmon, P., ed., *Intelligent Software Strategies,* Cutter Information Corporation, Arlington, MA.

Harmon, P., "Expert Systems, Job Aids, and the Future of Instructional Technology," *Performance and Instruction,* 1986, *25*(2), pp. 26–28.

Harmon, Paul, and David King, *Expert Systems: Artificial Intelligence in Business,* John Wiley and Sons, New York, 1985.

Harmon, Paul, Rex Maus, and William Morrissey, *Expert Systems Tools and Applications,* John Wiley and Sons, New York, 1988.

Haugeland, John, *Artificial Intelligence: The Very Idea,* MIT Press, Cambridge, MA, 1987.

Horn, Robert E., *Mapping Hypertext,* The Lexington Institute, Lexington, MA, 1989.

Horton, William K., *Designing & Writing Online Documentation: Help Files to Hypertext,* John Wiley and Sons, New York, 1990.

Kearsley, Greg, *Online Help Systems: Design and Implementation,* Ablex Publishing Corporation, Norwood, NJ, 1988.

Lewis, P. H., "I'm Sorry; My Machine Doesn't Like Your Work," *The New York Times,* February 4, 1990, p. F27.

Marcus, Aaron, *Graphic Design for Electronic Documents and User Interfaces,* ACM Press, New York, 1992.

McFarland, Thomas D., and Reese Parker, *Expert Systems in Education and Training,* Educational Technology Publications, Englewood Cliffs, NJ, 1990.

Morrison, J. E., and B. G. Witmer, "A Comparative Evaluation of Computer-based and Print-based Job Performance Aids," *Journal of Computer-Based Instruction,* 1984, *10*(3, 4), pp. 73–75.

Petterson, Rune, *Visuals for Information: Research and Practice,* Educational Technology Publications, Englewood Cliffs, NJ, 1989.

Rossett, A., "Job Aids in a Performance Technology World," *Performance and Instruction,* 1991, *30*(5), pp. 1–6.

Schmid, R. F., and V. S. Gorlach, "Instructional Design Rules for Algorithmic Subject Matter," *Performance Improvement Quarterly,* 3(2), 1990, pp. 1–14.

Schramm, W., and W. Porter, *Men, Women, Messages and Media: Understanding Human Communication,* 2d ed., Harper & Row, New York, 1982.

Seyer, Philip, *Understanding Hypertext: Concepts and Applications,* Windcrest Books, Blue Ridge Summit, PA, 1991.

Stolovitch, H. D., and E. J. Keeps, eds., *Handbook of Performance Technology,* Jossey-Bass, San Francisco, 1992.

Zagorski, S., "How I Created the Award Winning Job Aid," *Performance and Instruction,* May–June 1987, pp. 29–32.

Zuboff, S., *In the Age of the Smart Machine: The Future of Work and Power,* Basic Books, New York, 1988.

SECTION 4

Training Applications

28

Leadership Development

Donald K. Conover

Donald K. Conover, *now retired, has had an industrial career covering 40 years, divided between line and staff jobs, mainly at Western Electric which became part of AT&T with the breakup of the Bell System. His assignments included engineering supervisor, factory manager, Director of Engineering and Manufacturing at the Hawthorne Works, Director of Corporate Planning, and finally Corporate Education Vice President. During his tenure, the AT&T Corporate Education and Training organization had a full-time staff of 1200 people to provide management and technical education and product training to AT&T employees and customers. Conover's professional associations have included vice president, North American Society for Corporate Planning; chairman, Chamber of Commerce of the Princeton Area; board of governors, ASTD; board member, Thomas Edison State College Foundation, the Newgrange School, and the National Association for Industry-Education Cooperation. Conover participated in educational advisory committees at Columbia University, University of Pennsylvania, Manhattan College, The Conference Board, and the U.S. Chamber of Commerce. He has published many papers on corporate planning, education and training, and management, and has been a speaker at conferences in the United States, Europe, and China. He earned a bachelor's degree in engineering from Princeton University and a master's degree in industrial management from M.I.T. where he was a Sloan Fellow.*

When American troops landed at Omaha Beach in Normandy 50 years ago, they were met by withering machine-gun fire from the defending Germans. Thousands lost their lives in the first few hours, including a disproportionate number of the officers sent to lead the invasion. Those who managed to reach shore and cross the beach were pinned down at the base of a natural stone wall and threatened with annihilation unless they moved up the slopes to drive the enemy back from its fortified position.

We know the outcome. The beleaguered Americans did move out and eventually carried the day. The greatest military invasion in history was a success. But, as recalled by individuals who were there, tragedy was averted by soldiers (whose officers had been killed) who assumed command to get everybody moving again, up from that deadly beach.

Who were the leaders responsible for the Allied success? Certainly the generals who developed the strategies for Operation Overlord (as the invasion project was called) were important, as were the myriad officers and managers who brought together the huge array of ships and supplies and men. But ultimately, success depended upon the leadership of men who were not commissioned to lead but did so when it was needed.

This is only one example of the reality that is part of every organized enterprise, namely *that leadership is needed at all levels, whenever coordinated human behavior is essential to make something happen.* It is the catalyst for action which makes the difference between success and failure, and this is one of the reasons leadership development plays a central role in most corporate training agendas. The organization needs leadership to succeed!

The other reason is that leadership (or at least the presumption of leadership qualities) in individuals is still "the brass ring" for personal advancement in the organizational chain of command. People observe the cultural norms of their organizations and conclude that if they exhibit leadership, they will have an advantage in the competition to get ahead in their careers. Leadership is seen to be a major key to personal success!

With two such powerful incentives, it is hardly surprising that leadership development is one of the most sought-after training experiences. However, popular urgency doesn't explain the bewildering variety of training approaches to leadership development, and the training professional has the formidable task of choosing the approach that is best for a particular client.

In this chapter, we will begin with the premise that leadership is an attribute every organization needs to succeed and that, in varying degrees, everyone has the capacity to lead. Events in life may provide the spark to ignite leadership, but it is also something that can be learned, and that is the goal of leadership development. *The basic dimensions of leadership will be shown to be a recurring set of outcomes: purpose defined, direction provided, resources coordinated, and obstacles overcome.*

While such leadership fundamentals remain a constant, their application involves a wide variety of emphasis, style, and form to suit diverse circumstances. Thus, the relative importance of one or another aspect of leadership varies, and this fact explains the wide variety of training approaches. The challenge for the training professional is identifying the particular leadership needs that will help a client (organization or individual) to succeed.

Vignettes of successful leaders in large and small organizations will be provided to illustrate the variety of ways leadership is important in a changing environment. Finally, leadership training will be discussed as a diagnostic and prescriptive problem in which the trainer's job is to work with a client organization to ascertain what the leadership needs are and then choose (or develop) a training program tailored to such needs.

And, it deserves underscoring that the trainer rarely works alone. There is almost always someone in the client organization, often the organization head, who has perceived the need for leadership development and has called for a training intervention. This has both positive and negative aspects for the trainer.

The positive is that such a client (a sponsor?) represents a valuable resource, a touchstone with the particular needs of the organization to be served, and it is a wise training professional who takes the time to work with the client to learn what really needs attention and what training results will signal success in leadership development.

Unfortunately, dialogue with the client often begins with a prescription for what kind of training to do instead of what kind of leadership development is needed. If a team-building or some other training approach has caught the client's eye, the first interchange may be, "I want you to develop a program like the one used in the XYZ Company." It is the trainer's job to help the client revisit the circumstances which first prompted the need for leadership development and then take time, working with the client, to be sure that the training plan is right for the client's situation.

To help the trainer get ready to work with a client, this chapter is organized to present a review of leadership fundamentals, illustrate the variety of ways good leadership manifests itself in different real-life situations, and then provide a framework for translating a set of specific, leadership development needs into a training program that will be on target.

Leadership Dimensions

The underlying premise is that leadership is best understood as a set of outcomes which cause coordinated human endeavor to be successful. They are called *leadership dimensions* because they are seen to recur, in varying degrees, in different organizations facing different challenges, and they are the important things leaders do to make the difference between success and failure.

Defining Purpose

The first dimension of leadership is *defining purpose,* which includes formulating a vision, setting long-range goals, or redefining the organizational purpose when there is a fundamental change in the environment. The vision is the overarching statement which explains why an organization exists and how it intends to go forward. It is the most basic yardstick by which other organizational initiatives are evaluated. Closely related to the vision are long-range goals which become the distant targets to be achieved in order to fulfill the vision.

Over time it may be necessary to redefine the vision and establish new long-range goals. This event happens when the external environment changes profoundly or when some fundamental (often technological) change alters the basic premise on which the original vision was based. A prime example of such an alteration is the shift from a business outlook based on a national market to one that sees the world as the market.

Ironically, while the issue of organizational vision logically comes first in a discussion of leadership dimensions, it is the least active need for most leaders. The reason is because defining the purpose of the enterprise and setting long-range goals is an infrequent occurrence, and it is the leadership dimension reserved almost exclusively to the one top executive in the organization; hence, the trainer is much less likely to be involved in that phase of development when it does occur.

For the training professional, what is important about this first leadership dimension is understanding that the purpose and long-range goals for each different organization are unique and recognizing that they set limits on the way other leadership dimensions may be applied. Smaller organizations may not have the formality of a written mission statement, but they usually have a sense of who and what they are, which guides their action. If there is to be effective leadership development, in large or small organizations, it should be designed to fit within boundaries defined by the purpose of that organization!

Providing Direction

It might be said that the discussion of leadership dimensions should be divided into two categories: deciding why the organization exists (which is the *defining-purpose* dimension) and making the right things happen, which is what the other three leadership dimensions are all about.

Leaders at all levels of the organization are responsible for making the right things happen. The *purpose* and the *long-range goals* help define what is right for a particular business, in a particular era. *Providing direction, coordinating resources,* and *overcoming obstacles* are different aspects of making the right things happen.

An obvious but important point that bears repeating is that *leadership makes things happen through others.* Thus, leadership in all of the dimensions being addressed in this chapter manifests itself by gaining the respect, trust, and commitment of the people in the organization. (It is not enough for the leader to point the way; someone must be sufficiently persuaded to follow, to act!)

The most persistent responsibility of a leader, at all levels, is providing direction, and this is the second dimension of leadership. Providing direction means choosing strategies to both achieve long-range goals and realize the vision. It means setting policies to create a climate where people will commit their creativity and energy to the organizational purpose. It means choosing priorities that make the best use of resources. It means translating abstract goals into understandable objectives and then overseeing a measurement process that tracks progress and signals when an intervention is appropriate.

Whereas *defining purpose is discontinuous* (i.e., it doesn't happen all the time, and it tends to be the exclusive domain of the top executive), *providing direction is continuous*. It is needed all the time, and it is needed at all levels of the organization. It is not an exaggeration to state that this is an important dimension in any person's behavior, whether she or he is designated a leader or not. It is in this dimension that we all decide how we are going to conduct our lives, take care of our health, manage our time, interact with others, weigh self-interest versus group needs, behave ethically, etc. When the psychiatrist says we must take charge of ourselves, that is another way of acknowledging that in a very basic way, to be effective human beings means establishing a direction for our lives, being our own leaders.

The wide-ranging scope of this leadership dimension goes far to explain the variety of leadership training programs. There are so many legitimate areas for development and so many topics are part of providing direction, so the job of the trainer is to find out which area needs to be improved for a particular organization or individual.

Later, in the section "Leadership Training," the question of providing direction in the context of the organization's particular status will be taken up. Now, it may be more helpful to provide a more personally focused checklist itemizing the most common areas where the leadership dimension of providing direction is important and where a training need might be identified. As a further effort to identify valid learning objectives, the list is divided into four subsets which aggregate different levels of leadership responsibility (see Table 28-1).

Table 28-1. Providing Direction in Four Leadership Roles

Managing Self
▪ Define personal values. ▪ Set career objectives. ▪ Evaluate skills (strengths and weaknesses). ▪ Establish personal development plan. ▪ Monitor progress; make needed adjustments.

Supervising Others (e.g., First-Line Supervisor)
▪ Define personal leadership style. ▪ Identify priorities needed for organizational success. ▪ Evaluate resources, especially talent pool. ▪ Set organizational objectives. ▪ Delegate authority and responsibility. ▪ Monitor results and recognize performance of others.

Function Manager (e.g., Department Head, Middle Manager)
▪ Establish organizational norms (to guide how people relate to one another, to increase productivity of the work unit). ▪ Develop a business plan with clear objectives and schedule. ▪ Provide opportunities to develop and/or enhance the skills of people in the work unit. ▪ Monitor results and make appropriate adjustments to the business plan.

Top Manager (e.g., Business Unit Head, Executive)
▪ Set policies which balance the needs of customers, employees, and shareholders. ▪ Develop a strategic business plan which balances long- and short-range goals and objectives; monitor progress. ▪ Provide for the succession of key leaders. ▪ Ensure open communication between the enterprise and present and potential stakeholders.

Obviously, complexity and ambiguity increase at higher management levels in an organization, but note that there is a kind of natural progression to such levels of complexity and ambiguity. The leadership demands for effective self-direction or first-line supervision are reasonably straightforward. They can be addressed within limits already established by the existing norms, policies, and stated goals of the organization. As the focus moves to top management, the leadership demands are more complex, more ambiguous, and more often characterized in terms of balance, and are less constrained by clear boundaries.

Nevertheless, the continuity of leadership functions is important to the training professional. If there is continuity in the practical application and underlying values of leadership at different levels, leadership development training can be effective. (If the organization's approach to leadership lacks such continuity, the trainer might consider exercises in team building or sensitivity training to promote greater consistency in the way leadership is being exercised and values communicated throughout the organization.)

The good news about the inherent continuity of the leadership dimension of providing direction is that it lends itself to a consistent leadership curriculum applicable to all levels in the organization. A caution in these days of frequent corporate redirection: Be sure that the training provided to lower levels is based on the current directions from top management. Although this directive imposes an added vigilance to keep course material current, it ensures a positive learning environment to understand and adapt to the latest corporate directions. Such a curriculum helps build leadership consistency, which strengthens the organization.

Now that the issue of continuity in leadership has been raised, two caveats should be offered. The first is that this is not an argument for a single "style" of leadership. People do things in different ways, including the way they lead. Some effective leaders are autocratic; others lead with a less directive approach. Some use humor to make a point; others are more serious. Some are comfortable with an informal, open way of relating to others; others are not. Variations in behavior define personality, but they don't define effective leadership. The development of leadership must focus on helping each person understand the leadership dimensions and adopt personal, effective behaviors to bring about the right outcomes.

People can be taught the dimensions. They can learn by observing how other leaders have dealt with a situation, but in the final analysis they must develop their own style of leadership, how they might act to accomplish similar objectives. Training that takes a cookie-cutter approach to leadership style is doomed to fail, no matter how powerful the model on which it is based. The goal should be the development of leaders who accomplish real objectives, not people who have merely learned to posture as leaders.

The other caveat is that organizational circumstances may favor one style of leadership over others. For example, it is hard to imagine that the type of excellence required of a military combat leader would necessarily translate to the same type of excellence required of a leader of a university research organization. The environment, the mission, and the goals of the organization and its place among other competing organizations are just some of the extrinsic factors creating the demand for different approaches to leadership. Implicitly, this fact means that while individuals must adopt their own leadership style, it does not mean that those people are universally interchangeable. Sometimes it is better to have one person as leader than another.

The training professional is not usually consulted about leadership assignments; however, during prescription of a program to meet leadership development needs, *it is important to factor in what kind of leadership a particular organization needs.* This process involves looking at the organizational circumstances as a guide to the kind of leadership skills that will produce the best results. (A way to do this undertaking is a key part of the later section on "Leadership Training.")

In theory, these comments about providing direction, and the discussion of other leadership dimensions to follow, apply equally to large and small organizations. The reality is that the style of the top person in a small organization is usually more important than the style of the top person in a large one in shaping the interpersonal environment of the whole organization. In the small organization, day-to-day contact with top management is more frequent (because the top is closer to the bottom). Moreover, top management of the small company is more likely to be the owner-originator of the business, and hence that person is inclined to be more directive about such things as leadership style.

Coordinating Resources

Along with providing direction, coordinating resources is a constant leadership task applying to all circumstances. It is the "here's how we're going to do it" that follows the "this is where we're going." (It may be useful to think of these two dimensions as *planning* and *execution,* respectively.

Coordinating resources has as its objective the maximum productivity of all resources working together to achieve desired ends: fulfilling the organization's purpose, reaching its goals. This undertaking involves orchestrating all of the factors necessary to the desired outcome. Think of the organization's resources in four broad categories: capital plant, raw materials, people, and organizational climate.

Making decisions about the acquisition and employment of capital and raw materials are critical elements of good management; however, they are usually of more concern to process managers and engineers than to leaders who are more likely to focus on people and the organizational climate. Still, those elements are acknowledged here as a reminder that leadership is "where the buck stops"; even if the management of one or another resource is delegated to someone else, it is ultimately the leader's job to be sure that *all* resources are used in a way that produces the best overall results. For most leadership roles, in all kinds of organizations, in all kinds of circumstances, the most important responsibility of the leader is to make sure that all details of the operation are covered, that they are being managed well, and that they are being executed *in concert with the overarching directions* for the organization. This is the essence of coordinating resources.

A leader is most likely to be involved personally in supervising people and creating an organizational climate that fosters realization of the company's purpose and goals. The distinction between supervising people and creating an organizational climate recognizes a dual role: being a guide-coach-boss to others on a one-on-one basis, and being a creator of norms for working relationships among everyone in the organization. The more closely a leader directs the performance of another, the more important are the one-on-one skills. Conversely, if a leader directs the work of many others, with intermediaries handling most of the one-on-one duties, then establishing the organizational norms by which people are treated is more important.

Table 28-2 illustrates the range of areas where leadership makes a difference in the way individuals and organizations perform. The variety and range of possibilities is another reason for the multiplicity of courseware for leadership development. These are all legitimate subjects for training and development, and (to repeat a theme) it is the trainer's job to discover where to concentrate for the greatest benefit to the client.

The lists in Table 28-2 just begin to itemize the variety of ways a leader impacts the individual worker or the group as a whole. By definition, a leader has a positive impact on the individual performance of other individuals. By definition, a

Table 28-2. Areas Where Leadership Impacts the Human Environment

One-on-one leadership	Setting the climate
▪ Delegates authority and responsibility	▪ Communicates plans and schedules
▪ Provides learning and development opportunities	▪ Promotes a continuous-learning environment
▪ Encourages risk	▪ Open to alternative ideas
▪ Encourages excellence	▪ Promotes teamwork and quality improvement
▪ Provides performance recognition and feedback	▪ Communicates progress toward objectives
▪ Provides career guidance	▪ Communicates guidelines for career progression
▪ Recognizes individual needs	▪ Maintains fairness and ethical standards

leader sets the tone for the way the organization works together and sorts out the balance of personal and group objectives. Finally (and this is what distinguishes a leader from just being a cheerleader or kindred spirit), a leader can share, but never delegate, responsibility for advancing the purpose and goals of the organization. The Holy Grail of leadership is satisfying the needs of the enterprise, the organization, and each individual together.

Removing Obstacles

In an ideal world, a leader is a pathfinder boldly guiding the organization to new heights of achievement, inspiring others with new challenges, and encouraging breakthroughs in individual or team performance. In the real world, we may become a leader in an organization demoralized by a series of failures or squeezed by forces that challenge past models for success. If high costs, low productivity, an obsolete product line, adverse government regulations, a powerful new competitor, or any of the myriad threats to survival of the enterprise should be an issue, the effective leader concentrates on overcoming obstacles as a first priority.

The first task in overcoming obstacles is discovering what kind of problem is causing the trouble, so this dimension of leadership begins with the ability to distinguish cause from effect. The next task is finding a way to turn the situation around. First, identify the problem. Then, find a way to solve it. When you succeed, then you can become the pathfinder—for now, lead us out of the swamp!

To illustrate, here are some of the kinds of problems which can cause leaders to spend most of their energy removing obstacles:

- People are so busy competing against coworkers that no one "has time" to head off a real competitor.
- Following rules and regulations has become more important than serving the customer.
- Our product is no longer what the market wants.
- Our quality is not satisfying our customers.
- Our process technology is not as good as the competition's.
- We have too many unessential jobs.
- Our wages and benefits are too high for the level of productivity we are generating.
- There is no special reason for customers to choose our products or service.

As you read this, the names of some prominent companies will probably come to mind. Some of those companies are not so prominent now. Others may still be in the midst of a struggle to solve their problem, and some may have turned themselves around. For all those seriously committed to overcoming whatever adversity besets them, you can be sure their leaders have adjusted their own priorities. They are concentrating on identifying and overcoming whatever obstacle is preventing their company's growth and prosperity.

Overcoming obstacles takes a lot of self-discipline, and it isn't likely to win friends. It involves doing what is necessary to survive, not what may be exciting or fun. It often means making hard choices—to choose principle over expediency, change traditional practices, give up products that have had their day, reorder priorities, implement tougher performance controls, or reduce the workforce. It is lonely work, but it may be the only way to make it into the next round of growth.

To conclude discussion of this rather dreary aspect of leadership, it should be noted that this area is where most training programs are deficient. Part of the reason may be that organizations faced with severe short-term problems usually do not spend much time or money on leadership development which is inherently more future-oriented. However, leadership development curricula short-change our future leaders when there is no preparation for the time when they have to hunker down and give all their attention to finding a way out of a difficult situation.

Leadership Applications

As an introduction to leadership development, a course might begin with the sort of overview provided above. It is important to define leadership, but too much theory can be like describing how a clock works to someone who just wants to know the time. Students come to leadership development programs to gain knowledge or skills they can use in real life, so it is important to validate any theoretical approach with practical applications. And, that may be the best place to start (as long as you, the trainer, know that somewhere in the course it will be important to provide the structure to clarify some of the messiness of reality).

You might start by asking students to make a list of people who they consider to be outstanding leaders. Such a list will probably be heavily weighted with historical figures—Presidents, famous military leaders and public figures, and perhaps a tyrant or two. When you have a dozen or so names on your list, take a piece of paper and make four columns, headed (surprise, surprise):

Defined purpose   Provided direction   Coordinated resources   Overcame obstacles

Ask the students to identify what behavior-situation handled (i.e., what dimension of leadership) caused each person on their list to be identified as an outstanding leader. Of course, reality is rarely so neat that only one dimension will always be selected, but in most cases you will find it fairly easy to agree on the main reason each leader was chosen. (If, in a few cases, more than one dimension applies, that's part of reality too.) In this way, you can validate the lesson that leadership takes different forms to effect the outcome of different situations. Some great leaders will be seen as visionaries, some as directors of action, some as coordinators who brought people together, and some as problem solvers—corresponding with the leadership dimensions outlined above.

If there is plenty of time, a variation on this game would be to first make the list of leaders and then ask the students to develop their own labels to classify the different types of behaviors-situations handled into which the list might be subdivided. Thus, the students would generate the set of leadership dimensions in their own words. The words they choose may be different from mine, but the basic dimensions will be the same and will have added credibility for having been developed by the class.

To add emphasis to the point that leadership manifests itself in different ways depending on the situation, you might consider asking the students to make a second subdivision based on "leadership style" (e.g., list which leaders are thought to be authoritarian, coaching, manipulative, and/or charismatic). In all likelihood, the sublists of leaders by leadership dimensions will be different from the sublists by leadership style, thus reinforcing the notion that it is the outcome, not the way the result is achieved, that is the essence of leadership.

As an introduction to leadership development, you will have demonstrated that leadership is situational and that different leadership styles may be equally effective in producing a given outcome. Leadership development is not like making cookies; the object is not to product the same product every time. It is to develop the skills necessary to effect successful outcomes in the face of different challenges.

As a wrap-up to this exercise, you may want to ask the students to characterize the situation facing the organization(s) where they work. Ask them to describe the kind of leadership outcome (and even the leadership style most likely to succeed) which meets the organization's needs.

By way of illustration, here are some vignettes of leaders performing in different situations. A few are well known, but the main reason for these examples is to show how different situations call for different kinds of leadership, and how important good leadership is in every organization, at every level where people must work together to achieve a common goal.

Theodore Vail: Defining Purpose

In the telecommunications industry, the century seems to be ending as it began, with many different service providers competing for market share. Back in 1908, the president of AT&T was a man named Theodore Vail. Vail saw that the early telephone companies were expanding into one another's territory, creating overlapping (and incompatible) services as the new technology of voice communication inevitably bridged the different neighborhoods and communities of the United States.

The vision that Vail provided established both a practical and philosophical basis for the development of the Bell System which endured almost 75 years. It was "one policy, one system, universal service," and this was the vision that drove the hundreds of thousands of people who worked for the Bell System. AT&T was the parent company, but every one of the Bell Telephone companies had common policies to guide their business practices, their focus on customer service, and their relations with employees. The network of equipment and services was integrated so that every new product or extension of service was compatible and interconnected to work together. And, universal telephone service for every home and place of business was the goal driving the growth of the enterprise.

"Service First" was the way Bell System people described their mission, and it was a principle they lived by. It was the arbiter in deciding business strategy, and it was the bedrock of every policy or practice affecting customers, shareholders, and employees in every part of every affiliated Bell company.

Vail's statement of purpose defined a major American business. It lasted long after he died, and it obviated the need for generations of subsequent leaders to spend time or attention inventing a new mission. They, and everyone who worked in the Bell System, were keepers of the flame lit by Theodore Vail.

Not until recent years has an AT&T CEO had to concern himself with defining the purpose of the business. Now, Bob Allen at AT&T, and his counterparts in the seven "Baby Bells" are challenged by the need to redefine the purpose of the companies they head. The so-called MFJ (Modified Final Judgment) ended the Bell System as a corporate entity, but even before that, profound changes were eroding the basis for the old Bell System. In 1908 the separate neighborhoods of the United States were coming together to make up a national fabric. Today, the nations of the world are becoming a global fabric. In 1908, the technical challenge was how to build a universal voice communication network. Today we are building an information highway to move and manage information in every form.

The story of Theodore Vail, and the challenge facing Bob Allen and his Bell counterparts, is useful as an example of the leadership dimension of defining purpose. At the same time, the fact that the example goes back so many years underscores the observation that defining purpose is not a frequent part of a leader's job. Indeed, as the Bell System story attests, most leaders never have to do it at all. What most leaders, at all levels in the organization, are responsible for is upholding (interpreting, in the light of current events) the vision that gives enduring purpose to their company.

Ralph Cordiner: Providing Direction

In the early fifties, American business was riding the crest of growth which followed the Second World War. A concentration of the world's wealth, a huge new manufacturing base, new products for a vastly improved lifestyle, and a postwar American society hungry for "the good life" were creating opportunities for unprecedented growth for companies that could break out of the momentum of the past. Peacetime applications of new technology were creating new markets. Capital and labor were plentiful, so business was booming. A key issue for many companies was how to manage the rapid growth, how to encourage expansion and diversification without losing control.

From the earliest days of Thomas Edison and Charles Steinmetz, the General Electric Company (GE) had grown and diversified with the expanding applications for electricity. By the 1950s, GE not only was a leading supplier of heavy capital equipment for generating and transmitting electrical energy but it also was a leader in the production of all kinds of products driven by electricity: motors, industrial controls, large and small household appliances, and lamps. It had also established a strong position in the manufacture of aircraft jet engines and was taking a leading position in the manufacture of silicon products and various other chemicals and materials. The rapid and diverse expansion provided daily testimony to the company slogan: "Progress is our most important product."

In 1950, Ralph Cordiner succeeded Charles Wilson as president of GE and made his mark on GE by providing the direction that became known as organization by strategic business units (SBUs). The plan recognized that different markets imposed unique demands, that what was good for the large steam turbine business was not necessarily good for refrigerators or electric toasters. It recognized that to succeed on many fronts meant stimulating the entrepreneurial energies of many people while providing some necessary central governance and maintaining the synergy of certain common resources.

What Cordiner did was to divide GE into many businesses, each with the freedom to manage its own affairs subject to some overall guidelines which represented corporate interests and values. Each business was expected to take a leading position in its own market.

Although a central laboratory was retained, each business was free to develop new products and push the boundaries of its own technology. Corporate offices assured the continuance of uniform accounting and personnel systems, corporate advertising, etc., but to the rank-and-file GE employees, job identity became strongly associated with the business unit where they worked.

Also notable was the establishment in the fifties of the Crotonville facility for management training. All GE managers, from all business units, as they reached certain career milestones, were sent to Crotonville for leadership development. The Crotonville experience recognized two principles underlying the new organizational plan—that the fundamentals of leadership transcend business differences, and that a common, corporate learning experience provided bonding among GE managers which was part of the "psychological glue" to keep the company united.

Nothing was new at GE insofar as the continued development of new products and businesses, but everything was new because of the organizational directions provided by Ralph Cordiner.

Georges Perrier: Coordinating Resources

Somewhere in this chapter it is important to observe that leadership is not just doing the right things right; it also includes a passion to excel.

Georges Perrier is on his way to being a legend. He is the owner, creator, and chef of Le Bec-Fin, a restaurant in central Philadelphia which many have judged the best in the United States and among the top eating places in the world. No doubt, a part of his fame stems from his fabled eccentricities, his obsession about perfection, and fits of temper when the least detail is not up to his demanding standard. What most Le Bec-Fin customers see and care about is the result—a perfect orchestration of the best ambience, the best service, and the best food.

Passion is an integral part of Georges Perrier's leadership style. Obsessed with quality, dedicated to his customers, a creative artist, he is, at the same time, a very successful businessman. From redesigning the facade of his restaurant, providing an exquisite interior, and demanding perfection in both the preparation and presentation of every dish, Perrier is ever-watchful of the performance and the result of every aspect of his operation, every person in his employ. He has a reputation for violent verbal outbursts if the slightest detail is not to his exacting standards.

At first impression, he is hardly a leadership role model. Yet, not only is he successful, but he has trained chefs who are now successful restauranteurs in their own right. New, high-quality restaurants are opening in Philadelphia because Perrier has created the market demand for fine dining.

Certainly the obsessiveness, the passion for perfection, is a factor in his success. Without question, his creative talent as a chef is an important part of the equation. But, it is the total experience which he has planned (and orchestrates every day) which distinguishes Le Bec-Fin. Georges Perrier is more than a culinary artist; he is a leader who understands the importance and knows how to coordinate resources.

Frank Perdue: Overcoming Obstacles

One of the best, and more upbeat, examples of a leader overcoming obstacles is the man who made chickens a name-brand product, Frank Perdue. He is in a business where the customer was hard pressed to distinguish his product from someone else's. By focusing on how customers feel about the quality of chickens they eat and then describing the steps his company takes to meet or exceed those feelings, he made Perdue Chickens something more than a commodity. He created an identity where none had existed before.

Leaders such as Vail, Cordiner, Perrier, and Perdue are heroic figures. It is hard for most of us to imagine being on the same stage with them. We study what they have accomplished as a way of dramatizing the fundamentals which are part of every leadership experience. But, we need to look closer to home for the models who demonstrate the same truths on a scale that more of us might achieve. To illustrate, let me tell you about just one of my leadership heroes:

Cal Peters: Coordinating Resources

Cal Peters was a first-level supervisor in a Chicago factory where Western Electric made steel hardware (cable to hang telephone wire, forged steps for telephone poles, ground rods for electrical protection, etc.). Cal supervised three clerks, and together they planned the production and delivery of hundreds of different items involving many tons of material needed by the different Bell Telephone Companies.

There were no salespeople, just an annual program of production and deliveries that Cal negotiated with each company. Everything worked smoothly unless there was a hurricane somewhere that knocked down telephone lines, a transportation strike occurred so product couldn't be moved, or something else happened to disrupt the orderly manufacture and delivery of the annual program. Then, it was Cal's job to find a way to maintain service to the customer.

One wintery Friday night the TV news carried a report of a major storm hitting Mississippi and Louisiana. Telephone and power lines were down, and damage was widespread. I was manager of the factory and wondered if I could reach Cal to see about setting up an emergency shipment of supplies to the storm areas. His wife answered the phone, and she said Cal had heard the news, canceled a social engagement, and was at the plant. When I reached Cal, he had chartered two cargo planes. Two loads of cable and other outdoor hardware were already on their way to Midway Airport. He was still trying to get through to the local telephone company people to tell them what was coming, when it would arrive, and where they could pick it up. After using what they needed, they were to send the rest back, and we would work out the billing—after the emergency.

The phones were back in service by morning. That's what "Service First" was all about, but it depended on leaders like Cal Peters to know when to pull out the stops and coordinate all the resources necessary to make something happen.

Make your own list of leadership heroes. Then take a moment to reflect why they are heroes, what challenges they have faced (and how they are often the same challenges you face), and how their leadership manifests itself in different dimensions (and how you could be the same kind of leader).

Leadership Training

Because there are so many different ways leadership may assert itself, the trainer planning a leadership development program faces a double dilemma: doing the needs analysis to focus on the right leadership application, and recognizing that there is no simple formula for effective leadership. In this section, *a framework for leadership development* will be *structured around three situational issues: changes in the internal environment of the organization, changes in the external environment, and Why train now?* Change, whether internal or external, often dictates which dimensions of leadership should receive priority attention. Why train now? concerns when a student will apply the lessons learned. (Does the student have leadership responsibilities right now, or is the program part of a longer-range development process, training "tomorrow's leaders"?) The purpose of this section is to provide a diagnostic approach to help the trainer select from the vast array of available resources and plan a program targeted to achieve specific leadership development needs.

Changes in the Internal Environment

In most cases, the place to begin planning leadership development is based on meeting the internal needs of the organization. A model which may be helpful in generalizing the most typical issues of internal change are the familiar four stages of growth and development, as shown in Table 28-3.

Now, let's consider how the dimensions of leadership might apply to each stage of growth and development:

Formative Period. Although there is probably a founding vision (the idea for starting the business in the first place), it is too early to worry about a formal definition of purpose. Even providing direction has to be very flexible because this is a time for experimentation and innovation, and too much directing may hinder creativity and discovery. Likewise, coordinating resources has limited application because the directions are still so tentative. Discovering and overcoming obstacles is where the leadership action is likely to be, looking for breakthroughs.

Rapid-Growth Period. This is the phase where all the dimensions of leadership come into play. With rapid growth, it is time to define the purpose of the

Table 28-3. Growth and Development Stages

I. Formative Period
When a new business is just getting started and the organization and procedures are still in an experimental mode

II. Rapid-Growth Period
When the new business begins to grow and experimentation gives way to a concentration on expansion and evolution of standard procedures

III. Mature Period
When the business has its niche in an established market: sales and profits are stable, but the margin of difference among competitors is narrowing

IV. Declining Period
When the market begins to dry up, creating surpluses in facilities and organizational size as sales decline

business; otherwise, a continuation of the experimental mode will dissipate energy that should be focused on the mainstream business. Providing direction and coordinating resources add structure to the organization to sustain momentum and solidify gains. Since this stage has been achieved because breakthroughs were achieved in the formative period, discovering and overcoming obstacles no longer dominates.

Mature Period. By definition, this is a period of leveling off, where growth has slowed to the pace of the overall economy, and early successes have been consolidated. Now, the challenge is serving an established market and assuring maximum gain while the party lasts. There is still need for direction (more "fine-tuning" than "path finding"), and there may be some new obstacles to deal with, but the main effort will be the coordination of resources—being cautious about commitments which assume further growth, seeking improvements in efficiency, and being more directive about systems and procedures which experience has shown to be most effective.

Declining Period. This is the stage where being the leader isn't much fun. The action agenda is usually downsizing, reorganization, downsizing again, reorganizing again, etc. It calls for a special kind of direction (tough objectives, compassionate implementation) and constant coordination of resources. The hope is that out of the ashes of the old, something new will emerge and the process can begin again, but the leader has to deal with a lot of wounds (some of which are inevitably attributable to his or her actions).

Change and Leadership Style. Earlier in this chapter, the notion of *leadership style* was introduced with the comment that sometimes it is better to have one person as leader than another. Consider the preceding paragraphs, the discussion of how different dimensions of leadership may dominate in different stages of growth and development. Then consider leadership styles. Do you think the kind of leader who is successful guiding the emerging business through its formative period would be as successful (or satisfied) heading up a business in its mature period? Or how about assigning someone who successfully managed a period of rapid growth to "get in there and straighten out" a business that is in its declining period?

Large companies can take advantage of the differences in growth and development stages by assigning managers to jobs where their style is most compatible with a particular part of the organization and its special needs. What should be avoided, or at least handled with a "safety net," is haphazard rotation which mismatches the individual and the job in the belief that this is the way to develop better ideas. As this chapter is intended to show, there are better ways to develop leaders. In smaller companies, there are not the same options. The leaders must adopt to the changing phases of growth; otherwise, they, the company, or both may fail. What the trainer can do for each student and the client organization is help people understand what the new challenges are and where their strengths are most likely to be effective.

Change in Organizational Climate.   During the eighties, many established companies experienced profound changes which caused them to rethink their purpose, establish new directions, discard timeworn procedures, and adopt new ways of doing things. Wherever it happened, it was a bittersweet experience. Some celebrated the change, but a lot more mourned the passing of comfortable, old ways. Corporate education was called upon to help employees understand the change and align themselves with the new directions.

And many companies were schizophrenic about managing change. On one hand, there were moves to reduce the amount of supervision and promote teamwork, self-managing work groups, and risk taking. On the other, there was a push to become "lean and mean" where some very tough dictates treated people roughly and created a "one strike and you're out" climate of uncertainty and fear. Employees often perceived management as saying one thing but practicing something else.

Before starting a leadership development program, the trainer needs to find out how the organization is doing: Have there been changes in corporate direction? Where is the business in the growth and development cycle? What is the prevailing human relations climate? These are factors which determine where leadership development needs to start and where it should be headed. The surest way for leadership development to fail is to be out of touch with the organizational reality in which the new leaders are going to function.

A friend of mine, Lloyd Smigel, is a consultant who has been effective helping large and small organizations to do a better job managing people. When called into a new company, he employs a simple process to decide how to proceed. After being told what the problem is by the internal manager hiring him, Lloyd asks for some time to meet and talk with other managers and workers in the organization. Not infrequently, he hears a somewhat different story about what the "real problem" is and, before proceeding, goes back to the person who gave him the initial charge to revisit the question of what kind of intervention will be productive.

By making an assessment of what kind of internal change the organization is confronting and what the prevailing climate is regarding human relationships (i.e., attitudes about authority, delegation, trust, empowerment, risk, and responsibility), the trainer will have a better foundation on which to plan an appropriate leadership development program.

Changes in the External Environment

A few years ago, we might have focused only on the interplay of internal changes in the business and its impact on management style. Now, externally driven change is rearranging priorities and overturning many assumptions about business and the role of the leader. The preliminary needs analysis should not stop with internal change. External changes may be reshaping the business and may be important to recognize explicitly in leadership development.

As an example, consider what has happened to AT&T. The factory where Cal Peters worked had been regulated out of the business because steel hardware was not in the "talking path" for telecommunication (a regulatory dictate when the Bell System was a regulated monopoly). Then the Bell System was broken apart. The Bell Telephone companies were limited to their monopolies in regional telephone service. AT&T continued to provide long-distance service with competition from companies such as MCI and Sprint and was now free to manufacture any kind of product for any customer. Most recently, AT&T has initiated yet another corporate breakup, mainly involving the separation of service and manufacturing into two distinct corporations. With each change AT&T people have had to rethink what the business is and what the new priorities are.

In the "service first" world of the old Bell System, one leadership priority could be the best use of a "national resource" for the overall good of the telephone-using public (recognizing that this implies both a certain arrogance about what is best for the customer as well as the more laudable commitment to service before profit). After the Bell System breakup, the priorities became meeting the needs of each customer and expanding the business into new markets (e.g., wireless and computers) and new areas (the world). But some important customers of AT&T equipment saw AT&T service as a competitive threat, and this led to the latest decision to form separate service and manufacturing companies.

Change in the way the company operated, how decisions were made, how results were measured, and what constituted good leadership—change in virtually every job—were profound. Training was enlisted to help employees understand and adjust to the new business directions, and leadership curricula were extensively revised to reflect the revolution from bureaucratic monopoly to market-driven competitor.

The changes at AT&T are not unique; with variations, similar revolutions have affected many companies large and small. Consider the impact of personal computers on mainframe computer giants and typewriter manufacturers, of videocassette recorders and independent broadcasters on television networks, of shopping malls and chain retailers on local downtown retailers, of fast-food chains on local restaurants, of new interstate banking regulations on local banks, of government regulations from the Occupational Safety and Health Administration and the Environmental Protection Agency on businesses' operations—the list could go on and on. The changes from without may be emerging long-term trends or they may be sudden and unexpected. They may pose terrible obstacles to staying in business or huge opportunities for growth. Whatever the cause, whether the effect is seen as good or bad, the inescapable consequence is a reordering of priorities, practices, *and leadership.*

Another, greater and more profound impact affecting many, many U.S. companies has been the change from operating in a national market to becoming part of the global economic community. Consider the changes, not just as they affect operations, but also as they create new leadership challenges:

- In many markets, the government is a partner in development and expects to have a voice in certain management decisions. Particularly in developing countries, the business leader must balance the quest for market share and profit with social priorities.

- Different labor rates, different levels of skill and education in the labor pool, different work customs, and different languages must be integrated with traditional, domestic customs and values. The communication of directions and the winning of respect depends on acceptance by a new diverse population of managers, workers, and customers.

- Being global, not merely international, in scope implies the evolution of a global, as opposed to domestic, outlook by everyone in the company, but most people have had no preparation and little, or no, experience with such changes.

These just scratch the surface of changes taking place as the world becomes smaller, more interdependent, and less attuned to doing business "the American Way." Now, more than ever before, a priority in planning leadership development has to be the integration of global issues, communications, customs, and ethics.

If the client organization is changing as a result of external pressures, there is probably a mix of excitement about new opportunities and apprehension about "outsiders taking over." The trainer needs to evaluate how much importance to place on such change in planning a new learning experience.

One of the special niches for leadership development growing out of the globalization of business is the orientation of senior managers brought into the company as the result of mergers or as part of an effort to accelerate the globalization of company planning and operations. The trainer needs to know if the leadership development program is intended to introduce newcomers to the company or to help long-service employees expand their horizons and gain new perspectives; it makes a difference! If the new manager is being brought in as a change agent, the last thing a trainer wants to do is teach him to be an "old boy." It is more appropriate to try to borrow some of a newcomer's time to meet with traditional employees to talk about the kind of experiences and the outlook which made her necessary to the company.

Why Train Now?

Although training the newly hired manager is a special case, it leads into the last consideration the trainer needs to consider in planning a program of leadership development—namely, who is to be trained, or more to the point, why train now? As a generality, there are three major categories to consider: realigning the workforce to a major change, training a newly appointed leader, and preparing selected individuals for future leadership responsibilities.

Realigning the Workforce. The need to realign the workforce occurs when a major change (e.g., a merger, divestiture, globalization) necessitates the rearrangement of traditional procedures and roles to support new directions. The people and their titles may remain the same, but if their relationship to one another is different, if the standards by which their performance is evaluated are different, if the business goals and policies are new, there is a need to redirect leadership development.

A good example would be a commitment to Total Quality Management (TQM) which many companies have made. This process involves more than a few new procedures and reports; it involves a change in outlook, a change in relationships and priorities and, therefore, a change in the way leadership needs to operate.

What is special about realigning the workforce is the scope and timing, if it is to be effective. Virtually everybody needs to participate, and the sooner everyone is attuned to the new direction, the sooner they will begin to function as a team. This kind of training should have as a key design requirement speed of delivery to the widest possible audience.

Training Newly Appointed Leaders. The most straightforward leadership development plan involves training people newly appointed to a job they will be performing right away, e.g., newly promoted supervisors or new middle managers. As a rule, the job expectations are up to date, and doing the needs analysis is based on current knowledge and expectations. To a great extent, such training is a combination of functional skills to manage the business (e.g., how to budget, develop a business plan, monitor results) and the development of interpersonal skills to manage people (e.g., coaching, team building, giving feedback).

One shortcoming of many American companies is the tendency to shortchange leadership development and try to make up the gap with intensive pressure to perform. When this trend involves promoting people into positions of greater leadership responsibility than they once had, a too-frequent scenario is a last-minute decision designating a new manager, accompanied by tremendous pressure for said manager to be on the job, not in some classroom. This approach increases the risk that bad habits will be adopted, and it makes the new manager's team feel like guinea pigs in an experiment to see if the new supervisor is any good.

The prescription is obvious: plan ahead, and make time to help new leaders start with a lead, not a handicap!

Preparing Future Leaders.   The development of future leaders usually begins with a system to select a few high-potential people for executive development, people who someday may bear responsibilities substantially greater than what their current job entails. This is the most expensive kind of training because more development is required to bring the students up to the point where they appreciate the issues being addressed, because there is less certainty about which issues will be important several years hence, and because only some of the people selected will turn out to be the right choice for eventual promotion (or still be with the company when their potential is needed).

Despite these reservations, selective executive programs are often the best educational experiences the company offers. Assuming the executive program is not isolated from the rest of leadership training, a compensating advantage is having a program where more time and a bigger development and outside-speaker budget leads to a flagship model which may set the tone and direction of other more widely distributed programs.

Whether as an alternative or just a better way to piggyback the investment in selective executive development programs, new information technologies offer the promise of options in the development of future leaders that are especially appropriate for any company serious about becoming a continuous-learning organization.

Consider the development of a broader-based delivery system which allows everyone to become aware of emerging trends, stimulates everyone's thinking about how the company could or should react, and gives everyone a chance to be involved in adding to their skill bank so they will be ready when the time comes for them to lead.

New instructional technology has revolutionized what can be done to present issues, work across cultural barriers, and bridge constraints of time and distance. The techniques are being used in skill training. They should be tried as the way to educate (and involve) the whole workforce in the changing developments where the traditional goals are being challenged, where new directions must be charted, where new combinations of resources must be coordinated, and where new obstacles must be overcome. The training challenge is how to reach and develop the full measure of leadership inherent in the entire organization. (The technology that makes customized programs feasible in large companies can be adopted by colleges and independent training services to provide much improved, more convenient executive development opportunities for leaders in companies too small to support in-house programs.)

Wrap-Up

This final section is intended to distill the themes developed earlier and provide some suggestions about the form and substance of leadership training.

The argument has been made that leadership is best understood in terms of outcomes which make the organization more effective. Such outcomes vary according to the challenges the organization must handle to develop and prosper, and leadership is manifest to the extent that the organization's purpose is defined, directions sharpened, resources coordinated, or obstacles overcome. The examples of leadership are always in the context of a particular situation. And, though there may be similarities among cases, each one is different in the following ways: the organization (both its resources and its stage of development), the particular set of changes to be addressed (whether internal or external), and the individual attributes (style) of the leader. Thus, *the essence of leadership development is shared wisdom,* learning by example, then adapting to situations which are never exactly the same.

The learning experience aims at facilitating the impulse to lead, the desire to be in charge, and the need to make something worthwhile happen. It helps people interpret reality. It provides examples of how leadership has made a difference in the outcome. At its best, it helps people learn how to interpret reality and provides a catalog of examples that might be instructive in deciding what action to take. It does not assure the outcome any more than it prescribes a set response.

Leadership wisdom can be shared in a variety of ways: by using role models, case studies, simulations, action learning, or old-fashioned, stand-up presentations. Each technique has value, and a combination may be the best way to plan a curriculum. A few comments may be helpful in deciding which techniques to use:

- The *role model* works best in a stable situation where the experience of a leader is likely to be pertinent to students who aspire to leadership. The most valuable lessons from role models as educators come from their sharing their feelings about the qualitative side of a situation, what it was like to face a particular challenge, not just a rundown of the facts and the outcome of their actions. It may be as instructive to understand the actions they considered and ultimately rejected, or to gain some appreciation of the "political" issues and how they factored these into their decisions. For role models to be effective, they must be leaders who have confronted situations the students are likely to face and who are open to sharing their feelings about why they acted in a certain way.

- *Case studies* need little comment here because they are so widely used. To be most effective, they must be perceived as applicable to the kind of situation the students will face, and if they can be customized to incorporate some of the terms and conditions used in the student's world, so much the better. (See Chap. 24, Case Studies.)

- *Simulations* can be excellent learning experiences because they allow students to model future roles and interact with one another rather than just between student and instructor. The problem with simulations is the high cost of making them realistic and pertinent. On the other hand, there are some simple role-playing experiences that can develop a point very effectively.

  More elaborate simulations where a group of students are assigned roles to "manage a business" are expensive to develop and usually require continuing maintenance to keep them up to date. The advent of computer-based simulations with interactive video seems to be a breakthrough in this type of training. It is still expensive, but it has the potential of reaching a vast audience, which reduces the unit cost. For all the potential defects of various simulation techniques, the form of learning experience is the best way to permit someone to "move into" a new environment and practice new techniques for understanding and acting upon the kind of issues she or he may really face as a leader. (See Chap. 25, Instructional Games, Simulations, and Role-Plays.)

- *Action learning* has received much favorable attention because it builds the learning around real problems brought to the class by the students. The classroom experience gains credibility because people are working on real tasks. The problem is making sure the right kind of issue is brought to the class and that the instructor-facilitator has the skill to improvise his or her "lessons" to meet the planned learning objectives.

- *Stand-up presentations* still have an important place in leadership development programs. They are the fastest way to transmit information from source to receiver. They lend themselves to mass distribution (by video, audio, or the printed word) so they can reach more people, faster. To the student who controls when to watch, listen, or read, they are more user-friendly than a learning program that has to be scheduled and which disrupts the regular routine.

To summarize, the starting point for the trainer is an open exchange with the client about the leadership needs to be addressed. Then it is the trainer's job to plan learning experiences that will meet those needs, providing an understanding of the leadership dimensions, sharing wisdom about best practices for various situations, and helping each person to seek the most appropriate leadership style. A total development curriculum will probably include programs to align people with new company directions, train newly appointed leaders, and develop future leaders. The key to making such programs effective is the organizational commitment that makes the learning experience an integral part of career development, not an afterthought, not something to do if it's not too inconvenient.

This chapter began with the observation that leadership is important to both the organization and to every individual. Moreover, in organizations affected by rapid change, the need for leadership is greater than ever, from the individual responsible for his or her own career to the chief executive responsible for many. No one wants to be the victim of change. Leadership development is where people learn how to be masters of change.

Suggested Reading

Albrecht, Karl, with Steven Albrecht, *The Creative Organization*, Dow Jones-Irwin, Homewood, IL, 1987.

Bennis, Warren, *On Becoming a Leader*, Addison-Wesley, Reading, MA, 1989.

Champy, James, *Reengineering Management: The Mandate for New Leadership*, Harper Business, New York, 1995.

Kanter, Rosabeth Moss, *The Change Masters*, Simon and Schuster, New York, 1983.

Maccoby, Michael, *The Leader*, Simon and Schuster, New York, 1981.

McDermott, Lynda C., *Caught in the Middle*, Prentice Hall, Englewood Cliffs, NJ, 1992.

Rhinesmith, Stephen H., *Globalization*, ASTD, Alexandria, VA, 1993.

Senge, Peter M., *The Fifth Discipline*, Doubleday, New York, 1990.

Smigel, Lloyd M., *Management Plus*, Lowell House, Los Angeles, 1994.

Toffler, Alvin, *Power Shift*, Bantam, New York, 1990.

29

Organization Development and Change

Glenn H. Varney

Glenn H. Varney *is a professor of management, director of the Master of Organization Development program, director of the Institute for Organizational Effectiveness at Bowling Green State University, and president of Management Advisory Associates, Incorporated. He is also the founder of the Self-Directed Work Team Resource Center. Varney is nationally recognized in the field of organization development and change as an author, educator, and consultant. He has authored over 50 articles in professional journals and five books. His most recent books include* Goal Driven Management, *1988, and* Building Productive Teams, *1989. He has two new books in progress:* Productivity Improvement *and* Skilled Change. *He is the author of* Self-Directed Work Teams: A Concise Guide to Understanding and Implementing Self-directed Work Teams. *Varney has consulted internationally with major U.S. and foreign companies and is a frequent speaker at professional meetings including those of ASTD and the Association of Quality and Participation. He received the Organization Development Award for Excellence Leadership within the OD Professional Practice Area from ASTD in 1992 and 1994. His areas of specialization include building productive teams, designing organizational change strategies, designing and retrofitting world-class organizations, organization analysis and problem diagnosis, "visioning" for future organizations, assessing and developing management competencies, and implementing self-directed work teams.*

At no time since the industrial revolution have society's attitudes about work undergone such intensive scrutiny, debate, and change. Evidence of this change is everywhere and has been recorded and discussed in a flood of articles, books, and reports. The world we face in the future is well described as follows:

> Corporations based in the United States face increasing pressures in the 1990's. In industry after industry, senior managers are dealing with conditions that make success more elusive. The days of easy and effortless global dominance by United States firms clearly have passed, replaced by conditions that require executives to use every possible tool at their disposal to create and maintain effectiveness. These conditions create the need to develop new architecture of organizations.[1]

U.S. managers are facing major changes in the culture of organizations. To the dismay of many managers, they find that their knowledge, skills, and techniques are not in tune with what has been described by Allan Filley as the second "Great Age of Social Experimentation."[2] They are faced with acquiring new managerial competencies and skills which involve learning to manage in a way which will successfully change the nature of work. Thus, in virtually every organization, those persons charged with responsibility for organizational change are seeking new and improved skills as well as a better understanding of the complex and changing nature of organizations.

One of the visible recent responses is the emergence of organization development (OD) as a framework for study within which professional managers, researchers, and academics alike can come to grips with the complexities involved in organizing and managing human resources. Four factors are involved in the evolving practice of OD:

1. It is a long-range effort to introduce planned change on a diagnosis which is shared by the members of an organization.

2. An OD program usually involves an entire organization or a coherent system or parts thereof.

3. Its goal is to increase organizational effectiveness and enhance organizational choice in self-renewal.

4. The major strategy of OD is to intervene in the ongoing activities of the organization, facilitate learning, and to make choices about alternative ways to proceed.

Definition of OD

Describing OD has always been difficult to do, particularly for persons unfamiliar with OD. There are at least four accepted definitions:[3]

1. OD is a planned change effort evolving the total system managed from the top to increased organizational effectiveness through planned interventions using behavioral science knowledge. (Richard Beckhard)

2. Using knowledge and techniques from the behavioral sciences, Organization Development attempts to integrate individual needs for growth and development with organizational goals and objectives in order to make more effective organizations. (National Training Laboratories Institute)

3. OD is a process of planned organizational change which centers around a change agent, who in collaboration with a client's systems, attempts to apply valued knowledge from the behavioral sciences to client problems. (Warren Bennis)

4. Achieving an idea of corporate excellence toward which to strive and perfecting a sound system of management which can convert ideas into action. (Blake and Mouton)

The key words in these four definitions are:

Planned change

Total company

Increased organizational effectiveness

Interventions

Behavioral science knowledge

Individual needs and company goals

Change agent

All four of these definitions revolve around a common element: the concept of *change*. In short, OD involves an understanding and study of organizations to assure systematic change is followed, as opposed to just letting it happen.

OD makes use of the social and behavioral sciences. The change agent is the person who serves as the catalyst of the change process. She or he may be an internal or external consultant, a manager, in an organization. For purposes of this discussion, think of the manager as a change agent. Knowingly or not, every manager is responsible in some way for bringing about change in the organization.

A major corporation in the United States defines its OD approach as

> a plan for applying appropriate resources to organization revitalization....It is a planned intervention in the ongoing management process with the explicit intent of applying new knowledge, new technology, new resources, and new individual organizational authenticity to the achievement of the organization's goals in a dynamic and uncertain environment....[The objective of the program is to] increase earnings now...[and] to do so in such a way that the organization's capacity for continued growth and earnings is within its own control....[In addition, their OD program is] a means of changing the management process from one of dependence to one of autonomy based on the utilization of total technical and human resources.

This particular company does not think of OD as a programmatic effort. On the contrary, they see it as management in an organizational renewal effort being conducted on a continuing basis.

Many organizations throughout the world, such as Motorola, General Motors, Procter & Gamble, and General Electric, have OD departments and staff that manage systematic change. The OD functions in organizations come under many different banners such as organization effectiveness, change management, and continuous improvement. The core purpose of OD units is almost always to help the organization make smooth transitions from their current state to some desired future state.

Like other areas in the field of management practices, OD is based on a variety of different professionals' disciplines, the most popular being psychology, organizational behavior, sociology, and interpersonal communication. Because of this widespread basis, the practitioners in OD are required to have working knowledge of such subject areas as

Organization theory   Motivational theory

Learning process theory   Personality theory

Organization structure	Role theory
Power and authority	Leadership
Interpersonal dynamics	Small-group theory

A combination of forces stemming from societal, technical, and system changes require managers and practitioners in organizations to be more aware, responsive, and able to bring about change in accomplishing their organization's basic objectives and tasks as well as in meeting the desire for human fulfillment now being expressed throughout U.S. society.

History of OD

French describes the early history of OD as follows:[4]

> Organization development programs emerged about 1957 and have at least three origins. One origin centers around the late Douglas McGregor's work with Union Carbide in an effort to apply some of the concepts and insights from laboratory training to a large system.
>
> The second origin centers around a headquarters human relations research group at the Esso Company. About the same year Douglas McGregor was beginning to work with Union Carbide, the Esso group began to view itself as an internal consulting group offering services to field managers, rather than as a research group writing reports for top management. In addition, with the help of Robert Blake and Herb Shepard, this group began to offer laboratory training in the refineries of Esso.
>
> Certainly a third origin of OD stems from the experience that researchers were gaining at the Survey Research Center at the University of Michigan in the use of attitude surveys and in feeding back survey results in an effort to change organizations. For example, Howard Baumgartel reported some research in 1959 which, in retrospect, was an article of very good insight on OD. In his conclusions he stated,
>
> "The results of this experimental study lend support to the idea that intensive group discussion procedure for utilizing the results of an employee questionnaire survey can be an effective tool for introducing positive change in a business organization. It may be that the effectiveness of this method, in comparison to traditional training courses, is that it deals with the system of human relationships as a whole (superior and subordinate can change together) and it deals with each manager, supervisor, and employee in the context of his own job, and his own problems, and his own work relationships."[5]
>
> At the present time, OD efforts are becoming visible in England, Norway, Sweden, Holland, Japan, Canada and perhaps other countries, as well as in the United States. They are appearing in a wide range of kinds of institutions, including business firms, schools, police departments, and hospitals.

Models of Systematic Change

OD relies on orderly change—change which has been planned and thoughtfully executed thereby assuring that the end results have been achieved without unforeseen or undesirable results. Those who practice OD use what is commonly called "action research." Action research means systematic analysis of organizations in order to understand the nature of the problems and forces within the organization. Furthermore, it means using the organization's own resources to solve problems and to change the organization. An example of one such action research is as follows.

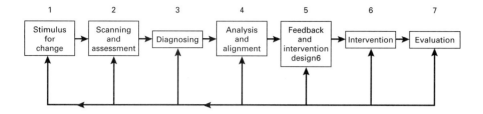

Models for organizational analysis abound in OD and they serve a very important function. They provide a framework for studying organizations based on known theories of how organizations operate. The practice of OD would indeed falter were it not for the models available in the field.

A Framework for Analysis

Models are used in most any endeavor or facets of our lives. For example, when an automobile is undergoing a new design, the architects always develop a model prior to the actual production process. Physicians doing diagnostic workups use a conceptual model of the illnesses using the symptoms as indicators of the illness. Models are used to design clothing. They are used to explain human activities; they're found in psychology to describe personalities. Models in general are very useful. They guide us in our search for information and understanding.

The value of a model for systematic change are many:

1. A model serves to guide a person through a series of steps. In this way one is assured of not overlooking some aspect or failing to carefully analyze or study some particular part of the problem.

2. A model assures that attention is given to each step in proportion to its value to the total result. It is not uncommon for humans to emphasize one aspect of life or a particular problem and to deemphasize another. The model also serves to place proper emphasis at the most important and least important points.

3. Management, like any other field, has a strong need for systematic analysis. Systematic analysis is applied rigorously in the technical aspects of business where we apply computer technology, engineering technology, and so forth. It often does not show up in management practice. Therefore, a model assures managers of a more careful analysis, resulting in more accurate and correct decisions relative to the social-technical equation.

4. As in project management, models serve a manager by providing a tracking method for following the progress of change. For example, well-conceived models can be used in developing critical-path plans for implementing change.

5. One of the least understood but most important values in a model is its utility in selling management on the need for change as well as the way in which the change is going to be managed. The advantage is the appearance of being organized and not "shooting from the hip." It gives the impression of doing your homework and having systematically examined the problem.

6. Explaining the need for change as well as exactly what is going to be done is more readily accomplished when a specific model of change is used.

Probably there are other reasons to justify the use of a systematic model for change; it suffices to say that any model used is better than no model at all.

Goals of Change: Improving Results and Outputs

Any time a change is made in an organization, it has the underlying purpose of improving the way the organization is functioning. In simpler terms, to increase productivity of a unit, group, or an organization is the primary basis for change. Without the end result of improved productivity, there would be no need to change.

The following model emphasizes effectiveness of the organization, both from the perspective of efficient technology as well as efficient human performance, resulting in both high productivity and high satisfaction. It involves a smooth intermeshing of technical-human management of the organization.

The Change Process Model

The model which we propose is laid out in Fig. 29-1. The following is a brief description of each of the stages and associated steps.

Stage 1. In stage 1 we have identified separate segments of change associated with assessing the need for change and selling change goals within the organization. The steps involve conducting a *preliminary scan* of the organization to generate a problem statement or hypothesis statement which results in a series of questions to be answered for a particular problem or change objective to be accomplished. In one client situation the manager was seen walking down the hall alone. As he progressed through the corridors, employees would step into their offices in order to avoid him. Then after he had passed they would come back out into the hall. It's the kind of observation that is important to note along with many other notable activities, all of which help the OD practitioner develop ideas about what's going on in the organization.

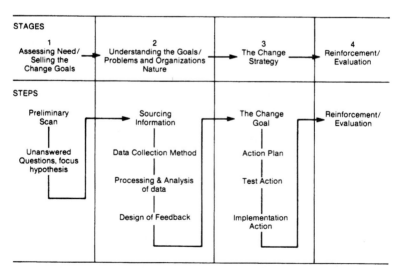

Figure 29-1. Change process model.

Stage 2.   Stage 2 attempts to understand the hypothesis and problems within the organization such that there is reasonable assurance that the correct targets have been identified and the problem clearly defined to avoid errors in the implementation of an intervention. This stage involves sourcing information within the organization—in other words, first, determining where the needed information is located; second, developing methods of obtaining and actually collecting the needed information; third, processing and analyzing the data; and, fourth, designing a feedback process for explaining what the data says and how it answers the specific questions outlined in stage 1.

Stage 3.   Stage 3 involves design of a change strategy designed to bring about the desired adjustments and changes within the organization. There are four steps involved:

1. Preparation of the change goal. Here we are attempting to clearly define what it is that we are trying to change in terms of behaviors, practices, and new assets.
2. Development of the action plan
3. Testing the action plan—to make sure that it is the correct action and that it meets the change goals
4. Implementing the action

Stage 4.   Stage 4 involves reinforcement and evaluation of the change. In this stage the change agent is required to develop reinforcing mechanisms and also to develop evaluation methods. The purpose of the evaluation is to assess the degree to which the change strategy has actually brought about the desired change. In other words, to what degree has the problem been solved or the goal met?

   The model at this point gives an overview of the change process. As each stage is presented, specific skills required for successful implementation of that stage will be cited.

   We stress that a practicing manager or a student of management need not be fully qualified to use all the skills required at each stage. It is common practice in organizations to ask for assistance in specific areas as needed. For example, if statistical knowledge is required, you could call upon a statistical quality-control analyst or a systems analyst to assist you. It is a commonly accepted belief, however, that managers must know enough about each of the skills to know when to seek assistance. All too often managers avoid a particular aspect of the change process because they do not have the needed skills and expertise.

How to Use a Change Model

The application of a model as a part of a systematic change management has been emphasized several times. Change must be carefully conceived and systematically implemented. Several points need to be made regarding how to use a model:

1. A model can serve as a basis for laying out a project for change or it can become the framework for a proposal for change.
2. The model can be used as a roadmap for change. It guides the manager and members of the organization through the change process in a step-by-step systematic way.

3. The model can serve as a reminder of the need for a systematic discipline of change. Frequently managers and students of change do not apply adequate discipline to the change process, dismissing rigor as unnecessary and not accepted within the organization. Other excuses for not being systematic include "it is too costly," "it leads to incorrect decisions," and "we don't have time to think through what we need to do."

4. Whenever change starts to take place, you must recognize that you are entering into a *destabilizing process*. This fact simply means that none of the variables, factors, or conditions will remain constant. Managers clearly see that there is a start and a finish to any change process—but its endpoints are illusive. Because of the abstract nature of our thinking, this beginning-ending conception is probably a necessary one. However, it is almost impossible to point to exactly where change starts and where it finishes.

As you work with the change process you must always keep in mind that when you initiate a particular aspect of change you are automatically affecting other aspects. In the process of using the model you need to recognize that factors are in a constant state of change and that the evaluation of each aspect or stage of the change process must be carefully reviewed. For instance, when you start to implement an action plan in stage 3, you begin immediately to change the definition of the problem identified in stage 1. The change agent must continuously reexamine the questions asked, the problem definition, and the resulting decisions.

Other Models

In the preceding section we introduced a change process model designed to assist change agents in systematic change analysis. OD abounds with diagnostic and explanatory models designed to guide practitioners in the process of change. Our purpose in this section is not to list all of these models, but to simply give you some other options.

Weisbord's Six-Box Model

Marvin M. Weisbord of Organizational Research and Development has designed a six-box diagnostic model. The model is portrayed in Fig. 29-2.[7]

The six boxes are purpose, structure, relationship, reward, helpful mechanisms, and leadership. These constitute the internal factors which the organization seeks to keep in balance. In general the organization as a whole, and each of its various subunits, must do something about each of these six factors. What it does and how it does it will depend to some extent on its environment. Basically the environment means forces difficult to control from inside that demand a response from the organization. Such forces include customers, government, unions, students, families, friends, and so forth. It is not always clear where the boundaries are between the external and internal environment. Basically the *purposes* of the organization include such things as goal clarity and agreement on goals by members of the organization. What is the organization attempting to do and where is it attempting to go? *Structure* has to do with the way in which the organization is put together. Common factors here include functions to be performed, products and services offered, and how they are to be combined into a cohesive organization which makes it possible to accomplish the goals stated under the heading of purpose.

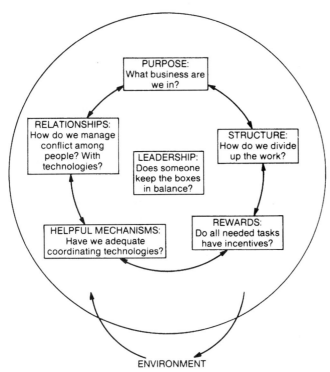

Figure 29-2. The six-box organizational model. Visualize this figure as a radar screen. Just as air controllers use radar to chart the course of aircraft—height, speed, distance apart, and weather—those seeking to improve an organization will observe relationships among the boxes and not focus on any particular blip.

Relationships are basically among people such as peers, boss, and subordinate; among units within the organization; and between people and their technologies.

Rewards have to do with satisfying the personal needs of people, including physiological safety, belongingness, esteem, and personal growth.

Helpful mechanisms simply mean having the technologies and systems in place within the organization to make it possible to accomplish things.

Leadership, as the word implies, means the ability the leaders have to direct the organization in a way which makes it cohesive, coherent, and able to perform the task needed to accomplish its goals.

A Social-Technical Model

Any organization is comprised of three basic components: the technical component, the linking component, the social component. These three major systems must interface and function efficiently and coherently for the organization to accomplish its objectives. The social-technical systems (STS) model is shown in Fig. 29-3.

Figure 29-3. Basic organizational system.

A *technical system* comprises factors such as the physical facility, the equipment, the materials, the manufacturing systems, the flow of materials, the layout of the plant, lighting, and the physical environment in general.

A *social system* comprises the individuals within the organization, the subgroups within the organization, the informal organization, interpersonal relationships, and the personal needs and wants of each individual.

The *linking system* is made up of the leadership in the organization, the procedures and practices and policies, the organizational structure and any factors needed to combine the technical system with the social system in order to achieve the objectives of the organization.

This approach to organizational analysis is a simple way of characterizing the factors which must be taken into consideration when one analyzes how a particular organization functions. A misfit between any one of the systems can create a problem with or an incongruity among organizational functions. The practitioner using a model such as the one in Fig. 29-3 looks for inconsistencies and breakdown. Also this model can be used for tracking or mapping to look for the cause-and-effect relationships of problems. The STS model provides a convenient way of going to the source of the problem. Or it can be used as an organizational planning model. When thinking about change, for example, of a physical layout of a plant, this model can be used to track the impact that the change will have on the social as well as the linking system.

STS is most valuable as changes are being planned. An example is when a major organization initiated an energy conservation program by turning off half the lights, cutting the heat back in the cooler months, and raising the air-conditioning level in the summer (change in technical systems) with no foresight of how the social system (people) would react. At the end of one year energy costs went up 10 percent, not down as planned. Why? Because people adjusted to the problem by bringing in lamps, heaters, and fans.

The two models we have presented represent only a fraction of the models available. Others are Hornstein and Tichy's Emergent Pragmatic Model, Lawrence and Lorshs' Contingency Models, Levenson's Clinical Historical Approach, and Nadler's System Model, to mention a few.

Organizational practitioners will find the STS model to be very helpful in two ways: (1) as a means of assuring that systems diagnosis is done in an orderly way, (2) it is a way to communicate clearly and concisely with the client organization.

OD Interventions and Techniques

In this section we will discuss various techniques and approaches used in OD. The approaches described are not the only ones available. Also, depending on the organization and the consultant using it, a given approach may be known by more than one name. The purpose is to give a general idea of the techniques and approaches. To assist in implementing changes, this section concludes by giving an example of how a strategy can be built using OD techniques.

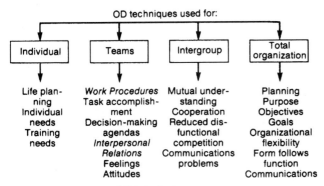

Figure 29-4. Use of OD techniques.

Fig. 29-4 illustrates a variety of OD techniques. Different approaches are recommended for different problems, groups, and levels within an organization. No attempt will be made to go into detail; however, the definitions and explanations which follow should help in understanding the techniques.

Interventions come in many shapes and sizes and they include programs like Diversity Training, TQM activities, Quality Circles, Team Building, etc. All interventions are designed and focused to help change something in the organization, most often in the social systems.

Descriptions of OD Intervention Technique

Six distinct OD intervention techniques follow.

1. Laboratory Training. This type of intervention ranges in length from two or three days to two weeks. It is aimed primarily at giving participants a better understanding of what makes them tick and what makes groups function as they do, as well as a greater understanding of interpersonal and intergroup communication. The focus can vary from great emphasis on organizational values and problems to great emphasis on inter- and intraindividual values and problems.

Strangers Laboratory. Participants are usually from different organizations and may include both men and women. Participants commonly have widely varying backgrounds, skills, professions, and trades.

Cousins Laboratory. Participants are from the same business, educational, and governmental organization, but usually no bosses are in the same group with subordinates and no two people are from the same work subgroup.

Family Laboratory. Usually includes the manager and the people reporting directly to him or her. It sometimes includes other key people in the manager's organization.

2. Team Building. The focus is on early identification and solution of the work group's problems, particularly the interpersonal and organizational roadblocks which stand in the way of the team's collaborative, cooperative, creative, competent functioning.

Establishing New Teams. The focus is upon the participants and the manager developing a common framework and common goals within which they can work, also on identifying problems which would prevent team members from working with one another. Examples of such teams are task forces and proposal teams.

Strengthening Existing Teams. This activity looks back over the recent past to determine what the strengths and the problems have been in the way the organization has conducted their business to develop action plans to solve the problems and to capitalize on the unit's strengths.

Reforming Teams. Much like establishing new teams, but here many of the participants have worked with or perhaps even for one another (e.g., because of mergers and acquisitions). The focus is on problems the participants anticipate will develop in working together.

3. Diagnostic Techniques. The main thrust here is diagnostic, i.e., to find out what the problems are with little emphasis on solutions.

Vertical Sensing. This activity involves interviewing, usually in small groups, an entire vertical slice of an organization to find out the nature of the main problems and the degree to which these problems are felt or make waves at the different levels within the organization. As nearly as possible the interviewers all report to one another in a vertical slice and should be able to discuss the impact of problems as they are understood and felt in the various levels in the organization. This procedure can be carried below the exempt-salaried level through the entire organization to the least-skilled employee.

Horizontal Sensing. This activity is usually done in small groups on a random basis but participants come from no more than three or four levels in the organization, as contrasted with vertical sensing. The focus is upon identifying problems most relevant for a general grouping of people such as middle-level managers, engineers, manufacturing specialists, etc. Though people at several levels are pulsed, participants in any one meeting are usually from only one or two organizational levels.

Division Consulting Teams. This type of team is usually made up of a division's general manager, its personnel manager, and an outside consultant. The latter is someone skilled in organizational development technology, usually on a university faculty or with a private consulting firm. Sometimes the outside consultant is an expert from within the company but not from the particular group or division utilizing the consultants. This team meets regularly, usually monthly, to discuss the current climate or health of the division, to review effectiveness of ongoing personnel programs, to spot new problems, and to plan future actions.

Organizational Mirroring. In this technique, people from a number of functional units within the organization are interviewed to gain a comprehensive picture of how one of those units appears in the eyes of the others. For example: A manufacturing organization wants to know more about how it is viewed by others—what its interface problems are. A sample of people in manufacturing are interviewed to determine how they see themselves and how they assess their relations with other units. Then people from the other organizations with whom manufacturing must work (sales, engineering, personnel, etc.) are interviewed to determine how they see manufacturing. When these results are combined, manufacturing can see from the data how they appear to the other organizations as well as how they see themselves.

4. Intergroup Meetings. This mechanism is primarily a problem-solving one. Such meetings are usually held when problems are known to exist and have become somewhat acute. The focus is on putting the cards on the table in such a way that the really difficult hang-ups are spotlighted and solutions, with time lines, are proposed.

Subgroups of an Organization. An example of a problem with subgroups would be when the sales engineers in a sales unit are technically trained as engineers but have been making promises to the customers about engineering changes in the product without the knowledge of the people in the engineering unit. The focus meeting would be on what kind of damage is being done and how this damage can be minimized or avoided.

Line and Staff. Examples of difficulties here are frequent and need not be cited. Because of the nature of their work, line and staff people frequently (though most inadvertently) step on each other's toes. From time to time, meetings are in order to help clear the air between them.

Customers. This is perhaps the most difficult intergroup meeting to design. Usually if the buyer is willing to talk, the customer is not—and vice versa. These meetings should be designed carefully, and a high level of skill is required. Potentially, however, its payoffs can be among the highest.

5. Third-Party Facilitation. This type of intervention involves the use of a knowledgeable, sensitive, and skilled third person to help diagnose, understand, and resolve the problems. Usually the helping mode is that of the consultant working intensively with the manager to help him or her work through some particularly difficult problems which he or she has encountered.

Improving Managerial Effectiveness. An example of this type of third-party facilitation would be a manager who is unsure of her impact on others, or perhaps of how efficiently she uses time, inviting a third person to be with her for half a day or a day. The manager's job is business as usual. The consultant's job is to observe and listen to the content and the process of everything the manager does during that time period. Then the consultant and the manager go back over the consultant's notes and the two discuss the manager's style and possible ways it could be improved.

Debriefing Staff Meetings. A manager should regularly use the last 10 or 15 minutes of staff meetings to ask those present what they thought of the staff meeting and how it might be improved. From time to time, the manager might find it helpful to ask a third party to sit in. Preferably the third party would be someone who knows the group and has a level of acceptance in the group. This person's job is to observe how the staff meeting is conducted and how the members of the staff interact. The observer often provides feedback to the group and to the manager at the end of the meeting.

In this section we have presented some commonly used interventions, techniques, and approaches used in organizational development. Sources of information listing the thousands of others can be found in the resources list at the end of this chapter.

Role of an OD Practitioner

In this section the role of an OD practitioner will be discussed. OD practitioners are those individuals who devoted most of their time to helping organizations improve and change. Cummings and Worley note that "although many authors have described the personal qualities of change agents, little empirical research has been done on OD practitioners."[8] OD practitioners may describe their experiences, conjecture what the traits of a successful OD professional are, and even define the appropriate styles individuals should use in varying situations. But there exists no detailed, empirically based analysis of the skills and competencies needed to succeed as an OD practitioner. The limited documentation of OD competencies falls largely into the category of defining dos and don'ts practices, specific traits or talents, and various rules of thumb for change agents.[9] In the absence of empirically based data we must rely on the judgments and opinions of experienced practitioners as our starting point.

Cummings and Worley identify the following eight personal styles and philosophies as important characteristics for OD professionals: (1) ability to assess themselves accurately; (2) objectivity; (3) imagination; (4) flexibility; (5) honesty; (6) consistency; (7) trust; and (8) stable and secure self-image. Cotton, Brown, and Golembiewski identify neutrality, open-mindedness, and flexibility of processing information as the personal qualities necessary to practice OD successfully.[10]

Margulies and Wallace suggest several aspects of the OD practitioner's behavior that are important to success. These include: (1) facilitating the diagnosis of problems; (2) assisting the clear statement and communication of problems; (3) pointing out those things not seen or said by the client; (4) facilitating the formulation of change plans; (5) acting as an integrator; and (6) providing internal continuity.[11]

A distillation of various perspectives of what OD practitioners do and of the skills and competencies necessary suggests two types of definition for competent OD professionals. We can define such people by, first, identifying the traits and characteristics they should possess, and second, by defining the activities they need to know. Based on the failure of the trait approach to predict successful behavior in other fields I believe it cannot succeed in defining or distinguishing competent performances in OD.

The definition of activities and knowledge holds more promise. A distillation of the literature yields the following list:

1. *Self-awareness and personal impact awareness.* Ability to sense organizational needs and generate organizational and individual awareness of need for change.

2. *Conceptual, analytical, and research skills.* Ability to link scientific and organizational information; ability to research and diagnose problems within the organization; ability to evaluate with the client the results of the change process.

3. *Change and influence skills.* Stimulating the organization to change; facilitating and assisting the organization to change; following up and providing continuity of direction.

Developing OD Competencies

The three categories cited in the preceding section represent a starting point for defining the major developmental areas. But what content should each area cover, and how is a learning sequence organized that provides systematic acquisition of both knowledge and skills? We can organize the three areas as illustrated in Fig. 29-5.

This diagram attempts to describe the three areas in relationship to the individual and the organization involved. Let us define the three areas in more detail.

Figure 29-5. OD knowledge and skills.

Self- and Impact Awareness

The skills which appear to fall into the self- and impact awareness category are listed below.

Self-Awareness.   Self-awareness refers to being aware of one's own set of values, beliefs, ideas, general emotional state, intellect, and all those things that make up the total person, being aware of how these things interact within the individual as well as how they are stimulated from outside the person.

Self-Awareness in Relationship to Others.   This skill area has to do with the impact an individual has on others and being aware of the other people's reactions.

Interpersonal Awareness.   This set of skills has to do with the awareness of transactional and associated consequences growing out of the interpersonal relationships.
  Personality Theory.   This set of skills involves being knowledgeable about personality models and how personality theories can be useful in understanding human behavior.
  Group Theory.   These skills comprise being knowledgeable of how groups of people work together and what group dynamics can contribute to OD practice.
  Organizational Theory.   Organizational theory attempts to integrate various behavioral theories. The line manager needs to develop an awareness of theoretical organizational constructs already developed.

Conceptual, Analytical, and Research Skills

The general category of conceptual, analytical, and research skills involved the following basic skills and competencies.

Theory Building.   Line managers need to be able to theorize about what's happening in organizations. Such theories help managers make predictions about the organization.

Theoretical Mapping.   Assuming that the line manager has knowledge about the organization, group, and personality theories, theoretical mapping simply takes that theory and applies it to the organization, describing the organization in terms of known theories.

Concept Model Building.   This skill involves the ability to conceptualize and design mental as well as graphic models of what an organization is like and in particular ways in which the organization can be conceptualized differently from what it is today.

System Analysis and Organizational Diagnosis.   As the title implies, this skill involves being able to analyze the interaction between systems such as the technical and social systems and being able to design methodologies and procedures for collecting information about the organization.

Data Processing.   Here a line manager needs to be able to assemble data which has been collected and apply statistical techniques to test hypotheses, thus assuring valid and meaningful information about the organization.

Feedback and Presentation.   This skill has to do with the ability that a person has to develop approaches to feed back information to the organization.

Organizational Change and Influence Skills

Finally, the basic organizational change and influence skills are as follows:

Change Strategy Design.   This skill involves the ability to design basic strategies for helping the organization change. This undertaking is to be differentiated from the actual use of specific interventions such as team building and confrontation meetings.

Intervention Design.   In this skill area we are referring to the specific activities which a manager uses to help the organization learn about itself and about the impact of change. This includes the full spectrum of experience-based exercises.

Persuasion-Power.   Managers need to develop skills as well as being able to know how to use the power of a consultant, either internal or external, to help the organization or to influence the organization to change.

Facilitation-Process Skills.   These skills are commonly thought of when one thinks about OD: the ability to "help" the organization and to facilitate changes. These are commonly referred to as "process skills."

Intervention Styles.   This skill area involves an awareness of the different styles which can be used to interact with the organization and the adaptability of the manager to the particular needs of the organization.

Teaching and Educative Skills.   These skills have to do with the ability to conduct "standup" teaching, both cognitively or experientially.

Although we have no doubt left out some areas which may be important to the well-rounded development of a manager, we have tried to cover the most important areas.

OD Assessment and Planning

Now that the basic skills that appear to be important to the development of OD competencies have been discussed, the question logically follows: "How do I know where I stand in my own development?" For your convenience, I have included a completed developmental skill-assessment scale in Fig. 29-6. You can use Fig. 29-7 to complete your own skill-assessment scale.

Caution should be used since you may misjudge your own skill levels. Thus it is suggested that those who are interested in a clearer picture of the level to which they are developing OD competencies and skills should invite comments from others who observe them in practice. In this way you will develop a broader perspective and develop a clearer picture of your level of OD skill development.

The skill-assessment scale also offers space for jotting down comments and suggestions on how you might develop your skills and competencies. There are four assumptions that typically underlie most individual development and these need to be questioned. These might be termed the traditional set of assumptions. They are as follows:

Figure 29-6. Completed skill-assessment scale.

Figure 29-7. Skill-assessment scale.

1. The most popular program is the best program to attend. By this I mean attending the program which most people attend.

2. It's good to way, "I've been there." It's nice to be able to associate with other OD managers, and say, for example, "I've been to the University Associates program on…"

3. All training is good and helpful regardless of whether it's directly on target or not.

4. Programmatic training is the main resource and should be utilized fully.

These assumptions lead to a rather fragmented developmental process which may be good for managers in terms of their association with other managers but tend to be weak and insufficient when it comes to professional development. For this reason I would like to pose another set of assumptions which seem realistic in terms of our day-to-day world:

1. Development of OD skills comes through a variety of different kinds of experiences. They are not limited to just programmatic experiences.

2. Developing OD skills involves a variety of different things. Individuals desiring to learn how to be more effective OD managers need to develop them-

selves through a variety of different approaches taking full advantage of all types of different ways of increasing their competencies and skills.

3. OD involves skills and behaviors specific to the activities where the skill and behavior is going to be applied. It is of little value to develop a set of skills which will never be used. It would be like learning how to speak Spanish and never having the opportunity to use it. Therefore, whatever skills you decide to acquire, they should be developed in an environment where they can be applied.

OD may or may not be regarded as a profession in the same sense as psychology, sociology, medicine, and so forth. However, it is highly likely that professionals in all fields will be required to develop organizational change skills. Whether or not the field of OD continues to grow may largely depend on its application to the general management of organizations, to the kinds of people who practice in the field and the ability they have to influence and successfully assist organizations in changing. What all this amounts to is that if you desire to practice in the field of OD, you need to be aware of the kind of skills and competencies required for success.

In this chapter we have attempted to provide the reader with a concise overview of organization development. The field is expanding rapidly, requiring a continuous updating of knowledge and skills. To keep abreast of these changes is the responsibility of a person professing to be a change agent, whether an OD practitioner or a manager.

Resources

Various universities and colleges throughout the United States have programs designed to train OD practitioners. Several are:

The American University
Institute for Human Resources Development
215 Ward Circle
Washington, DC 20016
Degree: AU/NTL Master's Degree in
Human Resource Development

Boston University
School of Management
685 Commonwealth Ave.
Boston, MA 02215
Degree: D.B.A. in OB or OD
Ph.D. in Social Psychology OD
Concentration

Bowling Green State University
College of Business Adm.
Dept. of Management
Bowling Green, OH 43403
Degree: Master's in O.D.

Brigham Young University
Dept. of Organization Behavior
790 TNRB
Provo, UT 84602
Degree: Master's in OB

Case Western Reserve University
Dept. of Organizational Behavior
Cleveland, OH 44106
Degree: M.S. in OD and Analysis
OD (open only to people who live and
work full-time in N.E. Ohio)

Columbia University
Teachers College, Box 6
525 W. 120th St.
New York, NY 10027
Degree: M.A. in Organization Psychology
(doctoral program planned)

Eastern Michigan University
Department of Management
504 Pray-Harrold
Ypsilanti, MI 48197
Degree: M.S.O.D.: Master's of Science in
Organization Behavior and
Development

The Fielding Institute
226 East de La Gucara
Santa Barbara, CA 93101
Degree: M.A. in OD (Ph.D. in OD planned)

George Washington University
School of Government and Business
  Administration
Washington, DC 20052
Degree: D.B.A., M.B.A.

Loyola University
Program in Community & OD
820 North Michigan Ave.
Chicago, IL 60611
Degree: M.A. in Community and OD

Massachusetts Institute of Technology
  (MIT)
Sloan School of Management
50 Memorial Dr.
Cambridge, MA 02139
Degree: Ph.D. in OB, M.S. in Management
  (Organization Studies)

New York State University
Graduate School of Business
  Administration
90 Trinity Place
New York, NY 10006
Degree: M.B.A. in OD

Pepperdine University
School of Business and Management
3415 Sepulveda Blvd.
Los Angeles, CA 90034
Degree: M.S. in OD

Purdue University
School of Management
Krannert Building
W. Lafayette, IN 47907
Degree: Ph.D. in Organization Behavior

University of New Hampshire
Whittemore School of Business
McConnell Hall
Durham, NH 03824
Degree: M.B.A. (OD Concentration second
  year)

University of West Florida
School of Business
Pensacola, FL 32514
Degree: Master's of OD

Associations and groups specifically involved in organization development are listed below:

Academy of Management OD/C Division
Ohio Northern University
P.O. Box 39
300 S. Union St.
Ada, OH 45810

*Academy of Management–OD Division
  Newsletter*
R. Wayne Boss, Editor
University of Colorado
Campus Box 473
Boulder, CO 80309

American Society for Training and
  Development
Curtis E. Plott, Exec. Dir.
1630 Duke St., Box 1443
Alexandria, VA 22313
Training and Development (monthly)

NTL Institute
P.O. Box 9155, Rosslyn Station
501 Wilson Blvd.
Arlington, VA 22092

The Organization Development Institute
Dr. Donald W. Cole, RODC
11234 Walnut Ridge Rd.
Chesterland, OH 44026
Organizations and Change
(monthly), *The OD Journal* (quarterly),
International Registry of OD Professionals
  (annually)

Organization Development Network
P.O. Box 69329
Portland, OR 97201
University Associates, Inc.
8517 Production Ave.
San Diego, CA 92121

References

1. *Work in America, Report of Special Task Force to the Secretary of Health, Education and Welfare,* MIT, Cambridge, MA, 1973.
2. From a casual conversation with Dr. Allan Filley at the Academy of Management meeting, 1976.

3. See *Bibliography of Organizational Development Literature*, ASTD, Alexandria, VA, 1992.

4. French, Wendell, "A Definition and History of Organization Development: Some Comments," *Proceedings of the 31st Annual Meeting of the Academy of Management*, Atlanta, August, 15–18, 1971. Used by permission.

5. Baumgartel, Howard, "Using Employee Questionnaire Results for Improving Organizations: The Survey Feedback Experiment," *Kansas Business Review*, vol. 12, December 1959, pp. 2–6.

6. Master of Organization Development Program, Department of Management, Bowling Green State University, Bowling Green, OH, 1994.

7. Weisbord, Marvin M., *Diagnosing Your Organization*, Organization Research and Development, Division of Petrella Associates, Inc., Wynnewood, PA, 1976.

8. Cummings, T., and F. Worley, *Organizational Development and Change*, 5th ed., West Publishing, St. Paul, MN, 1993.

9. Shepard, H. A., "Rules of Thumb for Change Agents," *OD Practitioner*, vol. 7, no. 3, November 1975.

10. Cotton, C., P. Brown, and R. Golembiewski, "Marginality and the OD Practitioner," *The Journal of Applied Behavioral Science*, vol. 13, no. 4, 1977, p. 493.

11. Margulies, M., and J. Wallace, *Organizational Change: Techniques and Applications*, Scott, Foresman & Co., Glenview, IL, 1973.

30
Executive Development

Lana H. Wertz

Lana H. Wertz *is head of her own firm, Lana Wertz Executive Development, having been a director of two learning institutes at Aetna Life and Casualty and Providian. She has had significant experience working with senior management in these companies in developing and implementing large-scale educational interventions supporting their highest priorities. At Aetna, she facilitated the change in management expectations set by the new CEO by establishing mandatory executive programs worldwide. At Providian, she facilitated executives in transforming the holding company to an integrated operating company through vision, values, strategy, and benchmarking programs. At Aetna, she also directed research focusing on distance and self-paced education and was responsible for equal opportunity. Wertz is a member of the ASTD Public Policy Committee and* The ASTD Training and Development Handbook *Advisory Board. She was the advisor on global workplace development for the U.S. delegation during the ILO (International Labor Organization) Annual Conference in Switzerland. She currently serves on the board of Berkana, a nonprofit research organization dedicated to the discovery of new organizational forms. She has an M.A. from Duke University and a B.A. from Depauw University. Wertz has written articles and been a speaker on the use of education in strategy implementation, educational technology, benchmarking, and equal opportunity in the United States and Europe. She is fluent in German and has studied French, Italian, and Russian.*

Executive development is a primary lever that a CEO uses to create and execute the company's vision, values, and strategies. The mission of executive development is to develop the organization's leaders, so that the strategic development of the whole company follows. Practitioners[1] of executive development work with the CEO and the direct reports to link development to the executive core.

This chapter will cover:

- Executive development policies
- Executive forums, curricula, and learning institutes
- Executive development support systems
- Links to HR systems

The author's experiences in heading up executive education and development at Aetna Life and Casualty and at Providian are the basis for this chapter. She was at Aetna from 1973 through 1991 and Providian from 1991 through 1995. The CEOs of both of these companies looked to executive development to communicate and engage the executives in a new vision for the company and to implement resultant new strategies in a changing world.

Executive Development Policies

Executive development becomes a critical issue whenever an organization undergoes a major change, such as a new CEO, a new vision, or new strategies to realize the vision. The CEO, understanding the necessity for education to effect transformation of people's thinking, establishes a development policy. This undertaking may require mandatory attendance at a series of executive development programs. Such programs address the critical issues and/or capabilities of the company, capture the intellectual attention and enthusiasm of executives, and facilitate their participation with senior management in resolving the issues of the organization.

An example of a strategic program is the *Aetna Management Process* (*AMP*), a program developed and implemented to facilitate a change in the critical thinking patterns of the company. The process was designed by the CEO and implemented, first, through a program attended by all 650 Aetna executives. Variations of this program were eventually delivered to all managers, supervisors, and employees of Aetna, an audience of 50,000. Selection, performance, appraisal, and development planning systems were changed incorporating this decision-making process. Eventually, the *AMP* became the language of the corporation.

This example illustrates the use of a "cascaded" model of training. Such a model, beginning with executives, is efficient and reinforcing. As the training moves through the organization each unit adopts the new process into their regular work routine. The executive leading the organization manages and rewards the change toward the desired outcomes.

Another example of a strategic program is Providian's *Creating the Future: Driving the Vision and Living the Values.* This program was developed to transform the former holding company, Capital Holding, to an integrated operating company. All executives attended the week-long program within a 24-month period and were introduced to the concept of an integrated company and requested to help in thinking through the implementation. These 200 executives, while reviewing their own leadership skills and values, engaged senior management[2] to recommend a new strategy for the company creating the integrated operating company. Following the program, the company changed its name. The transformation was complete.

Executive development policies also encompass individual assessment routines, development planning, senior management reviews of plans, and developmental placements in various positions throughout the company. These processes support and anchor strategic changes to the realities of the workplace. The processes are described later in this chapter.

Executive Forums, Curricula, and Learning Institutes

- Executives by nature are highly pragmatic, task- and goal-oriented. Executive development programs are, therefore, related strongly to business issues.
- Executives learn best when they are working on relevant business issues, problems, and processes.

Forums and learning institutes, built on the above principles, are generally successful. Topics for executive learning must come from the strategic needs of the business. Any forum directed at changing the corporation or business unit must demonstrate practical application and be seen to add value to the process.

Examples of strategic topics are: What's the role of technology in the competitive positioning of our business? What should our customer management strategy be? How can we manage the cyclical nature of our business? What should our vision be for the Asian Pacific? What's the best-in-class model for selling to our existing customers?

At Aetna, using a series of forums called *Strategic Management Seminars,* the company developed an understanding of the effect of varying business cycles on profits, highlighted the need for a corporate technology strategy, and developed a vision for the Asian region. Each seminar involved some 25 people in week-long events committed to produce results. In each case, recommendations arising from the seminars were implemented underscoring the fact of value added by the event.

At Providian, the second phase of their executive development effort was centered on benchmarking and was called *Creating the Future: Benchmarking for Excellence.* Senior managers chose topics of importance to the central strategy and set up benchmarking teams to investigate the "best-in-class" among business units. Through these teams executives were able to view one another's internal processes, compare them to external processes, and make recommendations. Further, a common method for benchmarking became a new tool for management. (Also see Chap. 19, Benchmarking for Best Practices.)

Using education strategically works at two levels, organizational and individual. Organizationally, senior management targets certain skills, models, and processes which they want the whole organization to use and around which a new language and culture is created. An experience is created that binds the organization together with a common goal, purpose, or standard of performance. Individually, each executive assesses the unique skills that she or he needs to develop in order to serve the organization. A practitioner of executive development needs to use organizational development techniques to strengthen the link between developing the organization and individuals simultaneously.

For example, at Providian, the *Creating the Future: Driving the Vision and Living the Values* program created a common understanding of an integrated operating company. At the same time, each executive was assessing his or her own skills at leading the organization toward the new vision. Designing events aimed at building both the organization *and* the individual together increases the strength of the outcome.

The Senior Managers' Role

The CEO and senior managers play the central role in such forums. They choose the topics and issues to be addressed, and they must be present as the executives work through the issue. They introduce the issue to the group in its kickoff, act as presenters of the current state of the problem, and are available for inquiry by the group as they "solve" the issue. They receive the recommendations of the group and respond to them. They should evaluate the work of the group candidly so that the importance of the learning is emphasized.

On learning events stretching over many months, they need to find ways of expressing their interest in the work of the group and of fueling the momentum by anticipating the results. There must be carrots (i.e., praise, money, more exciting assignments) and sticks (e.g., no bonus, loss of an assignment). They must communicate the results to the rest of the organization through the whole process so that others eagerly await their turn to work on critical business issues in this educational forum.

At Providian, benchmarking projects, cited earlier, demanded 10 to 20 percent of executives' time over an average of nine months per team. Executives resisted when this development objective was added to their business objectives. Therefore, these projects needed very careful attention from the sponsoring senior managers of the teams. The most effective instrument in this case was changing this development objective to a performance objective, ultimately rewarding each executive's effort on the team in their overall performance rating. The results of the benchmarking teams were reported to senior managers in regular meetings and communicated on a regular basis to all employees. As well, the CEO spoke often in meetings and in a written column of the value the company was deriving from these efforts.

Other examples of senior management involvement in forums are as faculty members who facilitate outdoor field exercises (such as orienteering), teaching leadership competencies, participating on expert panels (e.g., strategy and finance), leading discussions of values, sponsoring or leading benchmarking teams, endorsing strategic management seminars, and attending as an ordinary participant (highly recommended for all mandatory programs).

Developing an Executive Learning Event

After the senior managers define a strategic topic to be addressed, information and/or techniques must be made available which assist in the problem solving. Generally, this information comes from both external sources (e.g., consultants, academic faculty, reading, research, an executive from another company, or visits to other companies) and internal sources (e.g., senior managers, internal case studies, or reports which illuminate the issue from multiple perspectives). Executives tend to solve problems quickly with the information they have at hand, so getting them *new* information which stretches the mental models[3] they are currently using to solve problems is a critical part of the learning.

Such events need to be carefully orchestrated, remembering that the assessment of value-added will occur within a few hours of the opening. High-quality external faculty and well rehearsed internal faculty are critical to the event, as are carefully planned prework, program materials, and event planning details. There is not much room for error in an event designed to challenge executives.

Following Up

Equally important is the follow-up to the learning event. The changes described during the program need to be reinforced through multiple means. The strongest reinforcement is through the annual objective-setting, performance appraisal, and reward systems. Other methods include follow-up reports making specific recommendations; newsletters or memoranda to participants concerning organizational outcomes; regular senior management follow-up meetings at which conversations are continued that began during the event; and personal contacts between executives and senior managers to further inquire about the experience.

Ongoing personal attention to the topic by senior management is a very effective means of changing behaviors. Sometimes a CEO may feel frustrated with how much reinforcement is needed. However, the practitioner's job is to continue to encourage and find ways of helping the reinforcement to occur. As a strategic partner with the CEO, you cannot end your responsibility of supporting the change that is being implemented until the change actually happens, the responsibility is transferred to another part of the organization, or the goal is superseded by a new one.

A by-product of executive educational forums is creating an experimental space for a corporation to try out new ideas without committing either the organization or the individual to the direction that is being explored. Typically, people relax a bit and reflect. In that reflection comes the dawning of new ideas which really are useful to the direction of the company.

Executive Curricula

When an organization identifies competencies that are critical to creating more capacity for growth, excellence in operations, quality assurance, etc., a series of learning events can be developed which support, explain, and augment the competencies. These curricula become the cornerstone for executive development describing the multiple facets and priorities of the culture.

At Aetna, the *Office of the Chairman Educational Series* established a group of mandatory learning events for executives. The series was driven from 10 competencies[4] and described key behavioral changes the chairman wanted the organization to make as soon as possible. The mandatory programs were *AMP* (The Aetna Management Process): *Scanning and Describing the Environment; Executive Leadership; Selecting and Developing Managers; Managing the Information Technology Resource;* and *Project Leadership for Executives.* These programs supported 8 of the 10 competencies. Programs supporting the other 2 competencies were recommended. Variations of these programs were provided eventually for managers, supervisors, and all employees through the classroom, the Aetna corporate educational television network, and self-paced and on-the-job training packages. Essentially, this effort was aimed at developing the entire Aetna workforce toward a new and transformed "quick, flexible, and right" workplace. These words were chosen by the chairman to describe the culture he wanted the company to have.

The Executive Learning Institute

A very effective means of focusing senior managers and executives on changes that need to be made is to establish a learning institute. The institute is commissioned by the CEO and becomes the tool for overseeing and managing overall organizational development and change priorities. The CEO selects among his or her direct reports to form a board for the institute. Also included on the board can be one or two external representatives who either have experience with other corporate learning institutes or have information relevant to developing the company. These external representatives expand the perspectives of the senior managers and provide invaluable guidance on actions they need or want to take. The board meets regularly, three to four times a year for approximately a full day, to set direction, agree on strategic development needs, initiate learning events which close development gaps, and review progress of those programs and projects under way. These meetings become the natural forum for follow-up presentations by groups of executives on strategic topics they have been asked to address.

The institute has a charter which is clearly linked to the vision, values, and strategy of the company and is communicated to all executives. This charter serves as a message to the organization that development is a high priority for them and the organization. Participation in its events are a part of the success profile of executives. An example of a learning institute mission is:

> The Mission of the Providian Learning Institute is to enhance the corporation's ability to achieve its vision of competitive preeminence, domination of its chosen markets, and redefinition of what a financial services company can be. The Learning Institute will act as a catalyst for continuously increasing Providian Corporation's leadership capacity to foster collaboration and teamwork, innovation, change and mutual trust across the entire corporation.[5]

Managing the Learning Institute Board is one of the key objectives of the Director of Executive Development.

Supporting Executive Development Systems

- Competencies
- Assessments
- Planning
- On-the-Job Learning
- Development Planning Reviews
- Succession Assurance Development Discussions
- Selection and Placements

Competencies

Development systems are designed to assure the availability of a talented and capable pool of executives to lead the company. A prerequisite for these systems to be effective is a clear understanding of the current and future needs of the business which the pool is to serve. To meet these needs an organization must have leaders equipped with a set of specific competencies. The competencies are those behaviors required of an effective executive to lead the business, to lead associates in his or her work group, and to direct his or her personal work style activity. While a set of generic managerial behaviors can be helpful, a unique and specific set tailored to the company is likely to be needed to assure success.

Executive competencies need to be clearly linked to core competencies and capabilities of the company. These company core competencies relate to the competitive technologies and production skills integral to the company's value chain.[6] Competencies then become a combination of managerial, personal, and technical behaviors, knowledge, and skills, the benchmark for a capable executive in that company.

Competencies provide the basis for numerous functions in selecting, assessing, and developing executives and for succession planning and placement throughout the company. In some companies they are also being used for performance evaluations and outplacement decisions. Where this is the case, senior management needs to be clear for exactly what purpose the assessment tools will be used. Lack of clarity here may permit an assessment routine to become politicized and thus counterproductive to the company and harmful to the individual. Organizations new to using competencies may want to restrict their use for developmental purposes only, until the organization becomes more familiar with how competencies can aid the business.

Assessments

To begin the cycle of development, each executive should be assessed. Many methods are available for assessment. One highly useful technique is the so-called 360-degree assessment method. This method involves ratings by individuals who have working relationships as subordinates, peers, or bosses. The executive also rates himself. The instrument typically has numerous questions specific to the behaviors described in the competency set. The ratings from all individuals are combined and sorted so that the individual executive sees feedback from subordinates and peers—grouped, not individual—and from the boss, of course, as an individual. This feedback data is typically very powerful for the individual and provides motivation to take action on areas of development needs. This type of assessment routine can be done for one individual at a time or for groups of executives who are participating in an educational forum. Within a forum setting that is focused on leadership development, the data supports the executive in learning or renewing techniques that can enhance her performance. Such assessments need to be repeated periodically to let the executive know if she is improving or if other behaviors, knowledge, or skills need to be emphasized, particularly if the executive has changed positions. It hardly needs saying that a high level of sensitivity in the practitioner for the handling of such an assessment tool is essential.

For example, Providian has used a tailored 360-degree assessment instrument to start the development process of an executive who has either been hired new to the company or recently promoted from within. This assessment precedes their attendance at the company's *Creating the Future: Driving the Vision and Living the Values* program cited earlier and usually occurs within the first year of the selection or promotion. The feedback reports are distributed within the first 24 hours during the program's emphasis on learning. Competencies and their importance to the company are taught by the senior HR manager. Executives begin their development planning at the end of the five-day program and finish it when they return to work.

Other types of assessments can also be used. Some of those in use by companies today are

- Assessment centers, where certified internal and/or external assessors observe individuals as they carry out exercises tailored to the company or participate with a group in a generic simulation designed to challenge their skills. Executives are given feedback from the observers in written and oral form.
- Psychological assessments, where data on the individual is gathered through an interview with a trained psychologist and a battery of tests gauging one's intelligence, attitudes, etc. Executives receive feedback in written and oral form.
- Computerized assessments, where individuals answer numerous behavioral questions related to general or tailored competencies. Participants receive a psychological profile describing likely behaviors in certain settings, perceptions of others, strengths, and weaknesses. Some also provide developmental suggestions.

Planning

Critical to the planning process is the choice of areas for development. The executive is invited to choose priorities, first, to enhance his or her current performance, and second, to expand his or her capacity for performing. The executive reviews gaps in expected business outcomes, relates these to the feedback data received, and chooses those areas that are directly connected to the business. No more than three development areas are realistic for one development period. One of the development areas might be a strength to be leveraged in bridging one of the development gaps. For example, if an executive is particularly good in problem solving, but weak in technology, he might be assigned to a task force dealing with a technology issue of the company. In this activity, he will use the problem-solving skills to make a contribution while learning the necessary competencies.

On-the-Job Learning

On-the-job learning is preferable to classroom learning, both in discovering competency gaps and in implementing development activities. The difficulties of learning on the job, however, are related to an executive's desire to actually learn from the everyday situations in which she or he is involved. The mental models that are at work in an executive's successful skill set are sometimes powerful deterrents to trying out new skills. Regular reviews of a development plan with a learning partner or direct coaching from a boss or significant colleague can help maintain the motivation for improving the skill. Also helpful is establishing a learning environment within the company in which people talk openly of their development needs and ask for feedback from others at times when they have made a particular effort to change something. When the CEO and other senior managers can discuss their development plans, others will see this modeling behavior and adopt it.

An example of an executive learning on the job is as follows: Through an employee opinion survey, an executive discovered a need to provide more information to her large work group for them to be more effective. Feedback from an entire work group, rather than a few select raters, is a powerful motivator. During a development session with her boss, the executive committed to improving this competency gap. The executive deliberately set up methods to communicate that she had not used before such as regular unit meetings with direct reports, meetings for the entire work group, skip level interviews (interviews done by senior managers one level below their direct reports) or unit meetings, a computerized project reporting mechanism, "walk around management" routines, etc. The changes were noticeable to the work group. At the time of the next employee opinion survey, the executive was able to evaluate easily the impact of using these techniques.

Some companies have prepared unique development guides which direct executives and others to specific types of development activities relevant to the organization's competencies. For example, Aetna created guides for three levels of the organization: executives-managers, supervisors, and employees. The guides recommended educational events, on-the-job learning activities, and self-study materials (e.g., books, articles, videos) for each competency which were specific to each level's development. Mandatory courses were highlighted. These guides used the Aetna Management Process, the organizational critical thinking process, as the method for assessing significant development areas.

Development periods may go beyond one 12-month performance cycle. Frequently executives are attempting to improve lifelong performance gaps, such as lackluster presentation skills, poor interpersonal skills, ignorance of the strategic use of technology, and weak financial skills. The acquisition of certain technical skills such as database management or direct marketing skills may also require more than 12 months, even for an adequate understanding of function by a general manager.

Development Planning Reviews

Development planning reviews may be done annually to prepare and negotiate the coming year's objectives. This timing lets the individual and the boss see the direct link of the development to the delivery of the business objectives. When this link is strongly made, the possibility of the executive actually working on the objectives is more likely and, concomitantly, the boss is more likely to support the time spent on development activities. When development objectives are regarded as just "nice to have" rather than quite critical to the business, resistance by the boss is probable and the executive will suffer substantial conflict between his personal development work and his regular work on current objectives.

Development progress should be reviewed periodically throughout the year. If a coaching relationship exists between the boss and subordinate, these discussions are frequently spontaneous. Such discussions can also be a part of the annual performance appraisal or the negotiation on the coming year's objectives. Individual executives may also need to pursue discussions of their development with their boss, if no coaching relationship exists or if the boss is not likely to initiate such discussions. Executive development practitioners may need to encourage these discussions through the HR systems throughout the company.

Coaching is also key to actual changes in an individual's behavior. Coaching routines are accepted in the sports world as a means to achieve superior performance. In the corporate world, verbal feedback at the time of an occurrence is still very difficult, especially among executives. Senior managers need to become more comfortable with reflecting on performance (their own and those around them) and begin to provide to others valuable information which only they know from their experience. In this way the organization learns.[7] Senior managers and executives need to ask for coaching in areas of development gaps. Without this openness, coaching and instant verbal feedback will remain as an exceptional, soft skill practiced by relatively few executives. (Also see Chap. 20, Coaching for Growth and Development.)

Succession Assurance
Development Discussions

A powerful mechanism to review development progress can be established by the CEO and senior managers. Such a mechanism can become the cornerstone for discussions on succession assurance. At regular meetings, senior managers discuss the development strengths and needs of the executive pool. The goal is to review all executives over the course of the year. Some organizations have these discussions successfully in conjunction with the business planning cycle to assess what kinds of talent they already have to meet the coming year's critical business objectives. This timing provides the information needed to hire new talent or place internal executives in challenging developmental positions.

Discussions are supported by information on each executive's career history, education, volunteer activities, etc. The data also includes commentary on the competencies that a particular executive has already developed as well as the competencies she is currently developing. This information is provided by the senior manager of the business unit aided by the HR representative of the unit. Other senior managers than can ask questions, provide their own information on the person, suggest development activities, or offer a possible transfer to a position in another business unit. The aim is to create an understanding among the senior managers of the talent this person has to contribute to the successful leadership of the business.

The CEO has a unique accountability to the board of directors of the company to assure that the appropriate talent exists to ensure business success. These discussions when candid, provide the CEO with more complete knowledge of each executive. The CEO can also note when she or he does not know an executive well enough, so that this person can be placed in closer personal contact over the next few months. Most CEOs consider this activity as one of the highest priorities they have. The executive development practitioner needs to provide information and occasions for the CEO to achieve specific goals toward knowing the executive talent pool.

One of the problems in these senior manager discussions is the allegiance each senior manager has to the talent pool in his or her area of responsibility. The senior manager undoubtedly has detailed information about each executive and can choose to share his information or not. Sometimes the senior manager wants to protect her or his talented executives from being transferred to another business unit at severe cost to her or his own objectives.

Also problematical is that the senior manager may be unwilling to candidly assess an executive in such a meeting given the varying trust levels senior managers have with one another. If development gaps are shared, will this information be treated with the same nurturing attitude that the sponsoring senior manager has for the individual? Sometimes these sessions then become discussions of competing excellent talent pools—e.g., "My group is better and/or equal to yours."

Despite these problems an effort must be made to create the attitude among senior managers that the company owns the combined talent of all executives in the pool, so that they are seen as "corporate assets," not business unit assets. Practitioners can facilitate this attitude by providing occasions where senior managers work with executives from other business units, either in educational forums or cross-unit business teams. These experiences provide personal information for senior managers on other business unit executives—as well as opportunities for executives to form relationships with senior managers of other business units. Development review discussions become a sharing of information about individuals, rather than a presentation by one senior manager of all executives in his or her business unit.

Frequently, commitments are made during such discussions for certain actions to be taken. The practitioner can summarize these actions in written form to the business unit head, encourage follow-up feedback from the senior manager to individual executives concerning development suggestions made at the meeting, and record for future reference and relevant information in the executive development database. This information becomes the memory for subsequent discussions concerning these executives.

Selection and Placements

Sometimes succession assurance routines can become paper-driven. Detailed plans list names of individuals for numerous key positions who are ready *now* for promotion to various positions or *three to five years from now*, etc. It is common for these plans to lack real utility when a position becomes vacant. However, the process may be useful in alerting top management about competencies in which the resource pool is thin and needs attention, e.g., top-level financial skill. A more dynamic process views the whole pool as available for openings at the executive level.

Senior managers from all business units must first agree that the executive position openings will be brought to a meeting of senior managers before they are filled. A slate of candidates is prepared for an open position, looking at the unique managerial, personal, and technical competencies required for successful performance in the position. The executive development practitioner can facilitate this process by reviewing the executive database and discussing potential candidates with the business unit HR personnel and/or business unit head. The senior manager can veto an executive on the list if appropriate extenuating circumstances exist, e.g., if the executive has not been in the current position long enough or is on a key project that must be completed.

At the senior management meeting, the approved slate is discussed and the competencies of each candidate are reviewed. Other names may be proffered at that time. Challenges can be made to a senior manager who has not allowed a particular executive to be considered. The hiring senior manager expresses interest in certain candidates or can decide that no one on the slate has the sufficient level of competence to assure a fair chance of success. At this point an external search will be made. These discussions can bring to light the absence of a certain skill level throughout the organization, such as general managers or marketing managers, and the senior managers can agree to establish a goal to shore up this skill through internal development and external hiring.

Important to the success of this dynamic process is that the executive who accepts the position is expected to produce results from the time he or she takes on the responsibility. No position is merely developmental. This expectation puts pressure on senior managers and executives to assess the candidate's competencies and potential for success in the job accurately. How much development is actually needed? Can the candidate learn quickly enough to produce the needed business results? What activities will accelerate this development?

One might argue that this process deters building the competency base of the organization by expecting too much of transferred executives. However, with such an expectation of immediate results, the person being transferred to a position can add value from the competency strengths he or she already has while learning new products, production methods, etc., of the new organization. The value-added evaluation is a constant measure applied in this developmental process.

The process described above was applied at Providian as the senior managers were working to change the company from a holding company to an integrated operating company. Each business unit operated independently, hiring, promoting, and replacing executives as its own unique needs dictated. The strategy to reach the vision of an integrated operating company was to share and transfer unique skills across business units, thereby applying sophisticated operational techniques from one unit to another. The transfer of skills relied initially on the movement of executives, and secondarily, on an internal benchmarking process accomplished through cross–business unit teams. Over a period of three years key executives were reviewed for placement using the competency assessment routine. Immediate results were realized in the application of techniques to different market environments in which these executives were expert. The executives also recognized the increased career potential that this transferring procedure brought to them.

Integrating Executive Development Processes with HR

Executive development is most successful when its processes are linked with all other relevant HR systems. Business planning, organizational restructuring, results planning, selection and placement, and succession assurance are systems which rely on effective executive development to provide talented and capable executives to lead business efforts. Attention should be paid to integrating the timing and outcomes of these systems so that they support one another. The outcomes of these activities lead into selection and placement activities and succession assurance reviews. With some forethought, these systems can be optimally sequenced.

Performance appraisal, compensation systems, and development planning are interconnected. If executives see the link between closing their development gaps and their performance, they are more likely to take action on those gaps. As well, the organization reaps the benefit of an executive with expanded capacity.

Access to a central executive database system is useful for senior managers to make decisions on the capacity of the executive talent pool. Such a system can now be created by using a decentralized self-service data input system in combination with competency and corporate HR databases containing performance and compensation information. Typically, these systems are generated for other purposes. Integrating them into an executive database serves senior management's needs.

Strategic organizational change efforts are linked to results planning, development planning, educational activities, communications, assessment-feedback mechanisms, performance appraisal and compensation systems. At Providian, the process of creating an integrated operating company from a holding company used all of these systems. At Aetna, the process of instituting a new decision-making methodology and other critical competencies was started by educating all executives. It then quickly moved through changes in business planning processes, selecting and developing methods, educational events, communications, assessment and feedback mechanisms, and performance appraisal systems for all employees. In both cases persistent efforts produced highly successful results.

Measuring the executive development function is a crucial part of the senior manager's role in governing the development activities of the organization. The measures may take from one to three years of effort and will rely on senior managers playing their parts as vigorously as the practitioners play theirs. While specific, bite-size measures are necessary, the completion of a major change effort is the marker for the achievement, such as the shift from being a holding company to being an integrated operating one or the complete adoption of a new way of thinking and making decisions. It should be noted that these efforts involve many parts of the organization acting together to achieve the goal. When possible, specific measures relating to bottom-line monetary results should also be determined. Companies involved in the quality movement will be able to attach these measures with ease. Others should begin at whatever level of sophistication they can manage and hold themselves accountable for a specific result.

Critical Components of an Executive Development System

In summary, the following components are necessary for an effective executive development system:

- Development is linked to the vision, values, and strategies of the corporation.
- Systems to develop the organization and individual executives are integrated.
- Executive competencies are established as necessary to lead business efforts to meet the vision and strategies of the organization. These competencies are linked to the core capabilities of the organization.
- A developmental assessment routine is related to the competencies.
- The development plan is included in the performance objectives of the executives.
- Development plans are reviewed annually by senior management in general sessions.
- Educational activities for executives are linked to the development of the organization and governed by the senior management team.
- Educational activities involve senior managers as participants and faculty.
- Senior managers are involved in coaching and providing feedback to executives.
- A competency-driven process is used to fill executive openings.
- A database is established to provide information on competencies, credentials, transferability, development, results, performance, compensation, etc., of the pool of executives.
- The senior management team monitors the executive development progress.
- Executive development activities are integrated with all other key business systems, e.g., business planning, organizational restructuring decisions, results planning, performance appraisal, compensation, internal placements, and communications.

Competencies of Executive Development Practitioners

The competencies for an executive development practitioner include

- A belief that individuals and organizations can actually change
- Ability to inspire confidence and trust in working with the CEO, senior managers, and other executives when assisting them in developing and imple-

menting large-scale interventions aimed at carrying out the highest priorities of the company

- A system's perspective of how change occurs and courage to work on all parts of the system at once

- Polished communication and influence skills in order to work with decision makers throughout the organization

- A willingness to experiment and innovate in carrying out development responsibilities

- Expertise in building educational programs, in assessing individuals, and in creating individual development plans and organizational development systems

References

1. The word *practitioner* in this chapter refers to executive development staff or consultants.

2. The term *senior management*, or *senior managers*, in this chapter refers to the CEO and direct reports, and the term *executives* generally refers to those reporting to this group and one more level down. The target audience for executive development activities is both senior managers and executives.

3. To know more about "mental models," see *The Fifth Discipline: The Art and Practice of the Learning Organization*, Peter Senge, Doubleday, New York, 1990.

4. The 10 Aetna competencies established in 1989 were use of AMP—direction setting, leadership, selection of people, development of people, management of resources, communication skills, computer savvy and system building, business and organization knowledge, building teamwork, and adaptability.

5. The Providian Learning Institute mission was excerpted from a document called *The Learning Institute Strategy* produced by the executive development function of Providian.

6. For a more detailed understanding of competencies and capabilities, see the following two articles: Prahalad, C. K., and Gary Hamel, "The Core Competencies of the Corporation," *Harvard Business Review*, No. 90311, May–June 1992, and Stalk, George, Philip Evans, and Lawrence E. Shulman, "Competing on Capabilities: The New Rules of Corporate Strategy," *Harvard Business Review*, no. 92209, March–April 1992.

7. For more information on the art of reflecting and its connection to a learning organization, read Schon, Donald, *The Reflective Practitioner*, Basic Books, New York, 1983.

Bibliography

Davis, Brian L., Lowell Hellervik, and James L. Sheard, eds., *Successful Manager's Handbook*, Personnel Decisions, Inc., Minneapolis, 1989. This is a useful compilation of suggested development activities referenced to specific competencies.

Lindsey, Esther H., Virginia Homes, and Morgan W. McCall, Jr., *Key Events in Executives' Lives*, Center for Creative Leadership, Greensboro, NC, 1987. This is a technical report giving the results of a research study on executive competencies. This is one of many research reports on executives CCL can provide.

McCall, Morgan W., Jr., Michael M. Lombardo, and Ann M. Morrison, *The Lessons of Experience: How Successful Executives Develop on the Job*, Lexington Books, Lexington, MA, 1988. This is a book describing the lessons for executives. It grew out of the technical report *Key Events in Executives' Lives* by the Center for Creative Leadership.

Moulton, Harper W., and Arthur A. Fickel, *Executive Development: Preparing for the 21st Century*, Oxford University Press, New York, 1993. This book discusses competencies needed for the immediate future and how executives can equip themselves through life-long learning.

Quinn, James Brian, *The Intelligent Enterprise,* The Free Press, New York, 1992.   This book describes the importance of core competencies in managing the intellect of an organization.

Ready, Douglas A., ed., *In Charge of Change: Insights into Next-Generation Organizations,* International Consortium for Executive Development Research, Lexington, MA, 1995. Research presentation from a 1994 symposium of a remarkable group of practitioners and academicians.

Schon, Donald, *The Reflective Practitioner,* Basic Books, New York, 1983.   A unique book describing how reflection skills impact learning.

Senge, Peter, *The Fifth Discipline: The Art and Practice of the Learning Organization,* Doubleday, New York, 1990.   Required reading for all educators hoping to change organizations.

Walker, James W., *Human Resource Strategy,* McGraw-Hill, New York, 1992.   The chapter on "Developing Effective Managers," pp. 221–254, is very helpful in describing development systems for executives.

31

Management Development

Edward L. Brewington

Edward L. Brewington is Vice President, Human Resources, for Times Mirror Training, Inc. His responsibilities include recommending groupwide human resource policies, both domestic and international, including formulating executive and management development programs. He has dotted-line authority over the human resource offices in the individual training companies. Previously, he was responsible for the creation and implementation of a process for Times Mirror and its businesses which focuses on the development of executives to assume positions of greater responsibility. This initiative represents a major effort on the part of the organization to improve substantially in areas of promotions from within, succession planning, and executive and management development. Previously, he was Director, Leadership Development, at International Business Machines Corporation. His career at IBM spanned almost 25 years and included numerous executive and management assignments in human resources and marketing. Brewington received his B.A. from the City College of New York and his M.B.A. with distinction from Long Island University. He is a member of the board of directors of the Human Resource Planning Society; the Business Advisory Council; Business Development Entrepreneur Center, Los Angeles Urban League; and a member of the Industry Advisory Board, Executive Education, University of Southern California (USC). He is a former member of the Board of Trustees of Mercy College, Dobbs Ferry, NY, and former chair of the Academic Affairs Committee. He has served on the advisory boards of the Cornell University Extension programs, New York City; the New York State Police Leadership program, Albany, NY; and the William Patterson College School of Management, Wayne, NJ. He is a past guest lecturer at the New School for Social Research, Graduate Program, New York City, and he has presented at the University of California–Los Angeles Anderson Graduate School, Fully Employed M.B.A. Programs (FEMBA). In addition, he is a part-time faculty member at the USC Graduate Business School.*

The Need

Let's start by answering a few very important questions. Who are managers and what is management development? It seems almost superfluous to attempt to define a manager. Or is it? In many organizations individuals with similar duties and responsibilities are called different things: executives, managers, supervisors, and the latest to be widely used is team leaders. Therefore, the title of manager does not necessarily differentiate among the various roles. It is my recommendation to the practitioner to be somewhat flexible in dealing with these differences and to let the organization be the guide in determining who will be classified as a manager and otherwise.

The similarities in terms of duties of these positions far outnumber the differences. The most common element is having responsibility for providing direction to the organization's employees, or what is often called human resources. However, it is important to note that this does not necessarily mean that managers have employees reporting directly to them. The use of these titles often are simply indications of the importance of the responsibility to the organization. The actual work may require the cooperation of others who do not report to the management person leading the initiative. In the simplest terms: If the organization calls the person a manager, then we can expect to include that individual in our management development program.

If defining a manager is primarily the result of organizational decisions, can we apply similar logic to the definition of management development? The answer is simultaneously yes and no. The organization has as one of its key roles the development of its human resources. But on a higher level it has a greater responsibility for ensuring that those in positions of authority have the tools necessary to manage or lead the human resources of the organization. Starting with the legalities which protect and provide for employees and the need to be able to counsel employees on an ongoing basis, there is a wide body of knowledge which is required for managers to perform their duties effectively. It is therefore imperative that management personnel have knowledge and skills in the areas that affect the employees as well as the obvious skills in their functional areas. Therefore, management development is the education, training, knowledge transfer, and ultimately skills demonstration of those individuals who are defined as managers by their respective organizations.

If we accept the premise that supervisors are often individuals who gained their status by moving up through the line organization and managers are often professionals who have received extensive education and may be new to the organization, then we should ask, Why is there a need for management development? Many managers have college degrees and oftentimes a graduate degree. Surely with all this education they must be qualified to perform their duties and responsibilities.

This management development issue is a very complex one which once again is very organizationally dependent. In other words, some organizations insist on making the development of their managers a way of life. In contemporary terms this means that management development is a part of the organization's business strategy. On the other hand, there are many more organizations which do not require nor do they provide developmental programs for their managers.

If this discrepancy sounds like the need for these programs is questionable, let me set the record straight. There is beyond a reasonable doubt a great need for management development programs in all organizations. Stated another way, there should be a requirement that all managers pass a competency certification of some form which includes the opportunity to get and remain updated on how to manage their human resources. Very few would argue if this recommendation dealt with maintaining a certain skill level in a marketing, financial, or a technical discipline. Although managing human resources may require a great deal of common sense, it requires a lot more. It is this fact which establishes the need to impart to all managers the cultural norms of the organization and what is acceptable and expected of them as keepers of the most valuable assets available. "People make things happen" is a time-tested axiom.

The Effects of Change

Colleges and universities teach a broad array of subjects but often fall far short of transferring practical knowledge in many areas. Even if they did a better job in the human resource area, there would still be a need to educate managers on the application of many fundamental theories in managing people. Of course, since organizations are inherently different, the need for each to maintain their own skill set is imperative.

As mentioned, two reasons for having management development support for the management team are to help an organization impart its philosophy and values and to compensate for the lack of another reliable source of training for its managers. But there is another compelling reason to have MD support: constant change. Virtually all organizations today are undergoing significant transformation due to external economic pressures which in turn have triggered internal change. The world of management has been turned upside down by the new global economy in which global competition has wrecked stable markets and whole industries. The increased use of technology alone has enormous impact on the way we all conduct our business on a daily basis.

The manager has experienced an incredible increase in daily scrutiny just because the new information age has produced a daily steady stream of facts and communiqués which are real-time and often demanding immediate responses. The days of reflection upon receiving a memo and planning a response is often replaced by an audio voice-mail message or an electronic memo on-line which elicits an immediate response without the prior benefit of reflection and research.

The above example alone sends a powerful message to practitioners of management development to realize the need for important changes in the curriculum which stress both some of the old and the new competencies for managers of today and tomorrow. Although these changes will vary by organization, we will examine some of the implications by contrasting the more traditional management development content with ways in which it is changing. Much of the new thinking is often discussed under the subject of leadership development, which is covered in Chap. 28 of this handbook.

The Bottom Line

Regardless of where the skills or competencies are discussed, it is clearly the role of the management development function to understand and help disseminate information which is in support of the overall business strategy of the organization. In other words, the MD function must become a strategic partner in the organization or face the possibility of elimination or painful ongoing justification for its existence. Downsizing or rightsizing alone is enough to send a clear signal to all functions and individuals alike that the future offers little security and the survivors will likely be those who are clearly viewed as contributors to the bottom line. As any experienced practitioner of management development will attest to, this area of contributing to the bottom line has traditionally been one of the weaker areas of MD. It could be said that MD has often failed to work hard enough at demonstrating its real worth to the organization; instead it has relied on its intrinsic value.

The implications are clear, as outlined in Fig. 31-1; MD will have to transform itself along with the enormity of the changes affecting the organization. External forces will drive internal change at an astonishing rate. Managers will be expected to know when to apply the traditional command-and-control techniques while directing employees in traditional ways to get the job done. At the same time, they will be under increased pressure to encourage risk taking both for themselves and their subordinates. Organizations will be flatter, with fewer layers of management, and perhaps will be better able to respond in a more timely fashion to critical issues. The individual superstar will have to learn to be more concerned with the overall team's performance. The traditional information-withholding role played by the manager is rapidly giving way to information sharing due to a great extent to the new technological innovations and the increased deployment of teams and flatter hierarchical structures. Delegation will remain important, but empowerment will be the cry of the employees. All of these expectancies will require the MD function to teach both traditional and new skill sets.

TRADITIONAL	CONTEMPORARY/FUTURE
■ **MANAGE** Traditional Development IBMStory	■ **LEAD** 1990s Development
■ **CONTROL** "Span of Control"	■ **INFLUENCE** Span of Support
■ **DIRECT** "We Should Do"	■ **FACILITATE** "What are your thoughts on how we might approach this?"
■ **RISK AVOIDANCE** Kiss of Death	■ **RISK MANAGEMENT** Prudent Risk - "Wild Ducks"
■ **HIERARCHICAL ORGANIZATION** Layers of MGMT = Status	■ **FLATTER ORGANIZATION** Loss of Power Base
■ **INDIVIDUAL** Super Star	■ **TEAM** One of Many
■ **INFORMATION OWNED** Power	■ **INFORMATION SHARED** Often Difficult
■ **DELEGATE** Give Task	■ **EMPOWER** Give Task & Decision Making

Figure 31-1. Management skills transformation.

Management Careers

Thus far, the reader might be thinking in terms of the traditional training programs as the defining content of management development. This fact is probably true to a great extent, but one must not overlook the broader role of management development which is to influence the career development of the management team. Career development of course can include many components such as career-tracking models which include specific assignments leading to positions of higher responsibility. Many organizations include this type of activity in the organizational development function, but it is essential that MD be a major contributor to the career growth and development of management. It is very common to have educational and training interventions as a critical part of an individual's development plan, especially where managers are concerned.

The illustration in Fig. 31-2 is an intentionally exaggerated model of how education and training can and should be an integral part of an overall career development plan and execution. This model tracks a human resource career path over a period of time.

The key point for the reader is to recognize the importance of linking MD to an organization's overall strategic direction. The model might suggest an organiza-

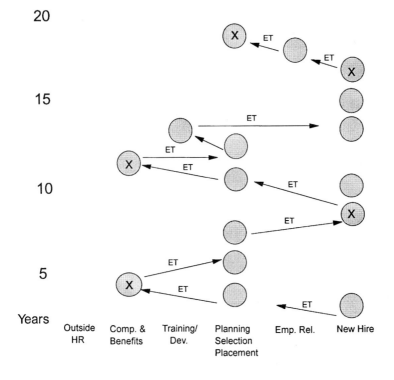

ET = Education & Training

(x) = Management Positions (Supervisor, Manager, Middle Mgr., Executive, Sr. Executive)

Figure 31-2. Sample human resource career path—development through specific assignments and regular education and training.

tion's commitment to developing its people to assume positions of greater responsibility or a similar desire to promote from within. Strategically linked developmental activities which include specific assignments along with education and training will undoubtedly go a long way toward the accomplishment of these kinds of goals.

The Role of Management Development in the Organization

How to Get Started

Getting started might imply several things to different people, and it is extremely important that we spend time on this subject before we go any further. The information in this section is relevant regardless of whether the management development function is new to the organization or is a long-established tradition. The need to have the commitment of the organization to MD beyond lip service is absolutely critical. In fact, long-established MD functions often run the risk of taking the organization's commitment for granted. Executive speeches which include an organization's commitment to MD may sound good for public relations and management morale, but the real test is often found in factors such as funding, participation by senior management, attendance, program evaluation, and ultimately whether or not MD is part of the overall strategic plan of the organization.

There is no one answer as to how to ensure the organization's commitment, and there are also numerous ways to display the lack thereof. Much is said and written today about the need for an organization to have a vision for its future—what it is striving to become. Similarly, there should be a documented vision or policy which is specific enough to make very clear the role and purpose of MD. Like most visions or statements of purpose or direction, it should help establish and give meaning to MD in the organization. This means that it should be in support of the organization's overall goals. Some examples might be:

Organizational vision: To become the recognized leader in our chosen field

Management development vision or goal: To develop the best managers to ensure our competitive position

Organizational vision: To develop a network of strong businesses led by a strong management team

Management development vision or goal: To become an acknowledged leader in developing our managers

Clearly, I have taken the most simplistic examples I could think of, but they help make the point for aligning the microvision of MD to the macrovision of the organization. However, mere statements without true support are meaningless. Management must be willing to go on record with specific examples of how their goals are being accomplished. It is equally important to have all levels of management in the organization accountable for attainment of these objectives, starting with top management which should lead by example. Accountability implies the need to have measurable ways to check on the progress. We will hear more about this subject later.

Customer Needs

Once management commitment is obtained, I recommend a thorough customer needs analysis to determine what the specific goals and objectives are for MD in support of the vision for MD and ultimately the organization. Clearly top management must be consulted as to their view of what needs to be done. However, limiting the needs assessment to top management eliminates the input of the broad customer base—the managers in the organization. Early involvement of the management population in determining the design of the program and the program content can go a long way toward ensuring overall management ownership of the initiative and a greater stake in the outcome. It is very important to avoid having the MD, organizational development, or human resource function be the sole owner of the management development initiative in the organization. We discuss this further under "Pitfalls to Avoid."

Customer Involvement

The "how" in gaining greater involvement by all management in the organization can be quite simple: ask them. One-on-one interviews, participation in management department meetings, management roundtables, and the use of a survey can all be potential sources of good information in determining what should be done. Personally, I advocate using as many of these opportunities as practical.

The use of a survey designed specifically for the purpose of determining the management development needs of the organization is a technique which I recommend with great enthusiasm. (See Fig. 31-3.) The payback can be enormous in terms of monitoring the progress of the deliverables and being able to reinforce periodically why the program exists—they asked for it! What better way to explain the content than to use the survey feedback material to demonstrate how you are responding to their wishes. I have used this technique in several organizations and can assure you that it has great potential for getting MD started on the right foot.

There are many more details to consider such as location, faculty, use of company executives to deliver content, the people who should attend and when, how large the class should be, how long the sessions should be, and of course the financial parameters that should be met. These and many other considerations are covered in other chapters in this handbook.

A checklist such as the one in Fig. 31-4, entitled "How to Delight Customers," can go a long way in keeping focus on the task at hand and can also help avoid some of the pitfalls which are so easy to succumb to.

According to one expert in the field, one of the major tasks of management development in the global enterprise is to provide the organization with "glue"—to "glue" or integrate subsidiaries and other units that need their own autonomy. The point is made that the role of management development is changing from a long-standing focus on "getting the right people into the right places at the right times" through recruitment, succession planning, training, and other forms of development. It is also becoming a tool for organizational development.

Pitfalls to Avoid

There is so much upside potential to influence the organization through management development initiatives, but there is the equally risky business of turning a well-intentioned effort into a disaster. Although this statement may sound like

1. I believe that an investment in management development activities will pay off over time on the bottom line:

   Frequencies (percentages)
   65.2% Strongly agree   1.5% Disagree   0.0% No answer
   33.0% Agree   0.4% Strongly disagree

   Statistics: Replies 267; Mean 1.37; Std. dev 0.54; Minimum 1.00; Maximum 4.00

2. I believe our company is now firmly committed to management development:

   Frequencies (percentages)
   3.0% Strongly agree   44.2% Disagree   3.0% No answer
   43.8% Agree   6.0% Strongly disagree

   Statistics: Replies 259; Mean 2.55; Std. dev 0.66; Minimum 1.00; Maximum 4.00

3. I believe our company sees management development as an important part of its future business success:

   Frequencies (percentages)
   4.5% Strongly agree   31.8% Disagree   3.7% No answer
   56.2% Agree   3.7% Strongly disagree

   Statistics: Replies 257; Mean 2.36; Std. dev 0.64; Minimum 1.00; Maximum 4.00

4. Development activities should be benchmarked and measured over time to determine an individual's progress:

   Frequencies (percentages)
   38.2% Strongly agree   3.7% Disagree   0.4% No answer
   57.3% Agree   0.4% Strongly disagree

   Statistics: Replies 266; Mean 1.66; Std. dev 0.57; Minimum 1.00; Maximum 4.00

5. I believe that part of the measurement of my performance affecting my compensation should include activities and efforts that develop the capacities and skills of my subordinates:

   Frequencies (percentages)
   53.6% Strongly agree   1.9% Disagree   0.0% No answer
   44.6% Agree   0.0% Strongly disagree

   Statistics: Replies 276; Mean 1.48; Std. dev 0.54; Minimum 1.00; Maximum 3.00

6. I believe the leadership skills of our managers can be significantly improved:

   Frequencies (percentages)
   54.7% Strongly agree   2.2% Disagree   1.5% No answer
   41.6% Agree   0.0% Strongly disagree

   Statistics: Replies 263; Mean 1.47; Std. dev 0.54; Minimum 1.00; Maximum 3.00

7. I currently have the coaching and management skills I need to help develop the potential of those for whom I am responsible:

   Frequencies (percentages)
   10.9% Strongly agree   29.2% Disagree   0.7% No answer
   58.1% Agree   1.1% Strongly disagree

   Statistics: Replies 265; Mean 2.21; Std. dev 0.64; Minimum 1.00; Maximum 4.00

Figure 31-3. Sample questions with responses for a management development needs analysis.

- Understand needs
- Provide total solutions
- Deliver responsively
- Have quality product and service
- Be a market leader
- Monitor and measure customers' satisfaction

Figure 31-4. How to delight customers.

pessimism at its zenith, it is very important to elaborate on some key pitfalls to avoid. Looking back at the notion of aligning MD with the strategic direction of the organization and ensuring broad ownership of the overall initiative, we find immediate clues to heed very carefully.

Management development, like many so-called soft disciplines, can easily be viewed as a nice-to-have effort but is easily expendable when there are other priorities such as cost reduction in the organization. I personally experienced the potential impact of not keeping managers' skills updated when, as a cost-cutting measure, an organization suspended management development. The erosion of management skills in terms of handling employee issues began to show up in the number of complaints to the chairman's office as well as in the content of these complaints. It became clear that managers were not "managing" according to the company's standards. But even more alarming was the obvious inference: MD was not viewed as key to the overall company strategy.

The implications are very clear and have been stated numerous times previously: MD must be viewed as a key element in the attainment of the overall organizational vision. It is the role of MD to make this connection as a part of the organization's commitment to its vision and thus to MD. This point cannot be overstated.

The obvious question at this point might be, "How can we make MD a part of the overall corporate strategy and vision"? The simplest answer is to reread the section above on "How to Get Started."

Product Design

One area where many mistakes are made is in the formal classroom program design.

Major pitfalls exist in the content development process, especially as the program matures. If the earlier advice for getting started is followed, then it is critically important to remember the need to remain "customer-driven" in all aspects of the follow-up activity. Receptivity to modifications to any aspect of the deliverables should be the modus operandi.

Regular feedback from the class participants should be reviewed very carefully with the intent of looking for ways to improve the sessions. Similarly, development of new curriculum should continue to involve the "customers." Many organizations have allowed themselves to develop additional and new course offerings which are the products of a select few individuals without making sure the offerings address customer needs. The records of corporate America are packed with product failures which neglected to assess customer reaction prior to product development. The same mistake in developing new programs and new course content will increase dramatically the chances of failure.

The simplest advice I can offer is to build in customer demand by involving the customer early in the cycle and on a regular basis. Many company sales training programs spend enormous amounts of money teaching their employees how to overcome objections to their products which might have been avoided if the product development had included real customer input. Likewise, many management development programs spend an enormous amount of resources trying to fill classroom seats because the "customers" simply view the offerings as of little, if any, value. Of course, this disinterestedness could be symptomatic of other problems such as a lack of organizational commitment. The key is to be able to build in customer demand and avoid this type of problem.

MD Evaluation

The last pitfall which will be discussed here (although there are many others) involves the use of evaluations or the lack thereof. Although this topic is covered in separate chapters (see Chap. 14, Evaluation, and Chap. 15, Measuring the Results of Training), it is an area where pitfalls are often overlooked.

The most common pitfall is not to attempt to measure the effectiveness at all. Imagine the following scenario:

> You are presenting your proposal for management development to the senior decision makers in your organization and you have covered the results of the management survey or needs analysis. You are then asked the question, "How are you going to prove these programs effective?"

Even if you have a sample of the participants' feedback sheet which you plan to use in the sessions, you may find that your plans are inadequate. Feedback or "happiness" sheets are very useful and probably should be used in most instances, but they fall far short of proving the effectiveness of MD programs in the long run. The various ways to measure such programs are covered in Chap. 14, Evaluation, and Chap. 15, Measuring the Results of Training, so I will only strongly recommend that evaluation information be a part of the MD overall design. Results which can reinforce MD's support of the overall business strategy will go a long way in keeping management development a part of the organization's main agenda. Measurements which provide data on a regular basis will help avoid the possible pitfall of constantly trying to justify the existence of the MD initiative.

The Management Development Function

A simple definition of the MD function is the organizational entity which has responsibility for coordinating or delivering the substance of the program. This entity may take many forms such as a department, a few individuals dedicated to MD, a vendor or supplier contracted to provide specific services, or some combination of internal and external teams who specialize in certain areas. No matter what form the entity takes, there should be *some* focal point for MD to ensure that it supports the organization's strategy, goals, and objectives. In most instances this role in the organization requires at least a dedicated resource. The amount of work required is enormous, from the conception of MD, to the selling of the initiative to senior management, design of the program, delivery of the content, measurement of the program's effectiveness, modification of its deliverables, reporting to management and to the organization, selection of "faculty" and contributors, etc. These plus many other duties and responsibilities are not a part-time endeavor.

This does not suggest that the MD role cannot be performed in conjunction with other similar duties and responsibilities such as executive, leadership, or supervisor development. The point is that these other duties have many common elements and offer opportunities for synergy. I would, however, guard against having the MD role assigned to an unrelated department or function. In the latter instance, much would be lost in terms of focus and expertise.

The Sourcing Issue: Internal versus External

One of the most important decisions to make is how to deliver the MD initiatives. The considerations are many and the implications equally numerous. The guidance offered here reverts back to our earlier comments on strategic alignment. For example, an organization undergoing downsizing might not be the place to recommend staffing up the MD organization. On the other hand, if the MD function is to be staffed by internal experienced personnel from other disciplines as a developmental assignment or as a permanent assignment, the decision is quite different. Fortunately, the options are plentiful and the decision must be made not solely on the basis of getting the job done but as a part of the overall organizational plan.

The use of internal personnel offers employees from other functional areas such as human resources, sales, engineering, finance, and administration the opportunity to learn new skills and contribute to the MD role. Experienced management personnel often lend enormous credibility to the practical side of what is being taught or implemented. On the other hand, having expertise in other areas does not automatically qualify the individual for an assignment in MD. The selection process and the career planning responsibility must be clear and well thought out. Often, individuals are selected to work in MD functions for a specific period of time as part of their own development and, of course, as a way to provide credible role models to the rest of the management population who will come in contact with them in their MD roles. In these cases, the organization must be willing to invest in the individuals' development and training to perform in the MD role. They may be expected to become experts in the classroom or in the development of curriculum which might require extensive training. On the other hand, for organizations which can afford this approach there are many models of success. My experience at IBM provided one of the best examples of how this approach can work extremely well.

Again, with the overall organizational plans taken into consideration, for those for whom staffing a separate function is not the appropriate course of action the good news is that there is a tremendous field of experts to choose from. Many organizations exist which specialize in all aspects of this field. Everything from program creation, curriculum design, classroom delivery, and follow-up activities are available from numerous sources. From independent consultants to training companies and universities, the choices are limitless. It would be advisable to invest in exploring these options carefully before deciding to staff internally. Of course, it is also advisable to examine several kinds of external providers in the process. Fortunately, many high-quality options are available. Just sending out a request for a proposal (RFP) to a variety of sources will quickly cause the "skies to darken" with "experts" eager for the opportunity to sell their wares. It is best to have someone knowledgeable in the field of MD to help in the evaluations of the various options. If this person knows a lot about the organization which is implementing MD, so much the better.

Gaining Commitment and Consensus Building

In the section of this chapter titled "How to Get Started" the focus is on gaining commitment from top management and from management throughout the organization for the MD initiative. The role of the MD function is to ensure an ongoing commitment to MD as a key part of the organization's agenda. An example of this comes to mind again from my many years at IBM. Every manager was required to participate in 40 hours of management development yearly. This followed the requirement to attend a formal MD session within 30 to 60 days of appointment to first-line management and 60 to 90 days of appointment to middle management. I am not suggesting that such a rigorous requirement is absolutely essential, but it does provide one model which worked well for many years.

Clearly, each organization is unique and must decide what is appropriate for its own culture. I would suggest some careful thought be given to institutionalizing the effort. The model cited is just one way to do so.

The MD function must be prepared to offer ways to keep the subject on the main agenda. Initiating and participating in surveys which ask employees key questions can provide very useful clues as to how MD can assist in the management of the entire organization. Problems which are attributable to management's behavior can often be corrected by teaching corrective actions through the MD function. It is recommended that the MD function constantly look for ways to improve the skills of the management team. There are many benefits to this approach, not the least of which is to keep MD in a role of adding value to the organization. Issues such as employee morale, employee-industrial relations, compensation, benefits, capital accumulation, performance appraisal systems, career development, succession planning, and diversity, are suitable agenda items for MD-led sessions. In net terms: teach what the organization needs, when it needs it; be able to show why it is needed; show the impact of the training; and do it continuously. The desired outcome of commitment and consensus building will follow.

The Value of Benchmarking

Since the topic of benchmarking is also covered in a separate chapter (see Chap. 19, Benchmarking for Best Practices), I will comment on it only briefly.

This obvious reason to benchmark the MD programs is to make sure that the best ideas from a number of sources are being put to use. Benchmarking in this context refers to the examination of MD programs in organizations other than one's own to learn what has and has not worked well there. This process can prevent insular and isolated thinking which can easily become a pitfall to the overall effort. The message is quite simple: Learn what others are doing and borrow the best ideas when possible. This is an expected part of your role and the payoff can be tremendous. The information gathered in this process can be invaluable in adding to the credibility of the MD function. Organizational management support of the overall effort is likely to be enhanced due to an increased confidence in the MD team.

The Importance of
Measuring Effectiveness

A brief discussion of areas whose effectiveness can be attributed to MD's contribution often reveals ways of measuring that effectiveness other than the traditional four levels of measurement covered in other chapters of this handbook. Obviously, the more one moves away from the traditional measurements, the more difficult it can become to show a direct correlation to an outcome attributable to the MD function. For example, an improvement in employee morale might be attributable to MD if specific actions have been taken to improve management's effectiveness. One such action might be an employee recognition program. On the other hand, an improvement in the stock performance of a corporation may not be directly attributable to the efforts of the MD function; the only correlation might be the fact that an effective management team is one of the goals of management development.

Similar observations may be made in terms of the organization's overall reputation in the world at large. It is not uncommon to see extensive references to an organization's succession planning in major business publications and Harvard case studies. The extent to which the organization is perceived as performing effectively, again, is a reflection on the management team. Major cultural changes in an organization are often attributable directly to the developmental functions such as management development. Many skills and tools to implement the changes are often developed and delivered by the MD team.

Another area which can benefit greatly from MD-led efforts is the diversity initiative. The success of such efforts depend on the cooperation of the entire organization, but the role of management in leading and showing commitment is critical.

Beyond such lofty measurements it can be said with certainty that the MD function should always be looking for ways to improve the effectiveness of the management team. Organizations by their very nature will continuously present opportunities to make managers better at what they do. The survival of individual managers and the collective management team is a compelling reason to measure whether or not the right support structure is in place. MD can be one of the most critical support systems. It is also obvious that the more MD can show in terms of its contributions to an organization, the more it is likely to survive as a key player in the overall organizational agenda.

Summary and Conclusions

This brief chapter on management development has attempted to outline certain principles and key actions which can be very useful in establishing and maintaining the vitality and usefulness of the MD function. However, I believe strongly that these suggestions can also be applied with similar success in other initiatives both related and nonrelated to management development.

The chapter begins by exploring the need for MD initiatives and suggests several reasons for this need: organizational effectiveness through the management of human resources; the unique nature of organizations; the lack of adequate training for managers by academic institutions; the need for a widely supported agent of change in the organization; promotion-from-within practices; the changing skills required for today's managers; and the career development role and the general need to function as a conduit for information.

The discussion of MD's function offers ideas on how to get started on developing an MD function and certain pitfalls to avoid. The importance of aligning

MD with the overall organizational vision and strategy is explored as is the importance of gaining true commitment. The crucial role of ongoing needs analysis in ensuring overall ownership of the initiative is shown to be helped greatly through the use of surveys. The adoption of a customer-driven approach is highly recommended.

In the discussion of some pitfalls to avoid, the need to have MD as a key player in the overall organizational strategy is reinforced along with the implications for failure to do so. Involving the "customer" or the organization's management team in future course or program development is shown to be key to remaining customer-driven. It can go a long way in helping to build in customer demand, which is a much desired ingredient. Evaluations, including the traditional class reaction or "happiness sheets," are vital to long-term success. A pitfall is to rely solely on this type of measurement or not to measure at all. MD must constantly and consistently "show cause" as to why it exists; it is wise not to forget this fact even in what seems like a safe environment.

The section on the MD function explores some of the options of internal versus external sourcing. Again, it is strongly suggested that these decisions should follow the overall organizational strategy. Considerations such as the use of the MD function as a developmental assignment are mentioned. The need to have management commitment and ongoing consensus building is reinforced. Making management development a requirement is an option which can be considered. The best scenario is to maintain a built-in customer demand at all times.

The section on benchmarking reminds us to keep the program vital by avoiding insularity and isolation by constantly keeping abreast of the best ideas and avoiding some of the mistakes of others.

Finally, in the last section on measuring effectiveness, the "why" of MD is explored as well as the difficulty of tying the organization's performance directly to management development, but there is a correlation: effective management. The role of MD in cultural change should be a given. Most important is the need to have some type of process for measuring MD's contribution to the organization. The survival of the MD function may depend on it. Tools for measuring MD are covered in other chapters as is more information on benchmarking.

Management development should be given careful consideration by all organizations regardless of their size. People need and expect to report to management personnel who understand the inseparable connection between organizational strategy and the role of human resources throughout the organization.

Bibliography

Berhnard, H. B., and C. A. Ingols, "Six Lessons for the Corporate Classroom," *Harvard Business Review,* September–October 1988, pp. 3–8.

Caudron, Shari, "HR Revamps Career Itineraries," *Personnel Journal,* April 1994, pp. 64b–64n.

Evans, Paul A. L., "Management Development as Glue Technology," *Human Resource Planning,* vol. 15, no. 1, pp. 85–106.

Huey, John, "The New Post-Heroic Leadership," *Fortune,* February 21, 1994, pp. 42–50.

Kiechel, Walter, III, "A Manager's Career in the New Economy," *Fortune,* April 4, 1994, pp. 68–72.

32

Supervisor Development

Lester R. Bittel

John W. Newstrom

Lester R. Bittel *is Professor of Management, Emeritus, and Virginia Eminent Scholar at James Madison University. He is author of the best-selling text* What Every Supervisor Should Know *(titled* Supervision: Managing for Results *in its seventh edition, 1996) and of* The Complete Guide to Supervisory Training and Development *and coeditor of* The Handbook for Professional Managers. *Before accepting his academic post, Bittel was an industrial engineer for Western Electric Company, a plant manager and training director for Koppers Company, and director of information systems for the McGraw-Hill Publications Company. He is a Fellow of the American Society of Mechanical Engineers and holder of its Centennial Medal.*

John W. Newstrom *is Professor of Human Resource Management in the School of Business at the University of Minnesota at Duluth. He has held several elective offices in ASTD and is an active consultant to industry. He is the author or coauthor of such well-known texts as* Games Trainers Play, More Games Trainers Play, Still More Games Trainers Play, Transfer of Training, The Manager's Bookshelf, *and, with Keith Davis, the classic* Human Behavior at Work.

The supervisory management force, two million strong, holds the power to turn on—or turn off—the productivity of organizations. These are the men and women who provide the tenuous interface between the management hierarchy in every organization and the vast body of employees who put their hands on, or apply their minds to, the real work of enterprise, public as well as private. These

651

unique hybrids are, in most instances, technically as well as legally, members of management. But their loyalties are strongly divided. Three out of four have risen from the ranks of labor—either blue-collar or white-collar. They rarely enjoy the privilege of establishing the goals of the organization they serve. Their upward mobility is severely limited. Yet their efforts ultimately ignite or defuse the productive spirit of the more than 70 million employees who generate the nation's output of goods and services.

Supervision: A Distinct
Segment of Management

Despite its linkage to management development, supervisory development remains in most instances clearly differentiated from it. The reason stems from the unique character of the supervisor's role in the organizational structure. Of all managers in the hierarchy, supervisors are the only ones who must function at a dual interface, relating on the one hand to rank-and-file operatives below them and on the other hand to the policy-oriented managers above them. Supervisors' employment origins are significantly different from other managers, too. As late as 1992 nearly three-quarters of all supervisors rose from the nether ranks rather than entering their managerial positions directly from college or from a high-level, professional, or specialized occupation. Both the unique nature of the supervisory job and the pre-management conditioning experienced by so many incumbents have acted to produce a supervisory segment of managers that is distinctive from other managers.[1]

Role Definition

While there are many popularly accepted definitions of the widely used title of supervisor, a simple one seems to serve best. It was developed by the International Labour Organization after considerable study of the literature:

> Supervisors are usually first-line managers whose major function is working with and through non-management employees to meet the objectives of the organization and needs of the employees.[2]

A modification of this definition is observed by the Opinion Research Corporation. It suggests that within the limits of this definition another distinction can be made: There are supervisors (*first-level supervisors*) who manage only nonmanagement employees, and there are also supervisors (*second-level supervisors*) who manage other supervisors in addition to nonmanagerial employees.[3]

Role Definition by Self-Analysis

While acknowledging inherent flaws in self-analysis, two major surveys conducted by the Center for Supervisory Research at James Madison University shed considerable light on how supervisors view their roles and responsibilities. Results from a 1981 survey of more than 8500 supervisors (*National Survey of Supervisory Management Practices*) were replicated in a similar (unpublished) survey of 2000 supervisors in 1992. Among the major conclusions drawn from these surveys were the following:

1. They see themselves as the boss, often operating independently on their own best instincts and judgment rather than according to policy. Their alignment with management is tentative at best. Only 40 percent say they "feel a part of company management"; 19 percent say they "feel closer to my employees than to company management." Another 17 percent "feel closer to other supervisors" and still another 18 percent say "I feel that I am on my own as a manager most of the time." Some 6 percent say "I feel that my boss and I are the company management."

2. Their thinking is in line with the traditional values of hard work and experience leading to achievement. The seniority principle, by which service is rewarded by promotion and security, appears to be "a good idea" to more than three-quarters of them. Performance appraisals as effective guides to motivation and discipline get the same degree of approval.

3. They are ambivalent about employee motivation. On the one hand, 93 percent of all supervisors say that "most employees want to do a good job," and 83 percent say that "most employees willingly accept responsibility for their own work." On the other hand, 66 percent say that "the main interest of most employees is to get enough money to do the things they want to do," while 61 percent say that "employees require close supervision," and 41 percent say that "most employees have to be pushed to produce."

4. All in all, however, supervisors are a vital, rather happy group. They are almost unanimous in saying (95 percent) that "what happens in my company or organization is really important to me." Only 24 percent say that "money is what's most important about my work." Eight out of ten (82 percent) say, "Generally speaking I am satisfied with my job."[4]

Historical Review

Much can be learned from (1) analysis of the supervisor's unique role in the organization, (2) reflection on the impact of environmental and organizational changes upon a supervisor's roles and responsibilities, (3) a review of the evolution of supervisor development programs, and (4) a critical examination of today's development practices. Emerging from these observations is a set of guidelines for effective supervisor development programs.

Ambiguity in the Traditional Role

Supervisors have traditionally performed a difficult balancing act in organized endeavors. This role is directly related to their position in organizations. In the United States and in many western societies, membership in structured organizations is legally divided vertically into two classes: management and employees. Managers occupy the upper strata and employees the lower. Both the implication and fact are that those in the upper strata of an organization have authority over those in the lower. Supervisors occupy the lowest level of the management strata and traditionally have been the ones who impose authority directly upon employees. Thus, supervisors perform at the interface of the two classes, acting as the connecting link between them. Placed in the middle this way, supervisors are assigned a highly ambiguous role in the organization. On the one hand, they must gain loyalty and acceptance from the employees with whom they have regular contact—in effect, to identify with, and protect, the goals and interests of employees. On the other hand, supervisors are expected to issue orders and instructions and to exert discipline in conformance with plans and policies, rules and regulations formed at the upper levels of management.[5] In preparing supervisors for their work, HRD professionals have struggled for decades to create programs that help supervisors perform effectively within this dichotomy of roles.

Impact of the Changing Environment

While the economic and cultural environments in which organizations function has changed radically in the last 40 years, the dichotomy of the supervisory role has changed little. Even the continuing erosion of structure within organizations (reengineered, horizontal, and virtual) and its attendant changes in relationships[6] has not had a significant effect upon this condition. Effective supervisory development programs must take into account the fact of this persistent dichotomy.

What has changed, however, and it has changed dramatically, is the range and versatility of performance expertise and competencies now expected of supervisors. Besides expanded technical knowledge and skill, they must demonstrate skills in counseling, team building, conflict resolution, information handling, and diversity accommodation. At the same time, supervisors face tightened reins upon their authority and their freedom to operate independently. These constrictions include conformance with labor laws and safety and health regulations, protection of equal-opportunity rights and of privacy, accommodation of disability-challenged employees, and the like. Contemporary programs for supervisory development must acknowledge these restrictions while addressing the very real needs for developing a greatly enhanced performance.

Evolving Changes in HRD Strategies and Techniques

Over the years, HRD professionals have, with varying success, attempted to match changes in the external environment and the internal structure of an organization with appropriate changes in the development strategy. In the early periods of supervisory development, for instance, the principal instructional technique was the lecture, augmented occasionally by experiential exercises such as those of job instruction training. Gradually, case-study analysis and discussion was introduced, and this was frequently enhanced by interactive role-play sessions. At the same time, the classroom gave way to the seminar and workshop, if sometimes in name only. Programmed learning had a brief fling, but mainly for the vocational aspects of the supervisor's job. During the 1970s and 1980s, however, supervisory programs became highly structured and comprehensive. Community colleges and technical institutes began to offer semester-length courses at the introductory and advanced levels. In many instances, the only difference between a company's internal management development and supervisory development programs was the status of the participants. In this same period, however, the impact of social legislation was being felt sharply at the supervisory levels. Accordingly, the comprehensive approach to supervisory development began to gradually give way to a wave of single-issue programs aimed at improving the supervisor's knowledge and ability to conform with Equal Employment Opportunity laws, to conduct nondiscriminatory performance appraisals, to enforce supportable discipline, to avoid and prevent sexual harassment, and the like. When supervisory development programs were not dealing with social and legally imposed issues, they were frequently diverted by nostrumlike, one-shot courses. Popular among these courses were transactional analysis, negotiating strategies, time or stress management, and career planning. From time to time, great faith was also placed in the effectiveness of experiential games and simulations and, especially, behavioral modeling as a basis for performance improvement.

The search by HRD professionals for the right match between occupational need and developmental approach continues today. The organizational scene as it affects supervision changes so rapidly, however, that development solutions have become dangerously eclectic, often eschewing a strategic rationale. Too often there is a frivolous interest in trying anything new, simply for the sake of change. Fundamentals are overlooked, or given short shrift, in the planning of development strategies. Continuity and consistency have become neglected. Development carried on in this fashion will not be effective. In view of the problems inflicted by the ongoing state of organizational flux, supervisors desperately need a strong conceptual base from which to view their responsibilities and to develop their competencies. This is something that a well-conceived developmental program can provide.

Toward the Future

In the most recent years, the supervisor's workplace environment has been assaulted by change from every quarter. Downsizing and dramatic corporate cost cutting have introduced new problems of employee productivity and motivation. Emerging beliefs in and demands for employee empowerment have challenged the traditional views of supervisory authority: Where, for instance, does the drive to create self-managing teams leave the supervisor? The astronomical advance in information handling and computer technology strikes at two levels. It shrinks the number of middle-level managers and support staffs that in the past have guided and bolstered a supervisor's efforts. And it removes or changes the nature of many operational decisions that were once in the supervisory sphere of control.

Significant changes have also occurred in the orientation of many organizations toward their customers and clients. Total Quality Management (TQM), with its diffusion of responsibilities, has removed the supervisor from center stage in the quality-control effort. On the other hand, customer-awareness programs have raised the supervisor's vision beyond the limits of the shop floor or office walls. As if these changes were not enough, there are the modern employees whom a supervisor is still expected to direct, motivate, and control. Not only do today's employees receive greater legal protection than ever before, they are also emotionally more sensitive than those of previous, authority-responsive generations, and their expectations are infinitely higher. Furthermore, many of them are likely to work only part time, or at "flextime" hours, or may even work at home. They may bring their children with them to work or be granted previously unheard of privileges to accommodate day care and other family-related responsibilities.

All of these changes will require the development of enlightened and viable attitudes on the part of all supervisors and new or enhanced competencies among the supervisory population in general.

Guidelines for Effective Supervisory Development

An effective supervisor development program will blend that which has been learned from the past with what is being experienced and viable today. A contemporary development program for supervisors should, at the least

1. Emerge from a well-thought-out strategic plan for development
2. Recognize and allow for the ambiguity, real or perceived, in the supervisory role, positioned as it is at the interface between management and employees
3. Provide a sound conceptual foundation of essential management knowledge, skills, and attitudes upon which to build specific competencies
4. Base the remainder of its content upon rigorously verified and precisely defined competency needs
5. Allow for flexibility in the program's implementation, while maintaining consistency and continuity
6. Introduce new developmental methods or techniques only after pretesting or otherwise verifying their suitability and effectiveness.
7. Guard against the inclusion of courses or subject matter that do not clearly meet an established competency need
8. Establish standards of participant assimilation and/or improvement that, while challenging, are demonstrably within the range of attainment for the particular supervisory population
9. Articulate and correspond with the organization's goals, policies, and prescribed relationships—as well as with the organization's beliefs and cultural norms
10. Provide for measurement and evaluation of the effectiveness of each element of the program, especially in terms of improved supervisory performance

Supervisory Competencies

Supervisory training programs should, of course, spring from a clear knowledge of the competencies required by employers of their supervisors. Here again, generalizations are not nearly so good as those that are compiled by each organization through observation and research. Nevertheless, many helpful hypotheses have been gathered by authorities close to the scene.

Basic or Traditional Competencies

In probably the most exhaustive research ever extended in the identification of competencies, AT&T isolated and ranked 14 principal duties of supervision as illustrated in Table 32-1. These are examined in detail as a guide for the development of supervisory training programs in Charles R. Macdonald's *Performance Based Supervisory Development.*[7] AT&T's analysis identified not only the 14 basic duties, but also the major tasks, decision points, skills, and related knowledge areas associated with each.

While the AT&T compilation of supervisory competencies remains the most significant, other studies add new or different dimensions to them. For example,

Table 32-1. Dimensions of Supervisor Competencies

Principal duties	Major tasks	Decision points	Skills	Knowledge	Total items
1. Planning the work	15	6	12	32	65
2. Controlling the work	9	6	13	36	64
3. Problem solving	11	4	14	17	46
4. Performance feedback	24	4	28	60	116
5. Coaching subordinates	22	1	22	25	70
6. Motivative atmosphere	13	3	10	19	45
7. Managing time	9	2	17	44	72
8. Communication	6	1	1	16	24
9. Informal oral communication	19	5	21	20	65
10. Self-development	8	1	7	17	33
11. Written communication	11	3	21	23	58
12. Representing company	5	1	—	3	9
13. Career counseling	17	3	2	32	54
14. Meetings	18	2	28	39	87
Total	187	42	196	383	808

SOURCE: Adapted from Charles R. Macdonald, *Performance Based Supervisory Development: Adapted from a Major AT&T Study*, Human Resource Development Press, Amherst, MA, 1982, p. 24.

Baker and Holmberg[8] analyzed data gathered by the American Management Association and found that the supervisory time spent on managerial functions can be ranked from most to least in this order: implementing, planning, organizing, delegating, evaluating, innovating, and staffing.

Researchers at one General Electric plant[9] singled out seven "dimensions" of the supervisor's job: technical knowledge and administrative skills, ability to develop a plan for achieving goals, ability to deal with the manager to whom one reports, communications ability, capacity for dealing with people outside the unit and the company, and ability to deal with employees reporting directly to the supervisor.

Cover,[10] however, takes issue with generalized managerial aspects of supervisory competencies and urges a "return to basics" such as production, quality control, sales support and customer relations, cost control, housekeeping, safety, administration, personal relationships, innovation, and identification and establishment of performance improvement objectives.

Additional competencies can also be inferred from the needs inventories shown in Figs. 32-1 and 32-2.

New-Wave Competencies

During the last decade it has become evident that supervisors are expected to have competencies far beyond and far more exotic than those basic ones identified by AT&T and others. Jones, Kaye, and Taylor,[11] for instance, have developed data that is especially relevant to contemporary or new-wave competencies such as facilitating, team building, working with self-managed teams, empowering employees, and managing diversity. Their research illustrates the difference in importance between the competencies required of a manager or supervisor and those required of people he or she may supervise (Table 32-2). According to this study of competencies, supervisors may be expected to outrank their subordi-

Respondents rate each item according to a scale of 3 "extremely important," 2 "fairly important," and 1 "not too relevant."

☐ Ability to set realistic goals and standards, define performance requirements, and develop action plans for achieving and for controlling (tracking) performance

☐ Skill in communicating effectively in face-to-face situations—with subordinates, peers, superiors, customers, etc.

☐ Ability to conduct selection interviews in a way that produces the information needed to make sound hiring decisions consistent with company policy and the law

☐ Skill in balancing daily activities between the demands of the task (production-oriented side) and of the employees (people-oriented side)

☐ Ability to challenge and motivate subordinates, thereby increasing their job satisfaction and developing a team of "turned-on" employees

☐ Skill in giving on-the-job training and counseling relating to behavior at work

☐ Ability to appraise performance objectively and to conduct regular, constructive performance reviews that are two-way dialogues

☐ Skill in writing letters, memos, and reports that are clear, concise, complete, and compelling…writing that gets action

☐ Ability to manage time (of self and others) effectively by prioritizing, controlling interruptions, measuring cost-effectiveness, investing rather than spending time, etc.

☐ Skill in cutting costs through methods improvement, work simplification or reallocation, flow charting, analysis of procedures, etc.

☐ Ability to hold meetings, briefings, conferences that are well-organized, crisp, and results-oriented

☐ Skill in negotiating and resolving conflict as it arises in interpersonal relations

☐ Facility in designing in depth, drawing out what is and isn't said, summarizing and clarifying, and organizing the speaker's message so that it can be acted upon

☐ Ability to identify problems, to separate causes from symptoms, to evaluate evidence, to weigh alternatives, and to select and implement appropriate solutions

☐ Ability to make effective presentations and to sell ideas in a persuasive, well-documented manner—to management, to subordinates, to users

Dept./Organization

Name

Figure 32-1. Needs inventory format. (*Adapted from Scott B. Parry and Edward J. Robinson, "Management Development: Training or Education?"* Training and Development Journal, *July 1979, pp. 8–13.*)

nates in sensitivity to events, social skills, emotional resilience, and self-knowledge, but their subordinates may be expected to match them in problem solving, proactivity, and creativity and to top them in command of basic facts (about the work) and relevant professional (job) knowledge.

Saul Gellerman[12] made a point years ago that also seems especially relevant today. He questioned whether many so-called competencies are a matter more of style than of substance. He considered this bias to be a consequence of studies asserting that workers are more collaborative—hence, more productive—under a supportive, or "employee-centered" style of supervision than they are under a style of distrust or low regard. Furthermore, Gellerman observed that what a supervisor *does* is often equally important. If a supervisor stresses and watches over output, quality, and cost, for example—which are paramount for most organizations—employees are likely to follow suit. Gellerman concluded that "the things to which supervisors give their attention largely determine what subordinates will channel their energies into. Hence, the choice of the "proper" priorities can also be said to be an important "company-specific" competency.

—1. Analyzing problems and making decisions:
  ☐ a. Identify the problem and describe it clearly.
  ☐ b. Determine whether or not the problem is worth spending time on.
  ☐ c. Use a systematic approach to collect information.
  ☐ d. Identify the most important characteristics that a solution should have.
  ☐ e. Generate a series of possible solutions and select the one which best meets the needs. Consider the characteristics of each possible solution.
  ☐ f. Prepare an effective action plan for the solution you select.

—2. Conducting fact-finding discussions:
  ☐ a. State the need or the information in such a way that the employee will be encouraged to provide what you need.
  ☐ b. Indicate clearly the kind of information you want.
  ☐ c. Probe for relevant information (both positive and negative) even though the employee may be reluctant to speak.
  ☐ d. Uncover all the relevant data without creating hostility or distrust.
  ☐ e. Record the facts you collect.
  ☐ f. End the discussion so that the employee feels he or she has made a significant contribution.

—3. Motivating:
  ☐ a. Identify situations that result from motivational problems rather than from lack of skill or organizational support.
  ☐ b. Identify causes of motivational problems.
  ☐ c. Indicate clearly the behaviors that you want to motivate.
  ☐ d. Develop a plan for removing demotivating elements from the work environment.
  ☐ e. Identify incentives in the work environment which can be used to motivate the employee.
  ☐ f. Demonstrate how to give effective motivational feedback.

—4. Dealing with emotional situations:
  ☐ a. Face up to, rather than avoid or be intimidated by, emotional situations.
  ☐ b. Recognize and avoid using "emotional blackmail" as a way of controlling others.
  ☐ c. Demonstrate respect for the feelings of others.
  ☐ d. Handle emotional situations by calming.
  ☐ e. "Defuse" the emotions of others so that the real cause of problems can be uncovered.
  ☐ f. Avoid responses that escalate emotional behavior.

Figure 32-2. Detailed items for a needs inventory. (*Adapted from Danny G. Langdon, "The Individual Management Development Program,"* Training and Development Journal, *March 1982, pp. 78–82.*)

Consideration of the research of Jones, Kaye, and Taylor and of Gellerman's observations point to enlightening conclusions about the evolving competencies expected of contemporary supervisors:

1. Some competencies represent personality rather than learned characteristics (e.g., leadership style, emotional resilience, and self-knowledge).

2. Some competencies require considerable personality change for those who do not innately possess the characteristics (e.g., social skills and a trust in, or high regard for, others).

3. Some competencies represent a learned orientation (such as the choice of company-specific priorities and a continuing sensitivity to events).

ers with each job requirement. Selection dimensions are derived from these studies. The selection process is then precisely prescribed and implemented. The better programs involve a combination of screening techniques—testing, multiple interviewing, in-basket exercises, and psychological evaluations.[16]

Training Needs Assessment

Ideally, the assessment of supervisory training needs should be the result of a comparison between (1) the required competencies of the position (AT&T calls these *mastery models*) and (2) the measured knowledge, skills, and attitudes of the incumbent supervisors or supervisory candidates. In actual fact, a great many organizations begin with generalized lists of competencies. They then use a number of techniques to establish the training gaps, or needs, between this list and presumed capabilities of their supervisory participants.

Capability Assessments

To establish the levels of capabilities already possessed or attained by an organization's supervisory population, human resource analysts commonly use as sources (1) *performance reviews,* from which specific and cumulative identification of less-than-satisfactory performance against appraisal criteria is gathered; (2) *critical incidents,* gathered from formal records or through interviews with supervisors, their peers in staff departments, and their superiors; (3) *attitude (or climate) surveys,* from which general indicators of unsatisfactory employee relationships are identified. In a relatively few instances, diagnostic instruments are also used. These are available commercially from a number of psychological test development organizations.

Needs Inventories

The most common approach in designing most supervisory training programs, however, is to rely upon an assessment of needs (made judgmentally) by the managers to whom supervisors report, by HRD professionals, by the supervisors themselves, or by some combination of these three.

A traditional, simplified needs inventory format and content is shown in Fig. 32-1. This form, developed by Training House,[17] asks that items be rated as 3, "extremely important"; 2, "fairly important"; and 1, "not too relevant." Other formats offer space for suggesting training needs not listed.

The trend in needs inventories is to expand definition of the items in order to more clearly specify the areas of deficiency, as shown in the excerpt in Fig. 32-2, developed by Langdon.[18]

Course Content

Typical course content for supervisory development can be inferred from an examination of established competencies and needs analysis inventory lists. Beneath the surface of the subject matter, however, it is important for the training coordinator to establish beforehand exactly what the learning thrust of each course or topic will be. Specifically, almost any subject or course may be approached with an objective of conveying *knowledge,* imparting or improving *skills,* or reinforcing or shaping *attitudes.* Many subjects, of course, lend themselves readily to classifications as knowledge or skill, but the deeper aspect of content should not be overlooked since it will have a significant impact upon the effectiveness of course material and subsequent evaluation of the training by participants and their sponsors.

Course Levels

The most common classification of course material has been according to level of experience of the participants rather than by course topic. Course content, emphasis, and technique may vary, but the great majority of supervisory topics might be taught at any level of experience. Many in-service programs and a great many institutional supervisory training programs are constructed, however, according to whether or not the participants are classified as (1) *presupervisory,* (2) *entering* or relatively inexperienced (1 to 5 years), or (3) *experienced* supervisors with more than 5 years of experience at that level.

Typical Supervisory Courses

One of the most comprehensive lists of separate course offerings for supervisors at all levels of experience was designed by the International Labour Office (ILO) in Geneva, as shown in Table 32-3. Extensive, detailed course outlines for instructors and trainees are available from ILO.

Supervisory Course Curricula

Many colleges, universities, community colleges, and technical institutes offer a for-credit supervisory curriculum and divide it into basic and advanced programs of a semester length for each. Typical elements of the for-credit curricula are shown in Table 32-4, with the division between basic and advanced supervision taking place with the sixth unit.[19]

Focus Clusters

It is popular in the in-service field to offer short courses that combine related topics that focus on a particular area of knowledge or skills. Typical clusters are interpersonal relations, counseling, and discipline; the four phases of the management process; staffing, training, and performance appraisal; productivity, quality, and cost control; leadership, communications, and team building; equal-employment opportunity, diversity, sexual harassment, disabilities, and right to privacy.

Special Interest Courses

There are always a number of topic areas that enjoy a brief popularity and relevance to current problems. Other courses hold high value periodically for any organization. Among both kinds of special-interest subject areas the following seem to retain perennial value: equal opportunity and related legal issues, performance appraisal, employee training, productivity improvement, quality

Table 32-3. Comprehensive List of Basic Courses

A Basic Modular Program for Supervisory Training
I.   Supervision
    1 The Organization and the Supervisor
    2 Principles of Supervision

II. Supervisory Techniques
    3 Planning and Scheduling
    4 Work Study and Organization
    5 Directing and Coordinating Work
    6 Controlling Work
    7 Quality Control
    8 Finance and Cost Control
    9 Decision Making and Problem Solving
    10 Role Analysis
    11 Introducing Changes
    12 Communications and Records

III. The Main Supervisory Areas
    13 Utilization of Equipment and Facilities
    14 Maintenance Supervision
    15 Material Handling
    16 Energy Utilities and Auxiliary Services
    18 Office Supervision
    19 Purchasing
    20 Marketing

IV. Supervising People
    21 Leadership
    22 Informal Organizations and Groups
    23 Individual and Group Discussions
    24 Staffing
    25 Motivating Workers
    26 Job Evaluation
    27 Performance Appraisal
    28 Salary Administration
    29 Training and Development
    30 Interpersonal Relations and Behavior in Supervision
    31 Industrial Relations
    32 Safety, Health, Security
    33 Maintaining Discipline and Morale
    34 Complaints and Grievances
    35 Supervising Special Groups

SOURCE: Adapted from J. Prokopenko and Lester R. Bittel, "A Modular Course-Format for Supervisory Development," *Training and Development Journal*, February 1981, p. 15.

assurance (TQM), time management, stress management, grievance handling, leadership, communications, variations of transactional analysis, and problem solving and decision making.[20]

Methods and Techniques

Supervisory development draws from the same array of locales, sources, methods, and techniques as do other training programs. Certain alternatives, of course, seem more appropriate and effective than do others, although documented evidence is scarce.

Table 32-4. Typical Course Elements Included in
Comprehensive Curricula for Supervisors

Unit 1:
1. Supervisor's Role in Management
2. Coping with a Dynamic Environment
3. Supervision and the Management Process

Unit 2:
4. Making Plans and Carrying Out Policy
5. Problem Solving and Decision Making
6. Information Management

Unit 3:
7. Organizing an Effective Workforce
8. Staffing with Human Resources
9. Training and Developing Employees

Unit 4:
10. Understanding and Motivating People at Work
11. Leadership Skills, Styles, and Qualities
12. Effective Employee Communications

Unit 5:
13. Appraisal of Employee Performance
14. Counseling Troubled Employees
15. Building Cooperative Work Teams

Unit 6:
16. Exercising Control Over People and Processes
17. Controlling Costs and Budgets
18. How and When to Discipline

Unit 7:
19. Stimulating Productivity and Innovation
20. Raising the Quality of Products, Services, and Performance

Unit 8:
21. Employee Safety and Health Under OSHA
22. The Supervisor's Role in Labor Relations

Unit 9:
23. Managing a Diverse Workforce
24. Contemporary Issues
25. Company Specifics

On-the-Job Training versus Off-the-Job Training

In a study by the Conference Board,[21] the implications were that 90 percent of all formal training for supervisors takes place off the job in a classroom, seminar, or workshop format. Only about 10 percent of all companies surveyed conducted formal supervisory training *on the job* that met a three-part criteria: (1) stated, written objectives for each participant, (2) one or more designated individuals (line managers or HRD professionals) to guide the experience of the trainee, and (3) a specific schedule setting forth the types of experience to be obtained and a timetable of intended progress. *Off-the-job classroom-type* training is obviously more convenient for the trainer and easier to control. The Conference Board survey showed a distribution of methods used in off-job classroom training for supervisors to greatly favor group discussion (95 percent) and formal presentation or lecture (90 percent), followed by case study (85 percent), role-play (60 percent), required reading (55 percent), and business games (40 percent). These figures do not tell the whole story, since other comments regarding this survey indicated that case studies and role-play were accorded less than 20 percent of the training time by those organizations using them. In a related study of off-site meetings attended by supervisors, McKeon[22] provides some specific insights into the elements of classroom methods that can make them effective. Participants observed that presentations and discussions accounted for about 60 percent of their training time and yielded 43 percent of the perceived learning value of the activity; working on problems in small groups took about 25 percent of the training time and accounted for about 27 percent of the perceived value. Interestingly, required reading and related outside work accounted for about 15 percent of the time and 16 percent of the value. The balance of perceived value was derived from incidental exchanges during meals and coffee breaks. The conclusion is that small-group assignments and self-paced learning for supervisors appears to be more effective, hour for hour, than formal presentations.

The Conference Board survey also indicated that HRD professionals provided the faculty with 75 percent of in-house, off-the-job classroom training for supervisors. The balance of the faculty was provided by line managers and other functional specialists in the organization.

Methods Selection

As with other training, supervisory training should use methods of a balanced variety to achieve the established objectives with the greatest simplicity and economy. The generally agreed-upon advice regarding choice of methods is this:

- To increase *knowledge,* consider especially assigned reading, lectures, guided discussions, observational tours, case studies, programmed learning, instructional films, and self-tests.
- To increase *skill,* consider especially modeling, role playing, demonstrations, case studies, behavioral games,[23] problem-solving conferences, job rotation, and supervised practice on or off the job.
- To influence *attitudes,* consider especially role playing, demonstrations, case studies, problem-centered conferences, job rotation, and interactive videos.

In general, supervisors tend to prefer and to learn more effectively from specific concrete examples, experience and reality-oriented practice, and interactive exercises than from abstract, conceptual presentations or from reading assignments.

Program Planning and Design

Once all the variables in competencies, selection, needs assessment, course content, and method selection have been reviewed and assembled, the trainer faces the major task of strategy determination and implementation. These two elements are encompassed by the planning and design phase of supervisory training. Coverage of subject matter in this section is mainly by example, since this phase is generic to all training and development.

Objectives

It is essential that the program objectives be clearly defined and put into writing. Agreement must be secured beforehand, *in fact* from the principal line managers, and *by inference* from the supervisors themselves. Objectives are typically expressed in terms of incremental improvements in knowledge, skills, and/or attitudes directly related to acknowledged competency requirements and an assessment of developmental needs. The more quantitatively these goals can be defined, the better, although the state of the art will leave many in purely qualitative terms.

Examples of Objectives

Some examples of both qualitative and quantitative objectives are

For a basic supervisory training program.   To provide the participant with
1. The essential knowledge of his or her responsibilities so as to make decisions that are compatible with company goals and policies
2. The knowledge essential to good management practices so that this knowledge—along with an understanding of appropriate attitudes—may guide day-to-day decisions
3. The skills to direct the work of department people in a positive and productive manner

For an introduction to supervision course.   To provide inexperienced supervisors with a basic understanding of management functions and of their special responsibilities in applying them in their organization

For an advanced supervision course.   To provide experienced supervisors with a review of job-related fundamental management practices and to introduce them to a selected variety of new concepts and techniques directly applicable to their work

For a time management course.   To instill in supervisors an awareness of the degree to which personal time may be controlled and to provide them with a number of specific tools and techniques for increasing the productive use of their time on the job

For a quality improvement course.   To provide supervisors in the record-keeping units of an agency with a number of tools and techniques for working along with employees to reduce the number of measurable errors in their departments by 5 percent within three months

For an impending methods change.   To provide supervisors in the shipping departments of a company's plants with the information and skills needed to accomplish a changeover from verbal to computer-directed loading procedures by October 1 of that year.

Format Choices

In addition, decisions must be reached as to what extent programs should be conducted (1) on the job or off the job (the great proportion occurs off the job in classroom settings); (2) on-site or off-site (most full-scale programs are conducted on the premises); (3) during working hours or after (most are held during working hours, although this choice varies widely); (4) continuously or on intermittent schedules, such as 2 hours per day for 2 weeks or 1 day a week for 10 weeks (schedules vary widely, but intermittent schedules prevail); and (5) by internal HRD faculty, line faculty, or outside organizations such as vocational-technical institutes, community colleges, university extensions, or independent consultants or professional societies.

Participant Selection

Another question to be resolved is whether or not for conference-type training to mix supervisors with those from other departments and with middle and upper managers. Most authorities agree that much is to be gained by placing line supervisors from different departments and divisions in the same classes as well as including equivalent-level staff supervisors. Interactions are likely to be democratic and vigorous with valuable exchanges of on-the-job as well as course-related information and perspectives. In general, however, there are risks involved in mixing widely separated echelons of management. The learning experience can be threatening to lower-level supervisors and their degree of participation in discussions inhibited. On the other hand, some courses may lend to exchanges of viewpoints for higher, as well as lower, levels. In a TQM environment, for instance, "vertical slice" training is chosen to ensure that all participants get the same message at the same time.

Traditional versus Modular Format

Because the number of subjects that might be judged as essential parts of supervisory development is so large, some authorities advocate a departure from this traditional approach to program design.[24] They believe that training is made more effective and less costly by targeting selected elements in modular fashion. Each module is thus integrated into a comprehensive, long-range program for supervisory development. There is considerable justification for this approach, as illustrated by the example in Table 32-5.

Planning Guidelines

Broadwell[25] cautions about a new generation of supervisors who are younger, better educated, and impatient with the ponderous, didactic methods used in traditional approaches to supervisory training. He also calls attention to the increasing number of white-collar, knowledge-oriented supervisors whose expectations and lifestyles differ from before the "baby boom." Fulmer[26] advises that the focus of supervisory training programs would not exclude the need to regularly familiarize supervisors with the internal workings of their own organizations. And Short[27] urges that program design allow for "unlearning" well-entrenched, ineffective habits on the part of supervisors. He observes that good design will entail discomfort or "disequilibrium" and its success will depend, in large measure, on the supervisor rather than exclusively upon the trainer.

Program Management

Management of supervisory development programs differs from others only to the degree that the supervisory population is more pliable (or manipulable) than the middle or executive levels of management and less manipulable than

Table 32-5. Traditional versus Modular Approaches to Supervisory Training and Development

	Traditional management development	Modular management development
Scheduling	Meetings are scheduled at the convenience of the instructor, usually same time each week (e.g., Tuesday mornings for eight weeks). Or, if many participants are required to travel, course may be held at hotel or conference center and run continuously (e.g., over one week)	Meetings are held as often as demand requires, at the convenience of participants. Thus, if 67 people sign up for "Time Management," it will be run four times (16–17 persons each time); a topic with 34 enrollees will be run twice. Offerings can be scattered throughout year
Length of sessions	Each class meeting is same length as others. Some topics are "rushed" or "crammed" to cover all the content; others fit comfortably	Length of meeting is determined by content and intent. Half day, full day, two days with two weeks between, and so on
Participants	Same people go through course cycle together. They become a group and function as such after the first meeting	Different faces at each meeting. Composition of group is based on need to know and availability to attend
Enrollment	Selection is usually done by personnel or training departments. Participants are drafted, with the approval of their immediate supervisor. Such programs usually try not to mix too wide a spectrum of grade levels in any one group: senior managers attend first, then middle, then first level	Selection is done by department heads, who fill out a "selection matrix" at start of year. They then confer with their subordinate managers (the participants) and enroll. A boss and subordinate can attend the same offering without disrupting their work flow or the group composition
Content	Over time, all members of the organization's management team get the same common core of concepts, skills, procedures, and policy. It becomes part of the "puberty rites" of passing into management in the organization. Once a manager has attended, there is often no further training within the organization	Different managers take different selections, based on their needs (e.g., some supervise people, others manage projects; some do a lot of writing, or negotiating, or presenting; or running of meetings; others don't). Of course, some matrix offerings can be required of everyone (e.g., those dealing with policy and procedures, budgeting, etc.)
Instructor	The instructor carries the burden of responsibility for making the course a success. Usually the same person(s) will teach all subjects and should speak with authority on all topics	Different instructors can be used for different modules, so the most qualified person (from within or outside) can be made available for a given topic
Follow-up	End-of-course activities are done on a group basis (e.g., graduation, postcourse evaluation, joining of supervisory association, follow-up meeting to report on composite action plans). Usually there is little or no follow-up	Follow-up is the responsibility of participant and immediate boss. There is more time to implement action plans after each module attended, and more commitment to do so. Better communication is possible between instructor and participant and boss, who can function more as a team

© 1978 by Training House, Inc./ P.O. Box 3090, Princeton, NJ 08543. Adapted from Scott B. Parry and Edward J. Robinson, "Management Development: Training or Education?" *Training and Development Journal,* July 1979, p. 9.

nonmanagerial trainees. Thus, in the main, the individual providing supervisory training can focus on program management mechanics rather than paying undue attention to the typical problems of attendance and out-of-class preparation.

Maximizing Outcomes

In any case, prudent trainers will seek to manage the program in such a way that results will be maximized. Rosenthal and Mezoff[28] suggest that supervisory development practitioners first make certain that the supervisors' managers understand the benefits to be derived from the training and then follow a series of steps during the development process to assure that what happens during the training occurs in the most favorable organizational atmosphere. Rosenthal and Mezoff suggest that trainers inform the supervisors' sponsors of the "ceremonial effects" of the development program: (1) it acts as a motivator and a builder of confidence and self-esteem, (2) it serves to remove stress and helps newly appointed supervisors to make the crossover to management more effectively, and (3) it facilitates improved working relationships between participants and their coworkers and employees. These two authors also suggest the following 10-point program for assuring the optimum learning environment:

1. Inform participants about training well in advance of the training event.
2. Conduct a pretraining interview with participants.
3. Encourage sponsoring managers to discuss the program beforehand with their participating supervisors.
4. Design the training to address issues of the supervisor's organizational role.
5. Provide ample opportunities for participants to discuss work-related issues.
6. Structure the program to include free time for social interaction and individual reflection.
7. Conduct training off-site or at a location that minimizes distractions and interruptions.
8. Structure the training to make it significantly different from the normal work routine.
9. Publicize the training in the organization's newspaper or newsletter.
10. Provide certificates of completion.

Certification

An attractive way to emphasize the importance, and lasting value, of supervisory training is to integrate it with the certification opportunities provided by the Institute of Certified Professional Managers. This organization, jointly sponsored by the National Management Association and the International Management Council, is located and operates independently on the campus of James Madison University in Harrisonburg, Virginia. It conducts a full-scale, recognized certification program based upon education, experience, and three certification examinations. The substance of the certification examinations parallels the range of subjects offered in a comprehensive supervisory training program, and participant and trainer's manuals are available for preparation purposes.

Program Monitoring

It is essential that training sessions begin and end at the stated time and that their conduct follow principles of good management. The HRD professional becomes an important role model in this regard. Rigorous attendance records should be kept; absences should be followed up (in a sensitive manner, of course) to determine their cause and to let individuals know that their participation was missed. If the program calls for out-of-class assignments, these, too, should be logged in, to indicate their importance to the training experience and to the trainee's progress. If assignments are optional, make certain that this is clear to all participants, although it is better for assignments to be an integral and required part of the program if they are to be included at all. It is often a good idea, too, to maintain contact with participants' sponsors during the program in order to receive ongoing, current feedback and also to sustain motivation at that end.

Program Examples

Supervisory training programs vary widely in content, length, and format. Most comprehensive programs, however, contain subjects and topics described earlier in this chapter. It will probably be more helpful at this point to look at how different aspects of supervisory development have been treated and at a few programs with distinctive features but with broad application elsewhere.

Policies

At a large diversified construction, design, and engineering firm, the supervisory program was constructed on explicitly stated policies and criteria, especially when vendor-supplied components were selected.[29] The policies state that all content must

- Be needs-assessment-based
- Employ performance task objectives
- Be how-to or skill-oriented
- Be highly interactive
- Incorporate behavioral modeling
- Utilize job aids, reminders that can be taken back to the job
- Concentrate on team effort
- Involve the supervisor's manager in the planning process
- Fit into an ongoing employee performance and career development program
- Be demonstrably cost-effective

Selection

At one food processing plant the success of its supervisory training program was founded on a complete redefinition of the supervisor's role in the organization and a more effective selection process.[30] Key elements in these phases included (1) differentiation between roles that were heavily weighted toward administration and those requiring technical know-how, (2) documentation of each position as to content and required skills, (3) redefinition and clarification of relationships between supervisors and staff department, (4) screening of supervisory candidates through an assessment center conducted by an outside consultant, and (5) changes in supervisory responsibility, authority, and method of selection made clear to the union.

On-the-Job Retail Supervisor Training Program

A major chain of retail stores designed and utilizes a comprehensive, trainee-paced, modular supervisory training program that "must take place on the job and complement, rather than interrupt, regular duties."[31] The program is divided into three phases: (1) learning experiences that are related directly to the company's products and processes, (2) management experiences that are oriented to aspiring or relatively inexperienced supervisors, and (3) management experiences for supervisory trainees and incumbent supervisors. Each of the latter two phases contains 12 management learning projects that direct the trainee through a series of step-by-step, on-the-job experiences. The procedure for each project encompasses several steps and takes about one year:

- A supervisor or manager trainee is assigned to a limited area of the store as a surrogate manager of that area. The trainee is encouraged to experience, observe, and participate in as many management activities related to that area as possible.

- A list of skills and knowledge (learning objectives) required and reference resources for self-study are provided.

- The trainee performs management learning exercises which provide an information base for the follow-up analysis and develops basic proficiencies in the assigned area.

- A management analysis of the assigned area is made by the trainee who creatively lists all areas with potential for improvement in that department. This is an indicator of the trainee's conceptual and creative depth.

- All the possible improvement activities listed in the above step are compared with store policies, budgets, inventory constraints, etc., and the listing is modified to allow for realistic implementation within the restrictions of the store's environment and management climate.

- The trainee prepares a plan of action which documents how improvement activities can be compiled, prioritized, and applied in the store to increase productivity, sales, and profits.

- The trainee implements those activities which will enhance, rather than interfere with, normal store operations.

- The store manager and/or district manager evaluate the trainee's plan of action, activities attempted, sales and efficiency results, and management effectiveness.

- When the trainee has satisfactorily completed all requirements in a project, the store manager certifies the trainee's ability to effectively manage that particular area. The trainee can then proceed to the next project as dictated by his or her job assignment in the store.

- If the trainee's results are not judged by the store manager as the best possible, the trainee is asked to repeat the learning project and plan of action until he or she achieves acceptable results.

- Once an employee completes all three phases of the program and has gained some expertise in all areas of store management, he or she is given an opportunity to manage an entire store for up to two weeks, often while the manager is on vacation.

- Assuming the trainee has met an acceptable standard of achievement throughout the program, he or she attends a six-day Management Candidate Seminar at the home site for an intensive week of review and additional management training.

Supervisors and Organization Change and Development

The supervisor's role in the organization is increasingly difficult to generalize about. Each organization places supervisors in a slightly different context from other organizations. Generally, however, the supervisors' role has emerged from one that was clearly defined for one-on-one authority relationships with subordinates, as shown in Fig. 32-3, to one requiring some form of team or group relationship not wholly dependent upon a concept of institutionalized authority.[32]

As mentioned earlier, nearly 20 percent of supervisors feel that they are miscast and ineffective in their current roles. Part of this dissatisfaction arises from the ambiguity of their position and the lack of a strong organizational support system.[33] Wolfe[34] observes that for supervisors to be effective, their roles must be established by a realistic organization strategy. He faults the present concept of the supervisor's role for the following conditions:

- Supervisors are expected to act as the linkage between management and non-management, which requires balancing two divergent viewpoints.

- Supervisors are expected to be action takers when change is required, even though their authority for introducing change is often nonexistent.

- Supervisors are frequently at a dead end in terms of promotability, even though they may be fully committed to the management team. Cummings[35] deplores this. He says, "To be promoted to a supervisory position early in one's career and never again be promoted can create a demotivating attitude....Career development and human resources planning programs can appear incoherent and paradoxical to these supervisors."

Wolfe also observes that "The supervisor's job has little real authority and, in a practical sense, is not viewed as a real management job." That is a harsh conclusion to draw, but it is one that should get greater attention from organization development people. Wolfe goes on to say that since supervisors have so little authority-related leverage, they must learn to exercise influence and to use available resources, especially through staff specialist groups. This influence, Wolfe says, should have two dimensions: (1) functional information which requires that supervisors know not only their own jobs but their subordinates' jobs well enough to supervise them effectively and (2) all the managerial-process and interpersonal skills needed to build an effective work group. As a consequence, Wolfe suggests a more functional definition of the supervisor's role:

> The role of the supervisor is to use influence and management work to maintain and measurably improve the return on the use of organizational resources at the point where physical work takes place.

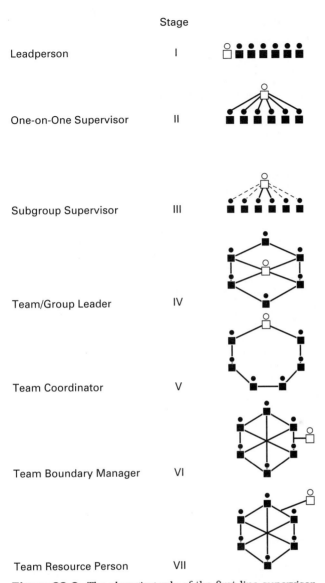

Stage

Leadperson — I

One-on-One Supervisor — II

Subgroup Supervisor — III

Team/Group Leader — IV

Team Coordinator — V

Team Boundary Manager — VI

Team Resource Person — VII

Figure 32-3. The changing role of the first-line supervisor. (*Adapted from Carl A. Bramlette, "Free to Change,"* Training and Development Journal, *March 1984, p. 39.*)

Such a definition would help to make supervisory training objectives more concrete. It would depend, however, upon (1) a specific articulation of how supervisors are to perform management work, (2) greater clarification of the kinds of relationships supervisors should have with management and nonmanagement personnel, and (3) improved reinforcement and support from middle and upper-level management.

Self-Development for Supervisors

Kur and Pedler[36] believe that the greatest improvement in supervisory performance will occur through self-development, using selected organization development techniques. They agree that self-development "is the most complex, difficult form of learning" but they emphasize that it "results in more mature, more competent individuals." They advise that such learning takes place at three levels: (1) participants first acquire the learning specified by the organization of which they are a part; (2) they then identify their own needs and the resources available and how to evaluate, monitor, and control their own learning processes; and (3) they learn to manage through egalitarian, people-centered means.

The OD approach that Kur and Pedler discuss includes several techniques such as action learning, field study and joint development activities, and body-mind approaches. The most appropriate OD techniques for supervisory development, however, would appear to be:

Structured experiences, which place the supervisor in a learning situation of accelerated experience, following a preprogrammed or structured set of activities requiring various levels of interaction. Emphasis is upon discovery of information and new ways of behavior leading to problem solving rather than upon expository learning. Structured experiences usually involve activity over relatively short intervals, seldom exceeding three hours.

Coaching, in which an informed helper assists the supervisor in problem solving or mastering new skills. In sales training, this is often called *curbstone coaching.* One variant used in supervisory development has the trainer "shadowing" a supervisor for several days, after which the two "process" or discuss each event, assessing the supervisor's handling of each event and identifying alternative approaches that might be used in similar situations in the future.

Experiential groups, including T-groups, sensitivity training, and encounter groups. Learning takes place as individuals discuss with group members the events that unfold during the life of the group. Though such groups were once very popular, results are often contradictory and nonproductive unless the learning sessions are conducted by professionally trained leaders under widely accepted professional guidelines.

Evaluation

Program evaluation encompasses five basic elements:[37] (1) identification of the decision makers who seek information and/or validation of the effectiveness of a particular training program (these people influence the budgets that support the program, and it is essential that their expectations be determined in advance); (2) clarification of the goals and objectives of the program, along with a specifically defined statement of their content; (3) translation of these objectives into criteria or standards for postcompletion evaluation; (4) a method of obtaining the measurements; and (5) interpretation of the evaluation information provided by the measurements.

Evaluation Criteria

Evaluation criteria can be classified as either objective or subjective, quantitative or qualitative. Often, they are a mixture of each. Among the most commonly used evaluation criteria, or methods, for supervisory training programs are the following:

Objective Criteria

- Testing (of course-related knowledge, skills, or attitudes) before and after training
- Records of production, costs, quality, safety, or other performance-related measures
- Records of absences, turnover, tardiness, grievances, or other employee behavior measures
- Comparative review of supervisors' performance appraisals prior to and after training
- Comparative study of before-and-after attitude surveys among employees supervised by the trainees
- Program evaluation studies conducted by an independent auditor
- Attainment of specified objectives

Subjective Criteria

- Trainee's reaction during or at close of program
- Trainee's reaction three to six months after training
- Appraisal of the program by the trainees' immediate superiors
- Impressions voiced by higher management
- Trainer's evaluation of the program
- Informal observations

For additional advice on evaluation criteria, see the previous section on "Objectives."

Evaluation Techniques

The more traditional evaluation methods are indicated in the list above. Swierczek and Carmichael,[38] however, enlarge upon these in a conceptual fashion. They suggest, for example, the following:

- *An open-ended questionnaire* distributed at the end of a program segment. Two questions are asked: "What skills did you learn at this seminar?" and "How will you apply these skills back at work?" No instructions are provided the respondent in order to reduce the bias inherent in conventional evaluation checklists.
- *Administration of standard "how-supervise" type of instruments* before and after the seminar. One that has proven to be particularly effective uses a series of questions based upon Likert's systems 1 to 4 by which he categorizes supervisory management styles as ranging from 1 (Autocratic) through 2 (Benevolent) and 3 (Consultative) to 4 (Participative). Instrument questions probe such things as confidence in subordinates, encouraging communications, acceptance of subordinates' ideas, responsibility for group goals, levels at which decisions are made, etc.

- *A follow-up survey checklist administered before the training as well as six months after.* Validated skill areas include: (1) identify and attempt to eliminate interruptions and time wasters, (2) assign tasks to subordinates, (3) provide subordinates with exact references to behavior in order to document performance problems, and (4) facilitate feedback from subordinates. This technique also uncovers supervisory resistance to, or failure to adopt, theoretically sound practices such as "setting priority tasks on a regular basis" and "keeping daily logs."

Environmental Influences

Almost all evaluations, other than those dependent exclusively upon performance documentation, are subject to uncontrollable influence in the supervisor's environment. Accordingly, Clement and Arand[39] remind trainers of three contingency variables that should be considered when evaluations are interpreted: (1) influence from the organizational setting (objectives, policies, practices, supervisor's authority to administer rewards and punishment, work-group expectations, etc.); (2) nature of the supervisor to be trained (education, experience, expectations, etc.); and (3) problems to be solved by the training program (ranging from simple, tangible, and immediate to complex, ambiguous, and long-term). The authors observe, for example, that supervisory training is more effective with young, relatively new supervisors, responsible for a small number of subordinates, and with a short period of total service.

Summary

The supervisor's job has been shaped by the changing and ever-intensifying pressures placed upon it by the environment. From what was once a simple emphasis upon the job and work requirements, factors external to the immediate job concerns have evolved to make the supervisor's job incredibly more complex and demanding. The implications for supervisory training are extensive and are reflected in contemporary development programs. Nevertheless, supervisory development remains a unique form of improvement activity, distinctive from the broader areas of management and executive development. It requires from the HRD professionals: (1) a practical recognition of the innate qualifications, limitations, and aspirations of the supervisors participating in such development, (2) a genuine knowledge of the specific competencies required of these supervisors in their work assignments, (3) a particular sensitivity to the roles and relationships imposed upon the supervisors by the organization structure and cultures in which they perform, and (4) a realization that supervisory development presents a moving target requiring that those who are responsible be open to and alert to the continuing evolution of the supervisor's role and the need to constantly modify programs.

References

1. Bittel, Lester R., and Jackson E. Ramsey, "The Limited, Traditional World of Supervision," *Harvard Business Review*, July–August 1982, pp. 26–36, and Lester R. Bittel and Jackson E. Ramsey, *Report of the National Survey of Supervisory Management Practices*, Center for Supervisory Research, James Madison University, Harrisonburg, VA, April

1982, and further replicated by an unpublished survey of 2000 supervisors in 1992 by Jackson E. Ramsey.

2. Prokopenko, J., and Lester R. Bittel, "A Modular Course-Format for Supervisory Development," *Training and Development Journal,* February 1981, pp. 14–22.

3. *Foremen Thinking: A Survey for the Foremanship Foundation,* Opinion Research Corporation, Princeton, NJ, 1970.

4. Bittel and Ramsey, op. cit. (no. 1).

5. Newstrom, John W., and Lester R. Bittel, *Supervision: Managing for Results,* Glencoe/McGraw-Hill, Westerville, OH, 1996, Chapter 1, "The Supervisor's Role in Management."

6. Newstrom, John W., and Jon L. Pierce, *Windows into Organizations,* AMACOM, NY, 1990, Chapter 13, "Organizational Culture"; Chapter 14, "Organizational Environment"; Chapter 15, "Participative Management."

7. Macdonald, Charles R., *Performance Based Supervisory Development: Adapted from a Major AT&T Study,* Human Resources Development Press, Amherst, MA, 1982, p. 24.

8. Baker, H. Kent, and Steven H. Holmberg, "Stepping Up to Supervision: Making the Transition," *Supervisory Management,* vol. 26, no. 9, September 1981, pp. 10–18.

9. "What's Ahead in Personnel?" *Industrial Relations News,* March 1978, p. 3.

10. Cover, William H., "Stepping Back to Basics," *Training and Development Journal,* November 1975, pp. 3–6.

11. Jones, Pamela R., Beverly Kaye, and Hugh R. Taylor, "You Want Me to Do What?" *Training and Development Journal,* July 1981, pp. 56–62.

12. Gellerman, Saul W., "Supervision: Substance and Style," *Harvard Business Review,* March 1976, pp. 87–89. See also W. Earl Sasser, Jr., and Frank S. Leonard, "Let First-Level Supervisors Do Their Job," *Harvard Business Review,* March–April 1980, pp. 50–60.

13. Bittel and Ramsey, op. cit. (no. 1).

14. Northrup, H. W., R. M. Cowin, L. G. Vanden Plas, and W. E. Fulmer, *The Objective Selection of Supervisors: A Study of Informal Practices and Two Models of Supervisory Selection,* The Wharton School, University of Pennsylvania, Philadelphia, 1978.

15. Benson, Carl A., "New Supervisors: From the Top of the Heap to the Bottom of the Heap," *Personnel Journal,* April 1976, pp. 176–178.

16. Byham, William C., "Assessment Center Method," in L. R. Bittel and Jackson E. Ramsey, eds., *The Handbook of Professional Management,* McGraw-Hill, New York, 1985, pp. 40–43.

17. Parry, Scott B., and Edward J. Robinson, "Management Development: Training or Education?" *Training and Development Journal,* July 1979, pp. 8–13.

18. Langdon, Danny G., "The Individual Management Development Program," *Training and Development Journal,* March 1982, pp. 78–82.

19. Fox, Gregory R., *Course Management Guide: What Every Supervisor Should Know,* 6th ed., ancillary to *What Every Supervisor Should Know,* 6th ed., Lester R. Bittel and John W. Newstrom, Glencoe, Westerville, OH, 1990, pp. 3–9.

20. Bittel, Lester R., *The Complete Guide to Supervisory Training and Development,* Addison-Wesley, Reading, MA, 1987. See Appendix 3, "Twenty-Five Model Course Outlines."

21. Wikstrom, Walter S., *Supervisory Training,* The Conference Board, New York, 1973.

22. McKeon, William J., "How to Determine Off-Site Meeting Costs," *Training and Development Journal,* May 1981, pp. 116–122.

23. Newstrom, John W., and E. E. Scannell, *Games Trainers Play,* McGraw-Hill, New York, 1980; Newstrom, John W., and E. E. Scannell, *More Games Trainers Play,* McGraw-Hill, 1983; Newstrom, John W., and E. E. Scannell, *Still More Games Trainers Play,* McGraw-Hill, 1991.

24. Parry and Robinson, op. cit. (no. 17).

25. Broadwell, Martin M., "Supervisory Training in the 80s," *Training and Development Journal*, February 1980, p. 44. See also "The Role of the Supervisor in the Organization," in Martin M. Broadwell, ed., *Supervisory Handbook*, Wiley, New York, 1985.

26. Fulmer, William E., "The Making of a Supervisor," *Personnel Journal*, March 1977, pp. 140–141.

27. Short, Ronald R., "Managing Unlearning," *Training and Development Journal*, July 1981, pp. 37–44.

28. Rosenthal, Steven M., and Bob Mezoff, "Improving the Cost/Benefit of Management Training," *Training and Development Journal*, December 1980, pp. 102–106.

29. Rosenthal and Mezoff, op. cit. (no. 28).

30. Doud, Ernest A., and Edward J. Miller, "First-Line Supervisors: Key to Improved Performance," *Management Review*, December 1980, pp. 18–24.

31. Kelley, Nancy, "Zale Corporation's Career Development Program," *Training and Development Journal*, June 1982, pp. 70–75.

32. Bramlette, Carl A., Jr., "Free to Change," *Training and Development Journal*, March 1984, pp. 32–40.

33. Bittel and Ramsey, op. cit. (no. 1).

34. Wolfe, Edward H., "Supervisory Development: The Need for an Integrated Strategy," *Training and Development Journal*, March 1983, pp. 28–31.

35. Cummings, Paul W., "Supervisory Expectations versus Organizational Reality," *Training and Development Journal*, September 1976, pp. 37–41.

36. Kur, C. Edward, and Mike Pedler, "Innovative Twists in Management Development," *Training and Development Journal*, June 1982, pp. 88–96.

37. Bakken, David, and Alan L. Bernstein, "A Systematic Approach to Evaluation," *Training and Development Journal*, August 1982, pp. 44–51.

38. Swierczek, Fredric William, and Lynne Carmichael, "The Quantity and Quality of Evaluating Training," *Training and Development Journal*, January 1985, pp. 95–99.

39. Clement, Ronald W., and Eileen K. Arand, "Evaluating Management Training: A Contingency Approach," *Training and Development Journal*, August 1982, pp. 39–43.

Additional Resources

Certo, Samuel C., *Supervision: Quality and Diversity Through Leadership*, Irwin, Burr Ridge, IL, 1994.

Comstock, Thomas W., *Fundamentals of Supervision: The First-Line Manager at Work*, Delmar Publishers, Albany, NY, 1994.

Imundo, Louis V., *The Effective Supervisor's Handbook*, 2d ed., AMA, New York, 1994.

Kirkpatrick, Thomas O., and Chad T. Lewis, *Effective Supervision: Preparing for the 21st Century*, Dryden Press, Troy, MO, 1995.

Larkin, T. J., and Sandar Larkin, *Communicating Change*, McGraw-Hill, New York, 1995.

Loen, Raymond O., *Superior Supervision: The 10% Solution*, Lexington Books/Macmillan, New York, 1994.

Napier, Rodney, and Matti Gershenfeld, *Groups: Theory and Experience*, 5th ed., Houghton Mifflin, Boston, 1993.

Newstrom, John W., and Keith Davis, *Organizational Behavior: Human Behavior at Work*, 9th ed., McGraw-Hill, New York, 1993. (Tenth edition is forthcoming.)

Pell, Arthur R., *The Supervisor's Infobank: 1000 Quick Answers to Your Toughest Problems*, McGraw-Hill, New York, 1994.

Robbins, Stephen P., *Supervision Today!*, Prentice Hall, New York, 1995.

Sholtes, Peter, *The Team Handbook: How to Use Teams to Improve Quality*, Joiner and Associates, Madison, WI, 1988.

Varney, Glenn, *Building Productive Teams: An Action Guide and Reference Book*, Jossey-Bass, San Francisco, 1989.

33

Career
Development

John E. McMahon

Stephen K. Merman

John E. McMahon *consults with organizations in the area of executive development and succession planning. His career has been in the field of human resources with his most recent industrial position as Director of Worldwide Management Development at Johnson Wax, Racine, Wisconsin. In this position, he directed the executive succession planning and management development for this global enterprise. He is one of the pioneers in executive succession planning and development for multinational organizations. McMahon joined Johnson Wax after 20 years with Union Carbide and 5 years with Smith Kline in the field of human resource development. He is most noted for his innovative life-career planning workshops and management development through the University of Michigan (Division of Management Education). He has introduced new programs for business, education, industry, and government and has contributed significantly to the field of career development. McMahon is an adjunct faculty member at the University of Wisconsin Management Institute in Madison. He served as the 1985–1986 Chairperson for the Career Development Professional Practice Area for ASTD. In 1983, he received ASTD's Professional Development Award for his contribution and commitment to career development and the HRD profession. In 1986, he received the Walter Storey Award for Leadership in Career Development. He has a bachelor's degree from St. Vincent College and a master of science degree from Canisius College.*

Stephen K. Merman *is with King Chapman Broussard and Gallagher, a Houston-based management consulting firm specializing in assisting organizations in implementing strategies to achieve competitive advantage. Merman has a national reputa-*

tion for his involvement and passion for career development and management systems for individuals and organizations. He is committed to the possibility of a generative organization where the worth and dignity of individuals are celebrated to gain competitive advantage. Merman has worked for both public and private organizations including the University of Colorado, U.S. Army, and more recently, Amoco Production Company. He has held numerous leadership positions with ASTD and served as its national president in 1992. He is the recipient of ASTD's Torch Award and the 1988 Walter Storey Award for Leadership in Career Development. A graduate of the University of Colorado, Merman completed his master's and doctoral programs at The American University in Washington, DC.

The effective management and development of an organization's workforce has received increasingly more attention in light of the emerging and rapidly changing and complex global marketplace. Technology, customer service, expanding global markets, changing workforce values, and the skill gap that emerges from what organizations need in terms of employee capabilities and what is available have all contributed to a dramatic change in how people manage and control careers.

Early career development efforts were built around the individual and programs were designed solely to help them achieve a sense of control and freedom in managing their careers. A shift has been dramatic, particularly in recent years. This shift is largely due to the following conditions:

- Organizations move toward quality and customer service
- Globalization of markets, delivery systems, and products
- Development of technology that speeds the delivery of products and services to customers
- Increased activity in restructuring, reengineering business processes, and work redesign
- Frequent reductions in the workforce with large-scale downsizings
- Growing numbers of nonwhite workers and women in the workforce
- Need for customization and specialization of products and services
- Need for a diverse, well-trained, and competitive workforce to sustain market advantage

These and other conditions forced organizations to take a hard look at how they manage their workforce and how they move people in, through, and out of the organization. Getting smart about how to do this and still sustain a competitive advantage became the desired outcome of career systems work in organizations.

This chapter offers a practical source of information regarding career development systems and practices in not only today's organization but tomorrow's as well. The information presented can be used to promote a healthy interchange of ideas and experiences related to how people interface with organizations in terms of movement within career disciplines. The information helps the reader understand how an organization can achieve key strategic staffing requirements to be competitive through the application of exciting new career development concepts.

High-performing organizations have discovered that the *investment* in employee growth and development through career development programs, policies, and practices is the competitive advantage they seek. Returns on shareholder *equity and dividends* can be directly linked to those processes that have helped individuals connect their individual career needs, interests, and values with the competitive requirements of the organization. In short, the career development field has "cracked the code" on how to help individuals and organizations align themselves to achieve an advantage in the global marketplace.

A Case for Career Development

A 1994 survey of HRD executives by the ASTD revealed several trends that will impact workplace learning and performance in the future. Among the top trends in this survey was the need for a "high-performance work organization, defined for the survey as organizations in which work is reorganized, redesigned, or reengineered to improve performance."[1] The condition of a high-performance work organization and the means of staffing it are not new concerns but they have emerged as the number-one developmental issue for organizations as we close out the twentieth century. Eric Vetter, an early pioneer in succession planning and staffing, defined manpower planning more than 25 years ago as "the process by which management determines how the organization should move from its current manpower position to its desired manpower position." Vetter positioned the often-heard notion of right person, right job, right skills, right time, and right place when he stated: "Through planning, management strives to have the right number and the right kinds of people, at the right places, at the right time, doing things which result in both the organization and the individual receiving maximum long-run benefit."[2] This formula has become the primary design for many career development programs in business, industry, government, and education.

Assessment of the capability needs of the workforce in terms of what is required to be competitive and what currently is in place reveals a gap that needs to be addressed with a flexible, responsive, and relevant development strategy to support an organization's financial and operational results.

Career Development as a Competitive Reason

Where does career development fit into this scenario? When an organization reorganizes, redesigns, and reengineers to sustain a high-performance work environment, the impact on individuals is both dramatic and, in some cases, traumatic. Individuals may be required to redesign themselves and perhaps reengineer and "reskill" their careers to meet the new and ever-changing requirements of the organization to remain employed.

Although the employee may have performed well in the past, there are often two pieces of information that can be disturbing. First, the organization needs the employee to do her or his job differently; consequently, there is a need to manage change effectively and adjust to the changing conditions of the workplace. Second, the employee may not have the new skills required. So the organization may decide to either (1) redeploy the employee to a position for which he or she can qualify, (2) realign the organization to either close facilities or eliminate certain lines of products and services, (3) significantly reduce the size of the workforce through layoffs or early retirements, or (4) retrain the workforce to require the necessary skills. The not-so-good news for the employee is that it may be more cost-effective for the organization to recruit in the necessary talent instead of retraining that person because (1) there isn't enough time to retrain given the speed of change in the market and (2) there aren't the investment dollars available to do extensive retraining.

What Now?

What is in place to help the organization effectively manage the workforce when these changes happen? What assistance is available to employees to help them sort through what is happening to them? What can an organization do to retain high performers, redirect mediocre performers, and assist poor performers in discovering work environments where they can be successful?

This is the context into which career development systems and programs seek to provide solutions. The key questions are

- Do we have the bench strength to fulfill the strategic needs of the organization?
- How can we retain the talent we have without cutting into the muscle of the organization via downsizing?
- How do we know we are keeping the right people?

Career Development: The Continuing Transformation

Webster defines *career* as a course of life for which one trains or prepares professionally and personally. A broad definition of career development is that it is a continuous process involving the individual's participation in her or his own professional growth and development. Modern views of this word (derived from the French *carriere*—a race course) have added career planning, career management, career engineering, career reengineering, and recareering as terms to describe how a person progresses through his or her work life.

As the word *career* itself evolves and takes on broader meanings, careers will be viewed in different ways. They are often associated with jobs, workplace learning, and training. Traditionally, career planning began to emerge from the notions of manpower planning that characterized management thinking in the 1960s and 1970s. During the 1980s, however, there was a significant shift from the responsibility being totally in the hands of the organization to the responsibility being with the employee working in partnership with the organization.

Recently we have seen an even further shift toward the individual, with the organization's role being one of providing information, third-party resources, consultants, and career development specialists to assist the individual in fulfilling his or her part of the partnership. This trend is largely due to the shifting nature of the individual-organization contract which has altered the way people view careers in organizations, particularly in the areas of entitlement, loyalty, and "being mobile" (the process of how people flow through an organization). For example, the expectation now is that a person may move from one organization to another without being loyal to just one or two particular organizations.

Professionals may have several jobs listed on their résumé. They may expect to change jobs several times during their careers or take on various roles that are not traditionally viewed as "jobs"; rather their position may be viewed as contributing necessary competencies to help organizations be competitive at certain points in time and place. As previously discussed, the organization's need to have the right person in the right place with the right job at the right time with the right skills has significantly altered work and careers. In some situations, the "right" person may become the "wrong" person very quickly—as in a matter of a few months.

What's Next?

The changing world of work has also altered how and where people do their work. By 2005, it is estimated that over 40 million people will be working at home. The notion of work at any time and at any place will require a whole new set of career competencies. For example, access to the information mainstream will be a necessary requirement for all jobs and people will have to create new disciplines to manage their responsibilities without direct supervision or direction.

The tracking of careers and performance will need to change as people work with less supervision and have greater responsibility and accountability with customers. A shift from managers and supervisors having direct control over the work activities of others to team leaders having that authority requires that all employees exhibit key leadership skills and qualities to be competitive.

Smaller and more intimate work groups dictate that careers will have to be managed in a more ambiguous way, with a "career path" defined to mean differentiated roles and value-added responsibilities versus job descriptions and upward movement to positions of greater responsibility.

Human resource systems and processes may need to be reengineered to reflect the ongoing dynamics of a changing marketplace. Policies and practices that were created in the past may need to be altered to match the speed and flexibility of the organization as it adapts to the marketplace.

Organizations: Individuals

The Organization of the Future

How will the organization of the twenty-first century operate? There are many answers and opinions regarding this intriguing question. Most futurists agree, however, that with the advent of the information age and the importance of an individual having the ability and competence to access and manage information, the possibility exists that work will happen *any time and at any place.*

The "work at any time and any place" scenario opens up incredible opportunity for careers and options for individuals. The organization becomes a source for information, resources, and direction. The individual becomes an independent contributor who either works alone or as a member of a *team* that strategically works to seek some competitive advantage. Regardless of their role, these teams would have direct access to their customers and rely on a small, yet cost-effective organization for leadership, learning systems, and strategic financial, technological, and human resources to maintain market share.

Employees now and in the future will need the interpersonal relationships and influencing skills to interface with a variety of teams formed to generate short-term strategic actions. This situation is very different from that of being a member of just one team and simply interfacing with a few customers.

The 7-S Model

The often used 7-S model created by Richard Pascal, Tony Anthos, Robert Waterman, and Tom Peters and utilized by McKenzie and Company to help organizations assess themselves can be useful in describing the organization of the future. The seven items making up the model (all beginning with the letter s) include *strategy, structure, systems, staffing, style, skills,* and *shared values.*[3] Once mission, vision, and values are established by the organization, the 7-S analysis helps to clarify what is required organizationally in carrying out the mission and fulfilling the vision.

The following is a summary of the 7-S's and the impact on organizations and individuals:

Strategy. The organization needs strategies that are consistent, yet flexible enough to meet the changing needs of the marketplace. Customer requirements are, in some businesses, moving targets and change frequently. An organization that can respond quickly and implements a strategy that meets those requirements can sustain the competitive edge.

Structure. Flatter organizational structures with the focus on customer contact is a growing trend. Corporate structures are reduced, with a combination of centralized and decentralized units, depending on the needs of strategic business organizations in meeting customer needs. Teams are developed with team leaders instead of managers.

Systems. If the strategy is flexible and can respond quickly, so should systems that support the structures. Centralized services as well as decentralized services can be organized quickly to have a delivery capability that meets the needs of a customer in a precise and accurate way better than can a competitor.

Staffing. "Contract" employees who are specialized in a particular area are increasingly being utilized to best meet customer requirements at the moment. Employees in such a system may be temporary and only serve for a short time period in one organization, then contract their services to another organization. The employee works for a temporary-services organization and receives benefits and services from this organization rather than the one supervising the work. Organizations need a flexible workforce and will staff according to the requirements needed to be competitive.

Organizations may contract out their workforce to others in times of reduced needs due to business cycles or downturns. This practice provides a way to reduce their need for downsizing and yet sustain a stable workforce that is well-trained and competitive. Organizations may also contract their workforce to their suppliers as a way to help improve the quality of goods and services provided.

Style. The cultural characteristics of the organization is one of sharing the power with those who are closest to the customer. A shift from top-to-bottom structures to bottom-to-top will mean a shift in how people are treated and empowered to do their work. Jobs as we know them will disappear and people will do work in a collaborative and cooperative manner to achieve the necessary results. As previously indicated, the team environment will require new and different skills and competencies in the area of relationship building, influencing, and working as a team player.

Skills.   The distinction between a "knowledge" worker and a "service" worker is more and more apparent. Employees have to participate fully in the learning environment in order to stay current and "marketable." The marketplace may require short-term applications of skills, then moving to another situation within or outside of the organization. Learning systems in organizations will have to be responsive to changing needs and prepared to train or educate employees at a moment's notice.

Employees are now required to have a whole new set of behaviors and competencies that include such generic skills as information management, team skills, influencing and integrity, interpersonal skills, and customer relations. Instead of laying off employees, organizations will focus on efficient methods to retrain the workforce in capabilities and competencies anticipated from market surveys and customer input.

Shared Values.   What people have in terms of values and beliefs about organizations and employee development is significantly changing now and it will continue to do so in the future. Organizations will have to continually review what they feel is important in operating their businesses. Employees will have to decide if those values are consistent with their own. For example, an organization totally structured and focused on customers and markets will endure a difficult transformation as they shift from a traditional command-and-control environment to one of employee accountability, empowerment, and control of product and service delivery. Employees will have to decide if they can endure the transition and cope with the gap in values between what is said and what is actually done.

Loyalty Redefined

Employees and organizations continually seek to define and redefine the nature of their relationship. For our purposes, loyalty refers to both the organization and/or the individual's profession or discipline. Expectations for both the individual and the organization remain the same in certain conditions (such as a day's work for a day's pay) while in others there are dramatic differences. For example job security continues to surface as a key issue. Employees want security; organizations are reluctant to provide it.

The essence of career development processes is to help individuals reassess priorities and take personal responsibility for their own development. From the organization's perspective, there are no guarantees, no certainty that the organization will or can sustain itself for an extended time period. There are always conditions out there that would lead to a merger, acquisition, closure, or buyout. Living in constant uncertainty changes the rules for an organization's commitment to lifelong employment for the employee.

Individuals must shift their attitude to one that allows them more freedom and control of choices. They must anticipate the future and communicate to the organization that "I will go to work and be loyal, committed, and productive for your enterprise. However, if I start getting cues that the organization may not be in business in the near future, then I will begin to exercise my options and may seek other opportunities."

A prevailing attitude is "I don't *need* to be here. I choose to be here because the environment is meeting my needs…but I don't *need* to be here because of other choices and options. This represents a sense of control over a career and in relation to the organization or my discipline."

What's New and What's Working?

During the years that organizations have been working with career systems we have learned a great deal about what works and what doesn't work.

Gutteridge, Leibowitz, and Shore conducted a survey in 1990[4] to report on the current state of the practice of career development. Of the many surprising results, what was most striking is that organizations are finally viewing career development as an integral part of their strategy. In other words, key line managers and executives are involving themselves in creating systems and programs that will assist them in meeting their operational results as well as assist individuals in the alignment of their special career interests and competencies to the needs of the organization.

What works in organizations? A review of the Gutteridge, Leibowitz, and Shore data, common experiences among practitioners in the field, and the survey literature shows that the following seem to work.

Organization Strategy

First and foremost, the career system should link directly to the business strategy. If the stakeholders in the organization cannot perceive how these programs will assist in achieving their operational and financial goals, then any career development activity may not work. Calibrating the initiative to a "strategy" will do wonders in selling the activity to employees at all levels. As new initiatives develop, the career systems *must* be tied to those initiatives and the value-added relationship demonstrated.

Employee Involvement

In the systems reviewed, what works is the direct involvement and ownership of employees at all levels in the design and development of the system. Their input and enthusiasm not only can help make the system work but also can promote its ongoing application. Usually, a strong employee-involvement culture within an organization contributes significantly in making the system work.

Operational Accountability

A common practice that has proven beneficial in most organizations is promoting the system as an operating responsibility. The system is viewed as an initiative within operations and not something that was created by the human resources department. Human resources involvement and commitment is critical; however, best practices indicate that organizations successful in career development should not locate the program within human resources.

Executive Sponsorship

What works best in career systems is the willingness of a senior-level executive officer to be the champion for the initiative. This person ideally should become involved in the design of the system as well as work to ensure its ongoing applications to the organization. Being the sponsor means not only attending meetings but also engaging oneself in making sure the initiative fulfills the competitive requirements of the organization.

Employee Accountability for Career Management

In most any system, its success depends on the willingness and capability of employees in taking full accountability for the management of their careers. In terms of the success of people aligning themselves to the needs of the organization, accountability should rest with the individual and a shared accountability with the organization. The organization provides resources, information, and programs, while the individual takes on the determination of career direction and choice.

Line and Staff Management Involvement. In successful systems, there is an opportunity for line managers to become involved in the actual design of the system as well as its ongoing operation. Through the use of steering committees, focus groups, career advisor roles, and advisory panels, the workable systems create ways in which these people stay involved and enrolled in the results produced by the system.

Assessment Tools. There needs to be a methodology by which people can engage in the act of self-discovery or self-awareness. In order to make intelligent decisions regarding one's life and career, the system must provide tools and exercises designed to uncover the true self. Assessments are generally in the area of behavioral traits, interests, values, beliefs, and identification of skills and competencies.

Resources for Supporting Discovery Process. One usually applies what one learns from self-assessment to the organization which provides various resources for doing so. For example, job posting, information interviewing, career advisors, self-assessment courses, opportunity centers performance management and developmental opportunities are just a few of the strategies provided in a career system.

Strategy to Sustain Program Visibility. Developing a communication strategy that will ensure the ongoing, day-to-day application of the system is likewise an essential ingredient. Bulletins, newsletters, frequent meetings, career advisors, advisory boards, etc., all help to keep the program visible. Continually stressing the benefits to key stakeholders is important, particularly if you can demonstrate positive results.

Manager's Role in the Organization of the Future

Top managers, middle managers, executives...all have careers and very critical career development needs. They are often overlooked, but they need to be involved if they are to own or champion career development.

The ongoing question facing all organizations is where will those who succeed the present leadership come from? For employees who have vertical aspirations in their career thinking, succession planning and development systems need to be rethought. Executive creativity is challenged to design infrastructure to identify the right talent for the needs. An example is the need to manage self-directed work teams and focus on the quality of products and services in the global arena.

Organizational changes have affected medium and large organizations in which traditional succession planning to ensure quality and quantity of management and career development systems has flourished. In the last few years, restructuring, resizing, and streamlining to be more "lean and mean" have cost several million jobs, especially in the middle-management levels.

On the other hand, in recent years, millions of new jobs have been created in smaller entrepreneurial organizations. Succession and career planning focus more on ensuring backup for specialty and professional as well as managerial talents. Different managerial skills, more facilitative as opposed to being high-control, are required to "manage" new structures. A smaller organization may be in a better position to accommodate these ever-changing requirements.

The needs of building future management and accommodating those with management career interest now demand that succession planning shift from a program focus to an ongoing, continuous process yet still retain its longer-range purview. For this reason, succession planning systems need to be reengineered to reflect the ongoing dynamics of a changing marketplace. What was true and relevant in terms of skills and competencies at one point in time may not be true and relevant six months later. Succession planning will shift from a process that is usually annual to one of being ongoing, depending on the needs of the market.

Those organizations still hierarchical and rigidly bureaucratic will be forced in time by global competition to either change and become more flexible or risk takeovers by someone who can. Does this mean there is no longer enormous opportunity for career growth and fulfillment? "Absolutely not," according to Stephen Covey, "but rather than being measured by how many rungs on the corporate ladder you have ascended, career growth will be found in significant responsibility, in task force acumen, team and project leadership and in having the opportunity to creatively develop and use a broad range of one's abilities and talents."[5]

Skills in managing task forces, self-directed teams, project leadership and downward empowerment, and diverse and dispersed workforces are among the new skills and attributes for the new leadership which will be quite different than those that have been adequate up to now. Sharpened communication and listening skills and rigorous attention to results are required more than ever.

To fulfill its end of the contract, however, every organization, no matter what size, will empower (delegate downward with trust) individuals at all levels to play an even more responsible role in building their own careers.

Career Development Specialists

The career development specialist will find the field ripe for innovation to provide and help manage ever-changing systems and techniques and to ensure that these processes are continually updated.

The continual reduction of middle management and supervisory ranks has taken its toll. Management employees must take on additional responsibility of employee work and career objectives, performance reviews, and development. We are seeing the emerging need for a third party, most likely a combination of line managers and human resource professionals to facilitate career processes and keep the function alive in the organization.

Often, operating managers did not particularly relish nor did they do a good job tending to these type of activities. Despite attempts to adequately train them, there was often little consistency in how programs were conducted, and managers were not very enthusiastic. For example, managers abhorred performance appraisals as well as any career counseling that required dealing with sensitive or personal issues. That was a job for someone else.

Leaders of the future, however, will have to take on a totally different attitude and perspective of this function. They will be held accountable for the development of the people for whom they are responsible. They will need help.

Enter the career development specialist. Our review of organizations indicates that this role is identified in a variety of different titles to include career advisor, business performance consultant, organizational capability consultant, or career specialist. The primary purpose of this role is to provide professional attention to the career development needs of employees in relation to the competitive requirements of the organization.

In particular, the role serves to "keep the initiative in the face of management and employees" in order to consistently relate the activities to the business outcomes desired. The career development specialist must keep the initiative alive and remind people of its importance in the day-to-day operational activities.

By focusing their activities on the performance, the career development specialist serves a critical role in helping employees align their particular career interests and competencies to the competitive requirements of the organization. This relationship to the goals and objectives is absolutely critical to sustain the initiative and create value-added results from the workforce.

Specific Role of the Career Development Specialist

Career development specialists are professionals trained in various techniques, processes, and programs to help facilitate the alignment of employees to operational and financial goals. They work in a three-way relationship with managers-supervisors or team leaders and employees and engage in a business conversation. They are not in an ombudsman role to work out differences between team leaders and employees nor are they engaged in any way in the performance review process. They are considered independent, third-party professionals who are trained to keep their eye on the ball of the business and coach or facilitate others in aligning with that business.

Figure 33-1 illustrates the relationship between the career discussion process and the operational goals for the organization. The following describes the role each must play in fulfilling the business context of their relationship:

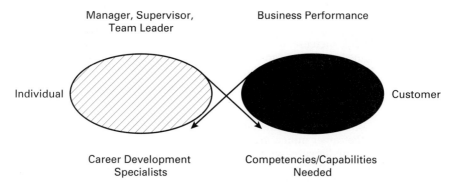

Figure 33-1. Relationship between business and career advisor role.

Individuals
- Be accountable for their own career management
- Utilize all resources to accomplish their career goals
- Review their progress periodically with the team leaders and career development specialists
- Implement actions on career plans
- Align career interests and personal competencies with the business requirements of the organization

Team leaders
- Communicate organizational capability needs
- Coach, mentor, and provide guidance as the business measures and results
- Coach direct reports in terms of options and mobility opportunities
- Implement and support career programs
- Provide business leadership

Career development specialist
- Know and understand business
- Manage the career system process
- Know and understand performance measures
- Provide organizational resources for employees
- Assist others in developing career skills
- Keep the process relevant to the business
- Conduct follow-up activities
- Liaison with the human resources department and top management

Five Career Development Criteria to Support CD Specialists

Five features or criteria important to the success of career planning are dialogue, guidance, the individual's involvement in the process, feedback to the individual, and the mechanisms by which the process operates.

Dialogue.   Dialogue represents the relationship between the individual and the organization. It might be between the individual and his or her immediate manager, the manager's manager, other interested parties, or the career development specialist. Often the career development specialist serves to facilitate the dialogue and helps increase the objectivity and vitality of the decisions. Through dialogue, openness and trust can be generated to the advantage of both the individual and the organization. Dialogue may be implemented in a number of ways, but the essential point is that without it, there is no possibility for career growth.

Guidance.   Guidance from management is, in essence, the provision of information about the career milieu in which the individual must function. An individual can plan intelligently with knowledge about options, opportunities, and goals available. The information can be provided by means of seminars or coaching from the career development specialist. It can be offered informally if no systematic program is available.

Individual's Involvement. A high degree of involvement must be established to allow individuals input into their career objectives, timetables, values, and other personally meaningful issues. Provision must be made to use this information once it is solicited to optimize the relationship between what the individual wants and what is needed.

It may be necessary to structure a sequence of events in order to obtain clear statements from individuals of what they, in fact, want. Doing so is not easy, since experience shows that individuals' desires are often poorly defined and are sometimes in conflict with the organization's goals. Special career planning workshops can be developed that will help identify and resolve career issues.

Feedback. Feedback to the individual is important in that it provides the basis for calibrating behavior or initiating appropriate changes in terms of what is learned. It may take the form of one-to-one discussions with team leaders and/or career development specialists; often it emerges from developmental experiences in which areas requiring change are pointed out.

Mechanisms of Career Planning. The mechanisms of career planning, or the processes and techniques, must interface with other human resource development subsystems. The potentially useful devices are numerous and are frequently the means by which the other four criteria are brought into being and sustained. In the following section, we describe selected approaches.

Techniques and Methods of Career Development Specialists

Career development discussions between managers, career development specialists, and employees are those links in the organizational career management process that facilitate employee growth and development. The interaction generates activity that can occur in the organization to help further assist the individual.

Career development programs take many forms, depending on the organization, the commitment, and a variety of other factors. Many devices are available, to assess skills, interests, values, beliefs, and behavioral traits. The following is a description of three of those devices: life and career planning, job posting, and interdependency.

Life and Career Planning

The life and career planning process is instrumental for career development activities in a growing number of organizations. It is a reasonably simple method to use and can be administered independently of any other program or system. Its costs are negligible, requiring only blank paper and a pencil for each participant for recording thoughts and reactions to stimulating questions about careers. An ordinary conference room can be used as long as chairs can be arranged in small circular groups of three or four. There are many variations of this process, but common to most is the idea that the individual is primarily responsible for his or her own career and that the result of the process is to have a written career plan in the individual's hands at the completion of the activity. This plan can be used to fit together the individual's purposes with the organization's.

Many people make the assumption that their future life or career is determined largely by their past or is controlled largely by people other than themselves. Career planning, dealing with a base of "here and now," often slips back into the past. It might be more effective if the process could slip more into the future. There is some credibility in "planning the future from the future." At times, it is useful to identify milestones in the future that are discussed as ways to get to the future.

The following sequence of exercises is a way of bringing the future of one's choice into being. Any of the exercises, or the entire sequence, could be done by individuals, pairs, or groups. The group method permits more sharing of one's plans with others and may generate more self-growth goals than could be achieved through self-insight alone.

Career by Objectives: A Hands-On Approach.   The following exercises should help participants confront various issues in their own lives and work to make choices that will lead to greater fulfillment of their potential. Career by Objectives helps the participants take stock of where they are now, what their plans are for the future, and how their career fits in with their situation. You might try this exercise yourself now or later with a group of peers.

Step One: Where I Am

This first step involves an examination of your current position in life and career and addresses the questions of where you are.

For a few moments, think about your entire life, from beginning to end, birth to death, womb to tomb. You might draw a line that represents your life from beginning to end (see Fig. 33-2). Your line may show peak experiences or events you remember vividly, important events that happened or may happen. Draw your line to include the past and present and draw it the way you think you would like it to go in the future. Draw the line out to the end of your life. Think about it! How would you like it to look?

Now put an X on your line to indicate where you are now.

Step Two: Who I Am

Think about who you are, the different roles you play. Ponder the question: "Who am I?" Think of as many answers as you can and write each one down on a separate slip of paper or 3 × 5 card. Use nouns (son, daughter, friend, sister, brother, names, woman, man), adjectives (quiet, talkative, active, athletic), or mixtures of the two (an active athlete, a loving son). You have many roles, responsibilities, and characteristics. Write statements if you feel it would help. Use a different card for each answer or statement.

Figure 33-2. Career by Objectives—where I am.

When you're finished, put the answers in order of importance to you. Think about which are temporary and which are permanent. Which would you like to take into the future with you? Which ones would be most valuable to your current organization? Which ones need to be left behind? Are there others you would like to add that are either important to you or to your organization?

Step Three: Where I Would Like to Be and What I Would Like to Have Happen

Spend the rest of the process on the part of your line from the X into the future. Now that you know where you are and who you are, look out to the very end of your line and think about where you would like to be or what you would like to have happen then. Think in terms of your career discipline, organization, and the industry in which your organization competes. What will be required in the future and how will you have to "be" in order to be competitive for jobs in the future?

Write a eulogy or autobiography to answer

What do you want to have accomplished?

What milestones were achieved along the way?

What do you want to be remembered for?

By writing answers to these questions, you are setting some goals regardless as to how specific or broad your thoughts may be.

Step Four: An Ideal Year in the Future

Come back to the present and select a 12-month portion in the future that you can arrange for yourself (e.g., see Fig. 33-3). Consider the following questions:

If you had unlimited resources, e.g., money or material, what would you do?

Allow yourself to fantasize and dream about the ideal environment. How would you look? feel? And what conditions are in place to support you?

Is this ideal environment in line with what you wrote as your life goals, or what you want to be remembered for, in the previous step?

Unlimited resources are difficult to imagine. We have found that even in this ideal environment, people put limits on their resources. Even though parts of the fantasy seem far-fetched, you may find many that are not so far from real and could be accomplished at least in part.

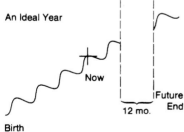

Figure 33-3. Career by Objectives—an ideal year in the future.

Step Five: An Ideal Job for You

Returning to the present and immediate future, think of an ideal job for you with your resources as you know them.

- Don't worry about titles or labels; rather think about a role you would like to play.
- Think of specific attributes about the job such as environment, people, tasks, working hours, location, etc.
- What kind of training or education will you need to do this role?
- How well are you qualified right now to do the role?

Step Six: Career by Objectives Inventory

Now let's take an inventory of how you view your current status using the following questions:

- In your life and career, what is your passion? What gets you up in the morning and excited about the day?
- What do you do well? What are you known for in your life?
- What do you feel you need in order to achieve your milestones and ultimate objectives—e.g., time, support, education, training, more resources?
- What would potentially keep you from achieving your objective?
- What actions should you put in place now to move forward?
- How would you describe your long-term career objective?

Summary

As illustrated in this exercise, there are a series of simplistic yet often difficult-to-answer questions. Essentially the exercise deals with the following questions: Where am I? Who am I? Where am I going? How can I best utilize my resources to get there? (See Fig. 33-4.)

The sequence requires periodic review. It is an educational process. Personal goals are desirable and worth working toward.

In management by objectives, goals are set for certain time periods. Strategies using available resources flow from the objectives. Specific actions and subsequent results achieved help input the objectives for the next time period. The career specialist must work to monitor these actions to ensure they are relevant to the operational and financial goals of the organization.

Experience has demonstrated that a one-day workshop is possible for a group of individuals. In between questions and group interaction on sharing responses, information is provided about the organizational career needs. When the first half of the workshop deals with life values and the second focuses on career issues and organizational needs, there is a helpful integration of individual and organizational goals. Although there are variations, this process is fairly consistent in career development work.

Job Posting

Job posting is the intraorganizational equivalent of publicly announcing position vacancies in the classified section of a newspaper. Candidates apply according to their aspirations and career plans. Individuals, motivated to apply for vacancies on their own, produce a vastly superior organizational climate for individual-organization (I-O) optimization than can be attained through any other single method of career planning. Systems combining job posting with other devices such as life and

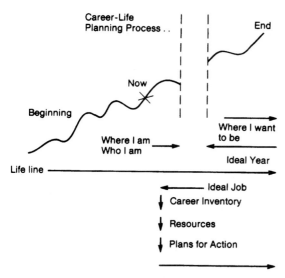

Figure 33-4. Career by Objectives—career life planning process.

career planning, assessment centers, organizational development, and management development are experiencing efficient and effective results. There is often a great deal of management resistance to the openness of announcing vacancies and their relative positions in the hierarchy, usually stated in terms meaning that individuals cannot be trusted to behave conveniently and rationally if they are given options. A solid career system can work to bridge the gap between what management knows and understands about employees and what is actually present.

Interdependency

One outgrowth of the I-O relationship is the increasing use of interdependency as a career management and development tool for individuals. The concept is simply the act of creating a positive, win-win relationship with another person for purposes of creating value for each. The idea goes beyond the traditional ideas of networking, which is usually reserved for information gathering and sharing. Interdependency requires much heavier involvement, participation, energy, time, and money to successfully complete.

Interdependency requires that an individual be quite selective in choosing another individual with whom to create the relationship. The choice must assure a relationship of benefit to both parties and must involve a project or program in which both can share acknowledgment and recognition equally. It may be a joint article, a book, a task force, or a special committee within an organization.

In terms of career management and development for an employee, interdependency becomes a powerful strategy used to enhance one's value, not only to the organization but also to one's profession. It is a strategy which can effectively increase a person's versatility or the options available to him or her. Finally, if done effectively, interdependency serves to enhance an individual's visibility to the organization as well as to the profession.

In terms of an organization's career and human resources planning systems, interdependent relationships among employees can produce significant benefits.

Not only are they motivating and rewarding for the employees, the relationships often produce increased productivity, new products and services, ways to decrease costs and increase profits, and new ways to produce collaborative problem solving among departments. The current focus on reengineering and work redesign illustrates an excellent example of interdependency when employees need to work cross-functionally as well as with various teams to produce operational results.

Organizations can promote the valuable strategy of interdependency among employees through innovative career management programs. Skills needed to create such relationships are often taught in career management seminars. These skills include the ability to build relationships, maundering, and determining self-marketing and presentation skills for seeking such opportunities. Organizations can also support interdependency among employees by open and supportive management styles that encourage, reinforce, and credit employees for their contributions.

What's Desired Next?

At the 1994 ASTD National Convention, a Career Development Professional Practice Area discussion facilitated by Marlys Hanson[6] revealed optimistic predictions about the field of career development. Among the items discussed, the following represents a look to the future of career development:

Viewed by senior management and employees as essential for performance

Bridges gap between present and future needs of the organization

Allows for a competitive strategy for both individuals and organizations

Integral part of every human resource development system or function

Focus on the integration of learning and work to enhance performance

Continuous lifelong process that applies to all

New culture, new norms, and new hope for the future

The session also addressed the types of payoffs for individuals, managers, and organizations for reaching the desired state of career development. The desired state is the integration and alignment of organizations and individuals to achieve competitive advantage. The following are some key points addressed:

Improved productivity, profits, morale, and performance

Employee retention and employability

A new and better way of life that is geared to the future

Trust built between employees and management

Community and society enhanced

Employee loyalty encouraged

Unwanted turnover and dramatic downsizings reduced

Organization is attractive to new hires

People provided with a sense of control, more energy, and improved job satisfaction

A well-trained, productive, and globally competitive workforce is generated

What's Possible for Career Development?

The future of the field is bright and full of opportunity. Given the ongoing changes in the workforce, the ever-increasing intensity of technology, information, and global competition, and pressures to accomplish more with fewer resources, the challenges facing our workforce will continue. Clearly, an infrastructure will be needed that helps people be resilient, productive, and motivated—systems that can assist people in moving cross-culturally to operate effectively in multinational organizations. The organization, in collaboration with the individual, will have to meet these challenges or risk being perceived as noncompetitive (individually as well as organizationally). We are rapidly learning that this risk is too great, and we have a strong need to apply our knowledge and expertise to create a well-trained, competitive, and motivated workforce. Career development will play a critical role now and in the future in creating that possibility.

References

1. *Training and Development,* vol. 48, no. 5, May 1994, pp. S-29–S-32.
2. Vetter, Eric, *Manpower Planning for High Talent Personnel,* Bureau of Industrial Relations, University of Michigan Graduate School of Business, Ann Arbor, 1967, p. 15.
3. Pascal, Richard, *Managing on the Edge,* Simon & Schuster, New York, 1991, p. 42.
4. Gutteridge, Thomas G., Zandy B. Leibowitz, and Jane Shore, *Organizational Career Development: Benchmarks for Building a World Class Workforce,* Jossey-Bass, San Francisco, 1993, pp. 14–15.
5. Covey, Stephen, "Career Wisdom for the 90s," *USA Today,* June 14, 1994.
6. Hanson, Marlys, "Survey: New Trends in Career Development," ASTD International Conference, Anaheim, CA, May 1994.

Additional Sources

Covey, Stephen, *The Seven Habits of Highly Effective People,* Fireside Press, Simon & Schuster, New York, 1989.

Felkins, Patricia K., B. J. Chakiris, and Kenneth Chakiris, *Change Management: A Model for Effective Organizational Performance,* Quality Resources, White Plains, NY, 1993, pp. 353–357.

Hanson, Marlys, "Job Fit and Creativity," *IEEE Potentials,* July 30, 1985.

McMahon, John, "Career Choices: A Hands-On Approach," *Engineering Horizons,* November 1985, pp. 11–12.

Merman, S. K., and B. J. Chakiris, *Best Practices in Career Development,* Infoline Series, ASTD, Alexandria, VA, 1994.

Merman, S. K., and Anne Clark, *Managing Toward Career Excellence,* King Chapman and Broussard, Houston, TX, 1987.

34

Continuing Professional Education

Donna S. Queeney

Donna S. Queeney is Director of Research and External Relations for Continuing Education and Distance Education and a faculty member in adult education at The Pennsylvania State University. She has conducted research, written, taught, and spoken internationally on continuing professional education, particularly in the areas of needs assessment and practice-oriented program development. She edited An Agenda for Action (1990), a series of reports on key issues in continuing professional education and is the author of Assessing Needs in Continuing Education (Jossey-Bass, 1995). She has been active in the National University Continuing Education Association, receiving that organization's 1991 Continuing Education for the Professions Individual Service Award. She has also received the 1995 Meritorious Service Award from the Association for Continuing Higher Education. She is founder of ATSD's Continuing Professional Education Network and for over 10 years has served as editor of The Journal of Continuing Higher Education. She earned a B.A. in liberal arts and an M.S. and Ph.D. in human development, all from Penn State.

Continuing professional education refers to the education of professional practitioners, regardless of their practice setting, that follows their preparatory curriculum and extends their learning, or assimilation of information and ideas that can contribute to the quality of their day-to-day performance, throughout their careers.[1] Ideally this education enables practitioners to keep abreast of new knowledge, maintain and enhance their competence, progress from beginning to mature practitioners, advance their careers through promotion and other job changes, and even more into different fields. Unlike much corporate training, continuing professional education focuses primarily on individual practitioners' growth and development. While application of learning to the work setting is a critical component of continuing professional education, such education emphasizes acquisition of knowledge, skills, and performance abilities that can be applied broadly rather than those that are task- or job-specific.

Although much has been written about the distinguishing characteristics of a profession as opposed to an occupation, when continuing professional education is considered the distinction between the two is not critical. The term *professional* generally is used broadly in this context to refer to any field of practice defined by a body of knowledge and requiring specific education for entry into practice. Hence many fields that might be regarded as occupations are encompassed in this definition. Similarly, the word *education* is used broadly and may overlap with *training*. However, some distinction is made between the more task-oriented approach connoted by *training* and the more conceptual orientation encompassed in *education*.

The Changing Role of Continuing Professional Education

According to Cyril Houle,[2] the lengthy first era of continuing professional education began some millennia ago in ancient times and continued through the apprenticeship systems of the Middle Ages and the Age of Enlightenment, right up to the present century. Professionals' curiosity as learners drove these informal educational processes, but formal, organized continuing professional education was unknown until it was prompted by the knowledge and technology explosions following World War II. By the 1970s, Houle contended, a large enough number of professions had become interested in their own continuing education to have formed a critical mass of professionals seeking learning. Thus began the possibility of a coherent, overarching field of continuing professional education, dedicated to providing practitioners across professions and practice settings with the education they need throughout their careers.

The Increased Call for Accountability

As Houle indicated, the concept of continuing professional education was not new in the 1970s. What was new was that professionals' accountability had become a widespread issue. Beginning in the late 1960s increased concerns about public health, safety, and welfare; changes within the professions (e.g., creation of specialty groups, escalation of litigation); societal changes that brought about a questioning of professional autonomy; and the emergence of new professions led to calls for more and more carefully structured education for professionals throughout their careers.[3,4] Longer life spans, combined with elimination of many employers' compulsory retirement age in the United States, resulted in continued practice by large numbers of older professionals whose preprofessional preparation had become obsolete in light of new knowledge and technology.

A primary factor in the increased demand for accountability is the very nature of professions. Any profession is a complex of configuration, represented not by a single entity but comprised of a group of practitioners, each expected to subscribe and adhere to a uniform set of standards and to operate within defined parameters. Yet within most professions, practitioners function with a high degree of autonomy despite the regulations to which they are subject and the organizational or institutional settings in which they practice. Perhaps it is this lack of central coordination or control that led to a mounting barrage of criticism concerning perceived practitioner incompetence and the accompanying demand for public accountability.

The demands for accountability, while stronger in some professions than in others, have spread across virtually all fields. The public expects its professionals to employ only appropriate practices, properly executed, and it knowingly tolerates not traces of obsolescence. State legislatures, professional associations, and consumer advocate groups all have joined the chorus of those determined to see these concerns addressed, noting that "the public perception of professional responsibility, accountability, and service has been called into question."[5] This increased public pressure for accountability has brought with it the growing realization that systems are needed to ensure at least minimum competence levels among professionals. Rightly or wrongly, continuing professional education often has been seen as the panacea. When properly designed, developed, and delivered to meet the educational needs of a carefully defined target audience, continuing professional education can be a major factor in stemming the tide of justifiable criticism. All too often, however, it is offered as an easy response, with no real attention paid to its actual potential for improving professional practitioners' performance.

The Effect of Knowledge Growth

At one time education for entry into practice was considered comprehensive and complete, and viewed as sufficient preparation for a lifetime of practice. The body of knowledge for any given profession was finite and manageable, so that students completing educational programs could be expected to master it. However, recent decades have brought exponential increases in the knowledge bases of all professions, with the body of scientific and technical knowledge doubling every five to seven years.[6] As Dubin[7] noted, "recent conditions have catapulted into prominence the issues of professional obsolescence and updating," substantially altering the expectation that a professional was once educated and henceforth forever competent. As a result, preprofessional education increasingly is being confronted with the need to focus on presentation of basic information, building of skills to pursue further knowledge, and the explicit understanding that practitioners must continue to learn throughout their careers. The type of learning or on-the-job training that typified the earlier continuing professional education that did exist has come to be recognized as valuable, but not sufficient. As Fisher and Pankowski[8] noted, "experience must be buttressed by more formal continuing education and self study."

Some professions, frequently but not exclusively those in which knowledge is expanding most rapidly, are ahead of others in recognition of the need for continued learning. Students completing preprofessional programs of study in accounting, engineering, dietetics, and medicine, for example, are inculcated with the understanding that only by participating in continuing professional education throughout their careers will they remain competent practitioners. As they prepare to enter these fields, the matter of their future education is not a question of whether or not they will continue to engage in some type of structured education, but rather a question of the ways in which they will obtain it.

The Need to Optimize Use of Educational Resources

Continuing professional education clients, be they individual professional practitioners or those organizations employing professionals (e.g., hospitals, schools, corporations, agencies, firms), look to this education to provide the knowledge, skills, and performance abilities professionals need to remain competent, enhance practice, follow a career path, and optimize their contributions to the organizations in which they work and the public they serve. Knowledge proliferation and the increased demand for accountability have forced them to turn to lifelong learning in order to adapt to their changing roles, public expectations, new technology, regulations, and globalization.[9] These continuing professional education clients are quite willing and even eager to invest their resources in educational activities from which they will benefit, but they also want to avoid expending time and money for education that is not well suited to their needs. Their intent is that each professional enrolled in an educational activity will benefit from participation and that the employer, individual, or organization who supports that participation will feel that the expectations for learning have been met. Participants should be able to transfer what has been learned in an educational activity to the work setting; continuing professional education should affect practice.

Conversely, continuing professional educators want to identify the educational activities or programs that will make optimum use of their resources and best meet their clients' needs. Since the 1970s, they have been confronted internally with increased financial pressures within their institutions and externally with clients' escalating performance and productivity expectations.[10,11] As their institutions have been less able to underwrite activities that failed to generate income and their clients have become more discerning, continuing educators have been forced to emphasize the use of systematic processes to identify and respond to professionals' educational needs and interests. Whereas they once offered continuing professional education programs because faculty members wanted to teach their favorite topic or a few clients requested programs of interest to them, for example, they now have less latitude to offer such programs without some assurance that they will draw enough participants to at least cover costs and be responsive to clients.

As described later in this chapter, needs assessment, a decision-making tool for identification of educational needs, arguably is the best option for use by both clients and providers of continuing professional education in determining what educational activities are appropriate. Even an excellent needs assessment cannot guarantee program success, but it can substantially reduce the chances that an activity will not be viable. Because most needs assessment is group assessment, this diagnostic measure most often has been used by continuing professional educators to obtain practical data and focus program planning in order to serve specific groups of professionals. Group assessment also is of use to employers and other groups that may be continuing professional education clients, for they can use it to pinpoint the needs of those professionals they employ or represent. On the basis of such an assessment, they can work with teachers of continuing professional education, giving them the information they need to provide meaningful educational activities.

Although not as common, use of individual needs assessment is growing. Because many educational needs occur as a result of individual experiences and personal characteristics, the uniqueness of individual needs, as opposed to group ones, cannot be ignored. Even when needs identified through group assessment are relevant to individuals, those individuals may not recognize that the needs apply to them. Although work in the area of self-assessment has been limited to date, the medical, architecture, and dietetic professions have developed some self-assessment programs. At least some of the instruments they have created incorporate individualized assessment and feedback, helping professionals understand their weaknesses and giving them information that enables them to seek appropriate educational interventions.[12,13]

All too often the teacher of continuing education is tempted to offer activities that appear to meet clients' needs and generate revenue without having any information to support such a decision. Similarly, professionals may select continuing professional education activities with little or no attention to the ways in which those activities might enable them to improve their performance. Both providers and consumers of continuing professional education tend to view educational activities as discrete events, failing to acknowledge the need for a curriculum approach to lifelong learning. Conscientious teachers of continuing professional education not only will avoid this pitfall in developing their programming but also will provide professional practitioners with the learning support services (e.g., education counseling, needs assessment) necessary to facilitate their educational planning.

The Advent of Distance Education

Among the greatest problems faced by those seeking continuing professional education are the time and money costs of participating in educational activities. Traditionally, continuing professional education has consisted of programs offered at a common location to which all participants traveled. This approach may not pose a major inconvenience when all program participants work for the same employer or can be expected to be in the same place, such as a conference, at a given time. However, even in these most ideal of situations, which do not require additional time and expenditure for travel, time away from practice may be problematic. In some situations, such as health-care facilities, essential services cannot be provided if many people are pulled away from their jobs for even an hour or two. Time is money for many other professionals, with the result that time away from the job means a lost earning opportunity. The problems associated with time away from the job are exacerbated when additional hours are required to travel to the site of a continuing professional education offering. In addition, travel costs can be significant, with the result that funds that could be used for additional or enhanced education are spent instead for transportation, meals, and lodging. *Distance education,* defined as "any formal approach to learning in which a majority of the instruction occurs while educator and learner are at a distance from one another,"[14] offers a range of attractive alternatives to site-based programs.

Given the constraints described above, the opportunities afforded by distance education, and the fact that "we have entered a new era that demands education for adults constantly, in a wider variety of ways, and at increasing speeds,"[15] the time has come to reevaluate the role of the traditional classroom in continuing professional education. Some topics are most effectively taught and learned in the standard classroom format, but many others can be presented as well or better with one of the many forms of distance education ranging from independent correspondence study to interactive computer and multimedia. Business and industry have been quicker to recognize and adapt to the opportunities presented by distance education than have many higher-education institutions, other employers, government agencies, and professional associations. They recognize that distance education not only makes possible the delivery of education and training to large groups of participants at locations and times convenient to participants but it also facilitates the widespread dissemination of excellent instruction. Professionals across the nation and the world can have access to leading experts through use of satellite transmission, for example, and videotapes can bring key presentations to the office or home of the most isolated practitioner.

A number of higher-education institutions and corporate education operations have large distance education components, including external degree programs, independent-study units, and electronic networks. Initially used primarily for delivery of college credit instruction, external degree study, and corporate training, distance education has only recently become a key factor in the delivery of continuing professional education.[16] However, it has the potential to revolutionize the ways in which professional practitioners learn throughout their careers. Sometimes viewed as high, the costs of distance education are properly evaluated by comparing them to the costs, including travel and related expenses, of participation in on-site programs. Use of print materials, audio- and videocassettes, and other easily reproduced materials can help control the costs of distance education. From the providers' viewpoint, much of the educational programming and supporting technology required for distance education is quite expensive, frequently leading educational institutions and others to "form consortia to share the costs and the risks of failure."[17]

Does Continuing Professional Education Make a Difference?

Recognition of professionals' needs to continue learning throughout their careers is almost universal, with educators, professionals, employers, and the interested public agreeing that continuing professional education has the potential to enhance and ensure practitioner competence. The challenge in providing education that makes a difference in professional practice lies in two areas: (1) motivating professionals to be active learners, and (2) providing continuing professional education that can affect daily practice.

Inherent in the concept of professionalism is an individual practitioner's commitment to remaining competent. Increasingly this obligation is defined in terms of continuing one's education, and ideally professionals will be "equip[ped]…with skills and competencies required to continue their own 'self-education' beyond the end of formal schooling."[18] They should enter professional practice with the ability to make wise decisions regarding their continuing professional education, decisions that will lead to learning that will have a positive impact on their practice. Providing the skills necessary for each professional to develop and continually revise a lifelong learning plan and employ sound criteria to choose educational activities in accordance with that plan should be an important component of their preparation. However, for most professionals such preparation is not yet reality. Currently they are not prepared to assume responsibility for developing a plan to guide their continuing professional education. When confronted with options, they may choose discrete activities in a random fashion because of convenience, attractiveness of the topic, the speaker's reputation, or other factors that have little or nothing to do with their learning needs. Unless these people are given the orientation and skills they need to be effective in assuming responsibility for their own education, continuing professional education may make little difference in their practices.

Providers of continuing professional education can help, not only by providing support for practitioners' self-directed learning but also by offering educational activities specifically designed to improve or enhance their performance. The responsibility to offer programming that will have an effect on professional performance presupposes an understanding that practitioners' educational needs will be identified, a step that most often requires a cooperative effort involving educators, representatives of the profession for which programming is to be developed, and, whenever feasible, employers of the professionals. And if continuing professional education is to have an impact on the manner in which professionals practice, provision of knowledge or demonstration of skills is not enough. Steps must be taken to relate the information provided to practice, to help program participants identify ways of transferring what they have been taught to their day-to-day operations.

The Role of Continuing Professional Education in Credentialing

In response to society's questioning the competence of professionals, the unprecedented growth of many professions' knowledge bases, and the changing contexts of professional practice, state legislatures, other regulatory bodies, and professional associations have been turning to credentialing processes that include a continuing-education component. Continuing professional education has emerged as one of the few options for addressing these issues, although its efficacy has not been proven. It is regarded as more acceptable than periodic testing, the other avenue frequently considered, since most practitioners balk at the concept of being subjected to examinations throughout their careers. Credentialing processes incorporating continuing professional education include those that give professionals the right (1) to practice, (2) to use a professional title, or (3) to earn and maintain specialty certification within their field. Mandatory continuing professional education occurs when education beyond that stipulated for entry into practice is required for continued license to practice. Continuing professional education required for use of a professional title or attainment of specialty certification also may be considered mandated, even though these are optional designations not required for practice of a profession, continuing education is required to earn and maintain them.

The entire concept of mandatory continuing education is one that has been fraught with controversy since the late 1970s. Its proponents argue that such requirements provide the only avenue for ensuring that professionals remain competent. They believe that it is necessary for competent practice, opining that individual professionals cannot be assumed to be responsible for pursuing their education without external motivation such as that provided by a practice, title, or certification requirement. They do not accept the assertion that professional practitioners are eager to pursue education for their professional growth. Those who oppose mandatory continuing education contend that it ensures only that professionals sign up for the requisite number of educational activities, emphasizing that real learning cannot be mandated.

Despite this controversy, continuing professional education often is used as a component of credentialing with the intention that it will help practitioners keep their knowledge, skills, and performance abilities current. However, use of continuing professional education "simply to extend the updated curriculum of professional schools to professionals in practice"[19] is only one facet of its potential for contributing to competent and enhanced practice. Continuing professional education also can be instrumental in enabling practitioners to maintain their existing knowledge, skills, and performance abilities at acceptable levels; avoid obsolescence;[20] and move to higher levels of specialization and accomplishment.

From two perspectives, access to education is an important issue related to the inclusion of continuing professional education in credentialing processes. First, all too often support for participation in continuing professional education is given to only a select group of people within an organization—those who control the budget, occupy positions of prestige, or show particular promise for the future, for example. Education requirements provide the impetus for all professionals, not just a favored few, to have access to education. Such mandates dictate equal access and can be instrumental in obtaining employer support or in justifying individual professionals' expenditures of their own resources for education.[21,22]

Second, required continuing professional education must be accessible to practitioners regardless of their work schedules, geographic locations, or other mitigating factors. The solo practitioner in a rural area needs ready access to continuing education just as much as the group practitioner in a major metropolitan area. Thus those organizations and regulatory groups requiring continuing education have a responsibility to see that the education is available to all who must have it. It is incumbent upon those people mandating continuing professional education to identify ways in which they can reach all professionals, not just a select few. Unfortunately, those who establish education requirements and those who provide programming most often are not the same people, necessitating cooperation between regulators and educational providers to ensure that appropriate educational activities are available in the quantities, levels, formats, locations, time frames, and price ranges that make them accessible to the entire group of practitioners they are intended to serve.

What Makes Continuing Professional Education Effective?

The notion that continuing professional education is the answer to updating competent practitioners and rehabilitating those who are less-than-fully competent is attractive. However, those who unquestioningly accept continuing professional education as a means to update knowledge, skills, and performance abilities and to remedy discrepancies between actual and desired levels of practice fail to recognize that enrollment in one or many educational activities cannot automatically be expected to ensure competence. Although it is the most readily available vehicle for enabling practitioners to remain current, address their weaknesses, and in general remain competent, it is far from a perfect solution. In reality, continuing professional education must build on the preprofessional education that precedes it and it must meet standards comparable to those of entry-level education if it is to be effective.

Continuing Professional Education as Part of a Continuum. In the early stages of the evolution of professions, preparation for entry into a profession was apprenticeship to an experienced practitioner, and later professional schools were deemed appropriate to provide lifetime preparation for individuals wishing to enter practice. It was not until the late 1950s that professionals, employers, and the public at large began questioning the assumption that preprofessional education could support a lifetime of practice; they then considered continuing education as a serious possibility for keeping professionals competent throughout their years of practice.[23] By the early 1970s substantial numbers of professionals and their educators, employers, professional associations, and legislators had turned to continuing professional education as a means of extending preprofessional preparation to provide lifelong education to practitioners.

Discrete or isolated continuing professional educational activities can and do provide updated information that may or may not have an effect on practice. Certainly the manner in which such activities are developed and the criteria professionals apply in selecting the educational activities in which they will participate are critical factors in determining the effectiveness of that education. However, continuing professional education that is an integral part of professionals' careers has its roots in their preprofessional education[24] and is designed specifically to serve as an extension of it. Education for entry into practice should provide the foundation for practice and for further education. Continuing professional education can be most effective if it builds on that foundation to address discrepancies between professionals' existing and desired practice patterns. Preprofessional education is most appropriately viewed as the "first step on an educational path spread over a lifespan,"[25] providing grounding in subject-matter areas and the development of critical thinking and study skills. The role of continuing professional education is to enhance and expand this entry-level learning throughout each professional's career.

As a result of this shift in thinking, graduates of preprofessional programs in several fields (e.g., engineering, accounting, architecture) now find themselves entering the workforce with a broad, general education in their discipline but with a need for specific training to perform the tasks that comprise their daily practice. In this characteristic they differ substantially from professional colleagues who may have entered the workforce only a few years earlier. Unlike their predecessors, they enter practices in which it is understood that their education will have to be expanded and updated regularly if they are to be competent, effective practitioners. For people in these forward-looking professions, their preprofessional education is only the first step in a continuum of education experiences. However, in many other fields the role of continuing professional education as part of a lifelong learning program is not fully acknowledged. Some of these professions are moving toward recognition of the criticality of practitioners' lifelong learning and inculcating their students with this expectation, while other professions have not yet come to view continuing professional education as an integral part of their practitioners' careers. Despite these variations, the era in which preprofessional education was regarded as comprehensive, complete preparation for a lifelong career in any profession has passed.

Professionals require assistance to help direct their continuing education in order to understand that education's importance to their careers. Some educators, professionals, and employers believe that preprofessional programs should shoulder full responsibility for teaching emerging practitioners to pursue the education they will need. Others argue that frequently these young, inexperienced students lack the long-range perspective and vision to be receptive to that message. They suggest that higher-education institutions, employers, and/or professional associations must provide ongoing learning support services beyond the preprofessional program to help practitioners develop continuing-education plans and select appropriate educational activities. Educational counseling, individualized needs assessment measures, and continuing-education curricula are among the support services that are needed, but their development has been slow, perhaps because few precedents for such support exist and such services are not without substantial costs. Those favoring their establishment suggest that professionals ideally not only will view lifelong learning as an important component of their careers but will also have available to them the resources necessary to develop their own lifelong learning curricula from entry into the profession through retirement and beyond.

Standards.   Setting of standards is critical to all education, and continuing professional education is no exception. Quantitative standards frequently focus on the processes employed to develop and deliver educational activities rather than on the value of the content provided. They may include such items as establishment of goals and objectives, instructor qualifications, and use of a program evaluation. Such standards are easy to establish and monitor, but they do little to ensure that the material covered is current, correct, or comprehensive let alone presented in a manner that will enable participants to apply it in their practice settings. Standards for *content, format, teaching strategies,* and *delivery modes* are more qualitative and more difficult to implement than other standards, but when properly defined and applied they are far more likely to result in an educational activity that is effective in meeting professional practitioners' needs.

- Appropriate *content* selection incorporates an understanding of basic and current issues in the professional field being addressed, and also considers practice-oriented learning needs of the program participants—What knowledge, skills, and performance abilities do they need to improve their daily practice?

- The *format* selected should be one that is compatible with the material to be covered. Communication skills might best be taught in an interactive format, for example, to allow participants to practice the skills being introduced.

- Good *teaching strategies* will incorporate adult learning principles and help participants identify ways in which they can integrate program content into their own practice settings, for information is of no use if it cannot be applied.

- Choice of *delivery modes* is governed by the effort to utilize the most effective means of providing the chosen content to participants in a manner that is readily accessible to them.

Standards establishing the expectations for each of these aspects of a continuing professional education activity can have a significant impact on the effectiveness of that activity. Rigorous standards can motivate use of a fairly structured program development process with the potential to encourage programming that will make a difference in practitioner competence. Such standards promote creativity and quality rather than strict adherence to quantitative measures that have little to do with the practice orientation or usefulness of continuing professional education.

Translating Education into Learning

Continuing professional education often is promoted as being synonymous with lifelong learning, but the two are not the same. Ideally continuing education does result in learning, but an automatic cause-and-effect relationship cannot be assumed. Unfortunately, continuing professional education not infrequently occurs with little corresponding learning. Practitioners may listen attentively and participate actively but learn little or nothing that they can take back to their workplace and apply. Lifelong learning, once recognized as a value-laden term connoting learning throughout one's professional and personal life cycle, has been cheapened by its repeated use to refer to activities and experiences that may be quite devoid of any real learning.[26] But while the words have become trite, the concept remains a viable and important one. True lifelong learning, in which professionals' knowledge, skills, and abilities continually are updated and refreshed, is the real goal of continuing professional education.

From kindergarten through postgraduate courses, it is entirely possible to obtain an education in the formal, documented sense (e.g., meet completion requirements, earn a degree, receive credits) without learning, or actually absorbing any knowledge, skills, or practice abilities beyond those already possessed. Continuing professional education can be either optional or required, but it cannot be guaranteed to result in learning. Assumptions that education can be equated with learning are dangerous because they foster an unwarranted sense of complacency, a false assurance that practitioners have been "cured" of any existing deficits or weaknesses. Although learning cannot be ensured, it can be supported and encouraged. It can occur serendipitously, and often does, particularly in informal contexts and on-the-job settings. However, through well-conceived program design, development, and delivery, continuing professional education can remove the element of chance and increase the likelihood that education will result in participant learning.

Some continuing-education activities fail to generate learning experiences because they do not properly address participants' content needs or practice constraints. Others fall short of their goals because individual participants are not receptive to learning or are not adequately prepared to process the material that is presented. Despite these potential pitfalls, in most cases at least a minimal amount of learning does take place, although it is not always immediately apparent; often time is required for new knowledge, skills, and practice abilities to find their way into daily practice.

The growing general acceptance of continuing education's potential to provide learning throughout professionals' careers carries with it implications for individual practitioners' commitments to the role of lifelong learning. Regardless of their orientation toward continuing professional education, most practitioners recognize that it can enable them to acquire the learning needed to remain competent throughout their careers, and some suggest that mandated education compels them to do so. The relationship between their education and learning is not a short-term one; rather it is one that must develop over time. If practitioners' continuing education is to result in learning, they must come to view it as an ongoing process guided by a plan, or curriculum; viewed in the context of their individual practice patterns and personal characteristics; and directed toward pursuit of lifelong improvement. They must be imbued with the desirability of ongoing learning from the earliest stages of their preprofessional preparation, and they must also be given the skills with which to pursue it. If this is to be the case with some degree of consistency, professionals need preparation not only as consumers of education, as suggested earlier, but also specifically for their roles as lifelong learners. As Candy[27] states, they should expect to take responsibility for their own learning and as self-directed learners learn to

- Independently pursue learning external to, as well as within, formal structures
- Organize their learning into a coherent whole, or curriculum, rather than randomly selecting discrete, isolated educational activities
- Demonstrate personal self-direction
- Exhibit self-direction in their learning

As self-directed learners, professional practitioners can anticipate accepting increasing amounts of responsibility for their learning as they move through their careers.

Educators in Continuing Professional Education

For many educators and would-be educators, continuing professional education is seen as a means of generating expanded demand for the products they produce. Some would argue that mandatory continuing education has been responsible for increased educational participation. As the numbers of professions having some form of mandated continuing education has increased, adult and continuing-education departments within higher education, employers' and professional associations' education departments, and other providers ranging from government agencies to private entrepreneurs have envisioned expanded opportunities. Some have imagined "the creation of a huge industry that satisfied the demands arising from extending compulsory education beyond the school walls and into the workplace."[28] In reality, the introduction of mandatory continuing education typically does not substantially increase practitioners' participation rates or generate significantly increased demand for educational activities. A study of nurses, for example, found that after regulations requiring continuing education were instituted the participation rates of over half of those surveyed remained the same as they had been prior to implementation of the mandate.[29] A study of counselors indicated that the participation rates of those required to obtain continuing education in order to retain certification were not measurably higher than those of their peers who were not subject to any requirement.[30] The growth of continuing professional education participation, which has been steady since the 1970s, is more accurately attributed to increased understanding of the necessity of such education than to its mandatory status in many professions.

In response to this increasing demand for continuing professional education, the number of program providers has grown somewhat and the profile of those providers has changed to include more individuals outside of higher education. Several large corporations have initiated their own training institutions, and others have significantly enlarged their education units. Many trainers and private entrepreneurs have moved into the continuing professional education arena. This expansion has brought some excellent new continuing professional education providers and offered practitioners a larger variety of continuing-education opportunities from which to choose. However, it also has broadened the range of providers to include some whose qualifications may be limited and whose motivation may be heavily weighted toward short-term financial gain rather than toward improved practitioner performance. In most such cases, organizations accrediting continuing-education activities and the practitioners themselves have been quick to recognize the charlatans and, by "voting with their feet," to put them out of business. Carelessly prepared but often well-marketed educational activities may draw an initial audience, but return business drops off rapidly if the quality is poor. Any organization or institution that enters the continuing professional education arena expecting it to be a solution for filling empty classrooms or a source of quick revenue quickly will learn that the ongoing provision of quality programs is not a high-profit business.

Who Is Responsible?

Many groups are quick to be heard regarding the importance of continuing professional education, and many providers are eager to offer those activities that utilize their existing resources and hold promise of revenue generation. However, this level of commitment does not automatically result in the comprehensive programming needed to support a continuing professional education curriculum and the support services that are required to ensure that continuing professional education will be a positive factor in promoting practitioner competence.

Within individual professions and across the professions, those organizations that are willing to take responsibility for overseeing or coordinating continuing education have been slow to step forward. The reason for this dearth of leadership is not clear, although it most likely is the result of a combination of factors. Accepted processes and parameters for building a continuing-education structure for a given profession have not been established, and in fact the components of such a structure have not been well defined or agreed upon. The linkages between preprofessional education and continuing professional education have not been well established, and the concept of a continuing-education curriculum is one that has not yet been raised, let alone been declared valid, in many professions. And not insignificantly, bringing coherence to continuing professional education can be a resource-intensive undertaking with little or no short-term revenue gains to offset the expenditures required.

Thus within a given profession various groups may bemoan their members' incompetence and decry the ineffectiveness of continuing professional education—but stop short of assuming the leadership that is necessary to correct the situation. Those who impose continuing-education requirements, be they regulatory agencies, professional associations, or other groups, too often do so with little or no attention to the options available to practitioners seeking to meet those requirements. With an almost pious attitude, they claim that having instituted regulations intended to protect the public and/or the profession, they have done their part.

Several groups have a potential role to play, arguably a responsibility in providing leadership for the development of meaningful continuing professional education. In some professions they are doing so, but to date these are more the exception than the rule. Institutions of higher education, professional associations, regulatory agencies, private entrepreneurs, and business and industry each bring different strengths, capabilities, and limitations with which to address the issue.

Institutions of Higher Education.   Colleges and universities, and the professional schools associated with them, provide entry-level education for practitioners across a great many professions. In the past their responsibility has been understood to end with presentation of the preprofessional degree or certificate. They launched new professionals into the world of practice with the assumption that they had properly prepared them and that the rest of their careers would take care of themselves. Clearly this has not been the case for several decades, and these institutions of higher education are left to wrestle with the realization that their graduates are representing them in the workplace, often with diminishing competence as the years go by. One factor in defining higher education's role in providing continuing professional education leadership is the argument that those institutions that prepare professionals have a responsibility—and an opportunity—to remain the lifelong learning home of those professionals. This role could encompass providing graduates with a continuing professional education structure or curriculum, at least some of the educational activities with which to pursue that curriculum, and the support services needed to enable them to direct their own learning.

A second factor pointing to the appropriateness of higher education's role in providing leadership for continuing professional education is that new knowledge frequently is created at colleges and universities. As the primary site for much, if not most, research in many professional fields, higher-education institutions have ready access to the most up-to-date information that can and should be applied in the work setting. They have the capability of helping professionals transfer research and theory directly into practice.

A third factor pointing toward higher education's responsibility in this area is the traditional instructional role of these institutions. Ideally colleges and universities have the expertise to develop curricula and educational activities to meet specified educational needs, the teaching skills necessary to convey information, and the delivery systems to bring continuing professional education to participants. However, having these latent capabilities and exercising them are two different things, and there are those who contend that higher education has abdicated its responsibilities, failing to respond to the education and training needs of the workforce. In a number of professions and work settings, other groups have filled this perceived void.

Professional Associations. Two primary factors motivate professional associations to provide continuing professional education leadership: (1) they wish to provide services to their members, and (2) they are eager to preserve and enhance the profession's reputation. One way in which professional associations can serve their members is through the establishment of a comprehensive continuing professional education structure, either a credentialing process or a process for identifying and addressing specific educational needs. Some professional associations address the issue from both perspectives. For these groups, the potential exists for a conflict of interest to arise since the same organization may be requiring and setting standards for education, then approving and even providing educational activities to meet those requirements. This is not an impossible situation, but it is one that requires care and integrity.

The American Dietetic Association, through its Commission on Dietetic Registration, has demonstrated the potential for a professional association to exercise leadership in continuing professional education. Having had a continuing-education requirement for registered dietitians for some time, this association determined that the requirement alone was not enough to promote and enhance practitioner competence. They recognized the importance of dietitians selecting continuing professional education activities that could address their identified learning needs and of their developing a coherent educational plan based on those needs. In partnership with The Pennsylvania State University, the American Dietetic Association's Commission on Dietetic Registration has developed a series of self-assessment modules that will enable individual practitioners to identify their educational needs by completing assessment instruments in their home or office.[31]

Regulatory Agencies. Regulatory agencies, be they government bodies, arms of professional associations, or special groups established to confer some type of credential, are those groups that establish the rules and regulations governing use of continuing professional education to fulfill certain requirements. Most commonly they specify a number of credits, hours, Continuing Education Units (granted for a wide variety of programs in accordance with standards set by the International Association for Continuing Education and Training), or other measure of continuing professional education (e.g., Category I or Category II continuing medical education hours, each granted for particular types of activities as specified by the American Medical Association) that must be completed within a given time frame, usually ranging from one to five years. In addition, some regulatory agencies may require that the continuing professional education be distributed among certain content areas. For example, the American Institute of Certified Public Accountants specifies that in order to maintain their designation, certified public accountants must complete some continuing professional education in accounting and some in tax subjects during each renewal cycle.[32] Many regulatory agencies accredit either individual educational activities, the providers of such activities, or both, thus stipulating those continuing-education activities that can be used to meet their requirements.

Beyond establishing regulations that include an educational component, however, these agencies rarely take an active role in the development and support of meaningful continuing professional education. They appear to assume that by establishing an educational requirement they have done their part toward ensuring competence among practitioners. One exception to this pattern has been the National Board of Certified Counselors (NBCC), which in 1983 initiated a certificate program that included a continuing-education requirement for certification maintenance. At the conclusion of the program's first five-year cycle, NBCC commissioned a study to examine their certificants' behaviors, experiences, and observations as related to continuing professional education and to compare the educational behaviors of certificated counselors to those of counselors not choosing to obtain NBCC certification.[33] In so doing, NBCC moved beyond simply instituting an educational component to considering the effects of that component on their program participants. While this type of action is a step in the right direction for regulatory groups, it cannot be viewed as providing the type of guidance that ultimately is needed to establish a continuing professional education structure to guide practitioners' education in a meaningful manner.

Private Entrepreneurs.   A number of private individuals, trainers, and organizations have entered the continuing professional education arena as the demand for programming and the dollars committed to education have increased. Because they most often are not bound by cumbersome bureaucratic procedures and red tape that may constrain other providers, they can move rapidly to respond to current trends, identified needs, and other programming opportunities. This flexibility permits them to meet professionals' educational needs in a timely and often creative fashion. However, these same assets also can be a liability when it comes to providing leadership in the field. Private entrepreneurs most often lack the organizational infrastructure and resources to mount a long-range project of the type that is required to build a continuing-education structure for a professional group. The pressure to sell new programs pushes many private entrepreneurs away from a leadership role.

Business and Industry.   Major employers have been investing in human resource development for some time, both by providing their own educational programming and by providing support, including tuition assistance, to enable employees to enroll in programs offered by other providers. Until the 1980s, few outside of the corporate world were aware of the extent to which business and industry, frustrated by the lack of available programming to meet their needs, were turning to development of their own corporate classrooms.[34] Much of the education they provide for their employees is decentralized, task-specific, and pragmatic, with programs offered as they are needed to enable employees to meet their job requirements. According to Eurich,[35] business and industry sometimes purchase educational activities from other providers, employ college professors to teach in-house courses, and use consortia for delivery of distance education programs. She notes that more frequently, however, major employers choose to develop their own programming over which they can maintain full control. In-house educational systems, including a staff of corporate trainers, enable large corporations to adapt both content and scheduling to their changing needs.

Such corporate education meets employers' immediate needs for a competent, updated workforce, and it provides practitioners with additional knowledge, skills, and abilities. However, it usually is not designed to support individual professionals in the establishment of continuing professional education plans that will span their careers. With some exceptions, most notably at the higher levels within an organization, business and industry's educational focus most often is on education and training for current job performance rather than on long-term competence and professional achievement.

The Need for Interorganizational Relationships

As the above discussion emphasizes, different groups bring different strengths to the continuing professional education arena. Interorganizational relationships can enable all of these continuing professional educators to be more effective and efficient, result in improved programming, and bring coherence in the field of continuing professional education. Relationships between the organizations they represent can vary greatly, from complete isolation and independence at one end of the continuum to merged organizations at the other. Through simple *cooperation*, two or more organizations can provide consultation and assistance to one another on an ad hoc basis. *Coordination* is a more involved relationship, calling for participating organizations to plan their activities in conjunction with one another, frequently dividing up a series of opportunities or a marketplace, for example. *Collaboration* is a fairly intense type of relationship in which two or more organizations work together and share resources to achieve a common goal. Continuing professional education provides the opportunity for any of these partnerships at two levels, among providers across professions, and among providers serving the same profession from a different perspective.

Relationships Across Professions. Continuing professional education today remains an emerging field, comprising people who have a commitment to meeting professionals' educational needs throughout their careers. These educators often focus on providing programming for a specific profession such as law, medicine, architecture, or accounting rather than serving a spectrum of professions. Because communication across these specialty areas has been minimal, until recently people in the field of continuing professional education operated in relative isolation—and many still do. Yet despite the differences in the content areas for which they provide educational activities, the problems these educators face and the issues they address are remarkably similar. Among the issues are budgeting, pricing, and funding continuing professional education; the need for and difficulty in providing quality educational programming; effective marketing of educational activities; and obtaining faculty participation in and commitment to continuing professional education. While an individual continuing-education operation can address these matters independently, the notion of isolated continuing professional educators, each wrestling with the same problems in his or her own setting, has come to be recognized as an inefficient, wasteful use of resources as well as a cause of substantial frustration and a serious impediment to progress in optimizing the effectiveness of continuing professional education.

These sentiments were documented by a group of educators in the field of continuing professional education meeting at The Pennsylvania State University in 1990.[36] Representing higher education, business and industry, regulatory groups, private entrepreneurs, and professional associations, they declared that steps were needed to bring together and provide support for educators in their field across practice settings and serving all professions. Toward this end they made two recommendations:

- A forum should be created in which all educators in continuing professional education could exchange ideas, learn of new developments and trends in continuing professional education, and share their solutions to the common problems they face. The group determined that a new organization was not required but that establishment of an interest group within an existing association could meet this need. The American Society for Training and Development (ASTD) was identified as an appropriate home for such an interest group, primarily because of its broad-based membership. Individual membership would be open to educators in continuing professional education from all practice settings. The ASTD Continuing Professional Education Network was formed in 1991, and since that time it has been serving as a forum for discussion of continuing professional education issues shared by various providers serving a wide range of professions.

- A program should be developed to provide continuing professional education to senior-level educators in continuing professional education from all practice settings and serving all professions. The Division of Continuing and Distance Education at The Pennsylvania State University collaborated with Harvard University's Graduate School of Education (HGSE) to offer the Leadership Institute for Continuing Professional Education. Modeled after other successful institutes offered through HGSE's Programs in Professional Development, the biannual institute was first offered in 1992. Its emphasis is on the conceptual issues surrounding continuing professional education.

From both the network and the institute it has become apparent that regardless of their practice settings, educators across professions in the field of continuing professional education confront the same or similar issues and are eager to join forces with colleagues to identify ways of addressing them. Many participants in both the network and the institute have spoken of the isolation they have felt as they have struggled with problems they now know are common to others in positions comparable to theirs. Information exchanges and discussions range from highly pragmatic and operational issues such as obtaining program approvals or establishing faculty pay scales to philosophical issues that include defining quality in continuing professional education. Both the network and the institute, while in their infancy, have begun to give shape and focus to the emerging continuing professional educational field.

Relationships Within Professions. Within any given profession, professional associations, regulatory agencies, employers, higher-education institutions, and/or private entrepreneurs work to meet the continuing-education needs of practitioners. These groups share the common goal of supporting the provision of meaningful educational activities to professionals within the field they serve, and they often have individual objectives as well. The professional association may wish to protect the integrity and reputation of the profession, for example, while an employing company's primary objective is improvement of its workforce capability. With common but not conflicting goals and objectives, two or more of the several organizations often can work together to accomplish more than any one of them could by working alone. They each bring different resources and strengths to a partnership.

- *Professional associations* represent both the profession and the practitioners. As representatives of the profession itself, they often are both spokesperson for and target of criticism of the field. They can be expected to have a clear perspective on their profession's strengths and weaknesses, internal and external politics, and members' characteristics and educational preferences. A professional association also can provide access to members to tap their expertise for needs assessment, program design, development, and delivery and to reach them for marketing purposes.

- *Regulatory agencies* understand the intent of any continuing professional education requirements and often are knowledgeable about the standards to be met in providing continuing education that can have an impact on professional practice.

- *Employers* frequently recognize the weaknesses demonstrated in professionals' daily practice, and they also are aware of the ways in which continuing professional education can be made relevant to their work settings. This latter knowledge is crucial, for without an understanding of the ways in which knowledge, skills, and performance abilities can be integrated into professional practice, the educator risks providing activities that cannot be applied to professional practice and hence will be of no benefit. Larger employers also may have facilities and technology to provide interactive and/or distance education.

- Because *higher-education institutions* are the traditional bases of both teaching and new-knowledge development, their potential contributions are in the areas of instructional design, teaching skills, learning support services, and up-to-date program content. They also may have access to technology that can be used to optimize educational delivery or to tailor it to a specific audience.

- *Private entrepreneurs,* including professional trainers, often bring a flexibility that is unmatched by the other groups. They usually are able to respond quickly to immediate educational needs, and sometimes they have the freedom to be more creative than their organization-bound colleagues in providing unique solutions to difficult or unusual continuing-education problems.

By joining forces, representatives of these various groups can bring a myriad of strengths and capabilities to bear on the continuing professional education of a profession they all serve. By working together, they have the potential to accomplish far more, in terms of both quantity and quality, than any of them might accomplish in isolation.

As demands for professional accountability continue to mount, knowledge increases exponentially, and technology continually opens new avenues, continuing professional education partnerships across and within professions will become even more important. Few, if any, educators involved with continuing professional education will have the expertise, funding, and facilities to provide much beyond single, discrete educational activities without some sort of partnership. Those educators in the field of continuing professional education who work together have the potential to be the leaders of the future. Only through such partnerships can they expect to have the breadth and depth of resources to push ahead the frontiers of continuing professional education.

Determining the Effectiveness of Continuing Professional Education

Nowlen[37] describes three models of continuing professional education, all of which can benefit from the range of perspectives available through partnerships:

1. The *Update Model* emphasizes practitioners' needs to keep up with their profession's knowledge base.

2. The *Competence Model* adds analysis of their job functions and preparation for new roles they may assume as their careers advance within their professions.

3. The *Performance Model* includes these factors and also allows for consideration of the environmental, professional, and personal contexts in which professionals practice.

Nowlen suggests that continuing professional education ideally is based on the Performance Model, which is "likely to generate the richest assortment of needs and responses."[38] He emphasizes that this model encourages, is enhanced by, and requires partnerships among providers. In addition, it requires careful analysis of professionals' practice-oriented educational needs and provision of educational activities that not only present needed information but also facilitate practitioners' application of that information to their daily practice. Such educational activities most often are developed through use of a comprehensive process or model.

The Needs Assessment–Program Development–Evaluation Process

Ostensibly the goals of continuing professional education are to disseminate new information, improve and enhance professional performance, contribute to the safety of professional practice, and increase the professions' public accountability.[39] Unfortunately, not all continuing professional education meets these goals, for in reality the effectiveness of such education is quite variable. One means of increasing continuing professional education's effectiveness is to implement a program development process that begins with identification of participants' educational needs and continues through an evaluation of the ways in which the educational activities offered have met those needs. By developing continuing professional education in the context of such a model one cannot ensure that the educational activities offered will address bona fide needs, but it is possible to increase the likelihood that steps will be taken toward meetings those needs.

The Practice Audit Model[40] developed in the course of the W. K. Kellogg Foundation–funded Continuing Professional Education Development Project conducted by Pennsylvania State University in the 1980s offered a comprehensive framework to guide collaborating groups in providing continuing professional education to meet the goals cited above. It has been used successfully with a number of professions ranging from architecture and accounting to medicine, nursing, clinical psychology, and dietetics.[41] The principles on which it was based remain valid and have proven to be sound guidelines. It is those principles, even more than the model itself, that merit consideration.

The Practice Audit Model emphasizes a collaborative process and a systematic approach to continuing professional education for a given profession. The model begins with establishment of a profession team comprised of representatives of all collaborating organizations; it is this team that guides the remainder of the process. The scope of practice of the profession to be served is delineated in the next step, defining the full range of professional practice. From this information, the team identifies those areas considered most important to practice, or most frequently used by professionals, on which to focus. Needs assessment materials to measure knowledge, skills, and/or performance abilities in these areas are designed in the third phase, and standards for defining need (e.g., At what level is an assessee's performance considered to be weak or below that expected or desired?) are established. The fourth step involves actually conducting the needs assessment, and during the fifth stage the results of the assessment are analyzed and compared to the established standards. In the sixth phase educational activities are designed to address the needs that are thus identified, and in the final step these activities are delivered and evaluated.

Such a needs assessment–program development–evaluation process is ongoing. Only a small area of professional practice can be addressed at one time, with the resultant opportunity to continually select new areas for needs assessment and the program development that follows. In addition, professionals' educational needs change over time, requiring that many areas be revisited during the career life cycle. If these needs are to be met, they must be identified; program design, development, and delivery must be based on them; and a program evaluation must be conducted as a step in determining whether or not the educational activities have been successful in addressing the needs they were intended to meet.

Assessing Needs

Continuing professional education can be interesting or entertaining, an opportunity to hear a renowned speaker or to interact with colleagues, but if it does not address participants' needs it most likely will not affect or improve their professional practice. Despite the fact that it is the educator's job in continuing professional education to identify clients' needs and expectations, many educators shy away from needs assessment. Perhaps they believe that needs assessment is a step that they can eliminate with little or no effect on the quality of their programming, or they may feel that they lack the necessary resources, particularly expertise, to conduct a valid needs assessment. Most often this type of reasoning is fallacious, for although needs assessment is no guarantee that an educational activity will be successful in improving practice, it can substantially increase the likelihood that an activity will meet its intended goals and be relevant to the improvement of professional practice. The expertise and resources required to conduct a needs assessment may be minimal, especially when compared to the costs of programs that fail because they do not meet educational needs.

Needs assessment is a diagnostic and a decision-making tool that uses questionnaires, interviews, observations, and other measures to identify the educational needs of a specific target population. It is not an examination or a punitive measure; no one fails a needs assessment. When employed as an integral part of the program development process, needs assessment allows educators in continuing professional education to make data-based decisions regarding all aspects of the educational activities they will provide for the professionals they strive to serve. It can be used to identify weaknesses, information gaps, or areas of educational need for professionals striving to achieve new levels of excellence.

Perhaps the greatest misconception regarding needs assessment is that it must be resource-intensive, rigorous research. Sound needs assessments can range from basic measures that are within reach of any educator's capabilities to highly sophisticated studies, from simply asking people what they consider to be their educational needs to employing complex assessment center methodology. However, the level of a needs assessment is less important than the thoroughness and care with which it is conducted.

Effective needs assessment at any level requires accuracy in collecting, recording, analyzing, and interpreting data. Valuable data can be obtained from the simplest of needs assessments, if they are well planned and executed.

Conversely, a poorly conducted needs assessment can be worse than no assessment, for it can result in decisions based on fallacious data.

Several factors are important in planning and executing any needs assessment. Defining the objectives of the needs assessment is the first step. Objectives might incorporate the needs assessment purpose, the scope of the proposed study, the target population, the resources to be allocated to the endeavor, and the level of complexity.

- In specifying the *purpose* of a needs assessment, the educator in the field of continuing professional education can choose one or more of the following issues on which to focus: the target population, content areas to be included, the level of education needed, learning styles of the anticipated audience, delivery modes that might be used, and scheduling preferences.

- The *scope* of a needs assessment describes both the breadth of the population to be assessed and the content to be considered. Population characteristics include range of professional practice levels, career stages, and specialties; geographical location; employment; and educational level, and all factors in determining the size and diversity of the population or sample to be assessed. The effect of content on the scope of a needs assessment relates to the magnitude of the content areas to be assessed and the level (e.g., knowledge deficits, performance weaknesses) at which they are to be examined.

- The *target population* is the group for which educational needs are to be identified. Their characteristics (as outlined above), motivation to pursue meaningful education, accessibility to participate in assessment, and ability to respond to assessment instruments affect the needs assessment objectives.

- The availability of *resources* for needs assessment can be the governing factor in defining needs assessment objectives. A realistic determination of what funds, facilities and equipment, expertise, and other resources can be committed to needs assessment is a critical component of needs assessment planning.

- The *complexity* of a needs assessment refers to the sophistication of the methods used and the number of participants to be included in the assessment. The detail of the data the assessment yields also is a factor.

The needs assessment methods available to the educator in continuing professional education can be categorized as follows.

- *Basic needs assessment methods:* self-reports, focus groups, nominal group process, delphi method, use of key informants, supervisor evaluations. These methods usually can be employed by teachers of continuing professional education with little or no assessment experience, particularly if some consultation is available to them.

- *Survey-based methods:* written on-site, mail, and media questionnaires; oral personal and telephone interviews. Because valid surveys are deceptively difficult to design and conduct, the educator wishing to use them will need to ensure that appropriate expertise and other necessary resources are available.

- *Performance assessment methods:* review of products of performance, performance observation, performance simulations, assessment centers. These methods, which access actual or simulated performance characteristics, almost always are more complex and more costly than other needs assessment methods. However, they are most effective in identification of needs reflected in professionals' daily practice.

Educators in the field of continuing professional education and others involved in the program development process must be committed to needs assessment if it is to be effective. They have to be prepared to accept data that does not support the viewpoint they espouse, to abandon an idea that is contraindicated by needs assessment data. Educators who are not used to conducting needs assessments may find that assessing needs delays their program development process. Because the process is new to them, taking the first steps in conducting a needs assessment can be somewhat awkward. However, each successive needs assessment will be somewhat easier, and as the value of needs assessment is demonstrated by increased enrollments and well-satisfied clients, the time and resources required will be justified.

Difficulties of Determining Impact

Professionals' patterns of practice develop over time, and changes in their practice are similarly slow to occur. Both basic practice patterns and alterations of those patterns result from a number of factors. While education certainly is key, other variables include the work environment, colleagues' influence, self-motivation, and other internal and external experiences that provide new insights and informal learning opportunities. Because of this multiplicity of factors, it often is difficult to isolate the impact of one or more continuing professional educational activities on professional practice. The knowledge, skills, and performance abilities presented through continuing professional education activities are melded with ongoing influences. The combination of these factors leads professionals to alter their practices gradually over time. For this reason, in many cases it is virtually impossible to document the direct effectiveness of a given continuing professional education activity. As Caplan noted in speaking about continuing education for physicians, "we may not see the outcome of any single [continuing medical education] activity, but its effect may appear in a different way, place or time, and connection to the original may be lost."[42] In these situations, continuing-education educators can strive to demonstrate that some learning has taken place, that needs identified through assessment have been lessened by participation in a continuing professional education activity. Only occasionally can they point with certainty to changes in practice that are the direct result of only an educational intervention.

Often measures similar to those used for needs assessment can be used to evaluate the effectiveness of a continuing professional education activity in addressing the needs identified. In most cases, the measures used do not relate directly to practice; instead they relate to deficits in the knowledge, skills, or performance abilities that are components of practice. Evaluations using these measures can be quite useful in the determination of the extent to which a documented need has been diminished, but they may provide little or no information regarding the educational activity's effect on practice. However, other measures such as supervisor observation, review of products or practice, or performance simulation do relate directly to the practice setting. They can be used first to assess needs and subsequently, within several weeks or only a few months of the conclusion of the continuing professional education activity, to evaluate that activity's effectiveness. Because they assess some aspects of performance, these measures can be indicators of actual changes in practice that have taken place. If a comparison of the scores obtained in the needs assessment and then in the program evaluation reveals some changes, it may be reasonable to conclude that the educational intervention did have an impact on practice.

A timely evaluation, occurring within a few months of the activity's completion, is most useful in demonstrating the impact of a single continuing professional education activity on practice. Yet if professionals engage in continuing education over time, as is encouraged and recognized to be an important factor in maintaining competence, there is another perspective. Measurement of the accumulated effects of continuing professional education may best be documented over extended time periods (e.g., at least five years). With such long-range measurement, ascertaining which changes are attributable to education and which were brought about by other influences does present problems, as noted above. However, by taking a longer view it is possible to examine changes not only in discrete skills and components of practice but also in the underlying philosophies and attitudes that help define the scope of competent practice. This type of evaluation is not simple or straightforward, but for a profession that has established a comprehensive approach to continuing professional education, it can provide highly useful information.

Minor changes in practice are far more difficult to identify and trace to an educational activity than are more major alterations. Competent professionals who participate in continuing education to enhance their practice or to address only small discrepancies between their current and ideal levels of practice are not likely to demonstrate readily documentable changes. Those professionals whose practice is minimally acceptable or substandard in some areas have more room for improvement—and hence greater opportunities to exhibit more substantial changes in their practice patterns as a result of even small amounts of continuing professional education.[43]

Research on continuing professional education's impact on practice is sparse, indicating that at best it has a minimal or small effect.[44] While the question of impact remains a highly valid one, the answers frequently are elusive. Continuing education may be a factor in improving professional performance, but it is difficult to separate the effects of education from those of the other factors that influence practice. Some changes, such as improved knowledge, can be measured. Dowling[45] reported that some studies have revealed knowledge changes but not changes in performance as a result of continuing-education participation. In many cases, the continuing-education educator may have to settle for evaluations that document reduction of educational needs and hope that these diminished needs do indeed result in improved practice.

Challenges for the Future

Educators in the field of continuing professional education strive to serve professional practitioners, the professions they represent, their employers, and the public that consumes their services, all in the course of fulfilling their own organizational, institutional, or individual mission. In so doing, it is important that they provide high-quality educational activities that meet practitioners' educational needs in an accessible manner and by utilizing formats that facilitate integration of new knowledge, skills, and performance abilities in daily practice. This is no small order. The temptation is great to bow to constraints on resources and offer continuing-education activities that ostensibly address pertinent topics for apparently appropriate audiences while avoiding the question of what impact those activities have on professional practice. Practice-oriented continuing professional education requires a focus on improving professional practice from preliminary planning through program evaluation. Fundamental to this approach is an understanding of the professionals to be served, the work settings in which they practice, the content that informs their practice, and the ways in which they learn. Partnerships among continuing-education educators most often are desirable, and even necessary, to amass this base for developing educational activities, and to build on it to develop programs that will benefit those people and professions they strive to serve.

Because continuing professional education remains an emerging field, it faces a number of questions that are as yet unanswered. These questions circumscribe the challenges for the future:

- What standards should be imposed, by individual providers, employers, professions, or regulatory bodies, to ensure at least a basic level of quality for continuing professional education?

- Who are the necessary partners in continuing professional education, and what are their roles? Educational institutions, professional associations, regulatory agencies, private entrepreneurs, employers, and practitioners themselves all bring different strengths to the continuing professional educational arena. Only by working together can they optimize the potential of continuing professional education.

- Who will provide the leadership to move continuing professional education from a series of isolated events to a component of lifelong learning curriculum?

- Under what conditions, and for which professions, should continuing professional education be required, and what is the appropriate form of such requirements?

- What activity formats, delivery methods, and teaching strategies can be used to engage professional practitioners in the learning process? What faculty development is necessary for those who instruct professionals?

- How can professional practitioners be supported to become and remain self-directed learners, assuming responsibility for educating themselves to optimize their professional performance? Who is responsible for providing that support?

- What continuing professional education outcomes can reasonably be expected? How can they best be achieved, and how can they be measured?

- How can all professionals be assured of equal access to continuing professional education so that they have opportunities to participate in educational activities regardless of their location, constraints of practice schedule, and personal responsibilities?

- Who is responsible for paying for continuing professional education? As costs of all educational activities, and of practice-oriented programs in particular, escalate, is it reasonable to expect individual practitioners to bear all financial responsibility?

Even if educators in continuing professional education were able to document that certain educational activities have an impact and others do not, it is not clear that the right question would be answered. The more important question is why some continuing professional education activities are more effective than others in generating learning and having an impact on practice. What are the factors that cause some continuing professional education activities to contribute to the knowledge, skills, and performance abilities that participants take back to their practice settings? They include participant readiness to learn, relevance to practice, appropriateness of presentation, and relevance to professionals' educational needs. These factors define quality in continuing professional education.

- *Participant readiness to learn* includes professionals' preparation as consumers of education and, more importantly, as self-directed learners. Motivation and positive earlier educational experiences also contribute to an openness to new educational opportunities.

- *Relevance to practice* is essential if the information presented is to be of any use to participants. The content must relate to the tasks of daily practice and be presented in a manner that facilitates and encourages its adoption and integration into practice.

- *Appropriateness of presentation,* or the way in which educational material is presented, can determine whether or not it is assimilated. Incorporation of adult learning principles is a key factor and should be supported by an engaging presentation style and use of delivery modes that enhance participant learning and program accessibility.

- *Relevance to professionals' needs* is the most important factor in relating continuing professional education to practice. Needs forming the basis of an educational activity may reflect minor or significant weaknesses in current practice or deficits that need to be addressed if a professional is to move up the career ladder.

Continuing professional education has the potential to enhance practitioners' competence, thereby increasing their own satisfaction and quality of practice and benefiting their employers, the professions they represent, and the public they serve. The opportunities are enormous, as are the challenges they bring with them.

References

1. Stern, Milton R., and Donna S. Queeney, "The Scope of Continuing Professional Education: Providers, Consumers, Issues," in E. Stephen Hunt, ed., *Professional Workers as Learners,* Office of Educational Research and Improvement, U.S. Department of Education, Washington, DC, 1992, pp. 13–34.

2. Houle, Cyril O., "Possible Futures," in Milton R. Stern, ed., *Power and Conflict in Continuing Professional Education,* Belmont, CA, 1983, pp. 254–261.

3. Houle, Cyril O., *Continuing Learning in the Professions,* Jossey-Bass, San Francisco, 1980.

4. Schuchman, H. L., *Self-Regulation in the Professions,* The Futures Group, Glastonbury, CT, 1981.

5. Azzaretto, John F., "Power, Responsibility and Accountability in Continuing Professional Education," in Ronald M. Cervero and John F. Azzaretto, eds., *Visions for the Future of Continuing Professional Education,* The University of Georgia, Athens, 1990, pp. 25–50.

6. Naisbett, John, *Megatrends: Ten New Directions Transforming Our Lives,* Warner Books, New York, 1982.

7. Dubin, Samuel S., "Maintaining Competence Through Updating," in Sherry L. Willis and Samuel S. Dubin, eds., *Maintaining Professional Competence,* Jossey-Bass, San Francisco, 1990, p. 9.

8. Fisher, F., and Mary L. Pankowski, "Mandatory Continuing Education for Clinical Laboratory Personnel," *Journal of Continuing Education in the Health Professions,* 12(4), 1992, p. 228.

9. Aslanian, Carol B., "Back from the Future," presentation to the National University Continuing Education Association Conference, New Orleans, 1990.

10. Cervero, Ronald M., *Effective Continuing Education for Professionals,* Jossey-Bass, San Francisco, 1988.

11. Nowlen, Phillip M., *A New Approach to Continuing Education for Business and the Professions,* American Council on Education and Macmillan, New York, 1988.

12. Klevans, Deborah R., Leonard E. Pollack, Wayne D. Smutz, and Robert Vance, "Self-Assessment, Phase II," presentation to the 74th Annual Meeting of the American Dietetic Association, Dallas, October 28, 1991.

Table 32-2. Comparative Importance of Rankings of
Competencies

Competency	Importance for Management	Technicians
1. Command of basic facts	Medium	High
2. Relevant professional knowledge	Medium	High
3. Continuing sensitivity to events	High	Medium
4. Problem-solving, analytical, and decision- and judgment-making skills	High	High
5. Social skills and abilities	High	Low
6. Emotional resilience	High	Low
7. Proactivity and inclination to respond purposefully to events	High	High
8. Creativity	Medium	High
9. Mental agility	Medium	High
10. Balanced learning habits and skills	Medium	Medium
11. Self-knowledge	High	Low

SOURCE: Adapted with permission from P. R. Jones, B. Kaye, and H. R. Taylor, "You Want Me to Do What?" *Training and Development Journal*, July 1981, pp. 56–62.

If these conclusions are reasonable, and they appear to be, both the selection of supervisory personnel and their development takes on an even higher degree of importance.

Selection of Supervisors

Roughly one in five supervisors in the NSSMP surveys volunteered that they would return to the ranks if they could do so without loss of face or reduction in pay.[13] This group of supervisors ranked significantly lower in every aspect of satisfaction and confidence than the others in the survey. It would appear, therefore, that prudent human resources management in this area should begin, not with supervisory development, but with a more careful and effective selection process.

Extensive studies reported by the University of Pennsylvania in 1978[14] conclude that employees with the greatest supervisory potential do not necessarily fill the key ranks. To begin with, selection systems are poorly planned and implemented. Preferences are traditionally given to friends and relatives. The seniority syndrome, too, carries over into supervisory selection. In effect, it says, give the longest-service employee a shot at the job first. But the selection system is only part of the problem. Many good workers will not move into supervision if it means shift work. Pay differentials between hourly employees and their supervisors are narrow. Hourly jobs are seen as more secure, supervisory work as full of frustrations. This view is supported by Benson,[15] who contends that "superworkers" continue to be rewarded by promotions to supervision, a position that is often inappropriate for their skills or without any promise of advancement. "We may be building failure into the selection process," warns Benson.

Good selection programs start with a study of the work to be performed. This is easier said than done. All too often it is the product of a facile job-description writer rather than a careful study of the work, especially its make-or-break aspects. Progressive organizations develop historical data that helps them to associate personal characteristics (measurable ones preferred) of successful perform-

13. Klevans, Deborah R., Wayne E. Smutz, Susan B. Shuman, and Carolyn Bershad, "Self-Assessment: Helping Professionals Discover What They Don't Know," in H. K. M. Baskett and Victoria Marsick, ed., *Professionals' Ways of Knowing: New Findings on How to Improve Professional Education,* New Directions in Continuing Education, Jossey-Bass, San Francisco, 1992.

14. Verduin, John R., Jr., and Thomas A. Clark, *Distance Education: The Foundations of Effective Practice,* Jossey-Bass, San Francisco, 1991, p. 8.

15. Eurich, Nell P., "Continuing Education and the Learning Industry," *The Journal of Continuing Higher Education, 39*(3), 1991, p. 2.

16. Friesen, Abram J. D., Doreen E. Zinyk, and Gloria Mah, "Mandatory Continuing Pharmacy Education in Alberta, Canada: The Response to Live Programs and Correspondence Courses," *American Journal of Pharmaceutical Education, 49,* 1985, pp. 156–159.

17. Verduin, op. cit., p. 53.

18. Candy, Philip C., *Self-Direction for Lifelong Learning,* Jossey-Bass, San Francisco, 1991, p. 15.

19. Nowlen, Phillip M., "New Questions for Continuing Professional Education," in Ronald M. Cervero and John F. Azzaretto, eds., *Visions for the Future of Continuing Professional Education,* The University of Georgia, Athens, 1990, p. 15.

20. Dubin, op. cit.

21. Fisher and Pankowski, op. cit.

22. Brockett, Ralph G., "Do We Really Need Mandatory Continuing Education?" *New Directions for Adult and Continuing Education, 54,* 1992, pp. 87–93.

23. Nowlen, op. cit.

24. Azzaretto, op. cit.

25. Morrison, A. A., "Resisting Compulsory Continuing Professional Education," *Australian Journal of Adult and Community Education, 32*(3), 1992, p. 146.

26. Collins, M., *Adult Education as a Vocation: A Critical Role for the Adult Educator,* Routledge, London, 1991.

27. Candy, op. cit.

28. Morrison, op. cit.

29. Cannon, C. A., and L. D. Waters, "Preparing for Mandatory Continuing Education—Assessing Interests," *The Journal of Continuing Education in Nursing 24*(4), 1993, pp. 148–152.

30. Queeney, Donna S., Wayne D. Smutz, and Susan B. Shuman, "Mandatory Continuing Professional Education: Old Issue, New Questions," *Continuing Higher Education Review, 54*(1), 1990, pp. 11–25.

31. Klevans, Smutz, Shuman, and Bershad, op. cit.

32. Queeney, Donna S., and Virginia M. Pearson, *Professional and Occupational Practice Requirements,* 5th ed., The Pennsylvania State University, University Park, 1991, p. 28.

33. Queeney, Smutz, and Shuman, op. cit.

34. Eurich, op. cit.

35. Eurich, op. cit., pp. 49–50.

36. Staff, "An Agenda for Action: A Report of the National Meeting of Continuing Professional Education Focus Groups," The Pennsylvania State University, University Park, 1990.

37. Nowlen, op. cit.

38. Nowlen, op. cit., p. 224.

39. Maple, G., "Continuing Education for the Health Sciences: The Voluntary/Mandatory Debate," *Australian Journal of Adult Education, 27*(2), 1987, pp. 22–28.

40. Office of Continuing Professional Education, "An Overview: Continuing Professional Education Development Project," The Pennsylvania State University, University Park, 1985.

41. Ibid.

42. Caplan, R. M., "A Fresh Look at Some Bad Ideas in Continuing Medical Education," *Mobius* 3(1), 1983, p. 43.

43. Phillips, Louis E., "Is Mandatory Continuing Education Working?" *Mobius,* 7(1), 1987, pp. 57–64.

44. Stross, J. K., and W. R. Harlan, "Mandatory Continuing Medical Education Revisited," *Mobius,* 7(1), 1987, pp. 22–27.

45. Dowling, C., "A Comparison Between Mandatory and Voluntary Continuing Education in Professional Performance," presentation at Annual Meeting of the American Educational Research Association, Chicago, 1985.

35

Training in Quality

Bruce J. Hayes

Bruce J. Hayes *is Director of the Motorola University Quality Center based in Schaumburg, Illinois. He has 19 years experience in manufacturing engineering, quality assurance, Total Quality Management, and operations management. Hayes is a Motorola Certified Malcolm Baldrige National Quality Award Examiner (1991) and a lead auditor for Motorola's Quality System Review (QSR) process. He has extensive international experience through various operations assignments at Motorola. Most recently, he was Director of Quality and Network Operations for Motorola's Communications Services Group. In his current rotational assignment at Motorola University, Hayes is responsible for managing quality and customer satisfaction research, courseware, and consulting for both Motorola and Motorola's strategic partners. He attended Northeastern University (engineering) and Fisher College (business), both located in his home state of Massachusetts. He is an active member of the American Society for Quality Control and holds university advisory board positions for quality-management programs, one at the University of Miami, Florida, and another at the Université de la Technologie de la Compiegne, France. He frequently serves as a subject-matter expert on quality and has assisted in many capacities for universities, state governments, and Motorola business partners.*

Overview

A basic fundamental in the successful implementation of a training process for quality improvement is that the training organization itself embraces and implements the strategies, tactics, and operational practices of Total Quality Management. After all, the business we serve, the students we teach, and the instructors who transfer the knowledge are all our "customers." We must therefore continually strive to understand their needs and requirements as well as the "best practices" in our customers' various functional disciplines to assure our unified success.

Training refers not simply to the operational task of courseware delivery, or knowledge transfer, but to the collective research, planning, design, development, testing, refinement, delivery, and continuous improvement of our respective curricula. The businesses, students, and institutions we (the training community) serve have many choices in the training marketplace. If we forget whom we serve or for what purpose, quickly our market will erode and the demand for our courseware evaporate. For these reasons we offer the model shown in Fig. 35-1 for reference.

This model is the essence of all quality-improvement activity at a strategic level. It is how most *successful* organizations define quality and customer satisfaction and, therefore, must be considered when planning training in quality.

As can be seen, an organization's primary purpose must be to satisfy our customer's needs and requirements prior to achieving long-term market or financial success. Some will argue that something unique, highly innovative, or one of a kind will violate the logic of this model. This is true, in the short term. Sooner or later patents or copyrights expire, another innovation emerges, or the next unique idea comes along and captures the business. In some regard this is a "survival" model, something to drive our own business by and something to teach (if longevity is one of our objectives). Quality is survival. Without it we slowly degrade to the point of average. In today's hungry global marketplace, average doesn't cut it! "Best in class" wins. For these reasons this chapter is based on the notion that best-in-class quality and customer satisfaction (not simply quality control of manufactured product) are the key drives to business, financial, and operational excellence.

The Perspective

The author of this chapter is not a formally trained academic professional. He is an operations manager with 20 years' experience—16 years with Motorola, Inc., a U.S. $20 billion electronics-communications company—on a planned 3-year rotational assignment at Motorola University, the company's corporate research

Figure 35-1. Customer/market-driven continuous-improvement model.

and training arm. In this capacity, his role is to lead a team of instructional designers, subject-matter experts (SMEs), and research associates in the quality topic area. Various outputs include research publications, workshops and/or seminars, and classroom and alternative-learning technology products (e.g., interactive CD-ROM, teleconferencing, and computer-based training). We felt this fact worth mentioning for several reasons. First, as an operations manager the author had very little real understanding of what training was all about—let alone learning behavior or instructional design. For those reasons, training was always viewed as something that took too long and had too little return (and usually the quality organization was blamed for these shortcomings). In fact, we (the operations managers and SMEs) were usually the root cause of the problem. We insisted—without any understanding of the reiterative process required for proper knowledge transfer—that course delivery times be slashed, in many cases by as much as two-thirds. What this resulted in was a little *awareness* training, not much *knowledge transfer,* and no time for *practice.* As a result of our learning this lesson the hard way, one of our important roles has become to teach managers and SMEs about learning behavior and instructional design (see Fig. 35-2). By establishing this platform we may then conduct constructive dialogue as to content, delivery, evaluation, and so on.

Conversely, we discovered that to a large degree the training community was not engaged to the same level in functional councils, strategic planning, operations reviews, and other activities where the *real* business issues and decisions were made. There was no network. Cross-functional rotation creates the communication channel and the synergy for pervasive quality-system implementation. Both the training communities and target populations must understand this fact to assure successful implementation of quality training and training in quality.

Aligning with Target Populations

Quality, customer satisfaction, and best-in-class performance are not accidents. They are the result of systematic, *arduous* planning and execution. For this reason students of quality methodologies (the target population) may be divided into structured categories for purposes of training planning. The model in Fig. 35-3

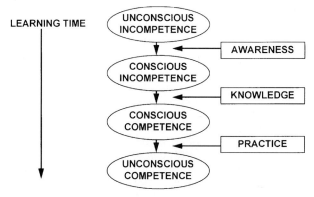

Figure 35-2. Learning behavior.

Figure 35-3. Organizational and functional depth of the target population.

indicates both the organizational and functional depth of the target population which may be useful in planning the scope of quality-training activities.

As you can see from Fig. 35-3, the learning objectives of senior managers are focused at a strategic level, middle managers at a tactical level, and individual contributors at an operational level. This arrangement is important because the scope of activities as it applies to the continuous-improvement process varies in application. While the tools of quality improvement applied at each level may be the same, their utilization and application will vary. Take a simple trend chart, for example. At a senior management level this "tool" will be used to display high-level results such as revenue, profit, market share, or customer satisfaction. At this level the data will be generalized in nature. The frequency of measurement intervals will be wide (weekly, monthly, quarterly). The results and conclusions drawn will drive "strategic" shifts and changes over relatively long periods of time. The same tool applied by a manufacturing associate on a production line will be applied at a very specific and detailed level—perhaps counting the quantity of successful assembly steps. The frequency of this measurement may be every second or minute. Actions will be triggered almost immediately, with the objective being to eliminate the cause of any anomaly immediately.

To maximize the learning which takes place in a quality-training curriculum, it is important to understand first the needs and then the required application depth of the target population, assuring a match of these two dynamics.

Quality-System Evolution

Another useful model when the organization is planning, developing, and implementing curricula for quality is the quality-system evolution model (see Fig. 35-4). The basis for this model is that successful quality systems do not materialize in a matter of days, but rather they evolve over a period of years. Quality systems may be classified against the model by observation of behaviors, measurements, practices, strategies, tactics, attitudes, and results. These observations are then compared to a known set of criteria for purposes of determining what phase of evolution the subject organization is in. From here we can determine the needs and identify knowledge gaps which are prohibiting the organization from moving in a positive direction.

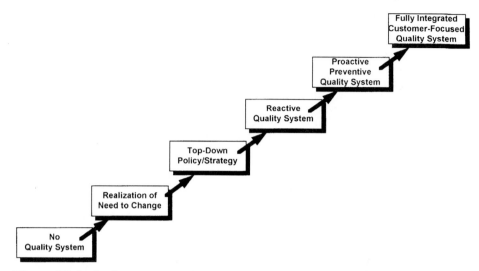

Figure 35-4. Quality-system evolution.

This model prompts several considerations when one is designing or delivering quality courseware. First, consider that an organization attempting to move from the first step (No quality system) to the second (Realization of need to change) will have vastly different training needs than an organization moving from the fifth step (Proactive preventive quality system) to the sixth (Fully integrated customer-focused quality system). An organization with no quality system is usually struggling from a business perspective and has yet to correlate the lack of business success with inferior quality, products, and services. Teaching Statistical Process Control (SPC) to this type of organization without first creating some general awareness of the ramifications of what poor quality means in business terms will not create an open learning environment. Another way to think of this concept is teaching the organization to crawl, then to walk, then to run, and so on.

Quality-Assessment Systems

There are many quality-assessment systems, quality-audit systems, international, local, and military standards with varying degrees of scope, depth, and purpose which organizations may use to evaluate and improve quality-system maturity. Examples include The United States Malcolm Baldrige National Quality Award (MBNQA) process, The International Standards Organization 9000 series of standards (ISO 9000), and Military Standard 9858. Exposure to these processes and standards may, in many cases, create behaviors in an organization not intended by their authors if administered in an inappropriate manner. In a panic to respond to an upcoming "audit," the training organization is often requested to "get everyone trained in a hurry." In this case, the audit result is usually not beneficial to either organization. Most of today's recognized standards' original intent was to foster a system of continuous improvement and confidence building over a period of time. Unfortunately, many companies took the approach that compliance to a given standard meant winning the business and noncompliance meant losing it (thus creating the "panic"). What is really important to a business is the long-term impact of committing to a quality system or standard. Once a commitment and strategy are in place, a logical training plan to follow the strategy may be implemented. Table 35-1 highlights training and target populations built around a general quality-assessment system.

Maturity models are usually a subset of an assessment system designed to assist and test for the "maturity" of a given element within a quality system. Table 35-2 illustrates a basic maturity model concept utilized by Motorola, Inc.'s *Quality System Review Process* which adopted the terms *approach, deployment,* and *results,* after winning The 1988 Malcolm Baldrige National Quality Award. On an element-by-element basis, the organization's approach to an element is reviewed for strategic linkage, appropriateness, and depth of application. Deployment is reviewed to determine the scope to which the approach is implemented—pervasive, companywide, or a "pocket of excellence"—and eventually the results are reviewed relative to appropriate benchmarks and rates of improvement.

In most of today's quality-assessment systems, the organization being assessed is consulted ahead of time. They are given a chance to have input to the process. When this opportunity occurs, the organization to be reviewed should request a comprehensive list of strengths (what they do well) as well as "opportunities for improvement" (where they will direct corrective action) as outputs from the process. In this case, a fair amount of learning will take place through the assessment process itself. *Once an assessment is complete, there is a significant opportunity for the training department to review the assessment output and build a training strategy and plan around the needed improvements.*

An example of one such success is the Motorola Quality System Review (QSR).[1]

> The Quality System Review is an assessment vehicle by which the corporation evaluates the continuing health of the quality system in each major Motorola business unit and Motorola supplier. It defines a vision of how our business should be conducted; it sets a common goal of perfection; and it provides an awareness of quality-system requirements across the total organization. These reviews also provide opportunity for cross-fertilization of ideas and serve to routinely refocus the organization on quality. Using the formally documented QSR assessment form and review procedures, the review team is able to reflect a macro view of the subject business unit-supplier, recog-

Table 35-1. Quality Training Matched to Target Populations

Time ───→					
Senior Executives	Basic awareness	Strategic quality planning	Conducting quality reviews	Motivating teams	Correlating results
Middle Managers	Basic awareness	Conducting self-assessment	Effective action planning	Implementing solutions	Managing quality improvement
Manufacturing Associates	Basic awareness	Quality tool training	Interpreting data	Team problem solving	Implement solutions
Administrative and Support	Basic awareness	Quality tool training	Interpreting data	Team problem solving	Implement solutions

Table 35.2 QSR General Scoring Maturity Matrix

Score	Evaluation		
	Approach	Deployment	Results
Poor	▪ No system and/or process evident ▪ No management recognition of need	▪ None	▪ Ineffective
Weak	▪ Beginnings of a system and/or process ▪ A few factors in place ▪ Management has begun to recognize the need	▪ Fragmented ▪ Deployed in some areas of the business	▪ Spotty results ▪ Some evidence of output
Fair	▪ Direction for system and/or process defined ▪ Wide but not complete support by management	▪ Less fragmented ▪ Deployed in some major areas of the business	▪ Inconsistent but positive results in areas deployed
Marginally Qualified	▪ A sound system and/or process in place with evidence of prevention activities ▪ Some management becoming proactive ▪ Evidence of eliminating organizational disconnects	▪ Most major areas of the business ▪ Mostly consistent	▪ Positive measurable results in most major areas ▪ Some evidence that results are caused by approach
Qualified	▪ Well-designed, proven system and/or process which is prevention-based with evidence of refinement and improvement and renewal ▪ Majority of management is proactive ▪ Total management support	▪ Pervasive and consistent across all major areas of the business	▪ Evidence that efforts are successful ▪ All requirements fulfilled ▪ Demonstrated positive and sustained results
Outstanding	▪ Exceptional well-defined innovative system and/or process that anticipates customer needs ▪ Management provides zealous leadership ▪ Recognized even outside the company	▪ Pervasive and consistent across all major areas of the business, both internal and external	▪ Requirements exceeded ▪ World-class results ▪ Counsel sought by others

Table 35-3. Sample QSR Worksheet

Evaluation Work Sheet: Quality System Management

No.	DESCRIPTION	POR (0)	WEK (1)	FAIR (2)	(3)	MARGINAL (4)	(5)	QUALIFIED (6)	(7)	OUTSTND (8)	(9)	(10)	APPLICABLE (A)	SCORE (R x A)
		FACTOR RATING (R)												
1.1	Is there a Quality function or well-defined organization which provides customer advocate guidance to the total organization and is this position fully supported by management?												9	
1.2	Does the organization have detailed goals, tactics, methods and tools to achieve Six Sigma standards in the required time frame, including administrative and non-manufacturing areas? Are the programs and results reviewed frequently?												9	
1.3	Does a quality measurement system exist with clearly defined metrics and is it utilized as a management tool?												10	
1.4	Are benchmark and customer satisfaction studies done to determine best in class for all products, services and administrative functions, and are goals set so that quality is a competitive weapon?												9	
1.5	Are there Quality Policies, Procedures Manuals and accepted standards which are currently maintained and utilized throughout the organization and is there a management representative or representatives with authority and responsibility for ensuring compliance to these policies and standards?												9	
1.6	Are there programs with sufficient resources assigned to support corrective actions and prevention in order to achieve best in class satisfaction for the customer?												9	
1.7	Are there regular management reviews of the quality system and it's elements, and are the results acted upon?												9	
1.8	Is management's support of ongoing training (including quality training) sufficient, and is it documented by an organizational training plan?												9	

ORGANIZATION: xxxxxxxxx 0
DATE: xx/xx/xx
SUBSYSTEM 1a: Quality System Management

This Page Score-> 0

nize achievements, point out shortcomings and opportunities, and offer recommendations for continuous improvement. The QSR process is designed to foster improvement and assure that the quality system is effective in achieving total customer satisfaction. (See Tables 35-3 and 35-4.)

As far as training in quality is concerned, any quality-assessment process provides an excellent structured approach to gathering the requirements of the organization, aligning them to the target population, and serving as a training effectiveness measurement. Therefore strong linkage between any formal quality assessment or audit activity is highly desirable and effective.

Table 35-4. Typical Motorola Internal Action Plan (as Presented to MCQC)

MOTOROLA

Division XYZ
QSR Action Plan

Subsystem/Element 1.4: Are benchmark and customer satisfaction studies performed to determine Best in Class for all products, services, and administrative functions, and are goals set so that quality is a competitive weapon?

QSR Team Comments: Benchmarking is done at the product level, and customers are regularly visited. However, benchmarking of specific processing needs to be improved (although some is done). For example, chip carrier processes could benchmark SPS facilities, board assembly against GSS or other PPG facilities, paperless manufacturing opportunities could be studied, employee benefits could be benchmarked against other Singapore companies, etc.

To Score 10: The benchmarking process has helped the organization establish world class quality leadership for all products, services, and administrative areas as well as internal and external processes. Customer satisfaction feedback and benchmark data are continuously validated and updated.

Actions:

	WHO	**WHEN**
• To benchmark Statistical Process Control at XYZ.	**J. L. Smith**	**Done**
• SMT equipment benchmarking.	**E. C. Jones**	**On-going**
- Solder printer		
- Chip mounter		
- Odd shape mounter		
- Reflow Oven		
- Robots		
• Benchmark Apple SMT processes.	**E. C. Jones**	**Q3'93**
• Benchmark Sony Manufacturing Lines.	**E. C. Jones**	**Q4'93**
• Benchmark Boynton Automation process.	**E. C. Jones**	**Q4'93**

Tactical Planning and Goal Setting

When planning or revitalizing a quality system, organizations often struggle with the goal-setting process. What do we improve? What rate of improvement is appropriate? Where do we start? All of these are common questions. Reflecting on the overview of this chapter, we find that many of the answers to these questions lie with our customers. They may also lie with our competitors or other organizations recognized with "best practices." In companies with mature quality systems, strategic planning usually encompasses the two inputs as shown in Fig. 35-5.

To facilitate the needed ongoing dialogue with our customers, as well as intelligence gathering on our competition, markets, and best practices, our people must develop specialized skills. Usually senior managers, middle managers, account managers, and engineers are involved in this ongoing process. In more mature quality systems, the entire employee population may engage in these processes at various levels. Important attributes in measuring, analyzing, and interpreting this data include

- Standards of measurement—to foster accurate comparisons

- Frequency of measurement—to track change over time

- Objective and quantitative data—to draw valid conclusions

Customer Satisfaction

Customer satisfaction is a very broad term. It is a fairly simple term to understand but very difficult to execute. In today's fast-paced environment, many are looking for the "quick fix" to customer issues. This quest may prompt an organization to attempt to address customer satisfaction in the least desirable way. For example, consider the organization which hires a firm to survey its customers (usually an expensive proposition) and receives several volumes of customer satisfaction results, indexes, comments, and ratings. An initial presentation of the results leaves the management team overwhelmed at the volume and scope of issues. The organization makes an attempt to prioritize the issues and takes action on the highest priorities. Action teams are assembled and begin to try and solve the problems. One year passes and the next survey result indicates no

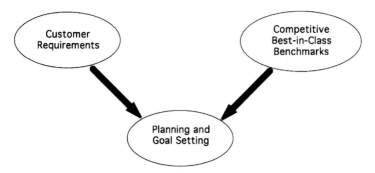

Figure 35-5. Tactical model.

improvement. The organization becomes frustrated with the lack of success and begins to question the value of this entire process. What went wrong?

This scenario is all too common. There are several flaws in this approach. Many can be addressed with proper planning and training. The first problem in the scenario is the entire process was reactive. It probably did not link to any of the "planned" activities of the organization. There was no overall strategy or quantitative goal for the project (e.g., improve market share by 3 points, or displace major competitor A). The problem-solving teams were attaching causes at a level too high to resolve root cause or systematic issues. Even the use of quality-improvement tools at this level will yield ineffective results. At the same time, the customers' expectations were rising and there was no incremental, frequent measurement system—such as daily feedback from the sales force—to supplement the annual survey. Consider the following steps when training in quality specific to customer satisfaction:

1. Begin with a strategy and quantitative goal.

2. Involve *people* in the process (especially the customer and front-line associates).

3. Assure external-to-internal measurement system linkage.

4. Measure often and track progress.

5. "Peel the onion" when problem solving (analyze "true" root cause).

6. Look for systematic issues.

7. Reward and recognize *incremental* accomplishments.

The above steps may prompt the training organization to offer several different types of learning interventions, depending on the target populations' needs and previous experience (see Table 35-5). Seeking out an internal expert (if one exists) will be beneficial in curriculum planning.

Benchmarking

Benchmarking is one of industry's favorite buzzwords in the 1990s. Many equate benchmarking to studying and copying best practices of others. While this description is somewhat true, it is a very shallow definition of a much more comprehensive and dynamic process. The term *benchmarking* means seeking a certain level, a comparison. There are many commercially available books (including this book's Chap. 19, Benchmarking for Best Practices), seminars, and training products built around the practice of benchmarking (see Fig. 35-6). But

Table 35-5. Possible Tactical Quality Training Curriculum

Gathering customer require- ments	Effective communi- cation	Quality function deploy- ment	Writing customer surveys	Under- standing customer survey results	Correlating customer results	Goal setting
Bench- marking	Database query	Measure- ment system standards	Measure- ment system analysis	Formatting results	Communi- cating results	Goal setting

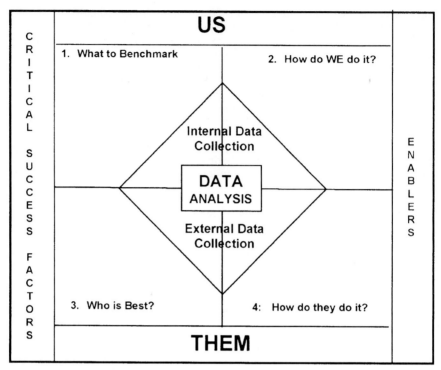

Figure 35-6. Benchmarking model—five phases. (*Copyright DEC, Motorola, Boeing, Xerox.*)

once again the strategy for how benchmarking is used, and what it is used for, that is of equal importance to the practice itself.

Benchmarking may be practiced by all levels of the organization and is a critical element in the quality goal-setting process. Senior management may benchmark results in certain businesses and compare them to their own as a function of strategic planning. Managers may benchmark certain functions such as training, finance, quality, or planning to assist in setting and achieving goals. Operations associates may benchmark individual work processes such as accounts payable, product assembly, or order fulfillment to gain insight into more efficient ways of doing their own work. Training for benchmarking usually requires basic tool skills (e.g., measurement and graphing) as well as "people" skills (e.g., effective interviewing and interpersonal skills). Benchmarking is usually a two-way process (except in the case of a direct competitor), making the interpersonal skills very important. The output of a benchmarking process will not always dictate immediate and drastic change; rather it will support the evolution of the business plan and the quality system.

Measurement Systems

The first several pages of this chapter deal with strategy and tactics. One cannot overstate the importance of strong linkage between the business strategy-plan-goals and the quality system. In fact, in MBNQA winning and other best-in-class organizations, they are one and the same. This situation exists because, through the evolution of the quality system (see Fig. 35-4), the entire organization has been through the learning curve on quality and accepts full responsibility for implementation and maintenance.

One of the keys to successful quality-system activities is the scope, depth, linkage, and pervasiveness of the quality-measurement system. Quality-measurement systems may be an inaccurate term. In effect, all the organizations' measurement systems are—or should be—in some way related to quality. Traditional thinking dictates quality to be measurements of goodness (or "badness") of certain process outputs. This concept translates quite easily in a manufacturing process whereby the quantity of good parts divided by the total number processed can quickly be measured (yield) and acted upon. As the quality system matures, the requirement for more dynamic data across a large part of the organization grows. The two basic types of data our organizations need to solve problems using quality tools include attribute data (e.g., go–no go and good-bad) and variable data (usually quantifiable measurements such as millimeters and degrees centigrade). Measurement systems may run the entire spectrum from simple checksheets to highly advanced computing platforms equipped with state-of-the-art statistical process control (SPC) software. The training community's most effective role relative to quality-measurement systems is probably not to develop training specific to quality-measurement systems but rather to conduct interventions geared toward helping the organization to discover, enhance, and relate existing measurements to new applications using quality-improvement tools. Training in certain software tools and/or computing platforms will help. However, there are no totally packaged quality-measurement systems suitable to every business. A more common path is to lead an organization to cross-functional process mapping to help identify the truly important process and product measurements required to drive the improvement process (see Fig. 35-7).

Process mapping is one of the most logical starting points in quality optimization and problem solving. Process mapping's value is as high for the process leading to its output as is the output itself. In addition, process mapping may lead to the critical measurement points in a given process and foster the refinement of the quality-measurement system. Process mapping works best when conducted in a team environment (and yields a much more accurate output).

A typical learning intervention for process mapping consists of bringing logical work groups together for the event. It is desirable that all organizational levels be represented and an actual process to be mapped is identified prior to the session. A period (two to four hours) of lecture-based teaching—to identify the symbols, process, and roles—followed by facilitation of an actual mapping session works best. Process mapping tends to surface many issues when it is performed properly. While initially the team involved may perceive this experience as a negative one, the facilitation is performing the function it is intended to.

Possible Process-Mapping Outcomes

1. Disagreement that the documented process is the same as the actual.

2. The team "sees" many non-value-added steps.

3. Early discussions occur on how to improve the process.

4. Agreement that everyone should follow the newly documented process.

5. Management wants to fix the process immediately.

6. Realization that the process cannot be mapped or reengineered in one facilitation.

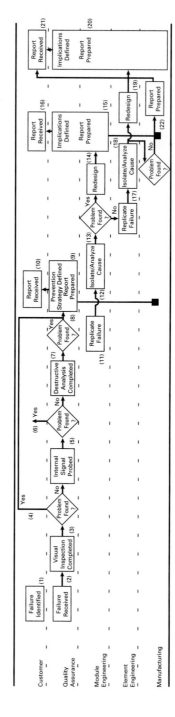

Figure 35-7. Motorola process map example.

As one can see from the above, process mapping will lead to more questions than answers. There will be attempts to undermine the process and temptation to give up. But, when properly facilitated, it will provide the documentation, guidance, and steering for far-reaching process improvement.

Defining Critical Measurements

Once an organization has begun and committed to a process-mapping activity, the ongoing, reiterative process of continuous improvement may begin. While many traditional thoughts on reengineering focus on the removal of non-value-added steps from a process, a simple removal of steps without proper understanding can be a very dangerous thing. In most cases, many steps must be undertaken to facilitate the removal of non-value-added steps.

Take, for example, a process whereby an inspection step has been identified as non-value-added. The inspection step was *originally* put there for a reason. Perhaps it was to prevent defective product from being shipped to a customer. If the root cause of these defects is not understood and eliminated, defective product will simply be shipped to the customer again (thus creating a new set of non-value-added activities).

The proper process for removal of non-value-added steps is a continuous process of measuring, analyzing, problem solving, and institutionalization of action steps. Through this reiterative process we may begin to identify the necessary actions to eliminate non-value-added steps from our core work processes.

In Fig. 35-8, the box labeled "Measure" is very important. Choosing the wrong measurement will almost certainly lead to wasted effort. To minimize this risk, process teams should examine—through tools such as brainstorming—the process, existing measurements, etc., and determine appropriate measurements.

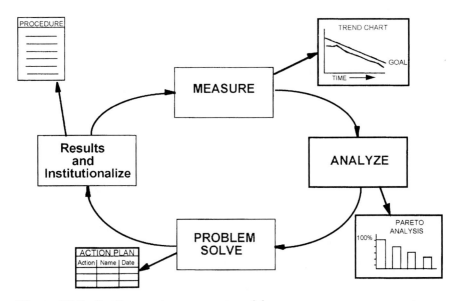

Figure 35-8. Continuous-improvement model.

Benchmarking of similar processes at other company locations or outside of the company may provide insight.

Training at this level begins to focus on the individual tools and the interrelationships of the tools to the continuous-improvement process.

Typical Tools to Assist in Measurement Definition

1. Benchmarking
2. Process mapping
3. Flowcharting
4. Brainstorming
5. Checksheets
6. Nominal group technique
7. Force-field analysis

Measurement System "Line of Sight"

Of equal importance to the continuous-improvement process is a level of synergy and a logical pattern to the measurement system and associated goals. Throughout the last several modules we have attempted to demonstrate the importance of integration between the various quality-improvement tools (see Fig. 35-8) and the improvement process. To initiate and sustain an improvement process there must be a system to reinforce the behaviors of the organization through feedback, reward, and recognition. It is best if some of this feedback be tied directly to quantitative performance against predetermined goals. In most any organization there is a hierarchy to the work being performed. Therefore, there should be a "line of sight" (see Fig. 35-9) from the operational measurement and goals as related to the various levels of the organization.

Too often, goal setting and measurement systems are top-loaded, i.e., they never cascade down through the organization, and therefore associates at the operational level cannot easily relate to the goals or performance measures.

When good line of sight exists in the measurement system, the operational associates clearly understand how their individual or team achievements support those of the total organization. Associates become highly motivated in a system where their individual and team results are captured and displayed in real time.

Analysis Techniques and Tools

There are several items to stress when one considers the scope and depth of analysis tools to be used by an organization:

- The relationship of the tools to the continuous-improvement process
- The functional discipline where the tool will be used
- The complexity of the process being analyzed
- The background and technical understanding of the people using the tools

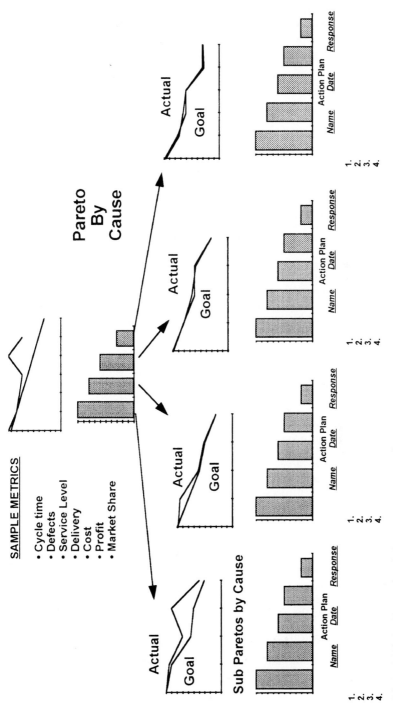

Figure 35-9. "Line-of-sight" improvement goals.

Table 35-6. Summary of Analysis Tools and Techniques

Basic	Intermediate	Advanced
■ Pareto diagram	■ Process capability study	■ Design of experiments
■ Histogram	■ Tolerance analysis	■ Failure mode, effect, criticality analysis
■ Control chart	■ $\overline{X}+R$	■ D-Optimal
■ Pie chart	■ Multivariable analysis	■ Robust design

Analysis tools and techniques range from fairly simple tools which most everyone can master (e.g., bar charts and Pareto diagrams) to the most complex techniques requiring a powerful computer and an individual with a degree in advanced statistics (see Table 35-6). The choice of tool is often left up to the improvement team leader who should be aware of the many tools available and their applicability to the given process.

There are many traditional sources for tool training available. Networking with reputable organizations such as the American Society for Quality Control or Motorola University Customer Supplier Training in Schaumburg, Illinois, can provide courseware to suit these needs. For the organization that desires this training from the ground up, a cadre of statistical subject-matter experts, instructional designers, and business unit sponsors will be required to design, develop, implement, and deliver the training.

Problem-Solving Tools and Techniques

As with analysis techniques, there is a wide range of possibilities for problem solving. Effective problem solving involves people working together to interact, analyze, discuss, and agree on items to be acted upon to drive improvement. While there are many tools and techniques available to assist in these efforts, the key becomes how well people work together. Many best practices indicate some form of an enabling process to motivate and reward the use of continuous-improvement tools. Quality Control Circles (QC Circles), with their roots in Asia, are one effective means. At Motorola, Inc., thousands of teams share their learnings, successes, and results through a process called The Total Customer Satisfaction Team Competition (TCS teams). There are many other examples of solid, proven enabling processes to create an environment whereby the utilization of appropriate tools and the improvement process is the preferred operating mode. The underlying message is simply this: *Training in the tools is not enough.* The training, combined with a compelling reason to use the tools, will create a synergy between the people, the core processes, the measurements, and the results.

Examples of Problem-Solving Tools and Techniques

1. Cause-and-effect diagram (Ishikawa or "fishbone")
2. Stratification
3. Brainstorming
4. Nominal group technique
5. Force-field analysis

Action Planning

An important attribute to the problem-solving process is to capture the agreed-upon action items in a clear and concise manner. The action plan must cover the who, what, why, and when as well as relate to a measure of performance. Action plans should attempt to predict or set a quantifiable expectation of the outcome of the action steps. This objective may sound simple but there are hundreds, probably thousands, of cases where quality-improvement efforts began with enthusiasm, yet, because the action plan was not crystal clear, no one followed up. Vital to the success of the action plan is the training of the team leaders and facilitators to ensure that this crucial step is performed properly.

Institutionalize ("Mistake Proof")

In Fig. 35-8, the box labeled "Results and institutionalize" is another very important step in the quality-improvement process. Institutionalization—or mistake proofing—is the action or series of actions which initiate and maintain a permanent change to a process. Examples of institutionalization include

- Establishing a procedure
- Modifying a procedure
- Changing a process flow
- Automating a manual step
- Changing a computer program

Institutionalization usually does not occur until the action steps have been proven effective by quantifiable means. Once a degree of confidence has been achieved, the improvement team's focus should shift to methods to make the changes permanent.

Summary

In this chapter we have explored the generic quality-improvement process and have attempted to examine it from several perspectives. First, at a macro level we covered the importance of quality at a *strategic level*—assuring that quality-improvement activities are tied directly to the strategies, goals, and tactics of the organization. Included in this activity is the guaranteeing of continuous improvement at all levels and functions of the organization, which is absolutely important to the business. For the training community, this objective creates several challenges and approaches to providing effective learning interventions. First, senior executives must be trained specific to their roles, responsibilities, and actions to drive an integrated quality-improvement strategy. It may be prudent for strategic quality training to co-exist in an integrated fashion with other "traditional" senior-management topics. In many cases, the time constraints involving senior executives prohibit training from occurring any other way. Second, the entire organization needs to have general awareness of the strategic importance of quality improvement to the total business. This knowledge helps in creating "buy-in" for the more intensive practical training which will ultimately follow the organizational commitment to excellence.

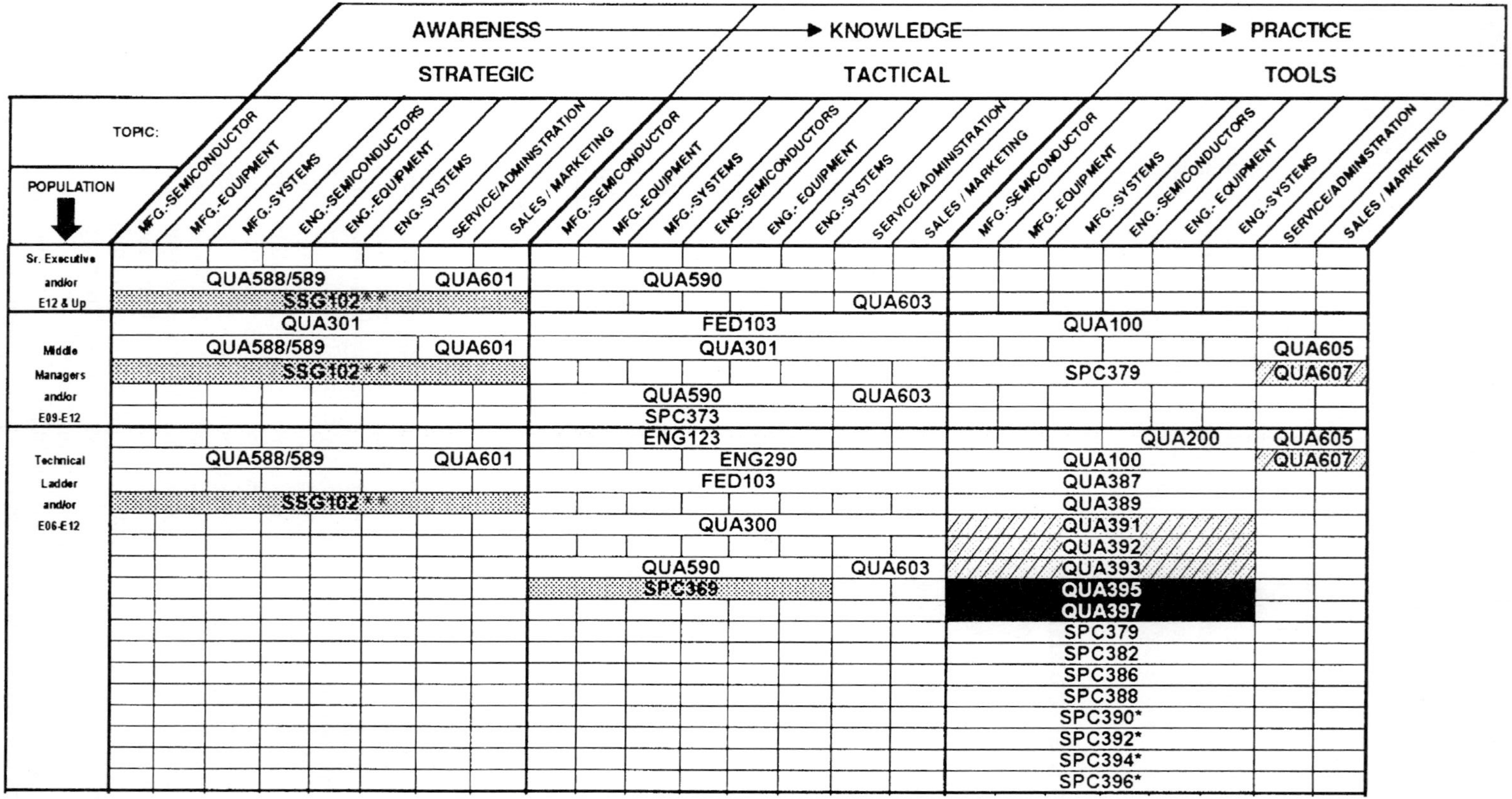

Figure 35-10. Training roadmap.

Row labels: Individual Contributors E06-Nonexempt | Customed | Supplier | & External | Programs

Table cell entries (as read): SSG102** · QUA601 · ENG123 · QUA100 · SPC369 · QUA605 · QUA607 · QUA588/589 · QUA601 · QUA590 · QUA100 · SPC369 · SPC379 · QUA605 · QUA607 · SSG102** · SPC373 · QUA603 · SPC386 · SPC388 · SPC390* · SPC392* · SPC394* · SPC396*

ENG123: Design for Manufacturability
ENG290: Six Sigma Design Methodology
FED103: Ethics Awareness: A Briefing on Procurement Integrity
QUA100: Customer Focused Problem Solving
QUA200: Quality Function Deployment
QUA300: Stds. Develop.: Creating & Promoting Motorola Strategies
QUA301: Strategic Standards Management
QUA387: JMP Fundamentals
QUA389: Intro to Design of Experiments
QUA391: Screening Designs of Experiments
QUA392: Systematic Approach to Problem Solving
QUA393: Optimization Using Response Surface Modeling (RSM)
QUA395: D-Optimal Design of Experiments

QUA397: Robust Design of Products & Processes
QUA588: Quality System Review (QSR) Overview - Windows
QUA589: Quality System Review (QSR) Overview - Mac
QUA590: Quality Systems Review, Subsystems 1-9
QUA601: Customer Focused Quality
QUA603: Organizational Quality Assessment
QUA605AG: Business Process Problem Solving
QUA607: Customer Care Tools/Techniques
SPC369: Applying Continuous Improvement Tools
SPC373: Intro. to Phased Techniques for Quality Improvement
SPC379: Statistical Process Characterization & Control
SPC382: Measurement System Analysis

SPC386: Precontrol
SPC388: Statistics II
* SPC390: Comparative Experiments B vs. C
* SPC392: Factorial Experiments
* SPC394: Fractional Fractorials
* SPC396: Component Search
** SSG102: Utilizing the Six Steps to Six Sigma

Available & supported
in development
Proposed
Required

SPC 390, & 396 to be replaced by QUA392;
SPC392 to be replaced by QUA389;
SPC394 to be replaced by QUA391

· available in CD-ROM

Figure 35-10. (*Continued*)

At a tactical level, the concepts of planning, goal setting, and evolving a quality system were presented. To a large degree these activities are the work of middle management. Installation of enabling systems, road maps, and reinforcement processes are important activities. The role of benchmarking and customer satisfaction assessment in the establishment at the operational plan is critical. Training of middle managers in quality improvement sometimes requires overcoming resistance to change in established practices and traditional norms. The training department often must partner with the quality organization to provide compelling reasons for managers to change. Once a receptive environment is created, skills-based training in topics such as benchmarking, problem solving, and leading teams may be introduced with a high probability of acceptance.

While the strategic and tactical levels of quality improvement are important, they are aimed at a relatively focused and small target population. When we apply both the implementation and training activities of quality improvement to the operational level, we face a wide range of functional disciplines. The size of the target population increases by an order of magnitude. Training organizations can easily be overwhelmed by the scope and depth of training required to achieve operational excellence utilizing quality-improvement methodologies. When faced with these challenges, we must recognize that world-class companies such as Motorola, Inc., have worked on these issues for 10 to 15 years! The change does not happen overnight. This fact is why the concept of quality-system evolution is so important. Rather than trying to list *all* the skills and tools needed and train "everyone in everything," the organization should focus on assessing, evaluating, prioritizing, and implementing "tuned" learning interventions.

Over time, the various functions and processes will develop an understanding of the operational improvement process and decide which specific skills and tools they need to be effective. In this context, the training organization's highest leverage is in facilitating assessments, organizing results, and aligning the "knowledge gaps" of the organization with appropriate training.

General training in team problem solving, statistical process control, and process improvement may then follow. The application of independent improvement tools vary greatly depending on the function of the people and their organization. Engineers will almost certainly require a curriculum that includes advanced statistical methods while administrative functions will utilize basic tools (see Fig. 35-10). As you can see, training in quality is not trivial and cannot be implemented in a few weeks or months. In world-class organizations it has evolved over many years and will continue to evolve over many more.

Reference

1. Motorola, Inc., "Motorola Corporate Quality System Review Guidelines," rev. 3, Schaumburg, IL, March 1995.

Bibliography

Motorola, Inc., *Motorola Corporate Quality System Review Guidelines*, Schaumburg, IL, March 1995, Rev. 3.

Motorola University, *QUA590: Quality System Review (QSR) Subsystems 1–9 Training*, Schaumburg, IL, 1995.

Motorola University, *Catalog of Training and Education Programs, Products, and Services*, Schaumburg, IL, 1995.

Motorola University, *BMK220: Benchmarking: Benchmarking Model/Five Phases*, Schaumburg, IL.

36
Job Training

Michael Nolan

Michael Nolan *is president of Friesen, Kaye and Associates, a 30-year-old training and consulting firm in Ottawa, Ontario, specializing in custom training programs and train-the-trainer workshops. He has over 20 years' experience in training, sales, and communications in both the public and private sectors. He has personally trained over 10,000 participants in various programs and worked with such clients as Digital Equipment Corporation, AT&T Communications, Oracle Corporation, Hewlett Packard, The Travelers, Cognos Corporation, Northern Telecom, Bell Northern Research, Southern New England Telephone, Canadian Airlines International, Motorola Codex, Glaxo, Pharmaceutical, and Microsoft. Nolan has presented at ISPI Conferences, Ontario Society for Training and Development Conferences, the Occupational Safety and Health Conference 1994, the Ninth Annual Autodesk University Conference 1994, and Ottawa Chapter sessions of the Ontario Society for Training and Development. Prior to Friesen, Kaye and Associates, Nolan was Director of Corporate Training and Development at Mitel Corporation, an international manufacturer of telecommunications systems. He has public-sector experience with the Department of Revenue as Head of Management Development and as a training consultant and specialist with the Department of Health. He is a sociology major from Carleton University and a member of ASTD, the International Society for Performance Improvement, and the Ontario Society for Training and Development.*

Whether it is Total Quality Management, new technology, teamwork, leadership, customer service, or just-in-time production, the workplace is changing and so are the skills that employees must have in order to change with it. As a result, training and on-the-job learning have taken a lead role in facilitating change and skill acquisition.

In this chapter there will be a review of what is meant by job training and the most common methods used today. An attempt will be made to summarize the benefit and identify potential barriers to job training, along with the key decision factors when job training is selected as a method of instruction. This chapter will also highlight events which have influenced modern job training and describe the critical steps of a structured on-the-job training process, and conclude with some general remarks on the future of job training.

The total dollars budgeted for formal training in 1994 by U.S. organizations reached $50.6 billion—an increase of 5 percent from the previous year. The total number of individuals receiving formal training from their employers in 1994 was 47.3 million.[1]

This data, although impressive, accounts for only *formal* training activities—structured away from the job programs, workshops, and courses—not the vast amount of informal instruction and learning which goes on every day in organizations called *job training*. It is estimated that more people have completed job training than any other form of training, and, that 60 percent of all training still occurs on the job.[2] Job training has been reported as the most frequently used training method across most job types and status levels including skilled and semiskilled industrial, sales, and supervisory-managerial positions.[3]

What Is Job Training?

Job training involves assigning the learners to work with a more experienced employee, either a supervisor, peer, or lead hand, to learn specific tasks in the actual workplace. The learner is usually a new employee who has been either recently hired, transferred, or promoted into the position and who lacks the knowledge and skill to perform some components of her or his job. The experienced employee normally demonstrates and discusses new areas of knowledge and skill and then provides opportunities for practice and feedback.

Throughout this chapter, the new employee will be referred to as the learner or the trainee, and the experienced employee, peer, lead hand, or supervisor who works with the learner during this job-training period will be referred to as the OJT instructor.

Three Methods of Job Training

There are several methods used in job training. The three most common methods are (1) structured on-the-job training (OJT); (2) unstructured on-the-job training; and (3) job instruction training (JIT).

Structured OJT. Structured OJT allows the learner to acquire skills and knowledge needed to perform the job through a series of structured or planned activities at the work site. All activities are performed under the careful observation and supervision of the OJT instructor.

The structured process is based on a thorough analysis of the job and the learner. The OJT instructor introduces the learner systematically to what he or she needs to know to perform competently and meet performance standards and expectations.

Unstructured OJT. Unstructured OJT often means sink or swim. Most activities in unstructured OJT have not been thought through and are done in a haphazard way. A common method of unstructured OJT is to have the learner "sit" with another employee or have him "follow the employee around" for a few days to see what that employee does and how she does it. This "sit-and-see" technique often leads the learner to pick up as much by trial and error as he does by any instruction given by the more experienced employee. The learner is typically inundated with reading assignments concerning policies, procedures, and other assorted documentation which, when not put into the right context, can cause more confusion than assistance.

The learner is often thrust on the experienced employee without notice and is seen as a hindrance, since this training time is interrupting the experienced employee's normal work load and performance outputs. The major drawback of the unstructured approach is that objectives, expectations, and outcomes are not defined in advance and, therefore, results are unpredictable.

Job Instruction Training (JIT). JIT was originally developed for use with World War II production workers and is based on a mechanical step procedure requiring the instructor to present the material in an orderly, disciplined manner. It is most frequently used in teaching motor skills.[4] Since there is a systematic approach to JIT, components of it are often found in today's structured on-the-job training initiatives.

Benefits of Job Training

There are many benefits of job training for the new employee. Understandably, the most powerful benefits of job training are from structured OJT rather than unstructured OJT. The major benefits of job training are that it

- Reduces unproductive periods of assimilation of new employees to the work requirements, therefore increasing individual productivity more quickly
- Ensures that employees learn how to perform tasks in line with the expectations and standards of the organization, the work unit, and the manager-supervisor
- Allows the learner to experience the day-to-day realities of the job which provides an opportunity to identify problems or discrepancies and enhance present job methods and procedures
- Eliminates the transfer-of-training problem experienced in other training methodologies since learning is done in the actual workplace
- Encourages the creation and maintenance of job and task descriptions and standards and procedures which support consistency and continuity in the job
- Increases learners' confidence and productiveness by allowing them to work at their own rate
- Establishes and strengthens relationships between learner and supervisor through positive reinforcement and feedback
- Increases the supervisor's understanding of the work done by individual contributors through the review and implementation of training plans
- Defines outcomes in advance, which increases the predictability of achieving results
- Requires active involvement by learners and OJT instructors, which is a cornerstone for any learning process
- Incorporates just-in-time training principles which support the concept of learning new skills as required
- Establishes a learning partnership between the new employee and the organization which reinforces joint training and development solutions

Potential Barriers to Effective Job Training

The most common drawbacks to effective job training can be grouped under three main categories: (1) instructor effectiveness, (2) environmental issues, and (3) unstructured process.

Instructor Effectiveness

- The OJT instructor lacks instructional skills and basic understanding of learning concepts.
- There is little or no interest on the part of the OJT instructor in training or improving the job performance of the learner.
- The OJT instructor is not a master performer and, therefore, has difficulty demonstrating the required performance.
- The level of the OJT instructor's interpersonal skills negatively impacts the understanding and motivation of the learner.

Environmental Issues

- Job training interferes or disrupts the normal work patterns and production schedules.
- The equipment needed for job training is required for production.
- There is significant production and material waste during job training.
- The total work unit is at risk if the tasks being learned require the use of hazardous materials.
- The workplace may be too noisy, stressful, or busy to be conducive to learning.

Unstructured Process

- The lack of a systematic approach results in unplanned and ineffective activities.
- Ill-defined outcomes give way to unpredictable results.

Criteria for Selecting Job Training

As part of the performance analysis–needs identification phase of most instructional design models, training is recognized as the appropriate solution only when there is a lack of knowledge or skills causing the performance discrepancy. Once this initial determination has been made, selection decisions on the specific methods of training should be considered. Job training is one of several methods of instruction that may be appropriate. Instructor-led (classroom) training; computer-based, multimedia training; self-directed learning; and job aids are other available training methods. Job training is appropriate for use in certain training situations but not in all. Figure 36-1 presents some selection criteria for considering the use of job training.

Factors	Consider job training when...	Consider alternatives to job training when...
Frequency	All key tasks occur on a regular basis	All key tasks do not occur on a regular basis
Permanency	The content does not frequently change	The content is frequently revised
Numbers	Not many trainees require training at the same time	Numerous workers share the same training needs at the same time so that cost savings can be realized by training them as a group
Equipment	Equipment not available in classroom (heavy, scarce, expensive)	Equipment can be brought into classroom
Environment	Work environment is conducive to a comfortable learning environment	Work environment is not conducive to a comfortable learning environment
Instructor availability	Qualified instructors are not available but master performers are	Qualified instructors are available
Risk	There is no physical risk involved	There is physical risk involved—risk can be simulated in classroom
Real world	Actual job conditions can be best simulated on the job	Job conditions can best be recreated in a classroom environment
Population variables	The population has diverse levels of experience	Population has similar background and experience
Motivation	Learners are well motivated and will work on their own with limited supervision	Learners are not motivated enough to work well on their own
Skills	The skills required to do the job can only be acquired over time and with practice	The skills required to do the job can be acquired quickly and with little practice
Completion time	Learner time to complete the course is not a factor	Learner time to complete the course is critical

Figure 36-1. Job training design table.

Skills versus Knowledge Criteria

Since many jobs in today's organizations are of a complex nature, the acquisition of the skills and knowledge needed to perform those jobs may be best addressed through the use of different instructional methods.

Job training seems best suited to skill or performance-based tasks. Some examples of skill-based tasks are (1) performing a simple, logical procedure of loading a software program; (2) conducting a 10-step quality inspection of a shop floor; and (3) performing troubleshooting procedures on a piece of equipment. Job training using JIT techniques may be very effective in unskilled or semiskilled jobs requiring motor skill development, and structured OJT could be used for routine jobs that require mastery of several skills.

Job training appears to be less suited to helping learners with knowledge-based tasks such as Total Quality Management (TQM) concepts or problem-solving and decision-making principles. In these cases, an off-the-job instructor-led method would be more preferable since this type of training would be provided to large numbers of learners across the organization.

Exceptions to the idea that skill-based tasks are best suited to job-training situations, are most often found in more complex skills such as interpersonal communications skills, presentation skills, customer service skills, management skills, sales skills, and conflict resolution skills. In these situations, off-the-job instructor-led programs using presentation methods such as demonstration, lecturette with video role modeling, and application methods using individual, small-group exercise, discussion, case study, role-play, and simulation would be most successful. The key to effective instruction in this type of skill training program is practice by the learners followed by constructive feedback by highly skilled facilitators.

Integrating Methods

Experience in developing job-training programs supports the literature which suggests that off-the-job training methods are better for attaining knowledge outcomes while on-the-job training methods seem better suited for skill outcomes.[5] Effective instructional strategy, however, can integrate knowledge and skill acquisition through use of a combination of methodologies. New employees, for example, may use some self-paced materials or computer-based training to learn critical knowledge items prior to beginning their structured on-the-job training that will develop skills and allow them to apply their newly acquired knowledge. Another combination often used is off-the-job instructor-led training, which develops generic knowledge and skills, supported with on-the-job training, which zeros in on the specific knowledge and skills required for the job.

Vestibule Training

Job training is conducted in the actual workplace with only a few exceptions. One such exception is vestibule training, a method in which a simulated work space is set up in a separate training facility or a designated area, usually adjacent to the workplace. Using the same kind of equipment and operating procedures as in the actual work situation, trainees learn to perform the job under the guidance of skilled instructors, not supervisors or other experienced workers. The research suggests that "vestibule training can be very effective in reducing the time required for training and in the resulting level of job proficiency."[6]

There are several advantages to vestibule training. Since its sole purpose is to train workers, there is no emphasis or pressure on production. The use of professional trainers also means that more personalized attention can be given to individual trainees. Trainees, too, do not have to worry about making costly or embarrassing errors in front of future coworkers. Nor do they have to be concerned about damaging equipment or slowing down the production process. Vestibule training also eliminates or reduces some of the other barriers listed earlier in the chapter, for example, allowing the total work unit to be at risk if the learner is handling hazardous goods and materials or having the actual workplace be too noisy, stressful, or busy. Vestibule training allows the new employee to be free to concentrate on learning the skills necessary for successful performance of the job.

The greatest disadvantage of vestibule training is the expense. The organization must equip a facility and maintain a staff of instructors. The cost may seem particularly burdensome when there are not enough new employees to make full use of the training facility.

As with most off-the-job training, if vestibule training does not closely match the actual working situation, there will be the problem of transfer of training. Without a close correspondence between the two situations, learners may need additional formal or informal on-the-job training when they actually begin to work.

The problem of transfer can be further aggravated by the common practice of using obsolete equipment, retired from the production floor, in the training program. If the equipment in actual use is sufficiently different from the training equipment, the net effect could result in a negative transfer.

Apprenticeship

Probably the earliest recorded training method in existence is the apprenticeship program for skilled crafts and trades. In today's work environment, apprenticeship programs are conducted in the workplace, but they differ from job training as defined in this chapter. A trade apprenticeship enables the individual to become skilled in one of many areas, as opposed to learning specific tasks within one job.[7] (Also see Chap. 38, Apprenticeship.)

Apprenticeships average four years, although in some skills they last as long as seven years. The standard procedure is for trainees to agree to work for a company for a fixed period of time in return for a specified period of training and a salary, usually about half that earned by a skilled craftsperson.

Typically the apprentice receives shop instruction from a master performer of that trade, called a "journeyman," while working with him. This instruction is supported by more formal instruction at a local technical school, which requires two to four years to complete, depending on the trade.

The combination of classroom instruction and actual work experience can provide excellent training in highly complex skills. However, if a company provides inadequate formal training, an apprenticeship program may be unsuccessful. This situation occurs when the organization's main goal is increased production with inexpensive labor as opposed to developing a skilled craftsperson.

The rapidly changing nature of organizations, specifically those incorporating the latest manufacturing techniques, sometimes renders a job obsolete by the time apprentices have finished the required period of training. For example, automation has completely altered the printing industry in recent years and has totally revised the skills requirements. Another example is the pressure found in the housing industry for factory-produced homes as an alternative to on-site construction. The skills required of a carpenter working on an assembly line to build one part of a house are different from those required of the on-site carpenter.

Apprenticeship programs must be capable of modifying their requirements and procedures in line with changes in today's industry. Although not defined as a part of mainstream job training, apprenticeship is generally an effective training method that is likely to remain useful for many years.

Background of Job Training

Vocational training and apprenticeship training were the forerunners of modern job training and can be traced back to ancient times. Like many other concepts, this form of training was brought to the American colonies from Western Europe. Not surprisingly, it has undergone significant changes from its earlier approaches.

It is suggested that today we find ourselves in the third stage of the industrial revolution.[8] The first stage was *mechanization*, when machines were developed to perform physical labor. The second stage was *computerization*, when new kinds of machines were developed to perform some of the mental work of human beings and to control the operation of other machines. For all the difference in sophistication, they share a concern with machinery and not with the people who run it. The third stage of the industrial revolution, *humanization*, focuses for the first time on people and their needs and aspirations. The development of job training has its roots in the first two stages of the industrial revolution and continues to flourish and evolve in the humanization stage.

There were several individuals, fields of discipline, and historical events that influenced the development of job training. Frederick W. Taylor and Frank B. Gilbreth, educators and organizational psychologists, and problems and solutions arising during World Wars I and II all contributed to the shape that job training would take over the decades to come.

Influences of Frederick W. Taylor and Frank B. Gilbreth

In the early 1900s, the philosophy of management was *scientific management*, an approach established by an engineer, Frederick W. Taylor, who was concerned primarily with ways to maintain or increase production levels. Through the use of time and motion studies, representatives of scientific management were interested in standardizing the production process—getting the machines and the workers who ran them to work faster and more efficiently. By experimenting with different shovel loads at Bethlehem Steel Company in 1898, he determined the optimum shovel size and introduced shovels of different sizes for handling different materials. Through a systematic approach, he studied the methods and equipment used and analyzed the steps required to do a job. By breaking down the work into simple steps and movements, he then observed the most productive workers and calculated the time it took them to do the job. By integrating the new shovels and key movements or steps, Taylor demonstrated that 140 men could now accomplish the same amount of work that had formerly required 500 men. This process enabled him to establish standards for quantity and quality, both critical components of effective job training.

A second pioneer in the time-and-motion area was Frank B. Gilbreth. Where Taylor had been concerned primarily with tool design, Gilbreth was concerned with the way in which workers performed their job. As an apprentice bricklayer at age 17, Gilbreth noticed that the bricklayers were engaged in many unnecessary motions in their work. He thought he could redesign the job to make it faster and easier, and within a year he was the fastest bricklayer on the job. He then increased the productivity of his coworkers from 120 bricks an hour to 350 bricks an hour, using a specially designed scaffold.

As a result of the efforts of Taylor and Gilbreth, many jobs, even those in hospital operating rooms, were revolutionized. Before Gilbreth analyzed the motions involved in surgery, surgeons had to seek out each tool they wanted to use. Gilbreth's recommendation that a nurse place the required tool in the surgeon's hand saved motions that reduced operating times by as much as two-thirds and still remains a key procedure in operating rooms today.[9]

Although Taylor, Gilbreth, and other early efficiency experts were accused of viewing workers simply as an extension of their machines, some cornerstones to the future of job training were laid. An emphasis was placed on standardization and the development and documentation of superior production methods. It was Taylor who believed that it was possible, scientifically, to select and train workers. Taylor also developed what was "probably the first training aid, an instruction (or method) card which gave a worker each specific part of the job to be performed together with the time required for each step or operation."[10]

Influence of Academic and Organizational Psychologists

Throughout the latter part of the nineteenth century and into the early part of the twentieth century, educators and psychologists had a profound influence on job training. The German psychologist Johann Friedrich Herbart shaped educational methods in the United States through a standard four-step format of instruction in the learning process. Other influences such as the human relations approach to management which began in the 1920s and 1930s under the impact of the Hawthorne and other studies focused on the workers instead of production. Concepts which are inherent in contemporary training, motivation, and learning theory were particularly influenced by the work of such psychologists as Abraham Maslow, Douglas McGregor, and Frederick Herzberg.

Several American educators also clearly influenced the development of industrial training methods. Horace Mann, Edward Thorndike, and John Dewey all supported the concept of "using procedural steps to condition the learner by presenting one step at a time, demonstrating and explaining it until it is done correctly."[11]

Training in World War I

World War I posed one unique problem to the United States, and training responded well as the solution. In 1917, the Emergency Fleet Corporation of the United States Shipping Board had an urgent need for 450,000 additional workers. The solution to the problem was to hire and train new shipbuilders. Charles R. Allen, as head of the program, "ordered that all training be done at the shipyards, and that instructors should be the supervisors...."[12] His adaption of Herbart's four-step method of instruction became show, tell, do, and check and was recognized as the main solution to this overwhelming problem. Figure 36-2 shows the four steps in a job instruction pocket card format used by C. R. Allen. One side of the card had the four steps of "How to Instruct" and on the reverse side, a four-step method on "How to Get Ready to Instruct."

Alice Bird McCord's research into Allen's work and that of the Army during World War I cites the following principles that developed as the basis for industrial training:

- Training should be done within industry.
- Training should be done by supervisors. (The ability to instruct is an important part of the supervisor's job.)
- Supervisors should be trained in how to instruct.
- The best group size for training is 9 to 11 people.

HOW TO GET READY TO INSTRUCT	HOW TO INSTRUCT
Have a Time Table - How much skill you need him to have, and how soon. **Break Down the Job -** list principal steps, pick out the key points. **Have Everything Ready -** the right equipment, materials, and supplies **Have the Work Place Properly Arranged -** just as the worker will be expected to keep it **Job Instructor Training** **WAR MANPOWER COMMISSION BUREAU OF TRAINING** TRAINING WITHIN INDUSTRY **KEEP THIS CARD HANDY** 16-26793-4 GPO	**Step 1 - Prepare the Worker** Put him at ease. Find out what he already knows about the job Get him interested in learning job. Place in correct position **Step 2 - Present the Operation** Tell, Show, Illustrate, and Question carefully and patiently. Stress key points. Instruct clearly and completely, taking up one point at a time - but no more than he can master. **Step 3 - Try Out Performance** Test him by having him perform job. Have him tell and show you; have him explain key points. Ask questions and correct errors. Continue until you know HE knows. **Step 4 - Follow Up** Put him on his own. Designate to whom he goes for help. Check frequently. Encourage questions. Get him to look for key points as he progresses. Taper off extra coaching and close follow-up. 16-26793-3 **If Worker Hasn't Learned, the Instructor Hasn't Taught**

Figure 36-2. Job instruction card.

- The preparation of a job breakdown is an important step before training.
- Break-in time is reduced when training is done on the job.
- When given personal attention in training, the worker develops a feeling of loyalty.[13]

Although training was viewed as a means to solving production problems for both supervisors and workers, and hands-on training or learning by doing resulted in significant savings in training time, job training did not become prominent again until 1940 and World War II.

World War II and the Establishment of Training Within Industry

As Americans registered for the draft in late 1940, thousands of others who had never worked in plants prior to this time were in the process of taking the place of those drafted into the armed forces. As the United States entered World War II in December 1941, these replacement workers needed to be trained as welders, machinists, and other plant and factory positions. Following the lessons learned from World War I, supervisors were identified as the job instructors by the Training Within Industry Service (TWI), established in 1940 by the National Defense Advisory Commission. In 1941, by presidential order, TWI became a part of the War Manpower Commission and operated under the Bureau of Training. When TWI ceased operation in 1945, it had been instrumental in training 23,000 persons as instructors and had issued nearly two million certificates to supervisors who had gone through TWI programs.

JIT, or job instruction training, was one of the TWI programs developed to train supervisors in defense plants in the skill of instructing their workers as rapidly as possible. JIT not only taught how to instruct but also emphasized the interpersonal relationship between the supervisor and employee and the determination of the best job methods.

Building on C. R. Allen's approach, jobs were broken down into key points, then training followed a seven-step method of instruction:

1. Show workers how to do it.

2. Explain key points.

3. Let them watch you do it again.

4. Let them do the simple parts of the job.

5. Help them do the whole job.

6. Let them do the whole job—but watch them.

7. Put them on their own.[14]

The emphasis on this form of job training was to break down each step of the job into separate discrete steps and allow the learner plenty of repetitive practice and drill. The instructor or supervisor prepared a job breakdown while watching an experienced worker perform each step of the job. She or he then recorded the breakdown on a blueprint or Job Breakdown Sheet (see Fig. 36-3), which showed important steps of the job (what to do) and key points (how to do it). Each step of the operation was documented in detail, in the right sequence.

Department_____ Job_____ Breakdown made by_____ Date_____	
Important Steps (What to Do) A logical segment of the operation, when something happens to advance the work	Key Points (How to do it) Anything that may ▪ Make or break the job ▪ Injure the worker ▪ Make the work easier to do
1. Place piece on plate against regulating wheel.	Knack—don't catch on wheel
2. Lower level wheel.	Hold at end of stroke (count 1, 2, 3, 4). Slow-feed, Watch—no oval grinding.
3. Raise level release.	
4. Gauge pieces periodically.	More often as approach tolerance
5. Readjust regulating wheel as required.	Watch—no backlash
6. Repeat above until finished.	

Figure 36-3. Job breakdown sheet for training purposes.

Job Training Today

Developing a Structured On-the-Job Training Program

The primary reason for developing and using a job-training program is to allow a new employee to acquire the knowledge and skills required to perform the job as quickly as possible. There are other situations where job training would also be appropriate: new standards may have been introduced to the job; new performance goals may have been assigned to the employee; new work procedures may have changed the way the job is presently being performed; or reengineering may have required the employee to now perform new or additional tasks along with present job requirements. Whatever the reason for undertaking job training, it should be developed using a systematic process similar to the way other training methods are developed. Figure 36-4 is an overview of the steps in a structured OJT process.

Step 1: Needs Analysis.   The first step of an instructional design process is a needs analysis. This step identifies a performance discrepancy, the cause of the discrepancy, a potential solution, and a cost to implement the solution. As stated earlier, training—including structured on-the-job training—is a solution to a performance discrepancy only if there is a lack of knowledge or skill or if there is a lack of practice. Figure 36-5 outlines some causes and solutions of performance discrepancies.

A number of diagnostic methods can be used to assess training needs. Since structured on-the-job training is performance-based, methods that measure against standards of performance are most appropriate. Jobs that have measurable units of output can use indirect examinations of performance or productivity measures. Direct observation and interview methods may be more suitable

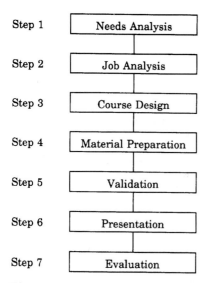

Figure 36-4. Structured on-the-job training process.

Cause	Solution
1. Task interference	Remove interference; modify procedures; subdivide tasks
2. Lack of feedback	Build in feedback loops
3. Performance standards not known	Make standards known
4. Lack of performance measurement	Develop performance indicators
5. Inaccurate performance measurement	Revise or develop performance indicators
6. Negative consequences for performance	Remove negative consequences; provide positive consequences; make nonperformance nonrewarding
7. Lack of positive consequences	Provide positive consequences
8. Positive consequences for nonperformance	Remove positive consequences for nonperformance; provide more positive consequences for performance; make nonperformance more punishing
9. Negative attitude	Change conditions or activities that reinforce
10. Wrong resource	Change selection criteria to reflect job requirements. Change resource.
11. Lack of knowledge or skills	Provide training: structured on-the-job training, instructor-led training; self-directed learning; CBT; job aids
12. Lack of practice	Provide practice; refresher training

Figure 36-5. Performance discrepancies—some causes and solutions.

for jobs where output may be more difficult to measure or where standards of performance do not exist.

Indirect Examinations of Performance or Productivity Measures. Indirect examinations, sometimes called *operational audits,* judge performance from such tangible indicators as quality-control rejects, production records, scrap notes, or other records about the quantity and/or quality of work performed. These examinations or audits, as a needs analysis tool, typically measure:

Output:

Units produced
Tons manufactured
Items assembled
Money collected
Items sold
Forms processed
Loans approved
Inventory turnover
Patients visited
Applications processed
Students graduated
Tasks completed

Output per person-hour
Work backlog
Incentive bonus
Commission
Shipments

Costs:

Budget variances
Unit costs
Cost by account
Fixed costs
Overhead cost
Operating costs

Number of cost reductions
Project cost savings
Accident costs
Program costs
Sales expense

Time:

Equipment downtime
Overtime
On-time shipments
Time to project completion
Processing time
Break-in time for new
 employees
Training time
Meeting schedules
Repair time
Work stoppages

Order responses
Late reporting
Lost-time days

Quality:

Scrap
Waste
Rejects
Error rates
Rework
Shortages
Product defects
Deviation from standard
Product failures
Inventory adjustments
Time-card corrections
Percent of tasks completed properly
Number of accidents

Operational audits may use a number of different record sources that take into account the following types of personnel-related data to be used for identifying training needs for on-the-job training:

Work habits:

Absenteeism

Tardiness

First-aid treatments

Violation of safety rules

Excessive breaks

Work climate:

Number of grievances

Number of discrimination charges

Employee complaints

Employee turnover

Disciplinary actions

Job satisfaction as determined through employee surveys

Direct-observation method. Observation or first-hand examination of what employees do to perform and how they do it, is another data collection method used to determine training needs for on-the-job training. The observations may be conducted by supervisors or individuals with highly developed observation skills. Most effective direct-observation techniques use a specialized form or checklist to record the actions or results of the performers. Observation may be continuous over a specific period of time or at various times of the day for a specified work period.

Questionnaires and Surveys. This method of data collections consists of written questions, to employees, about their training needs. The surveys also solicit opinions of the employees' needs from supervisors or other stakeholders. Questions are sometimes developed from interview results to verify or cross-check how many people share similar opinions or perceptions about the training needs. This can be a very effective data-gathering tool with new employees who have completed their initial training period and are able to articulate what other training is required.

Interviews. Interviews are structured conversations focusing on training needs. They are relatively simple to plan and conduct and can zero in on both the supervisor's and employee's perception about the performance discrepancy and the structured on-the-job training necessary to solve it. Focus-group interviews (groups of employees and/or supervisors) can also be used to help structure or validate questionnaires by listing problems and issues employees are currently facing, as well as determining exceptional and ineffective behaviors in job performance.

Mastery Model.   Mastery model is the process of gathering information which captures the performance of the job, in order to create an ideal or mastery model. The procedure involves a high-level systematic breakdown of the job into duties, tasks, subtasks, and knowledge and skills. It also reviews what tools or references are needed, to what standards the tasks should be performed, and under what circumstances and conditions they are performed. Through creation and use of a mastery model, employee's performance can then be compared (actual) to what should be (ideal). A more detailed analysis of the job is described in step 2 of structured on-the-job training—job analysis.

Other Diagnostic Measures.   There are several other data collection methods that are available when training needs for on-the-job training are analyzed. The following are the most common: skills inventories, tests, position descriptions, annual performance appraisals, problem logs, formal course evaluations, critical incident, assessment centers, and competency assessment.

Each data collection method has advantages and disadvantages. Figure 36-6 applies certain criteria to consider when the five methods described in this chapter are selected.

Step 2: Job Analysis.   The second step of structured on-the-job training is job analysis. This critical step involves an analysis of the learner, the organization, and the job. Figure 36-7 is an overview of this step.

Method	Incumbent Involvement	Management Involvement	Time Required	Ease of Development	Ease of Administration	Ease of Analysis	Sensitivity of Data	Cost	Relevant Quantifiable Data
Interviews	H	M	H	L	L	M	L	H	M
Observation	M	L	H	L	L	L	L	H	M
Questionnaires	H	H	H	L	M	H	H	M	H
Performance or Productivity Measures	L	M	L	M	M	M	L	L	H
Mastery Model	M	M	H	H	M	L	M	H	H

Legend:
L = Low
M = Moderate
H = High

Figure 36-6. Selection criteria for data collection methods.

```
┌─────────────────────────────────────────┐
│              Job Analysis                │
│  ▪ Learner analysis                      │
│  ▪ Organization analysis                 │
│  ▪ Task listing                          │
│  ▪ Task analysis                         │
│  ▪ Skills and knowledge analysis         │
└─────────────────────────────────────────┘
```

Figure 36-7. Overview of job analysis.

Learner Analysis.   The characteristics of trainees must be examined in order to target the on-the-job training accurately and develop effective instructional materials. Each trainee is different and should be approached with this difference in mind. What goes well for a new hire may not be as successful for an employee transferring from another part of the organization. This analysis of the learner helps guide the OJT instructor to deliver the training in a manner and style that is appropriate for the trainee. Some other terms synonymous with learner analysis include target group, audience analysis, student profile information, potential trainee profile information, and population description.

Figure 36-8, Learner Analysis Form, identifies essential learner information and should be completed for each potential trainee. The form can be used as a questionnaire and sent out to trainees or can be asked as interview questions. Questions surrounding age range may be asked in the context of how life experience will affect learning.

Organizational Analysis.   The purpose of an organization analysis is to review what aspects exist in the organization or the work unit that may influence the on-the-job training program. The responses to the questions in Fig. 36-9 will help structure or modify the training.

Task Listing.   Task listing is the systematic breakdown of the job. It identifies the duties or broad areas of responsibility that define the purpose of the job. A typical job might have from five to eight duties. As each duty is listed, the question "What do I do to fulfill my responsibility?" is asked and a series of tasks are listed for each duty. Figure 36-10 is a template that defines duties, tasks, and the frequency and importance of each task. Figure 36-11 is an example of a job titled "driver" or "chauffeur."

Task Analysis.   Task analysis is the systematic breakdown of the tasks. While each task describes what is done, there is not enough detail to describe how to do it or how to measure how well it has been done. In task analysis each task is broken down into a series of subtasks that describe the steps in performing the task. There is also a description of the parameters that surround the completion of a task such as tools and references, standards, and the conditions or circumstances under which the task is performed. Figure 36-12 is a template that defines the parameters, subtasks, and skills and knowledge of a task analysis–skills and knowledge analysis. Figure 36-13 is a continuation of the chauffeur example of a task analysis–skills and knowledge analysis surrounding the task of changing a flat tire.

Skills and Knowledge Analysis.   Skills and knowledge analysis is the final component of the job-analysis step and it comprises the systematic breakdown of the subtasks. It is the lowest and final level of detail required to perform each subtask. Tasks state *what to do,* subtasks state *how to do it,* and skills and knowledge are *the action and information needed to do it.* In training the skills and knowledge items represent the individual teaching points.

Learner question	Response(s)	How will this affect your OJT program?
1. How many years have you been with the company?		
2. How many years have you been in this job?		
3. Which of the following characteristics represent your last job? a) Full-time/Part-time/contract b) Technical/Nontechnical c) Management/Nonmanagement d) Similar job task/Varied job tasks		
4. Which of the following conditions exist? a) Rotating shifts b) Working with computers c) Working with machinery d) Customer contact e) Work with hazardous goods f) Work with noise/heat	Last job This job a) b) c) d) e) f)	
5. List your previous related training a) In-house ———— ———— ———— b) Vendor: ———— Off-site ————		
6. What is your knowledge of this job? a) Limited b) General c) High-level		
7. What education do you have that is related to the new job you must learn (e.g., accounting, diploma, apprenticeship program)?		
8. What experience have you had that seems related to the job or task at hand?		
9. How do you feel about your new job? a) Hostile b) Frustrated c) Indifferent d) Fearful e) Good f) Excited		

Trainee name: _____
Department: _____
Job: _____

Figure 36-8. Learner analysis form.

Consider	Response	Effect or result to OJT program
1. What company or work unit policies, if any, should the learner be informed about during training?		
2. What work standards are in place that should be communicated during training?		
3. What should the learner know about his or her supervisor's expectations concerning the job performance?		
4. Is the new employee likely to be influenced by existing coworkers? In what way?		
5. What company terminology or jargon should the learner be taught?		

Figure 36-9. Organization analysis.

Step 3: Course Design.   The course design step in structured on-the-job training is concerned with taking the job-analysis information and translating into a description of the training required to prepare the trainee to perform the job. This step will produce a course training plan that is the "blueprint" to be used to construct any training support materials. The course training plan should include a purpose statement, performance objectives, criterion tests (Fig. 36-14), presentation, application and feedback methods, course outline of content, a lesson plan, and training schedule.

Step 4: Material Preparation.   During the material preparation step, all training support materials are produced, as determined in step 3, course design. Figure 36-15 is an example of an OJT lesson plan used by bomb disposal experts and Fig. 36-16 a performance checklist used during training by the OJT instructor. These, along with the tracking system form (Fig. 36-17) would be examples of some of the materials produced at this stage.

Step 5: Validation.   After training materials have been developed for the OJT program, they must be tested to ensure they fulfill their mandate to train the individual to perform the job. Many organizations conduct "dry runs" of the training with selected individuals who are asked to assess the program. While this step may be useful in the editing of the course design, the program is really not validated until members of the target population have gone through the training.

Step 6: Presentation.   Effective instructional presentations incorporate a systematic learning process of *presentation, application, and feedback (PAF)*. Prior to actual delivery, the OJT instructor needs to review the structured process and

Job Title:

DUTIES	TASKS	FR.	·IMP.
These are the broad areas of responsibility or duties that must be met in order to perform the job. The duties should be separate and mutually exclusive. The duties are **not** activities. The list should consist of nouns, not verbs. The duties should be broad and **not** broken down into detail. There are seldom more than 8 duties for a job.	Each duty is broken down into its component tasks. The list of tasks is a breakdown of the broad activities to be performed on the job. These tasks should **not** be broken down into detail. Tasks should: - state what the employee will **do on** the job - begin with an action verb - have a noun following the action verb - be stated concisely - avoid overlap with other tasks.	How frequently is each task performed on the job? D - daily W - weekly M - once a month L - Less than once a month	How important is each task to overall job effectiveness? C - critical MC - moderately critical NC - not critical O - could be omitted

Figure 36-10. Task listing definition.

methods, collect all materials and tools necessary, and develop a schedule of training time.

Presentation	The OJT instructor

- States objective
- Motivates trainee
- Overviews key steps
- Presents tasks (tell and show)
- Tests for understanding

Job title: Driver/Chauffeur			
DUTIES	TASKS	FR.	IMP.
1. Routine maintenance	1.1 Change spark plugs	L	NC
	1.2 Change spark-plug wires	L	NC
	1.3 Adjust timing	L	NC
2. Appearance	1.4 Arrange work at service station	L	MC
	1.5 Inspect work done at service station	L	MC
3. Operation	1.6 Rotate tires	L	NC
	1.7 Change a flat tire	L	MC
4. Safety	1.8 Replace fuses	L	MC
	1.9 Replace bulbs	L	MC
5. Personal service	1.10 Top up fluids	M	MC
	1.11 Tighten fan belt	M	MC
	1.12 Charge battery	L	MC
	1.13 Clean battery connections	L	MC
	1.14 —		
	1.15 —		
	2.1 —		
	2.2 —		

Figure 36-11. Example of task listing for driver or chauffeur.

Application:	Trainee applies new knowledge and skill through
	▪ Directed practice
	▪ Undirected, yet supervised, practice
Feedback	OJT trainer observes and communicates to trainee
	▪ What was done well
	▪ What needs improvement
	▪ How to improve

Step 7: Evaluation. The final step in a structured OJT program is to evaluate it. Like other training methods, effective OJT programs may be evaluated using four distinct levels, as defined by Donald L. Kirkpatrick (see also Chap. 14, Evaluation, by Donald L. Kirkpatrick):

Level 1: Reaction: How did the learner react to the training?

Level 2: Learning: Did the trainees acquire the necessary knowledge and skills during the training period?

Level 3: Behavior: Did the trainees' performance and behavior change after training?

Level 4: Results: Has the performance discrepancy identified during needs analysis been solved?

By following the seven steps of a structured on-the-job training process—needs analysis, job analysis, course design, material preparation, validation, presentation, and evaluation—the learner will acquire the requisite knowledge and skills to perform the job in a systematic and effective manner.

Figure 36-18 summarizes the 12 major activities in structured on-the-job training.

Job training, specifically structured on-the-job training, can provide organizations with highly skilled, motivated, and competent performers. When inte-

	SUB-TASKS	SEQ	SKILLS AND KNOWLEDGE	JOB AID	ENT	SEQ
INPUT CONDITIONS What cues, events, orders or symptoms indicate that the task must be performed?	Each task is broken down into its component sub tasks. These sub-tasks should **not** be broken down into detail.		Focus on each sub-task and ask: "What does the learner need to **do or know** in order to perform this sub-task?" Include only things that are needed, not things that are merely nice to know.			
OUTPUT CONDITIONS What cues, events, orders or symptoms indicate that the task is completed? What has been produced?	Sub-tasks should: - state what the employee will do on the job - begin with an action verb - have a noun following the action verb - be stated concisely - avoid overlap with other sub-tasks		The skills and knowledge are the actual performance steps or teaching points to be learned. They are listed by breaking down the sub-tasks into their final level of detail for presentation to the learners. Skills and knowledge are detailed enough so that they do **not** need to be broken down or sub-divided further.			
TOOLS, REFERENCE What, references, tools, equipment or materials are used?						
STANDARDS How well must the task be performed (e.g., time, quantity, cost, safety, error rates, etc.).						
CIRCUMSTANCES What locations, situations, adverse conditions, obstacles, assistance, level of supervision, etc., exist when the task is being performed?						

Column note (SEQ, below SUB-TASKS): List the sequence in which the sub-tasks will be covered in the course.

Column note (SKILLS AND KNOWLEDGE / JOB AID): Check off (✓) skills and knowledge that will be covered by job aids.

Column note (ENT): Check off (✓) skills and knowledge contained in the learner's entry.

Column note (SEQ, rightmost): List the sequence in which the remaining skills and knowledge will be covered in the course.

Figure 36-12. Task analysis and knowledge analysis example definition.

Duty # 1 Routine Maintenance
Task # 1.7 Change a Flat Tire

Left (narrative) column

INPUT CONDITIONS
1. Looks flat
2. Unusual road noise
3. Steering irregularity

OUTPUT CONDITIONS
Spare is on, flat tire is in trunk, all equipment back in place in trunk.

TOOLS, REFERENCE
Jack and handle, wheel wrench, spare tire on rim, blocks, flares.

STANDARDS
1. All Safety precautions observed.
2. Spare is firmly seated.
3. Wheel nuts are tight.
4. Hubcap firmly in place.

CIRCUMSTANCES
Done alone and unsupervised. May be in garage or under adverse conditions on the road (at night, on curve, on hill, on rough terrain, heavy traffic, bad weather).

SUB-TASKS	SEQ	SKILLS AND KNOWLEDGE	JOB AID	ENT	SEQ
1.7.1 Determine when to change a flat tire.	1	1.7.1.1 Looks flat.			1
		1.7.1.2 Unusual road noise.			2
1.7.2 Identify necessary equipment.	3	1.7.1.3 Steering irregularity.			3
1.7.3 Remove equipment from trunk.	4	1.7.2.1 Spare tire.		✓	
		1.7.2.2 Scissor jack and handle.		✓	
1.7.4 Observe safety precautions.	2	1.7.2.3 Wheel wrench.		✓	
1.7.5 Jack up the car.	5	1.7.2.4 Wooden blocks.		✓	
1.7.6 Remove the flat.	6	1.7.2.5 Flares.		✓	
1.7.7 Install the spare.	7	1.7.3.1 Remove scissor jack, jack handle and wheel wrench from stowage compartment in trunk.			
1.7.8 Lower the car.	8	1.7.3.2 Remove spare tire from trunk.	✓		
1.7.9 Put equipment back in place.	9	1.7.3.3 Remove flares and wooden blocks from wheel well.	✓		
			✓		
		1.7.4.1 Move to right side of road as far as possible.	✓		4
		1.7.4.2 Stop on level ground.	✓		5
		1.7.4.3 Turn wheels to right if on hill.	✓		6
		1.7.4.4 Put transmission in park.	✓		7
		1.7.4.5 Put on emergency brake.	✓		8
		1.7.4.6 Exit on passenger side if traffic heavy.	✓		9
		1.7.4.7 Put flares on road.	✓		10
		1.7.4.8 Have someone flag traffic, if possible.	✓		11
		1.7.4.9 Block wheels.	✓		12
		1.7.4.10 Support jack with wood or stone if ground soft.	✓		13
		1.7.5.1			
		1.7.5.2			
		1.7.5.3			
		1.7.5.4			

Figure 36-13. Task analysis and knowledge analysis example for changing a flat tire.

DEFINITION	
PERFORMANCE OBJECTIVE #_____	**CRITERION TEST #_____**
The performance objective states what the employee must be able to do *on the job* after training is completed. The performance objective (PO) is constructed by combining the task statement with the items from the first column of the task analysis worksheet (input conditions, output conditions, tools, and references, standards and circumstances).	The criterion test is based on the PO. It should prove conclusively that the objective has been attained and that the trainee can perform the task. This test is a performance test and should duplicate or simulate the PO as closely as possible. If constraints make it impossible to simulate the PO during training, all items omitted in the criterion test should be listed later for reference.
EXAMPLE	
PERFORMANCE OBJECTIVE #1.7	**CRITERION TEST #1.7**

When the tire looks flat, unusual road noise is heard, or irregular steering is felt, the employee is required to change a flat tire by using the equipment from the trunk. This task may need to be done in bad weather, at night, with heavy traffic nearby, on a curve, on a hill, or on rough terrain. All safety precautions must be observed. When finished, all equipment and the flat must be put in place in the trunk. The tire must be firmly seated, the wheel nuts must be tight, and the hubcap must be firmly in place.	The OJT instructor will put two trainees together and provide each trainee with a checklist. Alternately, each will change a flat tire in the parking lot on a flat, level, paved surface. The rear driver's side tire will be changed with only the equipment from the trunk.
	
	Trainees will give feedback based on the checklist provided.
	
	NOT INCLUDED
	1. Input conditions
	2. Some safety precautions during the normal and adverse conditions.
	  - Uneven surface
	  - Parking on hill
	  - Exiting from car in heavy traffic
	  - Supporting jack in soft ground

Figure 36-14. Course training plan.

grated with off-the-job instructor-led methods, it enables the learners to more easily transfer what was covered in the classroom to the work site. When used as the primary method of instruction, structured on-the-job training not only helps trainees develop specific skills required for the job but it also can allow them to be actively involved in the training process. Through mutual discussion with their managers and OJT instructors, trainees can better understand the organization's expectations surrounding job performance and can potentially help set their own performance standards. The resulting benefit is that new employees and their managers work together more quickly to achieve both organizational and individual goals.

Figure 36-15. Sample lesson plan.

Trainer Lesson Plan	
Trainer's Guide	
Notes to Trainer	**Lesson**
Review what was achieved last session.	Link in: Last week you learned how to disarm the SL-39 bomb; this week we will address the type-A time bomb.
Explain what will be achieved in this session.	Objective: By the end of this OJT session you will be able to disarm type-A time bomb within a 3-minute time period to 100 percent accuracy in a pressure-filled environment until the bomb is disarmed and submerged in a sulphur solution.
Explain why he should learn the task.	Learn why a type-A time bomb is the most important popular bomb used by amateur (motivation) terrorists. Because you will spend much of your time dealing with this type, it is critical that you master it. Many of the skills you acquire in this lesson will make subsequent lessons easier. (If it is not done correctly, you and many others will be at risk.)
Place trainee at workstation.	Place trainee beside you. Ensure trainee can see clearly.
Explain conditions under which he or she will work and how well the task must be done. **(10 minutes)**	Standards and conditions ▪ Task must be completed in 3 minutes. ▪ Task must be completed to 100 percent accuracy. ▪ Task will be completed under extreme pressure because of the consequence of failure.

Give overview of task. What will take place? (High level)
 	
(5 minutes)
	Overview: We will deal with steps in the process of disarming the type-A bomb.
	    Knowledge
	    1. Identify equipment
	    2. Identify parts of bomb
	    3. Identify safety issues
	    Skill
	    4. Disassemble encasement
	    5. Diffuse timing device
	    6. Submerge in solution

First, review steps in the procedure to become familiar with them.	Subobjective no. 1.: Disassemble encasement in 1-minute time period to 100 percent accuracy in pressure-filled environment.

Figure 36-15. (*Continued*)

Notes to Trainer	Lesson
Explain what you will be doing. **(10 minutes)**	Steps: 1. Twist top of box counterclockwise until four screws exposed. 2. Identify the two screws with an X pattern on top. 3. Remove these screws using a Phillips screwdriver. 4. Identify the two screws with the square pattern on top. 5. Remove these screws with a Robertson screwdriver. 6. Remove top gently and place to the side. 7. Position bomb with half-moon closest to you.
Next, demonstrate the procedure.	
If possible, let trainee direct you through procedure again or ask questions to determine if an intellectual understanding has been acquired. **(5 minutes)**	
Direct trainee through procedure. **(5 minutes)**	
Have trainee disassemble type-A time bomb without direction but under supervision.	
Using the performance checklist, give feedback to the trainee. **(10 minutes)**	
Explain what was done well. **Explain what could be improved upon.** **Explain how to improve.**	Link out to next step. We have just finished disassembling the black box (encasement). Now we will tackle the most critical step in the procedure: diffusing the timing device.
Transition to next subobjective.	Subobjective no. 2: Diffuse the timing device within 1½ minutes to 100 percent accuracy in pressure-filled environment. Why it's important The diffusion stage is critical because…

Substep	Content	Yes	No	Comment
Identify all equipment	▪ Phillips screwdriver ▪ Robertson screwdriver ▪ Slot screwdriver ▪ Sulphur powder ▪ Water ▪ Reinforced disposal unit			
Identify parts of the time bomb.	▪ Black encasement ▪ Turnbuckle, screw right ▪ Timer dial ▪ Turnbuckle, screw left ▪ Arrow ▪ Anvil ▪ Main charge			
Observe safety precautions.	▪ Gently lift timing mechanism. ▪ Do not touch the timer dial. ▪ Carefully remove main charge.			
Disassemble time-bomb encasement.	▪ Twist top of box counterclockwise until four screws exposed ▪ Identify the two screws with an X pattern on top. ▪ Remove the screws using a Phillips screwdriver. ▪ Identify the two screws with the square pattern on top. ▪ Remove the screws with a Robertson screwdriver. ▪ Remove top gently and place to the side. ▪ Position bomb with half-moon closest to you.			
Diffuse timing device.	▪ Turn white screws counterclockwise using a slot screwdriver until red mark aligns with red dot. ▪ Carefully lift timing mechanism from casing using a slot screwdriver. ▪ Do not touch the timer dial. ▪ Remove the green wire. ▪ Simultaneously remove yellow and brown wires. ▪ Remove white wire.			
Submerge in sulphur solution.	▪ Pour water into the disposal-unit receptacle until it is half full. ▪ Mix in 3 tablespoons of sulphur concentrate. ▪ Mix for 30 seconds. ▪ Slowly immerse the bottom of box into disposal receptacle. ▪ Leave for 10 minutes. ▪ Send to examiner's office for evaluation.			

Figure 36-16. Performance checklist.

TRACKING SYSTEMS

(Must tailor to your own approach to structure OJT)

Forms Detailed Sign-Off Form

TRAINING COMPLETED

Dept: Explosives   Job: Explosive Expert IV   Duty: Operations   Task: 1.1 Disarm Time Bomb "A"

Name	Determine when to disarm bomb	Identify all equipment	Identify parts of bomb	Observe safety precautions	Disassemble Encasement	Disassemble Timing Device	Submerge in Solution	Sign Off
Jim	✓	✓						
Tracey	✓	✓	✓	✓				
Pat	✓	✓	✓					
Mary	✓	✓	✓	✓	✓			
Bill	✓	✓	✓	✓	✓	✓	✓	Michael Howe
Anne								

Figure 36-17. Tracking system form.

Activities in Structured On-the-Job Training	
1. Review (or prepare) the task listing for the job.	**A**
2. Analyze tasks for each major duty of general area of responsibility listed on the task listing form.	**N** **A**
3. Analyze: 3.1 The trainee population to determine what knowledge and skills they have which are required for the job or its tasks. 3.2 The organization to determine what issues are relevant to training.	**L** **Y** **S** **I** **S**
4. Prepare a structured OJT plan which includes 4.1 Instructional objectives 4.2 Teaching points 4.3 Method of delivery	**D** **E**

5. Apply components of the systematic learning process:
5.1 **Presentation**
  ▪ Motivation
  ▪ Outline
  ▪ Objective
5.2 **Application**
  ▪ Practice
5.3 **Feedback**
  ▪ What the learner did well
  ▪ What the learner should improve
  ▪ How the learner should improve
	S
	
	I
	
	G

6. Determine how to monitor progress of the trainee during structured on-the-job training.	**N**
7. Prepare the trainee for each job task: 7.1 Establish what the need and relevance of the task is to the trainee (motivation). 7.2 Use examples to clarify. 7.3 Use verbal and visual means to emphasize objectives. 7.4 Ensure that pace and sequence is appropriate. 7.5 Encourage trainee's questions and participation.	**D** **E**
8. Explain to the trainee 8.1 What the task is 8.2 What objectives are to be accomplished (results) 8.3 What standards the task should be performed to	**L** **I**
9. Demonstrate the tasks and subtasks to the trainee.	
10. Test intellectual understanding of the trainee.	**V**
11. Have the trainee perform the task and subtasks.	
12. Communicate to the trainee after he or she has demonstrated the task or subtask, taking care to 12.1 Detail what he or she did well 12.2 Give specific areas for improvement 12.3 Explain how to improve	**E** **R**

Figure 36-18. Major activities in structured on-the-job-training.

Job Training in the Future

More than ever before, job training will play a dominant role in the future success of organizations. In fact, there has been a consistent shift to the development of total performance solutions in which work and training become one.

With the present rate of technological change there will be increased need for constant adaptation of new information and the acquisition of knowledge and skills. The result once again will be an environment where the distinction between learning and work will disappear. There will be less emphasis on off-the-job instruction and more on integration of training and learning with on-the-job activities.

Electronic performance support system (EPSS) (see Chap. 27, Job Aids and Electronic Performance Support Systems) will combine such technologies as computer-based training, expert systems, hypertext, hypermedia, artificial intelligence, video disc, and database tools to allow workers immediate access to information and learning opportunities as required while they perform their jobs. This will be the new model for job training in the future.

References

1. "The Human side of Business," "Industry Report, 1994," *Training,* vol. 31, no. 10, pp. 29–74.
2. Wehrenberg, S. B., "Supervisors as Trainers: The Long-Term Gains of OJT" *Personnel Journal,* 66(4), 1987, pp. 48–51.
3. Jacobs, R. L., and T. D. McGiffin, "A Human Performance System Using Structured On-the-Job Training Approach," *Performance and Instruction, 25*(7), 1987, pp. 8–11.
4. McCord, Alice Bird, "Job Training," in R. L. Craig, ed., *Training and Development Handbook,* 3d ed., McGraw-Hill, New York, 1987, p. 364.
5. Rackham, N., "The Coaching Controversy," *Training and Development Journal, 33*(11), 1979, pp. 12–16.
6. Schultz, Duane P., *Psychology and Industry Today,* Macmillan, New York, 1982.
7. Jacobs, R. L., and T. D. McGiffin, op. cit.
8. Spencer, Metta, *Foundations of Modern Sociology,* Prentice-Hall Canada, Inc., Scarborough, ON, 1981.
9. Schultz, Duane P., *Psychology and Industry Today,* Macmillan, New York, 1982.
10. McCord, Alice Bird, op. cit., p. 365.
11. McCord, Alice Bird, op. cit., p. 366.
12. Miller, Vincent A., "The History of Training," in R. L. Craig, ed., *Training and Development Handbook,* 3d ed., McGraw-Hill, New York, 1987, p. 10.
13. McCord, Alice Bird, op. cit., p. 366.
14. McCord, Alice Bird, op. cit., p. 368.

37

Technical Skills Training

Donald W. Robbins

Thomas R. Doyle

Shahrashoob Orandi

Paul T. Prokop

Donald W. Robbins *is Manager, Supplier Education and Training at the Ford Motor Company's Fairlane Training and Development Center. He has worked for Ford for 12 years in a variety of training positions. Prior to this assignment, Robbins was Supervisor of Program Design, Development and Evaluation. He has also held positions in management and general business training and corporate training consulting. For approximately seven years, he held a variety of positions in Ford's technical training organization. Prior to joining Ford, he worked for IBM, Honeywell, and Control Data Corporation in various positions in the training, human factors, and product-testing arenas. Robbins holds an M.S. and Ph.D. from the University of Colorado in cognitive experimental psychology. He is the author of numerous technical publications and a wide range of courses. He has developed courses using media, including computer-based training, videotape, and interactive videodisc, and traditional print-based, instructor-led training.*

Thomas R. Doyle *is Supervisor of Technical Training, Ford Motor Company's Fairlane Training and Development Center. Prior to joining Ford, he taught on the secondary and junior college levels. For the past 15 years, he has been instrumental in the assessment, design, development, and delivery of both management and technical training programs for the Ford Motor Company. Within the last two years, he managed the design and delivery of* *a computer-disk-based needs assessment for the entire Ford North American automotive engineering community. Using data from approximately 11,000 respondents, Ford is developing a comprehensive corporate engineering curriculum. Doyle is a coauthor of the "Technical and Skills Training Suppliers" chapter in ASTD's Technical and Skills Training Handbook, 1994. He has been active in a number of national training organizations over the years and has presented at ASTD, International Society for Performance Improvement, Society for Applied Learning Technology, and Society of Automotive Engineers. Currently, Doyle is Director of the Automotive Industry Group (AIG) where he has been instrumental in obtaining support from auto-related organizations to help defray AIG expenses at both the International and National Technical and Skills conferences. He is director-elect of ASTD's Technical and Skills Professional Practice Area.*

Shahrashoob Orandi *is Instructional Technology Supervisor for Technical Training in Engineering and Manufacturing at Ford Motor Company. She has a master's degree in education and counseling from the University of Wisconsin and an Education Specialist certificate from Wayne State University. She is currently pursuing a Ph.D. in instructional design at Wayne State University. She has spent the last five years concentrating on managing the design, development, and evaluation of technical training courses.*

Paul T. Prokop *is Project Leader in Technical Training in the Engineering and Manufacturing Development Group, Ford Motor Company, Dearborn, Michigan. He has five years' experience in technical training. Past projects include development of technical and soft-skill courseware. The technical courses include various telecommunication and manufacturing programs, and the soft-skill courses include customer relations and leadership topics. Prokop has a master's degree in instructional technology from Wayne State University.*

The purpose of this chapter is to provide both new and experienced trainers with information on the current tools and techniques used in creating and delivering technical training. We have attempted to provide information for those engaged in training design and also those involved in the delivery of training. Many of the tools and techniques we will cover are similar to those used in nontechnical training. We have attempted to provide detailed information on those tools and techniques which are specific to the technical arena and to provide an explanation of how similar tools may differ slightly when applied to a technical topic.

This chapter is divided into 12 sections. We begin with an overview of the instructional design process as it applies to the analysis, design, development, delivery, and evaluation of technical training. The second section provides an overview of the tips and techniques that instructors should be cognizant of when delivering training that is technical in nature.

The following sections provide more detailed information on the major steps of the instructional design process as it applies to technical training. We have included sections on

- Front-end analysis
- Task analysis

- Design of training materials
- Design of job aids
- Development
- Implementation
- Evaluation

Finally, we conclude the chapter with three additional topics that we believe are critical to the success of training professionals yet which are often taken for granted in training books and courses:

- Outsourcing of training development
- Consulting relationships
- Project management

We have attempted to keep this chapter broad enough to be of value to a wide audience including corporate internal trainers and developers, external consultants, academicians, and those new to the field. At the same time, we have also included specific tools, lists, and tips that we hope will provide the experienced professional with a refresher on the most important topics and newcomers with an overview and orientation to the field of technical skills training.

Instructional Systems Design Considerations

The instructional systems design process differs little whether you are designing programs for general business skills or technical skills. However, a few important steps are specific to technical training. They deal with data gathering during the analysis of tasks.

In technical training, observation of job performance and interviews with subject-matter experts are the most commonly used procedures used to gather task data. In both procedures, it is imperative that the master performer be identified and employed in the process. When observing the performer, be certain that the person doing the observation is a skilled observer and that his or her presence does not interfere with or affect the actual job performance. A drawback to observation is that it can be time consuming and increase costs when compared to other methods of task data gathering.

Working with a subject-matter expert (SME) is a primary method and requires sound interviewing and interpersonal skills. To obtain good data, the interviewer must be able to accurately and objectively record, and properly interpret, what is being recorded. Because the subject-matter expert is so well versed in his or her job, it is critical that the interviewer probe and ask multilevel questions to identify the details of the job requirements which might otherwise be overlooked.

Of all the phases of the instructional design process (front-end analysis, design, development, delivery, and evaluation), the delivery or presentation of the course material often receives the lowest priority. This is especially true in instructor-led technical training. Ironically, quality delivery is of the utmost importance to the audience of technical training.

Instructor Delivery

A major role of the trainer in delivery is to establish an atmosphere or learning climate in which people are ready to participate in a meaningful way. This does not necessarily mean that everyone is committed to being an active participant. It does mean that most participants are in an open and cooperative frame of mind, are not unduly distracted, and are serious about committing their time and intellectual resources.

In most training situations, the climate should be one of controlled informality. A sense of formality or informality is a function of many things: the way people are dressed, the nature of the setting, the way furniture is arranged in the training room, the language used, or the way participants are treated. People don't readily experiment or try out new ideas in a completely formal setting. This fact does not imply that the setting must always be informal. The size of the group and complexity of subject often determines the formality of the presentation. The larger the group, the more formal and structured the process often must be.

Whether the setting is formal or informal, the participants should feel they are free to make mistakes and experiment with ideas and behavior. They should sense they will *not be punished* for incorrect answers but will be *supported* as individuals—even though you may comment on their responses or suggest possible adjustments in the way they approach certain tasks or solve problems. Try not to create the impression that you know it all or that you are an expert in everything. Avoid taking a posture that says "I am the expert, you are the student." If the learning climate is one of mutual anticipation, mutual exploration, and mutual respect, significant learning is more likely to occur.

From the beginning, try to adopt the language and actions that support a productive learning climate. Often the best approach is informal but businesslike, concerned about the participants as individuals and their individual reactions, but also committed to accomplishing the stated objectives.

Early in the program, describe your role as a guide, facilitator, and catalyst. Let participants know that, while you have ideas to present, you want them to share their ideas as well. If you portray the climate as one of mutual control, you create the expectation that learners take major responsibility for asserting and fulfilling their learning needs.

Describe and list on a flipchart or board the objectives for the program and provide a sense of how your time together will be managed. All participants appreciate knowing from the start where the session is going, how you envision getting there, and what is expected of them. Reference discussion and learning points to the objectives when appropriate, making the session more structured and cohesive for the participants. For instance, describe how the day is laid out and announce when coffee, stretch, and lunch breaks are scheduled.

If there are small-group activities, form the groups early and provide instructions only after they are formed into the groups. Participants perform small-group tasks more effectively when they have heard the task instructions as a group.

Let participants know how you prefer to handle questions. Some trainers like to hold questions until the end of a presentation to maintain the momentum of the session. Others prefer that participants ask questions as they come to mind. Whichever procedure you choose, let participants know early. Participants also need to know whether you recommend they take notes. If you plan to use a handout at the end, you may wish to suggest that participants only jot a few notes to themselves to capture important ideas as they occur.

It's a good idea to briefly review the major learning points and your work agenda immediately before the break (for example, "After the lunch break you'll begin to examine the five steps of…"). This helps maintain the flow of the session and bolsters the participants' sense of security because they will know exactly what will be expected following the break.

When possible, survey the group to gain a feel for the relevance of the session. The questions should be straightforward, such as, "Is what you have been covering useful to help you do your job more efficiently," being careful never to put anyone on the defensive. Getting agreement from the participants without putting anyone on the spot or defensive will help you maintain a climate of learner-focused training.

Here are two valuable pieces of advice that will help foster a comfortable and productive learning climate: (1) value the learner's individuality and experience, and (2) be conscious of your verbal communication—in tone and content.

Along with the instructor's guide and train-the-trainer experience, keep the following steps in mind both while preparing for and presenting your workshop.

1. Analyze your audience by identifying general and specific characteristics that could assist in conducting the workshop. Some examples are:

General Characteristics
- learning strategy
- reading ability
- subject knowledge
- technical vocabulary
- time on the job
- prerequisite knowledge

Specific Characteristics
- scientific notation knowledge
- troubleshooting skill
- specific problem-solving skills
- computer literacy
- flowcharting skill
- blueprint reading ability

2. State the workshop objectives in terms of learner action, conditions, and how you will evaluate transfer of knowledge and/or skills.

Purpose
- To inform learners what they should be able to do after the workshop that they could not do before
- To assist in planning and organizing your presentation and in determining the appropriate evaluation method
- To communicate to others what you are attempting to accomplish

Format
- To serve the purpose stated above, objectives must be communicated to and be understood by all participants
- A recommended format for objectives includes
  - *Action:* what the learner is going to be able to do

- *Condition:* circumstance under which the action will take place
- *Evaluation:* the level of performance you expect

Example:

Given the proper computer software (*condition*), the engineer will conduct a financial analysis (*action*) to determine three potential cost-saving areas (*evaluation*).

3. Utilize all course materials as designed within your presentation, always incorporating good training techniques and presentation skills.

Five basic steps leading to the workshop delivery or presentation

1. *Preview* the material.

2. *Practice* your presentation.

3. *Prepare* the environment.

4. *Prepare* the audience.

5. *Present* the course material.

Presentation Skills

Don't read from notes, present the material.

Don't apologize.

Be flexible.

Get the learners involved.

Speak up to be heard.

Use humor appropriately.

Use personal experiences when appropriate.

Facilitate rather than dominate.

4. Require learner response to keep the learners active and to facilitate learning the material presented.

Reasons for Requiring Learner Response

Increased learning

Increased interest

Motivation

Maintain attention

Enrichment

Gain learner input

Enjoyment

Ways to Get Learners Involved

Questions

Quizzes

Demonstrations by trainer

Demonstrations by learner

Group discussion

Group exercises and/or projects

Games

Role playing

Case studies

5. Evaluate your presentation with formal and informal techniques to assess both learning and presentation effectiveness.

Purpose of Evaluation
Measure learner achievement against stated objectives

Assess presentation and delivery skills

Improve future presentations

Improve course material

Types of Evaluation
Quizzes and self-checks

Demonstrations by learners

Group discussions

Formal and informal conversations (debriefings)

Let's look at some of the critical areas of the workshop in which you establish the lasting tone and climate for the course.

Preintroduction

Before the class begins, make sure that you have the appropriate number of pretests, course evaluations, handouts, manuals, and all associated materials. As participants arrive, ask them to complete a sign-in sheet or checkmark their name on the class roster. Another way of organizing the preintroduction is to list the orientation procedure on the chalkboard or flipchart. On the board or chart you would want to welcome participants to your class, identify tasks required of them prior to start of class, and ask them to pick up the class materials and handouts.

Introduction

Introduce yourself and give the participants some relevant information about yourself and the course. Ask them to introduce themselves and give a brief explanation of where they work and what they do. A good way to start is to say, "Good morning, my name is _____ and we'll be here for the next couple of days to cover_____(course name and topic). My background and experience in the field are _____. I hope you're all in the right room. If not we should resolve that right now. Let's get to know each other a little better. Why don't we go around the room and have each of you introduce yourself? Briefly tell us where you work and something about your work experience."

Logistics

Acquainting the participants with the locations of the restrooms and cafeteria at the beginning of the course is obviously necessary. Establishing a schedule for course activities, such as pre- and posttesting, morning and afternoon breaks, lunch, and completion of course evaluations, is also important.

Objective Setting

Before beginning your presentation, it is imperative to ensure that the learner understands and agrees with the objectives established for the workshop. This goal can be attained in a couple of ways. One is posting the course objectives on the wall, discussing them one at a time, and agreeing to refer to them throughout the presentation. Another way is to poll the participants on what they expect to get out of the course, formulate a list of objectives, compare them with yours, and establish a consensus list. Whichever method you choose, it is crucial that you become familiar with your presentation's stated objectives and can elaborate on them without having to read from the manual, course evaluation, or notes.

Reinforcement

Throughout the presentation, refer back to the objectives, ensuring that you remain on track with the presentation. Additionally, it's a good idea to summarize the key points and tie them to important concepts. This step helps the learner "see" the logical progression of ideas and how you are trying to build knowledge, block by block. By asking questions and obtaining feedback from the learner, you test for understanding and get an indication whether theory is being transferred to real-life situations.

Front-End Analysis

There is often confusion in the training field about the various terms used to denote the types of analysis performed in the instructional design process. Terms such as needs analysis, needs assessment, front-end analysis (FEA), task analysis, job-task analysis, goal analysis, and instructional analysis can frequently be found in the literature. To avoid confusion, we have limited ourselves to two terms. We refer to FEA as a phase in the instructional systems design process to identify the performance problem. This analysis is initially performed to determine whether a training solution is appropriate. Following the FEA, a task analysis is completed to determine the specific tasks that must be performed and the level of competency to which they must be performed.

A typical FEA determines whether or not training is the solution to the problem. If it is determined that training is the solution or part of the solution, then you would focus on *what* needs to be included in the training project and identify *who* the learners are. This process seems very straightforward, and often it has been. However, as technology advances and corporations become more global, training professionals are challenged with more complex issues than in the past. We are confronted with developing training for more complex systems and for a more diverse target audience, one with different levels of skills and knowledge who reside in various parts of the globe. To complicate matters further, training professionals are also challenged to deliver training solutions at a faster-than-ever rate using a variety of media.

The discussion of FEA will focus on the following:

- Definition
- Process
- Critical success factors

Definition

An FEA is a form of analysis conducted before a training project is started for the purpose of determining the solution to a problem. FEAs address questions such as: What is the performance gap? Who is affected by it? Where is the target audience located?

Process

Companies often look to their training organizations for support when they need solutions to performance problems. Many companies are undergoing globalization efforts to expand their business scope, thereby causing the existing training to be less robust. This situation creates a challenge for training professionals to understand and manage diversity and complexity. They must address issues such as

- What is the new process or system that has caused a need for this effort?

    Is this a new process resulting from a reengineering effort?
    Is this a new system that the employees must learn?

- Who is the audience for this training effort?

    What is the level of their skills and/or knowledge?
    How many people are affected by this?
    Where are they located?
    What type of medium is available to them?
    What languages do they speak?
    What are the cultural differences among them?

The FEA process must start with a project plan. The project leader must document the strategy for implementation of the project, and she or he must communicate this information to the customer and key stakeholders in the kick-off meeting. This communication provides a common understanding of the project scope. Typically, the information gained from the kick-off meeting, such as project deliverables, timetables, and resources available, are used to create a project timeline.

Figure 37-1 describes the information that must be included in a project plan.

Critical Success Factors

Certain conditions must be present for training to be successful. Before you embark on the development effort, as most customers insist on doing, it is critical to take a step back and examine the situation. The following is a list of questions to ask:

- Do the training-project objectives parallel the key business initiatives of the company?
- Has the new process or system been tried and tested?
- Is there any documentation available on the new process or system? Specifically, is a high-level description of what happens and what inputs-outputs are produced available?
- Are qualified SMEs available to the project?

Information	Description
Project description	A brief statement that describes the goal, scope, and timing of the project as communicated by the customer
Project deliverable	A description of the project outputs, with timetables
Methodology	A description of how the project team plans to collect the necessary data
Tools	A number of different resources ranging from hardware to software and worksheet templates.
Roles and responsibilities of the project members	A statement of who does what on the project
Input to training	A list of all necessary documentation for the start-up of the training project
Project assumptions	A statement declaring the team's understanding of certain factors
Critical success factors	A list of optimums that must be present to ensure the success of the project
Issues and concerns	A list of factors that can affect the achievement of project objectives in the given time frame

Figure 37-1. Project plan.

The first two questions are complex and critical.

Do the training-project objectives parallel the key business initiatives of the company?
Through interviews with the customer and project champion, the project leader must confirm that the training request is valid and supports the company's key business initiatives. When the training goals and objectives support the larger organizational objectives, the project receives the attention and support it deserves.

Has the new process or system been tried and tested?
In other words, are you focusing the training efforts on a process or system that you know is going to be successful? If you have doubts about this, it is time for the project team to initiate a dialogue with the project champion. You need to determine what is not working as well as what is working. This knowledge can help focus your attention on filling the information gap. If the project team fails to learn these facts, the training can become long and costly.

Task Analysis

As mentioned earlier, there is often confusion between the purpose of a task analysis and the purpose of a front-end analysis. In this chapter, there is a major distinction, in terms of both the scope of the analysis and the appropriate timing of the process in the instructional design cycle. In terms of scope, the distinction is simple: FEA is a macro-level look at the problem; task analysis is a micro-level look.

In an FEA, we are concerned with a high-level look at the problem and its solution. Is it a training solution, a nontraining solution, or some combined solution? Who is the audience? What are the outcomes we expect?

A task analysis typically follows an FEA, and will narrow down the focus to a specific task within a specific job which has been identified as an opportunity. It is an opportunity to improve organizational performance by improving the performance of individuals. It is an opportunity to improve individual performance through training and/or job-performance aids.

Both front-end analysis and task analysis are critical to the success of technical training. For most unsuccessful projects, you can trace the failure to inadequate time and resources devoted to this phase of the project. A good rule of thumb is between 20 and 40 percent of the time and budget allocated to a project should be spent in analysis. Similarly, when the analysis goes awry, it is often traceable to a lack of planning or, in a sense, the performing of an analysis of the analysis.

The process of planning the analysis includes consideration of the following six key topics.

1. Composition of the Project Team

We have already discussed the importance of SMEs in the project team for technical task analysis projects. In addition, a project leader role and an analyst role should be included in the project. For a small project, both roles may be performed by the same person. Larger projects require a team of individuals. Likewise, most projects of any scope will benefit from the inclusion of more than one SME. As the number of SMEs increases, the accuracy of the analysis will generally increase. Often, however, this increase in accuracy is accompanied by a marked increase in the project timeline. We have found that for most projects, a good trade-off is to have a maximum of three SMEs. It is critical to clarify the role of the SME early on in the analysis planning.

2. Length of the Project Timeline

Project timelines will vary with project complexity and, as we've pointed out, with the number of SMEs. We have seen projects range from a matter of days to over one year. In some of our technical training FEAs we have begun to use computerized FEA tools. For instance, we have just begun a major analysis in the area of machining and cutting technology. Initially, as we begin to use these software tools, we expect timelines and costs to increase, but we have the expectation that as we become more familiar with these tools, the cost and time needed will both be reduced significantly.

In general, expect that, of the total time spent on a task analysis project, less than 10 percent will be spent actually observing a task or interviewing task performers.

3. Availability of Existing Data

One of the most frequently missed steps in the task analysis process is a detailed analysis of existing documentation. Documentation to be reviewed includes historical data, personnel records, scrap rate data, troubleshooting and maintenance information, machine documentation, and problem reports.

4. Data Collection Strategy

Data collection strategy includes both identifying the technique used for data collection and planning the logistics for carrying out that technique. Just as with FEA projects, there are a number of techniques for collecting data. We will focus on five of the most common, and their strengths and weaknesses.

Task Observation (including time and motion studies). The major strengths of this technique are the opportunity to actually see and record what an expert does, and the outcome obtained. It is the best way to get the whole picture and a feel for what is actually going on. The major weakness of this method is that the act of observing can often influence the performer.

Reviewing Historical Data (personnel files, production reports, scrap results, etc.). The major strengths of this method are that there is less chance for bias—it is historical fact. Also, you can go over the material at your own pace and don't have to rely on other's schedules. The disadvantages include the fact that the data is always old—things may have changed since the data was collected. Also, it is often hard to determine what data may be relevant and what data is available.

Focus Groups. Focus groups are typically groups of 4 to 12 people who are brought together to focus on a single topic or task in a structured interview format, usually including a high level of interaction and discussion. Strengths of focus groups include the opportunity to collect several opinions or points of view quickly and the opportunity to simultaneously collect and verify data. They also provide a skilled facilitator an opportunity to probe responses and to bring the group to consensus. The weaknesses of focus groups include results that can be easily influenced by the facilitator or by a dominant individual in the group. Also, a focus group can be difficult to keep on track, and it requires an experienced facilitator to ensure that all points of view are heard.

One-on-One Interviews and Phone Interviews. The strengths of this technique are that you can get the same type of data as in a focus group, often without as much scheduling difficulty. Also, you can probe more deeply with an individual without feeling that you are wasting the group's time. The disadvantages of this technique are that you cannot obtain group consensus and do not have the opportunity for interaction between the interviewees. This method will often take more time for both data collection and data analysis.

Survey Instruments and Questionnaires. The strengths of this data collection method include the opportunity to obtain information from a lot of people quickly and the ability to tabulate and analyze the data more easily than in interviews or focus groups. Disadvantages include the lack of an opportunity for flexibility and "going with the flow" of the group. Also, it is often difficult to get a high rate of return on a survey.

While none of the data collection techniques is likely to provide you with all the data you need for a task analysis, a combination of these techniques should allow you to both collect and verify all the information you need to complete a task analysis. The point is to get as many different looks at the data through multiple data collection techniques as possible.

5. Data Collection Instruments

Once you have identified the techniques you plan to use for data collection, a plan must be made for creating data collection instruments. Some key tips to remember are

- Be clear about the role of team members, particularly the role of the SME. Know who is in a development role and who is in a review role. Make sure the reviewers know whether they are reviewing for content, clarity, format, and/or completeness.
- Plan to create "robust" data collection instruments. That is, create focus group and interview questions that will keep the interviewer supplied with value-added questions even if the responder is reticent or gives only short answers. Create survey questions that can be easily understood, even before they've had their morning coffee.
- Plan to pilot-test all survey instruments and focus-group and interview questions to make sure they are clear and get at the information you want.

6. Strategy for Data Analysis

It is important to discuss the data analysis strategy long before the first piece of data is collected. This is a valuable technique, as it prevents your collecting data in a format that is difficult or impractical to analyze. Keep in mind that the typical output of a task analysis is some form of task listing, which will be turned into enabling and terminal objectives as you move into the design phase.

Implementing Your Strategy

These six elements provide the key to successful task analysis. Once you have planned your process, the implementation has a high probability of success.

As mentioned, the most common format for task analysis data is a task listing. Four major steps are involved in creating a task listing:

1. Collect data from the SMEs by whatever data collection techniques you have selected. Arrive at a consensus of the steps performed to complete the task you are analyzing.
2. Describe each step in the process in terms of an action verb (e.g., install, press, or align).
3. Develop a hierarchy of tasks: i.e., Which are the main tasks, and which are the subtasks? Number the tasks according to their order of performance and their level in the hierarchy.
4. Recheck your information with your SME.

One of the most difficult steps in this process is to identify the level of detail you need. You can choose to stay at a very high level (e.g., start the robot, replace the worn drill bit) or you can get to a very fine level of detail. For example, pressing a single button can be broken down into many steps (e.g., open your eyes, identify the red button, move your arm so that your right index finger touches it). The best guideline is to stop when you reach the level of step complexity that you can safely assume everyone in your target audience knows how to do.

Once you have completed the task analysis, you are ready to move into the design phase.

Design of Training Materials

Tasks Completed Before the Design Process

At this point, it has been determined whether the project is or is not appropriate for an instructional solution. Other tasks that are completed before the design phase are the following:

- Needs assessment has been conducted.
- Learner characteristics have been identified.
- Setting and environment have been analyzed.
- Job, task, and content analysis have been completed.

Assuming the project is an instructional solution, the objective of design is to reduce the design time without lowering the quality of the training. The desired outcome is for the target audience to be able to get the just-in-time training that is needed to decrease cost, and, after transfer has occurred, to enhance profits. That is why a lot of today's companies are concerned with implementing an accelerated design and development process.

Design Terminology

Before discussing the design process, a baseline of terminology should be established. The following terms are commonly used in the design phase:

Design. In this document, design is defined as a plan of action that outlines the development of an effective and efficient program instruction.

Design document. This is the output or deliverable of the design phase which systematically outlines the program development. It establishes the learning outcomes, the practical framework, the content, and the instructional integrity of the program.

Evaluation plan. This is another output of the design phase and is a plan of action for the subsequent phases, including the preliminary evaluation instruments. Some criteria in the plan include an evaluation purpose, an audience, and methods.

Generic Design Process

Figure 37-2 represents a generic process for designing training solutions. This process is extremely effective in the creation of instructional course materials, especially technical training materials, because it can reduce the time it takes to design and develop deliverables. The process can also be applied to management-business training. Note that these are only guidelines; each design should be customized based on the project and customer request. The process should also follow quality principles by constantly searching for continuous improvements.

Step 1: Create Structure of Training Solution. Prerequisites to this step are to verify the customer request, complete the analysis phase, determine

Step	Description	Input	Tool(s)	Output
1	Create structure or outline of the training solution based on your performance-based training goals and objectives gathered from the analysis phase.	Performance-based training goals and objectives from the analysis phase	Content outline	High-level structure
2	Create high-level design or lesson outline. The design is directly related to the performance-based training goals and objectives by the creation of lesson or course objectives and/or design job aids.	High-level structure	Lesson design template and job aid template	Lesson/course objectives and high-level design of the solution and/or design job aid
3	Create lower-level design. This structure breaks down the high-level design into more detail and allows for the creation of specific objectives also known as enabling objectives.	Lesson/course objectives and high-level design of the solution and/or design of job aid	Topic and practice design templates	Detailed content of the solution and enabling objectives
4	Review training solution after each milestone. Reviews ensure the quality and integrity of the training solution.	Design deliverables	Instructional technology review checklist	Review of design deliverables and preparation for the development phase
5	Plan for the development and implementation phases.	Design deliverables and analysis information	Plan for development and implementation	Development and implementation plan and evaluation plan
6	Obtain sign-off for the design phase.	Design deliverables and other outputs of design	Sign-off template	Sign-off from customer

Figure 37-2. Design process.

the SME(s), and identify the performance-based training goals and objectives. The *performance-based training goals and objectives* are the real performance need of the customer's request or the gaps of skill and knowledge that are needed.

Step 2: Create High-Level Design.   After creating the high-level design of the training solution, use this structure as an input to initiate the design at a high level. Chunking the information into a high-level design helps the learner organize the information.

The high-level design is an iterative process that may be revised throughout the project. Breaking down the high-level design into more detail is the following step (step 3: creating a lower-level design).

Design of Job Aids

The topic of job aids is covered in Chap. 27, Job Aids and Electronic Performance Support Systems. However, because job aids are a critical element to the success of technical training projects, we will address a few points on the importance of job aids in technical training here. Job aids may be a tool and an adjunct to training or a replacement for training at other times. The key is to identify what task performers need to know and what they need to be able to quickly reference so that they can do their jobs. Job aids serve as reference materials, on-the-job reminders, or support for instruction, and they are often used for information that cannot be stored in memory. Job aids can be written, visual, verbal, or electronic representations of procedures such as tables, charts, and/or checklists. A job aid can be designed in tandem with the design of instruction.

Some of the key opportunities for job-aid use are

- When a task is complex and has many steps
- For troubleshooting and routine maintenance
- For retraining or cross-training employees on machine use
- When a task is performed infrequently
- When signals, cues, or reminders are needed to perform a task
- For updating a task or procedure

As the complexity of many technical tasks has grown, the need for job aids has increased. Fortunately, along with this complexity of machines and tasks, there has been an increase in the sophistication of job aids. Today, electronic job-performance aids are becoming commonplace. These systems generally take one of two forms: sophisticated delivery mechanisms for traditional job-aid information (e.g., computer displays, videodisc systems), and machine-based diagnostic, troubleshooting, and maintenance aids. The latter systems are essentially machines that will provide the information needed to repair or maintain them. The bottom line is that with the new capabilities of electronic job-performance aids, coupled with the traditional print-based job aids, there are many opportunities to save time and money, and increase efficiency, through the development of job aids as an alternative or addition to technical training.

Step 3: Create Lower-Level Design.   Create the lower-level design by using the high-level design as an input. By going into more detail in this step, design time is saved in development. When instructional materials are designed at the lower level, the chunking of content is called *topics.* Topics are detailed areas of content that are organized in a sequential manner and contain detailed information the participant must have.

Step 4: Review Training Solution.   The review is an iterative process and should occur after each milestone according to the project timeline that was created by the project leader. For example, suggested reviews for instructional materials include validation of course structure or outline, a validation of the course lessons and topics, and a review of the design document. There are three types of reviews:

Instructional Technology Review.   The IT review is done by the instructional designer and preferably another instructional designer not on the project. The reviewers look for instructional design principles to ensure instructional integrity and quality. For example, in a review of instructional material, the instructional designer considers the organization of materials, including the sequence and flow, the chunking of content, and consistency throughout the program.

Subject-Matter-Expert Review.   The *subject-matter-expert* review is done by the SMEs who specifically look for accuracy in the content, make decisions about content issues, and validate the deliverables.

Review Board Review.   The review board can consist of either and/or both external and internal reviewers. For example, an internal reviewer may be an editor on the project team and an external reviewer may be the stakeholder or the champion of the project.

Step 5: Plan for Development and Implementation Phases.   In this step, you prepare for the activities in the development and implementation phases. By planning for those stages in the design, the project manager is able to coordinate activities with foresight. For example, in the design phase the instructional designer determines that the SME for the project is needed as a facilitator in the implementation phase. By planning for the need of additional resources, the project manager is able to prepare for the addition of resources to be assigned in the implementation phase to deliver the material. A deliverable that should be completed during this step is the evaluation plan. The *evaluation plan* includes the preliminary evaluation instruments and also states the purpose of the evaluation plan, the description of the audience, and the strategies or methods for achieving the desired evaluation results (including an action plan for determining transfer of training). Examples of preliminary evaluation instruments include a course evaluation for implemented courses or a pilot evaluation.

Step 6: Obtain Sign-Off for the Design Phase.   After the above-mentioned steps are completed, the final step is obtaining sign-off approval from the customer and stakeholders of the project. This step is important because it provides the acknowledgment of progress on the project and also validates the design outputs or deliverables.

Design Tools

Tools are helpful in reducing the time to design instructional solutions. Tools save redundancy from project to project and ensure consistency. An example is the use of checklists. They are helpful in providing consistency and ensuring that all items are considered. By having a checklist created, time is saved by not reinventing the tasks previously accomplished in other projects. Another useful technique in designing instructional materials or job aids is the use of a template. A template is an electronic file that contains a preexisting framework. Examples of design templates include a lesson template, topic template, practice template, and a job-aid template.

Design Techniques

The following are suggestions that have come from experience and should be considered as time-saving design tips:

Design the Participant and Instructor Guide in Tandem.   Designing a participant and instructor guide ensures consistency between the instructor guide, the participant manual, and the overheads. Consider the instructor guide as the blueprint for all the deliverables.

No Need to Spend Formal Time to Educate the SME on Instructional Design Principles. The SME should be concerned with content, not instructional design principles. It is the instructional designer's responsibility to guarantee the integrity of the course. Time is better spent obtaining content information from the SME than teaching the SME instructional design principles. Another advantage is that the SME may be less defensive and more receptive to change if not constantly challenged.

SME Dedicated Time. The SME should be available for blocks of time rather than incremental periods (an hour here or there). This block of time should be uninterrupted and separated from the SME's working environment. This arrangement is one of the best ways to decrease design time. Be as thorough as possible when obtaining SME information. If the SME is unsure of the content or details of the content, make a placemark at that specific point and go on to the next piece of content, therefore maximizing the SME's time. Also, gather or placemark possible activities, practices, exercises, analogies, examples, etc.

Gather as Much Information as Possible During the Design Phase. The more complete the deliverables are in design, the faster the development time. With a concentration on completing the deliverables as close to a complete package as possible, the design can be validated during design reviews and instructional design issues may be resolved up-front in design rather than in development. This technique decreases development time by reducing redundancies (you won't have to go back to change the document) and duplication of effort.

Design Process Wrap-Up

After the design process is concluded, gather team members to reflect on the design process:

- What worked well in the design process? What did not?
- What accelerated the process? What lengthened the process?
- If you could do the design over, what would you do differently? What worked better than expected?

After brainstorming with the team, document the results into a process improvement folder, and communicate this information to your ISD colleagues.

Development

This section outlines a generic process for developing training solutions, the instructional strategies used in development, and proven development techniques gathered from experience.

Development Terminology

The following terms are commonly used in the development phase:

Development: In this document, development is defined as the phase which involves the construction of any instructional resources to be used by the learner in training

Accelerated learning: Philosophies that concentrate on individual learning styles and natural talents to maximize learner performance and retention

Reinforcement activity: An instructional strategy that increases the probability that a given response will reoccur in the same set of circumstances, events, or conditions

The Generic Development Process

Your design document provides you with a blueprint for the training solution. The design document and any approved prototypes or layouts are used as input into development. In development, all the information that the learner needs is constructed. For example, suppose a job aid has been blueprinted in the design phase. The next step may be to document a procedure by including all the necessary steps and actions needed to perform that procedure. Figure 37-3 shows a generic development process for an instructional solution. As in design, the objective is to accelerate the process while maintaining instructional integrity.

Phase 1: Finalize Design Document and/or Job Aid(s).   The design document consists of two main components: the high-level design and the low-level design. The input into this phase is the design document which includes all the lessons, topics, and/or job-aid(s) templates.

High-Level Design.   At this stage, the high-level design should be near completion. When developing the high-level design the instructional designer should focus on the introductions, purposes, objectives, summaries, the overall flow and logical sequence, transitions between lessons, and a constant theme throughout the intervention. The content should be viewed as a whole (sometimes called the big-picture perspective).

Phase	Description	Input	Tool	Output
1	Finalize design document and/or job aid(s).	Design document	Lesson, topic, and/or job-aid(s) templates	Draft of developed deliverables
2	Review the training solution for technical and instructional soundness of each deliverable.	Draft of developed deliverables	Instructional technology review checklist and technical review checklist	Prepared development deliverables for walk-through
3	Conduct walk-through of the development deliverables.	Development deliverables	Program quality assessment (PQA)	Final development deliverables
4	Obtain sign-off for the development phase.	Development deliverables and other output of development	Sign-off template	Sign-off from customer

Figure 37-3. Development process.

Low-Level Design. After finalizing the high-level design, finalize the low-level design. The inputs to finalizing low-level design include the topic and practice design templates. The lower-level design may require more work than the high-level design. The following should be completed when the low-level design is finalized:

- Incorporate all the information that participants must have. This information includes any relevant text that contributes to desired outcomes, graphics, figures, references, job aids, help screens (CBT), etc.

- Use any examples, nonexamples, analogies, scenarios, or transitions that the student may find useful. By your telling a story with different presentation formats or sharing various examples, the student is better able to retain the information and see relationships.

- Include a table of contents, list of acronyms, glossary of terms (especially unfamiliar terms), bibliography, and list of figures.

- Incorporate practices and reinforcement activities. Practices include every step needed to complete the task, solutions, and possible feedback. Reinforcement activities reinforce the information in a different format than the one already delivered.

- Use advanced organizers, topic introductions, and purposes. What's coming up, what's going to be learned, and why it's going to be learned is covered.

- Complete the test items to match objectives and/or finalize evaluation and validation materials.

Phase 2: Review the Training Solution for Technical and Instructional Soundness of Each Deliverable. The development deliverables are the input into phase 2. Reviewing the training solution for development is similar to reviewing for design and should be planned in the project timeline:

- Review for instructional integrity. The instructional designer should review for instructional soundness, organization of the deliverable, and content.

- Review for technical content. The subject-matter expert and instructor review the course for accuracy and validation of subject matter.

- Conduct any other internal and external reviews. Internal reviewers may consist of an editor or a member of a publishing team to format and edit. An external reviewer may include the customer, stakeholders, or champions of the training solution.

Development tools such as an instructional technology review checklist or a technical review checklist assist in standardizing the review process. After the reviews, the deliverables are ready for the development walk-through. The reviewed deliverables are the output of phase 2.

Phase 3: Conduct Walk-Through of the Development Deliverables. The project team and a member of the target audience should attend the walk-through as a good opportunity to see the training solution in action. Walk-throughs are especially beneficial for testing practices, participant activities, and facilitator or instructor delivery methods. The instructional designer and SME should each have their own checklist. Ford uses a detailed instrument called the Program Quality Assessment (PQA) as the checklist to validate instructional courseware. The output of this phase is finalized development deliverables.

Phase 4: Obtain Sign-Off for the Development Phase.   As in design, the last phase is to obtain sign-off from the customer and stakeholders of the project. By signing off, you obtain validation of development deliverables, and the project team is able to continue into the testing and implementation phase.

Next we will look at the two instructional strategies used in the development process: accelerated learning and reinforcement activities.

Instructional Strategies

Accelerated Learning.   Accelerated-learning strategies increase learning retention and accelerate the amount of material that can be covered. Accelerated-learning strategies can be as simple as the use of visuals, graphics, or color overheads instead of text. More complex strategies include the use of simulation games which can be incorporated into a lecture-style course or discovery learning activities. An example of a discovery learning activity is to ask participants what the answer is to a process and "discover" what they come up with and share the results with the class.

Other examples or ideas that are considered accelerated learning are the following:

- Various presentation techniques such as storytelling, computer animation, analogies and metaphors for different learning styles, backgrounds, and personalities
- Learner involvement and control, sharing ideas and experiences through collaboration, and a positive room environment
- Job-performance techniques such as problem solving, teaching others, self-assessments, and an opportunity to practice the acquired skills

Reinforcement Activities.   Another development technique is the use of reinforcement activities. Every reinforcement activity should be relevant to the training solution and tied to its objectives. Refer to Fig. 37-4 for the process of linking objectives to reinforcement activities.

Time-Saving Development Techniques

Use the following techniques to accelerate the time it takes to develop training solutions and enhance instructional materials:

Divide work between SMEs.   If you are working with more than one SME, divide the lessons and topics between SMEs. Have the SMEs review each other's material *before* the official review process. The instructional designer should review the SMEs' work after each topic.

Concentrate on how the information is presented.   Determine how the information may be more effectively presented to the participant. For example, if a block of text is difficult to understand, can it be put in a table or bullet format? If not, can a graphic be added or substituted for the text to complement the learning? If the training solution is facilitated, can a color graphic be used with color-coding schemes to demonstrate key learning points? The idea is to be as creative as possible to aid the learner.

Step	Action	Example
1	Review the objectives and determine the main points associated with each objective.	Using the objective: "Describe the design process." One of the main points may be to create a high-level structure.
2	Design and develop an activity with the SME for each objective. This activity should be different from the method used to teach the objective.	If the instructional material was presented by lecture-style instruction, then the reinforcement activity may be a paper-and-pencil puzzle or a group activity that requires interaction and physical movement.
3	Prototype the reinforcement activity.	Evaluate the activity to verify that it achieves the expected outcome and adds value to the training solution.

Figure 37-4. Linking objectives to reinforcement activities.

Use a user-friendly format. The learner should be able to find the information easily by using glossaries or indexes. Another example may be the use of headings to create a useful table of contents. Format training material so that it is obvious what information goes together and how new information is logically incorporated based on the information already presented.

Limit overheads. Some technical courseware has a tendency to be dry material and lend itself to use of too many overheads. Avoid this trap and be as creative as possible. For example, can a concept be roleplayed? A telecommunications example follows: A participant represents a bit that travels from network (participant) to network (participant). The bit or participant must communicate the proper password through a router (participant) to get to the other network. Other delivery strategies include scenarios, storytelling, analogies, and videos.

Development Process Wrap-Up

After the development process is concluded, gather team members to reflect on the process:

What worked well in the development process? What did not?

- What accelerated the process? What lengthened the process?
- If you could do it over, what would you do differently? What worked better than expected?

After brainstorming with the team, document the results into a process improvement folder, and share them with your colleagues.

Implementation

Earlier, we discussed tips and techniques for improving the delivery of technical training. We would like to add a few points about the overall implementation of technical training.

First, it is important to note that within many organizations the vast majority of technical training is not traditional classroom training or self-instructional training. Frequently, training is delivered as one-on-one, or one-on-few, on-the-job training. It is important to keep this fact in mind, as you plan technical training. A small increase in the effectiveness of this type of training can pay huge dividends. At Ford, we offer a one-day on-the-job training course which covers the process of one-on-one instruction and gives guided practice. This course has improved the effectiveness of several hundred employees who spend significant amounts of time training or cross-training fellow employees.

Second, when a technical training course is being implemented, it is important to have a clear and detailed process for piloting and validating courses. We typically offer only pilots of courses until we have validated the effectiveness. A common standard to use for validation is referred to as the 90-90 criteria. This criteria specifies that 90 percent of all course attendees must master 90 percent of the material before we will certify that a course is ready to run on an ongoing basis.

The final phase in the instructional design process is evaluation.

Training Program Evaluation

Evaluation is a much needed and demanding phase of instructional system design. It is often used to justify the training experience and, very often, the training function itself. Remember that evaluation does not and should not remain removed from the general design process—sitting on the periphery ready to catch mistakes and holes in the design and development of a program. This is a critical fact. Evaluation must be an integral part of the ISD process and considered from the very beginning during program analysis. In this way, evaluation is more objective and reflective of the actual learning experience.

The most commonly used procedure for program evaluation is the four-phase process developed by Donald Kirkpatrick in 1959. This process is often referred to as the four levels of evaluation. (Also see Chap. 14, Evaluation.) Ideally, the rationale for evaluation of a training program is to acquire data that demonstrates the efficacy of the program and value to the organization. It is no longer acceptable to believe in or accept on faith the intrinsic worth and value of training. It must be demonstrated through effective evaluation. An explanation of the four levels of evaluation follows.

Level 1

In this level, data is gathered on how much the participant enjoyed the training experience and whether program content and physical environment met his or her expectations. Data that is often gathered at this level includes demographics, learning-style preference, instructor capability, and program objective verification. A level-1 instrument should be designed to offer the participant a chance to give feedback on the training experience. After all, we give the learners feedback to help them in the learning process; designers should expect the same to help improve program effectiveness.

Level 2

Data is gathered on whether the participants learned the concepts and/or skills the program designers had planned. This data is usually gathered through use of pre-

and posttesting, which must demonstrate and embody the skills and knowledge stated in the course objectives. The pretest is also an excellent way of judging the incoming knowledge level of the learners and allows the instructor to adjust his or her presentation of the course materials to fit the learner's level of knowledge.

If the participant's knowledge level is low, the instructor may consider remedial instruction leading into the planned presentation. If the knowledge level is high, the instructor may be able to cover more information in more detail then originally planned.

The pretest must contain questions that reflect the stated objectives. Generally, the pretest will contain 20 to 25, but not more than 50, questions. The kinds of questions the test contains will be determined by the complexity of the concepts and/or principles presented. When the material is involved or complex, different levels of questions are needed. These various levels will indicate learner understanding and the ability to apply the learned concepts to real-life situations. By asking questions and obtaining feedback from the learner, the instructor tests for understanding and obtains an indication whether theory is being transferred to real-life situations.

Level 3

Data is gathered on whether the participants have transferred concepts or skills from training to their jobs. This evaluation is usually conducted three to six months after the initial training and is very often composed of a paper-and-pencil instrument asking for anecdotal and perception-based data. Some questions that may be asked are

- By attending this course, I learned skills which helped me on my job.
- After attending this course, I felt I could do my job faster and more efficiently.
- I learned practical skills in this course that allowed me to better perform my job.
- After attending this course, I now feel more confident about the job I am doing.
- The content of the course was too advanced for me to apply, and therefore, I am still performing my job at the level I was before the course.
- I apply the skills I learned in the course on my job.
- After attending the course, I am aware of tools and equipment that can help me do my job more easily and more efficiently.
- After attending this course, I have the ability to produce higher-quality work.
- I feel that after taking this course, my job performance has positively impacted my department.
- I do not perform my job any differently now than I did before taking the course.

Level 4

Data is gathered which demonstrates whether the training had an impact on the participant's department or organization. Level 4 usually takes the form of a paper-and-pencil instrument that is distributed at approximately the same time interval as the level 3 to the learners' respective supervisor and/or manager. The questions are commonly perception-based and may include the following:

- Error rates in the department have dropped after employees attended this course.
- Error rates were a consideration for sending employees to this course.

- As a result of employees' taking this course, productivity has increased.
- Employee productivity was a consideration for sending employees to the course.
- I have noticed that employees do their jobs more efficiently after having attended this course.
- Employees do their work more quickly after attending this course.
- Employee performance was a determinant in sending employees to this course.
- Attendance in this course appears to have a positive effect on plant-department goals.
- Attendance in this course appears to have a positive effect on the plant-department in general.
- Employees' attitudes toward their jobs have become more positive.
- The department as a whole has benefited as a result of this training.

Outsourcing or Insourcing

The most critical factor in determining whether to develop the identified training within the organization or go out to a supplier is one of competency. It must be determined that the internal resources have the core competencies to develop the specified training. With the current business climate of reorganizing and cost reduction, there may be a gap in a training department's ability that has not been previously uncovered. In other situations, the department may have begun to specialize in certain limited areas that would not lend themselves to developing a project in another content area. Additionally, timing can be a critical factor. If the program is needed in a short time, the internal organization may not be sufficiently staffed and resourced to deliver on time.

Besides ability, cost must be considered when the decision is being made whether to buy or produce the training. It is often difficult for internal-training departments to determine the actual cost of training program development because it is not normally an internal requirement to perform detailed costing analyses. This lack of understanding of all costs associated with program development frequently causes internal costs to be underestimated. The factors of time, material, and facilities must be considered by the internal developer when costs are compared with the external developer because the external developer is obligated to do so as a function of their doing business.

Technical Training Consulting

Again, the subject of consulting is covered in other chapters of this book (see Chap. 51, Consultants), but the topic, as it applies to technical training, deserves a few additional comments here.

First, if you are hiring a consultant, be clear on why you are doing so. Some of the common reasons we hear are

- Consultants possess specific expertise that you cannot always afford to keep around full time.
- The total cost of consultants, including benefits and payroll taxes, may be less than staff.

- Using consultants offers the flexibility to adjust for workload changes.
- Using consultants may reduce the managerial paperwork jungle.
- Finance organizations frequently restrict headcount, and it may be the only way to get things done.

Whatever the reason, be sure when you bring on a consultant, or are brought on as a consultant, that both sides are clear on why the consultant is being brought in and what benefit they will provide to the organization. For technical training, be sure to clarify whether the role of the consultant is one of content expert or process expert. Do you expect the consultant to know about a particular topic (that is, act as an SME)? Or do you expect an expert in design and development, or both?

Project Management

Process

Managing a training project requires a thorough understanding of the ISD process as well as managerial skills. A training leader or manager must be skilled in identifying critical tasks and resources for the project and also be able to determine roles and responsibilities of the project team members. This process requires a well-planned project timeline, a project book, adequate hardware platforms, software tools, worksheet templates, and sample forms. The project management process for a training effort is usually based on the phases of the instructional system design: front-end analysis, task analysis, design, development, implementation, and evaluation. Project progress is measured by whether the deliverables are produced on time and within budget.

After the initial customer contact, a project manager must create a project plan. The following is a list of recommended tasks the project manager must do:

- Identify roles and responsibilities of the project team members.
- Develop a project timeline.
- Confirm meeting, review, and delivery dates.
- Build into the project plan review meetings and sufficient time for all ISD phases.
- Hold regular meetings to review project progress and resolve issues.
- Obtain sign-off on all deliverables.
- Document the weekly meeting minutes.
- Document and communicate project progress with the customer.
- Hold a postproject meeting with all project team members to document and share lessons learned.

Tools

There are three main tools that promote the success of a project:

- A well-documented and tested methodology
- Worksheet templates
- Project book

Methodology. A successful methodology ensures that all the critical tasks and resources are identified in the planning stage of a project. Following a process consistently makes it easier to streamline future efforts and improve the quality of future projects.

Worksheet Templates and Sample Forms. Worksheet templates and sample forms are other tools that significantly accelerate the design and development process. For example, if worksheet templates exist for all project deliverables, the team can focus on conducting the critical tasks of the project instead of having to create worksheets.

Project Book. Finally, a well-documented project requires a project book which contains information such as the following:

- Project plan
- A list of all project members with their phone numbers and addresses
- Project timeline
- Meeting minutes
- Project status reports
- Change control sheets
- Project sign-off sheets
- Lessons learned

A project book ensures that all project activities are documented. It also ensures that all necessary information is accessible to all team members. After a project is completed, a project book serves as a good historical reference.

Many companies are investing in electronic performance support systems to help manage their training projects. The availability of such support ensures consistency and efficiency of work. Availability of such systems necessitates a uniform process for saving and converting files so that they are accessible to the project team. When a project is completed, all project documentation can be saved on a file server. (Also see Chap. 27, Job Aids and Electronic Performance Support Systems.)

Bibliography

Clark, R., *Developing Technical Training,* Addison-Wesley, Reading, MA, 1989.

Knowles, M., *The Adult Learner: A Neglected Species,* 2d ed., Gulf Publishing Company, Houston, TX, 1979.

Mager, R. F., *Making Instruction Work,* Lake Publishing Company, Belmont, CA, 1988.

Mager, R. F., *Measuring Instructional Results,* 2d ed., Lake Publishing Company, Belmont, CA, 1984.

Seels, B., and Glasgow, Z., *Exercises in Instructional Design,* Merrill Publishing Company, Columbus, OH, 1990.

Zemke, R., and Kramlinger, T., *Figuring Things Out: A Trainer's Guide to Needs and Task Analysis,* Addison-Wesley, Reading, MA, 1982.

38

Apprenticeship

A. H. Howard III

A. H. Howard III *is an instructional designer with Employee Training and Development at The Boeing Company. For the past five years he has been involved in the design and development of courseware supporting the 72,000 employees in the Boeing Commercial Airplane Group. These courses represent over 800,000 student-hours of training per year on subjects as diverse as forklift operations, cargo door rigging, office safety, hydrogen embrittlement, and team leadership. He has been instrumental in the development of performance-based alternatives to traditional classroom training including job aids, function guides, task guides, and multimedia courseware. Howard has been recognized for his contributions and leadership in the areas of safety and health, certification, computer-aided design, and industrial skills training. In addition to his individual contributions, he has been responsible for leading instructional development teams that include writers, editors, designers, illustrators, and subject-matter experts. Prior to his current assignment, the 17-year Boeing veteran worked in research and development for the Boeing Defense and Space Group and in manufacturing and engineering for the 747 and 767 airplane programs. Howard earned his degree in graphic design, with graduate studies in educational media, from Central Washington University in Ellensburg, Washington.*

History

The heritage of apprenticeship goes back to the beginnings of family life, with parents handing down basic craft skills to their children. As the complexity of economic life increased, craftspersons needed to specialize, and the practice of indenturing began. This meant that youths were bound to skilled craftspeople outside their family. Eventually apprentices became an integral part of the economic systems of many cultures. The practice of apprenticeship is evident in the records of ancient Egypt, Greece, and Rome.

Until the Middle Ages, apprentices were controlled by individual craft guilds. This control gradually moved to the state. In England, the first public apprenticeship law was enacted in 1562. America modeled its first apprenticeships after the English Guild, and in fact began by indenturing English youths to the settlers. The small scale of manufacturing and the social mores of the time helped foster the apprenticeship system. Youths were placed into the system for different reasons: the desire to continue a skill, a way of relief for the poor, a penalty for idleness, or a punishment for debt.

Apprentices were indentured to a master craftsperson for a specific number of years. The apprentices received room and board from the master in the space above the shop, and shared that space with the regular paid workers. The master also educated the apprentices in reading, writing, and arithmetic. This education was required by law and, for the youths, was the only alternative to expensive private schools.

The driving force for many young apprentices was the desire to learn a trade and become their own masters. Once they attained journey-level status, workers could go out and start their own businesses.

All craftspeople were not equal. At the bottom of the trade rankings were tailors, shoemakers, and candle makers, in the middle were carpenters and blacksmiths, and at the top were silversmiths and printers. These rankings were based on earning power, the difficulty of learning the trade, and the startup cost of a new business.

Two things came along to disrupt America's early apprenticeship system: the industrial revolution and the advancement of public education. Machinery pushed the move toward mass production and forced the relationship between the employer and the employee to a more impersonal level. After 1800, large shops and factories slowly displaced small crafts shops. This meant that apprentices no longer boarded in their master's house and now were paid cash wages. Public schools slowly took over most of the educational aspects of the apprenticeship system.

By the mid-1800s older skilled craftsworkers were supplanted by younger unskilled workers who basically tended machines. The trend was to use only apprentices, keep them until they reached journey status, and then discharge them and replace them with other new apprentices. To combat this trend and other matters, workers began to organize into trade unions. Starting in the 1830s, unions developed to help workers receive decent wages and working conditions and, ironically, restrict the number of apprentices they admitted. This last step was a means for workers to advance to journey level and maintain consistent employment. With the formation in 1886 of the American Federation of Labor and, later, the Congress of Industrial Organizations (leading to the present AFL-CIO), an association that included most of the larger U.S. unions, workers became a force in industry. Interest in a national system of apprenticeship training began to increase in the 1920s. The movement gained support from the federal government with the formation of the Federal Committee on Apprenticeship in 1934 and New Deal laws in 1935 and 1937. These laws helped mold and standardize the current registered apprenticeship programs.

Apprenticeship Today

Apprenticeship is a thorough system of training in occupations that require a wide range of skills and knowledge. It involves a combination of on-the-job training and technical instruction and is one of the most cost-effective and comprehensive methods of producing skilled workers. Programs are conducted by employers, often in concert with labor and management committees.

Purpose

Apprenticeship programs create competent, versatile workers who have developed skills that are in demand by industry. Apprentices learn to work with different kinds of people in an actual working situation and become familiar with a company's organization and operation. Apprenticeship programs offer efficient ways to learn skills and assess performance in a planned and organized manner, and they result in advantages for both employer and employee.

Advantages

In any apprenticeship program, there are advantages to both employer and employee. For an employer, apprenticeships

- Motivate the workforce
- Set a graduated pay scale in proportion to ability and skill
- Increase productivity
- Minimize the need for supervision by developing initiative and ability
- Assure a supply of skilled workers
- Improve employer-employee relations

  For an employee, apprenticeships provide

- The opportunity to develop skills
- Increased employability and security
- Versatility to adapt to technological changes
- A guaranteed wage with regular increases
- Improved employer-employee relations
- Recognition as a skilled worker

Standards of Apprenticeship

The sponsor or administrator of the apprenticeship program develops the standards for that particular program. The standards document sets the terms and conditions for wages, hours, conditions of employment, on-the-job training and related instruction, administrative procedures, and compliance with any applicable collective-bargaining agreement.

The programs registered by the Bureau of Apprenticeship and Training must provide the following basic apprenticeship standards:

- A starting age of not less than 16.
- Full and equal opportunity to apply for apprenticeship.
- A schedule of work processes detailing the training and experience an apprentice is to receive.
- A minimum of 144 hours per year of organized instruction in technical subjects related to the trade.
- A progressive wage schedule.

- Proper training facilities and supervision of on-the-job training.
- Periodic evaluation and documenting of apprentice's progress in job performance and instruction.
- Employer and employee cooperation.
- Recognition for successful completion.
- No discrimination in selection, employment, or training.

Qualifying and Selection

All applicants for an apprenticeship have to meet certain criteria which include age, aptitude, health, and education. They must also go through an interview process that determines whether they meet the minimum requirements and assesses such personal traits as initiative, honesty, ambition, attitude, and others. After the interview process is complete, the applicants are rated and placed on a register or waiting list. Applicants will be selected from this list or pool.

The selection method must be approved by the Department of Labor. Approved methods are

- On the basis of rank in scores
- At random from a pool of eligible applicants
- From a pool of current employees

An apprenticeship program may use one or any combination of methods as long as those methods are approved.

Skill Development

Apprentices become professional craftspeople. They agree to work for a certain length of time at lower wages in exchange for the opportunity to learn a trade. Skills are developed through a combination of on-the-job and classroom training. The training is supervised by experienced skilled workers—journey workers—assigned to the program. With the guidance of the journey worker, the apprentice gradually learns the trade and performs with less and less supervision.

At the end of the apprenticeship, apprentices become journey-level workers. Journey workers are recognized as skilled in their trades and earn full wages. Apprenticeship graduates can have considerable advantages over those workers trained by informal means. These apprenticeship graduates are generally

- More educated
- Better skilled
- Steadier workers
- Able to learn trades faster
- More productive
- Safer employees

Since employers retain better-skilled workers, apprenticeship graduates also experience less unemployment.

Machinist Apprenticeship

Hours	Weeks	Unit
240	6.0	Bench Work
360	9.0	Drill Press
240	6.0	Heat Treat
200	5.0	Elementary Layout
680	17.0	Turret Lathe (Conventional and Numerical Control)
800	20.0	Engine Lathe
320	8.0	Tool Grind
640	16.0	Advanced Layout
960	24.0	Milling Machine
280	7.0	Profile Milling
160	4.0	Surface Grinding
240	6.0	External Grinding
280	7.0	Internal Grinding
200	5.0	Thread Grinding
520	13.0	Horizontal Boring Mills
240	6.0	Jig Bore/Jig Grinder
160	4.0	Vertical Boring
600	15.0	Numerical Control Milling
240	6.0	Computer Numerical Control
640	16.0	Related Training
8,000	200.0	TOTALS

PROBATIONARY: The following hours are included in the totals above, but must be completed in the first 1000 hours of apprenticeship.

Hours	Weeks	Unit
80	2.0	Drill Press (Probation)
280	7.0	Lathe Work (Probation)
360	9.0	Milling Machine (Probation)
40	1.0	Elementary Layout (Probation)
80	2.0	Related Training (Probation)
840	21.0	TOTALS

Types of Programs

Currently, over half of all apprentices in this country are involved in the construction industry. Although traditionally seen as a training vehicle for construction and manufacturing jobs, apprenticeships have grown to encompass other major areas such as health care, service industries, and public-service occupations. It takes from one to six years to complete most apprenticeships and there are now registered apprentice programs for over 800 occupations ranging from aircraft mechanic to x-ray equipment tester.

Registered Apprenticeships

In 1937, the National Apprenticeship Act authorized the Secretary of Labor to work with state apprenticeship agencies, the Department of Education, and representatives of labor and management to support apprentices and promote establishment of apprenticeship programs.

Apprenticeship programs are commonly registered with a federally approved state apprenticeship agency or with the federal government itself. Twenty-seven

Tool and Die Apprenticeship

Hours	Weeks	Unit
40	1.0	Material Prep
400	10.0	Engine Lathe
400	10.0	Computer Numerical Control/Turret Lathe
800	20.0	Milling Machine
120	3.0	Rotary Head Mill Engineering
80	2.0	Profile Mill
240	6.0	Tool & Cutter Grind
60	4.0	Heat Treat
240	6.0	Surface Grinding/Computer Numerical Control
240	6.0	External Grinding/Computer Numerical Control
240	6.0	Internal Grinding
120	3.0	Die Form Grinding
160	4.0	Jig Grinding/Computer Numerical Control
80	2.0	Centerless Grinding
80	2.0	Thread Grinding
280	7.0	Horizontal Boring Mills
520	13.0	Jig Bore
840	21.0	CNC Mill
2,560	64.0	Bench Work (Tool Fabrication)
440	11.0	Manufacturing
240	6.0	Layout (Coordinate Measuring Machine, Dea)
80	2.0	Tool Inspection
80	2.0	Tool Insp. (Boice, Notes, Dea)
120	3.0	Spring Bench
200	5.0	Optical Tool Fabrication
240	6.0	Break Down
200	5.0	Electronic Discharge Machine
800	20.0	Related Training
10,000	250.0	TOTALS

PROBATIONARY: The following hours are included in the totals above, but must be completed in the first 1000 hours of apprenticeship.

Hours	Weeks	Unit
200	5.0	Lathes (Probation)
200	5.0	Mill (Probation)
240	6.0	Grinders (Probation)
240	6.0	Bench Work (Probation)
40	1.0	Break Down Area (Probation)
80	2.0	Related Training (Probation)
1,000	25.0	TOTALS

states plus the District of Columbia, Puerto Rico, and the Virgin Islands have apprenticeship agencies. In the states that do not have agencies, the U.S. Department of Labor oversees the apprenticeship functions through its Bureau of Apprenticeship and Training (BAT).

Registered programs meet federally approved standards on job duties, related instruction, wages, and safety and health conditions. When apprentices complete a registered program, they receive a certificate of completion from the approved state agency or the U.S. Department of Labor. Graduates of registered programs enhance their potential job mobility because employers across the country have confidence in the quality of their training.

The administrative part of registered apprenticeship programs is called an apprenticeship committee, representing the sponsors of the program. The committee reviews applications and conducts interviews of applicants. In order to comply with federal apprenticeship standards, equal employment opportunity, safety, and similar matters, apprenticeship committees consult with the state apprenticeship council and with the regional representative of BAT.

New-Generation Apprenticeships

Starting in the mid-1980s, and gathering momentum to the present, is a new type of job-training program—"youth apprenticeships." These nontraditional programs link high school, postsecondary education, and work experience for those youths who may not seek a four-year college degree. Students can start as early as 16 years of age to benefit from mixing school- and work-based programs geared toward broad career paths. Programs vary, but ideally employers pay the youth apprentices and serve as mentors for the work-site learning. Those who complete the programs receive nationally recognized certificates showing mastery of both academic and vocational skills. Between the Department of Labor and the Jobs for the Future agency, there are currently more than 20 youth apprentice efforts.

Business is also involved at a national level. The National Alliance of Business has opened a Business Center for Youth Apprenticeship to encourage the concept and give employers a stronger voice in the school-to-work transition by helping set standards and design curricula. The NAB system would have employers working with schools to recruit, hire, and educate youth with the emphasis on jobs that will have a productive future. Companies would hire youth as part-time employees with achievement standards designed jointly by employers and schools.

Over 170 companies now have youth apprenticeship programs. These are mostly small firms, but they get a choice of the best workers because of the strength of on-the-job learning.

"Tech-prep" is another model that balances a student's classroom and workplace experience. Although tech-prep efforts are on a local scale, the federal government does provide dollars for model programs. Students begin a prescribed course of study in their junior year in high school and finish with their associate's degree from a community or junior college. These programs offer training in areas such as electronics, computers, public safety, business services, and automobile repair. The scope of the program depends on the local market.

Administration

Administration of a registered apprenticeship program is done by a joint apprenticeship training committee with support from state and federal agencies.

Joint Apprenticeship Training Committees

Apprenticeship committees are made up of equal numbers of worker and employer representatives who together develop apprenticeship standards for a specific trade. The committees will screen and select applicants, approve training facilities, and help apprentices and employers if problems occur.

The committees will also try to maintain continuous employment during the training periods. Since many apprenticeship programs involve more than one employer, committees can rotate apprentices through different jobs to offset seasonal and economic fluctuations in demand for workers.

Federal Government

The U.S. Department of Labor supports apprenticeship through its Bureau of Apprenticeship and Training. BAT does the following:

- Sets federal standards for apprenticeship
- Registers programs that meet federal standards
- Monitors state apprenticeship councils to ensure they are in compliance with federal standards
- Oversees apprenticeship functions in states that do not have apprenticeship agencies
- Consults with the state apprenticeship councils and with joint apprenticeship committees
- Awards certificates for completion of registered programs
- Cooperates with other departments to help women gain better access to the skilled trades
- Help sponsors of apprenticeship programs

See the list of Department of Labor, Bureau of Apprenticeship and Training offices in the Appendix at the end of this chapter.

State Agencies

In the states that have apprenticeship agencies, administrative functions vary. Here are some functions that can be generally applied:

- Help employers, schools, and unions work together to provide high-quality training.
- Show employers how to establish standards and design cost-effective training programs to meet specific needs.
- Register and approve programs.
- Help employers locate training funds, if needed.
- Ensure that each program meets the requirements of the state agency.
- Assist in the program approval process.
- Make sure that programs meet the needs of local industry.
- See that the training is uniform and of high quality to ensure acceptance of apprenticeship graduates across the country.
- Guarantee that apprenticeship programs meet all applicable labor laws.

Apprenticeship can involve a number of different agencies or administrative bodies. Professional apprenticeship coordinators can help sponsors fill out paperwork and comply with state and federal regulations.

See the list of state offices that deal with apprenticeship in the appendix at the end of this chapter.

Union Views and Involvement

Led by the Congress of Industrial Organizations, labor reforms of the 1930s reorganized many unions on an industrywide basis, mixing skilled and unskilled workers in the same union. This arrangement strengthened the unions' bargaining power. Distinctions regarding the mastery of skills were dealt with through contract language which defined job classification and wages. Unions retain a leading role in defining skill levels associated with job titles or craft titles.

Unions in the United States are very active in the creation, implementation, and monitoring of apprenticeship programs. The craft orientation of many unions provides a natural vehicle for the transmission of skills related to the trade. Unions also foster pride and accomplishment associated with the mastery of skill levels within a certain trade. Many unions have established their own formal or informal apprenticeship programs in order to protect the integrity of the craft and to bargain effectively for the union members. In states where joint apprenticeship councils exist, unions are a major player in the process. Labor organizations continue to protect the integrity of the journey-level status within their trade.

Summary

Highly skilled workers are the result of extensive experience, on-the-job training, and technical knowledge; the strengths of apprenticeship programs. Apprentices have historically been a part of the economic system. The apprenticeship system has trained over 5 million workers since 1937 and continues to register about 100,000 workers per year.

A worker must qualify and be selected for an apprenticeship. The programs are structured systems of on-the-job training that are standardized, clearly defined, and commonly recognized throughout the industry. Apprenticeships involve manual skills, technical skills, and knowledge requiring a minimum of 2000 hours of on-the-job training with related instruction to supplement the training. Programs are strongly supported by the U.S. Department of Labor, employers, and labor unions.

Today's highly technical world is a perfect environment for apprenticeships in industry, commerce, or public service. Apprenticeship is one of the best ways to acquire the skills necessary for full qualification in the ever-increasing job market.

Bibliography

Kursh, Harry, *Apprenticeships in America*, Norton, New York, 1958.

Lobb, Charlotte, *Exploring Apprenticeship Careers*, rev. ed., Rosen Publishing Group, New York, 1985.

Rorabaugh, W. J., *The Craft Apprentice from Franklin to The Machine Age in America*, Oxford University Press, New York, 1986.

Shanahan, William F., *Guide to Apprenticeship Programs*, Arco Publishing, New York, 1983.

Acknowledgments

Robert A. McKenzie, Human Resources Development, The Boeing Company.
Doug George, Apprenticeship Program Manager, The Boeing Company.
Michal F. Settles, Department Manager, Human Resources, Bay Area Rapid Transit.
Virginia Roberts, M.S.W., Labor Educator, Aerospace Machinists Industrial District Lodge
751 AFL-CIO.

Appendix

Bureau of Apprenticeship and Training State Offices and State Apprenticeship
Councils, including Puerto Rico and the Virgin Islands.

Alabama
USDL-BAT
Berry Building, Suite 102
2017 Second Avenue North
Birmingham, AL 35203
(205) 731-1308

Alaska
USDL-BAT
Federal Building and Courthouse
222 West Seventh Street, Room 554
Anchorage, AK 99513
(907) 271-5035

Arizona
USDL-BAT
Suite 302
3221 North 16th Street
Phoenix, AZ 85016
(602) 640-2964

Apprenticeship Services
Arizona Department of Economic
  Security
438 West Adams Street
Phoenix, AZ 85003
(602) 252-7771

Arkansas
USDL-BAT
Federal Building, Room 3507
700 West Capitol Street
Little Rock, AR 72201
(501) 378-5415

California
USDL-BAT
Room 350
211 Main Street
San Francisco, CA 94105
(415) 744-6581

Division of Apprenticeship Standards
395 Oyster Point Boulevard
Fifth Floor
San Francisco, CA 94080
(415) 737-2700

Colorado
USDL-BAT
U.S. Custom House
721 19th Street, Room 480
Denver, CO 80202
(303) 844-4793

Connecticut
USDL-BAT
Federal Building
135 High Street, Room 367
Hartford, CT 06103
(203) 240-4311

Office of Job Training and Skill Development
Connecticut Labor Department
200 Folly Brook Boulevard
Wethersfield, CT 06109
(203) 566-4724

Delaware
USDL-BAT
Lock Box 36, Federal Building
844 King Street
Wilmington, DE 19801
(302) 573-6113

Apprenticeship and Training
Department of Labor
Division of Employment and Training
Sixth Floor, State Office Building
820 North French Street
Wilmington, DE 19801
(302) 571-1908

District of Columbia
District of Columbia
Apprenticeship Council
500 C Street N.W.
Suite 241
Washington, DC 20001
(202) 639-1415

Florida
USDL-BAT
City Centre Building, Suite 5117
227 North Bronough Street
Tallahassee, FL 32301
(904) 681-7161

Bureau of Apprenticeship
Division of Labor and Employment Sect
1320 Executive Center Drive
Atkins Building, Second Floor
Tallahassee, FL 32301
(904) 488-8332

Georgia
USDL-BAT
Room 418
1371 Peachtree Street N.E.
Atlanta, GA 30367
(404) 347-4403

Hawaii
USDL-BAT
Room 5113
300 Ala Moana Boulevard
Honolulu, HI 96850
(808) 541-2518

Apprenticeship Division
Department of Labor and Industry
 Relations
830 Punch Bowl Street
Honolulu, HI 96813
(808) 548-2520

Idaho
USDL-BAT
Suite 128
3050 North Lakeharbor Lane
Boise, ID 83724
(208) 334-1013

Illinois
USDL-BAT
Room 758
230 South Dearborn Street
Chicago, IL 60604
(312) 353-4690

Indiana
USDL-BAT
Federal Building and U.S. Courthouse
46 East Ohio Street, Room 414
Indianapolis, IN 46204
(317) 269-7592

Iowa
USDL-BAT
Federal Building, Room 637
210 Walnut Street
Des Moines, IA 50309
(515) 284-4690

Kansas
USDL-BAT
Federal Building, Room 256
444 S.E. Quincy Street
Topeka, KS 66683
(913) 295-2624

Kansas State Apprenticeship Council
Department of Human Resources
401 S.W. Topeka Boulevard
Topeka, KS 66603-3182
(913) 296-3588

Kentucky
USDL-BAT
Federal Building, Room 187-J
600 Federal Place
Louisville, KY 40202
(502) 582-5223

Apprenticeship and Training
Department of Labor
620 South Third Street
Louisville, KY 40202
(502) 588-4466

Louisiana
USDL-BAT
U.S. Postal Building, Room 1323
701 Loyola Street
New Orleans, LA 70113
(504) 589-6103

Apprenticeship and Training
Louisiana Department of Labor
Office of Labor
1001 North 23rd Street
Baton Rouge, LA 70804-9094
(504) 342-7820

Maine
USDL-BAT
Federal Building
P.O. Box 917
68 Sewell Street, Room 408-D
Augusta, ME 04330
(207) 622-8235

Apprenticeship Standards
Bureau of Labor Standards
State House Station #45
Augusta, ME 04333
(207) 289-4307

Maryland
USDL-BAT
Federal Building Charles Center
31 Hopkins Plaza, Room 1028
Baltimore, MD 21201
(301) 962-2676

Apprenticeship and Training
Department of Employment and Training,
 Room 213
1100 North Eutaw Street
Baltimore, MD 21201
(301) 333-5718

Massachusetts
USDL-BAT
11th Floor
One Congress Street
Boston, MA 02114
(617) 565-2291

Department of Labor and Industry
Division of Apprenticeship Training
Leverett Saltonstall Building
100 Cambridge Street
Boston, MA 02202
(617) 727-3488

Michigan
USDL-BAT
Room 304
801 South Waverly
Lansing, MI 48917
(517) 377-1746

Minnesota
USDL-BAT
Federal Building and U.S. Courthouse
316 Robert Street, Room 134
St. Paul, MN 55101
(612) 290-3951

Division of Apprenticeship
Department of Labor and Industry
Space Center Building, Fourth Floor
443 Lafayette Road
St. Paul, MN 55101
(612) 296-2371

Mississippi
USDL-BAT
Federal Building, Suite 1010
100 West Capital Street
Jackson, MS 39269
(601) 965-4346

Missouri
USDL-BAT
1222 Spruce, Room 9.102E
St. Louis, MO 63103
(314) 539-2522

Montana
USDL-BAT
Federal Office Building
301 South Park Avenue
Room 394, Drawer-10055
Helena, MT 59626-0055
(406) 449-5261

Apprenticeship and Training Bureau
Employment Policy Division
Department of Labor and Industry
P.O. Box 1728
Helena, MT 59626-0055
(406) 444-4500

Nebraska
USDL-BAT
Room 801
106 South 15th Street
Omaha, NE 68102
(402) 221-3281

Nevada
USDL-BAT
P.O. Building, Room 311
301 East Stewart Avenue
Las Vegas, NV 89101
(702) 388-6396

Nevada State Apprenticeship Council
505 East King Street, Room 601
Carson City, NV 89710
(702) 885-4850

New Hampshire
USDL-BAT
143 North Main Street
Concord, NH 03301
(603) 225-1444

New Hampshire Apprenticeship Council
19 Pillsbury Street
Concord, NH 03301
(603) 271-3176

New Jersey
USDL-BAT
Parkway Towers Building E
Third Floor
485 Route 1, South
Iselin, NJ 08830
(908) 750-9191

New Mexico
USDL-BAT
Room 16
320 Central Avenue S.W.
Albuquerque, NM 87102
(505) 766-2398

Apprenticeship and Training
New Mexico Department of Labor
501 Mountain Road N.E.
Suite 106
Albuquerque, NM 87102
(505) 841-8989

New York
USDL-BAT
Federal Building, Room 810
North Pearl and Clinton Avenues
Albany, NY 12202
(518) 472-4800

Employability Development
New York State Department of Labor
State Office Campus
Building 12, Room 140
Albany, NY 12240
(518) 457-6820

North Carolina
USDL-BAT
Aviation Building, Suite 375
4505 Falls of Neuse Road
Raleigh, NC 27601
(919) 790-2801

Apprenticeship and Training
North Carolina Department of Labor
Memorial Building
214 West Jones Street
Raleigh, NC 27603
(919) 733-7533

North Dakota
USDL-BAT
New Federal Building, Room 428
653 Second Avenue North
Fargo, ND 58102
(701) 239-5415

Ohio
USDL-BAT
Room 605
200 North High Street
Columbus, OH 43215
(614) 469-7375

Ohio State Apprenticeship Council
2323 West Fifth Avenue
Room 2140
Columbus, OH 43216
(614) 640-2242

Oklahoma
USDL-BAT
1500 S. Midwest Boulevard
Suite 202
Midwest City, OK 73110
(405) 732-4338

Oregon
USDL-BAT
Federal Building, Room 526
1220 S.W. Third Avenue
Portland, OR 97204
(503) 221-3157

Apprenticeship and Training Division
Oregon Bureau of Labor and Industry
State Office Building, Room 32
800 N.E. Oregon Street
Portland, OR 97232
(503) 731-4072

Pennsylvania
State Director
USDL-BAT
Federal Building
228 Walnut Street, Room 773
Harrisburg, PA 17108
(717) 782-3496

Apprenticeship and Training
Labor and Industry Building
7th and Forster St., Room 1303
Harrisburg, PA 17120
(717) 787-3687

Puerto Rico
Incentive to the Private Program,
Right to Employment Administration
P.O. Box 4452
505 Munoz Rivera Avenue
San Juan, PR 00936
(809) 754-5181

Rhode Island
USDL-BAT
Federal Building
100 Hartford Avenue
Providence, RI 02909
(401) 273-7640

Apprenticeship and Training
Rhode Island State Apprenticeship Shore
  Council
200 Elmwood Avenue
Providence, RI 02907
(401) 457-1858

South Carolina
USDL-BAT
S. Thurmond Federal Building
1835 Assembly Street, Room 838
Columbia, SC 29201
(803) 765-5547

South Dakota
USDL-BAT
Courthouse Plaza, Room 107
300 North Dakota Avenue
Sioux Falls, SD 57102
(605) 330-4326

Tennessee
USDL-BAT
Metroplex Business Park
460 Metroplex Drive, Suite 101-A
Nashville, TN 37211
(615) 736-5408

Texas
USDL-BAT
VA Building, Room 2102
2320 LaBranch Street, Houston, TX 77004
(713) 750-1696

Utah
USDL-BAT
Room 1051
1745 West 1700 South
Salt Lake City, UT 84104
(801) 524-5700

Vermont
USDL-BAT
Burlington Square
96 College Street, Suite 103
Burlington, VT 05401
(802) 951-6278

Apprenticeship and Training
Department of Labor and Industry
120 State Street
Montpelier, VT 05602
(802) 828-2157

Virginia
USDL-BAT
Room 10-020
400 North Eighth Street
Richmond, VA 23240
(804) 771-2488

Apprenticeship and Training
Division of Labor and Industry
P.O. Box 12064
205 North Fourth Street, Room M-3
Richmond, VA 23241
(804) 786-2381

Virgin Islands
Division of Apprenticeship and Training
Department of Labor
P.O. Box 890 Christiansted
St. Croix, VI 00802
(809) 773-1300

Washington
USDL-BAT
Room 950
1111 Third Avenue
Seattle, WA 98101-3212
(206) 442-4756

Apprenticeship and Training
Department of Labor and Industry
ESAC Division
925 Plum Street
Olympia, WA 98504-0631
(206) 753-3487

West Virginia
USDL-BAT
Federal Building
550 Eagan Street, Room 303
Charleston, WV 25301
(304) 347-5141

Wyoming
USDL-BAT
J. C. O'Mahoney Center
2120 Capitol Avenue, Room 5013
P.O. Box 1126
Cheyenne, WY 82001
(307) 772-2448

Wisconsin
USDL-BAT
Federal Center, Room 303
212 East Washington Avenue
Madison, WI 53703
(608) 264-5377

Bureau of Apprenticeship Standards
Department of Industry, Labor and
  Human Relations
7201 East Washington Avenue
Room 211-X
Madison, WI 53703
(608) 266-3133

39

Basic
Workplace Skills*

Jorie W. Philippi

Jorie W. Philippi *is the founder and executive director of Performance Plus Learning Consultants, Inc. (PPLC), an international consulting firm, with offices in Charleston, West Virginia, that has been providing training, product development, and evaluation services in workplace literacy since 1989. She is currently under contract to the U.S. Department of Labor to identify and articulate basic skills and cross-functional skills found in all occupations for the new, on-line version of* The Dictionary of Occupational Titles, *entitled the* Occupational Information Network *(O*NET). Philippi has worked in the private, public, and military sectors extensively, serving over 500 large and small organizations in the United States and abroad, including Fortune 500 companies; U.S. Departments of Labor, Education, Energy, and Defense; the Internal Revenue Service; and 32 state governments. She has authored numerous articles, customized training series and texts, including a how-to manual for Simon & Schuster,* Literacy at Work: The Workbook for Program Providers *(1991), and an interactive video and study guide series,* Retraining the Workforce: Meeting the Global Challenge *(1993). Philippi has taught graduate courses in workplace literacy for the University of Arkansas and the University of Delaware and is frequently a keynote speaker at conferences and meetings across the country.*

*Some of the material contained in this chapter has been published previously in another form in Philippi, J. W. (1993) *Retraining the Workforce: Meeting the Global Challenge*, Dallas County Community College District, R. Jan LeCroy Center for Telecommunications, Dallas, TX.

Why Basic Skills Training Is Necessary

The changing workplace has created new training needs. For years, workers needed to perform only a limited number of tasks in each job. Supervisors and forepersons monitored, inspected, and assumed full responsibility for the quality of work or services produced. The introduction of new equipment or procedures was spaced across wide increments of time. In today's world, things are different. Changes are now taking place in both large and small companies at an ever-accelerating rate. They center on improvements in product and service quality and increased worker responsibility. These shifts toward self-directed teamwork and emphases on the quality of production and services necessary for competing in a worldwide market have created new job tasks that employ numerous applications of basic skills.

To keep abreast of these changes, many employees must now perform a variety of new job tasks for which they have little or no previous experience. As a result, workers previously rated as competent may no longer be performing effectively, and employers have begun to realize that they need to provide workers with training in job-literacy skills to accomplish these new tasks effectively and improve job performance. Most employees also feel the need for a "brush-up" course or special training to prepare themselves to assume control of their work environment.

For every job there are tasks that are critical to its performance. The varying degrees to which workers can perform these critical tasks determine their job proficiency and, collectively, the quality of the workforce. Competent performance of job tasks requires more than technical knowledge of job content. The best workers also can identify job needs and efficiently use workplace basic skills such as reading, writing, computing, communicating, and problem solving.

Changes in Work and the Ways in Which It Is Accomplished

As jobs change, the traditional workplace applications of the basic skills that support task performance change, too. Even those workers who have mastered academic basic skills are seldom prepared for the ways in which they will need those skills to perform current and future job tasks competently. Changes now occurring in the workplace focus on continuous improvements in product quality and worker performance.

Organizational strategies undertaken to maximize profit often result in changing job duties in the workplace. These changes require workers to retool their skills to meet the demands of new procedures and equipment. Concurrently, a shift in demographics is occurring: fewer qualified people are available to enter the workforce without first completing extensive training or retraining. The number of women and minorities entering the workforce is growing rapidly; average age and seniority of workers are rising steadily; the labor pool is changing. Now, more than ever, there is a need to invest more resources in the workforce.

At one time, companies could replace underqualified employees with new, better-qualified workers. Now, they cannot find high-skilled replacement workers or entry-level hires so they often must hire workers who are less than fully qualified. It is apparent that in today's economy, there are no more "throw-away workers." A high school diploma or equivalency certificate no longer guarantees that workers have the necessary skills for competent job performance. Many graduates leave school with low skills or gaps in their ability levels. In addition, adults who have been away from the classroom for long periods may no longer be practicing the skills they learned, and basic skills are use-it-or-lose-it commodities.

The Conference Board of New York City.[1] reports that approximately 90 percent of the employed U.S. workforce are, in fact, academically literate. Only 10 percent of the employees of the companies surveyed were reported to be nonliterates or low-level literates, i.e., reading below a fourth-grade ability level. Yet, only one-quarter of all the workers were described as advanced-level literates, able to function in any situation. Of the remaining 65 percent of the employed U.S. workforce, many have high school diplomas or high school equivalency degrees but find themselves unable to perform new job tasks at fully competent levels.

A recent (1992) study by the international Organization for Economic Cooperation and Development indicates that other industrialized countries report similar findings. A 1989 Canadian government survey of their workforce showed that only 62 percent of Canadians met everyday reading demands and that one-third of Canadian firms have difficulty with introducing new technology because of poor labor skills. The German Commission for UNESCO estimates that there are between 500,000 and 3,000,000 illiterates in Germany. One in three factory workers in Sweden is reported to be in need of basic skills education. The Ministry of Defense in France estimates that 20 percent of the young men ages 18 to 23 called up for military service during 1990–1991 could not read a 70-word text.

For all countries in the global marketplace, a workforce that does not possess functional literacy skills severely handicaps economic performance in an industrial world. For years, workers have performed the same job tasks; but as their job responsibilities change with upgrades in technology and shifts in management structure, they find themselves no longer equipped with the skills needed to tackle new job tasks. Such workers may be classified as *intermediate-level literates,* no longer able to be completely functional in the workplace environment without additional basic skills training.

What Employers Want

Companies continue to look for ways to improve job performance so they can reduce costs due to accidents, waste, or unnecessarily poor quality. Leaner resources and tighter budgets make the need for rapidly achieved, long-term improvements even more acute. Many organizations are uncertain of the capacity of their current workforce and prospective hires to master the skills necessary for accomplishing these critical changes. They look for training that will enhance the return on their investments in new equipment or shifts in management procedures.

Increasingly, employers are facing the reality of now having enough qualified workers to fill the positions available. They find that qualified, retrainable entry-level and promotable employees are at a premium. These changes in the available workforce lead to a pressing need for applied workplace basic skills training, just as the changes in the workplace discussed earlier do. Both kinds of changes underlie the following indicators of workplace basic skills problems often noted by employers:

- Difficulties experienced by workers in technical training for upgrading or shifts in management structure
- Fewer qualified applicants and new hires

- Problems with introducing new equipment or procedures that need to be incorporated into the system quickly in order to remain competitive
- Seeming inability of lower-level employees to assume increased responsibilities resulting from downsizing or flattening of the organizational hierarchy
- Performance errors that cost time, money, or customers—or that result in accidents

---

Employers want employees who are able to:

✓ Learn new job tasks
✓ Perform competently
✓ Take on new responsibilities
✓ Help solve production and service problems

Effective training in applied workplace basic skills can enhance the likelihood of the success of organizational investments in change.

What Employees Want

Workers also express concerns about their changing work environment and how it impacts on job performance and job security. Until recently, the job tasks that most employees performed had remained fairly constant through many years. The current necessity to interact with competitors in a global marketplace and the resulting emphases on quality monitoring and self-directed management styles have caused workers to realize that their old skills and abilities may no longer suffice. The need to learn new job tasks and the skills required to perform them are sources of worry for many employees. Self-esteem and morale issues emerge, and rumors of potential dismissals or work-site closings frequently arise. The following indicators of workplace basic skills problems are often noted by employees:

- A lack of understanding of the purpose or procedures for required quality monitoring
- An inability to communicate adequately with, or give input to, supervisors, management, or coworkers
- Difficulty with mastering technical training sessions and applying new information to actual job-task performance, or finding training to be insufficient, too quick, or too advanced
- Frustration and feelings of inadequacy when engaging in many new tasks and procedures over a short period of time
- Difficulty passing the task performance tests tied to new "pay-for-skills" compensatory systems

To accomplish new workplace tasks effectively and to improve personal marketability, most employees feel the need for, and often ask for, a brush-up course or special training. They want to prepare themselves to contribute fully in their environment and assume control of their day-to-day responsibilities. Workers take pride in doing a good job; they recognize the skills required for the successful performance of the new workplace tasks. These skills are different from those they may have learned in academic settings. The new job tasks require specific applications of skills.

Employees want to be able to:

✓ Learn new transferable skill applications
✓ Take control of new responsibilities
✓ Perform tasks well and with pride
✓ Participate in company survival and improvement

Defining Applied Workplace Basic Skills

Performing job tasks requires specific workplace applications of basic skills. Competent workers must be able to use job-reading processes for locating information and for using higher-level thinking strategies to solve problems. They must be able to use occupational writing processes for organizing clear, readable writing and for mastering those thinking skills that enable analysis, elaboration, and extension of written ideas. They must be able to use workplace applications of mathematical processes for calculating information and solving problems that go beyond basic number concepts and computation and enable workers to acquire proficiency levels in reasoning and interpretation. These skills applications all require the use of cognitive strategies and are seldom used in isolation but instead generally cluster in combinations related to the performance of specific job tasks. The list below includes many basic-skills applications commonly identified through work-site investigations conducted with competent employees in organizations using Total Quality Management procedures, applying for International Standards Organization (ISO) certifications, or in the process of making a transition to pay-for-skills systems:

Communication Skills
- Formulating questions
- Requesting clarification of job information
- Presenting information to management or coworkers
- Conducting team meetings
- Writing summary statements
- Taking notes in group meetings
- Expressing rationale for process improvement suggestions
- Entering information into a computer

Reading Skills
- Locating information on computer screens
- Identifying relevant information in manuals or on job aids
- Interpreting schematics and graphics using gauges and symbols
- Following procedural directions
- Using multiple sources of information
- Matching alternate criteria to existing conditions

Mathematical Skills
- Collecting, graphing, and analyzing quality data
- Problem solving to troubleshoot
- Recognizing alternate conditions
- Estimating results or progress toward improved performance goals
- Computing cost savings
- Calculating specifications, tolerances, and machine calibrations
- Understanding and using statistics to make decisions

As restructuring occurs in the work environment, many new job tasks—and workplace basic skills applications such as those listed above which support their performance—emerge. Organizational changes in quality-monitoring procedures and shifts in responsibilities cause even the most competent workers to become intermediate-level literates temporarily. Successful workplace basic skills training needs to be built upon a solid understanding of today's organizational paradigms and the support skills required to perform changing job tasks competently. Providing an effective workplace basic skills program offers opportunities for employers and employees to work together for the good of both the organization and the individual.

Differences Between Academic and Workplace Uses of Basic Skills

Research provides strong evidence that the basic-skills applications employed in workplace contexts differ significantly from basic skills taught in academic environments.[2-4] Educational programs, such as *adult basic education* or *adult developmental education* teach academic applications of basic skills, such as reading paragraphs, writing essays, and solving mathematical word problems. The purpose for obtaining these skills may sometimes be to remediate deficiencies as measured by academic tests or to prepare to test for a high school equivalency degree [GED (general equivalency diploma)] or college entrance. Such programs do not teach participants how to transfer academic applications of basic skills to the performance of job tasks. *Adult literacy* programs refer to the field of instruction that targets nonreaders or very low level literates. The teaching of enabling skills, such as recognizing and combining letters in print to form words, is generally conducted by literacy tutors in a one-on-one setting. As with *adult basic education, adult literacy* does not address how to transfer such skills to the performance of job tasks.

Workplace applications of basic skills are not *technical training*, either. Technical training is content-specific. It is designed to teach particular organizational procedures or information related to performing a prescribed job action or series of actions, such as operating a piece of equipment or complying with a safety regulation. A workplace basic-skills program can be used to support or enhance the effectiveness of technical training, and, thus, it can be integrated with other company training. Because workplace basic skills directly benefit the organization, as well as the individual, they should be classified as *training* rather than as education. Placing workplace basic skills under the training umbrella also reduces the likelihood of them being perceived as remedial education efforts that acquire the negative connotations mentioned above.[5]

To provide appropriate and effective workplace basic-skills training that supports competent performance of job tasks, the information that follows on workplace applications of basic skills should be considered.

Workplace Reading Skill Applications

On the job, workers spend an average of 1.5 to 2.0 hours per workday engaged in reading print materials such as forms, graphs, charts, schematics, manuals, and computer screens.[6–11] The emphases of on-the-job reading are on locating information for immediate use and utilizing inferential processes for problem solving.

The act of reading, in which one acquires information from the printed page or screen, is primarily dependent upon the background knowledge the reader brings to the page. Understanding, or comprehension, relies on the reader's ability to make sense of what is being read by fitting the printed information into the context of what is already known about the topic. Without the interplay between the reader's stored prior knowledge and the new knowledge presented on the page, the printed words cannot impart meaning to the reader.

Reading comprehension is a constructive process in which the reader builds personal meaning or interpretation of what the writer is communicating. The reader must use prior knowledge held in memory in order to succeed in acquiring meaning from print materials. In the workplace, comprehension of printed job materials or computer screen displays is thus greatly dependent upon the worker's prior knowledge of the work environment and job tasks.

Workplace reading also often involves another layer of information processing. In text-search applications, which is a type of "reading to do" frequently used in the workplace to locate information for immediate use, the reader must perform cognitive operations that allow him or her to create categories and selectively search by rapidly scanning to identify and match requested information structures.[12–14] It is only by using innate language abilities for spelling patterns (orthography), word order (syntax), word meaning (semantics), and prior knowledge of the subject retrieved from memory (schemata) that the competent reader understands and interacts with the ideas on the page or screen.

Job reading tasks regularly require workers to be proficient in setting purposes, defining categories, utilizing self-questioning, summarizing information, and monitoring comprehension. Researchers have found that the ability to use these higher-level (metacognitive) reading processes correlates with superior job performance.[15] It is clear from these examples that specific applications of reading skills used in workplace reading are very different from the goals of traditional academic classroom remedial or developmental reading instruction.

Workplace Writing Skill Applications

Applications of workplace writing skills also differ significantly from those taught in the traditional classroom. In 1980, Diehl reported that the majority of occupational writing tasks involve completing simple forms or preparing brief memoranda.[6] A study by Mikulecky in 1982[16] confirms this. Mikulecky found that of 276 writing tasks required to perform jobs listed in the *Dictionary of Occupational Titles*, 42.4 percent involved filling out prepared forms and 22.5 percent required generating memoranda or letters. Another 25 percent of the job-writing tasks required recording, summarizing, or noting work completed. Task-related writing, such as producing blueprints, accounted for yet another 11 percent of job writing, and only 10.5 percent involved writing reports or articles like those students are taught to produce in academic settings.

In 1986, Rush, Moe, and Storlie[9] reported that, other than for those writing tasks performed by secretarial employees, clarity is the chief requirement of on-the-job writing. Information often must be translated into concise communication that contains only the essentials. For example, a production operator may have to enter information onto a computer problem log in 144 characters or use a specified format to send electronic mail to another department. In job-training situations, too, Rush, Moe, and Storlie found that accuracy of information is considered more important than the use of standard grammar.

One should not be misled about the nature of most occupational writing tasks by the seemingly simplistic style workers must use to complete forms or produce brief memoranda or summaries. Highly complex mental processing is required to perform such tasks successfully. To communicate effectively, whether in limited space on prepared forms, in summary statements, or in condensed, telegraphic terms, workers must employ a problem-solving process in which they activate mental schema to (1) define their anticipated audience and purpose, (2) determine what form of communication is appropriate, (3) generate and organize ideas, (4) translate their message to a concise, accurate form, and (5) review, evaluate, and revise the written product.[17]

Recent studies of the writing process have identified a prewriting period that may last for only as little as one minute but is a critical part of the writing process during which the writer utilizes mental strategies to activate topic background information (schemata), organize the writing task into manageable pieces, and select relevant information for the written product.[18] Other research findings support the writer's use of mental schema (established thinking patterns, categories, and connections built from experience and held in long-term memory) through the initial production and revision stages of the writing process as well as during prewriting.[19-21] As in the case of workplace reading, analysis of workplace writing skill applications shows them to go well beyond correct grammar or standard memo formatting. Rather, it indicates a strong undercurrent of cognitive strategies used by competent workers.

Workplace Math Skill Applications

In its recent report *Basic Skills in the U.S. Workforce,* the Center for Public Resources points out companies' constant need for employees who possess skills in reasoning and calculation. Executives reported that "medium to high levels of mathematical skills are required across job categories, with consistently high levels required in manufacturing, utilities and finance industries." Employees must use calculations to conduct inventories correctly, complete accurate reports of production and quality levels, measure machine parts specifications, and so on. They must be able to reason through problems logically in order to anticipate the consequences of their actions and assume the responsibilities of teamwork.

Employers frequently complain that their workers are deficient in computational skills, particularly those evidenced in miscalculations of decimals and fractions, which result in costly production errors.[22] However, upon further investigation, employers confirmed that workers can, in fact, perform basic computation algorithms (addition, subtraction, multiplication, and division). A report from the National Assessment of Educational Progress study, conducted by Kirsch and Jungeblut in 1986, supports this contention with the finding that approximately 75 percent of the tested young adults performed quantitative literacy tasks at the intermediate to adept levels or beyond.[23]

The real problem lies in the workers' inability to decide which computational algorithm(s) to apply to a particular job problem or to recognize errors resulting from inappropriate applications because they do not understand *why* specific computations are used.[24] Neither time-consuming computation skill drills nor the use of calculators is an effective remedy because, while both methods can correct the problem of computational errors, neither one assists the individual in knowing which computation is needed to solve an on-the-job problem.[25] The difficulty level of the computational task is also increased when workers must apply more than one numerical operation in an appropriate sequence or use information that is embedded in print materials.[23]

Workplace applications of mathematical skills require employees to acquire proficiency levels in reasoning and problem solving beyond the use of basic computational algorithms. Workplace problem solving can be defined as critical or logical thinking[26] that uses brainstorming, activates learners' schema, and involves group cooperation.[27] Good problem solvers are those who can clearly define the problem, state the goal, limit the "search space" for the solution, and access prior knowledge (schema) appropriately.[28]

Pratzner, in a 1978 report prepared for the National Center for Research in Vocational Education,[29] lists diagnosis, estimating, and problem solving (which includes determining relevant information and selecting alternative solutions) as "generic" or basic reasoning skills used in the workplace. Supporting his position with citations from studies by Singer in 1977[30] and Altman in 1976,[31] he points out that "application and practice of these skills under a variety of realistic life and work performance conditions should facilitate subsequent application or transfer of skills, knowledge and attitudes…to work settings" (pp. 34–35).

Wiant, in *Transferable Skills: The Employer's Viewpoint*, in 1977,[32] also identifies problem solving, analyzing, organizing, and decision making as skills most frequently mentioned as desirable by employers. Resnick, in 1987,[33] too, states, "In mathematics, recent research suggests the most successful learners…understand the task to be one of *interpreting* numbers, not just doing routine calculations.…Failure to engage in 'higher order reasoning' about quantities is related to failures in learning the 'basic' skills of calculation and number usage" (p. 10).

Teaching Basic Skills Within Functional Workplace Contexts

To have the most impact, a workplace basic-skills program should not just focus on the cannot-read-a-word or cannot-count-my-toes employees. Instead, the program should provide opportunities for the majority of workers needing help, that is, employees who are temporarily experiencing difficulty with transferring what they know to new job tasks. Special strands of training can be offered along with core workplace basic-skills training for those workers who are illiterate or who lack proficiency in English. It is not a good practice, however, to concentrate all resources on the highest-risk group. Those workers with severe reading and speaking problems will require long-term support; some may even have learning difficulties that prevent them from improving their skills to reach desired levels. Organizations want to see results—and often budget for only pilot workplace basic-skills programs that last for one or two fiscal quarters in order to determine if such training will prove to be effective. By focusing the majority of program efforts on the large percentage of workers who face changes in their job responsibilities and require training or brush-up on new or seldom-used skills, trainers can demonstrate higher rates of success in terms of job-performance improvement and thus build support for long-term programs for those workers with severe problems.

The most effective workplace basic-skills training programs are designed to facilitate maximum transfer from the learning situation to job performance.

These training programs are developed as a result of work-site investigations of job tasks identified as critical by employers and employees. The training activities are built on actual job scenarios and utilize job materials as a vehicle to teach the cognitive strategies that competent workers use.

The processing performed during instruction and in the tasks to which learning is to be transferred must be highly similar in order for subsequent retrieval and application of knowledge to take place. If the processes are not similar, procedures learned in basic-skills training yield no transfer or even negative transfer.[34,35] In a recent 1987 study of the cognitive basis of knowledge transfer, Gick and Holyoak[36] pointed out that "some of the most spectacular and widely decried failures of transfer—failures to apply knowledge learned in school to practical problems encountered in everyday life—may largely reflect the fact that the material taught in school is often disconnected from any clear goal and hence lacks a primary cue for retrieval in potentially relevant problem contexts" (p. 31). If workers are to transfer necessary basic-skills applications to competent performance of job tasks, the basic-skills training they receive should be conducted with the vehicles of actual job scenarios and materials. This form of instruction is known as a *functional context* approach.

Functionally, contextual workplace basic-skills training materials are built from analyses of job tasks determined to be critical to competent performance by employers and employees. Information about the job-task vehicles and the applications of skills used by competent workers is gathered through an interview-observation procedure called a *literacy task analysis*. Competent workers are observed as they perform critical job tasks and asked to share the mental steps they use to apply basic skills to the performance of the tasks. By probing to determine *how* competent workers think about moving step by step from questions to answers during daily work procedures, verbalization of their mental processes (*metacognition*) can be elicited. Awareness of mental processes is the essence of any basic-skills application that is transferable from task to task. A skill becomes "portable" when the user can abstract the mental-processing steps and apply them to any similar work situation. For example, a competent worker might describe *how* he or she locates information on a health benefits chart by, first, formulating categories to serve as locator phrases, such as "plan type" and "deductible amount," then using these locators to guide rapid scanning of the chart headings to spot the specific relevant rows and columns of information that are desired, and, finally, finding the cell containing the weekly deduction amount at the point where the selected columns and rows intersect. Awareness of this mental "process makes it available for retrieval from long-term memory and for application to similar new situations as they arise." This same cluster of "chart-reading" cognitive strategies forms a mental process that can be applied to any chart-reading task in the workplace. Information such as this about portable basic-skills application processes becomes the foundation on which workplace basic-skills training materials are designed and developed. The mental-processing steps, or portable skills, can be identified as competent workers apply them to performing job tasks, then taught to other workers. And, the use of actual job scenarios and job materials as the training materials for skills instruction provides learners with examples of and practice on immediate job applications, thus enhancing the transfer of training to job performance. Because the workplace materials and scenarios serve only as contextual examples of "portable" mental skill application processes, the basic-skills applications taught do not become obsolete or relate only to narrowly defined specific technical content that may change. Instead, they are the supporting skill applications that enable workers to cope with performance demands in a rapidly changing workplace environment.

Because functional context basic-skills instruction is an outgrowth of the way in which competent workers perform job tasks, its impact on learners' job performance can be measured. Employers and employees participate in identifying those job tasks that are deemed critical to the organization's survival and that employees need to perform. Baseline measures can be obtained for these indicators. Following the development and delivery of functionally contextual training built on literacy task analyses of these job tasks, transfer of learning from training to performance can be tracked and evaluated.

A Process Approach to a Workplace Basic-Skills Program

A functional context workplace basic-skills program requires careful planning. The training materials that form the core of instruction must be created to simulate skill applications used in performing job tasks. Unlike those for many other areas in technical training and education, materials to teach basic-skills applications and thinking strategies for specific job tasks are not readily available from commercial suppliers. They must be custom-designed to meet the needs of individual organizations.

After the decision has been made to provide workplace literacy basic skills and resources have been allocated to development, a plan must be devised for carrying out the essential steps to create the program. An awareness of the purpose associated with each activity in program development enables the beginning of concrete planning. The six identifiable steps in the process for building an effective workplace literacy training program are

- Selecting critical job tasks and identifying performance indicators
- Conducting literacy task analyses
- Assessing levels of employee need
- Designing a multistranded workplace basic-skills training program
- Delivering workplace basic-skills training
- Evaluating results

Selecting Critical Job Tasks and Identifying Performance Indicators

Critical job tasks are any for which the organization perceives imminent change, such as current or planned upgrades in technology or shifts in management structures, or areas needing improvement because of errors or accidents. The support skills used to perform these job tasks become the core of the training curriculum that is produced. Selecting critical job tasks to be addressed by the workplace basic-skills program that are shown to be priorities for improvement, based on analysis of baseline data, strengthens the role of the program in achieving organizationwide goals.

An important front-end activity in developing workplace basic-skills training is to assemble and convene an advisory committee. This committee creates a vehicle for maximizing input and support for the program development stages and implementation. It facilitates a group-process approach for determining training goals and contents that target organizational needs. An advisory committee with representative members from a cross section of the organization will recognize and focus on organizationwide concerns. The committee functions as an investigative and decision-making entity. It identifies those job tasks for which competent performance is critical and selects and prioritizes the critical job tasks to be targeted to support skills training in workplace basic-skills instruction.

The advisory committee should consist of people who can help select the high-priority job tasks. They should know about current and projected job duties, changes, problems, and training. Essential advisory committee members should be those people directly responsible for training functions.

Collecting baseline data enables one to benchmark existing conditions so that the impact of workplace basic-skills training on performance can be determined. If the program is a companion to specific quality or safety training courses, the measures of performance can be gathered before the program begins through use of organizational records previously collected. If the workplace basic-skills training program is to operate independently of other already-existing training programs and performance measures, supervisor focus groups are recommended for identifying observable, measurable behaviors that can function as performance indicators for various levels of worker competence. Collecting this information is the first step in the process for setting local standards against which to measure the impact of training.

Identifying performance indicators is an important part of the development of any workplace basic-skills program, too. It not only assists the program developer(s) in acquiring accurate and detailed information about actual job-performance needs, but it also provides the key elements for measuring program impact. Because supervisors or team leaders interact with other employees on a regular basis, they often are most knowledgeable about the ideal performance levels for job tasks within their area—and how their employees' performance ranks in relationship to the desired ideal. For this reason, it is beneficial to have supervisors or team leaders assist with identifying the indicators by which to measure changes in employee performance.

Convening focus-group meetings with the supervisors of the trainees is an expedient method for obtaining measurable, observable examples of employee behaviors evidenced in performing critical job tasks. Such indicators are excellent measures of program impact because they discriminate the levels of performance competency that are most meaningful to the organization; that is, behaviors exhibited by workers as they perform critical job tasks are observed and rated by the workers' supervisors. Targeted program participants and control groups can be rated with the instrument by their supervisors (or participants can self-rate when contractual agreements disallow such supervisor or coworker ratings) before and after a cycle of workplace basic skills training to determine the extent to which the program impacts positively on job performance (see Fig. 39-1).

Conducting Literacy Task Analyses

After critical job tasks have been identified, information must be gathered concerning how competent workers apply basic skills while performing those tasks. The simultaneous observation and interview technique called literacy task analysis (LTA) is used to obtain the needed information. Job materials used in performing critical tasks are also collected. Unlike the task analysis used for formulating job descriptions or for conducting time management or compensatory studies, an LTA is *not* a means for measuring or standardizing employee performance. Rather, it is a training materials developer's tool for identifying *how* thinking strategies are used by *competent workers* as they apply basic skills to

I. Meeting Participation		
Employee Name: _____		
Supervisor Code Number: _____		
Date of Rating: _____		
4		2
5	3	1
Demonstrates ability to listen well	Handles criticism well	Mumbles
Negotiates effectively	Seldom speaks	Falls asleep
Presents ideas clearly and objectively with appropriate support.	Is argumentative	Comes late to meeting and/or leaves meeting early.
Provides feedback	Complains	Is unorganized
		Shows lack of focus
		Constantly interrupts
		Offers no input or frequently offers negative input

Figure 39-1. Sample page from instrument for supervisor use in collecting performance data.

job-task performance. The documented results of LTAs become the training objectives for functional context instruction.

Each LTA requires approximately 20 to 45 minutes to complete. During the time spent with a competent worker, the analyst should ask questions about the critical job task or subtask being observed. Questioning techniques should be utilized that lead to clear, concise worker responses that focus on the *context* of the task procedure(s) and the mental *processing* used during skills application (see Fig. 39-2).

By focusing questions on these two categories, analysts get information about the nature of the thinking processes used by competent performers of the tasks and about the situations in which the tasks occur. Such information allows a competent training materials developer to design a credible unit or series of units of instruction that address portable basic-skills applications that are both specific to performance of currently identified critical tasks and transferable to new situations that may arise in the workplace.

Processing Information	Contextual Information
Thinking strategies used by competent workers while applying basic skills to the performance of specific tasks.	Actual tasks and job-situation details necessary for creating realistic basic-skills instruction training scenarios.

Figure 39-2. Questions about the job task should be based on processing and contextual information.

Materials used during performance of critical job tasks observed should also be collected.

Documented LTAs serve as visual bridges between job performance and workplace basic-skills training. When information is presented in a two-column format, it can be used as a graphic illustration of the relationships between elements of job procedures and those basic-skills applications required for competent job performance.

Documented LTAs provide a quick reference for developers when they prepare the functional context curriculum for workplace basic-skills training. The left-hand column embodies the workplace materials and scenarios that will be used as the instructional vehicle, or *context*. The right-hand column represents the skills that will be the instructional objectives of the workplace basic-skills training. An excerpt from an average length two-page documented LTA is shown in Fig. 39-3.

Job Title: Quality-control inspector

Job Task: Performing in-process inspection of products

Subtasks	Skill Applications
1. Completes top portion of in-processing inspection checklist form by entering required information from production job order (PJO) form attached to each operating machine on shop floor.	1.1 Scanning to locate information. 1.2 Using technical terms and abbreviations. 1.3 Entering information onto a form accurately and completely. 1.4 Distinguishing between relevant and irrelevant information. 1.5 Following sequential procedural directions.
2. Collects sample parts hourly from each of five machine operators; tests or inspects each sample part for compliance with standards, based on VP quality controls and on customer product specifications, checking for accuracy of precision measurements, shorts, sinks, scratches, humps, splays, and flash. Logs results onto in-process inspection checklist form. ▪ If product sample is in compliance, enters test type and results on traveler form and delivers form to machine operator. ▪ If product sample is not in compliance, analyzes problem to determine possible causes and notifies shift supervisor, then repeats product sample check every 10 minutes, communicating with machine operator until problem is resolved.	2.1 Following sequential procedural directions. 2.2 Using visual discrimination skills to recognize defects. 2.3 Comparing and contrasting. 2.4 Recognizing alternate conditions. 2.5 Categorizing to generate problem descriptors. 2.6 Identifying part-to-whole relationships. 2.7 Recognizing cause-effect relationships. 2.8 Drawing conclusions. 2.9 Predicting outcomes. 2.10 Making decisions. 2.11 Entering information onto a form accurately and completely. 2.12 Summarizing and paraphrasing information for verbal communication. 2.13 Telling time. 2.14 Sequencing by time order. 2.15 Interpreting increments on a scale. 2.16 Using linear measure. 2.17 Applying concept of greater than–less than. 2.18 Performing addition and subtraction computations with decimals (to .0001).

Figure 39-3. Sample of literacy task analysis documentation format.

Assessing Levels of Employee Need

The purpose of any test is to measure differences—differences between ability and standards, differences among test takers, or differences in ability over time. Many workers find being measured against a preset standard disconcerting, even if the standard is one's own past performance. Testing can have many negative ramifications if it is conducted with improper instruments or for inappropriate reasons. It is important to be well-informed about test purposes and options before deciding to implement any type of assessment of employee basic skills.

There are numerous reasons for obtaining information about the levels of employee competence in basic skills. The primary reason is to determine appropriate ability level(s) for which to provide technical training, job-supporting print materials, or instruction in workplace basic skills. This information is especially critical if materials are to be custom-written or if resources limit the amount of commercial materials that can be purchased. Assessing basic skills ability levels of targeted participants does not require a commercially developed standardized test. Normally, information about reading-ability levels can be obtained quickly by means of cloze exercises, i.e., fill-in-the-blank activities requiring comprehension of work-related passages written at specific reading levels.

Within the context of workplace basic-skills programs, the function of assessment is to aid instructional decision making about difficulty levels of the training materials and about who should be trained. It is critical to remember that assessment is *not* instruction. No instructional goal is realized by assessment. Assessment assists program decision making, but files of test scores serve no purpose unless a *specific* set of decisions to be made are identified before the assessment is conducted. For every workplace basic-skills training program there exists a variety of information that can be used in making program decisions. It is important for program developers to ask themselves if the information that testing would yield is necessary for making a particular decision. If it is agreed that the information is critical, then valid and reliable assessment instruments must be selected to provide the needed information at an appropriate level of precision. An assessment instrument should sample the same behaviors as those developed through the training program. Although assessment procedures do not necessarily have to match instructional procedures exactly, the skills and skill levels assessed should be identical to those contained in the workplace basic-skills training program.

Before implementing a testing program, program providers should become knowledgeable about the legal ramifications of conducting basic-skills testing in the workplace. This information should also be made available to workers who are to be tested. It is not an unlawful employment practice for an employer to give and to act upon the results of a professionally developed ability test, provided that such a test, its administration, or actions upon the results are not designed, intended, or used to discriminate because of race, color, religion, sex, or national origin. The key requirements imposed on an employer's use of a standardized test are that

- The test must be professionally developed
- The test cannot be designed, intended, or used to discriminate
- The test must be validated.

The U.S. Supreme Court and the lower federal courts have imposed additional "job-relatedness" requirements on such tests, which are that the tests must

- Not have the *effect* of discriminating based on race, color, religion, sex, or national origin
- Be shown to have been validated through professional validation studies, i.e., to ensure that the test accurately predicts or measures what it claims
- Be job-related, that is, it must measure a person's ability to perform a specific job
- Not exclude or disqualify a disproportionate number of protected minorities or women

If a test fails any one or more of these validation requirements, the employer is still entitled to show that use of the test is justified by "business necessity."

The Civil Rights Act of 1991 established new rules concerning "disparate impact" cases that charge discrimination based on the assertion that an employment practice impacts negatively on one group to a greater extent than on other groups. If an employer has utilized a device such as a basic-skills standardized test, an employee or applicant may attempt to show that its use has resulted in an "adverse impact" on the group or groups of which the plaintiff is a member. The employer must demonstrate that the challenged basic-skills test is required by "business necessity" and must also *prove* that the test is job-related for the position in question and consistent with business necessity. The job criteria must have a demonstrable relationship to successful performance of the jobs for which they are used.[37,38]

An employer who administers a standardized basic-skills test to employees and has knowledge of individual scores may also be held liable if an employee with documented low-level reading abilities is injured in an area where safety signs or information (such as material safety data sheets) are written at a higher difficulty level.

None of the commercially published standardized instruments currently available tests *applied basic-skills processes as they are used in performance of actual job tasks.* Instead, they test academic uses of basic skills. Some standardized tests include items that test knowledge of employability skills (e.g., résumé writing, interviewing, completing job applications) and many contain work problems about workers, but these tests measure knowledge of the *what* rather than the *how* of mental strategies for applying basic skills to job situations. It is risky for an employer to administer such tests because of the difficulties that would be incurred in attempting to *prove* that the tests were job-related. (Also see Chap. 9, Training and the Law.)

If the primary reason for conducting assessment of basic skills in the workplace is to determine which workers should participate in workplace basic-skills training, criteria other than the results of a standardized basic skills test should be considered. Optional procedures include employee self-evaluation and requests to participate, supervisor recommendations, job-performance ratings, or training test results.

Designing a Multistranded Workplace Basic-Skills Training Program

The development of functional context basic-skills training courses requires the creation of customized sessions that use actual job materials and situations to teach higher-level thinking skills and applied basic skills. The courses may also utilize commercial educational materials along with customized instruction to provide additional practice and to support basic-skills operations. Designing a blueprint for the development of basic-skills training materials can be accomplished through careful analysis of the results of literacy tasks analyses conducted in the workplace. Resulting courses of instruction address training needs categorized either by job functions or by skill applications that transect many varied job tasks. The courses should be made up of units of instruction that follow a standard format.

Gather Information. Before materials can be written, the information gathered from work-site investigations must be organized and analyzed so that course or session content can be determined. Specific training objectives and contextual vehicles for instruction need to be identified. The documented results of literacy task analyses are the primary sources of information to consider when a training plan is being organized. Because the job tasks analyzed are those that were identified as *critical* to job performance, they should be the focal points of training materials development. This analysis is the first step in creating an instructional blueprint. The remaining steps in the design process enable the training developer to refine the instructional plan.

Tailor Content. The second step in the design process is to tailor the training content to fit the time parameters for delivery. Many times the analyzed task(s) will be too complex to address in one session and will need to be broken into subunits. Examination of the subsets of cognitive activities that make up the basic-skills applications list derived from documented LTAs and job materials will suggest natural breaking points for dividing the training into manageable units. To facilitate training, it is recommended that complex tasks or subtask be treated in short, individual sessions. The content identified during step 1 must be trimmed or expanded and broken into the appropriate number of time blocks, or training sessions, available for use. Adjusting for actual ability levels is the next step of the design process. A good starting estimate for preliminary session planning is an average of 10 hours of delivered training for each complete task on an LTA, including all subtasks. This estimate must later be adjusted, since critical job tasks vary greatly in complexity and in the time needed for effective delivery of training in the applied skills that support them. Unless the scope of basic-skills training is extremely narrow, a minimum of 30 hours per course is generally necessary for measurable gains in job performance to be realized.

Assess Ability Levels. The third step is to determine the ability level(s) of the targeted user population. This assessment provides the information needed to ensure that time lines for addressing concepts, types of activities, and difficulty levels of any written directions are designed to maximize employee engagement and learning. Employee participants who are functioning at low ability levels in basic skills, or whose proficiency in English is limited, will need additional support and more time to master course content than intermediate-level trainees. If the majority of the population targeted for program participation is identified as belonging to a special learning population, such as those who lack English proficiency, the course will require adaptation for their use. Training sessions for that group should be planned in smaller incremental steps of content treatment for skills mastery. Such a design revision may result in a sequence of shorter, more focused courses that lead up to a skill mastery over a longer period of time. Special delivery techniques should be considered for training that population, such as use of concrete, manipulative materials, one-on-one or small-group tutorial sessions, or special learning strategies such as the "language experience" approach.

Select Media. The fourth step in the training materials design process is the selection of a delivery medium (or media) that facilitates initial learning and the transfer of learning to job performance. Basic-skills training should achieve a fine balance between training in portable mental-processing strategies for applied basic skills and using contextual examples that show employee-participants where and how skills might be used after initial training. The guiding role should always be to *develop training materials that most nearly resemble the context in which the basic skills are used to perform on the job.* The primary reason for developing functionally contextual materials is to facilitate the transfer of learning from training to skill application during job performance. The more closely instruction resembles actual performance conditions, the higher the expected level of learning transfer.

Create Format.   The final step in building a basic-skills training design is to create a session format for the training unit(s). The use of a standard organization for sessions makes possible quick, uniform development of all units; facilitates trainer preparation; and provides a vehicle for monitoring and, if needed, reworking materials to improve their quality and effectiveness. The choice of a session format often depends upon the options available for training delivery. If employee participants are to use materials independently in a self-paced or self-study program, the materials will need to contain explicit directions and feedback. The developer may or may not assume the role of trainer. Taking time to thoroughly script sessions offers wider flexibility in training delivery by multiple individuals and promotes replication or sale of a course to another company division or location. Session scripts also provide a permanent record of training expectations and/or activities that aid in program monitoring, evaluation, and revision. A structured session format also provides employee participants with an underlying framework that organizes activities and sequence of components subconsciously.

The similarity of the processing performed during training sessions and in the tasks to which learning is to be transferred must be high for subsequent retrieval and application of knowledge to be achieved. This similarity is accomplished by providing instruction in basic-skills applications and strategies as they are actually used in performing job tasks. The training materials developer assumes that employee participants' knowledge and life experiences can provide a bridge between new and old information.

Delivering Workplace Basic-Skills Training

Participants who achieve program goals and improve job performance as a result often comment that they value these achievements because they meet personal goals as well as those of the company. Research demonstrates that those participants who are attracted to such training programs and who complete instruction are the ones who perceive program content to be relevant to their needs.

The name given to a workplace basic-skills training program becomes its identity at the work site and in the community. It is how people will refer to the program. For this reason, it is important to select a name that connotes a positive program image. Unfortunately, the words *basic skills* or *literacy* or even *education* in the title project a negative image. Workers do not want to participate in training that may label them as deficient, dumb, or in need of remediation. They do not want to be looked down upon or pitied. To avoid such a stigma, choose a program name that denotes opportunities for growth and improved job performance.

A clear, concise presentation of program goals provides guidance to potential participants who may be deciding whether or not to enroll in or fully commit themselves to the program. Program overview presentations for workers and supervisory personnel should be scheduled and conducted to outline goals and contents of customized functional context instruction. Explanations need to demonstrate how workplace basic-skills programs are developed from real job situations and materials and how they will provide training in strategies used by the best workers to apply what they know to performing tasks.

During the start-up or pilot phase of a program, there may be only a limited number of course offerings available. To demonstrate results that prove the program can impact performance and is worth expanding and investing in on a larger scale, the developer should work with recruiters such as training managers or supervisors. It is possible to set separate goals for different strands of a program so that different progress outcomes are anticipated for participants of various departmental or ability levels.

Throughout program operation, monitoring activities should occur too. The effectiveness of training design depends not only on content but also on delivery. Any complete workplace basic-skills program should contain components that prepare and support trainers and enable participants to enter and exit the program based on levels of skill mastery.

The use of job materials as a vehicle for training in applied basic skills and the thinking strategies that accompany them during job task performance is more than likely a new concept for workplace trainers. Trainers assigned to deliver a basic-skills program bring with them a wide range of background experiences and abilities. To ensure successful program implementation, a comprehensive train-the-trainer program should be prepared to meet the needs of each training staff member.

Evaluating Results

Evaluation should be an integral part of any workplace basic-skills program. The evaluation design controls requirements for and methods of data collection. The data collected is used to determine the cumulative outcomes of program cycles in relation to the goals set during the program's design. Properly carried out, the process of workplace basic-skills training evaluation should provide information that improves the effectiveness of program design, development, implementation, and operation.[39] It also should provide hard data that identifies indicators of program effectiveness, measures change in terms of those indicators, and works toward establishing program standards from the results.[40]

A *quality indicator* is a variable that reflects effective and efficient performance. For example, if an applied math skills course were taught to support the use of statistical process control (SPC) in the workplace, a quality indicator might be a worker's ability to plot production-monitoring data on a run chart accurately. A *performance measure* is the datum used to determine the quantitative levels of performance. For example, the measure for the indicator of accurately plotting production monitoring data on an SPC run chart might be the number of errors found on data charts plotted by the worker. A *performance standard* is a measure with a specific numeric criterion or level of performance tied to it. Standards define levels of accepted performance on the measure. They may be established for a single point in time or to measure increases in performance over time. For example, a standard may be set for the maximum number of errors acceptable in plotted data on SPC run charts; or a measure may be established as a preprogram standard to be compared to a postprogram measure to determine whether a new standard for fewer errors can be set.

Quality indicators provide precise vehicles for evaluating the success of a workplace basic-skills training program in meeting its stated goals. Performance standards are more difficult to use because they compare program results to preconceived or preestablished levels of performance. For individual programs concerned with feedback on achievement of goals, they are primarily of use in comparing one program cycle to others over time.

Each workplace basic-skills training program designed in response to company or worker needs is unique because no two organizations have exactly the same set of critical job tasks to be addressed by instruction. For this reason, the evaluation of workplace basic-skills training needs to measure program effectiveness independently, that is, by comparing each actual program to its own stated goals, rather than comparing it to other training programs. When an evaluation model is being designed, it is important to consider the questions for which the evaluation is to help provide answers by supplying relevant information, the relationships of program activities and goals to those questions, and techniques that can obtain evidence to draw conclusions about the program areas under investigation. Selecting local program indicators and developing data collection instruments and procedures for measuring changes in those indicators are the core of any good workplace basic-skills training program evaluation. Analyzing, interpreting, and reporting the data obtained in ways that are meaningful to program decision makers and stakeholders is also an important component of evaluation. If the goal of workplace basic-skills training is to improve the productivity of the labor force, it should be viewed as an integral part of organizational human resource development—as a long-term investment in the building of a highly skilled workforce. Evaluation design, as a part of such a program, needs to determine program effectiveness according to the same value yardsticks that are applied to other training endeavors.

A means for costing changes in the workplace due to training can be found in the process of evaluating the value added to employees. The value-added approach assumes that there is a need for certain skills, e.g., basic skills, in areas relevant to the work performed, that there is motivation to do the job, and that there is an opportunity for the skills to be used to perform the job. With the value-added approach, pretraining analysis must be conducted to estimate the position of the individual targeted participants in comparison to levels of basic skills and motivation typical of employees who are doing the same kind of work. If employees are thought to have the motivation but lack some important basic skills, then the investment should be in employee basic-skills training. Postprogram measures of basic skills and motivation are collected and changes are calculated. Let's assume that managers and supervisors can accurately rate their employees, that participants are given opportunity and encouragement to use the newly mastered basic skills, and that the basic skills required for successful job performance have been accurately identified and are being taught in training; then value-added evaluation can be used to estimate the return on training investment.

Unlike cost-benefit analysis, which summarizes all outcomes in monetary terms and omits those things that cannot be expressed in dollars or other currency units, the value-added process describes outcomes in their own terms and then concludes that these do or do not imply significant increase in skills or motivation to perform work.[41,42]

The CIPP evaluation model is reported by ASTD to be receiving widespread use in a number of organizations.[43] The name is an acronym derived from the four areas of evaluation it addresses: *context, input, process,* and *product.* Developed in 1971 by educational researchers Daniel Stufflebeam and Egon Guba as part of Phi Delta Kappa's National Study Committee on Evaluation, the model is designed to provide feedback to program decision makers. It meshes well with traditional organizational training evaluation and with the value-added training evaluation model. Originally put forth as a means for evaluating reading

The CIPP Evaluation Model	
Context	Attempts to review and clarify the underlying philosophy and goals of a workplace basic-skills training program. Answers the question: *To what extent are the goals of key program players congruent or divergent?*
Input	Determines whether or not required resources exist. Answers the question: *To what extent are basic-skills training program resources adequate and appropriately utilized?*
Process	Compares workplace basic-skills training activities to program goals. Answers the question: *To what extent are program development and implementation being carried out in accordance with program goals?*
Product	Attempts to examine workplace basic-skills training program outcomes as defined by program objectives for participants and for the organization. Answers the question: *To what extent are program goals being met?*

Figure 39-4. The CIPP evaluation model.

programs, the CIPP model provides a framework for clarifying workplace basic-skills program goals and objectives, observing whether or not they have been achieved, and producing information that can be used by program decision makers to improve the basic-skills training program's capability to achieve its goals. The CIPP evaluation model has been used to evaluate numerous workplace basic-skills training programs across the country. The model poses a series of research-type questions in each of four areas (see Fig. 39-4).

Use of the CIPP model enables evaluation of workplace basic-skills training against its own goals, independent from comparisons with other programs. It also allows developers to conduct a responsive evaluation that provides feedback to all stakeholder groups.

A variety of data collection techniques can be used with these sources: To create effective data collection instruments, develop documents that are user-friendly for both respondents and evaluators. All items should be field-tested before they are used in instruments for gathering information. Preprogram evaluation planning is extremely important. Before implementing the delivery of a workplace basic-skills training program, it is critical to collect baseline data pertaining to the existing pretraining conditions. This data provides the evaluator with a point of reference with which to compare all posttraining results.

Workplace basic-skills training evaluation reports should be organized around the information needs of the users. The program stakeholders should be the recipients of interim reports; and their concerns should be addressed by the contents. When compiling information for an interim report, the compiler should remember that addressing current issues and providing progress updates are the main purposes for generating the reports. *The* final report should contain a description of the workplace basic skills program and evaluation design, along with data, conclusions, and recommendations.

Summary

Workplace basic-skills training programs that work meet the need for employee training in thinking strategies and basic-skills applications used to perform job tasks. They are different from traditional adult basic education because they provide training for skills in the context in which they will be used. They are also different from technical training because they teach the applications of basic skills used to perform job tasks and not the content of the tasks themselves. The most effective programs are those that link instruction with specific job materials and situations; that is, they teach skill applications as they are actually used on the job. This theory of instruction is referred to as the *functional context* approach. It works because the training in strategies and skills closely resembles their application to job situations. This approach enables almost direct transfer of basic-skills training to job performance and prevents attrition of newly acquired skills by building awareness of opportunities for their immediate use and practice on the job.

Functional context basic-skills training materials are not readily available off the shelf. That is, materials for workplace basic-skills training programs almost always must be custom-designed to fit the requirements of particular job tasks critical to a company's profit and competitiveness. They require time and resources to develop and implement. Critical company job tasks must be identified and then analyzed to determine how literacy skills are used in their performance. Training materials must then be developed based on the results of this analysis.

Developing a workplace basic-skills training program requires a substantial investment of time and effort. To be effective, training materials should contain information and exercises that assist workers with mastery of basic-skill applications for critical job tasks. These materials also need to match the ability levels of the employee participants who will use them. For this reason, it is important to determine the ability levels of potential training participants before beginning to design training content. Any instruments that are used for measuring basic-skills levels of employees need to be in compliance with legal guidelines for testing in the workplace. Formal testing with professionally developed standardized basic-skills tests should not be used unless the instruments have been validated for use in a specific workplace and have been determined to be an absolute necessity.

The goals of workplace basic-skills training target joint survival of the employer and employees. Participating employees who achieve program goals and improve job performance often comment that they value these achievements as meeting personal goals as well as those of the company. Research demonstrates that participants who are attracted to programs and who complete instruction are those who perceive course content as relevant to their needs. In addition to the relevance of instruction, other incentives used for recruiting and retaining workers frequently include full pay or partial pay for class time, bonuses and/or recognition for course completion, and so on. The most successful programs are those in which management and employees jointly commit themselves to the program to meet the emerging challenges of the workplace.

Each workplace basic-skills training program designed in response to company needs is unique because no two organizations have exactly the same set of critical job tasks to be addressed by training. For this reason, evaluation of workplace basic-skills training should measure program effectiveness by comparing the actual program to its stated goals and determining the value added to employee skills rather than by comparing it to other programs. The results of program evaluation can be used for various purposes, depending on the evaluation design. One good responsive evaluation model for measuring workplace basic-skills training program effectiveness is the CIPP (context-input-process-product) model. The CIPP model provides a means for clarifying program goals and objectives, observing whether or not they have been achieved, and producing information that can be used by program decision makers to improve the training's capacity to achieve its goals. Evaluation activities for investigating program effectiveness should examine program data from several points of view in order to corroborate results. Data collection forms and methods might include interviews, observations, surveys, participant scores on training exercises and tests, and so on. Reports resulting from workplace basic-skills training evaluations should present the data collected, draw conclusions using the data as evidence, and make recommendations for actions that can reasonably be undertaken to promote program continuation, expansion, and improvement.

References

1. Lund, L., and E. McGuire, *Literacy in the Workforce,* The Conference Board, New York, 1990.
2. Diehl, W., and L. Mikulecky, "The Nature of Reading at Work," *Journal of Reading, 24,* 1980, pp. 221–227.
3. Philippi, J. W., "Matching Literacy to Job Training: Some Applications from Military Programs," *Journal of Reading, 31*(7), 1988, pp. 658–666.
4. Sticht, T., *A Program of Army Functional Job Reading Training: Development, Implementation and Delivery Systems, Final Report,* HumRRO Report No. FR-WD (CA)-75-7, Human Resources and Research Organization, Alexandria, VA, 1975a.
5. Philippi, J. W., *Literacy at Work: The Workbook for Program Developers,* Simon & Schuster Workplace Resources, New York, 1991, pp. 211–329.
6. Diehl, W., *Functional Literacy as a Variable Construct: An Examination of Attitudes, Behaviors, and Strategies Related to Occupational Literacy,* doctoral dissertation, Indiana University, Bloomington, IN, 1980.
7. Mikulecky, L., N. Shanklin, and D. Caverly, *Adult Reading Habits, Attitudes, and Motivations: A Cross-Sectional Study,* Monograph in Language and Reading Series, No. 2, School of Education, Indiana University, Bloomington, IN, 1979.
8. Philippi, J. W., "Formative Evaluation of Basic Skills Education Program/Career Skills Education Program Reading, *Self-Evaluation of the HSCP and BSEP/CSEP Contract, 22 September '86–31 March '87,* a report presented to Army Continuing Education Services, U.S. Army Europe, Leimen, W. Germany (Contract No. DAJA37-86-D-008).
9. Rush, R., A. Moe, and R. Storlie, *Occupational Literacy Education,* International Reading Association, Newark, DE, 1986.
10. Sharon, A., "What Do Adults Read?" *Reading Research Quarterly, 9,* 1973–1974, pp. 148–149.
11. Sticht, T., *Reading for Working: A Functional Literacy Anthology,* Human Resources and Research Organization, Alexandria, VA, 1957b.
12. Dreher, M., and J. Guthrie, "Cognitive Processes in Textbook Search Tasks," *Reading Research Quarterly, 25,* 1990, pp. 323–339.
13. Kirsch, I., and J. Guthrie, "Prose Comprehension and Text Search as a Function of Reading Volume," *Reading Research Quarterly, 19,* 1984, pp. 331–342.
14. Kirsch, I., and P. Mosenthal, "Exploring Document Literacy: Variables Underlying the Performance of Young Adults," *Reading Research Quarterly, 25,* 1990, pp. 5–31.
15. Mikulecky, L., and D. Winchester, "Job Literacy and Job Performance Among Nurses at Varying Employment Levels," *Adult Education Quarterly, 34,* 1983, pp. 1–15.
16. Mikulecky, L., "Job Literacy: The Relationship between School Preparation and Workplace Actuality," *Reading Resource Quarterly,* vol. 17, pp. 400–419.
17. Mikulecky, L., J. Ehlinger, and A. Meenan, *Training for Job Literacy Demands: What Research Applies to Practice,* The Pennsylvania State University Institute for the Study of Adult Literacy, University Park, 1987.

18. Perl, S., "The Composing Process of Unskilled College Writers," *Research in the Teaching of English, 13,* 1979, pp. 317–336.

19. Hayes, J., and L. Flower, "Identifying the Organization of Writing Processes," in L. Gregg and E. Steinberg, eds., *Cognitive Processes in Writing,* Lawrence Erlbaum Associates, Hillsdale, NJ, 1980, pp. 3–30.

20. Rumelhart, D., "Schemata: The Building of Blocks of Cognition," in R. Spiro, B. Bruce, and W. Brewer, eds., *Theoretical Issues in Reading Comprehension,* Lawrence Erlbaum Associates, Hillsdale, NJ, 1980, pp. 33–58.

21. Stein, N., and C. Glenn, "An Analysis of Story Comprehension in Elementary School Children," in R. Freedle, ed., *New Directions in Discourse Processing,* vol. 2, Ablex Publishing, Norwood, NJ, 1979, pp. 53–120.

22. Henry, J., and S. Raymond, *Basic Skills in the U.S. Workforce,* Center for Public Resources, New York, 1982.

23. Kirsch, I., and A. Jungeblut, *Literacy Profiles of America's Young Adults,* National Assessment of Educational Progress, Report No. 16-PL-02, Educational Testing Service, Princeton, NJ, 1986.

24. Kloosterman, P., and H. Harty, *Need Sensing, Assessing, and Validation for Science, Mathematics, Computer, and Foreign Language Education in the State of Indiana: Final Report,* Indiana University School of Education, Bloomington, IN, 1986.

25. Kloosterman, P., and S. Gillie, "Basic Mathematical Skills for Vocational Education," in H. Harty, P. Kloosterman, L. Mikulecky, and J. Pershing, dirs., *The Impact and Potential of Basic Skills Applications in Vocational/Technical Education: The Basic Skills Work-Education Bridge,* Project No. 395-87-4700, prepared for the Indiana State Board of Vocational and Technical Education, Indianapolis, IN, 1987–1988.

26. Ibid.

27. Karmos, J., and A. Karmos, *Strategies for Problem Solving,* prepared for the Illinois State Board of Education, Department of Adult, Vocational and Technical Education, Springfield, IL, 1986.

28. Chi, M. T. H., and R. Glaser, *Problem-Solving Ability,* Research Technical Report No. LRDC-1985/6, prepared for the National Institute of Education, Washington, DC, 1985.

29. Pratzner, F., *Occupational Adaptability and Transferable Skills: Project Final Report,* Information Series No. 129, prepared for the National Center for Research in Vocational Education, The Ohio State University, Columbus, 1978.

30. Singer, R., "To Error or Not to Err? A Question for the Instruction of Psychometric Skills," *Review of Educational Research, 47,* 1977, pp. 479–498.

31. Altman, J., *Transferability of Vocational skills: Review of Literature and Research,* Information Series No. 103, prepared for the National Center for Research in Vocational Education, The Ohio State University, Columbus, 1976.

32. Wiant, A., *Transferable Skills: The Employer's Viewpoint,* prepared for the National Center for Research in Vocational Education, The Ohio State University, Columbus, 1977.

33. Resnick, L., *Skilled Workers Are Thinking Workers: The New Basics in American Education,* testimony before the Congress of the United States Subcommittee on Education and Health, Joint Economic Committee, October 5, 1987, Washington, DC.

34. Bransford, J., and J. Franks, "Toward a Framework for Understanding Learning," in G. Bower, ed., *The Psychology of Learning and Motivation,* vol. 10, Academic Press, New York, 1976.

35. Tulving, E., and D. Thompson, "Encoding Specificity and Retrieval Processes in Episodic Memory," *Psychological Review, 80,* 1973, pp. 352–373.

36. Gick, M., and K. Holyoak, "The Cognitive Basis of Knowledge Transfer," in S. M. Cormier and J. D. Hagman, eds., *Transfer of Learning: Contemporary Research and Applications,* Educational Technology Series, U.S. Army Research Institute for the Behavioral and Social Sciences, Alexandria, VA, 1987.

37. Douglas, B., and C. Williams, *Selected Legal Considerations Regarding Employee Literacy and Aptitude Testing,* Jackson and Walker, L.I.P., Dallas, TX, 1992.

38. Philippi, J. W., *Legal Considerations for Workplace Basic Skills Testing,* U.S. Department of Education, Office of Adult and Vocational Education, Washington, DC, 1992.

39. Sticht, T., *Evaluating National Workplace Literacy Programs,* U.S. Department of Education, Office of Adult and Vocational Education, Washington, DC, 1991.

40. Condelli, L., *Quality Indicators, Measures, and Performance Standards,* U.S. Department of Education, Office of Adult and Vocational Education, Washington, DC, 1992.

41. Bramley, P., *Evaluating Training Effectiveness: Translating Theory into Practice,* McGraw-Hill, London, 1991.

42. Philippi, J. W., *How Do You Know If It's Working? Evaluating the Effectiveness of Workplace Literacy Programs,* U.S. Department of Education, Office of Vocational and Adult Education, Washington, DC, 1992.

43. Galvin, J. G., "What Can Trainers Learn from Educators About Evaluating Management Training?" *Training and Development Journal,* August 1983, p. 52.

40

Computer Skills Training

Sam L. Warfel

Sam L. Warfel is National Technical Education Manager for AT&T's Professional Development Centers, a group which provides PC software training for over 70,000 employees and customers in more than 40 classrooms nationwide. He is responsible for the development of the instructors and curricula for the technical PC training offerings of the center. He began working with the AT&T Professional Development Centers in 1987. Dr. Warfel has developed an approach to teaching software which he calls concept-based learning, an approach which emphasizes the learning of concepts over keystrokes. More recently, he has been developing techniques for hands-on computer software training based on stimulating the right brain and creating a positive learning environment. His presentations on using right-brain techniques and multisensory experiences have been enthusiastically received at the Computer Training and Support Conferences. He has also made presentations to TechView, Price Waterhouse international conferences, the Silicon Valley Chapter of ASTD, and to the International Computer Training Association. More recently, he has been working with the Lotus Notes software, having become a Lotus Notes consultant and Lotus Notes certified instructor. He has also spearheaded the Bell Labs Technical Education Center's successful application for Lotus Authorized Center status. His undergraduate degree is in Biblical literature and he has master's degrees in English and linguistics and a Ph.D. in linguistics. He was a minister for 10 years, a university professor for 10 years, and for the past 12 years, involved in PC software training.

The personal computer, once a curiosity on the desk of that strange fellow down in Budgets and Results, now sits on most employees' desks and amplifies the productivity of everyone from the clerk to the president. E-mail (electronic mail) has grown to become as much an indispensable business tool (and sometimes nuisance) as voice messaging. No longer are presentations viewed with favor if illustrated with hand-lettered overhead transparencies; one must arrive at a meeting fully equipped with a laptop computer complete with a full-color, graphically enhanced, bullet-besplattered slide show to plug into a monitor projection system.

Software has also changed in the last decade. Most PC-based software has become simultaneously more complex and simpler to use. In 1981, the Lotus 1-2-3 spreadsheet software fit onto a single floppy diskette along with the operating system. Today's Windows-based spreadsheets consume over 30 megabytes of hard-disk space and require the latest and fastest central processing unit (CPU) to work effectively. While Windows has made the user interface simpler, maintaining a Windows system is much more complicated than altering a few lines in an AUTOEXEC.BAT or CONFIG.SYS file.

In like fashion, end-user computer training has come a long way since Lotus 1-2-3 training was done in three hours with a two-page handout in a spare conference room with two students to a machine by someone in the department who seemed to "have a knack" for computers. Today typical off-the-shelf courses for standard application software devote 6 hours to basic orientation and 18 to 24 hours beyond to learn the more powerful features of the software. The manual for the classroom student may contain 100 pages for a one-day course with desktop-published pages filled with screen captures, icons, tables, indices, and appendices. Today's training is most often done by an in-house dedicated computer-training professional or, increasingly, by an outside vendor who has been contracted to provide the manuals and instructors.

Many of the issues which face computer training are the same as those of any training program. However, computer training includes a number of problems which are unique. The following provides a path for anyone responsible for the success of computer training within an organization.

The following diagram indicates the relationships between the major phases of developing an effective training program for personal-computer skills and knowledge. As implied in the diagram, management support is essential in all phases of the planning and implementation of a training program. The importance of management support is discussed in detail below.

The significance of the sequencing of events in developing a training program cannot be overemphasized. Attempts to go directly to the design and delivery phases without laying a proper foundation of management support and conducting a thorough needs assessment are doomed to disappointment or outright failure from the outset.

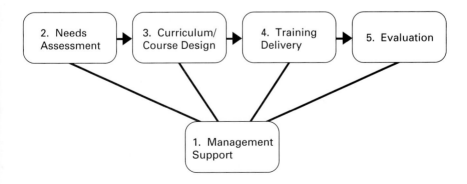

Phase 1: Getting Management Support for Training

The phrase "change management" as popularized by Daryl Connor[1] begins with the assumption that organizations will change and that it is possible to limit the negative effects of that change through enlightened management of the change process. Training stands as one of the major tools in effecting and managing change.

Because computers are at the forefront of technological innovation, changes involving computers require more careful and intensive management than most other types of organizational change. There are several reasons why this is so:

> While computers enable one employee to do work which would have required two or three employees in an earlier time, that productivity suffers while the employee is learning software or changing to new software.

> Software changes involve the fundamental tools which employees use to do their jobs. Employees naturally have an affinity to the tools they use and are often reluctant to change the habits they have painstakingly acquired, whether that involves a change from a manual to a computer-based system or from one software package to another.

> The use of computer tools is dependent on the acquisition of hardware and software. The timing of this acquisition is critical in planning any training and must be taken into account as part of managing the change.

Successful training also depends on good change management. At times training is given the lion's share of responsibility for organizational change. However, while training is certainly a major agent of change, managers must play their role as sponsors of the change.

Training departments most often are given the responsibility for training without having had any input into the decision to computerize or what software to purchase. The training department can be of enormous help in deciding whether, how, and when to make software changes.

The best training results when the trainee's supervisor has clearly defined his training objectives for sending the trainee to training and supports the trainee after the class with specific projects which require the skills learned. In a 1993 study by Logical Operations, Terry Boothman and Harvey Feldstein[2] determined that the best predictor of high performance after training was the support and clear direction of a trainee's manager. Those students who had managers who made clear what they expected from the training were significantly higher performers than those who attended training without clear management direction.

Training should be scheduled to coincide with software rollout. Training is often ineffective because a class has been given months before the software arrived or months after the software was installed and employees are expected to be using the software.

Phase 2: Assessing the Training Needs

As in all good training, it is essential to determine the needs of those to be trained in computers. The information from a good needs assessment not only helps to determine whether training is needed but also guides the type and extent of training. In particular, needs assessments serve the following functions:

Purpose of Analyzing Needs

Identify Needs.   As the phrase "needs assessment" implies, before a training program can be designed and implemented, the needs of the target audience of the training must be determined. This task is not as easy within the area of computer skills as in other skill areas. Oftentimes the potential computer users do not know enough about computers to know what they need to know or what a computer could do if they knew how to use one. There will be more on this problem later.

Provide Data for Evaluation.   There is increasing pressure on training departments to justify their existence. As organizations continue to tighten their budgetary belts, upper management requires more evidence of a return on their investment in training. The data collected in a well-designed needs assessment project can be used as a base for showing the improvement after training.

Build Participant Commitment.   Getting input on training needs helps build a buy-in on the part of the target audience. If computer users say they need to know a particular subject and the training offers this information, they have tacitly committed themselves to supporting the training initiative.

Generate Management Support.   As Connor indicates in his writings on change management, one of the most common reasons for the failure of a change program is a lack of effective support on the part of the sponsors of the change. By being able to document the need for training with the results of a needs assessment, training departments can get the sponsorship they need for the training.

Increase Training Department Credibility.   John Noonan, in his article "How to Escape Corporate America's Basement,"[3] accurately portrays the status of most training organizations in corporate America. His rule for finding the training department in any company is to go to the basement and look around the loading dock area. While this may be an overstatement, training departments are hardly the power brokers in most organizations. However, by doing a thorough needs assessment study and presenting the results in a succinct, usable form, training departments can build credibility with other departments.

The Nature of Needs Assessment

Simply put, a needs assessment involves calculating the following formula:

What the employees need to know	(Skill-knowledge requirement)−
What the employees know	(Current skill-knowledge)=
What the employees need to be taught	(Target skill-knowledge)

Thus, the needs assessment consists of two studies: the skill-knowledge requirement analysis (what they need to know) and the current skill-knowledge analysis (what they already know). Even under the best of circumstances, designing and implementing these analytic processes is difficult and time-consuming. However, in computer training there are several additional factors which muddy the requirement and skills-analysis waters.

Conducting Skill-Knowledge
Requirement Analysis

To do an adequate skill-knowledge requirement analysis requires information about the work done in each employee position within the training target group. In the case of computer training it also requires a knowledge of the capabilities of the various types of software in general and the specific software packages being used within the organization in particular. Doing this analysis raises special problems.

1. Gathering the Data.   Questionnaires are the most used instruments for gathering information from computer users about what skills they need to know to do their jobs. These are typically distributed among the employees in the hopes that a significant number will be returned and that the employees have enough information to complete the questionnaires intelligently.

The major advantage of using questionnaires for gathering skill-knowledge requirement information is that they are relatively easy and inexpensive to create and analyze. Properly administered questionnaires also ask the people who do the work what they need to know, thus gathering the data from the best source.

The major disadvantage of using questionnaires is that often employees don't understand enough about software to know how a particular type of software could help them do their job. Because of this problem, self-reporting questionnaires on training may not reveal real skill-knowledge requirements. Having a software expert do a task analysis of each job description can provide more accurate data but at considerable expense and time.

A less expensive approach to solving this problem is to conduct short demonstrations of software packages before distributing the questionnaires to give the employees some sense of the features and power of the software which they are expected to use. With this background the employees can then complete the questionnaires with a better sense of what they could do with adequate training.

Another technique for determining skill needs is the group interview. With this technique a software expert and a training professional meet with groups of 10 or 12 employees from each target organization. With a well-constructed interview plan which may include some demonstration time, these interviewers can gather a significant amount of data within an hour or so.

The interview results are very helpful in determining the overall needs of the target population, but they do not identify the needs of specific job functions. Often group interviews are used to decide how to phrase questions on the questionnaires in a two-step process.

2. Analyzing the Results.   An overview of the results may be represented by job function in a matrix something like the following:

Job description	Data entry and retrieval knowledge	Development skills	System design skills
Clerk	✓		
Secretary	✓	✓	
Supervisor		✓	✓
Manager	✓		

For example, in the instance of spreadsheet software, employees with data entry and retrieval knowledge would only need to be trained to launch the software, open files, close files, enter and edit data, and perhaps print reports. Employees who require development skills would need to be able to create spreadsheets with appropriate formula, functions, formatting, and report forms. A system designer would not only develop spreadsheets but write macros to download data from a network, consolidate the data, and print reports.

The job-description column would, of course, be more descriptive of the organization and might be subdivided by department. Additional skill-knowledge levels might also be determined given knowledge of specific software and of the general character of the organization.

Two warnings are appropriate when skill-knowledge requirements are being determined:

1. Given the culture of most corporations it is natural to assume that managers need only the skills to retrieve data from computers. However, the interactive nature and ease of use of the latest PC software makes it not only feasible but highly desirable for even upper-level managers to have development skills so that they can "play" with the data. The ability to do immediate "what if?" analyses often leads to more questions, questions which would never arise if the results depended on a subordinate doing the work and returning with answers days later. The end result is better analyses and better decisions. Therefore, how-to development training may be useful for even the highest-level manager.

2. Another pitfall in analyzing the results of skill-knowledge requirement research is to limit the training of employees to the bare minimum skill or knowledge required to do their jobs. A higher return on training investment may result from giving employees more skill-knowledge than absolutely required. If employees know additional features of the software, they may use the additional tools to create innovations beyond what management may expect.

Conducting Current Skill-Knowledge Analysis

While the assessment of skill-knowledge requirements are focused on job functions, the current skill-knowledge analysis focuses on the individual employee who performs the functions. The objective of the current skill-knowledge instruments is to determine what each employee already knows or, more importantly, can do. Remember that the training needs can only be determined by comparing the job-function skill-knowledge requirements with the current skill-knowledge of each individual who is responsible for those functions.

1. Gathering the Data. Determination of the current skill level of employees is usually done either through self-reporting questionnaires or through actual tests of ability. While tests give a truer picture of the employees' ability, they are usually more time-consuming and more threatening to the group which will become the training department's customers. For an example of a self-reporting questionnaire which incorporates some elements of skill-knowledge requirement, see Fig. 40-1.

Before deciding on the instrument for gathering this data, it is necessary to determine if the employee is not using the software as a result of a lack of skill-knowledge (which training can address) or a lack of performance (which training cannot address). The clearest method for determining the reason for nonperformance is to use the following rule: If the person could perform the task in question on penalty of death, the problem is a lack of performance. If the person could not do the task, even under the gun, the problem is a lack of skill-knowledge.

Dealing with lack of performance requires looking at incentives, working environment, morale, availability of adequate tools, conflicting goals, insufficient time, etc. Training will not solve these problems. For the training department to

Work Performance

Traditional programs offer schedules of work processes, wage increases, and periodic evaluation and recording of an apprentice's progress. Apprentices work as employees. An apprentice's pay generally starts at about half that of a journey worker and increases at prescribed amounts periodically during the course of the apprenticeship. If the programs are cosponsored by trade unions, the apprentices are usually offered union memberships.

Programs are sponsored by employers or employer associations and sometimes involve the union. The sponsor plans, pays for, and helps administer the program through an apprenticeship committee. Once accepted into a program, the apprentice with the sponsor sign an apprenticeship agreement. The apprentice agrees to perform the work and complete the related studies. The sponsor agrees to make every effort to keep the apprentice employed and to comply to the standards established for the program.

The work in any given program can be physically demanding and technically difficult. Apprentices must show they are learning the trade or they may be dropped during the probationary period. Also, there are periodic examinations of the work and instruction records of the apprentice to determine her or his progress.

At the beginning of the program, apprentices often feel the work is slow and boring; later they may feel that their pay is less than they could earn elsewhere with the skills they have acquired. By the end of the apprenticeship, however, workers are fully trained journey-level workers and have the security of knowing they are already well-paid employees, their skills are in demand, and those skills are transferable to jobs across the country.

Training

In any apprenticeship program there are two kinds of training: on-the-job training and related technical instruction. Both kinds of training are important; on-the-job training teaches hands-on skills, and the related instruction, often in a classroom, gives the apprentice the knowledge and theory necessary to understand the skills.

Employers select workers to teach the on-the-job portion of the apprenticeship. These workers are thoroughly skilled in the occupations they teach and generally proceed as follows:

1. Check the apprentices' knowledge of the operation or process.
2. Demonstrate each process or step, emphasizing key elements and safety issues.
3. Watch apprentices perform the same process, giving assistance as needed.
4. Have the apprentices repeat the process until you are satisfied they can do it properly, safely, and by themselves.
5. Continue supervision and encourage questions on the learned process as apprentices move on to new processes.

The related instruction, or classroom learning, is often done in conjunction with local vocational schools and community colleges. This practice allows the apprentices to gain the knowledge they need as well as the opportunity to earn credits toward an associate degree. Larger companies sometimes have their own training departments to handle classroom instruction.

The following are two examples of apprenticeship programs showing the hours and weeks to complete certain skill units.

THE WORD FOR WINDOWS 6.0
SOFTWARE SKILLS EVALUATION

At the AT&T Professional Development Center we are committed to long term increased productivity and excellence in software education. The following questionnaire will aid us in placing you into the appropriate class according to your skill level and experience. Please complete all questions so that we may effectively determine your needs.

	NAME:
	COMPANY NAME:
	DEPARTMENT:
	DATE:

	How long have you used a PC?
	How long have you used Word For Windows?
	How many hours do you use Word For Windows in an average week?
	Have you had formal training on Word For Windows?
	If yes, What type of training was it?
	How long ago did you take training?

In the right column rate your experience level in each skill. *(Scale 1 to 10, where 10 is expert & 0 is no experience)*

	1.) Describing and using PC hardware components.	
	2.) Distinguishing between memory and storage.	
	3.) Understanding DOS and application software.	
	4.) Formatting and copying floppy disks.	
	5.) Creating, Renaming, and Deleting file names.	
	6.) Understanding common file extensions.	
	7.) Viewing and explaining directory listings.	
	8.) Creating and removing Subdirectories.	

Figure 40-1. Current skill-knowledge analysis form.

accept the responsibility for correcting performance problems is to set itself up to fail. The solutions to performance problems lie with management.

Another complication of assessing current skill-knowledge is that most organizations have employees who are using various software packages to do the same task. For example, an organization may have employees using three different word processing packages, all of which do essentially the same tasks. To add to the confusion, there may be three software revisions of each word processor in use at any given point in time. Therefore, the skill analysis instrument has to question not only the general knowledge of each software package but also the particular quirks of each software revision.

2. Analyzing the Results. By comparing the current skill-knowledge analysis result for each employee with the skill-knowledge requirement analysis

Complete the following chart by answering "Y/N" in the second column if this is function or skill you currently use or would like to use. In the right-hand column rate your experience level in this skill. *(Scale 1 to 10, where 10 is expert and 0 is no experience)*

	FUNCTION or SKILL	UTILIZE	SKILL LEVEL
	1. Create, save, and open documents.		
	2. Modify and correct your documents		
	3. Navigate efficiently through long documents.		
	4. Send text to the printer.		
	5. Use bold, italics, and other features.		
	6. Copy and Move text between documents.		
	7. Find and Replace text.		
	8. Use the Speller to correct the spelling of a document.		
	9. Use tabs and control alignment.		
	10. Work with Page Setup.		
	11. Work with multiple pages.		
	12. Use the Tool Bar.		
	13. Create a simple mail merge.		
	14. Create a table.		
	15. Create and edit headers and footers for a document.		
	16. Using the Automatic Text Entry feature.		
	17. Using Templates and Wizards.		
	18. Understanding section breaks.		
	19. Using Styles.		
	20. Working with columns.		
	21. Change fonts multiple times within a document.		
	22. Insert a graphic image into a document.		
	23. Working with Frames.		
	24. Adding visual impact with drawing.		

Figure 40-1. *(Continued).*

of her or his job function, both the type and extent of training needed can be determined. The result should be a list of employees who need training in the various skills for each software package. A simple tallying of this list provides the number of employees who need various levels of training for specific software.

Phase 3: Designing the Training Plan

Now that the training need has been established, the training plan can be designed. At the outset some investigation should be made into the alternative delivery options. These options are based on three parameters:

Location of the training

Type of training

Source of training materials

While we will consider these parameters separately, any final choices must be made within the context of the organization's budget, culture, history, etc. It will also be obvious that choices made on one parameter will have implications for choices along another parameter.

Location of the Training

Let us look first at where the training should take place.

In-House Classroom. Many larger organizations have their own in-house training rooms fully equipped with personal computers. In other cases ad hoc classrooms are created from conference rooms and warehouse areas to which trainees bring their own computers. The first solution is preferable, certainly in most cases. In either circumstance, having the training at the place of work has several advantages: trainees can easily reach the training, the trainers have their support systems available, and familiar surroundings create a comfortable learning environment. On the other hand, having the training so near the trainees' offices can introduce interruptions. Colleagues stick their heads into the training room with "emergencies." Breaks can also drag on as trainees check their voice mail or pop into their offices to type up a memo. Not only do these interruptions take time away from training, but they distract the trainees' attention from the focus of learning.

Off-Site Classroom. Because of the expense of having in-house training rooms, many organizations are contracting with outside vendors to deliver training in the vendors' classrooms. This approach reduces the distractions and may be less expensive when compared to building and maintaining PC classrooms. However, it complicates the logistics of offering courses which are less than a day long because of the travel time required.

Learning Laboratory. If the training to be offered is delivered through technology such as computer-based training or video and audio presentations, learning laboratories may be the answer. Typically, a learning laboratory is equipped with the necessary technology and staffed by a technologist-trainer who can assist the trainees. The cost for equipping a learning laboratory is usually less than the cost for equipping a classroom and can be staffed with fewer people. The major advantage of learning laboratories is that employees determine when they want to learn and for how long. The major weakness of this approach is motivating trainees to set aside the time and make the effort to come to the learning laboratory.

Desktop. Increasingly, training can take place on the trainees' desktops. A number of computer-based training programs can run on the average office personal computer. In addition, many of the newest software application packages include excellent tutorials and pop-up aids which allow users to learn at their own computer as they work. This approach adds no extra training cost beyond the cost of the software.

Type of Training

In conjunction with the decisions regarding the location of the training, the type of training must be taken into consideration. With the increasing power of computers and the accompanying decrease in costs, training departments have a widening variety of choices for delivery of training. The following are some of the major possibilities.

Instructor-Led Classroom Training. Traditionally, technical training has been done in a classroom with an instructor. Most often the instructor lectures, directs hands-on exercises, and supervises self-paced lab activities. For most PC users, this approach is still preferred. In fact, most training professionals (including multimedia developers) agree that having a "live" human instructor is more effective than other methods of training for teaching software applications. The student-instructor interaction provides the emotional support which is important for learning. Also, in the classroom, the student has the opportunity to ask questions which an instructor can clarify if necessary. The social setting of the classroom can also provide reinforcement and motivation for more effective learning. However, there are several problems with instructor-led training. By its very nature, classroom training is not designed with the individual in mind. Each learner has a preferred learning style which cannot be satisfied in a group of students with other learning styles. Students arrive in class from varied experience levels with software and different skill needs. Therefore, the instructor must inevitably compromise in trying to reach each individual with the most efficient training.

Computer-Based Training. Computer-based training (CBT) has been around since early in the history of computers. As personal computers have become more available and more powerful, CBT is enjoying a resurgence. The latest programs engulf the student in speech, music, full-motion video, and complex access to more information than most care to know. These multimedia training programs raise the possibility that each student can tailor the training to her or his need and access the information at the moment it is needed for just-in-time training. While more expensive to develop than courseware for instructor-led training, technology-delivered training is relatively inexpensive to deliver since it does not require a "live" instructor. The primary problem is getting the user focused on learning the software. Without the social atmosphere of the classroom, some users find it difficult to concentrate on the learning process.

Video- and Audiotape-Based Training. Tape-based training attempts to provide the presentation skill of the instructor in a form which can be repeated as needed. Most of the packages are used in conjunction with the software. That is, the student works at the computer under the direction of the instructor on the tape. The primary advantage of this type of training is that the training packages are inexpensive and each copy can be used by scores of learners with a minimum of equipment required. The training method suffers from the same problems as the CBT and, additionally, does not have the interactive capabilities of the CBT.

There are several factors to consider in deciding whether to use classroom training, video courses, multimedia, or CBT for software training.

Comfort and independence level of the students. The more confident and self-confident and independent the student, the more likely he or she will do well with technology-delivered training. Beginning software users will probably benefit from the "hand holding" of a classroom instructor.

How much hands-on activity does the training provide? Like learning to ride a bicycle, learning to use software requires that the student experience the learning. Watching the CBT program or the video instructor flit through keystrokes is no match for actually performing the keystrokes or "mousestrokes."

Does the training provide concept training?   Most computer users think that they need to learn which menus to access or which control keys to press. However, with the ease of use of most Windows-based applications there is little need to memorize where to click. The major problems users have with application software are conceptual. They do not understand how to set up their spreadsheet or how to relate fields in their database. Training which does not include a clear explanation of basic software concepts will fall short of expectations.

How interactive is the material?   The concept of the student being a passive vessel into which information is poured is inadequate for trainers who must teach users to use application software which is essentially a tool. The trainers can never know all the keystrokes a student will need to make. The learner must instead be thought of as a detective, constantly interacting with the software to solve problems. Training materials that do not require the learner to react will not succeed in their goal of developing a user who can build what is needed with the tools.

Source of Training Materials

The third element in designing the training plan is to determine the source of the training materials. This decision will be affected by and will affect the decisions concerning the location and type of training. The following are possible sources for training materials.

Develop In-House.   The primary advantage to developing training materials in-house is the opportunity to target exactly the skill set which was determined to be needed through the needs assessment process. The major disadvantage is the time and, therefore, the expense of course development. While the expense may be acceptable for the development of support materials for classroom training, the expense of developing a multimedia program can run into the hundreds of thousands of dollars.

Off-the-Shelf Commercial Products.   An entire training industry has grown around PC-application software training. For the most popular software there are dozens of choices of courseware for instructor-led classroom training, CBT courses, and audio-video courses. These off-the-shelf products are aimed at teaching the most-used functions of the software in order to reach the widest user audience. Also the exercises and examples will deal with a fictitious company—say, Acme Widgets. However, in most cases the features chosen will apply to most users and the leap from the Acme Widgets situation to the user's real-life one is not great if the emphasis of the training is on the concepts instead of the keystrokes. That is, it doesn't matter that a spreadsheet course teaches students to add apples when the students work with oranges, provided that the general technique of summing numbers is taught.

Contracted Customized Materials.   Many of the companies which create off-the-shelf products will also customize their materials to fit the particular needs of an organization. Increasingly, they also offer their instructor-led materials on diskette with a license for the purchasers to customize the materials and print their own manuals. There are also companies which specialize in developing and delivering customized training. While there is a cost factor to consider in contracting customized materials, doing so may still be less expensive than developing materials in-house.

Designing the Curriculum

Before the courses to be taught are designed, it is essential to develop an overview of the entire range of courses. Decisions must be made as to which topics (software functions) will be included in each course and how long each course will be. With commercially available classroom training materials, the curriculum for a particular software package typically consists of beginning, intermediate, and advanced levels, or levels 1, 2, and 3. However, for custom-developed training, a beginning level overview might be followed with classes which focus on job functions or similar software functions in short two- or three-hour courses. Whether the courses are developed in-house, used off the shelf, or customized, care must be taken to ensure that the sequencing of courses is appropriate to the needs of the target audience.

Designing the Course

Once the courses have been defined in terms of which software functions they will include, each course must be designed with the following elements taken into consideration.

Concepts.   What concepts are most difficult to grasp for a given software package? While it may appear that the objective of the training is to teach trainees a series of keystrokes, most learners of software have problems understanding the more general processes incorporated into the software. The keystrokes can be retrieved from on-line help systems or keyboard templates. For example, students have considerably more problems understanding the concepts involved with the mail-merge function of Word for Windows than remembering which menu to choose to perform a merge. Therefore, once identified, the key concepts of the software should be given prominence in the design of a course.

Learning Styles.   Consideration should also be given to different learning styles in the design of a course. A number of approaches to learning styles have been developed over the years. There are implications for learning styles in the Myer-Briggs analysis of personality types which have been described in a number of works.[4] (See Chap. 11, The Behavioral Sciences.) The Learning Style Inventory from the McBer[5] company also provides tools for understanding how people prefer to learn. Successful training takes these differences into account by including activities which appeal to each learning style at least in part of the course.

Emotional Elements.   Effective elements of training have also risen to prominence in the last few years through the recognition that how learners feel affects how well they learn. Effective approaches usually collected under the rubric of "accelerated learning" have become standard training techniques in a number of large corporations. Most of these techniques are based on studies of left- and right-brain functions and involve the use of music, physical analogies, bright colors, games, simulations, props, etc.

Adult Learning Principles.   Good training design should also incorporate elements which recognize the special needs of adult learners. Malcolm Knowles[6] and others have done considerable work in the last three decades to determine how adult learning differs from juvenile learning. Two of the most important conclusions are that adults need to have practical reasons to learn and they need to have control of their learning. Thus, the training design should include demonstrations of the usefulness of the skills being taught—that is, how this knowledge will benefit employees in the performance of their jobs. The design should also provide options where possible so that the trainees can choose how they will learn a particular concept or skill. (See Chap. 12, Adult Learning.)

Type of Learning. The best training design will include an analysis of the type of learning which is required for each topic. Robert Gange[7] has classified learning outcomes as verbal information, intellectual skill, motor skill, attitude, or cognitive strategy. The most effective learning will take place when the course designer determines which of these outcomes is required of each topic and selects a learning activity which is appropriate for each outcome.

Sequence of Topics. The truism "learning must proceed from the known to the unknown" applies to the sequence of topics, which is crucial to the success of a training course. In many software courses the trainees build the project from unit to unit. For example, students start with data entry on a blank spreadsheet, proceed to add formulas which summarize the data, and then format and print the results.

Developing the Course

Once the design of the curriculum and the courses has been created, a decision must be made as to whether to develop the course in-house, find an existing course which meets the design criteria, or contract for the course to be developed based on the criteria. The following are some important points to consider in choosing or developing a course.

Exercises Which Illustrate. Be sure that the content of the exercise illustrates the point of the training unit. For example, if the purpose of the exercise is to show why secondary keys are important when data is being indexed, create data with duplicate first-key fields so that the results reinforce the concept. (First and secondary keys refer to index priority.)

Purpose of the Manual. Determine to what extent the manual will serve as an in-class tool for providing exercises and other instructional functions and to what extent it is intended as a reference tool for after class. This decision will affect the writing style and general layout of the materials.

Define Terms Before Using Them. Few instructional practices are more frustrating to students than to have the instructor lace a lecture with terms and abbreviations which the students do not understand. This problem can be avoided with a careful sequencing of topics and attention to defining terms carefully.

Use Analogies Liberally. It is impossible to emphasize too much the importance of using analogies for concepts. Training materials should be filled with phrases such as "this process is like…," "you can think of this process as…," or "if you did not have a computer, you might have to.…"

Both Directed and Self-Paced Exercises. While directed exercises in which the instructor "walks" the students through a process by demonstrating or directing the keystrokes, students will not have an instructor by their side when they return to their offices. Therefore, it is essential that students "solo" with the software as much as possible during the class while the "pilot" is available to help.

Generic Keystrokes. Too frequently keystrokes for particular functions are given in the student manual as part of the exercises. While this practice may make it easier for the student to complete the exercise, it makes it more difficult for the student to use the manual as a reference guide after the class. It is not clear to the learner which keystrokes were part of the Acme Widgets exercise and which are required whenever the function is used.

Phase 4: Delivering the Training

If the decision has been made to deliver training through computer- or tape-based courses, arrangements must be made to procure the necessary equipment or facilities for students to have access to the training. The details of establishing learning labs or checkout systems are beyond the scope of this chapter. If the decision has been to deliver training through instructor-led classroom training, there are a number of issues to be considered.

Establishing an Effective Learning Environment

The importance of creating a pleasant, inviting, comfortable classroom is essential to effective learning. Common sense as well as a number of studies link the quality of the physical environment to the quality of learning. Several factors contribute to creating the best learning environment. If the decision is made to create a computer training classroom, the planner should consider the following elements to create a classroom which meets the needs of both the students and instructor.

Layout. Typically, training activity during a computer software class includes lecture, demonstrations, hands-on practice, discussion, questions and answers, and group projects. Each activity requires a different classroom layout for optimum impact. The final design then will be a compromise which will depend on the predominant activity. The three most-used layouts are traditional, horseshoe, and cluster layouts.

Traditional. The traditional computer classroom layout places the students in rows facing the instructor as diagrammed in Fig. 40-2. The advantage to this arrangement is that the instructor can easily maintain eye contact with the students. Students can raise their gaze from the screen in a moment. Thus, the instructor can easily change from hands-on activities to minilectures, demonstrations, whiteboard examples, or questions and answers. The major disadvantage is that the instructor cannot see the students' screens without moving from the front of the room to a position behind the students.

Horseshoe. In the horseshoe classroom the students turn in their chairs to face the instructor during lectures and interaction with the instructor and other students. In some versions of this layout (Fig. 40-3) there is a large center table

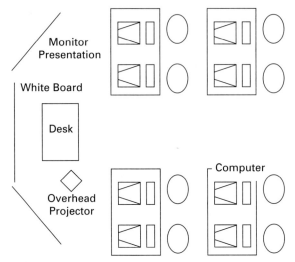

Figure 40-2. Traditional computer classroom layout.

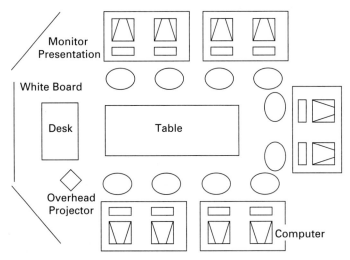

Figure 40-3. Horseshoe classroom layout.

which students gather around. This gives them writing space during the lecture or demonstration activities and faces them toward other students during discussions. They then turn to their computers during the lab portion of the class. The instructor can see all the students' screens from the front of the room in this layout.

Cluster. In the cluster layout (see Fig. 40-4) the computers are grouped together so that the students can see each other easily. Sometimes the entire class is "clustered" around a conference-sized table. This arrangement encour-

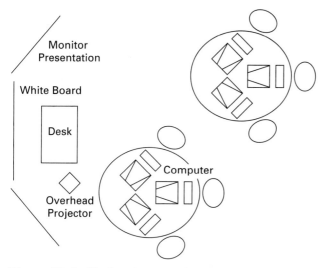

Figure 40-4. Cluster classroom layout.

ages student interaction. However, the instructor cannot see all the students' screens from one point in the room.

Expense and logistic considerations aside, the choice of classroom layout depends primarily on the style of training to be done in the classroom. The cluster arrangement works best when students spend most of their time working together on the computers. The horseshoe layout is ideal when the class time is carefully divided into periods of lecture, demonstrations, and student interaction and periods of hands-on lab activities. The traditional classroom works best when there are quick changes from lecture to demonstrations to hands-on questions.

Lighting.   Computer classrooms have their own lighting problems. The goal is to have enough light for students to read materials but not so much as to cause glare on presentation screens and monitors. In the best of computer classrooms, the lights can be easily controlled by the instructor to fit the needs of a given class. These installations include separate switches for different types of lights and the ability to dim arrays of lights.

Noise.   Computers and printers create a surprising amount of ambient noise. This noise is usually noticed more in its absence when the machines are turned off. However, this level of noise can cause student and instructor fatigue over the period of a class without their ever knowing the cause. Therefore, attempts should be made to muffle this noise as much as possible.

Temperature.   Nothing affects students more and is more difficult to regulate than room temperature. What constitutes a comfortable temperature for individual students varies all over the thermometer. Beyond the considerations of heating and cooling any room, special attention must be paid to computer classrooms because computer equipment generates a surprising amount of heat. Ignoring the additional heat load from the machines can make for a toasty classroom by afternoon just when the afternoon doldrums hit the students.

Electrical Service.   An obvious requirement of computer classrooms which is often overlooked is that computers, monitors, and printers require electrical outlets and the power to support their requirements. It can be a bit unnerving for the instructor when the lights dim as everyone turns on their computers.

Creating a personal-computer class environment is not a task to be taken lightly. In addition to the above considerations and accompanying expenses, classrooms must be continually upgraded for both hard- and software, considering the speed with which technology changes. Added to the initial and upkeep costs, computer training rooms are not readily useful for other types of training and may sit idle a great deal of the time.

Trialing the Courses

Before rolling out a course for the entire population, it is wise to test a course with a small number of participants from the target audience. This trialing is comprised of three phases:

Pretrial.   This phase involves gathering the students for the trial and setting their expectations. This process is often done through the distribution of a memo to the target population asking for volunteers and explaining how the test course will be conducted. Every attempt should be made to ensure that the people who attend the test course are legitimate students who do not know the material and have a need to learn the software. It is helpful to have experienced users of the software present for the trial, including instructors, course developers, managers, etc. They can provide insight into the effectiveness of the trainer and training materials. However, the focus of the trial must remain on the student who actually needs to learn the software.

Trial Class.   The primary purpose of holding a trial class is to check the flow and timing of the training activities. Therefore, the trial class should be taught as closely as possible to course materials. If the instructor wanders from the lessons or adds exercises on the spot, the results will not reflect the course as designed. This requirement also means that the class should not be interrupted by debriefing sessions. These sessions distract the "real" students and make it difficult to determine the effectiveness of the designed flow of activities.

Posttrial.   After the class, there should be some time to get feedback from the students. Every attempt should be made not to influence the opinions of the students but instead to gather information as objectively as possible. This session should first include time for the students to write their comments in response to specific questions. These individual responses can provide a corrective to later discussions in which a dominant personality may sway the group's opinion. After the written feedback, a discussion of the class should be conducted by someone other than the instructor. Every attempt should be made to clarify and expand on comments. That is, comments such as "I really like the unit on formulas" should be probed to determine specifically what the student liked about the unit. If time is available, a hands-on test of ability to use the software should be administered to determine if the goals of the course were met.

A caution! The life expectancy of PC software revision is currently from nine months to a year. The shelf-life of a course for any software is correspondingly short. Therefore, the needs of the students and the amount of time required to design and develop a course must be balanced with the realization that the course will have to be revised within a few months. Thus, while four or five months of trialing and revising a course might make for better training, such effort is impractical given the limited time the course will be useful.

Revising the Courses

The feedback from the trial class(es) should be taken into account in the final draft of courseware. If the original design and development have been well thought out by experienced developers, the revisions required are usually minor, involving the deletion, addition, or expansion of a unit or the reordering of units.

Scheduling the Courses

The most important principle for the scheduling of training is to provide the training when it is needed. Training which is scheduled to be delivered two months before the software is installed on the students' machines or two months after the students have begun using it will not be effective and may even be a disincentive for enrollments. Just-in-time training is more effective as the trainee receives the skill-knowledge at the time it will be used.

A secondary consideration when scheduling is the time interval between levels of classes. Because most training does not include a great deal of practice time within the class, students need to use the software at their job for several weeks before they are prepared to move on to new features and skill. Therefore, schedules should be arranged so that students can reenroll after an optimum interval from the previous class.

Some thought should be given to "selling" the training to the employees both to get them to register and to get their acceptance of the advantage of getting the training. This process may be as simple as making an attractive calendar to post and distribute or as elaborate as a kick-off presentation in the company cafeteria with music, balloons, and raffles.

Delivering the Courses

The key to effective delivery of courses is the instructor. Good instructors can create a successful class with poor, little, or no courseware. Bad instructors can make a shambles of the best-designed and written courseware.

The topic of selecting and training good instructors is beyond the scope of this chapter. Suffice it to say, instructors should know more about the software than the class requires, should have the ability to simplify the complex, and should treat students as people who happen not to know the subject at hand.

Following Up

A critical factor in the success of any training program is getting the students to practice what they have learned in class. Because using PC software is a skill, it must be practiced until the software functions learned in class can be applied easily to the tasks of the workplace.

One means to this end is to develop and implement a program which encourages trainees to use the skills acquired soon after the training. This program may be a "homework assignment" dealing with Acme Widgets or it may involve the trainee's immediate supervisor in assignments for "real work" using the new skills. Some companies have had success offering a small reward for completion of such projects as an incentive for the employees.

Another approach is for the instructor to call each student within two weeks following each class to offer assistance and encouragement. This proactive initiative reminds each student of the class and often elicits questions which the student has not taken the time and energy to ask about.

Phase 5: Evaluating the Training Results

Training is not complete until the results are evaluated. After all, training is done to effect a change in the skills and knowledge of employees so that they become more productive. Therefore, developing a continuing-evaluation process is a critical phase of the training cycle. In 1959, D. L. Kirkpatrick[8] developed a model which includes four levels of what can be measured in the evaluation of training (also see Chap. 14, Evaluation):

Level 1   Reaction—How did they like the training?

Level 2   Learning—What knowledge or skills did they acquire?

Level 3   Behavior—Do they use the new knowledge or skill on their jobs?

Level 4   Results—How does the changed behavior affect the productivity, profits, etc., of the organization?

As the level number increases, value of the evaluation increases as does the difficulty of gathering valid and reliable data. Most training departments provide some feedback mechanism, usually in the form of a "smile" sheet which checks the level-1 reaction to the training experience. A few test for acquired learning and fewer still get out into the workplace to look for behavioral changes in their students.

Gathering and evaluating data to show that training makes a significant impact on the "bottom line" is expensive, time-consuming, and tedious. Few organizations make the investment to do the study, relying instead on "common sense" to tell them that it must make a difference.

One way to provide a level-2 analysis is to use the skill analysis instrument used in the needs assessment discussed in phase 2. With a comparison of the "before" and "after" results, it is relatively easy to see improved knowledge and skill levels for each individual student.

Conclusion

PC application software training has become critical to business simply because there are millions of workers who need the training. Every indicator points to training becoming even more important to business into the twenty-first century. However, it will inevitably change from what we recognize as "standard" training today.

The seeds of these changes are already evident in the emerging expectations of those who "consume" and purchase training. The most recent attitudes are as follows:

Trainees and managers are more demanding, requiring better justification for the investment in training.

There is an increasing demand for just-in-time training, training which is administered when the user is attempting to do the task to be trained.

Because of the growth and availability of new educational technology, there is increasing pressure to replace or at least supplement instructor-led classroom training with interactive multimedia computer programs using audio and full-motion video.

With the growth of the computer training industry has come concerns for training standards with the attendant search for means to certify quality instruction and materials.

With these changes will come ever-greater challenges to the training community.

References

1. Connor, Daryl R., *Managing at the Speed of Change: How Resilient Managers Succeed and Prosper Where Others Fail*, Villard Books, New York, 1993.
2. Boothman, Terry, and Harvey Feldstein, *Training Evaluation and Impact: Maximizing, Measuring and Proving the Value of Training*, Logical Operations, Rochester, NY, 1993.
3. Noonan, John, "How to Escape Corporate America's Basement," *Training*, December 1993, vol. 30, no. 12.
4. Keirsey, David, and Marilyn Bates, *The Sixteen Types*, Prometheus Nemesis Book Company, Del Mar, CA, 1984.
5. *The Learning Style Inventory*, McBer and Co., Boston.
6. Knowles, Malcolm S., *The Adult Learner: A Neglected Species*, Gulf Publishing Co., Houston, 1990.
7. Gange, Robert, *The Conditions of Learning*, Holt, Rinehart and Winston, Orlando, 1985.
8. Kirkpatrick, Donald L., "Evaluation of Training," in *Training and Development Handbook*, 2d ed., R. L. Craig, ed., McGraw-Hill, New York, 1976.

41

Sales and Marketing Training

C. E. Hahne

David E. Schultze

C. E. (Gene) Hahne *is CEO of Intercom, The Woodlands, Texas. He was formerly Manager of Training, Shell Oil Company, Houston. Intercom creates and produces computer-based training for sales, management, and staff training. Hahne has received Shell Oil Company's Excelsior Award, ASTD's Distinguished Contribution to Employer Award, and ASTD's 1984 Torch Award. In 1989, he was awarded ASTD's highest award, the Gordon M. Bliss Award, which is a lifetime achievement award. He served on both the old ASTD board and its board of directors under the new governance structure; as Treasurer of ASTD; Chair, ASTD's Budget and Finance Committee; and on many national committees and task forces. He was Director of ASTD's Sales and Marketing Professional Practice Area and received the James R. Ball Award. His contributions to the community include work with Texas A&M University, University of Texas, Houston Baptist University, North Harris Community College, and the University of Houston. He helped design and implement a management development program for the state of Texas and has conducted workshops throughout the world. He has been named to* Who's Who in the South and Southwest, Who's Who in Finance and Industry, Personalities in the South, Personalities in America, Men of Achievement in the World, *and* Who's Who in the World.

David I. Schultze *is Director of Diversified Instructional Services, Houston, Texas. He presents and facilitates training programs for national and international clients in sales, management, customer service, and course design and development. He spent 27 years with Shell Oil Company in sales, marketing, and training. He has been a member of ASTD for 11 years and has served as Director of the Sales and Marketing*

Professional Practice Area. He has served on numerous national committees and was named the James R. Ball Award recipient in 1995. He has presented at international conferences and is listed in Who's Who in Sales and Marketing.

This chapter is a reference resource for sales trainers. It will help the sales trainer develop and maintain effective training programs. However, the principles of sales training will work with any type of training. More in-depth information can be found in the *Sales Training Handbook,* an ASTD-sponsored publication, edited by Robert L. Craig and Leslie Kelley.

Productive sales training increases sales permanently by enhancing the knowledge, skills, work habits, attitudes, self-confidence, and on-the-job behavior of an organization's sales force. The desired result is learning and the application of that learning. This result can occur only if there is a change in behavior for the better.

The bottom-line sales training goal is to support the organization's sales and marketing plan and maximize both current sales and long-term strategies for the success and continued growth of the organization.

Selling is not a natural gift. Successful salespeople are developed by their learning specific skills which, when properly employed and adapted, will allow them to identify opportunities when they arise. These experiences can be recalled in future situations and thus ingrained in the salesperson's behavior.

Selling is the process of human interaction to achieve the goal of persuading another person to make a decision that you support. In selling, you identify needs and wants and then create a fever through communication to convince someone that you can satisfy those needs and wants.

Everyone is a salesperson everyday! Whether you are selling a product to an outside customer, an idea to a manager in your department, or trying to convince your spouse or a friend to try a new restaurant, we all sell! All selling involves a learnable core of basic skills that apply to any sales situation, no matter what industry or field, and these skills will affect the outcome of the interaction and have impact, whether the salesperson is aware of them or not. For example, if you are unaware of the law of gravity and you stepped off a moving vehicle at 30 miles per hour, that law will still have impact on you. So, to reduce the chances of salespeople missing opportunities, we train them to change their behavior by exposing them to the knowledge and skills that allow them to communicate with others in a persuasive way. It is, in fact, the process of creating an environment in which individual sales personnel can feel motivated to develop effective sales skills and a productive attitude that can lead to achievement of personal and business goals.

Such training is an *ongoing process.* It is fed by a series of programs that expose the individual to key skills and knowledge. This exposure to personal communication skills is valuable to all personnel in any organization (purchasing, customer service, finance, etc.) who need to enhance behavior to persuade others to take action.

Any complete sales training process should include these knowledge and skill areas:

- Organizational philosophy, policies and procedures, structure, and strategies
- Business knowledge and skills
- Time and territory management
- Legal awareness

- Sales and negotiation skills
- Communication skills [e.g., presentation skills (including computer)]
- Planning and goal setting
- Self-awareness and personal development
- Computer skills (customer information, sales plan, competitive information, product information, etc.)
- Technical skills (cellular phone, fax, modems, etc.)

Each salesperson will possess specific experiences and skills as well as a unique set of needs. Ongoing programs to change behavior, therefore, must be adaptable to the various needs of the sales force. The long-term goal, however, is to field a sales team with the highest level of sales behavior so they may achieve the maximum personal and organization goals.

Benefits of Sales Training

The best-trained athletes are usually the best performers. This fact is also true with salespeople. Good training benefits both the salesperson and the organization.

The Salesperson Receives
- Greater self-confidence
- Ability to communicate more effectively
- Enhanced career opportunities
- Feeling of pride and satisfaction for company and customer
- Increased income potential
- Increased customer loyalty and rapport

The Customer Receives
- Solutions to immediate problems and needs
- Benefits of the product or service
- Better service
- A valuable resource for information and reliable supplier

The Company Receives
- Increased revenue from better sales
- Increased profits (return on training investment)
- Stability from repeat business because of satisfied customers
- Reduced employee turnover
- Improved employee morale
- More knowledgeable sales force
- Growth potential in the marketplace

The Sales Training Department Receives
- Greater credibility with management

- Greater support from sales managers
- Continued financial resources
- Enhanced job stability
- Increased job satisfaction

How to Create and Maintain Sales Training Results

Results are achieved by following *ten steps to productive sales training* (see Fig. 41-1).

1. Get and maintain management support and credibility.
2. Analyze and clearly identify the needs of both the organization and the sales personnel.
3. Develop a training action plan and present it to management.
4. Design and develop a criteria-based training program or find a suitable off-the-shelf program that meets your needs. In both cases, they should address the competencies needed for the job.
5. Design a comprehensive measurement-evaluation method and follow-up plan.
6. Select and train trainers.
7. Validate the program with a pilot group.
8. Collect data, analyze, and modify program.
9. Implement the training program.
10. Monitor and improve the program over the long term.

Before you start on the ten-part cycle it is very important to meet with the program sponsor, owner, or manager for whom the program is being developed to be assured that nothing has changed which will affect the desired outcome. Then, it is equally important to maintain constant communication with management during the entire cycle and inform them as to progress and direction of the program. This communication is vital to maintaining your credibility as a management resource for consultation and effective solution development. You will notice there are several management review spots on the flowchart (Fig. 41-1). These spots may be increased or reduced due to geographic constraints, but make sure some form of communication is maintained regardless of distance challenges.

The most critical phase of the whole process is usually *assessing needs and communicating them to management*. The problem is often a conflict in how the needs are perceived. The most difficult situation for the training person to handle is often having to tell management that the expected sales problem they thought they had was, in fact, not a sales problem but a management problem.

Managers tend to identify good training as that which provides what they want, based on their goals and their distanced view of their salespeople's needs. As a sales trainer, you must make sure your programs maintain a sensitive balance between what management wants and what the salespeople want. You must understand your organization's objectives and goals, its philosophy, and its strategic marketing plan in order to identify the most important needs. At the same time, you must also satisfy management with your solution.

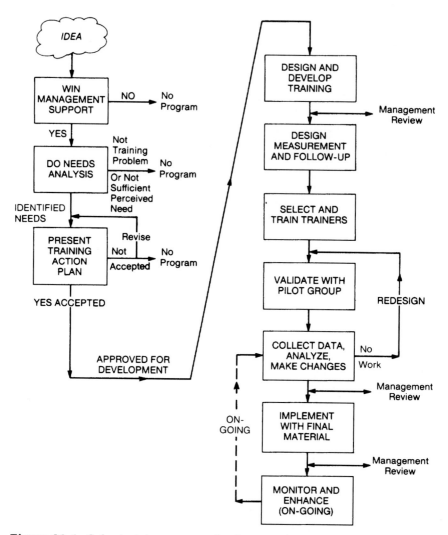

Figure 41-1. Sales training program development process.

Step 1: Gaining Management Support (Credibility)

Salespeople *respect* what you *inspect* not what you *expect!*

Winning management support is your first and most important job as a sales trainer. Maintaining that support is the result of successful implementation of selected programs.

Success in getting funds and support for training will be in direct proportion to your ability to develop and maintain credibility among management. The best training program ever developed can gather dust on the shelf if management doesn't support it and what it can do for the organization. Sales training succeeds best when you convince your management of the worth of each program, as well as your value as a sales training resource.

The most persuasive position you can take is to be visible, involved, and constantly communicating with all levels of the organization. The successful sales trainer develops workable programs by being a persistent diplomat who regularly communicates the bottom-line benefits of sales training to all members of the organization. This attitude provides the foundation for management support throughout the development process, gives you important positive communications, and enhances your position as training consultant and valuable management resource.

Two things that will help the successful implementation of sales programs are

1. Tie your management discussions to the proven results as measured through the evaluation methods;

2. Involve the sales manager with the evaluation step to inspect how the learning is being applied on the job. This supports the statement that salespeople will respect what they know will be inspected more than what is merely expected.

Step 2: Analyze Training Needs

To improve bottom-line sales results you must train your sales force in exactly the right skills. And you can't do that unless you know what their specific needs are.

That brings us to the second step in the sales training process which is analyzing and identifying the real-world needs of the sales force. This task can be done by the training staff, by a qualified outside consultant, or by a combination of the two.

Needs analysis is an objective look at the common processes, job tasks, problems, and challenges facing the salesperson. It is imperative to the success of any program and is worth spending the time and resources even when they are limited. If you have limited resources, spend what is necessary in this step to identify those specific needs and then present them to management in an in-depth training action plan.

A well-designed analysis instrument is absolutely essential for an accurate, objective picture of the needs. The survey questions should probe the following areas:

- Objective facts of the tasks, processes, and problems
- Feelings that might indicate attitude problems
- Weaknesses; areas in which the sales personnel feel a need to strengthen their skills (e.g., What skills would make them feel more confident?) or in which the supplied tools do not meet their needs
- What the respondents would change or teach if they were trainers

The needs analysis instrument (e.g., a survey or a questionnaire) should be exactly the same for all people interviewed and for all interviewers. Short questions are best. For getting objective information, ask short, direct questions that can be answered with only a few words. To get feelings and open the interviewee up to discuss hidden concerns, use open-ended questions that start with Why? or How? or What would you do if...? Try to design the instrument so that interview time is no more than an hour or so per person.

If a job description exists, study it to see if it is up to date and examine the tasks as to how they are perceived by the salespeople.

Other approaches include studying performance appraisals to look for performance problems which permeate the sales force, conducting group interviews, observing behavior by riding with some of the sales force, attending sales meetings, studying sales correspondence, and looking at turnover statistics and exit interviews.

On-the-job observation gives immediate feedback. You can see if the salesperson has planned the call or how he or she uses interpersonal skills to defuse anger or build rapport with customers. Convey the understanding with the salesperson that you are only an observer, not there to judge or inhibit their work but to understand their needs so you can help them achieve their goals.

While observing on-the-job behavior, you can begin to establish credibility for your training programs and generate enthusiasm. Salespeople enjoy talking to anyone who understands their business and feel comfortable with those who can relate to their world. Get them talking about training and themselves. When they are involved, you've created buy-in and ownership of the principles that the training is based on.

Be sure to interview management...and follow up with reports of results. Senior management responds best in one-on-one interviews. For middle managers and line managers you might try a group interview which will save time and is less taxing on your own communication skills. If you mail questionnaires, remember, you will get only about a 10 percent return at best unless it goes out under a senior management signature, so if you must do it by mail, keep that in mind.

In needs analysis, be careful not to blindly accept information on face value. Many will try to hide true feelings or tell you what they think you want to hear. They will also try to hide what they perceive to be limiting traits. Make sure you create a comfortable, trusting environment when talking with salespeople during the needs analysis.

There is a strong case for using an outside consultant for some of the one-on-one "bare-your-soul" sessions. Employees often feel safer with an outsider who assures them he or she will report the facts without disclosing the source. Even sales trainers are perceived as serving management as much as the employees.

The end result of a well-conceived and well-executed needs analysis will tell you exactly how to design your training:

- Who needs training
- When training should occur
- What exact skills and knowledge need to be learned
- What methods to employ in the training experience
- Who should be the instructor-trainer-facilitator, and what methods of delivery should be used
- What results management can expect in improved performance and how to measure them

What can salespeople learn in a good training program? They learn how a successful salesperson operates; product and service knowledge, company policies and procedures; internal organization, corporate strategy; how to plan, organize, manage time, manage a territory; etc. A formal training program also gives the trainer a chance to observe attitude of individuals and the group in general. This list will come from your needs analysis and will therefore be tailored to the specific needs of your sales force, both individually and collectively.

Manage the ongoing needs analysis process by

- Keeping a finger on the pulse of the sales force and its managers.
- Listening carefully at training sessions for needs
- Involving yourself in the management process
- Encouraging feedback through a confidential open-door policy

Step 3: Sell Training Action Plan to Management

After you have built lasting value into your training programs, the next important step is to convince management of your accomplishments. By producing a training action plan and selling it to management, you are basically saying, "Here's what I'm going to do, here's what I've done, and here's how you've benefited." This action will increase the credibility and value in management's feeling toward the worth of the training function.

An effective action plan includes the following parts:

1. *Target audience.* Who exactly needs the training and who doesn't, highlighting the variety of needs in the group to be trained

2. *Summary of results of needs analysis.* Prioritize specific needs and the net impact to the organization of meeting those needs. (Keep it brief; point out net impact, results, benefits, and the bottom line.)

3. *Establish objectives for the program.* There are three types of objectives for you to identify and explain:

- *Business objectives* that impact management's financial and strategic goals. In order for management to be aware of the proper business objectives, they must be met with in planning sessions. Business objectives are net tangible results in sales and profit—the company's return on its investment of money and resources for training.
- *Learning objectives* that describe what specific skills and behavioral change the participants can expect from the program.
- *Application objectives* that indicate how the participant will apply the new information or behavior change back on the job.

Training objectives identify the trainer's goals for creating and managing the learning experience. One of these objectives is to create the most stimulating, yet protective, learning environment possible. In such an environment trainees must feel that their performance during the learning experience will be treated with confidentiality and will not be reported back to management. They will then have the freedom to try new skills in a safe and trusting environment. You can't afford to allow intimidation to stifle participation, shut down candor, or curtail, honesty. Role-play video- and audiotapes should be for the participants and trainer's use only. They should be erased at the conclusion of the training session unless the trainees request to take them with them. Training isn't the time for management to observe and evaluate performance—it's time to experiment. Your commitment to your trainees must be total and your credibility will depend on it.

All objectives must be specific (exact, yet simple), realistic (challenging, yet achievable), and measurable (quantifiable, yet not limiting). For example, it isn't useful to tell management that you're going to teach salespeople how to probe a customer for information. Tell management instead that you're going to teach each participant how to increase sales by 10 percent—or improve the call closing by 25 percent—or boost sales to existing accounts by 5 percent in the next quarter. These are specific, realistic, and measurable goals that management wants to hear. Remember, to increase sales you must establish and maintain credibility with management. Set attainable goals, meet them with a finely tuned training program, and you will have successfully managed the expectations of a group of people very important to your future opportunities.

Most sales training will involve primarily cognitive (thinking) and affective (feeling) objectives; use high-level verbs with those categories whenever possible. Note that "understand" is not a specific measurable, doable skill and thus too vague to properly identify an important objective. Keep in mind that you are building criterion-referenced training with specific, realistic, and measurable learning objectives. In other words, each objective becomes a criterion upon which you'll build training exercises such that no important objective is left unfulfilled and no activity or concept is without direct relation to an objective. The danger of setting such specific objectives (especially business goals that relate to performance) is that others in the organization may want to share the glory and claim part of the credit for sales increases. Advertising will claim it was their campaign that made the difference; marketing will claim it was the consumer promotion, etc. Another danger is not achieving the results predicted. Here's where the successful trainer stands up and is willing to be accountable for the results. That's not so hard to do when you have a sound needs analysis that tells you exactly what needs to be done to increase sales and achieve those measurable results. You must trust the natural inclination of your participants to want to achieve goals and do well in order to receive the pride of recognition.

4. *Detailed tasks.* The fourth part of your training action plan should be a complete *task analysis.* This document lists job skills, by category, which are necessary for a salesperson to achieve the success expected and hoped for by management. A good task analysis often causes management to rethink job descriptions and update them to a more specific, measurable form, making them the vital criteria for performance upon which enlightened performance appraisals and career counseling are based. Whatever form you use to design your learning task outline, be specific with command verbs that specify action and identify doable tasks. Keep your tasks in parallel; that is, begin them all with command verbs.

5. *Use of available resources.* Management will want you to identify options for achieving the identified goals. You can cause the desired action on your training report and recommendations if you specify exactly what it will take in the form of *money, manpower,* and *management support* to accomplish the goals. It is also important to point out the return on investment in specific terms. Management will surely want to know the best training approach, challenging you to defend any one of a number of options:

- Use off-the-shelf program material intact (probably the most common solution to meet training needs)

- Customize material to fit your organization. When doing so, there will be additional cost involved, often significant.

- Update existing material (only if it does not involve copyright material)

- Develop an entirely new program which is exactly tailored to the needs of the current sales force.
- Hire consultant(s) to help do any of the above. Consultants are most valuable when (*a*) you have limited staff expertise, (*b*) your staff is too busy to meet the deadline, (*c*) the issues are so sensitive that an outside third party is the best answer, (*d*) management and the training staff feel they are too close to the problem to be objective. The consultant you select should
  - Have a successful track record and come with verifiable references
  - Be totally trustworthy for confidentiality and professionalism
  - Be able to relate well to your people and your organization
  - Contribute to the credibility of the training group

  Here's some valuable advice: Create a detailed, professional working contract with each consultant to outline specifically what each party's duties are, the consultant's availability, key deadlines, training approach to take, content of program, description of deliverable materials, approval cycles, what determines acceptable quality of deliverables, how to cancel the agreement, etc. (obviously carefully scrutinized by your legal department and purchasing, where applicable). You'll find that 99 percent of the time, this complete and careful agreement serves the sole purpose of managing expectations and making absolutely clear what's expected of each party; only rarely does it have to be enforced as a binding legal contract.
- Final option: *back off* and have no program at all—an option that management always has with any program proposal if there isn't sufficient *business and/or organizational value* identified.

Present your training action plan in a *formal stand-up presentation* to management.

- Net it out with bottom-line results and benefits.
- Use graphics, readable charts, computer slides, etc., to present a professional image.
- *Sell* your plan! Get management *commitment* to support the program with money, time, and verbal communication of support to people at all levels of the organization. Your goal is *management buy-in to your specific program plan recommendations.*

Be prepared to justify your findings and recommendations with facts at hand and detailed predictions of net impact. Then be prepared for approval and the opportunity to put your money where your mouth is!

Step 4: Developing Instructional Material

Once you have a specific, well-developed training action plan, developing instructional material should be a matter of following guidelines which can be found in many books and courses. Instructional design for sales training typically involves the following major components:

1. Completing the needs and task analyses
2. Choosing appropriate training media and methods

3. Identifying trainer's specific role

4. Developing the program material

The choice of media and methods is critical to your job of helping trainees change behavior. For example, *group discussion* is usually best for exploring decision making and behavior options that apply to the trainee's real world. *Role playing* is best for practicing concepts and techniques to create new behavior. *Slides* work well for audiences that are large and if you must repeat it many times. *Videos* can be used to supplement training programs or can be used as the main theme of the program. They are also useful in conjunction with role playing to capture and review the success the trainees are having in implementing newly learned techniques. *Audiotape,* especially combined with a graphic manual, helps people who are not especially print-oriented to step through a process in a way that simulates the actual experience. *Multimedia training* is another method of presenting learning to trainees. These aforementioned methods are effective and efficient ways to bring individual training to salespeople on site, on demand, thus saving time and allowing a faster knowledge transfer at the learner's own pace.

Special Considerations.   Consider the logistics of your sales organization's equipment and training facilities before making final decisions on training methods and media. Multimedia may be best for presenting certain tasks and objectives, but your sales locations may have video players instead of CD-ROM. You will have to decide which media to use and be prepared to justify your recommendations in dollars to management.

There are several key concerns in identifying the trainer's role in the program. The question is whether you want the trainer to "impart knowledge" or manage the learning experience. Selection of an instructor, trainer, or facilitator has a lot to do with the method of presentation. The instructor is charged with bringing the program to life for the participants. After all, the best-designed training program can be a bust if not properly presented with enthusiasm and skill by the instructor or facilitator. Stand-up lecture is the least effective way to teach adults. Training creates an environment (through provision of appropriate time and atmosphere) in which the individual is allowed and willing to learn. Trainers make best use of their time by supplementing a form of audiovisual presentation with concentrating on application, discussion facilitation, and one-on-one counseling.

For your choice of methods for sales training, consider the following approaches:

- *Seminars* and *workshops* provide opportunities for participating that are necessary for learning and change in behavior. They encourage the facilitator role for trainers, rather than stand-up lecturing.

- *Role playing* is a powerful means of reinforcing terms and concepts by giving the trainee the chance to practice techniques in realistic settings. *Audiotape* role playing is excellent for learning telephone sales techniques, with special emphasis on the impact of words (which convey only 10 percent of the complete message) and tone of voice (which conveys another 38 percent of the message leaving 52 percent to body language) on the sales process. *Videotape* role playing is excellent for the words and tone, as well as the body language so important to one-on-one relationships and sales effectiveness. *Trio group* role playing is a way to experience the sales situation from both sides; three participants in a group take turns acting out a situation as salesperson, customer, and observer.

- *Case studies* provide the real-world atmosphere within which to practice skills and techniques. The above role playing works best when, instead of using generic simulations, you provide an actual real-life situation with the opportunity to compare the trainees' solutions with what actually occurred on the job. Take plenty of care in writing case studies:
  - Keep them relatively simple with one major point or skill as a focus.
  - Use dialogue to simulate what went on before the trainee takes over the call.
  - Use real facts.

- *Exercises* are short activities designed to reinforce a single concept or technique through (1) definition, (2) example, (3) practice, and (4) reinforcement of proper technique. Keep exercises short and specific. Hand out the exercise instructions or forms only when it's actually time to do the exercise. Do one example with the whole class; then let individuals or small groups complete the actual exercise. Finish with a group discussion of key points learned.

- Multimedia and computer-based training gives the trainer some advantages when it comes to cost reduction and increased training effectiveness. Costs are reduced by the elimination of travel time and expense as well as time away from the job. Additional benefits of multimedia are
  - Flexibility.   Freedom of the user regarding pace and location
  - Availability.   Interactive training can be used 24 hours a day
  - Privacy.   Each individual can be self-paced and the process is less risky
  - Competency gates.   Tests can be built in to evaluate the trainees' learning and control their advancement to the next module

- *Special guest speakers* can add interest and valuable job-related knowledge and ideas to your program. Consider inviting especially successful salespeople, sales managers, and even customers to share their particular approach to achieving personal and company goals. Welcome discussion afterward as a valuable means of personal involvement and motivation.

- *Nonclass activity.*   Your program may well include such learning experiences as self-paced study, one-on-one counseling and tutorial guidance, and self-directed practice and development. These can also involve prework which is done in advance of attending a seminar or class. The value of prework is that the seminar can begin on a high level of knowledge since the participants have already done some reading or self-evaluation.

- *Self-analysis tools.*   The first step in communicating with others is to know yourself. A salesperson must be sensitive to the impact of his or her personal style on others, to avoid offending a prospect and to be the most persuasive salesperson possible. Consider two types of self-analytical tools in your sales training:
  1. *Style analyses.*   Numerous self-graded or computer-graded style analysis programs are available on the market. Each in some degree helps the individual see him- or herself clearly as others do. The result is often an increased sensitivity to behavior, to the needs of others, and to the use of words, tone of voice, and body language in order to create a desired impression.
  2. *Feedback from others.*   Commercial programs are available to provide questionnaires for a salesperson's coworkers, subordinates, managers, and customers to evaluate the individual's effectiveness as a communicator. The result is often an amazed new awareness of what others *really* think of the trainee, and more often than not an increased desire to listen to constructive ideas for improvement and to attempt to improve behavior.

The beauty of a good needs and task analysis is that it practically spells out the right method for each task to be learned. Your trainees, in effect, designed the program.

Developing program material is much easier if you have a well-executed instructional design. Materials development involves several key steps, as shown below.

Special Note.   Adults learn in different ways; visually, verbally, and kinesthetically. To appeal to all of your learners, you must build different exercises and vary these to appeal to different types of learners. This effort helps the entire group learn in the way that they best grasp new concepts and ideas. Use audio, video, hands-on, and group sessions as well as moderate lecture to satisfy those needs.

1. *Write copy (for exercises, case studies, workbook text, audiovisual scripts, etc.).*
   You'll need someone who specializes in writing training material and not simply an expert on the subject. The expert knows content detail but is too close to the subject; the writer is more of a layperson who knows how to package and present the key details in the clearest and most learnable style. Training copy should be

   - Clear and direct
   - Conversational in its verbiage
   - Logically organized with clear transitions
   - Aligned to the program's objectives, tasks, and the instructional design
   - Tied to the graphics and visuals
   - Checked by subject-matter experts for correctness (managers, salespeople, legal, etc.)
   - Final-edited by someone who knows the subject and the form in which it should be presented

   The best-designed program cannot withstand a mediocre writer, and an excellent writer cannot salvage a poorly designed program. Trust the subject-matter expert on content issues and trust the writer on presentation issues. Make sure that case studies and exercises are clear, without unfamiliar acronyms, and not confusing.

2. *Develop graphics and printed material.*   Almost everyone has a computer at his or her desk. They can be used to turn out top-quality graphics and text, with both illustrations and color. These printed materials can be reproduced professionally and bound into booklets or binders which will save you time and money. You might consider in-house production for the first pilot session. You can then modify the material before it is professionally printed and bound.

3. *Produce audiovisual segments.*   Training programs don't have to be Hollywood productions. They can be produced by local video companies who specialize in training. Keep the following things in mind:

   - Use a popular form of media based on the present equipment you have, unless it is outdated. Use ½-inch VHS tape systems, not Beta. If you are making slides, keep them simple and uncluttered. Make four to five key points, maximum, per slide, and use colors that stand out. Avoid pastels and washed-out colors.
   - Overhead transparencies can be generated by computer. Software is available to create excellent color overheads to supplement your exercises and lecture.
   - Consider using a computer program or CD-ROM program with an overhead scanner to present it on a screen. This method allows you to show up-to-date information to groups, large or small.

Special Note.   Among the many facets of multimedia available to the sales trainer is the computer-based *Internet* and the *World Wide Web*. These resources are available to any trainer who has a computer, phone line, and a modem. The software will be supplied by the specific network for a monthly or hourly user fee. These networks allow you to tap into a 30-million-subscriber resource of information and technology on the information highway. Some of these resources include electronic mail, file transfer, and information reproduction as well as teleconferencing and telecommunications.

Trainers can contact other subscribers on the Web or network through use of a bulletin board and may reach other trainers and vendors on specific services such as *ASTD Online, America Online, Prodigy,* and *CompuServe.* Sales trainers can talk to other sales trainers, retrieve articles, and even reproduce graphics. Information on these services are available through your computer store or supplier.

4. *Prepare trainer's teaching guide.*   Develop a compact summary of what the trainer needs to know to conduct the training. Include:

- Role of the trainer or facilitator
- Program objectives—business, learning, and application objectives
- Section-by-section lesson plan with times, location, and activity
- Exercises, case studies, and other class materials
- Answer keys to questions and examples and other support material
- Copy for flipcharts, overheads, slides, etc.

Well-prepared instructional material makes the rest of the training process much easier.

Step 5: Design Measurement and Follow-Up Plan

Measuring training results can be the difference between having management look on your efforts as an expense (burden) or an investment (asset). When times get tough and money tight, you'll want to be considered a wise investment to keep around.

The operative word is *payoff,* and measurability is your primary means of proving the bottom-line worth of your training programs to the long-term organizational business goals. You measure training results to

- Establish credibility, power, and commitment for your training group
- Help sell future programs to management
- Determine if you need to change your program and/or trainers to be more effective
- Make sure the program satisfies the organization's and individuals' needs and achieves objectives
- Determines if and when a follow-up program is needed
- Most importantly, prove to management that there is real benefit in spending money for sales training

A fail-safe way to measure the results of training depends on having specific, realistic, and measurable objectives—learning, business, and application objectives—originally developed in your needs and task analyses. The specific form and nature of each objective and task determines the measurement method you can use.

The implication behind all measurement of training results is *accountability:* your willingness as a trainer to identify specific objectives and put your credibility on the line in measuring how well your program achieved those objectives. Remember, however, that your objectives originally were the result of a joint effort with your sales force, management, and others in the organization. If your training program is true to the original objectives and tasks, it has an excellent chance of achieving its goals.

What Exactly Do You Measure?

Kirkpatrick's four levels of evaluation give feedback to the effectiveness of the training (see Chap. 14, Evaluation). They are discussed below.

Level 1. This form of evaluation measures the value of the information transferred during training as perceived by the participant. It is also known as "love notes," as it often measures enjoyment rather than learning. The methods used are generally questionnaire, program critique, or personal interview. The participants complete the critique at the end of training and it will reflect their attitude toward the program techniques and the perceived value of the information. The real proof, however, lies with behavior changes back on the job.

Level 2. Level-2 evaluation measures the mastery of the new material and concepts. Used as a pretest before the program starts to rate the knowledge level prior to the training, the evaluation instrument may be used to retest at the end of the training to measure change. The questions should relate directly to a major learning objective, and the test should present all major concepts in the program. Level-2 tests may also be used throughout the training in the form of quiz-show games (e.g., *Jeopardy!* or *Family Feud*) to check understanding and retention. They are called competency games when used with interactive video or computer games.

Level 3. This level pertains to the application of the new information to the job, or what behavior change has taken place as a result of the training. It should involve the manager and his or her opinion on what influence the training has had on the performance of the participant. As we said earlier, employees will respect what you inspect more than what you expect. Don't be afraid to involve the sales manager in the evaluation process. It gives the program more credibility.

Level 4. Finally, there is level 4. This measurement shows tangible results which can be quantified and linked back to impact on the bottom line. Things such as new clients, better sales numbers, more sales calls, and a higher closing rate are all examples of results of your training according to level 4 measurement. If you can establish control groups, you can show the impact of the training by comparing the performance of the trained group against a nontrained group.

Remember, set up the evaluation so it is based on specific, measurable, and realistic criteria upon which your training is based.

When should you measure for results? Level 1 should be done at the end of the formal training. Level 2 should be done during the training and also at the end. Level 3 initially should be done a few weeks after the participant has returned to the job, but after that it should be ongoing. Level 4 should be done two to three months after the training is complete and every two to three months continuously after that.

Design your measurement program early and you'll have the tools for proving the value of your work.

Step 6: Select and Train Trainers, Instructors, and Facilitators

Once you've decided on a training delivery system, you will define the role of your program's trainer(s), instructor(s), or facilitator(s). Assessing their experience, you can determine the preparation your trainer(s) will need.

It may be that a professional trainer has been involved throughout the design and development program and will now be the person to bring it to life. Or maybe you now must decide who is going to be that trainer. Will it be a salesperson or sales manager who might need training in delivery skills? It might be a non-sales-experienced trainer who will have to understand the sales function, or it might be an outside professional who needs to learn your company's products, services, policies, and culture. A few considerations to remember in selecting a potential trainer are

- Ability to sell themselves, their ideas, and their organization
- High level of enthusiasm
- Upbeat, positive, can-do attitude toward the task and life itself!
- Ability to implement new ideas and stick with the material
- Ability to deal with big egos
- A problem solver—someone who can read the group and deal with hidden agendas
- Flexible—not steeped in hard, rigid thought processes
- Ability to facilitate a group without being the dominant center
- Strong interpersonal skills
- Strong platform skills, comfortable in front of an audience and able to manage multiple visuals at one time

You want fast-track people who have proven accomplishment and will offer fresh ideas. They will bring credibility to the training group, the sales force, and themselves. Here are some sources to draw from in selecting trainers:

- *Training staff.* People in the training group but who have real-world selling experience
- *Sales management.* When involved, they bring ownership to the program and will support the training
- *Senior salespeople.* Experienced existing salespeople who can add key examples and who are well respected
- *Champions.* Senior executives who support the training process can be used to introduce the program and set the sense of necessity for the training

- *Outside consultants.* Use these people when you want fresh ideas, different experiences, and need added help

It is the responsibility of the program owner or developer to train each trainer via a train-the-trainer workshop, complete with the trainer's guide previously mentioned. Provide your trainers with

- Clear learning objectives and role guidelines
- Assistance in structuring the presentation
- A well-equipped facility and the best learning atmosphere, like break-out rooms, computer terminals, refreshments, etc.

The more you involve management in your program as coaches, cheerleaders, experts, and troubleshooters, the more credibility your program will carry.

Step 7: Validate Program with a Pilot Group

Your program can die with the test group if you don't choose one carefully. For your pilot program—the "litmus paper" test that management wants to see before committing major resources—you'll want to select participants who

- Have a high degree of motivation
- Feel positive about their jobs and the company
- Have pride in doing a good job
- Understand their role in helping refine and improve the program before it goes out to the rest of the field

You *don't* want troublemakers, skeptics, stubborn argumentative souls to destroy the credibility you've worked so hard to achieve. So pick a group that will help achieve your main goal of refining the program and getting it off the ground. You're not stacking the deck, because you want and will get honest feedback. What you're doing is making sure the participants will play the game and take this opportunity seriously.

The best system for a pilot program is to form groups or teams of five people, with a "one" (top performer) and a "two" (supportive performer) on each team. Use preliminary material (see step 4). Arrange the facility, equipment, etc., for maximum comfort.

Step 8: Collect Data, Analyze, Modify Program

Step 8 is your opportunity to get all the feedback you can and hone your program to its sharpest edge.

Collecting data is similar to *needs analysis.* Gather data on participants' reactions through (1) questionnaires, (2) one-on-one interviews with participants immediately after the program, (3) one-on-one interviews with participants' managers, and (4) comparison of notes among facilitators.

One of the best ways to collect data is to observe the same participants in the field that you observed before the program. See whether they are better able to handle the challenges of sales situations.

Use *questionnaires* as a quick and inexpensive means of polling participants and their managers on the value of the training. Look through *company records* for signs of improvement after the trainees have been at work in the field. Keep in mind that behavioral change is extremely slow and requires plenty of practice and positive feedback. One by-product of this communication process is letting the sales organization know that the training group cares about the impact of its efforts.

Once you've analyzed the data, put it into a formal report. Identify all recommendations for change. Then identify changes you've made as a result of this process. Make the alterations to audiovisual and printed material.

Next *present to management* the results of the validation and analysis. Find out what management expects the program to do at this point. *Sell* the benefits and results based on your collected data. Identify benefits to all managers present in the meeting. Close the sale! Your continued credibility depends on being able to say, "See, it's just as great as I said it would be!"

Step 9: Implement Training

Now that you have evaluated the pilot and done any modifying needed, you are ready to put your salespeople through the program. It is time to

- Follow the proven plan
- Stay on schedule
- Identify participants and mix up the groups so they will have the benefit of attending with different salespeople than those with whom they work daily
- Keep management involved and appraised on the program

All the hard work has been done and you now have a well-prepared approach to changing behavior in the sales organization. Implementation and evaluation will help you maintain credibility with management for future projects.

Step 10: Conduct Ongoing Monitor and Enhancement Process

Sales training needs change all the time. You must be open to modifying your existing programs as those needs change. What worked last year may not be valid this year. Also, management commitment and support may vary as management changes. To stay up to date, sales training needs to

- Continue to add new techniques to existing programs
- Follow up with reminders and published success stories to the sales training graduates
- Keep in contact with sales managers to make sure there is not a return to bad habits

Design follow-up activities to continually remind participants of program basics. Consider sending out regular training bulletins, newsletters, or electronic messages via computer if that medium is available. Hold periodic meetings with salespeople to discuss challenges and how they may be met with future training.

Benchmark against other companies by becoming involved with professional societies that address training issues. Some of these are ASTD, which has a sales and marketing forum, and the National Society of Sales Training Executives (NSSTE). Also, review new books on selling techniques and make these available to the sales force in the form of a reading list or reprints.

Use coaching and counseling skills to help individuals continue their learning experience and hone their skills.

Coaching is the process of encouraging the individual to improve both job skills and knowledge.

Counseling centers on helping each salesperson handle attitude and motivation problems and maintain a winning attitude toward the job.

When coaching and counseling, keep these key points in mind

- Be a good listener, ask open-ended questions.
- Observe performance strengths and weaknesses.
- Present ideas for improvement as positive alternatives rather than fault-finding criticisms.
- Help the salesperson list specific steps to take to improve personal skills and achieve greater goals.

Training is really self-development. People react more positively to encouragement and praise than to criticism. Catch someone in the act of doing things right! Create a climate where individuals feel confident and able to control their performance and make contributions to the long-term goals of the organization.

Sales Trainer's Checklist

How do you make sure you've followed the 10 steps to productive training programs?

Figure 41-2 is a suggested sales training checklist. Use it to check off each stage of a program as you complete it. Put the completion date so you can look back to analyze how well the development cycle went for each particular program. Such retrospection provides you with important feedback for improving your next training program. The checklist also gives a ready visual confirmation of your progress in response to management requests for an update.

Sources and Resources for Sales Training

Here's a recap of important concepts in the chapter regarding support for your training objectives.

Course Title/Subject: _____

Intended Participants: _____

Department: _____ Manager: _____

Training Deadline: _____ Budget: _____

PREDEVELOPMENT QUESTIONS:
— Is this training necessary? Is a new program necessary? Would an existing program serve the same purpose?
— Bottom-line value to organization:

10 STEPS IN DEVELOPING PRODUCTIVE TRAINING: DATES
    1. Win Management Support of the project.
    2. Analyze Training Needs:
       — Design analysis instrument.
       — Conduct analysis, study, and observation.
    3. Sell Training Action Plan (TAP) to Management:
       — Summarize results of needs analysis.
       — Define program objectives.
       — Prepare detailed task analysis.
       — Identify available resources.
       — Present TAP to management.
    4. Develop Instructional Material:
       — Choose training media and methods.
       — Identify trainer's role.
       — Develop program material:
         . . . Copy
         . . . Graphics, printed material
         . . . Audiovisual segments
       — Prepare trainer's guide.
    5. Design Measurement and Follow-Up Plan.
    6. Select and Train Trainers.
    7. Validate Program with Pilot Group.
    8. Collect Data, Analyze, Modify Program:
       — Send and gather questionnaires.
       — Study company records, etc.
       — Present results to management.
    9. Implement Training.
   10. Conduct Ongoing Monitor and Enhancement Process:
       — 3-month review
       — 6-month review
       — Ongoing long-term reviews
FINAL CHECKS:
Have I kept management informed at each step?
Has this program contributed to my group's credibility?
What would I do differently to improve performance next time?
What's my next step to monitor and improve this program?

Figure 41-2. Sales training checklist.

Training the Sales Manager

Companies are usually quite willing to spend money to train salespeople, but not so eager to spend it for training sales managers. Research has proven that a good salesperson does not always make a good sales manager. The set of skills required for the sales manager is different from the skills required for the salesperson, and a newly promoted salesperson may not possess these. He or she must learn how to

- Be more of a coach, not a cheerleader
- Develop management skills like planning, leading, delegating, and controlling
- Create and maintain a climate for motivation
- Reinforce sales skills
- Foster a teamwork mentality

Networking and Professional Development

Sales trainers have someone else to develop: themselves: One effective way to enhance personal skills and professional knowledge is called *networking*. This is the process of interacting with other trainers and organizations such as those we mentioned earlier.

By interacting, you learn what other companies are doing, how they are doing it, and how they are evaluating the results. It can save you from "reinventing the wheel" and save valuable time wasted on trial and error. So, to further develop yourself:

- Read and review new programs and preview videotapes
- Attend training programs yourself
- Share ideas with other trainers
- Attend local professional meetings such as ASTD chapters
- Establish your own network of training colleagues, or get online with your computer

Finally, understand your organization's needs. Develop specific training and business objectives, make professional presentations to management, and above all, evaluate your programs for bottom-line results.

Be a risk taker. Be proactive. Apply the checklist and modify it to fit your needs. Consider yourself a professional and an important part of the success of your organization.

42

Small-Business Training

Martin M. Broadwell

Martin M. Broadwell *is president of the Center for Manage-ment Services, Inc., a Decatur, Georgia, consulting firm special-izing in designing and conducting supervisory and trainer devel-opment programs. Broadwell is the author of a dozen books on management, supervision, and training and several hundred articles on the same subjects. He has conducted seminars at the University of Michigan's Executive Management Institute for over 27 years, being awarded their "Father of Training" award for his years of service to them. In 1990 he was inducted into the prestigious HRD "Hall of Fame." He has been recognized by the Mayor of Atlanta for "Outstanding contributions in writing and research in business and industry." Prior to founding the Center for Management Services, he was an engineer for the Bell System, serving not only as a field engineer and manager but also as Engineering Personnel Director and Director of Technical Training. Since then, his travels and training have taken him to over 60 countries from China to the Soviet Union to Nepal to India and most European countries. His writings and books have been translated into several languages. He considers himself a writer first and a trainer second, and he divides his time between skiing, writing, and traveling, frequently doing all in the same venture.*

Much of what is written and spoken about training in the adult world, in confer-ences, training books, and magazines, is from the standpoint of large or relatively large organizations. These references cite human resource directors or depart-ments or training directors and training departments under the human resources director. Actually, in absolute numbers, many more organizations do not even have a whole department—or even one person—dedicated to the training and development of their people. Yet, these smaller organizations not only have the same kinds of training needs as the larger organizations but they may also have greater requirements because of the diversity of assignments created by their small size.

These small organizations span the entire spectrum. They include small businesses—from the mom-and-pop delicatessens that grow and add one, two, three, or more nonfamily members, to the high-tech units started in a basement or a garage that suddenly "catch fire" and mushroom to 25, 50, or more employees. They also include nonprofit organizations (e.g., churches, charities), municipalities (e.g., towns, counties, small cities, water districts), and small not-for-profits (e.g., foundations, associations).

Training problems in these small organizations are frequently created or enhanced because of size. In a small business with no training department, per se, one person may be designated "the trainer" and given responsibility for training in addition to all her or his other assignments and responsibilities. While such an in-house "expert" usually has certain technical knowledge (which earned him or her the assignment), that person may lack any usable knowledge about training theory, design, or delivery—and all that goes before and after that. In small organizations often the only training offered is skills or technical training, taught by these "experts"; it may be neither well presented nor well received.

Small organizations seldom have enough employees who can be spared from their regular jobs to be students for a formal "training class." This fact precludes having consultants come in to conduct a formal program on the subject. As a final drawback, in most small organizations those in top management usually rose to their positions with little, or no, formal training (after high school or college). So they may have a lack of appreciation for formal industrial training; in turn, their unenthusiasm makes it difficult to generate either money, time, or interest for formal training, up and down the line.

The training that does go on in small organizations, which may be only barely better than nothing at all, may be "canned" or "off the shelf"—e.g., commercial programs purchased complete with leaders' guides and/or videos. While such programs may be designed for one particular industry, such as retail grocery or hardware businesses, they try to be generic enough to fit all kinds of situations. The generic situations seldom fit the specific problems of any single organization. An added problem with commercial programs relates to the lack of qualified trainers to conduct them. Training may fall upon the shoulders of whomever happens to be available, rather than a trained instructor. Again, the lack of an adequate number of people available to make up an appropriate training class further compounds the problem.

The solution most frequently used—other than to provide no formal training at all—is to use so-called public training programs or services. These courses are conducted in many cities by organizations or individuals, invitation is by mass mailings, and the price is per person attending. (And the primary objective of these programs is the sponsor's profit, not meeting the training needs of the attendees.) While public training programs can solve the problems of not having an in-house trainer or enough people to make up a class, the problem of the material not being specific enough for the organization still exists. Also, since all attendees bring their own needs and agendas to the session and have equal right to be heard, the class discussion often deals with problems and situations propounded by the most vocal attendee but of little or no relevance to others. Many times the only restriction on the number of people present is the number who respond to the mailings. A cutoff dictated by the room size, rather than by good training standards, can lead to large numbers of attendees in a ballroom setting, with a resulting decrease in the effectiveness of the program. Still, public programs remain a meaningful way to get certain types of training, although this type of training is much more expensive, per student, than in-house training.

So, are there solutions? In this chapter we will deal with some possible alternatives, including developing and presenting programs on an in-house basis. And we will see how to develop a practical "training philosophy" in any small organization, and how to make it work. Later, we will discuss who does the training, but for now we will look at what should be done to put together any kind of in-house training program.

But first, a word of caution: *training for the sake of training* must be avoided at all costs! The best way to discourage training at all levels is to put together a nonrelevant program and then urge (or force) employees to attend. Doing training is not nearly as important as doing the *right* training. So you must figure out what training is needed and set priorities, generally where the greatest payoff will be.

Start with a Training Needs Analysis

Training needs analysis simply means figuring out *if* training is needed and, if so, *what* training. Many ways of doing the needs analysis are fairly simple, though they may not be completely accurate.

Fortunately, many training needs are pretty obvious. For example, many technical jobs are unique to a business and must be learned in-house. If several people need to learn the job, because of expansion or newly developed technology, and no outside training sessions are available, sometimes equipment manufacturers or suppliers will conduct programs on their equipment or, at least, provide training guides for use by in-house instructors. Often, experts or specialists already on the business's payroll can be used—with proper train-the-trainer training themselves—for this training effort. The good part about this situation is that the initial job-skills deficiencies are so obvious that no "selling" of the training is necessary. Since these technologies are an integral part of the operations of the business, they are obviously top priority and will have the greatest immediate payoff.

Surveys

To develop a formal needs analysis, questionnaires are available commercially, but they can be made up in-house easily enough. Simply asking various groups if they feel their jobs would improve if they had some training, and, if so, what training they need is actually a need analysis. Another approach is to offer a list of possible subjects for training, then have the people check—possibly in some kind of priority order—which of the listed courses they would like to have. A third type of survey would be to ask supervisors where in their units they feel weaknesses lie that might be overcome with training. Each of these methods is really an opinion poll; we must remember that when we ask people's opinions, what we get are opinions, not necessarily facts!

Some training needs are not so obvious, and the payoff is not so immediate—with supervisory training, for example. We find that in small organizations less thought is generally given to formal supervisory training, especially at the first level of management.

Supervisory Needs

Many organizations assume that, because people know their jobs and have been doing them well, they should be promoted to supervise those jobs. The truth is that doing an operational job well does *not* mean that the person has the skills to be a good supervisor. Supervisory skills are very different from operational ones. And, people coming from outside the organization will be even less likely to fill the supervisory position adequately without training. (They have to learn the organization's culture as well as the technical and supervisory parts of the job.) Unfortunately, this situation is not always recognized as a training need. As a result, many new supervisors learn many things incorrectly and then carry these mistakes (mislearnings) for a long time. And, more importantly, if they have bad "people skills," these men and women too often may not be thought of as "bad supervisors" but as having poor-quality people working for them.

People brought in from outside the organization to supervise, or manage at higher levels for that matter, are usually selected because of their technical skills and knowledge, as opposed to their having good supervisory techniques. Frequently in small organizations, the atmosphere or climate is more friendly or "familylike," with a higher priority being placed on social skills than on performance skills. The hardship comes when it is necessary to take the proper action—especially if the supervisors have not received adequate training.

This lack of training also precludes any introduction to the newer managerial styles or approaches. Even if someone goes "outside" for a managerial development or training program, it is difficult to effectively bring this information into the organization in the absence of a training department or even a trainer.

Assessing Performance

A more sophisticated method of doing a needs analysis is available that will give us better information. We can deal in specific behaviors. Instead of asking for "courses," we can ask for behaviors that are absent or weak. For example: "When you begin to do your job, in what skills (or knowledge) do you find yourself most lacking? In which of these areas could training be the most help? This question could be asked of individuals suspected of needing the training or of their supervisors.

The most accurate way to determine training needs is to look at the operating results of the organizational unit. If sales are down in certain areas, with no market change but some newer salespeople—or a new product has been introduced (without training) and is not selling as well as projected—then training would seem to be a legitimate option. If safety is faltering, and new equipment or people are involved, training is a possible solution. In other words, look for places where the operating results show a need on the bottom line of that part of the operation.

Small organizations are often rapidly growing, an almost sure sign that training is, or will be, needed. Even if much of the growth is by moving skilled people in from the outside, training will be needed to get everyone doing their jobs the same way. This fact not only applies to technical skills but also to supervisory ones. The only way to get every supervisor treating subordinates the same way is through training; the same is true for customer relations, or accounting, or engineering design. People coming in from other environments bring different philosophies, views, and, certainly, skills. Training should be seen as the best way to get everyone on some common ground of behavior.

One thing is certain: the most productive training is that training which has the greatest payoff in the least time. If a training fad is going around and many organizations are apparently training their way into this new idea, this should not automatically establish a training need in another organization. The best approach is to investigate immediate results. If the results to be obtained by using this new and different approach are pretty well into the future, there is a good chance that other, more advantageous ways are available for using the limited training dollars available—dollars that will have much quicker payoffs.

Developing a Training Philosophy

Successful organizations have developed basic philosophies about various parts of their business. They have philosophies about customer relations, ethics, employee relations, minority hiring, etc. Many organizations are successful because they also have decided to put together a *training philosophy*. One of the first things small organizations must realize is that they *are* small. So they cannot compete with the larger organizations in most areas, including training. This fact means at least two things: (1) A full-scale, fully functioning training department is not much of a possibility; and (2) much of what is needed in the way of skills and knowledge will have to be learned on the job. As we've already seen, training often will be limited to the essentials and to those areas with the most immediate payoff.

Another limitation is that in small organizations, management styles tend to reflect the hierarchy. Hence, the management style may be set without training. In other words, those who survive in the organization must of necessity manage about the same way as top management does. Since there is frequently less distinction between levels in smaller organizations, this arrangement may be a means of stability—the organization not having to adjust to different styles. If the styles are roughly the same, less need exists for training in management or supervisory skills. This similitude may result in a stifling of initiative or imagination, but that's not a training problem!

Even with the above limitations and problems, it is still advantageous to have a training philosophy. It may come from the bottom to the top or from the top down, but however it comes into being, *it must be bought into by top management.* The reason is simple: training costs money, takes people away from the workplace, and requires expertise. If those doing the training must buck top management for every dollar of training cost and every minute of training time, the training cause will be lost. It's more than a matter of supplying the funds without any goals or direction. Top management must be willing to put their beliefs in writing and share them with their subordinates. The philosophy need not be elaborate, nor is there a form for it; it just needs to be a statement of how the organization is to approach training.

Policy Statement

The policy statement or philosophy should not only give an idea of the amount, quality, and budget for training but it should also state such things as the organization's view toward quality, customers, treatment of employees, handling good and bad performance, and regulations (e.g., of EEO, EPA, OSHA, ADA). The training policy can be put in terms of *how much* training or *what kind* of training is necessary. It might state that all new employees or new supervisors will have a certain number of days of training up-front, with refresher training of so many days per year. It may say a similar thing for the experienced employees and for the technical or production employees. An ample amount of specificity is needed avoiding general, nonmeasurable expressions such as "the customer comes first" or "people are our most valuable asset." Such statements offer no clue as to what employees are to do for customers or what the organization is to do for its people.

A more specific philosophy is preferable, because it puts things in measurable terms. It specifies not only the preferred management style but also how this style will be developed (through training, mentoring, osmosis, etc.). It should also tell the trainers what is defined as satisfactory performance—so training can be done to reach this end—and explain how those will be treated who do and don't meet these specifications.

Working with a Small Training Department or Staff

It is not unusual for either no one person to be actually designated as a trainer or for a designated trainer to have a very small staff. The most obvious point in such situations is that, to be successful, this "trainer" must be, or become, a multifaceted person. He or she must have multiple skills and must know much about operations in many parts of the organization. That person must be not only a talented classroom trainer but also a designer and producer of training programs, an administrator, a budgeteer, a seller of training, and, perhaps most importantly, a good politician.

Where does all this talent come from? Since rarely will such a person be found within the organization, the most obvious solution is to hire someone who has already demonstrated these skills with another organization. However, if it seems important to "raise up" someone from within the organization, *and time is available,* two things are particularly important:

1. These skills are best learned in seminar sessions where much practice is afforded.

2. Membership in an appropriate professional association is an absolutely essential activity. Joining local training groups is helpful. Participation in national or regional meetings and training sessions is also an immediate necessity, especially in the first months of having the assignment.

If someone is hired from the "outside," it must be remembered that the fact that he or she is not familiar with *this* organization results in two requirements: (1) No matter how much experience the person has—even in the same industry—*it is not with* this *organization.* Therefore, the new hire must take some time to become acquainted with the people, the needs, the policies, and philosophy where the training will be done. (2) Also, of necessity, considerable participation and cooperation will be required *from within the organization.* This intraorganizational interaction serves two functions: it not only gives the new person some knowledge of the organization in a hurry, but it also allows for some "selling" of training. Discussions with employees in various parts of the organization allows those people to see that there is a "new kid on the block" who is dedicated to helping them overcome some deficiencies within their work group. The new hire can make this attitude pay off by pointing out that, with a little assistance from these departments in the way of borrowed instructors or steering committee participation, some good things can happen in the way of training.

Steering Committees

It will be helpful to have a steering committee to help make decisions and supply information. These people should represent the decision makers, the potential users of the training, the budget control people, and the supervisors of those to be trained. A small group that doesn't have to meet often, it is a continuing source of help and information for the new trainer. It also becomes a part of the selling process. The more people who know about training plans and who assist in making decisions about training needs, possible participants, and where and how to get instructors, the more likely they are to support the training.

What do steering committee members do? They meet when the trainer needs them. They have no longevity promise. They supply information about when people can get off for training and how many can be spared. Above all, they offer assistance in the needs analysis and the knowledge and skills needed to do the job. What do they *not* do? They don't do the training design; they don't make training decisions about whether to use computers or overhead projectors in the training. They are not training experts! They are advisors on organizational considerations.

Professional Training Organizations

Another essential source of assistance for the one-person or small training organization is the professional training societies. ASTD, ISPI, and others are the obvious "generic" training organizations but also the discipline-specific organizations like sales-training, hospital-training, and insurance-training groups can be very helpful. As would be expected, the caliber of the local organizations may vary, which is also true of the national meetings and/or conferences. The best way to find out how good each group is, short of joining or going to meetings, is to talk with members who have similar needs for assistance and get their opinions on how much help is available through them.

"Borrowed" Training Staff

One very satisfactory solution to the small-size problem, in addition to the training steering committee, is to use a "borrowed" training staff. In talking with people from a small organization, finding out their needs, a trainer from an outside training organization can offer quicker training programs in return for some part-time help in developing the training and in the teaching to follow. If a good in-house train-the-trainer course is available that teaches good group interaction and gives skills for conducting dynamic meetings, many managers will want their people to become instructors just to get the additional training. It can be sold on the basis that "we'll make better potential supervisors out of these people you loan us in return for using them occasionally in our training." In addition, the actual classroom training experience will be invaluable to them in their poise and group dynamics. An obvious advantage to the "borrowing" concept is that people with excellent technical skills are available whereas they wouldn't be if they had to be on the training staff full-time. They bring not only a high degree of skills and competency, they bring credibility and respect to the training program.

The real key is to not overuse these borrowed instructors. Get more than one to teach the same sections so they can relieve each other and not be overburdened. A whole week of training can be put together with the use of several instructors. The same person may teach more than once but not necessarily on consecutive days. Two people can split a day, hence be away from their regular job only a half day. It is important to recognize these instructors as contributing to the success of the program. After all, they are holding down their own job and a portion of another.

Instructor Training

Instructor training is important, as we've seen, either as an in-house program or externally. Making sure it is an effective program, teaching people with high school competency but low teacher skills how to transfer learning in the classroom is vital. For a quick initial assessment as to the effectiveness of an instructor training program, examine the brochures and other advertising material to see what is promised and how they deliver. If the emphasis is on "platform skills," shy away; if it is on producing learning and student involvement and offers a solid set of objectives on what the participants will be able to do at the end of the training, it's worth further investigation.

The key to good training of trainers is to get them to understand that the training is being done because the learners have deficiencies on the job and the organization has decided to change that situation with classroom training. Therefore, the instructor's job is to produce *learning*—new skills—not just to "put the information out" for the students if they want it. The problem usually stems from the potential instructor's past experiences with academic role models who just lecture day after day. It's hard not to follow this easy practice, especially when one is blessed with a considerable amount of knowledge and skill in the subject to be taught!

Outside Help

If the concept of borrowed instructors doesn't fit the organization's philosophy or format and the training can't be done with the limited training staff, then the only alternative is to look outside the organization for people with the necessary expertise. This may range from a college instructor to a retired employee to a consultant who is well versed in the field of the deficiency. Any of these people are acceptable if they have not only the skills and knowledge needed but also the proven skills of instructing in that field. Retired employees can be a good choice, as they are familiar with the organization's policies and procedures and have actual experience in the subject. However, they may have an information lag if they have been retired too long or if there has been a rapid shift in technology. In most cases, they can catch up quickly, certainly more quickly than a nonemployee would.

College professors who most often avoid instructor training classes feel their experience already makes them good teachers. They may be in institutional classrooms, but they need to understand that training classes will be monitored by the training staff and the students will be evaluating the instruction as well. For the most part, such instructors aren't used to teaching the same students for several hours—even all day—and are also used to giving assignments at night (often to make up for lecture deficiencies during the day). Also they may not be accustomed to the concept that training objectives are for all students to *learn* the material or skill, not just for the instructor to cover the material.

University-based instructors frequently have experience in instructing outside the university and so may be an excellent choice. They may be familiar with the "eccentricities" of the business world. They may have even worked with a particular organization before in another training effort. Ideally you should look for those people with proven track records in industry rather than just look for those with technical competency. If good instructors are found, using them will work to your organization's advantage, increasing both its credibility and its employees' experience. (Incidentally, even large organizations use university-based training for their executive management personnel and it is not difficult to meet this need at a number of universities.)

Another resource for outside instructing is consultants. These people, more in supervisory and management instructing than in technical fields, usually do excellent instructing.

Also, consulting organizations may have people on staff for many instructing functions, including computer-based teaching and other technical areas. As with the academic-based help, consultants should be evaluated on their track record. Ask for the names of previous clients, then talk with them and see what results they had from the consultants. It's important to find out if the topic taught is close to the one needed by this organization. If so, then see if the students performed satisfactorily *on the job, not just in the classroom!* Another advantage of this kind of outside help is that most people are making a living at it and want to do a good job for the possibility of further work.

Whether outside help consists of former employees, college teachers, or consultants, it's a good idea not to make a long-term commitment. It's worth a little larger expenditure initially to get a one-time effort for evaluation. Just make sure the instructors will be available for the longer term, if they are satisfactory. If so, then give them as much support as possible and go for good training.

Pricing

"How much does one pay for this service?" The obvious response is, "How much is it worth to the organization to have employees able to meet the objectives promised?" A more realistic response is, "How much is the going price in the community?" This price can be determined by asking other trainers—perhaps at a local training society meeting. The important consideration is to be willing to pay enough to get good talent, doing a good job. (To facilitate a good job, it may be necessary to include some funds for development, remembering that if we did the course ourselves, we'd have development costs and people time too.)

Working with No Training Staff

Depending upon the size of the organization and the commitment and importance of training, the training activity will vary as to size, even in the small ones. While it isn't fair to judge commitment purely by size, it is usually a matter of priorities as to where the money goes and for what. A one-person training department isn't unusual but neither is a no-person function. Usually, it is a case where the personnel department or the benefits department or maybe even the human resource group will devote some time to training. The actual training may be "mandated" training such as safety or other compliance training. Since it's only a part-time responsibility, only those absolute necessities get handled in training. So other concerns such as career development, supervisory and management training, and perhaps even diversity and the "softer" skills get left behind.

A Training Coordinator

The first, and perhaps best, option is for someone to be assigned the responsibility for coordinating the training. Here, again, is the place for a good training steering committee. The declared purpose of the committee is to see that the necessary training is conducted and to make people available as needed. The work of the training coordinator is to provide data for the committee to work with, including any surveys or requests for training and perhaps suggestions for outside people who could conduct the training in-house.

Who's On the Steering Committee?

We've talked earlier about the makeup of the training steering committee; let's look at some specific members. First, someone needs to be designated as the training coordinator. This isn't a title; it is a responsibility. Then, someone from higher management is needed—someone high enough up to speak for policy, personnel, and money—in other words, someone with enough clout to see that the people are turned loose for training as needed and that enough money is provided in the budget to accomplish the training desired and decided upon. One or more people from first-line supervision are needed since most of the training is usually centered around this level or at least those who report to this level. If the training is to be for the first-liners, several (two or three) of them should be on the committee. If the training is to be below this level, several of the prospective trainees should represent that group.

One of the most important aspects of developing a valid training program in a small organization—whether a training department exists or not—is to keep the union involved, if there is a union. Getting their buy-in on programs that affect their population is important to the success of the program and they often can help by making certain concessions on time and pay during training. To do training without their involvement is to invite their intervention in a more hostile or challenging way.

Steering Committee Functions

How does the steering committee function, and what does it do when there is no real training department to give it direction? It sets its own direction, using the help of higher management for purpose and goals and the help of the other members for support and assistance. It generally works better if different people play different roles, take their own specific responsibilities, and be empowered to solicit additional people to help them. The work to be done and decisions to be reached include making some kind of needs analysis, selecting someone to design the training, picking instructors, determining costs, scheduling training, selecting training sites, determining priorities for who needs training, and working on how to evaluate the training.

Needs Analysis

Let's look at some of these functions, one at a time. First, the matter of a needs analysis. It's not nearly as complicated or as time-consuming as one might think. The whole thing can be done in two to three weeks. A simple survey, asking for what kind of training might be needed will often suffice. If 20 to 30 people respond, the information will be reasonably valid. The questionnaire can be a one-page document with places for a checklist or for one-word write-ins. The key is not to get overburdensome or people will put off filling it out and finally throw it away. The questions should be simple: In what areas do you feel you have strengths? In what areas do you think additional training would help? What new things would you like to know or be able to do that would help you in your job? Overall, what kind of training would be most helpful for the supervisors (or hourlies, computer operators, etc.)? The checklist could list specific or general courses and ask for a priority rating: Please rate the following on a priority basis; which would offer you the most benefit in your job? (Rate as high, medium, low, or on a scale of 1 to 5.) The same kind of survey could be sent to the supervisors or managers about their subordinates. The results can then easily be summarized and recommendations made.

Selecting and Training Instructors

Another responsibility has already been mentioned: selection of instructors. Good instructors are not limited to large organizations. For the most part, good instructors are trained, not born. They are usually picked for their knowledge and experience because that is a foundation to build upon, not a guarantee of success. They usually will need some form of "instructor training."

A simple instructor-training course may include basic steps in designing and conducting training. It would give the potential instructors a fundamental philosophy of a "learner-centered classroom." To be successful, the instructor must get much involvement from the students and the course must teach various involvement techniques including use of questions, subgroup activities, debating, agree-disagree exercises, the process of role-plays and case studies, and whatever other techniques the organization cares to use. (Determining what involvement technique to use is the job of the trainer, not the steering committee!) A number of practice sessions should be included in which the future instructors try out the techniques until they feel comfortable with *not* lecturing.

A final word of caution in selecting instructors: The training room, where a number of people are coming to learn a skill that they do not now have—and which the organization says they ought to have—is definitely not the place to put people who "just can't cut it" anywhere else. *It is the place for the best people, not the worst!*

The steering committee can also take on the responsibility of picking which employees have the greatest need for, or where there will be the most payoff from, the training. They can also work out the scheduling, deciding which people can be spared at which times during the week or month. This responsibility should also include picking training sites, making reservations, seeing to training equipment, notifying students and supervisors, even deciding what to do about lunches and breaks.

A final responsibility that cannot be taken lightly is the evaluation of training. Again, the philosophy must be that the true test of successful training is not how well the students *liked* the training or the teacher; it is a matter of how well they are able to meet the objectives when they walk out of the classroom—or more importantly—*when they get back on the job*. Here again, a questionnaire will help, given either at the end of the class or back on the job, or both. The questions aren't concerned with the respondents' happiness; they are concerned with changed behavior: What can you do now that you couldn't do before you came? What have you been able to do better now that you've been back on the job for X months? There will be more about the evaluation survey at the close of the chapter because it is the whole measure of how well the planning, the training, the instruction, and the students have done.

Training Administration

Incidentally, the steering committee must also make arrangements for the cost of all this activity. That's why someone needs to be on the committee who has the authority to make financial decisions and commitments. The overall function of the training steering committee is to take the place of a training administration staff. Members do not all have to meet all the time or be at all meetings. They do need to be there when their expertise or authority is needed. A successful committee will have its members doing what they do best and let others have the same privilege. They won't overlap or infringe on one another's territory but will assist as needed. Usually, the person wearing the "training hat" is the one to facilitate this happening. Let the committee be the sales force, let them solve the money, people, policy, philosophy, and procedure problems.

Training from Equipment Suppliers

We've talked about using outside training sources. Let's see how that works with training in both technical and people skills. Usually, vendors have some kind of training to go with their equipment and will offer it either as a condition of purchase or for a nominal fee. They frequently have training manuals that can be used in-house—but instructors are still required. It's always worth asking vendors for help even to the point of finding a qualified consultant to do the training. This is true for both new and presently owned equipment. The hazard in this effort is that not all vendors provide good trainers. It's an added expense to them and they may not have instructors who are well trained. As suggested earlier, it's a good idea to do your initial contracting on a short-term basis, rather than a long-term commitment, until the quality and applicability of the training is determined. Here again, asking previous users for their evaluations is usually a time- and cost-saving measure.

Because not all equipment vendors have training and not all of what is available is good or suitable, another possible source of help is the local vocational-technical school. If the technical skills are common to many people, courses may be available as may instructors who can come in and do the training on-site. Frequently, these instructors are people who are presently working on other jobs, doing what they're training on, giving them additional expertise and credibility. If you have some flexibility to meet their schedules, this alternative can be a viable solution to technical training needs.

Supervisory Training

Supervisory and/or management training is easily done by outside consultants. All the same rules apply as to choice and evaluation of these people. The following is a not-very-accurate rule of thumb: If a consultant is readily available ("next Monday"), it may be that he or she isn't much in demand. This availability, in turn, may suggest something about his or her ability. One thing is certain: If that person is ready to come in and run a generic program for the organization, it may be of questionable value. The criteria to look for is someone, or some organization, who immediately asks questions to find out something about your organization and makes an offer that includes needs analysis, measurable objectives, description of the training activities, and a suggested way of measuring the results. While a few things are generic in the people skills areas, the case studies and other action activities should be based on situations that *this* organization, not unrelated ones, would face.

Supervisory Training Should Fit Organizational Philosophy

One more thought about the choice of outside trainers and the kind of courses they run as far as people skills are concerned. It is imperative that the training fits the philosophy of the organization's management. Often an outsider gets better access to higher management than even a titled trainer in the organization. This opportunity should be used in determining the kind of training to be done. The ideal way of doing this is to present members of higher management with the case studies or other activities to be used in the courses and ask them for solutions. "Here is a case we'll be using. I'd like to make certain I'm echoing the organization's philosophy on the answer, so what should I tell them about this particular case?" Ask this question enough times and a pattern develops. It is a definite mistake to train first-line management people on a technique or style that is not practiced or believed in by their superiors. Put simply, if the organization doesn't practice participative management, it shouldn't be taught. If the organization says it believes in "empowerment" but higher management isn't willing to turn loose their control, it's a disservice to all levels to spend time trying to teach the skill. Asking them if they believe in it is one thing; asking them what to say in teaching several cases is another, more accurate way of finding out what to teach. In fact, this is one of the real problems with getting and using "canned programs." They often tout some current style or philosophy which may not have been accepted by the management of this organization. In the final analysis, it is still the role of the steering committee to approve the approach and style to be taught.

Evaluation Is Essential

Evaluation is a serious matter and needs a few more comments in addition to those already appearing in this chapter. The reason and the goals are simple. We found that there were performance problems in the organization which we feel training can and should address (needs analysis). We developed specific objectives to overcome these deficiencies. We designed (in-house or with outside contractors) a training program. We conducted the program. The measure of success is simple, though two-faceted. First, at the end of the training, determine if the students have met the objectives, i.e., can they do what we said they would be able to do when the course is over? Secondly, and harder to determine, see if the deficiency is gone from the job after the trainees have been back to work for a reasonable length of time.

All of this effort means that we'll have to monitor the training in some manner to make sure that the course is producing the correct and desired behaviors. We've talked about questions to ask at the end of the training and in surveys back on the job, for both the trainees and the supervisors. Another way of monitoring performance is to watch the training as it progresses. Primarily, we are watching the participants, not the instructors. If the training design is done correctly, the training will be using techniques that have the students "doing" the objectives as they go along. Watch them do their role-plays, conduct practice interviews or solve cases with poor-performing employees, give answers to action mazes, or progress through management games. These are indicators that the students at least know the right answers and right behaviors, whether or not they later apply them on the job.

Opinion Surveys

Three degrees of measuring can determine the success of our program. First, we've talked about *opinion surveys*. These are easy to do and quick to administer, and they give a lot of information in a hurry. The only drawback is that all we have when we are through is a lot of opinions. Opinions are just that: opinions. However, enough people saying the same thing is pretty good feedback if they are talking about training deficiencies, not how the training was done.

Behavioral Change

The next step up in reliability is measuring behavioral change. This task can be done with surveys but the information must deal with specific changes in behavior, not just, "Has the employee improved?" It still relies somewhat on opinions, but if we ask for examples of behavior changes we'll have a measure of how well the behavioral objectives have been met.

Operational Results

The higher order of evaluation is to look at *operational results*. This evaluation is the most reliable one but may be the most difficult to obtain. It is sometimes difficult to measure things like good supervision through reports but factors such as turnover, number of grievances, even tardiness and absenteeism are pretty good indications of effective supervision. Any significant changes will tell us that our training has brought results.

However, time is a factor. It takes longer for these things to get into a system and into the reports, hence longer to give us good data on our training. If the time and people are available to look at the aforementioned indicators, the results are well worth it.

One last caution: Any one of these measuring processes is solely dependent upon how well we did the initial needs analysis. If we don't keep good records on safety, we can't take much credit for our training with no beginning reference point. Without these records, we may have to go back to our "happiness ratings" and see if we've left the students feeling good. It's difficult to justify training for very long just on that basis!

Conclusion

Small organizations need training just as badly, or perhaps even more, than large organizations. With many people wearing many hats, with people changing jobs to keep the organization alive, training needs flourish. Waiting until the organization gets big enough to "justify" or afford training isn't the answer. No matter how small the organization, managers and supervisors still need help; customers still need good treatment and good service; people with potential still need to be developed; and there are constantly changing skill needs in technical jobs.

Problems exist in doing successful training in a small organization, but there are solutions, some of which have been brought forth in this chapter. Bad supervision destroys good people; bad managers destroy future business; bad customer relations destroy present business. The organization that wishes to survive and survive well has no choice: training can and should take place.

43

Customer Service Training

Chip R. Bell

Fran C. Sims

Chip R. Bell *is a senior partner with Performance Research Associates, Inc. (PRA), and manages the Dallas, Texas, office. PRA is a consulting firm which specializes in service quality training and consulting. Dr. Bell was formerly Vice President and Director of Management and Organization Development for NationsBank. He holds graduate degrees in organizational psychology and human resource development from Vanderbilt University and The George Washington University. He is author or coauthor of nine books, including* Service Wisdom *(Lakewood Books, 1989) and the best-seller* Managing Knock Your Socks Off Service *(AMACOM, 1992) both coauthored with consulting partner Ron Zemke;* Customers as Partners: Building Relationships That Last *(Berrett-Koehler Publishers, 1994); and his newest book* Managers as Mentors: Building Partnerships for Learning *(Berrett-Koehler Publishers, 1996). His articles have appeared in* Management Review, Executive Excellence, Training *magazine,* HR *magazine,* Supervisory Management, Mobius, Advanced Management Journal, Training & Development, *and many others. He has hosted three major training films on service management, and has served as consultant and/or trainer to such major organizations as IBM, Microsoft, GE, Motorola, Digital, Eli Lilly, Nabisco, Price Waterhouse, Aetna, Shell Oil, BF Goodrich, First Union, and Duke Power.*

Fran C. Sims *has been an independent management and training consultant, as well as a trainer, for the past 20 years. Her major focus has been in the field of helping organizations to evaluate and improve their customer relations. She has used her skills in government environments, corporations, health-care institutions, professional associations, and private enterprise. At the same time, Sims has been executive director of Suncoast*

Management Institute, a management development consortium affiliated with the St. Petersburg Area Chamber of Commerce. Prior to this work, she was responsible for management development within two major hospitals. She also served as Director of Volunteer Services, managing over 400 volunteers for one of those hospitals. She is also a former classroom teacher, having taught in a five-room schoolhouse in Alabama. Her first work after graduating from college 30 years ago was as Director of Christian Education for a 1000-member church. Sims' ASTD service spans over 20 years. In 1989 she served as the chairperson for the highly successful Region IX Conference. She has also served on a committee for selecting speakers for the Management Development Track of the ASTD National Conference.

"How many of you do customer service training in your organizations?" the master of ceremonies asked a management conference of 1000 attendees just before one of us was to speak on this topic. Almost every hand in the house went up! The MC had one more question for the audience.

"How many of you have formalized, organized classes on customer service?" Less than 10 percent of the hands went up! The room burst into laughter. All realized how ambivalent the phrase "customer service training" could be. Since we were working on this chapter at the time, the incident led us to conclude that some up-front definition of terms might be in order.

"Customer service training" will be the label used to refer to any planned (as opposed to haphazard), organized activity aimed at instilling the competencies (knowledge, skills, and attitudes) needed to ensure that customers are effectively being served. While the primary target of most customer service training is the front-line customer contact person, we will also explore customer service training for leaders (i.e., managers and supervisors).

Labeling customer service as we have excludes the "watch Nellie" method—an old-fashioned and too-often-relied-upon approach. It also rules out the "sink or swim" method which is even more misguided. We *will* include training which does not rely on a classroom setting but is nevertheless planned and organized. The effectiveness and growing pervasiveness of self-directed learning applies to customer service training as well.

Now, let's get started. We are making a few assumptions about you which we want you to know. And, we know the trouble assumptions can get one in. If you are really reading this chapter (rather than just scanning it), we will assume you are either a relatively inexperienced trainer, or a training supervisor seeking to learn more about this area, or an experienced trainer with limited experience in the customer service training area. Finally, you might be an experienced trainer seeking a few new ideas on the topic.

Be forewarned! There are complete books and countless articles on this topic. This chapter is just a sampler (or perhaps teaser). We will be successful if you get an overview you find useful, raise issues which keep you out of potholes and dead-end streets, and provide resources helpful to your continued learning.

What Is Customer Service All About?

We believe a few concepts about customer service are in order so we are all "singing off the same songsheet." Customer service is far more than a friendly "how may I help you?" Being fast, friendly, and helpful can be great attributes, but they are no guarantees of success. Customer service success requires a keen understanding of how best to manage a complex relationship with changing expectations and increasingly demanding requirements.

Effectiveness of customer service training starts with a recognition that service and product are very different. If there is one factor most impacting success in customer service training, it is this: If training is designed, delivered, or managed with the belief that customer service training is similar to other kinds of training, it will fail.

The stakes are high; over 72 percent of our gross national product derives from performing a service, not making a product. Similarly, more than three of four jobs in the United States, and more than 80 percent of the new jobs created in the decade of the 1990s are help-me, fix-it, value-added roles.

The output of the production world is an object; the output of the service world is a memory. This suggests that service training need be patterned more after Disney than Ford. While a product is a tangible commodity, a service is an intangible experience. Products can be inventoried and stored, stockpiled against the expectation that someday a shopper will call for them. They can be previewed or sampled to build a sense of security, tangible trust, and predictability. If found wanting, they can be returned for refund or replacement.

Services, on the other hand, have to be created as they are needed—you can't put haircuts, or appendectomies, or flights to Cincinnati on a shelf and ring them up when a customer comes through the door. Neither can you offer sample sizes or 10-day free trials with a money-back guarantee. And there's no way to return a service. It's an intangible exchange of effort for money that occurs in an interpersonal relationship that can't be recaptured, only repeated.

Consequently, the focus on training and the performance which follows must be on quality, not solely on quantity. As producing objects is a rational, concrete science, performing a service is an emotional, creative art. Subjectivity and perception rule out over objectivity and reality. So the training must zero in on sensitivity to customer needs and unique responses to consumer expectations.

This fact does not imply that customer service training is only relevant for memory-making industries like banks, hotels, airlines, and theme parks. Even manufacturers are affected. Service is what distinguishes one commodity from another. Whether that commodity is an automobile or a credit card is irrelevant. The consumer assumes that the car will start and the credit card will be accepted. Satisfaction comes from how the car is sold and serviced, how the credit card issuer responds to inquiries and solves problems.

In production, uniformity is a virtue; in service, it's often a disaster. The customer says, "Treat me as an individual. I want it my way." Whether the service at hand is accounting or medicine, suddenly an hour of production time is no better or worse than two hours. The issue is what the front-line worker is able to do for the customer. Because one size doesn't fit all in service work, doing business requires front-line people who have been trained and empowered to respond creatively and personally—people who can figure out and provide what the individual customer wants.

In the production world, buyers are viewed as end-users. Their input is collected, boiled down, filtered through market research and homogenized into a generalized understanding of the average prospect's tastes, preferences, and buying habits. They're not presented when the product is being designed and manufactured; they would just get in the way. But notice how things change when producing gives way to performing. Customers are there when the service is created and delivered. Very often, they share in that process. Service-seeking customers enter the factory and participate with front-line employees in creating an experience.

Production people never worry how customers feel about the production process for the simple reason that consumers are not involved in that process. But customer service employees make it or break it on customer relations because their consumers wander around the "factory" getting in the way of the work and the workers! Customers are cocreators—or partners—in the creation of the service experience. Successful customer service employees must be highly competent in partnering skills. Surly attitudes and body odor may not adversely impact the quality of widgets coming off the assembly line, but they dramatically impact the memory of the customer of service.

These three factors—a focus on *memories* which need to meet the *unique* requirements of buyers who *partner* in creating those memories—create a vastly different approach to training than a world in which the focus is on uniform objects required by end-users. Learners must be adaptable and creative and excellent listeners. They must possess skills of partnering and relationship management. Leaders must be able to model all these customer service skills. They must be able to support and direct on-the-job behaviors so that employees are positively reinforced to use what they have learned.

What Are the Attributes of Great Customer Service Training?

There is a lot of great customer service training occurring in organizations today. Unfortunately, there is also a lot of bad customer service training! So, what separates the winners from the also-rans? Below are the factors associated with success.

- The learners are the right ones—people who both need and want to increase their competence in customer service. Training is less than effective if attendees are not clear on why they are there, if they perceive they have no need for the training, and/or if they have little or no opportunity to quickly use what is learned after the training.

- The learning experience is crafted to be short enough for assimilation and application. Classes that last several days risk being data-overloaded and too far distanced from application for efficient learning to occur. Remember, the goal is not on what gets taught, but rather what gets learned. Also, marathon training—early morning to late in the day—is likely to be wasted.

- The learning experience matches the real world in tone, style, and philosophy. If learners are to partner with customers, the trainer must likewise create a partnership learning environment. Since customer service is interpersonal, the training should focus on the learning of interpersonal skills. This directive suggests that highly experiential methods like role-plays, simulation, and problem-solving exercises are likely to be heavily employed. Ask yourself the following questions: "If I made a movie of a customer service person performing effectively, what would I see? What would the person know, feel, and communicate? How can I create a learning experience which enables learners to ultimately perform effectively in all those realms?"

- The learning environment focuses on experimentation and risk taking. Remember, success with the customer turns on unique responses to individual needs and requirements. For learners to acquire the capacity and competency to creatively problem-solve and tailor on-the-spot reactions, they must experience the learning program as a laboratory of testing ideas and new behaviors.

This fact means that trainers must focus more on being authentic than on being perfect; more on being real than on being right.

- The learning experience is tailored to fit the needs of the organization. As service quality author and consultant Ron Zemke says, "To be effective, your training must be about the specifics of your own business and your customers, their unique problems, priorities, and demands." This statement is not an argument against generic, purchased training programs. Instead, it is intended to communicate that any program needs to be adjusted to fit the uniqueness of the organization.

- The learning experience is followed with opportunity to try new skills in a safe, supportive work environment. It is highly unlikely that learners will emerge from the training with mastery. More likely their new skills will be shaky and tenuous. It is important that the learner leave the training with tools and resources to assist in the transfer of the learning to the workplace. Ever notice how, as a customer, you lower your expectation and increase your patience with a front-line person wearing a "trainee" nametag? Such support encourages, enables, and empowers employees to stretch their new skills to enhance confidence and increase competence.

What does a front-line customer service training program look like? Service training comes in many forms. Some focus on a specific aspect, like "how to communicate with a customer who thinks her bill was inappropriately high." Some take a more general focus. Some programs rely on lectures (live or on videotape) coupled with discussion and exercise. Some use behavioral modeling plus a great deal of role-play or reality practice. The shape, length, and content of your customer service training program will depend on your need, your audience, your culture, and your philosophy regarding how people learn best.

Below is the outline for a typical, well-designed customer service program. It is provided, not to be duplicated, but to offer a sense of what a program might include.

Achieving Extraordinary Customer Relations*

1. Foundation for Customer Service

   Goals/Outcomes
   Exercise 1: Memorable Customer Experiences
   Lecture: About This Program/Key Points
   Exercise 2: Identifying Your Customers
   Lecture: Core Service and Customer Service
   Exercise 3: Core Service

2. Caring Customer Service

   Exercise 4: Situations That Cause Concern
   Exercise 5: Barriers to Service
   Lecture: The Caring Responses
   Exercise 6: Practicing Caring Responses
   Exercise 7: Customer Behavior

3. A Model for Customer Relationships

   Lecture: A Model of Behavior
   Exercise 8: Six Parts of Behavior

Achieving Extraordinary Customer Relations and *Managing Extraordinary Service* are training programs distributed by Kaset International, Inc., 8875 Hidden River Parkway; Suite 400, Tampa, FL 33637 (800/73-KASET). Used with permission.

Lecture: Choice
Exercise 9: Identify Parts
Video Exercise 1: Identify Parts
Optional Exercise 10: Practice Voice Tones
Lecture: Words to Use/Words to Avoid
Exercise 10: Body Language/Parts and Words

4. Your Impact on the Customer

Exercise 11: Identify Pet Peeves/Courteous Behavior
Lecture: Tapes/Discounting
Exercise 12: Discounting

5. Reducing Stress

Exercise 13: When Customers Hook Us
Lecture: Collecting Feelings
Exercise 14: Reducing Stress
Lecture: Staying Unhooked and Out of Stress
Exercise 15: Practice Reasoning Responses

6. Building Rapport

Lecture: Defusing Customer Emotions
Video Exercise 2: Write Responses
Lecture: Reflective Listening
Exercise 16: Reflective Listening
Lecture: Establishing Rapport
Exercise 17: Practice Empathy and Feel-Felt
Lecture: More Ways to Lead to Business

7. Creating Positive Outcomes

Lecture: Mistakes
Exercise 18: Develop Responses and Identify Skills
Lecture: Selective Agreement
Exercise 19: Practicing Selective Agreement
Lecture: Offering Options
Exercise 20: Situations That Cause Concern

8. Extraordinary Customer Relations

Lecture: Putting It All Together
Video Exercise 3: Identify Listening Skills
Exercise 21: Practice Listening Skills
Lecture: Responses for Creating PMCEs
Exercise 22: Positive Memorable Customer Experiences
Exercise 23: Planning to Return

What Are the Potholes of Customer Service Training?

All training is susceptible to potholes and dead-end streets. We wanted to share a few of the "lessons learned" from our mistakes so others would avoid them.

- Everybody knows how to smile and be nice to customers. If smiling and niceness are not occurring, training is not going to make a difference. Examine the real reason customer service people do not want to smile or be nice.

- Some people have customer-oriented aptitudes; some do not. Some people like working with customers; some do not. Both of these are selection issues, not training issues.

- All the training in the world is not likely to compensate for poor leadership. Will Rogers said years ago, "People learn from observation, not conversation." While he was talking about politicians, the adage fits service leadership. If leaders espouse "serve the customer" but reward or personally model contrary actions or philosophies, new customer service skills will quickly disappear in favor of what employees perceive to be more "valued" behaviors.

- Training is no substitute for poor systems and procedures. As Geary Rummler says, "You can take great people who are highly trained and highly motivated, put them in a lousy system and the system will win every time." Systems that make it difficult to get or give good customer service communicate how the organization views customers and employees.

- All training—especially customer service training—should be preceded by a thorough needs analysis. No competent physician would perform a surgical operation without a diagnosis, even if the preceding symptoms seem to obviously point to a particular treatment. No competent trainer would either. Just because you have customers and people who must serve those customers does not automatically mean training is needed. A needs analysis can inform you more than "if"—it can also inform "how" and "how not."

- The customer *is* always right—in the broadest sense of the word—since the customer is always the customer! However, the customer is not always correct. Customer service training which fails to assist people in dealing with incorrect customers in a manner which focuses on being effective (rather than being right) leaves learners vulnerable and ultimately insecure. Conflict resolution skills are not innate; they must be learned.

How Do You Get a Customer Service Training Design?

Training designs come in various forms. For some trainers, the design is a detailed set of instructions and directives that must be followed to the letter. For others, it is a sketchy outline that changes with each class. New training designs can range from generic to specific. A generic design for a customer service course might be one prepared for a wide range of service companies and to be taught by novice as well as experienced trainers. A tailored design for a customer service training program might be one prepared for a single company to teach people how to provide service to a unique customer. Such a program would be taught by specially trained instructors.

There are four ways in which your customer service training program design might be obtained:

1. A training design can be purchased from an outside resource.

2. A purchased design can be tailored or adjusted.

3. A training design can be assembled from various pieces.

4. A training design can be created from scratch.

We will now look at each of these four options in detail.

Buying a Training Design

Although buying a customer service training design may be the first option to come to mind, we would encourage you to avoid jumping to the "buy" option simply because it seems the easiest thing to do. In the long run, the design you purchase may not be the best for the learners or the organization. Only after examining the training need and all the other ways of getting to the final training design—tailoring, assembling, and making—can you be sure that the decision to buy a training design is a good one.

One valuable criterion in making this decision is the degree to which there will be satisfaction with generic training. Purchased programs (sometimes called "off-the-shelf" or "canned" programs) are by definition generic in that they apply generally, not exactly. Will a generic package meet your customer service training needs? Or does the training situation really require a design tailored for a specific problem, industry, or organization?

Another criterion is cost. Training is often bought because the other alternatives seem to be too costly. While it is initially more costly to assemble or create your own design, if the cost can be amortized over many years or many learners, tailored training may be a more cost-efficient and effective decision.

Ownership may be another issue in the "buy" decision. How important is it to own the customer service training design? It is not generally possible, for instance, to put your organization's logo on a packaged training program purchased from or developed by DDI, BTD, LI, ODI, Kaset International, or Bubba's We Train 'Em! Some vendors prohibit even minor modification without their permission. And copyright violation lawsuits are becoming very common.

Time is another critical factor. There may not be enough time to assemble, tailor, or make a training design. One major advantage of purchased programs is that they are generally turnkey systems, ready to use when one is ready for training. If an organization is faced with a short-fused training need, buying can typically allow implementation in a hurry.

Trainer priorities may also dictate the decision. By buying a customer service training program, in-house trainers can devote their energies to creating other training materials that *must* be tailored or made internally.

Remaining advantages to purchasing a customer service training design include:

- Many hours of thought and effort have gone into it.
- It is well-organized and complete.
- It can be easily and quickly implemented.
- It has worked in other organizations.
- It can be seen in its totality.

Tailoring or Adjusting a Training Design

Tailoring or adjusting can be a powerful way to convert a generic customer service training program into one more specific to an organization's learning needs, and more palatable to its culture.

Before you can tailor (or adjust) an existing customer service training program you must first identify a training program for purchase. Such an existing design will likely be oriented to a particular task, a specific skill, or a total job-role. A task-oriented design might attempt to teach trainees "how to properly complete an order form with the customer." A skill-oriented design might teach "how to handle a difficult customer." A design oriented to the total job might teach "how to serve as a concierge." Obviously, you will want to choose a program with an orientation close to your training goal.

With the proper permission, this training program is altered to suit a given organization. There are several ways you can tailor an existing design:

- Alter the *concepts, ideas,* or *content* of the purchased customer service training program. For example, a training program with a unit on service recovery may include a six-step process, one step of which is "offer symbolic atonement." In a given organization this step may be difficult, and certain gestures of atonement may even be illegal. Therefore, you might choose to delete that part of the content. Our experience has been that adding content is the more frequent route in alteration.

- Alter the *methodology* of the purchased program. One may buy a customer service training program that is primarily presentational and then elect to turn some of the presentations into group exercises. A training program with role-plays, for instance, may get altered to case studies. Or, more frequently, a program with case studies will greatly benefit from the addition of role-plays.

- Alter the *examples.* If the organization is a high-tech company and the examples are from the banking industry, the program may be more effective if the examples are altered to fit the high-tech form.

- Alter the *length.* Such alteration can be cutting, adding, or just reducing the amount of time spent on any single area.

When tailoring programs be careful that the integrity is maintained. Typically, great time and effort have gone into the design of purchased programs; enrich them, don't weaken them.

Appropriate permissions must be obtained for tailoring an existing design. Buying a training program is less like buying a book or record and more like buying the source code for computer software. Frequently there are copyright restrictions which limit how the programs can be used and the degree to which they can be altered.

If often takes more time to tailor or adjust a training program than initially may be apparent. Tailoring is far more complex than simply cutting and pasting. The trainer who attempts to tailor or adjust must first fully understand the intent of the original writer and be skilled in the area of design. This is not a job for a novice or a person whose principal experience has been as an administrator of training.

There are also administrative problems in altering or tailoring a training program. If one aspect is changed in the instructor's manual, for example, it may necessitate changes in the participant's workbook, in the later concepts, perhaps in the film. A minor change can have a snowballing effect.

Assembling a Training Design

Assembling is the process of putting pieces together. Most training programs contain the following pieces, all readily available in the marketplace.

- A conceptual framework around which ideas or steps are organized
- One or more lectures or presentations
- Structured activities (demonstrations, exercises, discussions, games, etc.)

- Some type of audiovisual support (sometimes used to deliver the lecture)
- Guidelines, plans, or instructions for the trainer
- Handouts, aids, or worksheets for learners
- Tests or instruments

The person assembling the training must see how such materials can fit together, like pieces of a puzzle, to make the best design. Not all the pieces will fit perfectly; it may be necessary to tailor or adjust all or some of them. Some of the advantages of assembling are

- It can save time.
- It requires the creativity of assembly—which is not as demanding as the creativity of design.
- Unlike tailoring or making the design, it frees trainers from the burden of researching the content of the training in exhaustive detail.

There are disadvantages as well. Assembling requires a higher degree of skill than the tailoring or adjusting of packaged programs. It takes great design skill to put generic training pieces together in a way that is job-focused and reflects job reality while meeting the specific learning goals previously identified. Other cautions follow:

- The prepackaged games or exercises can overwhelm the training mission. When this happens, training becomes a series of activities seemingly unrelated to the real job world. Learners often emerge from such training saying, "That was fun. I really enjoyed that"—but no change in performance follows.
- It takes both tailoring and a quest for specificity to truly integrate generic pieces. Transitional sentences or comments are usually not sufficient to produce this integration.
- Assembling a training design can be particularly seductive for new trainers in that it can give them the illusion that they are really designing training. There are several aspects of this seduction: (1) the value of the exercises seems self-evident; (2) the learners tell them that the exercises are fun; (3) although the trainers are putting together pieces which may or may not fit, to their eyes the result looks fine; and (4) with lots of pieces on the market, the "ideal" package can seem available at limited expense.

Making or Creating a Training Design

Making or creating a customer service training design is more difficult and requires more time and creativity than any other option. It is not necessarily more expensive. A designer must

- Know the content intimately
- Be skilled in identifying, adjusting, or creating appropriate concepts for the training situation
- Be able to develop learning activities designed to creatively help people master the intended content

The learning activities are more likely to produce results if they are nonanalogous and are developed for the specific learning the organization requires. Making or creating a design is the true role of the experienced designer of training. It generally requires a designer with experience, creativity, ability—and time.

Who will be doing the customer service training? The question directly affects the training design. The same designers would create substantially different programs for training situations where the trainers will be

- Themselves
- Other professional trainers
- Subject-matter experts skilled at delivering a particular training program but lacking professional background in training

The differences will arise not only because the designer will select different activities for different kinds of trainers but also because the designer will vary the amount and depth of documentation in an inverse ratio to the experience and maturity of the deliverers of training.

Despite the difficulties involved, designing training for an organization could end up being the least costly mode. It may be far more cost-effective to have a program specifically related to a particular group in content, culture, methodology, and learning needs. If a program is to be continued over two or three years for a hundred people, the development costs can be allocated to a larger number of learners.

Should the Trainer Be Internal or External?

There are advantages and disadvantages to using an external customer service trainer. A review of those advantages and disadvantages that fit a particular organizational situation can be extremely beneficial when a decision is being made as to whether to use an external customer service trainer.

The most common reason external customer service trainers are hired is the conclusion that an external resource can offer skills, perspectives, and/or credibility not available internally. There may be no one internally with the needed competence to design and/or deliver customer service training. Or competent internal trainers may be busy with other important activities so it may be easier to bring in an outsider on a project basis than free up a qualified person internally.

Sometimes the issue is one of internal standards. Decision makers may conclude that, while internal trainers may have the capacity and availability to design and/or deliver a customer service training program, it would not be up to the standards of quality required. External customer service trainers often bring a broad perspective borne out of working with a wide range of clients. As one training manager stated, "Our trainers teach communication, leadership, effective writing, and an assortment of other topics. They could probably do sales training as well. But I wanted someone who lives, eats, and sleeps customer service training—a true specialist."

What are the cons? External is external—consultants and vendors don't know the organizational culture, norms, and values. To be effective, an external resource must work extra hard to gather an understanding of the informal ropes important to program credibility.

In addition, external resources can be less committed to the outcome since they will exit the organization, leaving the internal person to "clean up the mess" and manage the follow-through, reinforcement, and maintenance. And the more tailored the program, the more expensive it can be to bring the external trainer up to speed on aspects an insider may have devoted years attaining.

One mythical disadvantage is cost. Clearly, there *are* consultants who over-price for their efforts and for the client's return on investment. However, the external resource called in to design a customer service training program is likely to be an expert in design *and* customer service content. Consequently, they can produce in days what might take an internal person months. Likewise, the external trainer called in to teach typically requires far less "prep" time to facilitate an effective customer service course.

External training resources can be great assets, bringing refreshing perspectives, innovative ideas, and new concepts. Uncluttered by historical baggage, they can offer important insights and objectivity. Because of this, they can speak with credibility that insiders might envy but find difficult to duplicate.

On the other hand, external training resources can be great liabilities. They can create dependence instead of fostering competence. They can subtly usurp the stature and popularity that rightfully belongs to the internal person. They can produce guruism or hero worship instead of making heroes of their client. Like all professions, the world of the external customer service trainer has its share of snake oil, charlatans, and ripoff artists.

What About Customer Service Training for Supervisors?

The issues of customer service training for supervisors focus far less on how, who, and when—and more on what. The potholes are the same as for front-line training, the design considerations are similar, and the delivery dimensions are the same. Trainers struggle with exactly what to include in the curriculum. At the core of the solution is the issue of the role of the customer service supervisor. Supervisors of customer service should be versed in all training their team members receive. While it is true that most customer service training relevant for the front line is relevant for supervisors, what additional training is likely to be needed?

It is important that supervisors learn that their actions must model the actions they want front-line people to demonstrate to customers. If "listening to the customers to determine needs and expectations" is important for front-line people, it is crucial for supervisors to model that behavior to customers. Supervisors must demonstrate strong listening skills through the manner in which they listen to employees

Bill Marriott, CEO of Marriott Corporation, once wrote, "Start with good people, train them and motivate them, give them opportunities to advance and the organization will succeed." People on the front lines need support, encouragement, affirmation, and mentoring. Partnerships with customers require front-line people who are carefully selected, well trained, provided the appropriate authority to go the extra mile when needed, and celebrated for excellence. Such a requirement is not likely to be provided or sustained with leadership that fails to treat employees as valued customers.

The role of the supervisor must be that of supportive partner, not surrogate parent. Great supervisors perpetually mentor front-line people to enable them to continually grow. Great supervisors have a clear vision of what service should look like, and their actions are consistent with that vision. As Max DePree wrote in his book *Leadership Is An Art:* "The first job of the leader is to create reality (or vision), the last job is to say 'thank you.' Everything in between is the act of servant leadership."

Effective customer service training programs for supervisors equip learners with skills of coaching, partnering, service system analysis, problem solving, strategic recovery, and "cheerleading!" Such programs assist supervisors in seeing the true meaning of empowerment (not unlimited license but rather responsible freedom) and to recognize their role as removers of obstacles to people acting empowered.

A typical service management course might look something like the following:

Managing Extraordinary Service*

1. Service is...

   Goals and Outcomes
   Lecture: Service "Report Cards"
   Exercise 1: Identify Your Core and Peripheral Services
   Lecture: Managing Service versus Managing Production
   Exercise 2A: How Service Management Differs from Production Management
   Exercise 2B: Video—Customer Perception Is All There Is.

2. Understanding Your Customer

   Lecture: What Is a Customer?
   Exercise 3: Customers' Interview Guides
   Lecture: Understanding the Customer

3. Service Strategies or Visions

   Lecture: What Is a Service Strategy or Vision?
   Exercise 4A: Developing a Strategy for Your Unit
   Exercise 4B: Announcement Video
   Lecture: Strategies into Actions
   Exercise 5: Management Action

4. Auditing the Delivery System

   Lecture: What Is a Service Delivery System?
   Exercise 6: Diagramming a Cycle of Service
   Lecture: Using a Moment of Truth Impact Analysis
   Exercise 7: Diagramming an MOT Impact Analysis
   Lecture: Service Recovery
   Exercise 9: Planned Recovery for a Key MOT

5. Focusing Through Service Standards

   Lecture: Service Deliverers
   Exercise 10: Self-Esteem
   Lecture: Setting Standards
   Exercise 11: Developing Service Standards

---

*Achieving Extraordinary Customer Relations and *Managing Extraordinary Service* are training programs distributed by Kaset International, Inc., 8875 Hidden River Parkway; Suite 400, Tampa, FL 33637 (800/73-KASET). Used with permission.

6. Empowerment

Lecture: Empowerment
Exercise 12: Empowerment
Lecture: Why Is Empowerment Difficult?
Exercise 12A: Empowerment in Recovery
Exercise 12B: Plan for Empowerment
Exercise 12C: Review (Video)
Lecture: Using Empowerment
Exercise 13: Levels of Empowerment

7. Celebrating Service Excellence

Lecture: Celebrating
Exercise 14A: Planning a Celebration
Exercise 14B: Planning for Return
Exercise 14C: Developing an Action Plan

The Future of Customer Service Training

We started our chapter with the position that effective customer service training needs to be planned and organized but need not happen in the classroom. This position offers a preamble to the future. With the availability of computer technology it is reasonable to assume that more and more customer service training will occur via interactive hookup.

Virtual-reality technology may enable the front line to learn real-time interpersonal skills by experiencing the realism of interacting with simulations. Customer service training will feel as real as flight simulators feel to pilots in training.

Such technologies, and the generations to come, may be a boon to the tailoring of learning—when I need it, in a form I can master on my own, and with diagnostic capacities that will enable me to quality-control and improve my own learning. Such programs will incorporate a component for the supervisor (or peer coach) to be able to pinpoint ways to support and mentor the new learner to ensure that shaky skills become habit and new skills are constantly added.

The learning environment of the future will often have front-line employees partnering with customers as they learn together. As organizations flatten, supervisors will have a much larger span of control. This arrangement will necessitate more peer coaching and colleague support and assistance. Internet-type systems will provide almost unlimited information. However, the challenge will be to find processes and relationships which will help transform data into learning and performance.

Whatever the future may hold, it is clear that customer expectations will perpetually climb. The one-on-one tailored response will come to be valued more than ever. Quickness and convenience will be customer requirements. All those characteristics will also fit the learning needs and expectations of customer service training participants!

We can also be certain of a few organizational outcomes. Organizations will become flatter, partnership will replace parentship as the preferred leadership style, and leaders will spend as much time mentoring as managing. Customer expectations of training (those who attend as well as those who fund) will be that the training they receive or buy increases competence, bolsters confidence, and makes a difference in the memories which graduates help create for their customers.

Bibliography

Anderson, Kristin, and Ron Zemke, *Delivering Knock Your Socks Off Service*, AMACOM, New York, 1991.

Bell, Chip R., *Customers as Partners: Building Relationships That Last*, Berrett-Koehler Publishers, San Francisco, 1994.

Bell, Chip. R., and Fran C. Sims, "Casting Customer Service People," *Supervisory Management*, June 1990.

Bell, Chip R., and Ron Zemke, *Managing Knock Your Socks Off Service*, AMACOM, New York, 1992.

Carr, Clay, *Front-Line Customer Service*, John Wiley & Sons, New York, 1991.

Clemmer, Jim, *Firing On All Cylinders*, Business One Irwin, New York, 1992.

Connellan, Tom, and Ron Zemke, *Sustaining Knock Your Socks Off Service*, AMACOM, New York, 1993.

Desatnick, Robert L., *Managing to Keep the Customer*, Jossey-Bass, San Francisco, 1987.

Disend, Jeffrey C., *How to Provide Excellent Service in Any Organization*, Chilton Book Company, Radnor, PA, 1990.

Lash, Linda M., *The Complete Guide to Customer Service*, John Wiley & Sons, New York, 1989.

Lee, Chris, "1-800-Training," *Training*, August 1990.

Margolis, Frederic H., and Chip R. Bell, *Instructing For Results*, Pfeiffer & Company, San Diego, 1986.

Meister, Jeanne C., "Retail U," *Training*, March 1992.

Zemke, Ron, and Chip Bell, *Service Wisdom*, Lakewood Publications, Minneapolis, 1989, pp. 155–163.

44

Occupational Safety and Health Training

Gerard F. Scannell

Gerard F. Scannell joined the National Safety Council as President in 1995. During 1992–1994, he was Vice President, Worldwide Safety Affairs, Johnson & Johnson, New Brunswick, New Jersey, and also served as that firm's Director of Corporate Safety/Fire/Environmental Affairs from 1979 to 1989. In 1989, he was nominated by President Bush to be Assistant Secretary of Labor for the Occupational Safety and Health Administration (OSHA). Earlier, he served in various positions at OSHA headquarters in Washington, DC; from 1971 to 1979 as Director of the Office of Federal Agency Safety programs, Director of the Office of Standards, and Special Assistant to the Assistant Secretary of Labor for OSHA. Other career positions included having been in safety management for Rohm and Haas, Thiokol Chemical Corporation, and Aetna Casualty and Surety Co. He is a member of the board of directors of the National Fire Protection Association and chairs the National Fallen Firefighters Memorial Foundation. Scannell graduated from the Massachusetts Maritime Academy with a bachelor of science degree in 1955 and took postgraduate training in epidemiology and environmental economics at The George Washington University. He served in the Navy as an explosive and nuclear weapons disposal officer from 1955 to 1958. In 1992, his alma mater conferred an Honorary Doctor of Public Administration on him.

In the field of medicine, it took thousands of years for the profession to move from an emphasis on "curative" medicine to one of "preventive" medicine. Similarly, in the field of health education, it took additional decades for many to recognize that what they should be teaching is how a person can ensure wellness rather than simply how he or she can recover from an existing illness.

Few things are more visible to the public than environmental disasters, product- or service-related problems, or occupational mishaps. Depending on how they are handled, these events can cause significant damage to a firm. Thus, it is essential that everyone in an organization, from the boardroom to the shop floor, have some knowledge of how such mishaps are caused and what employees' individual roles are in preventing or controlling them.

This chapter addresses some of the questions that training personnel might ask about the safety and health function. The intent is to provide for greater understanding between the two groups, which should result in a stronger bond between the training and safety and health staffs.

Change is the order of the day in the field of safety and health protection. It has been a long time coming, but it becomes more evident each day. We see it in the proactive stance that more and more employers and safety and health professionals are taking. We see it in the dissatisfaction with after-the-fact, postinjury-illness measures of program success (e.g., fatalities, disabling injuries and illnesses, workers' compensation costs, and various incidence rates). Now, we hear more managers and their safety and health staffs speak of "noninjury" measures of safety and health program effectiveness (e.g., numbers and types of critical incidents observed, the results of behavioral sampling of workers on the job, how many workers were removed from risk as the result of specific actions taken at the work site, and other measures that reflect a safety and health culture of "continuous improvement"). Perhaps most important, we have moved from an environment where the worker was the "culprit" who was blamed for incidents to one where employee input is aggressively sought on how to prevent workplace mishaps.

In this chapter, the term *safety* is explained, along with what safety staffs do. This is followed by a discussion of where the safety and health functions fit into the organizational structure and why training is an essential characteristic of an effective safety and health program. Next, the many dimensions of safety and health training requirements are reviewed, both those requirements necessitated by the job itself and those mandated from outside the organization. These requirements range from those needed to enable a worker to perform his or her tasks in an effective manner to those required to enable the worker to operate at minimal risk to him or herself, fellow workers, and the public. Then, some indicators of how well employers are fulfilling their safety and health training responsibilities are provided, along with some of the penalties that may result when they fail to do so. Following this are examples of some of the types of information and instruction on job safety and health that are being recommended and provided for managers. Attention is then focused on one of the mainstays of safety and health training programs (i.e., the job-hazard analysis, along with a few examples of how such an analyses is developed). This subject is followed by some observations on how job-safety and health training programs may be evaluated and by a list of references.

Background

What the Term "Safety" Means in an Operational Context

The word *safety* is an adjective used to describe a condition that, at its extreme, reflects the total absence of hazards. For example, an employer may be said to have a safe operation or a safe workplace when there are relatively few (preferably no) work-related deaths, injuries, or illnesses. Or, paraphrasing Section 5.(a)(1) of Public Law 91-596, the Occupational Safety and Health Act of 1970, one could say that a safe workplace is one where the "employer furnishes to each of his or her employees employment and a place of employment which are free from recognized hazards that are causing or are likely to cause death or serious physical harm to them...."

What Safety Professionals Do

Before addressing this question, it is necessary to distinguish between line and staff positions within an organization. Line positions traditionally are those in the direct chain of command with specific responsibility for accomplishing the production-related goals of the organization. Conversely, staff positions are outside the direct chain of command and are primarily advisory or supportive in nature. Normally, both the training and the safety and health personnel serve an organization in a staff capacity.

The safety function is an advisory or supportive activity. (See Fig. 44-1, which shows the functions of the professional safety position.) The functions of the safety professional are contained within four basic areas. However, application of all or some of the functions will depend upon the nature and scope of the existing accident problem and the type of activity with which the safety professional is concerned. These four major areas are (1) identification and evaluation of accident and loss-producing conditions and practices and appraisal of the potential for loss should an incident occur; (2) development of policy, programs, and procedures for accident prevention and loss control; (3) communication of accident and loss control information to those concerned; and (4) measurement and evaluation of the effectiveness of the safety and health programs and the modifications needed to achieve optimum results.[1] As shown in Fig. 44-1, feedback control is provided.

David MacCollum, an internationally recognized authority on construction safety, makes this observation about what the safety professional does:

> Too many people in management have the erroneous belief that a safety professional's only value to an organization is to conduct inspections and ensure OSHA compliance. They have never understood that a safety professional has the expertise to:
>
> 1. Identify hazards
> 2. Evaluate the risk of harm those hazards create
> 3. Inform management of the magnitude of the peril
> 4. Define safe design criteria or construction method and prescribe appropriate safeguards to avoid or reduce injury and prevent property damage
> 5. Define and arrange for appropriate training[2]

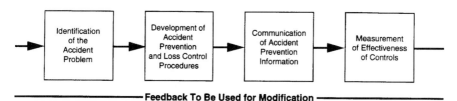

Figure 44-1. The professional safety task. (*Source: American Society of Safety Engineers.*)

The tasks performed by the safety professional may be found in the position descriptions developed and maintained by the employer. In addition to the guidance provided in Fig. 44-1, those tasked with the career development of occupational safety and health professionals will find extensive information on what these personnel do in the *Dictionary of Occupational Titles* (*DOT*) (Fourth Edition)[3], prepared by the U.S. Department of Labor's Employment and Training Administration, and available from the U.S. Government Printing Office, Washington, DC 20402-9328. Published in two volumes, the *DOT* is invaluable in providing general parameters of the types of tasks performed by various classifications of employees, from laborers to executives. Following are descriptions from the *DOT* for three of the several occupations that make up the safety profession; namely, (1) safety engineer, (2) safety manager, and (3) safety inspector.

012.061-014: Safety Engineer. Develops and maintains safety programs to prevent or correct hazardous working conditions, using knowledge of industrial processes, procedures, mechanics, chemistry, psychology, and industrial health and safety laws. Examines plans and specifications for new machinery or equipment to determine if all safety precautions have been addressed. Determines floor and storage-rack load limits. Tours plant to inspect fire and safety equipment, machinery, and facilities to identify and correct potential hazards and to ensure compliance with safety regulations. Determines requirements for protective clothing and devices, and specifies safety equipment and devices for machinery and facilities. Educates workers about safety policies and safe work practices, and conducts or coordinates safety and first-aid training. Investigates industrial accidents to minimize recurrence and prepares accident reports. May conduct air-quality tests for presence of harmful contaminants.

012.167-058: Safety Manager. Plans, implements, coordinates, and monitors programs to reduce or eliminate occupational injuries, illnesses, deaths, and financial losses. Identifies and evaluates conditions that could produce accidents and evaluates the extent of potential injuries and financial losses resulting from those accidents. Conducts or directs research studies to identify hazards and evaluates loss-producing potential of given systems, operations, or processes. Develops accident prevention and loss control systems and programs for incorporation into operational policies of the organization. Coordinates safety activities of managers to ensure uniform implementation of safety activities throughout the organization. Compiles, analyzes, interprets, prepares, and communicates reports of statistical data related to exposure and occurrence factors concerning occupational illnesses, injuries, and accidents in general. Maintains liaison with outside organizations, such as fire departments, mutual-aid societies, and rescue teams to assure information exchange. Devises methods to evaluate safety programs and conducts or directs evaluations. Evaluates technical and scientific publications concerned with safety management and participates in activities of related professional organizations to update knowledge for safety program development. May store and retrieve statistical data, using computer.

168.264-014: Safety Inspector. Inspects machinery, equipment, and working conditions in industrial or other setting to ensure compliance with occupational safety and health regulations. Inspects machines and equipment for accident prevention devices. Observes workers to determine use of prescribed protective equipment, such as glasses, helmets, respirators, and clothing. Inspects specified areas for fire protection equipment and other safety and first-aid supplies. Samples for noise, toxic contaminants, and other hazards using sound-level meter, gas detector, and light meter. Prepares reports of findings and recommendations for corrective action. Investigates accidents to ascertain causes for use in recommending preventive safety measures and developing safety program. May demonstrate use of safety equipment.

A movement within the safety profession which will have a dramatic impact on the training community is the move toward requiring certification of safety and health professionals. In the early 1980s, some 15 percent of those employers advertising vacancies for such personnel required or preferred the CSP (certified safety professional) or CIH (certified industrial hygienist) designation. By the mid-1990s, this figure had rise to some 55 percent of employers requiring such a designation as a condition of hire. To help their current safety and health personnel prepare for the qualifying examinations, many employers are conducting formalized training sessions to "prep" them for the rigorous examinations. Training staffs can be of inestimable value in this human resource development activity.

Where Job Safety and Health Fits into the Organizational Structure

Figure 44-2 shows how physical safety and health risks at the work site are recognized, evaluated, controlled, and prevented within the management structure. Note the prominent role that training programs play in the mix of management activities used to combat workplace mishaps.

The center of the illustration in Fig. 44-2 identifies the focus of all safety and health program efforts (i.e., the removal of safety and health hazards in the workplace).

The first ring out from the center of the illustration identifies the four conventional methods used by safety and health professionals, working through the management system, to eliminate or control workplace hazards. These methods include the recognition of such hazards and their evaluation, control, or removal where possible.

The second ring out from the center of the illustration is made up of three components, namely, (1) management, (2) the workforce, and (3) special staffs such as those made up of training professionals, occupational safety and health professionals, and others. Among the activities that take place at this level are effective management leadership and demonstrated management commitment; work-site analyses; hazard identification, control, and prevention; safety and health training programs tailored to the needs of the workforce in terms of both knowledge and skills and the hazards to which the worker is or can be exposed during the performance of his or her tasks; and program evaluation based on continuous feedback from both management and other employees.

The third ring out from the center of the illustration at Fig. 44-2 consists of those factors which impact any function of management: the mission and purpose of the organization; organizational goals and objectives; roles and responsibilities of management, staff, and employees; standards against which the performance of all members of the organization are to be measured; strategic, tactical, and operational planning; a control system; and the ability to effect change in a timely manner within the organization when necessary.

The fourth and final ring out from the center of the illustration identifies factors that impact any organization, including the corporate culture; internal-external environments; and the multitude of stakeholder organizations and their concerns such as public regulatory bodies, clients/customers, public interest groups, and the media.

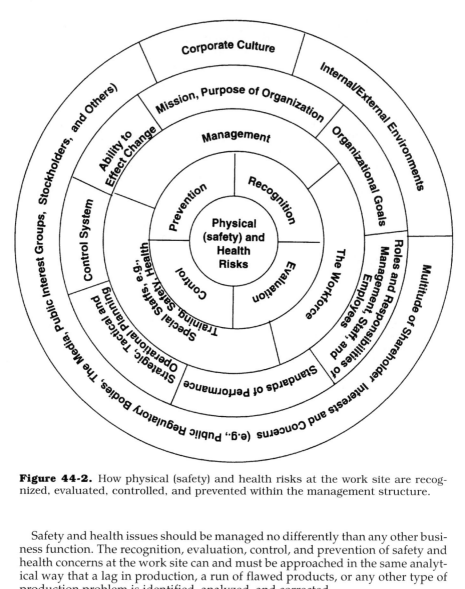

Figure 44-2. How physical (safety) and health risks at the work site are recognized, evaluated, controlled, and prevented within the management structure.

Safety and health issues should be managed no differently than any other business function. The recognition, evaluation, control, and prevention of safety and health concerns at the work site can and must be approached in the same analytical way that a lag in production, a run of flawed products, or any other type of production problem is identified, analyzed, and corrected.

Training as an Essential Characteristic of an Effective Safety and Health Program

Over the years, field staff of OSHA have seen many examples of exemplary workplaces where safety and health programs are well-managed and where injury-illness rates are exceptionally low. Common characteristics observed at these sites are (1) the use of organized and systematic methods to assign appropriate responsibility to all managers, supervisors, and employees; (2) a regular process to identify hazards; and (3) programs to train all employees in the ways and means on how to eliminate or control hazards.

OSHA found that the most successful programs look beyond only those hazards that have been addressed by legislation to address *all* hazards; the goal of these programs is to prevent injuries and illnesses and the attendant human and economic costs, whether or not compliance with the law is at issue. An effective occupational safety and health program will also be structured to anticipate ongoing changes in conditions and practices so that new hazards are identified and protective measures taken in time to prevent employee exposure.

In an effort to provide businesses with comprehensive guidelines for developing effective safety and health programs, OSHA identified four principal elements of effective safety and health management, namely, (1) management leadership and employee involvement, (2) work-site analyses, (3) hazard control and prevention, and (4) safety and health training. OSHA noted that "safety and health training need not be elaborate, formal or always solely related to safety and health. Safety and health information and instruction is often most effective when incorporated into other training about performance requirements and job practices, such as management training and performance evaluations, supervisors' training on the reinforcement of good work practices and the correction of poor ones, and employee training on the operation of a particular machine."[4]

One of the many organizations that offered suggestions to OSHA regarding safety program content was Procter & Gamble, a company which is consistently a top performer in job safety and health and is regularly found at or near the top of its Standard Industrial Classification, or SIC, category. Procter & Gamble evaluates its operations for job safety and health performance in terms of (1) organizational planning and support, (2) standards and practices, (3) training, and (4) accountability and performance feedback.

The author has yet to see a model for an effective occupational safety and health program that does not place extremely high priority on the training function. This goes for *Fortune* 500 companies as well as for smaller firms. Further, as will be pointed out later in this chapter, safety and health training is a requirement for safety and health programs of executive branch agencies of the federal government. Added to this, the principal voluntary safety organization in the nation, the National Safety Council, highlights training throughout all of its activities, as do the authors of the many texts on safety engineering and safety management.

The Role of Training in Job Safety and Health

Training is the process of transforming a known input into a desired output, with throughput representing the actual instruction. The existing knowledge and skills of a worker must be compared with the knowledge and skills required for the job. Training should involve reinforcement to ensure that tasks are performed safely.

In one of the first written accounts of the importance of job training and its relationship to workplace mishaps, Dewis, in Great Britain, reports the following:

> It has generally been accepted since the decision of Lord Wensleydale in *Weems vs. Mathieson* in 1861, that "a master is not less responsible to [his or her workers] for personal injuries caused by a defective system of using the machinery than for injuries caused by a defect in the machinery itself."[5]

Thus, to determine liability for negligence at common law and now to avoid criminal liability under Great Britain's Health and Safety at Work Act of 1974, employers in that country must see that their employees are instructed and trained in the intrinsic hazards of the job.[6]

It should be noted that the court decision referenced above speaks not of an absence of "safety training," but of a "defective system of using the machinery." This phrase has been interpreted to mean a system which, among other things, has failed to provide job-specific training (including information on physical and health risks on the job) to the worker. Subsequent safety and health legislation in Great Britain has included such requirements. For example, Great Britain's Shops and Railway Premises Act of 1963 contains the following requirement:

> 19. Training and supervision of persons working at dangerous machines. No person employed to work in premises to which this Act applies, shall work with any machine to which this section applies unless he or she has been fully instructed as to the dangers arising in connection with it and the precautions to be observed, and has received a sufficient training in work at the machine; or is under adequate supervision by a person who has thorough knowledge and experience of the machine.[7]

Clearly, the trend is for businesses to require workers to have some type of certification or competency designation in their chosen fields. The experience of the Construction Safety Association of Ontario, Canada,[8] is extremely impressive. It has achieved reductions in fatal and nonfatal injuries because of legislation enacted throughout the province. The legislation requires those in specific occupational classifications to establish a specified level of competency before they can work. One sees the same trend in other settings as well. For example, the National Aeronautics and Space Administration (NASA) requires all of its employees to take safety and health training commensurate with the hazards associated with their jobs. Critical skills jobs (e.g., propellant handlers, crane operators, and firefighters) require formal classroom instruction, testing, and certification.

In efforts to curb death, injury, and illness on the job, many safety and health practitioners speak of the "Three E's—engineering, education, and enforcement." These are seen as forming an interdependent relationship, with no one of them being able to do the job alone.

Engineering controls are the preferred method for reliable control of hazards since they are applied to the source of the hazard and don't require the worker to take preventive actions. Once implemented, engineering controls provide more permanent protection, provided they are adequately maintained. And while procedural controls are often an integral part of a program of worker protection, they rely upon employee behavior which, in turn, relies upon supervision, motivation, training, and education to make them effective.

An early model of the accident prevention process developed by the U.S. Department of the Army provided a key role for training (see Fig. 44-3). This role is one of three countermeasures for "hazard control" that make up the model (i.e., removing the hazard, guarding effectively against the hazard, and training workers to recognize the hazard and operate rationally in its presence until such time as it can be removed or guarded against effectively). The text accompanying the model states

> If it is not feasible to remove the hazard, or to guard effectively against it, the third type of action must be applied. It is to train personnel how to meet the hazard safely. We train men and women to take cover when fire is brought to bear upon them. The hazard is there, but the training has minimized it....Again, a loaded weapon always

Know the Hazards	Find the Hazards	Fight the Hazards
Problems	Test	Remove
Trends	Inspect	Guard
Types	Observe	Train
	Mission Accomplished Safely!	

Figure 44-3. Early model of the accident prevention process. (*Source: Office of the Deputy Chief of Staff for Personnel*, Safety and Command, *Department of the Army, Washington, DC, 1959, pp. 19–20.*)

represents a hazard, but training men and women how to properly handle loaded weapons has made the rifle range remarkably safe despite the hazards.[9]

The literature on accident prevention, occupational safety and health, and related subjects is replete with perceptions of what education and training can and cannot do to reduce workplace injuries and illnesses and associated costs.

At best, a well-designed and executed training program can produce workers who are better informed about physical and health hazards in the workplace and can identify hazards that need to be corrected. However, it is important to remember that the effective application of such knowledge is influenced by other factors (e.g., motivation, effective supervision, and other indices of management interest in, and commitment to, safety and health).

Safety and Health Training Requirements

How to Determine Safety and Health Training Requirements of the Organization and Its Members

Effective managers lead; they do not follow. Such managers do not wait to see whether OSHA or a state or local safety and health regulatory agency has promulgated a training requirement; rather, they constantly seek out and fulfill the training needs of their employees on their own.

A publication of the Man-Made Fibres Industry Training Board of Great Britain states: "Everyone working in industry needs some safety training; wherever possible this training should be integrated with job or specialist training. Safety in industry is a way of life, not a subject to be picked out for separate and special treatment."[10]

Of special importance is the board's identification of the scope of safety training for each of the following categories of employees: directors and senior executives, workers and functional managers, supervisors and foremen, professional engineers, scientists and technologists, laboratory staffs, engineering craftspersons, engineering trainees, process operatives, administrative, office and clerical staff, and safety officers.

In specifying safety training needs for these groups, the board suggested several questions which should be asked. These include

1. Who needs additional safety training (on the assumption that initial training has already been provided?)

2. What levels of performance are required and how will these be assessed?
3. How long will the training take?
4. What resources are required (e.g., money, people, equipment, and facilities)?
5. What are the expected benefits?
6. Is the training need urgent?
7. How many people are involved?
8. Who will undertake actual training?

Identification of training needs can be accomplished with the aid of the following techniques:

1. Use company injury and illness records to identify how mishaps occur and what can be done to prevent them from recurring.
2. Request that employees provide, in writing and in their own words, descriptions of their jobs. These should include the tasks performed and the sequence, tools, machines, equipment, materials, and processes used.
3. Observe employees at the workplace as they perform their tasks; ask about the work; and record their responses.
4. Examine similar training programs offered by other companies in the same SIC industry, or obtain suggestions from their insurer, the National Safety Council, OSHA full-service area offices, OSHA-approved state programs, OSHA-funded state consultation programs, or the OSHA Office of Training and Education.

The employees, themselves, can provide valuable information on the training they need. Safety and health hazards can be identified through the employees' responses to such questions as whether anything about their jobs frightens them, if they have had any "near misses" on the job, if they feel they are taking risks, or if they believe that their jobs involve the use of hazardous operations or substances.

Information and instruction on driving safety should be included in programs for employees. The latest data from the National Safety Council (for calendar year 1994) shows that, of 5000 work-related deaths, 2000 were work-related motor-vehicle accidents. An additional 100,000 work-related injuries were due to highway accidents also. When one realizes that motor-vehicle accidents claimed about 40 percent of all those killed on the job, it becomes apparent that employers should give far more attention to highway safety.

What Safety and Health Regulatory Legislation Requires of the Employer in Terms of Training

Many standards promulgated by OSHA explicitly require the employer to train employees in the safety and health aspects of their jobs. Other OSHA standards make it the employer's responsibility to limit certain job assignments to employees who are certified, competent, or qualified—meaning that they have previously had special training, in or out of the workplace. The term *designated personnel* means employees selected or assigned by the employer as being qualified to perform specific duties. These requirements reflect OSHA's belief that training is an essential part of every employer's safety and health program for protecting workers from injuries and illnesses.

The employer should obtain, study, and make readily available for study by managers and supervisors the following publications, depending on the employer's SIC:*

1. General industry standards (29CFR Part 1910)

2. Maritime industry standards (29CFR Parts 1915, 1916, 1917, and 1918)

3. Construction industry standards (29CFR Part 1926)

4. Agriculture industry standards (29CFR Part 1928)

5. OSHA Publication 2254 (Revised) Training Requirements in OSHA Standards and Training Guidelines

A good example of the trend in OSHA safety and health training requirements are those in the Process Safety Management of Highly Hazardous Chemicals Standard (29CFR Part 1910.119). The Process Safety Management Standard requires the employer to evaluate or verify that employees *comprehend* the training given to them. This requirement means that the training must have established objectives regarding what is to be accomplished. Subsequent to the training, an evaluation of each student is required to verify that the employee understood the subjects presented or acquired the skills required. If the established objectives of the training program were not achieved, the employer then would revise the training program to make it more effective, or conduct more frequent refresher training, or some combination of these requirements. The requirements of the Process Safety Management Standard follow the concept embodied in the OSHA training guidelines contained in OSHA Publication 2254 referenced above.

Typically, recent OSHA occupational health standards which contain a training requirement spell out the following with regard to the training: (1) who is to be trained; (2) date by which initial training is to be completed; (3) frequency with which training is to be conducted; (4) content of the training program; and (5) access to training materials.

Employer Responsibilities and Rights Under the OSHA Act

Figure 44-4 outlines employer responsibilities and rights as specified in the OSHA Act. They are essentially the same for employers in those states with OSHA-approved programs.[11]

The responsibilities and rights for both employers and employees are provided in detail, since they should be taught to each employer and each worker. Simply distributing copies is not satisfactory for such an important a body of information. The very knowledge of these responsibilities and rights and a desire to fulfill these obligations and exercise these rights are part of the foundation of any safety and health program.

---

*All of the publications listed are available from the U.S. Government Printing Office, Washington, DC 20402-9328.

Figure 44-4. Employer responsibilities and rights as specified in the Occupational Safety and Health Act of 1970. (*Source: Occupational Safety and Health Administration,* All About OSHA, *OSHA Publication No. 2056, U.S. Department of Labor, Occupational Safety and Health Administration, Washington, DC, 1992, pp. 34–41.*)

Employers have certain responsibilities and rights under the Occupational Safety and Health Act of 1970.

The checklists that follow provide a review of many of these. Employer responsibilities and rights in states with their own occupational safety and health programs are generally the same as in federal OSHA states.

Responsibilities

As an employer, you must:
- Meet your general duty responsibility to provide a workplace free from recognized hazards that are causing or are likely to cause death or serious physical harm to employees, and comply with standards, rules and regulations issued under the Act.
- Be familiar with mandatory OSHA standards and make copies available to employees for review upon request.
- Inform all employees about OSHA.
- Examine workplace conditions to make sure they conform to applicable standards.
- Minimize or reduce hazards.
- Make sure employees have and use safe tools and equipment (including appropriate personal protective equipment), and that such equipment is properly maintained.
- Use color codes, posters, labels or signs when needed to warn employees of potential hazards.
- Establish or update operating procedures and communicate them so that employees follow safety and health requirements.
- Provide medical examinations when required by OSHA standards.
- Provide training required by OSHA standards (e.g., hazard communication, lead, etc.).
- Report to the nearest OSHA office within 48 hours any fatal accident or one that results in the hospitalization of five or more employees.
- Keep OSHA-required records of work-related injuries and illnesses, and post a copy of the totals from the last page of OSHA No. 200 during the entire month of February each year. (This applies to employers with 11 or more employees.)
- Post, at a prominent location within the workplace, the OSHA poster (OSHA 2203) informing employees of their rights and responsibilities. (In states operating OSHA-approved job safety and health programs, the state's equivalent poster and/or OSHA 2203 may be required.)
- Provide employees, former employees and their representatives access to the Log and Summary of Occupational Injuries and Illnesses (OSHA No. 200) at a reasonable time and in a reasonable manner.
- Provide access to employee medical records and exposure records to employees or their authorized representatives.
- Cooperate with the OSHA compliance officer by furnishing names of authorized employee representatives who may be asked to accompany the compliance officer during an inspection. (If none, the compliance officer will consult with a reasonable number of employees concerning safety and health in the workplace.)
- Not discriminate against employees who properly exercise their rights under the Act.
- Post OSHA citations at or near the work site involved. Each citation, or copy thereof, must remain posted until the violation has been abated, or for three working days, whichever is longer.
- Abate cited violations within the prescribed period.

Rights

As an employer, you have the right to:
- Seek advice and off-site consultation as needed by writing, calling or visiting the nearest OSHA office. (OSHA will not inspect merely because an employer requests assistance.)
- Be active in your industry association's involvement in job safety and health.

Figure 44-4. (*Continued*)

- Request and receive proper identification of the OSHA compliance officer prior to inspection.
- Be advised by the compliance officer of the reason for an inspection.
- Have an opening and closing conference with the compliance officer.
- Accompany the compliance officer on the inspection.
- File a Notice of Contest with the OSHA area director within 15 working days of receipt of a notice of citation and proposed penalty.
- Apply to OSHA for a temporary variance from a standard if unable to comply because of the unavailability of materials, equipment or personnel needed to make necessary changes within the required time.
- Apply to OSHA for a permanent variance from a standard if you can furnish proof that your facilities or method of operation provide employee protection at least as effective as that required by the standard.
- Take an active role in developing safety and health standards through participation in OSHA Standards Advisory Committees, through nationally recognized standards-setting organizations and through evidence and views presented in writing or at hearings.
- Be assured of the confidentiality of any trade secrets observed by an OSHA compliance officer during an inspection.
- Submit a written request to NIOSH for information on whether any substance in your workplace has potentially toxic effects in the concentrations being used.

Section 405: Surface Transportation Assistance Act

Section 405 of the Surface Transportation Assistance Act (STAA) provided protection from reprisal by employers for truckers and certain other employees in the trucking industry involved in activity related to interstate commercial motor vehicle safety and health. Secretary of Labor's Order No. 9-83 (48 FR 35736, August 5, 1983) delegated to the Assistant Secretary of OSHA the authority to investigate and to issue findings and preliminary orders under Section 405.

Employees who believe they have been discriminated against for exercising their rights under Section 405 can file a complaint with OSHA within 180 days of the incident. The Secretary will then investigate the complaint and, within 60 days after it was filed, issue findings as to whether there is a reason to believe Section 405 has been violated.

If the Secretary finds that a complaint has merit, he/she also will issue an order requiring, where appropriate, abatement of the violation, reinstatement with back pay and related compensation, payment of compensatory damages, and the payment of the employee's expenses in bringing the complaint. Either the employee or employer may object to the findings. If no objection is filed within 30 days, the finding and order are final. If a timely filed objection is made, however, the objecting party is entitled to a hearing on the objection before an Administrative Law Judge of the Department of Labor.

Within 120 days of the hearing, the Secretary will issue a final order. A party aggrieved by the final order may seek judicial review in a court of appeals within 60 days of the final order.

The following activities of truckers and certain employees involved in interstate commercial motor vehicle operation are protected under Section 405.

- Filing of safety or health complaints with OSHA or another regulatory agency relating to a violation of a commercial motor vehicle safety rule, regulation, standard or order.
- Instituting or causing to be instituted any proceedings related to a violation of a commercial motor vehicle safety rule, regulation, standard or order.
- Testifying in any such proceedings relating to the above items.
- Refusing to operate a vehicle, when such operation constitutes a violation of any federal rules, regulations, standards, or orders applicable to commercial motor vehicle safety or health; or because of the employee's reasonable apprehension of serious injury to himself or the public due to the unsafe condition of the equipment.
- Complaints under Section 405 are filed in the same manner as complaints under 11(c). The filing period for Section 405 is 180 days from the alleged discrimination, rather than 30 days as under Section 11(c).

**Employee Responsibilities and
Rights Under the Job Safety and
Health Legislation**

Figure 44-5 lists employee responsibilities and rights as specified in the Act. As
with the responsibilities and rights of employers, this listing of employee responsibilities and rights may be used as a checklist to ensure that the employee has
received information on her or his responsibilities and rights.[12]

Differences in the Way OSHA
and MSHA State Their Training
Requirements for Employers

As we have seen, while many of the occupational safety and health standards
promulgated by OSHA contain training requirements, in most cases OSHA
provides wide latitude to the employer in terms of how he or she goes about
fulfilling these requirements. Conversely, the Mine Safety and Health Administration (MSHA) uses a significantly different approach in ensuring that employers provide the training required to their employees. Section 115 of the Federal
Mine Safety and Health Act of 1977 (Mine Act) requires each mine operator to
have a health and safety training program for miners, which must be approved
by the secretary of labor. Further, the secretary is required to publish rules
governing such programs. These rules set forth the requirements for obtaining
approval of training programs and specify the kinds of training, including
refresher and hazard training, which must be provided to miners. These rules are
intended to ensure that miners will be adequately trained in matters affecting
their health and safety, with the ultimate goal of reducing the frequency and
severity of injuries in the nation's mines.

Safety and Health Training
Requirements for Employees of
the Executive Branch of the
Federal Government

Title 29 of the Code of Federal Regulations, Part 1960, contains "Basic Program
Elements for Federal Employee Occupational Safety and Health Programs."
Subpart H of these regulations addresses the training required for six different
categories of personnel and is reproduced here to provide the reader with a
window on the type of training that is being provided for employees of the
federal public sector.

Subpart H - Training

1960.54: Training of Top Management Officials.   Each agency
shall provide top management officials with orientation and other learning experiences which will enable them to manage the occupational safety and health
programs of their agencies. Such orientation should include coverage of Sec. 19
of the Act, Executive Order 12196, the requirements of this part, and the agency
safety and health program.

Figure 44-5. Employee responsibilities and rights as specified in the Occupational Safety and Health Act of 1970. (*Source: Occupational Safety and Health Administration, All About OSHA, OSHA Publication No. 2056, U.S. Department of Labor, Occupational Safety and Health Administration, Washington, DC, 1992, pp. 34–41.*)

Although OSHA does not cite employees for violations of their responsibilities, each employee "shall comply with all occupational safety and health standards and all rules, regulations and orders issued under the Act" that are applicable.

Employee responsibilities and rights in states with their own occupational safety and health programs are generally the same as for workers in federal OSHA states.

Responsibilities

As an employee, you should:

- Read the OSHA poster at the job site.
- Comply with all applicable OSHA standards.
- Follow all employer safety and health rules and regulations, and wear or use prescribed protective equipment while engaged in work.
- Report hazardous conditions to the supervisor.
- Report any job-related injury or illness to the employer, and seek treatment promptly.
- Cooperate with the OSHA compliance officer conducting an inspection if he or she inquires about safety and health conditions in your workplace.
- Exercise your rights under the Act in a responsible manner.

11(c) Rights: Protection for Using Rights

Employees have a right to seek safety and health on the job without fear of punishment. That right is spelled out in Section 11(c) of the Act.

- Complaining to an employer, union, OSHA or any other government agency about job safety and health hazards
- Filing safety or health grievances
- Participating on a workplace safety and health committee or in union activities concerning job safety and health
- Participating in OSHA inspections, conferences, hearings, or other OSHA-related activities

If an employee is exercising these or other OSHA rights, the employer is not allowed to discriminate against that worker in any way, such as through firing, demotion, taking away seniority or other earned benefits, transferring the worker to an undesirable job or shift, or threatening or harassing the worker.

If the employer has knowingly allowed the employee to do something in the past (such as leaving work early), he or she may be violating the law by punishing the worker for doing the same thing following a protest or hazardous conditions. If the employer knows that a number of workers are doing the same thing wrong, he or she cannot legally single out for punishment the worker who has taken part in safety and health activities.

Workers believing they have been punished for exercising safety and health rights must contact the nearest OSHA office within 30 days of the time they learn of the alleged discrimination. A union representative can file the 11(c) complaint for the worker.

The worker does not have to complete any forms. An OSHA staff member will complete the forms, asking what happened and who was involved.

Following a complaint, OSHA investigates. If an employee has been illegally punished for exercising safety and health rights, OSHA asks the employer to restore that worker's job earnings and benefits. If necessary, and if it can prove discrimination, OSHA takes the employer to court. In such cases the worker does not pay any legal fees.

If a state agency has an OSHA-approved state program, employees may file their complaint with either federal OSHA or the state agency under its laws.

(Continued)

Figure 44-5. (*Continued*)

Other Rights

As an employee, you have the right to:

- Review copies of appropriate OSHA standards, rules, regulations and requirements that the employer should have available at the workplace.
- Request information from your employer on safety and health hazards in the area, on precautions that may be taken, and on procedures to be followed if an employee is involved in an accident or is exposed to toxic substances.
- Receive adequate training and information on workplace safety and health hazards.
- Request the OSHA area director to investigate if you believe hazardous conditions or violations of standards exist in your workplace.
- Have your name withheld from your employer, upon request to OSHA, if you file a written and signed complaint.
- Be advised of OSHA actions regarding your complaint and have an informal review, if requested, of any decision not to inspect or to issue a citation.
- Have your authorized employee representative accompany the OSHA compliance officer during the inspection tour.
- Respond to questions from the OSHA compliance officer, particularly if there is no authorized employee representative accompanying the compliance officer.
- Observe any monitoring or measuring of hazardous materials and have the right to see these records, and your medical records, as specified under the Act.
- Have your authorized representative, or yourself, review the Log and Summary of Occupational Injuries (OSHA No. 200) at a reasonable time and in a reasonable manner.
- Request a closing discussion with the compliance officer following an inspection.
- Submit a written request to NIOSH for information on whether any substance in your workplace has potentially toxic effects in the concentration being used and have your name withheld from your employer if you so request.
- Object to the abatement period set in the citation issued to your employer by writing to the OSHA area director within 15 working days of the issuance of the citation.
- Participate in hearings conducted by the Occupational Safety and Health Review Commission.
- Be notified by your employer if he or she applies for a variance from an OSHA standard, and testify at a variance hearing and appeal the final decision.
- Submit information or comment to OSHA on the issuance, modification or revocation of OSHA standards and request a public hearing.

1960.55: Training of Supervisors. (a) Each agency shall provide occupational safety and health training for supervisory employees that includes: supervisory responsibility for providing and maintaining safe and healthful working conditions for employees, the agency occupational safety and health program, Sec. 19 of the Act, Executive Order 12196, this part, occupational safety and health standards applicable to the assigned workplaces, agency procedures for reporting hazards, agency procedures for reporting and investigating allegations of reprisal, and agency procedures for the abatement of hazards, as well as other appropriate rules and regulations.

(b) This supervisory training should include introductory and specialized courses and materials which will enable supervisors to recognize and eliminate, or reduce, occupational safety and health hazards in their working units. Such training shall also include the development of requisite skills in managing the agency's safety and health program within the work unit, including the training and motivation of subordinates toward assuring safe and healthful work practices.

1960.56: Training of Safety and Health Specialists. (a) Each agency shall provide occupational safety and health training for safety and health specialists through courses, laboratory experiences, field study, and other formal learning experiences to prepare them to perform the necessary technical monitoring, consulting, testing, inspecting, designing, and other tasks related to program development and implementation, as well as hazard recognition, evaluation, and control, equipment and facility design, standards, analysis of accident, injury, and illness data; and other related tasks.

(b) Each agency shall implement career development programs for their occupational safety and health specialists to enable the staff to meet present and future program needs of the agency.

1960.57: Training of Safety and Health Inspectors. Each agency shall provide training for safety and health inspectors with respect to appropriate standards, and the use of appropriate equipment and testing procedures necessary to identify and evaluate hazards and suggest general abatement procedures during or following their assigned inspections, as well as preparation of reports and other documentation to support the inspection findings.

1960.58: Training of Collateral Duty Safety and Health Personnel and Committee Members. Within six months after October 1, 1980, or on appointment of an employee to a collateral duty position or to a committee, each agency shall provide training for collateral duty safety and health personnel and all members of certified occupational safety and health committees commensurate with the scope of their assigned responsibilities. Such training shall include: The agency occupational safety and health program; Sec. 19 of the Act; Executive Order 12196; this part; agency procedures for the reporting, evaluation, and abatement of hazards, agency procedures for reporting and investigating allegations of reprisal, the recognition of hazardous conditions, and environments; identification and use of occupational safety and health standards, and other appropriate rules and regulations.

1960.59: Training of Employees and Employee Representatives. (a) Each agency shall provide appropriate safety and health training for employees including specialized job safety and health training appropriate to the work performed by the employee; for example, clerical, printing, welding, crane operation, chemical analysis, and computer operations. Such training also shall inform employees of the agency occupational safety and health program, with emphasis on their responsibilities and rights.

(b) Occupational safety and health training for employees of the agency who are representatives of employee groups, such as labor organizations which are recognized by the agency, shall include both introductory and specialized courses and materials that will enable such groups to function appropriately in ensuring safe and healthful working conditions and practices in the workplace and enable them to effectively assist in conducting inspections. Nothing in this paragraph shall be construed to alter training provisions provided by law, Executive Order, or collective bargaining arrangements.

1960.60: Training Assistance. (a) Agency heads may seek training assistance from the Secretary of Labor, the National Institute for Occupational Safety and Health, and other appropriate sources.

(b) After the effective date of Executive Order 12196, the Secretary of Labor shall, upon request, and with reimbursement, conduct orientation for Designated Agency Safety and Health Officials and/or their designees which will enable them to manage the occupational safety and health programs of their agencies. Such orientation shall include coverage of Sec. 19 of the Act, Executive Order 1296, and the requirements of this part.

(c) Upon request and with reimbursement, the Department of Labor will provide each agency with training materials to assist in fulfilling the training needs of this Subpart, including resident and field training courses designed to meet selected training needs of agency safety and health specialists, safety and health inspectors, and collateral duty safety and health personnel. These materials and courses in no way reduce the agency's responsibility to provide whatever specialized training is required by the unique characteristics of its work.

(d) In cooperation with the U.S. Office of Personnel Management, the Secretary of Labor will develop guidelines and/or provide materials for the safety and health training programs for high-level managers, supervisors, members of committees, and employee representatives.

Industries and Occupations in Which Employees Are at the Highest Levels of Risk

This section identifies some of the industries and occupations where employees are at increased levels of risk.

Research Findings

Research has identified the following factors as being directly related to a high frequency of injuries and illnesses in the workforce:

- The age of the worker (younger workers have higher incidence rates)
- The length of time on the job (new employees have higher incidence rates)
- The size of the firm (medium-size firms have higher incidence rates than smaller or larger firms)
- The type of work performed (incidence and severity rates vary significantly by SIC code)
- The use of hazardous substances in the firm (by SIC code).

These are among the variables that should be considered when one identifies worker groups for training in occupational safety and health-related knowledge and skills.

Identifying Hazardous Occupations

One way to identify worker populations for training in safety and health is to develop a comprehensive list of specifically defined hazardous-type occupations, grouped by industry. Based on the presence of at least one of the three environmental criteria or factors (noise and/or vibration, physical hazards, and unsatisfactory atmospheric conditions affecting the respiratory system and the skin), the *Handbook for Analyzing Jobs* lists and defines 5194 occupational titles as being in a variable-risk category. Of these, 3599 occupations (69 percent) were marked for the presence of one environmental condition, 1260 (24 percent) for two of these conditions, and 335 (7 percent) for all three conditions present.[13]

Rating Injury Incidence and Employment by Occupation

The Bureau of Labor Statistics of the U.S. Department of Labor has developed a relatively new statistic which relates injury incidence and employment by occupation within economic sectors and industry divisions in the belief that such data should help target those workers who are at the greatest levels of risk and consequently more likely to sustain job-related accidents and illnesses. The statistic is computed as follows: The percentage distribution of injuries and of employment by occupation for a given industrial category is used to compute the ratio index. Specifically, the index is the percentage of injuries accounted for by an occupation, divided by the percentage of total employment that the occupation represents. The "universe" totals—100 percent of injuries and 100 percent of employment within the industrial category—yield an index of 1.0. An occupational index greater than 1.0 indicates that the percentage of injuries for an occupation is greater than the percentage of employment in that occupation, and a ratio smaller than 1.0 indicates the opposite. Thus, the index measures injury experience for a worker group against a base of 1.0 for all occupations within a given industry division or sector. Because absolute numbers are not used, the discrete indices are valid only within each industrial category.

Prioritizing Training, Should This Become Necessary

Occasionally, resources fall short of the need for occupational safety and health training. When this situation occurs, employers may be faced with the task of deciding which employees will receive training priority. The following information is designed to help managers make these difficult decisions. It should be remembered that the models shown are illustrative only; there is no single preferred training resource allocation model.

Models for Selecting Workers for Training

A model for prioritizing the selection of workers for training in occupational safety and health appears in Fig. 44-6. A worker selection matrix, using the logic of the branching model, appears in Fig. 44-7. The selection of workers to be targeted for job-safety and health information, education, and training is based on selection of the SIC as the operative element, limitation to areas where training is an appropriate solution (i.e., areas where a lack of skill and knowledge is a causative factor in the accident), and where existing training is not effective. Other groups targeted for training priorities are those exposed to significant safety and health hazards, especially where the number of persons exposed presents an unusually high potential for loss.

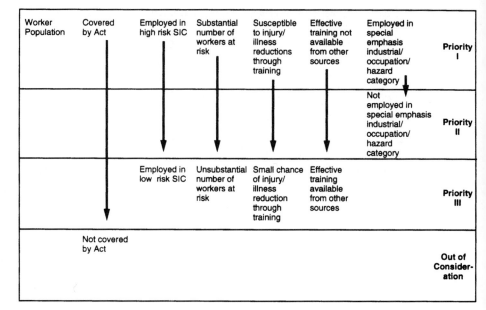

Figure 44-6. Model for the selection of workers for occupational safety and health training.

SIC identification	Covered by OSHA?	High risk?	Number at risk?	Is training an effective counter-measure?	Is there an effective employer OSHA training program?	Is other effective training available?	Is industry involved with special-emphasis or other program?	Training priority
xx	Yes	Yes	High	Yes	No	No	Yes	1
xy	No	No	Low	No	No	Yes	No	Out of consideration

Figure 44-7. Illustrative worker selection matrix for training in occupational safety and health.

How Well Are Employers Meeting Their Training Requirements?

Probably no one had a good handle on how well employers were meeting their responsibility to provide employees with safety and health education until the Bureau of Labor Statistics released its series of *Work Injury Reports* (WIRs). These surveys, conducted through 1991, reached out to the injured workers themselves for answers to specific questions directly related to causal factors in accident occurrences. The heart of the WIR surveys was the employee questionnaire, which focused on a particular type of accident resulting in injury to the worker. The questions were designed to isolate specific factors, such as the amount and type of training received, that were directly or indirectly responsible for producing the accident. An analysis of these WIRs revealed some shocking data. A few examples follow.

WIR data showed that 11 percent (a wholly unacceptable figure) of workers injured during welding and cutting operations said that they did not receive training for the tasks being performed at the time of injury. An astounding 73 percent of workers injured while using ladders said that they received no training. In the case of head and foot injuries, 71 percent of those injured reported never having received any safety training. Many other injured workers reported receiving little, if any, training on the safety and health risks of their jobs.

In addition to the above data, the WIR surveys had a number of other surprises. Significant numbers of injured workers reported the following:

1. Their employers reportedly provided training only following an injury-producing event.

2. The instruction employees did receive was perceived as being of little value in helping them to prevent the type of injury sustained.

3. The instruction provided by their employers was, for the most part, in lecture format with no written learning materials, lesson plans, instructional manuals, instructional aids, or provision for worker feedback.

4. Printed instructions were often simply distributed without further clarification or opportunity to query the instructor.

5. Workers rarely received feedback from their employers on what actions, if any, had been taken to prevent further incidents of the types that had resulted in their injuries.

6. Most of the information the workers did receive came not from their employer, but from fellow workers, employee representatives, salespersons for personal protective equipment, and other safety devices, and from the literature that accompanied tools, machines, and materials they used in their work.

The findings listed above should not be considered representative of American business; clearly, they are not. However, it would be a serious error not to take data of this type seriously and ensure that one's own employees are receiving the instruction they need to perform their jobs in a safe and healthful manner.

Penalties for Failing to Provide the Training Required by the Nature of the Job Itself, and by Federal and State Safety and Health Regulatory Agencies

Failure to ensure that one's employees are fully trained for their assigned tasks is grossly irresponsible since it places the workers at increased risk and reduces the possibility that they will perform their tasks in an optimal manner. Further, failure to provide the training mandated by regulatory agencies and by the nature of the job itself can be costly in terms of penalties meted out by OSHA (or by states which operate OSHA-approved programs). These penalties can be severe.

In the United States, in addition to being able to cite an employer for failure to provide the training identified in the occupational safety and health standards, an OSHA compliance safety and health officer (or state inspector in an OSHA-approved program) may invoke Section 5.(a)(1) of the Act, which states: "Each employer (1) shall furnish to each of his or her employees employment and a place of employment which are free from recognized hazards that are causing or are likely to cause death or serious physical harm to his or her employees...." An example of the application of this authority is the case where OSHA charged an employer with failing to adequately advise and supervise a new employee on the hazards of pressure vessels and hazardous material associated with the petrochemical industry. Evidence revealed that a new employee was killed when the phthalic anhydride melt tank which he was operating exploded. The employer contested the citation and penalty; however, the Occupational Safety and Health Review Commission (OSHRC) affirmed the citation and proposed penalty.

What Managers Need to Know About Job Safety and Health

Many of those who have studied the problem of occupational safety and health mishaps cite as a principal reason for these incidents the fact that employers have tended to rely too heavily on the expertise of specialists alone and, in so doing, have failed to enlist appropriate, ongoing management involvement. It is now generally recognized that environmental and occupational mishaps are caused by failures of control. As Great Britain's Health and Safety Executive (that nation's equivalent of our OSHA) puts it: "They (i.e., failures of control) are not, as is so often believed, the result of straightforward failures of technology; social, organizational, and technical problems interact to produce them."[14]

The sets of knowledge and skills required by managers to ensure optimal safety and health within their organizations are not intuitive; they must be acquired. But, the fact is that the scope and intensity of educational efforts are not provided at anywhere near the level required. In recent years, both the curricula and teaching methods of many schools of business have come under attack from groups as diverse as students on the one hand and corporations on the other. Among other criticisms, these schools have been faulted for failing to provide adequate instruction on safety and health problems despite the fact that surveys have repeatedly shown that these concerns rank high among executives of companies of all sizes.

The Joint International Labor Organization/World Health Organization Committee on Occupational Health and Safety had this to say about education and training methodology for supervisors and managers: "Many managers have backgrounds in economics, law, and engineering. In economics and law, there are seldom, if ever, any courses on occupational health and safety. Engineering courses may offer limited teaching on these subjects. Teaching curricula in schools preparing managerial staff should be revised in order to include occupational health, safety, and ergonomics."

Every effort should be made to impress upon all management levels the importance of occupational safety and health. Managers should understand that good working conditions and a good working environment are necessary for smooth, efficient production. Suggested topics to include in educational curricula are the role of management in safety and health activities; the functions of safety and health professionals; accident investigation; fire protection; ergonomics; productivity and health; and legal aspects of safety and health.[15]

Job Safety and Health Hazard Analysis: A Critical Tool When Developing Safety and Health Training Programs

One of the most valuable tools for identifying content for training programs in job safety and health is the job-hazard analysis (JHA). This analysis augments the task analyses which normally will already have been performed for each identifiable task the worker is scheduled to perform. Development of the JHA is a relatively simple procedure, yet it requires great care and insight to ensure that all actual and potential hazards associated with a job are identified. Hazard analysis requires studying and recording each step of a job, identifying existing and potential hazards, and determining the best way to perform the job in order to reduce, eliminate, or protect against the hazards. Information developed from such analyses should form the basis for identifying the needed safety and health training.

Figure 44-8 provides an example of such an analysis developed by OSHA to guide those who are required to have such analyses. In this instance, the analysis addresses the task of cleaning the inside surface of a chemical tank with top manhole entry.

There are a number of variants to the OSHA model shown in Fig. 44-8. One of the more thorough of these is one developed by the staff of the Labor Occupational Health Program (LOHP) at the University of California, Berkeley, as part of a special emphasis program to impact the ferrous foundry industry. This model is shown in Figs. 44-9 and 44-10. In this model, the processes associated with the foundry are identified and plotted on a flowchart by major function in the order of occurrence. Once this phase of the analysis has been carried out, hazards associated with each of these processes are identified. An added dimension to the LOHP model is the development of tables which identify the dusts, fumes, gases, and vapors produced in foundry processes and their effects, along with the threshold limit values for each.

Another format for JHA is to expand its scope so that it covers an activity in which two or more workers interact, thus making it possible for each worker to learn how individual actions impact fellow workers. Such activity analyses have been found to increase not only the camaraderie of a work group but also its safety and productivity.

Evaluating the Effectiveness of Job Safety and Health Training Programs

A frequent error when one tries to assess the effectiveness of a safety and health training program is to attempt to establish a direct causal relationship between completion of a training program and a firm's injury or illness experience, its workers' compensation costs, or some other criterion. If a direct causal relationship between training and mishaps is not possible with our current understanding of research design and manipulation of multiple variables, how, then, can the effectiveness of instruction designed to increase the levels of worker skills and knowledge be determined?

The evaluation of safety training programs is not unlike the evaluation of any other type of training program. The major difference is the nature of the knowl-

Figure 44-8. Sample job-hazard analysis: cleaning the inside surface of a chemical tank-top manhole entry. (*Source: Occupational Safety and Health Administration,* Job Hazard Analysis: A Tool to a Safer, More Healthful Workplace, *OSHA Publication No. 3071, U.S. Department of Labor, Occupational Safety and Health Administration, Washington, DC, 1981.*)

Step	Hazard	New Procedure or Protection
1. Select and train operators.	Operator with respiratory or heart problem; other physical limitation. Untrained operator—failure to perform task.	• Examination by industrial physician for suitability to work. • Train operators. • Dry run. [Reference: National Institute for Occupational Safety and Health (NIOSH) Doc. #80-406]

2. Determine what is in the tank, what process is going on in the tank, and what hazards this can pose.	Explosive gas
	
	Improper oxygen level.
	Chemical exposure—
	Gas, dust, vapor:
	      irritant
	      toxic
	Liquid: irritant
	      toxic
	      corrosive
	Solid: irritant
	      corrosive
		• Obtain work permit signed by safety, maintenance and supervisors.
		 • Test air by qualified person.
		 • Ventilate to 19–21% oxygen and less than 25% LEL of any flammable gas. Steaming inside of tank, flushing and draining, then ventilating, as previously described, may be required.
		 • Provide appropriate respiratory equipment—SCBA or air line respirator.
		 • Provide protective clothing for head, eyes, body and feet.
		 • Provide parachute harness and lifeline.
		 [Reference: OSHA standards 1910.106, 1926.100, 1926.21(b)(6); NIOSH Doc. #80-406]
		 • Tanks should be cleaned from outside, if possible.

3. Set up equipment.	Hoses, cord, equipment—tripping hazards. Electrical—voltage too high, exposed conductors Motors not locked out and tagged.	• Arrange hoses, cords, lines and equipment in orderly fashion, with room to maneuver safely. • Use ground-fault circuit interrupter. • Lock out and tag mixing motor, if present.
4. Install ladder in tank.	Ladder slipping.	• Secure to manhole top or rigid structure. • Empty tank through existing piping.
5. Prepare to enter tank.	Gas or liquid in tank.	• Review emergency procedures. • Open tank. • Check of job site by industrial hygienist or safety professional.

Figure 44-8. (*Continued*)

Step	Hazard	New Procedure or Protection
		■ Install blanks in flanges in piping to tank. (Isolate tank.) ■ Test atmosphere in tank by qualified person (long probe).
6. Place equipment at tank-entry position.	Trip or fall.	■ Use mechanical-handling equipment. ■ Provide guardrails around work positions at tank top.
7. Enter tank.	Ladder—tripping hazard. Exposure to hazardous atmosphere.	■ Provide personal protective equipment for conditions found. [Reference: NIOSH Doc. #80-406; OSHA CFR 1910.134] ■ Provide outside helper to watch, instruct and guide operator entering tank, with capability to lift operator from tank in emergency.
8. Cleaning tank.	Reaction of chemicals, causing mist or expulsion of air contaminant	■ Provide protective clothing and equipment for all operators and helpers. ■ Provide lighting for tank (Class I, Div. 1). ■ Provide exhaust ventilation. ■ Provide air supply to interior of tank. ■ Frequent monitoring of air in tank. ■ Replace operator or provide rest periods. ■ Provide means of communication to get help, if needed. ■ Provide two-man standby for any emergency.
9. Cleaning up.	Handling of equipment, causing injury.	■ Dry run. ■ Use material-handling equipment.

edge and skills taught to the individual. In a job-safety context, one may first, and fundamentally, examine the training program's administrative policies and instructional methodology to assure that these are in keeping with accepted educational values and standards on the assumption that desirable results are likely to follow. Second, one may attempt to evaluate those receiving the training based on their progress and achievement in terms of desired results. Third, and finally, one may seek to establish the "postgraduate" or continuing values for the training program completed by the worker insofar as these values are reflected by the primary criterion of improved performance on the job.

Let us briefly examine each of these three submeasures of a safety training program.

In examining the training program's administrative policies and instructional methodology, we are concerned with why the training program was developed, for whom, and what those receiving the training may reasonably be expected to

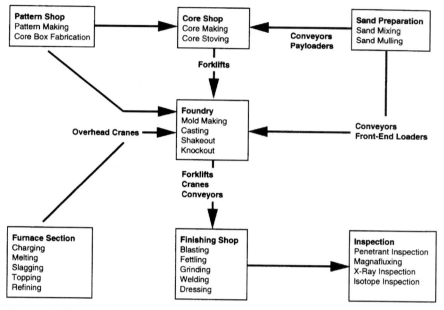

Figure 44-9. Flowchart of foundry processes.

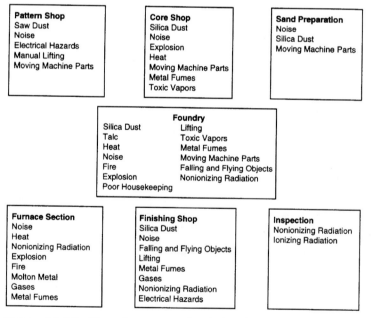

Figure 44-10. Hazards associated with foundry processes.

achieve from having completed the training. If an employer is given to looking to training as the panacea for most things that do not seem to be going according to plan, that employer will be disappointed. If, for example, an employee is committing a high number of errors, the remedy may be an improvement in job design, improved communication between the worker and his or her supervisor, or a more realistic goal of units to be produced or serviced. If the error causal factor is one or a combination of the preceding factors, even the best training program for the worker will not correct the situation. Similarly, if the employer wants to improve the skill levels of his workers, a training program designed to increase such skill levels is needed.

If the plan for evaluating the training program is designed to learn how well those receiving the training are achieving the desired results, the results (goals) must be specific, capable of measurement, and fully understood by the worker. Further, these goals must be realistic in terms of employer expectations. If the employer has neglected to develop his or her staff for years, a single or even a series of courses over a relatively short time span will probably not yield the level of improvement expected. Before attempting to measure worker progress and achievement, one must "test" the course itself in terms of whether it presents real-life situations or uses materials that will be readily recognized as relevant by the worker; whether course materials are free of ambiguous items or materials; whether the course is constructed so as to secure similar results from two applications of the same form (or equivalent forms) to the same group of workers by different instructors; whether it permits accurate and objective scoring by the instructor; and, where appropriate, whether it contains standards of achievement for the worker populations being trained.

The third element on which a training program can be assessed is what could be called the "postgraduate" or continuing values of the course. While one should not set a goal of a specific reduction in job-related mishaps for those completing a training program, one can establish before-and-after measures of factors such as the quality of cleanliness (or housekeeping) throughout the work area; the frequency with which unsafe acts are observed on the part of those workers who have completed the training; and/or the numbers of workers "removed from risk" within, say, six months following completion of the training program (on the assumption that if hazard recognition skills were taught and applied, additional risks would have been identified and corrected, thus removing workers previously exposed from such risks). Even measures such as these, however, should not be used as measures of training program effectiveness unless "improved housekeeping," "a reduction in specific types of unsafe acts," or "removing workers from risk" were stated objectives of the training, and the course content focused on how such objectives could be achieved.

It is well to remember that knowledge and skills, in and of themselves, are of little value, unless applied. And when one realizes that research has shown that the typical patient follows his or her physician's instructions regarding the taking of prescribed medication only 20 percent of the time, and that despite some 40 years of intensive publicity, only some 66 percent of the general driving population uses seatbelts regularly, one gets some idea of how difficult it is to get anyone, not just workers, to apply what they already know.

In summary, evaluation routines take many forms. Methods used to determine how effective certain facets of the training program are do not need to be elaborate or conducted according to any specific regimen to provide clues to its success. For example, many organizations, including OSHA, use survey questionnaires to gather data on how well specific training efforts are impacting the target populations. In OSHA's case, its survey instruments take two forms, one for employers and one for employees. These groups are polled to learn how well compliance officers are performing during site visits. Such feedback is valuable in that it provides one dimension of how the results of the compliance officer training are being applied at the work site and how the compliance officers, themselves, are perceived by the employer.

Many firms sample the knowledge and skills of their supervisors and employees by simply asking questions targeted to the level of knowledge and skills these employees have been taught. Questions are chosen on the basis of the hazards to which workers may be exposed throughout the work site.

Wellness Programs: How to Cut Costs and Reduce Accidents

Contrary to popular opinion, a wellness program does not have to cost a lot of money or involve an on-site exercise facility. Even a relatively small investment in the health of a company's employees can pay off tremendously in terms of fewer accidents, lower health-care costs, reduced absenteeism, and increased productivity.

What makes a good wellness program? First and foremost, a successful program requires support from all levels of an organization. "Mid-level managers are the ones who decide how employees spend their time on a day-to-day basis," according to Leigh Anne Jasheway, coauthor of *Adventures in Wellness: A Step by Step Guide for Implementing a Worksite Wellness Program.* "It's important for them to let employees know it's okay to take time for wellness."[16]

Of course, to really succeed, a wellness program needs support and participation from employees. That's why it's important to include wellness in your safety and health training programs. Be sure to ask employees for their input. Even if you don't have the training expertise to meet their needs, you can bring in a consultant to work with a variety of community resources.

A good wellness program focuses on prevention. A company-sponsored walking club, for instance, can encourage employees to exercise before or after work or at lunchtime. A health fair or a brown-bag lunch and health talk can provide a low-cost means to build health awareness at work.

To help employees address serious threats to their health—such as substance abuse, smoking, stress, domestic violence, and depression—an employee-assistance program or EAP is essential. To keep costs down, some companies outsource this function. But it's important for employees to know that they have resources to turn to—*before* things get out of hand.

Once a company has a wellness program in place, the safety and health manager can easily demonstrate its effectiveness. Here are several measurement tools from safety-director Donald E. McGowan:

- *Use beginning-of-program and end-of-program questionnaires.* Look for changes or patterns in absences, sick days, general well-being, occupational injuries, seat-belt usage, and smoking habits.

- *Perform health-care cost data assessment.* Compare health-care costs, workers' compensation claims, inpatient hospital days, and occupational-injury costs, etc., on an annual basis.

- *⸱t measurement.* Compare preprogram and postprogram statistics such as terol and weight.

- *cost comparison.* Establish cost-benefit from other professionally studies.[17]

Safety and health go hand in hand with wellness. To stay competitive, today's companies must make wellness a part of their overall strategy to improve safety and health performance.

References

1. American Society of Safety Engineers, *The Scope and Functions of the Professional Safety Position,* American Society of Safety Engineers, Des Plaines, IL, 1996.

2. MacCollum, David V., "Time for Change in Construction Safety," *Professional Safety,* February 1990, pp. 17–20.

3. *Dictionary of Occupational Titles,* 4th ed., U.S. Department of Labor, Employment and Training Administration, U.S. Employment Service, Washington, DC, 1993.

4. "Safety and Health Program Management Guidelines," *Federal Register* (54FR3908), January 26, 1989.

5. Dewis, M., *The Law on Health and Safety at Work,* MacDonald and Evans, Ltd., Estover, Plymouth, Great Britain, 1978, p. 94.

6. Ibid.

7. Ibid.

8. Construction Safety Association of Canada, 21 Voyager Court South, EITBICOKE, Ontario, Canada, M9W 5M7.

9. Headquarters, Department of the Army, *Safety and Command,* Office of the Deputy Chief of Staff for Personnel, Washington, DC, 1959, pp. 19–20.

10. Man-Made Fibres Industry Training Board, *Training Recommendation No. 8,* Man-Made Fibres Industry Training Board, London, 1980, p. 6.

11. Occupational Safety and Health Administration, *All About OSHA,* U.S. Department of Labor, Occupational Safety and Health Administration, Washington, DC, 1992, pp. 34–36.

12. Ibid., pp. 37–40.

13. Hilaski, H. J., *List of Hazardous Type Occupations: Job Listing by Selected Environmental Conditions,* PB 296-781-8, U.S. Department of Commerce, National Technical Information Service, Springfield, VA, May 1979.

14. Health and Safety Executive, *Managing Safety: A Review of Role of Management in Occupational Health and Safety by the Accident Prevention Advisory Unit of Her Majesty's Factory Inspectorate,* Her Majesty's Stationery Office, London, 1981, p. 6.

15. World Health Organization, *Education and Training in Occupational Health, Safety, and Ergonomics* (Technical Report Series 663), World Health Organization, Geneva, 1981, p. 37.

16. Rategan, Catherine, "Well? It's About Time," *Safety and Health,* July 1992, pp. 54–58.

17. McGowan, Donald E., "The Healthy Way to Reduce Accidents," *Safety and Health,* March 1992, pp. 46–49.

SECTION 5
Resources

45

Information Resources

Edith L. Allen

Edith L. Allen *is Director of the Information Center at ASTD where she is responsible for managing the reference and information services provided to members and the development of electronic networking and information services for the society. Prior to joining ASTD in 1988, Allen worked as a reference librarian for The College of William and Mary in Virginia and as an education specialist for The George Washington University. She received her M.S. in library and information science from the Catholic University of America, an M.A. in adult education with a concentration in human resource development from The George Washington University, and a B.A. in English from The College of William and Mary.*

Training practitioners have a unique challenge in keeping up with the information that supports their work. Trainers need to stay current in three distinct, yet interrelated areas of information. They need to be aware of new and changing information to support their roles and functions as HRD professionals. Trainers also need to find content information about the subjects on which they provide training, either to learn more about the subject so that they can design materials and present programs on it, or to identify and evaluate prepackaged training materials. Trainers also need to understand the trends in the industry or field in which they work and general business issues and trends that affect the workplace. This chapter provides an overview of the resources available to training practitioners to access information for all three areas of information needs, and it explains how to find and use these resources.

Organization of Information
for Training Professionals

HRD practitioners have several roles that they can hold during their career, or even within the same job. The *Models for HRD Practice*[1] identifies 11 roles for a training practitioner. Some of these roles—researcher, HRD manager, HRD marketer, organization change agent, career development advisor, administrator, and HRD consultant—require not only an understanding of the basic underlying principles of HRD but also a current understanding of general business trends to tie these roles into the needs of the organization. As the HRD profession changes and reinvents itself to meet the challenges of the changing business environment, HRD professionals will need to understand and adopt new roles, such as performance support technician, that require a broad understanding of a new field.

Other roles identified in the *Models* involve specific steps in the instructional design and delivery process which constitutes the backbone of training: needs analyst, program designer, HRD materials developer, instructor-facilitator, and evaluator. New theories and methods for performing these functions emerge with time, research, and the introduction of new technologies, requiring each practitioner to keep up to date with the new approaches while being grounded in the fundamental principles of each area of practice.

In addition to the roles of the profession, training practitioners need to stay current in the technology that supports their roles. To support their work, trainers increasingly will rely on technology such as human resource information systems that automate the scheduling of classes and maintenance of training records and skill inventories; interactive multimedia devices such as interactive video, simulators, and virtual-reality systems, for the delivery of training; and electronic performance support systems that will serve as both job aids and learning tools to improve performance. The Internet is evolving as a significant tool for practitioners, not only as a means of getting their information and conducting networking but also as a means of sharing training materials among themselves and delivering training to workers.

While training practitioners need to stay current with the tools for and principles of being training practitioners, they also need to find resources for the content on which they are developing or providing training. The need for obtaining content information can vary, depending on the involvement for the trainer. Information retrieval can be as simple as using a print directory or an on-line database to identify existing seminars or off-the-shelf materials to provide a ready-made solution to a training need. Or it can be as involved as obtaining resources for background reading, talking to other HRD practitioners who have developed training in the subject, or contacting an association that represents the subject for competency or certification requirements and the recommended curriculum to meet those requirements.

Line managers or other internal staff can serve as subject-matter experts to help design the content of a training program. Universities or community colleges that offer degree or certificate programs in the content area of training may also have curricula that they will share, or they may refer you to textbooks and other reading materials that will support course development.

Benchmarking is another method for identifying useful information. Benchmarking is an investigative approach to collecting the best practices that lead to the superior performance of a company.[2] (Also see Chap. 19, Benchmarking for Best Practices.) Some established institutions for benchmarking, such as the American Society for Training and Development's Benchmarking Forum and the American Productivity and Quality Center's Benchmarking Clearinghouse, have collected information about best practices. Although most of the information is available only to members of the forum or the clearinghouse, some limited information is available. But training practitioners can use the information in this chapter to identify sources of information to start their own benchmarking efforts.

Because training needs to be linked to the business function of an organization, trainers must keep up with general business trends and issues. These trends are often discussed in the journals and magazines that cover the HRD profession because training and organization development are closely connected to the work environment. But trainers should review other non-training-related publications to stay informed and to develop a well-rounded view of these general business issues so that they can be proactive in recommending solutions that improve overall performance within the organization.

The resources that best support these categories of information that trainers need often overlap. Instead of using a list of resources broken down into categories of information they provide, let's discuss the resources in terms of the format, how to obtain resources in that format, and how to use the particular resources.

Print Publications

Handbooks

For trainers not well versed in the academic knowledge base of training and development, a good place to begin is a handbook such as this one. Handbooks provide an overview of major theoretical issues and point out key research studies that have defined the field. Examples of other handbooks that provide a good academic overview include the following:

Dunnette, Marvin D., and Leaetta M. Hough, eds., *Handbook of Industrial and Organizational Psychology*, 2d ed., Consulting Psychologists Press, Palo Alto, CA, 1990.
Hampton, John J., ed., *AMA Management Handbook*, 3d ed., American Management Association, New York, 1994.
Nadler, Leonard, ed., *Handbook of Human Resource Development*, 2d ed., John Wily & Sons, New York, 1984.
Tracey, William R., ed., *Human Resources Management and Development Handbook*, 2d ed., American Management Association, New York, 1994.

In addition to handbooks that provide an overview to the field as a whole, several handbooks addressing a specific area of practice within training or performance support have been written. These handbooks include

Craig, Robert L., and Leslie Kelly, eds., *Sales Training Handbook: A Guide to Developing Sales Performance*, Prentice Hall, Englewood Cliffs, NJ, 1990.
Kelly, Leslie, ed., *The ASTD Technical and Skills Training Handbook*, McGraw-Hill, New York, 1994.
Stolovtich, Harold D., and Erica J. Keeps, eds., *Handbook of Human Performance Technology*, Jossey-Bass, San Francisco, 1992.

Research-Based Journals

Trainers seeking the most up-to-date academic knowledge in their field should consult academic journals. The typical academic journal article focuses on a single research study or synthesizes a group of such studies on a specific topic. Journal articles reporting the results of academic research often have a standardized format that includes

- Brief literature review
- Research hypothesis
- Experimental design
- Results
- Summary and conclusions

This format allows for easy initial scanning of the articles.

A sample of the major journals, both U.S. and international, that regularly publish academic knowledge relevant to trainers is listed below. New journals, however, are introduced and existing journals change their names or cease publication on a continuing basis. A thorough search of the literature requires a search of databases or print indexes and abstracts that will be described later in this chapter.

Adult Education Quarterly, American Association for Adult and Continuing Education.
Asia Pacific Journal of Human Resources, Australian Human Resources Institute.
California Management Review, University of California, Graduate School of Business Administration.
Education Communications and Technology Journal (ECTJ), Association for Educational Communications & Technology.
Educational Technology, Educational Technology, Inc.
Group & Organization Management, Sage Periodicals Press.
Human Resource Development Quarterly, American Society for Training and Development.
Human Resource Management, John Wiley & Sons, Inc.
International Journal of Human Resource Management, Routledge Journals.
Journal of Applied Psychology, American Psychological Association.
Performance and Instruction, International Society for Performance Improvement.
Personnel Psychology, Personnel Psychology, Inc.
Public Personnel Management, International Personnel Management Association.
Simulation and Gaming: An International Journal of Theory, Design, and Research, Association for Business Simulation and Experiential Learning.

Practitioner Resources

While the academic sources of information provide insight into the theories, research, and underlying principles that create the foundation of the field, practitioner-based information provides descriptions of trends that affect the field and an overview of how other organizations put the theories and principles into practice.

Books can provide a good discussion of a practical issue related to the field, many good examples of how the topic is practiced in organizations, or detailed checklists and "how-tos" to use for applying the theory to practice. The publication cycle for books, however, is long enough to keep them from being the most timely source of practitioner information. Books also convey new theories, trends, and other information that often have longer staying power, or are the foundation for magazine articles. Reading book reviews in both the research-based journals and practitioner magazines provides insight into which books will become the foundation for new theories and practices within the field.

A number of training-related journals and magazines are oriented to publishing practical information. The typical article in these journals is written by a practitioner and describes how a practical problem can be addressed in an actual training or organizational setting. Other articles provide how-to advice, checklists of steps to follow in conducting a training or organization development intervention, or news of issues, events, and new technologies in the field.

Trainers can also pick up useful information from advertisements, book and media reviews, letters and editorials, and events calendars, in addition to the articles. Major practitioner journals include

Bulletin on Training, Bureau of National Affairs, Inc.
HRMagazine, Society for Human Resource Management.
MicroComputer Trainer, Systems Literacy, Inc.
Monthly Labor Review, U.S. Department of Labor.
People Management, Institute for Personnel and Development.
Personnel Journal, ACC Communications.
T.H.E. Journal: Technological Horizons in Education, Ed Warnshius Ltd.
Training, Lakewood Publications.
Training and Development, American Society for Training and Development.
Training Directors' Forum Newsletter, Lakewood Publications.
Workforce Training News: The Newsmagazine for Employee Learning and Development, Enterprise Communications, Inc.

Performance Aids: Directories and Reference Materials

A wide variety of printed performance aids and reference sources are available to trainers for practical advice and assistance on the job. The following list provides examples of such resources. It is not comprehensive, as new titles emerge and existing titles may cease being published. But it does represent the types of resources that are available to help save trainers time.

Buyer's Guides and Suppliers' Directories

ASTD Buyer's Guide & Consultant Directory, published annually by the ASTD, provides references to training suppliers and consultants that offer products and services to training practitioners. These organizations are indexed by subject as well as by the services or products they offer and the industries they represent.

Bricker's International Directory, from Peterson's Guides, includes a selective listing of university-based executive development programs. The directory references both short-term (less than one week in length) and long-term (over one week in length) programs.

Buyer's Guide to Interactive Videodisc Products and Services, published in the May-June issue of *Instruction Delivery Systems,* focuses on interactive video products and developers and includes lists of authoring system products and vendors, delivery systems hardware, developers and consultants, production facilities, publishers, and videodisc sources.

Computer Training and Support Buyers' Guide, published irregularly by Ziff Institute, includes computer-skills training providers, computer-based training software suppliers, and computer training associations and regional organizations.

Consultants and Consulting Organizations Directory, published annually by Gale Research, lists more than 22,000 consulting firms and independent consultants organized by geographic region, consulting activities, personal name, and consulting firm name.

Equipment Directory of Audio-Visual Computer and Video Products from the International Communications Industries Association covers audiovisual production and projection equipment, furniture, and accessories.

The Evaluation Guide to Executive Management Programs is an annual publication compiled by Corporate University, Inc., and includes information on 150 executive programs offered by educational institutions throughout the United States.

Experience Based Training and Development: Domestic and International Programs is a publication of the Association for Experiential Education which appears irregularly. This directory focuses on programs that use experiential learning methods to train participants in finding creative solutions to group problems, and it includes many programs in the outdoor settings.

Personnel Software Census, an annual publication of Advanced Personnel Systems, lists software programs for human resource functions, including employment management, training management, performance management, and other areas.

Software Encyclopedia, published by R. R. Bowker, is a two-volume set that lists over 16,000 microcomputer software programs for business, professional, and personal use.

Tests: A Comprehensive Guide for Assessments in Psychology, Education, and Business, published by Pro-Ed, Inc., presents brief descriptions to thousands of tests from 437 publishers. Information on each test includes title, author, purpose, intended population, description, scoring method, price, publisher, and whether a test has administration time limitations.

Training and Development Organizations Directory, published by Gale Research, is an irregularly revised directory of firms, institutes, specialized university programs, and other agencies which offer training for managerial, professional, and technical personnel.

Videodisk Compendium for Education and Training, published by the Emerging Technology Consultants, Inc., covers almost 2800 instructional videodisk and CD-ROM titles from over 275 companies, as well as authoring systems, authoring tools, and multimedia presentation systems.

Reference Guides with Practical, How-To Information

The following reference sources were written specifically for the training field and provide practical, how-to information for specific tasks and functions within the profession:

Annual: Developing Human Resources, published by Pfeiffer and Company, includes practical exercises and readings for human resource development professionals, with each volume divided into three sections: structured experiences, instruments, and professional development.

ASTD Reference Guide to Professional Human Resource Development Roles and Competencies, by William Rothwell and Henry Sredl, serves as a companion to the ASTD competency study, *Models for HRD Practice.* The two volumes of the revised second edition expand on the 11 key roles of HRD professionals, describe the context of HRD, offer advice on planning HRD careers, review HRD ethical issues, and include a glossary of terms.

The Guide to National Professional Certification Programs, published by Human Resource Development Press, includes information for over 500 certification programs from a range of industries.

The Human Resources Glossary: A Complete Desk Reference for HR Professionals, edited by William R. Tracey, contains more than 3000 definitions as well as the names, addresses, purposes, and other pertinent information about more than 130 associations and societies of interest to HR practitioners.

Info-Line, published by ASTD, is a monthly booklet series with each issue devoted to a single topic related to training delivery. The booklets contain job-aid checklists, guidelines, and extensive resource lists.

The Trainer's Dictionary, by Angus Reynolds, is a glossary of HRD terms, abbreviations, and acronyms. It also identifies 100 of the most essential HRD terms and the basic terms associated with the field.

The Trainer's Handbook: The AMA Guide to Effective Training, by Garry Mitchell, is written as a field reference for trainers. It provides practical advice on the training function divided into three major functions of the trainer: delivering training, developing training, and managing the training function.

The Training and Development Strategic Plan Workbook, by Raynold A. Svenson and Monica J. Rinderer, offers a practical, step-by-step process to planning and building a comprehensive training system within an organization.

Literature Reviews

HRD Review: A Journal of Professional Opinion is a monthly newsletter that presents reviews of training materials and books in all areas of human resource development.

Training and Development Yearbook, published by Advanced Personnel Systems, provides an annual survey of HRD literature on training administration, program design and development, training technology, training techniques, training programs, and special features. Each yearbook includes a "Trainers' Almanac," a directory of professional organizations, training reference books, journals, newsletters, and conferences for trainers' professional development.

Unpublished Information

Although a wealth of information exists in published resources, sometimes the most valuable information has not yet been published or widely distributed. Valuable and current research is often being conducted by doctoral candidates and may appear only in the dissertation prepared by the candidate. Participating educational institutions submit copies of their dissertations to University Microfilms International for summarizing and indexing in *Dissertations Abstract International.* This print directory, and its related on-line database, *Dissertations Abstracts Online,* provide a subject, author, and title guide to all the dissertations. Researchers may order copies of a dissertation from University Microfilms International.

Other sources of unpublished information are the federal government, commissions and private institutions, and associations. These organizations produce white papers, positions statements, and background documents on topics that they have studied or that they represent. These reports often receive mention in newspaper or journal articles, allowing the reader to contact the organization directly to obtain a copy.

In addition to print materials, humans also serve as a good source for information. Whether at the informal level of one-on-one or group networking, or at the more formal level of a conference or symposium where authors and practitioners present their findings and experience, practitioners in the field have a great deal to share in terms of practical advice, recommendations for products and programs, and benchmarking information.

Accessing Information

Now that these resources for information have been identified, the question remains of where and how to find them. University, public, corporate, and association libraries and information centers are a good starting place and are often underutilized. Associations also contain a wealth of information and provide a targeted approach to obtaining information about a specific industry or profession. Electronic resources may be available to a trainer, either through a library or an association or directly from the trainer's personal computer through an account to the Internet or another on-line service.

Public and University Libraries

Trainers who work in organizations that do not provide a corporate library should visit their nearest public or university library to become familiar with its collection of magazines, journals, and other materials related to the field of human resource development. University and public libraries have extensive reference collections and professional reference librarians to help identify and use appropriate reference materials, including the directories of resources listed in this chapter. If a library does not have a book in its own collection, it will often provide interlibrary loan services to borrow the resource from another library. To identify books that are available from other libraries, librarians can check the *Online Computer Library Catalog (OCLC)*, which lists the books available at hundreds of libraries across the United States, and the information on books cataloged by the Library of Congress. Many libraries have public-access terminals to OCLC so that patrons can identify the books they need themselves. Public and university libraries also provide access to, or will perform brokered searches on, the electronic resources listed in the next section of this chapter.

Special Libraries and Information Centers

Corporate libraries and specialized information centers are often the most useful resources to trainers. Trainers working in organizations that provide a corporate library should become familiar with the collection and may even want to present this chapter's list of resources that the library may want to obtain to support the training function. Other special libraries and information centers collect information on training and human resource development as well as the content areas that trainers often need. These special libraries often use their own set of subject headings that are targeted to the subject area for indexing and organizing the information. They use this setup instead of relying on the more general Library of Congress subject headings that public and university libraries use for their catalogs. The targeted subject headings allow the librarians and patrons to access information within the field faster and customize it to specific needs more easily.

The *Directory of Special Libraries and Information Centers,* updated annually, lists over 21,000 of these libraries, information centers, and research facilities. This three-volume set, available at most public and university libraries, has supplemental subject indexes. The first volume of these subject indexes covers business, government, and law libraries; it includes subject headings for employee training and human resources as well as for the industries and content areas of business. Many government agencies and military institutions have libraries that have a concentrated collection. The Department of Labor has a strong collection on training, as does the U.S. Army TRADOC (Training and Doctrine Command) Headquarters Library. Government and military libraries are also included in the *Directory of Special Libraries and Information Centers.* Some of these special libraries have restricted access to the public, but many can accommodate the public by appointment or for a fee.

The ASTD Information Center is one of the leading special information centers on the field of training and human resource development. The ASTD Information Center has all of the resources referenced in this chapter as well as many other materials targeted to the training profession. Customized search services and unique databases that enhance networking among members, targeted access to literature on the field, and customized lists of training seminars or course materials are all available through the Information Center. ASTD members call in their requests for information, and professional information professionals tap the appropriate databases to compile the necessary information. The targeted collection of over 3000 books and over 70 magazine and journal subscriptions also provides a wealth of resources for conducting on-site research, including a vocabulary targeted specifically to the training-HRD field. The ASTD Information Center is an example of how associations provide information services to their members and society at large. Several of the associations listed in this chapter also have libraries or information centers.

Associations

In addition to their libraries and information centers, associations offer many other services that provide access to information, such as conferences and symposia, expositions, newsletters and journals, and opportunities for networking with colleagues. Associations convene the leaders of the profession to discuss trends, new developments, and practical techniques through conferences and symposia. Often the proceedings of these events, or a compilation of the papers presented, are available after the event. Expositions may accompany the conference or annual meeting and provide an opportunity to see the state-of-the-art products and services from suppliers in the field and to discuss with these suppliers how new technology and theory can be applied to the training and performance support process within a specific program or organization.

Associations also provide many avenues for networking with peers, whether through local meetings, colleague referral services, or special-interest groups that hold special meetings and focus on specific topics in their newsletters. Within the training and HRD profession, these special-interest groups may represent major content or practical areas of training, such as management development, career development, or technical and skills training, as well as specific industries, such as banking and finance, health care, and information management. These special-interest groups can provide practical content information and application to training and performance issues.

The following associations all specialize in training, performance, and human resources:

Accrediting Council for Continuing Education and Training
600 East Main Street, Suite 1425
Richmond, VA 23219
804/648-6742

American Association for Adult and Continuing Education
1200 19th Street N.W., Suite 300
Washington, DC 20036
202/429-5131

American Education Research Association
1230 17th Street N.W.
Washington, DC 20036-3078
202/223-9484

American Management Association
135 West 50th Street
New York, NY 10020
212/586-8100

American Society for Training and Development
1640 King Street, Box 1443
Alexandria, VA 22323
703/683-8100

American Vocational Association
1410 King Street
Alexandria, VA 22314
703/683-3111

Association for Business Simulations and Experiential Learning
Center for Business Simulations
LB 8127
Georgia Southern College
Statesboro, GA 30460-8127
912/681-5457

Association for Educational Communication and Technology
1025 Vermont Avenue, N.W., Suite 820
Washington, DC 20005
202/347-7834

Association of Experiential Education
2885 Aurora Avenue, #28
Boulder, CO 80303-2252
303/440-9344

Association for Supervision and Curriculum Development
1250 North Pitt Street
Alexandria, VA 22314-1453
703/549-9110

Council for Adult and Experiential Education
243 S. Wabash Avenue, Suite 800
Chicago, IL 60604
312/922-5909

ERIC Clearinghouse on Adult, Career, and Vocational Education
Center on Education and Training for Employment
The Ohio State University
1900 Kenny Road
Columbus, OH 43210-1090
800/848-4815

Institute of Personnel and Development
IPD House
Camp Road
London, WW19 4UX
United Kingdom
0181/946-9100

Instructional Systems Association
P.O. Box 1196
Sunset Beach, CA 90742-1196
714/846-6012

International Association for Continuing Education and Training
1101 Connecticut Avenue N.W., Suite 700
Washington, DC 20036
202/857-1122

International Board of Standards for Training, Performance and Instruction
102 South Hager Avenue
Barrington, IL 60010
800/236-4303

International Personnel Management Association
1617 Duke Street
Alexandria, VA 22314
703/549-8100

International Society for Performance and Improvement
1300 L Street N.W., Suite 1250
Washington, DC 20005
202/408-7969

National Organization Development (OD) Network
P.O. Box 69329
Portland, OR 97201
503/246-0148

Ontario Society for Training and Development
110 Richmond Street East, Suite 206
Toronto, Ontario M5C 1P1
Canada
416/367-5900

Organization Development Institute
11234 Walnut Ridge Road
Chesterland, OH 44026
216/461-4333

Organization Development Network
P.O. Box 69329
Portland, OR 97201
503/246-0148

Society for Applied Learning Technology
50 Culpepper Street
Warrenton, VA 22186
703/347-0055

Society for Human Resources Management
606 North Washington Street
Alexandria, VA 22314-1997
800/283-7476, 703/836-0367

Training practitioners can use the *Encyclopedia of Associations,* either to identify additional associations that serve the training and human resources or related fields or to identify associations that specialize in the profession or industry in which their organization is involved. This directory is a standard reference work that is available in almost every library, and it has a subject and key-word index for finding associations.

Electronic Resources

While the print and human sources of information will continue to be valuable, the distribution of information in the electronic format is growing rapidly and is fast becoming the preferred method for finding and sharing information. Whether through on-line database, on-line networking services, or CD-ROMs, electronic services are able to provide access to all the types of information listed above at a faster rate and with a more customized result than other types of information retrieval. More and more professionals are developing networking contacts through on-line services, finding the full text of articles and books readily available, and using the information to which the federal government is opening access via on-line services. Associations are using on-line services to publish their buyer's guides and magazines, provide news about the field, offer information about membership and activities within the association, and foster networking and dialogue among their members.

On-Line Services

Major on-line database vendors, such as Dialog, BRS, and Lexis/Nexis, provide access to references and the full text of articles from hundreds of magazines and journals, newspapers, wire services, television news transcripts, and other resources. Dialog and BRS offer access to hundreds of individual databases such as *ERIC* (Education Resources Information Center), the government-sponsored education database; *ABI/Inform,* a business and industry database that indexes and provides the full text of more than 800 publications; *A-V Online,* a database of more than 336,000 nonprint educational materials for all education levels, including 136,000 references to materials for use in workplace training and human resource development programs; *Grants* and *Foundation Directory,* which identify sources of grant funding by topic area; and hundreds of content-related or industry-specific databases. Most public or university libraries, as well as independent information consultants, offer brokered searching on one or more of the major vendors so that customers can pay to have someone else conduct the search.

Independent on-line services not included in a major on-line service can also provide access to a wealth of information, but they may be more difficult to identify and access. *HRIN* (*Human Resources Information Network*), a compilation of over 60 databases related to the human resources function, can be accessed without your subscribing to a major on-line service. *HRIN* also includes ABI/Inform; the *Training and Development Organizations Directory*; the *Consultants and Consulting Organizations Directory*; databases covering seminar information, such as *Seminar Clearinghouse International* and the *Business Education Seminar Training*; databases listing training videos, such as the *Training Media Database* (a subset of *A-V Online*); databases covering legal issues related to human resources, such as the Bureau of National Affairs' *Americans with Disabilities Act Manual* and their *Policy and Practice Series*; more general databases such as the *Official Airline Guide*; and other resources—all in a searchable format as part of its menu of services.

Private On-Line Networks. Associations are also establishing private on-line services that serve as an electronic gateway to the association. The American Society for Training and Development has established an electronic network, *ASTD Online,* to support its national members. ASTD Online offers electronic mail (e-mail) services and networking forums on specific topics such as organization development, technical and skills training, and instructional technology, and on more general topics such as trends in the field and how to use the Internet.

The service also provides access to information about publications, including the full text of association newsletters and magazines, catalogs of the books, audiovisual materials, and other publications distributed by the association, and their *Buyer's Guide and Consultant Directory* (searchable by key word), and access to the Trainlit literature database that references over 9000 books, journal articles, reports, and other materials on the topics of training, human resources, management, and general business subjects. Other features include a national job bank of positions open in the fields of training, human resources, and quality, news about the association, and access to the Internet through a gateway. Private networks sponsored by an association, such as ASTD Online, allow association members to tap into the benefits of the association 24 hours a day, often in such a way that an individual can easily customize the information to meet specific needs.

Government Information On-Line. Several government databases can also be accessed directly without the user going through a major on-line service provider. Many government agencies, such as the National Technical Information Service (NTIS), the Department of Labor, and the Office of Personnel Management, have their own on-line networks that provide information about grants that are available, regulations and laws, new products that are available for ordering on-line and downloading, and bulletin boards for discussion. The National Technical Information Services offers four databases: the Federal Applied Technology Database; the Federal Research in Progress; NTIS Alert: Foreign Technology; and the NTIS Bibliographic Data Base, which offers descriptions of over 1.5 million unrestricted reports available from the U.S. and non-U.S. government-sponsored research. The NTIS databases are available on the major on-line services as well as through the FedWorld network, either by direct dial or through an Internet telnet, which is described later in this chapter.

CD-ROMs

Some electronic databases are available in the CD-ROM format, which is easier to use than a print index and, for frequent users, costs less than paying for each search on-line and subscribing to a major database vendor. General literature databases, such as *ERIC* and *ABI/Inform,* offer subscriptions to their databases in CD-ROM format. ERIC is updated quarterly, ABI/Inform is updated monthly. Other databases in CD-ROM format that specialize in the human resources field are the Bureau of National Affairs' *Human Resources CD,* which includes the full text or summaries of state and federal employment laws and regulations, expert analyses of these laws and regulations, and sample company policies, employee manuals, job descriptions, checklists, comparison charges, and industry guidelines. Some resource directories, such as the *ASTD Buyer's Guide and Consultant Directory* and the *Linton's Training Sourcebook and Buyer's Guide,* are available in CD-ROM format for fast customization of a list of resources and enhanced directory information.

The Internet

A vast network of over 22,000 individual computers and computer networks, the Internet presents the individual who can connect to it with access to information at a speed and scope never before possible. The Internet is an international medium, allowing a broad distribution of information and communication capabilities worldwide. Usage rates are climbing at a staggering rate during the 1990s, with a high level of access from academic and business institutions. Because of the high media coverage and the new terminology surrounding the use of the Internet, many training practitioners and business professionals feel overwhelmed and confused about what the Internet has to offer and how it can be used.

At a basic level, the Internet makes three services possible: document or information transfer through file transfer protocol (ftp), communication with individuals and networking with groups through e-mail and discussion lists, and use of the resources of remote computer systems through the remote log-in or telnet functions. New software interfaces and hypertext linking programs, such as Mosaic and the World Wide Web, are making the Internet easier to navigate. Many books have been written about how to use the Internet, and several magazines are dedicated to tracking updates and new features. Instead of explaining how to use the Internet, this chapter will discuss how trainers are using the Internet to support their work and what resources are available on the Internet to support trainers.

Networking.   One of the easiest ways to use the Internet to support professional development and to stay on top of trends in the field is to subscribe to *list-servs.* Listservs are discussions that are exchanged in the format of a mailing list. Anyone with the ability to use electronic mail on the Internet can subscribe to a listserv. To participate, an Internet user would send a message to the mailing list to start a subscription. Then as a subscriber posts a message to the listserve, a copy is sent by electronic mail to every other subscriber. Many different listservs are available on topics related to training, human resources, and related fields. Here are a list of the most relevant listservs:

AEE-LIST@PUCC.PRINCETON.EDU   (Experiential education list)

ALTLEARN@SJUVM.STJOHNS.EDU   (Alternative approaches to learning)

ASAT-EVA@UNLVM.UNL.EDU   (Distance education evaluation group)

DISRES-L@RYERSON.BITNET   (Distance education research list)

EDNET@NIC.UMASS.EDU   (Educational usage, potential of the Internet)

EDTECH@MSU.BITNET   (Educational technology list)

HRD-L@MIZZOU1.MISSOURI.EDU   (Human resource development group)

HRIS-L@VM.UCS.UALBERTA.CA   (Human resources information, Canada)

OUTDOOR-ED@LATROBE.EDU.AU   (Outdoor-experiential educators)

TESLIT-L@CUNYVM.BITNET   (Adult education and literacy test literature)

TRDEV-L@PSUVM.PSU.EDU   (Training and development discussions list)

At the time of this writing, one of the most active listservs is the TRDEV-L listserv, with over 2700 subscribers representing over 44 countries. Seventy percent of the subscribers are corporate training professionals communicating on the cutting edge. Training practitioners use this listserv to discuss trends in the field such as outsourcing the training department and the need for certification in the field; to discuss ethical issues; to share ice-breakers and training techniques; to arrange to meet at conferences; or to develop lists of frequently asked questions (FAQs) about the training field and the appropriate answers. A training-related FAQ list that is updated every few months and includes lists of favorite books in the field, Internet sites and listservs that address training-related topics, and an overview of key or "hot" terms in the field is available for transferring as an ftp file on an ongoing basis.

Newsgroups, using the Usenet service, are similar to listservs in purpose, but they operate differently. Usenet newsgroups are discussion lists to which users post articles that are stored and read with a newsreader software package instead of having each posting mailed to the subscribers.[3] The following Usenet newsgroups related to the training and human resource development fields are available at the time of publication:

I ACT.RESEARCH   (Action research list)

ALT.ADULT.LITERACY   (Adult literacy learners, tutors, and instructors)

ALT.EDUCATION.DISTANCE   (Learning over networks)

I ALT.PSYCHOLOGY.NLP   (Neurolinguistic programming)

ALT.PSYCHOLOGY.PERSONALITY   (Personality taxonomy such as Myers-Briggs)

ALT.SUPPORT.LEARN-DISABLED   (Learning disabilities list)

BIT.LISTSERV.EDTECH   (Educational technology—moderated)

BIT.LISTSERV.ERL-L   (Educational research list)

BIT.LISTSERV.QUALITY   (Total Quality Management in manufacturing and service industries)

COMP.BENCHMARKS   (Benchmarking techniques and results)

COMP.COG.ENG   (Cognitive engineering)

COMP.GROUPWARE.LOTUS-NOTES.MISC   (Improving group work processes)

I MISC.CREATIVITY   (Creativity list)

MISC.EDUCATION.MULTIMEDIA   (Multimedia discussions)

Finding Published Information.	The Internet also allows practitioners to find published reference sources and other documents for either browsing on-line or for transferring back to their own computers for printing and storing. Many useful reference sources are available on the Internet through "gopher" services and through ftp. A gopher is a powerful system that allows users on the Internet to access many of the resources in a simple, consistent manner.[4] Hundreds of gopher services exist, and directories of gophers and other Internet sites and addresses are frequently published to help Internet users find what they need. Examples of the types of reference materials available on public gopher sites include the *CIA World Factbook,* which can provide basic facts about a country, including an overview of its economic condition; access to *CARL Uncover,* a service that allows users to order the full text of over six million journal articles for a fee; *AskERIC,* the on-line service of the Education Resource Information Center which includes a directory of tests for business, education, and psychology, files on disability information, and an Educator's Guide to E-mail Lists; standard reference books such as *Webster's Dictionary, Roget's Thesaurus,* and the Acronyms Dictionary; and access to the on-line catalogs of many libraries, including university libraries and the Library of Congress. The possibilities of what can be found through gophers are almost limitless, and they are growing every day. Many associations are establishing a presence on the Internet by setting up their own gopher sites that link their gopher users to the resources of specific interest within the profession or industry they represent.

One of the great myths of the Internet is that all the information on it is available for free. Copyright laws and royalty fees still apply to much of the information available on the Internet so that it is not free; nonetheless, that information is accessible through the network, for a fee. For example, the *CARL Uncover* service allows users to order the full text of articles to be faxed but requires a fee. The *Electronic Newsstand* allows users to subscribe to magazines to be received electronically via E-mail, but subscribers must still pay for the magazine. Major on-line vendors, such as *Dialog* and *Lexis/Nexis,* provide access to their services on the Internet at a reduced rate over their direct-dial services, but users still pay a fee for the connect time and for any citations or full-text publications they retrieve from the services over the Internet.

Government Information on the Internet.	Even though everything is not free on the Internet, a wealth of free information is available from one specific publisher—the federal government. Through the *FedWorld* network on the Internet, training practitioners can find a wealth of business and industry information from such agencies as the Office of Personnel Management, the Department of Commerce, the National Technical Information Service, the Office of Management and Budget, and the Office of Technology Assessment, to name only a few. The Department of Labor's bulletin board, *Labor News,* has information that is particularly pertinent to training practitioners. *Labor News* includes all the files from the Office of the American Workplace, an agency within the Department of Labor that focuses on supporting and promoting the development of high-performance workplaces by serving as a clearinghouse of information about high-performance workplaces and offering technical assistance to businesses that want to transform their workplaces. *Labor News* also includes summaries of articles published in the *Monthly Labor Review,* OSHA fact sheets and news on OSHA regulations that affect safety training procedures, help files on topics such as "An Employer's Guide to Dealing with Drug Abuse" and "Compliance Guide to the Family and Medical Leave Act," and information about grants available to support training programs and school-to-work programs.

Resources on the Internet. The Internet is constantly growing in the number of individuals who use it and in the resources and services available on it. New software enhancements continue to make it easier to navigate to find needed or useful information. Many books are available about how to use the Internet, and new books will continue to appear as the network evolves. At the time of publication, the following useful resources to the Internet are available:

Books About the Internet

Falk, Bennett, *The Internet Roadmap,* Sybex, San Francisco, 1994.
Hahn, Harley, and Rick Stout, *The Internet Complete Reference,* Osborne/McGraw-Hill, Berkeley, CA, 1994.
Kehoe, Brendan P., *Zen and the Art of the Internet: A Beginner's Guide,* 2d ed., Prentice-Hall, Englewood Cliffs, NJ, 1993.
Krol, Ed, *The Whole Internet User's Guide and Catalog,* O'Reilly and Associates, Sebastopol, CA, 1992.
Laquey, Tracy, and Jeanne C. Ryer, *The Internet Companion: A Beginner's Guide to Global Networking,* Addison-Wesley, Reading, MA, 1993.
Levine, John R., and Carol Baroudi, *The Internet for Dummies,* IDG Books Worldwide, San Mateo, CA, 1993.

Journal Articles About the Internet

"America's Information Highway: A Hitch-hiker's Guide," *The Economist,* December 25, 1993 through January 7, 1994, pp. 35–38.
Gleick, James, "The Internet and Your Business," *Fortune,* March 7, 1994, pp. 86–96.
Polly, Jean Armour, "Surfing the Internet: An Introduction," *Wilson Library Bulletin,* 66(6):38–42, 155 (1992).
Rubin, Bryndis A., "The Internet: Where Few Trainers Have Gone Before," *Training and Development,* 48(8):24–31 (1994).

Serial Publications About the Internet

Internet World, Meckler Publishing Corporation, Westport, CT.
Wired, Wired Ventures, Ltd., San Francisco, CA.

Conclusion

The pace of advancements in technology will continue to make the information available to the individual increase at an accelerated rate. Although much of the information in this chapter may soon be outdated, the concepts of what types of information are available and how to apply the information that is available will remain the same. The challenge will not be how to identify information, but how to assess its value and how to apply it to the profession. The successful training practitioners will learn how to evaluate information quickly and leverage it effectively in the workplace.

The best way for training practitioners to stay current in information is to develop a good relationship with a library or information service, visit it regularly to use its resources, establish a strong network of colleagues, learn about all the services of the professional associations that represent their professions and the industries in which they work, regularly read four or five magazines or journals that cover topics and issues related to training and to business in general to stay current with trends and developments, and become comfortable using on-line systems, especially the Internet. To get updated information on the resources mentioned in this chapter, readers may contact the Information Center at the American Society for Training and Development.

References

1. McLagan, Patricia A., *Models for HRD Practice: The Models,* American Society for Training and Development, Alexandria, VA, 1989, p. 49.

2. Camp, Robert C., *Benchmarking: The Search for Industry Best Practices That Lead to Superior Performance,* Quality Press, Milwaukee, 1989, p. xi.

3. Hahn, Harley, and Rick Stout, *The Internet Complete Reference,* Osborne/McGraw-Hill, Berkeley, CA, 1994, pp. 161–166.

4. Ibid., p. 430.

46

Higher Education as a Resource for Human Resource Development

Michal Foriest Settles

Michal Foriest Settles *is human resource manager at the San Francisco Bay Area Rapid Transit District (BART). Her responsibilities include labor relations, personnel services (recruitment, compensation, benefits, etc.), organizational development, and federal-state compliance (drug testing, etc.). Settles has served as adjunct faculty at the University of San Francisco, San Francisco Community College, and Saint Mary's College. Prior to joining BART, she was deputy general manager at AC Transit and Manager of Training and Organizational Development for the San Francisco Public Utilities Commission. Dr. Settles has been a board member and officer for the San Francisco School Volunteers and ASTD. She has presented papers and presentations at such national conferences as International Personnel Management Association, Northern California Human Resources Council, American Public Transit Association, and ASTD. She was one of three Americans at the October 1990 Fifth Annual Training and Development Conference in Singapore. The year before, she was a member of a 16-member U.S. delegation to China. Her master's degree in education is from Howard University, Washington, DC, and her bachelor's degree in history and psychology is from Morehead State University in Kentucky. She completed her doctorate in organizational leadership from the University of San Francisco. Her consulting clients include the U.S. Navy, Bechtel, USDA, Pacific Bell, San Francisco General Hospital, San Francisco International Airport, and San Francisco Veterans Hospital.*

In preparation for this chapter, several academic institutions were consulted and interviewed. The results of those interviews will be interwoven through this chapter, along with some material from some of the published literature on this topic. A profile on each of those institutions and industries are listed in Table 46-1.

All segments of American business and industry can benefit from the services of higher education. The keys to such benefits are found in the location and development of effective partnerships. Successful partnerships contain four components: mutual benefits to all parties, share of control, credibility, and integrity. This chapter will examine these components along with the building blocks for successful partnerships.

In addition, this chapter will provide insight into the creation, management, and assessment of academic partnerships. It will provide success stories as well as cautionary measures, along with dos and don'ts, concerning the establishment of effective partnerships. The most significant message is to alert both industry and academia that joint ventures can assist them in the attainment of their established missions and goals.

What Is a Partnership?

A partnership is a collaborative coalition process which brings together the right stakeholders who represent various parties on a mutual issue. In the case of industry and the academic community, the stakeholders could include the academic dean, faculty members, researchers, line managers, and human resource professionals. The partnership's purpose is to create focused dialogue, wrestle with common concerns, and advance a mutually beneficial agenda. Examples of such partnerships date back to the 1930s and 1940s with the Sloan Fellowship Program at MIT and the Wharton School at the University of Pennsylvania.

A partnership is an excellent example of synergy. The whole is bigger than the sum of its parts; to put it numerically, $1 + 1 = 3$. Synergy allows two or more parties to achieve goals greater than they could achieve separately. An example of the synergy is illustrated by A. J. Clark.[1] Through joint ventures, industries have provided corporate funding for literacy programs and donated equipment along with a new source of educational clients. The educational community brings reasonably priced programs, targeted training, on-time or quick response time, a wide range of courses, instructor expertise, geographic proximity, and quality content to the partnership. Each partner brings skills, knowledge, and know-how to the table. The combination can bring about a transformation of the industry's mission, organizational goals, and strategic planning into effective initiatives that result in productivity outcomes that keep the organization healthy and competitive.

Partnerships will, one hopes, extend beyond training programs to include such areas as technical assistance; small-business support centers; the attracting of new industries; linkages with state, federal, and private funding agencies; and the bringing together of various communities and industries to further expand the partnership model on a local or regional basis. The partnership extends to all levels of higher education, from junior colleges to major research institutions.

Beasley and Lowery[2] described a joint partnership (from August 1985 to May 1988) between Delco Remy (a division of General Motors in Anderson, Indiana) and Purdue University for the purpose of establishing an associate-degree training program for 37 employees. Ten recommendations, and the accompanying 10 planning questions,[3] resulted from this three-year venture. The 10 suggestions

Table 46-1.

Name of institution	Description of the institution	Contact person/interviewee
	Institutions	
University of San Francisco (USF)	The University of San Francisco is located overlooking downtown San Francisco and the Pacific Ocean. USF is San Francisco's first institution of higher education, established October 1855. This independent co-ed institution has a student body of over 7500 students.	Ms. Jan Wilson, Assistant Dean
Thomas Edison State College	Thomas Edison State College is located in Trenton, New Jersey. The institution is charged with expanding the educational opportunities of adult learners. The student enrollment is 8750 currently. The average age of a student is 39 years of age. Since 1972, over 10,000 degrees have been awarded.	Dr. Natale Caliendo, Vice President for Public Affairs Dr. Sonja A. Eveslage, Associate VP for Public Service
University of California–Berkeley	UC–Berkeley's extension was established in 1891, to provide continuing-education opportunities to individuals, companies, organizations, and school districts. The extension currently offers over 2216 courses and has over 53,890 student participants. In addition to contract education (The Berkeley Partnership for Professional Development), the extension offers executive education, international programs, public lectures, and the Center for Learning in Retirement (CLIR).	Ms. Barbara Pearl, Manager, Corporate Program
City College of San Francisco	The City College of San Francisco is the largest single college in the United States. With 7 schools and 55 departments, the student population is 30,000, with an average age of 27. The composition of the college reflects the demographics of San Francisco.	Ms. Linda Squires-Grohe, Contract Education Coordinator
	Industry	
Bethlehem Steel	Bethlehem Steel dates back to 1857. The company is the nation's second-largest integrated steel producer. Company products and services include the production and sale of coal and other raw materials, ship repair, mobile and off-shore drilling platforms, railroad cars, track work, and other types of manufacturing.	Merlin Davidson

Table 46-2.

Recommendations*	Planning questions† (suggested questions that can attribute to a successful partnership)
1. Identify the need.	What challenges are you attempting to solve? (Should be related to your mission and goals to keep you focused.)
2. Do not reinvent the wheel—locate existing programs.	Is there a program already tested that will meet your needs, or will you need a custom design?
3. Identify cost and seek funding.	Are there monies appropriated for the venture? If not, what are potential resources?
4. Sell to higher management.	Is this partnership viewed by senior management as a good venture? If not, what issues remain, and what is your strategy to address each?
5. Develop measurement standards for selection.	What criteria will you use for selection and evaluation? What are the performance indicators?
6. Provide tutors.	Are additional resources available to support trainees?
7. Address employees' concerns.	How will employee issues be addressed, e.g., through focus groups?
8. Monitor the program; be flexible.	Have you established benchmarks in the partnership which tie to critical paths in reaching each performance indicator?
9. Communicate to the organization.	What is your organizational communication system (newsletters, payroll stuffers, computer, e-mail, etc.)? What system will work for the partnership?
10. Identify university liaison and problem solver.	Do you have a designated academic contact who is responsive, creative, and flexible and who gets things done?

*From Beasley, J., and R. Lowery, "Technical Education for First-Line Supervisors," *Technical and Skills Training*, vol. 2, no. 4, May–June 1991, pp. 17–21.
†From Settles, Michal, "Joint Venture Partnerships," presentation at Golden Gate Chapter, ASTD, 1990.

and questions, shown in Table 46-2, can serve as guidelines for any potential partnership.

Interviewees Merlin Davidson of Bethlehem Steel and Jan Wilson of the University of San Francisco agree that a successful partnership is a win-win situation if both parties achieve benefit and satisfaction from a well-designed joint venture.

Why Should Joint Ventures Be Considered?

American industries, both public and private, have continuing demands (e.g., legislated mandates, competitiveness, and a constantly changing skill-knowledge base for its workforce). These demands and others challenge companies in light of outsourcing, downsizing, reorganizing, and merging. This chapter will focus on one strategy to address these demands—the creation of business partnerships with institutions of higher education. With stiffer competition, both nationally and abroad, and a need for constant cost containments, joint ventures between industry and academia are a type of partnership that can no longer be ignored. A partnership is not for just *Fortune* 500 companies but also for the small-business community. Both large and small companies share in the need for educational services that colleges and universities are equipped to deliver, both economically and "just in time."

In 1992, Barnshaw[4] wrote about the need for industries to look closely at local educational resources. Sometimes the solutions to problems are closer than we imagine. Higher-educational institutions come in several forms such as community colleges, junior colleges, technical colleges, and four-year, degree-granting, public-private colleges and universities. The specialties of higher education range from biomedical research to mechanical engineering and from supervisory training to English as a second language. The resources from these institutions historically have not been tapped to their potential by industry.

Interviewee Barbara Pearl of the University of California–Berkeley stresses the responsiveness (just-in-time) of the university. In addition, the partnering organizations can use their academic partner to complement internal staff with university faculty on specific organizational issues.

Interviewee Merlin Davidson of Bethlehem Steel cites numerous examples of the benefits of having employees in an academic setting. To name a few, it stimulates creativity and a receptive learning environment; removes the student-employee from the interruptions of normal business life (telephones, meetings, drop-ins, crisis of the day, etc.); exposes the participants to different viewpoints; gives participants time to focus on the issue(s) at hand; and enables time to be spent with colleagues or on skill enhancement or team-building planning.

Partnerships should be considered because they are a wise use of resources for all parties. The wisdom of formulating partnerships lies in tapping the resources of the academic community that has specialized in a particular phase of your business; their expertise could be technical (e.g., laser technology) or related to human resources (e.g., labor management initiatives). The exposure to the cutting-edge research and development that impact business trends is a key factor in the formation of academic partnerships. A successful academic partnership allows the application of state-of-the-art training expertise, faster response time, and lower training costs. Joint ventures of industry and the academic community can be economically wise and can result in a workforce being motivated to see the value of becoming a continuous-learning organization.

When Is a Partnership Appropriate?

Higher education and industry are traditionally perceived as having very distinct characteristics and uncommon goals. Many joint ventures between industry and education have demonstrated that this perception is full of fallacies. From a traditional viewpoint, education's defined role is theory while industry's strength is application or practice. Successful alliances can be of mutual benefit to all parties. Milheim describes benefits of such linkages: general research support (e.g., gifts, equipment donations, endorsements), transfer of knowledge, formal technology transfer (at research institutes), faculty consulting, new funding for labs, sites for student internships and employment, advisory committees, etc.[5] Business organizations also have much to gain by forming alliances with the academic community. The three main advantages are access to human resources (faculty, graduates, etc.), training, and new knowledge.

Interviewees Natale Caliendo and Sonja Eveslage of Thomas Edison State College report that the creation of a partnership is appropriate when three conditions are present:

1. Anytime there is mutual interest
2. Both parties see the benefit of setting aside differences and focusing on common needs
3. The partnership will meet the organizational mission of public service

Interviewee Jan Wilson of the University of San Francisco indicates that all parties in the partnership should fully understand the needs of one another. Through communication of needs, clearly and openly, the appropriateness of the potential partnership will be easier to identify.

Role of Organizational Culture in a Partnership

Each partner in the joint venture should be aware of the organizational culture and needs of their organization along with the potential partner. Factors to consider in the organizational culture include, but are not limited to,

Mission-goals	Formal-informal reward systems
Strategic plan	Reporting requirements
Organizational levels	Plans
Staff-line functions	Rules
Performance criteria	Procedures
Formal decision-making authority	Communication systems
Budgets	Informal systems
Chain of command	HRD policies and procedures
Task teams	Union or nonunion environments

If the above factors are not considered, the potential for creating a dysfunctional arrangement is quite high. Other issues proposed by Milheim are establishing a division of labor (Who will do what?), setting priorities (What is the work plan and resulting timelines?), identifying commercial value (Who owns the products—will they be marketed?), determining the value of the alliance to each partner (Is this partnership working?), determining the length of the venture, sharing of resources, and determining rights and responsibilities (legal considerations, code of ethics).[5]

When potential partners are considering entering into a partnership arrangement, it would be a good idea to develop an appropriate checklist of all the factors mentioned above that are reflective of your culture. Such discussions early in the process will decrease the chances of miscommunication and incorrect perceptions.

Pros and Cons of Establishing a Partnership

While the benefits of forming a joint venture are numerous, there are some disadvantages. Milheim cautions that a clear understanding of the treatment of results, time scales (academia is usually long range, while industry is usually short range), organizational structure (flat vs. hierarchical), lifestyles-values, and ethical considerations (collegiate procedures vs. propriety rights) will assist both partners in avoiding negative joint ventures.[5] Those discussions should include each of the areas listed below:

- Respect for others' roles, goals, and operating practices
- Responsibilities of each partner (Who will do what, by when, using what approach?)
- Right to discoveries
- Agreement between institutions versus individuals
- Transferring results
- Role of peer review, endorsement by outsiders
- Confidentiality

Obstacles blocking the creation and continuation of industrial and academic partnership(s) can be summarized in four categories: control, power, trust, and privacy. A Boston University study of these issues revealed that industry was weary of the educational bureaucracy and concerned about the proprietary nature of the information used in the training program. The educational community was fearful of compromising the integrity of the academic curriculum and research.[6] How can potential partners overcome these perceptions or realities? Harkins and Giber suggest several actions:

1. Academic community to demonstrate flexibility and a willingness to understand the needs of industry
2. Academic partners to learn the language of industry (cost-effective solutions to problems)
3. An academic liaison to be identified to assist industry across obstacles involving administrative bureaucracies and academic departments

Interviewees for this chapter (Bethlehem Steel, City College of San Francisco, the University of San Francisco, the University of California–Berkeley, Thomas Edison State College) each offered additional suggestions in this area. Table 46-3 lists a few of the recurring responses.

Reasons for Not Using Outside Resources

Harkins and Giber report that American industries have six primary reasons for not using outside partnerships for management training. The survey results should be of particular interest to the higher-educational community. By developing strategies for each of the six reasons, higher-educational institutions will be prepared to address each one effectively. Below are the six reasons reported in the survey why companies keep management training programs in house:

Table 46-3.

Dos	Don'ts
Deliver on your promises and commitments to industry (remain truthful and straightforward).	Make promises you cannot keep.
Deliver a quality product to industry.	Violate the trust (cut on quality, etc.).
Designate a liaison (cultural translator) for each partner.	Stake your educational partnership strategy on one alliance (cultivate several partnerships).
Continue to assess the partnership (what is or is not working) and take corrective action.	Assume anything, follow up on issues raised by your partner.
Identify all stakeholders up front and get them involved from the beginning.	Lose focus on the outcomes (keep your eye on the ball).
Listen to your industry partners.	Miscalculate time needed for successful coordination.
Keep your goals in mind, and keep your eye on the ball.	Ignore even the smallest problem.
Confirm you have the right players.	Underestimate the role of organizational culture.
Be flexible.	Fear to ask the "dumb" questions.
Communicate, then communicate again.	Ignore necessary follow-up.

1. Training is more specific to needs
   - For academic institutions to be competitive, faculty and staff need to understand and have expertise in the industry in question.
2. Costs are lower
   - With the economic times being what they are, cost-effectiveness measures will be considered as a top priority by industry. Higher-educational institutions have an opportunity to be quite competitive in this area.
   - It would be a mistake for the academic community to view industry as a source of unlimited resources. Academic institutions' knowledge and execution of effective costing models will serve them well when they are considering partnership with industry.
3. Less time is spent
   - Time is money, so responsiveness is a key to partnerships.
4. Material is consistent and relevant
   - Quality of service and delivery is a factor high on the list for industry.
5. There is more control of content and faculty
   - By forming a true partnership, all parties will, it is hoped, collaborate on program content along with faculty selection and retention.
6. Organizational culture and teamwork are helped to develop
   - The reason for keeping programs in house is a very compelling viewpoint. Successful partnerships can be viewed as an extension of the internal team effort if they are designed properly and continuous interface and collaborative communication is established.[6]

Reasons for Using Outside Resources

The work of Harkins and Giber revealed five major reasons for companies using outside training partnerships:

1. An outside perspective allows the company to obtain different insights on internal issues.

2. A new point of view infuses new opinions on existing organizational issues.

3. The removal of executives from the work environment is viewed as a plus for outside training. Such removal allows company personnel to potentially see their internal issues differently, resulting in improved creativity and problem solving.

4. There is exposure to faculty experts and research. Educational partnerships can be a rich exchange in cutting-edge technology and valuable research.

5. The vision can be broadened. By exposing your company's ideas to a broader audience, the vision can be sharpened and reflect valuable aspects that would otherwise not be considered.[6]

These five reasons should be assessed as any potential partnership is considered. Other recommended factors that should be part of your decision-making deliberations are

1. Availability of cutting-edge expertise, without the permanent investment of in-house staff

2. Educational partnerships' ability to develop, deliver, and evaluate the scope of services (training program) on-line faster than in-house resources can deliver the same product

3. The use of a neutral third party (as in an educational partnership) to deliver training programs can be extremely credible to American industries if their credibility has been established

Each of these additional factors are particularly significant since American industries are facing rightsizing, downsizing, reorganizing, outsourcing, and other factors that immediately impact human resources development efforts. While the challenges to industry are numerous, solutions are available.

Successful Partnership Models

Two American institutions, industry and higher education, that have historically viewed their missions as distinctive, are now joining forces to the benefit of both. Numerous industries view education as a continuous-learning process. Such an approach lends itself to partnership potentials.

Some of these partnerships go back decades and others are yet to be explored. *Technical and Skills Training News*[7] described a partnership where the Rock Valley College (Rockford, Illinois) designed a lunch and learning program for working mothers unable to remain after designated work hours for training due to child-care demands. In the same article, a major U.S. manufacturer, Whirlpool, was described as maintaining a 20-year partnership with a local community college for the following three reasons:

1. Flexibility of the local community to the business's educational needs

2. Proximity to the work site

3. High quality of the facility used for training delivery

Each of the five interviewees provided excellent examples of partnerships. Interviewee Linda Squires-Grohe of the City College of San Francisco has clients ranging from public utilities, to federal agencies, to private firms. Services include on-site classroom management development, computer support services, and the corporate college (offering an on-site associate applied degree program to businesses).

The University of California–Berkeley's Contract Education Unit has had partnerships with the following industries: utilities, telecommunication, health-care, transportation, and governmental entities. A recent partnership with AC Transit, a Northern California bus company, resulted in over 25 major projects implemented to achieve the organization's stated vision of collaboration at all levels of the organization.

The University of San Francisco uses a cohort four-degree model. The model is based on 15 to 20 adults starting and ending the degree program together. This model serves as a support for the students both academically and individually. This model started in the mid-1970s. Business partnerships included the telecommunication industry.

One of Thomas Edison State College's partnerships is with New Jersey's Public Service Electric and Gas (PSE&G) Nuclear Training Center. The partnership is a cooperative degree program which awards academic credit to PSE&G's employees. As of August 1994, 28 individuals completed degree requirements, with 57 actively pursuing degrees. Variations of this partnership model have included Omaha Public Power District, Garden State American Institute in Banking, and the National Registry of Radiation Protection Technologist.

From an industry perspective, Bethlehem Steel worked through a partnership established with Duke University from 1985 to 1992 in an executive development program involving 300 senior managers. This arrangement assisted the organization in accomplishing stated goals and targets. Why did the Bethlehem Steel industry take this approach? According to Davidson, Duke was able to meet Bethlehem Steel's strategic needs—and with a tailored approach versus a generic program. This customized method helped Bethlehem Steel to become a world-class competitor.

When asked why all the models previously mentioned were successful, the interviewees recurringly commented that the partnership was

1. Strategically linked to the organization's mission and goals

2. Able to address global competitiveness

3. An academic support system for industry participants

4. Convenient to industry participants (classes occurring at the work sites)

5. Delivering a combination of theory and application

Examples of partnerships can be located throughout the academic community. Van Pelt[8] describes a five-year (1986–1991) partnership between Glacier Vandervell Inc., Atlantic Iowa Plant, and Iowa Western Community College. Features of the partnership included training for 300-plus employees, on-site delivery of training, and a continuing-education instructor working at the plant 20 hours per week. The organization's move from an autocratic to a participative management style along with just-in-time (JIT) training and total quality initiative resulted in the plant receiving the 1991 Shingo Prize, a coveted award of excellence in American manufacturing.

A second example is described by Forsberg.[9] Business Link, used by Coast Community College District in Costa Mesa, California, is designed to provide customized training to over 60 local businesses (ranging from bakeries to ambulance services and hotels). The benefits of the Business Link include on-site delivery of training, no loss of employee productivity (because the training uses real-life issues facing the company), economically feasible services, and a process for employees to continue their education after attending a partnership program. Business Link is an example of contract education in academic institutions throughout the United States. Below is an expanded prototype of a process discussed by Forsberg.

Step 1: Contact	The contact can be made by the local businesses or the academic community contacting the business.
Step 2: First meeting	Identify the issues, desired outcomes, possible site visit, etc. How does this possible partnership link with the company's mission and strategic plan?
Step 3: Needs assessment	Based on the first meeting, an assessment tool or process is executed (focus group, surveys, etc.) to crystallize the specific content of the program. For example, a question to be explored might be: If computer training is identified as a need, what level of training is needed?
Step 4: Proposal	The academic institution submits a proposal which is to be in compliance with the company's contracting procedures. The final phase of this step is an agreement or contract (always in writing).
Step 5: Program design	Customized content is designed by an academic team in conjunction with input from industry.
Step 6: Training	Execute the scope of work, e.g., team building, management development, mechanical training.
Step 7: Evaluation	Reassessment or evaluation. This step should have milestones throughout the project and not just be considered at the end.
Step 8: Follow-up	Three- to nine-month follow-up. The academic team's contract is to return to the industrial site three to nine months following the last intervention (last training event) to assess the impact of the training on productivity, originally stated outcomes (which should be linked to the organization's mission), and strategic plan.

Interviewee Merlin Davidson of Bethlehem Steel offers several suggestions on establishing a partnership that reinforce the work of Forsberg:

1. The partnership should reflect the corporate mission and strategic issues.

2. Corporate participants should leave the educational experience with an action plan.

3. The partnership should have a built-in follow-up component three to six months later.

All five interviewees for this chapter were asked to identify key steps in creating a successful partnership. Below are the nine common responses:

1. Meet with partners to determine needs, challenges, etc.

2. Partnership to link with industry's mission and goals and strategic plan.

3. Develop a planning team (managers, faculty, end-users, union leadership, etc.).

4. Develop a negotiated agreement, e.g., deliverables, costs, time lines, responsibilities and roles.

5. Establish a rapport for a win-win arrangement.

6. Maintain open communication (celebrate the successes and take corrective action on mistakes).

7. Be available and accessible.

8. Be flexible and adaptable.

9. Follow up and have fun.

Summary

A successful partnership has four components: (1) mutual benefits, (2) credibility, (3) sharing control, and (4) integrity (see Fig. 46-1). The steps in the partnership will be influenced by organizational culture, vision, mission, and strategic issues. Numerous questions should be answered prior to your entering into an agreement; samples have been provided. Partnership models have applications both externally and internally.

Steps in building a partnership include identification of a need, identification of coalition participants (stakeholders, cosponsors, etc.), execution of agreement, implementation of the plan, monitoring of progress, taking corrective action, and conducting a follow-up assessment. The identification and selection of partnership participants is a key component. Figure 46-2 details suggested questions to

Mutual benefits	= Incentive, common denominator
Credibility	= Greatest strength (selecting participants; driving force in designing consensus building)
Sharing of control	= Centerpiece of credibility
Integrity	= Maintained at all costs

Figure 46-1. Partnership ingredients.

Note: The first question to ask yourself is "Why?" (not "Who?"). Finding a compatible partner requires figuring out what you have to offer that somebody else might want.

Suggested Questions to Ask:

- Why is this a good partnership?
- Which groups and/or individuals are driving the issue?
- Who else might be affected?
- What are their known or likely positions?
- How polarized are the extreme positions?
- Which are likely to be receptive to "our" point of view?
- Who are their opinion leaders?
- Where do we agree?
- Where do we disagree?
- Where can we work together?

Figure 46-2. Partnership participants.

1. Purpose of a Partnership
   - What are we trying to achieve? (vision)
   - Why should it exist? (purpose)
   - How will I know when the task is completed? (goals, objectives)
   - Who are the right people to include? (membership)
2. Communication
   - Different points of view
   - Hostility
   - Inclusionary vs. exclusionary
   - Noncommitment
   - Solicit involvement, buy-in
3. Decision Making
   - Problem solving
   - Reaching consensus
   - Open to all options
   - Ground rules—How will the group function?
4. Group Dynamics
   - Verbal-nonverbal communication
   - Hot buttons
5. Negotiation Skills
   - Win-win
   - Persuasion
6. Facilitation Skills
   - Logistics (comfortable facility, room setup, equipment, etc.)
   - All participants to be heard
   - Organizing data
   - Monitoring and tracking commitments
   - Meeting design skills
7. Timing
   - Commitments met
   - Time viewed as valued resource (not to be wasted)

Figure 46-3. Knowledge and applications of partnership skills.

ask when selecting a potential partner. Skills are needed to execute an effective partnership arrangement. Figure 46-3 outlines key suggested applications. Partnership development is good business.

References

1. Clark, Amy J., "Education and Training," *Technical and Skills Training,* vol. 2, no. 6, August–September 1991, p. 34.
2. Beasley, J., and R. Lowery, "Technical Education for First-Line Supervisors," *Technical and Skills Training,* vol. 2, no. 4, May–June 1991, pp. 17–21.
3. Settles, Michal, "Joint Venture Partnerships," presentation at Golden Gate Chapter, ASTD, 1990.
4. Barnshaw, John III, "Educational Resources in Your Own Backyard," *Training and Development,* vol. 46, no. 6, May 1992, pp. 53–55.
5. Milheim, N. D., "Linking Education and Industry: Reasons for Mutual Cooperation," *Technical Trends,* vol. 36, no. 4, 1991, pp. 15–18.
6. Harkins, P., and D. Giber, "Linking Business and Education Through Training," *Training and Development Journal,* vol. 43, no. 10, October 1989, pp. 69–71.

7. Editorial, "Companies and Community/Junior Colleges Forge Training Partnerships," *Technical and Skills Training News,* Winter 1988, pp. 1–4.

8. Van Pelt, D., "Education Drives Continuous Improvement," *Technical and Skills Training,* vol. 3, no. 6, August–September 1992, pp. 9–11.

9. Forsberg, M., "Custom Training on a Budget," *Personnel Journal,* April 1992, pp. 112–119.

Bibliography

Barnshaw III, John, "Educational Resources in Your Own Backyard," *Training and Development,* vol. 46, no. 6, May 1992, pp. 53–55.

Beasley, J., and R. Lowery, "Technical Educator for First-Line Supervisors," *Technical and Skills Training,* vol. 2, no. 4, May–June 1991, pp. 17–21.

"Companies and Community/Junior Colleges Forge Training Partnerships," *Technical and Skills Training News,* Winter 1988, pp. 1–4.

Clark, A., "Education and Training," *Technical and Skills Training,* vol. 2, no. 6, August–September 1991, p. 34.

Dervarics, C., "On Target: Community Colleges Mean Business," *Technical and Skills Training,* vol. 3, no. 6, August–September 1992, pp. 13–16.

Forsberg, M., "Custom Training on a Budget," *Personnel Journal,* April 1992, pp. 112–119.

Harkins, P., and D. Giber, "Linking Business and Education Through Training," *Training and Development Journal,* vol. 43, no. 10, October 1989, pp. 69–71.

Milheim, N. D., "Linking Education and Industry: Reasons for Mutual Cooperation," *Tech Trends,* vol. 36, no. 4, 1991, pp. 15–18.

"Retooling American Workers," *Business Week,* September 27, 1993, pp. 9–11.

Van Pelt, D., "Education Drives Continuous Improvement," *Technical and Skills Training,* vol. 3, no. 6, August–September 1992, pp. 9–11.

47

Meeting Facilities

Coleman Lee Finkel

Coleman Lee Finkel *is president and an owner of The Coleman Center, a meeting facility for groups of 10 to 150 participants in New York City. He has also been president and an owner of a 38,000-square-foot conference center and 204-room hotel in New Jersey as well as a 52,000-square-foot conference center and 300-room hotel in Williamsburg, Virginia. Lodging magazine described Finkel as "the nation's number one spokesman and most sought-after speaker on conference centers." With the American Management Associations for 10 years, he was responsible for a range of educational programs and was a director of divisions. He has been president of the Conference Center Development Corporation. He was awarded the Buzz Bartow Award by Meeting Planners International and the Torch Award by ASTD, the only person to receive both awards. He received the Kilmer Oak Award of Rutgers University and a citation from The Professional Communications Society of the Institute of Electrical and Electronic Engineers. Books he has authored include* How to Plan Meetings Like a Professional, The Professional Guide to Successful Meetings, The Total Immersion Learning Environment: Its Critical Impact on Meeting Success, *and* Powerhouse Conferences: Eliminating Audience Boredom. *He has been president, Mid-New Jersey Chapter, ASTD; chair, Construction/Development Committee, American Hotel and Motel Association; chair, Industry Advisory Committee, Graduate School of Technical-Vocational Studies, Rutgers University; and chair, Meeting Planners International Seminar.*

A significant change is occurring in the attention and concentration being given by human resource development (HRD) professionals to the places in which their training programs are held. With increasing frequency, they are showing greater recognition of the critical influence of the properly planned environment to higher levels of participant learning. The body of literature dealing with the design of meeting facilities is growing. For example, ASTD's Info-Line issued a publication on this subject, "Succeed in Facilities Planning."

However, in too many cases, there is a lack of critical and insightful judgment exercised by HRD professionals in evaluating, with realistic and thoughtful standards, the quality of the place in which their meetings are held. The objective of all meeting facilities is simple: to contribute to an increase in program results and participant learning, represented by improved job performance. However, there is no correlation between sophistication in the management of the HRD function and the ability to plan an "engineered learning environment." There may be a presumption of knowledge of conference room design, but HRD professionals are, generally, without specialized experience in planning meeting rooms. It is a specific and complex area calling for expert knowledge that relates learning goals to supportive environmental spaces. Programs will never reach their maximum learning potential unless greater judgment is exercised in evaluating the special environment necessary to achieve maximum program effectiveness. What is needed today is a set of guidelines that will help those who plan, use, or select meeting facilities to evaluate, with realistic standards, the degree to which these places contribute, or conversely, hinder, learning. In doing so, such standards can provide HRD professionals with another perspective for evaluating a meeting facility, whether it is one's own meeting rooms or an outside facility.

To that end, three subjects will be treated in this chapter:

1. What is the fundamental purpose of a facility in which training programs are held?

2. What are the premises upon which the planning of a meeting area should be based?

3. What is an approach that can be used to relate the principal activities of a 9-to-5 meeting day to the special design considerations of the environments in which those activities occur? And how, by applying these criteria to environments, can this evaluation contribute to maximization of the success of a program?

The Fundamental Purpose or Strategy of a Meeting Area

To fully appreciate the contribution of the properly designed learning environment, everyone must agree on the fundamental purpose of a meeting area. In Ben Tregoe and John Zimmerman's book, *Top Management Strategy*,[1] they define one facet of a company's purpose-strategy as "knowing what it is you want to be." Relating that definition to a modern learning facility, I see its strategy as "to contribute to an increase in the learning level of every meeting participant so that all of the person's time can be spent most productively, and to support the work of the meeting leadership so that they can communicate and guide the program with optimal effectiveness." This strategy sounds simple! It is not, in execution. Implementation of the purpose of a meeting area is a complex process. The work requires new thinking, concepts, and approaches different than that applied to any other structure, be it an office building, hotel, plant, research lab, or residential home.

Premises for Planning a Meeting Area

A framework is needed within which the planning of meeting spaces should proceed; there are several premises to be established as guidelines. They are as follows:

1. A meeting should be looked at as a continuous opportunity to educate participants throughout the entire meeting day. Beyond the formalized parts of the program (e.g., presentations, skill development sessions, small-group projects, individual study), learning should go on during the informal parts of the meeting day (at breaks; at meals; before, between, and after sessions). It is important, therefore, to examine every activity that goes on during the hours spent in a facility. Determine how the total time can be used to maximize learning. The environment should be a prime factor in determining how to relate the time management of meetings to greater participant learning. To the degree that you can keep the participants together in one group (throughout the formalized and informal times of the meeting day), you will more likely increase their interaction and, subsequently, discussion of meeting-related topics. Learning will, accordingly, increase.

2. The learning environment is a new and major consideration in increasing levels of participant learning. There is not one, but several different environments within which the activities of a training program should take place. Each of these environments should be considered separately and designed differently. In this way, there is a greater likelihood that participants will take advantage of the learning opportunities throughout the hours of the meeting. Desirably, all of the time in the program should be spent in one facility. Once the psychological and mental transition has been made to a learning orientation, it is interruptive to this important adaptation if participants move from the meeting to another geographical location for other portions of the program activities.

3. Subtle and complex factors of a psychological and physical nature affect participant learning in a facility. These factors take effect from the moment attendees arrive and continue throughout their stay. Weigh the impact of the following kinds of factors:

   a. How can attendees be helped to make a transition to another attitude and mood from the moment they enter the meeting place? Psychologically, you want them to free themselves from the pressures, anxieties, and problems of the outside, competitive world. The properly designed environment can help your participants sense a change to a place of tranquillity, calm, and relaxation. We are now in a different world—a world of learning and personal growth. Another mindset is necessary—one in which individuals are encouraged, mentally, to change their roles, from being activists to becoming thinkers, probers, and learners. It is difficult, in an office setting, to give participants the feeling that they are away from the "noise" of their own workplace.

   b. How can the facility increase the concentration levels of meeting attendees? The environment, and the details within it, can help participants make an adjustment to the more "passive" role of sitting, listening, absorbing, and taking notes. It is a difficult change for the typical attendee whose job requires him or her to be the "doer" and activist. That person has been away from the disciplines necessary for maximum concentration in a classroom setting. Consideration and help, from a facility standpoint, must be given to eliminate distractive elements in the environment and provide a place where fatigue can be reduced and interactivity encouraged. Think of how to avoid such negative influences as noise, uncomfortable chairs, glare from reflective surfaces, poor lighting, sight obstructions, and inadequate air circulation.

4. The design of a learning environment is different in its requirements and objectives than that of any other structure. The work involved in planning a meeting area today has become a whole new specialty. The base begins with an understanding of the processes involved in adult learning. Within this framework, we need to analyze how learning is influenced by the way in which individuals listen, take notes, participate, interact, concentrate, study, eat, move, read, relax, and play. When these functions are identified and analyzed, and detailed specifications are written by the facility professional, then the architect, interior designer, and engineers can make their critical and essential contributions. It is paramount though, that the functions of the meeting spaces take precedence over architectural aesthetics and interior design considerations. With the uses of the environment spelled out in detail, the other professionals can creatively discharge their responsibilities with a common understanding of the learning goals to be achieved and with a uniform set of specifications to guide their important contributions.

The Principal Activities of a 9-to-5 Meeting Day

Over a period of six years, I conducted sessions in groups of 25 to 35 with over 600 individuals. They were people involved with human resources development. During the course of discussions, an exercise was held in which these participants were asked to indicate the number of hours allocated in their programs for the different activities in the hours of a typical meeting day. The type of training program they were asked to evaluate had these characteristics: held for one day or longer; group size of 15 to 30; the program scheduled for morning and afternoon sessions. Six activities were identified by these individuals. Obviously, the application of these broad guidelines will vary depending upon such factors as program objectives, learning design and schedule, and the level of the participant. However, these time allocations, within the meeting characteristics noted above, provide some numbers against which other programs can be compared.

There was a surprising consensus as to the range of hours individuals allocated to the six activities they identified. Though there were some variations from day to day, results for the average day were as follows:

Form 1

Various activities	Range of hours allocated to the six activities
1. Presentation and discussion in main meeting room	4–6
2. Work in small-group projects	1–2
3. Individual work related to the program	½–1
4. Meals	1–2
5. Two breaks	½–1
6. Informal socializing with other participants (before, after, between sessions)	½–1

Relationship of Six Activities to the Environments in Which Those Activities Occur

The six activities listed in form 1 are related to four environments in an optimum layout. Note that, within several of the four environments, more than one activity can take place, depending on the design of your program. Because of space constraints, all activities may have to occur in one, two, or three different areas rather than four. That need to adjust can certainly work. But, to the degree possible it is desirable to give meeting participants various sensory experiences by changing the environment for different activities.

Form 2

Meeting environments	Activities possible to place in various environments (see form 1 for numbered activities)
1. Environment of the principal meeting room where instruction, talks, and discussions take place	1, 2, 3, 4, 5
2. Environment of the break-out rooms where project work occurs in small, team groups	2, 3
3. Environment where participants relax, take breaks, attend cocktail receptions, and informally socialize with other members of the same training class	2, 3, 4, 5, 6
4. Environment in which the meals are eaten.	2, 3, 4, 5, 6

Four Elements Necessary for Program Success

There is another perspective that relates the contribution of environment to program success. This perspective relates environment as one factor, among four elements. In a subsequent part of this chapter, there are percentages which indicate the importance that each of these four elements contribute to an optimally productive meeting.

First, let me identify the nature of the four elements.

1. *The program.* This element involves the care with which the problems, interests, and needs of your audience are properly identified and, also, the creativeness of the meeting design which permits the participants to develop their skills in the application of the knowledge communicated.

2. *The meeting leadership.* This factor reflects the effectiveness of the individuals who will lead discussion and make presentations at the program.

3. *The administrative input.* This factor refers to the efficiency with which the details of the meeting, such as facility arrangements, transportation, registration, and workbooks, are executed.

4. *The meeting environment.* This element includes the quality of every detail in the environments within which the activities of your program are held and how they contribute to attendee learning.

Relative Importance of the Four Elements in the *Formalized* Parts of the Program

For the "formalized" activities, the structure for learning is imposed by the design of the program. HRD professionals have carefully selected the subjects and program design and they also control the time schedule. They know what they want to have happen in the main meeting room, the break-out rooms, and during the individual work and study assignments. The percentages that follow are based on my informal survey among HRD professionals. I asked a dozen of them to give me their best evaluation of the percentage importance of these four factors to program success. As shown below the consensus of their opinions was collated into the numbers suggested by these individuals. The percentage of importance of each of the four elements in the formalized part of your program is as follows:

Formalized parts of the program	Percentage importance of each element to maximize participant learning
1. The program	35
2. The meeting leadership	45
3. The administrative input	5
4. The meeting environment	15

Relative Importance of the Elements in the *Informal* Parts of the Program

As contrasted to the formalized parts of the program, the environments for the informal activities provide the key structures that will dictate whether additional learning will or will not take place in a meeting. It is here that so many programs fall down. They do not take advantage of the extra hours of learning that are potentially inherent during the informal hours of meetings (breaks, meals, before and after sessions). If you plan the right environments for the informal activities, the likelihood of fruitful interchange and cross-fertilization of ideas is immeasurably increased. Many HRD professionals have observed that the learning that goes on among participants during the informal times of a meeting can be as valuable as the information presented in the classes. Why shouldn't we, therefore, use every effort to make those informal times as productive as possible? Thus, the percentage of contribution of each of the four elements to greater learning, as shown below, stresses the critical nature of the environment to achieve learning results, during the informal hours of a program.

Elements of a meeting	Percentage importance of each element to maximize participant learning
1. The program	10
2. The meeting leadership	10
3. The administrative input	5
4. The meeting environment	75

Implications of Meeting Environment on Participant Learning

Programs are not helped by a space which has been simply provided. There is increased awareness of a body of knowledge about how advanced concepts in the field of an "engineered learning environment" can be applied to meetings so that they can be even more successful. By applying learning concepts to the selection of a meeting facility, organizations can attain a greater return on their enormous investment in participant time and out-of-pocket costs.

Small-group meetings, particularly in training, are applying greater and greater sophistication in presentation methods, participation projects, training techniques, and participant involvement. The environment is the last frontier that needs to be explored by meeting planners to make breakthroughs in terms of higher participant impact. We should not repeat the past approaches which follow traditional thinking to develop a facility layout and design using the model based on college classrooms or which concentrate on aesthetics. These approaches will inevitably result in meeting rooms that reduce program effectiveness.

Environmental Factors

Michelangelo wrote that "perfection is made of trifles." In a meeting facility, perfection is made of the meticulous attention to dozens of details. These details will influence the degree to which participants will be able to spend their time most valuably and meeting leadership can communicate and guide the program most productively.

As indicative of the details to be considered in an environment, I have selected the principal meeting room as an illustration. The listing of details that follows is not intended to be exhaustive. It is typical, though, of the kinds of considerations that should be thought through in *every* space of your meeting facility.

Principal Meeting Room: Detail Considerations

Noise.   Listen for either intermittent or continuous noise from these sources: heating, ventilating, and air-conditioning system; from adjacent rooms or corridors; from outside the building.

Colors.   Variations of white are cold and sterile. Blacks and brown shades will close in psychologically after prolonged viewing and become fatiguing. Select such pastel hues as oranges, greens, blues, or yellows—happy, warm, pleasant colors to view.

Room structure.   Look out for long, narrow rooms that stretch participants apart. It is harder for individuals in the back to see, hear, and feel a sense of identification with the discussion. Try to use rooms that are squarer in shape.

Lighting.   The main source of lighting should be fluorescent lights. Incandescent lighting should be spread throughout the room and used with dimmers, when projection is required. Sconces on the walls or chandeliers in the ceiling are poor sources of light and are distracting.

Wall and floor covering.   Carpeting should be placed throughout the meeting area. Do not use floral, striped, or vivid colors on the wallpaper or carpets. They will be distractive. Solids shades are preferable—neither too light nor too dark.

Meeting-room chair.   Do not utilize stack chairs or chairs with a rigid back. Chairs should have wheels, swivels, and backs that provide support in the lower lumbar region of the participant. There should also be a reclining back that permits only the chair's back to move when the person leans on it. The seat should not move, however.

Pictures, clocks, sculpture.   There should be no objects on the walls that will attract the eye of the participants, taking the mind off the program. Only meeting-related material should be on the walls of the meeting room.

Glare.   Glare will be produced from such sources as metal surfaces, television monitors, and mirrors. As they reflect light, the glare will induce eye fatigue. Check and eliminate glare sources.

Ceiling.   Try to get at least 9 feet, preferably 10, in ceiling height.

Windows.   Some individuals find that windows are desirable in a meeting room. Others feel that windows should not be in the principal meeting room. Among the negative influences, the latter group lists the following factors:

- Participants will stare out of them, offering an undesirable distractive feature.
- They take up space that can be better used for hanging meeting-related materials.
- The light from the outside changes throughout the day. It affects the shadowing in the room and alters light levels. If the day is a rainy one or overcast, it is a depressant to view the weather. On a sunny day, the strong light will be annoying and tiring to participants who are facing the windows.
- Noise penetrates from the outside.

However, I have seen both schools of thought applied effectively.

Electrical outlets.   Outlets should be spread around the walls every 6 feet. Desirably, a telephone jack should be placed next to the outlets. With this arrangement, you have available the electrical connections needed for computer hookups. Also, place one outlet in the floor 8 feet from the instructional wall. The overhead projector can be plugged in there without its trailing wires.

Acoustics.   Check on the bounce or absorption of sound from the walls, ceiling, floors, and furniture. Try voice checks with three or four people, monitoring voice clarity and level.

A Numerical Evaluation of Three Environments in a Meeting Facility

The meeting facility you use may only have one or two areas available for your program, although there are three separate environments noted below. Yet, the evaluative scales shown can still be related to and are valid for the fewer areas in which your meeting is held.

As you study each item in the three environments, rate it by encircling a number, including 0, from the range shown. A 0 is the lowest rating, and the highest number for each item is the best. The number you circle should represent the degree to which you feel the facility rates on that item. The different gradations of numbers on items are a factor of the importance of that item in the total environmental setting. Add your total for each environmental area. At the end, there is a category of quality-level categories. Check to see how your evaluation measures.

1. Main Meeting Room Environment

A. Square or slightly rectangle. Not long and narrow so that
participants in rear are removed from the trainer.   0-1-2

B. Lighting is bright and evenly spread throughout the room.
No spots of light. No high and low shadows on walls or
ceiling. No sconces or chandeliers.   0-1-2-3-4-5

C. No reflections from mirrors, glass, TV monitors, crystal,
chrome. Will cause eye fatigue and reduce perceptual levels.   0-1-2-3

D. Wall colors of bright, solid shades of blue, orange, yellow,
green. Not whites, browns, blacks which are depressing after
long exposure or bright reds or similar loud colors, plaids,
or stripes which are distracting.   0-1-2-3

E. Solid colors on floor covering. No plaids or stripes which
are fatiguing to the eye.   0-1-2

F. Ceiling at least 9 feet, preferably close to 10 feet. Avoid feeling
of compression. Difficult also for projection.   0-1-2-3

G. Comfortable chairs with arms, swivel, wheels, and recliner.   0-1-2-3

H. Tables that provide 2½ feet between participants, with
modesty panel at front. Rich-looking top requiring no covering
and hard enough to write on.   0-1-2

I. No pictures or clocks on walls.   0-1-2

J. Light controls on front wall operated by communicator.
Dimmers in room.   0-1-2-3-4-5

K. Audiovisual controls at front which communicator can
operate easily.   0-1-2-3

L. Air-conditioning controls in each room. Quiet system with good
ventilation capabilities.   0-1-2-3

M. Comfortably sized room for number of people in group.   0-1-2-3

Maximum total: 39

Your total: ———

2. Break-Out Room Environment

A. Room appropriately sized for number in your group.
Not too large or small.   0-1-2-3

B. Room specially designed for small meetings. Not a "make-do" room.   0-1-2-3

C. Comfortable seating.   0-1-2-3

D. Subdued lighting. Need not be too bright.   0-1

E. Quiet area.   0-1

Maximum total: 11

Your total: ———

3. Environment for Breaks and Informal Socializing

A. Separate area.   0-1-2-3-4

B. Comfortable lounge seating in groupings of two, three, or four
people. Chairs easy to move. No immovable seating arrangements.   0-1-2-3

C. Refreshments self-service and easy to obtain.　　　　　0-1-2-3

D. Cheerful decor.　　　　　0-1

E. Quiet area.　　　　　0-1

Maximum total:　12

Your total:　　　———

Rating Scales for Three Areas

1. Main meeting room:

Quality	Rating
a. Superior	36–39
b. Very good	32–35
c. Good	28–31
d. Fair	24–30
e. Poor	Below 23

2. Break-out room:

Quality	Rating
a. Superior	10–11
b. Very good	8–9
c. Good	6–7
d. Fair	4–5
e. Poor	Below 3

3. Breaks and informal socializing:

Quality	Rating
a. Superior	11–12
b. Very good	9–10
c. Good	7–8
d. Fair	5–6
e. Poor	Below 4

Conforming with the Americans with Disabilities Act (ADA)

Bathrooms must have an appropriate number of stalls with doors wide enough for wheelchairs. There should be supports for standing.

Doors to meeting rooms should be wide enough to permit wheelchair entry.

If there are steps to reach a floor or a meeting room, a ramp is needed to allow wheelchair access.

Carpeting should not have high piles that make it harder for wheelchairs to maneuver.

Meeting Facilities of the Future

The changes being introduced into business today through technological advances are staggering. Human resources development is being affected by this progress. Interactive computer instruction, video conferencing, multimedia systems, distance learning, network software and equipment, and videodisks are tools that have become a part of our learning resources. In our desire to ensure that development programs are keeping up to date with the improvements in technology, we must not overlook the caution that John Naisbitt pointed out in *Megatrends 2000*.[2] He referred to "high-tech, high-touch." No matter how sophisticated we become in using electronic and audiovisual systems, we cannot forget that we are dealing with people. These devices are tools. Nothing will replace the exchanges, the understanding, the support, the attitude that can be positively transferred when individuals are able to get together and to touch and sense one another face to face in relaxed circumstances. Televised pictures, computer screens, and amplified long-distance voices have a place among our arsenal of training designs and techniques. However, the training program that involves a meeting of a group of people is an irreplaceable and powerful force for many subject areas and meeting types. The skills, knowledge, and attitude of people that can be enhanced in a meeting, through its unique intimate dimension and through personalized "touches," reaching all of our senses, cannot be duplicated in any other way. You cannot send a handshake by fax.

Our need is not to replace meetings as a learning medium, but to make them more effective in conjunction with other, newer training techniques.

Summary

In this chapter, I have set forth the importance of the properly designed environment as one critical factor that can significantly improve the amount of learning that it is possible for participants to achieve in a meeting. I have seen differences that happen when programs are held in environments specially designed for knowledge and skill enhancement.

It is encouraging to see an emerging appreciation that recognizes the nuances, complexities, and major differences resulting from applying the fundamentals, concepts, and approaches related to the planning of meeting areas such as the following:

1. The purpose of a meeting facility is to add greater levels of learning for every program participant.

2. Learning should go on continuously throughout all the hours of a meeting—not just in the formalized parts of the program, but during the informal times as well.

3. The properly designed meeting facility is based on an understanding of the processes of learning. This knowledge is related to the ways in which learning can be affected by every detail in meeting spaces—colors, ceiling height, room structure, lighting, air-conditioning, noise, type of meeting room furniture, and the variety of spaces.

4. The different activities of the meeting day should desirably *not* be held in one unvarying environment. They should be planned for multienvironmental spaces, specifically analyzed and planned to provide participants with a vari-

ety of sensual experiences. They should permit the opportunity to take advantage of the learning inherent in all the activities within those environments.

5. Maximum learning for any one group will occur when the participants in the meeting are able to be together as much as possible. The sharing of ideas, the exchange of information, the clarification of questions, and the testing of application are much more likely to occur when people, going through the same learning experiences, are readily able to meet and interact with familiar faces.

6. If organizations hold many meetings scheduled for more than two hours, consideration should be given to isolating the meeting rooms and their related areas from the environment of the typically busy, crowded, noisy office or plant. If the meeting facility is an integral part of the business activity, it is too easy for participants to go back to their offices to continue work at breaks, reducing the effectiveness of the meeting. Once attendees have made the mental and psychological adjustment to a learning mode, that total concentration should be maintained for maximum productivity.

In B. F. Skinner's book, *Beyond Freedom and Dignity*,[3] he says, "We are all simply a product of the stimuli we get from the outside world. Specify the environment completely enough and you can exactly predict individual actions." We may not be able to predict the *exact* reactions we will get from meeting participants through the careful planning of the meeting environment. However, I am firmly convinced from the successful results I've seen in programs that the thoughtful consideration of what should be included into a learning-effective meeting environment will have predictable increases in participant and leadership satisfaction. And, in the final analysis, there will be a greater feeling by attendees that their time has been well spent learning information that will help in making better decisions and acquiring knowledge that will improve their performance back on the job—most desirable objectives for any meeting.

References

1. Tregoe, Benjamin B., and John W. Zimmerman, *Top Management Strategy*, Knopf, New York, 1980.
2. Naisbitt, John, and Patricia Auberdene, *Megatrends 2000*, Morrow, New York, 1990.
3. Skinner, B. F., *Beyond Freedom and Dignity*, Bantam/Vintage, New York, 1972.

48

Academic Programs for HRD Professionals

Neal Chalofsky

Cynthia A. Larson-Daugherty

Neal Chalofsky *is the director (and a professor) of the Human Resource Development Graduate Program at The George Washington University and president of Chalofsky Associates, an HRD consulting firm. Previously, he was a professor and director of HRD graduate studies at Virginia Polytechnic Institute State University. He has been an internal HRD practitioner, manager, and researcher for several federal and corporate organizations. Chalofsky has consulted with such organizations as Mobil Research and Development Corporation, the U.S. Department of Education, Computer Sciences Corporation, the U.S. Chamber of Commerce, The Smithsonian Institution, Ernst and Young, Inc., World Bank, the National Alliance of Business, and Bell Atlantic. He has been on the national board of directors and chaired several national committees for ASTD as well as been past president of the Washington, DC, chapter. He organized the first meeting of academics for ASTD and was a founding member and past director of the HRD Professors' Network in ASTD. Chalofsky currently chairs the Select Committee on the Status of HRD Academic Programs for the Academy for Human Resource Development. He is on the Review Panel of the* Human Resource Development Quarterly *and has been a speaker at numerous national and international conferences. Chalofsky is coauthor of* Effective Human Resource Development *and* Up the HRD Ladder *as well as numerous chapters of edited works and journal articles.*

Cynthia A. Larson-Daugherty is in charge of corporate commu- nications, Human Resource Division, Chevy Chase (MD) Bank. She is an adjunct faculty member of the Psychology Department at Towson (Maryland) State University and a graduate teaching assistant in the Human Resource Development Program, The George Washington University. Her work history includes Human Resources Associate/Administrative Assistant in Execu- tive Administration, Chevy Chase Bank's Human Resource Divi- sion; marketing and communications manager for an accounting and finance interim staffing organization; and varied positions with Giant Food, Inc., Landover, MD. Larson-Daugherty has a consulting firm, the Center for Career Management, specializing in individual and organizational career development, planning, and management services. She is completing research for The George Washington University HRD Program on Career Develop- ment/Career Management Practices, including surveying aca- demic institutions and practitioners on the delivery of career development core competencies. She received her bachelor's degree, with a mass communications major, and a master of arts–liberal studies, with a focus in mass communications, human resource development, and human resource manage- ment, from Towson State University. She is completing her doctoral work in human resource development with an emphasis in career development at The George Washington University. She received the ASTD Washington Chapter "Ben Bostic/Human Resource Development Professional" Award in 1993.

There used to be only one way to learn to be a trainer—"by the seat of your pants." There was no theory, no process, no exercises. You learned by one of two ways: you were either handed a lesson plan and went into the classroom "cold turkey" or you apprenticed yourself to an experienced instructor and watched his or her approach. Your choice of instructional technique consisted of lecture, demonstration, or discussion.

In the 1950s, three streams of theory and practice began to emerge that would provide the foundation for a body of knowledge for this new field of practice: adult learning theory, behavioral science, and programmed learning. Initially, these three areas were primarily the province of academics and consultants (who were often one and the same). As the research and theory was translated into practice, alternative instructional processes, approaches, and techniques were designed and developed. This process began to provide a structure for this field that, up to this point, operated primarily by trial and error.

In 1958, The George Washington University in Washington, DC, developed the first master's degree program, which was called "employee development." It was designed primarily for federal government training officers and essentially was based almost entirely on practical knowledge.

In 1967, Leonard Nadler and Gordon Lippitt coauthored what is now consid- ered a seminal article in the field, "The Emerging Roles of the Training Director."[1] This article, which identified the roles and subroles being performed in the field, represented the first attempt to provide a framework for the field to begin to develop from an occupation into a profession. In 1970 Nadler, who at the time had been the director of the Employee Development Graduate Program at The George Washington University for five years, published his first book, *Developing Human Resources*.[2] This book popularized the term "human resource development" (which also became the new name for The George Washington program).

In 1975, ASTD formed a national committee on professional development to nurture and guide the evolution of the profession. By 1979 there were enough academic programs to warrant this committee organizing a conference to bring professionals together to discuss issues of mutual interest. In 1981, at the second annual conference of HRD academic programs, the professional development committee spun off a separate committee to organize the professors of these programs and the HRD Professors Network of ASTD was established. In 1993, the professors formed a new independent group called the Academy for Human Resource Development.

Much of the body of knowledge and practice in these programs was (and still is) borrowed from other disciplines: organization and management theory, organization behavior and group dynamics theory, adult-learning theory, instructional technology, and industrial and organizational psychology. And most of the students enrolling in these programs through the 1970s and into the 1980s were men who were already in the field and were interested in advancing in this emerging profession by learning the theories, concepts, and processes underlying the practice of the profession.

During the 1980s, people in other professions who wanted to change careers started to enroll in HRD graduate programs. In addition, people who were staying in their primary professions (e.g., nurses and engineers), but who had responsibility for professional education and staff development enrolled in master's programs. Some of these same people subsequently became attracted to the HRD field and eventually changed professions.

The 1980s was an era in which the discipline matured and solidified its knowledge base around the areas of adult learning and instructional design, consulting and organizational development, and (to a lesser extent) career development. Numerous doctoral programs were established and the dissertation process began to produce scholarly HRD research by students as well as faculty. There was also a tremendous increase in female enrollment, and to this day approximately 80 percent of the students in master's programs are women. The end of the 1980s and the beginning of the 1990s also saw an increasing number of young people enrolling in master's programs in order to begin a career in human resource development.

The practitioners and leaders that graduate from these programs and the research that is produced by them continue to be the catalysts which further professionalize the HRD field. Faculty have been engaged in developing new theory, and doctoral dissertations have been testing that theory. For the first time, new knowledge is being produced within the field rather than borrowed or adapted from other disciplines. And graduates from HRD academic programs are translating this new knowledge into practice.

The Scope of Academic Programs in HRD

"HRD degree programs are offshoots of various university departments and tend to be shaped by the preferences of the professors who founded them."[3] Since there has been no generally accepted body of knowledge or set of accreditation criteria, academic programs have usually been started by an entrepreneurial faculty member who had some expertise in adult learning and/or experience doing training and recognized the market value of an HRD-related program to the university. So, in a sense, academic programs developed much the same way HRD practitioners developed—more by happenstance than by planning.

A reflection of the growth in the field is the tremendous increase in higher-education programs in HRD.[4] In particular, there has been a rise in professional certificate programs and master's degree programs. Business and industry are now demanding the educational expertise to support the professional practice of the field.

ASTD maintains an *Academic Directory of Programs in HRD* database which lists undergraduate, graduate, continuing-education, certificate, and specialist programs. The information below has been synthesized from the various programs listed in this database.

HRD academic programs are most often found in one of three schools of study: business and management, psychology, and education. Certificate and specialist programs can be found in both academic settings and professional associations. Although all schools of study offer some foundational coursework in human resources development, the focus of the program is often dependent upon which school of study an HRD program is housed in. For example, in schools of business the coursework is often centered around organization development, training and development, career development, human resource management, and industrial and labor relations. Within schools of psychology, coursework focuses on organizational and industrial psychology, organizational behavior, and personnel development. Schools of education offer coursework in adult learning, leadership, distance learning, and instructional technology.

Certificate Programs

HRD certificate and professional designation programs are offered by both academic institutions and professional associations. Some professional associations offer both precertification and continuing-education programs. Colleges and universities offer an array of select core competency certificates and specialist certificates. The *Academic Directory* currently lists approximately 30 academic certificate programs.

Certificates can be found in such categories as labor-management, technical writing, training and development, human resource management, professional trainer series, training, training design and development, organizational quality transformation, industrial training, train-the-trainer, and psychology. These programs range in credit hours from as few as 9 to as many as 84. The format for delivery also ranges from a traditional classroom setting to a workshop design. To accommodate the vast majority of students who work full-time, a majority of these programs are offered weekday evenings, on weekends, or in week-long formats.

Certificates serve a variety of purposes, providing opportunity for both personal development and professional growth. Practitioners in the field use them to add to their existing knowledge, as well as to educate themselves in areas outside of their given expertise. A certificate program can also be a preliminary step to pursuing an advanced degree in the field.

Undergraduate Programs

A bachelor's degree in human resource development provides students with an interdisciplinary amalgam of coursework in the behavioral and organizational sciences. This foundational education prepares students for careers in human resource development, employee development, management and supervision, technological instruction and training, employee relations, and general human resource management. An HRD undergraduate major is also excellent preparation for graduate work in the applied behavioral sciences. Because of the applied nature of the field, it is necessary to gain and apply practical knowledge in order for the learning experience to have significance. Often HRD undergraduate programs will have cooperative educational-workplace experiences and internship tied into their credit hours in order for students to gain relevant experience.

An undergraduate major in human resource development offers broad-based learning in the liberal arts and depth in the applied behavioral sciences. These programs can be found across the United States and in Malaysia, Spain, and Canada. Most often undergraduate HRD programs are found in the following classifications: human resource development, human resource management, industrial psychology, instructional technology, organizational communication, organizational development, and vocational-technical education.

The *Academic Directory* currently lists approximately 60 undergraduate programs in HRD or HRD-related academic programs. Most schools offering undergraduate programs in HRD offer three options for a course of study: daytime, evening, and weekend coursework options. However, there are some schools that offer only daytime study options.

Graduate Programs

Masters.   A master's degree in HRD both provides a broadening of theoretical knowledge and prepares participants to improve their performance in organizations.[4]

A graduate degree in HRD serves a variety of purposes. For practitioners in the field it provides an opportunity to augment their experience with theoretical knowledge. For new workers, or professionals with a background in another field, graduate study in HRD provides professional entry.

Master's programs can be found in the following categories: administrative-educational leadership, adult education, career development, human resource development, human resource management, industrial psychology, instructional design and development, instructional technology, evaluation and program management, organization communications, organization development, and vocational-technical education. The programs tend to be interdisciplinary in nature, providing students with a set of core HRD competencies. These programs typically integrate classroom experience with internship and independent studies. This comprehensive learning is designed to prepare graduates for the rapidly changing workplace.

The *Academic Directory* currently lists over 150 graduate programs in HRD or HRD-related academic programs. These programs can be found across the United States, and also in Canada, Singapore, and Spain.

Most schools offering undergraduate programs in HRD offer three options for a course of study: daytime, evening, and weekend. However, there are some schools that offer only daytime study options.

Doctorate.   A doctorate degree in HRD focuses in depth on the theoretical and philosophical foundations and contemporary concepts and issues. Although interdisciplinary in nature, the linkages between the different disciplines are brought together to form a tightly knit web of theory, understanding, and knowledge for both practical application and new theory building.

Doctorate programs can be found in the same categories as master's programs. The *Academic Directory* currently lists approximately 85 doctoral programs in HRD or HRD-related academic programs. These programs can be found across the United States and also in Singapore and Spain.

Schools offering doctoral programs in HRD offer three options for a course of study: daytime, evening, and weekend in both full-time and part-time study options. However, there are some schools that offer only daytime study options and have full-time study requirements.

Issues Concerning Academic Programs in HRD

Curriculum (Program Design)

While the school or department that houses the HRD program certainly has an influence on the curriculum, there are other factors that tend to differentiate the design and delivery of academic programs. The following are four significant considerations that you should take into account in choosing a program:

Focus. What is the purpose, vision, mission, and/or outcome of the program? Is it to develop generalists or specialists; technical experts or managers; organization development consultants or performance engineers? Like any other program in our field, academic programs should (and most do) have specific goals and objectives.

Competency versus Subject. When ASTD's *Models for Excellence* competency study[5] was issued, many programs used the roles and competencies to redesign their existing curriculum. Others have a subject-centered list of courses based on the focus of the program. Still others have a hybrid of the two. No matter what framework is used, a prospective student needs to ask two questions concerning this issue: "How current and future-oriented is the course content?" and "What skills, knowledges, understandings, values, and beliefs will I be equipped with when I finish?"

Theory versus Practice. Although all programs would probably consider themselves to have a mixture of theory and practice, programs tend to fit into numerous points along this continuum. A program with more practical information will give you skills and techniques that can be used immediately but less understanding of the "why's" behind the techniques and less of a foundation for building competence in the future; and vice versa. Usually, the higher the degree, the more theoretical and less practical the learning.

Structure and Format. This issue relates to whether a program is offered in a traditional open enrollment, a format of one class a week for a semester (or quarter); or a number of other options. Open enrollment means that a student can enter the program at the start of any semester; closed enrollment refers to programs that only admit students once (or twice) a year. A program may have closed enrollment because they use a cohort (learning group) format and everyone starts together. Or it may only offer its introductory courses once a year and wants everyone to start the program during that semester. Another aspect of structure and format is whether classes are offered on weekday evenings, weekends, intensive week-long sessions, or other variations. There are also several "programs without walls" that do not require formal coursework. They may offer several seminars but the primary learning is accomplished by working on a major project with the support of a committee of experts. Structure and format are areas in which academic institutions have been experimenting lately. Because of the advances in video and telecommunications technology, the next "wave" of new formats will be different versions of distance learning via interactive television combined with communications through the Internet.

Part-Time versus Full-Time Study

In terms of defining the "right" option from a career development perspective, selecting between part-time and full-time study is situational. There are numerous issues, both personal and professional, that impact this decision.

Part-Time Study.   For all practical purposes, part-time study is an excellent option. Part-time study allows students-professionals to continue to work in the field while entering into a structured learning environment. This situation enables the academic experience and the workplace experience to complement each other because they are taking place simultaneously. As the student gains more theoretical knowledge, he or she can pull from relevant workplace experiences to interpret theory and assign meanings to practical experience.

Part-time study is becoming more readily available as an option as academic institutions cater to the changing workplace and diverse circumstances of working professionals. Going to school full-time has become less of an option and more of a luxury. The expense of leaving the workforce for two or more years to acquire a degree can be costly, both personally and professionally. Even if financial implications were not a factor, the workplace keeps changing so rapidly that leaving the workforce for any extended amount of time could be detrimental to career growth. In addition, the labor pool of skilled professionals is relatively high as organizations and industries continue to downsize.

From a career development perspective, cooperative study arrangements and part-time study with internships are highly recommended for people interested in changing fields. Upon completion of study, they will have both new knowledge and new experience in the field and will have an easier time finding a job than someone who went to school full-time but has no HRD work experience.

Full-Time Study.   The essence of full-time study most often comes into play at the doctoral level. The learning experience at this level is much more theory-based, which requires a great deal of intensive field research in a variety of settings: academic, laboratory, and organizational. In the past, a professional with a full-time position had difficulty meeting the requirements of academic institutions' residency requirements for doctoral study. But the trend has been to adjust doctoral study requirements for the working professional who seeks a scholarly education beyond the master's level. At the same time, there are professionals who are leaving work to pursue full-time study because the intensity of these programs has not changed, even if the residency requirements have. Often working professionals can only take one or two courses a semester because the demand of doctoral work is much greater than master's or undergraduate work. If you want the full measure of learning at the doctoral level, you need to go full-time. Full-time study allows you time not only to take more courses and complete your degree faster but also to interact with faculty, do research, and experience the academic lifestyle that is so intellectually stimulating and rewarding.

Therefore, selecting part-time or full-time study really depends on the student and his or her experience, professional and career goals, the academic program options, changing dynamics of the workplace, and financial constraints.

The Value of a Doctorate in HRD

There are three reasons to get a doctorate: professional growth, the career opportunities, and the credential. The first two reasons are legitimate the third is justifiable only if one accepts the enormous amount of work that is required to get those three letters after one's name—and that only 30 to 50 percent of those who start a doctoral program get beyond the ABD stage. (ABD means "all but degree" and refers to people who finish their coursework but never complete the dissertation.)

The value of the doctoral program for people who want to be academics or researchers is obvious. Less obvious but equally important is that the HRD doctoral program, especially as part of the offerings of a professional school (such as business or education), is designed to develop leaders in the field.

Many people enter a doctoral program because they recently switched to an HRD position from another profession, they have a master's degree in this other discipline, and they are at a high enough organizational position to warrant an in-depth and sophisticated level of learning. Others who are in "line" management or consulting are looking for this same level of learning in order to understand how to help organizations be more effective (from a people and learning perspective). For some, it is a matter of continuing professional and career advancement in the HRD field.

At this time it is probably safe to say that it may be a while, if ever, before employers require a doctorate for HRD positions. Yet doctoral program enrollments are increasing because of the desire for increased professional competence, deeper understanding of the theories underlying the field, and an interest in research. And for some it is simply the enjoyment and challenge of continual life-long learning.

Choosing the Best Program for You

There are no standard guidelines for evaluating the quality of HRD academic programs, although as of this writing a committee of the Academy of Human Resource Development is starting to develop such a list. The following are suggested factors that you may want to keep in mind as you investigate programs:

- Ratio of full-time faculty to students (lowest is best)
- Number of full-time faculty to part-time and adjunct faculty
- Percentage of time faculty are expected to teach and advise versus percentage of time they are expected to do research
- Number of full-time faculty devoted directly to the HRD program (teaching 100 percent in the program)
- Number of full-time faculty with relevant degrees and HRD experience
- Quality of support for program from the dean, vice president–provost, and president
- Quality of support and/or involvement from alumni
- Quality of support and/or involvement from employers
- Reputation of program in the HRD community
- Reputation of program among other HRD academic programs

- Quality of financial support for faculty professional development
- Quantity and quality of financial aid for students (especially at the doctoral level)
- Research (and development) efforts that bring in funds for graduate assistant-ships and professional development
- Scholarly contribution of faculty
- Service contributions of faculty

We need to constantly remind ourselves of the parable of the shoemaker's children who had no shoes; continuous professional development is not just for everybody else. We need to stay ahead in order to provide the learning interventions which organizations need to maintain effectiveness.

References

1. Nadler, L., and G. Lippitt, "The Emerging Roles of the Training Director," *Training and Development Journal, 21*(8), August 1967, pp. 2–10.
2. Nadler, L., *Developing Human Resources,* Gulf Publishing, Houston, 1970.
3. Geber. B., "HRD Degrees," *Training, 24*(7), July 1987, pp. 48–55.
4. Harris, D., and R. DeSimone, *Human Resource Development,* Harcourt Brace College Publishers, Chicago, 1994.
5. McLagan, P., *Models for Excellence: The Conclusions and Recommendations of the ASTD Training and Development Competency Study,* ASTD Press, Alexandria, VA, 1983.

49

Business-Education Partnerships

Edward W. Bales

Edward W. Bales *is Director of Education, External Systems, Motorola University, Motorola Corporation, Schaumburg, Illinois. Bales is a leader, nationally and internationally, in developing education-business partnerships focused on the systemic transformations of learning and teaching. Beginning in 1990, Bales has continuously expanded the role of his corporation in the application of principles which have made Motorola a leader in world-class education. He is the U.S. representative to and vice chairman of the Education Committee of the Business Industry Advisory Committee (BIAC) of the Paris-based Organization for Economic Cooperation and Development (OECD). In this capacity, Bales has been involved in developing several publications on global educational change. He is a member of the National Science Foundation Education Advisory Council, the National Conference Board Education Committee, the National Alliance of Business Education Committee, the Research and Education Advisory Panel of the U.S. General Accounting Office, and past member of the National Academy of Sciences Corporate Council on Math and Science Education. Prior to 1990, Bales was director of operations for Motorola University, managing the design, development, and delivery of Motorola University programs and was responsible for North American operations of the university. He is one of the founders of Motorola University in 1980. He has been with Motorola for 32 years, in engineering, marketing, and national sales management. Before joining Motorola, he was an officer in the U.S. Navy, receiving three decorations. He holds a B.S. degree in electrical engineering from the Illinois Institute of Technology and an M.B.A. from the University of Chicago.*

Is Change in the Education System Necessary?

In the past decade the world has changed dramatically with the demise of communism, growth in international trade relations (NAFTA and GATT), and development of technology which provides an "information superhighway" to share learning on a worldwide network. The world of business has changed from an "industrial" model to an "information" model. This shift is not much different from what took place over 100 years ago when society changed from an agricultural model to an industrial mode. Figure 49-1 is useful in defining the components of these shifts and the implications for both the present and future workforce.

The information age was christened in the late 1940s with the invention of the transistor. This device has provided us with the ability to store, process, and generate information and data at ever-increasing rates. Information, as is seen in Fig. 49-1, is the output of this new age. Today the axiom "knowledge is power" is seen in such terms as the "knowledge worker" who is becoming the basic foundation in most new enterprises today. Since knowledge is the basic strategic resource for the information age, it becomes obvious that the driving energy source for this age is the mind. Figure 49-1 is also useful in explaining some other shifts which have taken place in society. In the agriculture and industrial ages, the physical strength of the male was a natural advantage to being successful. Both farming and manufacturing required extensive physical labor. Women were the nurturers and family raisers. When they did venture from the home, they were confined to intellectual endeavors in teaching, health care, and libraries. However, the transistor and computer have leveled the playing field. Computer-controlled robots and machines do most heavy labor. Intellectual labor is now the foundation for work, and it is no longer gender-biased. Thus we see the dramatic shift of women moving into the workplace and becoming successful in formerly male-dominated work.

Another significant point demonstrated by Fig. 49-1 is the time frames involved in the shifts we are discussing. The agriculture-based society lasted at least 10,000 years. The industrial age began in the mid-1800s and is now rapidly being phased out. The information age is about 45 years old. The rate of change has accelerated (10,000 years–150 years–45 years) and continues to increase. The primary constant in today's society is change.

While we acknowledge that great change in society and the workplace has taken place, is the same true in the system of education? The system in place today was developed over 100 years ago to meet the needs of the industrial age. At that time the school year was established around the needs of the farm—with spring break to help in the planting and summer break to assist in the harvest. We have the same school year today as 100 years ago! While society has shifted, the school year has not. In a similar way, school was designed around the industrial model of mass production and standardized and specialized tasks. Time

	Agriculture	Industrial	Information
Dominant technology	Plow	Machine	Computer
Output	Food	Goods	Information
Strategic	Land	Capital	Knowledge
Organization	Form Family	Corporation	Networks
Energy source	Animal fossil	Fuel	Mind
Nature of production	Self	Mass	Individualized

Figure 49-1. Societal shifts.

was a major factor in measuring work (time and motion studies). The industrial model of school we have in place today is also designed around the concept of "time as the constant." School days are broken into 47- to 50-minute periods, each period having a specific subject taught. All children spend the same number of days in school. There are separate departments focused on English, math, science, history, and other major subject areas. All children in a class use the same book and are covering the same page on the same day. In the present system, time is the constant and performance is the variable. Children are allowed to fail, get poor grades, and drop out of school. The system forces them to sit quietly and listen to the teacher, even though, biologically, children are in school during their most physically active years. Research also shows that listening alone is not an effective way of learning. School today is designed to be efficient (the mass production model), but it is not effective. Just as the workplace has moved from the industrial model to the information model, schools must shift from treating all children the same to determining the needs of each child's mind (and body) and adjusting the system to meet these needs.

What Skills Do Young People Need to Develop to Be Successful in the Present and Future "World of Work"?

In 1993, a report was issued by a commission of the U.S. Department of Labor, Secretary's Commission on Achieving Necessary Skills (SCANS), which describes the key competencies required to be successful in the workplace today. This commission met for over a year to articulate the attitudes and skills that young people need to develop to be successful once they leave the formal education system.

When the summary of the SCAN skills is reviewed (see Fig. 49-2), it becomes obvious that they are much more complex and broad-based than what the education system is prepared to deliver. The SCANS skills are necessary for survival in the information society. The skills in Fig. 49-2 are also quite different than those most readers of this chapter will have experienced in school. Work is being done by the Department of Labor to transfer the SCANS competencies into curriculum guidelines that can be used by educators to redefine school.

Figure 49-3 provides a shorter summary of both the SCAN skills and those developed by ASTD several years ago. The most important skill that all children must develop is the ability to be continuous lifelong learners. Since a basic assumption of the information society is that change is continuous and accelerating, continuous learning must take place if the workforce is to remain effective. It is generally acknowledged today that children are taught to memorize facts and do not really learn the process of continuous learning.

An Education System Which Develops SCANS Skills in All Children

A school must begin by becoming student centered. The teacher is no longer the center of information but is a facilitator of learning. A "model school," as generically described by recent studies, would have these major components:

The know-how identified by SCANS is made up of five competencies and a three-part foundation of skills and personal qualities that are needed for solid job performance. These are:

Workplace competencies: Effective workers can productively use

- Resources—They know how to allocate time, money, materials, space, and staff.
- Interpersonal skills—They can work on teams, teach others, serve customers, lead, negotiate, and work well with people from culturally diverse backgrounds.
- Information—They can acquire and evaluate data, organize and maintain files, interpret and communicate, and use computers to process information.
- Systems—They understand social, organizational, and technological systems; they can monitor and correct performance; and they can design or improve systems.
- Technology—They can select equipment and tools, apply technology to specific tasks, and maintain and troubleshoot equipment.

Foundation skills: Competent workers in the high-performance workplace need

- Basic skills—Reading, writing, arithmetic and mathematics, speaking, and listening
- Thinking skills—The ability to learn, to reason, to think creatively, to make decisions, and to solve problems
- Personal qualities—Individual responsibility, self-esteem and self-management, sociability, and integrity

Figure 49-2. Workplace know-how.

- Learning to learn
- Reading
- Writing
- Computing
- Listening
- Speaking
- Solving problems
- Thinking creatively
- Setting goals and staying alive
- Cultivating self-esteem
- Fostering interpersonal relations
- Developing personal and career skills
- Promoting teamwork
- Negotiating
- Understanding your organization
- Leadership

Figure 49-3. Workplace basics. (*Source: ASTD/U.S. Department of Labor.*)

- Since each child learns in a different way and at a different rate, each child requires an individualized education plan. This requirement involves having an education system that adapts to meet the needs of each child rather than forcing all children to meet the needs of one system.

- Each child develops a "portfolio" of accomplishments which includes individual and group work, skill assessments, attitudes toward self and others, and those other SCANS competencies required to be successful.

- The focus of curriculum (what is taught) is on material that is relevant and engaging to the students. (*A major role of industry is to be able to describe the needs of the workplace so that educators can develop materials that are relevant to meeting the needs of that workplace.)*

- The focus of instructional methods (how the curriculum is taught) must be on cooperative learning among students facilitated by collaborative teams of teachers. In this system, both children and adults are learners.

- The focus of the system of assessment (what students have learned) must be on what students accomplish, not what they have memorized. Students must be able to show they are able to do something with the knowledge they have gained.

The role of technology is absolutely vital in the engagement of young people in curriculum and instructional methods. Today in many classrooms the highest level of technology remains the pencil and the chalk. Computers must be integrated as learning stations through use of data networks as pathways to information. (*Business can provide valuable input to educators on the development of data and computer networks. Software selection, current technology, and systems applications are all areas of expertise for business.*) A model school invests heavily in the training and development of teachers and administrators. Teachers need continuous development on new learning theories and instructional methods.

Principals and other administrators need training on leadership and management skills. A principal as middle manager must also understand the process of change, enterprise management, the development of trust within the organization, and the many other middle-management skills required to be successful in this role. (*The training and development professionals can provide access for principals to many of the skills being taught to first-line and middle-level managers in industry. These programs are not traditionally taught in colleges of education or other education administrator development programs.*) The superintendent of the school district functions in a way similar to the chief executive officer of a corporation. The district has its board of directors (school board or school committee) as well as responsibility for most of the functions that a CEO and the board would have in the private sector. (*Training and development professionals can provide superintendents access to the senior executive development programs available to business CEOs.*) School superintendents need to understand the process of boardsmanship as well as communicating with the community that supports the education of the young.

Roles and Responsibilities of the Training and Development Professionals and the Improvement of Schools

A major role of business partnership with schools is to be able to describe the "real world of work" that students will be entering. Students, teachers, and administrators need exposure to real-world problems that exist in the workplace. Teachers require understanding of workplace needs so they can provide a relevancy to the material being taught to their young students. A critical need in education is for career counselors to fully understand the different aspects of careers in the private sector. They need to be aware of the workplace opportunities and future trends in jobs for which students must begin to prepare themselves early in life. Business must offer students practical work experience during the summer so they can fully understand the implications of their education. Training and development professionals have the ability to provide organizational and leadership development programs for school administrators.

Business-Education Partnership Models for Training Professionals

The National Alliance of Business has developed a useful model of the different levels of partnerships between business and the education systems. Figure 49-4 demonstrates that different partnerships will have varying levels of impact and investment based on the focus of the relationship. The most important feature of Fig. 49-4 is that it demonstrates that every organization, regardless of its size or type, can be involved with the restructuring of the education system.

Level 1: *Partners in policy* are those that shape the public and political debate, bring about substantive change in state or federal legislation or local school governance, and affect the overall direction of the education system.

Level 2: *Partners in systemic education improvement* are those in which leaders identify the need for reform or improvement in the education system and then work over the long term to make those major changes happen in the system.

Level 3: *Partners in management* are those that provide school leadership with management support and business expertise in a broad range of areas.

Level 4: *Partners in professional development* are those that provide opportunities for school personnel to update, upgrade, or maintain their skills or learn more about the labor market, industries and businesses, in the community, workplace needs, and career opportunities.

Level 5: *Partners in the classroom* are those that provide business volunteers who improve the learning environment either by bringing their business or occupational expertise directly into the classroom for students and teachers or by bringing the classroom to the business.

Level 6: *Partners in special services* are those who provide short-term, project or student-specific activities or resources to help with a specific problem or need.

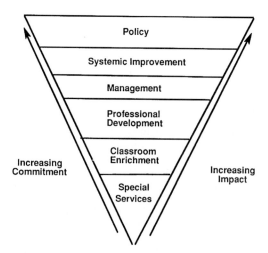

Figure 49-4. Business-education partnership levels.

There are numerous examples of the different levels of partnerships described in newspapers, trade journals, and books. Collaborative partners have begun the transformation of the education system to the new model required by the information age. However, much more must be done before all schools become student-focused. There are many things the training professional can do at every level of the partnership triangle. Some examples follow:

Level 1: *Partners in policy*
Become involved with other businesses in your area through the Chamber of Commerce, National Alliance of Business, The Business Roundtable, or other organizations that have policy issues in education as a major initiative. It is very difficult for one business to have much impact in this area, but networks of business are impacting public policy and have the potential to be a major force in the improvement of school rules and regulations.

Level 2: *Partners in systemic improvement*
These partnerships, as with those in the policy area, work on a significant scale over the long term and require a collaborative effort on the part of many organizations. Training professionals, because of their knowledge of change processes in business, can be valuable advisors to the larger groups involved in systemic change. In the United States, the school district is considered to be the "strategic unit" of change because it is at this level the curriculum is designed, instructional methods are defined and supported and the assessment process is managed. The school is the focus of change because it is here that changes must be implemented. But until any change is designed and/or supported at the district level, school-based change will be episodic and short-lived.

Training professionals can provide expertise to school boards and superintendents as the system develops a new vision and mission for the district. The systemic issues in education are similar in form to those in business, only the context is different. Business is further down the learning curve on systemic organizational change, and this experience must be shared with the education system. The training professional can be a major factor in this transfer of experience.

Level 3: *Partners in management*

Level 4: *Partners in professional development*
These two levels are discussed together since the training professional can have a major impact on both. So much work in training is directed at the improvement of management technologies and processes through the training and implementation of new skills that the possibilities for education partnerships are boundless.

Strategic planning, financial management, employee relations, building design and management, technology integration and management, quality measurement, and management and leadership development are only some of the areas for partnership. The marketing of school successes, development of teacher training programs, team problem solving, management coaching skills, and meeting management are still areas in which the training department can provide valuable services to educators.

Simple things like providing one or two seats in a training program will provide educators access to knowledge and skills not available in the traditional education development process. Providing job aids and "toolkits" to teachers for use in their personal development is another example. Hiring teachers as summer interns in the training department is an excellent way to introduce educators to the "world of work" in an area where they can contribute their expertise. Some training departments have assisted in the design of development plans for school principals based on the knowledge and skills required by middle managers in business. Others have developed job models of the educators' jobs through a collaborative process used for business job models.

The training professional must realize that almost all teacher development is provided through the university system. Just as in business, a workplace-based component must be included for skill development. Business can provide this workplace training.

Level 5:   *Partners in the classroom*

Level 6:   *Partners in special services*

These two levels are the most traditional in the history of business-education partnerships. Mentoring and tutoring programs are the most common forms of these levels. Sharing expertise in a particular area with students in a classroom is an example of a special service. Young people are isolated from real-world requirements in the classroom and are dependent upon business to reduce this isolation. In many cases, business provides technology to the school or becomes involved in the planning for technology through participation on design committees. Formal "adopt-a-school" programs are often driven out of the training department because of the similarity in the purpose of both functions (developing human resources: The present generation by training departments and the next generation by schools).

Summary

Business is the eventual "customer" of the school system in that most students will be entering the private sector after they leave the formal education system. Business therefore has a responsibility to articulate the needs of the workplace and work in partnership with the suppliers (schools) to develop learning systems that develop young people to be successful in the workplace. Business can only be "world class" if it has a world-class workforce. This future workforce is being developed in the education system today. Evidence shows that this system is no longer world class. It becomes incumbent on all members of the community to be involved in the renewal of education to ensure a bright future for children.

The training professional has many opportunities to be a key component in this renewal. Whether it's partnering with other businesses involved in the systemic changes in education, or providing training programs for educators, or making a presentation to a fifth-grade class on the products or services of their business, the training professional is an important player. All that remains is for the professional to take the initiative and reach out to an education partner to begin the redesign of the system upon which children (and this society) is so dependent.

Bibliography

The Business Roundtable, *The Business Roundtable Participation Guide: A Primer for Business on Education*, The Business Roundtable, New York, 1991.

Chubb, John E., and Terry M. Moe, *Politics, Markets, and America's Schools*, The Brookings Institution, Washington, DC, 1990.

The Commission on the Skills of the American Workforce, *America's Choice: High Skills or Low Wages*, National Center on Education and the Economy, Rochester, NY, 1990.

National Education Commission on Time and Learning, *Prisoners of Time*, Washington, DC, 1990.

Rigden, Diana W., *Business-School Partnerships, A Path to Effective School Restructuring,* Council for Aid to Education, New York, 1991.

Rosow, Jerome, and Robert Zager, *Allies in Educational Reform* (Work in America Institute), Jossey-Bass, San Francisco, 1989.

Schargel, Franklin P., *Transforming Education Through Total Quality Management: A Practitioner's Guide,* Eye on Education, Princeton Junction, NJ, 1994.

Schleshty, Phillip C., *Schools for the 21st Century: Leadership Imperatives for Educational Reform,* Jossey-Bass, San Francisco, 1990.

Secretary's Commission on Achieving Necessary Skills (SCANS), *Blueprint for Action: Building Community Coalitions,* U.S. Department of Labor, Washington, DC, 1992.

Secretary's Commission on Achieving Necessary Skills (SCANS), *Learning a Living: A Blueprint for High Performance,* U.S. Department of Labor, Washington, DC, 1992.

Siegel, Peggy, and Sandra Byrne, *Using Quality to Redesign School Systems: The Cutting Edge of Common Sense,* Jossey-Bass, San Francisco, 1994.

Tucker, Marc, *A School-to-Work Transition System for the United States,* National Center on Education and the Economy, Rochester, NY, 1994.

50

Outsourcing in Training and Education

June Paradise Maul

Joel D. Krauss

June Paradise Maul *is director of Business Education World-wide, AT&T School of Business. She directs a global education program providing AT&T business managers and customers with education across a wide range of key business strategy areas. Internationally known as an innovative business educator, Maul has been recognized and lauded for creating training and educational programs that teach by solving real problems in a classroom setting. Under her aegis, AT&T has taught its managers how to run their organizations like small businesses as well as how to lead global businesses. Her latest innovative efforts include creating a series of virtual office training programs. She is a 14-year veteran with AT&T and has served in a variety of management posts at the district and division manager level. Early in her career, she was responsible for the programs orienting all middle-level managers and executives in AT&T's Long Lines transition from a monopoly to a competitive business environment. She holds a B.S. degree from MIT in geophysics and Asian studies and a Ph.D. from Rutgers University in science and humanities. Dr. Maul also holds an honorary M.B.A. from Western International University in London. Prior to joining AT&T, she was an assistant professor at the Rutgers Center for Coastal and Environmental Studies. She is well known as a consultant and speaker on business planning, financial management, and operations improvement.*

Joel D. Krauss *is managing partner of OmniTech Consulting Group, Inc., a Chicago-based global management and marketing* *consulting firm serving Fortune 1000 companies, specializing in high-tech arenas. Krauss has assisted companies in the telecommunications, computer, pharmaceutical, financial services, and information technology industries. In recent years, he has served a large number of consumer packaged-goods firms. His clients have included AT&T, Ameritech, Baxter, BellSouth, Dell, Digital, Motorola, PacificBell, Pepsico, Sears, US West, and Warner Lambert. Krauss has more than 20 years' experience in the development of custom and broad-based training programs. He has created and directed education and training across a wide spectrum, from high-technology quality control to sales-force techniques. As OmniTech principal, he leads an organization of professionals whose expertise covers strategic management and marketing, reengineering, new-product introductions, sales-force training and development, business education and leadership. Prior to cofounding OmniTech in 1985, Krauss was a principal at the international management consulting firm of Harbridge House, Inc. He holds a B.S. degree in computer science from The Illinois Institute of Technology and an M.B.A. degree in finance and statistics from The University of Chicago.*

You're in a meeting with your company's executive committee. Changes are accelerating. Customer service centers are being consolidated into megacenters and equipped with a new generation of automated solutions. The sales organization has been realigned and moved into a virtual workplace environment. Several layers of middle management are being redeployed to flatten the management hierarchy. New leadership paradigms to make empowered workers a reality are taking shape. And the new-product development process has been substantially overhauled so the firm can launch new products in 9 months rather than 24.

All of this presents you, the training organization, with a myriad of complex, challenging, and very fast-paced opportunities to assist. But these are new expectations for your organization. Management expects you, the training function, not only to meet these new and ever-changing needs but also, like each of the other work groups, to reinvent yourself, taking bold new steps to improve the learning process. You have been challenged to offer new learning methods, slash development times, expand the business knowledge and expertise of your training professionals, and, at the same time, bring your cost structure in line with what your industry and market conditions allow.

If your organization is typical, you probably face one or more of these pressures. If you do, outsourcing is one mechanism you should consider for selected portions of your training function.

What Is Outsourcing?

Your first question, of course, is what is outsourcing all about? You have relied on vendors, external faculty, and all sorts of outside resources for many years. So is this really anything new? Or is it simply more of the same?

Literally, outsourcing is the use of external agents to perform one or more specific functions of importance to your business. As we discuss later, outsourcing options provide a spectrum of choices, from minimal outsourcing of a handful of functions to a total outsource of your entire training organization. So to some extent it is *not* new.

	Internal sourcing	Subcontracting	Comprehensive sourcing
TIME	1970s	1980s	1990s
Motivation	Leverage internal expertise	Financial	Strategic objectives
Vendors	Few	More	Outsourcing training management companies
Vendor measures	—	Contract fulfillment	Customer success based on performance metrics

Figure 50-1. Training sourcing time line.

But what *is* new about outsourcing is its systematic nature. This is no longer an ad hoc, occasional decision to use vendors here and there. Rather it's a careful, precise review of all aspects of your training business with a focus on breakthrough improvements (e.g., capability, responsiveness, expense) achieved by creating new sources for work you now do via traditional internal personnel.

Outsourcing itself has changed considerably in recent years. As Fig. 50-1 illustrates, outsourcing in the 1970s was highly motivated by a need to leverage and extend resource capabilities. In recent years, outsourcing has taken on a more strategic role, offering strategic value not otherwise attainable.

A question often asked about outsourcing is whether it leaves management without a role. While it is widely believed that management is left without a role, this opinion is in fact untrue. Outsourcing shifts the role of management. It is liberation from a firefighting mode to a concentration on what is core and strategic to the business.

Outsourcing is often connected to a reengineering or quality initiative that focuses on new performance norms or metrics. Its best results come from "radical" rather than traditional thinking. Even if an outsourcing analysis suggests that no changes in sourcing are desirable, this "fresh-look" analysis will often offer powerful insights into where your organization could improve.

Outsourcing analyses intentionally challenge traditional approaches, cultural norms, and almost everything else associated with work in a training organization. Certainly, open-minded thinking is a key prerequisite. You will find that engaging an outside facilitator—from elsewhere in your company or from an outside firm—will add value. Facilitators suggest, coach, prod, but never decide. Their role is to help you advance, tear down walls of tradition, and open-mindedly consider new sourcing approaches.

The remainder of this chapter provides answers to the key questions many of us ask as we proceed with outsourcing training for the first time. In particular, it addresses these questions:

- What is the range of outsourcing options?
- What benefits can be obtained, and what risks are present?
- How can I systematically assess my business to determine (1) what, if anything, should be outsourced and (2) how should it be outsourced?
- How can I implement outsourcing in my organization?

Each of these points is discussed below.

Benefits of Outsourcing

Outsourcing part or all of your training operation can provide distinct advantages for you, your training organization, and your business. Before going forward, you should consider your goals and determine how outsourcing might assist you in meeting them. Usually outsourcing can offer *one or more* of the following benefits (see Fig. 50-2).

Flexibility.   Outsourcing can allow you to extend your resource team, augmenting your in-house team, as needed. It can give you the advantage of added resources without increasing your fixed payroll costs.

Capability Advantage.   Outsourcing can be motivated by a desire to obtain new and different capabilities not now available within your organization. For example, experts in specific businesses, markets, industries, or training technologies are often outsourced rather than hired.

Enhanced Quality.   Outsourcing is often an implementation strategy associated with a Total Quality Management (TQM) initiative. *Very often this initiative stimulates "breakthrough thinking" about new directions.* Often new sourcing strategies are developed to fulfill these new needs.

Refocus of Management's Energy and Resources.   Although outsourcing doesn't take management "off the hook" relative to the role of the training organization, it does recast their roles for increased productivity. Rather than focusing on day-to-day firefighting, management can focus on core business issues and training solutions that add real value. In effect, the management team is able to reinvent its role without sacrificing overall quality.

Strategic Directions.   New strategies, new markets, or new products can all create requirements that are better met via outsourcing. For example, many telecommunications organizations, when moving toward sales and deployment of data solutions, have outsourced their data training needs.

Resizing.   Bringing fixed labor costs and associated headcounts in line with corporate cost initiatives is often a driver of outsourcing efforts. For example, one organization outsourced its desktop publishing operation since demand for their services was highly variable and cost savings could be achieved in the open market.

- Flexibility
- Capability advantage
- Enhanced quality
- Refocus of management's energy and resources
- Strategic directions
- Resizing
- Competency development
- New perspectives
- Cost

Figure 50-2. Benefits of new sourcing strategies.

Competency Development.   Outsourcing is often a wise way to obtain talents and know-how not available within your organization and to rapidly transfer that capability to your team over time. Many companies began their initial experimentation with multimedia training development by outsourcing to vendors, teaming with them on assignments and then learning from their partners.

New Perspectives.   In many cases outsourcing helps a company identify new and improved ways of doing things. These new perspectives can be minor (e.g., format of training materials) or major (e.g., new training technologies). In any event, they can be incorporated to improve the organization's overall performance.

Cost.   The traditional motive for outsourcing has been to save money—both in terms of annual expenditures (e.g., labor and materials) and assets (e.g., physical plant). The long-term savings in the brick-and-mortar expense of physical facilities, in particular, makes outsourcing highly attractive. Several major corporations have plans to pool their facilities, outsourcing management of the facilities to a third party, who would then offer services to the sponsoring companies, as well as others.

Options of Outsourcing

Outsourcing of training today offers a wide range of options. As Fig. 50-3 illustrates, depending on your needs, you may (1) continue to source internally, (2) partner with outside capabilities, or (3) comprehensively outsource specific functions to a third party. As its name suggests, partnering melds your capability with that of your partner, allowing you to extend resources, obtain capabilities, and obtain specialized expertise. A comprehensive outsource is a situation where you turn over some aspect of your business to the third party to operate on your behalf. This arrangement is often desirable in situations where the capability needs rejuvenation, or where you feel the capability is not relevant strategically and should ultimately be harvested or divested.

Another key option is the *breadth* of your outsource. As Fig. 50-4 illustrates, you may choose to outsource a narrow or a broad range of services. In effect, a specific element of work, such as materials production, may be sourced via a comprehensive outsourcing relationship. Another, possibly broader set of responsibilities, such as responsibility for all classroom training, might be outsourced via a partnering relationship.

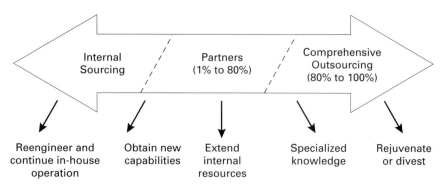

Figure 50-3. A continuum of choices.

Outsourcing Focus:

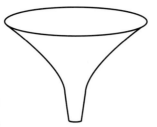

- Total Outsourcing

- Product Line
  Outsourcing

- Capability Extension

- Operational Support

Example:

- Establish third party that
  supports *all* training

- Outsource all *sales*
  training to a team of
  partners

- Vendors extend your
  development or delivery
  team

- Materials Production

- Facilities Management

Figure 50-4. Breadth of outsourcing.

The degree of outsourcing that makes sense in a given situation must be carefully assessed. The next section illustrates how to make that choice.

Evaluating Your Outsourcing Needs

Outsourcing decisions should be based on a systematic analysis of your needs and capabilities as well as the availability of outside resources. What follows is a framework for you to consider as well as an illustrative example.

Define Your Business

An early step in the outsourcing question is to define (1) the business your training operation is now in and (2) the business it *ought* to be in. Very often, simply answering this fundamental definition question offers great insight into the direction you should take and the role outsourcing should play. But this is only a preliminary step.

The next major step is to enumerate the activities that your training organization performs. Create a function wheel like that shown in Fig. 50-5.

Assess Strategic Criticality and Your Relative Capability/Cost

Not every function your training business performs is critical to the success of your enterprise. To assess outsourcing direction possibilities, you need to evaluate both the strategic importance and the total cost of each activity in terms of out-of-pocket expenses, investments in assets, use of staffing, etc. These are shown graphically in Figs. 50-6 and 50-7.

In doing this assessment, we suggest you use the following assessment scale to evaluate strategic importance:

1 Limited Value	2 Important Tactically	3 Mission Critical	4 Vision-Critical Strategic

Decreasing ⇦ **Relative Importance** ⇨ *Increasing*

- Adds little to the value perceived by end customers.
- Key to tactical success, but not mission or vision critical.
- Activity whose absence would jeopardize successful daily operation.
- Critical to the <u>future</u> success of the business.

   You should consider the dynamics of the importance of each activity over time. Some activities that are of limited value today may be critical to you in the future. Several years ago, many organizations saw little value in developing multimedia capabilities. Today, those same organizations may not be able to support the companies' strategies.

   With respect to capability costs, the following scale may be utilized:

1 Minimal Capability	2 Moderate	3 High	4 Extremely High Capability

Decreasing ⇦ **Relative Capability/Costs** ⇨ *Increasing*

- Low effectiveness or satisfaction
- High level of satisfaction

- High-cost provider
- Low-cost provider

   Each of the services can be "sized" relative to its strategic importance to the organization and its costs. The more important an activity is strategically, the larger its size. Likewise, the higher an activity's cost, the larger its size. You should be actively managing the larger pieces of the pie.

Assess Corporate Capability

This step is a critical one and extremely difficult to do objectively. But it is essential to assess your capability relative to that of other organizations which *could* be sourced to perform this function. A rigorous assessment of relative performance involves establishing a series of performance metrics and comparing your capability with best-in-class and third-party providers.

Choose the Best Sourcing Strategy

Figure 50-8 illustrates the range of sourcing strategies that result from this assessment. As the figure illustrates, your decision is based on both the strategic relevance *and* your relative capability in each function under consideration.

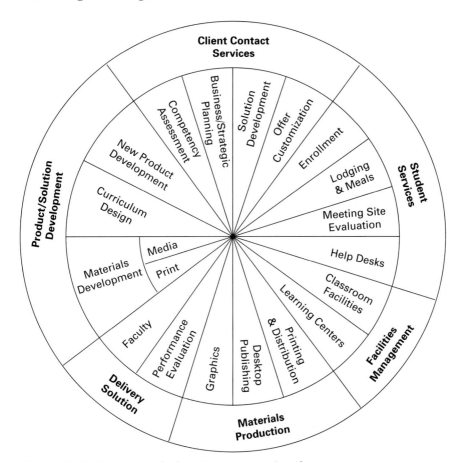

Figure 50-5. Training and education services identification.

For example, at ABC Corporation (see Fig. 50-9), training, new-product development, and custom solution development are areas of great importance in helping the organization respond to future needs of the business. But these areas are where ABC's capability is evolving; thus ABC's own training function has limited relative capability. In these areas, a partnering sourcing strategy makes sense as a mechanism to allow ABC to ramp up quickly to respond, grow its internal capability over time, and remain competitive.

In addition, ABC has traditionally provided overnight lodging as part of its training effort. Management's assessment suggests that being in the hotel business is neither strategic nor something the company is very good at. As a result, a decision has been made to *discontinue* lodging services, allowing students to make their own individual arrangements.

Other operations, such as student enrollment, help desks, and materials development, are areas where ABC has a relatively strong capability, but they offer limited strategic advantage. While the organization plans to continue these services over the near-term, each will be part of the training team's spin-off strategy. For example, the training registration system, while efficient, is time-consuming to manage and operate. At ABC, the marketing operation has shown

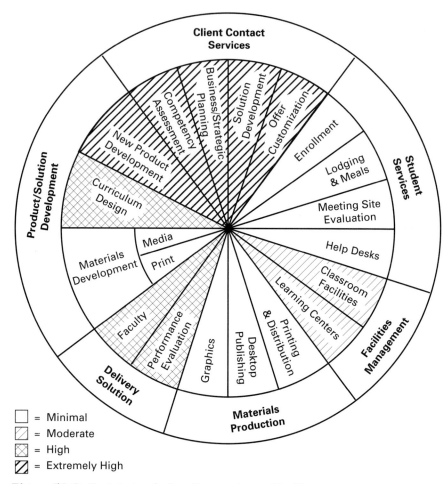

Figure 50-6. Training and education services criticality.

interest in taking on this operation and refocusing it to outbound selling and customer support. Having this additional center is key to their strategic needs. A "commercial contract" has been agreed to between training and marketing to transfer the registration telemarketing unit, while preserving its role as a registration service for education and training.

While ABC has competency in materials development, new training technologies (e.g., multimedia) are rapidly overtaking their in-house know-how. Similarly, the proportion of print-based training being developed is expected to diminish in future years. ABC has therefore chosen to outsource this capability. It has offered this development unit an opportunity to spin off as a separate business, with a guaranteed contract for ABC's training development business over the next three years.

Lastly, areas ABC finds critical, and where its capabilities are high, are *not* candidates for outsourcing. Rather, ABC plans to further develop these areas internally. For example, ABC's business leadership finds real value in the way

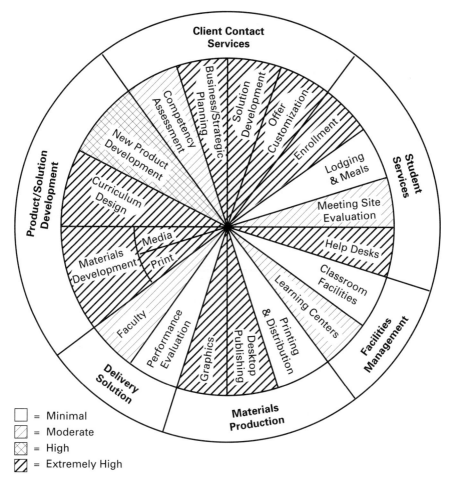

Figure 50-7. Training and education services identification of relative capability.

the training organization creates customized interventions to meet short- and long-term business needs. Given the value of these efforts, they are in high demand. Attempts to use third parties have not been as successful, since these parties lack both an understanding of ABC's strategies and, more importantly, *real* commitment to the effort. ABC has decided to expand its internal capability so that twice as many interventions can be handled in the next 12 months.

Evaluating the Risks

While outsourcing offers many potential benefits, it poses risks as well. Naturally, the risks increase as your outsourcing plans become more ambitious. Most risks, however, can be minimized through careful analysis, planning, and contingency development. You should consider the following when evaluating the risks of outsourcing.

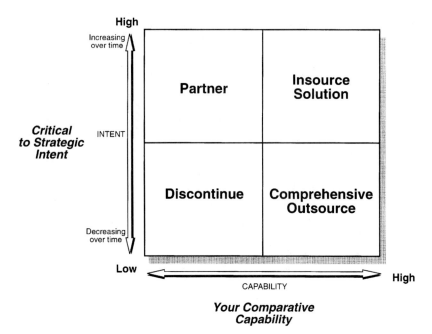

Figure 50-8. Sourcing strategies.

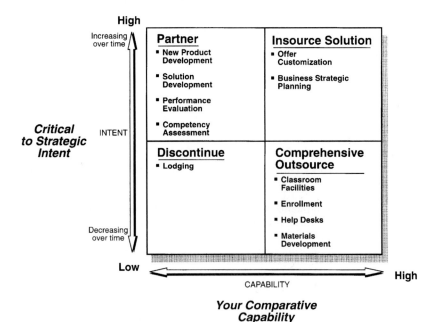

Figure 50-9. ABC Corporation illustrative example.

Reliability and Commitment. Care must be taken to ensure that an outsourcing firm will actually be able to meet your needs. The chances of poor performance increase if the outsourcing firm (1) is small and inexperienced, (2) is unprepared or lacks the skills to meet your expectations, or (3) considers your work requirements to be small compared to their total work mix.

Developing a Competitor. As your outsourcing partners' know-how increases, the chances of their becoming a future competitor can increase as well. Should you perceive this to be a real risk, demand a noncompete clause in all your contractual agreements.

Lose Motivation. This "slow down after we win the contract" phenomenon is quite typical in most situations. The best method of avoidance is to create incentive contracts, where compensation is tied to specific performance goals.

Seeking Employee Status. In situations where personnel obtained via a third-party provider mingle with your personnel and work on your premises, there may be requests to treat them like regular employees. That is, they may seek wage increases, benefit increases, or participation in other programs your full-time employees receive. Given the fact that these personnel work for a third party, it is likely you cannot meet these requests. It is wise to require the third party that manages these personnel to clarify expectations before their personnel begin serving your organization.

Ramp-Up Time and Learning Costs. It may take longer than you expect for your outsource partners to become fully effective at their roles and responsibilities. During this time you could unknowingly risk slow, inadequate, or poor performance. It should be expected that the first six months will be a learning period for any outsource you select. Plan for ramp-up time; if feasible, continue your operation in parallel with the outsourcing firm's for the first months.

Impact on Your Present Workforce. The type of impact that you experience will depend on whether the outsourcing firm's personnel will replace your people, augment your people, or absorb your people into their operation. You should anticipate personnel issues in any case. Even if the outsourcing firm simply augments your team, situations often arise in which your employees or the outsourcing firm's personnel feel like second-class citizens. Most notably, situations involving transfer of employees to the outsourcing firm present complex interpersonal and compensation issues.

Making a Bad Financial or Performance Deal. Nothing is worse than a long-term agreement that is unfavorable to your business. Bad deals often set mediocre performance targets, overcompensate the outsource partner, or both of the above. The more significant the outsourcing effort, the greater the need to create an incentive contract tying the outsourcing firm to substantial (but doable) performance objectives, and linking fees to realization of these objectives. The contracts should be win-win, allowing the outsourcing firm to do well financially, but only if they far exceed your present performance and add significant new value.

Differences in Basic Values. Every firm may not share your firm's commitment to business ethics, fundamentals, values of respect, honesty, and the like. It's very important to sound each vendor out on this issue and, prior to beginning work, develop a common code of conduct that both parties can follow.

Ineffective Conflict Resolution. Every arrangement between businesses involves conflicts, and the resolution of these conflicts must be rapid and unemotional. To avoid this risk, in each agreement, discuss and decide in advance what your conflict resolution methodology will be. And, of course, prescreen potential outsourcing partners to ensure that they have good conflict resolution skills.

Lack of Direct Control. While you will retain ultimate responsibility and authority for this outsourced role, you will no longer have the same hands-on control that was possible prior to outsourcing. The broader the role being outsourced, the less day-to-day control you will have. Prepare yourself for this change. You may find this to be a difficult adjustment.

Note, however, that the lack of day-to-day control does not imply a total loss so much as a shift of control. While you cannot run your outsourced business, you can establish frequent checkpoints enabling you to monitor progress and jointly plan for operational changes. The *style* of control changes considerably, but the smart training organization recognizes that it always has both responsibility and control.

An All-Around Bad Choice. Finally, one of the most disastrous of outcomes is to learn that you have indeed selected the wrong vendor and need to cancel the contract. The best way to avoid this outcome is through careful screening, reference checks, establishment of a trial period, identification of a fallback vendor should the first choice fail, and negotiations in advance of what will happen in situations of nonperformance.

Steps in Implementing Your Outsourcing Strategy

The decision to outsource all or a portion of your training function is probably one of the most significant choices you will make. Like all other strategies, it is far easier to determine what direction to take than it is to successfully guide your organization down that road. Strategic decisions to outsource usually fail because the leadership team falls short on the job of successful implementation.

The exact approach you will need to take in terms of fulfilling your outsourcing strategy will depend on exactly what you plan to outsource and how you expect that outsourced operation to work with your remaining organization. Regardless of what you outsource, your implementation should involve consideration of each of the following implementation steps:

- Creating an outsourcing plan
- Building internal support
- Identifying resource options
- Resourcing partner evaluation criteria
- Obtaining assistance
- Establishing win-win process and performance objectives
- Issuing a very specific request for proposal
- Outsourcing firm and negotiation
- Creating the outsourcing contract

- Launching a pilot phase
- Ongoing monitoring and evaluation performance

Each is described below.

Create an Outsourcing Plan for Your Training Business

While this may seem like an obvious step, many organizations falter because they lack a clear understanding of their outsourcing plans. As with any plan, your approach to outsourcing will change as common sense dictates. But by creating a written plan and program, the risk of confusion, and inadvertently contracting for something other than what you really need, will be minimized. At a minimum, your outsourcing plan should address the key sections shown in Fig. 50-10, many of which have been described in previous sections of this chapter.

Building Internal Support

The success of your outsourcing strategy will depend very much on whether it is embraced by your key internal clients and leadership team as the best direction for the training organization to take. Having an outsourcing strategy approved by senior management is a reason to redouble this effort, not discontinue it.

Part I: Purpose and Vision
- Specific outsourcing goals and objectives
- Benefits to your organization
- Key services to be provided to your organization by the outsource provider
- Type of outsourcing relationship sought

Part II: Financial and Risk Analysis

- Financial analysis of outsourcing program
- Contingency plans and exit strategies in event of nonperformance

Part III: Impact on Organization and Personnel

- Service improvements and operating changes that will be experienced by training function clients, suppliers, and others
- Impact on current employee base
- Transformation strategy for affected *internal* training personnel whose role will be affected by outsourcing

Part IV: Evaluation, Negotiation, and Contracting Strategy

- Outsource evaluation criteria
- Contractual obligations and performance incentives to be developed with outsourcing partner
- Expert resources (internal and external) to be involved in the selection and negotiation process

Part V: Work Plan and Timetable

Part VI: Ongoing Performance

- Key performance measures
- Process for ensuring satisfaction
- Process for discussing and resolving conflicts and differences
- Process for mutual planning for strategy for the outsource relationship

---

Figure 50-10. Key elements of outsourcing plan.

To build support for your recommended outsourcing approach, create a brief presentation illustrating your plan. Do this immediately after approval and even before the actual actions have been completed. Obviously, you will not be in a position to explain the details of the new operation, since an outsourcing partner has not yet come on board. But you will be able to begin the critical job of preparing those involved so they can begin to adjust to the change and embrace it. Your goal is to (1) build awareness across the organization about what is about to happen, (2) explain why the new approach makes sense, and (3) explain what the change will mean to each of the stakeholders, including clients, education and training personnel, and current suppliers. The more ambitious your proposed outsourcing, the more significant your effort to build support must be.

Identifying Resource Options and Resourcing Partner Evaluation Criteria

Recently a senior executive interested in outsourcing his entire training operation told us that his organization backed off, not because they changed their minds, but because they couldn't find any organizations *interested* in meeting their needs. His view was that "there are lots of organizations willing and able to outsource our Information Technology function, but fewer who are *really* set up for and interested in taking on major portions of our training effort."

Indeed, the more significant your proposed outsourcing strategy, the more difficult it is to find top-notch partners. This doesn't mean that partners aren't available, only that the job of scanning, screening, and selecting is a difficult one that must be pursued aggressively. Unlike the classic selling process, where vendors beat a path to your door, you must be the proactive participant in this effort. Think of it not as a vendor selection, but as a partner selection. If you were doing a large-scale merger for your corporation, it is doubtful you would consider only those firms you know or that approach you. Rather you would be the aggressive hunter, seeking out the best capability, the best fit for your needs. This approach, when applied to outsourcing, will help ensure your success.

While only a small number of firms will actively seek you out to outsource, don't assume that no one will do so. For example, it is likely that some of your current vendors will approach you seeking to be your outsourcing partner. These could include firms that have developed or delivered training programs for you in the past. And it can include a few megacorporations that have recently turned their training departments into profit centers—and sent them out into the world to hunt for firms such as yours that seek to outsource training. While these firms are worthy of consideration, they are also worthy of a word of caution. Before selecting any of these new-to-training firms, find out if they can *really* meet your needs. It is important to create a list of evaluation criteria and to live by the list as you actively pursue your potential opportunities. Look for the following attributes.

Resourcefulness. The training organizations of megacorporations are often saddled with the same kind of bureaucracy, morale issues, and inflexibility you may be trying to move away from. Very often these organizations are nimble only if you seek the exact solution they have been providing their parent corporations for decades. And it is likely that in the 1990s, if that solution had been effective, they would be protecting it like a trade secret, not trying to offer it to your organization. Be careful about assuming that a large-scale company is resourceful. It may not be resourceful; rather, it may be deep in expensive, unproductive resources that you could wind up subsidizing.

A Demonstrated Record of Creativity. Have all prospects illustrate to you how they have responded to changing requirements. Get a sense of how they staff and manage their assignments. Do they "put an army on it" or a small, nimble team? Are they limited to the range of people they have on staff, or do they consistently engage thought-leaders from both within and outside their organization?

Intellectual and Business Range. When considering your current vendors, it is important to recognize that they may or may not have the range of expertise you need to meet your outsourcing needs. Even if you consider your outsourcing requirements to be narrow in focus, remember you will be entering into a long-term relationship. The last thing you need is to invest substantial time (not to mention money) in a partner only to conclude after a year or so that the partnership is failing because the partner isn't able to respond to changing circumstances because of a lack of vision, intellect, and business acumen.

The current vendors you do business with should be scrutinized carefully in this regard. For example, if you decide to outsource your sales training to the vendor now supporting you, be sure to determine if they can go beyond their current training offerings. Can they adapt to changing market conditions your sales personnel face, benchmark their performance and offer new programs aimed at giving your organization a competitive advantage? Or will they simply be rehashing the same selling techniques for years to come? In short, do they have the intellectual vision and the business range to really add value?

Optimum Financial Viability. Obviously you don't want to partner with a firm that will go bankrupt. Hence you seek a viable organization. And you probably don't want a firm whose viability hinges solely on your business, since that suggests a lack of performance elsewhere. However, it would be wise to select a firm whose financial success will depend on your business. In short, you will have more leverage and buying power if your purchase is a significant portion of the potential partner's revenues—perhaps 20 to 30 percent. That way, you are sure you will be well served and not ignored.

Proven Track Record. Evaluation should include the most careful analysis of references and prior experiences you have ever performed. Given the long-term nature of this relationship, your evaluation should be conducted as if you are an investigative reporter. Seek out all the facts (don't simply accept prima facie statements and testimonials offered to you). A full investigation of potential partners will thoroughly address their long-term track record in terms of customers, suppliers, and employees.

Be bold about your requests. Ask for the names of customers they haven't done business with in several years, not just current customers. Seek out prior employees, not just current employees. Evaluate financial performance over five or six years, not just the current year. Get the truth about each potential partner, not just the hype.

Consistency in Strategy. Firms with zigzag strategies may be risky outsource partners. There is little value in establishing an outsourcing relationship with a company, only to find two years later that the firm has decided to refocus and no longer considers your needs important to its long-term direction.

Quality and Depth of Managerial Talent. The ability of the management team of a potential outsourcing firm will directly influence your satisfaction and their performance. Are the managers hands-on "player-coaches" who will actively participate in meeting your needs? Or are they the old-style hierarchical managers seated in their offices waiting for you to call? Is there sufficient backup and an appropriate mix of management and operational personnel?

Best-in-Class Performance.   Does the potential outsourcing organization exhibit characteristics that others would seek to emulate? Do they have talents and abilities that you have always wished could be developed within your own organization? Or are their talents about the same as those your organization possesses? Even if you consider your own team's talents to be superior, you should strive for an outsourcing partner who can outperform your organization on the dimensions you consider vital. Now is not the time to be myopic. Don't settle for any firm that you don't wish you could emulate.

Willingness and Ability to Absorb Your Personnel.   In many outsourcing situations, the potential vendor's ability to absorb segments of your organization's internal staff becomes an issue. Are the firms you are considering willing and able to participate in this way? What financial or nonfinancial opportunity can they make available? Have they a track record of satisfying employees they have absorbed in this way from prior engagements? Is there willingness to negotiate arrangements like this for a win-win outcome?

Obtain Assistance

Selection of the outsourcing firm is one of the most far-reaching decisions you can make, involving a broad range of experts with diverse experience, and input can only improve the partner identification, evaluation, and selection effort. The exact choice of personnel you need to call on for assistance will depend on your situation and what is available. However, you should at least seek out professionals with expertise in

- Scanning the marketplace for potential firms with which to outsource
- Establishing win-win agreements that meet the expectations of both parties
- Issuing Requests for Proposal for outsourced service
- Addressing legal and taxation issues
- Creating the guiding principles that will bind the relationship with the outsource company
- Creating a contract between your firm and the outsource firm

Addressing these issues is key to the success of the venture. Several are discussed further in subsequent sections.

Establish Win-Win Processes and Performance Objectives

The key to a successful outsourcing relationship is to focus on performance, not just on the proposed fee structure being offered by the possible outsource firms. The more significant the outsourcing in question, the more this performance focus is required. Even if you are outsourcing simply to cut costs, you need to ensure that the work being outsourced does not suffer in order to meet these cost objectives.

Performance objectives can best be defined if the business process being outsourced is clearly documented as it currently exists. Around this process, current and desired performance metrics can be defined in terms of (1) time to complete and (2) desired level of performance in terms of customer satisfaction, targets for defect rates, and the like. Obviously the specific measures will depend on what you are outsourcing.

Issue a Very Specific Request for Proposal (RFP)

Specificity is the key to a successful request for proposal (RFP) in an outsourcing effort. You must be extremely specific in writing about the following issues:

1. What service you seek
2. The performance objectives you require
3. Level of management involvement you expect from the outsource firm
4. Role expected of your organization in managing and interfacing with the outsource firm
5. Economic incentives offered to the outsourced firm for different levels of performance
6. Follow-up audit processes to be used to gauge levels of satisfaction, service, defect rate, and efficiency achieved
7. Process to be used to terminate, should the outsourcing arrangement become unworkable
8. Responsibilities of the outsourcing firm for insurance, indemnity, and other issues of exposure
9. Business process the two parties will use to resolve conflicts that arise as part of the outsourcing relationship

While you should be as specific as possible, also solicit from the respondents specific changes to your RFP that improve the nature of the working relationship. In fact, we recommend that one of the evaluation criteria be the degree to which the respondent can *improve* upon the working framework you have set forth in the RFP.

Outsourcing Firm Selection and Negotiation

Probably the one distinction between this kind of procurement and most others is the need to pay special attention to creating both upside (and downside) performance incentives (disincentives) that both parties can commit to and live by. True, you want to get the best buy for your company. But that best buy may in fact come from the firm offering the highest, not the lowest, bid.

What you need to evaluate is the cost savings of each bid compared to your present method of doing business. For price analysis purposes, that is your benchmark comparison. For example, if it costs you two dollars per head to register a student, any and all bids below that price should be considered. But price is not the only issue. What additional services will the outsource partner provide? What level of service will be offered? Will additional analyses of your enrollment population (e.g., buyer demographics) be provided that you do not now have, and are they of value? The entire service and value proposition must be considered.

In the case of commoditylike services, very often the thrust of the outsource effort should be on how the service, when outsourced, can be transformed into a market advantage. Perhaps this involves using reservationists to provide snippets of information on new course offerings to enrollees. Or perhaps it involves telemarketing during slow periods to present relevant offerings to your company's customers, increasing the leverage of existing training programs. Whatever the specifics, your move into outsourcing should allow you to begin all those things that up to now were on the "can't be done" list.

Create the Outsourcing Contract

Many of the points discussed above should be included in the outsource contract. In particular, your outsource contract should be sure to address incentive performance provisions that are negotiated, the responsibilities of your outsourcer to meet all obligations of the Internal Revenue Service for personnel working on this assignment, insurance and indemnity requirements, and exit processes should the outsourcing arrangement fail.

Remember again, the issue is not one of beating down the vendor, but one of achieving a win-win outcome. After the California earthquake, the California Department of Transportation determined that the cost of not having their highways repaired quickly outweighed other factors. They entered into an incentive contract, tying payment to the speed (e.g., number of days) with which work was completed. As a result, the road was repaired in a time frame that almost everyone thought was impossible. While the construction firm did very well financially, the economic benefits of rapid repair on the state economy far outweighed the incentive costs.

This is an excellent example of a win-win contract. Such contracts should be the goal of your outsourcing. Paranoia about the fees being paid are unfounded if the value created by the outsourcing relationship outweighs the cost. Strive for a contractual relationship that motivates your outsourcing firm to create lots of incremental value and then reward them accordingly.

This notion of incentive win-win relationships is truly effective as long as you can be sure that real value is being created. For example, if you decide to outsource your product and sales training to a third party, establishing an incentive win-win relationship is quite possible. But the focus must be clear. Minimal performance could be defined in terms of student satisfaction with the training they are receiving, as measured by postworkshop evaluations. But there should be minimal incentive premium associated with that metric. Rather, significant upside performance should be tied to real-time actual performance in the field by trained sales personnel. This real-time performance, continuously monitored by a qualified third party, should gauge such key actual measures as

- Number of customers who find that their sales teams can accurately explain product features

- Number of customers who find that sales teams can accurately pinpoint and address business requirements

- Increases in win-backs driven by customer realization that sales personnel offer cost-effective solutions

- Number of times customers accurately understand the economics of your organization's product over its life cycle, going beyond the purchase price

Metrics such as these, if they improve, suggest that your outsourced training provides your firm with a competitive advantage and increased revenue, and, therefore, your outsource partner is worthy of some incentive premium.

The common counterargument made about such situations is that there are many nontraining factors that also influence these metrics. Thus an outsource partner may be disadvantaged in such an arrangement. Many believe this argument is a cop-out. In truth, an incentive program will lead a worthy sales training partner to fully explore the kind of interventions that will improve performance where it matters—with the end-customer. It will motivate the firm to refocus and reframe both training and related interventions so that real value is created. Your training outsourcer will rightfully seek a place at the sales organization's planning table, with you, to offer suggestions, stay up-to-date on new product developments, and offer market intelligence. In effect, this incentive moves the firm from a vendor role to a more true partner role.

It is worth noting that third-party monitoring of real-time actual customer reaction can provide an accurate barometer as to how your sales team is performing compared to the competition's. That investigation can be carefully structured to separate results attributable to the training initiative from other factors such as favorable pricing, advantageous products, and the like. Thus, the risk of rewarding your outsource partner for serendipitous results is minimized.

Conversely, your outsourcing partner may accurately argue that its performance is hindered by a number of factors beyond its control, nontraining factors that affect performance. Two remedies should be considered. First, your partners should be engaged as fully as possible in the business process so they actually do have an influence on the factors they perceive as beyond their control. To some extent, these uncontrollable factors can be minimized simply by giving the outsource partner access to the issues—and an opportunity to contribute input and influence the outcome. Second, be practical about the incentive you negotiate. If there are numerous uncontrollable events, don't try to negotiate performance penalties, only performance improvement rewards.

Effective incentives are simple incentives that both parties agree on. And they are incentives that reach win-win not only in theory but also in practice. Testing the feasibility of these win-win incentives is an important goal of the pilot phase of the effort.

Launch a Pilot Phase

No product or system would go to market without a thorough shakedown period. The same is true for a well-conceived outsourcing effort. In fact, the more significant the outsourcing effort, the more stringent and carefully monitored the pilot phase must be. It must be clear to the outsourcing firm that this period is not simply a "best behavior trial." That is, you cannot live with a situation where the outsourcing effort proceeds well during the trial and falls apart thereafter. The trial is used to ensure that the outsourcing relationship *meets* or *exceeds* the minimally acceptable performance standards for the relationship.

Ongoing Monitoring and Evaluation

Implicit in the outsourcing contract is the continuous monitoring and evaluation of the outsourcer's performance. Such measures can be simple or complex. Simple measures include meeting critical dates for deliverables, posttraining evaluations and the like. More complex measures can include ongoing analysis of performance for individuals who have attended the training and those who have not. Such measures may only be available in the short term, since training that is deemed to be beneficial should be provided to all personnel for whom the training is appropriate.

It is also important that performance measures be reevaluated over the life of the outsourced work. In this way, the changing expectations of both parties can be met over time. This is especially important in outsourced work where fees are a function of performance.

Summary

In the first few paragraphs of this chapter, you learned that outsourcing is not new. What is true, however, is that today it is entering a new, expanded, highly sophisticated era as a business practice. Indeed, as this is being written, business leaders in the United States are predicting that most or all major companies will be outsourcing multiple business functions within the next two to three years. As companies today strive to excel at core competencies, reinvent themselves, and be more competitive, it's a safe bet that outsourcing will continue to accelerate in all areas, including the training function.

In the foregoing pages, you've been prompted to look at the myriad of challenges and complex issues facing those considering the outsourcing of company training and education. How do you evaluate outsourcing needs? What can and what should be outsourced? What are the benefits? How do you develop an outsourcing strategy and properly structure and implement a program? And, since not all outsourcing is successful, you've also been prompted to evaluate the risks involved and be leery of certain pitfalls. Most important, there are sections on how to select the best outsourcing partner and contract and manage the relationship for optimum results.

Whether, or how, outsourcing makes sense for your company or organization training is today a strategic determination requiring careful study. This chapter has been designed to focus on the right questions—for those seeking the right answers.

Appendix

The following examples are provided as illustrations of outsourcing:

Example 1: A Global Electronics Firm (Partner)

A global electronics firm located in an exurban midwest community had developed a very capable internal staff of developers and presenters. Because of the technological nature of the company's products, it was necessary to provide training in close proximity to the company's R&D labs. Because of the company's location, there were not enough "business hotels" nearby and training participants were forced to drive long distances between the hotel and the training center. In addition, the training facilities were simple meeting rooms, not designed for training.

The company partnered with a national conference center company which agreed to manage the development and operations of a residential training facility (named after the company) paid for by the electronics firm. For its investment, the electronics firm would have priority in using the facility and be allowed to keep a percentage of the total revenues of the facility.

Benefits

- Obtains the use of a "convenient" residential training facility
- Receives a return on its investment in the facility
- Becomes known for its training expertise and facilities

Example 2: A Computer Services Firm (Outsource)

During a recent economic downturn, a large midwestern heavy equipment manufacturer decided to "sell" the services of its internal computer services support team to other organizations. This move would allow the company to keep its team intact while it weathered the economic storm. For legal reasons, the team became a subsidiary of the manufacturer.

Although the support team had the necessary technical skills to perform for external customers, they did not know how to sell their services. The company hired an outside sales training organization to perform a needs analysis as well as develop and deliver the sales training.

The ultimate result: The support team performed so well the subsidiary was sold for over $10 million. As part of the sale, the manufacturer was provided with a long-term "at cost" contract for the new computer company's services.

Benefits

- Much more effective than developing the training internally
- The training organization provided a turnkey solution
- The company made money by ultimately selling the expertise it had purchased

Example 3: A Canadian Generic Pharmaceutical Manufacturer (Partner)

As part of its strategy, a Canadian generic pharmaceutical manufacturer wanted to sell its product line in the United States. Although the products were successfully being sold in Canada, the company understood that in order to sell in the United States, it needed to comply with Food and Drug Administration (FDA) regulations.

The company knew that the window of opportunity was going to be open for only a short time and it needed to "get smart" on the FDA's Good Manufacturing Practices. Rather than develop its own program, the manufacturer decided to contract with an American company that had developed and delivered similar training to many U.S. pharmaceutical firms. The costs of materials and delivery were under $10,000. This amount was less than 20 percent of the company's estimate to develop the materials and deliver the training internally.

Not only was the training delivered on target, but it was delivered within days of initial discussions.

Benefits

- Savings were significant.
- The company was able to do business within the window of opportunity.
- The company improved its own training capability.

51

Consultants

Scott B. Parry

Scott B. Parry is chairman of Training House in Princeton, New Jersey, and consultant to more than 50 of the Fortune 500 organizations. Active in ASTD, he is a frequent speaker at national conferences and regional meetings. Prior to founding Training House in 1971, Parry was president of Training Development Center, a division of Sterling Institute, in New York. He worked with the ASTD Metropolitan chapter and New York University to set up an adult education program of 10 courses for training and development professionals, and served on the faculty of NYU as principal instructor of the program. Parry's speaking and consulting engagements have taken him to 6 continents and 39 countries. He holds a B.A. from Princeton, an M.S. from Boston University, and a Ph.D. from New York University.

According to the membership list of ASTD, one out of every seven members is a training consultant. A growth in the number of books, articles, and workshops on the subject of HRD consulting is further evidence that more and more organizations have turned to outside resources for help in training and developing their employees. The hiring of consultants must be done on the same basis that any sound purchasing decision is made: through cost-benefit analysis. A client invests in training to help people perform in ways that benefit them and their enterprise. Consultants who cannot earn an organization more money than they cost should not be retained.

Consultant Defined

Let us start by agreeing on what a consultant is—and is not. Most trainers are familiar with one or two of the negative, tongue-in-cheek definitions that abound:

- A consultant is someone who borrows your watch, tells you the time, then keeps it.
- A consultant is someone who can help you go wrong with confidence.
- A consultant is an expert, which comes from the Latin *ex* meaning "has been" or "former," and *spurt,* meaning "a large drip or gush."
- Those who *can do* will do; those who *can't do* will consult.
- A consultant is anyone farther than 50 miles from home and carrying an attaché case costing more than $100.

Fortunately, similar derogatory comments are made about doctors, lawyers, and other professionals, and so we need not take them too seriously. They are, in fact, symptomatic of a universal problem that all of us face: knowing when we do and do not need outside help, be it the help of a consultant, doctor, lawyer, or TV repairperson. Because we lack the knowledge and experience that professionals bring us, we are uncertain about how to utilize their services and how to evaluate their performance.

For our purposes, let's agree to define a training consultant as any outside individual or firm who is paid primarily to deliver professional training advice, instruction, or customized development of material. Notice that this definition excludes outside suppliers of films, public seminars, cassettes, audiovisual hardware or software, tests, and other training products or services that are purchased "off the shelf." Of course, our definition does not bar consultants from having a product line. Indeed, those who have been in the consulting business for at least several years are likely to have favorite activities and exercises that they bring to new clients. Experience in using these is one of the consultant's main assets provided they fit the client's needs. Many publishers of instructional systems have a capability and interest in customizing their products to meet their user's requirements. It is here that their publishing activity ends and consulting begins.

In short, a consultant may offer both products and services, but the primary focus must be on the client's needs and not on the sale of existing products. This requires an ability to carry out a needs analysis, to customize, and to provide the supportive service needed to enable a client to get the performance that was specified at the start.

Although our definition and discussion so far have been based on the assumption that the consultant is an outsider, an increasing number of organizations now have internal consultants—specialists in organizational development, human resource utilization, technical training, and so on. An increasing trend is to charge their services to the using department through a system of cross-budget credits and debits. These staff specialists often have more in common with the outside consultant than they do with the training director.

When to Use a Consultant

Three major reasons, or needs, prompt companies to use training consultants:

- The need to expand capability on an ad hoc basis—when time is short and stakes are high. Many organizations keep a lean training department whose staff members are problem solvers, internal consultants, or project managers who call on outsiders to create and/or deliver courses.
- The need for specialized *expertise* or *facilities.* The design or selection of needs analysis instruments and/or specialized instructional techniques may require

professional skills that can be purchased from an outsider as needed for much less than it would cost to recruit or develop and maintain this expertise internally.

- The need for the "intangibles" of *objectivity* or *corporate leverage* to get a job done. This is a political reason for using an outside consultant whose neutrality and/or credibility is an asset in terms of seeing the problem in a fresh perspective and getting top management to listen. Training managers know all too well that prophets are never heeded in their own country. Outsiders may command attention and be catalysts in getting things done, whereas insiders would have difficulty (either because their personal stakes in the outcome render them suspect or simply because they lack experience, credentials, or leverage).

Given these reasons for employing outside help, let us examine some of the major types of client engagements that consultants accept. Some training consultants are specialists, and others are generalists who have competence in a broad range of activities. Surveying the range of firms and individuals that identify themselves *primarily* as training consultants, we find their activities falling into one or more of the categories listed in Fig. 51-1.

Note that we have avoided any reference to the consultant's area of expertise—sales management, bank teller training, etc. A company seeking outside help should look for a consultant with experience in the same industry or functional area (sales). Of course, it is often not possible to find a consultant who is both the subject-matter expert (SME) and the behavioral technologist. In most engagements, the client provides the SME who works with the outside consultant. This kind of partnership usually produces a more satisfactory and more cost-effective

---

a. ANALYSIS—analysis of human performance and assessment of organizational and individual needs. Includes task analysis, systems analysis, behavioral analysis, establishing behavioral objectives and performance criteria, and use of tests and survey research.

b. DESIGN—design of training programs. Includes research to determine course content and a design rationale for selecting methods and media, instructional strategies, criterion tests, and decisions on administering the instruction—when, where, how often, for whom, by whom, etc.

c. PRODUCTION—preparation of instructional materials. Writing of training manuals, programmed instruction, cases, role plays, instructor guidelines, games and simulations, assessments, script for tape, creation of slides, film, videotape or disc, computer-based training, etc.

d. INSTRUCTING—presenting in-company courses (either public, tailored, or homegrown) in such areas as sales training, management by objectives, problem solving, management development, transactional analysis, sensitivity training, "train-the-trainer" workshops, and dozens of other topics.

e. IMPLEMENTING—installing instructional systems, pilot testing, revising as needed, and training of client's instructors in how to administer the course(s) on a continuing basis.

f. EVALUATING—evaluation and/or design of performance development systems. Performance appraisal, job analysis, preparation of job descriptions, assessment labs, skills inventories, placement, career planning succession programs, and OD work.

Figure 51-1. Major types of activities of training consultants.

end result than is possible when the client and consultant work separately on the assumption that the consultant possesses all the subject-matter expertise needed to fill the engagement.

Defining the Job

From the client's viewpoint, our "inventory of activities" listed in Fig. 51-1 should help to identify the nature and scope of services you are looking for. Thereafter, it is much easier to *select* the type of consultant who can best meet your needs and to agree on the division of labor between your staff and the consultant's.

Let us illustrate this:

- If you are interested in carrying out a needs analysis and in receiving professional advice on systems design (items a, b, e, and f in Fig. 51-1), then you should seek a consultant who has problem-solving skills, research design experience, maturity, and a following of clients for whom these services have been performed satisfactorily.

- If you are interested in finding outside help in putting together a course (items b and c), then you should find a consultant who has experience and creative skills in the various instructional methods and media, including both *presentation systems* (video, slides, overhead, etc.) and *practice and feedback systems* (role-play, case method, games and simulations, etc.).

- If you are interested in finding a consultant to teach in-company courses for you (item d), then you will look for someone with a dynamic personality, subject-matter expertise, and a catalytic teaching style that produces a high degree of learner interest and participation.

These three examples illustrate the same point: You must know what you want done before you seek out a consultant, and you should look for and be able to identify a consultant who has the skills to do the job. This sounds like a truism, and yet we could all point to examples of firms that have engaged consultants without first establishing the nature and scope of their involvement and the performance criteria against which they would be evaluated. Figure 51-2 might be useful to client and consultant alike in helping them to define what work is to be done and by whom.

Guidelines for Selecting Consultants

Unlike the purchase of tangible goods, the selection of a consultant carries with it a mystique that often finds buyers putting their trust in the seller's hands. To a certain degree this is true—much as you trust your doctor, lawyer, or TV repairman. What we are discussing, of course, is *trust*, and *confidence*. This is perhaps the first quality to look for.

Does your consultant inspire confidence, or do you think twice about giving out information and being completely candid? A professional consultant will protect the interest of your company; a nonprofessional may carry tales outside

PLANNING AND DEFINING	1. Specify organizational objectives.
	2. Perform a needs analysis. (Identify the knowledge, attitudes, skills needed to perform.)
	3. Specify performance objectives for the workplace.
	4. Specify terminal behaviors (learning objectives).
	5. Specify entering behaviors of trainees.
	6. Develop a criterion test.
STRUCTURING AND ENLARGING	7. Determine course content: facts, skills, procedures, attitudes, concepts, principles, rules, techniques, etc.
	8. Organize material in a "teachable" way: a. Progression from simple to complex. b. Relate the new to the old; build a web of learning. c. Organize material in a "logical" way: chronological and psychological, in addition to the "logical" order in which it has always been done.
	9. Flesh out the content outline: draw examples from the real world of behavior, illustrations, anecdotes to bring things to life.
	10. Ask management to review materials developed to this point: make revisions, if necessary, and obtain go-ahead.
STRATEGY AND METHOD	11. Determine instructional strategies—concepts vs. rote, inductive vs. deductive, etc. Keep in mind, "We learn not by being told, but by experiencing the consequences of our actions."
	12. Decide on instructional methods—lecture, text, slides, photos. Both presentation and response methods must be built into the instructional system, so that the learner may respond in an audial mode (discussion, question and answer, cases) or a visual mode (draw diagram, make visual discrimination).
	13. Determine the media and packaging of the course.
DEVELOPMENT AND TESTING	14. Write the course (or supervise the writing of it).
	15. Review by management and SMEs of the material in as close to finished production form as possible. (This review is for content—not format.)
	16. Developmentally test the course with 1, 2, or 3 trainees at a time.
	17. Revise accordingly.
	18. Prepare a field tryout edition of the course.
	19. Select a sample of the population of trainees to try out the course.
	20. Train the administrators of the field test.
	21. Conduct the field test.
	22. Analyze the data from the field test.
	23. Revise accordingly (another tryout necessary?)
PRODUCTION AND INSTALLATION	24. Prepare final version of course, using professional narration, artwork, etc. Order in quantity (or schedule seminars, etc.).
	25. Distribute materials and train the trainers (provide instructor guidelines, test score key, data collection forms).

Figure 51-2. Steps in the design of an instructional system. (*Training House, Inc.*)

the company, steal key people from you, or work for your competitor immediately after completing your contract. (You may want to include a "noncompetitive work" clause in your contract.)

The client should examine the consultant's desire for a long-term relationship—many consultants develop a pattern of going from client to client rather than building longer relationships with a base group of clients.

A second quality you should look for in a training consultant is a solid *understanding* of your problem or need. Listen to the questions your consultant asks and the manner in which he or she goes about testing you and your assumptions relating to the need. Some consultants have one or two techniques, instruments, or methods which, they will assure you, are just what you need. Others may focus on the abilities or experience of key persons in their firm. Still others spend much of their time describing specific problems they solved for other clients relating an impressive array of success stories.

However useful it might be to have a consultant that can bring you proved methods, key people, and success stories, the real test of professional consultants is their ability to listen, probe, test, analyze, and thereby come to grips with *your* problem. Listen to see how much time the consultant spends discussing his or her capabilities versus your needs. What is the ratio between the two? Which does the consultant want to talk about first? The answers to these two questions can be quite revealing, and they may help you to separate professionals from those who have solutions in search of problems.

The outstanding training consultants are those who have sold their services and proved their worth on the basis of their understanding of the client's problems, needs, resources, and constraints. In entering a new engagement, they bring with them experience, but they reserve judgment on what is called for until they have first listened to the client and done their own independent data gathering. Professionals know that their objectivity is a major part of their value.

A third quality to look for is the consultant's ability to *reduce uncertainty.* Uncertainty always accompanies change. Often the solving of one set of problems or needs may produce another set. We identified earlier the three most common reasons for engaging a consultant: shortage of *time,* shortage of *expertise,* and shortage of *objectivity* or *corporate leverage.* Behind each of these is the client's desire to reduce uncertainty. This is the fundamental service that the experienced, professional consultant can provide. The novice can bring specialized knowledge and skills to a client, but an inexperienced consultant is often unable to reduce risk for the client (and, in many cases, may actually increase the probability of failure).

In selecting a consultant, find out how he or she proposes to reduce risk or develop benefits. What controls and checkpoints will be used to measure progress? What prior successes and failures (with reasons why) has the consultant had with other clients? Does the consultant talk about results and successes, or does the talk center on products and services to be provided? In selecting a consultant, you should check with two or three current clients to get the answers to these questions.

There are many other factors to look for in selecting consultants, of course. Here are a few:

- Is your consultant concerned with making you and your program a success, or is he or she on an ego trip, using your organization to meet personality needs? (Many consultants have strong ego needs; the issue is whether these needs are satisfied as a by-product of meeting the needs of your organization.)

- How fast does the consultant grasp your operations, the opportunities and constraints, and the nature of the interpersonal relations (company politics, personal rivalries, etc.)? Are the consultant's people-handling skills equal to the task-handling skills?

- How will your fellow managers perceive the consultant? Will the consultant make friends for you in making contacts with other employees, or is there a danger that the consultant will embarrass you or cause others to wonder why you brought in such a person?

- How much time will the principal or principals in the consulting firm be spending with you? Do you know who will be assigned to the contract? Are you getting the "first team" or "second stringers"?

- Are you seeking a "bargain" or a "value" in selecting a consultant? Can the consultant contribute in ways that will build the success of your own organization? Is the consultant a good businessperson?

- What successful projects has the consultant handled? What is the quality of the samples of work submitted? What references can the consultant give you, and what do they have to say?

- Does your consultant have back-up capability? Or are you putting all your eggs in one basket? Is the consultant an individual or an organization? If the latter, what depth?

- What interest does the consultant show in your business? How important is your project to the financial vitality of the consultant?

- How does the consultant go about managing projects? Deadlines and control of the "critical path"? What evidence do you have of the consultant's planning, scheduling, and controlling skills (PERT, CPM, Gantt charts, etc.)?

Once an organization has determined the qualities needed in a consultant, a decision matrix can be drawn up and numerical ratings assigned to each candidate. This is illustrated in Fig. 51-3. The qualities listed are not all of equal importance. Hence, each one has been assigned a "weight" from 1 to 10 to reflect its relative importance. Each option (in this case, three candidates) can then be rated on a scale of 1 to 5. By multiplying the *weight* of each quality by the *rating* assigned to each potential consultant and adding the resulting products, we arrive at a "bottom-line" evaluation that identifies the best-qualified consultant...in our example, William Smith and Associates.

The Needs Analysis

When we select a doctor, lawyer, accountant, architect, or other professional, their work for us usually begins with a needs analysis. Questions are asked and data is collected and analyzed. So it is with training consultants. Sometimes the organization will have already completed a needs analysis before locating a consultant, although experience suggests that the client-consultant relationship and the quality of the information obtained will be better if both parties work on the needs analysis as a team.

Since it is sometimes difficult to agree on a contract for services to be rendered until the needs analysis is complete, many consulting firms will undertake this phase of a project on a per diem basis, billing only for labor and out-of-pocket expenses until the nature and scope of the consultancy has been defined. The major kinds of methods and tools used in conducting a needs analysis are listed in Fig. 51-4. Typically, a needs analysis may last from several days to several months. It gives both client and consultant the opportunity to see each other at

There are five major methods for collecting data in a needs analysis. Each is listed below, along with examples of the tools that can be used to generate new information (as in 1 and 2) or to capture existing information (as in 3). In a typical needs analysis, no more than two or three are employed. Organizational audits (3) are best when they yield *reliable, valid,* and *sufficient* data, since 3 does not take employees away from their work. However, these criteria are often not present in 3, and trainers must use survey research (1) and simulation assessments (2) to generate information that cannot be captured via organizational audits (3).

1. SURVEY RESEARCH
   - interviewing—present job holders, new trainees, supervisors, customers
   - questionnaire—mailed or filled out at work, alone, or in researcher's presence
   - "climate survey"—to measure morale, commitment, work environment, attitude
   - tests of proficiency—writing skill, knowledge of supervisory practices, circuitry
   - attitude survey—management style, communication style, etc.
   - "critical incident" research ("Recall a recent situation in which . . .")

2. SIMULATION ASSESSMENTS
   - assessment lab in managerial skills, via videotape or live experience
   - in-basket and managerial appraisals
   - role playing (e.g., selling skills, interviewing, supervisory skills)
   - case analysis (e.g., in problem-solving and decision-making skills)

3. ORGANIZATIONAL AUDITS
   A. TASK ANALYSIS AND SYSTEM ANALYSIS
   - flow charting of procedures and work flow
   - work distribution study and analysis of time sheets
   - methods improvement and work simplification
   - "present vs. proposed" analysis of work elements
   - operation analysis, person-machine analysis

   B. OBSERVATION ON THE JOB
   - participant observer (as "coworker")
   - nonparticipant observer: obtrusive and unobtrusive research
   - "shopping survey"—retail sales, banks, airlines, etc.
   - telephone shopping of employees at work

   C. RECORDS CHECK
   - reports on file: call reports, incidents reports, grievances, etc.
   - systems and procedures documentation (flowcharts, etc.)
   - methods and procedures manuals, training guides, etc.
   - complaints, error rates, "squeaky wheel" data
   - job descriptions, performance appraisals, etc.
   - library research—trade association data, competitor's data, studies by industry, use of experts, commercially available courses, etc.

Figure 51-4. Needs analysis methods and tools. (*Training House, Inc.*)

analysis may make use of a combination of research techniques (see Fig. 51-4) and may require many months. In such cases, the client and consultant usually enter into contract to cover the needs analysis phase of the work (with a subsequent contract to cover the materials development phase). Their preliminary per diem time is then spent together in determining what information they want and why and how they plan to get it during the needs analysis.

A word of caution regarding the needs analysis: Many training managers (or their top management) are action-oriented and do not enjoy seeing a lot of time and money spent on research to determine the need. "We *know* we need training," they are quick to tell the consultant. "So why spend a lot of time carrying out a needs analysis?" A little selling (educating, if you prefer) may be called for to make sure that client and consultant are agreed on the values obtained. A list of the major reasons for doing a needs analysis is shown in Fig. 51-5. But all these reasons can be summed up in Bob Mager's delightful parable of the seahorse who observed that "if you don't know where you are or where you want to be, you're not very likely to get there."[1]

Note our seventh reason in Fig. 51-5. This is the one that enables client and consultant to make decisions regarding the design and implementation of the instructional system: Who will be trained? Where, when, and in what sequence will they be trained? What criteria, standards, objectives, etc., will be used to measure performance? What course content, methods, media, and instructional strategies will be employed? How will the system be administered? Who will teach, who will collect performance data, who will promote the program and enroll the trainees, etc.? These are the questions that should be answered at the end of the needs analysis phase. These answers mark the beginning of the materials development and systems design phase.

Those who have been in the field of training for some time have learned, often painfully, that not every problem is a training problem. We could point to courses we have put together which were very good training programs (from an instructional systems design standpoint) but which failed to produce the desired terminal behavior in the trainee. A consultant who has (1) experience working with many firms, (2) a behavioral scientist's outlook, and (3) an understanding of the many organizational factors affecting human performance can be especially helpful in counseling a client on the degree to which training per se will and will not be useful in producing behavior change. The research tools used to carry out a needs analysis are valuable in helping a firm to identify the factors that are at work in producing or hindering the desired performance (organizational climate, reinforcement and feedback systems, work-station design, work flow, design of forms and procedures, recruitment and placement policies, and so on).

Contracts and Agreements

Once the nature and scope of the work to be performed have been determined by client and consultant, a contract or letter of agreement can be drawn up. Some consultants write their proposal in such a way that it can be signed by both parties and serve as the agreement. However, a proposal is mainly written to sell, and it may lack protections that the client wants (e.g., noncompetitive assurances, nondisclosure warranty, terms of nonacceptability).

Organizations that make frequent or recurring use of consultants to deliver seminars, conduct interviews, handle needs analyses and assessments, etc., have found it convenient to use a standard consulting agreement (see Fig. 51-6) that can be kept on file as an "umbrella contract." Each new assignment is treated as

1. To find out <u>what</u> the present level of performance is. By establishing a "bench level" of present behavior (performance), we can measure change over time. That is, a needs analysis will give us pretraining measures which we can compare with our posttraining measures (assuming we give training. . . there may be other ways besides training to improve performance).

2. To determine <u>why</u> present performance is what it is. Why are those whom we'll be training performing as they are? What reinforcers are maintaining their behavior? What contingencies and constraints are preventing better performance? What is the relative strength of each of the factors affecting human performance, both positively and negatively? What can be done to increase the positive and reduce the negative?

3. To find out <u>who</u> the trainees are. What entering behavior do they bring to the job? What strengths can we build on? What deficiences do they possess? How universal are these? How homogeneous or heterogenous is our population of trainees? Should they be subgrouped for ease of administering different modules of training to deal with individual differences?

4. To assess the <u>organizational climate</u> or work environment within which the trainee operates. Will it support and nourish the behavior we will shape through training, or will it discourage and cause it to die? What can we do to improve climate? How can we prepare the trainee, his or her boss, customers, etc., to maintain a supportive climate?

5. To examine the <u>systems and procedures</u> employed with a view toward identifying ways of working smarter instead of harder. Can steps, tasks, forms, etc., possibly be eliminated, resequenced, combined, simplified to produce better behavior (increased output, reduced error, easier work, etc.)? Methods improvement and work simplification should always be examined as a possibility throughout your study of tasks performed, work stations, work flow, and who does what.

6. To establish <u>behavioral objectives</u>. . . measurable, observable, specific performance goals that each trainee must achieve as a result of training and/or whatever other changes (e.g., organizational, motivational) you identify as essential to producing and maintaining the desired behaviors. These objectives can be analyzed and sorted into subcategories for convenience in designing our subsequent behavior-shaping strategies. For example, behavior might be classified as cognitive, affective, and psychomotor (knowing, feeling, doing). . . or as knowledge, attitudes, skills (since not all skills are psychomotor—e.g., interviewing, proofreading). Skills might be further classified as task-handling and people-handling.

7. To establish <u>policy and make decisions</u> regarding the length, scope, format, location, cost, frequency, etc., of training. Examples of these decisions: initial vs. continuation (i.e., how much or how little to teach initially vs. subsequently); formal vs. OJT (i.e., "vestibule" and classroom vs. training by supervisor on the job); make vs. buy; head vs. book (must know "cold" vs. can look up or ask someone); centralized vs. decentralized training; individual vs. group (self-instruction vs. group-based); etc.

8. To <u>involve line managers</u> and others in your organization whose support and whose inputs are important to the success of your training efforts (e.g., the bosses of your trainees, the subject matter experts, the influentials. By getting them ego-involved at the start and forming a "partnership" with them you can rely on them to promote and sell training (or make changes in procedures, systems, reinforcement schedules, etc.).

Figure 51-5. Reasons for conducting a needs analysis. (*Training House, Inc.*)

an addendum and referred to in the agreement as an exhibit. This can be a one- or two-page description of the assignment, the time frame, and the costs and payment schedule.

A major advantage of the standard consulting agreement is that training managers to not have to wait for the legal department to draft or approve contracts for each new consulting engagement, which can be time-consuming. The training manager can usually draft a letter for each new engagement (Exhibit A, B, C, etc.) without legal approval.

THIS CONSULTING AGREEMENT (the "Agreement") made and entered into this —day of —, 19— by and between _____ ("Company") and _____ ("Consultant").

WITNESSETH:

WHEREAS, Consultant is in the business of preparing and conducting seminars and providing training services relating to the business of Company; and

WHEREAS, Company desires Consultant to present such seminars and/or perform related services for Company, on the terms and conditions hereinafter set forth;

NOW, THEREFORE, in consideration of the premises and the mutual promises and agreements contained herein, the parties hereto, intending to be legally bound, hereby agree as follows:

SECTION 1.   *Consultant Undertakings.*
a. Consultant shall prepare for and carry out each Assignment (seminar, survey, assessment, etc.) according to the guidelines set forth in this agreement and the terms and conditions contained in a supplemental letter agreement ("Supplemental Agreement"), which, when signed by Consultant and Company, will become an exhibit to this agreement and will be incorporated herein. The Supplemental Agreement will set forth the specifics of each Assignment, including but not limited to, the description of work, dates, and fees to be paid to Consultant in connection with the services rendered.

SECTION 2.   *Confidentiality.*
In conjunction with the rendering of services by Consultant, it is anticipated that Company has disclosed or may disclose to Consultant or Consultant may come in contact with or observe certain confidential information, including trade secrets, that is the property of the Company. Such information shall be held in strict confidence by Consultant and, from the date hereof through two years following the termination of this Agreement, shall not be disclosed to any third party without the prior written permission of Company.

SECTION 3.   *Fees.*
a. The fees to be paid to Consultant ("Consulting Fee") for each Assignment conducted by Consultant during the term of this agreement will be specified in the Supplemental Agreement mentioned above. In the event of the cancellation of any scheduled Assignment, Company shall give Consultant thirty (30) days prior written notice of such cancellation. Subject to the Company's timely notification of cancellation, Company shall not be obligated to pay Consultant the Consulting Fee for the seminar cancelled. Company and Consultant may mutually agree upon a rescheduled date during the same calendar year for any Assignment cancelled without any liability to either party.
b. The Consulting Fee is payable within thirty (30) days of receipt by Company of Contractor's invoice and is subject to the provisions of Section 4 hereof.
c. Company shall reimburse Consultant for reasonable out-of-pocket expenses and traveling expenses (tourist class only) incurred at the direction of Company. Consultant shall submit invoices with documentation satisfactory to Company in order to receive reimbursement for such expenses.

SECTION 4.   *Term of Agreement.*
a. This Agreement shall have an initial term of one (1) year, automatically extending for renewal terms of one (1) year unless either party gives written notice to the other of its intention not to renew the agreement at least thirty (30) days prior to the end of the initial term or any renewal term.
b. The Agreement may be terminated as follows:
   (i) At any time by the mutual consent of the parties;
   (ii) By Company, unilaterally by, and effective upon, the giving of written notice to Consultant, if Consultant breaches any warranty contained in the Agreement;
   (iii) By Company, unilaterally for any reason by, and effective upon, the giving of thirty (30) days' written notice to Consultant.

Figure 51-6. Standard consulting agreement.

c. If the Agreement is terminated at any time after the date hereof pursuant to subsection 4b(i) or 4b(ii) of this Section 4, Company's sole obligation shall be to pay Consultant any amount properly accrued to the account of Consultant under Section 3 hereof to the date of termination, and Consultant shall have no right to receive any other payment of any nature whatsoever.

SECTION 5. *Representations and Warranties.*

Consultant represents and warrants that it has the experience, ability and expertise to carry out the Assignment as described in the Agreement; that Consultant's services hereunder shall be performed in a good, professional and workmanlike manner; that the services furnished hereunder will be suitable to Company's purposes; that no part of the services furnished hereunder will in any way infringe upon or violate any rights whatsoever of any third persons; and that Consultant is authorized to enter into the Agreement and that the undersigned is authorized to sign the Agreement on behalf of Consultant.

SECTION 6. *Indemnification.*

Consultant agrees to indemnify and hold Company, its divisions and subsidiaries and agents, representatives and employees thereof, harmless from and defend same against every claim, damage, loss, liability and suit (including interest and attorneys' fees) caused or alleged to have been caused by any breach of warranty or by acts or omissions of Consultant in connection with performance under the Agreement or arising out of any contractual obligations of Consultant to third parties in connection with the services to be provided pursuant to the Agreement.

SECTION 7. *Miscellaneous.*

a. *Independent Contractor.* Consultant is and shall be an independent contractor, and it has no authority to bind Company in any way.

b. *Governing Law.* The Agreement shall be interpreted, construed and governed by and in accordance with the laws of the State of _____, where Company is located.

c. *Headings.* The section and paragraph headings contained in the Agreement are for reference purposes only and shall not affect in any way the meaning or interpretation of this Agreement.

d. *Waivers.* All waivers must be in writing, and the waiver by either party of a breach or violation of any provision of this Agreement shall not operate as or be construed to be a waiver or subsequent breach hereof.

e. *Assignment.* The Agreement shall not be assigned in whole or in part without the written consent of Company.

f. *Entire Agreement.* The Agreement embodies the full and complete understanding of the parties hereto and supersedes any previous agreement, written or oral, relating to the subject matter hereof. The Agreement may be modified only by written instrument signed by each of the parties hereto.

IN WITNESS WHEREOF, Company and Consultant have executed this Agreement under seal as of the date first above written.

COMPANY: _____
By: _____
Title: _____

CONSULTANT: _____
By: _____
Title: _____

Figure 51-6. (*Continued*) Standard consulting agreement.

Many organizations have made use of consultants over the years without entering into contracts with them. Both parties may feel that a contract is unnecessary...perhaps even a statement of distrust, a step backward in their relationship. These are the same feelings that managers experience when an organization embarks on a management by objectives (MBO) program and now requires managers to put down on paper the things they plan to accomplish, with time frames and costs. "Haven't I been doing a good job?" is their natural reaction. "Don't you trust me?"

Although issues of trust are addressed in a contract or letter of agreement, their primary purpose is to make sure that both parties have given enough thought to the assignment that it will be performed to the satisfaction and benefit of both parties. Contracts are a form of self-discipline; they force clearer and deeper thinking than is usually present in face-to-face (oral) agreements. As such, they minimize the chance of a "win-lose" outcome in which one party benefited at the expense of the other. In short, a contract is the proverbial "ounce of prevention, worth a pound of cure."

Fees and Billing

As discussed earlier, consultants generally charge for their services on either a project basis (i.e., fixed-fee) or a time-plus-expenses basis (i.e., per diem). Either way, charges are based primarily on the consultant's time. When the nature and scope of the work to be done can be defined very specifically in advance, with agreement between consultant and client on the amount of time each will spend on the project, then it is appropriate to have a fixed fee for the project. However, many consulting engagements are subject to the "iceberg" phenomenon: Neither client nor consultant knows what lies beneath the surface—they can see only a small fraction of the mass. Projects of this nature should be priced on a per diem basis; otherwise, one party will inevitably end up being "short-changed."

For this reason, many consulting engagements are planned in two phases, with Phase 1 being the needs analysis phase (the activities described in Fig. 51-4). Here it is appropriate for the consultant to bill on a per diem basis. One of the objectives of a needs analysis, of course, is to define in precise terms the kinds of activities (courses, materials, etc.) that are needed. Once client and consultant have defined these, a fixed-fee contract is usually desired by both parties: *Clients* must budget specific amounts and are glad to have the "open-ended" phase 1 behind them, and *consultants* like the incentive of performing within the time estimates on which the fixed fee was based, thereby increasing the profit margin.

Both client and consultant have cash-flow needs, and it is important for both to agree on how and when fees are to be paid. Some contracts simply divide the total contract price into equal payments payable monthly (or at equal time intervals) throughout the contract. Others will make payments contingent on delivery of the specified products or services. Thus a contract covering the production of a course to be done in eight modules (lessons, cassettes, weeks, locations, etc.) might be billed in nine equal payments: the first is payable upon signing the agreement, the second is payable upon delivery of module 1, and so on. However, if the course is useless until all eight modules are delivered, the payment schedule might be weighted toward the back end of the contract. For example, there might be nine payments, as just noted, but the last one might constitute one-fourth of the cost of the contract. Such a schedule helps to protect the client from a consultant who may lose interest during the contract or be lured into a more profitable assignment elsewhere.

Epilogue

Nowhere in the preceding comments have we addressed one of the major benefits that client and consultant enjoy from working together. It is this: professionals want to continue their growth and development and to stay on the cutting edge of their discipline. Many training departments are relatively small and lack the perspective that an outsider brings to the table. Similarly, consultants need the structure and framework of an organization as their "laboratory" in which new courses, techniques, instruments, etc., can be refined and brought to life. In short, each party needs the other, and the professional growth of both should be a major by-product of any consultancy.

Reference

1. Mager, Robert F., *Preparing Instructional Objectives,* Lear Siegler, Inc./Fearon Publishers, Inc., Belmont, CA, 1962, preface.

Bibliography

Block, Peter, *Flawless Consulting: A Guide to Getting Your Expertise Used,* Pfeiffer & Co., San Diego, 1981.

Connor, Richard A., and Jeffery P. Davidson, *Marketing Your Consulting and Professional Services,* John Wiley & Sons, New York, 1985.

Edwards, Paul and Sarah, *Making It on Your Own,* Jeremy P. Tarcher/Perigee Books, New York, 1991.

Gallessich, June, *The Profession and Practice of Consultation,* Jossey-Bass, San Francisco, 1986.

Geoffrey, M., *The Consultant's Calling: Bringing Who You Are to What You Do,* Jossey-Bass, San Francisco, 1990.

Greenbaum, Thomas L., *The Consultant's Manual: A Complete Guide to Building a Successful Consulting Practice,* John Wiley & Sons, New York, 1990.

Gendelman, Joel, *Consulting 101: A How-to Guide for Successful Training Consulting,* ASTD, Alexandria, VA 1995.

Johnson, Barbara L., *Private Consulting: How to Turn Experience into Employment Dollars,* Prentice-Hall, Englewood Cliffs, NJ, 1982.

Montgomery, Daniel J., Judith F. Vogt, and Laura B. Pincus, "Process Contracting: Legal and Relational Considerations in Developing Consultant-Client Contracts," *Organization Development Journal,* vol. 11, no. 1, Spring 1993, pp. 23–30.

Petrini, Catherine M., ed., "Putting a Price on Your Head," *Training and Development Journal,* vol. 44, no. 7, July 1990, pp. 15–22.

Robinson, Dana G., and Bob Younglove, *Making Your Career Transition into External HRD Consulting,* ASTD, Alexandria, VA, 1986.

Shenson, Howard L., *The Contract and Fee-Setting Guide for Consultants and Professionals,* John Wiley & Sons, New York, 1990.

Tepper, Ron, *Become a Top Consultant: How the Experts Do It,* John Wiley & Sons, New York, 1985.

Weiss, Alan, *William Dollar Consulting: The Professional's Guide to Growing a Practice,* McGraw-Hill, New York, 1992.

Index

Qualities Desired and weight of each (on a 1-10 scale)		Options (consultants being considered)					
		The Optima Group		Wm. Smith & Associates		Klein, Fraser, and Co.	
1. Trust and confidence	10	4	40	5	50	5	50
2. Fast learner quick to understand	8	4	32	5	40	2	16
3. Experience in our industry	8	1	8	3	24	1	8
4. Evaluation by references	9	5	45	5	45	5	45
5. Back-up capability (depth of orgn.)	6	5	30	4	24	4	24
6. Desire to have our business	5	5	25	5	25	5	25
7. Prior work of a similar nature	7	3	21	4	28	2	14
8. Writing and organizing skills	6	4	24	3	18	4	24
9. Needs analysis skills	4	2	8	4	16	2	8
10. Project management skills	8	3	24	4	32	1	8
			257		302		222
			Second choice		First choice		Third choice

Figure 51-3. Decision matrix for selecting a consultant.

work, to decide how they can work together to best advantage, and to establish criteria for evaluating the success of the project. It is extremely important that this be a joint activity of both parties; the consultant should not be expected to go back to the office and write up a program or proposal until this dual investment is made.

The end product of the needs analysis is a blueprint—a plan of action that both parties feel is appropriate to pursue. This plan of action usually lists the behavioral objectives (terminal behaviors, performance criteria) that trainees will have reached upon completion of their training. In smaller engagements, the needs analysis may take only a few weeks to complete and may be paid for under a per diem arrangement. (Fees and billing will be discussed later.) When the consulting engagement and training project are more ambitious in nature, the needs

About the Editor

Robert Craig, a leading T&D professional for more than 30 years, has edited the three previous editions of the *Training and Development Handbook*. He established the *National Report for Training and Development*, a key source of information about the field. He is the recipient of ASTD's highest award—-the Gordon M. Bliss Memorial Award.